Our Own Backyard

Our Own Backyard

The United States in Central America, 1977–1992

William M. LeoGrande

The University of North Carolina Press *Chapel Hill & London*

© 1998 William M. LeoGrande

All rights reserved

Manufactured in the United States of America

The paper in this book meets the guidelines for

permanence and durability of the Committee on

Production Guidelines for Book Longevity of the

Council on Library Resources.

Library of Congress Cataloging-in-Publication Data

LeoGrande, William M.

Our own backyard: the United States in Central America,

1977–1992 / William M. LeoGrande.

    p. cm.

ISBN 0-8078-2395-3 (cloth: alk. paper)

ISBN 0-8078-4857-3 (pbk.: alk. paper)

1. Central America—Foreign relations—United States.

2. United States—Foreign relations—Central America.

3. United States—Foreign relations—1977–1981.

4. United States—Foreign relations—1981–1989.

5. United States—Foreign relations—1989–1993. I. Title.

F1436.8.U6L453   1998

327.730728'09'048—dc21   97-18198

CIP

03   02   01   00   99   6   5   4   3   2

Brief excerpts from the following journal articles are used in this
book: William M. LeoGrande, "The Revolution in Nicaragua:
Another Cuba?" *Foreign Affairs* 58 (Fall 1979): 28–50, and
William M. LeoGrande and Carla Anne Robbins, "Oligarchs and
Officers: The Crisis in El Salvador," *Foreign Affairs* 58 (Summer 1980):
1084–1103. Reprinted by permission of *Foreign Affairs*; copyright 1979
and 1980 by the Council on Foreign Relations, Inc. William M.
LeoGrande, "From Reagan to Bush: The Transition in U.S. Policy
toward Central America," *Journal of Latin American Studies* 22, no. 3
(October 1990): 595–621. Reprinted by permission of Cambridge
University Press.

Contents

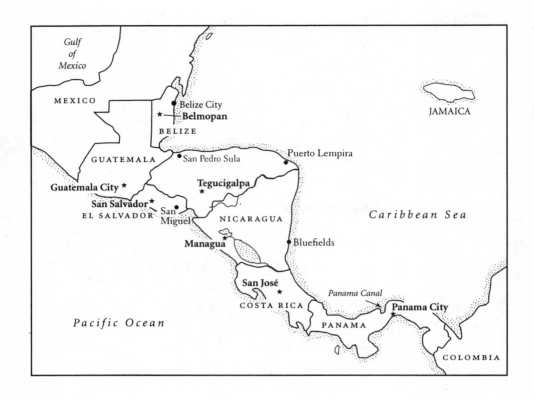

Preface

When I began this book, I intended to write an account of the domestic opposition to Ronald Reagan's Central America policy, focusing on the Congress. Not since Vietnam had Americans been so bitterly divided over a foreign policy issue as they were over Central America. I soon realized, however, that investigating the domestic debate was like pulling on a loose thread—it lead inexorably to other questions.

To understand the political struggle between the Reagan administration and its critics, it was first necessary to examine what was happening in Central America. As U.S. involvement deepened, a tension arose between the instinct of many U.S. policymakers to preserve Washington's traditional hegemony in the region, and the desire of Central Americans to control their own destiny. On this issue, Washington discovered adversaries not only among Marxist guerrillas on the left, but also among military officers and businessmen on the right. Maintaining even tenuous control over allies such as the Salvadoran armed forces or the Nicaraguan contras proved as difficult for Washington as plotting strategy against the Salvadoran guerrillas and the Sandinistas.

In the United States, the tempo of the debate between the Reagan administration and its critics waxed and waned with the rhythms of the war on the ground. As the region's civil strife escalated, Reagan's opponents charged that his policy was failing to achieve its stated objectives; Reagan replied that the critics' caviling tied his hands, preventing success.

I was also compelled to look at how policy was formulated inside the Reagan administration. From the beginning, it was beset by a severe internal schism between self-described "hard-liners" and "pragmatists" who struggled with one another for control over foreign policy in general and Central American policy in particular. On Central America, the hard-liners were inclined toward military solutions, and they bitterly opposed any diplomatic accord that gave Washington less than total victory. For the pragmatists, Central America was *not* the most important place on the globe, and the wars there were less a test of ideological mettle than a challenge to traditional U.S. security interests. If those interests could be reasonably safeguarded by diplomatic compromise, the pragmatists were willing to pursue it.

The policy differences between hard-liners and pragmatists were often reinforced by rivalries of ambition and personal animosity. It was not uncommon for different officials to describe U.S. policy in hopelessly contradictory ways within a few days—or even hours—of one another. Both camps leaked continually in an effort to gain the upper hand in the internal tug of war. With a president reluctant to resolve conflicts among his senior advisers and notoriously inattentive to the details of policy, the administration's internecine conflict over Central America was never definitively resolved. Every policy decision bore the scars of it.

On one issue, however, the hard-liners and pragmatists could agree: both regarded the policy prescriptions of the liberal Democrats in Congress as anathema. The biggest battles fought in Washington over Central America pitted the Reagan administration against Congress, and most administration officials regarded the Democrats' efforts to promote an alternative policy as ill informed and illegitimate.

Finally, I had to look beyond Central America at the behavior of U.S. allies and adversaries. For Ronald Reagan and his conservative loyalists, Central America was not intrinsically important. Its significance derived from its place in a global context; it was a theater in the Cold War struggle with the Soviet Union. Indeed, Central America was the last major battle of the Cold War. Reagan's policy cannot be understood outside that context, and the opposition to his policy from liberal Democrats reflected their rejection of Reagan's Manichaean conception of international affairs. While Reagan invariably pointed to Soviet and Cuban machinations as justification for his approach, liberal Democrats pointed to the nearly universal opposition to U.S. policy among allies in Latin America and Western Europe—opposition that manifested itself in active efforts to resolve Central America's armed conflicts diplomatically, despite persistent resistance from Washington. No one caused the Reagan administration more headaches than Costa Rican president Oscar Arias, whose regional peace plan won him the Nobel Peace Prize.

For me, then, what began as a relatively bounded project examining the domestic debate over Central America evolved into a comprehensive history of U.S. policy toward the region during its decade of crisis—how policy was made, how it worked, and how the administration tried to sell it to the American people. From the overthrow of the Somoza dynasty in Nicaragua and the outbreak of the civil war in El Salvador in the late 1970s, to the final regional peace settlements negotiated a decade later at the end of the Cold War, this book chronicles the struggles—both in Central America and Washington—that shaped the region's destiny. I have tried to give a reasonably full account of how the regional crisis unfolded on the ground, but the principal venue of this story is Washington, D.C. For good or ill, Central America's fate during this crisis depended fundamentally on decisions made in Washington—decisions over which Central Americans themselves had little influence.

The narrative is predominantly chronological. Within that basic framework, I have tried to weave together four thematic elements corresponding to the dynamics described above: (1) the conflicts on the ground in the region;

(2) the conflicts within the U.S. administration over what policy should be; (3) the domestic debate between administration supporters and critics, especially in Congress; and (4) the role played by other countries in Latin America and Europe in alleviating or exacerbating the crisis.

Part I begins by exploring the roots of the Central American crisis that erupted during the later years of Jimmy Carter's presidency. Ronald Reagan came to office determined to reverse the basic thrust of Carter's foreign policy, and Central America became a symbol and test case for demonstrating Reagan's new hard line against international Communism. During Reagan's first year in office, U.S. policy shifted from Carter's attempts to seek a negotiated settlement in El Salvador, and coexistence with the Sandinista government in Nicaragua, to Reagan's effort to achieve military victory for the Salvadoran government, and the ouster of the Sandinistas by covert proxy war.

Part II focuses on El Salvador, which became one of the most controversial foreign policy issues of Reagan's first term. As U.S. military support for the Salvadoran government increased, the civil war escalated dramatically. Congressional Democrats bitterly opposed Reagan's apparently uncritical and unlimited support for a government that engaged in widespread and egregious violations of human rights. Under pressure from Congress, the administration tried to entice the Salvadoran government to reform, only to discover that managing the internal politics of the regime was as difficult as fighting the war.

Part III shifts the scene to Nicaragua. Although Reagan launched the covert war against the Sandinista government shortly after assuming office, it became a focus of public debate only toward the end of his first term. When Congress cut off U.S. support for the contras in 1984, senior administration officials led by National Security Council staff aide Oliver North conspired to keep aid flowing. The revelation of this effort to circumvent Congress, which came out during the Iran-contra investigation, shook the Reagan presidency to its foundations.

Part IV carries the narrative into the Bush presidency, when both the Nicaraguan and Salvadoran wars were finally settled by negotiations. In Nicaragua, the implementation of a regional peace agreement led to a free election in 1990 that was won by the Sandinistas' civilian opponents. In El Salvador, after a surge in fighting in 1989, both sides concluded that a negotiated peace was preferable to endless war. With help from the international community, including the United States, they were able to reach a peace agreement in 1992. The book concludes with an assessment of what the decade of turmoil in Central America has meant for U.S. relations with Latin America, and for the Central Americans, who are left to recover and rebuild after long years of brutality and war.

Finally, the book looks at the consequences of Ronald Reagan's policy for our own political process. Like the domestic turmoil unleashed by Vietnam, the struggle over Central America was so divisive that it damaged the fabric of democratic politics at home. It weakened the ties of comity between Democrats and Republicans in Congress, inflamed the tug-of-war between Congress and the executive branch over control of foreign policy, and ultimately led some administration officials to circumvent the law. Just as domestic dissent over Vietnam led to the White House plumbers and Watergate, domestic opposition to Reagan's Central American policy led to Oliver North and William Casey's secret intelligence apparatus and the Iran-contra scandal.

To readers especially interested in Guatemala, I apologize for giving it short shrift. Although the war in Guatemala in the 1980s was no less intense or bloody than those in Nicaragua and El Salvador, Washington's role was more peripheral. An ongoing congressional ban on military aid, which lasted until late in the decade, prevented the United States from becoming the arsenal of the Guatemalan army the way it did in El Salvador. Moreover, Guatemala's guerrillas never achieved the strength to threaten the survival of the regime, so Washington had less impetus to intervene. Still, I would have liked to include several chapters on Guatemala, but considerations of space precluded it.

During the early 1980s, I had the good fortune to work on the staff of the Democratic leadership in both the United States Senate and the House of Representatives, dealing specifically with U.S. policy toward Central America. From 1982 to 1984, I worked with the Democratic Policy Committee, chaired by Senator Robert C. Byrd, and from 1985 to 1986, I worked with the House Democratic Caucus Task Force on Central America, chaired by Congressman Mel Levine. From these vantage points, I was able to witness and participate in many of the key battles between the administration and its congressional opponents.

In reconstructing events and conversations, I have relied, where possible, on official documents, published (e.g., presidential and congressional papers and hearings) and unpublished (e.g., declassified documents). During the debates on Central America, a surprising number of classified documents were leaked to the press by one or another faction inside the administration. For most key decisions, the record of internal deliberations available from journalistic sources is unusually complete. In citing documents, I have tried, to the extent possible, to direct readers to the most readily available published source when there is one. Some of the documents cited, mostly ones from Central American sources, have never been published. Almost all of these are in my possession.

Most of the unpublished U.S. government documents cited are available at the National Security Archive in Washington, D.C.

In addition to documents and contemporary journalistic reports, my account is also based on several hundred interviews conducted over the course of a decade with executive branch officials, members of Congress and their staff, and Central Americans on all sides of the region's various conflicts. When interviews were conducted formally, with set ground rules, I have cited the sources appropriately. Conversations that occurred in the course of my work in Congress are cited anonymously, since people then were speaking to me as a colleague, not with the expectation that their views would eventually show up in print.

Aficionados of Congress will find that the notes contain additional detail on various procedural maneuvers. I banished this material to the notes because it is too arcane for most readers, but as a former congressional staff member, I couldn't bring myself to edit it out completely.

Careful readers will also notice the frequency of citations to the daily press. One reason is simply that the narrative style I use frequently quotes comments in press briefings and interviews not reproduced in official documents (although I rely on official transcripts when available).

A second, more substantive reason is that the press played a crucial role in how the story unfolded. From the coverage of human rights violations in El Salvador to the revelations of the Iran-contra scandal, the press had a profound effect on the formation of both elite and mass opinion. And in Washington, warring factions inside the Reagan administration regularly used the press as a weapon in their internecine combat.

Finally, as the adage goes, journalists write the rough draft of history, and I wanted to show what a good job most of them did with the Central America story. In many notes, I juxtapose contemporary press accounts with documentary evidence that only became available much later, showing that reporters had the facts essentially right early on. The documentary evidence may be more authoritative, but it seemed to me only fair to give credit to those who had the story first. A number of reporters consistently filed high-quality reports, both from Central America and Washington—people such as Alan Riding, Karen DeYoung, Christopher Dickey, Raymond Bonner, Stephen Kinzer, Clifford Krauss, Don Oberdorfer, Alfonso Chardy, Roy Gutman, Dennis Volman, Sam Dillon, Julia Preston, Joanne Omang, Brian Barger, and Robert Parry.

Projects of this length and duration invariably accumulate debts to many people along the way, some of whose contributions are so great that they should be formally acknowledged. My thanks go first to friends and colleagues who read parts of the manuscript and provided valuable comments on it: Ken Sharpe, Janet Shenk, Alex Wilde, and Pete Vaky.

Peter Kornbluh at the National Security Archive gave me invaluable assistance finding my way through mountains of declassified government documents on Central America. Jim Lobe, Griffin Hathaway, Pat Bodnar, and Marshall Yurow were all kind enough to share with me interviews and documents collected in the course of their own research. Former Speaker of the House Jim Wright allowed me to see his memoir when it was still in manuscript. My editors, Elaine Maisner, Pam Upton, and Eric D. Schramm, were as skilled as any I have encountered.

Both the Council on Foreign Relations and the Open Society Foundation helped launch this project, without realizing it, when they provided me with fellowships to take time off from teaching in order to work as a congressional staff member. Financial support for writing the book was provided by the Arca Foundation, the Everett McKinley Dirksen Congressional Center, American University, and W. H. Ferry and Carol Bernstein Ferry. My thanks to all for their generosity.

The burdens of writing a book are shared, unavoidably, by an author's family. In my case, I owe a special debt of gratitude to my wife and partner, Martha Langelan. She tolerated my spending untold hours hunched in front of the computer screen, she read the whole manuscript when it was even longer than it is now and gave me editorial advice second to none, and she remained ever optimistic (outwardly at least) that this book would, in fact, get finished. That it did is in no small measure a result of her support.

Abbreviations Used in the Text

ACLU	American Civil Liberties Union
AID	U.S. Agency for International Development
AIFLD	American Institute for Free Labor Development, AFL-CIO
ANSESAL	Salvadoran National Security Agency (Agencia Nacional de Seguridad Salvadoreña)
ARENA	Nationalist Republican Alliance (Alianza Republicana Nacionalista), El Salvador
CBI	Caribbean Basin Initiative
CIA	Central Intelligence Agency
CONDECA	Central American Defense Council
CORDS	Civil Operations and Revolutionary Development Support
COSEP	Superior Council of Private Enterprise (Consejo Superior de la Empresa Privada), Nicaragua
CPPG	National Security Council Crisis Pre-Planning Group
DCM	deputy chief of mission
DIES	Directorate of Special Investigations (Directorio de Investigaciones Especiales), Honduras
FAO	Broad Opposition Front (Frente Amplio Opositor), Nicaragua
FDN	Nicaraguan Democratic Force (Fuerza Democrática Nicaragüense)
FDR	Revolutionary Democratic Front (Frente Democrático Revolucionario), El Salvador
FMLN	Farabundo Martí Front for National Liberation (Frente Farabundo Martí para la Liberación Nacional), El Salvador
FSLN	Sandinista National Liberation Front (Frente Sandinista de Liberación Nacional), Nicaragua
FY	fiscal year
GAO	General Accounting Office
GOP	Republican Party
IMF	International Monetary Fund
ISA	U.S. Army Intelligence Support Activity
LRRPS	Long Range Reconnaissance Patrols
NATO	North Atlantic Treaty Organization
NED	National Endowment for Democracy
NHAO	U.S. Department of State Nicaraguan Humanitarian Assistance Office
NIO	National Intelligence Officer
NSC	National Security Council

NSDD	National Security Decision Directive
NSPG	National Security Planning Group
OAS	Organization of American States
ORDEN	Nationalist Democratic Organization (Organización Democrática Nacionalista), El Salvador
OSS	Office of Strategic Services
PCN	National Conciliation Party (Partido de Conciliación Nacional), El Salvador
PDC	Christian Democratic Party (Partido Demócrata Cristiano), El Salvador
PLO	Palestine Liberation Organization
RIG	Restricted Inter-Agency Group
RMTC	Regional Military Training Center
SEALS	U.S. Navy Sea, Air, and Land special forces
SELA	Latin American Economic System
South-Com	U.S. Southern Command, Panama
UCLAS	Unilaterally Controlled Latino Assets
UCS	Salvadoran Communal Union (Unión Comunal Salvadoreña)
UDN	Nicaraguan Democratic Union (Unión Democrática Nicaragüense)
UNO	National Opposition Union (Unión Nacional Opositor), Nicaragua
UNO	United Nicaraguan Opposition (Unidad Nicaragüense Opositor)
UNTS	National Unity of Salvadoran Workers (Unidad Nacional de Trabajadores Salvadoreños)
UPD	Popular Democratic Union (Unión Popular Democrática), El Salvador

1 Origins

We do control the destinies of Central America and we do so for the simple reason that the national interest absolutely dictates such a course. . . . Until now, Central America has always understood that governments which we recognize and support stay in power, while those we do not recognize and support fall.

—Undersecretary of State Robert Olds, 1927

CHAPTER 1

A New Beginning

As if on cue, the sun broke through the gray blanket of clouds over the city of Washington just as Ronald Wilson Reagan was sworn in as fortieth president of the United States. The sunshine pushed the temperature into the mid-fifties, making January 20, 1981, one of the warmest inauguration days on record. The rainstorm forecast for the afternoon never came.

On the inaugural platform, Reagan looked relaxed and resplendent in morning coat and striped pants. At sixty-nine, he was the oldest man ever to assume the presidency, but he looked vigorous next to Jimmy Carter. The outgoing president had not slept for three days, trying in vain to arrange the release of the fifty-two American hostages in Iran before the final hours of his presidency ticked away. Carter, who refused the suggestion by Reagan's staff that he, too, don formal morning dress, looked weary and plain in his ordinary business suit.

A southern populist, Carter had tried to demystify the institution of the presidency by bringing the president closer to the people. After his own inauguration, he walked down Pennsylvania Avenue to the White House rather than ride in a limousine. He insisted on being called "Jimmy" Carter, not James Earl. He was everyman, and after the Byzantine Court politics of the Nixon years, Americans found him reassuring. But people were not entirely comfortable with a president who seemed so common. Americans liked having some pomp and ceremony associated with the presidency. The office was no ordinary one, and it demanded an extraordinary person to fill it. Despite his intelligence and a real compassion for the less fortunate, Jimmy Carter, the peanut farmer from Georgia, never projected a heroic persona.

An engineer by profession, Carter approached the presidency as a problem solver—clear-headed, unemotional, matter-of-fact. He appealed to the American people for support by explaining issues, trying to persuade them by dint of logic. Coming to office in the aftermath of Vietnam and Watergate, during the Middle East oil crisis, Carter believed the days of U.S. military and economic global dominance were over, and he said so. To many Americans, it was an unwelcome message. Carter was not wrong when he observed, in his infamous "malaise" speech, that the country was plagued by self-doubt, but in the end it was easier to blame the messenger.

Ronald Reagan, a successful film actor for over twenty years, approached politics as if it were theater. He understood instinctively that the first task of the leading man is to form an emotional bond with the audience. Once the hero wins the audience's loyalty, it will stick by him, rooting for him, even if he displays a few minor faults and even if the story line has an occasional hole in it. This was the secret of Reagan's "teflon" presidency—a willing suspension of disbelief. He could make factual mistakes, he could advocate policies that most people disagreed with, but he was so warm and engaging, both in person and in front of the camera, that the audience was always on his side. He played the hero to perfection.

And he cast Jimmy Carter as the villain. When Carter told the American people that they had entered an era of limits, Ronald Reagan reassured them that it was not America that was unequal to the challenge; rather, Jimmy Carter was unequal to it. "It is time for us to realize that we are too great a nation to limit ourselves to small dreams," Reagan said in his inaugural speech. "We're not, as some would have us believe, doomed to inevitable decline. We have every right to dream heroic dreams."[1]

People liked Ronald Reagan because he told them they lived in a shining city on a hill and that the nation's greatest days were still ahead. He told them that their traditional values—the belief in hard work, love of country, dedication to family, and the small-town sense of community—were not obsolete. Reagan's appeal was classically conservative; he recognized people's discomfort with the rapid economic, social, and cultural changes that had pounded the nation like a succession of hurricanes since the early 1960s—the assassinations of John F. Kennedy, Robert F. Kennedy, and Martin Luther King Jr., the civil rights movement, the women's movement, Vietnam, Watergate, stagflation. He held out the promise that fidelity to the old virtues could form the basis of a moral revival and make America great again, both at home and abroad. The lost tranquility of Norman Rockwell's America could be recaptured. America would have "a New Beginning."

Central America and the Legacy of Vietnam

In foreign policy, Reagan aimed to recapture the bipartisan unity and self-confidence that were shattered in Vietnam. Over the next eight years, he would pursue a foreign policy diametrically opposed to Jimmy Carter's. Where Carter had sought to expand detente with the Soviet Union, Reagan would return to a Cold War posture of distrust and animosity, punctuated by the largest peacetime military buildup in American history. Where Carter had sought to craft a new relationship with the Third World based on tolerance for ideological pluralism and a presumption against intervention, Reagan viewed the Third World primarily through the prism of the East-West struggle and, under the rubric of the "Reagan Doctrine," would launch half a dozen covert paramilitary wars against perceived adversaries. Where Carter promoted human rights as a cornerstone of U.S. foreign policy, Reagan would renew U.S. alliances with anti-Communist authoritarian regimes.

The foreign policies of these two presidents were as different as any in the post–World War II era, and nowhere were the differences clearer than in Central America. When civil conflicts erupted in Nicaragua, El Salvador, and Guatemala in the late 1970s, Carter's instinct was to limit Washington's direct involvement and promote diplomatic settlements. Despite the growing strength of Marxist guerrillas, he refused to commit the United States to the defense of the status quo by resuming military aid to dictatorial regimes. From his first day in office, Ronald Reagan repudiated Carter's approach in favor of active U.S. military support for Central America's anti-Communists.

For the next decade, the Central American crisis would dominate America's foreign policy agenda and polarize domestic politics. During the first Reagan administration, the civil war in El Salvador held center stage. Despite fervent opposition from congressional Democrats, who opposed aiding a regime guilty of massive human rights abuses, Reagan never wavered in his support for the Salvadoran military. In eight years, he poured nearly $4 billion in U.S. assistance into the country. During Reagan's second term, El Salvador receded from Washington's political agenda (though the war continued unabated), only to be replaced by Nicaragua. As part of its global campaign to roll back the tide of international Communism, the Reagan administration organized an exile army to wage a proxy war against Nicaragua's revolutionary government. Here, too, Reagan met with stiff congressional resistance, but he would brook no opposition. When Congress finally voted to prohibit further U.S. aid to the exiles ("contras"), senior administration officials, led by National Security Council staff aide Oliver North, continued to support the contras clandestinely. The revelation that they had circumvented the law produced a political scandal reminiscent of Watergate and nearly destroyed Reagan's presidency.

Why did such a small region loom so large in the American psyche during the 1980s? The debate over Central America was, in large measure, an extension of the debate over Vietnam. For the Reagan wing of the Republican Party, Central America was, first and foremost, an arena of struggle between Communism and Democracy. Those who, like Ronald Reagan, regarded Vietnam as "a noble cause" worried that the "Vietnam syndrome" was interfering with America's ability to resist Soviet encroachments in the Third World.[2] Central America was a test of America's mettle after the defeat in Southeast Asia, and conservatives were determined to win a clear victory to reinvigorate the nation's will to use force abroad.

Much of the general public shared the Republican right's distress about America's position in the world. Defeat in Vietnam seemed to mark the end of America's global preeminence. The 1970s oil crisis, the Soviet invasion of Afghanistan, and the revolution in Iran all seemed to confirm that the United States was sliding downward toward the status of a second-rate power. Ronald Reagan pledged to stop the march of the "Evil Empire" of international Communism by restoring the United States to its rightful place as world leader.[3] Central America was the place that Reagan would draw the line.

If anti-Communism was a unifying force for Republicans, it divided Democrats. The Democratic Party never fully recovered from the political trauma of Vietnam. The war split the party from top to bottom along ideological lines: The "doves" of the left-liberal wing backed Eugene McCarthy's and Robert Kennedy's insurgent challenges to Lyndon Johnson; the "hawks" stuck with their president and Hubert Humphrey. After Johnson's withdrawal from the race and Kennedy's assassination, the party convened in Chicago for a fratricidal bloodletting that paved the way for the election of Richard Nixon. Four years later, the Democrats nominated antiwar candidate George McGovern.

Although McGovern lost as decisively as Barry Goldwater had almost a decade earlier, the ideological center of the national Democratic Party moved to the left, just as the center of the Republican Party had moved to the right after 1964. Outside the South, Democrats who had been Cold War liberals became antiwar liberals. The few who resisted this evolution either migrated as neoconservatives to the Republican Party, or tried in vain to fight a rear-guard action against the Democrats' ideological shift. In the South, however, most Democrats remained supporters of the war and a tough anti-Communist foreign policy. The shift of majority sentiment in the national party to an antiwar, anti-interventionist posture widened the chasm between southern Democrats and their northern colleagues, reinforcing the split over civil rights. Liberal Democrats regarded Vietnam as a mistake and were always on guard to be sure the mistake was not repeated in some other faraway land. To them, Central America looked like another Vietnam in the making—another benighted Third World region where America would run afoul of history by casting its lot with authoritarian military regimes defending an anachronistic social order. They were determined not to start down the slippery slope.

The American people—from the average citizen to the foreign policy elite—were as divided about the lessons of Vietnam as were the Republican and Democratic Parties. Among the elite, Vietnam shattered the bipartisan consensus constructed by Harry Truman at the onset of the Cold War. That consensus rested upon several basic premises: that the Soviet Union (and later, Communist China) was an aggressive power that had to be contained or, like Hitler's Germany, it would subjugate others relentlessly; that the United States, as the leader of the free world, had primary responsibility for standing up to the Soviets; and, after Korea, that no corner of the world was too far away or too insignificant to defend from Soviet encroachment, lest aggression appeased become aggression repeated.

An unwritten corollary to this containment doctrine held that revolutions in the Third World created opportunities for Communist penetration. Instability was incompatible with U.S. security interests. With this precept as rationale, the United States took on the role of global policeman. In its zeal to block the advance of Communism, Washington often committed itself against the aspirations of revolutionary nationalists and social democrats in developing nations around the world. The war in Vietnam brought the limits of U.S. power into sharp focus. If the United States was no longer willing or able to "pay any price, bear any burden" in the international struggle against Communism, then debate was inevitable over what price should be paid, and where. Central America became the arena for that debate.

Among the general public, the war in Vietnam increased isolationist sentiment substantially, but it also split the "internationalist" public into two camps: those who thought Vietnam was justified and those who did not. Throughout the 1970s and 1980s, these two groups disagreed fundamentally over the most basic issues of American foreign policy. The antiwar group opposed virtually all U.S. military involvements abroad, especially if they involved sending American advisers or troops and therefore raised the specter of "another Vietnam." Those who supported the war in Vietnam evinced no such fears and no reluctance about new adventures abroad.

These policy differences within the public and the political elite tended to follow partisan cleavages, especially as the Republicans became more conservative and the Democrats more liberal. Partisan politics no longer stopped at the water's edge. For any post-Vietnam American president, the combined political weight of anti-interventionist and isolationist sentiment would have been a formidable obstacle to military commitments abroad. The simultaneous shift in institutional power between the president and the Congress made foreign commitments even harder to sustain.[4]

Until Vietnam, Congress, the press, and the public had left control of foreign policy to the president. Without the normal checks on executive power that keep domestic politics on a relatively even keel, the Imperial Presidency became powerful enough to wage war with little regard for public opinion, until discontent erupted into massive antiwar protests at home. In reaction to what Senator William Fulbright (D-Ark.) called "the arrogance of power" came the "democratization" of foreign policy—the reassertion by Congress of a more active role. In 1973, Congress tried to recapture its constitutional power to declare war by passing the War Powers Resolution over President Nixon's veto. Later that same year, Congress ended America's role in Indochina's wars by prohibiting all U.S. military and paramilitary combat operations "in or over Vietnam, Laos, or Cambodia."[5] In 1975, the Clark amendment (named for Senator Dick Clark, Democrat from Iowa) prevented Henry Kissinger from extending Washington's covert role in the Angolan civil war. Revelations of the CIA's misdeeds—including spying on Americans, conducting medical experiments on unwitting subjects, and plotting to assassinate foreign leaders—led Congress to create permanent committees to oversee the intelligence community and require that they be notified of all covert operations.[6] Finally, in the late 1970s, Congress passed a series of laws prohibiting the United States from providing foreign assistance to governments that were "gross and consistent violators of internationally recognized human rights."[7]

The legacy of Vietnam—public uncertainty about America's proper role in the world, partisan division over foreign policy, and institutional conflict between Congress and the executive branch—was not something Ronald Reagan could simply wish away, even though he had been elected on a platform that promised to make America great again. The Reagan Republicans sometimes liked to think that the Vietnam syndrome could be exorcised easily, that the restoration of American preeminence was simply a matter of political will.

Certainly, as the sun shone down on Ronald Reagan riding along Pennsylvania Avenue in his inaugural parade, everything seemed possible to the Republican faithful who lined the route, eagerly straining for a glimpse of their conquering hero. Patriotic songs filled the air—"God Bless America," "Anchors

Aweigh," "The Battle Hymn of the Republic"—and Reagan sang along as the marching bands played. A red, white, and blue float carrying young girls in tight outfits passed the presidential reviewing stand, releasing hot-air balloons that carried aloft an American flag. "Oh, it's so good it made me cry," gushed Maxine Hinkle, a Republican from West Virginia. "I can't believe how everything is coming out a happy ending."[8]

Only about a thousand demonstrators marred the carefully staged celebration, trying to puncture the festive bubble. Standing in clusters at various points along the inaugural parade route, they carried placards proclaiming their opposition to the new president on a variety of issues. They were not disruptive, but their mere presence was an unwelcome intrusion, an unpleasant reminder that outside the Republicans' cocoon of good feeling, America was still deeply divided and unsure of its future. Reagan pointedly looked away as he passed the demonstrators, so he probably didn't see the signs held up by some of them demanding, "U.S. Out of El Salvador."[9]

CHAPTER 2

The Dragons' Teeth of War

Perhaps it was inevitable that Americans would have to finish the debate over Vietnam in Latin America, where the United States had long been the predominant power. Vietnam was 12,000 miles away, but Latin America was our own backyard. El Salvador was closer to Miami than Miami was to Washington, D.C., as Ronald Reagan regularly reminded us. Harlingen, Texas, was just a few days drive from Managua, Nicaragua.[1] If Washington's commitment in Vietnam was a mistake because it was too far away, because the culture was too alien for Americans to understand, or because the interests at stake did not justify the sacrifice, none of these reasons applied in Central America.

The isthmus of Central America stretches from Mexico's southern border to Panama, encompassing five former Spanish colonies—Guatemala, Honduras, El Salvador, Nicaragua, and Costa Rica. Nicaragua, the largest, is about the size of Michigan; El Salvador, the smallest, is the size of Massachusetts. Only about 23 million people live in the entire region, whose average gross national product per capita in the 1980s was well below $1,000.

Central America has always been among the most underdeveloped regions in Latin America. Even during the colonial period, it was a sparsely settled backwater. Unlike the colonial centers in Mexico and Peru, Central America had few precious minerals to attract the Spanish and, except in Guatemala, there were too few indigenous people to work the mines or the large landed estates. Central America's subsistence economies were not fully integrated into the world market until the late nineteenth century, when the coffee and banana booms spurred a rapid expansion of export agriculture.[2]

Contemporary Central American society was built on coffee and bananas. Most of the banana plantations were owned by U.S. businessmen, but coffee was locally controlled. Successful entrepreneurs joined with the traditional landed aristocracy to form powerful "coffee oligarchies" that dominated society and politics in Guatemala, El Salvador, and Nicaragua. They built their plantations by forcing small peasant farmers off the land, and they built modern armies to suppress the resulting unrest.

Despite stark inequities, these societies survived virtually intact into the second half of the twentieth century, held together by repressive force. By the mid-1970s, however, the oligarchic regimes had begun to decay. In Nicaragua and El Salvador, the established order broke down in the face of popular revolution, confronting the United States with brushfire wars in its own backyard.

Nicaragua: Autumn of the Patriarch

The history of U.S. involvement in Nicaragua stretches back to the California Gold Rush in the middle of the nineteenth century. In 1848, as a result of the war with Mexico, the United States acquired the western territories of New Mexico, Arizona, Nevada, Utah, Colorado, and California, thereby fulfilling its "Manifest Destiny" to control all the territory between the Atlantic and Pacific Oceans. To reach the West, however, required months of perilous journey across the plains and the Rocky Mountains, so the prospect of establishing a passage across the isthmus of Central America began to attract serious interest. The Gold Rush of 1848 set off a stampede of people into the western territories and gave new urgency to the idea of a Central American canal.

Like Panama, Nicaragua was always regarded as a logical site for a canal. By traveling up the San Juan river and across Lake Nicaragua, a shallow-draft boat could get within twelve miles of the Pacific coast. In 1853, Cornelius Vanderbilt established a lucrative business transporting travelers across Nicaragua by building a decent road over that twelve-mile finger of land.

With U.S. business came the gunboats of the U.S. government, intent upon preserving the honor and interests of its citizens. The first of eleven U.S. interventions in Nicaragua came in 1853 when a contingent of Marines landed on the Atlantic coast to settle a dispute between Vanderbilt's transit company and local Nicaraguan authorities. They resolved it in Vanderbilt's favor, of course. A year later, a U.S. diplomat was grazed by a bottle thrown from an angry crowd during a fracas with the mayor of San Juan del Norte, a small

Atlantic coast port. In retribution, a U.S. naval gunship bombarded the town until hardly a building remained standing. A landing party of Marines then looted the ruins and put them to the torch.[3]

All this was mere prelude, however, to one of the most amazing and, for Nicaraguans, most galling episodes in the history of relations with the United States. In 1854, the Nicaraguan Liberal and Conservative Parties were engaged in a civil war. The Liberals appealed to a North American named William Walker to raise a contingent of "filibusters"—mercenaries—to bolster their forces. Walker's troops managed to capture the Conservative capital of Granada and, by holding hostage the wealthy families of the Conservative leaders, Walker forced them to surrender. Calling himself "the Grey-Eyed Man of Destiny," Walker then took control of the Nicaraguan government, had himself elected president, made English an official language, and legalized slavery.

The occupation of Nicaragua by Walker and his filibusters had one salutary effect: it led the states of Central America, who were engaged more often than not in fratricidal conflicts with one another, to set aside their differences and unite to oust this Yankee interloper. In 1856, the combined armies of Central America drove Walker out of Nicaragua. When he tried to return in 1860 to resume the war, he was captured in Honduras and shot.[4]

The first two decades of the twentieth century were no less traumatic for U.S. relations with Central America. These were the years of gunboat and dollar diplomacy. Behind this interventionist impulse was the rapid expansion of U.S. interests, both economic and strategic. The closing of the U.S. frontier marked the fulfillment of Manifest Destiny, but not its satiation. As U.S. economic power grew, entrepreneurs began to seek profitable investment opportunities beyond the bounds of North America. They were drawn to the regions lying on the geographic periphery of the continental United States—Mexico, Cuba, Central America, and the Caribbean. As the economic interests of U.S. business extended into these regions, so too did their stake in political stability. When that stability appeared tenuous and investments were in jeopardy, the U.S. government was not hesitant to deploy gunboats and Marines to protect them.

The turn of the century also marked the emergence of the United States as a world power. At the same time, the Great Powers of Europe were busy carving up the Third World into colonial domains. Latin America was safe from European depredations by virtue of the 1823 Monroe Doctrine, in which the United States declared its willingness to fight to prevent European recolonization of the New World. But as the United States itself entered the ranks of the Great Powers, the Western Hemisphere seemed its logical domain. To justify the subordination of Latin America to the United States, the doctrine of Manifest

Destiny was resurrected in a new form: it was the natural right of the United States to expand its influence throughout the hemisphere, just as it had been its natural right to span the continent. The Roosevelt Corollary to the Monroe Doctrine, articulated in 1904, declared Washington's right to exercise "an international police power" to maintain order and stability when Latin American governments exhibited "chronic wrong-doing."[5]

Nicaragua was among the countries most often victimized by the new Manifest Destiny.[6] In 1912, Nicaragua became a virtual protectorate of the United States when three thousand U.S. troops landed, ostensibly to protect American lives and property during a period of civil strife. A contingent of Marines stayed for thirteen years to guarantee the survival of the Conservative Party government. Asked in 1922 what prospects Conservative president Adolfo Díaz would have if the Marines left, W. Bundy Cole, a New York banker who managed the National Bank of Nicaragua, answered, "I think the present government would last until the last coach of Marines left Managua station, and I think President Díaz would be on that last coach."[7]

In 1925, the Marines did leave briefly, and Cole's prediction was proved right. The Liberals immediately took up arms against the Conservatives, and in 1927, six thousand Marines returned to restore order. But the United States never quite succeeded in pacifying Nicaragua during the second occupation. Augusto César Sandino, a Liberal Party leader, refused to accept Washington's imposition of a Conservative president. Leading a rag-tag "Army for the Defense of Nicaraguan National Sovereignty," Sandino fought a six-year guerrilla war against the U.S. Marines, achieving international stature as a nationalist and anti-imperialist.[8]

The U.S. war against Sandino left a bitter legacy. "Today we are hated and despised," wrote an American coffee planter in Nicaragua in 1931. "This feeling has been created by employing the American Marines to hunt down and kill Nicaraguans in their own country."[9] Despite President Calvin Coolidge's warning that Sandino was an agent of Bolshevik Mexico and that Mexico was intent on extending Soviet-style Communism to all of Central America, opposition to the futile war rose in the United States. Entertainer Will Rogers began asking in his act, "Why are we in Nicaragua, and what the hell are we doing there?"[10] In 1932, Congress refused to finance any additional troop deployments.

When Washington finally withdrew in 1933, it left the task of ensuring Nicaraguan stability to a U.S.-trained constabulary, the National Guard. The Guard was commanded by Anastasio Somoza García, who had been the liaison between the U.S. Marine commander and the Nicaraguan government. One of Somoza's first achievements was to lure the legendary Sandino to Managua on the pretext of arranging peace, only to have him assassinated. In 1936, Somoza forced the civilian president from office, arranged his own election, and thus initiated the family dynasty that ruled Nicaragua for the next forty-two years.[11]

The Somoza dynasty rested upon two pillars: the National Guard, transformed by patronage into the Somozas' personal gendarme; and the support of the United States, ensured by the Somozas' anti-Communism and their ability to maintain order. Occasionally, Washington pressured the Somozas to be more tolerant of their political opponents and move toward democratic rule, but it was never willing to risk destabilizing such a reliable ally by pushing too hard. President Franklin D. Roosevelt's apocryphal but oft-repeated description of Somoza captured the flavor of Washington's attitude: "Somoza may be a son of a bitch, but he's our son of a bitch."[12] When the United States took on the task of training Latin American military officers after World War II, more soldiers from Nicaragua's National Guard were trained than from any other Latin American army.[13]

The elder Somoza was succeeded by his sons, Luis and then Anastasio Somoza Debayle, the latter a West Point graduate who spoke better English than Spanish and who always seemed a bit anachronistic; he peppered his conversation with English slang that had disappeared in the 1950s. His enemies called him "the last Marine."

Though their reign did little to alleviate the tremendous poverty of Nicaragua, one of the hemisphere's poorest countries, the Somozas proved adept at personal enrichment. At the end, Anastasio Somoza Debayle controlled an economic empire worth nearly $1 billion, including one-third of the nation's arable land, the meat-packing industry, the construction industry, the fishing industry, the national airlines, the only television station, radio stations, banks, and more. So complete was his economic control that foreign investors avoided Nicaragua for want of reasonable investment opportunities.[14]

During the first three decades after World War II, opposition to the Somoza dynasty was weak and divided. The middle-class and upper-class moderates of the traditional opposition political parties were paralyzed by the Somozas' close ties with the United States. Time after time, Somoza lured them into unequal "alliances" with the government—alliances that gave them little real power, but branded them as opportunists and collaborators in the eyes of the public. The slang expression for such politicians was *zancudos*—blood-sucking mosquitoes. Radical opposition in the lower classes, on the other hand, was controlled by ferocious repression. Thus the future of the dynasty seemed secure when, on December 23, 1972, the earth began to move, changing not only the physical geography of Nicaragua, but its political geography as well.

The political aftershocks of the earthquake that destroyed the capital city of

Managua in December 1972 fatally weakened the structure of Somoza's rule. Turning adversity to advantage, Somoza and his cronies enriched themselves shamelessly by stealing international aid intended for earthquake victims. With Somoza in charge of reconstruction, Managua was rebuilt on Somoza's land, by Somoza's construction companies, with money funneled through Somoza's banks.

The corruption, together with the expansion of Somoza's economic empire after the earthquake, alienated both the middle and upper classes. Among Nicaragua's lower classes, the economic adversity caused by the earthquake stimulated radical opposition, manifested in a wave of strikes, demonstrations, and land seizures that swept the country in 1972–73.[15] The moderate opposition coalesced around the leadership of Pedro Joaquín Chamorro, a reformist member of the Conservative Party and editor of the opposition newspaper, *La Prensa*. The radical opposition was led by the Sandinista National Liberation Front (Frente Sandinista de Liberación Nacional, FSLN), named for nationalist hero Augusto Sandino.

Founded in 1961, the FSLN was one of the many guerrilla organizations spawned in Latin America by the example of the Cuban Revolution. It had scant success during its first decade; it was routed by the National Guard in its only two serious military ventures.[16] Throughout the 1960s, the FSLN received arms and training from Cuba, though the amount of Cuban assistance was circumscribed by the FSLN's small size—fewer than fifty members—and its inability to establish a guerrilla base against the well-trained and well-equipped National Guard.[17]

One of the Sandinistas' most dramatic actions took place on December 27, 1974, when a band of guerrillas invaded a Managua Christmas party and captured a dozen of Nicaragua's most prominent business and political leaders. The guerrillas exchanged their hostages for fourteen political prisoners, $1 million in ransom, and safe passage to Cuba. The boldness of the operation brought the Sandinistas national recognition.

Somoza's embarrassment over the Christmas raid led him to embark upon a war of extermination against the FSLN. He declared a state of siege, created an elite counterinsurgency force within the National Guard, and secured an 80 percent increase in U.S. military aid. The National Guard then proceeded to conduct a reign of terror in the northern provinces of Matagalpa, Jinotega, Estelí, Zelaya, and Nueva Segovia, where the FSLN had been most active. "We want to be sure no new guerrilla focal point will rise in those hills," a National Guard officer told journalist Bernard Diederich. "We want to eliminate the contaminated peasants."[18] For two years, people in the northern provinces were subjected to a systematic campaign of torture, murder, and forced relocation. Such gross violations of human rights appalled Nicaragua's moderates and earned the Somoza government well-deserved international opprobrium. When the Carter administration unveiled its new human rights policy in 1977, Nicaragua became one of its principal targets.

A Policy as Good and Decent as the American People

Jimmy Carter made a conscious effort to break with the traditional habit of U.S. policymakers to view Third World conflicts through the prism of the Cold War. With the East-West conflict dampened by detente, he sought a policy more sensitive to North-South issues and more cognizant of the regional forces shaping the Third World independently of superpower machinations. In a major foreign policy address at Notre Dame University just a few months after taking office, Carter promised that the "inordinate fear of Communism" that had been the hallmark of past policy would be replaced by a tolerance for ideological diversity and a heightened concern for human rights.[19]

From the outset, Carter presented his human rights policy in moral terms: it was an approach to the world "as good and honest and decent" as the American people themselves. In the international arena, Carter sought to repair the damage done to the image of the United States by the ferocity of the war in Vietnam, while simultaneously posing a sharp moral contrast between the United States and the Soviet Union. At home, Carter hoped to reconstruct bipartisan domestic support for foreign policy by grounding it in principles to which no one could easily object.[20]

Yet the Carter administration never saw its human rights policy in exclusively moral terms. It was also intended to distance the United States from the brutal excesses of decaying autocracies. Right-wing dictatorships bent on preserving anachronistic social orders were regarded as bad security risks. The more they relied upon force to sustain themselves, the more rapidly they mobilized and radicalized their opponents, hastening their own demise. For the United States to enlist in support of such regimes would endanger national security, for ultimately they would collapse and an angry populace would not soon forget that the United States had sided with the tyrants.[21]

Though global in scope, Carter's human rights policy found its most consistent expression in Latin America. In 1977, there appeared to be no immediate security threats in the hemisphere, so the policy was not diluted by fears of political instability, as it was in Iran and South Korea. The few guerrilla movements still active in Central America appeared to be little more than feeble remnants from the 1960s, incapable of posing a serious challenge to existing regimes.

Carter's human rights policy was applied full force in Central America, where the four nations of the northern tier—Nicaragua, El Salvador, Guatemala, and Honduras—were all ruled by military dictatorships, most of them notorious for their systematic and brutal repression. Rather than submit to U.S. scrutiny on human rights, Guatemala and El Salvador preempted Washington in 1977 by refusing to accept further military assistance.[22]

Nicaragua constituted a near-perfect showcase for Carter's human rights policy. The long history of Somoza's ties to the United States suggested that he might prove especially malleable to U.S. influence. In addition, Nicaragua appeared to be a relatively safe laboratory in which to experiment since repression had apparently eliminated the Sandinistas.[23]

During Gerald Ford's brief tenure in the White House, the United States had already begun to gently distance itself from Somoza, partly as an antidote to Richard Nixon's close embrace of the dictator and the sycophancy of his ambassador, Turner Shelton.[24] But no real sanctions were imposed against Somoza until the advent of Jimmy Carter. Carter withheld economic and military aid on human rights grounds, and although the material effect was insignificant, the symbolic impact was enormous. Historically, Somoza's moderate opponents had been paralyzed by the unflagging U.S. support he enjoyed. With the power of Washington behind him, Somoza seemed unassailable, and he was a clever enough politician to actively foster this perception. By suspending aid, the Carter administration galvanized the moderates into active opposition by suggesting that Somoza's support in Washington was no longer secure.[25]

The Nicaraguan situation became more complicated for U.S. policymakers in October 1977, when the supposedly defunct FSLN launched a series of small-scale attacks on National Guard garrisons in five cities. Although the attackers were easily driven off, the assaults shattered the myth of Somoza's invulnerability. Coincident with the attacks, twelve prominent Nicaraguan professionals in exile (el Grupo de Los Doce) praised the Sandinistas' "political maturity" and asserted that the FSLN would have to play a role in any permanent solution to Nicaragua's problems.[26]

The willingness of moderate progressive forces to open a dialogue with the Sandinistas was due both to their exasperation over the ineffectiveness of electoral opposition and to a significant shift in strategy by the FSLN. Ideological differences emerged within the guerrilla movement in 1975. After the FSLN's founder, Carlos Fonseca Amador, was killed in combat in 1976, the Sandinistas split into three factions. The traditional strategy of rural-based guerrilla warfare was upheld by the Prolonged People's War Tendency (Guerra Popular Prolongada), while the Proletarian Tendency (Tendencia Proletaria) advocated a shift to political work among the urban proletariat. Both groups agreed, however, that the time was not ripe for major military actions, and both rejected extensive cooperation with "bourgeois elements."

A third group, the Insurrectional Tendency (Tendencia Insurreccional, known popularly as the Terceristas), shared neither of these views. Believing that opposition to Somoza had become nearly universal, they favored exemplary military action to spark popular insurrection. Most significant, they also advocated the unity of all opposition forces around a program of social reform and democracy.[27] It was the Terceristas who carried out the October 1977 attacks, and it was they who set about building links to the moderate opposition through Los Doce. Still, as 1978 began, the Sandinistas had neither the political nor the military strength to offer a serious challenge to the Somoza regime.

Sandino's Revenge: The Revolution in Nicaragua

On January 10, 1978, Pedro Joaquín Chamorro, the popular opposition leader and editor of La Prensa, was assassinated in Managua. The city erupted in a paroxysm of outrage and spontaneous violence. After several weeks of riots, Nicaragua's business leaders called a general strike with a single demand—Somoza's resignation. The two-week strike was 90 percent effective. Midway through it, the Terceristas added their endorsement and launched military attacks in several cities. The insurrection against Somoza had begun.[28]

For the next twelve months, the country was rocked by sporadic violence—strikes, demonstrations, and street fighting—most of it uncoordinated, organized by a widely disparate array of opposition groups. During this crucial period, the political initiative slipped inexorably from Somoza's moderate opponents to the guerrillas. The Sandinistas spent those months gathering their forces, stockpiling arms, and organizing the urban and rural poor.[29] The moderates waited for the United States to push Somoza out of power. Paralyzed by their inability to bring down Somoza by themselves and by their fear of the Sandinistas' radicalism, the moderates expected the United States to act for them. They were encouraged in this belief by the Carter administration's earlier condemnation of Somoza's human rights record and by the shared interest in avoiding a Sandinista victory. Yet Washington, too, seemed paralyzed during those crucial months. Its ambivalent response dashed the moderate's hopes and drained their political strength, leaving them to play second fiddle to the FSLN's military might.[30]

As Nicaragua's stability slipped away, U.S. policy was caught in the pull of opposing imperatives. The assassination laid bare the fragility of Somoza's rule. Faced with the specter of political chaos, the administration's desire to promote human rights was forced to compete with resurgent concerns about national security. Should the United States stand by its advocacy of human rights and democratic reform in the face of Somoza's deteriorating political position? Or should human rights be relegated to second place behind political stability, long provided by a brutal but reliable U.S. ally?

Within the administration, conflicting evaluations of the situation reflected both bureaucratic divisions and differences in outlook between career professionals and political appointees. In the State Department's Latin American Bureau, Assistant Secretary Terence Todman and his staff of foreign service officers were skeptical that much good could come of Carter's human rights policy. Todman argued that it was largely responsible for Somoza's difficulties and that the United States could ill afford to further undermine him. This view was echoed in the Pentagon, where the uniformed military was chagrined that Carter's preferred punishment for human rights violators was to withdraw military aid.[31] To these traditionalists, Somoza was a loyal ally and the most reliable bulwark against the Marxist guerrillas.

Carter's political appointees, on the other hand, resisted any backsliding on the policy of distancing the United States from Somoza. At the State Department's Bureau of Human Rights and Humanitarian Affairs, Assistant Secretary Patricia Derian regarded the Latin American Bureau's warnings about Nicaragua as little more than an excuse to abandon a human rights policy that the bureau had never really liked. Anthony Lake (the State Department's director of policy planning), Richard Feinberg (Lake's specialist on Latin America), and Robert Pastor (National Security Council staff specialist on Latin America) all opposed an active U.S. role in the growing Nicaraguan crisis. One reason was President Carter's expressed commitment to nonintervention. They saw Nicaragua as a test of whether Washington could resist the traditional temptation to take charge whenever events in Latin America began to go awry. The other reason was more practical. If the administration became deeply involved in trying to resolve the Nicaraguan conflict and failed, Carter would be blamed for the resulting bloodshed or, worse yet, a Sandinista triumph.[32]

The administration was unable to reconcile its conflicting priorities into a clear, coherent policy. It could not bring itself to jettison such an old and reliable ally by breaking completely with Somoza, but neither was it willing to become an accomplice in Somoza's repression by resuming military aid to the National Guard. So Washington equivocated.

While the administration wrestled with this dilemma, it was also buffeted by powerful congressional factions: liberals urging a complete break with the decaying regime, conservatives demanding that Carter come to the aid of a loyal ally. The "Nicaragua Lobby"—a small but powerful group of legislators whom Somoza had cultivated as friends and supporters—was the most influential. It was led by Representative John Murphy (D-N.Y.), a boyhood friend of

Somoza and his classmate at LaSalle Military Academy on Long Island. Murphy was in constant contact with Somoza during the entire Nicaraguan crisis, speaking with him several times a week and traveling regularly to Nicaragua to give Somoza advice. When newly appointed U.S. Ambassador Lawrence Pezzullo met Somoza for the first time at the height of the crisis in June 1979, Murphy was there, sitting on the edge of Somoza's desk, acting as his adviser and "witness."[33]

The interplay of forces, both within the executive branch and between the executive branch and Congress, resulted in a policy that was more a product of bureaucratic compromise than of a clear assessment of U.S. interests. Washington's contradictory actions confounded and demoralized Nicaragua's moderates, destroying their confidence in the United States and driving them, in desperation, into open alliance with the Sandinistas. In this regard, nothing was more damaging than the letter President Carter sent to Somoza in July 1978.

Carter wrote Somoza congratulating him on his recent promise to improve human rights and urging him to carry it through.[34] It was arguably the worst policy error made by the United States during the Nicaraguan crisis. The letter was leaked to the press almost immediately and was interpreted as an endorsement of Somoza's rule. It stiffened Somoza's resistance to compromise with the opposition and convinced his moderate opponents that their strategy of relying on the United States to force him out was hopeless.[35] Their only practical alternative, then, was to join forces with the radical opposition. The result was the creation of the Broad Opposition Front (Frente Amplio Opositor, FAO), the first coalition uniting the moderate and radical wings of the anti-Somoza movement.

In August 1978, guerrillas commanded by Edén Pastora, Comandante Cero, seized the National Palace while the Congress was in session, taking 1,500 hostages. The Sandinistas' audacity captured the popular imagination and with it the leadership of the anti-Somoza struggle. As the attackers and fifty-nine newly freed political prisoners drove to the airport for a flight to Panama, thousands of Nicaraguans lined the streets to cheer their triumph.

The palace assault was followed swiftly by a new general strike, and in September the Sandinistas repeated their action of the previous October by launching small-scale attacks on National Guard garrisons in several cities. This time, however, the attacks sparked insurrections in half a dozen cities, all of which fell under guerrilla control. To retake them, the National Guard bombed the cities indiscriminately. It took nearly two weeks and over three thousand dead before the Guard prevailed. When the Sandinistas withdrew, taking thousands of new recruits with them, the Guard "mopped-up" with hundreds of summary executions of teenage boys. After the carnage of September 1978, no compromise that would retain Somoza in power was possible.[36]

The spectacle of Somoza's National Guard waging war against its own citizenry convinced the State Department that Somoza would never be able to restore stability and thus prompted a reevaluation of U.S. policy. The FSLN's unexpected strength and support raised the specter of an eventual Sandinista victory unless some sort of "political solution" could replace Somoza with a moderate government. Nicaragua was no longer just a human rights problem. The debate within the U.S. government became more urgent.

Assistant Secretary of State Todman's obstructionist attitude toward the administration's human rights policy led Carter to replace him in August 1978 with Ambassador Viron P. "Pete" Vaky. Vaky came to his new post from a long and distinguished career in the Foreign Service, having served as U.S. ambassador to several Latin American countries. Vaky supported Carter's human rights policy, but he also shared the Latin American Bureau's belief that Washington needed to get more directly involved in the Nicaraguan crisis. The longer Somoza stayed, the more his presence would radicalize the opposition, increasing the likelihood of a Sandinista victory. Vaky argued strenuously for Washington to exert whatever pressure was necessary to force Somoza's resignation and engineer a moderate succession.[37]

Robert Pastor and Anthony Lake, on the other hand, were even more determined to prevent the administration from being drawn into the Nicaraguan vortex. After the bloodshed of September, they agreed that Somoza ought to leave, but Vaky's proposal that Washington force Somoza out quickly smacked too much of old-style intervention. Moreover, even if it succeeded, the consequences were unpredictable. Since the whole Nicaraguan regime, especially the National Guard, was built around the Somoza family, there was no guarantee that it would not simply disintegrate after Somoza left. The moderate opposition was fragmented, poorly organized, and had virtually no experience governing. There was reasonable doubt as to whether they could fill the political vacuum left by Somoza's departure. They might simply play Kerensky to the Sandinista's Bolsheviks—a particular worry of National Security Adviser Zbigniew Brzezinski.[38]

Whatever happened, though, Washington would be held responsible. "In my own mind was the experience of the American-approved coups in Saigon in late 1963 and 1964, which had ushered in a period of severe instability," Lake wrote later.[39] A collapse in Nicaragua, brought on by Carter forcing Somoza out, would have serious domestic political implications; Carter was already under attack from conservatives for selling out U.S. allies in the Third World.[40]

The debate between Vaky's activism and the caution of Pastor and Lake was never fully resolved. U.S. policy after September was to ease Somoza out, as Vaky wanted, but not to coerce him into leaving or even to say publicly that this was Washington's preference—far short of what Vaky thought necessary to accomplish the task at hand.[41] But one overriding fear gave some coherence to U.S. policy during the last eight months of the Somoza dynasty—the fear that Somoza's demise would herald victory for the Sandinistas, who, week by week, were capturing the political initiative. The Carter administration's unambiguous objective was to prevent the Sandinistas from coming to power. The disagreements were always about how best to do it.[42]

At Washington's initiative, the Organization of American States (OAS) met in late September to assess the Nicaraguan crisis and authorized the United States, Guatemala, and the Dominican Republic to undertake a mediation effort between Somoza and his opponents. Washington's aim was to devise a formula for peaceful transition to a new government of moderates that would either exclude the Sandinistas or restrict them to minimal participation.[43] Initially, Somoza and the Broad Opposition Front (FAO) would not even meet together; proposals had to be carried back and forth by the mediators. The FAO demanded Somoza's immediate resignation and exile, followed by an interim government dominated by the opposition. Somoza countered by calling for a plebiscite on who should govern—a plebiscite that he and the National Guard would conduct.

Despite Vaky's conviction that Somoza's offer was a stalling tactic, Secretary of State Cyrus Vance, along with Brzezinski and the president, thought the idea had merit, so long as the plebiscite was internationally supervised to guarantee its honesty. U.S. mediator William Bowdler dutifully talked the skeptical FAO into accepting such a plan, though not before several of its constituent organizations quit in disgust. "A river of blood separates us," one FAO member said of Somoza. "How can we sit down and negotiate with a man who has just slaughtered three thousand Nicaraguans?"[44] In the end, Somoza would not agree to anything but a "traditional" election that he could manipulate; his advisers had warned him that he would lose a fair contest. On January 18, 1979, the mediation collapsed in failure.[45]

The mediation process severely damaged the moderate opposition. By pressuring the FAO to abandon its call for Somoza's immediate resignation and to negotiate directly with the regime, the United States undermined the moderates' unity and credibility. The Sandinistas, fearing that a mediated settlement would exclude them and leave the National Guard intact, denounced the idea as "*Somocismo sin Somoza*"—the maintenance of the Somoza regime without the dictator himself.[46] By the time Somoza finally rejected the plebiscite proposal, the moderate opposition was so fragmented and demoralized that it could play no more than a subsidiary role in the climactic battles to come.

Somoza played the mediation masterfully. For nearly three months, the United States tried to cajole him into making meaningful concessions while publicly repeating over and over that it did not seek his resignation. By stalling for time, he was able to reinforce the National Guard and fracture the moderate opposition. His gamble, in essence, was that if the United States faced a clear and unequivocal choice between Somoza and the Sandinistas, it would eventually come to his aid. "I think he felt that if he could polarize [the situation] and make it . . . Somoza versus the Marxists that the United States and everybody else would rally to him," Pete Vaky recalled. "And he always used the argument of *après moi le déluge.*"[47]

Despite U.S. warnings that a collapse of the mediation would affect the "whole gamut" of relations with Nicaragua, the sanctions imposed when Somoza rejected the final mediation proposal were relatively mild. The Peace Corps and the four-man U.S. military mission were withdrawn, military aid (already suspended) was terminated, and the embassy staff was cut by half. Economic aid was unaffected, however, and Washington still refused to publicly call for Somoza to resign.[48]

Washington's weak response was due in part to Somoza's apparent strength. By May 1979, his moderate opponents were in disarray, the Sandinistas were relatively silent, and the National Guard had doubled in size. United States intelligence analysts were predicting that through sheer firepower the Guard could defeat any offensive the FSLN could launch.[49] It looked as if Somoza might be able to survive after all. Brzezinski, for one, felt safer sticking with an unpopular but powerful Somoza rather than pushing him out in favor of the politically divided and isolated moderates. In May, the United States supported $65 million in loans to Nicaragua from the International Monetary Fund (IMF)—loans that Washington had blocked in November 1978 because Somoza refused to cooperate with the mediation.[50]

When the FSLN launched its "final offensive" in late May 1979, any illusions about the viability of the regime quickly melted away. Within weeks, the Sandinistas controlled the nation's major cities, virtually all the countryside, and half of Managua. Bowdler was dispatched to Latin America in search of some multilateral formula for reviving the mediation, but found many of Washington's allies supporting the FSLN.[51]

As the fighting intensified, the Nicaragua Lobby stepped up pressure on Carter to come to Somoza's aid. One hundred members of the House and five senators signed full-page advertisements in the *New York Times* and *Washington Post* in late June denouncing the administration's indifference to Somoza's plight and calling on Carter to resume military assistance.[52]

After June 20, however, most of the domestic political pressure on the administration came from the opposite direction. That morning, ABC News correspondent Bill Stewart and his crew were out covering the war when they came upon a National Guard outpost. Stewart approached the guardsmen, who forced him to kneel and then lie facedown on the ground. While Stewart's crew filmed the scene from their van, one of the soldiers nonchalantly raised his rifle and shot Stewart point-blank in the head, killing him. The murder was shown that evening on the news, and the outpouring of public emotion was intense—"unlike anything I had seen since I had been in the White House," Pastor wrote.[53] After Stewart's murder, few members of Congress were willing to publicly defend Somoza or his National Guard.

At Washington's initiative, another special OAS meeting was convened June 21, to discuss the Nicaraguan crisis. Secretary Vance outlined the U.S. position, beginning with Washington's first public call for Somoza's resignation. The rest of the U.S. proposal, however, was largely oblivious to political realities in both Nicaragua and the OAS. Making no mention of the Provisional Government for National Reconstruction appointed only days earlier by the Sandinistas and their allies, Vance called for a "broad based representative government," and an OAS "peace-keeping force" to restore order and enforce a cease-fire. Not incidentally, such a force would also have prevented the Sandinistas from winning the war and retained the National Guard intact.[54]

The reaction to Vance's proposal marked a nadir of U.S. influence in the OAS. The call for a peacekeeping force was widely condemned as a transparent effort to justify intervention against the FSLN.[55] The efforts of the U.S. delegation to raise the specter of Cuban involvement as justification for the peace-keeping force convinced no one, since at least half a dozen other Latin American states were also providing aid to the Sandinistas.[56]

After the September 1978 insurrection, the cast of foreign powers entering the Nicaraguan fray had increased rapidly. Costa Rica, Venezuela, Panama, and Cuba undertook a loosely coordinated effort to provide the Sandinistas with arms. Mexico, Peru, Ecuador, and Bolivia added their diplomatic support for the insurgents. On the other side of the battle lines, Israel, Spain, Argentina, Brazil, Honduras, Guatemala, and El Salvador came to Somoza's aid, replenishing his depleted military stocks.[57]

Until the last few weeks of the war, the Cubans' role was limited. They increased their training of FSLN combatants, provided a few arms shipments, and helped the Sandinistas establish contact with other international arms sources.

Their most important contribution was to mediate the differences between the FSLN's three factions.[58] As a result, Sandinista leaders concluded an agreement in March 1979 that reunified the movement by creating a nine-member National Directorate with three members drawn from each faction.[59]

Most of the arms for the final phase of the war were provided by Venezuela and Panama, which shipped them to Nicaragua through Costa Rica. Cuban arms shipments only became significant in the last few weeks, replacing Venezuelan support, which declined after Christian Democrat Luis Herrera Campins replaced Social Democrat Carlos Andrés Pérez as Venezuela's president.[60] Cuba had good reasons for pursuing what the Central Intelligence Agency described as a "low-key approach" to aiding the FSLN. Foremost among them was the fear that significant Cuban involvement would trigger a resumption of U.S. military aid to Somoza, thereby doing the revolutionary cause more harm than good.[61]

Nevertheless, it was the Cuban presence that most concerned Brzezinski. To him, the importance of the Nicaraguan crisis lay in its implications for the East-West conflict; it was a test of U.S. credibility "in our own backyard." If Washington failed to intervene, Fidel Castro would fill the "vacuum," he argued. "We have to demonstrate that we are still the decisive force in determining political outcomes in Central America and that we will not permit others to intervene."[62] A more concise rendition of the Roosevelt Corollary to the Monroe Doctrine would be hard to find.

After the OAS repudiated Washington's "peacekeeping" proposal, Brzezinski argued for a unilateral U.S. intervention to block a Sandinista victory. President Carter refused to consider such a step in the face of unanimous Latin American opposition.[63] In the Carter White House, both the instincts of the Roosevelt Corollary and the spirit of Franklin Roosevelt's Good Neighbor Policy could be found in uneasy cohabitation.

From Washington's perspective, the one positive outcome of the OAS meeting was the passage of the final resolution calling upon member states to "facilitate an enduring and peaceful solution of the Nicaraguan problem."[64] The United States took this as sufficient mandate to try once again to fashion a mediated settlement. With all of Nicaragua engulfed in battle, the United States began an attempt to construct a "constitutionalist" solution. Somoza would resign in favor of a constitutional successor who would then appoint an "executive committee" of prominent, independent Nicaraguans and turn power over to them. The committee would mediate between Somoza's Liberal Party, the National Guard, and the opposition to create an interim government composed of all these forces. The interim government, with a reformed National Guard intact, would then hold elections in 1981.[65]

While the Sandinistas' strength was obviously too great to completely freeze them out of any post-Somoza government, the goal of U.S. policy was still to minimize their influence. The key was keeping the National Guard as a military bulwark against the Sandinista guerrilla army. "With careful orchestration, we have a better than even chance of preserving enough of the GN [Guardia Nacional] to maintain order and hold the Sandinistas in check after Somoza resigns," Ambassador Pezzullo optimistically reported in late June.[66]

The main difference between the "executive committee" plan and the U.S. position during the earlier mediation was Washington's willingness to force Somoza's resignation. "We don't see a solution without your departure," Ambassador Pezzullo bluntly told Somoza when they first met on June 27. "We don't see the *beginning* of a solution without your departure." Surprisingly, Somoza seemed to accept the inevitable. On June 28, he told Pezzullo he was willing to resign and asked when he should leave.[67]

Had the United States been willing to demand Somoza's resignation nine months earlier, a constitutional solution might have been feasible. By July 1979, however, even the most conservative Nicaraguan opposition groups had already endorsed the Sandinistas' Provisional Government, which rejected the U.S. plan outright. Washington could find no prominent Nicaraguans to serve on the governing council it sought to construct; they were all supporting the Sandinistas. "You raised our hopes during the mediation, but you failed us," moderate Ismael Reyes replied when Pezzullo tried to recruit him to the U.S.-backed council. "It is too late, way too late to be devising schemes."[68]

The universal rejection of the constitutional succession plan finally convinced U.S. officials that the Provisional Government would inevitably come to power. Washington shifted gears and sought to negotiate terms of transition that would limit the Sandinistas' influence. In this endeavor, the United States had two levers: its ability to control the timing of Somoza's departure, and its willingness to provide economic aid if the new government was acceptable to Washington.

In exchange for Somoza's resignation, the Carter administration wanted two moderates added to the Provisional Government's five-member junta and a guarantee that neither Somoza's Liberal Party nor the National Guard would be dismantled. Recognizing full well that Washington was negotiating with them only because its attempts to supplant them had come to naught, the junta flatly rejected the U.S. proposal.[69] Despite pressure from the United States and several Latin American countries which had aided the FSLN, the junta would do no more than guarantee the lives of Somoza's cronies and National Guardsmen and leave open the possibility that "honest" members of the Guard might join the new national army. The battlefield situation, plus the moderate tenor of the Provisional Government's program and cabinet, finally led the United States to accept its terms. "The problem," a U.S. official lamented, "is that you cannot take away from the Sandinistas at the conference table what they have won on the battlefield."[70]

On July 17, 1979, President Anastasio Somoza Debayle and the senior command of the National Guard flew into exile in Miami.[71] The Guard proceeded to disintegrate ignominiously and within twenty-four hours had ceased to exist. Even the face-saving transition crafted by Pezzullo collapsed when Somoza's successor, Congressman Francisco Urcuyo, refused to play the role scripted for him. Instead of immediately turning power over to the Provisional Government, Urcuyo declared his intention to stay in office. This farcical performance ended abruptly when Somoza called from Miami and told Urcuyo to resign, lest the United States deport Somoza back to Nicaragua.[72] Urcuyo followed Somoza into exile as Sandinista troops rolled into Managua. Thus was realized the very eventuality U.S. policy since January 1978 had sought to avoid—a complete Sandinista military victory.

An "Acceptable Model" of Revolution

The Government of National Reconstruction that took power on July 19 represented an unlikely alliance of conservative businessmen and Marxist guerrillas. The partnership was fragile from the outset, resisted by people on both sides, but consummated by their common hatred of Somoza. The guerrillas needed the private sector's prestige and influence to legitimize their revolution both at home and abroad; the businessmen needed the guerrillas' guns to defeat the dictatorship.

In the euphoria of victory, guerrillas and businessmen alike pledged to sustain their partnership, dedicating themselves to the task of rebuilding an economy devastated by war. Both the program and the composition of the new government were delicately balanced between the new partners. A social democratic program promised a mixed economy, political pluralism, and a foreign policy of nonalignment, but it remained purposefully vague on what these would mean in practice. The platform's ambiguity reflected its origins as a compromise between the radicalism of the FSLN and the conservatism of the private sector. It was not the product of a consensus for social democracy.

As in every postrevolutionary regime, the victorious coalition began to show signs of strain almost immediately. While formal power was shared—representatives of the private sector sat on the executive Junta of Government and predominated in the cabinet—it soon became clear that real power lay in the nine-member National Directorate of the FSLN.[73] The businessmen, who had opposed Somoza because he froze them out of government and encroached upon their business ventures, began to wonder if they had gained much. The Sandinistas seemed no more willing to share political power, and their commitment to improving living conditions for the poor threatened the private sector's economic interests. Before the revolution reached its first anniversary, most of the private sector had gone into opposition.

The Sandinistas' "popular project" was socialist. At a minimum, it entailed a radical redistribution of wealth and income and the creation of an extensive social welfare system. The government conducted a national literacy campaign, made basic health care and education free, and initiated agrarian reform. Beyond this basic program, however, the FSLN was divided over the shape of things to come.[74]

Moderates in the National Directorate, led by brothers Daniel and Humberto Ortega, hoped to reach a lasting accommodation with the private sector in which it would contribute to economic development in exchange for the right to make a modest profit and the right to limited participation in politics.[75] The moderates were motivated by necessity; the government did not have the technical capacity to centrally plan a nationalized economy, and no major international donor—including the Soviet Union—was willing to provide the external financing required to sustain a Cuban model of development. On the other hand, Sandinista radicals, led by Tomás Borge and Bayardo Arce, doubted that a long-term accommodation with the private sector was possible. They regarded the bourgeoisie as a class enemy and advocated doing away with it in order to build Nicaragua in the image of Communist Cuba. Ironically, Fidel Castro himself cautioned against such a strategy. "He warned us not to repeat Cuba's mistakes," recalled a Sandinista official who met with Castro within days of Somoza's fall. "He told us to avoid a confrontation with the United States, to maintain good relations with the church, [and] to preserve a private sector."[76]

The Sandinistas held a near monopoly on political power. The defeat of the National Guard left the FSLN as the only effective military force, and it soon organized its combatants into a new national army. The FSLN was also the best organized political party, the only one able to mobilize mass popular support through its ancillary "mass organizations" of workers, farmers, women, and students. The FSLN's most important political advantage was the least tangible: the legitimacy that derived from having defeated a hated dictator. When teenagers in Nicaragua's cities held off the National Guard with hunting rifles, they called themselves Sandinistas, and when victory was won, the cheers and banners that filled the plaza in Managua were the slogans and emblems of the FSLN.

The Sandinistas never outlawed other parties, but their vision of the polity was less than pluralistic. They conceived of themselves as a political vanguard that would hold hegemony while directing a revolutionary transformation of Nicaraguan society.[77] The Sandinistas tried to use their control of the state to force the private sector to cooperate with the government's economic plans, offering tax incentives and cheap credit for compliance, while threatening expropriation as the penalty for decapitalization.

The private sector, for its part, sought to regain enough political power to safeguard its economic interests. Few of its members were willing to accept the Sandinista prescription that they play a passive role in a one-party state. The business community also had its moderates, who were willing to reach an accommodation with the FSLN based on democratic socialism, and its hard-liners, who regarded the Sandinistas as unreconstructed Communists who would have to be overthrown.[78]

Fragmented in a welter of civic and business groups, the opposition was badly disorganized. It had to rely on the same weapons it used to good effect against Somoza: control over the economy and enough foreign contacts to make or break the international reputation of the regime. The private sector tried to use its economic muscle to extract political concessions from the Sandinistas, warning that the "rules of the game" both economically and politically had to be codified in law before business confidence would improve enough to spur production. Despite their tenuous political position, most businessmen were nevertheless determined to stay in Nicaragua and struggle with the Sandinistas for the right to define Nicaragua's future. "We are not like the Cuban upper class," vowed one Nicaraguan businessman. "We are not going to Miami."[79]

The United States decided to make the best of the Sandinista victory. "The worst alternative took place, but maybe it was still a ball game," Pete Vaky recalled. "The options were not good, but there were other options that were bad and worse."[80] In the wake of Somoza's defeat, U.S. policy shifted 180 degrees, from an attitude of outright hostility toward the Sandinistas to an attitude of cautious acceptance. The change was no less stark for having been forced by circumstances, since it implied that even radical social and political change did not necessarily endanger the vital interests of the United States.

Nevertheless, considerable mistrust lay below the surface of this peculiar friendship. The long history of U.S. support for Somoza could not be wholly forgiven or forgotten by Nicaragua's new leaders, nor could they shake the fear and suspicion that the United States might yet concoct a counterrevolutionary scheme to rob them of their victory. In Washington, policymakers could not ignore the Marxist origins of many Sandinista leaders, even though Somoza's defeat had been engineered by a politically heterogeneous multiclass coalition. There was always the possibility that the guerrillas, having won power, would shed their moderate garb, dump their middle-class allies, and steer the revolution sharply to the left, down the road of Cuban-style Marxism-Leninism.

Yet the interests of both Nicaragua and the United States lay in maintaining friendly relations. Nicaragua was in desperate need of foreign assistance to help rebuild its shattered economy. International assistance from Western Europe and the international financial institutions would tend to follow the lead of the United States. A deterioration of U.S.-Nicaraguan relations would have economic ramifications far beyond the aid dollars from Washington alone.

For the United States, maintaining cordial relations was a means of salvaging something from the failure to keep the Sandinistas out of power. From Washington's perspective, the struggle to control the succession to Somoza had been "lost," but perhaps Nicaragua itself need not be. The Carter administration set out, quite consciously, to avoid repeating the errors of 1959–60, when U.S. hostility contributed to the radicalization of the Cuban revolution and its alignment with the Soviet Union.[81] "We should stay out of the 'foreign devil' role, which they'd just love to put us in," Ambassador Pezzullo said of Washington's new relationship with the Sandinistas.[82] Administration officials resolved to create an environment in which the incentives would impel the Sandinistas to follow the least radical path. "The Sandinistas are wearing a moderate mask," observed a senior State Department official. "Our job is to nail it on."[83]

In the immediate aftermath of the insurrection, the United States provided $10 million to $15 million in emergency relief to help feed and house the thousands of people displaced by the war. This was followed in September 1979 by $8.5 million in "reprogrammed" economic assistance—money reallocated to Nicaragua from other foreign aid accounts.[84]

In addition, the State Department drew up an $80 million supplemental foreign aid request for Central America for fiscal year 1980, $75 million of which was for Nicaragua. Although the proposal was ready in August 1979, it was not sent to Congress until November.[85] The delay was due partly to debates within the administration over whether to resume military aid to El Salvador, Guatemala, and Honduras. By submitting a request that included both economic aid for Nicaragua and $5 million in renewed military aid for right-wing governments, the administration hoped to disarm both its conservative and liberal critics.[86] Another reason for the delay was more political. With the U.S. election campaign getting under way, the administration sought to minimize its vulnerability by waiting a few months to be sure the Sandinistas did not immediately steer the revolution to the far left.

The aid bill passed the Senate in January 1980 with only minor amendments. The battle in the House was much tougher. Conservative Republicans succeeded in attaching sixteen conditions to the bill. Aid would be terminated if Nicaragua engaged in a consistent pattern of gross human rights violations, aided or abetted acts of violence in another country, allowed Cuban or Soviet combat troops to be stationed in Nicaragua, violated the right of unions to organize and operate, or violated the rights of free speech and press.[87]

On February 27, 1980, after four days of debate, the aid bill passed the House by only five votes, 202–197. The most persuasive lobbyists in its favor were members of the Nicaraguan private sector, who argued that without U.S. aid, their economic and political position in Nicaragua would be untenable. On May 19, the Senate adopted the House version of the supplemental because the House leadership could not muster the votes needed to send the bill to the joint conference committee to resolve the differences between the House and Senate versions.[88]

But even after the aid bill became law, the odyssey was not over. Before the funds could be disbursed, the president was required to certify that Nicaragua was not exporting revolution to its neighbors. Conservatives in the CIA and Defense Intelligence Agency were convinced that the Sandinistas were supporting the Salvadoran guerrillas. Intelligence information collected during 1980 indicated quite clearly that some Nicaraguans had been aiding the Salvadorans and that arms were being shipped from Costa Rica through Nicaragua and Honduras to El Salvador. A summary CIA report of the available intelligence concluded, "There is a very high likelihood that such support . . . represent[s] official FSLN policy."[89]

The Department of State's Bureau of Intelligence and Research did not believe that the evidence against the Nicaraguan government was so definitive. After all, the Salvadorans were smuggling arms through Costa Rica, Honduras, Mexico, and Guatemala, too, but no one suggested those governments were implicated.[90] State Department officials still held out hope that a conciliatory policy from Washington would convince the Sandinistas to restrain their involvement in neighboring countries.

On September 12, Carter certified that Nicaragua "has not cooperated with or harbors any international terrorist organization or is aiding, abetting, or supporting acts of violence or terrorism in other countries."[91] Nevertheless, the evidence of Sandinista involvement was suggestive enough that Ambassador Pezzullo issued a stern warning and reminder to Sandinista officials that U.S. aid would remain contingent on their good behavior. Deputy Assistant Secretary of State James Cheek made a special trip to Nicaragua to repeat the warning.[92] With the certification duly made, aid to Nicaragua finally began to flow—over a year after the aid proposal had first been drafted.

The Carter administration's objectives in post-Somoza Nicaragua were modest, realistically suited to a situation in which the United States had limited leverage. Everyone expected the Sandinistas to have friendly relations with Cuba, which had consistently supported them during their years of struggle against Somoza. The administration had no illusions that it could block such a relationship, but hoped to minimize it in the military field, so that it would not threaten Nicaragua's neighbors.[93] Washington also expected the Sandinistas to provide some aid to the Salvadoran guerrillas since the Salvadorans had contributed funds to the insurrection against Somoza. But the administration hoped to restrain the Sandinistas so they would not become a major factor in El Salvador's revolutionary war.

Finally, Washington recognized that Nicaragua's revolutionary coalition was inherently unstable. The Sandinistas' radical plans could only be pursued at the expense of their upper-class and middle-class allies, which would inevitably generate political conflict. The administration's objective was to keep this conflict within reasonable bounds, avoiding a radicalization of the revolution that would eliminate the private sector and any vestige of political pluralism.[94]

For a year and a half—until Ronald Reagan's election—Carter's strategy worked reasonably well. None of the worst fears of either side materialized. Despite conflicts between the Sandinistas and the private sector, capitalism was not abolished and political pluralism, though not robust, survived. On occasion, Ambassador Pezzullo acted as mediator between the government and the opposition to prevent their disputes from escalating into apocalyptic confrontation. The United States provided emergency economic assistance and offered neither aid nor comfort to the Somocista exiles plotting a return to power from Honduras.[95] A year after the fall of the dynasty, Ambassador Pezzullo could declare that Nicaragua was an "acceptable model" of revolution.[96]

Nevertheless, the Carter administration's strategy of engineering a moderate transition to keep the Sandinistas out of power was a dismal failure, largely because of Washington's inability to realistically assess the balance of political forces in Nicaragua and the depth of popular animosity toward Somoza. Nicaragua had been under U.S. influence for so long that policymakers badly overestimated their ability to manage events. Washington was, as Pete Vaky said, "always behind the curve."[97]

Yet in the year and a half after the Sandinista victory, Carter managed to chart out a policy that was both realistic and successful, as far as it went. In November 1980, when he lost the presidency to Ronald Reagan, U.S.-Nicaraguan relations were constructive and the radicalization of the revolution that Carter sought to avert had not happened. Nicaragua had not become another Cuba.

El Salvador: Oligarchs and Officers

In Washington, the fall of Somoza conjured up images of toppling dominoes in Central America and prompted a major review of U.S. policy to prevent similar guerrilla victories in El Salvador and Guatemala. At issue was the question never adequately addressed during the Nicaraguan crisis: How could the Carter administration reconcile its commitment to human rights with its desire to preserve political stability?

Advocates divided roughly into two camps, paralleling the divisions that existed over how to respond to the insurrection against Somoza.[98] Hard-liners in the Department of Defense and on the National Security Council staff argued that these objectives were inherently contradictory. They pointed out that Washington's criticism of Somoza's human rights record had undermined his rule by encouraging his opponents and depriving him of the military means to maintain order. Central America, so the argument went, was not as stable as it had appeared in 1977, and the spread of insurgency brought the issue of U.S. national security back to the top of the policy agenda. The hard-liners argued for restoring military assistance to the region's anti-Communists, even at the expense of human rights—in essence, a return to Kissinger's policy of supporting friendly dictators.

Defenders of the human rights policy replied that military aid could not buy stability. The oligarchic social order and dictatorial politics of Central America's ancien régimes were anachronisms that could not long survive mounting popular demands for change. The old policy of supporting traditional elites was fruitless, for it could neither contain nor resolve the growing crisis. Rather than enlisting on the side of military regimes fated for extinction, they argued, the United States should seek to manage the inevitable process of change, pursuing fundamental reform through evolutionary means. This view was most forcefully articulated by Assistant Secretary of State Vaky. "Change cannot be avoided," he told the Congress. "Defense of the status quo cannot prevent it or cap instability for long; it can only radicalize the dynamics at work. . . . The central issue is not whether change is to occur, but whether the change is to be violent and radical, or peaceful and evolutionary."[99] Vaky's view prevailed, although like most bureaucratic victories, its triumph was incomplete. Military aid was resumed to El Salvador and Honduras, but at low levels, and, in the Salvadoran case, was restricted to nonlethal materials.

Implicitly, the management of change meant—as it had during President John F. Kennedy's Alliance for Progress—a search for "openings to the center" combined with policies designed to contain the left. Once again, the United States would prescribe reform as the antidote to revolution. The unspoken dilemma in this formulation was the dilemma that had doomed the Alliance two decades before. By arming existing regimes to contain insurgency, Washington would end up arming the very conservative elites it sought to replace with reformers. Once armed, incumbents would have little incentive to accept even modest change.

The clearest test of the Carter administration's policy of promoting reform came in El Salvador, a country burdened with one of the most rigid class structures in all of Latin America.[100] For over a century, the social and economic life of the nation had been dominated by a small landed elite known popularly as "the fourteen families" (*Los Catorce*), though their actual number was larger. The family clans composing the oligarchy included only a few thousand people in a nation of nearly five million, but they owned 60 percent of the farmland, the entire banking system, and most of the nation's industry. The richest 8 percent of the population received 50 percent of the national income.[101]

The tensions inherent in this social structure were exacerbated by severe population pressure on the land. With over 600 people per square mile, El Salvador's population density was the highest in Latin America. Over a quarter of rural families (26.1 percent) were completely landless, and another 60.6 percent owned too little land to support a family.[102] Unlike most of its neighbors, El Salvador had no undeveloped land for surplus agricultural labor to settle; cultivation extended up the slopes of active volcanoes. Illegal emigration to less populous Honduras acted as a safety valve for the potentially explosive situation in the countryside, until the 1969 "Soccer War" between the two countries forced some 25,000 impoverished peasants back to El Salvador and closed the border.[103] An expanding manufacturing sector offered another alternative to rural laborers, but the war with Honduras also pushed the economy into a recession from which it never fully recovered.

The dominance of the oligarchy and the persistence of rural poverty produced an immense potential for class conflict. For decades, the oligarchy's primary political objective was to prevent this latent cleavage from erupting into class war. Despite its economic preeminence, the Salvadoran oligarchy exercised political hegemony indirectly. The military ruled El Salvador from 1932 onward, serving as the guardian of the oligarchy and suppressing by force any challenge to the established order. The history of Salvadoran government was largely a history of the twists and turns in the political alliance between oligarchs and officers.

The alliance was forged in 1932 when the armed forces under General Maximiliano Hernández Martínez took control of the government, suppressing a peasant uprising at a cost of between 10,000 and 30,000 dead—a bloodletting known in El Salvador as *La Matanza* (the Slaughter).[104] The psychic scars left by this abortive revolution and its brutal suppression disfigured the nation's political culture in ways that were still visible in 1979. For the oligarchy, the growth of even moderate opposition always raised the specter of 1932. A strong current of belief persisted among them that the threat of revolution could only be effectively met by bloody suppression.

The military shared the oligarchy's fear of revolution, though it occasionally opted for reform rather than repression as a more reliable bulwark against the left. The oligarchy tolerated a bit of reformism because it promised modernization without structural change. The army retained its monopoly on political power for half a century through alternating periods of reform and retrenchment, but two things held constant: the modernizing policies of the regime never threatened the social and economic foundations of oligarchic power, and the military never allowed the political system to become so open that reformist civilians might actually win control of the government.

This practical partnership between the oligarchy and the army gave birth to an electoral system that was largely a charade. Moderate opponents could vent their views in periodic elections, but control of the government was reserved for the military's own National Conciliation Party (Partido de Conciliación Nacional, PCN). Perpetual electoral victory for the military was guaranteed by the simple expedient of having the army count the ballots.[105]

In 1960, El Salvador joined with its four neighbors to form the Central American Common Market, creating a free trade area in the region and erecting regional tariff barriers to protect developing industry. After 1961, the efforts of the Common Market were boosted by assistance from the United States under the Alliance for Progress. Together, the Common Market and the Alliance were highly successful at promoting economic growth and industrialization, but yielded no gains in equity. Although El Salvador was touted as the Alliance showcase in Central America, by the early 1970s it was the only country in Latin America without even a semblance of agrarian reform legislation, and it was still illegal for peasants to organize politically.

In fact, economic growth proved to be destabilizing. As export agriculture expanded to earn hard currency to pay the costs of imported inputs to new industries, peasants were forced off the land. The living conditions of the poor deteriorated not just in relative terms, but absolutely.[106] Economic development also produced demographic growth in the urban middle class and working class, both of which bridled at the military's monopoly on political power. At issue was whether the military and its wealthy partners would allow the creation of a system of politics—that is, an institutional process for reconciling conflicting demands among the nation's significant social groups. The oligarchs preferred the security of authoritarianism to the uncertainty of electoral competition.

The brief but disruptive 1969 war with Honduras derailed the Salvadoran economy and thus set the stage for political turmoil in the 1970s. The proximate cause of political disorder, however, was the military's determination to maintain its monopoly on politics. By 1970, the Christian Democratic Party (Partido Demócrata Cristiano, PDC) had emerged as the principal focus of opposition. The opportune time for a "centrist solution" to El Salvador's social ills came in 1972 when the Christian Democrats stood at the summit of their popular support. The coalition headed by PDC presidential candidate José Napoleón Duarte and social democratic vice presidential candidate Guillermo Ungo won the 1972 presidential election. The military was able to snatch victory from the jaws of defeat only through blatant fraud and brutal suppression of the subsequent protests.

In the wake of this electoral fiasco, the army unleashed a wave of repression against the moderate opposition parties, destroying both their effectiveness and the viability of electoral opposition. Many civilian opposition leaders were driven into exile, while their rank-and-file supporters turned to the radical left. Three guerrilla organizations began operating during the 1970s and expanded as the center was demolished. The Popular Liberation Forces (Fuerzas Populares de Liberación) was founded in 1970 by radical university students and dissident Communist Party members, including the party's former general secretary, Salvador Cayetano Carpio. In 1972, another group of dissident Communists joined with radicals from the Christian Democrats to form the Revolutionary Army of the People (Ejército Revolucionario del Pueblo), which split in 1975, producing the rival Armed Forces of National Resistance (Fuerzas Armadas de Resistencia Nacional). The most impressive gains on the left were made by the "popular organizations." Begun at mid-decade, these coalitions of peasant, worker, and student unions pressed demands for immediate social improvements by staging militant mass demonstrations and acts of civil disobedience. Until early 1980, the popular organizations rarely mounted joint actions because of political disagreements that reflected rivalries among the armed groups, with which the popular organizations were affiliated.[107]

The Catholic Church also played a crucial role in mobilizing mass opposition to the regime. Historically, the church had been a pillar of the established order, pacifying the peasants with promises of paradise in the afterlife for those who stoically accepted misery on earth. But the role of the church began to change after the 1968 Conference of Latin American bishops in Medellín, Colombia. There, the bishops charted the applicability of the Second Vatican

Council to Latin America and accepted a new responsibility to minister to the poor. This new ministry soon evolved beyond the spiritual to engage social issues. The church became an advocate for the poor—criticizing governments and social classes who did nothing to alleviate the suffering of impoverished masses. When the authorities resorted to violence to suppress peaceful demands for change, the church spoke out in defense of human rights.[108]

In remote rural areas, the church organized peasants into local religious groups (Christian Base Communities)—a movement that touched a sensitive political nerve. Organized peasants with a growing sense of their own dignity inevitably began to make economic demands on their landlords. El Salvador's main peasant union in the 1970s grew out of such church-based rural communities.[109] Peasants demanding land reform were seen by landlords as subversive and were dealt with in the traditional way: they were murdered or "disappeared." The church was regarded as a promoter of such subversion, and activist priests began to be targeted as well; in the late 1970s, six priests were murdered by Salvadoran death squads with names such as the White Hand (El Mano Blanco) and the White Warriors' Union (Unión Guerrera Blanca). The squads operated with the active collaboration of the government's security forces (the National Guard, National Police, and Treasury Police).

The archbishop of San Salvador, Oscar Arnulfo Romero, was particularly outspoken in his defense of the poor, eloquently defending their right to a decent standard of living and to organize politically without fear of state violence. Romero had originally been selected as archbishop by the Vatican because he was more moderate than the other leading candidate. But as alternative voices of dissent were silenced by repression, Romero emerged by default as the leading critic of the regime.

As the violence mounted, he became ever more adamant in his criticism of the government's repression and ever more insistent on the need for peaceful social change. Romero's constant condemnation of human rights abuses and his insistence that the rich surrender some of their wealth in the name of social justice made him a hero to the poor and anathema to the far right. Oligarchs denounced him regularly. Despite a constant stream of death threats, he refused to accept any bodyguards—though most prominent figures in Salvadoran politics were surrounded by small armies of them.[110]

As the 1977 Salvadoran presidential election approached, the reign of the military modernizers showed unmistakable signs of decay. The government's sporadic attempts to enact a modest agrarian reform law between 1973 and 1976 were blocked by the oligarchy and the defense minister, General Humberto Romero (no relation to the archbishop). The moderate opposition, led by the Christian Democrats, was in retreat under the drumfire of repression, while both the armed and popular wings of the left were gaining strength. In the face of this growing crisis, the military signaled its determination to hold fast rather than compromise by nominating the conservative General Romero for the presidency. He won, of course.

With General Romero's "election," the regime of the military modernizers became a regime of military conservators. Despite popular demands for access to the political process, the armed forces refused to create a political order it could not control. By that refusal, it produced instead political disorder which no one could control. The deterioration of El Salvador's moribund polity commenced in earnest.

Avoiding Another Nicaragua

A small nation of little inherent strategic or economic importance, El Salvador seldom attracted much attention in Washington. Bilateral relations were ordinarily governed by regional policies the United States fashioned in response to exigencies elsewhere. The result was not always wholly sensible. When counterinsurgency was thought to be the antidote to Cuban-style revolution in the 1960s, the United States lavished military assistance on Latin America. El Salvador received some $4 million of this aid between 1961 and 1970, even though it had no revolutionaries to speak of at the time.[111] Naturally, the military government perceived the flow of arms as an endorsement.

Military assistance to El Salvador was interrupted when the Congress introduced human rights concerns into the allocation of foreign aid. In early 1977, El Salvador joined Guatemala, Brazil, and Argentina in rejecting further military assistance rather than submit to an evaluation of their human rights records. Previously authorized aid continued to flow, but no new authorizations were made until 1979. Economic aid was cut by half, from approximately $20 million to $10 million annually.[112]

El Salvador first attracted high-level attention from the Carter administration in June 1977, when one of the right-wing death squads, the White Warriors' Union, accused the Salvadoran Catholic Church of promoting Communism and threatened to kill all the Jesuits in the country. Leaflets appeared exhorting, "Be a Patriot! Kill a Priest!"[113] Since several priests had already been assassinated, the threat could not be ignored. Washington warned General Romero that relations with the United States depended upon preventing the prospective massacre. The wholesale slaughter of the Jesuits never materialized (though half a dozen more priests were assassinated over the next two years), and the activities of the death squads subsided temporarily (reinforcing suspicions that they operated with official sanction).[114]

In late 1977, however, the rising tide of popular opposition prompted the military government to enact a draconian Law for the Defense and Guarantee of Public Order, which effectively made it illegal to oppose the government in any fashion whatsoever. It instituted full press censorship, banned public meetings, outlawed strikes, and suspended normal judicial procedures. Mere suspicion was specified as grounds for arrest.[115] The day after the law's passage, U.S. Ambassador Frank J. Devine, speaking to Salvadoran businessmen at the Chamber of Commerce, explicitly endorsed the government's right to do whatever necessary to maintain order. Devine was no fan of Carter's human rights policy; increasingly fearful for his personal security as the Salvadoran insurgency grew, he thought Washington should resume military aid.[116]

Far from restoring stability, the Public Order Law accelerated the spiral of political violence. The clandestine guerrilla organizations proved to be beyond the reach of the government's security apparatus or the paramilitary right, so the brunt of the repression fell upon the more accessible moderates. The resulting human rights abuses further radicalized the population and attracted widespread international condemnation. In late 1978 and early 1979, a series of human rights reports from Amnesty International, the International Commission of Jurists, the Organization of American States, and the U.S. Department of State unanimously condemned General Romero's government for its systematic torture, murder, and persecution of political dissidents. According to the archbishop's Legal Aid office, 727 people were killed by death squads and the government's security forces in 1978 and 1979.[117]

The wave of official violence brought new recruits to the radical left, which in turn stepped up its bombings, assassinations of government officials, and kidnappings of businessmen, both foreign and domestic. The popular organizations began occupying government offices and foreign embassies to demand the release of prisoners newly arrested under the Public Order Law.

Torn by escalating political violence, El Salvador moved quickly to the top of Washington's policy agenda once the Nicaraguan insurrection came to an end. The Carter administration resolved not to repeat the mistakes it had made in Nicaragua, where it failed to break fully with Somoza and enlist wholeheartedly on the side of the moderate opposition until the eleventh hour—several hours too late. Throughout the summer of 1979, Washington pressured General Romero to move El Salvador's political conflicts back into the electoral arena where the Christian and Social Democrats could retrieve the political initiative from the revolutionary left. Two high-level delegations carried this message to San Salvador, one headed by Special Envoy William Bowdler and the other headed by Assistant Secretary Viron P. Vaky.[118]

General Romero responded with promises of reform, but he adamantly refused to reschedule the presidential election, which was not due until 1982.

Convinced that the tattered fabric of El Salvador's polity would not hold together until 1982, the United States was not satisfied. Neither was the opposition. Even the moderates refused to confer with the government on its promised reforms until the violence of the security forces ended. Romero would not or could not end it.

The October Coup

On October 15, 1979, General Romero's government was ousted in a bloodless coup led by young, progressive officers. Charging the regime with corruption, electoral fraud, and human rights violations, the young officers committed their new government to a thorough reform of the nation's "antiquated economic, social and political structures." The oligarchic system, they charged, had not offered the people even "the minimal conditions necessary to survive as human beings."[119]

The young officers moved quickly to establish a popular base by inviting the moderate opposition into the government. Three civilians joined two colonels in a ruling junta, and the cabinet was drawn almost entirely from the centrist political parties. In a dramatic break with the past, the junta also asked for support from the country's militant left, beseeching the radicals to "understand that the government is no longer their enemy." To gain the left's support, the junta promised to end the repression, create a democratic political system, and institute a wide range of policies to help the poor. Most important, it promised agrarian reform to break the socioeconomic dominance of the oligarchy.

The popular response to these proposals was mixed. The moderate opposition parties joined the new government immediately, but Archbishop Romero was more cautious in his endorsement. Acknowledging the junta's good will, he warned that the nation's new rulers could rally popular support only by demonstrating that their "beautiful promises are not dead letters."[120]

On the left, reaction to the coup was even more skeptical. Refusing to believe that the military would or could break with the past and displace the oligarchy, two guerrilla groups greeted the new government with calls for insurrection. But within a few weeks, the junta's reform program and its avowed intention to seek an opening to the left convinced the popular organizations and armed groups to suspend their attacks on the government, giving it an opportunity to make good on its promises.[121]

The junta did not use the time well. The pledge to investigate human rights abuses led to no arrests; the pledge to reorganize the government's security apparatus led only to a cosmetic reshuffling of personnel; and the pledge to conduct an agrarian reform led nowhere. Most important, the government could not even rein in its own security forces. Although the colonels had condemned the Romero government's indiscriminate use of lethal force against civilians, the practices of the police and National Guard did not change.

More than mere indecision lay behind the junta's failure to act, as the issue of the "disappeared" illustrated. Despite its promise to discover the whereabouts of some three hundred missing political activists, two weeks after coming to power the junta claimed that it could not account for any of them. In fact, the junta dared not look too closely at the excesses of the Romero regime for fear of what it might find—that senior police and military officials were culpable in the disappearances. Such a discovery would have shattered the fragile unity of the armed forces, something the progressive officers refused to risk.[122]

The same obstacle confronted the new government at every turn. Whenever the progressive officers and their civilian allies proposed reforms of any significance, rightists within the armed forces blocked them. The result was paralysis. The deadlock might have been broken if the progressive officers had been willing to confront their rightist brethren and take full control of the ideologically divided military. But that they were unwilling to do—partly because of institutional loyalty and partly because the United States was unwilling to stand behind them.

From their first days at the military academy, all Salvadoran officers were trained to put loyalty to the armed forces and their brother officers ahead of loyalty to the government or the constitution.[123] Bound together with their conservative compatriots by this ethos, progressive officers could alter the status quo only in ways the conservatives were willing to tolerate. This was why three decades of military modernizers had failed to produce any significant change in El Salvador's outmoded social and political structure.

At first, the centrist, reformist October junta seemed the perfect vehicle for Washington's new regional policy. Ambassador Devine cabled Washington that the people in the new government were "highly acceptable figures" and that its program was "very much in keeping with our own ideals and objectives."[124] But while Washington favored social reform, it balked at the junta's willingness to bring elements of the radical left into partnership with the government. The Carter administration's strategy was to isolate the radical left, not allow it to share power. Ambassador Devine reinforced the reluctance of the conservative officers to accede to civilian demands and explicitly warned the progressive officers against destabilizing the military by challenging their conservative colleagues.[125]

The stalemate between the junta and the rightists in the military revealed in bold relief the historic dilemma of Salvadoran politics. In a closed political system that had never allowed significant civilian participation, public policy was the exclusive preserve of the armed forces and its patrons in the oligarchy.

Reforms were inevitably limited by the government's need to preserve at least a rough political consensus within the officers' corps. On every important issue, the progressives caved in to conservative resistance rather than risk a split in the armed forces.

The government's paralysis demolished any hope of accord with the radical left. By December 1979, all three of the guerrilla groups had gone back on the offensive, and even the moderates within the government had become deeply discouraged. In a final bid to break the deadlock, the civilians sought a showdown with the officers, demanding that the rightist defense minister, General José Guillermo García, be removed. Forced to choose between their commitment to change and their loyalty to the armed forces, the progressive officers chose loyalty. Backed by a majority of senior officers, García stood fast, the civilians resigned, and the government moved sharply to the right.[126]

At this critical juncture, the United States did nothing to preserve the government's broad-based character. Despite a fundamental shift to the right in the balance of forces within the regime, the Carter administration continued to support and defend it as a centrist government under attack from extremists on both the left and the right. Encouraged by Washington, the Christian Democrats rejoined the government, arguing that there was no other alternative to civil war. A new junta was formed in January 1980 and, under intense U.S. pressure, the military finally accepted a set of reforms—including nationalization of the banking system and an agrarian reform—that went further than anything the October junta had been able to achieve.

Yet the moderation of the new government was more chimerical than real. Its strategy for resolving the political crisis differed profoundly from its predecessor's. The October junta tried to combine structural change with a political opening to the left in order to resolve El Salvador's crisis through dialogue and reconciliation. The January government's strategy was to assuage the right's fear of reform by combining it with repression of the left. The goal of building a center-left social base for the government was abandoned. Instead, the government sought to consolidate, as best it could, a political consensus for reform within the armed forces—even if that left it utterly isolated from the civilian populace.

In this, the new government was no different from the military modernizers of the past. The reforms it advocated were more extensive, but it approached politics in a familiar way—an authoritarian regime centered in the armed forces and buttressed by repression of those who dared to challenge the military's hegemony. This strategy of "reform with repression," as Archbishop Oscar Romero called it, was considerably more repressive than reformist.

The strategy of reform with repression destroyed what little chance the

January junta had to build a popular base of support. The reforms alienated the right and the repression alienated the left. The government stood isolated and precariously dependent upon the United States. When rightists in the armed forces mounted coup attempts in February and May, no significant social or political group in El Salvador rallied to the government's defense. Only the influence of the United States preserved it.[127]

A Clean Counterinsurgency War

Fearful that El Salvador was quickly becoming another Nicaragua, the Carter administration stood determinedly behind its rickety ally. If the admittedly weak regime could be sustained by the United States in the short run, U.S. officials believed, its program of social reform would eventually attract support, rebuilding a political center where none now existed. The reforms would break the dominance of the oligarchy and then erode the left's popular base. Eventually centrist democratic politics would predominate.

To implement this ambitious strategy, Carter picked Ambassador Robert E. White. A twenty-five-year veteran of the diplomatic corps who had served most of his career in Latin America, White was appointed ambassador to El Salvador in January 1980, brought in on emergency reassignment from Paraguay. Whereas Ambassador Devine had been unsympathetic to the administration's efforts to promote reform, White was tapped for the Salvadoran post because he had distinguished himself as an "activist" ambassador in Paraguay, meeting regularly with opposition leaders and pressing hard (albeit without much success) for human rights improvement. He was willing, in his own words, to "ruffle feathers" if that was what it took to get the job done.[128]

In fact, White was one of the few strong proponents of human rights in the State Department before Carter's election in 1976 put the issue high on the diplomatic agenda. Human rights did not merit much esteem in the geopolitical designs of Henry Kissinger, and vocal advocates of human rights could not expect much career advancement in the Foreign Service while he was secretary of state. Robert White, however, was an outspoken man. In 1976, while serving as deputy representative to the Organization of American States, he got himself in trouble by criticizing the human rights practices of the Chilean government during an OAS General Assembly meeting in Santiago. White was officially reprimanded for his comments, allegedly at the order of Kissinger himself, but the reprimand was withdrawn when White threatened to resign. It was not the last time that White's determination to speak his mind would get him into difficulty with a Republican administration.

"What Latin America desperately needs is a non-Communist model for revolution," White explained.[129] Under his stewardship, the U.S. embassy in El

Salvador tried to craft one by pursuing four objectives: (1) pressure the government into implementing social reforms designed to undercut the left's popular support and build legitimacy for the regime; (2) urge the government to reduce the level of official violence by reining in its own security forces, even if that required firing some rightist officers; (3) protect the government from a coup by the extreme right; and (4) entice the moderate left away from its alliance with the guerrillas, thus opening the way for a negotiated settlement that would leave the radicals isolated on the political periphery.

The pivotal issue was whether the Christian Democratic politicians and the progressive military officers could take control of the armed forces away from the right. Only then could they begin to remove extremist officers from command positions, punish those guilty of political murder, crack down on the death squads, and effectively carry out the reforms. White judged that the government was not in any immediate danger of military defeat by the guerrillas, so he opposed any significant increase in U.S. military aid, lest it strengthen the conservative military at the expense of the civilians.[130]

White's opposition to military aid quickly put him at odds with the Pentagon. Since the October 1979 coup, officials in the Defense Department had been pressing for a resumption of the military assistance program. A December 1979 defense survey left the Pentagon appalled at the poor quality of the Salvadoran armed forces.[131] In January 1980, the Pentagon began drawing up a full counterinsurgency plan for El Salvador. President Carter agreed to reprogram $5.7 million in nonlethal military aid (trucks, communications equipment, and uniforms), despite a personal appeal by Archbishop Romero warning that U.S. aid would merely sharpen the regime's "injustices and repression."[132] The purpose of the aid, U.S. officials insisted, was to give the embassy greater political leverage over the armed forces. "What we have to do," one official explained, "is wean the military off the teat of the oligarchy and onto ours."[133]

In late February, rightist officers tried to overthrow the government. Ambassador Devine had been recalled to Washington and replaced by Deputy Assistant Secretary of State James Cheek, who was filling in until the U.S. Senate confirmed White's appointment. Cheek thwarted the coup by warning the military that all U.S. assistance would be cut off if the government was ousted and by promising them new military aid if they remained loyal.[134] When White was finally confirmed a few weeks later, Cheek returned to Washington. From there, he argued that Washington should deploy military advisory teams and send the Salvadoran army six helicopters on a no-cost lease basis in order to maintain U.S. credibility. U.S. influence would ensure that the Salvadoran military fought "a clean counter-insurgency war," Cheek argued.[135]

White, however, adamantly opposed the introduction of U.S. advisers, lest

Washington come to be identified with what he called "the right-wing Murder Incorporated." Cheek insisted that Washington had a "genuine commitment" to send the advisory teams; White argued that the United States did not owe the Salvadoran armed forces anything just because they had agreed not to overthrow the government.[136] The plan to send the advisers was shelved.

But the Pentagon was not about to let the proposal die so easily. In May, the U.S. Southern Command in Panama ("South-Com," the U.S. military headquarters for Latin America) revived the program, casting it as one in which the U.S. advisers would improve the Salvadorans' human rights practices. "The idea," said a U.S. military official in Panama, "is that if a guy is standing with a protest sign, you don't have to cut him down with a machine gun. You can use tear gas." Both the State Department's Human Rights Bureau and Ambassador White opposed the plan.[137] White was the pivotal figure in keeping the training program out of El Salvador, threatening to resign if the advisers were sent over his objection.

As ambassador, White brooked no disagreement. Shortly after arriving in San Salvador, he engineered the reassignment of the CIA station chief, who was an inveterate Cold Warrior, too friendly with commanders of the Salvadoran security forces. To prevent even the appearance of U.S. identification with the military, White repeatedly deferred requests by South-Com commander General Wallace H. Nutting to visit El Salvador. "White is the guy that is calling all the shots in El Salvador," lamented a U.S. military official.[138]

Eventually a compromise was struck. Rather than send U.S. advisers to El Salvador, three hundred Salvadoran officers would go to Panama to take a three-week course, entitled "Human Rights Aspects in Internal Defense and Development." Especially designed for the Salvadorans, the program was a basic military training course with a human rights component added on.[139]

Slowly but surely, the Pentagon continued to chip away at the limitations on its role. In October 1980, a team of logistics advisers was sent to El Salvador on a training mission. In November, a U.S. Army survey team went to assess the military's weapons needs, even though the Carter administration had declared that it had no intention of resuming lethal military aid. That same month, a five-man U.S. Army Operational and Planning Assistance Team was dispatched to help the Salvadorans organize counterinsurgency operations, codenamed Operation Golden Harvest, to defend the upcoming coffee harvest from anticipated guerrilla efforts to disrupt it.[140]

Additionally, in October the Pentagon finally won approval of the program to lease six helicopters to the Salvadoran military at no cost. Washington demanded a series of human rights reforms as the price for the aircraft, including a clampdown on the extreme right and the transfer of officers implicated in the death squads. Instead, it got only a new code of military conduct, which was as worthless as the one it replaced. The Pentagon argued that this was sufficient progress, and the helicopters were sent.[141]

While the Pentagon gradually expanded U.S. support for the Salvadoran military, the center-left elements of the government were losing what little influence they had. The right-wing coup that White labored diligently to prevent occurred slowly, by degrees in the high councils of the officer corps. As moderately conservative officers lost patience with reform, they slipped quietly into agreement with their more extreme compatriots, becoming convinced that the only way to meet the challenge of the left was with violence—another *Matanza*.[142]

The steady stream of resignations by Christian Democrats over the year gave testimony of the rightist character of the regime. Each letter of resignation told the same story—frustration with the intransigence of the military and the inability of the moderate civilians to overcome it. "We have not been able to stop the repression," lamented junta member Héctor Dada, "and those committing acts of repression . . . go unpunished."[143]

The main split in the government came in March, prompted by the February 23 assassination of Attorney General Mario Zamora by a right-wing death squad. Zamora had tried to act as a bridge between the Christian Democrats and the left. After his murder, the progressive wing of the Christian Democratic Party resigned from the government, formed a new party called the Popular Social Christian Movement (Movimiento Popular Social Cristiano), and went into opposition.

Then, on March 24, Archbishop Romero was assassinated while saying mass. He had just finished a homily on the need to dedicate one's life to striving for peace when a gunman in the back of the chapel fired a single shot through his heart. He died on the altar. A morbid calm settled over the nation as word of Romero's death spread. Traffic stopped and businesses closed in homage to the slain prelate—and in fear of what might happen next. Thirty thousand people marched in Romero's funeral procession, which erupted into chaos when gunshots and explosions at the edge of the crowd triggered a panicky stampede. Thirty people were killed and hundreds injured.[144]

Even the progressive officers could not halt the rightward drift of the regime. Their leader, Colonel Adolfo Majano, was the key to Washington's efforts to consolidate the Salvadoran regime. In the words of Ambassador White, Majano constituted "80 percent of the respectability of the junta."[145] Majano was also someone who might broker negotiations between the government and the opposition—something White favored as the only chance to avoid a full-scale civil war. But the role of interlocutor between left and right was a dangerous one. Two people had tried to play it before—Mario Zamora and Archbishop Romero—and by April 1980, both of them were dead. The right had the same fate in mind for Majano and his supporters in the army.

In May 1980, Majano discovered a coup plot by the extreme right and ordered the arrest of the conspirators, chief among them ex-Major Roberto D'Aubuisson, former chief of intelligence for the National Guard and principal spokesman for the far right. The plot was intended to culminate on May 5, with D'Aubuisson announcing that the coup had saved El Salvador from a Marxist takeover perpetrated by Ambassador White, the Catholic Church, and the Trilateral Commission. The plot was foiled and D'Aubuisson was arrested along with twenty-three co-conspirators.[146]

He did not stay in jail long, however. Although the Christian Democrats threatened to resign from the government if D'Aubuisson was not prosecuted, eight of the nation's fourteen military garrison commanders voted to free him, thereby overruling the civilian-military junta that supposedly led the government. D'Aubuisson was released, and the Christian Democrats, their bluff called, stayed in the government. Majano was demoted from his position as armed forces commander.[147]

In midsummer, rightist officers began to systematically strip the progressives of their command positions, demoting them or reassigning them to diplomatic posts. Shortly thereafter, several of the most prominent progressive officers were assassinated by death squads. In November, after a failed assassination attempt, Majano himself was removed from the governing junta by a vote of the officers corps. When he refused an order to go into diplomatic exile as military attaché to Spain in February 1981, he was arrested and forced to leave the country. By late 1980, the progressive officers, who had been powerful enough in 1979 to overthrow General Romero's government, had ceased to be a significant political force.[148]

On the left, the climate of repression forged unprecedented unity. In early 1980, the popular organizations joined together with center-left trade unions and political parties to form a broad coalition, the Revolutionary Democratic Front (Frente Democrático Revolucionario, FDR). The armed groups were also coming together. The three major guerrilla organizations were joined by two smaller ones, the pro-Moscow Communist Party of El Salvador (Partido Comunista de El Salvador) and the newly founded Central American Workers Party (Partido Revolucionario de los Trabajadores Centroamericanos). The five groups called their coalition the Farabundo Martí Front for National Liberation (Frente Farabundo Martí para la Liberación Nacional, FMLN), named for the Communist leader who had launched the 1932 peasant uprising that was prelude to the *Matanza*.

Finally, the FDR and FMLN joined together in a grand coalition to form a unified opposition. The political platform of the FDR-FMLN represented a compromise between the traditional reformist demands of the FDR's constituent parties and the revolutionary socialist demands of the armed groups. It called for far-reaching socioeconomic changes that would break the economic dominance of the oligarchy, but promised a long-term role for the private sector. It also called for a pluralist political system, excluding the oligarchy, and a foreign policy of "nonalignment."[149]

The Major Bob Show

The strength of the far right was growing, too. Major D'Aubuisson was its symbol and inspiration. A dashing, charismatic figure who bore an uncanny resemblance to the singer Eddie Fisher, D'Aubuisson was fanatically anti-Communist. He chain-smoked, drank heavily, and never seemed to relax. He spoke in a rapid fire staccato that reminded some listeners of a machine gun, and he could not sit in a chair without fidgeting. People who met him came away with the feeling that he was on the verge of exploding, like a coil wound too tight. In some ways he was almost comical, a parody of himself. Embassy officials referred to him derisively as "Major Bob." But D'Aubuisson was capable of unfathomable violence. His other nickname was "Blowtorch," for his interrogation technique.[150]

D'Aubuisson had spent most of his twenty-year military career as an intelligence officer in the National Guard, where he was a protégé of General José Alberto Medrano, longtime Guard commander and the father of Salvadoran counterinsurgency. Medrano once referred to his three top aides—one of whom was D'Aubuisson—as "*mis tres asesinos*" (my three murderers).[151]

In the mid-1960s, Medrano founded the Nationalist Democratic Organization (Organización Democrática Nacionalista, ORDEN), a nationwide network of government informants and rightist paramilitary groups that, at its peak, included 100,000 people. With CIA assistance, he also organized the Salvadoran National Security Agency (Agencia Nacional de Seguridad Salvadoreña, ANSESAL)—a centralized intelligence unit staffed by officers drawn from the various armed services.[152]

ORDEN and ANSESAL functioned in tandem: intelligence collected by ORDEN was transmitted to ANSESAL, which kept elaborate files on alleged "subversives." In some cases, ANSESAL would direct ORDEN members to murder suspected dissidents; in others, the intelligence section of the National Guard or ANSESAL itself would dispatch special elite units (*especiales*) to do the killing. It was from this network established by Medrano that the first death squad, the White Hand, emerged. Medrano was unapologetic about the extralegal killings. "All the guerrillas are traitors to the Fatherland," he said. "And the law against that is the death penalty. So we applied the law against them."[153]

D'Aubuisson helped Medrano build ORDEN and eventually became ANSESAL's deputy director, under the command of Colonel Roberto Eulalio Santiváñez. Santiváñez, no stranger to dirty work, remembered D'Aubuisson as "an anarchic psychopath."[154] D'Aubuisson himself spoke openly of his involvement with death squads, describing to a reporter the military's frustration with normal judicial processes during the late 1970s. "We began to act incorrectly, and not take them [suspected subversives] to the judge, but make them 'disappear' instead," he explained. Just as Salvadorans associated Medrano with the White Hand, they came to associate D'Aubuisson with the second death squad to appear in the mid-1970s—the White Warriors Union.[155]

After the October 1979 coup, D'Aubuisson was forced out of the armed forces because of his death squad connections. Covertly, however, he continued to work for senior military commanders intent upon destabilizing the new reformist government.[156] He also became a regular feature on Salvadoran television, using intelligence files taken from ANSESAL to denounce alleged traitors and Communists during shows paid for by wealthy Salvadoran exiles. An unsettling pattern developed: the people denounced by D'Aubuisson on television were murdered by death squads shortly thereafter. D'Aubuisson's old friend and mentor, General Medrano, interpreted D'Aubuisson's televised accusations simply and straightforwardly: "D'Aubuisson was pointing out the Communists so the troops could kill them."[157]

In February, D'Aubuisson accused Attorney General Mario Zamora of being linked to one of the guerrilla groups. Zamora sued D'Aubuisson for libel. A few days later, a death squad broke into Zamora's house during a dinner party, took him into the bathroom, and shot him a dozen times in the face—the trademark of the White Warriors Union. When D'Aubuisson was arrested in May 1980 for trying to overthrow the government, documents captured with him described a paramilitary operation resembling the Zamora assassination.[158]

D'Aubuisson also denounced Archbishop Romero on television a few weeks before Romero was murdered. When a short-lived Salvadoran investigation pointed to the ex-major, the presiding judge began receiving death threats. He fled to Costa Rica, where he voiced his conviction that D'Aubuisson was responsible for the killing.[159] The U.S. embassy was also convinced of D'Aubuisson's guilt. In April 1981, Ambassador White told Congress that there was "compelling, if not 100 percent conclusive evidence" that D'Aubuisson ordered the archbishop's murder.[160] Among the documents captured at the time of D'Aubuisson's arrest in May 1980 was one describing Operation Pineapple.

The details of the operation—the equipment used, the number of people involved—matched the details of the archbishop's assassination almost exactly.[161] The embassy also had a "highly reliable" informant in D'Aubuisson's inner circle who claimed to have participated in a meeting of a dozen men, mostly active-duty military officers, in which the participants drew straws for the privilege of killing the archbishop. D'Aubuisson chaired the meeting.[162]

D'Aubuisson and his supporters spent much of 1980 and early 1981 building an organizational network to save El Salvador from Communism. According to one of D'Aubuisson's aides, they set out to build an organization with three tiers: "a political or propaganda level . . . to encourage and protect the military level; . . . a financial system where we would always have the money to attack; and a military level—what the United States called right-wing death squads—people who go out and kidnap and kill communists."[163]

The financial apparatus for D'Aubuisson's network was composed of wealthy Salvadorans living in Miami. In January 1981, Ambassador White sent the State Department a cable charging that a group of expatriate millionaires in Miami were responsible. The "Miami Six," as White dubbed them, "organize, fund and direct the death squads through their agent, Maj. Roberto D'Aubuisson." Subsequent CIA reports also concluded that D'Aubuisson was funded by wealthy expatriates.[164]

As Salvadoran politics polarized, most senior military officers abandoned their flirtation with reform and lined up with D'Aubuisson and the extreme right. The government then degenerated into a brutal military regime hiding behind a civilian facade. Despite the pleas of the Christian Democrats, the reign of official terror was much worse than it had been under the openly reactionary government of General Humberto Romero. In 1980, more than eight thousand people were killed—eight times the number murdered in 1979— the vast majority either by the government's security forces or the paramilitary right. Christian Democratic Party leaders were often among the victims, though they were supposedly partners with the military in the coalition government. And no one was arrested for any of the killings.[165]

The Search for the Elusive Center

The vision of Central America developed by the Carter administration after the fall of Somoza was both sophisticated and naive. Its sophistication lay in the recognition that Central American reality had changed so fundamentally that maintaining the status quo was no longer a real option. The politicization of the poor, both urban and rural, augured inevitable change in the narrowly based, closed political systems that historically dominated the region. Carter also recognized that change in Central America would inevitably endanger the privileges of existing elites, provoking fierce resistance. Nevertheless, he was willing to break the traditional alliance between the United States and the oligarchies in order to reconstruct political stability in the region on a foundation of socioeconomic reform and political democratization.

The naivete of Carter's policy lay in the belief that the United States could conjure up a moderate reformist political center to act as the instrument of evolutionary change, a center strong enough by itself to overcome the intransigence of the right and recapture the political initiative from the radical left. Central America's reformist center had reached its zenith in the early 1970s, only to be demolished thereafter by the hammer blows of official repression. The collapse of the center precipitated insurgency. By 1978, the guerrilla movements in Nicaragua, El Salvador, and Guatemala had grown from small bands isolated in remote rural areas to powerful political movements capable of seriously challenging the existing regimes. Few centrists from the early 1970s remained in the center.

The inability of the Carter administration to find a successful strategy for managing the Central American crisis was rooted in the administration's basic objective: not only to keep the radical left out of power, but to keep it from wielding any significant influence in a postoligarchic order. Thus Washington was forced to rely upon the debilitated political center to carry the mantle of change in the face of oligarchic resistance—a task the center did not have the strength to accomplish. When Washington confronted the choice between assisting a rightist regime battling insurgency, or risking guerrilla victory, it could not, in the wake of the revolution in Nicaragua, bring itself to allow a guerrilla triumph. To prevent another Nicaragua, the Carter administration, its commitment to human rights notwithstanding, armed the reactionary military. The facade of reform, rather than its substance, became sufficient justification for U.S. support.

Ronald Reagan would inherit from Jimmy Carter a region in crisis and a policy seemingly incapable of containing it. The incoming conservatives took Carter's failures in Central America as evidence of the righteousness of their own vision—one instinctively less convinced of the benefits of reform. Reagan's Republicans were more inclined to resume Washington's traditional policy of allying with existing elites in their struggle to restore order. Human rights could come later.

CHAPTER 3

From Carter to Reagan

Jimmy Carter tried to adapt U.S. foreign policy to a world increasingly beyond the control of the United States, but to many Americans, he simply looked weak and ineffectual. The "give-away" of the Panama Canal, the Soviet invasion of Afghanistan, and the impotence of America during the hostage crisis in Iran—all appeared to represent a retreat by the United States from the summit of world power. Ronald Reagan was elected president in part because he promised to restore the nation's global preeminence, and with it the sense of national pride and security that characterized "the American Century" before it was cut short in the jungles of Vietnam.

The Soviet threat loomed as the centerpiece of Reagan's worldview and became the cornerstone of his foreign policy. The recurring theme of Reagan's political attack on Carter was that he neglected national security. By pursuing detente single-mindedly, Carter had allegedly allowed U.S. strategic superiority over the Soviet Union to be lost and failed to meet the challenge of Soviet expansion in the Third World. By advocating human rights and ideological pluralism, Carter purportedly obscured the distinction between allies and adversaries, criticizing traditional anti-Communist friends while improving relations with hostile leftist regimes. Carter was, according to Reagan, "totally oblivious to the Soviet drive for world domination."[1]

Though Reagan's campaign rhetoric often posed these issues in simplistic terms, his complaints reflected a profound division within the foreign policy elite over the status of East-West relations. Carter's foreign policy was premised on detente—the reduction of East-West tensions conceptualized by Henry Kissinger and the eastern Republican establishment during the Nixon and Ford presidencies and supported by liberal Democrats. Reagan's critique, shared by the Republican right and the neoconservative Cold War Democrats, began from the premise that detente was a fraud. Reagan's supporters did not see themselves as the initiators of a new Cold War; for them, the Cold War had never ended. The United States, deluded by its desire for peace, had simply stopped fighting.

The Reagan coalition saw the Third World as little more than an arena of East-West struggle. Washington's strategic objective should be to strengthen the global network of U.S. allies while striving to weaken that of the Soviet Union. During the 1980 presidential campaign, Reagan routinely blamed all Third World conflict on Soviet conspiracies. "The Soviet Union underlies all the unrest that is going on," he told the *Wall Street Journal*. "If they weren't engaged in this game of dominoes, there wouldn't be any hot spots in the world."[2]

Here, too, the real policy debate was deeper and more complex. The advocates of detente had understood it to encompass certain "rules of the game" in the Third World—neither superpower would actively seek to expand its influence at the expense of the other. In effect, this meant freezing the international status quo, in which most of the Third World was more closely "nonaligned" with the West than with the East.

The Soviet Union, however, never understood detente in these terms. To the Soviets, detente, or "peaceful coexistence" as they called it, meant a reduction of bilateral tensions and increased cooperation on issues of mutual interest. It did not mean accepting in perpetuity an international status quo in which the Soviet position was inferior. The death of detente in the late 1970s could be traced to these conflicting interpretations, which materialized in real crises when Cuba and the Soviet Union collaborated to send thousands of Cuban combat troops to Angola in 1975 and Ethiopia in 1978. To Washington, Soviet policy in these conflicts violated the rules of the game. After the Soviet invasion of Afghanistan in December 1979, U.S. relations with Moscow reverted to familiar patterns of the Cold War, and the Carter administration's policy toward the Third World gravitated back toward traditional notions of containment. Carter's disillusionment with Soviet behavior in the Third World was gleefully seized upon by conservative enemies of detente, who proceeded to attack its entire structure.

Attack on the Americas

The Republican critique of Carter's Latin American policy was particularly sharp. Roger Fontaine, Reagan's principal foreign policy adviser on Latin America, denounced Carter's tolerance for ideological pluralism as nothing but "a cant phrase with no precise meaning other than accepting various Marxist and pseudo-Marxist ideologies that abound in the Third World."[3] Under this dubious rubric, Carter had allegedly embraced anti-American regimes such as Omar Torrijos's Panama and Michael Manley's Jamaica and even pro-Soviet ones such as Fidel Castro's Cuba.

At the same time, Carter had distanced the United States from its traditional friends, leaving them to fend for themselves in the face of rapidly advancing insurgencies backed by the Cubans and Soviets. Carter's reduction of military aid to the dictatorships of Central America and the Southern Cone (Argentina, Chile, Brazil, and Uruguay) on human rights grounds appeared to be nothing less than the willful dismantling of Washington's alliance structure in Latin America. To cast off traditional anti-Communist allies for the sake of some vague moral idealism seemed reckless in the hostile international environment of realpolitik, the Republicans charged. To contrive such a policy when those allies were beset by leftist insurgency—as they were in Central America— seemed the height of folly, or worse.

Two documents provided the intellectual wellspring of Reagan's Latin American policy. Jeane Kirkpatrick's *Commentary* article, "Dictatorships and Double Standards," was a sophisticated, albeit contentious, critique of the underlying premises of Carter's policy toward the Third World. A monograph by conservative Latin American specialists, *A New Inter-American Policy for the Eighties*, gave an apocalyptic litany of Carter's errors in Latin America and provided an aggressive agenda of remedies. Its authors (Roger Fontaine among them) dubbed themselves "the Committee of Santa Fe," and most of them eventually appeared in midlevel foreign policy posts within the Reagan administration.[4]

Kirkpatrick's broadside, which first attracted the attention of candidate Reagan to the acerbic professor, argued that Carter's policy of promoting human rights and reform in the Third World was not only ineffectual but downright dangerous. She rejected the argument that change in the Third World was inevitable or necessarily in the interests of the United States. Carter simply lacked the will to resist malevolent changes fostered by our enemies. The "deep historical forces" of change that Carter officials were always trying to accommodate "look a lot like Russians or Cubans," Kirkpatrick wrote.

The idea that the United States could successfully promote democratic change was little more than an imperial conceit, Kirkpatrick argued. Instead of providing stability, Carter's policy "facilitated the job of insurgents" by causing social disruption while simultaneously restricting the ability of the existing regime to use force to preserve order.[5] Strong friendly governments, however cruel, were thus replaced by moderate weak ones that would soon fall prey to Communists.

The obvious solution was for the United States to resume its traditional policy of providing military aid to friendly rightist dictatorships. Such a policy was justified, Kirkpatrick insisted, because traditional dictators were more "moderate" than revolutionaries. "Moderately authoritarian" governments might eventually evolve into democracies, whereas "totalitarian" regimes never changed. There was a happy coincidence between this theoretical distinction, which made it possible to support dictators of the right with a somewhat easier conscience, and the fact that so-called "moderate" authoritarians tended to be pro-American.

Kirkpatrick's article was widely criticized among academics as both historically inaccurate and logically unsound, but it caught the eye of Richard V. Allen, Ronald Reagan's top foreign policy adviser, who passed it along to the candidate. After meeting with Kirkpatrick several times, Reagan asked her to join the campaign and, subsequently, she became his ambassador to the United Nations.[6]

The Santa Fe report repeated the right's critique of Carter's policy, but did so in a tone that verged on hysterical. "Containment of the Soviet Union is not enough," the report began. "Detente is dead. Survival demands a new U.S. foreign policy. For World War III is almost over." Carter's "indecision and impotence" had abandoned Latin America to Soviet attack and thereby "placed the very existence of the Republic in peril."

The report portrayed the Soviet Union as everywhere on the march, most especially in the Western Hemisphere: "The Americas are under attack," it warned, and Jimmy Carter was guilty of "accommodation" to this aggression. Carter had helped overthrow Somoza in Nicaragua by refusing to give him military aid and had destabilized El Salvador by forcing it to accept reforms and by preventing "nationalist elements" (i.e., ex-Major Roberto D'Aubuisson and his allies in the military) from taking over the government.

To recover from the disaster of Carter's policy, the United States had to "abandon" its human rights policy and stop trying to force reforms on reluctant friends. In practical terms, this meant restoring military assistance to Argentina, Brazil, Chile, El Salvador, and Guatemala. If necessary to halt the spread of Communism, the United States had to be ready to intervene directly with its own military forces. "Only the United States," the report concluded, "can . . . protect the independent nations of Latin America from Communist conquest and help preserve Hispanic-American culture from sterilization by international Marxist materialism." The recommendations enumerated in the Santa Fe report proved to be the best guide to what Ronald Reagan would do once he came to office.

The Santa Fe report was also a harbinger of another aspect of Reagan's policy—the right's practice of impugning the loyalty of liberal Democrats, casting them as conscious allies of America's foreign enemies. Liberals had "engineered the end of the American presence in the Caribbean," the report charged. Carter exhibited "strategic indifference" to Cuban and Soviet expansion in Latin America because "the norms of conflict and social change adopted by the Carter administration are those of the Soviet Union."[7]

Just before the 1980 election, Reagan adviser Roger Fontaine wrote a scathing attack on Carter's policy, citing what he called its intentional "bias in favor of the extreme left" that ran "parallel" to the interests of Cuba and the Soviet Union. The reason for this, Fontaine suggested, was that some of the people responsible for Carter's policy were, consciously or unconsciously, under the influence of the Cuban and Soviet intelligence services.[8] Jeane Kirkpatrick struck a similar theme in "Dictatorships and Double Standards," where she charged that Carter had "actively collaborated" in the replacement of U.S. allies with adversaries in a policy reminiscent of the one that "lost" China.

Such attacks were not merely the overheated rhetoric of a sharply contested campaign. They reflected a real and deep animosity not just toward the people running Carter's Latin American policy, but toward the whole liberal wing of the Democratic Party that had reacted to the Vietnam experience by developing a robust skepticism about new interventionist adventures. The Republican right's animosity would not dissipate after Carter left office. On the contrary, when liberal Democrats raised their voices in opposition to Reagan's policies in Central America, the rhetoric would became even more vituperative.

Central Americans for Reagan

No U.S. presidential campaign ever captured the attention of Central Americans as did the contest between Jimmy Carter and Ronald Reagan. All across the political spectrum, there was a sense that the fate of the region was being decided by an electoral process that the Central Americans could only watch from afar.

The traditional right—the wealthy businessmen, landowners, and military officers—hated Jimmy Carter. Carter had betrayed and abandoned them by criticizing their human rights practices and cutting off their lifeline of military aid just when they needed it most. Their complaints were essentially the same as those leveled against Carter by his conservative critics in the United States, but for the Central Americans, the issue was not abstract. Their way of life was under attack, their wealth and privilege at stake. Nicaragua stood before them as a terrifying example of what could happen. In just a few months, a small Marxist guerrilla band—smaller than the guerrilla armies in both El Salvador and Guatemala—had taken over the leadership of a mass movement and swept the Somoza regime from power. The United States stood idly by, doing nothing to save its oldest friend in the region. Even worse, Washington itself had given Somoza the final shove and then rushed to embrace his usurpers. Or so it appeared from the balconies of the wealthy neighborhoods of San Salvador and Guatemala City.

Carter's policy seemed so naive, so wrong-headed, so incomprehensible that many rightists in Central America became convinced only a conspiracy could explain it. "Most of the elements in the State Department are probably pro-Communist," complained Guatemalan businessman Roberto Alejos Arzu. "Either Mr. Carter is a totally incapable president or he is definitely a pro-Communist element." The president of Guatemala, General Romeo Lucas García, held a similar opinion; he referred to Carter as "Jimmy Castro."[9]

To Central American rightists, Ronald Reagan appeared as a savior. Though Reagan himself said little about Central America during the campaign, his attacks on Carter's human rights policy and his pledge to resist Soviet advances in the Third World gave the Central Americans reason to believe he would come to their rescue. In El Salvador, rightists routinely picketed the U.S. embassy and Ambassador Robert White's residence, carrying protest signs that read, "Reagan Is America's Last Hope," "Only Reagan Can Halt Communism," and "Reagan for President."[10]

In the wealthy neighborhoods of San Salvador and Guatemala City, the oligarchs rejoiced with lavish parties that lasted long into the evening on election night, November 4, 1980. "When Reagan won, we celebrated in Guatemala just like New Year's Eve, with mariachis, marimbas, and firecrackers," recalled Lionel Sisniega Otero, a leader of Guatemala's rightist National Liberation Movement who sported a Reagan bumper sticker on his car.[11] The reaction in El Salvador was much the same. "In the posh residential neighborhoods of Escalon and San Benito," wrote New York Times correspondent Raymond Bonner, "homeowners stepped onto manicured lawns and squeezed off a few rounds from their automatic rifles to register their joy."[12]

Carter's Central American policy collapsed immediately. Throughout the region, both right and left began to act in anticipation of the drastic changes soon to overtake U.S. policy. The right no longer felt compelled to pay any attention to Jimmy Carter and his blather about human rights. In Guatemala and El Salvador, the toll of death squad murders began to rise. In the province of San Miguel in El Salvador, just a few days after the election, two bullet-riddled bodies were found on the side of the road with signs around their necks, reading: "With Ronald Reagan, the miscreants and guerrillas of Central America and El Salvador will be finished."[13]

As the bloodshed mounted, seventy-one U.S. religious leaders appealed to President-elect Reagan to speak out against "widespread arrest and imprisonment, torture and murder," and to reaffirm Washington's commitment to human rights. Reagan refused on the grounds that the appeal was "one-sided" because it did not denounce human rights violations in Communist countries.[14]

Reagan's election prompted an acute crisis in El Salvador. The right had been struggling since October 1979 to regain control of the government from the reformist coalition of progressive military officers and moderate civilians and had made considerable headway. But despite coup attempts in February and May 1980, the right had been unable to depose the regime, largely because of the unflagging efforts of Ambassador White to prop it up. With Reagan's election, the right launched yet another attempt. White was so closely identified with Carter's policy that Carter's electoral defeat weakened White considerably—enough, the right hoped, to cripple his ability to keep the army in line behind the government.

White's commitment to Carter's reform policy and his repeated success at thwarting coups made him a special nemesis of the Salvadoran right. When D'Aubuisson was arrested after his May 1980 coup attempt, three hundred of his supporters lay siege to White's residence, barricading it with automobiles and vowing to hold the ambassador hostage until D'Aubuisson was released. With loudspeakers and placards they denounced White as a Communist, chanting "White is Red," and "Reagan sí, Carter no." After several days, the siege was ended when White's Marine guards fired tear gas at the crowd and broke through the blockade with an armored Cadillac. Later that day, unknown gunmen threw two bombs at the embassy and sprayed it with heavy-caliber machine-gun fire.[15]

Carter's fragile policy in El Salvador was not helped by the outspokenness of Reagan's transition team. In a press conference two days after the election, Reagan himself seemed to confirm his intent to resume military aid to El Salvador when he said, "I don't think that you can turn away from some country because here and there they do not totally agree with our conception of human rights."[16]

Later in November, four of Reagan's Latin American aides, Kirkpatrick, Fontaine, James Theberge (a former U.S. ambassador to Nicaragua), and Constantine Menges (a hard-line conservative academic), met with a visiting delegation from El Salvador's private sector. They promised that Reagan would resume shipments of lethal military aid, although they warned against a rightist coup ousting the Christian Democrats.[17]

Reacting to stories about the right's meeting with the Reagan team, Christian Democratic leader José Napoleón Duarte decided to come secretly to Washington to tell his side of the story. Meeting with Kirkpatrick, Menges, and Richard Allen (soon to be appointed Reagan's national security adviser), Duarte got a decidedly colder reception than the businessmen who preceded him. He was shocked by the hostility of the Reagan people, especially toward his land reform program. "Their attitudes ranged from skeptical to rude as they interrogated me," Duarte recalled.[18]

In El Salvador, events were moving fast. The rising power of the right within the officers corps meant that the war of extermination against "subversives" was increasingly a joint venture between the semiprivate death squads of the oligarchy and the regular armed forces. Evidence of the shift was not long in coming. On the morning of November 27, the leadership of the Revolutionary Democratic Front, the broad coalition of left-wing civilian opposition parties, was meeting in a Jesuit high school in San Salvador. Two hundred armed men, some in the uniforms of the National Police and the Army Commandos, arrived at the high school and set up a secure perimeter around the building. Two dozen more heavily armed men in masks and civilian clothes (but still wearing their military combat boots) burst into the school and ordered everyone to lie face down on the floor. Five of the six members of the FDR's executive committee, including FDR president Enrique Alvarez (himself a prominent member of the oligarchy and former minister of agriculture), were taken away. The next day, their tortured and mutilated bodies were found dumped along a road outside the city. A note pinned to one of the corpses read, "Long live El Salvador! Long live the massacre of 1932!"[19] Responsibility for the killings was claimed by a new death squad, the Maximiliano Hernández Martínez Anti-Communist Brigade, named after the Salvadoran general who conducted the 1932 *Matanza*. The Central Intelligence Agency's report on the killings concluded unequivocally that they were "the work of the security forces."[20]

The killing of the FDR leaders derailed any remaining chance of negotiating a way out of El Salvador's escalating conflict. Since his arrival in the spring, White had been trying to convince the FDR leaders to rejoin the government. In this way, he hoped to reconstitute a broad-based government of the center-left that could effectively compete for power with the oligarchy and at the same time undercut the popular support of the leftist guerrillas. White was making progress when the FDR leaders were killed—in all likelihood, precisely to sabotage any chance of negotiations. "Who am I going to talk to now?" White muttered when told of the FDR leaders' deaths.[21]

In Washington, Jeane Kirkpatrick was less troubled by the killings. "It's a reminder that people who choose to live by the sword can expect to die by it," she said evenly.[22] A U.S. diplomat who served in Central America during the Reagan years tried to explain such apparent callousness on the part of Reagan's advisers: "Unless they see a guy like D'Aubuisson running a machete through somebody, they're inclined to ignore it. . . . There is absolutely zero conception of what these people are really like, how evil they really are."[23] The victims were never limited to those who lived by the sword.

Roses in December

Salvador was unusually tense on December 2, the day before the funeral of the murdered FDR leaders. A large turnout by the popular organizations was anticipated, and everyone remembered the violence that had erupted during Archbishop Romero's funeral in March, when thirty people were killed. Maryknoll sisters Ita Ford, Maura Clarke, and two other missionaries were due back in El Salvador from the Maryknolls' annual regionwide gathering in Nicaragua. Ford and Clarke were both natives of New York City and worked together in the war-torn province of Chalatenango distributing food and clothing to refugees displaced by the fighting. Ford had come to El Salvador in March after working for six years in Chile. Clarke had just arrived in August, though she was no stranger to Central America, having worked for seventeen years in Nicaragua.

The Maryknoll Order was well known for its commitment to fighting for social justice on behalf of the poor—a mission that was often interpreted by the authorities as subversive. Relations between the church and the local armed forces in Chalatenango were strained. "The colonel of the local regiment said to me the other day that the church is indirectly subversive because it's on the side of the weak," Ita Ford told an interviewer in November. That same month, someone nailed a note to the door of the parish house where Ford and Clarke lived. "In this house are Communists," it read. "Everyone who enters here will die. Try it and see." The note was illustrated with a drawing of a knife stuck in a skull, dripping blood.[24]

Late in the afternoon on December 2, Ursuline sister Dorothy Kazel and lay missionary Jean Donovan drove out to El Salvador's international airport to meet Ford and Clarke's flight from Nicaragua.[25] Kazel and Donovan, both from Cleveland, worked in the city of La Libertad, where they, too, ministered to the needs of the poor, with the help of Father Paul Schindler. Donovan was appalled at the poverty and brutality suffered by Salvadoran peasants, but even as the level of political violence increased, so, too, did her determination to stay in the country and continue her work. After all, she wrote in her diary, "Where else would you find roses blooming in December?"[26]

Kazel and Donovan had to make two trips to the airport in their white van because the four Maryknoll sisters arriving from Nicaragua did not all come on the same flight. Early in the afternoon, they picked up Sisters Madeline Dorsey and Teresa Alexander and drove them safely home to La Libertad. Then they returned to the airport just before dusk to meet Ita Ford and Maura Clarke. The comings and goings of the white van caught the attention of a National Guardsman stationed at the airport, who informed his superior, Subsergeant Luis Antonio Colindres Alemán, that the American women were behaving suspiciously. Colindres Alemán ordered his squad of five guardsmen to change into civilian clothes. At the traffic checkpoint outside the airport, he ordered uniformed guardsmen to hold up all traffic for ten minutes, but to let the women's white van go through. Then he had his squad take up positions just down the road.

The squad stopped the van, searched it, questioned the four women, and then forced them to follow the guardsmen into the countryside toward the small village of Santiago Nonualco, fifteen miles from the airport.[27] Just outside the town, the guardsmen ordered the women out of the van and raped them. When the soldiers were finished, they shot the women at point-blank range and left the bodies on the roadside where they fell. The soldiers then drove the white van twenty miles away, in the opposite direction from the airport, removed its license plates, and burned it. Later, Sergeant Colindres Alemán explained why he had ordered the women's murder, saying simply, "They were subversives."[28]

Father Schindler knew something was wrong when Dorothy Kazel and Jean Donovan failed to appear at a meeting the next morning. When he couldn't locate them, he immediately informed the U.S. embassy that the women were missing, and the embassy asked Salvadoran authorities to begin a search. Schindler spent the rest of the day searching on his own, driving through the region around the airport, looking for some clue as to what had happened. That evening, he found the burned-out van.

In Santiago Nonualco, villagers had heard gunshots during the night of December 2, but they knew better than to investigate. The next morning, they found the bodies of the four women lying on the roadside. Finding bodies like this was not uncommon; these corpses were distinctive only because they were foreigners. The authorities were duly informed, and on orders from the local National Guard, the women were quickly buried in a common grave. Word of the dead foreigners reached the local parish priest, who told the vicar of the

San Vicente diocese the following day. The vicar, in turn, informed the U.S. embassy. Ambassador White drove immediately to the scene, where he found Paul Schindler, who had been contacted by the parish priest.

As the women's bodies were pulled out of the narrow grave by ropes, one at a time, three other American nuns knelt in silent prayer at the graveside. Reporters circled the scene, photographing the grisly tableau. White stood by in quiet rage, muttering over and over, "This time they won't get away with it. . . . The bastards won't get away with it."[29] The women had been stacked on top of one another, and as they were exhumed, the small circle of onlookers could see the evidence of their trauma. Jean Donovan's face had been destroyed by the high-velocity rifle bullet that killed her, fired into the back of her head.

"We already knew they would be dead," White said later, remembering the moment, "but when you saw the flies, the ropes, when you saw them uncovered, it was horrible and pitiable. . . . You see people you love beaten and broken, and you realize something important about El Salvador. They'll kill anybody."[30]

President Carter reacted to the killing of the churchwomen by ordering the suspension of $25 million in economic and military aid to the Salvadoran government, pending the outcome of an investigation.[31] In private, U.S. officials had no doubt that the Salvadoran armed forces were involved in covering up the murders if not in actually committing them.[32]

Carter also appointed an investigating team to go to El Salvador. To head it, he named William G. Bowdler, who had replaced Viron P. Vaky as assistant secretary of state for Latin America in late 1979, and William D. Rogers, who had held the same post in the Ford administration. Rogers was included in order to make the team credible to the incoming Reagan team and to the Salvadoran right, which no longer cared what Jimmy Carter thought.

The investigators' agenda, however, was considerably broader than just the murder of the churchwomen. They were to examine the overall diplomatic and political situation in El Salvador and assess, according to Rogers, "what kind of government can exercise power effectively now in El Salvador's conditions."[33] D'Aubuisson and his allies on the right were using the killing of the churchwomen and the consequent cut-off of U.S. aid as the occasion for yet another coup attempt. The Christian Democrats, in a last-ditch effort at self-defense, threatened to resign unless the military agreed to transfer rightist officers out of key command posts and opened a dialogue with the surviving moderates in the FDR.[34]

The Carter administration used the occasion of the murders to carry out a plan originally devised before the 1980 election, but shelved as impractical because of Reagan's overwhelming victory. Carter had intended to pressure the Salvadoran government to bring the armed forces under civilian control, transfer extreme rightists out of command positions, and halt the political murders being carried out by death squads—an agenda almost identical to the actions the Christian Democrats were now demanding. The killing of the churchwomen gave the administration an unassailable reason for suspending aid and insisting on major changes in the Salvadoran government as the price for releasing the funds. The Bowdler mission's aim was to extract those concessions from the armed forces.[35]

The mission was a success in some respects; it kept the right from overthrowing the government and persuaded the military to accept the Christian Democrats' demands. The junta was reorganized in December with Duarte as its president, and the armed forces agreed to shift a dozen notorious rightists out of senior command posts. Only a few were ever actually reassigned, however; once Carter left the White House, nothing more was heard about the military's promises. The price of this reorganization was the political head of the progressive military leader, Colonel Adolfo Majano, who was forced off the junta and sent into exile.[36]

In exchange for the military's concessions, the Carter administration resumed economic assistance on December 17—less than two weeks after the churchwomen were killed. But the real payoff for the army was Washington's private pledge to resume military assistance, including military advisers and helicopters. The aid would arrive on a "phased" basis beginning in late December, so long as the Salvadoran government made "tangible progress" on its promises to reassign officers suspected of human rights abuses, reduce political killings, and conduct a serious investigation of the churchwomen's murder.[37]

The Reagan camp was strongly opposed to even a brief suspension of aid.[38] Kirkpatrick was the most vocal, declaring it "utterly irresponsible . . . tantamount to turning the country over not to the infamous right-wing coup that keeps being talked about, but to a rapid victory of the revolutionary left." The idea that the Salvadoran armed forces were especially brutal was simply untrue, Kirkpatrick insisted. "I think the degree of commitment to moderation and democratic institutions within the Salvadoran military is very frequently underestimated in this country. And I think it's a terrible injustice to the government and the military when you suggest that they were somehow responsible for terrorism and assassination."[39]

Kirkpatrick's view of the murdered churchwomen, however, was less charitable. Shortly after their bodies were discovered, Kirkpatrick caused a furor by stating flatly, "The nuns were not just nuns. The nuns were also political activists. We ought to be a little more clear about this than we usually are. They were political activists on behalf of the Frente [the leftist FDR-FMLN] and somebody who is using violence to oppose the Frente killed these nuns."[40] The accusation was completely unfounded. Neither the Bowdler mission nor any subsequent investigation turned up any evidence of such an affiliation. On the contrary, the State Department acknowledged it had "no evidence that the four American missionaries were engaged in political activity as we define it. Rather, as we understand, their activities were what we would regard as religious and social welfare work."[41]

When asked whether she thought the Salvadoran government was responsible for the killings, Kirkpatrick replied, "The answer is unequivocal. No, I don't think the government was responsible." That, too, proved to be mistaken.[42]

Kirkpatrick's efforts to preserve the reputation of the Salvadoran government and armed forces were in vain. Nothing could blunt the visual impact of the women's bodies being dragged out of the shallow grave and lying on the ground, half naked and covered with bits of brush for modesty's sake. The murders put El Salvador on the evening news and in the headlines in the United States, focusing the attention of ordinary Americans on the small country as never before. Like the 1979 murder of ABC News correspondent Bill Stewart by Somoza's National Guard, the murder of the churchwomen shocked the public and discredited the government that was purportedly a U.S. ally.

Pretend Emissaries

The Reagan team was divided on what its new policy toward El Salvador should be. Conservatives viewed Duarte's government as inclined toward socialism and too weak to adequately resist the left. A government of the right would be more coherent and, with help from Washington, better equipped to prosecute the war.[43] Roger Fontaine criticized Carter for collaborating in the replacement of the "pro-U.S." and "economically viable" government of General Romero with the leftist Christian Democrats, who had "brought the country to near economic ruin by desperate and sweeping reforms." It was intervention, Fontaine argued, for Washington to block the efforts of conservative Salvadorans to overthrow Duarte's junta and replace it with a government of the right.[44]

Reagan's more pragmatic advisers were convinced that the United States had no alternative but to support the Duarte government, imperfect as it was. In this view, the reforms forced on the Salvadorans by the Carter administration, for good or ill, were now an established fact that could only be reversed at great political cost. A rightist coup that rolled back the reforms and drove the Christian Democrats out of the government would simply bolster the recruiting efforts of the guerrillas and accelerate their drive for power.[45]

But Duarte still had to survive until inauguration day. If a government of the right was already in power when Reagan came to office, the hard-right conservatives on his staff were certain he would support it rather than allow it to fall to the guerrillas. In early December, the conservatives leaked the State Department transition report on the Latin American bureau to the press, further undermining White's authority.[46]

The transition report argued that the bureau needed a "basic reorientation." No longer should ambassadors "function in the capacity of social reformers and advocates of new theories of social change." Ambassador White's promotion of reform in El Salvador was singled out as an example of what should be avoided. The report also blasted Carter's human rights policy, recommending that human rights be balanced against security concerns, that public criticism of human rights violators be curtailed, and that the authority of the Human Rights Bureau within the State Department be limited to prevent it from blocking aid to U.S. allies. Also leaked was a "hit list" of sixty ambassadors slated for immediate replacement when the new administration took office. At the top were Robert White in El Salvador and Lawrence Pezzullo in Nicaragua.[47]

White, his authority eroding rapidly, was finally moved to speak out after a visit to El Salvador by Cleto DiGiovanni, a former CIA officer and coauthor with Fontaine of an article criticizing Carter's support for Duarte. While in El Salvador and Nicaragua, DiGiovanni reportedly represented himself as an official in the Reagan transition team and told the Salvadoran right that the team's public statements of opposition to a coup should be ignored. Livid, White called in reporters from the *New York Times* and the *Washington Post*. The leaked transition report, combined with the statements of various Reagan aides such as DiGiovanni, "weaken my authority to carry out the policy of the administration," White said. He accused the transition team of "malice and stupidity."[48]

The Reagan transition team disavowed DiGiovanni. "We have about half a dozen pretend emissaries all over the world who are complete hoaxes," complained Robert E. Neumann, head of the State Department transition team.[49] But a few days later, Pezzullo in Nicaragua weighed in, echoing White's complaint. "This has been going on for a long time and for the Reagan people to now say that 'these guys don't speak for us' is kind of lame. I don't buy that for a second."[50]

Assistant Secretary of State for Human Rights Patricia M. Derian also backed up White's complaint. "Imprudent statements" by the Reagan transition team playing down the importance of human rights had encouraged the escalation of death squad activity in Central America, she charged. The killings of both the FDR leaders and the U.S. churchwomen were partially the result of the right having been "emboldened" by the Reagan team's attitude.[51]

The depth of animosity the Reagan team harbored toward Carter was demonstrated by the preinaugural meeting Reagan scheduled with Mexican President José López Portillo. Reagan's advisers refused to consult with the State Department or the U.S. ambassador to Mexico prior to the meeting, and they refused to invite a State Department representative to attend. Embarrassed by such a breach of protocol, the Mexicans urged Reagan's advance men to find some embassy official who could attend the meeting. Impossible, said the Reaganites; there was no one at the embassy who could be trusted. "[They had] an amazing degree of suspicion and hostility toward the Carter people," a senior Mexican official recounted. "It's incredible, as if they were public enemies." A career diplomat in the U.S. embassy in Mexico City was equally amazed: "We were completely cut out. . . . It's total surrealism."[52] Day by day, the atmosphere in Washington was becoming more poisoned around the issue of Central America. In El Salvador, the death toll kept mounting.

Late in the evening on January 3, 1981, Michael Hammer and Mark Pearlman were having dinner with José Rodolfo Viera in the coffee shop of San Salvador's Sheraton Hotel. Hammer and Pearlman worked for the American Institute for Free Labor Development (AIFLD), an agency of the AFL-CIO that specialized in organizing anti-Communist labor unions in Latin America. Financed jointly by the labor movement and the U.S. government, AIFLD was often charged with being little more than a disguised instrument of U.S. foreign policy. At times in its history, it had served as a front for CIA covert operations.[53]

Pearlman, one of AIFLD's two local representatives, had been working in El Salvador for seven months on a $1.5 million contract from the U.S. Agency for International Development (AID). He was assisting the Salvador Communal Union (Unión Comunal Salvadoreña, UCS), a Christian Democratic peasant group, to set up cooperatives on the large landed estates nationalized in the first phase of El Salvador's agrarian reform. Strengthening peasant and labor groups affiliated with the Christian Democrats was a key element in Washington's strategy of building a constituency for the civilian-military junta and undercutting the popular appeal of the left. Hammer, the director of Agrarian Union Development for AIFLD, had just arrived from Washington that morning, but he was no stranger to El Salvador. He had served there for four years in the late 1960s, helping to found the UCS.[54]

José Rodolfo Viera was one of the few truly popular figures remaining in the Salvadoran government. In March 1980, when the junta promulgated the agrarian reform, Viera left his job as head of the UCS to accept the presidency of the Salvadoran Institute of Agrarian Transformation (Instituto Salvadoreño de Transformación Agraria), the agrarian reform agency. But after nine months of struggling with a divided government that was unable to prevent the armed forces from killing agrarian reform workers, Viera was preparing to resign. It was this impending political crisis that brought Hammer back to San Salvador.[55]

As Hammer, Pearlman, and Viera sat talking in the deserted restaurant at about 11:30 P.M., two men entered, walked over to their table, and opened fire with submachine guns, pumping some forty rounds into them. The killers then turned and walked calmly out of the building, unmolested by hotel security. Hammer and Viera were killed on the spot; Pearlman died on the way to the hospital.

The assassins were soldiers who later testified they had been ordered to commit the murders by two officers: Lieutenant Rodolfo Isidro López Sibrián, deputy director of intelligence for the National Guard, and Captain Eduardo Ernesto Alfonso Avila. According to the triggermen, a wealthy businessman, Hans Christ, was also part of the plot.[56] Both officers were close associates of D'Aubuisson: López Sibrián had been his aide and Avila his colleague when D'Aubuisson was in the National Guard. Both were with him when he was arrested in May 1980 for plotting to overthrow the government.[57]

Though the murder of the AIFLD advisers was no more gruesome than the murder of the churchwomen, it was more surprising. The army suspected the missionaries, like it suspected everyone associated with the Catholic Church, of harboring guerrilla sympathies. But AIFLD's anti-Communist credentials were impeccable. It was a full-fledged partner in Washington's efforts to help the Salvadoran regime win the hearts and minds of the peasants.

The Best Defense Is a Good Offensive

The Central American left was also watching the presidential transition in the United States. Sandinista officials reacted angrily to the Republican platform's call for a cut-off of U.S. aid to Nicaragua and its veiled encouragement of counterrevolution.[58] Ambassador Pezzullo cautioned them, both publicly and privately, to be more restrained, noting that they might well have to deal with Reagan as the next U.S. president. Presidents, once in office, did not always adhere strictly to their campaign promises or their party platform, Pezzullo pointed out. The Sandinistas took Pezzullo's advice, but they were not convinced, especially since Reagan's advisers kept repeating that aid to Nicaragua should be halted.[59] "Economic aid won't work," Roger Fontaine argued during the campaign. "The hard-line Sandinistas are in control, and money would entrench the Marxists in power." Making the same argument on another occasion, he concluded, "I think Nicaragua is lost . . . for the moment."[60]

In El Salvador, the FDR-FMLN planned a "final offensive" to depose the Salvadoran government on the eve of Reagan's inauguration, thus presenting the United States with a fait accompli. "The situation in El Salvador will be red hot by the time Mr. Reagan arrives," promised guerrilla commander Fermán Cienfuegos in a rare interview with U.S. reporters. "I think Mr. Reagan will find an irreversible situation in El Salvador by the time he reaches the presidency."[61]

For the arms to mount such an offensive, the guerrillas turned to Nicaragua, Cuba, and the Soviet bloc. The Soviet Union and its Eastern European allies were not very responsive. Cuba, on the other hand, was willing to help. Prior to Reagan's nomination and election, Cuba provided very little material aid to the Salvadoran guerrillas, instead following the precedent of cautiousness established during the Nicaraguan revolution. Castro's most significant contribution was mediating the ideological differences among the disparate factions of the Salvadoran left and getting them to unite.[62] The logic behind Cuba's restraint was similar to what it had been in Nicaragua. Although the Carter administration was supporting the Salvadoran government politically, it was not providing large-scale military assistance. A significant influx of weapons from Cuba would likely bring forth a counterescalation by the United States. Cuba's policy changed during the U.S. election campaign. Reagan's tough rhetoric convinced the Cubans that if he won, the United States would certainly escalate its military role in Central America.[63]

For the Sandinistas, the request for aid from their Salvadoran comrades posed an especially difficult dilemma. They themselves had faced a similar supply problem before their own final offensive in 1979. Cuba, along with Panama and Venezuela, had helped fill the breach. Moreover, the Salvadoran guerrillas had given the Sandinistas $10 million to buy weapons on the international arms market.[64] On the other hand, the war in El Salvador was the single most sensitive issue in Managua's relations with Washington. Though the Sandinistas had turned a blind eye to the FDR-FMLN's use of Nicaraguan territory as a way station in its arms-smuggling operations, they had refrained from making a major commitment in El Salvador. "They were torn in this," said Ambassador Pezzullo. "They were pressured by their so-called friends or colleagues in Salvador, yet there was a desire to have a relationship with the United States."[65]

In the end, the Sandinistas, like the Cubans, decided that Reagan's policy toward them would be one of hostility, regardless of how they behaved. That expectation diminished the incentive for moderation that the Carter administration had so carefully crafted. According to U.S. intelligence reports, arms shipments began arriving in Nicaragua from Cuba during the late summer and early fall of 1980 and began moving into El Salvador after the November election.[66]

In its last few weeks in office, the Carter administration was forced to respond to the unraveling of its Central America policy. As evidence of the Nicaraguan arms transfers to the Salvadoran guerrillas accumulated, Carter came under intense pressure to halt economic aid to Nicaragua and to resume military aid to the Salvadoran armed forces. On January 6, 1981, the CIA sent the White House a new intelligence report on Nicaragua's complicity in arms smuggling. Robert Pastor, the National Security Council senior staff member for Latin America, later wrote, "That report, for the first time in my opinion, provided conclusive proof that the Nicaraguan government was providing significant amounts of aid to the insurgency in El Salvador." The most compelling evidence was aerial photographs of an airfield in Nicaragua being used to resupply the Salvadorans.[67]

On January 16, Carter's crisis management committee, the NSC's Special Coordinating Committee, met to review the evidence of Sandinista complicity in arms smuggling and decided to recommend that Carter suspend aid. He agreed.[68] "I had no alternative but to cut off aid to the Sandinistas before I left office," Carter said, "because there was evidence that was clear to me that the Sandinistas were giving assistance to the revolutionaries in El Salvador, and the law required me to stop the aid."[69]

The suspension of aid was the first step in dismantling the constructive relations with Nicaragua that Carter had tried to maintain for eighteen months. By only suspending aid rather than canceling it, Carter left open the possibility that it might be resumed if Nicaragua ceased its support for the Salvadoran guerrillas. But that determination would fall to Ronald Reagan.

The Camel's Nose

In early January, the FDR-FMLN began its promised final offensive. "It is necessary to launch now the battles for the great general offensive of the Salvadoran people," the guerrillas declared, "before that fanatic Ronald Reagan takes over the presidency of the United States."[70] But the final offensive did not unfold as the guerrillas had anticipated. The military did not split. A handful of progressive officers defected to the guerrillas, but most were too loyal to the institution of the armed forces to go over to the other side. Moreover, there was no mass urban insurrection of the sort that sounded the death knell for the Somoza regime in Nicaragua. The popular organizations that might have led such an uprising had been demolished by the bloody work of the death squads and the security forces. A general strike called in San Salvador failed, leaving the military free to devote its full energy to repulsing guerrilla attacks on outlying army posts. Although the scale of the FMLN offensive strained the army's logistical capabilities, it came nowhere near overthrowing the regime.[71]

Nevertheless, the final offensive reopened the debate over military aid for El Salvador that had been raging within the U.S. government for over a year and tipped the balance in favor of those who wanted to escalate the U.S. military role. Concern about the Salvadoran army's ability to weather the offensive, and the evidence of an increased arms flow to the guerrillas from abroad, led the State Department's Latin American bureau to recommend the resumption of military aid. The Pentagon and the NSC concurred, and on January 13, 1981, Carter agreed.[72]

The decision was made, the Department of State announced, because the Salvadoran government had made "progress in areas of concern to us"—specifically, the investigation into the murders of the churchwomen and the reorganization of the government to reduce human rights abuses. In fact, progress had been meager. As Secretary of State Edmund Muskie noted in his memo to Carter, "It is too early to assess progress in controlling indiscriminate violence." Regarding the murders, Muskie wrote that the investigation was moving forward, but "what remains to be seen is whether the investigation will be pressed to the point of identifying those responsible because of the possible linkage to higher officers."[73]

The overriding reason for resuming military aid was the battlefield situation, along with a plea from Duarte that Washington restore military aid in order to give him some leverage with the armed forces.[74] But the fiction of progress in the churchwomen's case had to be maintained for political reasons. As late as December 22, Secretary Muskie had assured the families of the churchwomen that military assistance would continue to be withheld if the United States was not satisfied with the Salvadoran investigation.[75]

Once the dam was broken, the Pentagon moved quickly to escalate its request. On January 14, the day after Carter decided to resume nonlethal aid, the NSC approved $5.9 million of additional lethal aid, thereby lifting the ban on lethal aid that had been in force since 1977. In order to get the aid to El Salvador quickly, Carter invoked emergency provisions in Section 506(a) of the Foreign Assistance Act, enabling him to send the aid without congressional approval.[76] By resorting to this emergency power, Carter set a precedent that Ronald Reagan would not overlook when the war in El Salvador began to escalate.

The final days of the Carter administration set the stage for the entrance of Ronald Reagan. On more than a few occasions, Reagan administration officials would remind their critics, especially congressional Democrats, that it was

Jimmy Carter who cut off economic aid to Nicaragua and resumed military aid to El Salvador. But while circumstances finally forced Carter into policy decisions that were, if not alien, at least uncomfortable, Ronald Reagan would pursue the policies of hostility toward Nicaragua and military buildup in El Salvador with relish and on a scale that no one in January 1981 could have imagined.

CHAPTER 4

The Vicar Draws the Line

Nothing better symbolized Ronald Reagan's aggressive new foreign policy than his choice for secretary of state: General Alexander M. Haig Jr. It was a controversial appointment, for few people had been more intimately involved with the momentous and troubling events of the 1970s—the war in Vietnam, the coup in Chile, Watergate. Democrats worried about putting a career military officer in charge of the Department of State, especially in light of the general's reputed inclination to seek military solutions to most foreign policy problems.

Al Haig was a politician's general. After graduating an undistinguished 214th in his West Point class of 310, he spent most of his career as an aide to senior officers or civilian policymakers.[1] His forte was maneuvering on the bureaucratic battlefield. Haig's political career began in 1963 when, as a young lieutenant colonel, he was selected to serve on a Pentagon task force on Cuba, where the CIA's secret war against Castro was in full swing.[2]

In 1969, Haig became National Security Adviser Henry Kissinger's military aide on the NSC staff, and within two years the "can-do" colonel had out-maneuvered all the bright young civilians to emerge as Kissinger's deputy. With the patronage of Kissinger and President Nixon, Haig jumped over 230 more senior officers in his two-year rise from the rank of colonel to four-star general, the highest peacetime rank attainable. Fellow officers remarked that they could think of only two parallels for such a meteoric career: George C. Marshall, President Truman's secretary of state from 1947 to 1949, who authored the Marshall Plan for postwar reconstruction in Europe, and George A. Custer, who was killed along with his entire command at the Battle of the Little Big Horn in 1876. Haig liked to compare himself to Marshall.[3]

The World According to Haig

Haig flirted briefly with the idea of running for president in 1980—not enough to be taken seriously as a contender, but just enough to make Ronald Reagan's inner circle suspicious of his ambition and his loyalty to the new president. Only the support of Richard Nixon, who lobbied the president-elect on Haig's behalf, enabled the general to beat out Reagan loyalists Caspar W. Weinberger and William J. Casey for the job of secretary of state. As consolation prizes, Weinberger got Defense and Casey got the CIA.[4]

Haig was an outsider to the Reagan team. Most other senior officials were members of the "California Mafia" who had been with Reagan since his time as governor, or had worked closely with him during the presidential campaign. Haig had done neither. Moreover, Haig was not Ronald Reagan's sort of person. Reagan preferred low-key, cooperative team players who evinced more concern for the common goal than over who received credit for it. Al Haig was just the opposite—extremely jealous of bureaucratic "turf," sensitive to the smallest slight to his authority, and volatile to the point of belligerency. It sometimes seemed that there were two Al Haigs, a White House adviser observed. "One is the smooth-talking diplomatic machine who represents this country most capably. The other is an angry man who becomes unraveled whenever his mandate is challenged."[5]

From the start, Haig feuded openly with rivals or potential rivals: White House Chief of Staff James Baker, National Security Adviser Richard Allen, and U.N. Ambassador Jeane Kirkpatrick. "At Cabinet meetings," recalled one White House official, "he seemed almost like a gunfighter in a hostile saloon."[6] When decisions went against him, Haig was quick to threaten resignation.

"He was a very fragile fellow in a lot of ways, but he got this appearance of toughness and macho," said a colleague in the State Department. "He always used to say, with distressing frequency, that a particular event or a particular problem was or was not 'a test of our manhood.' "[7]

Haig's public persona was also unsettling. There was a certain theatricality about him that left the impression he was always posturing. In speech, he was prone to hyperbole and such contortions of grammar that his "Haigisms" became a standing joke.[8] His image was not helped by his imperious demeanor in the White House after the March 30, 1981, assassination attempt against Reagan. A breathless Haig appeared before television cameras and, gripping the podium tightly, announced, "I am in control here," going on to confuse the constitutional succession by placing himself third in line to the presidency. As one journalist wrote, "By his quavery, Queeg-like demeanor," Haig managed to "suggest that he was far from in charge—even of himself."[9]

Reagan was well aware of Haig's mercurial and suspicious personality. "It's amazing how sound he can be on complex international matters," Reagan wrote in his diary after a briefing from Haig in early 1982, "but how utterly paranoid with regard to people he must work with."[10]

That Al Haig survived as secretary of state for any length of time at all was remarkable, but survive he did. He declared himself "vicar" of foreign policy and immediately tried to subordinate all the various institutions of the executive branch that dealt in one way or another with events abroad. On inauguration day, Haig attempted a putsch of sorts by presenting Reagan with a plan for the new administration's foreign policy decisionmaking process—a plan that gave Haig primacy over Weinberger, Casey, and Allen. "We're going to strip them of their underwear before they even realize that their belt's been unbuckled," Haig bragged to a State Department official. But James Baker stepped in and blocked the maneuver.[11]

"I discovered only a few months into the administration," Reagan recalled, "that Al Haig didn't want anyone other than himself, including me, to influence foreign policy while he was secretary of state."[12] Yet Reagan put up with Haig's egomania and tantrums because, among the senior officials on the Reagan team, only Haig had any substantive knowledge or experience in foreign affairs. Moreover, Haig's policy views fit neatly into the ideological mold Reagan had cast during the campaign.

Haig had long since repudiated the policy of detente that earned his mentor Henry Kissinger the enmity of the Reagan Republicans. The central theme of Haig's speeches during the final years of the Carter administration had been the "relentless" growth of Soviet military power and Washington's dangerous lack of resolve to stand up to the Soviets' "imperial foreign policy," especially in the Third World. "Soviet diplomacy is based on a test of wills," Haig explained. "Since Vietnam, the United States has largely failed these tests."[13] To Haig, it was absolutely imperative that this erosion of power and influence be reversed and that U.S. credibility be restored. One way to do this was a program of rearmament. The other was to turn back the Soviet offensive in the Third World.

Haig saw the world in Manichaean geopolitical terms—a simple vision, devoid of nuance. Although he paid obeisance to the complexity of the modern world, the heart of Haig's view was that things had not really changed very much from the early days of the Cold War—except that the Soviets were stronger and bolder, the United States weaker and more timid. Central America was simply the latest Soviet challenge. The war in El Salvador was a Soviet "probe" designed "to test the strength of Western determination," he wrote.[14]

The Gang That Couldn't Shoot Straight

Haig wasted no time taking control of the State Department. As soon as he was confirmed, he summoned Reagan's State Department transition team and fired them. The team, heavy with Reagan campaign advisers, had become controversial because of its intense conservatism, unpolitic public statements, and leaking of classified documents. It had also terrorized the professional bureaucracy at State by intimating that deep purges were in the making. When the transition team's "hit list" of sixty ambassadors to be fired was leaked to the press, the State Department's worst fears were confirmed.[15]

If the foreign service officers in the Latin American bureau thought the new secretary had saved them from a blood-letting, they were mistaken. Like the Reagan conservatives, Haig had a deep distrust of the people who carried out Carter's Central America policy. Haig only parted company with the conservatives when it came to choosing a new team. Rather than picking "movement conservatives" who had spent their entire careers in opposition and would be neophytes in government, Haig wanted seasoned professionals who knew how to get things done.

Starting on inauguration day, Haig began the most thorough purge suffered by the Department of State since the hysteria over who lost China. The aim, Haig told one of his deputies, was to "clean out" the Latin American bureau.[16] The first to go was Assistant Secretary William Bowdler, who was told unceremoniously to empty his desk by the close of business on January 20. A change in assistant secretaries was normal with a change in administrations, but the shabby treatment Bowdler received certainly was not. A thirty-year veteran of the Foreign Service, Bowdler had served as U.S. ambassador to El Salvador, Guatemala, and South Africa, as director of the State Department's Bureau of Intelligence and Research, and finally as Carter's assistant secretary for Latin America. Such a distinguished officer of long service would normally have been entitled to a major ambassadorial appointment. Instead Bowdler was told there was no longer a place for him in the government and forced into retirement. He had earned the enmity of conservatives by helping arrange the final transition from Somoza to the Sandinista government and was thereby fixed in the minds of the Reagan team as one of the people who "lost" Nicaragua.

Two of Bowdler's deputies, John Bushnell and James Cheek, were kept on temporarily until a new assistant secretary was confirmed. Normally, the forward assignment for someone of their rank would be an ambassadorship. Bushnell, who of all the Carter officials was the most sympathetic to the new Reagan policy, had his ambassadorship vetoed by the White House. He was left to languish for over a year as "ambassador to the hallways"—that is, without any assignment at all—before he was finally sent as deputy chief of mission to Argentina.

James Cheek had spent most of his career in Latin America, serving in Chile, Brazil, Uruguay, Nicaragua, and, most recently, El Salvador. Highly respected for both his insight and his courage, he had won an award for his reporting on the corruption and venality of Somoza in the early 1970s. During the last six months of the Carter administration, Cheek headed the State Department's task force on El Salvador. Haig sent him into exile as deputy chief of mission in Katmandu, Nepal.

Jack Binns, the U.S. ambassador to Honduras, had been acting as an intermediary between the United States and the Salvadoran left, trying to broker a negotiated settlement of the war in the closing months of 1980.[17] Although he had been in Honduras less than a year when Reagan came to office, within a few months he was sent off to be diplomat-in-residence at the University of California, Berkeley. He was never given another ambassadorship and retired a few years later.

Despite the transition team's recommendation, and to the surprise of many people, Lawrence Pezzullo in Nicaragua was not fired immediately, but his policy recommendations were ignored. Discouraged, he left the embassy in Nicaragua at midyear. Pezzullo was sent off to be a diplomat-in-residence at the University of Georgia, after which he too resigned from the Foreign Service.[18]

Robert White was the first career ambassador replaced by the new administration. Haig fired him within a week after the inauguration. White's removal was announced before he had been given an onward assignment, and when an offer was finally forthcoming, it was a midlevel post in the inspector general's office—a dead-end job beneath the stature of a veteran ambassador. White refused to take it and so was forced to retire.[19]

The State Department explained that White's removal was intended to signal the coming change in U.S. policy. As a temporary replacement, Frederic Chapin was sent to San Salvador as chargé d'affaires. Chapin had been deputy assistant secretary of defense for inter-American affairs under Carter. He was the official who designed the Pentagon's proposals for a major military buildup in El Salvador—the very proposals Bob White had spent the past year fending off.[20]

The people Al Haig put in charge of the Latin American bureau were people like himself—ambitious, "can-do" managers who were willing to bend a few rules if that was what it took to get the job done. They were the "five-percenters," the best and brightest in the Foreign Service. And most of them had gotten their first big career boost in Southeast Asia. "We assigned a lot of people to Vietnam who were action-oriented because it was the highest national priority," explained one official, describing his own career path. "It's not surprising that they find themselves now in Central America."[21]

Few of these people knew anything about Central America, but regional expertise was not highly prized. In fact, subordinates who insisted on pointing out the divergence between Haig's globalist assumptions and regional realities were worse than useless. They were not team players; they were always wringing their hands and lamenting the limits of U.S. influence. Having no experience in the area came to be seen as an advantage, because it meant an officer had not been infected with "regionalitis."[22] Not surprisingly, officers who had built their careers in Latin America resented the sudden influx of crisis managers. Noting the Southeast Asian experience of many of the interlopers, one Latin American specialist described their arrival as "the gang that couldn't shoot straight gets another chance."[23]

Haig chose Thomas O. Enders to be assistant secretary of state for inter-American affairs. Enders had never served in Latin America and did not speak Spanish, but Haig was unconcerned. He chose Enders because he was "a demonstrated performer who can cut through the system."[24] Enders did not formally assume his post as assistant secretary until five months after inauguration because Senator Jesse Helms (R-N.C.) worked furiously to block his nomination. Helms regarded Enders as dangerously liberal and hoped to convince the White House to force Haig to accept Lewis Tambs, a conservative academic, instead. (Tambs was finally appointed ambassador to Colombia and later Costa Rica.) This delaying maneuver became Helms's favorite ploy whenever the State Department nominated someone he thought was from the Kissinger wing instead of the Reagan wing of the Republican Party—"Kissinger retreads," he called them.[25] But Helms was not acting alone. Because Helms was one of Ronald Reagan's earliest and most avid supporters, his views carried weight with the president's closest advisers. The Enders appointment was held up not in the Senate but in the White House. He was not even officially nominated for more than a month after Haig asked him to take the Latin American post, and then his name went forward only when Haig forced the issue by announcing the appointment before the White House had cleared it.[26]

Tom Enders was not often mistaken for a liberal. Born into a wealthy Republican banking family in Connecticut, he had the credentials of the American upper class: Exeter, Yale (where he finished first in his class), Harvard, and a touch of Europe from his time at the Sorbonne. He was a towering figure, both physically (at six foot eight inches) and intellectually. "Of all the people in the Foreign Service of his generation that I knew, he was the brightest of the lot," said former supervisor George Kaplan. But Enders's stature was matched by his ambition and arrogance. He made no secret of his desire to be the first career foreign service officer to be appointed secretary of state, and in his climb up the career ladder, he never suffered fools lightly.[27]

Arrogance got Enders into trouble midway through his career. After a decade of rapid promotions, he was appointed in 1969 as deputy chief of mission (DCM) in the U.S. embassy in Yugoslavia. There, Enders clashed with another strong personality, Ambassador William Leonhart, who had Enders recalled to Washington after only a year at the post. With his promising career in a tailspin, Enders went willingly as DCM in Cambodia in 1971, a time when most diplomats were avoiding service in Southeast Asia. In 1972, he was the target of an assassination attempt that killed his chauffeur and three bodyguards, but Enders himself escaped unscathed.[28]

Enders quickly became Al Haig's favorite officer at the embassy in Pnomh Penh because of what Ambassador Emory C. Swank called his "can-do personality." Swank was not highly regarded by Haig and Kissinger; he lacked enthusiasm for a policy that was wreaking destruction on Cambodian society. Enders, on the other hand, did his job with élan. "We were delighted with him," recalled a Kissinger aide. "He was strong, aggressive, and exuded confidence."[29]

When control over the secret bombing of Cambodia was shifted to the U.S. embassy in February 1973, Enders took charge of it, selecting targets for B-52 strikes using maps so crude and outdated that it was impossible to know whether civilians were in the target area. "I began to get reports of wholesale carnage," recalled embassy political officer Bill Harben. The raids continued.[30]

Enders was not one to let outsiders such as the press or Congress interfere with getting the job done. When the Senate Foreign Relations Committee sent two staff members to Cambodia in April 1973 to investigate the embassy's role in the bombing, Enders did his best to mislead them. First he told them the embassy had no detailed knowledge of air operations. That line of defense became untenable after *Newsweek* correspondent Sylvana Foa showed the investigators how, with a cheap transistor radio, she could hear U.S. embassy personnel giving bombing instructions to warplanes on their way to target. Confronted with this evidence, Enders told the Senate staffers that the embassy had special instructions that prevented him from discussing the bombing. In fact, Enders himself had written the instructions, sent them to Washington for approval, and then invoked them as a rationale for refusing to cooperate with the congressional inquiry.[31]

When the Senate Foreign Relations Committee finally got to the bottom of the Cambodia bombing, it concluded that Enders had been "grossly misleading." But troubles with Congress were not a black mark for Enders as far as Haig and Kissinger were concerned. The following year he was appointed assistant secretary of state for economics and business affairs and then ambassador to Canada, one of the most sought-after posts in the Foreign Service. He was back on the fast track.

When Reagan officially nominated Enders to be assistant secretary of state for inter-American affairs, no one in the Senate mentioned his scrap with Congress over the Cambodia bombing. Senate liberals were relieved that Haig had picked a career foreign service officer and not one of Jesse Helms's movement conservatives.

As his chief assistant on Central America, Enders chose L. Craig Johnstone, another action-oriented career officer who earned his reputation in Southeast Asia. Although Johnstone spent much of his childhood in Latin America, he had not served there during his foreign service career.[32] In the late 1960s, he had been special assistant to William Colby in Vietnam, working in the Civil Operations and Revolutionary Development Support (CORDS) program—a pacification program run jointly by the Agency for International Development and the CIA. Colby, on leave from the CIA to serve as the program's director, helped set up the most infamous part of CORDS—the "Phoenix" counterterror operation designed to uproot the National Liberation Front's political infrastructure. Some 20,000 suspected Viet Cong cadres were killed by Phoenix hit squads, dubbed Provincial Reconnaissance Units.[33] When the Saigon regime collapsed in 1975, Johnstone returned to Vietnam on his own initiative to help evacuate two hundred "high risk" Vietnamese who had worked with the United States, most of whom were members of Phoenix's Provincial Reconnaissance teams and their families.[34]

To mollify Senator Helms, the White House saddled Enders with two hardline conservative special advisers: retired general Gordon Sumner, one of the authors of the Santa Fe report, and retired general Vernon A. Walters, a veteran of both the Defense Intelligence Agency and the CIA. Sumner had been a vocal opponent of the Panama Canal treaties, and during the 1979 insurrection in Nicaragua, he advocated U.S. support for Somoza right to the end. He believed that the burgeoning toll of murders by the death squads in El Salvador was exaggerated.[35]

In Honduras, Ambassador Binns, who had spent most of his career in Latin America, was replaced by John Negroponte, who had served there only once. Negroponte had been a political officer in the U.S. embassy in Saigon during the early stages of the Vietnam War and was assigned to the Paris peace talks in 1968. From there, he moved up to the National Security Council staff to become Kissinger's expert on Vietnam after several NSC aides resigned over the invasion of Cambodia. Like Haig, Negroponte broke with Kissinger over the Paris Peace Accords, arguing that the United States had given away too much. When Kissinger became secretary of state, he took revenge by banishing Negroponte to Ecuador.[36]

In El Salvador, Deane R. Hinton replaced Robert White. Hinton, a highly regarded generalist with thirty-five years of service, had spent only four years in Latin America—two tours with AID during the late 1960s and early 1970s. He was in Guatemala from 1967 to 1969 when AID was working closely with the Guatemalan armed forces in their counterinsurgency efforts, and in Chile from 1969 to 1971 when AID participated in Nixon's effort to destabilize Salvador Allende's government.[37]

When Lawrence Pezzullo left Nicaragua, he was replaced by Anthony C. E. Quainton, who had never served in Latin America and spoke no Spanish. For the Reagan team, Quainton's chief attraction seemed to be his previous post as head of the State Department's Office for Combatting Terrorism.[38]

"Any one of the former ambassadors has more years in Central America than all three of the new ones combined," commented one State Department official.[39] "It isn't embarrassing that the Secretary of State doesn't know anything about Central America," commented another who served in Central America during the Reagan years. "And it is only moderately embarrassing that the assistant secretary doesn't know very much. But it is very bad when the deputy assistant secretaries and even the office directors know so little."[40] The dearth of regional expertise among the key officials handling Central America, both in Washington and in the field, meant that there was no one to temper Haig's unremitting globalism.

Making El Salvador a Test Case

Al Haig was convinced that Central America was the place for the United States to finally "draw the line" against the spread of international Communism.[41] A tough new policy would constitute a test of Washington's ability to manage events in the region and, more important, of Washington's will to turn back the tide of Soviet expansion. "The fires of insurrection fed by the Soviets and fanned by their surrogates, the Cubans, spread unchecked in Central America," Haig explained. The Soviets had targeted the region with wars of national liberation because it was a "strategic choke point" and therefore "a hinge area for vital American interests."[42]

As an arena for demonstrating American force and will, Central America seemed to offer a number of advantages. The crisis there was already acute, and President Carter himself had paved the way for a tough U.S. response by renewing military aid to El Salvador in his last days in office. Moreover, the war in El Salvador looked winnable. By the time Reagan entered the Oval Office, the guerrillas' final offensive had already petered out. A significant increase in military aid would enable the army to go over to the offensive and make short work of the insurgency. A few months, Haig expected, was all it would take. "Mr. President," he told Reagan in an early NSC meeting on Central America, "this is one you can win."[43]

Geography also worked in Washington's favor. Haig did not believe the Salvadoran guerrillas could survive without substantial external aid from Cuba and the Soviet Union. Since Central America was of marginal importance to the Soviets, the risk of a superpower confrontation seemed slim. But even if El Salvador did become the focal point of reciprocal escalations by Washington and Moscow, Washington's supply lines were short, whereas Moscow's were long—almost as long as Washington's had been in Vietnam. Politically defensible, militarily winnable, and geostrategically advantageous—El Salvador seemed like an ideal place for a showdown.

A victory in Central America would be Reagan's first foreign policy success and its ramifications would be global. By defeating the Soviet challenge in Central America, the United States would demonstrate to the Kremlin and its Cuban proxies that the new president would not tolerate Soviet adventurism in the Third World. Such firmness would reduce the likelihood of Soviet troublemaking elsewhere. It would also send a message to Western Europe that the United States was once again committed to world leadership. And most important, it would demonstrate to the American people that the United States could project military power into the Third World without becoming entangled in another Vietnam.[44]

This last objective was especially vital. Reagan's conservatives came to Washington convinced that the United States had been paralyzed by the trauma of Vietnam and that the security of the nation depended upon overcoming the reluctance to use military force. A quick victory in Central America would begin purging the national psyche of the Vietnam syndrome, rebuilding the pre-Vietnam consensus for aggressive containment.[45]

Shortly before Reagan's inauguration, his new National Security Council met at Blair House to review the most urgent foreign policy problems—Iran, Poland, and Afghanistan. As the meeting was coming to an end, Haig raised Central America, arguing passionately that the Communist threat there demanded immediate action. "The thrust of his argument and the principal target of his emotion was Cuba," Caspar Weinberger recalled. Asked what Washington ought to do in response to this threat, Haig told his stunned colleagues that they would have to invade Cuba and put an end to the Castro regime. To Haig's chagrin, no one else on Reagan's team was eager to begin the new administration with a foreign war.[46] Other officials generally agreed that the Central American crisis was a serious escalation of Soviet and Cuban adventurism, but, Haig recalled, the issue "did not arouse high passions."[47]

On January 23, the NSC devoted an entire meeting to El Salvador—the first in a series of meetings marked by sharp debate over what, precisely, the new administration should do. Easy agreement was reached on increasing economic aid, shifting the emphasis of policy from human rights to combating Communist subversion, and replacing Ambassador White. Everyone also agreed on the need to increase military aid, but the consensus broke down over how much should be sent and whether U.S. advisers should accompany it.[48]

For Haig, the reluctance of his colleagues was "anguishing." His desire to make El Salvador an exemplary battle in the Cold War required a high public profile and a quick victory. The whole point of meeting and defeating the Soviet challenge in Central America was to demonstrate to the world that America was back, standing tall at the barricades against Communist expansion. It made no sense to move slowly or quietly. Moreover, Haig was convinced that Washington must not dispense its military aid with an eye dropper. One of the lessons he drew from Vietnam was that incremental escalation allowed the enemy time to adapt. The key to victory was for Washington to apply its overwhelming power early.[49]

But aiding the Salvadoran government was not enough. The other lesson Haig took from Vietnam (and Korea before it) was that to win a guerrilla war you had to "go to the source"—cut off the guerrillas' logistical supplies by carrying the war to their rear bases. In El Salvador, "going to the source" meant taking the war to Cuba. "There could not be the slightest doubt that Cuba was at once the source of supply and the catechist of the Salvadoran insurgency," Haig wrote later. "Cuba, in turn, could not act . . . without the approval and material support of the USSR. I believed our policy should carry the consequences of this relationship directly to Moscow and Havana."[50]

In March, at another NSC meeting, Haig raised the issue again. "You just give me the word," he told Reagan, "and I'll turn that fucking island into a parking lot." Deputy Chief of Staff Michael Deaver was appalled at Haig's bellicosity. "It scared the shit out of me," he told a colleague after the meeting. Deaver, who controlled access to Reagan, resolved never to let Haig see the president alone.[51]

"Haig had this real [thing] for Castro," recalled one senior administration official. "He kept saying, 'Give me a Cuban policy,' which was really some way to knock off Castro. He wanted to 'defang' him."[52]

Haig believed Cuba could be punished with impunity. When he complained about Cuban adventurism to Soviet Ambassador Anatoly Dobrynin, Dobrynin insisted that the Soviet Union was not masterminding Cuban policy in the Western Hemisphere and that Cuba's actions were a matter between Washington and Havana. Haig interpreted this as a signal that the Soviets would allow the United States a "relatively free hand" to take punitive measures against Cuba.[53]

Proceeding on his own, Haig put together an inter-agency task force to develop policy options. "You put together a strategy for toppling Castro," Haig told them, "and in the process, we're going to eliminate this lodgement from Nicaragua and the mainland." Directed by Robert McFarlane, who worked for Haig's deputy, William Clark, the task force included General Paul F. Gorman, a staff officer for the Joint Chiefs, Nestor Sanchez, chief of the Latin America operations division at the CIA, and Francis West, from the Pentagon's Office of International Security Affairs.

Their first report concluded that ousting Castro wasn't feasible. Haig was apoplectic. "This is just trash," he raged, "limp-wristed, traditional cookie-pushing bullshit." They went back to the drawing board and eventually developed a set of options ranging all the way up to military blockade. But most of the options still relied on diplomatic and economic instruments rather than military ones. Although the options paper came to be known as the "Haig plan," Haig himself didn't think it was tough enough.[54] Other senior officials continued to disagree. "It was a plan that might best and most fairly be described as folly," said Richard Allen. "If we give Al Haig his way," James Baker mused, "the next thing you know, we'll be carpet-bombing Central America."[55]

Haig proposed a naval blockade of Cuba to interdict the flow of arms to Nicaragua and El Salvador and assigned Enders to draw up the plans.[56] Initial steps were taken by sending two nuclear-powered carrier battle groups into the Atlantic for maneuvers around Cuba. In addition, NATO exercises were staged in Puerto Rico, and the Key West military task force was upgraded to the status of Caribbean Command.

But no other senior administration official supported Haig's blockade proposal. The president was sympathetic, but everyone else thought the venture too risky.[57] They did not share Haig's belief that Dobrynin was giving Washington a green light to punish Cuba. A blockade could well be interpreted by the Soviets as a violation of the 1962 agreement that ended the Cuban Missile Crisis, thus precipitating a major superpower confrontation. Senior White House officials were appalled that Haig was willing to risk war over Cuba. Despite his isolation, Haig continued to press his blockade proposal for several weeks, even sending Reagan an options paper on it in the hope that he could win the president over.[58] Reagan, too, had a particular dislike for Castro, so the idea of some military action against Cuba appealed to him. On the campaign trail, Reagan had called repeatedly for a blockade of Cuba in retaliation for the Soviet invasion of Afghanistan.[59] When he first took office, Reagan was inclined to launch an invasion of Cuba to rid the island of Castro, but was dissuaded by advisers who pointed out that the large and well-trained Cuban army would turn the country into another Vietnam, this time on America's doorstep—not to mention the risk of war with the Soviet Union.[60]

Opposition from both the Pentagon and the senior White House staff ultimately proved fatal for Haig's blockade plans. Like the White House, the Department of Defense was not eager to risk a superpower confrontation over Central America. Neither the Joint Chiefs of Staff nor the new secretary of defense, Caspar Weinberger, was willing to involve the armed forces in a conflict unless there was a clear national consensus behind it. This was the principal lesson that the uniformed military drew from Vietnam.[61]

Moreover, Ronald Reagan had come to office promising a major strategic military buildup, and opinion polls showed that the public believed a buildup was necessary. The Pentagon had no interest in risking this consensus by taking on another unpopular brushfire war. When the Caribbean military exercises were completed at the end of February, the Pentagon insisted that the carrier battle groups were needed elsewhere and reassigned them despite Haig's urging that they be left permanently on station in the Caribbean.[62]

While the military was loath to pick a fight with the Soviet Union, they were eager to get into El Salvador and show that they could win a counterinsurgency war—not with American troops, but with advisers and large-scale military aid. Unlike Al Haig, however, the Pentagon had no illusions about the prospects for quick victory. Several military survey teams had been in El Salvador over the preceding year, so the Pentagon knew all too well the manifest deficiencies of the Salvadoran armed forces.[63] Winning the guerrilla war there would be a long-term task.

Even the prospect of a significant increase in military aid met some resistance inside the administration, however. "Very nearly the first words spoken on this subject in the councils of the Reagan administration made reference to the danger of 'another Vietnam,'" Haig recalled ruefully.[64] At the White House, a "troika" of senior staff members—Edwin Meese, James Baker, and Michael Deaver—dominated administration decisionmaking. This inner circle of Reagan advisers was leery about raising the stakes over El Salvador because it was so controversial. "These men were intensely sensitive to the public mood and reluctant to take any action that might alter it in the president's disfavor," Haig recalled. "Every day [they] put their finger to the wind to see what the people wanted."[65]

The troika's top priority was Reagan's domestic program, particularly his budget and tax bills. With a new Republican majority in the Senate and a potential ideological majority of conservatives in the House of Representatives, a profound alteration of domestic priorities—a Reagan Revolution—was within reach. The White House inner circle wanted nothing to interfere with that agenda.

The debate over what to do in El Salvador stretched on for a month. Ronald Reagan's style of governing was to wait until his principal advisers reached a consensus before he made a decision. When his advisers disagreed, as they did initially on El Salvador, Reagan simply deferred deciding.[66] While the debate dragged on inconclusively, a reorientation of policy was already under way, emanating from the Department of State. On January 28, Haig gave his first press conference, setting the new tone: The Soviets were involved in "unprecedented . . . risk-taking" in the Third World, he said, and Washington would no longer sit still for it. "International terrorism will take the place of human rights" as the administration's special concern, Haig promised.[67] The practical meaning of this for policy toward El Salvador was soon spelled out. In February, State Department spokesman William Dyess announced that Washington regarded the left as the main danger in El Salvador and that U.S. aid would no longer be conditional upon the government's human rights practices or its investigation of the murders of U.S. citizens.[68]

Acting on his own, Haig took small measures to convey the new tough line to America's adversaries. He spurned an offer by the FDR-FMLN to open a private dialogue, via Mexico, about the possibility of a negotiated settlement in El Salvador. He berated the Nicaraguan ambassador, Rita Delia Casco, at a Washington cocktail party when she expressed her hope that relations between Nicaragua and the United States would be cordial under the new administration. Towering over the diminutive Nicaraguan, Haig bluntly told her that there would be "no business as usual" (one of Haig's favorite phrases) as long as Nicaragua was committing aggression against its neighbors. The United States would cut off economic aid and "do others things as well," he threatened, if Nicaragua did not relent.[69]

In every conversation with Soviet officials, Haig raised the issue of Cuban support for the Salvadoran insurgency, insisting that there could be no business as usual between the superpowers unless the Soviets reined in their proxy. He invoked a policy of "linkage," in which bilateral issues such as arms control were "linked" to Soviet behavior in the Third World, especially Central America. There would be no dialogue on arms control, Haig informed the Soviets, until the Cubans stopped subverting El Salvador.[70]

After several weeks of stalemate in the policy debate over El Salvador, Haig began to worry that a golden opportunity was being lost. Anxious to establish himself as the administration's foreign policy "vicar," he decided to force the issue. In mid-February, Haig unleashed what one former Carter official called a "political blitzkrieg," turning El Salvador into a high-profile East-West issue whether his colleagues in the administration liked it or not.[71]

The White Paper

Haig's blitzkrieg began in earnest on February 12, 1981, when the press was told in a background briefing that El Salvador was going to be a "test case" to establish Reagan's tough new foreign policy. Not only would the administration draw a clear line against further Communist subversion, it would also turn El Salvador into an "early barometer" of the loyalty of U.S. allies.[72] Washington had obtained conclusive evidence that El Salvador was the victim of an international Communist conspiracy, the press was told.

The centerpiece of Haig's public relations offensive was a State Department White Paper, *Communist Interference in El Salvador*, released on February 23, 1981.[73] Based on captured documents and other intelligence information gathered during the final months of the Carter administration, the report claimed to present "definitive evidence" that "over the past year, the insurgency in El Salvador has been progressively transformed into a textbook case of indirect armed aggression by Communist powers." At the center of this conspiracy were Nicaragua, Cuba, and the Soviet Union, all accused of serving as arms conduits for the guerrillas and turning El Salvador into a Cold War battleground. The campaign to arm the FMLN was allegedly global, involving Hungary, Czechoslovakia, East Germany, Bulgaria, Vietnam, Ethiopia, Iraq, and the Palestine Liberation Organization (PLO). Based on the captured documents, the White Paper charged that Communist countries had promised eight hundred tons of arms to the guerrillas and delivered two hundred tons in late 1980.

The heart of the White Paper, the section that had the most dramatic impact, was a six-page summary of the contents of nineteen captured documents, complete with photographs, chronicling the efforts of the Salvadoran rebels to obtain arms abroad. This section carried the burden of proving that the war in El Salvador was an East-West conflict in microcosm. On the face of it, the narrative seemed to clearly establish that significant quantities of weapons had been provided to the Salvadoran guerrillas by the Soviet Union and its allies. "We have clear evidence of catching the Communists' hands in the cookie jar," boasted White House Press Secretary James S. Brady.[74]

The White Paper inevitably called forth memories of Lyndon Johnson's 1965 White Paper on Vietnam, *Aggression from the North*, which was also designed to make the case that the United States needed to expand its military commitment to a Third World ally beset by internal conflict.[75] Both White Papers asserted that the conflicts were not civil wars but instances of external aggression by the Communist bloc. Both insisted that internal opponents of the U.S.-backed regimes were nothing but puppets of foreign powers. Both argued that there had recently been a qualitative increase in the degree of external involvement, necessitating a U.S. response. And both insisted that the evidence was "incontrovertible."

With great fanfare, the State Department dispatched briefing teams armed with the White Paper to Western Europe and Latin America, hoping to enlist allied support. The allies were generally noncommittal. They were willing to voice their opposition to foreign interference in El Salvador, if that was what the White Paper proved, but they were not willing to endorse an aggressive U.S. policy that had not yet been fully formulated.[76]

Congressional leaders were more credulous. Accepting the White Paper at face value, they hurried to voice support for strong measures to hold back the Communist tide. Emerging from a briefing by Haig, Senator Charles Percy (R-Ill.), the new chairman of the Foreign Relations Committee, declared, "I think those outside forces should be on notice that this nation will do whatever is necessary to prevent a Communist takeover in El Salvador." House Majority Leader Jim Wright (D-Tex.) echoed Percy's sentiments: "Central America is probably more vitally important to us than any other part of the world," he said. "Our response to what is happening there requires a bipartisan, unified approach and I fully expect that is what the president and the secretary of state will receive."[77] Even the staunchest liberals did not challenge the White Paper's basic premise.

The press also took the White Paper at face value. Administration officials calculated, correctly, that harried journalists writing on deadline would rely upon the White Paper and not look too closely at the supporting documentation. Among journalists who regularly covered Central America, the White Paper was widely disbelieved, though few questioned it in print.[78] John Dinges, writing for Pacific News Service, was the first to actually look at the captured documents to see if they supported the White Paper's conclusions. He discovered they did not. A great many claims in the White Paper were nowhere to be found in the documents. When he asked about these discrepancies, the State Department "declined further elaboration on its conclusions," Dinges reported in March, "and has stopped providing copies of the original documents."[79]

The critique by Dinges had little immediate effect on the policy debate, but it prompted the *Wall Street Journal* and the *Washington Post* to take a closer look at the White Paper.[80] Those investigations were not concluded until June, after the administration's first fever over Central America had subsided, but the resulting critiques devastated the administration's credibility. They showed in detail that much of the White Paper's argument was, in the words of a U.S. intelligence analyst, "a castle of sand."[81]

The White Paper documents did show that the Salvadoran guerrillas enjoyed political and some material support from Nicaragua, Cuba, and the Communist bloc. The flow of weapons to them through Nicaragua appeared to increase in the last two months of 1980 as the rebels prepared for their January "final offensive." But the documents also showed guerrillas who were poorly armed and desperately searching for additional supplies—"a disorganized rag-tag rebellion," in the words of Wall Street Journal correspondent Jonathan Kwitny—not an army flush with modern equipment as the White Paper suggested.[82]

Moreover, the Sandinistas were hardly eager sponsors of the Salvadoran insurgency. The FMLN used Nicaragua as a conduit for arms smuggling with the connivance of some senior Sandinista officials. But the documents clearly showed the Sandinistas' reluctance to become too deeply involved in logistical support for the Salvadorans. The Sandinistas were skeptical of the FMLN's strength, critical of its operations, and on the whole leery about risking the security of their own revolution to promote one next door.

The documents also showed that the FMLN got help from Cuba, but was generally disdained by the Soviet Union. The Soviets were hardly the puppet masters behind the arms supply effort, as the White Paper claimed. The picture painted by the documents themselves was one of Soviet indifference and reluctance to become involved even in transporting arms, let alone providing them. Above all, the documents did not support the White Paper's central thesis— that massive external interference by the Communist bloc had transformed the Salvadoran conflict from a civil war to a case of indirect external aggression.[83]

Even some State Department officials were dismayed at the propagandistic character of the White Paper. It had gone through several hurried drafts, becoming more argumentative and less nuanced with each revision. Haig wanted the report to make a stronger case, while foreign service officers in the Latin American bureau argued that the report should reflect the real ambiguities in the evidence. By the time the final version was done, even officials who had worked on it thought it "overreached the evidence" and had become "too ideological." The White Paper was, in the words of one official, a "selling" document.[84]

In fact, the evidence arrayed in the White Paper was no different from what had been available to the Carter administration, but it had not altered Carter's assessment that the Salvadoran insurgency was an indigenous movement largely independent of foreign powers. What changed from Carter to Reagan was the ideological prism through which the evidence was viewed and the political agenda for which it could be used.[85]

Though the critiques of the White Paper were devastatingly thorough, they did not get nearly as much attention as the report's original release, or have nearly the impact. The White Paper's February 1981 unveiling came at a critical juncture, when Haig was intent upon changing the thrust of policy toward El Salvador despite significant opposition in Congress and reluctance within the administration itself. The White Paper changed the framework of the debate at a key moment. From February 1981 onward, the issue was not whether the United States should provide military aid to El Salvador, but how much should be given and under what conditions. When the White Paper was fully dissected four months later and its core arguments thrown into doubt, it hardly mattered. The White Paper had done its job by helping smooth the way for a policy change, and once the new policy was established, no after-the-fact debunking of the White Paper could turn back the clock.

The Decision to Engage

On February 27, 1981, the NSC finally settled on a policy toward El Salvador, approving $25 million in new military aid—more than El Salvador had received in total since 1946 and more than all the rest of Latin America and the Caribbean received in 1981.[86] Of these funds, $20 million were to be sent immediately, without congressional approval, under the same special emergency powers Carter had used. Reagan's use of emergency powers to send the first booster shot of military aid was indicative of the administration's penchant for resorting to unilateral actions to circumvent congressional opponents.[87] Most of Reagan's Republicans scorned the hard work of building broad bipartisan support through consultation and compromise. Congress was seen not as a partner in the foreign policy process, but as an obstacle to be overcome.

Reagan also decided to deploy twenty-six more U.S. advisers, bringing the total to fifty-four. Most of the new advisers were in Mobile Training Teams that would train special rapid response battalions of Salvadoran troops. Planning was also begun for a hefty increase in economic assistance.[88] Two weeks later, on March 9, Reagan signed a "Presidential Finding on Central America," authorizing CIA covert operations in support of the Salvadoran government. The program, devised by CIA Director William Casey, had a budget of $19.5 million. It included regional political operations and a paramilitary component designed to "interdict" arms supplies flowing into El Salvador from Nicaragua and Honduras.[89]

These initial decisions on El Salvador were a classic example of bureaucratic compromise. After a year of agitation, the Pentagon finally received permission to send Mobile Training Teams into the field to train Salvadoran infantrymen. It also received a large enough increase in military aid to cement the administration's political commitment to the survival of the Salvadoran government. But because of the White House's domestic political worries, the package of military aid was substantially below the level the Pentagon thought was needed to win the war. In another move to limit the negative political fallout, the advisers were prohibited from entering combat zones.

Although the increases in military aid for El Salvador were couched in terms similar to those used by the Carter administration to justify its commitment to the Duarte government, they nevertheless constituted a significant reorientation of U.S. policy. Carter, seeing the war as essentially an internal conflict that had to be resolved politically, limited the amount of U.S. military aid as a way of trying to strengthen the hand of the reform-minded Christian Democrats. Aid was at least nominally contingent upon the human rights practices of the government. By bolstering the centrist civilians, Carter hoped to politically defeat the Salvadoran oligarchy and then foster a political dialogue between the Christian Democrats and the "democratic" (that is, the unarmed) elements of the Salvadoran left.[90]

Reagan, like Haig, instinctively saw the Salvadoran war as Soviet meddling in Washington's sphere of influence. Defeating this Soviet incursion militarily was the administration's principal aim; a political settlement was inadequate. When the FDR-FMLN offered to negotiate after the failure of its January 1981 offensive, Reagan was not interested.[91] Nor was the new administration particularly committed to the reforms Carter had tried so hard to impose on a reluctant Salvadoran military. "You do not try to fight a civil war and institute reforms at the same time," said President-elect Reagan. "Get rid of the war. Then go forward with reforms."[92]

Washington's militant new posture had political consequences inside El Salvador that the Reagan team did not fully anticipate. By delinking military aid from reforms and human rights, the Reagan administration inadvertently convinced the far right that they no longer needed the Christian Democrats as a fig leaf to guarantee the flow of U.S. aid. On March 3, D'Aubuisson called on the armed forces to oust the Christian Democrats from the government, asserting that Reagan advisers Roger Fontaine and Daniel O. Graham had assured him Washington would "favor" such a move.[93]

The White House press office quickly denied D'Aubuisson's claim that Fontaine had ever "stated or implied" U.S. support for a rightist coup. Shortly thereafter, the U.S. embassy was machine-gunned. "This incident has all the hallmarks of a D'Aubuisson operation," Chargé Frederic Chapin remarked.[94]

Still, Reagan did not want to be trapped into cutting off aid if the right went ahead and ousted the Christian Democrats anyway. Winning the war was still the top priority, so administration officials began to equivocate. State Department spokesman William Dyess again denied that Washington had signaled support for a coup, but he repeatedly refused to say that the United States would oppose one. At the White House, Press Secretary Brady was asked how Reagan would view a rightist takeover. "We just don't have a view on that," he replied.[95] When Reagan himself was asked if he would cut off aid in the event of a coup, he reaffirmed his support for the existing government, but refused to rule out a continuation of U.S. aid regardless.[96]

The Democrats Respond

The dazed Democrats straggled back into Washington in January 1981 like a beaten army, their overwhelming defeat in the 1980 campaign all the more bitter for having been unexpected. Everyone had recognized, of course, that with the hostages still held in Iran, Carter might lose his bid for reelection. But few Democrats had anticipated the magnitude of his defeat. Until election eve, it appeared that Carter might eke out a narrow victory. But in the harsh light of morning, the enormity of Reagan's triumph was inescapable. The Republican ticket carried forty-four states, winning 50.7 percent of the popular vote to the Democrats' 41.0 percent.

The greatest shock for the Democrats, however, was the loss of the Senate. Going into the election, they had held what seemed to be an unassailable majority of 59 seats. In just a few hours, that margin melted away as the Democrats lost 22 of 34 Senate races—their worst reversal since 1946. For the first time in a quarter of a century, the Republicans would control the Senate, vastly enhancing President Reagan's ability to move his legislative proposals through the Congress. The Reagan Revolution was about to begin.

The demoralized Democrats were immediately thrown on the defensive by Haig's public relations campaign over the Soviet menace in Central America. They had no grounds to challenge the authenticity of the State Department's White Paper or the contention that the Salvadoran rebels were getting outside aid, especially since the Carter administration had acknowledged as much in its closing days. But congressional liberals were skeptical of the administration's conclusion that outside aid had transformed the Salvadoran conflict into an East-West confrontation. That argument seemed like a convenient justification for Reagan's plan to escalate U.S. military involvement in the conflict—a prospect the liberals uniformly opposed.

But there was not much they could do to slow the administration's rush to war. None of the basic decisions taken by Reagan in late February required approval of the full Congress, and only a few were subject to any congressional review at all. Moreover, the Democratic leadership simply didn't have the stomach for a fight with the new president on foreign policy. Carter's defeat cast a long shadow over the Democrats, many of whom blamed the debacle as much on Carter's foreign problems—Iran, Afghanistan, and the Panama Canal—as on his difficulties with the domestic economy. In the Senate, liberals who survived the electoral decimation of their colleagues were cowed, fearful of being tarred with the brush of weakness abroad. "The last election changed things," explained Senator Paul Tsongas (D-Mass.). "Not only did we lose Democrats and liberals, but those who are left are so weary. Everyone is running for cover from Reagan and the conservative trend."[97]

Liberal Democrats in the Senate faced the added liability that Minority Leader Robert C. Byrd (D-W.Va.) was a moderate conservative on foreign policy issues and a traditionalist who preferred to leave the initiative with the president. "I fully agree with President Reagan that Cuban interference and arms supplies to that country [El Salvador] are totally unacceptable," Byrd said in reaction to the White Paper. "I don't believe we should be forever paralyzed by what happened in Vietnam."[98]

In the House of Representatives, the liberals were more numerous and a bit better organized, but they, too, faced a reluctant leadership. Speaker Tip O'Neill (D-Mass.) refused to take a position on the administration's aid requests for El Salvador, preferring to keep his powder dry for the momentous budget battles to come. When Gerry Studds (D-Mass.), one of the most vocal opponents of administration policy, introduced a bill to cut off military aid to El Salvador, even the senior liberals on the Foreign Affairs Committee would not support it, arguing that the timing was not right for a confrontation with the new president.[99]

The only real leverage Reagan's congressional opponents could exert was to hold hearings to express their worries and grill administration officials. Their star witness was former ambassador Robert White, who argued passionately against increasing military aid or introducing U.S. combat advisers into El Salvador. In appearances before three different committees, White focused on the basic objection that liberal Democrats had to the military cast of Reagan's policy: that it would encourage the most intransigent rightist elements in the Salvadoran armed forces to pull back from the reforms fostered by Carter and move ahead without restraint in the "dirty war" of extermination against the left.[100]

"Do you want to associate yourself with this kind of killing?" White asked a Republican congressman. "Are we really going to send military advisers to be part of that kind of machinery?"[101]

To defuse the human rights issue, administration officials tried to minimize the government's abuses or to blame them on the guerrillas. "I think it is safe to say," Acting Assistant Secretary of State John Bushnell told the Senate Foreign Relations Committee, "that the number [of civilians] who are killed by unauthorized activities of the security forces . . . are certainly not as great as the number that are killed by the forces of the left."[102]

This claim, however, was contradicted by all three human rights organizations inside El Salvador (including the Archdiocese of the Catholic Church) and by the assessment of international human rights organizations like Americas Watch, Amnesty International, the OAS Inter-American Commission on Human Rights, and the United Nations Human Rights Commission. All of these groups attributed the overwhelming majority of killings of noncombatants to the government. When Assistant Secretary Bushnell was asked to account for the discrepancy between his portrait of El Salvador and that of the Salvadoran Catholic Church, he suggested that the church had been infiltrated by Communists.[103]

Administration officials argued that more military aid would improve the human rights situation by increasing the "professionalism" of the army and by reducing the combat role of the security forces, which were acknowledged to be the source of most government atrocities.[104] This same argument had been used for years to justify military assistance to regimes with poor human rights records, despite slim evidence of beneficial effects. Since the 1940s, the United States had trained 1,971 officers from the Salvadoran armed forces, and they still had one of the worst human rights records in the hemisphere.[105]

Of all the killings in El Salvador, the murders of the U.S. churchwomen and the AIFLD labor advisers crystallized congressional fear that there were no limits to the slaughter. If the Salvadoran government could not prevent the security forces from murdering U.S. citizens and then could not or would not bring the killers to justice, how could it even pretend to create democracy? And how could Washington even begin to justify military aid to such a government?

Administration officials constantly reassured Congress that the Salvadoran government was conducting full and serious investigations in the two cases.[106] Actually, the Salvadorans were working overtime to cover up the fact that the churchwomen had been killed by members of the National Guard. Within days of the murder, the sergeant commanding the patrol that committed the murders confessed to senior officers. The killers were transferred to new assignments and their weapons were switched in order to make ballistics detection more difficult. The Salvadoran government did "everything possible to conceal the perpetrators of the crime," an investigation by U.S. Judge Harold Tyler later found. The Salvadoran officer supposedly investigating the killings directed the cover-up.[107]

In February 1981, the U.S. embassy acquired a highly classified source that, over the next two months, allowed Washington to identify the killers and alerted the embassy to the cover-up. The guardsmen were finally detained only after the embassy supplied their names to the Salvadoran military and insisted that they be arrested.[108] The administration was less than forthcoming to Congress about the discovery of a cover-up by the same armed forces that were slated for big increases in U.S. military assistance.

The administration's most potent answer to criticism about the human rights record of the Salvadoran regime was the message of the White Paper: El Salvador was no longer an internal conflict; Soviet intervention had transformed it into a superpower confrontation. In the face of this challenge, such parochial concerns as human rights had to take a back seat. Even though "a great deal of violence" originated from the government, Washington still had to support it. "If we stick with what we would like to do in accordance with our moral principles," Bushnell explained, we would "allow the Communists to support their friends and win a victory."[109]

As a counterpoint to Haig's bellicose rhetoric, lower-ranking State Department officials did their best to mollify Congress, reassuring it that U.S. policy had really not changed very much from the days of Jimmy Carter. The chief of policy planning in the Latin American bureau, Luigi Einaudi, called Reagan's policy "Carter plus," meaning Carter's policy of reform plus a large dose of military aid.[110] Undersecretary of State Walter J. Stoessel assured two Senate committees that the administration recognized the domestic causes of the conflict and stressed Washington's continued commitment to reform. "El Salvador is not another Vietnam," Stoessel declared. "We are proceeding in a measured, careful manner."[111]

The decision to send U.S. military advisers was by far the most contentious because it rekindled memories of Vietnam. But there was little congressional liberals could do other than to beseech the president not to carry out the program he had already decided on. Sending advisers to El Salvador was a purely presidential prerogative so long as they were not sent into combat or into areas where they were in danger of "imminent involvement in hostilities"—the operative language of the 1973 War Powers Resolution.

When Reagan decided to deploy advisers to El Salvador, the Pentagon went to great pains to avoid triggering the War Powers Resolution, since that would have given Congress the right to review and approve the deployment.[112] The advisers' rules of engagement were written to minimize the danger that they would be caught up in any fighting. They were stationed in the city of San Salvador and a few "carefully selected" regional garrisons, making only day trips to outlying areas to conduct training. They were prohibited from carrying weapons other than side arms for personal defense so that they would not be, in the language of the law, "equipped for combat." And they were prohibited from accompanying the units they trained on combat operations. Based on these limitations, the State Department insisted that the War Powers Resolution did not apply.[113] Over the next two years, all of these limitations except the prohibition on engaging in combat operations would be quietly lifted. To emphasize that the personnel sent to El Salvador had a different role than their predecessors in Vietnam, the administration insisted on calling them "trainers" rather than "advisers." Everyone else called them advisers, and even administration officials occasionally slipped.[114]

Regardless of their job titles, the Defense Department began giving the advisers in El Salvador "hostile fire" pay—a special monthly bonus paid to members of the armed forces who attested that they had been "subjected to small arms fire" or were "close enough to the trajectory point of impact of hostile ordinance" so that they were "in danger of being wounded, injured, or killed."[115]

The administration also denied the applicability of another law, Section 21(c) of the Arms Export Control Act, which required a report to Congress if "significant hostilities" erupted in a country hosting U.S. advisers.[116] Senator John Glenn (D-Ohio), for one, did not understand how the administration could deny that there were "significant hostilities" in El Salvador. Reagan's refusal to comply with this simple reporting requirement was not momentous in itself. As Senator Glenn admitted, even if a report had been filed, "not a blooming thing" would have changed.[117] But like Reagan's initial use of emergency powers to send military aid to El Salvador, the refusal to report was indicative of the administration's hostility toward any congressional role in the formulation of foreign policy. Reagan was determined not to admit anything that could be interpreted as triggering statutory constraints on his discretion.

Reagan's use of special emergency authority to send $20 million in military aid was another echo of Vietnam. The only other time that power had been used extensively was in Southeast Asia during the late 1960s and early 1970s, when the growing unpopularity of the Vietnam War made Congress reluctant to fund it.[118] Reagan, however, could legitimately claim he was simply following the precedent set by Jimmy Carter, who had sent the Salvadorans $5 million in military aid during his last week in office. There was not much the Democrats could say in reply, and in any event, there was nothing they could do about it.

The other $5 million in new military aid for El Salvador, along with the entire $63.5 million proposed increase in economic aid, had to be reprogrammed—shifted from the foreign aid accounts of other countries. When the president wants to reprogram funds, thereby changing appropriations made by Congress, he must notify the Appropriations Committees fifteen days in advance, giving them an opportunity to review the reallocation. By tradition, either the Senate or House committee (or their relevant subcommittees) can block a proposed reprogramming by a simple majority vote.

The Democrats raised no objection to reprogramming additional economic aid. Some even regarded it as a hopeful sign that despite Haig's Cold War rhetoric, the administration understood it would have to ameliorate the social and economic roots of Salvador's discontent.[119] That left only the reprogramming request for $5 million in military aid as a focal point for the Democrats' opposition to Reagan's new policy. Although the amount of money was negligible in light of the fact that almost $30 million in military aid had been sent since January 1, the reprogramming request became a symbolic test—an opportunity for the liberal Democrats to put an early brake on the administration's instinct to escalate the war.

In the Republican-controlled Senate, the Appropriations Subcommittee on Foreign Operations easily approved the reprogramming request. In the House subcommittee, with its liberal majority, the administration faced a more formidable task. The subcommittee was chaired by Clarence "Doc" Long, a seventy-two-year-old Democrat from Baltimore with a Ph.D. in economics (hence the nickname) and a reputation for being both outspoken and a bit eccentric. He was the only member of Congress who had a son wounded in Vietnam, and he was adamantly opposed to letting the United States slip into a similar war in Central America. When Haig declared El Salvador a "test case" for Reagan's new foreign policy, Long decided to go there and see the country for himself. Fearing that El Salvador was too dangerous, the full Appropriations Committee refused to pay for the trip. Long went anyway and paid for it himself.[120]

The administration's new policy was "gunboat diplomacy all over again," Long said. "I wish to God presidents would read a few books. If Johnson had read some, we wouldn't have been in Vietnam. If Reagan would read some, we wouldn't be here now." Long absolutely opposed the deployment of U.S. advisers to El Salvador, believing that they would inevitably suffer casualties, thereby providing the administration with an excuse to escalate the war—"a kind of Gulf of Tonkin resolution," he said.[121]

As the vote in Long's subcommittee approached, the administration began making concessions. On March 13, Undersecretary Stoessel promised that the number of advisers in El Salvador would not exceed the fifty-four already there. A few days later, the State Department announced that about a dozen of the advisers would return to the United States in July, and the rest would be home by September (in fact, the advisers would still be there in 1989 when Ronald Reagan left office).[122]

On March 24, Long's subcommittee approved Reagan's reprogramming request by a single vote, 8–7. "It's awfully hard to beat the president," Doc Long said ruefully when it was all over.[123] The vote was an important victory for the administration, and especially for Haig, who was facing White House criticism for the congressional ferment stirred up by his hard-line pronouncements. But the narrow margin of victory was a warning that the administration would not have an easy time selling the war in El Salvador on Capitol Hill.

Reactions at Home and Abroad

Despite Ronald Reagan's popularity and his electoral mandate, the Democrats were not alone in their uneasiness over the administration's escalating commitment in Central America. Haig's aggressive rhetoric produced a public backlash that grew in intensity until it became a serious political worry among the White House guardians of Ronald Reagan's image. A Gallup poll in May found that 38 percent of the public disapproved of Reagan's policy in Central America and only 30 percent approved. Mail at the White House ran ten to one against the policy and presidential pollster Richard Wirthlin found Reagan's popularity falling off sharply because of Haig's war scare.[124] State Department officials traveling around the country defending the policy in public forums reported hostile receptions, particularly at universities. Even conservative business associations were unwilling to back the policy. To help its spokesmen on the stump, the department's Foreign Service Institute began teaching special classes on how to defend Reagan's Central America policy to the public.[125]

Washington's allies in Latin America and Europe were also alarmed by Haig's tough talk. The most significant international opposition came from Mexico, whose economic and cultural ties with the United States were extensive and growing. A wide range of bilateral issues, from immigration to oil, were of vital importance to both countries, but their disagreement over Central America threatened to poison their relationship.

Mexico's policy toward Central America was based on an assessment of the crisis wholly at odds with Ronald Reagan's. The Mexicans were convinced that the military governments of El Salvador, Guatemala, and Honduras could not long survive growing demands by the poor for social and political change. Regional stability required replacing these regimes with popular governments willing to dismantle the oligarchic land-owning system and distribute the benefits of economic development to a broader cross-section of the population. "We have a greater interest in the stability of the region than the United States," a Mexican diplomat reminded Washington. "But we recognize that the pressures for change can no longer be smothered. These countries have to find their own solutions, even if this means revolutions. Otherwise they will never be stable."[126] Having lived through a social revolution of their own from 1911 to 1917, the Mexicans tended to see revolutionary change as positive. In official Washington, it was invariably seen as dangerous.

The Mexicans certainly did not favor the establishment of pro-Soviet Marxist-Leninist regimes in Central America, although, based on their experience of peaceful coexistence with Cuba, they were confident they could live with whatever revolutionary governments might emerge. They believed the best strategy for blunting Cuban and Soviet influence was to support the social democrats among the region's revolutionaries rather than side with the forces of conservatism. By trying to hold back the process of social change in Central America, the United States would only make the inevitable break with the past more cataclysmic and radical. By introducing large amounts of military aid, Washington itself was turning Central America into an arena of East-West conflict, drawing Cuba and the Soviet Union in. "The United States will not make the Vietnam syndrome disappear by repeating it," warned one Mexican official.[127]

Mexico's diplomatic strategy was to urge restraint on Washington and dampen the fires of war by pressing all parties to negotiate their differences. Within hours of Reagan's election, Mexican President José López Portillo publicly warned the incoming administration against intervening in Central America. Mexico's diplomatic protests escalated as Washington expanded military aid to El Salvador.[128]

In April, Presidents López Portillo of Mexico and Luis Herrera Campíns of Venezuela launched a mediation effort of their own, which was quickly endorsed by the European Social Democrats. The Mexican-Venezuelan proposal was particularly unsettling to the administration because Venezuela had been the Latin American country most supportive of Washington's policy. During his exile in Venezuela, José Napoleón Duarte had developed personal ties to many Venezuelan Christian Democrats, including Herrera Campíns. For Venezuela to join with Mexico in support of negotiations highlighted Washington's isolation.[129]

The North Atlantic allies also had difficulty understanding Haig's decision to make Central America a major battleground of the Cold War. When Assistant Secretary of State for European Affairs Lawrence Eagleburger was dispatched to brief the allies on the White Paper, he was not well received. Most Western European governments spoke out against outside interference in the Salvadoran conflict, but in the same breath called for a negotiated political solution rather than an escalation of the war. The Swedish government was so vocal in its opposition to U.S. policy that the Reagan administration was moved to lodge a formal protest—the first such protest made to a Western European nation since the war in Vietnam. Even conservative governments generally regarded Reagan's East-West vision of the conflict as simplistic.[130]

The Europeans were especially dismayed that the first issue on the new administration's agenda was El Salvador, and they resented having it cast as a test of alliance solidarity. When they politely registered their disagreement with U.S. policy, the Reagan administration's instinct was to ignore or berate them.[131] El Salvador became a symbolic issue within NATO, seized upon by Social Democrats as proof of Reagan's dangerously confrontational approach to international affairs. As such, it strengthened the hand of those who opposed cooperation with Washington on such issues as the deployment of intermediate-range nuclear forces (the Pershing II and cruise missiles).[132] The Reagan administration itself aggravated this problem by advocating "linkage"—conditioning bilateral relations with the Soviet Union on Soviet behavior in the Third World. On February 24, Reagan said explicitly that there could be no arms control negotiations and no summit meeting with Soviet President Leonid Brezhnev unless the Soviet "invasion" of El Salvador was ended.[133] To the Europeans, caught geographically between the two superpowers, linking East-West relations to far-off El Salvador seemed manifestly absurd.

Many European countries were themselves actively involved in the region. The Socialist International provided political and financial support to both the FDR-FMLN in El Salvador and the Sandinista government in Nicaragua.[134] The Europeans, like the Latin Americans, also tried to fashion a negotiated settlement in El Salvador. The German Social Democrats and Christian Democrats teamed up to cajole their Salvadoran counterparts to accept mediated negotiations. The Socialist International undertook several mediation efforts as well. By mid-May, as many as ten different countries were actively trying to broker negotiations.[135]

This was not the sort of response the Reagan administration had sought from the allies, and its frustration began to show. Administration officials reacted with hostility to all these diplomatic initiatives. During congressional testimony, Undersecretary of Defense Fred C. Iklé, one of the administration's hard-liners, blasted the Europeans for being "much too insouciant and cavalier about the growing military threat in the Caribbean."[136]

The Vicar Muzzled

The controversy generated by Haig's hot rhetoric and his conspicuous unwillingness to be a team player angered the White House troika of Meese, Baker, and Deaver. Like any good military tactician, Haig had sought the advantage of surprise, stealing a march on his rivals by launching his El Salvador publicity campaign unilaterally.[137] "It was Haig who galvanized the government, above all," explained a displeased senior official. "He spent much of his first six months on this area, with no encouragement from the rest of the government." Haig had "gone off like a one-man band."[138]

When polls showed the Central America issue damaging Reagan's popularity, the troika sought to downplay El Salvador and bring the focus of attention back to domestic policy. They tried to prevent Central America from becoming a "presidential issue" by keeping the president away from it; Reagan did not deliver a single speech on Central America in 1981. But Haig's campaign caused such a public stir that El Salvador invariably came up in presidential interviews and press conferences. At every turn, Reagan had to reassure the press and the public that he was not planning to send American troops to Central America or get caught up in another Vietnam. "It didn't matter what we decided," lamented a senior White House aide, "because El Salvador kept coming back."[139]

In early March, Baker showed the president Wirthlin's polls (which Baker had commissioned) indicating that Haig's rhetoric was damaging him. "People got afraid of what Reagan would do," reflected White House official David Gergen. "We were losing control of the agenda. Important as Central America was, it diverted attention from our top priority, which was economic recovery, which we wanted to be the only priority. Haig didn't understand that. We decided we had to cut off his story." With the president's blessing, Baker told Haig to "knock it off" so they could get El Salvador off the front pages.[140]

But just a few days later, while testifying before the House Foreign Affairs Committee, Haig was back in form, baldly asserting that the war in El Salvador was part of a "four-phased operation" by the Soviet Union, in which Phase One was the "seizure of Nicaragua," Phase Two was the attack on El Salvador, to be followed by assaults on Honduras and Guatemala. Asked if he was resurrecting the domino theory, Haig replied, "I wouldn't call it necessarily a domino theory. I would call it a priority target list—a hit list if you will—for the ultimate takeover of Central America."[141] El Salvador was back in the headlines.

Haig stirred even greater controversy with his response to a question about the investigation of the murders of the U.S. churchwomen. "I would like to suggest to you," Haig said, "that some of the investigations would lead one to believe that perhaps the vehicle that the nuns were riding in may have tried to run a roadblock or may have accidentally been perceived to have been doing so, and there may have been an exchange of gunfire."[142]

In fact, there was no evidence at all that the women had been armed or run a roadblock. Quite the contrary; they were abducted to a remote area, beaten, raped, and executed. No sooner had Haig made his remarks than the State Department began trying to explain them away.[143] Haig himself made light of his remarks subsequently, denying he had claimed the women tried to run a roadblock or that they might have been armed. "I haven't met any pistol-packing nuns in my day, Senator," he quipped. It was all a big misunderstanding, he insisted.[144]

The White House staff's unhappiness with Haig reached a climax shortly after these congressional performances. The troika concluded that Haig was "a loose cannon" who needed to be tied down.[145] Their first opportunity to discipline him came in late March over the issue of who would be in charge of crisis management. Haig presumed that, as the "vicar" of foreign policy, he should be. The White House was loath to give the mercurial general any more authority, so Vice President George Bush was put in charge of the crisis management committee.[146] Haig threatened to resign, but then relented. He seemed, however, to have finally gotten the message about Central America. He kept quiet until the summer.

With Haig holding his tongue, El Salvador disappeared from the headlines almost as quickly as it had come. The March 30, 1981, assassination attempt on President Reagan and his convalescence dominated the news in April. With the entire administration observing a discrete silence about Central America, there was little news to report out of Washington. Nor was there much out of El Salvador, where the army was contentedly drinking from the new fount of U.S. military aid, and the guerrillas were quietly trying to regroup after their disastrous January offensive. To the relief of the White House, the press stopped writing about Central America, the pollsters stopped asking about it, and the general public stopped thinking about it.

Waist Deep in the Big Muddy?

In its first foray into foreign policy, the Reagan administration unwittingly let loose the ghosts of Vietnam, both at home and abroad. Al Haig had "opened the jar," one of his senior aides admitted, "and he didn't, perhaps, realize how many genies were in it."[147]

The parallels with Vietnam were obvious enough. Once again, in the name of the global struggle against Communism, Washington was embarking on a major military commitment to a Third World ally of dubious legitimacy. A small, poor nation of little inherent significance was suddenly thrust onto center stage because the United States decided to wager its prestige and credibility on the outcome of a civil war. If the U.S. investment of "blood and treasure" was not great to begin with, the incrementalism of the commitment nevertheless failed to reassure because of the memories it conjured from the past. "For both the opponents and proponents of the Reagan administration's policy toward Salvador," wrote veteran journalist Don Oberdorfer, "Vietnam provides the emotional kindling, the passion, as well as the frame of reference for a new national debate."[148]

Across the political spectrum, Vietnam held different lessons for different people. For members of Congress, especially liberal Democrats, the lesson of Vietnam was that they should be more jealous of their constitutional prerogatives and less willing to blindly follow the president's lead. For journalists, the lesson was that they should be more aggressive in deflating official mythology. For the military, it was not to let civilians embark on a foreign war without adequate support on the home front.

Administration officials were deeply frustrated by the comparisons between El Salvador and Vietnam, knowing as they did that nothing was a greater political albatross. "We can't help it if there are similarities," a White House official lamented after an NSC discussion of the Vietnam analogy. "That does not mean we should not act in this case."[149]

When officials insisted that El Salvador would not become another Vietnam, they did it in ways that gave cold comfort. Haig explained that El Salvador would not be another Vietnam because this time, vital U.S. interests were truly at stake and we would "go to the source." His deputy, John Bushnell, argued that El Salvador was different because our supply lines were shorter than our adversaries'—just the reverse of the Vietnam situation. General Ernest Graves, director of the Defense Security Assistance Agency, distinguished El Salvador from Vietnam by maintaining that the Salvadoran guerrillas were nothing more than terrorists and had no base of support—a claim that only convinced critics the general knew as little about Central America as his predecessors had known about Southeast Asia. The problem in Vietnam, Reagan himself averred, was that the troops had been "denied permission to win."[150]

The common thread in all these declarations was not reassurance that Washington would avoid entanglement in a major Vietnam-style war, but an almost blustery self-confidence that this time we would win. In truth, no reassurance could lay to rest the anxieties unleashed by Reagan's policy, because all the same reassurances had been offered in the 1960s during the early phases of Vietnam and had proved hollow. Every time Ronald Reagan insisted that El Salvador would not become another Vietnam, more people who had never heard of El Salvador began to worry that it would.

The public's convulsive reaction to Haig's early declarations put the White House on notice that the Vietnam syndrome was not limited to the carping of a few cowardly liberals. The war had left a deep and lasting scar, not just in the political establishment, but reaching all the way down to the man and woman in the street. In office for just three months after a landslide victory at the polls, Reagan and his White House team beat a hasty retreat on El Salvador. Forging an effective political consensus for military engagement in Central America was going to be a tougher fight than they expected.

CHAPTER 5

A New Policy for Nicaragua

While El Salvador dominated the headlines during Ronald Reagan's first few months in the Oval Office, another policy shift was quietly taking place behind the scenes. Two days after Reagan's inauguration, Al Haig recommended that the president reaffirm the suspension of economic aid to Nicaragua imposed by President Carter a few days before he left office. Reagan agreed.[1] This surprised no one and drew little comment. After all, congressional Republicans had bitterly opposed Carter's Nicaraguan aid package, and the Republican Party platform explicitly called for ending it. The new administration seemed determined to replace Carter's policy of coexistence with one of hostility.

Ambassador Larry Pezzullo was not willing to give up so easily. For a year and a half, he had labored to build a constructive relationship between the United States and the revolutionary government in Nicaragua, and he was convinced the policy was working. The Sandinistas seemed genuinely interested in avoiding a break with Washington, and they had been responsive to Pezzullo's warning the previous September about exporting revolution to El Salvador.[2]

Pezzullo saw the Sandinistas' aid to the Salvadoran guerrillas in the months leading up to the January 1981 final offensive as an anomaly. The Nicaraguans had great solidarity with the Salvadorans, of course, but through most of 1980, they had resisted providing them with any significant material support. Pezzullo thought that perhaps Fidel Castro had talked the Sandinistas into changing their policy, or that some of the Sandinista *comandantes* decided to send arms to El Salvador without telling the others. In any event, Pezzullo wanted to give the Sandinistas a chance to reconsider their actions before the United States took reprisals.[3]

In early February, Pezzullo was called to Washington to participate in a policy review. Acting Assistant Secretary of State for Inter-American Affairs John Bushnell had drafted an options paper for Haig that included three alternatives, all of which began with a permanent cut-off of U.S. aid to Nicaragua. Asked for his recommendation, Pezzullo rejected all three options as essentially the same. Instead, he proposed a "zero option"—continuing aid because it provided the only real leverage Washington had over the Sandinistas.[4]

Pezzullo insisted that it was possible to restore the implicit understanding Washington had had with Nicaragua before Reagan's election: the United States would provide economic aid if the Sandinistas showed restraint in El Salvador. He argued forcefully that the proper mix of diplomatic pressure and the threat to cut off badly needed economic assistance could persuade the Sandinistas to curtail their material support for the Salvadoran guerrillas. But if U.S. aid was actually stopped, Pezzullo pointed out, the Sandinistas would no longer have any incentive to limit their role in El Salvador or maintain a moderate domestic policy. The only instrument Washington would then have to modify Sandinista behavior would be military pressure. "They're tough kids," Pezzullo warned Haig. "You'd have to mount one hell of an operation to get them out of there."[5]

Haig's interest in Nicaragua was peripheral to his concern about El Salvador. His instinct was to cut off aid to punish the Sandinistas for supporting the Salvadoran guerrillas, but his principal objective was to halt the arms flow. Dry up the enemy's logistics—that was the key to defeating a guerrilla insurgency.[6] "[Haig] never considered the Nicaraguans the major factor in this drama," Pezzullo recalled, "and was perfectly willing to see if he could use diplomatic measures to end the flow of arms to the [Salvadoran] rebels."[7] Pezzullo convinced Haig to give diplomacy a chance. "I'll buy the zero option," Haig said, and took Pezzullo to the White House to make his case directly to the president. Reagan agreed, and the zero option became policy.[8]

Pezzullo returned to Managua in mid-February and informed the Sandinistas that they had thirty days to halt their material support for the Salvadoran guerrillas. At the end of that time, Washington would assess whether or not to resume economic aid. He gave the Sandinistas a list of specific actions the

United States expected them to take. Among these were closing an airfield that was being used to resupply the Salvadorans and a clandestine FMLN radio station broadcasting from the outskirts of Managua.[9]

For the Sandinistas, Pezzullo's offer was an attractive proposition. The Salvadoran final offensive had failed dismally, demonstrating that there was no hope for a rebel victory in the foreseeable future. The Sandinistas were angry at the Salvadorans for having misled them about their strength, and top Sandinistas had begun urging a negotiated solution to the Salvadoran war. The Nicaraguans were also worried that a permanent cut-off of U.S. aid would cripple their battered economy, which was still recovering from damage sustained during the insurrection against Somoza.[10]

Daniel Ortega, chairman of the governing junta, assured Pezzullo that Nicaragua would refrain from aiding the Salvadorans and would take firm measures to prevent them from using Nicaraguan territory for arms smuggling. Ortega acknowledged that the Sandinistas had been "very permissive" in allowing the Salvadorans to mount smuggling operations in the past, but he pledged that "not a single round" would transit Nicaragua thereafter.[11]

Pezzullo's strategy began to show results almost immediately; the Sandinistas shut down the airstrip and the clandestine radio station. "Washington's message has been received loud and clear," a senior Sandinista official told the *New York Times*.[12] On February 23, less than a week after Ortega had given Pezzullo his assurances, Acting Assistant Secretary Bushnell announced that the arms flow from Nicaragua to El Salvador appeared to have stopped.[13] Testifying to Congress a week later, Bushnell said that the administration was "pleasantly surprised" at how positively Nicaragua was responding to U.S. demands. If the arms flow remained halted, he said, U.S. aid to Nicaragua would be resumed.[14] As the end of Haig's thirty-day trial period approached, events seemed to have proved Pezzullo right. "Every bit of evidence we had, every indicator, showed that there was a cutoff," he recalled. "If we had that much progress with other countries in similar situations, we would have applauded it."[15]

But administration hard-liners were not willing to concede the issue. Senior officials met in mid-March to review Nicaragua's compliance with U.S. demands. The meeting was chaired by Deputy Secretary of State William P. Clark and attended by National Security Adviser Richard V. Allen.[16] The hard-liners, led by Allen, advocated a permanent cut-off of aid to Nicaragua, pointing to the Republican platform as their rationale. They acknowledged that the arms flow to El Salvador had stopped, but interpreted this as merely "seasonal," due to the guerrillas' reduced logistical needs in the wake of the final offensive. There was no guarantee that the smuggling would not resume. The hard-liners also argued that the Sandinistas might have shifted to new smuggling routes that U.S. intelligence had not yet detected, or perhaps they would establish new channels in the future. There was, of course, no way to disprove such speculation.[17]

Weak though these arguments were, they carried the day because no one was willing to defend Pezzullo's strategy of using aid as diplomatic leverage. The State Department, which logically should have argued Pezzullo's case, was represented by Deputy Secretary Clark and the new assistant secretary for Latin America, Thomas Enders. Unlike Haig, Clark was a longtime friend of Reagan with strong connections to the White House staff, and a foreign policy hard-liner. Enders, though he would soon develop a reputation as one of the administration's leading pragmatists, was a staunch anti-Communist—and a wise enough bureaucrat not to defend the policy of the previous administration. Pezzullo was in Washington when the decision was made, but he was not allowed to argue on behalf of his strategy. The decision to end aid was a foregone conclusion.

Although the Sandinistas' compliance made Pezzullo's argument all the more compelling, the internal balance of the administration had changed. In February, Haig was in full stride as the new vicar of foreign policy and willing to take the issue of Nicaragua directly to the president. By March, Haig's outspokenness and his disinclination to coordinate with the White House had soured his relations with Allen and the troika of James Baker, Michael Deaver, and Edwin Meese. When policy toward Nicaragua came up for review, Haig was unwilling to further complicate his relations with the White House by fighting over it.

Pezzullo pleaded with Haig not to abandon a proven strategy. "You're throwing away your chips," he warned.[18] Washington had made demands on the Sandinistas as the price for keeping U.S. aid, and they had complied. If the administration was to retain any credibility with the Nicaraguans, it would have to fulfill its part of the bargain. At a minimum, Pezzullo argued, food aid should be restored. Haig was unmoved. Rather than contest the decision to terminate aid, Pezzullo recalled, Haig "just let it happen."[19]

The decision was announced on April Fools' Day, before Pezzullo could get back to Managua to give the Sandinistas the bad news in person.[20] The U.S. action prevented the shipment of $9.6 million in food aid and canceled disbursal of the final $15 million of Carter's $75 million aid package, except for a few million dollars destined for the Sandinistas' opponents in the private sector.

The wording of the official announcement conveyed the odd logic behind the decision. It noted that the United States had made "strong representations to the Nicaraguans to cease military support to the Salvadoran guerrillas," and acknowledged Nicaragua's "positive" response. "We have no hard evidence of arms movements through Nicaragua during the past few weeks, and propaganda and some other support activities have been curtailed," the statement continued. Nevertheless, the president had determined that Nicaragua was supporting violence in another country and was therefore was no longer eligible for aid.[21] "The reason the wording of the termination notice came out the way it did," Pezzullo recalled, "was that everyone had to admit—and I insisted that they admit—that indeed the arms were cut off."[22]

The Sandinistas described the aid decision as "interventionism, blackmail, and Yankee economic aggression." Within a few weeks, the Soviet Union offered to provide Nicaragua with twenty-thousand tons of wheat to make up for the canceled U.S. shipment, Libya offered a $100 million loan, and Cuba agreed to provide $64 million in technical aid.[23]

The announcement that aid to Nicaragua was being terminated prompted little congressional reaction. Senator Clairborne Pell (D-R.I.) and Congressman David E. Bonior (D-Mich.) both lamented the decision, pointing out its incongruity with the evidence that Nicaraguan arms shipments to El Salvador had ceased. Congressman Tom Harkin (D-Iowa) saw it as something more sinister: "There are elements in this administration that are geared up to create economic chaos in Nicaragua," Harkin warned. "[The aid cut-off] is no more than the first step in this destabilization process, the same destabilization process our CIA engaged in [in] the Dominican Republic, in Guatemala, and in Chile." The real objective of the policy, he predicted, was "to overturn the Nicaraguan revolution."[24]

The Origins of the Covert War

After the decision to cut off aid, Pezzullo was virtually alone in arguing for continued engagement with Nicaragua; the debate had shifted to disagreements over the extent and modality of U.S. hostility. The Reagan team began with a fundamentally different conception of the Sandinista government than the one that had guided Pezzullo and the Carter administration. Pezzullo assumed that Nicaragua's revolutionary government was malleable. If Washington crafted a proper set of incentives, it could affect the direction the revolution would take.

The Reagan team did not accept this view. To them, the Sandinistas were Marxist-Leninists. If they stayed in power, they would guide Nicaragua inexorably toward a one-party Leninist dictatorship, alliance with the Soviet Union, and active subversion of their neighbors. No incentives from Washington or anywhere else would dissuade them from this trajectory. Even if the Sandinistas seemed responsive to U.S. demands, the Reaganites regarded such moves as merely temporary and tactical—designed to buy time while the

Leninists consolidated themselves. Nothing the Sandinistas did could penetrate this seamless web of ideological certainty. The threat to U.S. interests, in the hard-liners' view, stemmed from the very existence of the Sandinista regime. The only choice for the United States was to find a way to dislodge the Sandinistas from power, or acquiesce in the creation of a "second Cuba."[25]

The idea of overthrowing the Sandinistas was a popular one among the Reagan team. The Republican platform pledged to "support the efforts of the Nicaraguan people to establish a free and independent government," a thinly veiled reference to ousting the Sandinistas, according to an aide to Senator Jesse Helms, John Carbaugh, who wrote the passage.[26] Roger Fontaine, Reagan's key campaign adviser on Latin America and top NSC staff aide on the region, repeatedly dismissed the idea that economic aid could moderate the Sandinistas. He advocated getting rid of them, as did Constantine C. Menges, who became the National Intelligence Officer for Latin America at the CIA.[27] But how, exactly, was that to be done?

The review of policy toward Nicaragua fell to the inter-agency group on Latin America—a group of senior and midlevel officials representing each of the principal executive branch agencies dealing with Latin American policy (State, Defense, the National Security Council, and the CIA). This group referred to itself as the Inter-Agency Core Group and, after 1983, as the Restricted Inter-Agency Group (RIG). Throughout most of the Reagan administration, it was the place where U.S. policy toward Central America was hammered out.

Although it was nominally subordinate to three Senior Inter-Agency Groups that dealt with foreign policy, defense, and intelligence matters, in practice the Core Group operated with an astonishing degree of autonomy.[28] This was possible because of the chaos that characterized the Reagan administration's foreign policy decision-making process. After White House Chief of Staff James Baker blocked Haig's inauguration-day attempt to get Reagan to approve a structure that would make the secretary of state predominant, foreign policy decisionmaking was handled on an essentially ad hoc basis. Even for senior officials like Haig and Allen, access to the president was severely limited. Normally, management of the foreign policy decision process would fall to the president's national security adviser, but Richard Allen was so weak that he was regularly ignored. Instead, foreign policy was coordinated through Ed Meese, who proved to be a poor manager.[29]

The strategy Enders devised for managing Latin American policy was first to achieve consensus on a proposal among the key midlevel officials in the Core Group and then to have each of them individually get their bosses to approve it. Using their personal connections throughout the national security bureaucracy, members of the Core Group would then manage policy implementation. In this way, it was possible for midlevel officials to conceive and execute major policy initiatives without top officials ever sitting down together and making a decision.[30]

Through the spring and early summer of 1981, two approaches to the Nicaragua problem were actively debated within the Core Group. As described by a participant, one option was "long-term rollback" by gradual economic destabilization. This would involve economic pressure combined with limited negotiations "to get Cuba and the Soviet Union out of there" and to extract guarantees from the Sandinistas allowing maximum freedom for their internal opponents. "We always figured they'd self-destruct over time if there was an opposition," the official explained.[31] The other option was "short-term military rollback" to be accomplished by direct assault. In some scenarios, the invasion would be a joint venture by Nicaraguan exiles and the armies of Honduras and Guatemala, with the United States providing logistical support. In other scenarios, U.S. combat forces would carry the brunt of the invasion themselves.[32]

The State Department, particularly Enders, became the leading advocate of "strangling" the Nicaraguan economy—cutting off U.S. aid and blocking loans from international financial institutions and private banks. Enders also favored providing military aid to Nicaraguan exiles who were launching hit-and-run attacks across the Honduran border. "I was one of those who took the lead in proposing the contras," he acknowledged.[33]

The exile attacks would drain economic resources, demolish infrastructure, and disrupt transport and communications. If economic misery eventually triggered an uprising against the Sandinistas, the exiles (who came to be known as "contras"—short for *contra-revolucionarios*) would sweep across the border to lead the new insurrection. Failing that, the damage done by contra attacks would weaken the Sandinistas' hand at the bargaining table.[34]

Direct military action was the alternative for those with less patience. The option of an exile invasion was modeled on the CIA's Operation Success, which overthrew the elected government of Jacobo Arbenz in Guatemala in 1954, and on the less successful effort to overthrow Fidel Castro in 1961 at the Bay of Pigs. Backers of the military option included Undersecretary of Defense Fred C. Iklé and, initially, CIA Director William Casey. They argued against the long-term destabilization plan on the grounds that it would allow the Sandinistas to consolidate internal security and expand their armed forces to the point that no internal opposition would stand a chance of removing them.[35]

The principal weakness of the plan for quick military action was that no one seemed willing or able to undertake it. The exile forces by themselves were so small and disorganized that they had no hope of defeating the Sandinista army.

Some elements of the Honduran military were willing to go to war with Nicaragua to create an excuse for canceling upcoming elections. But Guatemala was unwilling to join the crusade, and Honduras was not up to the task by itself.

Most important, the U.S. military was as adamantly opposed to getting entangled in Nicaragua as it was to getting entangled in El Salvador. "I know of no plans to put U.S. combat troops into El Salvador," said one administration official during the debate over what to do about the Sandinistas, "and sure as hell not into Nicaragua." The advocates of quick military action were thus forced to argue that a small exile invasion would trigger a spontaneous uprising against the Sandinistas. This seemed far-fetched to most of the key policymakers. Indeed, it was a bit too much like the Bay of Pigs, where faulty CIA predictions of a Cuban uprising convinced President Kennedy to go forward with a plan that turned out to be a fiasco.[36]

The long-term and short-term options had one practical element in common: both envisioned a role for Nicaraguan exile forces. For the hard-liners, supporting the contras was a first step toward removing the Sandinistas. For those who favored a long-term policy designed to extract concessions, the contras were an asset because they would magnify other forms of pressure. "There was a unity of interest between those who wanted to develop a bargaining chip and those who wanted them to do the [rollback] job," recalled an administration official. "It was a total convergence."[37] While Pezzullo was still debating the issue of whether to continue economic aid to the Sandinistas, the CIA was moving quietly to open contacts with the contras.

The Last Great Buccaneer

U.S. support for the contras was given additional impetus by the Reagan administration's commitment to revitalizing covert operations on a global scale. Covert operations had been out of favor during the Carter administration. Skeptical of their value, CIA Director Stansfield Turner scaled them down considerably, firing or retiring hundreds of "old-timers" from the Directorate of Operations, the Agency's covert branch. The "housecleaning," as it was called, came as a direct consequence of the revelations in the mid-1970s of wrongdoing by the CIA. A series of congressional investigations uncovered a plethora of illegal and quasi-legal activities, including plots to assassinate foreign leaders, spying on U.S. citizens both at home and abroad, and experiments with psychokinetic drugs on unwitting subjects. The airing of these secrets, which CIA veterans referred to as the "family jewels," demolished morale at the Agency and led Congress to impose a new regime of congressional oversight, both to keep a tighter legislative rein on covert operations and to hold presidents accountable for them.[38]

The House and Senate established intelligence committees with oversight responsibility and the right to unlimited access to classified material. By law, the president was required to keep these committees "fully and currently informed of all intelligence activities" carried out by any agency of the government.[39] The most stringent requirement for notification, however, concerned covert operations. Before any covert operation could be undertaken, the president was required to sign and submit to the Congress a "finding" that the operation was "important to the national security of the United States." By requiring the president's explicit endorsement of covert operations, the law sought to prevent him from evading responsibility for them.[40]

On the Republican right, these events were seen as disgusting episodes of self-flagellation: the United States, in a fit of naive moralism, had dismantled the only instrument that allowed it to compete with the Soviet Union on the covert battlefields of the Cold War. Members of Congress such as Senator Frank Church (D-Idaho), whose 1976 Church Committee investigation uncovered many of the CIA's misdeeds, were vilified by the right. "Frank Church—when you talk to Frank Church, you might as well be talking directly to the KGB," said former CIA official Osborne Day.[41] A 1979 Republican National Committee study of the intelligence community headed by Richard Allen (in which Osborne Day participated) concluded that the reforms of the 1970s had been "drawn up by a small group of people who seem more bent on the old anti-CIA crusade than in creating an effective intelligence community." This report became the basis of the 1980 Republican Party platform plank on intelligence, which called for "the repeal of ill-considered restrictions sponsored by Democrats, which have debilitated U.S. intelligence capabilities."[42]

After election day, Reagan selected his campaign manager, William J. Casey, to be Director of Central Intelligence. Casey was very much one the "old boys" himself—a veteran of the Office of Strategic Services (OSS), forerunner to the CIA, where he had worked directly with the legendary William J. "Wild Bill" Donovan. In the words of Casey's deputy director for operations, Clair George, "Bill Casey was the last great buccaneer from the OSS."[43]

Casey's admiration for Donovan was rooted in their backgrounds. Both were devout Catholics, fervent Republicans, and men who prided themselves on getting results by any means necessary. "You didn't wait six months for a feasibility study to prove that an idea could work. You gambled that it might work," Casey said approvingly of Donovan's style in running the OSS. "You didn't tie up the organization with red tape designed mostly to cover somebody's ass. You took the initiative and responsibility. You went around end, you went over somebody's head if you had to. But you acted."[44]

Casey worked the same way. "Bill had a healthy contempt for bureaucracy, for form and protocol," one of his oss comrades recalled. "He was a feet-on-the-desk, get-the-job-done-I-don't-care-how-you-do-it executive." During World War II, Casey rose to become chief of American intelligence operations in Europe. He recruited German prisoners of war as spies, even though the practice violated the Geneva Convention. His rationale was that when his oss recruiters interviewed German POWs, they waited until the prisoner made some disparaging remark about the Nazis and then asked if the prisoner was volunteering to fight Hitler. Thus Casey's spies were "volunteers" rather than "recruits."[45] Such circumvention of the spirit of the law came to be a Casey trademark.

After the war, Casey left the oss to make his fortune as an attorney. He had a gift for digesting complex laws and summarizing them in ways that laymen could understand. Casey invented both the concept and the term "tax shelter." By showing businessmen how to do the bare minimum necessary to comply with the letter of the law, he soon became a millionaire. Laws, Casey explained, were "written by guys like you and me. Not by geniuses. . . . There was nothing God-like to me about a piece of legislation. Interpretation was everything. And I interpreted them in the best interests of our business subscribers."[46]

William Casey, a lover of books and student of history, was one of the most intelligent members of the incoming Reagan administration. He was also one of the most hard-line conservatives. "Bill, from the beginning, was to the right of Attila the Hun," said longtime friend Leo Cherne. In the 1930s, Casey supported the fascist general Francisco Franco during the Spanish Civil War because the Catholic Church backed Franco and the Loyalist side included Communists. In the 1950s, Casey defended Senator Joseph McCarthy. "This isn't patty cake we're playing with the Russians," Casey explained. "You need a McCarthy to flush out the enemy."[47]

In early 1980, with Ronald Reagan's presidential campaign floundering and running out of money, Casey was brought in to replace campaign manager John Sears. Casey's absent-mindedness, slouching posture, slovenly personal appearance, and incomprehensible mumbling created the impression of a man perhaps too elderly for the rigors of a national political campaign. Both reporters and senior campaign staff derisively called him "Spacey Casey."[48] But it was Casey who made the major managerial decisions and got the campaign out of debt.

As Carter and Reagan prepared for their televised debate, someone inside the Carter campaign slipped copies of the president's briefing books to the Reagan camp. A subsequent investigation of "debate-gate" concluded that the purloined papers, which had been kept in Casey's safe, had probably "entered the Reagan campaign through its director, Casey." Casey denied knowing anything about it.[49]

Casey had hoped to become secretary of state, but his droopy, unkempt appearance simply did not evoke the dignity requisite to such high office. When Reagan offered him the CIA instead, Casey agreed to take it on the condition that he be given cabinet rank and thus a role as policy advocate as well as intelligence officer. Such a confounding of roles was unprecedented, but Reagan agreed without a second thought.

Revitalizing the CIA's Operations Directorate was high on Casey's agenda. Maintaining good relations with the congressional oversight committees was not.[50] "If Bill believed in something, he often did what he damn well pleased," recalled Senate Intelligence Committee Chairman Barry Goldwater. "Casey just said to hell with Congress."[51]

Shortly after arriving at CIA headquarters, Casey held a meeting of the operations staff. "Here's the trouble," he said, holding up the Agency's 130-page booklet of guidelines covering the conduct of covert operations. "We're too timid. The attitude is, 'Don't stick your neck out. Play it safe.' This kind of crap is smothering us," the director railed. "You practically have to take a lawyer with you on a mission. I'm throwing this thing out." And he did. Casey's attitude toward covert operations was guided by his experience as a successful venture capitalist. You had to take risks to get results.[52]

When Casey was briefed on the CIA's covert war in Afghanistan, he was thrilled. "This is the kind of thing we should be doing—only more," he exclaimed. "I want to see one place on this globe, one spot where we can checkmate them and roll them back. We've got to make the Communists feel the heat."[53]

Within six weeks of Reagan's inauguration, Casey proposed a sweeping program of covert operations, many of them targeted against governments regarded as pro-Soviet: Afghanistan, Cambodia, Laos, Grenada, and Nicaragua. Operations were also planned in Iran, Libya, El Salvador, and Guatemala. Reagan approved Casey's blueprint for reinvigorating the Directorate of Operations, and soon its burgeoning staff—some one thousand new positions—displaced the entire Soviet analysis division from the headquarters building in Langley, Virginia.[54]

Central America held a prominent position in Casey's plans. Early in March, he presented the president with a proposed operation aimed primarily at supporting the Salvadoran government of José Napoleón Duarte. The plan included covert media and propaganda work inside El Salvador, improved intelligence gathering on the sources of the guerrillas' arms supply, and a paramilitary operation designed to "interdict" arms supplies flowing into El Salvador from Nicaragua and Honduras. The plan also affirmed an existing program begun by President Carter to provide assistance to internal opponents of the Sandinista government—opposition parties, trade unions, the press, the private sector, and the Catholic Church.[55]

On March 9, 1981, Reagan signed a presidential finding authorizing Casey's plan. The congressional intelligence committees supported the finding, even though it was so short on details that it was hard to know exactly what was being authorized.[56] Shortly thereafter, 150 new operatives were dispatched to Central America to lay the groundwork for the Agency's expanded role. CIA officers made contact with the bands of Nicaraguan exiles in Honduras and at paramilitary training camps in Florida.[57] One of the groups approached was the Nicaraguan Democratic Union (Unión Democrática Nicaragüense, UDN), a small coterie of conservative middle-class Nicaraguans involved more in political agitation in the United States than in military operations. José Francisco Cardenal, head of the UDN, met with CIA officials often in Washington and Miami and traveled with them to Honduras to confer with armed bands of former members of Somoza's National Guard. He also began receiving payments from the CIA, with promises of more to come.

"He was told that the United States Government was prepared to help us remove the FSLN from power in Nicaragua," said Cardenal's former colleague in the UDN, Edgar Chamorro, "but that, as a condition of receiving this help, we had to join forces with the ex–National Guardsmen." A number of UDN members were adamantly opposed to any alliance with the Guard. "We were well aware of the crimes the guardsmen had committed against the Nicaraguan people while in the service of President Somoza," Chamorro recalled, "and we wanted nothing to do with them." But the prospect of enlisting Washington as an ally in the fight against the Sandinistas proved too tempting to resist. That spring, the UDN agreed to join the guardsmen, who called themselves the 15th of September Legion.[58] The Defense Intelligence Agency, which had been tracking the guardsmen's pillaging of villages on both sides of the Nicaraguan-Honduran border, called them "terrorists."[59]

Washington was not the only potential patron urging unity among the exiles. The Argentine military government had been helping the former guardsmen since late 1980, and when UDN officials traveled to Buenos Aires in May 1981, Argentine officers told them they were prepared to train and finance UDN combatants if they would unite with the Legion. By some accounts, the United States had already begun channeling funds to the contras through Argentina.[60]

In June, Reagan's ambassador-at-large Vernon Walters, former Deputy CIA Director and confidant of various Latin American military officers, traveled to

Argentina himself as part of the new administration's effort to upgrade ties with the military regime. Though U.S. diplomats on the scene denied that Walters struck a deal with the Argentines, other officials in both Buenos Aires and Washington reported that he did precisely that. In any event, shortly after his trip, large numbers of Argentine military advisers began arriving clandestinely in Honduras.[61]

The partnership between Washington and Buenos Aires was finalized in November 1981, when General Leopoldo Galtieri, chief of staff of the Argentine armed forces, visited Washington and concluded a secret agreement with Casey on joint support for the contras. Washington agreed to provide military supplies and finance the contra operation if Argentina would provide advisers and manage it.[62]

The Honduran armed forces were another potential partner. In early 1980, Emilio Echevarry, a former member of Somoza's National Guard, prevailed upon an old classmate from Argentine military school, Honduran colonel Gustavo Alvarez Martínez, to help the contras smuggle military equipment from the United States. As commander of the National Police, Alvarez was one of the most powerful officers in Honduras and a vehement anti-Communist. He arranged to have contra arms shipments sent through the Honduran armed forces.[63]

With the arrival of Ronald Reagan, Alvarez hoped that the United States might act in concert with him to rid the region of the Sandinista plague. In April 1981, shortly after the CIA began contacting various contra groups, Alvarez traveled to Washington to meet with CIA Director Casey and NSC staffer Major General Robert Schweitzer. Alvarez proposed that Honduras and the United States build the contras into a formidable military force and launch them against Nicaragua in the hope of provoking retaliation. If the Sandinistas fell into the trap of striking at Honduras, then the Honduran military backed by the United States would invade Nicaragua and get rid of the Sandinistas once and for all.[64]

Although a full-scale military invasion of Nicaragua was judged impractical, Casey moved ahead with preparations for a major covert effort. In August 1981 he replaced thirty-year veteran Nestor Sanchez as division chief for operations in Latin America because Sanchez, though a hard-liner, was skeptical about the contra army. "When the option paper was being pulled together," said one intelligence community source, "Sanchez was reluctant to plunge in."[65] Sanchez moved to the Pentagon as deputy assistant secretary of defense for policy in charge of Latin American affairs—the Defense Department equivalent of Enders's post at State. In his new job, he remained a member of the

Inter-Agency Core Group and, ironically, ended up with significant responsibility for managing the covert war once it got under way.[66]

To replace Sanchez, Casey chose Duane R. "Dewey" Clarridge, the CIA station chief in Rome. Clarridge was a flamboyant, aggressive operative with the "can-do" attitude that was so popular everywhere in the Reagan administration's national security apparatus. The "Lawrence of Arabia School of Management," he called it—"give the right officer clear tasks and adequate resources and then stand back." Clarridge had impressed Casey during the director's European trip in early 1981 by arranging an elegant late night dinner. "Dewey's the only really impressive guy I met out there," Casey told Deputy CIA Director Bobby Ray Inman when he returned to Washington. "I'm going to bring him back here for something big."[67]

Within the Agency, Clarridge was best known for his unconventional dress. "Dewey was a very 'spiv' dresser," said a senior CIA veteran. "Pastel jackets. White shoes. Kerchief in the pocket. I don't know where he got all his clothes, but everybody was quite amused by Dewey." Clarridge had served in Nepal, India, Turkey, and Rome, but never in Latin America. No matter—Casey liked him because he was "a real doer, a real take-charge guy." Clarridge also shared Casey's contempt for congressional oversight. Most congressional staffers, he averred, couldn't pass a counterintelligence polygraph, and their bosses catered to organized groups who were sometimes "under the influence of foreign interests."[68]

"If you have a tough, dangerous job, critical to national security, Dewey's your man," said Robert M. Gates, a career CIA officer who held several top positions under Casey and became Director of Central Intelligence under President George Bush. "Just make sure you have a good lawyer at his elbow—Dewey's not easy to control." Casey set up a direct line of communication with Clarridge, bypassing both Inman and John Stein, the new head of the Operations Directorate, neither of whom was enthusiastic about the Nicaragua program.[69]

On August 11, contra representatives from the UDN and the 15th of September Legion, along with Argentine and perhaps CIA officials, met in Guatemala City to sign the unity pact that Argentina and the United States had been urging on them. They dissolved the UDN and the Legion, creating a new organization, the Nicaraguan Democratic Force (Fuerza Democrática Nicaragüense, FDN). "The name of the organization, the members of the political junta, and the members of the general staff were all chosen or approved by the CIA," recalled former FDN official Edgar Chamorro. The FDN set up offices in a safe house in Tegucigalpa, Honduras, rented for them by the Agency.[70]

Just a few weeks after the Guatemala meeting, Clarridge traveled to Honduras to see General Alvarez. He took with him Colonel Mario Davico, the vice chief of Argentine military intelligence. Clarridge was unequivocal about U.S. aims. "I speak in the name of President Ronald Reagan," he affirmed. "We want to support this effort to change the government of Nicaragua." Out of this meeting came "La tripartita"—a three-way agreement among the United States, Argentina, and Honduras to support the creation of a contra army. The agreement, as described by FDN military commander Colonel Enrique Bermúdez, provided for a division of labor: "The Hondurans will provide the territory, the United States will provide the money, and Argentina will provide the 'front.' "[71]

The Enders Initiative

During the summer of 1981, the first rumors of U.S. support for military action against Nicaragua began filtering through Central America. Larry Pezzullo was appalled and immediately cabled Washington with his strenuous objections. The contras, Pezzullo warned, were "poison" and it was foolhardy for the United States to ally with them. It would be equally disastrous for the United States to entice Honduras into a war with Nicaragua. "What the hell are you doing?" an exasperated Pezzullo asked Enders. "Are you giving these fellows [the Hondurans] a green light to come into Nicaragua?"[72]

In an attempt to avert the coming conflict between Nicaragua and the United States, Pezzullo prevailed upon Enders to take a last stab at diplomacy.[73] Enders, in turn, had to convince a skeptical Al Haig that the effort was worth making. He also ran into serious opposition from hard-liners like Casey, Allen, Sanchez, and even Haig's deputy, William Clark, all of whom saw diplomacy as pointless and wanted to move straight to a policy of military support for the contras.[74]

With so little backing for a diplomatic initiative and with the foundations of a covert paramilitary program already being laid, the Enders initiative was very much an eleventh-hour effort. "Few people thought the Sandinistas would talk to us seriously," said one member of the Core Group. "But we had to try."[75] Part of the argument for making the attempt was cosmetic. When the administration went to Congress with its program of covert operations against Nicaragua, it would be able to say that diplomacy had been tried and had failed. As one Pentagon official explained, "I certainly felt we should make every effort possible so that the audit trail showed we went every step of the way."[76]

On August 11, as the contras were meeting in Guatemala City to form the FDN, Enders arrived in Managua. His strategy, as he later described it, was to see "if you could use the threat of confrontation rather than confrontation itself" to make the Sandinistas abandon their support for the Salvadoran revolution. In two days, Enders met six times with top Sandinista officials—

meetings that were "very confrontational," according to one U.S. official. Enders presented the "stark realities" to the Sandinistas. "He was frank to the point of being brutal," another official recalled.[77]

Enders accused the Sandinistas of smuggling arms to the Salvadoran guerrillas. They denied it, arguing that, at most, some smuggling might have been done by low-level Sandinista officials without the government's knowledge. Enders replied that such a notion was "patently ridiculous." To Enders's complaint that Nicaragua's military buildup was a threat to its neighbors, the Sandinistas replied that the buildup was defensive, designed to protect the revolution from outside attack. Enders ridiculed the idea that they could possibly defend themselves against the United States: "You can never forget that the United States is exactly 100 times bigger than you are."[78]

Tempers flared frequently during the two days of talks. Pezzullo, who knew how sensitive the young, inexperienced Sandinistas were about national dignity and independence, winced at some of the exchanges. The Sandinistas responded by railing against the history of U.S. intervention in Nicaragua.

Yet, as the talks went forward, the outline of an agreement seemed to take shape. Enders raised four issues: the Sandinistas' continued support for the Salvadoran guerrillas; the buildup of their military forces; their increasingly close ties with Cuba and the Soviet Union; and the restrictions they had placed on economic and political pluralism within Nicaragua. The first two issues, however, had priority. Enders summed up the U.S. position the first day in an angry exchange with Comandante Bayardo Arce, reputed to be the most militant member of the Sandinista National Directorate. "You can do your own thing," Enders said, "but do it within your borders, or else we are going to hurt you."[79]

However indelicately phrased, this was not different in principle from the attitude taken by the Carter administration: Nicaragua's relations with the United States depended mainly upon Nicaragua's foreign policy, not on how it conducted its internal affairs. If the Sandinistas were willing to make concessions on the issue of El Salvador and their arms buildup, rapprochement with the United States was still possible.

"I think you've got a deal," Pezzullo told a discouraged Enders at the end of the first day. "The deal is that if they commit themselves to no export of revolution and to limiting the size of their armed forces and their weaponry, we would on the other hand be willing to guarantee that we would not invade."[80] Specifically, Washington would ask Congress to restore economic assistance, make an effort to close the paramilitary training camps for Nicaraguan exiles that had sprung up in the United States, and sign a nonaggression pact with Nicaragua under the terms of the Rio Treaty of Reciprocal Assistance signed by Latin America and the United States in 1947.[81]

Enders presented this formula to Daniel Ortega in their last round of discussions.[82] He tried to reassure the Sandinistas that the United States did not intend to overthrow them. "Just as you consider your revolution irreversible, we do also," Enders began. "We recognize that the defeat of Somoza is an accomplished fact."

"We are revolutionaries," Ortega asserted firmly. "We will not surrender to the imperialist and aggressive attitudes of the United States. But we are certainly looking for a better relationship with the United States, in exchange for which we are left alone to make our revolution. . . . We do not want to become a threat to what the United States calls hemispheric security."

Enders then proposed a six-week course of action leading to another meeting with Ortega in Managua. Washington would submit a series of proposals dealing with the issues that concerned the United States, and the Nicaraguans would do the same. In the meantime, both sides would agree to reduce the level of public rhetoric. More important, Washington expected the Sandinistas to halt the flow of arms to the Salvadoran guerrillas, "as you did in March," Enders added.

"We are at a fork in the road," he warned, "and if we do not take these actions, we are not going to achieve a reduction in tensions. I do not think it is necessary to explain in detail the alternative." There were circumstances, he continued, under which the United States would intervene directly in the region with military force, even though the political cost throughout Latin America would be severe.

"We, too, have seen the crossroads," Ortega replied. "We are resolved to defend this revolution by force of arms, and if we are crushed, to carry the war to all of Central America. . . . But we are not suicidal," he added. "I regard your proposal as reasonable." Ortega agreed to proceed as Enders had suggested.

When Enders returned to Washington, he found that selling the deal to the rest of the administration was harder than selling it to the Sandinistas. Haig remained deeply skeptical. In the margin of Enders's memo describing the possibility of an agreement, Haig wrote, "I'll believe it when I see it, and meanwhile let's not hold up on the other plans."[83] Enders also came under attack from the hard-liners, including Allen and his assistant for Latin America, Roger Fontaine. They accused Enders of giving short shrift to the issue of democracy. Indeed, though democracy had been discussed, Enders had put much greater emphasis on security issues. The hard-liners opposed this tack because it might lead to an agreement that would leave the Sandinista regime in power. The demand for democracy, on the other hand, became a code for ousting the Sandinistas because they refused to negotiate about Nicaragua's internal affairs.[84]

One of the tactics adopted by the hard-liners in order to scuttle the Enders initiative was to insist that the draft proposals submitted by the United States be as uncompromising as possible. On September 8, Enders forwarded to Daniel Ortega the first of five draft position papers on the issues they had discussed in Managua. The first focused on Nicaragua's concerns over contra training camps in the United States. If agreement could be reached on the other issues, Washington would make a unilateral statement affirming that it would "vigorously enforce" existing neutrality laws that make it a crime for individuals to mount military attacks from the United States against foreign governments.[85]

The Sandinistas did not find the proposal very impressive. After all, as one Sandinista official pointed out, Washington was "merely promising to do what it should be doing already—enforcing its laws."[86] In the past when Nicaragua had protested the training camps, U.S. officials contended there was no clear evidence that the contras were violating the law. The Sandinistas were not confident that a pledge of "vigorous" enforcement would actually close the camps.

An even worse omen for the future of the negotiations came attached to Enders's letter. It was final notification that $7 million in economic aid halted in April was being permanently cut off. The earlier decision to halt aid had left open the possibility that it might be restored if Nicaragua stopped supporting revolutionary movements abroad. The September 8 notification marked the end of that possibility.

Ostensibly, the notification was made because the State Department wanted to reprogram the funds for use in another country before the authority to spend them expired at the end of the fiscal year on September 30. But it could hardly have been a coincidence that the notification was sent along with the first U.S. negotiating proposal, especially since the cut-off of economic aid was one of the main complaints raised by the Sandinistas when Enders was in Managua. Back in Washington, the hard-liners were doing everything they could to sabotage the dialogue from the outset.[87]

A week later, on September 16, Enders sent Ortega a second draft proposal concerning nonintervention. Intended as a joint statement by Nicaragua and the United States, it affirmed the principles of nonintervention and peaceful settlement of disputes set forth in the U.N. Charter, the OAS Charter, and the Rio Treaty. Once again, it seemed to the Nicaraguans that Washington was offering to do nothing more than comply with existing obligations.[88]

Just two days later, the Pentagon announced that it would conduct three days of joint naval maneuvers with Honduras, code-named *Halcon Vista* (Falcon View), in early October. The exercise would involve three U.S. patrol boats, about four hundred U.S. military personnel, and a comparable contingent from the Honduran side. It was intended to improve the Hondurans' ability to intercept arms shipments to El Salvador passing through Honduran waters. The idea for the exercises originated with NSC staffer General Schweitzer, who intended the exercises to be provocative—"a deliberate attempt to stick it in their eye," said a military officer at the U.S. Southern Command in Panama.[89]

He succeeded. Although the exercises were relatively modest, Nicaragua denounced them, warning that they would "seriously affect" the bilateral discussions. Enders tried to smooth over the problem by assuring Nicaragua that the exercises were routine and offering to invite Nicaraguan observers.[90] The Sandinistas were not reassured. In public they condemned the exercises as practice for an invasion of Nicaragua and announced plans to put the entire country on alert.[91] On October 3, they launched an "anti-imperialist campaign" of mass mobilization and street demonstrations against the exercises. Although none of the demonstrations were targeted at the U.S. embassy, the U.S. chargé d'affaires, Roger Gamble, became so fearful the embassy would be attacked that he ordered the destruction of classified documents and readied contingency plans to evacuate dependents and nonessential personnel. "This will not be another Teheran," Gamble warned the Sandinistas. They assured him the embassy would be protected.[92] It was a good thing they did. Under the guise of preparing for an emergency military evacuation of the embassy, hardliners at the Pentagon developed a full-fledged invasion plan.[93]

Amid this inauspicious atmosphere, the United States tentatively presented Nicaragua with its most important negotiating proposal—the paper on security concerns. The process of drafting the proposal had set off a major battle between hard-liners and pragmatists. "We had some difficulty in defining the arms control questions," Enders recalled. "We ultimately got agreement on a set of principles that would be very demanding."[94]

That was an understatement. The U.S. proposal demanded that the Sandinistas reduce their armed forces immediately from 23,000 men to between 15,000 and 17,000 and eventually limit their military to the "traditional size" of 8,000 to 10,000. They would have to forswear the acquisition of any additional heavy weapons and return to their suppliers any weapons systems that other Central American countries did not possess—such as their recently acquired Soviet tanks. To verify their compliance, Nicaragua would have to allow OAS inspectors into the country. The provisions on weaponry, in particular, were much tougher than the proposal Enders had put on the table during his meetings in Managua. They were, a senior administration official conceded, "something in excess of what was reasonable."[95]

The proposal was presented informally to Arturo Cruz, who was then Nicaraguan ambassador to the United States. "I was flabbergasted by the demands," he recalled. "If that was my reaction as a moderate, think of what the reaction would have been in Managua. I told them this sounds like the conditions of a victorious power." Cruz asked Enders's assistant, Craig Johnstone, to withdraw the proposal for fear that transmitting it to his government would kill the dialogue.[96] Nothing further was done with the proposal and the two remaining proposals on cultural exchanges and economic assistance were never presented to the Nicaraguans, either.

On October 31, the Nicaraguans wrote another letter to the Reagan administration expressing their desire to "continue the dialogue." The Nicaraguan letter went unanswered.[97] Within the administration, Enders had run out of maneuvering room on the negotiating track. The furor over the *Halcon Vista* exercises, combined with a new Sandinista crackdown on domestic opponents, had poisoned the atmosphere.[98] When Ambassador Cruz wrote to the *New York Times* in mid-October that his government felt that the Enders visit in August had "paved the way for closer and more friendly relations between our two governments," the Department of State upbraided him, insisting that U.S. relations with Nicaragua were bad and getting worse.[99]

The Nicaraguans, however, had not given up hope of reviving the dialogue. At Mexico's urging, Haig agreed to meet with Nicaraguan Foreign Minister Miguel D'Escoto during the OAS General Assembly meeting on the island of St. Lucia in December 1981. The two talked for ninety minutes, but there was not much communication. Haig complained of Nicaragua's support for the guerrillas in El Salvador, its military buildup, and its lack of democracy. Washington would take "reciprocal measures," Haig warned, unless Nicaragua stopped supporting subversion. D'Escoto, in turn, blasted Washington's intervention in El Salvador and its threats against Nicaragua. He denied that the Sandinistas were shipping arms to the Salvadoran guerrillas, and he reproached Haig for raising the issue of Nicaragua's internal politics. In August, D'Escoto recalled, Enders had said Washington was concerned about Nicaragua's international behavior, not its internal policies. Enders, sitting beside Haig, demurred. "No, I didn't precisely say that."[100] Washington's agenda had begun to shift.

The Reagan administration was too divided to undertake a serious diplomatic effort and see it through to conclusion. Every step of the way, the hard-liners conspired to derail the dialogue. The Sandinistas, on the other hand, had no trust whatever in Washington's good faith—especially after the diplomatic fiasco in March, when they had made concessions to U.S. demands only to have the administration cut off economic aid anyway.

Inexperienced and overly sensitive to slights from Washington, the Sandinistas were too quick to denounce the insulting rhetoric in which Enders's proposal came couched—even though the substance of the proposal was the same as the understanding they had had with the Carter administration. Although the United States had left open the door to reconciliation, said Daniel Ortega, it was "so small that in order to pass through we would have to do so on our knees."[101] Later, when Reagan's hard-liners had effectively destroyed any possibility of a negotiated settlement between Nicaragua and the United States, the Sandinistas would look back longingly to Enders's proposals, chagrined that they had not taken them more seriously.[102] "There are magic moments," Pezzullo reflected later, ". . . little windows of opportunity, and then they close, and everybody's caught with their prejudice in place."[103]

By August, momentum was building on the paramilitary track and flagging on the diplomatic one. Just as the hard-liners envisioned El Salvador as the test case for a new, more aggressive, U.S. counterinsurgency policy, they envisioned Nicaragua as the test case for reinvigorating CIA covert operations. In El Salvador, the United States would demonstrate that it could halt the tide of Communist insurgency in the Third World; in Nicaragua, it would demonstrate that it could roll back the Communists even after they had come to power. The difference between the two policies was that policy toward Nicaragua, both diplomatic and paramilitary, was being conducted in secret. For the time being, at least, it was immune to the firestorm of opposition Haig had stirred up on El Salvador.

CHAPTER 6

Tough Guys

Alexander Haig had promised the president that winning in El Salvador would be easy. If Washington would simply take a strong stand, Cuba and the Soviet Union would back down, Latin America and Western Europe would fall into line, and the Democrats in Congress would acquiesce. With U.S. hardware and expertise in abundance, the Salvadoran army would make short work of the guerrillas, and Ronald Reagan would begin his presidency with a dazzling foreign policy triumph.

When Thomas O. Enders was sworn in as assistant secretary of state for inter-American affairs in June, Haig's rosy scenario was already fading. Allies abroad were skeptical of Washington's approach and in some cases were actively working at cross-purposes. Buoyed by opinion polls showing that Reagan's Central America policy was enormously unpopular, the Democrats were becoming bolder in their challenge, and even moderate Republicans were questioning the wisdom of Haig's approach. In El Salvador, the rapid infusion of arms and advisers seemed to make little difference in the military balance, and the coalition government between the Christian Democrats and the military remained as shaky as ever.

Enders Takes Control

The public backlash and congressional resistance that followed Haig's war scare did not bode well for a policy based exclusively on anti-Communism. Enders believed the policy needed a sounder political footing—a more positive message. It had to be *for* something. Democracy and free elections, Enders suggested, were the symbols that would resonate best for a conservative Republican administration. With deft argument, the liberal values of human rights and social justice could even be subsumed under the rubric of democracy. Free elections, after all, offered the best guarantee that a government would respect basic human rights and be responsive to popular demands for social change.[1]

In dealing with Congress, Enders believed gradual, conciliatory persuasion would produce the best results. If the administration assured legislators that it shared their concerns, they could be cajoled into providing the dollars needed to wage the war. Enders's style was to be solicitous of members' views, profess sympathy with their underlying anxieties, but hold tenaciously to the essence of administration policy. Unlike Haig, who sought to overpower dissident Democrats by sheer force of will and decibel level, Enders sought to prevail by the power of his intellect. With impeccable logic, if not always impeccable facts, he argued that the administration's policy was the only reasonable course of action and the one most likely to achieve the goals that all Americans wanted. His usual demeanor was cool and aloof. Flashes of temper came only occasionally, when someone was unable or unwilling to grasp the compelling logic of his argument.

Enders's plan to promote democracy as the ideological centerpiece of the administration's Central America policy ran into immediate opposition from hard-liners like Haig's deputy, William P. Clark, National Security Adviser Richard V. Allen, and Undersecretary of Defense Fred C. Iklé. They feared that putting too much emphasis on democracy might limit the administration's options.[2] Echoing Jeane Kirkpatrick's thesis from "Dictatorships and Double Standards," the hard-liners argued that reform was dangerous, weakening friendly regimes at the very moment they were confronting insurgency. Enders's emphasis on democracy sounded uncomfortably like Jimmy Carter's human rights policy. Better to defeat the insurgents first and then worry about democracy and reform. The hard-liners wanted to continue military aid to El Salvador, even if the far right was finally successful in one of its perennial coup attempts, and they wanted to restore U.S. military aid to the military dictatorship in Guatemala, regardless of its human rights record.[3]

The hard-liners were also much less tolerant of Congress. Whereas Enders favored conciliation, they wanted confrontation. Convinced that the public's reluctance to use military force abroad was the fatal weakness of American foreign policy, the hard-liners wanted to confront the Vietnam syndrome head-on by provoking a major battle with Congress over Central America. If Reagan won this war at home, he would have a free hand to turn back the Communist tide in Central America and around the globe. If not, the blame for losing Central America could be put squarely on the doorstep of the Democrats.[4]

Enders prevailed over the hard-liners by winning the support of White House Chief of Staff James A. Baker, who still wanted to prevent Central America from derailing the president's domestic agenda. Baker believed that no policy could succeed without a reasonable level of support from the Congress, the press, and the public.[5]

Enders unveiled his new policy with considerable fanfare in a speech to the World Affairs Council in Washington, D.C., on July 16, 1981. Although it opened with a familiar condemnation of Cuban support for the Salvadoran guerrillas, it was otherwise devoid of the Cold War fulminations that had been a staple in Haig's early pronouncements. Stealing the rhetoric of Reagan's critics, Enders endorsed a "political solution" to the Salvadoran war rather than a military one. Only Salvadorans could solve their nation's problems, he said, and all parties should join in a political process to end the conflict. The process, however, was elections, and the guerrillas would have to "renounce violence" in order to participate. Washington still opposed the sort of settlement most people meant when they spoke of a "political solution"—a negotiated end to the war.[6] By posing elections as an alternative to negotiations, the administration sought to make a negotiated settlement appear undemocratic.

"El Salvador's leaders will not—and should not—grant the insurgents, through negotiations, the share of power they have not been able to win on the battlefield," declared Enders, coining one of the administration's favorite slogans. "But they should be—and are—willing to compete with the insurgents at the polls." For most members of Congress, whose stock-in-trade was getting elected to office, the allure of "free elections" in El Salvador was hard to resist.

Modernizing the Oligarchy

Enders's July speech was also designed to reaffirm U.S. support for José Napoleón Duarte against his enemies on the far right.[7] The Salvadoran business community was convinced that Reagan Republicans did not really support the Christian Democrats, whom the businessmen regarded as barely distinguishable from the Marxist guerrillas. "Duarte is just a Communist who happens to believe in God," explained Herbert de Sola, a member of one of El Salvador's wealthiest land-owning families.[8] The attitude of the Salvadoran armed forces was not much different.

Opposed by the right and by much of the military, the Christian Democrats were unable to move ahead on the reforms promised in 1980. The agrarian reform sputtered to a virtual halt. The human rights practices of the army and the security forces did not improve. The investigations of the murders of the U.S. churchwomen and the labor advisers stalled. As soon as the Carter administration left office, the military even reneged on the concessions agreed to in December 1980 as a condition of U.S. aid.[9] Reagan's failure to object to such backsliding only added to the right's conviction that Washington was on their side.

The impotence of the Christian Democrats was a major obstacle to the strategy Enders envisioned. Skeptics in Congress would not long support Reagan's policy without progress on the reforms and the murder investigations. A rightist coup would spark a serious congressional move to cut off military aid entirely, leaving U.S. policy in shambles. So in his July speech, Enders reemphasized Washington's support for the Christian Democrats. Much as the hard-liners might dislike Duarte and the agrarian reform, Washington was now committed to them both. "Duarte is all we have," a U.S. official explained.[10]

Nevertheless, the Reagan administration was much more sympathetic to the Salvadoran private sector than Carter had been. Whereas Carter had seen the rightist business community as a political enemy that had to be defeated in order to make reform possible, Reagan saw it as an essential ally in the battle against the left. Carter had tried to break the political and economic power of the oligarchy, and it responded by decapitalizing the economy and trying to overthrow the government. Reagan, by contrast, tried to foster reconciliation between the right and the Christian Democrats in order to restore business confidence.[11] So Enders's speech combined an endorsement of agrarian reform with strong support for compensating previous owners—a key demand of the right—and he cautioned the government against any "new economic changes" until there was "assurance that the existing reforms will be made to work."

As the price of reconciliation, the private sector demanded a role in the government, so that it could further blunt the reforms. In June and July 1981, the Reagan administration pressured the Christian Democrats to share power with the right by bringing private sector representatives into key economic ministries. The Christian Democrats resisted, the right mounted yet another coup attempt, and the U.S. embassy once again had to save the government from falling.[12]

Washington's strategy in El Salvador was a complex one, the pieces of which were not entirely consistent. The first priority was to provide the Salvadoran armed forces with the military aid necessary to defeat the guerrillas. Large-scale aid had the side effect of further strengthening the armed forces at the expense of the Christian Democrats. On the other hand, it also increased Washington's influence over the officers corps, enabling the embassy to hold in check the army's instinct to rid itself of the bothersome civilians.[13] And keeping the Christian Democrats in the junta was essential to retaining congressional support to finance the military buildup.

Some State Department officials believed that implementing the agrarian reform, reducing the number of political killings, and gradually democratizing the Salvadoran political system were necessary to build a viable popular base of support for the regime and ensure its long-term survival. They saw the military effort as only one part of the conflict, and not the most important part. U.S. military aid was "only enough to give the government a breathing space," explained one official. "The war cannot be won militarily; it must be won politically."[14] This view was essentially an expression of the classic counterinsurgency model developed by the United States in Greece, the Philippines, Guatemala, and Vietnam. Not coincidentally, it was L. Craig Johnstone, a veteran of the pacification program in Vietnam, who was the most consistent advocate of applying this model in El Salvador. In the 1980s, counterinsurgency doctrine underwent something of a revival at the Pentagon as well, under the new label of "low intensity conflict" or LIC. Pentagon officials such as General Paul F. Gorman, the Joint Chiefs of Staff representative on the Core Group, regarded El Salvador as a testing ground for the new doctrine.

Elections for a constituent assembly, scheduled for 1982, were a key element in Washington's counterinsurgency plan. Because of the ongoing violence of the security forces, no one expected the left to participate in the elections, so there was no possibility that the balloting would end the war. In that sense, Enders's July speech was disingenuous when it posed elections as a "political solution" to the conflict. But the elections could enhance the regime's legitimacy and serve as a nonviolent means of resolving the conflict between the Christian Democrats and the far right. If the right could be persuaded to channel its efforts to oust the Christian Democrats into an election campaign rather than fomenting a coup, one of the main dangers to U.S. policy would be defused.

Traditionally, the Salvadoran oligarchy never had to bother with politics directly, other than assuring that its ties to the military high command were in good repair. For the most part, members of the oligarchy left the task of governing to the army and paid it well to safeguard their interests. Elections would force the right to learn more modern means of translating their wealth into political power. They would have to master political skills like campaigning, bargaining, and perhaps even compromising. In short, Washington hoped elections would modernize the Salvadoran oligarchy, making it a more effective and acceptable political partner both in El Salvador and in Washington.

The outcome of elections would almost certainly be a division of power between the Christian Democrats and the right, thereby giving the right the role in government it had been demanding. The process of reform might be slowed, but that could be justified in Washington as the consequence of a free election.[15] If all went according to plan, the Salvadoran regime would be consolidated around a center-right coalition anchored in the armed forces. The elections, along with modest reforms, would assure continued congressional support for administration policy. These efforts would buy time for U.S. military aid to give the Salvadoran army the upper hand on the battlefield, eventually limiting the guerrillas to isolated pockets of resistance in the depopulated northern provinces.

Seeing the hopelessness of the war, the civilian politicians of the Revolutionary Democratic Front (FDR) might be enticed to break with their more radical guerrilla comrades in the Farabundo Martí National Liberation Front (FMLN) and join an electoral process controlled by the government.[16] The most recalcitrant fighters might remain in the hills, but without domestic or international legitimacy, they would eventually be eradicated. At the State Department, this scenario was dubbed "the Venezuelan solution" because of its superficial similarity to the way in which the insurgency there had been defeated in the 1960s. Ambassador Deane Hinton summed up his marching orders more pithily: "Save the economy, stop the violence, have the elections and ride into the sunset."[17]

Certification

The reasonable tone of Enders's July 16 speech was welcome on Capitol Hill, but it was not enough by itself to dispel the doubts about Reagan's policy. Even before Haig threw down the gauntlet on El Salvador, congressional liberals, led by Christopher J. Dodd (D-Conn.) in the Senate and Steve Solarz (D.-N.Y.) and Michael Barnes (D-Md.) in the House, had anticipated that Central America would be a major point of conflict with the new administration. With the Senate Foreign Relations Committee under Republican control, the House Subcommittee on Inter-American Affairs was the principal congressional forum for contesting Reagan's policy. When Congress reconvened in January 1981, House liberals chose Barnes to replace Inter-American Subcommittee chairman Gus Yatron (D-Pa.), whom they considered a conservative and lethargic chairman.[18]

A lawyer by training, Barnes was energetic and thoughtful, a rising star in the House despite his relative youth. He was firmly convinced that Reagan's policy was fundamentally wrong and would prove disastrous for the United States. Yet his style was never brash or confrontational; he fought political battles with more civility than was the norm on either side of the aisle. Under Barnes's leadership, the Subcommittee on Inter-American Affairs (later renamed Western Hemisphere Affairs) became the focal point of Democratic opposition to Reagan's policies.

In the Senate, Chris Dodd took on a similar role, even though he was a freshman. Dodd began his political career as one of the "Watergate babies," elected to the House in the Democratic tidal wave of 1974. After six years there, he easily won an open Senate seat in 1980—one of the Democrat's few Senate victories that year. Despite his junior status, Dodd spoke out aggressively on issues that were important to him. That earned him a reputation for stridency among older members who still believed that newcomers should be seen but not heard, at least for a year or two.

On Central America especially, Dodd insisted on being heard. Having served as a Peace Corps volunteer in the Dominican Republic, he had a first-hand understanding of the harsh poverty Latin American peasants endured. Social injustice combined with government repression—not guns from Havana, Managua, or Moscow—were behind the crisis in El Salvador, Dodd was certain. Reagan's bellicose approach to the region appalled him. Over the next decade, he would be one of Reagan's most persistent critics.

In March 1981, just a few weeks after Reagan announced his emergency military aid package for El Salvador, the State Department submitted its fiscal year 1982 foreign aid budget with big increases for El Salvador. "Because El Salvador has been most affected by outside interference, it has our largest proposed aid program [in Latin America]," explained John Bushnell. "Externally armed guerrillas cannot be defeated by fertilizer alone."[19] Reagan requested $26 million in additional military aid (almost five times Carter's request the previous year), $51.2 million in economic development aid (more than twice Carter's request), and $40 million in Economic Support Funds (Carter had requested none).[20] Unlike Reagan's emergency aid package, over which Congress had little say, the fiscal year 1982 request was subject to all the scrutiny of the normal budgetary process. In a rare instance of coordination between the House and Senate, liberal Democrats devised a strategy to force Reagan to continue Jimmy Carter's policy of promoting reform in El Salvador. Senator Dodd and Congressmen Solarz and Jonathan Bingham (D-N.Y.) drafted a bill making U.S. military aid conditional upon human rights, land reform, and a negotiated end to the war.

The Bingham-Solarz proposal required that within thirty days after the foreign aid bill was signed into law and every six months thereafter, the president would have to certify to Congress that the government of El Salvador met five conditions: (1) that it was not engaged in "a consistent pattern of gross violations of internationally recognized human rights"; (2) that it had achieved "substantial control" over its armed forces; (3) that it was making "continued progress" in essential reforms, including land reform; (4) that it was committed to holding free elections at an early date; and (5) that it had "demonstrated its willingness to negotiate" an end to the war. If the president could not certify that these conditions were being met, military aid to El Salvador would cease.[21]

In April, the Foreign Affairs Committee attached these certification conditions to the foreign assistance authorization bill. To guarantee victory, however, the sponsors made significant concessions: they agreed to drop language limiting Reagan's ability to use emergency authorities to send aid to El Salvador without congressional approval; and they agreed to drop a provision that gave Congress the right to vote on whether to accept the president's certification. By giving up this "legislative veto," the Democrats surrendered to Reagan the ultimate judgment on whether the conditions had been met.[22]

Certification was a way for Congress to force the administration to pay greater heed to human rights and social reform in El Salvador, as the price of obtaining an increase in military aid. In effect, the liberals' strategy was designed not to prevent Reagan from escalating U.S. involvement in the war, but to control the circumstances under which the escalation would take place. Certification represented a "middle ground" between cutting off aid and giving it unconditionally.[23]

In the Senate Foreign Relations Committee, Dodd worked closely with moderate Nancy L. Kassebaum (R-Kan.) to forge a bipartisan certification bill. Like the proposal finally adopted by the House Foreign Affairs Committee, Dodd's proposal did not include a legislative veto provision, and Dodd also agreed to soften the conditions. Rather than having to certify that the five objectives had been achieved, the president only had to certify that progress was being made toward them—a substantially less stringent and more subjective standard. But the concessions assured a solid victory; Dodd's proposal was adopted, 12–1.[24]

In September, with Senate action on the foreign aid bill coming up, José Napoleón Duarte came to the United States to plead for continued aid. The Reagan administration had mixed feelings about his visit. The State Department, facing a tough battle in Congress over the certification proposal, hoped Duarte could help muster the votes to defeat it. The White House, on the other hand, still saw El Salvador as a political liability and was not anxious to put it back on the front page. Duarte's visit therefore was kept "unofficial," which meant that there was no honor guard, no state dinner, no public appearances with President Reagan, and no joint communiqué. Duarte met with Reagan, but to the extent that the president's image makers in the White House could manage it, the visit was a nonevent. The State Department had to argue long and hard with the White House just to schedule a photo opportunity.[25]

Duarte's reception on Capitol Hill was a bit warmer, although the Democrats remained skeptical about his ability to deliver on his promises of reform. His bid for aid was hobbled by the fact that his government had still taken no action against the National Guardsmen accused of killing the U.S. churchwomen. He had a hard time explaining why.[26]

When the full Senate took up Dodd's certification proposal, Duarte joined the administration in a last ditch effort to defeat it, arguing in a letter to the Senate that the conditions were "unwarranted" and an "unacceptable imposition to a government friendly to the United States." But Duarte's position was ambiguous enough to leave some doubt about his real views. In meetings with members of both the House and Senate, Duarte acknowledged that he agreed wholeheartedly with the substance of the conditions because they corresponded closely with his own aims. According to one report, he actually endorsed the certification conditions in a private meeting with the Senate Foreign Relations Committee, only to reverse himself the following day in the letter.[27]

When the issue came to the Senate floor on September 23, 1981, liberal Democrats praised Duarte and argued that certification would strengthen his hand by giving him leverage over the armed forces. "The fact is the Duarte government's record to date is less than encouraging despite their good intentions," said Senator Dodd. "He needs all the help he can get. I do not take a back seat to anyone in my continued support and admiration for José Napoleón Duarte."[28]

Conservative Republicans responded that certification was a just a backdoor means of cutting off aid to El Salvador, abandoning it to the Communists. Its purpose was "to make certain we get out," charged Senator Richard G. Lugar (R-Ind.), and it infringed on the president's right to conduct foreign policy.

Senate Foreign Relations Committee chairman Charles Percy spoke for a number of moderate Republicans when he noted that there had been "very strong protests in the country" against aid to El Salvador, especially by the religious community. Percy argued in favor of certification on the grounds that it would be "reassuring" to the public. More than a dozen moderate Republicans, including Senate Majority Leader Howard H. Baker (R-Tenn.), joined almost all the Democrats in voting to keep the binding certification conditions. Despite furious lobbying by the administration, including a special White House session with the president for wayward Republicans, the Senate refused to reverse itself on two additional votes the following day.[29]

Apart from the provision on El Salvador, the State Department was pleased with the overall foreign aid bill. Knowing that the bill would pass the House only if a significant number of Democrats supported it, Reagan chose to avoid floor fights over controversial issues that might alienate them. The certification issue was one of the battles foregone. Thus, the foreign aid bill passed the House without controversy and the certification conditions on military aid to El Salvador were signed into law.[30]

Since the law gave Reagan the exclusive right to determine whether or not the Salvadoran government was making the requisite progress on reforms, the administration was only mildly displeased at its passage. White House officials failed to recognize what a serious political liability it would be to have Congress conduct an exhaustive public review of Reagan's policy every six months in conjunction with the president's certification reports. The White House troika had a hard enough time keeping Al Haig quiet. Keeping Congress quiet would be a problem of an entirely different order of magnitude.

The Nine-to-Five War

The Reagan administration's plans for a quick victory in El Salvador were not progressing too well on the ground. After the failure of the January 1981 "final offensive," the Salvadoran guerrillas withdrew for several months to regroup. Their offensive had been premised on two expectations: that the urban population would rise up against the regime and that the army would split, with a significant number of young progressive officers bringing their troops over to the insurgent side. When neither the insurrection nor the mutiny materialized, the final offensive quickly collapsed, and the guerrillas were forced to revise their hopes for an early victory.[31]

They replaced the strategy of mass insurrection with a war of attrition targeting the economy. They cut power lines to cripple manufacturing, burned export crops to deprive the regime of foreign exchange currency, and blew up bridges to disrupt transport. To wear down the army, the guerrillas attacked small outlying garrisons and ambushed relief columns, if and when they came. As the army gradually abandoned indefensible outposts, the guerrillas expanded their "zones of control"—areas where they could operate freely.[32]

The Salvadoran military was unable to cope with these classic tactics of guerrilla warfare. Nearly two-thirds of its seventeen thousand troops were tied down guarding roads, bridges, and towns and were too poorly trained to serve as more than static defense forces. The troops available for offensive operations were led by an officer corps riddled with corruption and political intrigue. So few officers remained after the political purges of 1979 and 1980 that army units regularly went into combat led by noncommissioned officers.[33]

In any event, many of the regular officers were not very skilled or very brave. They followed their troops into battle more often than they led them. On weekends, many left their commands unattended and returned to San Salvador to be with their families. "A nine-to-five war," U.S. advisers called it. The rank-and-file troops were peasant conscripts, most of them shanghaied by army press-gangs; their training was rudimentary, their morale abysmal, and their will to fight nil. The army lacked the ability to evacuate the wounded, so even minor wounds often proved fatal. The armed forces suffered 1,300 casualties in the first six months of 1981—12 percent of their forces.[34]

Given the army's limited capabilities, the Salvadoran high command developed a very cautious strategy for fighting the war—"search and avoid," U.S. advisers called it. The military had no plan for eliminating the guerrillas. Its primary objective was simply to prevent them from capturing any cities or towns, even if that meant conceding control of the countryside. Consequently, the army spent most of its time "sitting in garrisons abusing civilians," according to one U.S. official.[35]

If the army engaged the guerrillas, it did so reactively—when the guerrillas made a move, it chased them. But its response was ponderous and slow. Since the air force had only a dozen helicopters, the army's mobility was severely limited. When the Salvadoran army went into the field, it went on foot or riding in the backs of pickup trucks, traveling down the main roads. To avoid ambushes, the army advanced only in large units; U.S. advisers called the ineffectual sweeps "walks in the sun."[36] Salvadoran officers acted as if they feared the army might disintegrate under the pressure of a more aggressive approach. "We have to move slowly and carefully so we do not suffer many losses," explained a Salvadoran major. "That is the system. Those are our orders."[37] Because the army's command and control were so poor, units involved in the same operation were not usually coordinated, so the army's numerical advantage over the guerrillas could never be exploited. Time after time, the guerrillas simply slipped away.

A February 1981 Defense Department assessment of the Salvadoran army's performance concluded that it had "no hope" of winning the war unless it underwent radical changes. It was "not organized to fight an insurgency," or even a conventional war for that matter; it was "more like a 19th century constabulary than a 20th century army," the report said. "The guerrillas can last indefinitely," a Pentagon official lamented. "This thing could go on as a war of attrition forever."[38]

Even the pessimists were surprised, however, when the FMLN went back on the attack in May and June 1981, less than four months after the debacle of the January offensive. The army always responded to guerrilla attacks by sending large columns of troops to sweep the remote northern provinces of Chalatenango and Morazán, reclaiming occupied villages. The rebels would melt away into the hills, sniping at the army but avoiding any direct engagement. Meanwhile, guerrilla units in other parts of the country would invariably take the offensive while the army was occupied in the north. The army would then cut short its sweeping operation in order to respond to guerrilla actions elsewhere, lest it face the political embarrassment of the guerrillas seizing a major town.[39]

U.S. military advisers roundly criticized the army's tactics, arguing that the remote areas seized by the guerrillas were depopulated and economically worthless. But while the army was chasing the rebels around the mountains, serious economic damage was being done in other departments like San Vicente, Usulután, San Miguel, and La Unión. Don't fall into the trap, the U.S. trainers advised; let the guerrillas take a few isolated villages. Keep the army's best troops available to defend the economically vital regions.[40] For the Salvadoran high command, however, it was a point of honor that the guerrillas not be allowed to keep control of any town, even in the north. The armed forces responded as usual to the guerrillas' June offensive, moving to retake the towns seized by the guerrillas. But instead of withdrawing, the guerrillas stood and fought. The army took heavy casualties.[41]

The FMLN's early summer success shook the complacency about El Salvador that had settled in among Washington policymakers during the late winter and spring. A Special National Intelligence Estimate in June concluded that the war was stalemated, and it would take the government at least two years to get the upper hand.[42] U.S. worries mounted in August when the FMLN stepped up its sabotage campaign and launched a new round of attacks on army garrisons. The guerrillas took control of Perquín (population three thousand), the largest town in northern Morazán province, and held it for more than a week before the army was able to win it back. Hinton belittled the fall of Perquín, calling it "a speck on the map that doesn't amount to a hill of beans," but its temporary loss was a psychological blow to the army.[43]

The guerrillas' August offensive also showed just how little U.S. military aid had changed the balance of forces. At the height of the fighting, all ten of the Huey helicopters Washington had provided were grounded by damage from small arms fire. Washington promised to send more.[44] The Atlactl battalion, an elite Salvadoran rapid response unit trained by U.S. advisers, was simply inadequate. No sooner was it deployed to one area than the guerrillas would take the offensive somewhere else. Atlactl spent weeks dashing from one province to another, never able to trap the elusive guerrillas. It was like punching smoke.[45]

The FMLN's offensives were a serious disappointment to Al Haig, who had expected U.S. aid to turn the tide of war before year's end. Undaunted by the timidity of the Defense Department, Haig ordered his special counselor, a retired Marine colonel, Robert C. McFarlane, to undertake an in-house study of military options for Central America. McFarlane's options paper reflected Haig's enduring conviction that the key to winning in El Salvador was to stem the flow of outside aid to the guerrillas. Entitled "Taking the War to Nicaragua," the study focused mainly on ways the United States could prevent Cuban arms from reaching Nicaragua, which was seen as merely a way station en route to El Salvador. The options discussed included a naval blockade of Nicaragua, sinking Cuban ships headed for Nicaragua, and shooting down Cuban planes.[46] "We'll see who the tough guys are in this administration," Haig bragged as he prepared a new campaign to sell his hard-line strategy to skeptics in the White House and the Pentagon.[47]

The Department of Defense took this new crisis as an opportunity to re-open the debate about how much military aid El Salvador should receive. The war would remain stalemated, Pentagon analysts argued, unless Washington resolved to provide significantly more arms and advisers.[48] Privately, some Pentagon officials worried that the war might actually be lost unless the United States acted swiftly.[49] In early September, the Defense Department undertook a comprehensive study (a Defense Requirement Survey) of what it would take to win the war. Brigadier General Frederick F. Woerner Jr., one of the U.S. Army's top specialists on Latin America, was put in charge of a seven-man Military Assistance Strategy Team tasked to prepare the survey. They spent eight weeks working with a team of Salvadoran officers to produce a highly classified report several hundred pages long. The Woerner report, as it came to be known, was the most comprehensive study of the Salvadoran military situation ever done.[50]

The survey was very tough on the Salvadoran military. It argued forcefully that the war could not be won merely by increasing the amount of U.S. aid and advisers. The problems of the Salvadoran officer corps were so fundamental that major changes would have to be made—removing incompetent and corrupt commanders, curbing human rights abuses against noncombatants, and revising the army's strategic approach to fighting a guerrilla war.[51]

On human rights, the Salvadoran officers were so intransigent that Woerner's team could not even discuss the issue with them. "The existence of any significant threat from extreme rightist terrorism and institutional violence is generally dismissed by the Armed Forces," Woerner reported. "[Their] belief is that punishment [for human rights abuses] . . . would erode individual morale, breed internal dissension, and divide the institution in the face of its greatest common threat."[52]

The Woerner report also spelled out the resources required for alternative U.S. objectives over five years. The first option was essentially a continuation of the status quo, in which U.S. assistance was too limited to stem the tide of the guerrillas' "protracted war." Under this scenario, the government "will not be able to guarantee the economic infrastructure . . . [or] the 1982 electoral process," the report warned. In short, the first option was a recipe for defeat, included not as an option to be seriously considered, but rather to demonstrate that the existing level of aid was inadequate.

The second, more modest option called for strengthening the Salvadoran army enough to take the initiative away from the guerrillas, but not enough to eradicate them. Even then, it was not cheap; the estimated cost was $277 million in additional military assistance.

The third option, the one recommended by the Woerner team, was entitled "Strategic Victory." Its objective was "the destruction of the insurgent forces and their capability and will to continue fighting." Winning the war, the report estimated, would require $400 million in additional military assistance, ten new U.S.-trained rapid response battalions of a thousand men each, dozens more U.S. advisers to train them, and tripling the size of the Salvadoran army to some 40,000 men in order to approximate the 10-to-1 ratio of troops to guerrillas that counterinsurgency experts regarded as a prerequisite for victory.[53]

While the Woerner report was still being prepared, the FMLN struck again. On October 15, 1981, to celebrate the anniversary of the 1979 military coup that ousted the Romero dictatorship, FMLN commandos blew up the *Puente de Oro* (the Golden Bridge), El Salvador's largest and most strategically important span, linking the eastern and western halves of the country. The destruction of the bridge was a disaster for the government. It struck a blow at Salvador's export economy because it made transporting cotton and coffee produced in the eastern provinces to market in the capital more costly and difficult. It also reduced the mobility of the Salvadoran army. Perhaps most important, the loss of the heavily defended bridge was yet another major setback for an army whose morale was always tenuous.[54]

The Showdown with Castro

With the eruption of the FMLN's October offensive, the Reagan administration's worry over the direction of the Salvadoran war turned to panic. The guerrillas effectively controlled a quarter of the country and were threatening to isolate the eastern half of it. Their campaign against the economic infrastructure was tremendously successful, with thirty-two bridges destroyed in 1981 alone. The war was stalemated and, as Haig pointed out, "Stalemate could ultimately be fatal."[55]

The deteriorating military situation prompted a new policy review. The timing was opportune; the guerrilla offensive in El Salvador coincided with the failure of Enders's diplomatic initiative toward Nicaragua. Administration officials were convinced that Nicaragua was fast becoming a consolidated Communist regime, "right in the heart of Central America," as one official put it. If that happened, it would be a bastion from which the Sandinistas could subvert the whole region.[56] The Cubans, for their part, had been rapidly expanding their armed forces as well. Soviet military assistance was running at more than double the amount given in 1980, approaching the record levels set before the 1962 missile crisis.[57] Administration officials began envisioning a nightmare in which all of Central America fell to Marxist-Leninist guerrillas, who would then take aim at Mexico and the Panama Canal. But on the question of what to do, agreement proved elusive.[58]

Haig was still obsessed with Cuba. Amid the growing sense of urgency that something had to be done to prevent El Salvador's collapse, Haig convinced the Pentagon to draw up plans for a range of military actions that went beyond even McFarlane's options paper. In addition to a blockade of Nicaragua and an arms quarantine of Cuba, the Pentagon was tasked to develop contingency plans for a full blockade of Cuba and a joint U.S.–Latin American invasion of the island.[59] The Pentagon's final report outlined a series of escalating sanctions and threats designed both to punish Fidel Castro and frighten him into a less activist foreign policy.[60]

On October 29, Haig announced that the administration had completed "extensive studies" on how to respond to Cuban intervention in Central America and that decisions were imminent. Washington would act to alter the calculus behind Cuban adventurism, Haig promised—"to make the risks seem to be more costly than the advantages." As the announcement was being made, a U.S. naval task force began maneuvers off the Cuban coast. Fearing imminent attack, Castro put his entire armed forces on full alert—the first such alert since the U.S. invasion of the Dominican Republic in 1965.[61]

Less than a week later, Haig confirmed press reports that the options being considered against Cuba and Nicaragua included direct military action. At a hearing before the House Foreign Affairs Committee, he called Cuban and Soviet adventurism "a profound danger to world peace and stability," and warned that the risks of their behavior exceeded any possible gain.[62] Haig also denounced "the growing totalitarian regime in Nicaragua" and warned that the United States would have to act to prevent establishment of "another Cuba in this hemisphere." When asked by Congressman Gerry Studds whether he could assure the Congress that the administration would not undertake any effort to overthrow the Nicaraguan government, Haig replied, "No, I would not give you such an assurance."

"If I were a Nicaraguan," commented Congressman Michael Barnes, "I'd be building a bomb shelter."[63] Washington's new war scare was in full bloom.

In part, Haig's threats were intended as psychological warfare. Whether or not the administration had any intention of following through on them, they might frighten Cuba and Nicaragua into reducing support for the Salvadoran insurgency. Haig's tough talk the previous February had been followed by just such a response.[64]

It was hard, however, to talk tough enough to scare the Cubans without scaring the American people, too. To the dismay of the White House staff, the public reacted to Haig's bellicosity just as it had the previous winter. Opinion polls again registered a sharp decline in the public's rating of how Reagan was handling the situation in Central America, along with rising fears that the United States was headed for "another Vietnam." By early 1982, Gallup found that opposition to Reagan's policy in El Salvador had burgeoned from 32 to 50 percent. A Harris poll found that 64 percent of the public rated Reagan's handling of the problem as "only fair" or "poor." The polls consistently showed broad opposition to any deeper U.S. involvement in the region, whether it meant sending more aid, advisers, or troops.[65] To calm people's anxieties, Reagan was again forced to deny explicitly that he had any plans to deploy U.S. troops in Central America. One administration official succinctly summed up the problem: "Al Haig scared everyone."[66]

Washington's allies in Latin America and Europe were also quick to voice opposition to any direct U.S. military action. During a state visit to Washington in November, Venezuelan President Luis Herrera Campíns warned against intervention and urged greater tolerance for Nicaragua.[67] Mexican President José López Portillo called for an end to the "verbal terrorism" on both sides, but strongly implied that he held Washington more to blame than Cuba or Nicaragua. At the Mexicans' insistence, Haig traveled to Mexico City in late November, where López Portillo warned him that a direct U.S. intervention in Cuba or Nicaragua would be "a gigantic historical error."[68]

Secretary of Defense Caspar Weinberger returned from a European trip in the fall of 1981 convinced that a shooting war in Central America might also jeopardize his plans for strengthening U.S. nuclear forces in Europe. Tensions in the Atlantic alliance were already high over the production of the neutron bomb and the deployment of intermediate-range nuclear forces. The unpopularity of Washington's Central America policy had spilled over into the nuclear issue, projecting an image of Reagan as a trigger-happy Cold Warrior.[69]

The surge of domestic and international opposition produced by Haig's "beating the drums of war," as one Pentagon official described it, reinforced Weinberger's conviction that military action was politically unwise. "Nobody [in the Pentagon] is going to go with military activity where we don't have public support," explained a Defense Department official. "We're not going to be put in a situation like we were once before."[70]

In an unusual reversal of roles, the Pentagon was convinced that the State Department was underestimating the political uproar that would be caused by sending U.S. forces to war and overestimating the efficacy of military action. "A purely military solution just doesn't exist," explained a Pentagon spokesman. "There just is no quick fix. I know that makes us sound like diplomats at just the time that the State Department sounds like warmongers, but that's how it is."[71] In an obvious rebuke to Haig, Weinberger told NBC News, "We are well away from the syndrome of drawing a line in the sand and saying thus far and no farther." In private, he called Central America "a tar baby."[72]

The Pentagon again blocked Haig's war plans, just as it had in March and June. The debate within the administration over what to do about El Salvador, Nicaragua, and Cuba settled back into a review of less apocalyptic options. The Pentagon continued to argue that the war in El Salvador could be won in the long term if the administration would simply increase the military assistance program, lift the fifty-five-man limit on the number of U.S. advisers, and relax the rules of engagement that kept the advisers off the battlefield.[73] The CIA was developing plans for a more active, covert U.S. military role in the region. But no one was burning the midnight oil devising diplomatic initiatives.

Nicaragua Moves to Center Stage

Nicaragua was more vulnerable to pressure than Cuba. The Sandinistas had not yet fully consolidated political control, the economy had never fully recovered from the ravages of the insurrection against Somoza, and Nicaragua was surrounded by U.S. allies. Moreover, an instrument for exerting pressure on the Sandinistas was at hand. With the help of Argentina, the CIA had already begun knitting together Nicaraguan exile groups into a single organization, and Honduras had eagerly offered its territory as a base of operations.

Throughout September and October, the Inter-Agency Core Group of mid-level officials dealing with Latin America discussed policy options for Nicaragua. Gradually, as other options were discarded as ineffective or politically unacceptable, covert action came to the top of the list. Administration hardliners such as Jeane Kirkpatrick, Edwin Meese, and William Clark favored covert action to force the Sandinistas out of power. Weinberger supported it because it was an alternative to direct military action and did not involve the Pentagon in a way that would damage its prestige if the operation went awry. In the White House, James Baker and Michael Deaver supported covert action precisely because it was covert and would not tarnish Reagan's political image. CIA Director William Casey supported it because it gave him operational control of the policy.[74]

Among Reagan's top foreign policy advisers, only Haig opposed going covert. "In order for covert activity to be effective in this situation," Haig recalled, "it would have to be of a scope that by its very nature could not remain covert." But most important, as a way of dealing with a vital national security interest, it was a "cop-out."[75] The Soviets would escalate their commitment to the Sandinistas, and Washington would be unable to match them effectively by operating through proxies. Moreover, the administration could not hope to rally Congress and public support for a showdown with the Soviet Union in Nicaragua when the foundation of Washington's policy was secret. Growing opposition was already limiting the options. "People turned to covert action because they thought they could not get congressional support for more overt activities," Robert McFarlane conceded.[76]

There were other skeptics, but none were in a position to challenge the policy. In October, Lieutenant General Wallace H. Nutting, commander of the U.S. Southern Command in Panama, convened a group of political and military experts at the U.S. Army War College to assess U.S. options toward Nicaragua. Their report concluded that military pressure would be ineffective and counterproductive. "Based on their role in the overthrow of Somoza, the Sandinistas are still supported by a wide spectrum of the Nicaraguan populace," the report concluded. "Moreover, the Somocistas are not likely to gather sufficient support within Nicaragua to manage a successful counter-revolution."

The army report anticipated most of the arguments that would later be leveled against the covert war: It would rally the population behind Sandinista appeals to nationalism, unify the Sandinista leadership behind a more radical program, force Nicaragua into closer alignment with the Soviet bloc, prompt a Sandinista crackdown on the internal opposition, and damage U.S. relations with the rest of Latin America. As an alternative, the army report called for a return to political and diplomatic efforts to cajole and compel the Sandinistas to live up to their promise of political pluralism, a nonaligned foreign policy, and noninterference in their neighbors' affairs. In short, it prescribed a resumption of the strategy pursued by Jimmy Carter.

Coming from the army—hardly a bastion of liberalism—such a critical assessment might have been expected to slow the rush toward a covert paramilitary program. But it had no apparent impact on the policy debate. The basic decision to support the contras had already been made.[77]

Even at the CIA, there were serious doubts about the contra program. To Casey's deputy director, Admiral Bobby Ray Inman, it seemed like a subterfuge designed to avoid a bruising domestic political debate. Inman reflected the concerns of many younger CIA officers on the analytic side of the Agency. For them, the collection and analysis of intelligence information was the CIA's main function. They were loath to see a return to the bad old days of dirty tricks. "They worry that secret operations, especially when they are exposed and criticized, impact adversely on the more important job of foreign intelligence collection and analysis," Inman explained.[78]

Casey was not interested in listening to such naysayers. Their concerns were nothing but a symptom of the timidity that had paralyzed the Agency since the mid-1970s. That was an attitude that needed to be eradicated. In the meantime, Casey would find a few stalwarts such as Dewey Clarridge to run the Nicaragua program, even if he had to circumvent the CIA's own bureaucracy and direct the operation himself.[79]

National Security Decision Directive 17

The National Security Council met on November 16, 1981, to consider a ten-point plan developed by the Core Group to respond to the worsening situation in Central America.[80] Enders presented the program and defended his strategy of making democracy and elections the cornerstone of U.S. policy. "It is the only way to gain legitimacy for them and for us," he argued.[81] Legitimacy was a crucial issue, since Washington would have to significantly increase both military and economic aid to El Salvador to keep the Duarte government afloat until the scheduled election in March 1982. At least some of the new aid would require congressional approval, and getting it would not be easy.

The NSC approved three aid proposals. It decided to seek an additional $250–$300 million in economic aid for Central America and the Caribbean under the auspices of the administration's regional economic plan, the Caribbean Basin Initiative (CBI). It decided to send additional military aid to El Salvador and Honduras, drawing the money from the president's special emergency fund, as Reagan had done in March, in order to avoid the need for congressional approval. And it decided to expand the U.S. military training program in El Salvador, as the Pentagon had been urging all year. To avoid breaking the administration's pledge to limit the number of U.S. advisers in El Salvador to fifty-five, Salvadoran troops and officers would be brought to the United States for training. As a consolation prize for Haig, who remained preoccupied with "going to the source," the NSC directed the Pentagon to draw up further contingency plans to deal with "unacceptable military action" by Cuba, particularly any Cuban effort to deploy combat troops to Central America.[82]

The center of discussion at the November NSC meeting was the proposal for covert action against Nicaragua. Enders remained skeptical about the prospects for ousting the Sandinistas; he presented covert action as a way to force them to the bargaining table. Covert paramilitary action would weaken the Sandinistas enough to extract the concessions Washington wanted—particularly a termination of aid to the Salvadoran guerrillas.[83]

The Core Group's proposal called for the United States to "work with foreign governments as appropriate" in order to "support and conduct political and paramilitary operations against the Cuban presence and Cuban-Sandinista support structure in Nicaragua and elsewhere in Central America."[84] This emphasis was consistent with the priority that both Haig and Enders put on ending Cuban and Nicaraguan support for the Salvadoran guerrillas.

The options paper developed by the CIA, however, described much broader objectives than merely interdicting arms by hitting the Cuban and Nicaraguan logistical apparatus. The CIA proposed to do the following:

> Build popular support in Central America and Nicaragua for an opposition front that would be nationalistic, anti-Cuban, and anti-Somoza.
>
> Support the opposition front through the formation and training of action teams to collect intelligence and engage in paramilitary and political operations in Nicaragua and elsewhere.
>
> Work primarily through non-Americans to achieve the foregoing, but in some circumstances CIA might (possibly using U.S. personnel) take unilateral paramilitary action against special Cuban targets.[85]

The CIA options paper included proposals that ranged from expanding Carter's program of aid for internal opponents of the Sandinistas, to mounting a large-scale paramilitary effort designed to overthrow them. One of the more ambitious proposals called for the United States to organize a commando army of five hundred Latin Americans, mostly Cuban exiles, to operate out of base camps in Honduras, attacking Nicaraguan military installations and economic targets such as bridges and power stations. The first-year cost of the operation was set at $19.95 million, but the CIA proposal advised, "The program should not be confined to that funding level or to the 500-man force described. . . . More funds and manpower will be needed."[86]

By aiming at economic targets, the CIA hoped to cause maximum damage with minimum risk to its combatants. The rationale for hitting "soft" targets was that it would divert the attention and resources of the Sandinista government away from their program of aid for the guerrillas in El Salvador.[87]

Some officials also hoped that the resulting economic damage would produce enough popular discontent to destabilize the Sandinista regime. This strategy was consciously designed to mimic the economic warfare begun by the FMLN in El Salvador the year before—a strategy that administration officials regularly denounced as cynical terrorism.[88]

A second CIA proposal, which was presented as a complement rather than an alternative to the five-hundred-man force, called for the United States to provide financial support to a thousand-man force of Nicaraguan exiles already being trained by Argentina. Washington's role in this operation would be merely supportive; Argentina would continue to supervise the force.[89]

Convinced that the operation would be "too large to hide," Haig insisted that the United States avoid direct involvement and operate as much as possible through Argentina and Honduras. That would give Washington a measure of deniability if—or when—the operation became public.[90] Another concern raised in the NSC meeting was the role of former members of Somoza's National Guard. The ex-guardsmen were widely hated in Nicaragua and therefore constituted an enormous political liability for any exile movement. "There was a very clear understanding in discussions in the National Security Council that it would be counterproductive to work with Somoza supporters," said an administration official who participated in the debate. The NSC decided that the United States would not give support to the ex-guardsman, although this proved impossible to avoid in practice since management of the contra army was handled by the Argentine military. The Argentines had no scruples about supporting ex-guardsmen; on the contrary, their support had been brokered by former guardsmen trained in Argentina. Besides, the guardsmen were the only trained military men around whom a clandestine army could be built.[91]

President Reagan was one of the least enthusiastic supporters of the covert action proposal at first—not because it appeared overly ambitious, but because it was not ambitious enough. "It took some persuading" to get Reagan interested in the contra program, according to a senior administration official. Plans for a small force to harass the Sandinistas or interdict arms did not interest him. He was only convinced the plan had merit when it was presented as a way to roll back the Nicaraguan revolution. The contra army would be Washington's answer to Soviet support for wars of national liberation.[92]

This was not a new idea to Ronald Reagan. A decade earlier he had suggested that the United States should respond to brushfire wars in allied countries by launching similar wars against pro-Soviet states. "Maybe part of the answer in a hot spot such as Vietnam is to give the enemy something to worry about in another corner of the world," Reagan argued. "Maybe he ought to have some unrest in some corner of his realm to worry about."[93] Reagan had gladly extended Jimmy Carter's covert aid to the mujahadeen guerrillas fighting against the Soviet-backed regime in Afghanistan. Now Nicaragua would be added to the list of secret wars fueled by Washington, and others would soon follow in Cambodia and Angola. The Reagan Doctrine was taking shape.

On November 23, the NSC reconvened to finish its deliberations on Central America. Reagan approved the plan to give covert financial support to internal opponents of the Sandinistas, as well as a CIA paramilitary plan that included both the five-hundred-man Latin American force to be organized by the United States and support for the thousand-man Nicaraguan exile force being organized by Argentina. Reagan also approved National Security Decision Directive (NSDD) 17, formalizing his approval of the ten-point policy plan for Central America.[94]

On December 1, the National Security Planning Group (NSPG) met to draft a presidential finding for Congress justifying the covert action program against Nicaragua. Reagan signed it later that day.[95] Formed during the summer of 1981, the NSPG was the apex of Reagan's national security apparatus, the place where the key foreign policy decisions were made. In addition to the president, it included Vice President George Bush, Secretary of State Haig, Secretary of Defense Weinberger, Director of Central Intelligence Casey, and the White House troika of Baker, Deaver, and Meese.[96]

The decisions made at the November NSC meetings established a framework for U.S. policy toward Central America that remained essentially unchanged throughout Reagan's two terms in office, despite dramatic shifts in rhetoric and personnel. Its basic elements included extensive economic and military aid for U.S. allies, with the lion's share destined for El Salvador; an increased U.S. military and intelligence presence, focusing especially on military exercises; a covert war against Nicaragua; and a concerted "public diplomacy" effort designed to sell the policy to a reluctant Congress and public.

To the chagrin of the White House staff, Central America had been a major issue during Reagan's first year. The policy reviews were now completed and the program set, but the experience of 1981 demonstrated that prevailing in the region would be tougher than expected. Despite having been trounced in the 1980 elections, the Democrats were putting up surprisingly stiff resistance to Reagan's policy, and they had the public on their side. Washington's allies were an even greater disappointment. Instead of falling into line behind a more assertive U.S. policy, they were caviling and, in some cases, promoting negotiations that Washington opposed. On the ground in El Salvador, the guerrillas were proving to be far more resilient, and the government far more brittle, than anyone had anticipated. The light at the end of the tunnel was not very bright.

II El Salvador

It is time the people of the United States realize that under the domino theory, we're the last domino.

—Ronald Reagan

CHAPTER 7

The Tonic of Elections

By 1982 it was clear that winning in El Salvador would take a long time and require a huge investment of resources. What had begun as an effort by Al Haig to establish his predominance with a quick, easy victory, now looked like a quagmire in the making. Once the prestige and credibility of the administration had been committed, however, there was no turning back. Much of NSDD 17 could be implemented simply on the decision of the president. Washington's intelligence capabilities in Central America were expanded exponentially, military exercises were accelerated, and the covert operation against Nicaragua got under way. If the policy was to succeed over the long run, however, the administration would have to sustain high levels of economic and military aid over a number of years. For that, congressional support was essential, and winning it preoccupied the administration throughout 1982.

Washington Ups the Ante

The reaffirmation of Washington's military commitment in Central America was soon apparent. To enhance intelligence collection, CIA stations in the region were augmented, Spruance-class destroyers were stationed off Nicaragua's coasts to gather signal intelligence, and overflights of both Nicaragua and El Salvador were carried out by secret army and air force Special Operations units based in Honduras, El Salvador, and Panama. U.S. officials bragged that coverage of Nicaragua was so complete that they could "hear a toilet flush in Managua."[1]

The Pentagon expanded its Caribbean Command at Key West and increased the number and size of military exercises in the region. In March 1982, it initiated the first major NATO naval exercise in the Gulf of Mexico and Straits of Florida.[2] In April, the Navy began a five-week Caribbean readiness exercise, "REDEX 2-82," involving two carrier battle groups—twice the size of a similar exercise conducted in 1981. Even before REDEX 2-82 concluded, a larger exercise, "Ocean Venture 82," began in the same area. It involved two carrier task forces, Marine amphibious units, B-52 bombers, and Special Operations forces—45,000 troops in all, the biggest Caribbean exercise ever conducted. Its objective was to destroy the offensive military capacity of an imaginary country, "Brown," a hostile Caribbean island that was exporting terrorism to Central America in conjunction with its regional ally, "Yellow." U.S. forces practiced punitive saturation bombing of Brown's ports and airfields.[3]

On land, the army expanded the number of military advisers in Honduras to nearly one hundred, and the air force developed plans to build or upgrade several Honduran airfields to assure that it would have adequate facilities to conduct operations in Central America should the need arise.[4] During the summer of 1982, forces involved in a small U.S.-Honduran exercise built a permanent Honduran military base at Durzuna, just twenty-five miles from the Nicaraguan border. The base soon became a logistical staging area for the expanding covert war against the Sandinistas.[5]

In February, Reagan again invoked presidential emergency powers to send an additional $55 million in military aid to El Salvador without congressional approval. Congressional Democrats complained that Reagan was misusing the emergency law to circumvent the normal budgetary process, but there was nothing they could do about it, short of passing a law to strip Reagan of the power to invoke emergencies in Central America (which they subsequently tried to do without success).

The excuse Reagan used to justify the emergency aid presented itself in late January, when the Salvadoran guerrillas launched a dramatic attack on Ilopango air base. With help from soldiers inside the base, a guerrilla commando team destroyed most of the Salvadoran air force on the ground. The audacity of the devastating raid reminded some U.S. officials of the 1965 Viet Cong attack on Pleiku air base in Vietnam. Since U.S. advisers were trying to convince the Salvadoran army of the wisdom of air mobile rapid response to guerrilla attacks, the loss of nearly the entire helicopter fleet was a crippling blow to the counterinsurgency effort.[6] Four days later, Reagan announced he would send the $55 million aid package.

Damage from the raid totaled only about $25 million. The extra $30 million in aid was used to expand the air force and pay for training Salvadoran troops in the United States: 490 attended officer-training classes at Fort Benning, Georgia, while 1,000 infantry troops took basic training at Fort Bragg, North Carolina.[7] Though costly, bringing the Salvadorans to the United States was judged less politically explosive than exceeding the administration's self-imposed limit of fifty-five U.S. advisers in El Salvador.

Just a few weeks after announcing the $55 million emergency military aid package, Reagan unveiled his Caribbean Basin Initiative (CBI)—a major new economic and military aid program for the countries in Central America and the Caribbean. Congressional Democrats were inclined to support the economic elements of the CBI because it responded to their conviction that poverty and underdevelopment were the truly subversive problems in the region. However, the heavy allocation of CBI funds to El Salvador proposed by Reagan made them suspect that the program was a cover for funding the war. Although the CBI included twelve countries, El Salvador was slated for $128 million of the total $350 million in Economic Support Funds. Of the $65 million in military aid requested, more than half ($35 million) was for El Salvador. This seemed excessive since, as Senator Edward Zorinsky (D-Neb.) reminded his colleagues, "not one inch of El Salvador's shoreline or territory lies anywhere near the Caribbean Basin."[8]

So the CBI was subject to a bit of trimming on its way through the legislative process. In the end, Reagan got $10 million in military aid for Honduras and $3.5 million for military training regionwide, but none of the $35 million he wanted for El Salvador. The full $350 million regional economic aid package eventually won approval, but the House Appropriations subcommittee chaired by Clarence Long limited El Salvador's share to $75 million.[9]

With no new military aid for El Salvador in the CBI, the Pentagon's plans for building the armed forces into a capable counterinsurgency force were still badly underfunded. And the more the U.S. military saw of the Salvadorans, the more pessimistic it became about their chances. U.S. advisers were as close to the fighting as the War Powers Resolution would permit, and often a lot closer.[10] They judged that the military situation was deteriorating, and the CIA agreed with them. The Pentagon pressed the administration to look down the road and make some fundamental judgments about how far the United States was willing to go to fend off a guerrilla victory. Was the White House prepared to fight Congress for the resources needed to prevail?[11]

At the State Department and among the senior civilians at Defense, such pessimism was seen as alarmist. Not coincidentally, a grim picture of the situation on the ground better justified the military's demand for more money and advisers. The optimists thought that the military situation was improving, or had stabilized.[12] But they too had self-interested reasons for their view. Civilians at the Pentagon—Secretary Caspar Weinberger, Undersecretary Fred C. Iklé, and Deputy Assistant Secretary Nestor Sanchez—were among the most ideologically committed conservatives in Reagan's foreign policy apparatus. They had a stake in believing that the Reagan hard-line could turn the tide against Communist expansion where Carter's liberalism had failed—that Washington could successfully apply military force in the Third World without being drawn into a quagmire.

At State, more pragmatic officials like Assistant Secretary Thomas Enders had a different but no less psychologically compelling reason for seeing the bright side. If the situation was deteriorating as rapidly as the military claimed, Enders's strategy of cajoling Congress into gradually escalating the U.S. commitment was not viable. Washington would have to drastically increase support to shore up its Salvadoran client—a move that would inevitably provoke a major confrontation with Congress at a time when public opposition to administration policy was on the rise. The logic of Enders's strategy for managing the domestic politics of the Salvador crisis virtually required that the pessimists be wrong. And so he believed they were. But the truth of the matter was that nobody really knew for certain whether things were getting better or worse.

The Algebra of Death

Whatever the battlefield situation, the Salvadoran regime's human rights performance wasn't getting any better, and it was hurting Reagan's policy at home. Apart from the fear that the United States would become entangled in "another Vietnam," the most potent source of public antagonism toward U.S. policy was what administration strategists called "humanitarian" concerns— the Salvadoran military's bestial human rights record.

That record was the central focus of debate when Reagan submitted his first certification report on the Salvadoran government's progress on human rights and agrarian reform.[13] The administration did not take the report very seriously. Submitted on January 28, 1982, it was only six pages long and contained little evidence to support the declaratory judgments that progress had been made in all of the areas required by law. The report refused to acknowledge any government complicity in human rights violations, instead blaming the guerrillas for creating the "chaos" that prevented the government from ending abuses. Moreover, the report flatly denied that the paramilitary death squads were linked to the government, even though a report on political violence prepared by the U.S. embassy and released during the certification review concluded that the squads were comprised of "both on and off-duty members of the security forces." The embassy report was also more candid about the role of the government security forces themselves, acknowledging that they were responsible for "many hundreds, perhaps thousands" of political killings.[14]

The administration's claim that the human rights situation was improving rested almost entirely on the body count produced by the embassy's "grim-gram"—a weekly report on the number of political killings compiled by the embassy from Salvadoran press reports.[15] According to these statistics, which the embassy acknowledged included "only a tiny portion" of the killings, the trend line on political murders was down. Fewer people were killed in 1981 than in 1980 (5,331 as compared to 9,000), and fewer people were being killed monthly at the end of the year than at the beginning (665 in January, 349 in December). Moreover, the embassy insisted it was impossible to tell who was responsible for the vast majority of the murders. According to the embassy's statistics, of the deaths for which one group or another claimed responsibility, the guerrillas actually killed more people than the armed forces or the rightist paramilitary groups.

The main weakness of the embassy's body count, as it readily admitted, was that the Salvadoran newspapers "only report deaths in areas where they momentarily have correspondents." That rarely included the most conflicted rural areas. As a consequence, in 1981, the papers reported 1,449 people killed in the relatively peaceful department of Santa Ana, but only 247 and 47 killed in the "battleground departments" of Morazán and Chalatenango. That, obviously, was absurd.

The rightist ideological hue of all the surviving Salvadoran newspapers introduced another source of bias into the embassy's data. They simply didn't report rightist terrorist attacks very often; only thirteen were cited in 1981, only one outside the capital. This statistic, the embassy warned, "should in no way be construed as evidencing an absence of rightist terrorist violence."[16] Moreover, one element of the CIA's covert operations program approved under Reagan's March 9, 1981, finding was a press operation in El Salvador designed to promulgate a negative image of the guerrillas and a positive image of the government. In all likelihood, the embassy's human rights reports were distorted by Washington's own covert propaganda.[17]

No independent human rights group agreed with the Reagan administration's portrait of the situation. In a January 1982 report, Amnesty International concluded: "A systematic and brutal policy of government-sponsored intimidation and repression has characterized the past year in El Salvador." A detailed report by the American Civil Liberties Union (ACLU) and Americas Watch came to a similar conclusion. Americas Watch Vice Chairman Aryeh Neier excoriated the administration's certification as "misleading" and "preposterous."[18] For the first time in its history, the ACLU took a public stance against continuing U.S. aid to a specific country because of its human rights record. The United Nations Human Rights Commission accused the Reagan administration of understating the number of political murders in El Salvador by half.[19]

The reports by international human rights agencies were based in part on the work of three Salvadoran human rights groups: the Catholic Church's Legal Aid Office (Socorro Juridico); the Central American University's Documentation Center; and the Salvadoran Human Rights Commission. All of them recorded between two and three times the number of killings cited by the embassy—a minimum of 13,000 in 1981 compared to the embassy's estimate of just 5,300. They also concluded that many more people were murdered in 1981 than in 1980 and that government forces and the paramilitary death squads linked to them were responsible for most of the killings.[20]

Even though they counted the killings differently, the three Salvadoran groups agreed with one another on the basic pattern of the violence. They showed a terrible surge in killings during the first four months of 1981, at midyear a return to the levels prevalent in late 1980, followed by another bloody surge in the last three months of 1981. The pattern of killings recorded by the embassy looked nothing like that; it showed a steady gradual decline in the number of killings throughout the year. "There is something fishy with the embassy's numbers," Congressman Stephen Solarz (D-N.Y.) observed. "It's like the estimates of enemy strength in Vietnam. These figures have such an implication for policy that the officials who compile them can't give an honest estimate."[21]

The administration sought to explain the discrepancy between the Salvadoran reports and its own by impugning the motives and accuracy of the Salvadoran human rights workers. According to Enders, the Central American University Documentation Center had an "ideological bias," the Salvadoran Human Rights Commission was "not a human rights organization at all," but "a propaganda vehicle for the insurgency," and the Legal Aid Office of the Archdiocese had been disowned by the archbishop.[22]

Archbishop Rivera y Damas had, indeed, criticized Socorro Juridico for not reporting killings by the guerrillas, and he subsequently reorganized the office (which became known as Tutela Legal). But at no point did he repudiate Socorro's human rights reports; on the contrary, he affirmed their accuracy.[23]

It was also true that the faculty at the Central American University was generally sympathetic to the social democrats in the Revolutionary Democratic Front (FDR) and that the Human Rights Commission was sympathetic to the guerrillas, but they were no less self-interested nor were their methods any more suspect than those of the U.S. embassy.

To the administration's embarrassment, on the eve of the certification report both the *Washington Post* and the *New York Times* ran stories describing a major massacre in and around the village of El Mozote, in Morazán province. On December 11, 1981, the army's elite Atlactl battalion, the first rapid response unit trained by U.S. advisers, swept through El Mozote, killing everyone they found and then blowing up the peasants' houses. According to the Catholic Church, 926 people were massacred. The villagers themselves compiled a list of 733 dead, over half of them children under fourteen.[24]

As if that were not bad enough, just three days after Reagan certified El Salvador's progress, security forces rousted over two dozen people from their beds in San Salvador's lower-class neighborhood of San Antonio Abad. After raping several teenage girls, the troops lined up twenty-seven of their captives in the street and executed them. The armed forces insisted that the victims, many of whom were wearing nightclothes when they died, were guerrillas killed in a gun battle with the security forces. The military's victory, said the official communiqué, was a testament to the effectiveness of the "training and professionalization" that the troops had recently undergone.[25] Such behavior was hard to explain away. Defending the certification in congressional hearings, Enders minimized the massacre at El Mozote, claiming that it had been exaggerated for propaganda purposes. He had to admit, though, that the killings in San Antonio Abad looked suspicious.[26]

The administration also had a difficult time convincing Congress that the Salvadoran government was making a serious effort to solve the murder cases of the U.S. churchwomen and the AIFLD labor advisers. Six enlisted members of the National Guard had been detained in connection with the churchwomen's case, but in eight months no further progress had been made. The guardsmen had not even been remanded to the courts so that the legal process against them could begin. Junta leader José Napoleón Duarte later admitted that he had great difficulty convincing the military that prosecuting the killers was the sine qua non for additional U.S. aid.[27] Moreover, the Salvadorans made no effort to discover if any officers were involved in the murders or the subsequent cover-up. "There was less than a total effort to get at the truth," conceded a senior American diplomat in San Salvador.[28]

The status of the AIFLD case was even more discouraging. The two triggermen had been arrested, but every effort to charge the military officers and civilians who ordered the killings came to naught. The administration insisted that the Salvadoran government was making "a good faith" effort in the cases as the law required, even though all the suspects except for the two enlisted men had been released.[29]

Reagan's certification report did not even address the requirement that the government of El Salvador be willing to seek a negotiated solution to the war. This was the trickiest of all the certification issues, because administration policy opposed talks between the government and the guerrillas. Some Christian Democrats confided in private that they wanted to open negotiations, but the armed forces would not allow it.[30] Enders argued in his congressional testimony that the law merely required "discussions"—as distinct from negotiations—and that these need only be held pursuant to elections. Therefore, since the government had offered to talk with the guerrillas about their participation in the March elections if they would lay down their arms and renounce violence, it had met the letter of the law.[31]

The guerrillas had refused such talks, seeking instead a "comprehensive" negotiation "without preconditions." They wanted to discuss economic reforms, a reorganization of the armed forces, and the creation of an interim government in which the guerrillas would be represented. The necessary conditions for a free election did not exist, argued FDR vice president Rubén Zamora, brother of the Christian Democratic attorney general slain by a death squad in 1980. For the guerrillas to lay down their arms, after the armed forces had murdered thousands of people, would be "naive, suicidal."[32]

Congressional reaction to the certification report split predictably along liberal-conservative lines. Conservative Republicans readily accepted the administration's case; liberal Democrats didn't believe a word of it. Fifty-five House liberals wrote Reagan a letter charging that the certification was "contrary to the documented facts," and called on him to withdraw it.[33] Congressman Jonathan Bingham (D-N.Y.) called the certification "a fraud, pure and simple. We should not allow the Reagan administration to swear a duck is an eagle in order to support repression in the name of anti-Communism in El Salvador."[34]

Congressman Gerry Studds (D-Mass.) and thirty-two other House members introduced a bill declaring Reagan's certification null and void and cutting off military aid. "The president has just certified that up is down, and in is out, and black is white. I anticipate his telling us that war is peace at any moment," Studds railed at Enders during hearings on Reagan's certification.[35]

Defending Reagan's policy before the Senate Foreign Relations Committee, Enders faced growing concern from moderate Republicans as well. When he explained that the war was going to require more resources and that no ceiling had been set on the amount the administration might ultimately request, Senator Nancy Kassebaum (R-Kan.) quipped, "Can you see the light at the end of the tunnel?"

"I'm fundamentally on the optimistic side," Enders retorted.[36]

Despite their vocal complaints against the administration, the liberal Democrats did not have the votes to interrupt the flow of resources fueling Reagan's policy. Studds's move to cut off aid sputtered and died, while the administration's requests for more assistance slowly made their way through the legislative maze, never emerging unscathed, but always emerging.[37]

Congressional moderates, both Democrats and Republicans, had not yet given up on either the Duarte government or the Reagan administration. Most of them had voted for the certification requirement in 1981 as a way to fortify Reagan's uncertain resolve to defend reforms. They did not intend the certification law to be a mere prelude to ending military aid, and they were not willing to declare the process a failure on the first review. They were therefore prepared to accept almost any evidence of progress, however meager, rather than face the implication of terminating U.S. assistance. The administration played effectively to their fears, arguing that an aid cut-off meant "abandoning El Salvador" to the Communists.[38] That was probably right; if Washington halted military aid, the guerrillas would probably win the war. Senator J. James Exon (D-Neb.) succinctly summed up the moderates' dilemma: "If we turn down additional aid, we could be helping the Communist guerrilla takeover of the country. But on the other hand, we'll be aiding a government we're not happy with. The bottom line is: which is the lesser of two evils?"[39] As matters stood, Duarte was very marketable as the lesser evil.

The liberals' hope of passing tougher legislation to further constrain the administration's options was doomed by the fact that moderate Democrats held key leadership posts in the House. "I agree with the administration position and I very actively oppose any effort to withhold assistance to the moderate government of Duarte," declared Majority Leader Jim Wright of Texas. Privately, Wright told colleagues he feared that the Democratic Party would be "McGovernized"—tainted with the political stain of softness—if it opposed military aid.[40]

Speaker Tip O'Neill of Massachusetts was sympathetic to the liberals, but he was unwilling to divide the party over El Salvador. He was fighting too many other battles whose outcome depended upon keeping conservative Democrats (nicknamed the "boll weevils" because so many were southerners) from falling permanently in love with the Reagan Revolution.[41] In February, O'Neill sent his friend, moderate John P. Murtha (D-Pa.), to El Salvador on a fact-finding trip. Murtha came back impressed with Duarte's sincerity, and he warned that

Congress must guard against deciding policy toward El Salvador "on the emotions of Vietnam." Murtha urged the Democrats to support the Constituent Assembly elections the Duarte government had scheduled for March 1982, provided that they were "free and open" and that the centrists won.[42]

In the Senate, even liberal Clairborne Pell (D-R.I.), the ranking Democrat on the Foreign Relations Committee, returned from a trip to El Salvador convinced that "we shouldn't rock the boat until after the election."[43] For Congress as well as for the administration, the Salvadoran elections came to be seen as a turning point upon whose outcome much else would depend.

El Salvador's Election

El Salvador's March 1982 Constituent Assembly elections would demonstrate, one way or another, the effectiveness of Reagan's political and military strategy. Successful elections would curtail congressional criticism of the Salvadoran regime, help fend off calls for negotiations, and justify the huge increases in military aid that the war required. The new government would enjoy the legitimacy of having been "freely elected," which was how Western Europeans and Americans believed governments should be chosen.[44]

"The elections will indicate very clearly that the vast majority of the people of this country are in favor of something different than these five or ten or fifteen thousand misguided individuals that are trying to destroy the country," U.S. Ambassador Deane Hinton predicted. "How are they going to go around the world saying they represent the people of El Salvador if the people of El Salvador are on record as supporting somebody else?"[45]

A few potential flaws marred this strategy. The center-left civilians of the Revolutionary Democratic Front (FDR) remained unwilling to participate in the election, fearing that they would be murdered if they returned from exile to run, just as their leadership had been in November 1980.[46] Duarte himself admitted he could not guarantee the safety of FDR candidates. Hinton suggested that the FDR campaign in absentia by using videotapes and radio broadcasts, but the larger problem, as Hinton himself acknowledged, was that the military opposed any electoral participation by the left. If the left boycotted the election, the election would not stop the war.[47]

The electoral strategy's major risk was uncertainty about whether the election could actually be held. If the guerrillas decided to disrupt it, election day might prove to be a public relations disaster. Rather than highlighting the popularity of the Duarte government, a failed election would highlight its isolation and impotence. Rather than shifting international sympathies away from the FDR-FMLN, a failed election would accelerate international recognition of the guerrillas as a legitimate political force and increase pressure for a negotiated settlement.

It was critical, therefore, that the election be held as scheduled, that guerrilla efforts to disrupt it be effectively contained, and that a significant portion of the voting public turn out at the polls. As 1982 began, it was not clear that these conditions could be met. The FMLN was vowing to stop the balloting. "We will defeat the elections, not by attacking voters or polling places, but by making the war felt at all levels everywhere," said Roberto Roca, one of the five top FMLN commanders. Fermán Cienfuegos, another senior guerrilla commander, promised that the FMLN would call for a nationwide "popular uprising" that would make the elections impossible. Intelligence estimates indicated that the guerrillas had the capability to make good on their threat.[48]

As election day approached, a new danger began to emerge. Members of the Salvadoran oligarchy, together with ex-Major Roberto D'Aubuisson, had founded a new political party in 1981: the Nationalist Republican Alliance (Alianza Republicana Nacionalista), or ARENA as it was known. Built on the foundation of the clandestine network of death squads that had terrorized El Salvador since the late 1970s, ARENA was modeled after Mario Sandoval Alarcón's fascist National Liberation Movement in Guatemala and organized with his help.[49]

While ARENA drew its structure from the far right in Guatemala, it borrowed its public face from the Republican right in the United States. Influential Republicans had urged D'Aubuisson and his backers to organize a party to contest the 1982 elections, and they gave him advice on how to present himself. It was no coincidence that D'Aubuisson's party was the Nationalist *Republican* Alliance. Significant elements of its program were drawn from the 1980 U.S. Republican Party platform, and its campaign was run by a U.S. public relations firm, McCann Erickson. D'Aubuisson's flair for the dramatic, combined with plentiful funding from the Salvadoran oligarchy, made him a formidable candidate. With the backing of local garrison commanders, D'Aubuisson campaigned in areas that the Christian Democrats were afraid to enter.[50]

"Is your life better now than it was two years ago?" D'Aubuisson's standard stump speech began, stealing from Ronald Reagan's famous line in the 1980 campaign. Christian Democrats were like watermelons, D'Aubuisson charged, as he held a melon aloft and then hacked it in half with a swing of his machete: "Green on the outside and red on the inside!"[51] The Christian Democrats were simply "the right wing of the Communist Party," and Duarte was "an agent of international Communism." D'Aubuisson pledged that if ARENA was victorious, it would put all the Christian Democrats on trial for treason.[52]

In addition to financial support from the oligarchy and logistical support from armed forces, ARENA benefited from the longing by some voters for a charismatic *caudillo*—a strongman who promised a quick end to the war. The problem, D'Aubuisson insisted, was that the Christian Democrats, with the connivance of the United States, had shackled the armed forces with human rights requirements. If the full force of the army was unleashed against the guerrillas, the war would be over in three months. "We don't believe the army needs controlling," said ARENA party secretary Mario Redaelli. "Civilians will be killed—war has always been that way."[53]

By mid-February, ARENA was making strong headway against the Christian Democrats, whose political infrastructure had been eroded by years of repression and defections to the left. Duarte's party, Hinton acknowledged, had "all the liabilities of having been the party in power during a period of violence, sharp economic decline, and rising unemployment."[54] Fear was a factor, too. After decades of fraudulent elections in which landowners had marched their peasants to the polls to cast votes en masse for the right, it was hard to convince people that this election would be different. "In the hamlets, there is the widely held suspicion that authorities know who you voted for," warned former ambassador Robert White.[55]

Hinton began to worry that ARENA might win the assembly elections, even though the party had been in existence only six weeks. If D'Aubuisson, the reputed death squad leader, became provisional president, Congress might well cut off military aid. The embassy started signaling its electoral preference in none too subtle ways. Washington had been "very comfortable" with the coalition government between the Christian Democrats and the armed forces, Hinton said. A government of the extreme right "could complicate the problem of public support in the United States." Still, Hinton promised, the United States would try to work with whatever government emerged.[56]

Behind the scenes, the CIA spent $2 million to help the Christian Democrats. Some of the money was sent via sympathetic Salvadoran trade unions. Some was spent on a multicolored comic book that portrayed ARENA supporters as fat cats in limousines and guerrillas as torturers of children. The CIA airdropped the comics into areas where support for the government was weak.[57]

On the eve of the balloting, with ARENA looking strong, the administration's characterization of D'Aubuisson shifted to prepare public opinion in the United States for the unpleasant prospect of a rightist victory. D'Aubuisson's past history as a death squad leader was no longer disqualifying. "We must not prejudge him," Hinton said. "He denies the rough stuff. He should be judged on his future actions and performance and not his past performance."[58] In cables back to Washington, Hinton was more blunt: "Whether we like him or not is [the] wrong question," he said of D'Aubuisson. "We must deal with him. Now and in the future." Two U.S. intelligence agencies, in their biographical profiles of D'Aubuisson, dropped references to his suspected involvement in death squad activity and the 1980 assassination of Archbishop Oscar Romero.[59]

By all accounts, election day in El Salvador was inspiring. Turnout was far heavier than expected, with some 85 percent of eligible voters reportedly going to the polls. People willingly traveled great distances on foot and stood in line for hours waiting to cast their ballots. Sporadic efforts by the guerrillas to intimidate voters and disrupt the elections were unsuccessful in all but a few areas.[60]

The various guerrilla organizations had been unable to agree on a common strategy in response to the election. Some called upon their supporters to stay away from the polls, others told them to deface their ballots (11.4 percent of voters did so), and others launched military attacks to disrupt the voting.[61] None of the strategies proved effective. Moreover, the FMLN's actions were so obviously contrary to the popular desire to vote that the attacks seriously damaged the guerrillas' international image. For the next six years, whenever Ronald Reagan talked about El Salvador, he always told the story of a woman who, though wounded in a guerrilla attack on her polling station, refused to leave her place in the voting line to get medical attention.[62]

But the election did not consolidate the Salvadoran regime or resolve the conflict between the far right and the Christian Democrats. The Christian Democrats won a plurality of votes (40 percent) and of seats in the Constituent Assembly (twenty-four of sixty). Five rightist parties divided up the rest of the seats. ARENA won the most with nineteen; the National Conciliation Party (Partido de Conciliación Nacional, PCN), the military's old party, won fourteen; and three smaller rightist parties split the remainder.[63] The rightists had no fundamental ideological differences with one another and were united in their hatred for the Christian Democrats. They quickly formed a majority coalition and pledged to throw the Christian Democrats out of the government. D'Aubuisson, as leader of the largest party on the right, was their logical choice for provisional president.

This was not the outcome the Reagan administration had planned. Publicly, it tried to accentuate the positive, lauding the record turnout and calling the election a clear rejection of the guerrillas.[64] But behind the scenes, U.S. officials were deeply worried that a government led by ARENA would roll back the agrarian reform, escalate the level of violence, and knock the footings out from under Reagan's policy on Capitol Hill. The task of keeping D'Aubuisson out of the presidency, keeping the Christian Democrats in the government, and preventing the right from rescinding the reforms fell to Ambassador Hinton.

Deane R. Hinton was one of the top members of the Foreign Service when Al Haig personally asked him to take the embassy in El Salvador in early 1981. Several other candidates had refused the dangerous and controversial post, but that was not Hinton's style. "I'm a soldier's son and a professional foreign service officer," he explained. "When you're asked to take on a hard one, you do it."[65]

Hinton was used to the hard ones. He had served in a variety of assignments all over the world—in Europe, Africa, the Middle East, and Latin America—often appearing at moments of crisis. He was AID director in Guatemala from 1967 to 1969, during an intense and bloody counterinsurgency war, of which U.S. AID–sponsored "civic action" was an integral part. From there, he went to Chile as AID director at a time when the CIA was actively subverting the elected Marxist government of Salvador Allende, in part by sabotaging the economy and bribing trade unions to go on strike. During Hinton's tenure (1969–71), AID funding for Chile fell by 96 percent, from $35.4 million to $1.5 million.[66]

President Ford appointed Hinton ambassador to Zaire in 1974, just as the United States was moving covertly to arm pro-Western factions in Angola at the outset of its postcolonial civil war. Supply lines for the operation ran through Zaire. Hinton was expelled after only a year in Kinshasa for allegedly plotting to assassinate President Mobutu Sese Seko. "Total nonsense," Hinton replied. "My defense has always been that if I had been out to get him, he'd have been dead." Hinton's penchant for turning up in hot spots convinced some observers that he was actually a CIA officer. He denied it, but as journalist Christopher Dickey wrote, "the aura of the spook" followed him around the world.[67]

Hinton and Enders had been friends for years. They saw the Salvadoran problem in the same terms and agreed on the prescription, despite their markedly different temperaments.[68] Enders always remained cool, aloof, and totally in control, even under the most acerbic congressional interrogations. Hinton, by contrast, was gruff and less studied in his reactions. He could be surprisingly frank about El Salvador's problems, even though his candor sometimes contradicted the State Department's official optimism. But he was no less diligent than Enders in defending the essential correctness of U.S. policy, and he was not above losing his temper if it served his purpose.

Whereas Enders usually couched his defense of policy in terms of the national interest, Hinton was more likely to address the morality of it, insisting that the potential evil of the other side was greater than the evil of ours. He could flash righteously indignant at any suggestion to the contrary. At fifty-eight, Hinton had about him an air of quiet bravado and machismo that, along with ample jowls and thinning hair, reminded people of an aging Marlon Brando. And he always enjoyed a good cigar.

Hinton demanded high-caliber performance from everyone on his staff, and he raised hell when he didn't get it. "Members of the country team used to trade jokes about who got chewed out worse by Deane Hinton," recalled one aide. "It's part of the folklore there. He was such a tough son of a bitch to work for, we figured we all had to stick together or we would get sent home separately." But Hinton's toughness and intelligence inspired respect as well as fear. "We'd march to hell with him," the aide added.[69]

Hinton, like Robert White before him, was not averse to flexing the muscles that came with U.S. assistance. He denied being Washington's proconsul in El Salvador—"I've got a lot of influence, but I don't run it," he said at one point. "If I were running the place, a lot of things would be different." But he was always at the center of the action, even when it wasn't politic to admit it. "I'm moving them in the right direction," he reflected in early 1983. "Or, rather," he quickly corrected, "they're moving in the right direction while I sit here and watch."[70]

No challenges were tougher than the ones Deane Hinton faced in the first half of 1982—first, trying to keep D'Aubuisson out the presidency, and later trying to keep the rightist parties from gutting the agrarian reform. The day after the Salvadoran election, Hinton assembled leaders of all the parties and urged them to form a broad-based coalition government. He also implored them not to raise any charges of electoral fraud, lest they tarnish the regime's newly won legitimacy.[71] All agreed, even though officials later admitted that 15 to 25 percent of the votes cast were fraudulent. "We didn't denounce it because we didn't want to foul up the good results and the good image of the election," ARENA's Hugo Barrera admitted.[72]

Keeping D'Aubuisson out of the presidency and keeping the Christian Democrats in the government were crucial to preserving congressional support, but members of the Salvadoran right were unimpressed with Hinton's warnings. They simply did not believe that Ronald Reagan would cut off aid. They were convinced that the demands for reform emanated, unbeknownst to Reagan, from liberal bureaucrats in the State Department, or were simply posturing for the sake of domestic U.S. politics. "The United States has never cut off aid anywhere for very long or even entirely," explained one D'Aubuisson ally. "Reagan will never let the Communists win here. It's just a complete bluff."[73]

Nothing Hinton said could shake their conviction. He even began passing out copies of the certification legislation—a law he had once called "stupid"— to show the right that an aid cut-off would be required if the reforms were reversed or if the human rights situation deteriorated markedly.[74] The administration also solicited help from Congress to convince the right that aid could be forfeited if they did not heed Washington's concerns. A large delegation of House members headed by Majority Leader Jim Wright traveled to San Salvador two weeks after the election to deliver the warning in person. "They really put the heat on us," said a leader of one of the rightist parties.[75]

The postelection maneuvering focused on the National Conciliation Party (PCN), which had come in third in the balloting. Although the PCN was ideologically close to ARENA, its ties to the military made it especially sensitive to the need for U.S. aid to fight the war. The PCN therefore became the target of embassy pressure aimed at inducing it to break with ARENA and support Washington's formula for an all-inclusive "government of national unity."[76]

Hinton forced the rightist parties to stay at the bargaining table with the Christian Democrats through four weeks of fruitless negotiations, but he could not make them give in to Washington's terms. ARENA refused to relent. After all, they argued, they had played by the rules of the democratic game as Washington demanded, and they had won. It was unjust for the United States to now insist that the hated Christian Democrats be allowed to share power. Three times, ARENA scheduled Constituent Assembly meetings for the purpose of electing D'Aubuisson provisional president; each time they were thwarted by their inability to keep the PCN on board.

Gradually, the armed forces became fed up with the inability of the civilians to form a government. Rumors of a coup began to circulate, but a coup would have squandered the legitimacy produced by the election and made the Salvadoran regime thoroughly unpalatable on Capitol Hill. In the face of U.S. opposition, the coup rumors dissipated, but the army began to echo the embassy's warning that a rightist government excluding the Christian Democrats would be unacceptable.[77]

The monthlong deadlock was finally broken when the United States appealed to the Salvadoran military to force a settlement on the bickering civilians. On April 20, a U.S. envoy, General Vernon Walters, arrived in San Salvador with a letter from Secretary of State Haig warning that the stalemate was jeopardizing continued U.S. assistance. The letter also reminded the Salvadorans that U.S. aid was contingent upon the new government's commitment to continue the reforms, its human rights practices, and its inclusion of the Christian Democrats. "Help us to help you," Walters said to the military high command, in asking that they support the U.S. conditions.[78] Walters was accompanied by John Carbaugh, aide to Senator Jesse Helms, whose job was to convince the Salvadorans that the danger of a congressional cut-off of assistance was real, not just a chimera invented by the State Department.

Hinton then gave the armed forces a list of nine possible presidential candidates whom Washington could support.[79] Convinced that military aid was endangered, the army summoned the politicians to military headquarters to face a solid phalanx of the high command. The officers ordered them to choose a president. "They said, 'Here are three names. Pick one,'" related one of the civilian politicians present. But the officers made their preference clear: Alvaro Magaña, an apolitical mortgage banker with close ties to the armed forces.[80]

ARENA tried various devices to block Magaña's election, including postponing Constituent Assembly meetings repeatedly. Members of other parties received death threats warning them not to vote for Magaña. On the day of the vote, ARENA supporters filled the galleries of the Constituent Assembly and passed out leaflets denouncing Magaña as "a little Jew" whose election would amount to treason. Nevertheless, the PCN and Christian Democratic deputies did as the armed forces had ordered and elected Magaña provisional president. In the end ARENA accepted the army's imposition of Magaña because, as one ARENA official put it, "They had a gun to our head." As a consolation prize, D'Aubuisson was elected to head the Constituent Assembly.[81]

Hinton had, in his own words, "weighed in heavily" to resolve the postelection crisis and succeeded. He prevented the extreme right from capturing control of the regime, but at the expense of reinforcing rather than reducing the dominant role of the army. Looking back on it a year later, Hinton judged that the only "downside" to Magaña's selection as president was that to achieve it, "one had to resort to the military."[82]

"Perfecting" the Agrarian Reform

Once the postelection crisis had been resolved, Washington's next step was to ensure that Magaña cooperated with U.S. policy. The incoherence of his administration complicated that task considerably. The new Government of National Unity was hardly unified; the cabinet and subcabinet were divided among the Christian Democrats, ARENA, and the PCN. A forceful president might have used the resulting interparty squabbles to establish a strong role for himself, but Magaña was not forceful. He aspired to be nothing more than the administrator of decisions made by the Constituent Assembly, and as such, he was peripheral to the real policymaking process.[83] One joke that made the rounds in San Salvador compared Magaña's office to a public phone booth: anybody could walk in and nobody ever called.

Washington worried that this bizarre hybrid government would be unstable and ineffective.[84] The first item on the State Department's agenda was to have Magaña schedule regular presidential elections as quickly as possible. In the meantime, Washington urged him to take steps that would make it easier to certify to Congress that progress was being made on human rights and social reform.

"You should indicate that we need by the end of June a program of concrete proposed GOES [Government of El Salvador] actions which we could use in defending certification and [the] maintenance of requested economic and military assistance," Haig instructed Hinton.[85] In the area of human rights, Haig wanted the armed forces to stop resorting to violence against the civilian population, such as "the failure to take prisoners, the killing of real or apparent guerrilla followers . . . [and] the execution of suspected guerrilla supporters or sympathizers. We recognize that this program represents a major change, and that it will be difficult to implement immediately," the cable to Hinton said, in a rare acknowledgment of how common political murder by the armed forces was.

In the area of negotiations, Haig wanted the government to "seize the initiative from the FMLN-FDR by offering opportunities for elements of the extreme left to return to the political mainstream and by seizing the high ground in contesting international opinion on the issue of dialogue with the left."

Finally, Washington insisted that Magaña's government be steadfast in carrying out the agrarian reform, which came under fierce attack from the right in the months after the election. During the campaign, ARENA and the other parties on the right regularly blamed the moribund state of the Salvadoran economy on the reforms introduced by the Christian Democrats in 1980—the nationalization of the banks, the creation of a state monopoly on marketing agricultural exports, and the agrarian reform. To avoid alienating voters and antagonizing the United States, the right rarely called for the outright repeal of the reforms; instead, they promised to "perfect" them. It did not take long to see what such perfection would look like in practice.

To the landed oligarchy that constituted the political backbone of ARENA, nothing was more noxious than agrarian reform. For decades they had managed to successfully derail or dilute every reform proposal. Then in March 1980, Ambassador Robert White arrived in San Salvador and flatly told the armed forces that assistance from Washington was directly contingent on the adoption of economic reforms, including agrarian reform. Faced with a mounting insurgency that they could not manage without Washington's help, the army agreed.

In March 1980, the government promulgated a two-phased agrarian reform law and added a third phase the following month. Phase One expropriated large estates in excess of 1,250 acres and transferred ownership to the resident workers, who ran them as cooperatives. Under Phase One, 328 farms were taken over, constituting about 14.7 percent of the nation's arable land, and about 30,000 families benefited. With a few exceptions, this was not the best land; much of it was used for cattle grazing or was lying fallow.[86]

Phase One was carried out within a few months, but it was hardly trouble-free. Landowners resisted violently, often with the aid of the local security forces. In the first year of the reform, 184 government agrarian reform workers and leaders of peasant cooperatives were murdered by the right.[87] An evaluation prepared by U.S. AID concluded that the pervasive violence had produced "an atmosphere of uncertainty, insecurity, and fear among the people on intervened farms throughout the country."[88]

Phase Two called for expropriating estates between 250 and 1,250 acres, creating cooperatives similar to those under Phase One, or distributing the land in the form of family farms. This would have affected some 1,700 farms, comprising about 12 percent of the arable land, and about 50,000 families would have benefited. Phase Two was the most significant part of the reform because it was aimed at the most modern farms producing for export—the heart of the agricultural economy and the foundation of the oligarchy's power. The affected farms produced 35 percent of El Salvador's coffee, 40 percent of its cotton, and 20 percent of its sugar.[89]

Phase Two was never carried out. It was postponed indefinitely because the owners of the affected farms constituted "a considerable element in the country's political power structure," a 1981 U.S. AID study acknowledged.[90] The United States opposed Phase Two because it would have antagonized the right and reduced foreign exchange earnings, further weakening the already shaky economy (not to mention requiring more U.S. aid).[91]

The third phase of El Salvador's agrarian reform was not part of the original plan; it was drafted by the United States and enacted in April 1980 by Decree 207. It gave all renters and sharecroppers the right to own the land they worked, up to a maximum of seventeen acres. The peasants would pay for the land over a period of thirty years, during which time they were allowed to sell it only to the government. Decree 207 potentially affected about 12.3 percent of El Salvador's arable land and could have benefited approximately 100,000 families if everyone eligible had applied.[92]

The principal aim of Decree 207 was explicitly political rather than economic—to create a base of political support for the government by quickly distributing small parcels of land to landless peasants.[93] Designed by Professor Roy Prosterman, Decree 207 was often referred to as "Land to the Tiller," after Prosterman's earlier effort in South Vietnam, which served as a model for the Salvadoran reform. As in Vietnam, land reform was to be an integral part of Washington's counterinsurgency strategy.

Few Salvadorans outside the high command of the armed forces were consulted before the adoption of Decree 207, with the result that many regarded the law as "misguided and U.S. imposed," according to an AID assessment. A U.S. diplomat in San Salvador was more blunt: "It had to be shoved down their throats," he said.[94]

Decree 207 was not well adapted to Salvadoran conditions. Most renters worked plots of less than three acres of very poor land—not nearly enough to support the average family of six. Moreover, the land's low quality required frequent rotation of crops to avoid soil exhaustion, so peasants rarely rented the same plot two seasons in a row. Under Decree 207, however, beneficiaries would be locked into producing on the same plot year after year, with considerable risk of declining productivity.[95]

In a fit of optimism, the authors of Decree 207 described it as "self-implementing," a view they amended after nearly a year had passed with no discernible implementation.[96] Six months after the law was adopted, a survey conducted by the American Institute for Free Labor Development (AIFLD) found that 93.4 percent of the potential beneficiaries thought they were still renters rather than owners, and 86.9 percent did not think the decree had altered their status on the land. By the terms of the decree, all these people owned the land they were working, but almost none of them were aware of it. Rental arrangements were continuing, according to an AID official, "as if the law had never been announced."[97] Even worse, the first instinct of many owners was to forcibly drive renters off the land so they could not claim title to it. Since over 80 percent of rental arrangements were verbal, a peasant not occupying a plot had no way to prove his right to it.[98] As of January 1982, some 25,000 potential beneficiaries had been evicted.[99]

ARENA pledged during the 1982 election campaign that it would not reverse Phase One of the reform, but it opposed both Phase Two and Decree 207.[100] On May 18, 1982, the Constituent Assembly struck a major blow against Decree 207, voting to suspend for one crop cycle the right of tenants to acquire title to rented land. President Magaña had originally proposed suspending Decree 207 just for cotton and sugar lands in order to stimulate export production. Land was lying fallow, Magaña explained, because owners were afraid that if they rented it, the tenants could simply file claim to take possession. The Constituent Assembly, however, expanded the proposal to apply to cattle-grazing and grain-producing lands as well. Together these four categories of land included virtually all of the farms subject to Decree 207. Moreover, owners would only have to put a few head of cattle in a field to claim exemption from the law.[101]

In the countryside, the new laws were interpreted by landlords and peasants alike as signaling the end of agrarian reform. Rightist politicians openly hailed the "repeal" of Decree 207, and the Ministry of Agriculture instructed its officials to stop accepting applications for title.[102] As a result, new applications fell 90 percent from the preelection period and provisional title grants fell nearly 75 percent. In a new wave of violence, landowners forcibly evicted between 4,000 and 10,000 peasants.[103]

Congressional reaction to the suspension of Decree 207 was swift. By happenstance, the Senate Foreign Relations Committee was meeting to mark up the fiscal year (FY) 1983 foreign aid bill the week that suspension was imposed. "If the Salvador government is reneging on the land reform program," Senator Charles Percy (R-Ill.) said angrily, "then it is the expressed opinion of this Senator that, under the law, not one cent of funds shall go to the government of El Salvador."[104]

Administration officials begged the senators not to act precipitously until the meaning of the Salvadoran law could be clarified. The senators were not mollified. It was clear enough where the government was headed on agrarian reform, said Senator Christopher Dodd (D-Conn.). "They are out to destroy it."[105] On an amendment sponsored by Dodd and Nancy Kassebaum, the committee voted unanimously to freeze security assistance to El Salvador (military aid and Economic Support Funds) at FY 1982 levels, thereby cutting $100 million from the administration's request (slashing it from $166.3 million to $66 million). And that was not all. Dodd and Kassebaum sponsored another successful amendment cutting off the remaining aid to El Salvador if the government "modifies, alters, suspends, or terminates any provisions of the land reform program in a manner detrimental to the rights of the beneficiaries under those decrees."[106]

In the House, Foreign Affairs Committee Chairman Clement Zablocki (D-Wis.) canceled the scheduled markup on the supplemental economic aid destined for El Salvador under the Caribbean Basin Initiative. "If the new regime in El Salvador believes it can dismantle the land reform program with impunity, it is sadly mistaken," Zablocki warned. Speaker Tip O'Neill commented that aid to El Salvador should be cut off because the suspension of the agrarian reform violated the certification requirements.[107]

In San Salvador, Ambassador Hinton was working furiously to reverse the Constituent Assembly action or convince President Magaña to veto it. The best he could do was to get the Constituent Assembly to clarify the suspension decree, declaring that it would not prejudice the rights of anyone who had been eligible to apply for land prior to its adoption. This was better than nothing, but with evictions rising rapidly, the letter of the law appeared less important than the malevolent spirit behind it. "You've heard all this propaganda . . . that the reforms continue," Duarte said. "But the truth is that the law has stopped the reforms."[108]

Having done his best with the Salvadorans, Hinton rushed to Washington and spent three weeks trying to reassure angry members of Congress. He argued that the changes in the reform law did not mean what everyone seemed to think they meant. The reform had not been suspended at all, he insisted. The Constituent Assembly had merely exempted certain lands for a time. "I don't think it's dead and I don't think it's going to be killed," Hinton declared. There had been "a lot of hullabaloo up here," he lamented, all based on "misperceptions" caused by mistaken news reports. However, when President Magaña was asked whether Phase Three had been suspended, he answered, "Yes, definitely." And even Hinton had to admit that evictions had become a serious problem.[109]

The army's initial reaction to the controversy over Decree 207 was indifference. The sharp reaction in Congress, however, changed the military's outlook. Just as the postelection efforts of the right to elect D'Aubuisson president had threatened the interests of the military by endangering the flow of U.S. aid, now the efforts of the right to cripple the agrarian reform posed a similar threat.[110] Urged on by the U.S. embassy, the armed forces moved in June to defend the agrarian reform by actively reinstating evicted peasants. Though not everyone in the high command approved, Defense Minister José Guillermo García convinced most senior officers that U.S. aid was directly dependent on reviving Decree 207. Over the next month or so, 1,900 renters were reinstated.[111]

When it became clear that the United States and the armed forces would not tolerate the overt demolition of the reform, ARENA settled on a more subtle approach. By taking control of the administrative agencies involved with agriculture, the right was able to slowly strangle the agrarian reform program by neglecting its implementation—for example, by withholding credit or neglecting extension services.[112] But the right's bitterness toward the military for first blocking D'Aubuisson's accession to the presidency and then saving agrarian reform would be long-lasting.

In Hinton's maneuvering against the Salvadoran right, an odd symbiosis developed between the Reagan administration and its congressional opponents. The administration hated the certification requirements and bitterly opposed the aid cuts that its opponents were always threatening. Yet in Hinton's battles with the Salvadoran right, it was precisely the onerous certification and the threat of reduced aid that, time after time, gave him the crucial leverage he needed to keep the armed forces on the side of the embassy.

Certification: Round Two

The Reagan administration took its second required certification more seriously than it had taken the first, producing a twenty-one-page report with thirty pages of appendices. The July 1982 report was more balanced than its predecessor, admitting that there was a dark side to the Salvadoran reality as well as a bright one, that there had been setbacks as well as improvements. Making the certification was "a close call," admitted Assistant Secretary of State for Human Rights Elliott Abrams.[113]

Administration officials wanted to focus the July certification hearings on the Salvadoran election, which they touted as a great triumph for democracy. The election was invoked as evidence that the military was being brought under control (because they allowed it to take place), as evidence of human rights improvement (because democracy was "the best guarantee" of human rights), and as evidence of progress toward a peaceful political settlement to the conflict.

On human rights issues, the tone of the certification was more subdued. "Progress on human rights has not been as great as we would have liked," Enders acknowledged. "Serious violations of human rights continue." Unlike the first certification report, this one was straightforward in attributing some of the blame to the government's own military and security forces. Still, Enders insisted, things were getting better. "Deaths attributable to political violence are on a slow downward trend," he reported. In the first five months of 1982, the State Department's "grim-gram" counted only 1,573 political murders, compared to 2,692 in the first five months of 1981. But Enders did not mention that even the embassy's data showed a higher death toll for the first six months of 1982 (the second certification reporting period) than for the immediately preceding six-month period, when 1,313 people were murdered.[114]

Not surprisingly, the issue of land reform generated the most congressional interest. Here, too, a forthright approach served the administration best. Rather than trying, as Hinton had done in June, to pretend that there had not really been an attack on the reform, Enders acknowledged the obvious. But thanks to the Magaña government and the army, he concluded, "the agrarian reform process is today back on track."[115]

The second set of certification hearings followed the same pattern as the first. Administration witnesses testified that the situation on all five certification requirements was improving. Congressional critics grilled them about the more dubious aspects of their claims, which irritated the witnesses. The witnesses stuck to their lines, though, conceding nothing even in the face of contrary evidence, which irritated their interrogators. Whether or not progress was being made in El Salvador, there was no discernible progress in the dialogue between the administration and the Congress. Three senior liberal Democrats, Joseph Biden (D-Del.), Paul Sarbanes (D-Md.), and Alan Cranston (D-Calif.), didn't even bother to attend the testimony by State Department witnesses in the Senate hearings. "We've won," said one administration official wryly. "We've succeeded in making the issue of human rights in El Salvador boring."[116]

The problem was not boredom so much as frustration. The State Department was frustrated because its entire policy rested upon being able to certify progress every six months. Otherwise, military aid would cease and the policy would collapse. "We are asked to make an up or down judgment. Reality is of course a mass of positives and negatives," Enders complained. "[Certification] requires us to threaten to cut off military assistance to achieve the goals of our policy when we know that an actual cut-off would defeat the goals of those policies."[117] A U.S. diplomat in El Salvador was more pointed: "It forces the president to overstate things in order to get the aid that must be sent. What choice did he have?"[118]

To congressional liberals, on the other hand, the administration's version of events was not just overstated, it was unreal. Reagan's apparent willingness to certify anything to keep the aid flowing was exasperating. If Reagan would not obey the certification law by reporting honestly, Congress was left with only two alternatives: sit quietly, accepting the farce; or use the blunt instrument of the purse by cutting aid drastically.

The consequences of cutting aid were unpredictable. If the extreme right took an aid cut as an opportunity to move against the government, the U.S. embassy would no longer have the leverage with the army to stop it. A rightist coup would probably be followed by an intensification of the war, more bloodshed, and an eventual guerrilla victory. And, of course, the Democrats would be blamed for it all.

Alternatively, a cut in aid might convince the army that a negotiated settlement was the only rational way out of the quagmire. Many of the liberals were willing to risk cutting off aid because if Washington continued to pretend that the situation was improving when it wasn't, the right would never believe the United States was serious about promoting change. The army would keep on killing innocent civilians while upholding only the barest pretense of reform, and eventually the guerrillas would win anyway. "At some point we have to be willing to cut off aid," Congressman Studds argued. "[If] the cut-off of aid is unthinkable because of the consequences which would flow from that . . . then nothing we do by way of conditions will have any credibility down there."[119]

This view appealed to the liberals, but moderate Democrats, not to mention conservatives, thought it too risky—both for El Salvador and for the domestic political fortunes of the Democratic Party. So Studds was stuck, just as he had been since the outset of the Reagan administration. He could raise nearly one hundred cosponsors on a bill to end military aid to El Salvador, but he could not get the backing of his own party leadership. "Congress protests now and then," Michael Barnes said in frustration, "but essentially supports the policy . . . of military and economic aid to that government, speeches to the contrary notwithstanding."[120]

El Salvador's March elections were a huge political success in Washington, but they could have easily been a disaster if Hinton had been less skillful in keeping D'Aubuisson out of the presidency. The survival of the agrarian reform program was a close thing, too. Hinton blunted the right's effort to gut the program, preserving enough of it to convince Congress it was still viable. Despite the Salvadoran regime's unremittingly atrocious human rights record, support for it on Capitol Hill edged marginally higher in 1982. For most members of Congress, the television pictures of Salvadorans standing in long lines waiting to vote made up for a multitude of shortcomings. Public support for Reagan's policy also increased slightly in the wake of the elections, but the gain proved short-lived, eroding by August, when opinion stood almost exactly where it had in March 1982: 66 percent opposed to Reagan's handling of El Salvador, 23 percent in favor.[121]

Reagan's modest progress in selling his policy at home was not matched, however, by much success in El Salvador. In 1982, the administration learned just how ornery its Salvadoran client could be. Certainly the March election dealt the guerrillas a severe political setback, but the balloting did nothing to stabilize the regime. A weak junta led by the Christian Democrats and dependent on the army was replaced by a weak conservative president heading a fractious coalition government, also dependent on the army. The agrarian reform was technically alive, but the far right was dismantling it slowly by administrative neglect.[122] Whatever reforms remained on paper, the Magaña government was even less likely than Duarte's junta to redress the social and economic grievances that gave rise to the guerrilla insurgency in the first place.

Finally, to avert the twin disasters of a D'Aubuisson presidency and repeal of the agrarian reform, Hinton had to rely on the armed forces. Faced with a threat to the military's institutional interests, the high command imposed its will on the civilian politicians in a manner long familiar to Salvadorans. The March 1982 balloting demonstrated that El Salvador could be forced to go through the motions of holding an election, but its aftermath demonstrated with equal clarity that the election had not changed the basic dynamics of Salvadoran politics. The army was still the ultimate power behind the regime, and the guerrillas were still in the mountains fighting to overthrow it.

CHAPTER 8

The War Party Takes Control

Alexander Haig spent his first year in the cabinet feuding with Secretary of Defense Caspar Weinberger, U.N. Ambassador Jeane Kirkpatrick, and White House Chief of Staff James Baker. Yet despite his paranoia about intrusions on his turf, Haig had no real rival for control over foreign policy so long as Richard V. Allen was President Reagan's national security adviser. Allen and his staff were pitifully weak and unskilled in the arts of bureaucratic warfare.[1] When Reagan's old friend William P. Clark took over Allen's post in January 1982, however, Haig was suddenly faced with real competition. Clark didn't know much about foreign policy, but he knew Ronald Reagan.

After Haig's shuttle diplomacy failed to avert the April 1982 South Atlantic war between Argentina and Great Britain over the Falklands/Malvinas Islands, he felt his influence slipping. In June 1982 he clashed with Clark and Weinberger over Israel's invasion of Lebanon and threatened to resign unless Reagan reaffirmed his primacy—a threat Haig had made several times before to get his way. This time, the president took him up on the offer, much to Haig's surprise.[2]

Reagan immediately named George P. Shultz to succeed Haig. Shultz was quickly and unanimously confirmed by the Senate, partly because he was a picture of calm and reason at his confirmation hearings—a welcome relief from Haig's histrionics. The policy positions Shultz marked out were not fundamentally different from Haig's, but he defended them so judiciously that Senate Democrats felt reassured. On Central America, in particular, Shultz struck a moderate tone. He reiterated the administration's charges that the Soviets were aiding the Salvadoran guerrillas, but he also emphasized the social and economic roots of the insurgency. Instability, he acknowledged, was the result of "poverty and the sense of hopelessness that comes with it."[3]

Shultz came from an academic background and retained something of a tweedy professorial style—thoughtful, relaxed, and sensible. He had been a business professor at Stanford University and dean of the School of Business at the University of Chicago before joining the Nixon administration as secretary of labor in 1969. His background in labor-management relations made him more comfortable with negotiated solutions to conflicts than military ones, though he believed in showing the sword occasionally to improve one's bargaining position. His willingness to deploy military forces for essentially political motives soon put him at odds with top military leaders, who, after Vietnam, recoiled at committing troops without a clear military objective.

Shultz became the first director of the Office of Management and Budget when it was created in 1972 (Caspar Weinberger was his deputy) and was appointed treasury secretary a year later. Though his manner was low-key, he developed into a tough bureaucratic infighter who prevailed by dint of dogged persistence. "Knowing he is a Marine who has a [Princeton] tiger tattooed on his butt tells you more about him than any State Department biography," said a friend. In 1974, Shultz left government to become president of the Bechtel Group, Inc., a multinational construction firm, where Caspar Weinberger was general counsel. They didn't get along, and time did not dispel their mutual animosity.[4]

Unlike Haig, Shultz paid little attention to Central America during his first six months in office. His top priorities were the Middle East crisis and the friction in NATO caused by U.S. economic sanctions aimed at halting construction of a natural gas pipeline between the Soviet Union and Western Europe.[5] A transition report on Central America entitled "Where Do We Go from Here?" prepared for Shultz by Thomas Enders's assistant L. Craig Johnstone indicated that the policy was proceeding relatively well. "The trend of events is now running in our favor," Johnstone wrote. "Assuming that Cuba and Nicaragua do not substantially increase the stakes in Central America, the secret to success will be a steady and sustained effort." The most serious obstacle was Congress, where "human rights concerns" and "fears of a Vietnam-style escalation" threatened to curtail the resources required for the policy. "We must build a stronger constituency on the Hill if we are to succeed over the long run," Johnstone concluded.[6]

Taking on the "Mafia"

With the Salvadoran elections out of the way, Alvaro Magaña safely installed in the presidential palace, and the land reform alive if not prospering, Enders and Deane Hinton began looking ahead to the next stage of their strategy—significantly reducing the military's murderous violence against the civilian population. No single action was more important, both for building congressional support and for strengthening the Salvadoran regime at home. An end to death squad operations was a necessary prerequisite for splitting the social democratic civilians of the Revolutionary Democratic Front (FDR) away from the guerrillas in the Farabundo Martí National Liberation Front (FMLN). No sane politician would return from exile while the death squads had a free hand to exterminate anyone suspected of leftist sympathies. So the first order of business was to bring the death squads under control. The second was to open some sort of dialogue with the FDR leaders to entice them into returning to participate in the next round of elections, thereby further legitimizing the regime. The third was to achieve enough progress in the cases of the murdered U.S. citizens to satisfy Congress at certification time.

In pursuit of this agenda, Hinton found himself confronting the same adversaries he had battled over the appointment of Magaña and the preservation of the agrarian reform—Roberto D'Aubuisson and the far right. Once again, Defense Minister José Guillermo García was Hinton's principal ally. Throughout the fall of 1982, the struggle over Washington's policy agenda was waged deep inside the Salvadoran officers corps between García and D'Aubuisson's allies led by Colonel Nicolás Carranza. Their battle for the loyalty of their fellow officers focused on two issues: the AIFLD murders and whether any "dialogue" should be allowed between the government and the FMLN.

The AIFLD killings had always been of special interest to the administration because Michael Hammer and Mark Pearlman had worked closely with the embassy's AID staff. "It was like losing family members," explained one official. "We knew these guys."[7] For Hinton, the case became a test of the government's willingness to control death squad violence and prosecute those responsible. Not only was the case highly visible and crucial to assuring continued U.S. military aid, it was also clear cut. In the churchwomen's case, the enlisted men arrested for the killings denied acting on higher orders, and there was no hard evidence to contradict them. In the AIFLD case, on the other hand, the trigger-men identified two National Guard officers, Lieutenant Rodolfo Isidro López

Sibrián and Captain Eduardo Ernesto Alfonso Avila, as having organized the shootings. The U.S. embassy and the AFL-CIO developed additional evidence against the two. "There is no question that López Sibrián is the guy who ordered the murder," Hinton said flatly.[8]

Would the army allow the prosecution to go forward, breaking the unwritten code that military officers were immune from punishment for crimes against civilians? The embassy pushed hard, threatening privately that the administration would have difficulty certifying to Congress that progress was being made on the AIFLD case unless the two officers were arrested. "If the Salvadoran court system allows these killers to go free because of political pressure, there is no way that we can certify human rights progress, or that we would be credible if we did," warned one State Department official.[9]

Even though Avila and López Sibrián were friends of D'Aubuisson, García pressed for action against them because the embassy insisted on it. When the two were finally charged with the Hammer and Pearlman murders in September 1982, D'Aubuisson publicly came to their defense, turning the case into a test of strength with García.[10] "They are my colleagues and my friends, just like those who through twenty years of military service I knew and lived with," D'Aubuisson said of the accused in a television appearance. "I feel honored to be their friend and I know they are good soldiers."[11]

Avila escaped the prosecutor by fleeing the country, but López Sibrián was detained. Less than a month later, however, two courts ruled that the evidence against him was insufficient and dismissed the case. Witnesses to the killings had been unable to pick López Sibrián out of a police lineup because he had been allowed to shave off his mustache and dye his flaming red hair black. At the U.S. embassy, officials were appalled at the miscarriage of justice. "We spent a lot of political capital, a lot of time, and had a major investigation," an embassy official said bitterly. "Justice was about to be done, and it blew up in our face."[12] Hinton brought in General Wallace H. Nutting from South-Com to warn the Salvadoran high command that U.S. aid was at risk—hoping that they would take the message more seriously if it came from another officer. It did no good. "If they can't get that son of a bitch in jail, then fuck'em, let's go home," a U.S. military adviser said in frustration. "We're wasting our time here."[13]

The right was equally intransigent when it came to any hint of dialogue with the FDR-FMLN. After the 1982 election, Washington urged Magaña to "seize the initiative" on the issue of negotiations by appointing a special commission to discuss how the left might be included in the next round of elections.[14] Magaña did as he was told, creating a Peace Commission in September to open contact with the FDR-FMLN about the conditions under which they might lay down their arms. Shortly thereafter, the FDR-FMLN responded with a call for "immediate dialogue without any prior conditions." The two sides, it appeared, were edging warily toward talks. Publicly, Hinton praised the government's openness and predicted that the left might participate in the 1984 presidential elections.[15]

The right denounced the idea of dialogue—D'Aubuisson called it "the most vile treason and an unqualifiably absurd policy"—and denounced both Enders and Hinton for proposing it.[16] Faced with the danger that peace might break out, the right turned to its traditional weapon—paramilitary violence. As rumors of negotiations increased, so did the ghoulish activities of the death squads. Murders became more conspicuous and ghastly—mutilations, disembowelments, beheadings. The right was sending a message.

In late October, the message got stronger. Over a two-day period, heavily armed men in civilian clothes seized seventeen labor leaders and politicians affiliated with parties in the FDR coalition.[17] The sweep took every major leftist leader who had not already gone into exile. Hinton immediately called the disappearances "thoroughly regrettable," but pronounced himself certain that the government had nothing to do with it. "This is not what the government wants to have happen," he insisted.[18] Perhaps it was not what Hinton's friends in the government wanted, but two days later the armed forces acknowledged that they were holding eight of the missing men for "conspiracy against state security." The others simply disappeared, never to be heard from again.[19]

The kidnappings were reminiscent of the November 1980 slaying of the FDR's national leadership, both in method and intent. Once again the right sought to block the initiation of a dialogue by murdering the most senior leftist leaders it could lay its hands on. The kidnappings gave weight to the FDR-FMLN's claim that its people would be slaughtered if they gave up their arms and trusted their fate to the good will of the armed forces, as the government was asking.

Within the Salvadoran regime, the audacity of the far right and the collaboration of the armed forces tipped the political balance against peace. General García rejected talks, proclaiming, "The only dialogue open to the leftists is the dialogue with the people at the next election." Magaña quickly followed García's lead and rejected the FDR-FMLN proposal. The door to peace talks, which had opened a crack, swung closed again.[20]

Hinton was thoroughly disgusted. First the setback in the AIFLD case, then FDR kidnappings—Washington's strategy seemed to be at a dead end. With death squad killings on the rise and the government refusing to talk to the left, the administration would be hard pressed to certify to Congress that El Salvador was in compliance with the conditions for continued aid.

On October 29, Hinton vented his frustration, in a calculated way, in a speech to the American Chamber of Commerce in El Salvador. It was an annual tradition for the U.S. ambassador to address the group, which constituted a virtual assembly of the Salvadoran oligarchy. On this occasion, Hinton delivered a blistering attack on the far right—a blast designed to bolster García in his struggle with D'Aubuisson and to force some movement on the AIFLD and churchwomen's cases.[21]

"I would no doubt be well advised to talk of other things," Hinton began. "But for better or worse, today I want to talk of a subject so many of you . . . leave in eloquent silence." As many as thirty thousand people had been "murdered, not killed in battle, murdered!" Hinton said sharply. "Is it any wonder that much of the world is predisposed to believe the worst of a system which almost never brings to justice either those who perpetrate these acts or those who order them?"

"The 'Mafia' must be stopped," Hinton declared. "Your survival depends upon it. The gorillas of this Mafia, every bit as much as the guerrillas of Morazán and Chalatenango, are destroying El Salvador." Despite the reduction of political killings since 1981, Hinton continued, "by no stretch of the imagination can current levels be considered acceptable by any civilized person." Hinton concluded by reminding the audience that unless El Salvador made progress in the human rights field and brought the killers of U.S. citizens to justice, U.S. aid would end, regardless of Washington's concern about Communist expansion.[22]

The Salvadorans were stunned by Hinton's blunt language, and their reaction was a measure of how wedded the oligarchy was to violence. A dozen people walked out on the speech. Those who stayed fired a barrage of hostile questions at the ambassador, accusing him of "blackmailing" El Salvador by threatening to cut off aid. The Chamber of Commerce took out a full-page newspaper advertisement denouncing the speech as "an act of arrogant imperiousness . . . a slap in the wounded and bloodied face of our country."[23]

The Salvadoran rightists were not the only ones outraged by Hinton's speech. Ronald Reagan didn't like it either. Hinton was kicking an ally when he was down, Reagan thought. The speech had been cleared at the State Department by Enders, but not by the White House.[24] "They thought it was not in keeping with a quiet diplomatic approach," Hinton explained later. "They thought it was a little loud, public diplomacy. I thought the basic policy is quiet diplomacy but there is provision for exception. I decided the time had come to go public, and I went public."[25]

Hinton was muzzled—told to curtail public criticism of the Salvadoran government—and National Security Adviser William Clark leaked word of the rebuke to the press. The White House was especially unhappy about Hinton's explicit threat to withhold military aid unless the human rights situation improved. Never mind that the certification law *required* such conditionality.[26] The unspoken implication of the rebuke to Hinton was that the White House had no intention of cutting off military aid, regardless of the human rights situation—an implication that the Salvadoran right was quick to grasp.

President Reagan himself seemed to confirm this interpretation a few weeks later during his December trip to Latin America. After visiting Brazil and Colombia, Reagan met for an hour with President Magaña in Costa Rica (security concerns precluded actually going to El Salvador). Speaking with reporters after the session, Reagan was asked whether he would certify in January that El Salvador was continuing to improve its human rights record. "On the basis of everything we know now, yes, of course," he replied. Just the day before, a Salvadoran judge had dismissed all charges against Lieutenant López Sibrián in the AIFLD murder case.[27] (Two months later, in February, Hinton recommended that Washington "play hardball" on the AIFLD case by refusing to certify, thereby cutting off military aid. His recommendation was ignored.)[28]

Next Reagan stopped in Honduras, where he met with President Roberto Suazo Córdova and General Efrain Ríos Montt from Guatemala. Ríos Montt had come to power in 1982, overthrowing the brutal military government of General Fernando Romeo Lucas García. Ríos Montt's government had not improved Guatemala's horrific human rights record; if anything, the level of military violence against Indian peasant communities had gotten worse. But after meeting with the general, Reagan pronounced him to be "a man of great personal integrity," and insisted that Guatemala had gotten "a bum rap" from international human rights groups.[29]

General García Outlives His Usefulness

The White House's repudiation of Hinton's speech reverberated through the Salvadoran officers corps, weakening General García. The D'Aubuisson faction led by Colonel Carranza portrayed García as Hinton's puppet, willing to sacrifice the interests of the army and the nation just to satisfy the gringos. The rightists tried twice, in August and September 1982, to unseat García as defense minister by seeking votes of no confidence from the high command. On both occasions they failed because the provincial commanders were García's friends and classmates from his graduating class (*tanda*) at the Salvadoran military academy.[30] Coup rumors continued through October and into November, but García's association with the United States was a source of strength as well as vulnerability. At a critical moment in early November, Hinton let it be known that if D'Aubuisson ousted García, military aid from Washington would be cut off. Wavering officers got back into line.[31]

By late November, García felt strong enough to take revenge against those who had plotted against him, demoting them from command positions and sending them into diplomatic exile. Colonel Carranza was removed as head of the telephone company, ANTEL, which despite its prosaic title was a powerful post for intelligence collection through wire taps and for capital accumulation through corruption. The only senior commander among the conspirators who was not reassigned was Lieutenant Colonel Sigifredo Ochoa, the commander in Cabañas province.[32]

For all his political acumen, García suffered from a serious failing. Like many of his contemporaries, he was a lousy soldier. As the guerrillas grew stronger, the deficiencies of García's command became increasingly apparent. Most of the provincial commanders he appointed were incompetent and corrupt. They had no combat experience and no desire to risk getting any. They regularly ignored the advice proffered by U.S. military advisers, insisting on conducting large sweeps rather than small-unit operations; their jobs were sinecures, and they could reap more profit in graft from large maneuvers than from small patrols. U.S. advisers referred to them as "the warlords."[33] The Pentagon tried to get García to replace these crooks with officers willing to actively engage the guerrillas in combat, but he would not. The regional commanders were García's base of political support, critical allies in the struggle with D'Aubuisson and Carranza.[34]

All the old problems that had plagued the army from the beginning of the war—the lack of training, the shortage of competent officers, the corruption—remained unremedied. The FMLN, estimated at five to seven thousand full-time troops with perhaps another ten thousand part-time militia members, was improving faster than the armed forces. The result was a dangerous erosion of government control over the countryside. "The guerrillas own the night," acknowledged one U.S. military adviser.[35]

In October 1982, the guerrillas launched their annual fall offensive, just at the height of the army's internecine struggle. The offensive was larger, better coordinated, and more successful than the army or the embassy had anticipated; in a few weeks, the rebels seized two dozen towns. The army's response began predictably with large sweeps. But as in June 1981, the counteroffensive met stiff guerrilla resistance that inflicted heavy casualties on the army.[36] Although the army had grown to twenty-two thousand men, supported by eleven thousand armed members of the security forces, there were only thirty-eight hundred troops in the U.S.-trained rapid response battalions—the only units capable of effectively engaging the guerrillas in combat. For the first time, García decided to heed his U.S. advisers and not commit major units to retaking the northern towns, a decision that may have been influenced by his desire to keep his most loyal commanders close to the capital to defend him against a potential coup. In any event, the army's counteroffensive was broken off.

U.S. military advisers praised García's decision as "the first faint stirrings of maturity."[37] But what may have been good military strategy was not good politics. To many Salvadorans, the army's failure to challenge the expansion of guerrilla-controlled territory appeared to be proof of the government's weakness. D'Aubuisson and his allies quickly seized on the issue. Not only was the overall war effort going badly, they charged, but García had in effect ceded part of the national territory to the Communists. In December, García succumbed to the political pressure and pledged an all-out offensive that would eliminate the guerrillas once and for all—exactly what D'Aubuisson had been demanding. When the army's offensive failed to score any major victories, García's political position deteriorated further.[38]

In January 1983, García made a fatal miscalculation. To complete his retribution against the plotters on the right, he ordered Colonel Ochoa into diplomatic exile as military attaché in Uruguay. Sensing García's weakness, Ochoa refused to obey, declaring a mutiny and vowing that he would not leave Cabañas province until García resigned as minister of defense.[39]

Sigifredo Ochoa was popular with U.S. advisers because he had successfully pacified Cabañas using small-unit tactics—and a strong dose of brutality. Politically, Ochoa stood on the far right with D'Aubuisson. But he was also on good terms with commanders of the new U.S.-trained rapid response battalions, an increasingly powerful cohort of younger officers who did not identify with either the D'Aubuisson faction or the older traditionalists who backed García.[40] This younger group bore the brunt of the war and were proud of their professionalism. They called themselves "praetorians" and had only contempt for commanders who stayed in their garrisons or in San Salvador. The praetorians were the officers most unhappy about General García's conduct of the war, and it was to them that Ochoa appealed for support.

In the showdown the previous fall, the praetorians had backed García against D'Aubuisson because the U.S. embassy lobbied them vigorously on García's behalf. As commanders of the U.S.-trained battalions, the praetorians interacted frequently with U.S. advisers and had a closer relationship with the U.S. embassy than any other group in the army. They represented a new generation of officers—one that was not so beholden to the Salvadoran oligarchy and, Washington hoped, would not simply act as its servant the way earlier generations of officers always had. Instead, they would be the guardians of the new political order Washington was building. And, of course, their rise to power enhanced the ability of the United States to control events.

In January, the praetorians switched their allegiance from García to Ochoa because the U.S. embassy declared itself neutral in the mutiny, which it termed a "strictly internal" affair of the Salvadoran army. Washington deserted its long-term ally García because he was losing the war. In 1982, García had played an invaluable role in blocking D'Aubuisson's presidential bid, reviving the agrarian reform, and pressing for prosecution in the cases of the U.S. church-women and the AIFLD advisers. His political utility outweighed his military incompetence. By 1983, with the military situation deteriorating, García's military shortcomings could no longer be overlooked.[41]

Ochoa's mutiny ended when he agreed to accept a diplomatic post in the United States—a "golden exile"—and García agreed to resign as defense minister in ninety days, when he completed thirty years of service—the traditional retirement deadline for Salvadoran officers. Ever the wily politician, García tried to renege on the deal just before the deadline ran out by engineering a vote of confidence for himself from the high command. But it was to no avail. Anxious to get García out of the way so that his cronies could be replaced with officers willing to fight the war Washington's way, the U.S. embassy moved from its stance of neutrality to actively pushing for García's replacement. When the ninety-day timetable for García's resignation ran out, the commander of the air force, Colonel Juan Raphael Bustillo, another D'Aubuisson ally, followed Ochoa's example, declaring he would no longer accept García's orders. With no gambits left to play, García retired.[42]

General Carlos Eugenio Vides Casanova, commander of the National Guard, was named García's successor. Vides was a compromise candidate. As a member of García's *tanda*, he was acceptable to García's allies. As former commander of the Guard, he also had ties to D'Aubuisson's faction, which tended to be concentrated in the security forces. Vides had only two liabilities. First, he had no field experience as a troop commander, which led his detractors to refer to him as "señorita Casanova."[43] This problem was solved by shifting control over most operational matters to the armed forces chief of staff. That post went to a praetorian, Colonel Adolfo O. Blandón. Vides's other shortcoming was his image in the United States. During his tenure as commander, the National Guard had killed both the U.S. churchwomen and the AIFLD labor advisers, not to mention countless thousands of Salvadorans. The Guard had tried to cover up its role in the killing of the churchwomen, and it was hard to believe that Vides had not known it.

The solution to this problem was a matter of public relations. The embassy touted Vides as a military moderate who was honest and reform-minded and had cleaned up the National Guard. That was hype. In fact, while the embassy was publicly extolling Vides as a reformer, it was reporting to Washington that he represented a "shift to the right." As soon as Vides took over, D'Aubuisson ally Colonel Carranza was rehabilitated and given command of the feared Treasury Police, the security force most often associated with the death squads. Another rightist, Lieutenant Colonel Mario Denis Morán, whose bodyguard was one of the triggermen in the AIFLD killings, was given command of a major regional garrison.[44]

The FMLN took advantage of the disarray in the army caused by the Ochoa revolt to launch another round of attacks in January 1983. In Morazán, guerrillas closed in around the provincial capital of San Francisco Gotera, overrunning a three-hundred-man government garrison in the small town of Jocoaitique and a five-hundred-man garrison at Meanguera. The army rushed six thousand troops, including all three U.S.-trained battalions, into the Morazán battle, leaving other areas virtually undefended. The guerrillas, as usual, countered with new attacks in Chalatenango and Usulafter. But they also met the army's counteroffensive in Morazán head-on and fought the U.S.-trained troops to a standstill.[45]

Just as the army seemed to have regained the upper hand in Morazán, the guerrillas attacked and captured Berlín, the second largest city in Usulután, with a population of forty thousand. It was their biggest victory of the war, and though the guerrillas held Berlín for only three days, its capture was a stunning psychological blow to the armed forces.[46]

The Sky Is Falling

The Ochoa revolt and the fall of Berlín in January 1983 touched off a panic in Washington. The State Department had been assuring the White House that the military situation in El Salvador was gradually improving and the political situation was at least manageable. Suddenly events seemed to be dangerously out of control. Back in 1981, the FMLN's fall offensive had dashed the administration's complacent belief that the war could be won quickly and had sparked a major review of policy leading to the plans for increased U.S. involvement that Reagan approved in NSDD 17. These new guerrilla offensives dispelled the illusion that the war was being won at all. A new, more frantic policy review was hurriedly launched.

The 1981 policy review had been controlled by the State Department. The Inter-Agency Core Group, which Enders chaired, had drafted policy options and then presented them to the National Security Council for decision. The 1983 review was ordered and directed by the White House. Shortly after the fall of Berlín, National Security Adviser William Clark suggested that Reagan send

Jeane Kirkpatrick on a trip through Central America to give the White House a fresh view of the crisis. Kirkpatrick, as the only senior foreign policy official in the administration with any claim to expertise on Latin America, was highly regarded by both Clark and Reagan. She gave their instinctive anti-Communism a veneer of intellectualism.

Jeane J. Kirkpatrick was an unlikely person to find in a Republican administration that represented the triumph of the Barry Goldwater wing of the party. A self-described "Humphrey-Jackson Democrat," Kirkpatrick was a university professor long active in Democratic Party politics. But when Vietnam opened the great schism between Cold War liberals and antiwar Democrats, Jeane Kirkpatrick stood to the right with the Cold Warriors. Distressed by the nomination of George McGovern in 1972, she joined with other conservatives to found the Coalition for a Democratic Majority—a refuge for lapsed Democrats who came to be known as neoconservatives.[47]

Kirkpatrick harbored deep animosity for New Left activists and liberal intellectuals, whom she held responsible for hijacking the Democratic Party. In a revealing interview with the *New York Post* in 1983, Kirkpatrick blamed the loss of national will in the 1960s and 1970s on the "manipulation" of the public mood by the liberal media, on the "corruption of thought and language" by intellectuals who had lost religious values, and on the machinations of Soviet disinformation agents who were waging "ideological aggression" against the United States.

The antiwar movement and the counterculture of the 1960s were opaque to her, inexplicable and seemingly frivolous. "Truths about politics and society became a category of fashion," she said, "something more akin to the values of the entertainment industry than to thought and scholarship." She seemed not to grasp the irony of her commentary; she was, after all, ambassador for an ex–movie actor in a White House run largely by public relations professionals.[48]

By virtue of her *Commentary* articles about Central America and her Ph.D. dissertation on Argentina, Kirkpatrick gained a reputation as an expert on Latin America. It was not wholly deserved, for Kirkpatrick's academic research focused primarily on U.S. domestic politics. Apart from her dissertation, she published no scholarly work on Latin America during her two decades as a political scientist.[49] But among the senior officials of the Reagan administration, none of whom knew anything about Latin America, Kirkpatrick's slim credentials gave her a comparative advantage.

At first, Kirkpatrick did not carry the sharply polemical style of her writing into her post as ambassador to the United Nations. While Alexander Haig was secretary of state, she maintained a relatively low profile both in public and inside the administration. Even after Haig left, Kirkpatrick was still frozen out of decisionmaking on Central America by Enders. She was unhappy enough to tender her resignation in December 1982, but it was rejected, and thereafter her influence grew apace.[50] She was ushered into the administration's highest foreign policy circles when Reagan invited her to begin attending meetings of the National Security Planning Group (NSPG) in early 1983. An uncompromising hard-liner, Kirkpatrick settled quickly into an alliance with Clark, William Casey, and Weinberger—a group that pragmatists at State dubbed "the War Party." Kirkpatrick's special concern was Central America and she was, according to one official close to her, "the most militant figure in the administration."[51]

Kirkpatrick left on her fact-finding trip to Central America on February 3, 1983, and spent ten days traveling to countries in and around the region. While on the road, she publicly disparaged any notion that the Salvadoran army was in serious trouble. "The guerrillas are not winning anything," she insisted. "They do not even expect it."[52]

But upon her return, Kirkpatrick gave Reagan and Clark a hair-raising private report. El Salvador was in danger of collapse, she told the White House, and U.S. allies in the region were terrified. "She said, in effect, if we don't get with it in El Salvador, we'd better write it off," a senior administration official related.[53] Kirkpatrick recommended an immediate increase in military aid for El Salvador and big increases in economic aid for the entire region—a "Marshall Plan" for Central America. She rejected the idea of talks with Nicaragua or Cuba, or dialogue between the Salvadoran government and the FDR-FMLN.[54]

Both the CIA and Pentagon echoed Kirkpatrick's dire warning. The CIA's intelligence estimates on El Salvador were pessimistic, and Casey's hard-line instincts put him firmly in the camp of those advocating drastic action. An inspection tour by South-Com commander General Wallace H. Nutting led the Defense Department to conclude that the war was being lost and that heroic measures would be needed to save the situation. "I told Judge Clark that if we did not step up our effort . . . the thing was going to go down the tubes," Nutting recalled.[55] The Pentagon prescription: a large infusion of additional military aid. Even then, the Pentagon estimated it could take up to seven years before the government would show any significant progress on the battlefield, and the war would stretch on long after that before the FMLN was finally defeated.[56]

Implicitly, this developing consensus about the impending disaster in El Salvador cast doubt on the skill of the State Department's stewardship. Until the Ochoa revolt and the army's debacle at Berlín, State had been purveying a relatively upbeat assessment. As recently as November 1982, the U.S. embassy had reported that the Salvadoran armed forces were so much improved that they might win the war in 1983.[57] If suddenly the government was on the verge of collapse, the State Department had obviously not been doing its job.

In fact, the State Department was not entirely to blame for this disjuncture between its assessments and Kirkpatrick's trip report. State had focused on attaining specific operational goals: holding the 1982 election, keeping the extreme right from taking over the government, carrying out the agrarian reform, gradually improving human rights, and forcing action in the cases of the murdered U.S. citizens. It was slow going, but State could claim some progress in all areas, and several potential disasters had been averted. On the battlefield, the Salvadoran army was growing and becoming more capable, so there, too, the operational goals of policy were being accomplished.

Unfortunately, the operational goals were inadequate to the core strategic aims of stabilizing the regime and winning the war. The elections and the reforms did not resolve the basic political, social, and economic problems that had produced the war, and the training and equipment that Washington gave the Salvadoran army were not enough to make it fight with the same commitment and courage as the guerrillas. The State Department was doing its job about as well as it could be done, but the job, as the Reagan administration had conceived it, was Mission Impossible.

Nevertheless, the State Department was held to blame for the crisis in early 1983, because it had monopolized control over the policy. When William Clark took over from Richard Allen as national security adviser in January 1982, he brought no particular interest in Central America to his new post; until 1983, he was content to let control of the policy stay with the Department of State.[58]

The transition from Haig to Shultz did not reduce Enders's autonomy any more than the transition from Allen to Clark had. If anything, it enhanced it. Shultz had worked with Enders during the Ford administration, when Shultz was treasury secretary and Enders was assistant secretary of state for economic and business affairs. The new secretary had confidence in Enders and was happy to leave Central America in his hands.[59]

For his part, Enders continued operating as he had before—convening his Core Group of midlevel officials, setting policy, and implementing it without necessarily having the decisions regularly brought before the National Security Council. He limited the disruptive influence of Reagan hard-liners who were midlevel political appointees by simply neglecting to invite them to critical meetings of the Core Group, or by convening informal rump sessions with the people he trusted. When Kirkpatrick went on her trip to Central America, Enders tried to blunt its impact by cabling ahead to U.S. ambassadors in the region, advising them that her views did not necessarily represent the direction in which U.S. policy was headed.[60]

The autonomy with which Enders was able to operate made it possible for him to craft and carry forward a strategy for Central America despite the general chaos that characterized foreign policymaking in the Reagan administration. "It was like he had his own little State Department," said one official.[61] But the very autonomy that gave Enders so much clout also made him vulnerable. When the hard-liners finally decided to go after Enders, it was easy to accuse him of being a renegade, of not clearing policy decisions properly, and of assuming powers that rightfully belonged to his superiors. Enders had had a free hand in Central America, so there was no one to share the blame when things went wrong. "It was like what happens when a baseball team is on a losing streak," explained one senior official. "You get a lot of agitation to fire the manager, and Enders was regarded throughout the government as the manager on Central America."[62]

In January 1983, things seemed to have gone very wrong in El Salvador. Surveying the mess, administration hard-liners such as Clark and Kirkpatrick lost faith in Enders's ability to effectively manage the crisis. The policy review initiated by Kirkpatrick's trip to the region quickly became a struggle by the hard-liners to wrest control of the policy away from Enders and the Department of State.

Two Tracks

The right's unhappiness with Enders was not new, but it had grown more intense over the preceding months. The schism first opened when Enders and Hinton maneuvered Alvaro Magaña into the Salvadoran presidency in April 1982, blocking the aspirations of Roberto D'Aubuisson. As the principal representative of the Salvadoran private sector, D'Aubuisson's ARENA party held a continuing attraction for the Republican right. Within the Reagan administration, hard-line conservatives had reluctantly accepted the State Department's strategy of backing the Christian Democrats, but they would have preferred to let D'Aubuisson claim the mantle of provisional president. When Enders and Hinton went to work once again during the summer of 1982 to defend the agrarian reform against ARENA's efforts to repeal it, the conservatives in Washington were even more aggrieved.[63]

But the issue that worried conservatives most was negotiations. The very thought of forcing the Salvadoran government to sit at the same table with the Communist guerrillas made hard-liners apoplectic. From the outset, official policy had been to oppose negotiations over "powersharing" (that is, giving the guerrillas or their civilian allies any role in the government), while supporting talks intended to entice the left into laying down its arms and participating in government-sponsored elections.

That policy did not change when George Shultz became secretary of state, but its rhetoric changed markedly. Whereas Haig spoke constantly of the Soviet and Cuban menace, Shultz was more apt to speak of the need to address the social and economic problems that had given rise to the Central American crisis. "Haig saw the problem as Communist infiltration and the solution as increased military aid," explained one administration official. "Shultz in contrast is more conscious of the economic and social roots of the crisis. He even worries about human rights. But I'm not sure the White House is with him."[64]

Conservatives feared that behind Shultz's change in tone, a reorientation of policy was under way as well—that the "striped pants boys" at the State Department were preparing to negotiate with the Communists in El Salvador.[65] This was no more than half true, at best. In the wake of the Salvadoran election, Enders and Hinton did urge Magaña to open talks with the civilians in the FDR about what sorts of procedural guarantees might lure them into the next election campaign. But this was well within the bounds of existing policy.

To administration hard-liners, however, convening any negotiations between the government and the left was seen as a step down the slippery slope toward surrender. The hard-liners always displayed a disconcertingly low opinion of Washington's allies. They seemed convinced that if Salvadoran officials sat down with the FDR-FMLN, they would leave the bargaining table without their shirts or their country. Even the hint that Washington was interested in a settlement short of victory, the conservatives warned, might set off panic in San Salvador. "The problem is, you run the risk of breaking the morale of the Salvadorans if they think we're going to run out from under them and leave them to the mercies of the guerrillas," explained one administration official. "If the sense spreads that the U.S. will desert them, I don't know what they'll do. It's Vietnam all over again."[66]

The hard-liners wanted to win the war, so any talks that went beyond setting the terms for the FDR-FMLN's surrender were unacceptable. Enders, on the other hand, was telling Congress that the aim of U.S. policy was *not* to win the war. "We're trying to do two things in El Salvador," he explained in January 1983. "We're trying to give [the government] enough military assistance to hold off the insurgents—not to defeat them militarily, but to prevent them from prevailing—while we get on with the reforms."[67]

The disagreement between Enders and the White House hard-liners extended beyond the substance of policy. They also fought bitterly over how best to sell the policy to Congress. Enders's strategy had not changed much since mid-1981: listen patiently, evince sympathy for congressional concerns, but stick doggedly to the administration's agenda of remedies. Over two years, this strategy had worked reasonably well getting Congress to go along, albeit reluctantly, with the essential elements of Reagan's policy.[68]

The key, of course, was resources. Enders had to fight each year to get Congress to approve the increases in economic and military aid necessary to finance his strategy. And he had to keep Congress from weighing down the policy with too many "barnacles"—conditions, like the certification requirement, that limited how aid could be spent. From Haig's counterproductive war scares in 1981, Enders drew the lesson that it was better not to alarm Congress by giving Central America too high a profile. A quiet, incremental approach was more fruitful. The Pentagon complained constantly that this gradual approach was inadequate. Hard-liners Clark and Kirkpatrick agreed. Enders, they thought, did not have the stomach for confronting Congress head-on and demanding that it fund Reagan's policy.[69]

By the beginning of 1983, circumstances had conspired to defeat Enders's gradualist approach. A year earlier, in the fiscal year (FY) 1983 budget request sent to Congress in the spring of 1982, the administration had intentionally asked for substantially less aid for Central America than it needed. It planned to seek an additional $300 million later in the year as a supplemental request.[70] By breaking up the aid requests rather than asking for a huge increase all at once, Enders hoped to avoid aggravating public and congressional fears of another Vietnam.

By year's end, however, the situation in El Salvador had deteriorated considerably. Fighting in late 1982 was more intense than expected, depleting the Salvadoran army's stores of ammunition and leaving a shortfall in military assistance. Moreover, Congress never got around to passing a new foreign aid bill in 1982, so funding levels for FY 1983 were frozen at the FY 1982 level—well below even the artificially low amount the administration had requested. The result was a huge gap between the resources available for implementing Enders's Central America policy and the resources it required.

Hard-liners, joined by the Pentagon, began pressing in late 1982 for the State Department to submit a large supplemental aid request to Congress, but Enders felt the political climate was wrong, both in San Salvador and in Washington. By the time the Ochoa revolt ended in January 1983, the situation had deteriorated even further. By March, less than halfway through the 1983 fiscal year, the entire $26.3 million military aid budget for El Salvador had been spent.[71]

The amount of aid needed just to stabilize the Salvadoran military was too enormous to be passed off as merely a routine adjustment of aid levels. The urgency of the situation made it impractical to continue coddling Congress to extract incremental increases—there just wasn't time to raise the ante by nickels and dimes. Enders's gradualist approach had, ironically, produced the opposite of what he intended; the resource gap had grown so large that closing it would now look like a qualitative escalation of Washington's commitment.

To cushion the political shock of a large aid request, Enders proposed a new diplomatic offensive. In an internal memorandum reviewing U.S. options, he set forth a "two-track" policy for Central America. The first track involved continuing support, including increased military aid, for the Salvadoran regime. The second track called for new U.S. efforts to promote regional peace talks among the Central American governments, to test the possibility of resuming negotiations with Nicaragua, and, most important, to push for the beginning of a political dialogue in El Salvador. In the scenario Enders sketched out, the United States would importune a third country, perhaps Spain, Mexico, or Venezuela, to act as intermediary in getting a dialogue started. Washington would help sell the idea to Magaña and the Salvadoran armed forces.[72]

Enders, who spent a great deal of time on Capitol Hill testifying and lobbying for Reagan's aid packages, was acutely aware of how shaky congressional support had become. He feared that unless the administration launched a diplomatic initiative of its own, Congress might mandate negotiations in El Salvador that would be much harder for either the administration or its clients in San Salvador to swallow.[73]

Enders didn't have much hope that his gambit would actually produce peace, but he did think that it would allow the administration to plausibly claim that it wanted a diplomatic settlement. Having made the diplomatic gesture and failed, the administration would then be better positioned to extract the necessary military resources from a reluctant Congress.[74] "The feeling never was that we could negotiate an agreement on El Salvador or Nicaragua," a senior U.S. official explained. "Notwithstanding, we decided in February that we needed to move on the diplomatic side to deflect the perception of our only going for a military solution."[75]

Although the "two-track" memo did not propose any change in basic policy objectives, its new emphasis on diplomacy struck administration hard-liners as dangerously soft. What to Enders seemed like a clever way to mollify Congress looked to the hard-liners like pandering. What Enders regarded as a genuflection to diplomacy, necessary to pave the way for greater military aid, the hard-liners feared was the first step toward craven surrender. "That's what you might expect from a Carter ambassador to Canada," sneered a White House aide.[76]

When Enders traveled to Spain in early February to confer with Prime Minister Felipe González, a social democrat and advocate of negotiations in Central America, conservatives were certain that Enders was racing ahead on the negotiating track. Kirkpatrick and Clark maneuvered to turn Enders's two-track proposal against him by leaking it before Enders had developed a consensus around it. That would force the president to deny that any change of policy was being contemplated, repudiating the memo and Enders along with it. Kirkpatrick's office leaked word of the two-track memo to the *Washington Times*, which accused Enders of "advocating a coalition government" with the Communists—a willful misreading of the proposal.[77] The story was guaranteed to get conservatives' blood boiling; it touched off howls of "betrayal" and "surrender," and fueled conservative demands for Enders's head.[78]

Enders tried to fight back as best he could. A ranking State Department official called the press reports "an extraordinary distortion of the situation." The leaks, this official explained, were designed to "demonstrate that there was a move afoot to change basic policy. That's not the case at all."[79] Secretary Shultz, testifying on Capitol Hill, insisted that press reports implying the administration was willing "to bring the guerrillas somehow into the government" had "no foundation in fact."

In a heated exchange with the congressional panel, Shultz sounded every bit as hard-line as Alexander Haig. "The guerrillas are busy upsetting people in El Salvador, creating hell, shooting their way around. They are responsible for the level of violence there," Shultz charged. "Let them shoot their way into government? No dice."[80] Rhetoric alone could not salvage Enders's position, however. Not only did he have Clark and Kirkpatrick gunning for him, but Ronald Reagan was also outraged by the two-track proposal. "Reagan hit the roof," said one official. The president felt that any talk of negotiations signaled a weakening of Washington's resolve, demoralizing its allies and emboldening its adversaries. The hard-liners had the president on their side.[81]

The White House in Command

In any crisis, control over decisionmaking flows to the top of the national security bureaucracy. In the case of El Salvador, it moved straight into the White House. After Kirkpatrick raised the alarm, senior administration officials began meeting regularly to manage the crisis, often with President Reagan himself attending. Clark and Kirkpatrick, backed by Weinberger and Casey, took day-to-day management of the policy away from the Department of State. Enders's bureau, American Republic Affairs, was being "reintegrated" into the administration, as one official phrased it. In fact, it was really being locked out. "The upshot of it all was that Clark was taking charge," recalled NSC consultant Michael Ledeen. "Clark had had it with the State Department."[82]

Judge William P. Clark's rise to the pinnacle of the foreign policymaking apparatus of the United States was astonishing, to say the least. Like Edwin

Meese and Michael Deaver, he was part of Ronald Reagan's "California Mafia." After dropping out of Stanford Law School and flunking out of Loyola, Clark managed to pass the bar and set up a modest law practice. In reward for his work as Reagan's campaign chairman in Ventura County during the 1966 gubernatorial race, he was appointed cabinet secretary to Governor Reagan. Though shy and introspective, he won promotion to the top staff position as Reagan's executive secretary in 1967.[83]

Clark and Reagan got along well. Like the president, Clark made no pretense of being an intellectual. What Clark lacked in brilliance, he made up in efficiency, thoroughness, and unquestioning loyalty. He managed the flow of paper into and out of the governor's office and devised the famed "mini-memo." Before any issue, no matter how complex, went to Governor Reagan, it had to be boiled down to just four paragraphs that would fit on a single page: one paragraph to state the essence of the problem; one to summarize the facts; one of commentary; and one for recommended action.[84] The same format was adopted in Reagan's White House. Governor Reagan was so appreciative of Clark's good work that he appointed him to the California bench in 1969 and later elevated him to the California Supreme Court, an appointment that appalled the legal community because of Clark's scant qualifications.

Clark loved being a judge and resisted leaving the bench. He turned down Reagan's offer to manage the 1980 campaign and refused several cabinet-level posts in the new administration. But when Reagan called personally and asked Clark to become deputy secretary of state to facilitate White House relations with the mercurial Haig, Clark could not refuse his old friend.[85]

Clark knew nothing about international affairs. "I had to start pretty much from ground zero and educate myself on subjects I'd never thought about before," he admitted. His confirmation hearings before the Senate Foreign Relations Committee demonstrated an embarrassing lack of basic knowledge.[86] Nevertheless, Clark acquitted himself fairly well at the State Department. His main contribution was to serve as a back channel between Foggy Bottom and the White House staff, interpreting and defending Haig's supercilious behavior to the troika of Baker, Deaver, and Meese. Had it not been for Clark's good offices, Haig might well have been fired even sooner.

In January 1982, Reagan brought his old friend to the White House as his national security adviser, replacing Richard Allen, whose overly academic briefings bored the president.[87] Clark interpreted his new role as seeing to it that the State Department carried out the president's policy even when it conflicted with the preferences of the department bureaucracy. His experience at State had taught him that the bureaucracy could be deadeningly slow when it disliked its marching orders. Clark was not shy about laying down the law to enforce the president's policy. He still liked to be called "Judge," and he kept his grandfather's sheriff's badge and old six-shooter in his office.[88]

In mid-1982, Clark cooperated with James Baker to replace Haig because Haig's increasingly argumentative style had led Clark "to wonder about the man's mental balance." But Clark was instinctively a hawk, siding with Weinberger, Casey, and Meese on most foreign policy issues, against Baker and Michael Deaver. "The White House staff was split right down the middle between the moderates and the conservatives," Deaver recalled.[89] Clark's hardline stance also brought him into conflict with Shultz, especially over Central America. To Shultz, Clark was "obsessed" with the region and intent on "micromanaging" policy, with "disastrous" consequences. "Clark had stubbornly strong opinions," Shultz wrote later, "but lacked the depth of judgment and experience to back them up."[90]

To Clark and his fellow hard-liners, Enders and the State Department seemed unenthusiastic about arguing the administration's case to Congress and the public. As an antidote to Enders's pacifism, Clark arranged the appointment of former Democratic senator Richard Stone, a Florida conservative, as special adviser on Central America. Nominally, Stone's new job was to be the administration's "super-spokesman" heading up a new "public diplomacy" operation to sell the administration's Central America policy. He would wage the ideological battle that the State Department seemed loath to undertake.[91]

In practice, however, Stone acted as the National Security Council's assistant secretary for Latin America, reporting directly to Clark rather than to Shultz. The public diplomacy job gave Stone a seat in the Core Group and a perfect listening post from which he could keep his friends in the White House well briefed on the machinations of the State Department.[92] Stone began taking on operational responsibilities almost immediately. In late February 1983, Clark sent him on a special diplomatic mission to El Salvador to convince the Magaña government to move the next presidential elections up from March 1984 to October 1983. The 1982 election had given the regime's credibility a big boost in Congress, but the effect of that tonic had begun to wear off. The White House prescribed another dose of elections as soon as possible, and Stone convinced the Salvadorans to go along.[93]

On the commercial flight back to Washington, however, Stone was indiscreet. A reporter sitting nearby overheard him discussing the mission with a White House aide who was just beginning to get involved with Central American issues—Major Oliver L. North. "North chortled that he had arranged things so that it would appear that the Salvadorans had thought up the idea," said local television reporter Mark Feldstein, who spent most of the flight furiously taking notes on cocktail napkins. "It was North who had done most of the blabbing." The resulting publicity was embarrassing for both the Reagan administration and President Magaña, who appeared to be little more than a puppet of the United States. The Salvadorans changed the election back to its originally scheduled date.[94]

With Enders under growing attack, his ability to manage policy melted away. Day by day, the White House usurped control, leaving Enders with little more than his title. Toward the end, he did not even have the power to choose his own deputies. When he proposed Myles Frechette, a career foreign service officer who had been director of Cuban affairs, the White House vetoed the selection.[95] Poor Frechette was a victim of circumstance. He dutifully echoed the Reagan administration's tough line on Cuba, but White House conservatives had not forgotten that he had also loyally supported Jimmy Carter's policy of normalizing U.S.-Cuba relations in 1977–78. Notwithstanding the fact that supporting the policies of the incumbent president was his duty as a professional, Frechette's record on Cuba, along with the fact that Enders wanted him, made him unacceptable to the hard-liners.

In April 1983, Clark recommended that Reagan fire Enders, but Shultz resisted, so Enders was temporarily spared. The situation was obviously untenable, though. A few weeks later, Enders himself initiated the final showdown by telling Shultz that while he wanted to stay on as assistant secretary, he could not function effectively without a reaffirmation of the president's confidence in him. On May 25, Shultz had a long meeting with Reagan during which he hinted he would resign unless policy control returned to State. "Mr. President," Shultz said, "you have a fed-up, frustrated Secretary of State on your hands." Professing to be "absolutely unaware" that there was any problem, Reagan reaffirmed the State Department's primacy. But the price Shultz had to pay for wresting control back from Clark was to fire the very people who had been running it—Enders and Hinton.[96]

"You don't handle Central American policies with tea and crumpets on the diplomatic circuit," a White House aide said, explaining why the two diplomats had been sacked.[97] Another White House official said bluntly that the ouster of Enders and Hinton was just the beginning. The administration was contemplating broad personnel changes in the State Department, "all of it designed to bring in people the White House can trust. No longer are we going to leave our policies in the hands of people who are only interested in their careers and who undermine our interests in Central America."[98]

The only other casualty of the purge, however, was Ambassador Frank McNeil in Costa Rica. McNeil, the sole remaining ambassador in Central America appointed by President Carter, had helped Enders design the "two-track" options paper. The White House had been trying to replace McNeil for over a year with Curtin Winsor Jr., a fanatically right-wing Republican political appointee who was president of the Winsor Pittman Coal Company of West Virginia. Enders managed to delay McNeil's departure until his own position became untenable.

McNeil was bitter about the way the White House was politicizing the Foreign Service and impugning the loyalty of anyone who didn't share its unadulterated conservatism. "To suddenly find out that senior people in the White House are charging the Foreign Service with being soft on Communism—that's McCarthyism," he said angrily. McNeil left Costa Rica in June and was packed off to the Fletcher School of Law and Diplomacy at Tufts University as a diplomat-in-residence.[99] But it would not be his last run-in with Reagan's conservatives.

The replacements for Enders and Hinton envisioned by the White House belied the notion that the hard-liners were going to let Shultz's State Department run anything. Langhorne A. "Tony" Motley, a real estate entrepreneur and Republican fundraiser, was selected to replace Enders as assistant secretary for Latin America. Motley was a friendly and informal fellow, with a politician's sense of how to work a room. He was not a deep thinker; he learned by doing rather than studying. Since 1981, Motley had been Reagan's ambassador to Brazil, a political appointment that turned out unusually well. Born and raised in Brazil, Motley spoke fluent Portuguese and got along nicely with the Brazilian generals who ran the government. He did not speak Spanish, though, and came to his new post with little knowledge or experience of the rest of Latin America. Loyalty was his chief qualification. Long active in Republican politics, Motley was a Reagan loyalist with easy access to the White House staff. He was to be Clark's man inside the belly of the State Department beast.[100]

To replace Hinton, the White House proposed the U.S. ambassador to Guyana, Gerald E. Thomas, a retired admiral who was an old friend of Clark and Admiral John M. Poindexter, Clark's chief military adviser. Thomas was also a political appointee, and that was too much for the career Foreign Service. A delegation of senior officers met with Shultz and told him that morale was plummeting because of the White House's blatant effort to undermine the Foreign Service.

Shultz himself was reportedly irritated by unnamed White House officials disparaging the loyalty of Enders and Hinton. He refused to accept Gerald Thomas for the Salvador embassy, insisting that Hinton be replaced by a career officer. He chose Thomas Pickering, one of the most senior members of the diplomatic corps. In an unusual press briefing, Shultz personally announced Pickering's selection and went out of his way to praise both Enders and Hinton.[101] Privately, he told Pickering to "raise hell" about Salvadoran human rights abuses, whether the White House liked it or not.[102]

At the Pentagon, senior military officers worried that the advent of the hard-liners was the prelude to a shooting war in Central America—one that they would be sent to fight without solid political support. In the weeks following the ouster of Enders, the "never again" school of officers who had commanded troops in Vietnam launched an extraordinary public campaign against the use of U.S. combat forces in Central America.

Army Chief of Staff Edward C. Meyer, who was about to retire, acted as principal spokesman. "I am just concerned about having American soldiers at the end of a string without having the support of the American people," Meyer said. "I wouldn't even know how to design, right now, a military solution to the problem. If I thought the 82nd Airborne going in there would be a solution . . . I'd probably recommend that right now. I don't think it would be."[103] In the days that followed, several four-star generals and admirals sought out reporters to express similar views and actively lobbied their colleagues to join them in opposing any troop deployment. General Bernard W. Rogers, supreme commander of NATO, and General William C. Westmoreland (ret.), former commander of U.S. forces in Vietnam, publicly echoed Meyer's warning.[104]

The furor caused by this highly unusual politicking by senior military men led the chairman of the Joint Chiefs of Staff, General John W. Vessey Jr., to declare, "Neither I nor any member of the JCS, nor the civilian leaders in the Department of Defense, advocate introducing U.S. combat forces to try to implement an American military solution to the problems of Central America."[105] At a press conference on June 28, President Reagan again denied that he had any plans for sending U.S. troops to war, though he prudently kept his options open by noting, "Presidents never say 'never.' "[106]

No Exit

At the State Department, a few career officials thought that the administration's fears of collapsing dominoes were exaggerated and that U.S. interests in Central America could be adequately safeguarded with a settlement short of military victory. But after Enders and Hinton were fired for much milder heresies, no one dared speak up. To suggest that Washington settle for less than victory over the left was regarded by the hard-liners as tantamount to treason. Even questioning the effectiveness of existing policy, despite its obvious failings, was seen as disloyal. Criticism provided ammunition to congressional liberals who were demanding a broad reassessment of U.S. aims. Anyone who suggested that the policy was not working was, objectively, giving aid and comfort to the enemy at the other end of Pennsylvania Avenue.[107]

Hinton and Enders, the principal architects of Reagan's policy in El Salvador, were ultimately undone by the contradictions inherent in their own strategy. In the short and medium term, the survival of the Salvadoran government depended upon large-scale military aid from the United States. Providing such aid inevitably strengthened the armed forces politically as well as militarily, reinforcing the army's predominant role in the regime. Few military officers had much use for civilian politicians, democracy, or agrarian reform. Some, like García, were willing to grudgingly accept limited reforms to keep aid flowing from Washington. Others, like Carranza, resisted. But no one in the military really supported building a full-fledged democracy in which the armed forces would be subordinate to civilian control by freely elected politicians.[108] Hinton could maneuver at the margins, winning a concession here and there, but he could not change the fundamentally reactionary character of the military or make it release its grip on political power.

This recalcitrance had dangerous side effects both in El Salvador and in Washington. In El Salvador, the military's continuing murder of civilian opponents and its opposition to any dialogue between the government and the left meant that the war could not be settled at the bargaining table. Meanwhile, the government's neglect of social and economic problems provided the guerrillas with a steady stream of new recruits. An effective counterinsurgency program was impossible under such conditions, and prospects for the regime's long-term survival were doubtful.

In Washington, the Salvadoran regime's resistance to reform undercut congressional support. Every step forward (like the 1982 election) was followed by a step back (like the assault on the agrarian reform). To many members of Congress, the Salvadoran regime looked as fatally flawed as the Saigon regime before it. With skillful diplomacy, Enders could wheedle a few extra million dollars in aid, but he could not build a bipartisan consensus to assure a consistent and adequate flow of funds. Without enough resources, the situation on the ground got predictably worse, the need for assistance became more acute, the administration's requests for money grew exponentially, and Congress became ever more worried that Washington was headed down a slippery slope.

Drastic action was necessary to break out of this vicious circle. Either the administration would have to force the Salvadorans to change their behavior to please Congress, or it would have to force Congress to accept the Salvadoran regime, warts and all. Enders and Hinton tried to compel the Salvadorans to change and were fired for it. Now the War Party would try to move Congress.

CHAPTER 9

The President Moves to Center Stage

By 1983, Ronald Reagan's credibility on Capitol Hill had eroded considerably. The visible failure of his Central America policy to achieve results, its growing price tag, and his apparent determination to escalate U.S. involvement frightened moderates from both parties. Moreover, the Democrats' gains in the 1982 midterm elections tarnished the mantle of invincibility Reagan had acquired in the budget battles of 1981. Nervous Democrats were reassured that Reagan's 1980 landslide had simply been a rejection of Jimmy Carter, not the first step in a national realignment that would make Republicans the majority party. The Ninety-eighth Congress convened in January 1983 with the Democrats eager to take on Ronald Reagan over Central America—just as White House hard-liners were taking control of the policy away from Thomas Enders and the Department of State. Neither side harbored much faith in the possibility of bipartisan compromise.

Rounding Up the Usual Suspects

One of the first issues to come before the new Congress was the now doggedly routine semi-annual certification of progress in El Salvador. Everyone played their appointed role. Enders announced the certification in January and made the rounds on Capitol Hill defending it. Critics denounced it. "I do not believe that we should bestow a medal of good conduct on them because they are killing a few less people," Congressman Stephen Solarz (D-N.Y.) argued. "It is self-evident that the government is not trying to stop it."[1]

Both the House and Senate held lengthy hearings at which church groups, human rights organizations, and liberal academics testified that the certification was wrong; things had not improved. Administration witnesses and conservative academics testified to the contrary.[2] Often, the witnesses jousting with one another were the same people who had made the pilgrimage to the hearing rooms six months before, and six months before that. "We're rounding up the usual suspects," said a staffer tasked to recruit witnesses.[3] At the U.S. embassy in San Salvador, a diplomat deluged with visiting delegations of Americans dubbed the resulting chaos "the semi-annual pre-certification flying circus and hootenanny."[4] On all sides, there was a growing feeling that the certification ritual had exhausted whatever purpose it might have served originally.

For its congressional sponsors, certification had had three aims: to prevent Reagan from ignoring reform and human rights while he escalated U.S. military involvement in El Salvador; to pressure the Salvadorans themselves to improve their behavior on pain of losing U.S. aid; and to provide a means for periodic review and debate of the policy.[5]

The administration mastered the certification process by transforming it into a numbers game in which the State Department got to pick which statistics would count as indicators of progress. If the number of people killed by death squads went down, the administration argued that progress had been made toward safeguarding human rights—even though thousands were still being murdered and no one was ever punished for it. Similarly, if the number of applications for land titles went up, that was proof of progress on the agrarian reform, even though peasants were still at constant risk of being evicted from their new land.[6]

Faced with irreconcilable disagreements among the experts who testified at certification time, some members of Congress found the apparent solidity of the administration's numbers reassuring. It did little good to criticize the methodology that lay behind the numbers, though human rights groups tried.[7] The attraction of the numbers was that they gave people a point of reference, a yardstick, and the illusion that they were measuring El Salvador's elusive reality. Even as a means of keeping the debate over El Salvador alive, certification had been reduced to a charade—everyone reading their old familiar lines on cue semi-annually. If the Democrats were going to impel Reagan to adopt a Central American policy less reliant on military action, more sensitive to human rights, and more open to negotiations, they would need something more potent than the existing certification law to do it.

Reagan Joins the Fray

As William Clark and Jeane Kirkpatrick assumed day-to-day control over Central American policy, determined to embark on a major military buildup in El Salvador, they had to confront the same problem Enders had been struggling with for over a year: how to sell the package to a reluctant Congress. "Unless we get the Congress in gear, we lose the war," one administration official said tersely.[8] With Congress in revolt and public opinion running strongly against administration policy, Clark and White House Chief of Staff James Baker knew they stood little chance of winning massive aid increases unless Ronald Reagan himself joined the battle.[9]

During 1981 and 1982, Reagan had stayed away from the unpopular issue of Central America, at Baker's insistence. By early 1983, however, it was clear that without Reagan, no big aid package would survive the congressional gauntlet, and without a big increase in aid, El Salvador would be lost, perhaps sooner rather than later. So the administration committed its greatest asset to the battle—the president himself.[10]

On February 22, 1983, in a speech to the annual Washington conference of the American Legion, Reagan delivered his first major address on Central America since unveiling his Caribbean Basin Initiative to the Organization of American States (OAS) a year earlier. Unlike the OAS speech, which argued for promoting economic development as an inoculation against Communism, the speech to the American Legion focused on Central America's wars. "We face a special threat in Central America, where our own national security is at stake," he warned. "The specter of Marxist-Leninist controlled governments in Central America with ideological and political loyalties to Cuba and the Soviet Union poses a direct challenge to which we must respond."[11] The following week, Reagan summoned congressional leaders to the White House to impress on them the urgency of sending more aid and advisers to El Salvador without delay.[12]

The presidential full-court press continued. Speaking to the Commonwealth Club in San Francisco a few days after meeting with congressional leaders, Reagan said that El Salvador was "on the front line of the battle that is really aimed at the very heart of the Western Hemisphere, and eventually at us." In response to a question from the audience asking if El Salvador was not a replay of the early years of Vietnam, Reagan was adamant: "There is no parallel whatsoever with Vietnam." But he proceeded to describe the importance of El Salvador with a vintage recitation of the domino theory that could have been lifted directly from a speech by Lyndon B. Johnson in the 1960s, with only the names of the countries updated: "The threat is more to the entire Western Hemisphere than it is to any one country," Reagan said. "If they get a foothold, with Nicaragua already there, and El Salvador should fall as a result of this armed violence on the part of the guerrillas, I think Costa Rica, Honduras, Panama, all of these would follow."[13]

On March 8, Reagan brought the congressional leadership to the White House for a second time to lobby for more aid. While describing the various needs of the Salvadoran army, Defense Secretary Caspar Weinberger offhand-edly revealed that the administration's earlier call for $60 million in military aid had now been superseded by a new request for $110 million—a 400 percent increase over the amount Congress had already approved for fiscal year (FY) 1983. The congressional leaders were stunned.[14]

Two days later, Reagan gave a major speech to the National Association of Manufacturers devoted entirely to Central America. The Soviet Union, Reagan argued, was behind the war in El Salvador, hoping to conquer all of Central America. From that Marxist-Leninist bastion, the Soviets could then endanger Mexico, Panama, and the vital sea lanes of the Caribbean. Mocking those who argued that Central America and the Caribbean were too small to be so impor-tant, Reagan pointed to the growing Cuban military presence on the tiny island of Grenada—a major producer of nutmeg. "It isn't nutmeg that's at stake in the Caribbean and Central America," the president said sharply. "It is the United States' national security." But as soon as he asserted that Central America was "vital" to national security, Reagan quickly answered the question that was on everybody's mind: "Are we going to send American soldiers into combat? And the answer to that is a flat no."[15]

The pattern of earlier war scares was taking hold. As soon as the administra-tion declared that vital interests were at stake in Central America and upped the ante of military aid or advisers, Congress and the public began seeing visions of Vietnam. To calm these fears, Reagan was forced to deny that he had any intention of sending U.S. troops to fight. This put him in the odd position of arguing that vital interests were at risk, but that he would limit his response to sending more aid and perhaps a few more advisers. The inconsistency was obvious. Liberal members of Congress scoffed at the administration's dire warnings of impending disaster, arguing that both the threat and the U.S. interests at stake were being grossly inflated.

Round One: Reprogramming

How could Reagan get an additional $110 million in military aid for El Salvador? If he sought it through the normal budgetary process by submitting a supplemental aid bill, it would take months before any new aid was ap-proved. In light of the difficult military situation in El Salvador, a long delay was deemed too risky. The administration's only alternatives, therefore, were to reprogram funds already approved for other countries or have the president invoke his emergency powers to bypass Congress altogether.

Reprogramming had two drawbacks. First, the money had to be taken away from the security assistance program for some other country. Second, reprogramming requests had to be approved by all the relevant congressional committees—approval that was by no means assured. In particular, reprogramming meant placing U.S. policy in the unpredictable hands of Congressman Clarence Long, chairman of the House Foreign Operations Subcommittee of the Appropriations Committee.

For these reasons, some White House officials favored using the presidential emergency powers, just as Reagan had done in 1981 and 1982. Under Section 506(a) of the Foreign Assistance Act, Reagan could send up to $75 million in military aid immediately, without congressional approval. On February 22, Secretary of Defense Weinberger told the House Foreign Affairs Committee that Reagan would probably use this authority to give the Salvadorans an additional $60 million in military aid.[16]

Congress was intensely opposed to Reagan using this device again to circumvent its control of the purse strings. In 1981 and 1982, 68 percent of military aid to El Salvador ($80 million out of $118 million) had been sent this way. Congress was so angry about Reagan's use of 506(a) in 1982 that it rejected a routine proposal to reimburse the Pentagon for the $55 million sent to the Salvadorans.

As word circulated that the emergency option was being considered once again, congressional pressure against it mounted rapidly. Warned by both Democrats and Republicans not to use the emergency authority lest its whole policy be put at risk, the White House decided that discretion was the better part of valor.[17] Instead, the administration decided to reprogram $60 million in emergency military aid and seek another $50 million in a supplemental appropriation. Consequently, Reagan's confrontation with Congress manifested itself in two major battles: one over reprogramming and a second over the supplemental bill and the regular FY 1984 foreign aid bill, which moved through the legislative process in tandem.

The reprogramming battle was fought first. Once the request was submitted to the relevant congressional committees, they had fifteen days to disapprove the request or the administration was free to go ahead with the reprogramming. Reagan had to fight on three separate battlefields—the House and Senate appropriations subcommittees on Foreign Operations and the Senate Foreign Relations Committee.[18]

In the Senate, the huge size of the administration's new aid requests led several prominent moderates from both parties to break with the president.

Senator Nancy Kassebaum was the first. A thoughtful, middle-of-the-road Republican from Kansas, Kassebaum was often a swing vote on the Senate Foreign Relations Committee, where the GOP held only a one-vote majority. In 1981, she was a key supporter of Senator Christopher Dodd's certification proposal—support that assured its passage in both the committee and on the Senate floor. Recognizing her influence, the Reagan administration had selected her as a member of the official observer team to the 1982 Salvadoran elections. The enormity of the turnout and the evident enthusiasm of Salvadorans for the election impressed the senator, and she returned ready to support Reagan's policy.

A year later, however, Kassebaum's confidence had begun to wane. Even before the administration's request for $110 million in new military aid, she had become convinced that the policy led to a dead end. Like many of her colleagues, she considered negotiations the logical alternative. "We need to find some framework for talks with the guerrillas," she said in February, announcing that she would not support further increases in military aid.[19]

The other prominent defector from the ranks of administration supporters was Senator Daniel K. Inouye of Hawaii. Inouye, the senior Democrat on the Senate Foreign Operations Subcommittee, had initially supported Reagan's Central America policy because he believed that foreign policy was primarily the prerogative of the president. An even-tempered man of considered judgment and honesty, Inouye had great influence among his Senate colleagues. Democratic leader Robert Byrd, in particular, looked to Inouye for guidance on foreign policy issues where Byrd himself felt ill at ease.

So when Inouye rose on the Senate floor on March 14 to say he would oppose further military aid unless negotiations began, it was a severe blow to administration prospects. "I agonized over this," Inouye explained. "One cannot easily forget Vietnam, especially if you had to live through that experience." A World War II hero who lost an arm from his wounds, Inouye had supported the war in Vietnam until 1969. He was also moved by the mail he received from his constituents. "In my mailbag, for each letter of support for our involvement in El Salvador, perhaps twenty-five are in opposition," Inouye said. Some of the letters came from fellow veterans of the 442nd Infantry. "These are from men who seldom write," he noted, but now they were asking him, " 'Don't you think one Vietnam is enough?' "[20]

When Reagan announced the new aid request for El Salvador, Senator Dodd set about building a coalition with Kassebaum and Inouye to limit and condition any additional military aid. With Inouye on Foreign Operations and both Dodd and Kassebaum on Foreign Relations, the three were well situated to give the administration headaches.

On none of the three committees reviewing the reprogramming request were there enough votes to either approve or reject the administration's request outright. The Senate Foreign Operations Subcommittee was the most amenable to Reagan. Chaired by conservative Robert Kasten (R-Wis.), most of its Republican majority were Reagan loyalists. Yet even here, Secretary of State George Shultz met vigorous criticism when he came to explain the policy. Even senators who had been supporting Reagan were getting fed up, especially after the Salvadoran courts again postponed the trial of the guardsmen accused of killing the U.S. churchwomen. "They're thumbing their nose at us," Senator J. Bennett Johnston (D-La.) complained.

Shultz was uncomfortable in the role of advocate on behalf of the Salvadoran regime, given its atrocious human rights record. "You cannot defend what has happened under the judicial system of El Salvador," Shultz admitted. "I will not do it. I do not do it. I do not think it is defensible. . . . In the end, if they do not clean up this act, the support is going to dry up. They have been told that. They know that, and it will happen." But on the essentials of the policy, Shultz was unyielding. "We will not support negotiations that short-circuit the democratic process and carve up power behind the people's back."[21]

Personal lobbying by the president convinced wavering Republicans not to reject his request outright, and Inouye was forced to compromise. In what Kasten called a "modified victory" for the administration, the committee approved all $60 million as requested, but tied the money to a series of conditions. It demanded that the administration agree "in writing" to limit the number of U.S. advisers to fifty-five; "begin a new and immediate effort" to strengthen the Salvadoran judicial system and to press for progress in the cases of murdered U.S. citizens; and to "take the initiative" in bringing about "unconditional discussions between the government of El Salvador and its adversaries on the holding of free, fair and safe elections, and any other subject of concern between the parties." Only the two most liberal senators on the committee, Democrat Patrick Leahy of Vermont and Republican Mark Hatfield of Oregon, refused to go along with the compromise.[22]

In the Senate Foreign Relations Committee, Dodd and Kassebaum labored hard to win over as many of their colleagues as possible. In the end, all the Democrats and all but five Republicans signed on to a compromise that cut the reprogramming request in half, approving only $30 million, and added a series of nonbinding policy recommendations echoing the conditions that had been imposed by the Foreign Operations Subcommittee.[23]

That left only the House Foreign Operations Subcommittee—Doc Long's committee—to rule on the reprogramming request. With a majority of Democrats, Long's committee was the most hostile to Reagan's policy. But Long himself, who had opposed military aid to El Salvador in 1981 and 1982, had begun to change his mind. "I shifted from being totally opposed to more military aid to being open-minded," Long said after a trip to El Salvador in early 1983. "But the administration has to understand that without a move toward a broad-based political solution, they're not going to get the money. I'm not going to support throwing money down a bigger and bigger rat hole." Long himself thus became the key swing vote on the subcommittee. "There is no question Mr. Long is a very powerful man in this situation," said a senior administration official. "He holds his finger on our jugular vein."[24]

Several factors contributed to the softening of Long's opposition. One was the 1982 election in El Salvador. Another was the U.S. embassy's success in convincing Long that the likely result of cutting off aid would be a rightist coup. "If we said, 'No money,' I don't think the guerrillas would take over. The right-wing military would move in and there would be a bloodbath."[25] Of equal importance in the conversion of Doc Long was the solicitous effort Enders invested in him and the red-carpet treatment Long received in El Salvador—no doubt stage-managed by the U.S. embassy. Shortly after Long visited the blasted buildings of Berlín, the Salvadoran government announced that a new school being built there with U.S. AID funds would be named the Clarence D. Long Nursery School and Kindergarten.[26]

Enders worked so hard on Long that conservatives in the administration charged Enders with pandering to the chairman. "He treats Doc Long as though he was deputy assistant secretary of state," groused one White House aide.[27] But Enders knew what he was doing. Doc Long wanted to influence policy. If treated seriously, and if his views were listened to, he was amenable to compromise.

For all his eccentricities, Long was a smart enough politician to know that outright, uncompromising opposition would yield nothing in terms of policy change. You had to give a little to get a little. What Long hoped to get was a series of commitments from the administration on human rights and negotiations. George Shultz, Long warned, had better come "loaded with hard stuff to please me" if he wanted any more military aid.[28] And Long demanded his assurances in writing.

After six weeks of bargaining, a deal was struck. On human rights, Long demanded that the Salvadoran government free political prisoners; President Magaña agreed to undertake a case-by-case review and free those charged with minor offenses. Long demanded that the government allow the International Red Cross unrestricted access to its prisons; Magaña agreed. Long demanded that the Reagan administration allow the families of the murdered churchwomen to review the FBI's evidence in the case; the administration agreed to appoint a high-level independent jurist to review the case (Judge Harold R. Tyler Jr.). And Long demanded that the Salvadoran government abolish the Treasury Police and the Civil Defense forces, both of which were notorious for their abuse of civilians. This was the one demand that the Salvadoran government flatly rejected.[29]

The drama, however, centered on the issue of negotiations. Long wanted the administration to change its attitude toward a negotiated settlement of the war, and he insisted that Reagan appoint a special envoy to broker talks between the Salvadoran government and the guerrillas. Long wanted an envoy of such eminence that he could operate virtually independent of administration control. As Long himself put it, "I think we need somebody whose stature is so great that once they appoint him they can't pull the rug out from under him."[30] Not surprisingly, the administration's initial reaction was decidedly hostile.

But as the bargaining with Doc Long dragged on, the idea of a special envoy began to seem less noxious. In the first place, Ronald Reagan, not Doc Long, would appoint the envoy, and he would report to the president, not Long's committee. The appointment of an envoy would give weight to Reagan's insistence that he was not seeking a military solution to the war, but it would not require any substantive change in policy. The envoy could be tasked to try to bring the Salvadoran guerrillas into the electoral process, and nothing more. This finesse was possible because Long himself did not challenge the core premise of the administration's position on negotiations—that "powersharing" was unacceptable. Once that was conceded, the distance between Long's position and the administration's was relatively small—or at least it could be made to appear so.[31]

The administration came around to accept Doc Long's demand for a special envoy, thus assuring his support for half of its reprogramming request. On April 26, the House Foreign Operations Subcommittee voted 7–6 to approve the reprogramming of $30 million in additional military aid for El Salvador, with Doc Long casting the deciding vote.[32] To Long's chagrin, Reagan then appointed Richard Stone, the hard-line former senator who only a few weeks earlier had been appointed chief salesman for the Central America policy. Nothing better exemplified the administration's attitude toward the congressional demand for negotiations in El Salvador—it was a public relations problem.

As a result of the reprogramming debate, the administration publicly accepted the idea of "unconditional dialogue," which it interpreted to mean talks about elections, in which either side could "raise any issue they wish," Shultz wrote to Doc Long. Nevertheless, he added, "The U.S. will not support negotiations for powersharing."[33] Ironically, this was exactly the sort of cosmetic shift in policy that Enders had gotten into such trouble for advocating in January. He had been proved right after all, but it did not save his job.

The Limit on Advisers

The issue of the U.S. military advisers was exemplary of how the Reagan administration dealt with the rising tide of congressional opposition to its policy in El Salvador. Rumors that Reagan might increase the number of advisers put the issue high on the agenda of the congressional committees that reviewed Reagan's reprogramming request. The Pentagon, of course, had long been pushing to deploy more advisers than the White House felt was politically wise. Under Jimmy Carter, the military wanted several dozen, and Ambassador Robert White earned the Pentagon's enmity by holding the number down to just a handful. When Reagan escalated the U.S. military role in early 1981, the Pentagon pressed for upward of 150 advisers, but had to settle for just 55. In a statement that administration officials would later come to rue, Undersecretary of State Walter J. Stoessel promised the Senate Appropriations Committee in March 1981 that the administration would not exceed this "cap" without consulting Congress.[34] Thus the number of fifty-five advisers became a kind of talisman, a mystical marker that Congress used to reassure itself that the administration was not sliding down the slippery slope.

When the war in El Salvador proved more difficult than anticipated, the Pentagon chafed under what it regarded as an artificial limit. "The number has taken on a life of its own and has become much more important than it should be," a senior Defense official complained in 1983. "Any increase, no matter how insignificant in actual numbers, would be portrayed as a major American escalation. That's foolish."[35]

When administration hard-liners decided to expand the U.S. commitment in 1983, the first item on the Pentagon's agenda was to lift the ceiling on the number of advisers and to relax their rules of engagement so they could get into the field and watch their students in action. In practice, the advisers' operational rules had already evolved considerably. Sometimes they ventured into the field in contested areas carrying their M-16s, though their original rules of engagement limited them to side arms so they would not be "equipped for combat," and therefore trigger the War Powers Resolution. Sometimes the advisers actually engaged in combat operations. "The trick is not to get caught," one of them explained.[36]

In February 1983, Staff Sergeant Jay T. Stanley became the first U.S. military casualty of the war when his helicopter took ground fire, wounding him. The original account of the incident—that the helicopter was ferrying Stanley and other advisers to repair a radio relay station—proved to be a cover story. After an investigation, the U.S. embassy admitted that two helicopters carrying U.S. advisers had been directing Salvadoran combat operations from the air during the final phases of the battle of Berlín. Three advisers responsible for the incident were ordered out of El Salvador.[37]

The wounding of Sergeant Stanley did not long delay the Pentagon's drive to change the limits on the advisory mission. By the end of February, Secretary Weinberger was once again telling Congress that fifty-five advisers were inadequate and that it would be "useful" to have ten to twenty more.[38] Behind the scenes, the military was pushing for a larger increase. General Wallace H. Nutting wanted three hundred advisers immediately and an open-ended commitment to send as many more as necessary. Some officers thought that five hundred would eventually be needed.[39]

A few days later, National Security Adviser William Clark, speaking on background, told the press that the president was considering whether to lift the fifty-five-adviser ceiling and relax the advisers' rules of engagement.[40] That sparked a quick and largely negative reaction on Capitol Hill—so much so that administration officials spent the next several days denying that any change in the number or role of the advisers was contemplated.[41] But in fact, the White House was reviewing the Pentagon's request to let advisers be assigned to brigade headquarters in the provinces in order to exert greater influence over the intermediate level of command, where the Salvadoran army was weakest. The advisers would still not be sent into combat, but they would get a lot closer to it.[42]

Both of the Senate committees that considered Reagan's reprogramming request explicitly opposed any change in the number or status of the advisers. The Senate Foreign Operations Subcommittee conditioned its approval on "a reaffirmation, by the President . . . that the number of advisers and trainers will not exceed fifty-five persons."[43] The administration deftly refused to give such an assurance, instead reaffirming an earlier pledge to "consult with the Congress on changes in the number of U.S. military personnel."[44] This was not what the committee had demanded, but it never called the administration to account for this willful misreading.

The issue of advisers became even more sensitive on May 25, 1983, when Lieutenant Commander Albert A. Schaufelberger, a naval officer and deputy commander of the Military Group, was assassinated by guerrilla commandos. *Newsweek* put Schaufelberger on its cover under the headline "The First Casualty," but both Republicans and Democrats were restrained in their response to the killing.[45] Democrats did not want to appear disrespectful of the dead soldier by reminding the administration that they had warned this would happen. Republicans did not want to draw further attention to the anomaly of an adviser in a supposedly noncombat situation getting killed. Schaufelberger's death put an effective end to any possibility that the administration might decide to openly discard the fifty-five-adviser limit. Even after administration hard-liners consolidated control over Central America policy, senior White House officials rejected a new Defense Department proposal to increase the number of advisers to 125.[46]

Instead, the administration devised several ways around the limit. One was to simply expand the size and mission of the advisers without admitting it. While the press was reporting that Reagan had rejected a proposal to formally change the advisers' operational guidelines, in practice the guidelines were changing. As early as May 1983, Mobile Training Teams were stationed outside San Salvador, training infantry troops in the fiercely contested provinces of San Vicente and La Unión. In San Vicente, U.S. advisers began to accompany Salvadoran units on training missions in the field. By August, operations and training teams were stationed in brigade headquarters outside the capital as well. In 1984, advisers began making field trips to front-line command posts during army offensive operations against the guerrillas.[47]

The size of the advisory mission more than doubled during the same period by the simple expedient of changing the definition of who was a military "trainer," so that fewer of the personnel assigned to El Salvador would count against the fifty-five-man limit. In 1981, all U.S. military personnel in El Salvador counted. By mid-1983, the embassy's Marine guards, the military assistance group, the military attaché's office, a twenty-six-member military medical training team, and advisers in administration and communications had all been excluded from the category of "trainer." In total, there were 102 military personnel stationed in El Salvador in August 1983 and dozens more who regularly flew in on temporary duty from their official posts in Honduras and Panama. In effect, the Pentagon managed to achieve and even exceed its goal of putting 125 advisers in El Salvador, while insisting that the fifty-five-man ceiling had not been breached. Administration spokesmen insisted with a straight face that they were not playing "a numbers game."[48] But officers in the field joked about who was and who was not a "counter"—who counted against the limit.[49]

The administration's principal solution to the shortage of U.S. advisers in El Salvador was to train the Salvadorans (or "Salvos," as the advisers called them) next door in Honduras. In May 1983, the Pentagon unveiled a plan to open a Regional Military Training Center there staffed by 125 U.S. advisers.[50] Some Hondurans ("Hondos") were slated for training too, in order to soothe the nationalist sensitivities of the Hondurans, for whom El Salvador was a traditional enemy.

Tripling the number of advisers in Honduras did not cause much furor in Congress because there was virtually no risk that any of them would get killed. In addition, training Salvadorans in Honduras was vastly cheaper than bringing them to the United States. By keeping training costs down, the Pentagon could stretch its limited military aid dollars a lot farther.[51]

Unfortunately, the Regional Training Center violated the Honduran constitution, which prohibited the presence of foreign military troops on Honduran soil unless explicitly approved by the Honduran Congress. Neither the United States nor Honduran military commander General Gustavo Alvarez had bothered to even inform the Honduran Congress, let alone seek its approval. This proved momentarily embarrassing, since Washington had been lauding Honduras's progress toward democratic civilian rule. The dilemma was resolved when the Honduran military redefined the Salvadorans as "students" rather than "soldiers," and then sought congressional agreement.[52] By that time, the base had already been set up, the U.S. Green Berets and their Salvadoran "students" had arrived, and the training program was under way. The Honduran Congress gave its consent. But regardless of what they were called, the Salvadorans' presence in Honduras angered many Hondurans, including some key members of the officer corps who had fought the Salvadoran army in the 1969 "Soccer War."[53]

One final device for getting around the adviser limit was to send in additional advisers covertly, financed not by the Defense Department but by the CIA. If advisers were sent as part of an intelligence operation, only the intelligence committees of Congress had to be informed. One such program involved training special Salvadoran military units for Long Range Reconnaissance Patrols (LRRPs). These units undertook deep-penetration operations into guerrilla territory, located concentrations of rebel troops, and called in airstrikes on them. Not only did U.S. advisers train Salvadoran LRRPs, but they also accompanied them on combat missions until 1985.[54] Throughout this period, administration officials regularly assured Congress, falsely, that U.S. advisers were not involved in combat. If any of the regular contingent of military advisers had been assigned combat duty, the administration would have been compelled to report to Congress under the War Powers Resolution. By sending advisers into combat under the cover of an intelligence operation, the administration could claim the War Powers Resolution did not apply.

The issue of advisers was indicative of the Reagan administration's attitude toward congressional efforts to restrain its policy. Administration officials saw Congress as interfering in the president's prerogatives. Congressionally imposed limits were largely ignored, circumvented whenever possible, or obeyed only in a technical sense. Never did the administration allow them to seriously interfere with its conduct of the war.[55]

Reagan Charges Up Capitol Hill

As the smoke cleared from the reprogramming battles in March and April 1983, the administration had won only half the money it requested, and even that was weighed down with numerous conditions. Yet given the rising tide of opposition, President Reagan had to count himself lucky to have gotten anything at all. Even before the reprogramming battle ended, Congress gave other indications that the hard-liners' plans to escalate the war in Central America would meet stiff resistance. On April 12, Congressman Michael Barnes's subcommittee (renamed Western Hemisphere Affairs in the Ninety-eighth Congress) rejected the administration's entire request for $50 million in supplemental military aid for El Salvador (for FY 1983). At the same time, the subcommittee began work on the FY 1984–85 foreign aid bill by cutting the administration's request for military aid for El Salvador from $86.3 million annually to $50 million, capping the number of U.S. advisers at fifty-five, cutting military aid to Honduras by half, banning military aid to Guatemala entirely, and prohibiting U.S. support for the contra rebels in Nicaragua.[56]

And that was not the worst of it. The committee also adopted a new certification bill proposed by Congressman Solarz that tightened the conditions required of the Salvadoran government and gave Congress the right to approve or reject President Reagan's certification reports. Whereas the existing certification legislation called for progress in various areas, the Solarz bill demanded accomplishments, among them an end to human rights abuses by government forces, trials of officials guilty of previous abuses, and negotiations with the guerrillas. If Congress found the president's certification unconvincing, within thirty days it could pass a concurrent resolution disapproving the report, thereby terminating military aid. In that event, the bill also prohibited the president from invoking his emergency authority to circumvent the ban.[57]

Solarz himself admitted that mandating such a complex, restrictive set of conditions was perhaps not the ideal way to conduct foreign policy, but he defended it as Congress's only option. "We are not on the same wavelength as the administration," said Solarz. "We have no alternative."[58] On April 19, the full House Foreign Affairs Committee upheld the subcommittee's recommendation that the entire $50 million in supplemental military aid for El Salvador be denied.[59]

While the Foreign Affairs Committee was demolishing the administration's overt foreign aid program, the House Intelligence Committee was preparing to prohibit further U.S. aid to the Nicaraguan contras. "We are on a downward roll with Congress right now," one administration official glumly admitted.[60]

The day after the full House Foreign Affairs Committee gutted the supplemental military aid request for El Salvador, the White House decided that the president should appear before a joint session of Congress to appeal for support on Central America. Apart from the annual State of the Union address, presidential appearances before Congress were rare and dramatic events, reserved only for issues of the gravest importance. By going to the Hill, Reagan would guarantee himself a broad national television audience as well as the concentrated attention of the lawmakers. "He's giving the speech," explained a White House official, "because he thinks that the fate of American policy in the region hangs in the balance."[61]

The gambit was risky. By identifying himself so directly with such an unpopular issue, Reagan might damage his own popularity. If his appeals failed to stem congressional efforts to upend his policy, the failure would be his alone. In politics, where the appearance of power is very much part of its substance, a president could be crippled by confronting Congress head-on and losing. "There is a high risk to this," a senior official conceded, "but it's a higher risk not to do it."[62]

Republican congressional leaders were initially against the idea of a presidential speech to a joint session, fearing that it would further polarize the House along partisan lines. Even a presidential appearance, they warned, would not assure that they could muster the votes to turn back the liberal Democrats' challenge. But in the White House, the president's top political advisers were confident that a major speech by Reagan would have a significant impact. Their polls told them that the president's television address in March (known as the "Star Wars" speech because in it Reagan had announced his commitment to a space-based ballistic missile defense system) had energized new public support for the administration's defense buildup. Perhaps a repeat performance on Central America would work equally well.[63]

On April 27, 1983, when Reagan went before Congress, he emphasized U.S. support for democracy, reforms, human rights, and negotiations. Military aid, the president assured Congress, was not an end in itself, but "a shield for democratization, economic development, and diplomacy." Moreover, he was not asking for much; his entire aid budget for Central America was only $600 million. "That's less than one-tenth of what Americans will spend this year on coin-operated video games," Reagan beseeched. He invoked the memory of the Truman Doctrine, the cornerstone of bipartisan foreign policy in a bygone era. "The national security of all the Americas is at stake in Central America," Reagan warned. "If we cannot defend ourselves there, we cannot expect to prevail elsewhere. Our credibility would collapse, our alliances would crumble, and the safety of our homeland would be put in jeopardy."

In addition to the heavy emphasis on national security, the speech contained a new theme—the threat of blame. Only one sentence in the speech carried the warning, but it was the last sentence, and it was pointed. "Who among us," the president intoned, "would wish to bear responsibility for failing to meet our shared obligation?"[64] Lest the import of this be missed, administration briefers were more direct. If Congress did not give Reagan the resources he needed for Central America, then he would blame it for the policy's failure.[65]

Reagan did not concede any fundamental points of policy, so his critics were not impressed. Most Democrats sat quietly through the speech, joining the Republicans in applause only when Reagan pledged, "Let me say to those who invoke the memory of Vietnam, there is no thought of sending American combat troops to Central America." To the president's chagrin, it was the biggest hand he got all evening.[66]

In the days following the speech, administration officials honed their "politics of blame" barbs by directing them at Senator Christopher Dodd, who had delivered the Democratic response to Reagan's speech. Jeane Kirkpatrick called Dodd's reply "demagogic" and "an irresponsible attack on administration policy."[67] Soon, the attacks became broader and, once again, Kirkpatrick led the charge. "There is a plan to create a Communist Central America," she wrote in an op-ed piece for the *Washington Post*. Congress was unwilling to prevent it because "a very well organized lobby" had made the anti-Communist side seem "unbearably unfashionable." Opponents of administration policy were not simply people with a different assessment of the national interest or the nature of the problem. They were part of "well-orchestrated international campaigns" defaming the Salvadoran government. If Congress cut off aid to the Nicaraguan contras, Kirkpatrick said in conclusion, it would become "the enforcer of the Brezhnev doctrine of irreversible Communist revolution."[68]

"There are people in the U.S. Congress who do not approve of our efforts to consolidate the constitutional government of El Salvador and who would actually like to see the Marxist forces take power in that country," Kirkpatrick told an interviewer a few weeks later. When outraged members of Congress demanded that Kirkpatrick name whom she had in mind, she demurred, insisting that she had been quoted out of context—the same explanation she used in 1980 after accusing the four U.S. churchwomen murdered in El Salvador of having been political activists on behalf of the guerrillas.[69]

A few days later, William Clark called Reagan's opponents advocates of Marxism who "dishonor our country."[70] Shortly thereafter, the administration released a background paper on Central America, in which it described international opposition to U.S. policy as a product of Communist intelligence operations.[71]

Undersecretary of Defense Fred C. Iklé blasted Congress on the day it returned to Washington from summer recess: "As long as Congress keeps crippling the president's military assistance program, we will have a policy always shy of success," Iklé declared. Clearly and defiantly, Iklé spelled out the hard-liners' agenda in Central America: "We do not seek a military defeat for our friends. We do not seek a military stalemate. We seek victory for the forces of democracy."[72]

"We've had it with the opposition in Congress," a senior official said. "We're fed up with their interference on the one hand and their lack of support on the other."[73]

Congress Gives In

Within a few days of Reagan's speech to the joint session of Congress, amid administration attacks on the patriotism of its opponents, congressional moderates who had been leaning against Reagan's policy began falling into line—or at least seeking political cover. "That last question of the Reagan speech hangs heavy over their heads," explained an aide to the Senate Democratic leadership.[74]

House Foreign Affairs Committee Chairman Clement Zablocki was frank: "I certainly don't want to be accused of losing El Salvador by voting against more aid."[75] On May 11, Zablocki's committee voted 13–10 to reverse its earlier rejection of the president's request for $50 million in supplemental military aid for El Salvador. It only approved an additional $8.7 million, but the vote was a clear signal that the liberals were going to be outvoted on the committee by a coalition of Republican stalwarts and moderate Democrats who were suddenly running scared.[76]

Compromise and bipartisanship suddenly became watchwords among moderate Democrats. On the House Foreign Affairs Committee, Dante B. Fascell of Florida, the second-ranking Democrat, began trying to fashion a compromise on El Salvador. After much horse trading, Fascell was able to patch together a package that passed the Foreign Affairs Committee by a vote of 36–1. The Republicans accepted Fascell's compromise because it gave the administration $65 million in military aid (about 75 percent of the requested level of $86.3 million) for each of the next two years. The liberals accepted it because it required Reagan to certify that the government of El Salvador was making continued progress on human rights, agrarian reform, and trials for the killers of U.S. citizens and, most important, that it had begun "a dialogue, in good faith and without preconditions, with all major parties to the conflict." Moreover, the compromise gave Congress the right to reject Reagan's certification reports.[77]

The Republicans ranted and raved during the debate over the details of the bill. Congressman Henry Hyde of Illinois denounced the restrictions placed on the administration, charging, "We have taken the president, put him in a straitjacket, locked him in a trunk, and dropped him in the river." But when all was said and done, Hyde was not unhappy with the outcome. "If you can't get dinner," he shrugged, "you get a sandwich." Another senior Republican on the committee, Robert J. Lagomarsino of California, was also pleased. "The president is getting what he wants. Congress, two weeks ago, was against the whole thing. . . . The president's speech made a difference."[78]

In the Senate, where the Democrats were in the minority, compromise had always been the order of the day. After long negotiation, the Foreign Relations Committee came up with a formula that both Republicans and Democrats could accept. Much milder than the House bill, the Senate package extended the existing certification requirement with only minor modifications. It also gave Reagan 88 percent of the funds he requested.[79]

The 1983 congressional battle over aid to El Salvador ended anticlimactically. Neither the House nor Senate enacted a foreign aid authorization bill for FY 1984, so there was no dramatic floor debate over El Salvador to test the relative strength of Reagan's supporters and opponents. Instead, funding for El Salvador had to be handled once again by continuing resolution, which provided $64.8 million in military aid (75 percent of the $86.3 million requested), and did not extend the 1981 certification requirements. Instead, 30 percent of the military aid could not be distributed until the Salvadorans had reached a verdict in the trial of the National Guardsmen accused of killing the U.S. churchwomen, and 10 percent was withheld pending a presidential certification that the agrarian reform was making progress.[80]

The relative weakness of these constraints resulted from the Democrats' submissiveness in the wake of Reagan's invasion of the small Caribbean island of Grenada—a quick military strike that had the dual virtue of being both successful and enormously popular. The October invasion came just a few weeks before the continuing resolution was enacted, and it gave a big boost to public support for Reagan's handling of foreign policy generally and his handling of Central America in particular.[81]

Vox Populi

Why Reagan's speech and the Republicans' threats of recrimination set off such panic in the ranks of Democratic moderates was not self-evident. Opinion polls were unanimous in recording broad opposition to the administration's policies in El Salvador. Ever since Alexander Haig had first put the issue of Central America in the headlines in 1981, the trend in public opinion had run consistently against the administration, and every time the issue flared up, the polls got worse. In dozens of polls taken from 1981 to 1984, public support for Reagan's "handling of the situation in El Salvador" never rose above 40 percent and averaged only about 28 percent. A private poll for the White House by pollster Richard Wirthlin confirmed the findings of the public surveys.[82]

On the face of it, the politics of the Central America issue seemed to favor Reagan's opponents, yet there was a deep reluctance among the Democratic leadership to do battle head to head with the president. The Democrats simply didn't trust the polls. Opinion could change, and on foreign policy issues about which people had little knowledge, it could change very fast. Although every poll showed strong opposition to Reagan's policy, most people did not regard Central America as very important, and they knew little about it. A third of the public did not even know which side the United States was backing in El Salvador or Nicaragua.[83] When attitudes are so shallowly rooted, sudden events can produce dramatic shifts in opinion. This is especially true in foreign policy, where the president can evoke a surge of patriotism (the "rally 'round the flag" effect, as the pollsters refer to it) with dramatic action in a moment of crisis.

The Democrats' anxieties were exacerbated by the active role Reagan took in the 1983 debate on El Salvador. For most of the first two years of his administration, he had stood aloof from the issue. Once he joined the fray, Democrats worried that his political muscle might produce a major shift in public views. When the White House began threatening recriminations, the Democrats became even more reluctant to press their attack. Speaker Tip O'Neill might have rallied the Democrats to stand firm; he thought Reagan's Central American policy was a disaster. But after losing the budget battles of 1981 because of the defection en masse of southern conservative Democrats, he was unwilling to further divide his party by leading the charge on Central America.

Ideologically, the southerners tended to agree with Reagan's assessment of the threat. Even when the moderates among them began having doubts about the efficacy of Reagan's strategy, they still worried that the deeply imbued patriotism of their constituents made them politically vulnerable if they opposed a popular president over foreign policy. Their concern extended beyond their own votes, which they normally cast in favor of Reagan's aid proposals. If the national Democratic Party itself was seen as battling the president, the boll weevils would be hurt politically at home, and their personal voting records might not be sufficient safeguard. Within the House Democratic caucus, the moderate and conservative southerners consistently urged caution on their northern liberal colleagues. The national polling results, the southerners insisted, meant nothing in their constituencies.

Throughout 1983, the Democrats' tried to extract an ironclad pledge that the administration and the government of El Salvador would honestly try to settle the war by negotiation. In the end, they settled for mere promises that the administration would be more supportive of talks and that the Salvadoran government would continue to make progress on human rights and agrarian reform. The Democrats remained trapped in a familiar dilemma, summed up perfectly by Congressman Solarz: "We do not want to see a guerrilla victory, but we do not want to see the United States provide assistance to a government whose security forces remain responsible for the abduction and torture of thousands of people."[84] Yet in 1983, these were precisely the choices.

Despite the best efforts of the White House troika to keep Ronald Reagan insulated from the issue of Central America, the president was forced to lead the battle for his policy lest it be lost on Capitol Hill. Committing Reagan's formidable political skills to the debate stemmed the tide of congressional rebelliousness, but only because the president followed the advice of administration hard-liners and turned Central America into a loyalty test.

The president's high profile was at best a temporary expedient. Like the 1982 election in El Salvador, its chief virtue was that it bought some time before congressional doubts reasserted themselves. Yet public opinion remained hostile to U.S. involvement in Central America, and the divisiveness of Reagan's confrontational style did nothing to build a broad bipartisan consensus behind his policy. Without such a consensus, the policy would never be self-sustaining; every year, the administration would have to find some new gimmick to extract the necessary resources from a reluctant Congress. Confrontation virtually guaranteed that Congress would disburse funds only grudgingly, never giving the administration enough to fully finance its strategy. With the situation on the ground getting worse rather than better, more and more money was needed just to maintain equilibrium.

The hard-liners had set out to take control of administration policy, believing that its problems were due principally to Enders's temerity. Once in charge, they expected to sweep away congressional opposition by dint of sheer political willpower and Ronald Reagan's skill in front of the camera. Enders and the State Department pragmatists were vanquished soon enough, but the hard-liners discovered that making Reagan's policy work, either in El Salvador or on Capitol Hill, was not so simple.

CHAPTER 10

The Politics of Murder

Despite the power of the hard-liners, George Shultz sent Ambassador Thomas Pickering to El Salvador in August 1983 with a mandate to continue the policy that Thomas Enders and Deane Hinton had designed. Pickering was to guide Alvaro Magaña's government toward presidential elections as soon as possible, pressure it to improve human rights, resist rightist attempts to cripple the agrarian reform, and support those military officers willing to follow U.S. advice on how to fight the war. Even Enders's "two-track" policy of combining increased military aid with talks between the Salvadoran government and the guerrillas was still official U.S. policy.

The resilience of Enders's strategy, despite his departure in May 1983, was due to the short-lived character of the hard-liners' dominion. Although Shultz was unable to protect Enders from the wrath of William Clark and Jeane Kirkpatrick, he did get Reagan to reaffirm the basic outlines of the State Department's approach, especially the need for reforms in El Salvador to sustain public and congressional support for military assistance.[1] The key to the resurgence of the State Department pragmatists, however, was the sudden departure of William Clark as national security adviser.

Musical Chairs

Although the alliance of Clark, Kirkpatrick, Casey, Weinberger, and Meese handily defeated Shultz and Enders in the spring of 1983, their strategy of making Central America a high-profile issue sparked resistance from the pragmatists on the White House staff, especially James Baker and Michael Deaver. The schism in the White House opened in early 1983 when Clark, heady with success at having displaced Shultz on Central America, proposed that James Baker's post as chief of staff be abolished and that he (Clark) be given co-equal status with the three members of the original troika (Baker, Deaver, and Meese). Baker and Deaver regarded Clark's rising influence as a threat, and together they blocked Clark's reorganization plan.

There were substantive differences between the two camps as well. Clark and Baker disagreed on how foreign policy issues should be managed politically. Clark reinforced Reagan's anti-Communist instincts and urged the president to speak out more forcefully and more often. Baker saw the power and popularity of the president as a finite resource, to be husbanded rather than squandered on unpopular causes. Clark's approach to Congress was confrontational. Baker was inclined toward flexibility and conciliation; he regarded Clark as ideologically rigid and politically naive.[2]

Central America became a central point of contention between the Clark and Baker factions. "Clark really felt strongly about Central America," said a senior foreign policy official. "He was instrumental in drawing the lines and getting the president excited about it."[3] Baker and Deaver were not so enthused. Baker had reluctantly gone along with the decision to have Reagan address a joint session of Congress in April 1983, but he was not comfortable elevating this contentious foreign policy issue to the top of the president's agenda. He worried that it would revive the image of Reagan as, in the words of one White House official, "a jingoistic warmonger."[4]

The returns on Clark's high-profile campaign on Central America started coming in right away from pollster Richard Wirthlin's surveys—Baker was right. Central America was still dangerous for Ronald Reagan. The tough line rekindled public concern about the "war and peace issue," which had dogged Reagan all through 1981 and into 1982.[5] (The hard-liners' schemes were so frequently stymied by the political verdicts of Wirthlin's polls that they began referring to him as "Richard Worthless.")[6]

Clark's close relationship with Reagan made it impossible for Baker and Deaver to challenge him directly, but the animosity between the two factions was palpable. Baker and his allies waged the same kind of "guerrilla war" of deprecating leaks against Clark that they had used to good effect against Alexander Haig. Clark was so ignorant of international affairs, one White House aide quipped, that his management of foreign policy was "content-free."[7]

Baker and Deaver worried that Clark, in one of his private meetings with the president, might talk Reagan into approving some wild foreign policy adventure. They set up an elaborate system to track both Clark and William Casey's meetings with Reagan, after which Deaver would casually drop in on the president and debrief him. "The crazies want to get us into war," Baker warned Deaver. "We cannot get this economic recovery program going if we get involved in a land war in Central America." Since Reagan had a habit of agreeing with whomever spoke to him last, Deaver and Baker could usually talk him out of whatever scheme Clark or Casey had proposed.[8]

Clark also had to contend with the State Department. Though Clark had vanquished the pragmatists, George Shultz had not surrendered unconditionally. When Shultz met face to face with Reagan in May 1983 over the direction of policy on Central America and the fate of Tom Enders, the deal they struck was straightforward. In exchange for Enders's head, Reagan agreed to give control over the policy back to the Department of State. But the hardliners at the NSC were not prepared to part so easily with their newly won power. Shultz tried to reassert control, but found his adversaries at the White House unwilling to yield. When Shultz tried to reaffirm the agreement he thought he had reached with Reagan, he was rebuffed. The National Security Council staff, Reagan said, would continue to play the role it had been playing.[9]

Shultz reached his breaking point in early August. Clark and Weinberger had convinced Reagan to launch massive air and naval exercises around Nicaragua to intimidate the Sandinistas, without informing Shultz. The secretary of state was the one taking most of the flak from Congress. On August 4, Shultz appeared before the Senate Foreign Relations Committee and apologized for the absence of prior consultation. Always the good soldier, he dodged questions as to whether he himself had been consulted. But that same day, Shultz took his complaints directly to Reagan once again.

Shultz recited a long list of grievances about Clark's management of foreign policy, which he called "a disgrace," concluding with an offer to resign. "Mr. President," he said, "you don't need a guy like me for Secretary of State if this is the way things are going to be done."[10] Shultz was usually so low-key that his threat to resign came as a surprise—and a very unpleasant one, since the 1984 presidential campaign loomed on the horizon. "The day Shultz roared," as the confrontation came to be known at the State Department, was a turning point. From then on, Shultz was gradually able to reassert control over policy toward Central America.[11]

Clark had no stomach for such bitter and prolonged infighting. In the summer and fall of 1983, he spoke often to friends about leaving Washington and retiring to his ranch in California. Life in the White House had become "a living hell," he said. In October, when Secretary of the Interior James Watt was forced to resign after making a racial slur, Clark asked Reagan to let him take the vacant cabinet post, and Reagan agreed.[12]

Both inside and outside the administration, conservatives were crestfallen. Without Clark, who would counter the schemes of the White House and State Department pragmatists? "The hard-liners are demoralized," said one senior official. "There are no Reaganites left any more."[13] Of course, there were plenty of hard-liners still at the barricades; Shultz was outnumbered by Casey, Kirkpatrick, and Weinberger. But the conservatives always imagined themselves under siege.

Not surprisingly, a battle immediately erupted over who would replace Clark. He favored his deputy, Robert "Bud" McFarlane, but the other hard-liners worried that McFarlane, who had always held staff positions rather than policymaking ones, was too subdued and colorless to contend with Baker, Deaver, and Shultz.[14] Movement conservatives outside the administration disparaged McFarlane as a "Kissinger protégé," not a real conservative. The hard-liners' favorite was Jeane Kirkpatrick. "She had her heart set on the job and told me so," Reagan wrote later, but she was unacceptable to both Baker and Shultz.[15]

With the decision over Clark's successor deadlocked, Baker and Deaver attempted something of a palace coup. They convinced Reagan to appoint Baker as the new national security adviser and move Deaver into Baker's job as chief of staff. Reagan signed off on the idea without consulting anyone else in the national security bureaucracy, but happened to mention it to Clark before the deal was consummated with a public announcement. Clark quickly gathered hard-line stalwarts Casey, Weinberger, and Meese, and together they confronted the president and talked him out of the idea. Baker was a moderate, they argued; his appointment would send a message of accommodation to the Soviets and to U.S. allies. Reagan seemed genuinely surprised. "I had no idea the fellas would be so adamant," he said when he told Baker the deal was off.[16] Instead of the politically savvy Baker, Reagan picked McFarlane because he was the least objectionable candidate. McFarlane's own military adviser, Admiral John M. Poindexter, moved up to become his deputy.

McFarlane, a retired Marine lieutenant colonel, was a graduate of the Naval Academy (class of 1959). In 1965, he led the first U.S. combat troops ashore at Danang, South Vietnam. In 1973, he joined the NSC staff as Kissinger's military assistant, following in the footsteps of Al Haig. After President Gerald Ford lost to Jimmy Carter in 1976, McFarlane moved to the staff of the Senate Armed Services Committee.[17]

In 1981, he joined the Reagan administration as a special counselor to Haig. When Clark replaced Richard Allen as Reagan's national security adviser, McFarlane went with Clark to the White House as his deputy. Haig's resignation in June 1982 left McFarlane as the senior administration official with the most experience in foreign affairs.

But McFarlane was not a powerful figure. Terribly insecure, he tried to hide his anxieties behind a facade of unemotional, businesslike efficiency. He always spoke in a monotone, using big words and convoluted syntax—as if trying to imbue his thoughts with an aura of profundity. "I think he constructed the McFarlane persona," said colleague Richard Fairbanks. "It's something he worked on. A protective thing."[18] Despite his extensive experience, he lacked self-confidence, and it showed. The other senior players in Reagan's national security bureaucracy did not regard McFarlane as an equal because McFarlane did not see himself as one. "This job is way beyond me," he confided to a friend after he was appointed national security adviser. His enemies in the White House referred to him derisively as "Henry Kissinger Jr."[19]

Clark's departure was not the only blow to the conservative cause. Jeane Kirkpatrick was a casualty of the battle over Clark's successor, undone by the unseemly public way in which she and her allies pursued the job and by her openly bitter complaints to the press when she was passed over. By implication, she was faulting the president's judgment, an act of disloyalty that constituted the highest crime in Reagan's inner circle. Kirkpatrick, it appeared, was willing to be a team player only if she could be one of the captains.[20]

The latest round of musical chairs had come to an end with Kirkpatrick left standing. In the wake of the Clark affair, her influence shriveled. When she left the United Nations in 1985, Reagan did not offer her a position in his second administration that she deemed suitably senior, so she returned to academia.[21]

The National Plan

The problems Ambassador Pickering faced upon arrival in San Salvador were familiar ones. The Magaña government was an artificial coalition held together only at the insistence of the U.S. embassy. A cautious man with no independent base of power, Magaña's instinct was to conciliate everyone, which meant that paralysis was the norm. Magaña's weakness led Washington to push for new elections, which also promised to have a salutary effect in Washington. The 1982 elections had been so favorably received by the U.S. media and Congress that the administration enjoyed a temporary respite from congressional badgering. By 1983, however, the critics were becoming vocal once again. "The euphoria of the Salvadoran elections has worn off," observed Congressman Michael Barnes.[22] The administration was eager to revive it. "One thing Congress can't resist is an election," said a senior administration official, "and assuming we have a fair and open one that elects Duarte, we should be able to prevail in getting more aid for El Salvador."[23]

No real progress was being made at the negotiating table. Through the good offices of Colombian President Belisario Betancur, the FDR-FMLN finally met with representatives of the Salvadoran Peace Commission that Magaña had created in September 1982 at Washington's urging. Still, their positions were irreconcilable, and neither side showed any inclination to bargain. The Peace Commission was under orders from the military to make no concessions, and after two meetings, the government broke off the dialogue.[24]

One reason for the government's intransigence at the bargaining table was its new optimism on the battlefield. The replacement of General José Guillermo García as minister of defense cleared the way for the adoption of a new military strategy—the National Plan. Designed by U.S. counterinsurgency specialists, the plan was modeled after the Civil Operations and Revolutionary Development Support (CORDS) program instituted in South Vietnam in the late 1960s. L. Craig Johnstone, Enders's principal assistant for Central America, had worked in the CORDS program for two years as a district-level senior adviser and in 1968 had become a special assistant to CORDS director William E. Colby. Johnstone was one of the main advocates of the National Plan.[25]

The plan's basic strategy was to concentrate the army's best battalions in a single province to clear it of guerrillas. Behind this wall of troops would come money and civilian advisers to reactivate the local economy. Roads would be built, electrical power restored, schools and health clinics opened, and refugees would return home. Meanwhile the army would train local civil defense forces to rebuff any new encroachment by the guerrillas. When the region had been successfully pacified, the main force units of the army would move to another province and begin the process all over again. In as little as six months, if all went according to plan, the guerrillas would be penned into their mountain redoubts, far from any population centers. Then victory for the government would simply be a matter of time and attrition. "This strategy is a turning point in the war," said a military man involved in it. "We win or lose on this operation."[26]

San Vicente in central El Salvador was selected for the first application of the National Plan. Strategically located between the two main FMLN strongholds, Chalatenango and Morazán provinces, San Vicente was a guerrilla logistics hub and also one of the nation's main cotton-growing regions. The pacification of San Vicente would disrupt FMLN operations, secure the Pan-American highway (the main east-west route), and allow a revival of cotton production to boost badly needed foreign exchange earnings.[27]

In June 1983, six thousand troops launched Operation Well-Being to clear San Vicente. Warned by the advance publicity surrounding the National Plan, the thousand or so guerrillas who normally operated there dispersed into neighboring provinces. The army found nothing but the remnants of their dismantled encampments. This, however, was not regarded as a setback. The point of the plan was not to engage the guerrillas militarily, but to separate them from the population. If the guerrillas faded away without a fight, so much the better. Pacification would go faster.[28]

The initial success of the National Plan produced a certain giddiness in some quarters. The dire warnings of imminent collapse sounded in Washington in the spring of 1983 gave way in the fall to predictions of imminent victory. In August, a new intelligence estimate concluded that the National Plan was working and that the armed forces had seized the initiative.[29] "Right now the army's got it all their way," said Ambassador Hinton just before his departure, "and it's damned encouraging."[30] It all seemed too easy. For nearly three months, the FMLN did not challenge the National Plan. More cautious observers agreed that the real test would come when they did.

Within two months of the beginning of Operation Well-Being, the FMLN began reinfiltrating combatants into San Vicente and setting small ambushes for government patrols. Gradually, the guerrillas reestablished their base camps and reclaimed control over the rural areas. The key to the rebels' resurgence in San Vicente was their fall offensive everywhere else. In September, approximately seven hundred guerrillas attacked San Miguel, capital of an adjacent province and the third largest city in the country. It was the biggest single guerrilla operation of the war. FMLN troops, including an artillery unit, rode to the battle on trucks.[31]

Over the next two months, the FMLN attacked some sixty towns and villages, killing eight hundred government troops and capturing four hundred. "The guerrillas have the initiative now, no one can question that," said a U.S. adviser.[32] In Washington, Enders's successor, the affable Tony Motley, tried to deflect the growing sense of alarm with black humor. "What do El Salvador and Costa Rica have in common?" he asked jokingly. "Neither has an army."[33]

Washington blamed the army's inability to cope on familiar weaknesses: low morale, poor communications, lack of training. But a senior Salvadoran military commander had more insight, or at least more candor. "These troops have nothing to fight for," he explained, "and subsequently, they do not fight."[34]

To meet the FMLN offensive, the army's U.S.-trained rapid response battalions were withdrawn from San Vicente, and the plan to extend Operation Well-Being into Usulután province was delayed.[35] The war was returning to familiar patterns: a guerrilla thrust, a government parry, with the guerrillas seemingly stronger after each engagement.

With San Vicente defended only by regular garrison troops, it was easy for the FMLN to reestablish itself in the province. By December 1983, the army controlled only the largest towns and the main roads, and only in daylight. Before beginning a civic action project funded by U.S. AID through the government's counterinsurgency program, local mayors asked the FMLN for permission. "To keep our schools open and our AID work projects functional, we have to accept the terms that the guerrillas set," explained Guadalupe Montano, the mayor of Santa Clara. In one town, the FMLN approved the opening of a school with the proviso that one hour be set aside for them to conduct political education classes. Even U.S. businessmen working on contracts in the province paid war taxes to the FMLN to keep the guerrillas from destroying their equipment. "It doesn't take a genius to say that we're not in an up phase," said a frustrated U.S. official working on the counterinsurgency plan.[36]

In December, the FMLN routed 400 government troops defending the Cuscatlán bridge, the only remaining span connecting the eastern and western halves of the country. The government troops fled at the first attack, leaving the bridge to be demolished at the guerrillas' leisure.[37] But the army's biggest defeat came at El Paraíso, its forward fire base for operations in the province of Chalatenango. A modern garrison designed by U.S. military engineers in 1981, El Paraíso was supposedly impregnable. On December 30, 1983, 800 guerrillas attacked and overran the base, killing more than 100 government troops and taking 162 prisoners. The government buried its dead hastily with bulldozers, lest the magnitude of the debacle shatter the army's morale nationwide. "We are losing the war," lamented a senior Salvadoran officer, "and the only way to salvage the situation is to give the troops something to fight for. Until that time, we cannot be saved, no matter how much military equipment arrives from the United States."[38]

Reining in the Death Squads

Fall 1983 was a virtual replay of the previous fall in another respect as well. The death squads went on the offensive again in hopes of derailing the agrarian reform program and blocking any move toward negotiations.[39] Since its election in March 1982, the Salvadoran Constituent Assembly had been trying to write a new constitution. In September 1983, it came to the issue of agrarian reform. Christian Democratic trade unions and peasant associations belonging to the Popular Democratic Union (Unión Popular Democrática, UPD) mobilized twelve thousand people to pressure the assembly not to gut the existing reform. It was the largest demonstration in San Salvador since the left's mass mobilizations in 1980.[40]

No sooner had the debate opened than one of the death squads, the Secret Anti-Communist Army, began murdering union leaders. Constituent Assembly president Roberto D'Aubuisson went on television to accuse UPD director Samuel Maldonado of being a guerrilla collaborator.[41] On five occasions in 1979–80, such public denunciations by D'Aubuisson were followed by death squad murders. Ambassador Pickering met with D'Aubuisson and expressed Washington's displeasure with such behavior, but to no avail. A week later, D'Aubuisson repeated the accusation. In early November, rightist officers tried to organize a coup, but were stymied by more moderate colleagues.[42]

The assembly debate stretched on for three months. Assembly members who spoke in favor of the agrarian reform received death threats. The intimidation took its toll, and in the end the right won. The new constitution specified that only farms larger than 605 acres could be expropriated for agrarian reform, which exempted 97 to 99 percent of privately owned land. Moreover, the owners of farms larger than 605 acres were given three years to dispose of their excess property before it could be expropriated.[43]

Ambassador Pickering, like Hinton before him, was outraged by the surge of death squad killings. The murders were especially galling because the victims were mostly Christian Democrats and trade unionists allied with Washington. "It was a direct challenge to the government here . . . and to the United States," Pickering said. "It absolutely could not go undealt with."[44] He recommended that Washington launch a concerted campaign against the death squads, beginning with a clear repudiation of them by President Reagan and culminating in a threat to cut off military aid unless key death squad leaders were removed from the armed forces. "The right here thinks that we are infiltrated by Communists," explained an embassy staff member. "We want the *president* to say he's fed up with this."[45]

Pickering's recommendations were received sympathetically at the State Department. In a July 1983 policy review, State had complained to Reagan that the Salvadoran government had "not been motivated to take the minimal actions required to help us sustain our support." The department recommended confronting the Salvadorans and extracting from them "a new and reliable contract . . . that outlines for the Salvadorans what they must do to win and what we will do to help." If the Salvadorans wanted enough money to win the war, they would have to meet U.S. demands, including "elimination of military participation in death squads." If such a contract could be obtained, State argued, congressional resistance would give way to bipartisan support.[46]

With the hard-liners in control, Reagan chose not to act on the State Department's prescription in July. By November, however, Clark was gone from the White House, and Shultz had begun to regain control over Central American policy. Pickering was given the go-ahead.[47] At first, he tried quiet diplomacy, urging Magaña to remove just a handful of officers most directly implicated in the death squad violence. When Magaña raised the issue with Defense Minister Vides, the armed forces refused to accede.[48] "I am absolutely convinced that the death squad members do not exist within the armed forces," Vides affirmed.[49] Magaña was more candid: "All of the death squads are related to the army or paramilitary [security forces]," he acknowledged, but there was nothing he could do about it. "I have had no power, no authority. The extreme right here is incredible."[50]

After Pickering's private proposal was rejected, U.S. officials went public, discussing the death squads much more candidly with journalists, even naming officers involved. In early November, the embassy announced that a twenty-three-year-old student the Salvadoran government had arrested for the murder of Lieutenant Commander Albert A. Schaufelberger was not guilty and had been tortured into confessing.[51]

On November 25, 1983, Pickering addressed the Chamber of Commerce, the same group to which Hinton had given his famous speech about the death squad "mafia" a year before. It was Pickering's first speech since arriving in San Salvador, and he was just as blunt as Hinton had been. "No one wants to live in a country where no efforts are made to find who dumps bodies in gas stations and parking lots," he warned. The death squads were "murderers, torturers and kidnappers" who deserved "nothing less from society than open and honest punishment for such crimes."

"Too little has changed," Pickering said, recalling Hinton's speech the year before. "Where are the condemnations? Why hasn't the private sector . . . publicly condemned such outrages? Why haven't the daily papers done so?" he demanded. Asked after the speech if Washington might cut off military aid over the issue of the death squads, Pickering replied that there was an "extremely serious risk" of that happening.[52]

Yet even as Pickering labored to get the Salvadoran military to take seriously the need to clean up the death squads, other administration officials, including Ronald Reagan himself, were working at cross-purposes. On November 20, Reagan undercut Pickering's campaign by pocket-vetoing legislation that would have extended the 1981 certification requirements on El Salvador for another year.[53] Certification had originally been part of a two-year foreign aid authorization passed in 1981, which expired on September 30, 1983. Although even Reagan's critics had become discouraged by the semi-annual certification ritual, they feared that ending it would send the Salvadorans the unintended message that Congress no longer cared about human rights, agrarian reform, and negotiations. Therefore, as the fiscal year drew to a close, Congress rushed through a bill that extended the existing certification for another year. The Republicans mounted no opposition to it.

To everyone's surprise, Reagan killed it with a pocket veto. In fact, the administration had been planning at least since July to scuttle any renewal of certification.[54] Certification posed no immediate threat to the military aid program, so long as Reagan was willing to endure criticism for certifying progress even when there wasn't any. But certification posed other dangers; every six months, it brought El Salvador to the top of the congressional agenda and focused a media spotlight on it.

Nevertheless, the decision to veto the legislation was not a unanimous one. The State Department argued against it, fearing that it would further poison relations with Congress and make it harder to win new increases in aid. Hard-liners in the NSC prevailed, however, insisting that Reagan should cut away legislative restrictions on his authority in foreign policy whenever possible.[55]

Finally, doing away with certification was a way to avoid a bruising internal debate over whether or not certification could be made in January 1984. The rising tide of death squad violence and the constitutional restrictions on agrarian reform made it hard to argue that there had been any progress; if anything, things seemed to be deteriorating. "If you look at the situation," said a diplomat in El Salvador, "it would have been a joke [to certify]."[56]

Congressional reaction to Reagan's rejection of the certification bill was predictably negative. Senator Christopher Dodd threatened to filibuster against any additional military aid for El Salvador until the certification was restored, though he never carried through on the threat. Even Senate Foreign Relations Committee Chairman Charles Percy, usually an administration stalwart, complained that Reagan's action "sends a confusing signal to El Salvador just at a time when we are trying to send a strong, clear signal that political violence must cease." To blunt the negative reactions, the administration promised to submit a voluntary report covering the certification topics.[57]

If the administration was largely indifferent to the reaction in Congress, it did worry about how the veto would be perceived in El Salvador. Obviously, the veto could derail the campaign to convince the Salvadorans that Washington was finally serious about stopping the death squads. The administration's problems were exacerbated when Reagan was asked about the veto during a meeting with high school students on December 2. He admitted that "so-called murder squads" existed on the right, but their persistence, he argued, was due to the inability of the government to combat them and the guerrillas at the same time.

"I'm going to voice a suspicion I've never said aloud before," Reagan continued. "I wonder if all this is rightwing, or if those guerrilla forces have not realized that . . . they can get away with these violent acts, helping to try to bring down the government, and the rightwing will be blamed for it."[58]

By accusing the left of masquerading as rightists and killing its own leaders and activists, Reagan echoed exactly the Salvadoran far right's public explanation of the death squads. In so doing, he convinced D'Aubuisson and company that their instincts had been correct all along; Ronald Reagan was as fervent an anti-Communist as they, and he understood what had to be done. The hand-wringing about human rights emanating from the embassy was either the work of Communists in the State Department, or it was just public relations designed to pacify the American Congress. In either event, it was not anything the right needed to take seriously.[59]

Notwithstanding the president's remarks, Washington had to counter this impression quickly, or all Pickering's efforts would be undone. In December, Vice President George Bush was sent to El Salvador to forge the sort of "contract" that the State Department had advocated in July. Bush carried a letter from Reagan, so there would be no doubt that he spoke for the president. It proposed a series of specific actions the administration wanted from the Salvadoran government, including the removal of nine high-ranking individuals involved with the death squads. If the government complied, Reagan would seek major increases in military and economic assistance from Congress.[60]

Bush got right to the point. In the formal toast opening the state dinner given in his honor, he was careful to bolster Pickering's influence by endorsing his tough speech to the Chamber of Commerce. "Tom Pickering's remarks—which I greatly admire and which the president and I fully endorse—were right on the mark," Bush began. The "rightwing fanatics" of the death squads were undermining the anti-Communist cause, Bush said. "Every murderous act they commit poisons the well of friendship between our two countries." Bush closed with a clear warning: "If these death squad murders continue, you will lose the support of the American people, and that would be a tragedy."[61]

Then Bush held three private meetings—two with top military commanders and one with civilian party leaders. He met first with Defense Minister Vides, deputy minister General Raphael Flores Lima, and Chief of Staff Adolfo Blandón and then repeated his message to the full high command. He laid out a series of demands; foremost among them was reining in the death squads. "The main point is the death squad issue," he said. "The president has asked me to come to express that point to all here. This is no smoke screen. This is a reality." Specifically, Bush demanded that the military officers on his list of death squad participants be relieved of their commands and expelled from the armed forces and that the civilians on it be exiled for at least three years. Furthermore, he insisted that the high command issue a forthright condemnation of death squad activity, arrest Captain Eduardo Ernesto Avila in the AIFLD murder case, hold a trial of the soldiers accused of killing the U.S. churchwomen, reorganize the armed forces in order to improve its combat capacity, assure the extension of Phase Three of the agrarian reform, and guarantee the 1984 election. In exchange, the United States would boost military aid enough to finance what Bush called "a winning effort."[62]

The army, not accustomed to being held accountable for its behavior, at first resisted Bush's demands. "The reaction was terrible," President Magaña recalled.[63] The far right bitterly opposed the U.S. effort to cashier its friends in the armed forces. D'Aubuisson came to the defense of those whom the embassy was naming as complicit in the death squads, denouncing the United States for denigrating loyal officers.[64] But the promise of enough military aid to win the war, combined with the threat of an aid cut-off if they did not comply, finally led the Salvadoran high command to accept Bush's proposition. "We know that improving our image is worth millions of dollars of aid for the country," Defense Minister Vides said.[65]

Still, the initial results of Bush's démarche were rather modest. None of the officers on Bush's list were expelled from the military. Three of them were sent to diplomatic posts abroad, although two had already been slated for transfer before Bush's visit.[66] The civilians on the list, including Hector Regalado, chief of security at the Constituent Assembly, all worked for D'Aubuisson. They lost their jobs when D'Aubuisson resigned from the Constituent Assembly leadership to run for president against José Napoleón Duarte in the March 1984 election. None were exiled.[67]

The high command promptly issued a proclamation condemning the death squads, though its impact was muted by the fact that half a dozen of its signatories were officers whose own units were responsible for gross human rights violations.[68] Death squad killings dropped by almost 50 percent in December 1983 and January 1984, but by February they were edging back up. At the urging of the army, the Constituent Assembly approved a six-month extension of the "land to the tiller" phase of the agrarian reform. And Captain Avila was arrested on December 19, 1983, although he was released again a few weeks later.[69]

Salvadoran compliance with U.S. demands was "mainly verbal," concluded a January 1984 CIA assessment of the impact of Bush's trip. "We believe efforts by the civilian government and military high command to crack down on rightwing violence seemed almost exclusively aimed at placating Washington. . . . Defense Minister Vides—whose room to maneuver is limited—appears both personally disinclined and professionally unable to effect a major cleanup within the armed forces any time soon."[70]

Despite such minimal compliance, Pickering seemed genuinely pleased. "A very constructive and excellent start has been made," he declared.[71] The Bush visit seemed to finally convince the military that the United States was serious about conditioning military assistance on human rights progress. That was a breakthrough and a necessary first step toward actual improvement. The Salvadoran election scheduled for March 1984 would provide an opportunity for further steps—so long as D'Aubuisson did not win.

See No Evil

George Bush was able to hand the Salvadoran high command a list of people intimately connected with the deaths squads because in 1983 the CIA had begun to actively gather intelligence on the murderous network. Astonishingly, it paid little attention to them earlier, even though they played a major role in Salvadoran politics and threatened the Washington-backed government. The intelligence community conducted only one major analytic study of the far right before 1983. That report, done in mid-1980, concluded that "there is scant intelligence on rightwing terrorist organization membership and the groups' relationship to each other, to the wealthy elite, or to the military."[72] Yet nothing was done to remedy this intelligence gap until the absence of reporting on the far right was criticized by the House Intelligence Committee in late 1982.

Why did the intelligence community turn a blind eye to violence by the far right? Most simply, the right was not a priority. Resources were "devoted almost exclusively to the insurgency," according to the House Intelligence Committee.[73] Despite the administration's rhetoric that it was trying to protect a centrist Salvadoran government from violence by both the extreme left and the extreme right, when it came to allocating intelligence resources, only the left was really regarded as a threat.

Another reason for Washington's reluctance to look too closely at the death squads was a fear of what it would find. When the intelligence community finally did focus on them, it discovered what Salvadorans had known all along—the people responsible for "extreme rightwing terrorism" were "an integral part of the government of El Salvador."

"It is undeniable . . . that significant political violence—including death squad activity—has been associated with elements of the Salvadoran military establishment, especially the security service," the Senate Intelligence Committee concluded after reviewing the fruits of the intelligence community's 1983 investigation of the far right. "Numerous Salvadoran officials in the military and security forces as well as other official organizations have been involved in encouraging or conducting death squad activities or other violent human rights abuses." A 1985 National Intelligence Estimate reached the same conclusion.[74]

U.S. officials on the ground in San Salvador knew this perfectly well, even before the CIA's assessment. Colonel John D. Waghelstein, commander of the U.S. Military Group in El Salvador in the early 1980s, spoke of the military's death squad killings euphemistically as "night visits," and boasted of how he had convinced one signal corps unit to stop killing people after their activities came to his attention. No one from the unit was punished, however.[75]

After the 1983 intelligence assessment, the administration could no longer maintain the fiction that the death squads were private thugs, distinct from the regular government forces. Nor was it possible to contend that members of the security forces involved in the killings were rogues suborned by right-wing oligarchs—an explanation that left the armed forces as an institution guilty of nothing worse than poor discipline. Although members of the oligarchy, some in exile in Miami, helped finance the death squads, the unsettling truth was that most of the squads were clandestine units of the security forces acting on intelligence information and orders transmitted down the regular chain of command.[76] They were not rogues; they were the dirty underside of the army's war against the left.

This, in turn, posed a political problem for the administration, which was trying to convince Congress that the regime in El Salvador was a fledgling democracy that deserved hundreds of millions of dollars in military aid. In such a politically charged atmosphere, the administration was better off not knowing who was responsible for the killings. At each six-month certification, its assessment of rightist violence was confined to the cumulative reports of the "grim gram," the embassy's weekly compilation of death listings from the Salvadoran press. During the two years the certification law was in force, the Reagan administration never tasked the intelligence community to conduct an assessment of political violence in El Salvador.[77]

So many midlevel and senior officers of the army and security forces were involved in the death squads that embassy officials could not avoid doing business with them. They were Washington's allies, and the administration did not dare press them too hard for fear of weakening the military institution on which the regime depended for its survival.[78] "We all made our compromises, but you have to view everything in the context of a civil war," said one U.S. official in retrospect. "Maybe we were too cautious [about pressing the death squad issue], and maybe we can be criticized for that. But we were excruciatingly conscious of the danger of running a very fragile system."[79]

Some U.S. intelligence officials developed close relationships with officers implicated in the death squads.[80] The most notorious case was that of Colonel Nicolás Carranza, D'Aubuisson's most senior ally in the officers corps and commander of the dreaded Treasury Police. Ambassador Pickering called Carranza a "fascist," and another U.S. diplomat said of him, "He's not a thug, he's the Gestapo."[81]

According to Colonel Roberto Eulalio Santiváñez, the former head of Salvadoran military intelligence, both Carranza and Defense Minister García worked with D'Aubuisson in late 1979 and early 1980 to establish the paramilitary network of death squads around the country.[82] Yet for five years, through the worst of the death squad killings, Carranza was a paid CIA informant, receiving $90,000 annually to provide intelligence on the left, not on the activities of his colleagues in the death squads. "You can't always do business with honorable people," said a former U.S. intelligence officer, explaining the rationale for such a relationship. "In such cases, the less you know, the better it is."[83]

The rot reached so deep into the Salvadoran armed forces that even officers Washington regarded as moderates, relatively free from the taint of murder, were culpable by the strict standards of the rules of war. In 1946, the United States tried, convicted, and hanged Japanese general Tomuyuki Yamashita for war crimes because troops under his command murdered civilians and prisoners of war in the Philippines during World War II. Yamashita argued in his defense that he had neither ordered nor participated in the killings, so he should not be held responsible for them. The U.S. Supreme Court rejected this reasoning on the grounds that officers were always responsible for controlling the behavior of troops under their command.[84]

By that standard, virtually the entire Salvadoran officers corps was guilty of murder. Defense Minister Vides, whom the administration touted as a moderate, was commander of the National Guard when its troops killed the U.S. churchwomen, the AIFLD labor advisers, and countless Salvadorans. Colonel Domingo Monterrosa, whom American advisers hailed as the army's best field officer, was the commander of the Atlactl battalion when it massacred hundreds of peasants at El Mozote in December 1980. Army Chief of Staff Colonel Adolfo Blandón, who helped depose García as defense minister to facilitate Washington's counterinsurgency plans, had command responsibility for the intelligence departments of the General Staff, which conducted their own murderous special operations. "There's no way the government can purge itself," said one U.S. official. "Too many people have blood on their hands. The government itself is a rightwing death squad."[85]

There was one last reason for the administration's reluctance to peer too closely into the charnel house of the death squads. It was a reason rarely mentioned, but everyone was aware of it: the death squads worked. "The horror years of '80 and '81 had a lot to do with breaking the FMLN in this city," admitted a U.S. diplomat in San Salvador. "[Death squad killing] wasn't indiscriminate."[86]

Between 1980 and 1983, the deaths squads acting clandestinely and the regular security forces acting openly killed over thirty thousand civilians, utterly destroying the left's organized political base in the cities.[87] The popular organizations, which had been the core of the left's political strength in 1979, had been exterminated by 1983. Their demise had considerable military importance. With no infrastructure in the cities, the FMLN could not launch a popular insurrection to accompany its "final offensive" in 1981. Throughout 1982 and 1983, though the military prowess of the FMLN grew phenomenally, its inability to combine military operations with an urban uprising prevented the guerrillas from dealing the regime a fatal blow.

The apparent success of George Bush's visit to El Salvador and the ultimatum he delivered on the death squads proved that Washington could force some compliance from the Salvadoran army by brandishing the big stick of military aid. When the United States made a credible threat to cut assistance, the Salvadorans would do as they were told—just as they had in 1981 when Robert White forced them to adopt the agrarian reform, and in 1982 when Deane Hinton foiled D'Aubuisson's presidential ambitions.

But did such obedience, given grudgingly under coercion, signify permanent changes in attitude and behavior? Did the shuffling of personnel and modest decline in political killings that followed Bush's visit represent a fundamental shift in the armed forces' view of civilian opponents, or was it just a temporary expedient necessary to open the cornucopia of U.S. military aid? The record of the agrarian reform did not inspire confidence that the changes were very deep. It had been on the books for almost four years, but the armed forces had never embraced it or tried to make it work. At best, they tolerated it.[88]

Early signals suggested an equal lack of enthusiasm about stopping the death squads. The number of killings fell, but they did not stop; they became more selective. Labor organizers, peasant leaders, and student activists still had good reason to fear for their lives. As Archbishop Arturo Rivera y Damas pointed out, the apparatus of state-sponsored murder was still largely intact, available to resume the carnage if and when those who ordered it to desist should change their minds. "The problem is that the people running the death squads are also running the country," said a church official. "Removing a few infamous offenders does nothing to dismantle the structure."[89] Not a single military officer had been prosecuted for any of the political killings, not even the AIFLD murders. The army was still above the law.

To the United States government, however, the concessions Bush extracted during his visit seemed to be a major victory. At last, Washington was getting movement on the human rights issue, whereas before it had always run into a stone wall. That seemed like progress. The improvements were incremental, to be sure, and there might be backsliding unless Washington kept up its guard. But things were moving in the right direction. New civilian political institutions were being built, the agrarian reform was still on the books, and now the violence was being reduced. If the 1984 election went as well as the 1982 election had, it could be the vindication and crowning achievement of four years of U.S. policy.

Of course, the election would not make the guerrillas go away; the army would still have to win the war. But with the political situation on the ground stabilized, the prospects for victory would depend largely on the beneficence of Congress. That, in turn, would depend on the Reagan administration's ability to convince members that its optimism about El Salvador's bright and shining future was not just a pleasant fantasy.

CHAPTER 11

From Conflict to Consensus

Having promised the Salvadoran military that Washington would reward them for curbing the death squads by providing enough military aid to win the war, Ronald Reagan faced the conundrum of how to convince Congress to appropriate the funds. Reagan would have to wage another political struggle against congressional Democrats, this time in the midst of a presidential election campaign when partisan passions on both sides would be higher than usual. To assist him in this battle, Reagan placed great hopes on the National Bipartisan Commission on Central America, which he had established in July 1983.

The Kissinger Commission
The commission was the brainchild of United Nations Ambassador Jeane Kirkpatrick and the late Senator Henry Jackson (D-Wash.). Both neoconservatives, they hoped an endorsement of Reagan's policy from a bipartisan blue-ribbon panel would undercut liberal Democrats' opposition.[1] Reagan appointed the Central America commission with the aim of recreating the political marvel of the 1983 Scowcroft commission on the MX missile. When Congress halted production of the MX, Reagan created a putatively bipartisan commission stacked with members certain to support building the missile.

237

The authority of their report was then used to win back enough moderate Democratic votes in Congress to resurrect the MX. The Central America commission began with a comparable mandate and membership. Its purpose, one administration official candidly admitted, was to "provide a rationale" for current policy, not to design a new one.[2] As a bonus, the mere existence of a bipartisan commission would defuse Central America as an election issue in the 1984 campaign.

Henry Kissinger was appointed to chair the Central America commission, a selection that displeased people at both ends of the political spectrum. Liberal Democrats remembered Kissinger as the man who ordered the Christmas bombing of Hanoi after telling everyone that peace was at hand in Vietnam. They also recalled, as did Latin Americans, that Kissinger presided over the CIA's successful destabilization of President Salvador Allende's democratically elected government in Chile.

For the right, Kissinger conjured up the demons of detente. In 1976, running against Gerald Ford in the Republican primaries, Ronald Reagan himself condemned Kissinger, noting that his stewardship "coincided precisely with the loss of U.S. military supremacy."[3] But whatever his past sins, in 1983, Henry Kissinger still had stature. Polls showed that his credibility with the general public was high—a key ingredient if the Central American commission was to have an impact on public and congressional opinion. Kissinger's other virtue was that he agreed completely with Reagan's Central America policy.[4]

The Kissinger Commission, as it came to be known, was nominally divided equally between Republicans and Democrats, but its bipartisanship did not extend past party labels. Among the twelve commissioners, only one moderately liberal Democrat was included intentionally—Henry Cisneros, mayor of San Antonio and a prominent Hispanic-American politician. Another liberal, Yale economics professor Carlos Díaz-Alejandro, was appointed by mistake only because he was a Cuban-American. White House officials wrongly assumed that his heritage carried with it an appropriately conservative ideology. The error was quickly pointed out by the real conservatives in the Cuban-American community, who denounced Díaz-Alejandro as a Cuban agent and demanded that he be fired because he favored normalizing relations with Cuba.[5] White House hard-liners were ready to throw him off the commission, but cooler heads prevailed. James Baker argued that it would not be an auspicious start for the bipartisan commission if Reagan fired one of its members just because he turned out to be more liberal than expected. So Díaz-Alejandro got to stay, and Henry Cisneros had someone to talk to.

The rest of the Democrats were Cold War liberals: AFL-CIO president Lane Kirkland, Boston University president John Silber, former Democratic Party chairman Robert S. Strauss, and professional election observer Richard M. Scammon. It was a group designed to appeal to moderate and conservative Democrats. The Republicans were all conservatives of varying hues: former Supreme Court justice Potter Stewart; former New Jersey senator Nicholas F. Brady, a close friend of James Baker; former Texas governor William P. Clements; former director of Project Hope William B. Walsh; and businessman Wilson S. Johnson.

The one thing all the commission members had in common was their ignorance of Central America. Díaz-Alejandro was the only one who had any professional expertise or experience, and he specialized in South America rather than Central America. Kissinger aide William D. Rogers described the members' initial knowledge as "Zero. . . . They were appallingly ignorant of the realities of Central America."[6]

With no knowledge base of their own, the commissioners were heavily dependent on the information presented to them. Controlling the flow of that information was one way Kissinger sought to mold the commission's deliberations. On the sensitive political and security issues, Kissinger sought to limit presentations to government officials, past and present, few of whom would present a fundamental critique of U.S. policy. Commission consultant Gregory Treverton was assigned to organize a day and a half of hearings, but found that the staff kept rejecting all the liberals he proposed to have testify, including even former attorney general Elliot L. Richardson, a Republican. As a result, not only were Cisneros and Díaz-Alejandro outnumbered by the conservatives, but they were unable to gather enough ammunition to argue their case. "My sense is that the commission never had access to balanced analysis," Cisneros complained afterward. "It was very clear what the ideological bias was going in."[7]

Neither Cisneros nor Díaz-Alejandro was temperamentally disposed to be very aggressive in defending their point of view anyway. The politically ambitious Cisneros worried about being branded a liberal and kept denying that he was one.[8] Díaz-Alejandro was by nature a mild-mannered professor with no experience in politics. Neither of them was any match for Henry Kissinger's skills at bureaucratic maneuver. "On a project like this, Kissinger's mind splits in two," a U.S. official said admiringly. "One half is writing the report, and the other half is coopting the other members of the commission."[9]

With Kissinger in charge, there was never any doubt that the commission's report would frame the Central American crisis in East-West terms and call for increased military assistance. It was equally certain that the report would recommend a "mini–Marshall Plan" of economic aid to address the region's social and economic ills, which both moderates and liberals identified as the root cause of the crisis. The economic plan was the sugarcoating to induce congressional moderates to swallow the bitter pill of deeper U.S. military involvement.

In January 1984, the commission dutifully produced the report expected of it, with only a handful of polite dissents. Cisneros and Díaz-Alejandro dissented on the most central issues—whether the United States should pursue serious negotiations in El Salvador and whether it should continue the secret war against Nicaragua—but they did not have the courage to craft a separate report of their own, a move that would have destroyed any political benefit the commission had for Reagan.

The liberals' dissents did not lessen the importance of the consensus Kissinger was able to assemble around the underlying logic of the report—a logic that paraphrased exactly the Reagan administration's justification for its Central America policy. The report, like the policy, was based on four premises: that Cuba and the Soviet Union were behind the crisis, posing a challenge to vital U.S. security interests; that the United States was supporting democrats and democracies in the region; that the United States favored social and economic reform to remedy historic injustices; and that the United States was seeking political rather than military solutions to the crisis. The Kissinger Commission report was a sophisticated brief for administration policy and gave it the imprimatur of bipartisan truth.

Yet the Kissinger Commission had surprisingly little impact on the congressional debate over El Salvador, perhaps because the battle lines were already so clearly drawn. Reactions to the commission report were predictably partisan. Reagan exclaimed that the report was "magnificent." Liberal Democrats were highly critical of the report's premise that the Central American conflict was an East-West struggle and its call for major increases in military aid.[10] The public, too, was apparently unmoved by the authority of Dr. Kissinger. Opinion polls showed that 66 percent of the public opposed providing El Salvador with economic aid and only 27 percent supported it, even when people were informed that the aid had been recommended by the National Bipartisan Commission.[11]

The Senate Debates Central America

On February 3, 1984, President Reagan announced how he planned to translate the report's recommendations into policy. For the current fiscal year, FY 1984, he wanted an additional $400 million in economic aid and $259 million in military aid for the region, doubling the amount of economic aid already approved and tripling the military aid. Of this new money, El Salvador was to get $134 million in economic aid and $179 million in arms (on top of the

$199 million in economic aid and $65 million in military aid Congress had already granted). To provide these new funds, Reagan requested a supplemental appropriation.

Reagan's proposal also included budget requests for the upcoming 1985 fiscal year: $1.8 billion in economic aid and $256 million in military aid for Central America, with the bulk of it again going to El Salvador, including $133 million in military aid.[12] Both of the two principal legislative vehicles Reagan submitted to implement the Kissinger Commission's recommendations—the supplemental foreign aid bill for FY 1984 and the regular foreign aid bill for FY 1985—would take months to make their way through the legislative gauntlet on Capitol Hill. Thus, neither of them solved the administration's most immediate problem: the acute shortfall in military aid for El Salvador. The Salvadoran army had grown from 12,000 in 1980 to 33,000 by 1984, with plans to add another 6,500 men within a year.[13] Congress, however, had not appropriated enough money to bankroll the army's growth.

Administration officials were especially exasperated at the outcome of the 1983 budget debate over El Salvador. In the continuing resolution passed at the end of 1983, Congress had approved $64.8 million in military aid rather than the $86.3 million the administration had requested, and 30 percent of that ($20 million) could not be spent until a verdict was handed down in the trial of the National Guardsmen accused of killing the U.S. churchwomen. Thus the administration had gotten only about half of what it had requested.[14] The heavy fighting during the fall 1983 offensive had left the military short of supplies, just as in late 1982. By February, most of the FY 1984 military aid budget for El Salvador had already been expended.[15]

Reagan could be reasonably certain that at least some of the $179 million in additional military aid that he requested in February 1984 would eventually be approved. In the meantime, however, the logistics of the Salvadoran armed forces would be stretched thin—perhaps so thin that the army would be unable to protect the upcoming March presidential election. The White House was also anxious to strengthen the army enough to prevent the guerrillas from launching an embarrassing offensive on the eve of the U.S. presidential election in November. In fact, the Pentagon was so worried that an FMLN offensive might precipitate the collapse of the Salvadoran army that they drew up contingency plans for U.S. airstrikes to bail it out.[16]

Reagan's first instinct was to resort to the special emergency powers he had used in 1981 and 1982 to send military aid with no congressional approval. In fact, National Security Decision Directive (NSDD) 124, signed by Reagan on February 7, 1984, specifically approved the use of emergency powers if necessary.[17] On March 21, Deputy National Security Adviser John Poindexter directed the State and Defense Departments to reassure the Salvadorans that additional military aid would be forthcoming, "no matter what happened on the Hill."[18]

But rumors that Reagan might use his emergency powers again provoked vigorous opposition in Congress, even from Republicans. On February 20, Clarence Long and twenty other House members sent Reagan a letter warning that if he used these powers to bypass Congress, he would jeopardize passage of his entire foreign aid bill.[19] Since every dollar in aid that Congress approved for Central America had to go through Long's subcommittee, Reagan backed off.

The White House hit upon a clever maneuver to get both emergency military aid for El Salvador and additional aid for the Nicaraguan contras (who were running low on funds because of a $24 million ceiling Congress imposed on them in 1983). Administration allies in the Senate would add the funds as riders to two emergency appropriations bills that had already passed the House. That way, no meddlesome House committees would have an opportunity to mangle the aid programs. If the Senate passed the bills, they would go to conference committee with the House, where a compromise would probably produce at least some of the funds the administration needed.

In a surprise move early in March, Republicans on the Senate Appropriations Committee added $93 million in military aid for El Salvador to an urgent supplemental appropriation bill (H.J. Res. 492) that included emergency funds for Africa famine relief, domestic child nutrition programs, and summer jobs. At the same time, they also tacked on $21 million for the Nicaraguan contras. Democrats on the committee argued that the aid for El Salvador should be delayed pending the outcome of the election there, lest Congress end up funding a government headed by Roberto D'Aubuisson and the death squads. Republicans countered that the money was needed immediately to prevent the guerrillas from disrupting the election. The Republicans had more votes.[20]

Naturally, the House leadership resented the administration's effort to short-circuit the normal legislative process. Ordinarily, its recourse would be to refuse any compromise in the conference committee. But the administration was gambling that the need for famine relief was so urgent that the House would cave in and accept the Central America funds. In effect, starving Africans would be held hostage to the administration's battle with Congress over Central America. But Senate Democrats managed to upend Reagan's strategy with a surprise of their own. They added money for Africa famine relief to a different supplemental appropriation, thereby eliminating the urgency of the bill containing Reagan's Central America funds. Then they used the Senate rules to block the Central America bill.[21]

This deadlock was finally broken when the Republican leadership struck a deal with Minority Leader Robert C. Byrd and Senator Daniel Inouye to reduce the amount requested for El Salvador by a third, from $93 million to $61.75 million. In exchange for this reduction, the Democrats would allow the bill to come to the floor just after the first round of voting in the Salvadoran election. By playing to Inouye's instinct for compromise, the Republicans managed to split the Democrats almost exactly in half—staunch liberals on one side, moderates and conservatives on the other. With the Democrats divided, the Republicans were assured of an overwhelming Senate vote in favor of aid, which they could then use as leverage in the conference committee with the House.[22]

On March 28, 1984, the Senate began its first floor debate on Central America since the certification requirements on El Salvador were adopted in 1981. The debate lasted six days, with liberal Democrats offering amendments on three issues: the amount of military aid destined for El Salvador and the conditions under which it would be provided; the amount of aid for the Nicaraguan contras; and limitations on the president's power to send U.S. troops into combat in Central America.

Senator Edward Kennedy sponsored most of the liberals' amendments. Senators Christopher Dodd and Patrick Leahy worked closely with him and spoke often during the debate. On the Republican side, Senator Robert Kasten, the floor manager for the emergency appropriations bill, led the administration's forces. But for the most part, the Republicans abstained from the debate, leaving it to moderate and conservative Democrats like Inouye, David Boren, and Lloyd Bentsen to argue with their liberal colleagues.

The liberals, abandoned by their leadership and vastly outnumbered, lost every contested vote. Both Inouye and Senator Nancy Kassebaum spoke against the liberals' efforts to cut the administration's request. A year earlier, they had agreed to join with Dodd to limit military aid in FY 1984 to just $50 million.[23] Now they voted to increase it to at least $126.55 million. Inouye justified his turnaround by arguing that without additional money, the "hotheads" of the death squads would unleash a "bloodbath." In 1932, Inouye recalled, the Salvadoran army killed almost thirty thousand people during the *Matanza*, and it could happen again. "I do not want that on my conscience," he said, apparently unaware that since 1981, the armed forces he wanted to fund had already killed *more than* thirty thousand noncombatants.[24]

The debate on El Salvador was lengthy but desultory. The liberals too often based their case on peripheral issues, arguing, for example, that the funds for El Salvador should be rejected because the Senate Foreign Relations Committee had not been adequately consulted, that there was really no emergency requiring quick action, that too much aid was being siphoned off in corruption.[25] Occasionally, some speakers went to the heart of the matter—whether the government of El Salvador deserved Washington's military assistance and whether Reagan's policy was working. But much of the time the liberals seemed reluctant to grasp the nettle.

Not so the other side. The Republicans and their conservative Democratic allies hammered on Reagan's basic themes, as echoed by the Kissinger Commission. Central America was vital to U.S. national security, the Cubans and Soviets were on the march there, and only quick action by Washington stood between them and the Texas border. Moreover, the argument went, Washington's allies in the region were building democracy. The first round of the Salvadoran election, held just days before the Senate debate opened, was repeatedly invoked as living proof. Several senators who had been members of the official observer delegation gave moving accounts of the Salvadorans' desire for peace and their hopes of achieving it through the ballot box.

"I will never again take for granted the privilege of voting in an election," said Senator Boren. To cut aid now, he argued, would be "a criminal break of faith with people who desire democracy, who want the ballot, not the bullet to determine their destiny."[26]

The liberals' reticence on El Salvador stemmed from a fundamental dilemma that most of them could not resolve. They believed that the government of El Salvador was so brutal and corrupt that it was beyond reform and would never win the support of its own people. It was impossible to build a strong and capable military on such a flawed foundation, so regardless of how much aid Washington poured in, the army would never win the war. Washington's role would simply continue growing until the United States was dragged directly into the fighting by the weight of its own commitment—just like Vietnam.

If Washington ended its aid program, however, few senators doubted that the Salvadoran government would fall. Though many liberals doubted that such an outcome would pose a serious security threat to the United States, few thought it was desirable. Moreover, no Democrat was prepared to say publicly that an FMLN victory was an acceptable outcome, lest they be accused of being soft on Communism. Such was the dilemma that ensnared the Democrats: staying in El Salvador looked like a policy disaster in the making, but getting out carried mortal political risks.

The liberals mounted a much more robust debate over keeping U.S. combat troops out of Central America. On that issue, they were not at all ambivalent. They wanted to make Reagan come to Congress for approval before he sent U.S. forces into combat in the region. In passionate appeals, they beseeched their colleagues not to allow another Vietnam, but to no avail. The Senate voted 72–23 against Kennedy's amendment requiring prior approval before U.S. troops could be sent into combat in Nicaragua or El Salvador.[27]

Toward a Showdown in the House

The House of Representatives refused to even convene a conference committee on the urgent supplemental for over a month, until after the runoff election in El Salvador.[28] With the urgent supplemental bill stalled, the regular foreign aid program—the FY 1985 request—became the main arena of battle between the administration and House Democrats. The first test for this package came on March 1, in Michael Barnes's Western Hemisphere Subcommittee, where a large liberal majority rejected every facet of Reagan's plan. They deleted the entire request for $179 million in additional military aid for El Salvador in FY 1984, cut Reagan's FY 1985 military aid request by two-thirds (approving just $64.8 million instead of the $189.5 million requested), and placed extremely strict conditions on FY 1985 military aid.

The new certification requirement, authored by Congressman Stephen Solarz, was similar to the one the subcommittee approved in 1983, but which never became law. For any military aid to be provided, the president would have to certify that the government of El Salvador had "achieved" (1) the removal of people connected with the death squads from the armed forces and the elimination of human rights abuses by the military; (2) an end to the detention of political prisoners; (3) the establishment of an effective judicial system as demonstrated by trials in the case of murdered U.S. citizens and of "substantial numbers" of those responsible for the murder of Salvadorans; (4) freedom of the press and association; (5) participation of the government in negotiations, "in good faith and without preconditions," with its opposition; (6) compliance with the Geneva Convention in the treatment of prisoners and noncombatants; and (7) progress in carrying out the agrarian reform program. Even if Reagan certified that all these conditions had been met, military aid could be provided only if Congress passed a joint resolution agreeing with him. If either the House or Senate disagreed, military aid would be cut off.[29]

The intention behind such tough provisions was to close the loopholes in the original 1981 certification law that had allowed Reagan to certify progress in 1982 and 1983 even when there wasn't any. Two years of experience with Reagan's efforts to evade congressional constraints on his policy had destroyed whatever shred of trust existed between the administration and its Democratic opponents. If the president could not be trusted to see that the laws were faithfully executed, then the law would have to be rewritten so as to leave him no choice.

The subcommittee also voted to limit the number of U.S. military advisers in El Salvador to fifty-five; prohibit Reagan from using any special emergency powers to send additional military aid to the Salvadorans; prohibit most military aid or sales to Guatemala; prohibit joint military exercises with Honduras or Guatemala; limit the number of U.S. personnel in Honduras to three hundred; and end all funds for the Regional Military Training Center in Honduras.

The administration was bitter about the wholesale rejection of its approach by Barnes's subcommittee, but not panicky. The subcommittee's action was only the first step in a long process, not the last. After Barnes's subcommittee reported its Central America package, Democrats on the full Foreign Affairs Committee began conferring among themselves to find a compromise they could all accept. Chairman Dante Fascell and a handful of conservative Democrats wanted to give Reagan much of what he had requested, especially for El Salvador.[30] Liberals backed the subcommittee bill. The compromise they worked out was much closer to the subcommittee recommendation than to anything the administration had in mind. Like the subcommittee bill, it rejected additional military aid for El Salvador in FY 1984 and imposed stringent conditions on most military aid in FY 1985. It, too, gave Congress the power to reject Reagan's certification and retained the limits on advisers, joint exercises, and the use of emergency powers in the subcommittee bill.

The foreign aid authorization bill went to the House floor with the Foreign Affairs Committee's compromise Central America plan in it. The Republicans, for their part, drafted a full-blown alternative of their own. Although the House of Representatives had been arguing about El Salvador since 1981, the issue had never been subject to full-fledged floor debate. The battles had always been fought in hearings on Reagan's certification, in committee reviews of reprogramming requests, or in committee markups of foreign aid bills that never passed. The floor debate on the FY 1985 foreign aid bill loomed as a decisive test of strength between the administration and its Democratic opponents. The Democratic leadership scheduled the foreign aid bill, quite intentionally, for the week after the final round of voting in the Salvadoran presidential election.

The Salvadoran Election

Although Washington had wanted a new presidential election in El Salvador as quickly as possible because of President Magaña's weakness, U.S. officials were nervous about how it might turn out. As the preelection maneuvering began in mid-1983, ARENA was poised to nominate D'Aubuisson as its presidential candidate, and the Christian Democrats were likely to pick José Napoleón Duarte. D'Aubuisson and Duarte were the undisputed leaders of their parties—experienced, charismatic, and well known. But they were also, as one U.S. official put it, "the most hated" of the possible nominees—D'Aubuisson because of his role in the death squads, Duarte because his populist antagonism toward the private sector bordered on demagoguery. A campaign between them would be bitterly divisive, making it all the more difficult for the United States to assemble a unified governing coalition for the struggle against the guerrillas.

Indeed, the embassy worried that a victory by either of them might provoke a military coup. If Duarte won, the private sector would urge its allies in the army to overthrow him. If D'Aubuisson won, the army might step in on its own, fearful that the U.S. Congress would halt the flow of desperately needed military supplies.[31] Either way, a military coup would shatter the regime and precipitate a battle royal in Congress to cut off military aid.

For Washington, the best outcome was one in which neither D'Aubuisson nor Duarte emerged victorious. In early 1984, the embassy tried to discourage ARENA from nominating D'Aubuisson by signaling his unacceptability. Twice his requests for a visa to visit the United States were turned down. U.S. officials frequently told the press on background that his election would endanger U.S. aid because Congress would refuse to fund a government headed by a reputed death squad leader. The CIA even sponsored trips to El Salvador by unwitting European journalists and fed them derogatory information about D'Aubuisson.[32] The strategy almost worked; at one point, ARENA leaders considered replacing him at the head of the ticket, but they had no one else who could match Duarte on the stump.[33]

Among the Christian Democrats, Washington's first choice was Fidel Chávez Mena, a businessman who got along well with both the private sector and the army. Unlike Duarte, who seemed to revel in antagonizing his adversaries, Chávez Mena was conciliatory by nature. Duarte, however, was a founding member of the Christian Democratic Party. When it came to maneuvering inside the party, Chávez Mena was no match for him. "I know we pushed at the highest levels," said one U.S. official in San Salvador, explaining the embassy's effort to secure the nomination for Chávez Mena, "but it came down to the convention and Duarte won."[34]

Having failed to block either D'Aubuisson or Duarte, Washington quietly bestowed its blessing on a dark horse, Francisco Guerrero of the National Conciliation Party (Partido de Conciliación Nacional, PCN)—the old traditional party of the armed forces that controlled the government during the 1960s and 1970s.[35] Guerrero was a veteran politician acceptable to both the private sector and the army, but he was not exactly reform-minded. In 1976, when moderates in the military government proposed a limited agrarian reform, Guerrero was one of its toughest opponents. As the 1984 campaign got under way, he refused to endorse the existing agrarian reform and defended the security forces against charges that they harbored death squads.[36]

The administration hoped that Guerrero would siphon off enough votes from D'Aubuisson to place second behind Duarte in the first round of balloting. With D'Aubuisson eliminated, ARENA supporters would flock to Guerrero, who would then defeat Duarte in the runoff election. To Washington's dismay, however, Guerrero proved to be a lousy campaigner—affable, but colorless and uninspiring. The CIA provided almost half a million dollars to boost his campaign, but when the ballots were counted in the first round on March 25, 1984, Guerrero came in a disappointing third with only 19.3 percent of the vote. Duarte took a commanding lead with 43.4 percent and D'Aubuisson came in second with 29.8 percent.[37]

The runoff campaign lasted five weeks, during which Duarte and D'Aubuisson hurled invective at one another. D'Aubuisson accused the Christian Democrats of being Communists, referring to them as the "Cretin Democrats" and to Duarte as "Crazy Duarte." Duarte gave as good as he got, calling ARENA the "ARE-Nazis." He also made a pun on D'Aubuisson's name to evoke his connection with the death squads, calling him "Roberto Escuadrón."[38]

On the serious side, Duarte ran on a platform that called for a "social pact" among classes to get the nation moving again. He pledged to end the death squad violence and bring the armed forces under civilian control. On the issue of negotiations, Duarte was circumspect. He spoke repeatedly of his support for a "national dialogue" with the FDR-FMLN, but he also swore not to concede a share of power to them.

D'Aubuisson defended the military's conduct of the war and called for human rights constraints to be lifted so that the soldiers could get on with their job. "This is a dirty war," he said. "Human rights prohibits the army from winning against the subversives." And he was adamantly opposed to any sort of talks with the guerrillas. "We are never going to negotiate, we are never going to dialogue, we are never going to surrender," he declared. "We will only have peace through victory."[39]

Between Duarte and D'Aubuisson, the Reagan administration's choice was easy. Duarte was highly regarded in Washington and in Europe as an authentic democrat, despite his participation in the civil-military junta that presided over the bloodletting in 1980–82. Most observers were willing to accept Duarte's own assessment of those years. "I was just a member of the junta," he said. "My power came from the military." Things would be different when he had the mandate of a popular election behind him, he insisted. People believed him—or at least, they believed he would try.[40] D'Aubuisson, on the other hand, still carried the burden of Ambassador Robert White's terse characterization of him as "a pathological killer."[41]

The CIA had been helping the Salvadoran Christian Democrats for a long time. One of the first covert actions launched by the Reagan administration in 1981 was a program of political aid to them. Duarte himself had been a CIA asset, complete with code name, for many years, although it was unclear whether he realized he had been providing information to the CIA or whether he received payments. The CIA had spent nearly $2 million on the 1982 Salvadoran election, trying to boost the Christian Democrats and blunt the appeal of the far right.[42]

The Agency spent another $2.1 million during the 1984 campaign to keep D'Aubuisson out of the presidency. A million went to the Christian Democrats, much of it laundered by the Konrad Adenauer Foundation in West Germany, which channeled it to a private Venezuelan foundation, the Institute for Popular Education. The Venezuelans then conducted polls and produced radio and television spots for Duarte at no cost. The Venezuelans also gave extensive advice and financial support to the Salvadoran Elections Council (a nonpartisan government agency responsible for administering the election), paying the salaries of three hundred staff workers.[43]

In addition to covert support, Washington also provided over a million dollars in overt assistance through the U.S. Agency for International Development (AID) to AIFLD-backed trade unions that were campaigning for Duarte. Although it was against the law for unions to participate in Salvadoran elections, the unions belonging to the Popular Democratic Union (Unión Popular Democrática, UPD) federation openly canvassed on Duarte's behalf. U.S. advisers also organized the entire election process from start to finish, and the State Department footed the $10.5 million bill for it.[44]

As expected, Duarte won the May 6 runoff election handily, getting 53.6 percent of the vote to D'Aubuisson's 46.4 percent. At first, ARENA denounced the result as fraudulent and claimed D'Aubuisson had actually won. The Elections Council dismissed ARENA's complaints, however, and the army did not respond positively to discreet soundings about the possibility of a coup. "The CIA, not the PDC [Christian Democrats] won the election," complained D'Aubuisson's vice presidential candidate Hugo Barrera.[45] But there was not much ARENA could do about it.

The Salvadoran right was understandably bitter about Washington's covert support for Duarte. Since 1981, State Department officials had been urging the right to disband the death squads and make their political case in the electoral arena. When they took up this challenge, Washington conspired to keep them from winning—first in 1982, when Ambassador Hinton lobbied the armed forces to impose Magaña instead of D'Aubuisson as provisional president, and now in 1984 when the CIA did its utmost to assure Duarte's victory. As usual, the U.S. ambassador was the lightning rod for the right's discontent. The right hated Thomas Pickering almost as much as they had hated Robert White.

In Washington, the Salvadoran right's anger was voiced by D'Aubuisson's friend Senator Jesse Helms. In a letter to Reagan, Helms demanded that Pickering be fired for trying to "rig the electoral outcome." The White House reaffirmed the president's confidence in Pickering and defended its aid to El Salvador's "democratic institutions."[46] Helms refused to relent, however. On May 8, he spoke on the Senate floor, accusing the CIA of interfering in the Salvadoran election to assure Duarte's victory. "This covert funding has been going on for two years," Helms charged. "The State Department and the CIA bought the election for Duarte. Mr. Pickering was merely the purchasing agent."[47]

The accuracy of the accusation was confirmed by the response. Senators Barry Goldwater and Daniel Patrick Moynihan wrote a letter on behalf of the entire Intelligence Committee formally rebuking Helms for releasing classified information. One committee member, Senator David Durenberger, acknowledged the CIA's role, but said the CIA "gave us the impression there had been some involvement, not with any particular candidate but with various parties" (referring, no doubt, to the fact that the CIA had aided both Guerrero and Duarte).[48]

Helms's denunciation of Ambassador Pickering had unintended reverberations in El Salvador. It confirmed the right's suspicion that Pickering, like Deane Hinton and Bob White before him, was soft on the Communists. It also misled them into thinking they could take action against Pickering without retribution.[49] In May 1984, just after Duarte won the runoff election, U.S. intelligence uncovered a plot by D'Aubuisson supporters to assassinate the ambassador. The plot was far advanced by the time it was discovered; the killers had been recruited, the necessary weapons had been acquired, and Pickering's movements had been charted. To foil the plot, the administration dispatched troubleshooter Vernon Walters to confront D'Aubuisson.

Senator Helms received word of the assassination plot from an NSC official who tipped him off because Helms was then in a tight race for reelection, and the White House did not want him caught out on a limb defending D'Aubuisson just before news of the assassination plot became public. Helms's staff promptly warned D'Aubuisson that Walters was on his way to El Salvador with proof of the conspiracy. By the time Walters arrived, D'Aubuisson had his denials well prepared, insisting he knew nothing about the plot. Few officials in Washington believed him.[50] "General Walters read the riot act," said one administration official. "The message was that we knew what was going on and it had better not happen."[51]

"We wouldn't want anything to happen to the ambassador," Walters warned. If it did, Washington would hold D'Aubuisson "personally accountable" and he would "regret it."[52]

Astonishingly, just a few weeks after the assassination plot was thwarted, Washington reversed its policy against granting D'Aubuisson a visa to visit the United States. The rationale for this turnabout was to show D'Aubuisson that the United States was not unalterably hostile to him. Perhaps if Washington proffered a little respect, D'Aubuisson would behave himself. "It was to try to get him to be a good opposition leader," an administration official explained. "We told him, 'Those days [of assassinations] are gone—they are gone permanently. You are to be recognized as a politician. And you have the right, as a politician, to go shopping in Miami.'"[53]

The administration's strategy of trying to wean D'Aubuisson from the practice of violence was not notably successful. In October, Washington discovered that the assassination plot against Pickering was back on track. A few weeks later, the State Department warned both congressional and executive branch officials to avoid traveling to El Salvador because of the danger of death squad attacks by rightists still angry over Washington's support for Duarte.[54]

To protect Ambassador Pickering from D'Aubuisson's friends, the White House pulled him out of El Salvador. Nevertheless, D'Aubuisson was again granted a U.S. visa in December, just a few weeks after the administration denied visas to four Salvadoran women from the Mothers of the Disappeared (Co-Madres) who wanted to come to the United States to receive the 1984 Robert F. Kennedy Prize for human rights. The State Department insisted that the Mothers were nothing but a front for the guerrillas and therefore allowing them to enter the country would endanger national security.[55] D'Aubuisson, it seemed, was only a danger to Ambassador Pickering.

Despite his reputation for violence, D'Aubuisson had a devoted following among grassroots Republican conservatives. Republicans tended to identify with El Salvador's besieged private sector, sympathizing with its antagonism to agrarian reform and social welfare programs. After all, they themselves were struggling to undo fifty years of government interference with the free market in the United States. As Senator Helms was fond of pointing out, Americans would never stand for the government nationalizing farm land at home on the scale that Washington was advocating in El Salvador. The Salvadoran Christian Democrats, with their talk of "communitarianism" and programs to improve the lives of the poor, sounded like liberals at best, perhaps even socialists. The principles of ARENA, affirmed Senator Helms, "are the principles of the Republican Party in the United States."[56]

Even the assassination plots against Ambassador Pickering did not dampen the Republican right's enthusiasm for D'Aubuisson. When he came to Washington in June 1984, the Young Americans for Freedom organized his press conference, and the YAFers who squired D'Aubuisson around town wore ARENA T-shirts. During another D'Aubuisson trip in December, over a dozen conservative groups sponsored a dinner in his honor. They presented him with a commemorative plaque expressing their appreciation for his "continuing efforts for freedom in the face of Communist aggression which is an inspiration to freedom loving people everywhere." Among the presenters of the award was White House official Faith Ryan Whittlesey. Sponsors of the dinner included the Young Americans for Freedom, the Moral Majority, the Viguerie Company, the *Washington Times* newspaper, and the National Pro-Life Political Action Committee.[57]

Such expressions of admiration played havoc with the State Department's efforts to control D'Aubuisson and his friends in the security forces. "We can spend weeks, even months, trying to convince somebody like D'Aubuisson that we mean what we say about human rights," said a veteran U.S. diplomat in frustration. "Then somebody like [former Helms aide John] Carbaugh or [Senator Jeremiah] Denton comes down here, puts his arm around him and gives him a sly wink, and it's all undone."[58]

D'Aubuisson and ARENA were not the only big losers in the 1984 election. As in 1982, the FDR-FMLN boycotted the balloting but was unable to forge an effective political response. Civilian FDR leaders Rubén Zamora and Guillermo Ungo argued that El Salvador's violent and repressive atmosphere was incompatible with free elections.[59] But even if that was true, the exclusion of the left from the election did not make the remaining choice between Duarte and D'Aubuisson meaningless. It was hard to ask people to boycott an election when the differences between the two principal candidates were so stark and so portentous. Ungo pledged that the FDR-FMLN would "fight the elections politically, not militarily."[60] Yet he offered no new political initiative.

Despite Ungo's promise, the guerrillas launched major attacks on election day with the obvious intent of disrupting the voting. President Reagan relished drawing attention to the contrast: the common people of El Salvador lining up to vote in free elections; the Marxist guerrillas trying, literally, to shoot their way into power.[61]

On June 1, 1984, Duarte finally achieved his lifelong ambition when he was inaugurated president of El Salvador. He had learned a great deal about Salvadoran politics since his first election victory was stolen by the army in 1972. In his inaugural address, he praised the armed forces effusively.[62]

The House Votes on El Salvador

The House leadership scheduled the foreign aid authorization bill for floor debate during the second week in May. The Democrats would make their most concerted effort yet to constrain Reagan's options in El Salvador, and if the president failed to turn back their challenge, his Central America policy would no longer be viable.

In the weeks leading up to the House debate, the administration and its allies lobbied feverishly. Because 1984 was an election year, Reagan's political advisers wanted to keep him away from issues that might identify him with war. But the danger to Reagan's Central America program was too grave for him to sit on the sidelines. As in 1983, the president would have to use all his powers of persuasion to save it.

On May 9, with the House debate in full swing, Reagan gave a prime-time television address to the nation, asking Congress and the American people to support his policies in Central America.[63] It was a strong performance, reminiscent of the president's April 1983 speech to the joint session of Congress both in tone and intent. Reagan portrayed the Central America crisis in stark East-West terms, attributing it to "Cuban and Nicaraguan aggression aided and abetted by the Soviet Union." He invoked the domino theory, warning, "This Communist subversion poses the threat that 100 million people from Panama to the open border on our south could come under the control of pro-Soviet regimes," bringing "hundreds of thousands of refugees fleeing Communist oppression" into the United States.

El Salvador, Reagan argued, was "struggling valiantly to achieve a workable democracy," and while it had some trouble with the violent right wing, "they are not part of the government" (though his own CIA was reporting just the opposite). "Will we support freedom in this hemisphere or not?" Reagan asked. "Will we defend our vital interests in the hemisphere or not? Will we stop the spread of Communism in this hemisphere or not?"

When the foreign aid bill came to the House floor on May 9, 1984, members had three Central America proposals to choose from: the package authored by Steve Solarz and approved by the Democratic caucus of the House Foreign Affairs Committee; an administration-approved package offered by Michigan congressman William Broomfield, the ranking Republican on the Foreign Affairs Committee; and a liberal amendment sponsored by Gerry Studds that was even tougher than the Solarz proposal. The Studds amendment did not significantly alter the substantive conditions or procedures in the Solarz proposal; it just had them take force sooner.[64] Few people thought it had any real chance of passage, but it served an important purpose: it covered the left flank of the main Democratic package, positioning the Solarz proposal as the middle alternative—a coveted spot in a confrontation where moderates would determine the final outcome.

The Solarz proposal was very similar to the plan originally approved in Barnes's subcommittee. President Reagan would have to certify that the Salvadoran government had achieved effective control over the military and the death squads and had made a good-faith effort to negotiate an end to the war.[65] The Democratic proposal reflected the liberals' utter distrust of Reagan and sought to reduce his discretion as much as possible. When Republicans charged that the Democrats' plan would "tie the president's hands," Geraldine A. Ferraro (D-N.Y.) shot back, "This president's hands need to be tied."[66]

The Republican alternative, on the other hand, left control of the policy to Reagan. The Broomfield amendment fully authorized all the aid Reagan had requested for both fiscal years 1984 and 1985 and encumbered it with no binding conditions.

Debate began just two days after Duarte won the runoff election. The Democrats' most compelling argument for tough new conditions was the failure of the old certification law to significantly change the Salvadoran government's behavior. Republicans countered that the election of Duarte marked the dawn of a new day; now, real improvements would begin. Duarte was much heralded by both sides, each arguing that its proposal was best suited to helping him succeed. The Republicans argued that Duarte's election was proof of the enormous progress that El Salvador had made. "What a showcase of democracy," Henry Hyde (R-Ill.) exclaimed. "Thousands of civilian deaths by the army?" he scoffed. "It is the guerrillas who kill the civilians, not the army."[67] Congress should respond to the successful election by increasing aid and reducing restrictions to demonstrate Washington's confidence in Duarte.

Democrats countered that although Duarte would assume the presidency, real power would still lay with the armed forces. To fulfill his campaign promises, Duarte would need leverage against the recalcitrant military. The tough conditions offered by the Democrats would give him that leverage. "The whole purpose of the committee bill is to strengthen the hand of President Duarte in bringing the security forces under control," Solarz avowed.[68]

The Democrats mocked the Broomfield proposal as a "blank check" that gave the Salvadoran armed forces huge increases in military aid with no strings attached. Without tough conditions, the Democrats argued, the Salvadoran army would never stop violating human rights. And if it continued abusing the population, it would eventually lose the war. "My amendment is not intended to terminate U.S. military aid to El Salvador," insisted Studds. "It is, rather, intended to spur reforms that must occur if a military victory by the left is to be avoided."[69]

Republicans didn't believe a word of it. The conditions required in the Solarz and Studds amendments were "unrealistic" and "unachievable," they charged. What the Democrats really wanted was to prohibit military aid, abandoning El Salvador to Communism. "If you want America to pull out completely from El Salvador, then cast your vote for the Studds amendment," said Broomfield. "If you want to turn that country over to the Marxists, and Cuban-Nicaraguan dominance, vote for this approach. You will be casting a vote for a program which will push El Salvador off the cliff."[70]

Eight members of the House had just returned from serving on the official U.S. observer delegation to the Salvadoran election, and they had nothing but fulsome praise for the process. The State Department picked its observers well, using the same strategy that guided the composition of the Kissinger Commission. It put a few moderate and conservative Democrats from Congress in with conservative Republicans and neoconservative private citizens. Not a single liberal was included. Having witnessed the election with their own eyes, the observers took on special authority in the House debate. And every one of them favored the Broomfield amendment.

A speech by Majority Leader Jim Wright marked the climax of the debate. This was "an agonizing moment," Wright said, but he felt compelled to break with his Democratic colleagues and endorse the Broomfield amendment. "We need steady, emphatic commitment to freedom in El Salvador—not a tenuous, tentative, hesitant or begrudging commitment," Wright began. "It is almost as though we had sat by and encouraged this decent man, José Napoleón Duarte, to undertake the monumental task of building a democratic society in a swamp and then denied him the wherewithal to dredge the swamp. . . . El Salvador needs help now. While we temporize, brave men and women die."[71]

Wright's endorsement of Broomfield gave other moderate and conservative Democrats permission to desert the party position, too.[72] First, the House rejected the Studds amendment, 287–128. The next vote was on Broomfield's proposal, and the Republicans scored a narrow victory, 212–208. All but 8 of the 164 Republicans were joined by 56 Democrats to make up the winning coalition. All but 7 of the Democrats were from the South. Liberal Democrats forced a second vote on the Broomfield proposal, losing again 211–208, and then fought a last-ditch battle to defeat the entire foreign aid bill. But conservative Republicans who normally denounced foreign aid as a giveaway of tax dollars to ungrateful foreigners suddenly saw the wisdom of the program and voted for it. The bill narrowly passed, 211–206.[73]

Realistically, the Republican victory on the Broomfield amendment was just one step in a long legislative process. The Senate had not yet completed work on its version of the foreign aid authorization, and both the House and the Senate still had to pass appropriations bills. There were still plenty of pitfalls for the administration's program, especially since the Democrats had lost by only four votes. Nevertheless, the Broomfield vote was a critical symbolic victory for Reagan and the turning point in the debate over El Salvador. In the House of Representatives, the stronghold of Reagan's liberal opponents, the president had eked out a victory. With Duarte coming to office, these votes would prove to be the high-water mark for Reagan's critics.

The Consensus Consolidated

House Democrats were not yet willing to give up the fight. Once action on the foreign aid bill had been completed, the next battlefield was the long-delayed conference committee on the urgent supplemental bill to which the Senate had added $61.75 million for El Salvador and $21 for the Nicaraguan contras. A majority of the House conferees opposed any additional military aid, and they refused to give in. That sent the issue back to the House and thereby set the stage for another showdown just two weeks after the vote on the Broomfield proposal.[74]

Duarte himself came to Washington to lobby the House and made an overwhelmingly favorable impression. He pledged to stop the death squads and to investigate their most infamous murders. He promised to resume the agrarian reform program, calling the guerrillas a "symptom" of El Salvador's social and economic problems, not their cause. He offered to open a dialogue with the FMLN (though they would have to lay down their arms first; he would "not negotiate with rifles over the table"), and he pledged not to ask for American troops.

Duarte was irresistible—the newly elected president of El Salvador, a man who had fought for democracy and social reform all his life and had endured beatings and exile at the hands of the military. He conveyed a vision of El Salvador's problems and an agenda of remedies that closely matched what the liberal Democrats had been saying for four years. But when it came to U.S. policy, Duarte stood foursquare with Ronald Reagan. "We agree with the objectives and intentions of those who would condition aid," he said, but he opposed the imposition of any actual conditions as a violation of Salvadoran sovereignty. "I am here to ask that you have faith in me."[75]

There was no gainsaying Duarte's impact. "Duarte's election has changed the atmosphere of Congress," said Mike Barnes. "His case is a strong one and he makes it well." Many liberals remained skeptical, not about Duarte's good intentions but about his capacity to carry them out. "The question is not whether we trust Duarte—we do—but whether we trust the military to let him go ahead and do the job," explained Clarence Long, whose Foreign Operations Subcommittee controlled how much money Reagan would actually get for El Salvador.[76]

Duarte's cause was aided by the fact that the National Guardsmen charged with killing the U.S. churchwomen finally went on trial on May 23. All five were convicted the following day, just hours before the House voted on the $61.75 million in the urgent supplemental. The House approved the aid overwhelmingly, 267–154. Only the staunchest liberal Democrats opposed it.[77] (The AIFLD case, however, did not fare as well. In March 1984, Captain Avila was released from prison, and in May, on the same day the churchwomen's case went to trial, an appeals court dismissed the charges against Lieutenant Rodolfo Isidro López Sibrián, freeing him as well. Rank-and-file soldiers might be convicted for killing Americans, but officers were still above the law.)[78]

After winning a decisive victory in the House on the urgent supplemental, the administration sought the remainder of its request through a regular supplemental appropriations bill (H.R. 6040). In the Senate, Robert Kasten's subcommittee on Foreign Operation's approved the administration's full request—$565 million in additional economic and military aid for Central America (as compared to the $131 million approved by the House), including $117 million in military aid for El Salvador. The full Senate concurred.[79]

In the House, Doc Long's subcommittee approved some economic and military aid for Central America, but no additional military aid for El Salvador. Long noted that with only two months remaining in the fiscal year, the administration had not yet used all the military aid funds already available; obviously it did not need any more.[80]

Again, the House-Senate conference committee deadlocked, just as it had over the urgent supplemental, and the House conferees again brought the issue back to the full House to resolve. With the support of Republicans and Jim Wright's Democrats, a proposal providing El Salvador with $70 million in military aid passed 234–161.[81]

With the $64.8 million in military aid originally appropriated for fiscal year 1984, $61.75 million approved in the urgent supplemental, and $70 million approved in the second supplemental, the Reagan administration had a grand total of $196.6 million at its disposal for the war in El Salvador in fiscal year 1984—almost two and a half times as much as it had the year before.

As Congress moved to adjourn for the 1984 elections, it had one last set of decisions regarding El Salvador—how much foreign aid to provide in the *upcoming* fiscal year, 1985. The decisive votes on the Salvador portions of the urgent and regular supplemental appropriations left little doubt that sentiment in the House favored helping Duarte as much as possible. "The wind has been taken out of Congress's sails to a certain degree," Assistant Secretary of State Langhorne Motley said happily.[82]

Since no foreign aid authorization or appropriations legislation for FY 1985 had passed, aid to El Salvador was once again included in the continuing resolution. The House approved $123.25 million in military aid for FY 1985, just $9.25 million less than Reagan's request. Of those funds, $5 million was set aside pending a verdict in the 1981 AIFLD murder case. The set-aside was little more than a symbolic remembrance since it was hardly enough to coerce the Salvadorans to reopen the case. No certification conditions were imposed on the FY 1985 military aid, not even the mild ones contained in the Broomfield amendment. Instead, the continuing resolution simply required that the president "consult with the Committees on Appropriations in regard to the reduction and punishment of death squad activities, elimination of corruption and misuse of government funds, development of an El Salvadoran plan to improve the performance of the military, and progress toward discussions leading to a peaceful resolution of the conflict." The House did, however, add a provision terminating both economic and military aid to El Salvador in the event of a military coup.[83]

When the continuing resolution went to conference, the small discrepancy between the House and Senate military aid levels for El Salvador was resolved by simply splitting the difference. In the end, Congress approved $128 million. The conditions the House placed on the aid were so mild that the administration did not oppose them.[84]

Amid the euphoria over Duarte's victory and the subsequent legislative maneuvering, Congress hardly noticed when, less than a month after Duarte's inauguration, the rightist majority in the National Assembly repealed Decree 207, ending the agrarian reform. A few moderate Republicans drafted a sense of the Congress resolution urging the Salvadorans to extend the reform, but the Reagan administration talked them out of introducing it. U.S. aid was no longer conditioned on reform.[85]

The House votes on El Salvador constituted a major victory for the Reagan administration. It had taken four years, but the president finally managed to get Congress to provide the high level of military aid the Pentagon said was necessary to win the war. General Paul Gorman, commander-in-chief of the

U.S. Southern Command, predicted that the armed forces would have control over 80 percent of the country within two years. National Security Adviser Robert McFarlane was even more optimistic, declaring that the war would be over within a year.[86]

José Napoleón Duarte had done what Henry Kissinger and his bipartisan commission failed to do—build a solid majority coalition in the Congress behind virtually unlimited military aid. In the end, it was not so much fear of Communism that carried the day as it was hope that Duarte would be able to convert El Salvador into something resembling a real democracy. Even for members of Congress who were skeptical about Duarte's chances, he still represented the lesser evil. He was far better than D'Aubuisson and could hardly be worse than Magaña. Moreover, if Duarte failed, the actors waiting in the wings were rightist military officers and leftist guerrillas. Duarte's prospects for success might be grim, but he was still the best bet available.

A negotiated settlement might have been a viable alternative, but try as they might, the Democrats could not convince Ronald Reagan to take it seriously. With Reagan unwilling to press for talks and the Salvadoran military violently opposed to them, there was little that congressional Democrats could do to bring about negotiations. Their only alternatives, then, were to support Duarte with economic and military aid, or not support him. Most moderate Democrats and many of the liberals concluded, albeit grudgingly, that they could not turn their back on the new president. Flush with virtually unlimited funds, the Reagan administration's policy toward El Salvador would now get a real test. If Duarte could not control the armed forces, if he could not press ahead with reforms as promised during his campaign, and if the army could not win the war, the miserly Democratic Congress could no longer be held to blame.

CHAPTER 12

El Salvador Disappears

Ronald Reagan's landslide reelection in 1984 returned him to the White House with a mandate few presidents ever enjoy. He had won 58.8 percent of the popular vote to Walter Mondale's 40.6 percent, and he carried forty-nine states—all except the District of Columbia and Mondale's home state of Minnesota. Although the victory was more personal than partisan, congressional Democrats were not eager to pick an early fight with a president who seemed invincible. The Democrats' timidity, combined with José Napoleón Duarte's election, accelerated the disappearance of El Salvador from the U.S. policy agenda. Duarte, however, still faced formidable opposition at home. If Reagan's policy had finally overcome the resistance of congressional Democrats, it was not yet clear whether it could overcome the resistance of Salvadorans, both left and right.

From La Palma to Ayagualo

Despite his solid electoral triumph, Duarte assumed the presidency with very little freedom of action. A coalition of rightist parties still controlled the National Assembly, from which they could block any executive initiative that required legislation or funding. Since the assembly appointed the Supreme

260

Court, it, too, was dominated by the right. The armed forces, which had never trusted Duarte, allowed him to assume office because aid from the United States depended on it, but they retained a veto over any initiative they disapproved. Fearful of a backlash in the private sector and the armed forces, Washington pressed Duarte to go slow on all fronts.[1]

In the human rights field, Duarte tried to follow through on the process Washington had set in motion with Vice President George Bush's December 1983 visit. He had some success pressuring the armed forces to reassign officers suspected of death squad activities, but even when he was successful, offenders were sent into "golden exile" rather than being punished. Two, Lieutenant Colonel Mario Denis Morán and Lieutenant Colonel Adalberto Cruz, came to the Inter-American Defense College in Washington, an assignment normally regarded as a reward. Colonel Nicolás Carranza, head of the Treasury Police, was slated to be sent to West Germany as military attaché, but the Germans wouldn't take him. He went to Spain instead.[2]

Carranza was replaced by Lieutenant Colonel Rinaldo Golcher, a favorite of the U.S. embassy, who had been in charge of the National Plan in San Vicente. He immediately abolished the Treasury Police intelligence unit, admitting that it had been the source of death squad operations. "Even the other soldiers here feared it," Golcher said. A similar unit in the National Police was disbanded as well. To oversee the cleanup of the security forces, Duarte created the new post of vice minister of defense for public security and appointed a military lawyer and reputed moderate, Colonel Carlos Reynaldo López Nuila, former head of the National Police, to fill it. Duarte also abolished the private security forces attached to various state agencies, such as the power company and telephone company, many of which had become death squads. Death squad murders fell to less than a dozen monthly, down 90 percent from their high point in 1981. Still, no one was punished for the 37,000 people killed since 1979.[3] A year after his election, the CIA concluded that Duarte had had only "modest" success and was "approaching the limits of his ability to control extremist elements."[4]

On the economic front, Duarte was stymied by the right's control of the National Assembly. Within a month of his inauguration on June 1, 1984, the assembly refused to extend Decree 207, thus ending Phase Three of the agrarian reform. Washington, meanwhile, urged Duarte to maintain business confidence, lest a new hemorrhage of capital further depress the crippled Salvadoran economy.[5]

The conditions for negotiating peace were not auspicious, either. Both the armed forces and the U.S. embassy opposed negotiations, and their combined power appeared irresistible. During his first few weeks in office, Duarte's hard-line rhetoric seemed to rule out talks with the guerrillas unless they surrendered.[6] Then, during a speech to the United Nations General Assembly in October 1984, Duarte shocked everyone by proposing to meet with representatives of the Farabundo Martí National Liberation Front (FMLN) to begin an unconditional dialogue for peace. He had not advised either the army high command or Ambassador Thomas Pickering of his intention to make the proposal until just before departing for New York.[7]

Pickering tried to talk Duarte out of making the proposal, but to no avail. Washington feared that the armed forces might overthrow the government, thereby demolishing the bipartisan congressional majority Reagan had finally managed to assemble. But once Duarte made the dramatic announcement, the administration had no choice but to support him publicly—especially since the proposal came in the closing weeks of the U.S. presidential campaign.[8]

The right denounced Duarte as a traitor, and Colonel Sigifredo Ochoa, commander in Chalatenango province where the talks were to take place, sent troops to occupy the area that Duarte had promised would be demilitarized.[9] By the appointed day, however, the troops had been withdrawn. On October 15, 1984, the first face-to-face dialogue between the government and the FDR-FMLN took place in the little town of La Palma. Three thousand people flooded the town, some bused in by the Christian Democrats to cheer for Duarte, others drifting in from the surrounding countryside to show their support for the FDR-FMLN. FDR leaders Rubén Zamora and Guillermo Ungo flew back from exile for the talks and were joined by two senior FMLN commanders, Fermán Cienfuegos and Facundo Guardado, who came down from the mountains. Duarte and Defense Minister Carlos Eugenio Vides Casanova represented the government, and Archbishop Arturo Rivera y Damas mediated. They talked for almost six hours, agreeing only to continue the dialogue, but most people shared Duarte's sentiment when he said, "Just being here is an advance."[10]

The opening of talks was enormously popular in a country that had endured half a decade of war and economic privation. Both sides recognized immediately that it was politically crucial not to be seen as an obstacle to progress at the bargaining table. In the first dialogue session, both sides were on their best behavior. Neither pressed its core demands too vigorously, but neither retreated from them, either.

"Our thesis is still that there can be no real settlement unless there is a sharing of power to guarantee its implementation," Ungo said after La Palma. "Powersharing remains one of our fundamental goals."[11] Duarte, on the other hand, reiterated his long-standing demand that the guerrillas simply join the existing political process. "I guarantee the necessary political space so that those who are currently up in arms can incorporate themselves into society," he pledged. But opposition leaders still were not willing to bet their lives on Duarte's ability to control the armed forces and the death squads.[12]

The La Palma talks took place before the far right could mount any effective opposition, but once the first session was over, it immediately launched a campaign to block any subsequent meetings. D'Aubuisson began traveling from garrison to garrison trying to rally the army against the talks.[13] Although no one in the military was enthusiastic about the dialogue, the praetorians were willing to allow it to proceed as long as Duarte did not retreat from his position that the FMLN simply lay down their arms. Army Chief of Staff Colonel Adolfo Blandón and Lieutenant Colonel Domingo Monterrosa were the key figures supporting Duarte.

On October 23, 1984, Monterrosa and his entire staff were killed when their helicopter exploded and crashed during military operations in Morazán. His death seriously weakened those officers who were willing to support the peace talks. Blandón, in particular, began to back away from the negotiations, especially in light of Washington's obvious ambivalence about them.[14] As the second dialogue session approached in late November, the high command met repeatedly, trying to reach some consensus on how much leeway Duarte should be allowed. They finally informed him that the military would not accept any agreement on a truce, cease-fire, or any limitation of military operations unless the armed forces itself approved the proposal. Faced with such severe opposition and rumors of a coup, Duarte chose not to attend the second dialogue meeting in the town of Ayagualo, sending his political aide, Julio Adolfo Rey Prendes, instead.[15]

The meeting was a disaster. The FDR-FMLN demanded an end to U.S. military aid, the removal of U.S. military advisers, the formation of a new government, constitutional revisions, the reorganization of the armed forces, and the prosecution of human rights violators.[16] The government's position was equally extreme. It refused to consider any solution other than the FMLN's acceptance of the status quo. Although both sides agreed to continue the dialogue, no new meeting was scheduled. As one foreign diplomat observed, "There does not seem to be much they can talk about beyond talking about more talks."[17] As 1985 began, Duarte was once again guarding his right flank. The timing was bad for further talks, he said.[18] It would take three more years of war before the two sides would sit down across the bargaining table again.

Although Duarte's abortive dialogue yielded no progress toward an armistice and strained his relations with both the armed forces and the United States, the talks were not a total loss. They touched a deep desire for peace in the Salvadoran population, bolstering the Christian Democrats as they entered the campaign for National Assembly elections in March 1985. Most observers expected the coalition of rightist parties led by ARENA to retain their assembly majority because of the sagging economy and Duarte's failure to undertake any of the social reforms he promised during the 1984 campaign.

Publicly, the United States declared itself neutral in the legislative election; privately, embassy officials voiced their hope that the right would win, thereby maintaining "a good solid check on Duarte's reformist tendencies."[19] Duarte's surprise announcement of the La Palma talks reinforced Washington's concern that he was a loose cannon who needed to be constrained. Moreover, Washington feared that another defeat for the right might destroy its tenuous commitment to electoral politics, leading to an upsurge in death squad violence.

To the surprise of most observers, the Christian Democrats won a sweeping victory on March 31, 1985, taking 54 percent of the vote and winning thirty-three seats in the sixty-seat assembly.[20] Together, the National Conciliation Party (PCN) and ARENA won only 37 percent of the vote and twenty-five seats. Stunned, the rightist parties accused the Christian Democrats of fraud and demanded that the Election Commission annul the balloting. ARENA even went so far as to accuse the armed forces of complicity in stealing the election. That was a mistake. Defense Minister Vides, flanked by the entire high command, appeared on television to denounce ARENA's attack on the honor of the army. The PCN, sensitive to its military heritage, quickly withdrew its electoral complaint, leaving ARENA isolated.[21]

In the aftermath of this fiasco, ARENA replaced D'Aubuisson as chief of the party. Ever since Washington had helped Duarte win election in 1984, some ARENA leaders had argued that the United States would never accept an ARENA government so long as D'Aubuisson remained in charge. After the 1985 electoral defeat, these voices prevailed. D'Aubuisson was replaced by Alfredo Cristiani, scion of one of the nation's wealthiest families and head of the coffee growers association. Educated at Georgetown University in Washington, D.C., Cristiani spoke perfect English and knew how to talk to gringos. His name had never been linked to the paramilitary violence of ARENA's origins. Soft-spoken and urbane, he was everything that D'Aubuisson was not.[22]

Although the election had not come out as Washington hoped, U.S. policy benefited nevertheless. ARENA's alienation from the army greatly reduced the chances of the far right fomenting a military coup. The Christian Democratic victory also solidified congressional support for the U.S. aid program.

For José Napoleón Duarte, the 1985 election was a great triumph, demonstrating that his appeal for peace and social change resonated with the Salvadoran electorate. The Christian Democrats were now in full control of the presidency, the legislature, and the judiciary. Duarte was well positioned to begin the transformation of Salvadoran society that he had argued and struggled for all his life—if the army and the U.S. embassy would let him.

The Air War

The army was growing more confident. By 1985, U.S. military assistance had begun to have an effect. The regular army, which numbered 7,000 men in 1981, had expanded to 40,000. The security forces (the Treasury Police, National Police, and National Guard) had grown from 5,000 to 13,000, for a total of 53,000 men under arms.[23] Estimates of the size of the FMLN were imprecise—ranging from 5,000 to 13,000 combatants—and the administration was not above inflating them when pleading with Congress for more aid. The FMLN had also grown considerably, doubling or perhaps tripling in size since 1981, but it could not keep up with the rapid growth of the armed forces.[24]

The army's quality was much improved as well. The United States had trained three full-size rapid response battalions and over a thousand new officers, and it was in the process of training a dozen smaller "hunter-killer" battalions for search-and-destroy operations. But the most significant U.S. contribution was hardware. Washington refitted the Salvadoran army from the ground up—boots, uniforms, weapons, ammunition, trucks, jeeps, artillery. Washington gave El Salvador a navy (which it never had before) to interdict arms smuggling by sea and a new air force to fly combat support for the troops in the field.

The air force had the biggest impact on the military balance. When Ronald Reagan came to office, the Salvadorans owned two dozen World War II–vintage training aircraft and four helicopters. The Pentagon immediately set about building an air force designed for counterinsurgency. Progress was slow because new aircraft were expensive and Congress kept trimming Reagan's aid requests, but 1984 was a watershed. When Congress approved virtually all of the funds the administration requested, the Pentagon was able to double the size of the Salvadoran air force virtually overnight.

By 1985, the Salvadorans had forty-nine "Huey" (UH-1) helicopters for transporting troops, along with half a dozen A-37 "Dragonfly" jet aircraft and AC-47 gunships for close air support of troops in combat.[25] The helicopters gave the rapid response battalions unprecedented mobility. Before the helicopters arrived, these elite battalions moved by truck (which confined them to the roads and made them vulnerable to ambush) or on foot (which made them no more "rapid" than the guerrillas). With their new mobility, large numbers of troops could be inserted by surprise into rebel territory, or could be positioned to block the escape of guerrilla units during the army's perennial sweeps. "For the first time," admitted a guerrilla commander, "the immediate reaction battalions are actually reacting immediately."[26]

The AC-47 was especially effective for combat air support. Designed during the war in Vietnam and nicknamed "Puff the Magic Dragon," the AC-47 could fire 18,000 rounds per minute, blanketing a football field with bullets in the time it took to fly over it. The firepower of the AC-47 was so enormous that the planes sent to El Salvador were initially fitted with fewer and less powerful guns than usual, for fear that the Salvadoran air force might use them indiscriminately in populated areas producing horrendous civilian casualties.[27] U.S. pilots also flew clandestine AC-47 combat missions over El Salvador from bases in Panama, the War Powers Resolution notwithstanding.[28]

The A-37 jets were used mainly for bombing. During 1984 and 1985, the air force bombed extensively in the rebel-controlled zones of Chalatenango, Morazán, and the Guazapa Volcano to demoralize the guerrillas and their supporters. The armed forces generally regarded the guerrilla areas as free-fire zones. "The people who move in zones of persistence are identified as guerrillas," an army spokesman said. "Good people—the people who are not with the guerrillas—are not there."[29] In fact, tens of thousands of civilians still lived in the rebel zones, and many of them were, indeed, sympathetic to the guerrillas. The distinction between guerrilla combatants and civilian sympathizers was never one that the armed forces was very good at making.

The bombing, combined with increased army sweeps, was designed to make life so miserable that people would migrate into government-controlled areas, thereby depriving the guerrillas of logistical support.[30] In 1986 the armed forces launched a revised version of the failed 1983 counterinsurgency plan, Operation Well-Being. The new plan, dubbed "United to Reconstruct" ("Unidos Para Reconstruir"), envisioned massive army sweeps to clear a region of guerrillas, followed by the forcible relocation of civilians in outlying areas into resettlement towns where the army could keep an eye on them. If the people cooperated with the military, civic action programs would be started in the community.[31] Army psychological warfare specialists lectured the refugees in order to "give them the idea that they were not captured but rescued."[32] That was what the army called these forced relocations—*rescates*, rescues.

The strategy of depopulating the guerrilla zones owed a great deal to the experience of the Guatemalan armed forces, which had nearly defeated its own insurgency by using air attacks and scorched-earth military sweeps to ruthlessly eliminate any village suspected of harboring guerrilla sympathies. Although this forced depopulation damaged the logistical base of the guerrillas, it also created an ever-expanding dependent population of internal refugees living at government expense—an added strain on El Salvador's already moribund economy. By 1986, 500,000 Salvadorans were internally displaced and over a million had fled the country, most of them going to the United States. In all, 30 percent of the population had been uprooted by the war.[33]

The reconstruction part of the counterinsurgency plan did not work with the same efficiency as the *rescates*. The central government proved incapable of rebuilding civil administration in the countryside, so resettlement areas received little in the way of services or aid. Money earmarked for civic action was stolen by corrupt government officials. The agency responsible, the Committee for the Restoration of Areas (Comité Nacional de Resturación de Areas) was, according to a report by U.S. military officers, "notorious as a black hole, swallowing up U.S. money without evident result."[34]

In many areas, the refugees vigorously resisted being sent to resettle in conflicted zones. And even when they were enticed into such areas, they resisted the government's entreaties to form Civil Defense units. Civil Defense forces became targets for guerrilla attack, the peasants knew, and the Civil Defense forces were never skilled or numerous enough to successfully resist; they were always overrun and killed. Consequently, many "fortified" villages were not fortified or defended at all. The guerrillas moved through them at will.[35] "It is the same as always," said a peasant in San Vicente, the heart of the counterinsurgency effort. "The army comes and goes. The guerrillas come and go. We hide under our beds."[36]

Although the army's various pacification schemes never seemed to make much headway, the army's new firepower changed the battlefield situation considerably. Sustained operations involving large concentrations of guerrillas became impossible in the face of the military's new air power.[37] The FMLN's June 1984 attack on Cerrón Grande dam was a bellwether. Modeled on earlier spectacular successes like the attacks on the Golden Bridge in 1981, Ilopango air base in 1982, and the Cuscatlán bridge in 1983, the Cerrón Grande attack was intended to knock out the dam's hydroelectric plant. But unlike the earlier assaults, this one was only partially successful because the armed forces responded so quickly, flying in elite troops to reinforce the guard garrison at the dam. In March 1985, a similar FMLN assault on a hilltop communications facility failed when the army reinforcements and AC-47 gunships drove the attackers off.[38] Such successes soon brought forth new predictions of imminent victory from officials in Washington.

By early 1985, the FMLN general command had begun to reassess its strategy. Since 1981, it had sought to build a powerful, professional guerrilla force capable of engaging army troops on the battlefield and defeating them. By striking "decisive blows," the FMLN believed it would spark a general insurrection in the cities. The army would then collapse and the revolution triumph.[39]

The army's improved capability forced the FMLN to reevaluate. Military victory, which seemed within reach in late 1983, was impossible by early 1985. The FMLN was forced to abandon major offensives using battalion-size units, turning instead to small-unit operations involving only ten to twenty men, against which air power was ineffective. Rather than trying to expand control over territory, the FMLN sought to inflict maximum casualties on the army in small hit-and-run attacks. If the army was no longer vulnerable to decisive blows, it might still be bled to death by a thousand cuts. The FMLN's earlier strategy of preparing for imminent insurrection gave way to a "war of attrition."[40]

Economic sabotage, which had been an element of FMLN military strategy since 1981, assumed greater prominence. The guerrillas were more assiduous about burning trucks and buses, blowing up electrical pylons, and destroying export crops. Inevitably, many ordinary people were economically injured by the stepped-up sabotage campaign, which had never been popular.[41]

As the FMLN settled into its war of attrition, it was determined to defeat the counterinsurgency scheme the army had been testing in San Vicente and Usulután provinces. The guerrillas had retained their military presence in the disputed areas during 1984 and forced many local government officials to cooperate with them. But as their military fortunes receded in 1985, the guerrillas became less tolerant. Rather than coexist with the regime's local officials, they decided to eliminate the civil government's presence wherever they could. They burned town halls and kidnapped over two dozen mayors, some of whom they held and some of whom they released after warning them to resign or face execution. Two who failed to heed the warnings were murdered. The threats against the mayors had the desired effect; many resigned, many others fled to the safety of the provincial capital. In contested towns and villages, the machinery of government, rudimentary as it was, ground to a halt.[42]

Here, too, there was a political price to pay. Most of the kidnapped mayors were Christian Democrats who won office in the March 1985 elections. They were reformers, not local oligarchs or rightist paramilitary thugs. And, being new to their jobs, they hardly seemed to have done anything to justify being kidnapped or killed. The FMLN's ruthlessness proved that the government did not control the contested areas, but it did not endear the rebels to the population.

Finally, a key element of the FMLN's new strategy was to rebuild its military capacity and base of political support in the cities. Between 1980 and 1983, the security forces and the right-wing death squads had exterminated the urban popular organizations. Thereafter, FMLN officials spoke often of the need to rebuild their urban base, but little was done before 1984, in part because the terror of the death squads continued unabated and in part because the FMLN general command was preoccupied with building an army. Duarte's 1984 victory opened some space for renewed political activity in the cities just as the FMLN's chances for a battlefield victory began to fade.

The result was a new emphasis by the FMLN on urban organizing. Looking back on past experience, the guerrillas concluded that the failure of the revolutionary movement in the cities in the late 1970s was due to the absence of an effective military arm to respond to state repression. Conversely, the failure of the revolutionary army in the 1980s was due to the absence of an effective urban movement that could spark a popular insurrection to tie down government troops in the cities. The FMLN strategy for the late 1980s, therefore, was to husband the strength of combatants in the countryside while rebuilding the urban movement.[43] Urban military actions consisted mostly of assassinations of military and government officials. In 1985, on the anniversary of the assassination of Archbishop Oscar Romero, four urban guerrillas gunned down the legendary José Alberto "Chele" Medrano—D'Aubuisson's mentor and the former commander of the National Guard who had laid the foundations for El Salvador's paramilitary right during the 1960s and 1970s.[44]

Death in the Zona Rosa

Despite occasional assassinations by FMLN commandos, the city of San Salvador had been relatively peaceful since death squad violence subsided in 1984. A bit of nightlife had revived in an area known as the Zona Rosa, a string of sidewalk cafés and discotheques that catered to wealthy Salvadorans and foreigners. Security regulations forbid U.S. embassy personnel from patronizing the Zona Rosa because its open-air cafés were so vulnerable to attack. But it had been two years since Commander Albert A. Schaufelberger was killed, and security consciousness had once again grown lax. Off-duty Marine guards from the embassy were regulars along the strip.

Half a dozen Marines were there on June 12, 1985, when an army truck carrying ten men in uniform pulled up in front of their table. No one paid much attention as the soldiers climbed down; troops were a normal sight in the city, especially after dark. But these were not government soldiers. They were guerrilla commandos who opened fire point-blank on the Marines, killing four of them, along with two U.S. civilians. When other patrons fired back at the commandos with pistols, the guerrillas sprayed the crowd with their automatic weapons, killing nine and wounding fifteen.[45]

Ronald Reagan, George Bush, George Shultz, Caspar Weinberger, and Robert McFarlane all stood on the tarmac at Andrews Air Force Base when the Marines' caskets came home. Reagan pledged that the United States would "find the jackals and bring them and their colleagues in terror to justice."[46] Inside the administration, hard-liners such as new White House communications director Patrick Buchanan argued for massive retaliation, including U.S. airstrikes against the guerrillas and their alleged training camps in Nicaragua. Other officials advocated a relaxation of the legal ban on assassinations so that the CIA could target both FMLN and Sandinista leaders. In the end, Reagan decided against launching any air attacks for fear of civilian casualties, and the ban on assassinations remained intact.[47] But according to several reports, a special squad of U.S. Rangers was dispatched on a retaliatory raid that wiped out an entire FMLN training camp, killing eighty-three people.[48]

The administration also used the Zona Rosa attack as an opportunity to launch a new police training program. The killings occurred at a time when the administration was already searching for ways to improve the ability of the Salvadoran security forces to combat the growing FMLN presence in the cities. The main obstacle was the prohibition on U.S. aid to foreign police forces, written into the law in 1974 because so many foreign police trained and supplied by the United States had engaged in systematic campaigns of torture and murder.[49] In El Salvador, the security forces (Treasury Police, National Police, and National Guard) had always been among the worst human rights violators and were home to many of the death squads.

In fact, Reagan did not wait for the ban to be lifted before beginning police training. In early 1985, U.S. military advisers trained a special counterterrorism unit of the Treasury Police to act as a SWAT team. When the U.S. role in creating the special unit was revealed, the administration argued that it had not violated the law against training police because the unit involved had been transferred from the Treasury Police and placed under the command of the armed forces chief of staff. That made it a military unit rather than a police unit and therefore eligible for training. The transfer, however, occurred only on paper. The head of the security forces, Colonel Carlos Reynaldo López Nuila, not the armed forces chief of staff, continued to exercise direct command authority over the special unit. President Duarte was not informed that such a unit even existed.[50]

The attack on the Marines in the Zona Rosa in June 1985 gave the administration an unprecedented opportunity to press Congress to lift the ban on police aid. A rash of international terrorist incidents against Americans—the Zona Rosa attack, the hijacking of TWA flight 847, and the bombing of a café in Germany frequented by U.S. soldiers—had made terrorism the issue of the day.

When the 1985 foreign aid bill came to the floor of the House of Representatives just a few weeks after the Zona Rosa killings, Bill McCollum (R-Fla.) proposed an amendment to lift the ban on police training for El Salvador and Honduras.[51] In the antiterrorist fever of the moment, not many Democrats had the courage to oppose it. George Miller (D-Calif.) reminded his colleagues that between 1957 and 1974, before the ban on police aid was enacted, the United States had spent $2.1 million to train 448 officers of the Salvadoran security forces, with no noticeable improvement in their respect for human rights. D'Aubuisson himself was a graduate the old program's International Police Academy.[52] Miller urged the House to vote against lifting the ban, but even he conceded that some sort of police program was needed to combat terrorism. McCollum's amendment passed easily.

Lifting the ban did not automatically create a police aid program, but the administration immediately reprogrammed $9 million for training in El Salvador and requested another $54 million for the Central America region. This latter request was blocked only by Senator Tom Harkin's single-handed filibuster late in the congressional session.[53]

Duarte's Daughter

On September 10, FMLN urban commandos kidnapped President Duarte's daughter, Inés Guadalupe Duarte Duran, outside the university where she was taking courses. The guerrillas spirited her out of the capital, into guerrilla territory in Chalatenango, and then offered to trade her for thirty-four political prisoners, including Américo Mauro Araujo, the second in command of the Communist Party, arrested just a few weeks before.[54]

The kidnapping of Duarte's daughter was a shattering personal blow to the president. In an emotional speech, Duarte berated the kidnappers, declaring they had "crushed the most sacred part of my being, fatherly love, the love of my children." Then he broke down and wept.[55] Duarte's first and only concern was to get his daughter back safe and sound. He ordered the air force to stop bombing in Chalatenango and the army to stop search-and-destroy operations for fear Inés might be injured. He began negotiations by radio with the kidnappers as soon as they made their demands.

Everyone sympathized with Duarte, but his eagerness to comply with guerrillas annoyed both the armed forces and his colleagues in the Christian Democratic Party. The army felt Duarte's reaction was weak and self-centered. "Duarte must think as a father, but he must act as a president," commented one officer.[56] After all, military men had lost many friends in the war, but that was no reason to capitulate to guerrilla demands. Duarte added insult to injury by sending the rest of his family to the United States, implying the armed forces were incapable of safeguarding them.

Other Christian Democrats noted that Duarte had done nothing to free the three dozen Christian Democratic mayors and municipal officials kidnapped by the FMLN since 1985. Only when his own daughter was taken did he suddenly become willing to negotiate an exchange. After six weeks of discussions mediated by the Catholic Church, the FMLN agreed to release Inés and thirty-three local PDC officials in exchange for twenty-five political prisoners held by the government and the evacuation of ninety-six wounded FMLN combatants to hospitals abroad.[57] Leaders of the two sides also agreed not to target each other's families in the future.

Though it lasted just over a month, the kidnapping of Inés Duarte inflicted lasting political damage to her father. His relations with the armed forces, never good, worsened because he was so quick to release senior FMLN prisoners. In the midst of the negotiations, rightist officers led by Colonel Sigifredo Ochoa wrote a memo to the high command arguing that Duarte was a danger to national security and should be overthrown. The memo provoked an all-day debate at the highest levels of the army.[58]

For the FMLN, the political harm done to Duarte by the kidnapping did not come without cost. Internationally, it was widely condemned as terrorism. In the United States, it further consolidated the bipartisan congressional majority behind Duarte's government. No Democrat was about to offer any proposal that could be interpreted as sympathetic to the guerrillas after they killed six U.S. citizens in the Zona Rosa and then kidnapped Duarte's daughter.

The kidnapping also diminished the possibility of a negotiated settlement to the war. By weakening Duarte's standing with the armed forces, the kidnapping made it more difficult for him to overcome the military's resistance to dialogue, had he wanted to continue it. But he didn't; the residue of personal bitterness left by the kidnapping ended any real prospect for negotiations as long as Duarte remained president.[59]

Finally, the kidnapping exacerbated divisions between the FMLN guerrillas and their civilian allies in the FDR. From the beginning, there had been ideological differences between the two coalitions. The guerrillas were fighting for a socialist revolution, whereas many of the civilians in the FDR were struggling for radical social reform in a mixed economy presided over by a democratic government. The repressive violence of the Salvadoran regime submerged the differences on the left in the early 1980s and united it behind the common belief that only armed struggle could force any significant change.

The first cracks in the united front became visible when the guerrillas attacked the 1982 elections. Both the FDR and FMLN agreed that the elections were illegitimate, but the civilian politicians were nevertheless uneasy about disrupting the electoral process by force. These concerns were heightened when the guerrillas tried to derail the 1984 and 1985 elections as well. The FMLN saw the elections in black-and-white terms: so long as their supporters continued to suffer repression, the elections were not free. They were simply an element of Washington's counterinsurgency strategy, a facade designed to legitimize a regime based not on popular sovereignty but on coercive force. The elections were therefore a legitimate target for attack.

The politicians of the FDR took a more nuanced view. They agreed that the elections were not fair, but they also recognized that the reduction of death squad violence and the increased political space available for trade unions and other popular organizations after 1984 meant that the elections were not totally a charade, either. At a minimum, they were a political challenge that the left was failing to meet.[60] When the FMLN burned voting records in rural townships, FDR President Guillermo Ungo publicly criticized the practice. In 1985, senior FDR officials began openly criticizing FMLN military actions that they regarded as human rights abuses, particularly the kidnapping and assassination of mayors, the shooting of civilians in the Zona Rosa, and the kidnapping of Duarte's daughter.[61]

Congress Acquiesces

By 1985, there was not much fight left in Congress when it came to El Salvador. Despite the constraints Duarte labored under, his first year in office appeared successful. The right was in disarray after ARENA's defeat in the National Assembly elections, human rights violations continued to decline, dialogue had begun (albeit fitfully), and the armed forces finally seemed to be gaining the initiative on the battlefield. No one doubted that there was still a long way to go, but few congressional Democrats were still willing to argue that the direction of Reagan's policy was fundamentally flawed. Those who had feared that reform in El Salvador was impossible and that U.S. involvement would lead inexorably to another Vietnam seemed to have been mistaken. Even liberal critics who were less sanguine about Duarte's progress had to face political reality: Most moderate Democrats believed U.S. policy was working and were not about to challenge it.

With the rising federal budget deficit forcing cuts in virtually every domestic program, Reagan proposed only moderate increases in his fiscal year 1986 foreign aid request for Central America. For El Salvador, Reagan asked somewhat less than the previous year's record levels: $132.6 million in military aid (down from the $146.25 million approved for fiscal year [FY] 1985) and $352 million in economic aid (down from $433.9). In recognition of Duarte's efforts, the administration asked that the aid be approved with no conditions. Past conditions had "served a useful purpose," Assistant Secretary of State Tony Motley acknowledged, but with Duarte's election, "the need has passed."[62]

House Democrats had little stomach for another fight over El Salvador, but sought to revive the certification requirements for El Salvador that passed originally in 1981. For military aid to be released, Reagan would have to certify every six months that the Salvadoran government was willing to dialogue with the FDR-FMLN, that it was in control of its armed forces, and that it had made demonstrated progress in implementing agrarian reform and establishing an effective judicial system.

In committee, liberals, led by Peter H. Kostmayer (D-Pa.), tried unsuccessfully to prohibit the provision of additional aircraft to El Salvador because of the large number of civilians killed or left homeless by air attacks.[63] The Republicans argued that accounts of human rights violations in the air war were fabrications. They acknowledged that there had been excesses in 1983 and 1984, but in September 1984, Duarte had issued rules of engagement that prohibited air attacks in civilian areas. The Republicans would not countenance the idea that perhaps the Salvadoran air force, long a bastion of the far right and "an autonomous fiefdom" according to U.S. officers, might be less than scrupulous in hewing to the president's orders.[64]

When the foreign aid bill went to the House floor, the only real debate over El Salvador came on an amendment offered by John Conyers Jr. (D-Mich.) that would have replaced the weak conditions on military aid with much tougher ones. Conyers wanted to suspend military aid immediately, restoring it only if the government agreed to negotiate an end to the war, carried out the agrarian reform, and prosecuted people for the thousands of political murders that had been carried out.

The first member to rise in opposition to Conyers was Mike Barnes. The conditionality already in the bill addressed all the same concerns, Barnes argued. Suspending military aid, however, would be "a mistake." With Barnes and the rest of the Democratic leadership against it, the Conyers amendment was crushed, 375–47.[65] If the close vote on the Broomfield amendment in 1984 marked the zenith of the Democrats' opposition to Reagan's policy in El Salvador, the vote on the Conyers amendment marked its nadir. The defeat was so total that for the next three years, no one even tried to raise the issue of El Salvador on the floor of the House of Representatives.

Moderate Democrats congratulated themselves that they were "building a broad base for a bipartisan policy toward El Salvador."[66] In fact, this new bipartisanship was almost entirely on Reagan's terms. In the House-Senate conference on the foreign aid bill, the weak conditions on aid to El Salvador passed by the House were transformed into mere "expectations." Aid would not be contingent upon their achievement. The conference report included no specific amount of aid for El Salvador, leaving the administration free to provide funds up to the full level of its request. Except for retaining the condition that aid would be cut off in the event of a military coup, the FY 1986 foreign aid bill gave Ronald Reagan a blank check.[67]

As Reagan's second term began, his policy toward El Salvador looked more successful than ever. On the military front, massive U.S. aid had dashed the left's hope of a military victory. The armed forces might not be winning war, but they were no longer losing it. On the political front, three elections had been held despite guerrilla efforts to disrupt them. Washington had enticed the far right to join the electoral process, but had kept it from winning the presidency. Instead, the Christian Democrats were firmly in place at the helm of the civilian part of the government. And the number of civilian noncombatants killed by the military and the death squads had gradually been reduced from over 12,000 in 1981 to 1,500 in 1985.[68] On the home front, Reagan had won the showdown with liberal Democrats in 1984 and built a comfortable majority behind his policy.

Despite its apparent success, Reagan's policy still had a few weak spots. El Salvador's new electoral institutions had not displaced the army from its position of privilege, or broken its immunity. The armed forces remained an institution apart, bound together by its own traditions, laws, and loyalties, impervious to civilian control. Justice, a scarce commodity even in Salvadoran civil society, did not extend into the armed forces. Duarte could not govern against them; he could only maneuver within the bounds of their tolerance and the protection afforded by the U.S. embassy.

Duarte's other albatross was the war. The war dragged on in protracted stalemate, bleeding the economy and making it all but impossible for Duarte to improve people's lives. Campaigning on a platform of social reform was easier than delivering it. So long as the United States had a law that automatically cut off aid to El Salvador in the event of a military coup, Duarte was secure in office. He was not, however, secure in power. Salvadoran voters elected Duarte because he promised a brighter future. The U.S. Congress supported him because he was better than all the plausible alternatives. On the strength of his promises, the exuberant, charismatic Duarte enjoyed a honeymoon in 1985 with both his domestic and his foreign constituencies. But honeymoons do not last forever.

Out of Sight, Out of Mind

For the next three years, Ronald Reagan had a free hand to pursue his strategy for victory in El Salvador. In 1986 and 1987, Congress approved the administration's aid requests without significant debate or condition. Only a single constraint remained in force—U.S. aid would be cut off if the elected government was overthrown. Experience had taught that this gave the U.S. ambassador valuable leverage when the right periodically threatened a coup, so the administration did not oppose the condition.[69]

Despite the severe U.S. budget constraints imposed by the Gramm-Rudman-Hollings deficit-reduction requirements, El Salvador was one of a handful of countries that received more aid from Washington in FY 1987 than in FY 1986.[70] Congress continued to balk at providing large-scale police aid, for fear that U.S. dollars would end up directly subsidizing death squads. But the administration was able to get around this reluctance by continuing to finance a modest police training program with reprogrammed funds.[71]

Besides Duarte's popularity, a variety of factors contributed to the disappearance of El Salvador from the congressional agenda. In 1986, Mike Barnes gave up his safe House seat to run for the Senate and lost the Democratic primary to Congresswoman Barbara Mikulski. Barnes was replaced as chair of the Western Hemisphere Subcommittee by George W. Crockett, an elderly former judge from Detroit. One of the most progressive members of the House, Crockett was even more ideologically opposed to Reagan's Central America policy than Barnes—so much so that some hard-right conservatives charged that he should be denied the chairmanship because he would be a security risk. Henry Hyde (R-Ill.) defended Crockett—sort of—by quipping, "He's no more a security risk than anyone else on his side" of the aisle.[72] Unlike Barnes, Crockett was neither energetic nor highly respected by his colleagues. Under his direction, the level of subcommittee activity declined noticeably.

Another prominent Reagan opponent, Clarence Long, was defeated for reelection in 1984. Long was succeeded as chair of the Foreign Operations Subcommittee by David R. Obey (D-Wis.). Obey was no less liberal than Long, but whereas Long had no compunctions about using his chairmanship to force policy concessions from the administration, Obey took a more traditional view of the appropriations process: its role was to set the level of funding, not make policy. Obey was reluctant to weigh down appropriations bills with policy language and conditions that properly belonged in authorizing legislation. Even when Congress failed to pass foreign aid authorizations (as it frequently did), making the appropriations bills the only vehicle through which Congress could assert any influence over policy, Obey resisted.

Despite the unencumbered flow of U.S. aid, the military situation on the ground in El Salvador remained essentially unchanged from 1985 to 1988. The armed forces seemed to have regained the initiative after weathering the crises of 1982–84, but they were unable to deal the guerrillas a fatal blow. The FMLN continued to rely on hit-and-run attacks that cumulatively took as great a toll on the army as the guerrilla's major offensives had in earlier years. From July 1983 to July 1984, the armed forces admitted suffering 2,208 casualties. From mid-1984 to mid-1985, the casualty rate was 2,834, and the following year it was 3,003. Economic damage from the war continued to run at about $250 million annually, for a total of $1.5 billion by the end of 1985.[73]

Occasionally, the FMLN demonstrated it still had the ability to launch large-scale attacks. In June 1986, several hundred guerrillas attacked the headquarters of the army's 3rd Brigade at San Miguel, killing or wounding dozens of soldiers. The five U.S. advisers living in the camp managed to escape injury.[74] Staff Sergeant Gregory Fronius was not so lucky in April 1987, when guerrillas attacked the army's modern fire base at El Paraíso, which they had overrun in December 1983. Fronius was killed in the attack, along with at least sixty-nine Salvadoran soldiers. None of the Salvadoran casualties were officers; when the attack began, the entire base command abandoned the field and took shelter in an underground bunker.[75] Six more U.S. advisers, including the deputy commander of the Mil-Group, were killed a few months later when their helicopter crashed. But none of these incidents caused much of a stir in Congress or the press, and none led the administration to alter its rules of engagement for the advisers, even though they routinely came under enemy fire.[76]

In Washington, U.S. officials continued to insist that the war was being won, but as the decade wore on, they seldom repeated the confident predictions of imminent victory that were so common after Congress approved massive increases in military aid in 1984. By 1986, U.S. military experts were admitting that it would be another four to six years before the guerrillas were beaten. By 1987, the horizon of victory had been pushed back to a decade or more.[77] "Officers in El Salvador today have difficulty knowing whether or not American policy is any closer to achieving its purposes than it was half a dozen years ago," four U.S. colonels wrote in a scathing 1988 report on the war's progress.[78]

If the army was not becoming more capable, it was at least becoming more pliable as younger officers close to the U.S. embassy gradually gained control of the institution. By 1987, most key commands were held by members of the *Tandona*, the largest graduating class (*tanda*) from the Salvadoran military academy. Colonel René Emilio Ponce, who ranked first in the class of 1966 and became its acknowledged leader, succeeded Colonel Adolfo Blandón as army chief of staff in 1988. As was the tradition in the army, Ponce then appointed his classmates to senior posts. Like all *tandas*, the *Tandona* was by no means ideologically homogeneous; it had its share of extreme rightists. But Ponce was generally regarded as a moderate, even though he supported D'Aubuisson in the early 1980s and was linked to death squads operating in the National Police.

As his chief of operations, Ponce chose one of the most liberal officers in the army, Colonel Mauricio Ernesto Vargas, whose father had been a founding member of the Christian Democratic Party.[79]

As the war dragged on inconclusively, a new division emerged within the Salvadoran officers corps between the moderate right, led by Ponce, and the extreme right, led by air force commander General Juan Raphael Bustillo. Ponce and his allies, like Blandón before him, accepted Washington's counterinsurgency strategy of "low intensity conflict" with its emphasis on winning hearts and minds through civic action and improved human rights performance. Bustillo and the extreme right resented Washington's meddling. Aligned politically with D'Aubuisson and ARENA, the rightists advocated a strategy of "total war"—an all-out military campaign against not only the FMLN but also peasants and urban activists suspected of supporting the guerrillas—that is, anyone demanding social reform. Even if 100,000 people had to be killed, the hard-liners reasoned, at least the war would be over quickly. Less fanatical officers, on the other hand, recognized that the carnage of "total war" would likely provoke an end to U.S. military aid, without which the armed forces could not sustain operations.[80]

With the war seemingly under control, Washington's attention turned to the economy, the regime's most serious vulnerability. From 1979 to 1983, El Salvador's gross domestic product had fallen 22 percent, back to the level of the 1960s. Thereafter, sluggish growth just kept pace with the population increase. Real per capita wages had fallen 27 percent, due to the combined effects of some $3 billion in war damage and capital flight. By 1985, unemployment had hit 30 percent, with another 30 percent underemployed, and inflation was running at 22 percent as well. Despite a doubling of coffee prices on the world market, El Salvador's trade deficit in 1985 was $376 million.[81]

After the Christian Democrats won the 1985 National Assembly elections, Washington began pressuring Duarte to devise an economic stabilization plan to reduce the government's annual $100 million deficit, which Washington had to finance. Austerity meant cutting public sector spending (in nondefense areas, of course), so Duarte would have to hold firm against state employees' demands for wage increases, his campaign promises notwithstanding. Duarte resisted, knowing that the people who would be hit hardest by austerity were his constituents—the urban middle and lower classes. But Washington threatened to curtail economic aid. "Without U.S. aid, we would be absolutely broke and inflation would be totally out of control," admitted Planning Minister Fidel Chávez Mena.[82] Duarte had little choice but to comply.

In January 1986, Duarte unveiled his economic "package." It devalued the currency, raised import taxes, limited imports of luxury goods, and proposed a "war tax" on the wealthy. To cushion the blow for the poor, the package also raised public sector wages, froze the price of basic foods, and increased the minimum wage (which few producers actually paid anyway). The impact of the package was immediate. The prices of all goods with any imported component rose dramatically. Gasoline prices went up 50 percent, and bus fares rose 25 percent. The poor opposed the package because it aggravated inflation and further eroded their standard of living. The rich opposed the package because most of the new tax burden fell on them. For Duarte, the package was a political disaster—just as he had anticipated.[83]

The right was so angry that they tried to foment a military coup. "Anonymous letters have been circulating clearly inviting a coup, and some officials have received visits in their homes from people interested in destabilizing the government," admitted Army Chief of Staff Adolfo Blandón. But once again, Washington's threat to close the aid spigot kept the military in line.[84]

The package also provoked bitter protests from organized labor, which was already disenchanted with Duarte. Six months earlier, in mid-1985, trade unionists from one hundred labor organizations had formed a new umbrella federation, the National Unity of Salvadoran Workers (Unidad Nacional de Trabajadores Salvadoreños, UNTS). It united leftist trade unions that were in the process of rebuilding after having been demolished in the bloodletting of 1980–83 and pro-Christian Democratic trade unions that had grown to fill the vacuum when the leftist unions were destroyed. In February 1986, the UNTS mounted the largest street demonstration since 1980 to protest the austerity program. Twenty thousand people marched through San Salvador chanting, "Abolish the package," and, "Dialogue yes, war no."[85]

The emergence of the UNTS marked a watershed in Duarte's presidency— the point at which the organized base of the Christian Democratic Party began to desert the government because of Duarte's failure to fulfill his campaign promises of peace and social reform. The willingness of Christian Democratic unions to cooperate with leftist unions was especially disconcerting for Washington. Disparaging and eventually demolishing the UNTS became a priority for the U.S. embassy and its allies in the AFL-CIO's American Institute for Free Labor Development (AIFLD), which had helped build the Christian Democratic unions over the preceding five years.[86]

As labor unrest mounted, both Duarte and the U.S. embassy denounced opposition unions as Communist-inspired. "All of the union strikes—all of them—correspond to the unions managed by the Communists," Duarte charged.[87] Captured documents showed that the FMLN was, indeed, trying to build support inside the resurgent unions and was encouraging them to press economic demands on the government. The guerrillas judged that Duarte's inability to meet such demands would expose him as a fraud and speed the decay of his political base.[88] But the idea that all the labor unrest was entirely guerrilla-inspired was absurd, as even some of Duarte's closest advisers acknowledged. "He doesn't seem to realize we are losing our base of support," lamented one veteran Christian Democrat.[89]

Both AIFLD and the embassy worked diligently to woo back the Christian Democratic unions. AIFLD formed yet another new labor federation—the National Union of Workers and Peasants (Unión Nacional de Obreros y Campesinos)—to compete with the UNTS and offered new funding to its old allies if they would break with the center-left federation. The strategy worked. In November 1986, the Christian Democratic unions quit the UNTS and rejoined the AIFLD family. The U.S. embassy was "overjoyed" at its success in breaking the alliance between leftist and centrist unions, and, in a cable to Washington, it reported its intention to continue to "pick-off" other UNTS member unions "one by one."[90] For the rest of the decade, the Salvadoran labor movement remained fatally divided between left and right. The absence of effective organized labor opposition to Duarte did not mean that working people were happy with his policies, however. The U.S.-engineered demolition of the UNTS treated one symptom of Duarte's declining popularity, but it did not cure the disease.

On October 10, 1986, all of Duarte's political problems were suddenly multiplied when an earthquake hit San Salvador, killing over 1,000 people and leaving up to 300,000 homeless. Washington sent $155 million in supplemental economic aid as disaster relief, but it could not begin to cover the damage.[91]

Among the many hundreds of buildings destroyed by the earthquake was the U.S. embassy. Surrounded by a twelve-foot-high, three-foot-thick concrete wall dubbed "Reagan's Ramparts" and "the Berlin Wall" by staffers, the embassy compound occupied a full city block in downtown San Salvador. Inside the wall, the three-story embassy building was draped in metal netting to stop rocket-propelled grenades, and its bullet-proof windows were outfitted with blast curtains and metal plates. At all four corners of the compound and on the roof, Marines stood guard in sandbag emplacements. The staff called it Fort Apache; Salvadorans referred to it simply as "El Bunker."[92] The embassy was not toppled by the initial shock of the earthquake, but like a behemoth trapped in a bog, it began to sink slowly into the ground.[93]

As Duarte entered the final year of his presidency, even his biggest boosters had to admit he was more beloved in Washington than in San Salvador. Constrained by the army's unwillingness to negotiate an end to the war and the Reagan administration's insistence on economic austerity, Duarte had been unable to fulfill his two main campaign pledges—to improve the standard of living of the poor and to end the war. The human rights situation remained much improved from the early 1980s, but occasional murders, disappearances, and massacres by the armed forces reminded everyone that the government's infrastructure of violent repression had not been dismantled. What to do in El Salvador after Duarte was not an issue that overly concerned the Reagan White House, however. Ronald Reagan would be leaving the presidency and retiring to California four months before the end of Duarte's term in office.

The Lessons of El Salvador

The Reagan administration drew certain lessons from its experience in El Salvador. First, events there confirmed the Republicans' belief that they were right about Central America and the liberal Democrats were wrong. The liberals had criticized Reagan's effort to prop up the Salvadoran regime, arguing that reform was impossible, the guerrillas were unbeatable, and negotiations were the only alternative to another Vietnam. Reagan rejected such defeatist counsel, stood fast against negotiations, doggedly backed Magaña and Duarte, and poured vast sums of money into the armed forces. By 1985, the formula seemed to be working.

Once Reagan's policy began to produce results, the resistance of congressional liberals was decisively defeated by a solid majority of conservatives and moderates. This was the second lesson of the Salvadoran experience: If the White House refused to waver in the face of liberal objections, if it refused to accept hobbling conditions on its policy, eventually the opposition would melt in the face of the policy's success. A bit of red-baiting was an effective way to throw the Democrats into disarray in the meantime.

The main problem, however, was keeping the policy alive long enough for it to succeed. The most pressing danger had been that the liberal Democrats in Congress would win an early victory, strangling Reagan's policy with impossible conditions. The third lesson that the Reagan administration took from its experience in El Salvador was that this danger could be averted if the White House was willing to do whatever was necessary to keep the policy going until a congressional majority could be assembled behind it—even if that meant circumventing legal restrictions imposed by Congress in the meantime.

A great deal of Reagan's policy toward El Salvador was conducted on what former senator Sam Ervin called "the windy side of the law." The president used his emergency powers, even when there was no emergency, to send $80 million in military aid to El Salvador without congressional review. He reprogrammed large amounts of aid to avoid sending requests through the gauntlet of the regular budget process. And when the committees reviewing the reprogramming requests put conditions on them, Reagan simply ignored the ones he didn't like. Overt military aid was supplemented by covert aid sent via the CIA for the sole purpose of avoiding normal congressional review.

The administration also ignored statutory restrictions on the role of U.S. military advisers in El Salvador, refusing to report to Congress under either the War Powers Resolution or the Arms Export Control Act. Some advisers were detailed to the CIA so they could be sent into combat without being subject to these laws. Even the administration's own informal limit of fifty-five advisers was circumvented by constantly changing the rules about who counted as an adviser.

After Congress imposed the certification requirement, Reagan certified progress when there was none in order to keep military aid flowing. Despite a statutory ban on police training, the administration opened a training program using the transparent dodge of having the prospective police trainees temporarily reassigned to the armed forces.

In the end, this concerted effort to avoid any congressional restriction on administration policy succeeded. Congress never called Reagan to account for flouting the spirit and letter of the law because the Democratic leadership was so ambivalent about El Salvador. Liberals did the best they could, challenging Reagan's preposterous certifications, proposing tougher conditions on aid, and threatening to repeal Reagan's emergency powers. But after the passage of the first certification law in 1981, the liberals never had the votes to beat the president in a head-on confrontation on the floor of the House or Senate.

The issue of El Salvador became such a crux of partisan animosity that Republicans regarded any criticism of Reagan's methods as ill motivated. When Democrats complained that the administration was ignoring the law, Republicans took it as just another liberal stratagem for killing the president's policy. They rallied behind their leader, even though it sometimes meant undermining the authority of their own institution. Thus the final lesson that the Reagan administration learned from its battle with Congress over El Salvador was that it could ignore the law to keep the policy alive and not have to suffer any consequences.

El Salvador faded from the American political agenda in the late 1980s, slipping out of sight and out of mind. But the lessons learned from it guided the Reagan administration in the new foreign policy struggle that replaced El Salvador as the focal point of conflict between Congress and the executive branch, between liberal Democrats and Reagan Republicans—Nicaragua.

III Nicaragua

I'm looking for a place to start rolling back

the Communist Empire.

—Director of Central Intelligence William J. Casey

CHAPTER 13

Launching the Not-So-Secret War

While El Salvador dominated the foreign policy agenda during Ronald Reagan's first term, his policy of hostility toward Nicaragua was accelerating, largely out of public view. At the outset, even most members of Congress had only the vaguest notion of what was happening. But the escalating war against Nicaragua could not be kept secret for long. As El Salvador slipped off the policy agenda, Nicaragua moved to center stage.

Although the CIA laid the groundwork for the covert war against Nicaragua during the spring and summer of 1981, the operation was formally launched in November and December when Reagan approved National Security Decision Directive (NSDD) 17 and signed the December 1, 1981, presidential finding authorizing the CIA to build a paramilitary army of Nicaraguan exiles. Within a few days of those decisions, CIA Director William Casey went to Capitol Hill to brief the congressional intelligence committees. The finding he presented was only three sentences long. The operation, it said, was intended to interdict arms flowing from Nicaragua to El Salvador, compel the Sandinistas to "look inward," and pressure them to negotiate with Washington. The CIA would work "primarily" through third parties, but CIA personnel might take direct action "in some circumstances."[1]

Casey presented the program as small and modest. Washington would work through Argentina and Honduras. The exiles would not target the Nicaraguan economy, only the "Cuban support structure" that was nurturing the revolution in El Salvador. "The committee . . . was told the effort would involve a small number of paramilitary fighters who would be trained and armed to conduct raids against the Sandinistas' supply of arms to the Salvadoran guerrillas," House Intelligence Committee Chairman Edward Boland explained later. Casey said nothing about the political aim of building a broad opposition front to the Sandinistas, which was included in the scope paper for the operation.[2]

Despite the program's limited objectives, the House committee was shocked by it and asked Casey some tough questions.[3] How could the United States control the paramilitary army once it had been created? How could the operation avoid jeopardizing innocent civilians? What if Nicaraguan troops chased the insurgents into Honduras and clashed with Honduran forces? What if the Sandinistas requested Cuban troops to defend themselves? And what if Washington's role was discovered? Wouldn't that just strengthen nationalist support for the Sandinistas? "It's as if nobody ever read about the Bay of Pigs," complained one committee member.[4]

Casey did not have good answers, which upset the Republicans as much as the Democrats.[5] Five days after the briefing, Chairman Boland wrote Casey a letter notifying him that the committee would require briefings at regular intervals to monitor the operation. Casey agreed to brief the committee every two months.[6]

On the Senate side, Casey had an easier time since the Republicans controlled the Intelligence Committee. Still, several members were skeptical about the program, particularly its arms interdiction rationale. "You can't get people to fight for interdicting arms," one observed. But Casey presented the program as an accomplished fact. Argentina and Honduras had already begun building the exile army; Washington was simply "buying in" to an ongoing operation.[7]

Congressional complaints had little effect on Casey's plans. Although the CIA abandoned the scheme to build an army of five hundred Latin American commandos, the army of Nicaraguan exiles exceeded the thousand-man limit within two months.[8] The intelligence committees could do little more than voice their worries and insist that the administration keep them fully apprised. The law mandating congressional oversight of covert operations required only that the president inform Congress; it did not give the committees the power to block an operation by rejecting a presidential finding. Congress's only recourse was to prohibit the administration from spending any money on an operation—a drastic step bound to provoke a confrontation with the president. Members of the intelligence committees had been selected to serve by their parties' congressional leaders precisely because they were moderate and cautious. Many of them held the old-fashioned view that the president should take the lead in foreign policy. By temperament, they were the members least likely to seek confrontation.

Opposition was also stifled by Casey's description of the operation as a simple arms interdiction program. Intelligence briefings had convinced the oversight committees that Cuba and Nicaragua were still supplying arms to the Salvadoran guerrillas. Most members were willing to accept a program designed to halt what they regarded as illegal arms smuggling.

But Casey's portrayal of the program wasn't accurate. Certainly one objective was to pressure the Sandinistas into ending aid to the Salvadoran guerrillas. For Alexander Haig and Thomas Enders, who saw El Salvador as the main event in Central America, this was the principal aim. But even they did not conceive of the covert operation as literally intercepting arms shipments. It was intended to build an insurgent force that would hurt the Sandinistas and force them to make concessions at the bargaining table.[9]

"I was absolutely stupefied when I heard how it had been described to Congress," said Craig Johnstone, Enders's deputy for Central America at the State Department. "No one thought that we were going to send a group out and capture some guy running across with weapons." Looking back on it, Johnstone regarded Casey's arms interdiction story as "a major blunder" in the administration's effort to sell the covert operation to Congress—one that "cost us dearly down the line" when the cover story came unraveled.[10]

For administration hard-liners, Nicaragua's foreign policy toward El Salvador was never the key issue. From the outset, they saw the operation as a way of overthrowing the Sandinistas. That, however, was not an objective they shared with Congress. "It was hard to spell out what we wanted to Congress," explained an administration lobbyist. "They wouldn't have gone for it then."[11]

The López Portillo Plan

In a speech on February 21, 1982, in Nicaragua, Mexican President José López Portillo offered a peace initiative to loosen the "three knots of tension" in Central America: the war in El Salvador, the conflict between Nicaragua and the United States, and the animosity between the United States and Cuba. He repeated the warning, first given to Haig in November, that direct U.S. intervention in Central America would be a "gigantic historical error" provoking a "continental convulsion" of anti-Americanism. As an ally of the United States, López Portillo offered Mexico's good offices for mediation.[12]

The White House was not enthusiastic about the Mexican plan; for several days the only response was official silence. Finally, Haig criticized it for lacking "one fundamental ingredient"—an end to Nicaragua's involvement in El Salvador.[13] Others, however, responded favorably. The Nicaraguans and the Cubans accepted the mediation proposal immediately, and the Salvadoran guerrillas followed suit a few days later. The European Parliament passed a resolution endorsing the Mexican plan, and even the Soviet Union announced its approval. Over a hundred members of the House of Representatives sent Reagan a letter urging him to accept López Portillo's offer.[14]

The Mexican plan posed a problem that continuously plagued Ronald Reagan over the next seven years. If his White House dismissed the plan too quickly, it would appear uninterested in diplomacy, and congressional support for his policy would fade. Yet if Washington entered into negotiations in good faith, willing to make reasonable compromises to reach agreement, the administration would have to sacrifice its hopes for victory. When Mexico explicitly asked for a meeting with U.S. officials in order to discuss the initiative, the administration felt politically compelled to accept. "As you know, we were cool to the initiative from the beginning," explained one U.S. official, "but we were effectively ambushed by Congress and public opinion. We had to agree to negotiate or appear unreasonable."[15]

A policy paper prepared for an April 1982 meeting of the National Security Planning Group (NSPG, the executive committee of Reagan's NSC system) revealed what administration officials really thought of Mexico's role in the region. "Mexico continues public and covert support for the extreme left with propaganda, funds and political support," the paper asserted. Fearing "congressionally mandated negotiations, which would work against our interests," the paper recommended "co-opting the cut-and-run negotiations strategies by demonstrating a reasonable but firm approach to negotiations and compromise on our terms."[16]

Abruptly, the administration's public tone toward the Mexican initiative changed from frosty to friendly. Haig met twice with Mexican Foreign Minister Jorge Castañeda to discuss the López Portillo plan and agreed to have Mexico convey Washington's concerns to Nicaragua and Cuba. Castañeda engaged in some shuttle diplomacy, reporting back to Haig that both Cuba and Nicaragua were willing to begin talks. Privately, administration officials doubted that talks would be fruitful, but they were willing to let Castañeda try—if only to "massage the Mexican ego a little," explained one official.[17] Administration hard-liners went along only grudgingly.[18]

The Mexican proposal for negotiations between the Salvadoran government and the guerrillas was stillborn. In the midst of the March 1982 Constituent Assembly election campaign, Duarte rejected the Mexican proposal out of hand. Nor was Washington willing to even consider negotiations in advance of the election.[19] The administration was no more forthcoming about opening a dialogue with Cuba. A November 1981 meeting between Haig and Cuban vice president Carlos Raphael Rodríguez in Mexico City had accomplished little. Haig had repeated to Rodríguez the administration's standard position: Washington wanted actions, not words.[20]

José López Portillo's peace plan was most specific regarding Nicaragua. It proposed three steps: (1) the United States would renounce the use or threat of force against Nicaragua and close contra training camps in U.S. territory; (2) the Sandinistas would renounce the acquisition of sophisticated weapons and reduce the size of their armed forces once the contras had been disarmed; and (3) Nicaragua would conclude nonaggression pacts with the United States and with its neighbors.

At Enders's urging, Haig agreed to resume talks with the Sandinistas.[21] The Reagan administration's negotiating position was essentially the same proposal Enders had delivered to the Sandinistas in Managua the previous summer: (1) a bilateral nonaggression pact between Nicaragua and the United States embodied in a "mutual, high-level reassertion of our Rio Treaty engagements"; (2) a U.S. commitment to apply the Neutrality Act to Nicaraguan exiles engaged in military training in the United States; (3) a regional agreement to ban the import of "heavy offensive weapons" and to reduce the number of foreign military and security advisers; (4) an administration pledge to propose renewed economic aid for Nicaragua to the Congress; and (5) the "sine qua non": Nicaragua had to "get out of El Salvador—to wind up the command and control, the logistics, including weapons, ammunition, and training camps."[22] Absent from the list was any mention of Nicaragua's internal political arrangements.

The resumption of high-level negotiations between Nicaragua and the United States seemed imminent. At the White House, spokesman Larry Speakes thanked Mexico for its help, noting, "We have indicated a readiness to discuss relaxation of tensions with the Nicaraguans." Various U.S. officials told the press that talks would begin in early April 1982.[23]

But administration hard-liners, called the "War Party" by State Department pragmatists, still opposed any negotiation. They sought to delay the talks as long as possible while insisting, as they had the previous summer, on an agenda of demands the Sandinistas would reject. The issue of Nicaraguan democracy became pivotal in this internecine debate. Enders opposed adding democracy to the list of U.S. demands because he saw it as preempting any chance for an accord. Proud and nationalistic, the Sandinistas would never agree to negotiate with Washington about Nicaragua's internal affairs. Hard-liners had a similar assessment. They wanted to add democracy to the agenda in order to scuttle any chance for an agreement, thus clearing the way for a full-fledged military effort to drive the Sandinistas from power.

Two unexpected developments bolstered the hard-liners' position. First, the March 1982 election in El Salvador proved to be a bigger success than anyone had anticipated, thereby reinforcing those who were convinced that Washington could win the wars in Central America if only it would show some constancy. Then on April 2, 1982, Argentina invaded the Falklands/Malvinas Islands, triggering war with Great Britain, which for the next three months consumed the time and attention of all the Latin American specialists in the government. While the British and Argentines were fighting in the South Atlantic, Enders was too busy to go to Mexico to negotiate with the Sandinistas. The delay proved fatal.

In early April, Lawrence Pezzullo's replacement as U.S. ambassador to Nicaragua, Anthony C. E. Quainton, presented Nicaragua with a preliminary list of eight topics Washington wanted to discuss. Two new demands had been added to the agenda that Haig had outlined only three weeks earlier: Nicaragua would have to allow on-site inspections of military installations to guarantee that it was not shipping arms to the Salvadoran guerrillas; and the Sandinista government would have to make good on its commitments to pluralism, a mixed economy, and nonalignment. Fulfilling these commitments, particularly the promise to hold free elections, would be "essential elements of the political context of future relations between our two countries," Quainton told the Sandinistas. Despite Enders's resistance, the hard-liners, led by Bill Casey, had succeeded in adding the "democracy issue" to the agenda.[24] From this point on, the conflict between Nicaragua and the United States no longer turned on Sandinista foreign policy. The nature of the Sandinista regime itself was at issue.

The Nicaraguans reacted harshly to the demand that they satisfy Washington's standards of democracy, but nevertheless were prepared to talk, even about their sovereign rights. Nicaragua agreed to discuss all the issues raised by Washington, submitted a fourteen-point agenda of its own, and urged that formal negotiations begin as soon as possible.[25]

The administration, however, had decided not to talk. "We don't think it is a serious offer," one administration source said of the Sandinista reply, "and we don't intend to give it any priority." Until the Sandinistas ended their assistance to the Salvadoran guerrillas, the administration would do no more than "study" the Nicaraguan offer. This delaying tactic would give the contras time to "soften the Sandinistas up and make them more inclined to negotiate seriously on the terms we've proposed."[26] On April 29, the State Department informed Managua there would be no negotiations. Until the Sandinistas halted all support for the Salvadoran guerrillas, Quainton told the Sandinistas, "we believe these conversations ought to take place within normal diplomatic channels."[27]

In a major speech on Central America on August 20, 1982, Enders denounced the Sandinistas as "hardcore Marxists" and "new caudillos" who had betrayed their promise of pluralism. He reiterated the demand that Nicaragua halt its support for revolutionaries elsewhere in the region. Moreover, for the first time publicly, he said that this by itself was not enough. "We have raised a second issue," he explained, "the fulfillment of the Sandinistas' own original commitment to democracy." Other countries had a legitimate interest in Nicaragua's internal politics, Enders argued, because no one could trust Nicaragua to keep its international commitments if it remained "the preserve of a small Cuban-advised elite of Marxist-Leninists." Peace in Central America required that Nicaragua, like the other countries in the region, establish democracy.[28]

The Falklands/Malvinas

The Argentine invasion of the British atolls just off Argentina's South Atlantic coast ignited war between one of Washington's oldest and closest NATO allies and its newest and most cooperative Latin American ally. From his first days in office, Ronald Reagan had been eager to restore the traditional security ties between the United States and the military governments of Latin America. In its first two months, the new administration hosted military delegations from Chile, Brazil, Argentina, and Bolivia. In July 1981, the administration decided it would no longer oppose, on human rights grounds, loans by international financial institutions to Argentina, Chile, Paraguay, and Uruguay.[29]

Reagan's geopoliticians had a special interest in Argentina. Believing that the South Atlantic was a strategically vital nexus of sea lanes, they advocated a military alliance between the United States, Argentina, and South Africa to safeguard the lanes from any Soviet threat.[30] Administration officials evinced no concern that it might appear unseemly for Washington to jump so eagerly into bed with a military regime notorious for its "dirty war" against dissidents in the 1970s. From 1976, when the military overthrew the government of Isabel Martínez de Perón, until the end of the Carter administration, the Argentine armed forces "disappeared" nine thousand people.[31]

A few officials in the Reagan administration displayed a certain admiration for the efficiency with which the Argentine military had solved the problem of leftist insurgency. After an August 1981 trip, U.N. Ambassador Jeane Kirkpatrick suggested that the military regimes in Argentina, Chile, Uruguay, and Brazil were really not so undemocratic. They had "more elements of constitutionalism" than many countries, she explained, and could provide the Central

Americans with valuable lessons on internal security.[32] In 1979, Reagan himself belittled the horror of the dirty war, saying, "Today, Argentina is at peace, the terrorist threat nearly eliminated. In the process of bringing stability to a terrorized nation of 25 million, a small number were caught in the crossfire, among them a few innocents." But, Reagan assured his audience, the average Argentine was quite satisfied with the result.[33]

The Argentine generals, with their doctrine of the "national security state" and their experience in the dirty war, saw themselves as experts fighting Communism. Even without prodding from Washington, they had ambitions of spreading their doctrine and expertise throughout the hemisphere. The war against international Communism, they avowed, was a "war without frontiers." They sent military advisers to Honduras to train the contras and provided advisers and money to the Salvadoran government.[34]

In the fall of 1981, when Washington began to discuss with other Latin American countries a hemispheric anti-Communist military force, the administration looked first to Argentina. The Argentines, said one U.S. official, would play a "cutting edge" role.[35] Joint support for the contras was by far the most important element in this new partnership. The United States provided money and intelligence information, including satellite photographs of potential targets inside Nicaragua, but left the day-to-day management of the war to the Argentines. "It was convenient to run the operation through the Argentines," said a high-ranking U.S. intelligence official. "We didn't have to ask questions about their goals that we couldn't escape asking about our own goals when we took over."[36]

The new partnership between Argentina and the United States came crashing down when Argentina invaded the Falklands/Malvinas Islands. Argentina had long claimed sovereignty over the small, sparsely populated islands lying 300 miles off its southern coast, but they had been under British control since 1833, and seventeen years of effort to resolve the dispute had been fruitless. Facing growing labor unrest and popular opposition at home, the Argentine generals thought a stiff dose of nationalistic fervor would be good politics; the one thing all Argentines could agree on was that the Malvinas belonged to Argentina. Britain would have little stomach for fighting a war over a few barren rocks thousands of miles from home, the generals calculated. They did not reckon that British Prime Minister Margaret Thatcher's political need for a rousing military triumph was equal to their own.

The outbreak of the war took Washington by surprise. As relations with Buenos Aires warmed, the Argentines often mentioned the importance of the Malvinas, but U.S. officials did not take the issue seriously. The Argentine generals interpreted Washington's silence as sympathy.[37] When U.S. intelligence finally determined that Argentine forces were moving on the Falklands/Malvinas, the administration tried frantically to stop them. Reagan himself spoke on the telephone for forty minutes to Argentine president General Leopoldo Galtieri, but it was too late; Argentine troops were already on the beaches.[38]

For three weeks, as the British fleet steamed toward the South Atlantic, Alexander Haig shuttled back and forth between London and Buenos Aires trying unsuccessfully to broker a diplomatic solution to the conflict. Once Haig's mediation collapsed, Washington sided with Great Britain. Indeed, Thatcher was the Western leader with whom Ronald Reagan was closest, both ideologically and personally. In NATO, she staunchly supported Washington's new tough line on the Soviet Union and the deployment of intermediate-range nuclear weapons in Europe. At bottom, the choice came down to which alliance system was more important to the United States: NATO or the budding new relationship with the military governments of Latin America. NATO, not surprisingly, ranked first with most officials in the administration. Haig, for example, as a former allied commander of NATO and a disciple of Henry Kissinger, was a confirmed Atlanticist. But Jeane Kirkpatrick and others on the right saw the Communist threat in Latin America as more immediate and the new anti-Communist alliance with Argentina as too valuable to lose.

Kirkpatrick's interest in Argentina had deep roots; she had written her doctoral dissertation on the Peronist movement.[39] From the beginning of the war, her sympathies were with Buenos Aires. On the day of the invasion, she attended a dinner given in her honor at the Argentine embassy. Kirkpatrick argued determinedly that Washington should stay neutral in the war, taking her case directly to Reagan and National Security Adviser William Clark. If Washington sided with Britain, Kirkpatrick warned, it would engender a hundred years of animosity in Latin America.[40]

Through her post at the United Nations, Kirkpatrick kept up friendly private communications with Argentina while Haig was trying to hammer together a settlement. According to Haig, Kirkpatrick was guilty of "undermining" U.S. policy by leading the Argentines to believe that the United States would remain neutral if the mediation failed. Kirkpatrick denied doing any such thing, but it was clear that Argentina did not take seriously Haig's warnings that Washington would side with Britain.[41]

Haig won the policy debate, though it proved to be his last. Washington sided with its NATO ally, forsaking its newfound friend in the South Atlantic and thereby forfeiting plans for a hemispheric anti-Communist strike force. The Argentines had been certain that their cooperation in Central America would guarantee U.S. support for their crusade in the Malvinas. They were stunned at the betrayal. A billboard went up in Buenos Aires reading, "United States, Judas of America."[42]

The armed forces of Argentina, which had spent the previous half century waging war against civilians rather than other armies, were no match for the British. On June 15, 1982, after six weeks of fighting, the last elements of the Argentine expeditionary force surrendered. The defeat so discredited Argentina's military leaders that they were compelled by public contempt to return control of the government to civilians. After investigating the "dirty war" of the 1970s, the democratically elected government of Raúl Alfonsín tried and convicted five top military officers, including the Reagan administration's erstwhile partners, junta leaders General Roberto Viola and General Jorge Raphael Videla, for ordering the disappearance, torture, and murder of thousands of people.[43] So ended Washington's scheme to groom its own proxy forces for use in Latin America. "We've lost our spear carrier," lamented one administration official.[44]

In appreciation for Nicaragua's diplomatic support during the war, Argentina promised to end its Central American operations. Most of the two hundred or so Argentine military advisers in the region went home soon thereafter, although about thirty-five stayed in Honduras training the contras, probably because of the Argentine military's close ties with Honduran armed forces commander General Gustavo Alvarez. The CIA supplanted Argentina as the principal architect of the contra war as well as its financier.[45]

Our Man in Tegucigalpa

No sooner had the Falklands war ended than the United States began to have trouble with its other partner in the contra war, Honduras. This was no coincidence. General Gustavo Alvarez Martínez, who spent three years attending Argentina's military academy (class of 1961), was almost as angry as the Argentines over Washington's support for Britain.[46]

Washington's difficulties with Alvarez began in the spring of 1982, when the CIA's division chief for operations in Latin America, Dewey Clarridge, set out to recruit Edén Pastora to be the leader of the armed opposition to the Sandinistas. Pastora, the legendary Sandinista military hero Comandante Cero, was an adventurer. He had joined the Sandinista movement in the early 1960s, not because he shared much affinity for the movement's Marxist ideology, but because of his hatred for Somoza.

Although Pastora was never part of the political leadership of the Sandinista movement, he commanded the August 1978 attack on the National Palace—an exploit that catapulted him to international prominence. Pastora's vague nationalism and social democratic inclinations made him Venezuela and Panama's favorite Sandinista. Most of the aid they gave the rebels during the insurrection was channeled to Pastora's forces. As the end of the war drew near, Venezuela, Panama, and the United States all urged Pastora to forsake his Sandinista comrades and join a moderate successor regime that would freeze out the radical revolutionaries. When the revolution triumphed, these same countries urged Pastora to keep his troops intact as a counterweight to the nine-member FSLN National Directorate. In the flush of victory, Pastora ignored the overtures.[47]

The Sandinista National Directorate made Pastora vice minister of the interior under Tomás Borge, then shifted him to the Ministry of Defense to organize the militia. Excluded from the top ranks of power in the new Nicaragua, Pastora was uncomfortable as an administrator and gradually grew disaffected. He left the country in July 1981, ostensibly to join the revolution in Guatemala, but went first to visit his friend and idol General Omar Torrijos in Panama. There he stayed until Torrijos was killed in a plane crash just a few weeks later. From Panama, Pastora went to Cuba, where he was held under house arrest for five months because he refused to return to Nicaragua and mend his breach with the Sandinistas. The Cubans finally released him in January 1982, at the insistence of the Panamanians.[48]

Shortly thereafter, Clarridge met Pastora in Acapulco, Mexico, and recruited him to the counterrevolution. The CIA would provide Pastora with funds, taking care to be discreet so that his credibility as a nationalist would not be damaged. The money would be laundered through an elaborate network of intermediaries in Venezuela, Colombia, Panama, and Costa Rica.[49] At first, all Clarridge asked for was Pastora's political support. "What he wanted me to do was to criticize the Sandinista regime so the war in the north would be legitimized," the expatriate *comandante* explained.[50]

But that was just the beginning. Clarridge saw in Pastora a charismatic leader who, unlike the other exiles, had a popular following inside Nicaragua. The contras in Honduras were still led mostly by former members of Somoza's National Guard who were feared and hated by the Nicaraguan population. Clarridge envisioned Pastora taking over the leadership of a unified contra army operating on two fronts—from Honduran bases in the north and Costa Rican bases in the south. Washington would make Pastora the star of the second Nicaraguan revolution. It was a vision the *comandante* could not resist.[51]

On April 15, 1982, Pastora surfaced in Costa Rica to hold a press conference denouncing his old comrades-in-arms as "traitors and assassins," and appealing to the army and the militia to overthrow them. In a speech written with the help of Arturo Cruz (former member of the governing junta and Nicaraguan ambassador to the United States until his resignation in November 1981) and Alfonso Robelo (junta member until 1980), Pastora claimed the mantle of "true Sandinismo" for himself. He echoed all the conservative opposition's complaints against the Sandinistas: they had ruined the economy with arbitrary seizures of private business; they had involved Nicaragua unnecessarily in the East-West conflict by striking too close a friendship with Cuba; and they were persecuting the church. Unless the Sandinistas straightened things out, Pastora warned, "I will drag them with bullets from their Mercedes Benzs."[52]

The following month, Pastora traveled to Honduras to open negotiations with the Nicaraguan Democratic Force (FDN) about forming an alliance. At this point, he had yet to assemble any army of his own; his support consisted entirely of a few subordinates who left Nicaragua with him and a few civilian politicians like Robelo and Cruz. He had no strategy other than the hope that his declaration of opposition would provoke a coup.[53] Yet Pastora approached the meeting in Honduras as if he were about to assume command. As a condition for any alliance, he demanded that every former officer of the National Guard be removed from the FDN.

General Alvarez was not impressed. To him, Pastora seemed egotistical, unreliable, and politically suspect. Any number of his camp followers could be Sandinista agents (in fact, his mistress was one).[54] Indeed, Alvarez thought Pastora himself might be an agent, sent to disrupt and divide the contra movement. He refused to support any of Pastora's demands and even tried to hold him hostage in Honduras to keep him from making mischief. In a dramatic showdown with Alvarez and a top CIA official, Pastora pulled his pistol and threatened to kill himself if he was not released. He seemed just crazy enough to do it, so Alvarez let him go.[55] But since Washington needed Alvarez's cooperation to run the war, the FDN could refuse to make any concessions to Pastora so long as Alvarez backed them up. Dewey Clarridge's grand design of a united contra movement led by the legendary Pastora remained just a dream.

General Alvarez was a problem of Washington's own creation. Trained in Argentina, he was a great admirer of the how the Argentine armed forces had exterminated the left. Rising rapidly through the ranks, then-Colonel Alvarez became chief of Honduran Public Security Forces (Fuerza de Seguridad Pública) in August 1980, a post from which he could begin practicing "the Argentine method" himself. For the first time in Honduras, people began to disappear.[56]

Until the 1980s, Honduras had been lucky. Guerrilla insurgencies flourished all around it in Nicaragua, El Salvador, and Guatemala, but Honduras remained relatively calm. It was the poorest and most backward country in Central America, a condition that ironically proved beneficial. During the

1960s and early 1970s, rapid economic growth stimulated by the Central American Common Market had destabilizing effects in much of the region, unleashing a torrent of political and economic demands from the lower classes. Underdeveloped Honduras, however, attracted little investment, so the pace of economic growth and modernization was slower there than in neighboring countries. Traditional social patterns and political habits remained largely undisturbed.

At the same time, the Honduran government reacted to popular demands for reform with less intransigence and brutality than regimes in neighboring countries. Though the military ruled throughout the 1970s, it tolerated organized dissent from political parties, trade unions, peasant organizations, students, and the press. There were no waves of indiscriminate official violence, no plague of disappearances, and no death squads. In the early 1970s, the military regime even undertook some limited reforms, including land distribution.

With Washington's encouragement, the Honduran armed forces held elections in 1981 to return the nation to civilian rule. The opposition Liberal Party won an upset victory, and although the armed forces accepted the results, the transition to democracy was far from complete. As the price for returning to the barracks, the army insisted that it retain considerable power behind the scenes. The civilians had to give the military a veto over all cabinet appointments, a dominant role in foreign policy, and exclusive control over military affairs.[57]

Although both the Carter and Reagan administrations backed the Honduran transition to civilian rule, another aspect to U.S. policy undermined it. Washington saw Honduras as "an oasis of peace amidst the storm" of Central American turmoil and the logical place to increase the U.S. military presence.[58] At the same time that Washington was pressing the Honduran armed forces to relinquish power to civilians, it was increasing military assistance, which had the countervailing effect of strengthening the armed forces relative to civilian institutions.

This contradiction in U.S. policy was aggravated when Washington enlisted General Alvarez's help in building a secret army of contras. To run the war, the U.S. embassy established direct liaison with Alvarez, circumventing civilian authorities. As a reward to the Honduran armed forces for their cooperation, military aid increased astronomically. As the Hondurans received new weapons from the United States, they passed their old ones to the contras.[59]

Military aid jumped from $8.9 million in fiscal year (FY) 1981 to $31.3 million in FY 1982, then to $48.3 million in FY 1983, and finally leveled off at $77.4 million in FY 1984. That made Honduras, a country with only 4.2 million people and no insurgency, the second largest recipient of U.S. military aid in Latin America (behind El Salvador). By 1984, the number of U.S. military advisers in Honduras had swelled to 224.[60]

In addition to being the point man for the covert war against Nicaragua, Alvarez also played a crucial role in U.S. efforts to strangle the Salvadoran insurgency. Although the contras were not organized to interdict arms shipments from Nicaragua, Washington did have a regionwide interdiction program in place in 1982 under the authority of Reagan's March 9, 1981, intelligence finding on Central America. In Honduras, the program was called Operation Quail Shooter. The CIA, along with Argentine and Chilean military advisers, helped Alvarez organize the Directorate of Special Investigations (Directorio de Investigaciones Especiales, DIES), an elite unit that gathered intelligence on arms traffickers and dissidents and then eliminated them.[61]

The initial contingent of DIES troops was trained in Texas, and the unit's operations were supervised by CIA officers in Honduras. With U.S. financial support, the DIES built a network of safe houses, clandestine jails, and interrogation centers. CIA officers regularly visited the facilities where "disappeared" people were held, and the U.S. embassy was given access to the intelligence reports based on their interrogations.[62]

U.S. advisers taught the Hondurans to avoid physical torture in favor of psychological pressure to break a prisoner. "Make him stand up, don't let him sleep, keep him naked and isolated, put rats and cockroaches in his cell, give him bad food, serve him dead animals, throw cold water on him," recalled DIES interrogator Florencio Caballero, reciting what the CIA had taught him. But the Hondurans had their own ways of doing things. "When we had someone important, we hid him from the Americans, interrogated him ourselves, and then gave him to the death squad to kill," Caballero admitted.[63]

Alvarez gave command of the DIES to his most trusted subordinate, Major Alexander Hernández, who was also the chief liaison between the Honduran military and the contras. Working with Ricardo "El Chino" (the Chinaman) Lau, a former intelligence officer in Somoza's National Guard and the chief of contra counterintelligence, Hernández recruited contra troops to carry out political killings and kidnappings on behalf of the DIES. Honduran military officials later estimated that the contras were responsible for about a hundred kidnappings and murders.[64] By the end of 1981, the DIES had crushed the Salvadoran guerrillas' logistical support network inside Honduras by murdering dozens of Honduran and Salvadoran nationals.[65]

When Roberto Suazo Córdova became president of Honduras in early 1982, he appointed Alvarez chief of the armed forces. Alvarez won the top post over more senior officers because he had the backing of the CIA station chief and the defense attaché in the U.S. embassy. "He was dynamic, aggressive and disciplined. He had a clear chain of command. He fit our mold of a military leader. He was our candidate," said a U.S. military source.[66] General Alvarez quickly became the most powerful man in Honduras and began to dream of rescuing all of Central America from Communism. On his desk, next to the plastic model of an assault helicopter, he kept a bust of Napoléon Bonaparte.[67]

With Alvarez in charge of the armed forces, the number of disappearances and political assassinations accelerated. The DIES grew into a special military intelligence unit, Battalion 316, and after eliminating the arms traffickers, it turned its attention to ordinary dissidents. "The arms network was broken fairly early," recalled a senior Honduran military officer several years later, "but then the unit got into other things."[68] Between 1980 and 1984, there were 247 unsolved political killings and disappearances.[69]

Although the Hondurans had orders to keep their CIA advisers in the dark about the torture and murder of suspects, the embassy was aware of what was going on. "The CIA had nothing to do with picking people up," explained a U.S. official who served in Honduras at the time. "But they knew about it and when some people disappeared, they looked the other way."[70] In 1983, Ambassador John Negroponte complained to the Hondurans about the killings, but to no avail. Some U.S. officials were deeply disturbed at the morality of what was happening, but more than one argued that the Honduran strategy "worked"—it broke up the Salvadoran rebels' support infrastructure and demolished the small Honduran left.[71]

In public, the Reagan administration downplayed reports of Honduran human rights abuses. When a former military rival of Alvarez, Leónides Torres Arias, denounced him in 1982 for running death squads, a senior U.S. official scoffed that the charge was "preposterous."[72] By 1983, when the disappearances had become too numerous to ignore, the State Department was still giving Honduras a relatively clean bill of health in its annual human rights reports. Killings and disappearances were explained away as the result of private vendettas based on "personal and political rivalry," not actions by the state. "Government authorities did not order any of these murders," the State Department concluded.[73] When human rights activists from the Commission for the Defense of Human Rights in Honduras spoke out against the disappearances, U.S. officials denounced them as Communists and terrorists.[74]

The First Boland Amendment: A Shot across the Bow

With each new briefing on the burgeoning size of the contra army, the congressional intelligence committees' anxiety grew apace. In December 1981, Casey had led the committees to believe that the contra force would not exceed five hundred commandos, slipping quietly across the Honduran border in the dead of night to blow up bridges and attack Sandinista army depots.[75] This sketch of "The Project," as the CIA called the war, began to wear thin almost immediately. When the House Intelligence Committee convened in February 1982 for the first of its special bimonthly briefings on the operation, Casey and Clarridge caused consternation when they informed the committee that the contras had already grown to a thousand men, and more were on the way.[76]

Each subsequent briefing eroded the trust between the intelligence committees and the CIA a little more. Casey simply did not approve of intelligence oversight by Congress. He thought Congress leaked too much and turned intelligence operations into political footballs. He referred to congressional critics as "those assholes on the Hill," and if highly sensitive matters were involved, Casey's instinct was not to brief the committees at all.[77]

When he did give briefings, he never volunteered anything. Famous for mumbling incomprehensibly, he could answer a direct question without conveying anything intelligible. His voice had "a built-in scrambler," joked Defense Secretary Caspar Weinberger. Goldwater called him "flapper lips," adding, "Much of the time, I never knew what the hell he was talking about. Neither did anyone else on the committee. That was just the way Bill wanted it." Casey couldn't even manage to pronounce "Nicaragua" correctly; it kept coming out "Nicawawa." The Democrats joked that Casey shouldn't be allowed to overthrow the government of any country he couldn't pronounce.[78]

Dewey Clarridge's briefings were even worse. Clarridge had as much contempt for Congress as Casey did, and he flaunted it. He was flippant and sarcastic in his responses to questions, secure in the knowledge that he was working directly for Casey, and Casey had the trust and confidence of the president. Clarridge had no compunction about giving the committees a version of events that was contradicted by the next day's news reports. "It got to the point where I wouldn't believe a word Dewey Clarridge said," recalled committee member Norman Mineta. "We are like mushrooms. They keep us in the dark and feed us manure."[79]

The intelligence committees were also distressed at how quickly the Nicaragua operation became public and how blithely unconcerned Casey seemed to be about the revelations. Hints of the secret war began appearing in the press almost as soon as the plan was approved. On December 4, just a week and a half after Reagan signed NSDD 17, William Beecher reported the essentials of the directive in the *Boston Globe*, including the authorization of covert action against Nicaragua. In February, Don Oberdorfer and Patrick Tyler published a full account of NSDD 17 in the *Washington Post*, but the covert operation against Nicaragua was only one item in the long list of NSDD 17 decisions.[80]

The first detailed account of the incipient war came from Tyler and Bob Woodward, writing in the *Washington Post* in early March. "Everything in the *Post* story was true," said Goldwater when asked if he could confirm the report. "They didn't have everything, but everything they had is true."[81]

Tyler and Woodward got the story from administration sources who opposed the plan, but when Casey was contacted for confirmation, he evinced no particular concern that one of his most important covert operations was about to be revealed. Casey's calm and the speed with which the television networks were able to confirm the story suggested that the administration was not unhappy about the publicity.[82]

Like Haig's rumors of war, the public discussion of planned paramilitary attacks had value as psychological warfare to intimidate the Sandinistas into meeting U.S. demands. Whether or not the revelations frightened the Sandinistas, they certainly worried members of Congress, especially since the *Post*'s sources were describing an operation much more expansive than the one Casey had outlined to the intelligence committees.

When the House Intelligence Committee took up the fiscal year 1983 intelligence authorization bill on April 5, 1982, liberal Democrats failed in a bid to close down the Nicaragua operation by deleting its funding. But concern on the committee was great enough to prompt a compromise. In an effort to hold the CIA to its purported objective of arms interdiction, the committee added language to the bill's classified annex that limited the uses to which funds could be applied. "The program was to be directed only at the interdiction of arms to the insurgents in El Salvador," the committee specified. No funds could be used "for the purpose of overthrowing the government of Nicaragua or provoking a military exchange between Nicaragua and Honduras."[83] Senate committee members were worried enough about the direction of the program to accept the House restrictions. In September, the bill was signed into law.

The restriction imposed by Congress was not designed to bring the covert operation to a halt. On the contrary, it was intentionally crafted to register the committees' growing uneasiness *without* interfering with the limited arms interdiction operation Casey purportedly wanted. The Reagan administration could interpret the law as allowing support for the contras so long as the purpose of the United States was not one of those proscribed. The intentions of the contras were irrelevant, legally at least.[84] Because of this statute, the Reagan administration vehemently insisted during 1982 and 1983 that it was not trying to overthrow the Sandinistas, despite mounting evidence to the contrary.

Just as Congress was moving to put the first limits on the covert war, the CIA was trying to expand its scope dramatically. Although General Alvarez and the former National Guardsmen who led the contras in Honduras refused to go along with Dewey Clarridge's scheme to make Edén Pastora the contras' commander, Clarridge did not give up on Comandante Cero. With Washington's help, perhaps Pastora could build a formidable army of his own in Costa Rica and open a southern front in the war against the Sandinistas. Washington began financing Pastora at a rate that eventually reached $500,000 monthly.[85]

The recruitment of Pastora posed a problem for the CIA's cover story that the contra war was aimed at interdicting arms. As Admiral Bobby Ray Inman, deputy director of the CIA, pointed out, there was no arms flow to interdict on the southern front.[86] Inman argued, unsuccessfully, for a new presidential finding that would more accurately describe the administration's intent. But a new finding might evoke even more congressional resistance. Vice Admiral John M. Poindexter, then military adviser to the NSC, argued that a new finding was unnecessary.[87] Instead, Casey and Clarridge simply didn't tell Congress that Pastora had been added to the program.[88]

In November 1982, Newsweek put the contra war back in the headlines. The operation was not just aimed at interdicting arms, Newsweek reported, but it was also intended to harass and undermine the Nicaraguan government. Casey, who agreed to be interviewed for the piece so long as he was not quoted by name, acknowledged that although the original rationale for the program did not include destabilizing the Sandinistas, "there are secondary and tertiary consequences which you cannot control."[89] The rest of the article left little doubt that ousting the Nicaraguan government was more than a secondary objective in the rapidly expanding project.

A new wave of revelations followed the Newsweek article and reverberated in Congress. Over the summer, Casey had told the House Intelligence Committee that the contra army had grown to 1,500 men. Press reports in November put the number at 4,000 and rising.[90] "The numbers went up, the arms increased, and nobody could say why that was happening or what they would do if the conflict widened," a House Intelligence Committee source recalled.[91] The number of contras was not the only guideline the program had exceeded. Originally, the CIA was supposed to exclude former members of Somoza's National Guard from the contra force, yet virtually the entire senior command of the secret army was composed of Guard officers. They were the only ones willing to fight, Casey explained.[92]

Originally, the contras were supposed to attack only military targets. "They told us that the thing was designed to be specifically targeted on military installations, bridges and so forth, and that the CIA did not anticipate any loss of life of civilians," recalled Wyche Fowler (D-Ga.).[93] Yet most contra raids hit farms, villages, and granaries, taking a heavy toll of civilians. Such "soft" targets were lightly defended and therefore easy prey.

But the committee was most disturbed by the accumulating evidence that the covert war was not an arms interdiction program at all. In the first place, the contras had not interdicted any arms.[94] Second, the contras themselves denied that they were trying to. "It is not acceptable to us to carry out missions to interdict Cuban and Russian supply lines to El Salvador," declared FDN military commander Enrique Bermúdez. "We are Nicaraguans and our objective is to overthrow the Communists and install a democratic government in Nicaragua."[95]

On December 8, 1982, Congressman Tom Harkin (D-Iowa) offered an amendment to the FY 1983 defense appropriations bill (which included appropriations for the intelligence community) to prohibit U.S. assistance to any group "carrying out military activities in or against Nicaragua." The contras, Harkin argued passionately, were "vicious cutthroat murderers . . . remnants of the evil, murderous National Guard. In the name of all that is right and decent, we should end our involvement with this group."

A long line of liberals followed Harkin to the microphone to denounce the contra war. Supporting the contras would give the Sandinistas a "propaganda bonanza" and an excuse to crack down on their internal opponents, they argued. It would destabilize Honduras, either by provoking war between Honduras and Nicaragua, or by strengthening the already powerful hand of General Alvarez. And it risked drawing the United States into a wider war. "Some of us came here to stop Vietnam," George Miller (D-Calif.) reminded his colleagues. "And here is a chance to stop the new one."

After letting the liberals vent their outrage, Edward Boland, chairman of the Intelligence Committee, took the floor to reassure them that he was carefully monitoring the situation. "Your intelligence committee is as concerned . . . as all of you who have spoken here this afternoon," Boland assured Harkin. "I can say that the committee certainly does understand its obligations to rein in activities which can get out of control or which could threaten to involve this nation or its allies in a war."

The Harkin amendment was unnecessary, Boland said. He then revealed for the first time that the Intelligence Committee had already placed limits on the program in the FY 1983 intelligence authorization. As a substitute for Harkin's amendment, Boland offered the same language that had been included in the classified portion of that earlier bill. This would reaffirm Congress's desire that the program be kept within strict limits. One advantage of the existing language, Boland pointed out, was that the administration had accepted it. "They do not like it, but it is agreeable to them," he explained. The Republican leadership, seeking to avoid a vote on the Harkin language, supported Boland's substitute, which passed 411–0.[96] The Senate accepted the Boland language in the House-Senate conference committee on the defense appropriations bill. The first of the famous Boland Amendments was signed into law on December 21, 1982, prohibiting the use of funds "for the purpose of overthrowing the government of Nicaragua."[97]

Although the Boland amendment merely reaffirmed existing law and had a built-in loophole that minimized its practical effect, the White House should have recognized it as a warning to rein in the contra program. Instead, most administration officials interpreted the amendment in narrow legal terms, treating it as virtually meaningless. "That doesn't prevent anything," Casey mumbled when he heard about it.[98] Only CIA general counsel Stanley Sporkin seemed to appreciate the political danger lurking in this seemingly toothless statute. Congressional opponents would be watching for the slightest hint that the CIA was violating the Boland amendment, Sporkin warned. "This thing is going to come back and bite us in the ass like nothing you've ever seen."[99]

Nineteen eighty-two was a year of definition in the Reagan administration's relations with Nicaragua. The covert war became the central element of U.S. policy, supplanting any serious effort at diplomacy, and Washington took over primary responsibility for the war from the Argentine generals. The pragmatists at the State Department, who initially backed the war as means of pressuring the Sandinistas into making concessions at the bargaining table, found that the war's momentum made negotiations less likely. Under attack, the Sandinistas moved closer to Cuba and the Soviet Union, increased the size of their army, and restricted the political liberties of domestic opponents—all of which made them appear more menacing and reinforced the hard-liners' argument that only removal of the Sandinistas from power would safeguard U.S. interests.

Reagan's anti-Communism was so intense that it overwhelmed any scruples about the character of Washington's allies. In El Salvador, the United States made common cause with a murderous military establishment to prevent Marxist guerrillas from winning the war. In Nicaragua, the United States teamed up with the Argentine military dictatorship, the megalomaniacal General Alvarez, and the remnants of Somoza's National Guard to prevent the Sandinistas from consolidating their revolutionary government. Such policies were the logical consequence of the Kirkpatrick doctrine that called for befriending pro-American dictators to reinforce the bulwarks of freedom against totalitarianism.

As the contra war expanded, both the public and Congress grew restive about where the policy was ultimately headed. The mild restrictions of the first Boland amendment were the result. But the Reagan administration was no more willing to accept congressional restrictions on its policy toward Nicaragua than it had been on its policy toward El Salvador.

CHAPTER 14

Gunboat Diplomacy

By the time Congress returned to Washington in January 1983, the Reagan administration had decided to treat opposition to its Nicaragua policy as a public relations problem. The contras projected an image of military weakness and moral turpitude. They had yet to attack anything other than small, lightly defended communities along the Honduran border, and they routinely killed more civilians than soldiers. In November 1982, the CIA tried to give the main contra group, Nicaraguan Democratic Force (FDN), a facelift by recruiting a new civilian directorate of exiles with no discernible ties to the Somoza regime. One of the people the CIA approached was Edgar Chamorro, a former Jesuit seminarian who had dropped out to become an advertising executive. Chamorro met in Miami with the head of the CIA's Central America Task Force, who went by the name of Tony Feldman. "He assured us that this was a commitment from the United States government to overthrow the Sandinistas," Chamorro recalled. "He said the Sandinistas must go." Feldman promised victory by July 1983, December at the latest. Chamorro signed on.[1]

The new directorate was patched together hastily. Most of its members had never met one another before they convened for their inaugural press conference in December. The urgency, Feldman told the new directors, came from the need to counter growing congressional disillusionment with the contras—

to "repackage the program for Congress."[2] Feldman and another CIA official calling himself Tomás Castillo (his real name was Joseph Fernandez) came to Miami to help the new FDN directors prepare for the press conference. The CIA men didn't like the statement of principles the directorate had drafted; it was too starkly anti-Communist and dwelt too much on restoring the sanctity of private property. Feldman and Castillo junked it and brought in another CIA official to write something more uplifting.[3]

The intelligence officers also coached the Nicaraguans on how to handle questions from the press. They were never to admit that they met with U.S. officials or received money from the U.S. government. Above all, they were never to admit that their aim was to overthrow the Nicaraguan government. Instead, they were supposed to say that their purpose was merely to "create conditions for democracy." In private, however, their CIA handlers reassured them that Washington ardently shared their dreams of victory. "In private . . . they always said, 'The president wants you to go to Managua,'" Chamorro recalled.[4]

Some of the FDN's new directors, Chamorro among them, were discouraged to discover that neither the CIA nor the FDN military command took them seriously. Enrique Bermúdez, a former colonel in Somoza's National Guard, never regarded the directorate as having any authority over his army; he referred to it as the FDN's "political branch" and treated it like a facade.[5] Real control of the organization remained with the CIA and was exercised through a triumvirate of Nicaraguans: Bermúdez, Aristedes Sánchez, a former political ally of Somoza's, and Adolfo Calero, the former manager of Managua's Coca-Cola bottling plant. Before going into exile, Calero served as defense attorney for a number of Somoza's guardsmen who were tried for war crimes after the insurrection. His relationship with the CIA reportedly went back a number of years, and when he left Nicaragua in early 1983, he was immediately added to the FDN directorate.[6] A few months later, Dewey Clarridge talked the directorate into electing Calero chairman. Together, Calero, Sánchez, and Bermúdez were so impervious to influence from the directorate that disgruntled directors began referring to them as the "Bermúdez triangle."[7]

The CIA envisioned the directorate lobbying in Western Europe and the United States on behalf of the contra army. Congress was a top target, and the CIA briefed the contra lobbyists for their assault on Capitol Hill just as thoroughly as they briefed Bermúdez's combatants for forays into Nicaragua. They told the contras which members of Congress were swing voters, coached them on how to talk to members, and gave them key contacts of influential people in the members' home districts. "The CIA men didn't have much respect for Congress," Chamorro recounted. "They said they could change how representatives voted as long as we knew how to 'sell' our case and place them in a position of looking soft on Communism."[8] When members of Congress visited the contras in Central America, the CIA briefed the Nicaraguans on the members' views ahead of time, "so that we could use a tailor-made approach to each visit." With friendly, conservative members the contras were candid about their ultimate aim of overthrowing the Sandinistas. With liberal members, they stuck to their cover story.[9]

One of Chamorro's jobs as head of press relations for the FDN was to build a positive public image for the contras in Honduras and Costa Rica. His task was simplified by bribery; the CIA had someone on the payroll at virtually every major newspaper, radio, and television station in both countries. In Honduras, Chamorro distributed bribes to over a dozen journalists.[10]

Chamorro also briefed U.S. journalists and arranged trips for them to contra base camps. In early 1983, the contras started allowing reporters to visit their camps in Honduras, so long as the journalists maintained the fiction that the camps were *not* in Honduras. The decision to allow reporters to visit the camps was made by the CIA, and every journalist invited had to be cleared first by the Agency to assure that no one hostile to the contra cause would get in. "The contra leaders won't invite you on trips, won't take you into their camps, and won't talk to you if your articles are too critical," explained *New York Times* correspondent James LeMoyne.[11]

Opening the contra camps to the press indicated that the administration was trying to muster popular support for the war rather than maintain any vestige of secrecy. That did not seem consistent with the limited character of the operation that Casey kept describing to the intelligence committees. In addition, the contra army continued to expand at a phenomenal pace. In February 1983, the intelligence committees were told that it was 5,500 strong; by May, it had jumped to 7,000, and by July, to nearly 10,000 men. Casey refused to set any upper limit on how large the army might become.[12]

In early 1983, the CIA assumed closer operational control of the war in hopes of spurring greater military success. Increased intelligence collection in the region, including photo reconnaissance and electronic intercepts, enabled Washington to pinpoint Sandinista military units and follow their every move. With this data in hand, U.S. advisers selected targets for contra attacks, planned the operations, and then debriefed the troops when they returned.

In April, Edén Pastora announced his decision to take up arms against the Sandinistas, opening a southern front, and the CIA also began providing direct assistance to insurgent Miskito Indians operating on the Atlantic coast.[13] The Miskitos, like Pastora, were operating nowhere near any conceivable arms smuggling routes. Even the FDN had not yet interdicted any Sandinista arms shipments—"not a *pistole*," admitted Ambassador Deane Hinton.[14]

The contras staged their first major offensive in March 1983; between 1,400 and 2,000 combatants infiltrated Nicaragua and launched attacks on the town of Jalapa, near the Honduran border, and on various hamlets in Matagalpa province, a hundred miles from the frontier. The Matagalpa attack marked the first time the contras were able to mount a campaign in the interior of the country. At Jalapa, the contras hoped to capture the town, use its airstrip to fly in supplies from Honduras, and perhaps even declare it liberated territory. Throughout the war, the contras dreamed of capturing a large enough town or slice of territory to establish a provisional government and then seek recognition and aid from the United States. They never managed it.[15]

Although the March offensive produced few results, the contras and their CIA advisers exuded nothing but optimism. "We'll be in Managua by December," they boasted to members of Congress and journalists alike.[16] Implausible as it seemed, the CIA had actually drawn up a planning memo in 1982 that set Christmas 1983 as the date for the fall of Managua. The scenario for this lightning victory was based on an analogy with the Sandinistas' own triumph. Contra attacks would show people, by example, that the Sandinistas could be successfully resisted. As the contras' triumph appeared more and more likely, more and more people would rally to their banner. Finally, a popular uprising would erupt, the Sandinista army would disintegrate, and the contras would march into Managua, triumphant. "The contras were going to be the spark for the tinderbox," recalled a U.S. official involved with the program.[17]

Missing from this scenario was any sense of politics. The rapid collapse of the Somoza regime was the result of its political frailty. After years of repression and unbridled larceny, the entire population despised it. Despite the Sandinista government's conflicts with the private sector, the middle class, and the Catholic Church, in 1983 it could still rely on a deep well of support from workers and peasants who had benefited materially from the revolution. And the Sandinistas still enjoyed the legitimacy that came from ousting Somoza. The idea of a popular uprising against them was fanciful—as fanciful as it had been at the Bay of Pigs in 1962—and administration officials needed to read no further than the cables from their own embassy in Managua to know it.[18]

But in Washington, propaganda and psychological operations were regarded as an adequate substitute for a popular base. Rather than forcing the contras to supplement their military strategy with a real political program, Pentagon and CIA planners thought it was enough for the contras to simply appear to be winning. "If the contras can obtain the mantle of inevitable success," explained a top U.S. military strategist, "they can create a popular revolution." It wasn't necessary for them to actually be popular.[19]

By early 1983, it was clear that the contras would not be celebrating Christmas in Managua. Nevertheless, the logic of bestowing on them the "mantle of inevitable success" still had its attractions—especially in Congress. As opposition to the covert war mounted, administration officials grew more expansive about the contras' prospects. In May, Casey and Enders hinted to the intelligence committees that the December deadline for victory might still be met. "They were telling us that, in effect, if we cut off assistance to the rebels now, we would be responsible for aborting a great chance to reverse Communist gains in Central America," a committee member recalled.[20] A June 1983 National Intelligence Estimate, "Nicaragua: Outlook for the Insurgency," was more realistic: it doubted they could even hold any major population centers, let alone defeat the Sandinista army.[21]

Congressional concerns about the military ineptitude of the contra army were exacerbated by reports of their human rights abuses. The contras were still attacking mostly farms and villages and killing civilian public officials—mayors, justices of the peace, literacy volunteers, and public health workers. They routinely murdered prisoners and kidnapped teenagers to augment their ranks. The CIA operatives running the war were aware of the contras' depredations and quietly tried to control them, but to no avail. The legacy of the National Guard's brutality and contempt for the civilian population was all too apparent in the behavior of the new army.[22]

The intelligence committees were also distressed by the shifting rationales they were given for the contra operation. By late 1982, State Department officials were outlining a broader purpose than arms interdiction: contra attacks were intended to punish the Sandinistas until they behaved. "By supporting the Nicaraguan rebels," a senior intelligence official explained, "we create a symmetrical situation in which the Sandinistas have an incentive, namely the withdrawal of the rebels from Nicaragua, to stop their aid to El Salvador."[23]

Symmetry became the metaphor justifying the war, and Congress was even told that the CIA was fine-tuning attacks in Nicaragua to respond, tit for tat, to attacks by the Salvadoran guerrillas. By the logic of symmetry, the contra war would continue as long as the Farabundo Martí National Liberation Front (FMLN) pressed the war in El Salvador.[24]

Symmetry was more a rhetorical device than a principle that guided policy. The hard-liners were not really willing to trade the war in Nicaragua for the war in El Salvador. It was Enders's willingness to do precisely that—to call off the contras if the Sandinistas would halt aid to the Salvadoran guerrillas—that made him persona non grata on the right. The hard-liners wanted to win both wars. Nor were they interested in symmetrical negotiations. They opposed negotiations in El Salvador and had Enders fired for merely suggesting them. But the hard-liners were certain that the Sandinistas would never agree to negotiate with the contras, so their insistence on symmetry in the negotiating arena was a convenient way to deflate liberals' demands for talks in El Salvador. These new rationales for the contra operation did not make the intelligence committees any more sanguine about it; they simply intensified members' feeling that Casey would tell them anything to keep the war going.[25]

Congress Turns Against the War

Both intelligence committees sent delegations to Central America in early 1983 to see the war firsthand. Senator Patrick Leahy (D-Vt.) went on behalf of the Senate committee. In Honduras, he met with the director of the contra operation, Chief of Base Ray Doty ("Colonel Raymond"), a former master sergeant in the U.S. Army who had run the CIA's paramilitary training in Laos. Doty described how FDN troopers would soon be marching south from their bases in Honduras to link up with other contras moving north out of Costa Rica. The two forces would meet by midyear, effectively cutting Nicaragua in half.

Wasn't this a plan aimed at overthrowing the Nicaraguan government? asked Leahy. "Absolutely not," Doty assured him. It was just arms interdiction, designed to cut off the populous Pacific coast from the east coast ports where much of Nicaragua's military aid was being imported. Of course, the plan might have other consequences for the Sandinistas. "If they fall of their own weight," Doty said, "we don't care." Leahy then met with Honduran military strongman General Gustavo Alvarez Martínez, who boasted, "We'll have our soldiers in Managua by Christmas."[26]

Next, Leahy traveled to Panama, where the CIA had convinced General Manuel Antonio Noriega, a longtime CIA asset, to set up a secret training camp for the contras. Dewey Clarridge got there ahead of Leahy and directed the CIA station chief not to speak with the senator. When Leahy tried to cable CIA headquarters to get Casey to countermand Clarridge's orders, the CIA station refused to send the cable, relenting only when Leahy threatened to call Washington on an open line.

Leahy finally got his briefing, but he returned to Washington convinced that the contra operation violated the spirit if not the letter of the Boland amendment. "We must ask ourselves bluntly," he told the Senate, "whether there is any practical difference between aiding insurgents who want to take power in Managua, while saying that is not our purpose, and giving them that aid because we unequivocally share that aim."[27]

Leahy wrote a lengthy report for the Senate Intelligence Committee, detailing how elaborate the operation had become. It was much larger and more ambitious than the committee had been led to believe, and at times the contra program appeared to be "preceding policy rather than following it." In short, the operation was out of control.[28]

Wyche Fowler (D-Ga.) went to Central America in March for the House committee and returned with essentially the same conclusion. His report convinced Chairman Edward Boland that the administration was violating the law. "The evidence is very strong," Boland said shortly after Fowler's return.[29] Something would have to be done.

Elected to Congress in 1952, Edward Boland was the quintessential House insider—quiet, unassuming, hard-working, and very well connected. He had been a good friend of President John F. Kennedy and was close with Speaker Tip O'Neill, with whom he shared a Washington apartment. Among colleagues and constituents alike, his reputation for personal integrity was unsurpassed. In 1982, he spent just $47 on his reelection campaign. "He has absolute integrity and no personal interest," Senator Daniel Patrick Moynihan said of Boland, "only the interest of his district and his country."[30]

Boland was also a foreign policy traditionalist, believing that the leading role in foreign affairs belonged to the president, not the Congress, and that policy should be bipartisan. That, combined with his collegiality and aversion to speaking to the press, made him an ideal chairman for the House Intelligence Committee. But Boland's strong sense of principle and respect for the law also meant that he took the duty of intelligence oversight most seriously. "The reason this whole strategy of the administration unraveled," said colleague George Miller later, "is that they decided to lie to Eddie Boland rather than to tell the truth."[31]

On April 27, 1983, Boland and Clement J. Zablocki (D-Wis.), chairman of the House Foreign Affairs Committee, formally introduced H.R. 2760, a bill to prohibit funding "for the purpose or which would have the effect of supporting, directly or indirectly, military or paramilitary operations in Nicaragua by any nation, group, organization, movement, or individual."[32] On May 3, the Intelligence Committee approved the bill in a 9–5 vote that split along party lines.

In reporting the Boland-Zablocki bill to the full House, the Intelligence Committee noted that the covert operation was supposed to be bound by two legal constraints: (1) the first Boland amendment, which prohibited aiding the contras for the purpose of overthrowing the Nicaraguan government or provoking a conflict between Nicaragua and Honduras; and (2) the conference report to the fiscal year (FY) 1983 intelligence authorization act, which directed that the funds be used "only for the purpose of the interdiction of arms."

"The Committee has reached the point where it is unwilling to assure the House that the present program meets both these requirements," their report said. "Developing a sizeable military force and deploying it in Nicaragua . . . strains credibility as an operation only to interdict arms."

Moreover, the committee concluded, the operation was a failure. It had not interdicted any arms, it had not convinced the Sandinistas to reduce their support for the Salvadoran guerrillas, it had not led them to reduce their ties to Cuba and the Soviet Union, and it had not bolstered democracy inside Nicaragua. On the contrary, "entirely opposite results have been produced."

The bill proposed by the committee had two provisions. The first prohibited further funding of the covert war and the second allocated $80 million (the amount Reagan had requested for the contras for FY 1983 and FY 1984) for overt aid to friendly governments in Central America so that they could interdict any arms being smuggled through their territory.[33] If the administration wanted to interdict arms, the committee would give it a real arms interdiction program.

The overt aid provision was included to win the support of moderate and conservative Democrats who believed that Washington needed to do something to stop Nicaragua's support for the Salvadoran guerrillas. It was also designed to provide "political cover" for Democrats so their Republican opponents in the 1984 election could not accuse them of doing nothing to stop the Communist menace in Central America.

Republican members of the Intelligence Committee bitterly opposed Boland-Zablocki. They took some solace from the fact that the committee report affirmed unequivocally that the Salvadoran insurgency "depends for its lifeblood—arms, ammunition, financing, logistics and command-and-control—upon outside assistance from Nicaragua and Cuba." But they derided the overt arms interdiction provision as unworkable.[34]

President Reagan called the Boland-Zablocki bill "irresponsible." The contras were "freedom fighters," struggling against an illegitimate government, he declared in a White House interview with selected reporters. But Reagan's performance was confused and incoherent, as sometimes happened when he was tired. Moreover, he plainly did not understand Boland-Zablocki, thinking it allowed the United States to send contra aid to third countries who could then pass it along to the contras. In fact, the bill expressly prohibited that.[35]

In early July, as the House floor vote on Boland-Zablocki approached, the entire U.S. foreign policy community was drawn into the debate. On the right, commentators began to argue that the president would be justified in simply ignoring the Boland amendment—both the one that was pending and the one that was already law. The *Wall Street Journal* called the 1982 law "sophomoric" and mocked the Democrats for being "more frightened of the dreaded CIA than of the Russians." But on the whole, editorial opinion was with the Democrats. The *New York Times* called for an end to contra aid on the grounds that it "mocks the very principle of nonintervention that the president invokes against Managua and Havana." The *Miami Herald* called the contra war "un-American," arguing, "It differs not one whit in principle from what the Soviet Union did when it invaded Afghanistan."[36]

Grassroots opposition to the contra war was also growing apace. When pollsters asked whether the United States should be aiding the contras to overthrow the Nicaraguan government, opinion was uniformly hostile. Throughout 1983, half a dozen public polls found opposition to Reagan's policy running between 60 and 80 percent and support at only 15 to 25 percent. Private polls taken for the White House by Richard Wirthlin showed about the same results.[37]

On July 19, 1983, the fourth anniversary of the triumph of the Nicaraguan revolution, the House of Representatives convened for only the fourth secret session in its history to discuss Washington's not-so-secret war against the Sandinistas. Democrats and Republicans from the Intelligence Committee gave their respective views of the war, and administration officials, led by Casey himself, briefed the House. Casey did his cause more harm than good. He continued to insist that the whole purpose of the rapidly escalating war was simply to interdict arms to El Salvador. Nobody really believed him.[38]

The administration's credibility suffered a more fatal wound the next day. The story of the secret House session was supplanted by another, bigger Central American story that dominated the news throughout the week leading up to the House vote on Boland-Zablocki. Ronald Reagan was sending thousands of U.S. soldiers and sailors to Central America in a massive show of military force, code-named "Big Pine II."

Preparing the Battlefield

The idea for the Big Pine II military exercises began when administration hard-liners ousted Tom Enders in early 1983. After seizing control of Central America policy, they wasted no time laying plans for a major escalation of U.S. military involvement. In the spring, Defense, State, and the CIA were all tasked to draw up new policy options for bolstering Washington's allies and intensifying pressure on the Sandinistas. Casey and Clarridge devised a plan to double the size of the contra army from seven to fifteen thousand.[39]

The most elaborate proposals, however, came from the Department of Defense, drawn up by General Paul F. Gorman, who had just been assigned to replace General Wallace H. Nutting as commander-in-chief of the U.S. Southern Command in Panama. Gorman, who had sat in the Inter-Agency Core Group on Latin America for the previous two years as the representative of the

Joint Chiefs of Staff, thought the military should play a more aggressive role in Central America. He saw himself as the man to lead the way. "While others dawdle over economic aid and negotiating strategies," said a Pentagon colleague, "Gorman will be getting military things done."[40]

Though he looked like a kindly, bespectacled grandfather, Gorman was one of the toughest and most uncompromising hard-liners in the administration. Even his friends referred to his ideological views as "hard right," and he had no tolerance for those who disagreed with him. One of his fellow generals described Gorman as "absolutely brilliant, but a man with czarist tendencies."[41]

Gorman blamed the weakness of the U.S. military position in Central America on Jimmy Carter's "strategic disinvestment"—his policy of halting aid to military dictatorships. Like the other hard-liners, Gorman believed that the revolutions in Central America were the result of a Soviet thrust into the region that Washington had to counter with a military buildup of its own.[42]

Besides a "hard-charging" attitude, Gorman went to Panama in May 1983 with a number of advantages. He was well versed in the labyrinths of the national security bureaucracy, having served not only in the Core Group, but also as a National Intelligence Officer for conventional military forces at the CIA during the late 1970s. The Panama command was upgraded from a three-star to a four-star post when Gorman was assigned there, giving him greater influence at the Pentagon, where he already had close ties to the Joint Chiefs of Staff.[43]

General Gorman was not averse to using his influence in Washington to run roughshod over uncooperative U.S. ambassadors. In Guatemala, Ambassador Frederic Chapin objected to Gorman's efforts to solicit the military's cooperation in revitalizing CONDECA (the old Central American Defense Council that broke up after the 1969 war between Honduras and El Salvador) for fear it would give the generals the impression that Washington was content with their unremittingly terrible human rights record. Gorman got Chapin recalled to Washington. In Nicaragua, Gorman clashed with Ambassador Tony Quainton, who was insufficiently anti-Sandinista. In Honduras, Gorman developed a very close relationship with General Alvarez and began to battle Ambassador John Negroponte over who would supervise U.S. operations there. By 1984, both Quainton and Negroponte were on their way to new jobs, and General Gorman was being called "Mr. United States" in Central America.[44]

In May 1983, Gorman submitted to Washington a plan to rapidly raise the U.S. military profile throughout the region. He proposed to expand upcoming exercises with Honduras to several times their normal size and duration, deploying a significant U.S. military force for at least several months. The exercises, however, were merely the prelude to a more permanent military presence. Gorman also called for building new air and naval bases in Honduras and pre-positioning supplies there to facilitate direct U.S. military intervention if need be. He also wanted to build military access roads and airstrips in Costa Rica near the border with Nicaragua, but the Costa Ricans resisted for fear of being drawn into a war with the Sandinistas.[45]

The decision to launch the Big Pine II exercises grew out of a National Security Council meeting on July 8, 1983, called to review various policy proposals developed in the wake of Enders's removal. Secretary of State George Shultz regarded it as so important that he traveled for twenty-four hours from the Middle East in order not to miss it.[46] The background paper drawn up for the meeting reflected the apocalyptic vision of administration hard-liners. Unless Washington acted quickly, it argued, all the countries in Central America were likely to collapse, followed by the destabilization of Mexico. The briefing paper also reflected the hard-liners' preference for military measures. It said little about economic assistance or diplomacy, but recommended increased military aid regionwide and endorsed General Gorman's plan for expanded military exercises and base construction.[47]

Reagan found the hard-liners' arguments convincing. "The security situation in Central America is deteriorating" because of "inadequate resources" and "a persistent lack of public understanding of our interests," he concluded. To address these difficulties, Reagan ordered three actions: the creation of a presidential commission (later known as the Kissinger Commission) "to develop requisite bipartisan support for our policies"; the development of a detailed plan of "appropriate military actions, exercises and contingency measures designed to curtail and eventually halt Cuban/Soviet bloc assistance and presence in Nicaragua"; and the launching of a revitalized public affairs and legislative action program.[48]

On July 13, 1983, Defense Secretary Caspar Weinberger submitted the Pentagon's blueprint for Central America. It included an increase of $168 million in military aid for FY 1984 (a 120 percent increase over the initial FY 1984 request) and an increase of $120 million in military aid above the levels planned for FY 1985. It also included Gorman's plan for expanded maneuvers and the construction of several new airfields, a new radar installation, and a $150 million air and naval base at Puerto Castilla, Honduras. Weinberger noted that contingency plans were being developed for setting up a naval blockade of Nicaragua and for interdicting arms being smuggled into El Salvador. And for good measure, he threw in a recommendation that the 55-man limit on U.S. military advisers in El Salvador be raised to 125.[49] The Pentagon was going for broke.

George Shultz thought the proposals submitted in response to Reagan's general decisions at the July 8 NSC meeting would be reviewed through the normal inter-agency process before any final decisions were made. But on

July 15, just two days after Weinberger submitted his memo, Reagan approved the expanded military maneuvers on the advice of National Security Adviser William Clark. The hard-liners were so distrustful of the State Department that Shultz was not informed of the decision, for fear he would try to talk Reagan out of it. Shultz first heard that the exercises had been approved when he read about it in the *Washington Post* on July 21. "I was totally blindsided . . . totally out of the loop," he recalled.[50]

Instead of involving sixteen hundred U.S. troops and lasting a few days, as the Big Pine I exercise had in January 1983, Big Pine II involved upward of four to five thousand U.S. ground forces and lasted six months, from August 1983 to January 1984. The land exercises included amphibious landings by U.S. Marines and mock bombing runs by jets from carriers offshore. In addition to the USS *Ranger*, two other carrier groups and the battleship *New Jersey* also participated in the exercises—nineteen ships, over two hundred jet fighters, and twenty thousand personnel in all. Big Pine II was the longest and the largest U.S. military exercise in Central American history.[51]

As administration officials described it, this military muscle flexing had several purposes. One was to "intimidate" the Sandinistas into withdrawing their support for the Salvadoran guerrillas.[52] Another was to reassure Washington's regional allies—especially Honduras—who reacted nervously to Congress's growing resistance to Reagan's policy. The exercises "signal our friends that we can move in with greater force if necessary," Undersecretary of Defense Fred Iklé explained. "[We] have established an attitude of caring."[53]

The presence of U.S. combat troops in Honduras also provided a tangible deterrent to dissuade the Sandinistas from striking across the border at contra base camps—a "shield" behind which the contras could operate.[54] As a side benefit, when the exercises were over, the improved facilities and leftover supplies could be given to the Hondurans and the contras, thereby supplementing the regular military aid program without the aggravation of seeking congressional approval. Such use of the Pentagon's training funds was not strictly legal, and Pentagon officials promised that no equipment or supplies would be left behind. But they were.[55]

The exercises in Honduras were a key part of Washington's psychological warfare against the Sandinistas—"perception management," the Pentagon called it. The aim was to convince the Sandinistas that they were constantly on the verge of being attacked. "We're playing a little cat-and-mouse game with them," a Defense Department official explained, "putting a little squeeze on, making them wonder what's going to happen next."[56]

Time and time again, the Sandinistas, believing Washington's deceptions, appealed to the United Nations that an invasion was imminent. The assaults never materialized, and U.S. officials dismissed the Sandinistas as paranoid lunatics. Like the Little Boy Who Cried Wolf, the Sandinistas' warnings gradually came to be ignored by the international community.[57] Meanwhile, the repeated mobilization of Nicaragua's national defenses in anticipation of attack interrupted normal economic activity, enervated the public, and let the Pentagon take a measure of what resistance Nicaragua could offer to an actual intervention. "[We] push very close to the border, deliberately, to set off all the alarms," a senior administration official acknowledged. Invasion jitters also tended to soften up the Sandinistas' negotiating position. "Every time there's an invasion scare, they make some concessions," the official continued. "We do our best to keep them concerned."[58]

Nor was the invasion threat entirely hypothetical. U.S. army engineers on maneuvers in Honduras built or improved bases, roads, airfields, and storage depots—the physical infrastructure necessary to support a large-scale U.S. presence in Honduras, or the use of Honduras as a staging area for intervention by U.S. combat forces in El Salvador or Nicaragua.[59]

During Big Pine II, military engineers built or substantially upgraded four Honduran airfields—at San Lorenzo, La Trujillo, Aguacate, and Tiger Island. Follow-on exercises in early 1984 (called Granadero I) also included an agenda of military construction projects, including two more airfields. During the two sets of exercises, U.S. military engineers also built barracks, hospitals, and training camps.[60]

All of this construction was financed out of the Pentagon's "operations and maintenance" funds—its general operating budget. That was illegal, according to the General Accounting Office (GAO); the law required explicit congressional approval for any permanent military construction project costing more than $200,000, which most of the Honduran projects did.[61]

Congressional Democrats denounced Reagan for deploying U.S. combat forces into Central America and accused him of violating the War Powers Resolution. "He thinks he's John Wayne," said Speaker Tip O'Neill. "He thinks he can go down there and clean the place out." In both the House and Senate, Democrats introduced legislation to prohibit the deployment of U.S. military forces in Central America without the prior approval of Congress.[62]

Ironically, the job of damage control fell mainly to George Shultz, who was widely regarded on Capitol Hill as the most moderate and reasonable member of Reagan's foreign policy team. Shultz, frozen out of the decision to launch the exercises, now had to pacify an angry Congress. He invited key members to breakfast, visited the Hill, and testified in the Senate. He apologized for the failure to consult, not letting on that he himself had not been consulted. He swore that U.S. forces were "absolutely" not going to attack Nicaragua, and he pledged that if hostilities broke out, U.S. troops would withdraw. "They will defend themselves," he said, "but they will withdraw."[63] Nevertheless, he defended the administration's policy tenaciously, rejecting suggestions that the exercises be scaled down.

Administration hard-liners were unimpressed with the harsh congressional reaction. At one of Shultz and Weinberger's weekly breakfast meetings amid the tumult over Big Pine, Weinberger suggested that they simply "ignore Congress," and his deputy, Paul Thayer, was openly contemptuous of the legislative branch. "Congress," Shultz reminded them, "is provided for in the Constitution."[64]

The White House staff was less sanguine about the flood of press reports and growing political furor. In hopes of calming the waters, President Reagan gave two news conferences. The first, on July 21, 1983, unintentionally exacerbated the war fever. Reagan began by insisting, against all evidence, that the exercises were routine. Then he refused to rule out the possibility of a naval blockade of Nicaragua, saying only that he hoped that would not be necessary.

The headline from Reagan's press conference, however, was his statement that it would be "extremely difficult" to achieve a regional settlement of the Central America crisis if the Sandinistas remained in power.[65] For a year and a half, administration officials had been insisting that the covert war was not intended to overthrow the Sandinista government, which the 1982 Boland amendment prohibited. In one offhand remark, the president put the lie to it. If there could be no regional peace while the Sandinistas were in power, how could one escape the conclusion that U.S. policy must be aimed at getting them out? Reagan's admission, coming while the fleet steamed toward Nicaragua, did nothing to calm the fears of those who thought the hard-liners in the War Party were finally going to get a chance to live up to their nickname.

Less than a week later, on July 26 (the eve of the House debate over contra aid), the White House staff decided to hold another press conference, this one carefully staged to convey a message of peace. "We have no military plans for intervention," Reagan said in response to the first question, adding later, "There is no comparison with Vietnam and there's not going to be anything of that kind." Reagan insisted, a bit implausibly, "We are not seeking a larger presence in that region."[66]

It was by now a familiar pattern. Hard-line policies touched off a war scare that began to have corrosive political consequences. Reagan himself was inclined out of ideological instinct to go along with the tough anti-Communist line. But when the political costs of the incipient crusade began to mount, the White House pragmatists and keepers of the presidential image stepped in and put a stop to it. Under their guiding hand, Reagan tried to reassure the public that war was not imminent, that he would not send U.S. troops into another Vietnam. The public, according to the polls, was not very reassured.

Boland-Zablocki

For Reagan, the timing of the leak about the military exercises could not have been worse. Front-page stories about the exercises and Casey's plan to double the contra army appeared just before the House debate on the Boland-Zablocki bill, wrecking administration efforts to forge a compromise on contra aid with moderate Democrats. The exercises made Reagan appear two-faced—feigning moderation to avoid an aid cut-off, while secretly planning a massive escalation of the war. "This show of power turns off people who might be thinking of compromise," Republican House leader Robert Michel (R-Ill.) acknowledged. "It's really undercutting us."[67] Before news of the exercises broke, Democratic leaders in the House conceded that they did not have the votes to pass the Boland-Zablocki bill. After a week of scary headlines, the Democrats' whip count showed them narrowly ahead.[68]

The Boland-Zablocki bill came to the House floor on July 27, 1983, and was bitterly debated for two days. The Democrats repeated the arguments first laid out by the House Intelligence Committee. "This secret war is bad U.S. policy," said Boland, leading off, "because it does not work, because it is in fact counterproductive, because it is illegal."[69] The covert war had not succeeded in either interdicting arms or intimidating the Sandinistas into better behavior. On the contrary, it had led them to impose a state of emergency curtailing civil liberties and to seek closer military ties with Cuba and the Soviet Union.

The Republicans adamantly denied that the contra operation violated the Boland amendment. From the beginning, the amendment had been intended to let the operation go forward, they noted, even though everyone understood perfectly well that the goals of the contras and those of the United States might not be exactly the same. Regardless of what the contras wanted, President Reagan was not trying to overthrow the Sandinistas, so the operation was perfectly legal.

The Republicans also insisted that the covert operation was succeeding. Even if no arms had been intercepted, the flow had diminished and the contras deserved credit for it. The decay of political freedom in Nicaragua and the growing military relationship between Nicaragua and the Soviet bloc was not a result of the covert war; it was the natural trajectory of the Sandinistas' Marxist-Leninist revolution. If anything, the contras had slowed the march toward totalitarianism.

The debate turned more emotional as it dragged on. Republicans lauded the contras as freedom fighters; Democrats denounced them as "thugs, brigands, and thieves" left over from Somoza's National Guard. Republicans warned that failure to support the contras would lead to the collapse of Central America and Mexico, producing a "tidal wave of refugees, both feet people and boat people," twelve million strong, "swarming into our country."[70]

The most rancorous exchanges were produced by a coterie of hard-line Republican conservatives who accused the Democrats of being unpatriotic cowards who were soft on Communism. Donald L. Ritter (R-Pa.) compared the Democrats to Neville Chamberlain appeasing Adolf Hitler at Munich. In an op-ed piece published shortly before the debate, he accused the Democrats of "making the world safe for Communism." Bob Livingston (R-La.) denounced Boland-Zablocki as "an abomination" and asked why the Democrats insisted on ignoring Central America's pleas for freedom. "Is it naivete? Is it isolationism? Is it partisan politics? Or is it worse?"[71]

Calling the Boland-Zablocki proposal the "Trust Nicaragua Amendment," Henry Hyde (R-Ill.) accused the Democrats of wanting to make Americans "impotent spectators, paralyzed" in the face of Communist aggression. It seemed to Eldon D. Rudd (R-Ariz.) that advocates of Boland-Zablocki "wish to see [the United States] reduced to impotence so that we could experience the misery of slavery under the Soviet Union." "Impotent" was the adjective most often invoked against the Democrats.

Newt Gingrich (R-Ga.) argued that the vote on cutting off contra aid would draw the line "between radicals who want unilateral disarmament and the rest of us." He went on to charge that some Democrats "believe the CIA is more dangerous than the KGB," a charge that brought forth cheers from the Republicans and a chorus of hissing from the Democratic side of the isle.

Ted Weiss (D-N.Y.) rose in response, excoriating the Republicans for questioning the loyalty of other members of the House: "I think that is reprehensible, shameful, despicable, and has no place in this body." The Democrats stood and applauded. Toward the end of the two-day fracas, Republicans strained the comity of the House by objecting to routine unanimous consent requests to allow liberals such as Mike Barnes and Tom Harkin a few additional seconds to finish their remarks when they ran short of time.

The escalating partisanship of the debate ultimately favored the Democratic majority in the House. On July 28, 1983, the House approved the original Boland-Zablocki bill with minor changes, by a tally of 228–195, with only eighteen Republicans voting in favor and fifty conservative Democrats voting against.

Reacting to the vote, a senior NSC official expressed the administration's disdain. Boland-Zablocki was merely a display of "partisan politics," he said. "It requires no modification in our plans."[72]

Old Wine in a New Bottle: The September Finding

A challenge to the covert war was also brewing in the Republican-controlled Senate. Senator Leahy's report on his January 1983 trip had disturbed moderates on the Intelligence Committee from both parties. Vice Chairman Moynihan warned of a "crisis of confidence" between Congress and the administration because there was "evidence every night on television" that the administration's policy in Nicaragua was breaking the law.[73]

When the FY 1984 intelligence authorization bill came before the Senate committee in May 1983, Senator David Durenberger (R-Minn.) planned to offer an amendment to cut off the contra aid program immediately.[74] He and Senator Leahy were confident they had the votes to prevail. But they had not counted on Chairman Barry Goldwater's cleverness. When the issue arose on May 6, Goldwater offered a compromise. Rather than give the administration its full request of $50 million for FY 1984 or give it nothing, Goldwater proposed postponing a decision until Reagan submitted a new presidential finding that clarified the aims of his Nicaragua policy.

Under Goldwater's proposal, the contra program would continue uninterrupted through September 30, 1983 (the end of FY 1983), but no funds would be approved for FY 1984. Instead, the committee would put $19 million aside in the CIA's contingency fund. The administration could draw on those funds only if Reagan submitted a new finding and the committee approved it. "We want him to tell us in plain language just what it is he wants to do relative to Nicaragua and the other countries," Goldwater explained.[75]

Goldwater, of course, had cleared this proposal with Reagan and Casey beforehand. Casey, who was at the Senate committee meeting when the issue arose, admitted that the goals of the Nicaraguan operation had evolved beyond those originally specified in the December 1, 1981, presidential finding and that a new one was called for. The Democrats, and Moynihan in particular, regarded it as a great triumph that they would get to vote on the new finding, since normally the intelligence committees had no such power. And Goldwater's proposal seemed to cut the administration's request by more than half, freezing the operation at its current size. Anxious to avoid polarizing the committee along partisan lines, as had happened in the House, most of the Democrats accepted Goldwater's compromise.[76]

The CIA drafted a new finding in July and Casey met with the Senate committee on August 3 to discuss it. The senators were not pleased. The draft resolved the contradiction between the war's expansive character and the narrow objective of arms interdiction by defining broad new aims for the operation—aims that most members thought were overly ambitious.[77] According to the draft, U.S. aid to the contras was intended to pressure the Sandinistas into halting their support for regional insurgencies, reducing their ties to Cuba and the Soviet Union, and building a democracy with freedom of the press, freedom of religion, and free elections. In short, the war would continue until Nicaragua met the full panoply of U.S. demands.[78]

Moynihan criticized the draft for demanding democratization, which he regarded as "undue interference in the internal affairs of Nicaragua." An expert in international law, Moynihan took U.S. obligations seriously. He was confident that a covert operation designed to halt Nicaraguan aid to the Salvadoran guerrillas was legally defensible. Nicaragua's aid was itself a violation of international norms, and Washington had the right to respond in kind. But Moynihan was equally certain that a covert war designed to bring democracy to Nicaragua was indefensible. International law clearly and unequivocally forbade the use of force to change another country's form of government. Durenberger thought the draft finding was so vague and general that the CIA "could do just about anything and never have to prove they were successful."[79]

Casey went back to the drawing board to revise the draft. Reagan approved the new finding at an NSPG meeting on September 16 and signed it on September 19, 1983. Shultz and Casey presented it to the Senate Intelligence Committee the following day. The final document was a grab bag that included every rationale the administration had ever tried on the skeptical Congress. It authorized the CIA to "provide for support, equipment and training assistance to the Nicaraguan paramilitary resistance groups as a means to induce the Sandinistas and Cubans and their allies to cease their support for insurgencies in the region; to hamper Cuban/Nicaraguan arms trafficking; to divert Nicaragua's resources and energies from support to Central American guerrilla movements; and to bring the Sandinistas into meaningful negotiations and constructive, verifiable agreement with their neighbors on peace in the region."[80]

Moynihan took heart from the fact that the explicit goals of the revised finding seemed "more precise and much more limited" than those in the first draft. David Durenberger, the leading Republican opponent of contra aid on the committee, was so pleased with the new finding that he changed sides and became a defender of the program (thereby amplifying his reputation for eccentricity). Reassured, the committee voted 13–2 (with Democrats Leahy and Joseph Biden of Delaware dissenting) to approve most of the $50 million the administration had requested for the covert war during FY 1984.[81]

The atmosphere was totally different the following day when Casey and

Shultz appeared before the House Intelligence Committee. Battle lines had already been drawn in the House, and the strength of the two sides had been tested in the floor votes on Boland-Zablocki. The House committee was not at all convinced by Shultz's performance. "The scope of activities which are authorized is very broad, and in no way limited to arms interdiction," Boland said of the new finding. "Its bottom line is the continuation of the war."[82]

The September finding bought the administration some time by reassuring moderates on the Senate committee, but it treated the symptom rather than the disease. Although much of the debate had focused on the disjuncture between the arms interdiction rationale of the December 1981 finding and the full-scale war that evolved over the subsequent two years, the real problem was not merely definitional. Many members of Congress, especially but not exclusively the liberal Democrats, were upset that the war was escalating. Their worries could not be assuaged by defining broader aims that better fit the reality of an expanding war. It was the reality that troubled them.

As a free-standing piece of legislation, the Boland-Zablocki bill that passed the House had no chance of becoming law. The Republican leadership in the Senate could simply prevent it from being considered there, and even if the Senate did somehow pass the bill, Reagan would veto it. So, House Democrats added a prohibition on contra aid to the FY 1984 intelligence authorization bill and the defense appropriation bill (containing the intelligence community's appropriations).[83] These funding measures, in one form or another, had to be passed. By using them as vehicles for a contra aid ban, the House Democrats posed a real threat to the program.

In the Senate, where liberal Democrats were the minority, the intelligence and defense bills contained continued funding for the contras. The House-Senate conference committee on the intelligence bill deadlocked. Boland, reinforced by Tip O'Neill's directive that the conferees "hold firm" against contra aid, was determined to prevail.[84] In the conference on the defense bill, however, contra aid was but one issue among many, and the House conferees tended to be more conservative than the House as a whole. The conference agreed to a compromise which provided $24 million for the contra war in FY 1984 (about half of what the administration had originally requested) and prohibited the president from supplementing that by using the CIA contingency fund or reprogramming. This compromise was then included in the intelligence authorization as well.[85]

"We seem to be stuck with this," Boland lamented. Later, he tried to make the best of it, pointing out that the amount approved was too little to run the war for more than six months at its current level. The administration would either have to wind it down, or come back to Congress early in 1984 for more money.[86]

The Reagan administration, on the other hand, was very pleased. The House had taken nine votes on contra aid—seven during the debate in July and two in October. Although the administration had lost eight of them, the program was still alive. Officials attributed their good fortune to the surge of public support for Reagan produced by the invasion of Grenada on October 25, 1983, just three weeks before the conference committees resolved the deadlock on contra aid. If the Democrats were going to halt the covert war, they would have to do it during the 1984 election year.

CHAPTER 15

Bringing the War to a Head

In late 1983, in the wake of the House votes against contra aid, Reagan's new national security adviser, Robert C. McFarlane, set up a Special Inter-Agency Working Group to review Central America policy. One of the policy's main impediments, the group concluded, was Congress. "Given the distinct possibility that we may be unable to obtain additional funding in fiscal year (FY) 1984 or FY 85," the group argued, "our objective should be to bring the Nicaraguan situation to a head in 1984."[1] Inevitably, that meant bringing the domestic debate over Nicaragua to a head as well.

Reagan approved McFarlane's recommendations at a January 6, 1984, National Security Planning Group (NSPG) meeting and codified his decisions by signing National Security Decision Directive (NSDD) 124 on February 7. NSDD 124 called for further military exercises in Honduras to "maintain steady pressure on the Nicaraguans," diplomatic pressure on Mexico to curtail its support for both the Sandinistas and the Salvadoran guerrillas, a review of possible economic sanctions against Nicaragua, and a stern warning to Cuba and the Soviet Union that the United States would "not tolerate the introduction into Nicaragua of advanced fighter aircraft or Cuban ground forces."[2]

The contras remained the linchpin of the policy. The White House would have to make a concerted effort to obtain additional funding. "We must make this a matter of the highest priority," Reagan instructed his foreign policy team. "I am determined that this program should continue."[3]

New funds were needed quickly. The $24 million approved by Congress in late 1983 would not last much past April 1984. To protect a new aid request from being mangled by hostile committees in the House, the White House decided to use the same strategy for contra aid that it devised for sending supplemental military aid to El Salvador in early 1984: add the funds to a Senate appropriations bill that the House had already passed and hope that administration allies in the Senate could extract at least some funds from the House in conference committee.

Since this strategy short-circuited the normal legislative process, it had to be executed with considerable political finesse to avoid irritating Congress any more than necessary. That proved to be beyond the administration's competence. On March 8, Senator Ted Stevens (R-Alaska), acting at Reagan's behest, tried to add $21 million in new contra aid to an emergency supplemental appropriation containing $200 million to help low-income citizens with winter energy costs.[4] Appropriations Committee Chairman Mark Hatfield (R-Ore.), an opponent of Reagan's Nicaragua policy, was not warned of the maneuver until the last possible moment for fear he might block it.

Worse yet, the administration did not clear the request with the Senate Intelligence Committee—an egregious blunder since Casey had promised the committee in September that he would seek its approval before expending any additional funds on the covert war.[5] The result of this ineptitude was defeat. After more than two hours of bitter argument, the Appropriations Committee, despite its Republican majority, rejected the contra aid amendment, 15–14. Hatfield cast the deciding vote.[6]

The administration managed to recover from this initial debacle by striking a deal with the moderate Democrats. Just as Senator Daniel K. Inouye brokered a compromise between the administration and his moderate colleagues on the El Salvador portion of the bill, Inouye and Senator Daniel Patrick Moynihan, vice chairman of the Intelligence Committee, arranged an agreement on contra aid. When the administration sheepishly brought the request for $21 million to the Intelligence Committee on March 23, Moynihan proposed that only $7 million be approved immediately. The other $14 million would be placed in the CIA's "reserve for contingencies" fund. That way, the administration would have to consult the committee before allocating any of it. The purpose of this exercise, as Moynihan explained it, was to allow the committee to closely monitor the contra operation to assure that it remained within the guidelines set down in the September 1983 presidential finding.[7]

In truth, although Reagan had changed the language of the September finding to pacify the senators, his policy had not changed one whit. As NSDD 124 made perfectly clear, "democracy"—which to the White House meant ousting the Sandinistas—remained at the top of Reagan's agenda. But in the Senate Intelligence Committee, the moderates convinced themselves that they could keep the administration honest. Democrats, trying to be bipartisan, agreed to the Inouye-Moynihan compromise, 14–0, with only Senator Patrick Leahy abstaining.

A few days later, with the blessing of the Intelligence Committee now in hand, the administration returned to the Appropriations Committee in hopes of adding the $21 million in contra aid to another urgent supplemental appropriation, which included funds for Africa famine relief, child nutrition, and summer jobs.[8] Reagan personally lobbied for the proposal, and this time the committee approved it.

When the urgent supplemental moved to the Senate floor, it sparked the first extended Senate debate on Central America since the 1981 debate over the El Salvador certification bill. Just as the debate was beginning, Reagan gave an interview to the *New York Times* in which he seemed to admit that his aim was to overthrow the Sandinistas after all. The Sandinista government was illegitimate, Reagan contended, because "it was set up by force of arms and the people have never chosen it." He went on to specify, in embarrassing candor, what it would take to stop the contra war: "We have made it plain to Nicaragua—made it very plain, that this would stop when they kept their promise and restore the democratic rule [*sic*] and have elections."[9] This was exactly the position that the Senate Intelligence Committee had rejected in the first draft of the September 1983 finding.

Exasperated, Moynihan went to the Senate floor to respond to what he called "this extraordinary, wholly unexpected, and deeply troubling turn of events." The Congress had not authorized a covert action program to bring about democracy in Nicaragua, Moynihan reminded the president. The aims of the program were supposed to be much more limited. "Has the president deceived us?" Moynihan asked rhetorically. "I doubt this; it is not in his nature, nor that of his associates." What, then, was the explanation? "The president has misstated his own policy," Moynihan concluded. "If we vote today or tomorrow to approve the additional $21 million recommended by the committee, we do not vote to do what the president says he would like to see done. We vote simply and exclusively for the provisions of the presidential finding of September 20."[10]

Reagan's penchant for gaffes made it just plausible that he might misstate the fundamental aims of one of his highest priority policies. But in light of the escalating war and the contras' declared intention to rid Nicaragua of the Sandinistas, Reagan's version of the program's goal seemed a lot closer to the mark than Moynihan's. Senator Edward M. Kennedy (D-Mass.) scoffed at the "willful blindness" of senators who eagerly accepted the administration's reassurances despite overwhelming evidence to the contrary.[11]

Most of the weeklong Senate debate in April focused on El Salvador. Liberal Democrats offered over a dozen amendments on Central America, but only three dealt directly with the contra war in Nicaragua: Kennedy proposed to delete the $21 million in contra aid; Christopher J. Dodd (D-Conn.) proposed a prohibition on using the $21 million "for planning, directing, executing, or supporting acts of terrorism" against Nicaragua; and Inouye proposed a prohibition on using the funds to aid any movement which had as its intention "the violent overthrow of any government in Central America."[12]

The floor debate on the three contra aid amendments was severely onesided. The liberal Democrats spent a total of about six hours running through all the arguments against the covert war. As a result of the Inouye-Moynihan compromise, the Republicans knew they had the votes to defeat the liberals' efforts to kill or cripple the aid request. Rather than join the debate, they just let the liberals hold forth until their time had expired. Most moderate Republicans and Democrats followed the lead of the Intelligence Committee and voted with the administration. Both Kennedy's and Dodd's amendments were defeated.

Inouye's amendment prohibited using any of the $21 million to support groups whose intent was to overthrow the Nicaraguan government. "We cannot innocently provide money knowing that that money will be illegally spent," Inouye reasoned. "If we know that the contras are out to overthrow the Government of Nicaragua, we have no business providing funds to that group."

This argument was sensible enough, though it was odd for Inouye to be the one making it. He had helped build the coalition that guaranteed Senate approval of the $21 million. Now he was saying that the money should not be used to support anyone who intended to overthrow the Sandinistas. Yet no one disputed that this was precisely the contras' intention; they themselves said as much. So why had Inouye supported the $21 million in the first place? His instinct for seeking political compromise was keener than his sense of logic. The Republicans again declined to debate, and the amendment was tabled, on a 51–44 vote that split the Senate mostly along party lines. Shortly thereafter, the entire urgent supplemental was approved.

The administration had won the first round, but its difficulties were just beginning. For almost two months, the House refused to even convene a conference committee with the Senate on the urgent supplemental, mainly because the House was awaiting the outcome of the Salvadoran presidential election (the bill included military aid for El Salvador, too). In the interim, the contra aid program suffered its worst setback to date with the revelation that the CIA had been mining Nicaragua's harbors.

Admiral Dewey and the Motley Crew

It was no secret that Nicaragua's harbors had been mined; the Nicaraguans themselves announced it on January 3, 1984. The first major press reports of the mining did not appear in the United States until mid-March, however, after several European and Latin American ships had been damaged. Then on March 21, a Soviet oil tanker approaching Puerto Sandino hit a mine and sustained serious damage. Five seamen were injured. The Soviet government denounced the mining as a "grave crime" and "an act of banditry and piracy." Foreign Minister Andrei Gromyko personally delivered a strong note of protest to the U.S. ambassador in Moscow.[13] The United States refused to accept the protest, denying that it had placed the mines. The contras, on the other hand, were eager to take credit. "We are responsible for placing the mines, not the United States," said Nicaraguan Democratic Force (FDN) leader Adolfo Calero.[14]

Over the next several weeks, more than half a dozen merchant ships from Japan, Panama, Liberia, the Netherlands, and the Soviet Union were damaged by mines in Nicaragua's three major ports—Corinto, Puerto Sandino, and El Bluff. Fifteen sailors were injured, and two Nicaraguans were killed when their fishing boats hit mines and sank.[15]

The issue of whether the contras or the United States had placed the mines was one of those fine distinctions that matter only in Washington politics. No one seriously believed that the contras had the technical expertise or resources to manufacture and deploy mines by themselves. At a minimum, Washington was an obvious accomplice. As Senator Clairborne Pell (D-R.I.) said during the Senate debate on the $21 million contra aid package, "Maybe the people laying the mines are not American citizens. . . . But the fact remains, which we all know, that those mines originated in the United States."[16]

Nevertheless, the administration insisted on the fiction that the mining was the work of the contras. "The United States is not mining the harbors of Nicaragua," Secretary of Defense Caspar Weinberger flatly declared.[17] In fact, the mining was a CIA operation from beginning to end.

The decision to mine Nicaragua's harbors was made by President Reagan in late 1983, but its roots stretched back to the battle earlier that year between Thomas O. Enders and administration hard-liners. Mining the harbors was proposed in the Inter-Agency Core Group in the spring of 1983, but Enders, sensitive to the diplomatic repercussions it would have in Europe, opposed it. Shultz also opposed it when it was raised at an NSPG meeting on May 31, calling it "dangerous" and "outrageous." After Enders was fired and control over Central America policy shifted into the White House, the hard-liners revived the mining idea.[18]

First, however, the administration decided to supplement contra operations with direct sabotage attacks by the CIA itself. The contras' own military efforts had been disappointing. Something had to be done to increase the pressure on the Sandinistas and improve the contras' image. "There was a push to have some kind of success in Nicaragua, something that would quell the congressional criticism. To show that we were doing things," explained a senior intelligence official. "I suppose some of Casey's impatience was that neither the FDN nor Edén Pastora were having any political effect."[19]

Casey wanted to attack the economy, to hit the Sandinistas where they were most vulnerable. "Let's make them sweat," he told Dewey Clarridge, his division chief for operations in Latin America. "Let's make the bastards sweat." Clarridge came up with the idea of creating a special commando force of CIA contract agents—Unilaterally Controlled Latino Assets, or UCLAS—to attack vital economic installations.[20] "Our mission was to sabotage ports, refineries, boats and bridges, and try to make it look like the contras had done it," one of the UCLAS later explained.[21]

The CIA outfitted two oil rig servicing ships as platforms for the UCLAS, who were mercenaries recruited from all over Latin America. Operating out of a secret CIA base on Tiger Island, Honduras, in the Gulf of Fonseca, these "mother ships" sat off the Nicaraguan coast, just outside the twelve-mile limit. From there, they launched speedboats and helicopters to attack Nicaraguan ports. CIA officers managed the operations from the mother ships. Heavy Chinook helicopters ferried the UCLAS and their speed boats to the Nicaraguan coast; light Hughes 500 helicopters strafed and rocketed Nicaraguan coastal defenses. Sometimes, especially difficult sabotage operations were carried out by U.S. Navy SEALS (Sea, Air, and Land special forces).[22]

Between September 1983 and April 1984, the UCLAS and U.S. Special Forces carried out nineteen attacks, most of them targeted at Nicaragua's three oil storage facilities. On October 10, the commandos blew up oil storage tanks at Corinto, causing the loss of over 3.2 million gallons of gasoline and diesel fuel. One hundred and twelve people were injured and some 20,000 had to be evacuated from the city. Three days later, frogmen blew up mooring facilities on the oil pipeline in Puerto Sandino. Shortly thereafter, Exxon Corporation informed Nicaragua it would no longer provide tankers to transport Nicaraguan oil.[23]

Casey was thrilled. He pressed Clarridge to come up with new ideas for crippling the Nicaraguan economy. Clarridge, who had studied the effectiveness of naval mines in the Russo-Japanese War while he was at Columbia University, suggested mining Nicaragua's harbors.[24] Assistant Secretary of State for Latin America Tony Motley was all for it, and so was the National Security Council staff. The Nicaraguan economy was highly dependent on trade. Choke off shipping, and the economy would die.[25]

To avoid the diplomatic headaches that would come from sinking ships and killing seamen from third countries, the CIA had "firecracker" mines specially made—mines supposedly not big enough to sink a vessel or kill anyone (although some contained 300 pounds of plastic explosive), but big enough to damage ships and, as one official put it, "wake up folks at Lloyd's of London."[26] By driving up the insurance rates on vessels that dared to call in Nicaraguan ports, the country's trade could be severely curtailed. Mexican ships were specifically targeted, because Mexico supplied almost all of Nicaragua's oil.[27]

The mining proposal was discussed at length by the National Security Planning Group (NSPG) in late 1983, with Reagan present. But there was no serious effort to assess the potential costs of the operation. "This was not one of the happiest episodes of decision-making," National Security Adviser Robert McFarlane recalled ruefully. "There was some disagreement on it, and then some people kind of waffled and said this and that, but that is normal."[28] George Shultz, who had blocked the mining proposal in May 1983, was absent this time—attending the annual NATO foreign ministers meeting in Europe. He didn't realize the mining decision had been taken until news of it broke in the press four months later.[29]

One factor that inhibited frank discussion of the pros and cons of a proposal like the harbor mining was the atmosphere that developed after Enders was fired. Anyone who raised questions about the policy was suspected by the hard-liners of being a closet liberal. "You had to be careful," said Nestor Sanchez, himself a hard-liner. "To raise a question was to be a negative thinker." Skeptics kept quiet, but among themselves, they referred to the mining operation's boosters derisively as "Admiral Dewey and the Motley crew."[30]

The mining began in January 1984 and continued until Washington's role became public in early April. The mines, about seventy-five in all, were laid by speed boats and helicopters piloted by UCLAS and U.S. Special Forces. Since one purpose of both the mining and the UCLA commando raids was to convince Congress that the contras were becoming more effective, it was not in the CIA's interest to be entirely forthcoming about the fact that the contras themselves had nothing to do with the operation—especially when Congress was about to consider the $21 million contra aid package.

The House Intelligence Committee was briefed on January 31, 1984, and after persistent questioning managed to get the full story. Some members still felt that they had not been adequately informed, especially about the UCLA commando raids that had been going on for months. When members asked why the committee had not received prior notice of an initiative as important as the mining of Nicaragua's main port at Puerto Sandino, Casey replied that it was not a port, but an "anchorage."[31]

The Senate committee was not briefed until March 8. When Casey finally appeared, most of the meeting was devoted to members venting their anger at the administration's effort to sneak the $21 million in contra aid into the urgent supplemental without first clearing the proposal with the committee. Casey did not divulge the CIA's role in either the UCLA attacks or the mining. In fact, during the two-hour hearing, the transcript of which ran to eighty-four pages, Casey uttered only one sentence about the mining of Nicaragua's harbors: "Magnetic mines have been placed in the Pacific harbor of Corinto and the Atlantic harbor of El Bluff, as well as the oil terminal at Puerto Sandino."[32] Perhaps Casey's use of the passive voice should have tipped off the senators that they needed to probe a bit deeper to get at the facts, but none did.

Casey next met with the committee on March 13, to get its formal approval for the $21 million aid package. Again, he mentioned the mining only once, repeating the same sentence almost verbatim. Again, no one asked for details. Later that month, Senator Pell, who was not a member of the Intelligence Committee, asked the CIA for information on the mining, and the Agency's response mentioned the UCLAS. That tipped off the Intelligence Committee staff that something was amiss; they requested another briefing, which the CIA provided on April 2. The briefing officer fully detailed the U.S. role in both the UCLA commando raids and the mining of Nicaragua's harbors. The staff immediately prepared a memorandum for committee members that summarized the briefing, but few read it prior to the April 4 and 5 floor votes on contra aid.[33]

Senator Joseph Biden (D-Del.) happened to read the report while he was on the Senate floor listening to the contra aid debate. He couldn't believe his eyes. He showed it to Senator William Cohen (R-Maine), who hadn't seen it either. Cohen took it to Senator Goldwater. "Is this true?" Cohen demanded. "Why haven't I been told?" Goldwater, taken aback, looked at the memo. It was the first he had seen of it, too.[34]

Then, to the horror of the Intelligence Committee staff, Goldwater began to read the classified memo aloud on the Senate floor. The staff stopped him and his remarks were expunged from the printed record, but the cat was out of the bag.[35] David Rogers of the *Wall Street Journal* heard Goldwater's remarks and the following morning, April 6, broke the story that the CIA was responsible for the mining.[36] Just as the mining story broke, the administration compounded its political problems by notifying the United Nations that the United States would refuse to accept the jurisdiction of the World Court in a case that Nicaragua was preparing against it for mining its harbors and arming the contras.

Over the next few weeks, administration officials tried to cope with three public relations disasters: the Senate Intelligence Committee's outrage over not being adequately informed of the CIA's role in the mining; negative reactions from both Congress and the general public over the mining; and an even greater revulsion at the administration's refusal to defend itself in the World Court.

Barry Goldwater had always been a loyal defender of Reagan's Nicaragua policy, and he was mad as hell that Casey had launched a major covert initiative without telling him. "I feel like such a fool," Goldwater told an aide. "I feel betrayed."[37] As chairman, Goldwater also felt compelled to publicly accept responsibility for the Senate Intelligence Committee's failure to do the job of oversight the Senate had entrusted to it. "I am forced to apologize to the members of my committee because I did not know the facts on this case," he said on the Senate floor. "And I apologize to all members of the Senate for the same reason."[38]

It made no sense for Casey to keep Goldwater's committee in the dark about the harbor mining, and Goldwater sent Casey a scathing letter telling him so. "All this past weekend, I've been trying to figure out how I can most easily tell you of my feelings about the discovery of the president having approved mining some of the harbors of Central America," Goldwater began. "It gets down to one, little, simple phrase: I am pissed off!"

The letter continued: "Bill, this is no way to run a railroad. . . . The president has asked us to back his foreign policy. Bill, how can we back his foreign policy when we don't know what the hell he is doing?" The mining, Goldwater advised, "is an act violating international law. It is an act of war. For the life of me, I don't see how we are going to explain it." The mostly likely result, Goldwater warned, was that the $21 million aid package for the contras would now be defeated. The letter immediately leaked to the press.[39]

Casey met with the Intelligence Committee to brief them on the mining on April 10, the day after Goldwater sent his letter. Casey's instinct was to stonewall. The senators had certainly known about the mining; many of them had referred to it during the floor debate on the $21 million contra aid proposal the week before. Their sudden outrage was just so much hypocrisy. How could they have thought the United States was not involved? And if they wanted to know the details of the CIA's role, they should have asked.[40]

Casey insisted that his one-sentence references to the mining during testimony on March 8 and March 13 fulfilled the CIA's statutory obligation to keep the committee fully informed. When members objected that a passing reference buried in two hours of testimony did not meet the spirit or letter of the law, Casey replied, "If you ask me the right question, I will respond."[41] That attitude did not sit well with the senators. "On a zero to ten scale, Casey rates a two on the trust factor," said Republican David Durenberger afterward. "There is no use in our meeting with Bill Casey. None of us believe him."[42]

Outraged by Casey's intransigence, Senator Moynihan resigned as vice chairman of the committee. Without a relationship of trust between the committee and the intelligence community, he could not continue to serve, he said in his letter of resignation. In private, he was harsher: "Casey was running a disinformation operation against our committee."[43]

Like the Vichy police prefect in *Casablanca* who professed shock at discovering gambling in Rick's café, Moynihan's protest was a bit disingenuous. He must have surmised that the mining was not strictly the contras' doing. In fact, he had asked the State Department for a legal opinion on the mining on March 27 (more than a week before the CIA's role was revealed)—something he would have had no reason to do if he really believed the contras had mined the harbors all by themselves.[44] He also acknowledged that staff members had told him of the April 2 meeting where CIA officials spelled out the details of the mining, though he insisted he had not read the full report of that meeting until later. Had he known the mining was done exclusively by the United States, he claimed, he would have opposed the $21 million.[45]

The mining revelation was especially embarrassing for Moynihan. After all, he and Inouye had convinced their dubious colleagues to support Reagan's $21 million request on the grounds that the program would be strictly limited and closely supervised by the Intelligence Committee. The mining proved that Casey was not willing to abide by such limits. Moynihan, it appeared, had been played for a fool. Resigning was a way for him to recoup his dignity as a stalwart defender of the committee's prerogatives. Amid the drama of it, perhaps no one would recall that it was Moynihan who had been so easily sold a bill of goods in the first place. "If we didn't know, we should have known," Moynihan later admitted. "I lost a lot of skin on this one."[46]

At first, the CIA steadfastly defended itself, even in the face of Moynihan's threatened resignation. Spokesman George Lauder released a statement insisting that Casey had kept the committees fully informed. From the December 1981 finding to the end of March 1984, Casey or his deputy had briefed Congress thirty times on Central America. In the months since the September 1983 finding, lower-level CIA officials had briefed members or staff twenty-two times, eleven of them on the mining of Nicaragua's harbors. "The only thing more we could have done is install a teletype down there and let them see the daily cables," complained CIA congressional liaison Clair George.[47]

Casey himself made light of the furor. "I think that people in the long run are less concerned about reports of mining Nicaraguan harbors than they are about the danger of creating a wave of immigration into this country if Central America or any part of it should fall under Communist domination," he told the press.[48]

But stonewalling Congress was a no-win strategy. Even if Casey got the better of the argument, he would poison what little was left of his relationship with the senators. Since they controlled the CIA's budget, he might win the battle, but he would surely lose the war. If the moderates on the Senate committee became so disenchanted with Casey that they voted to stop funding the contras, the full Senate would probably follow their lead. With the House already committed to killing the program, that would be the end of it.

Much as it pained him, Casey had to give in for the good of the policy. A peace agreement was negotiated by Senators Richard G. Lugar (R-Ind.) and Lloyd Bentsen (D-Tex.), contra supporters who feared that if Moynihan actually resigned, the new vice chairman might be a Democrat who opposed the war. The terms of Casey's surrender required him to apologize, admit that the Intelligence Committee had not been adequately informed, and agree to guidelines governing notification of future covert actions.[49]

First, Casey apologized privately to Moynihan and asked him not to resign; Moynihan agreed. Then Casey apologized to Goldwater with a handwritten note that read, "I'm as sorry as I can be about the misunderstandings and failure in communications which have developed to impair an activity which I thought we were handling well together."[50] The next day, April 26, Casey met with the full committee and acknowledged that it was his responsibility to keep the senators informed. If they felt he had not done so, it was his failure. For that, he said, "I apologize profoundly."[51]

Apologizing was bitter medicine for Casey. "I sure as hell didn't want to do it. I gagged on it," he told his deputy John McMahon afterward. "But I don't have to tell you, the Nicaragua operation was on the ropes. I only apologized to save the contras."[52]

In addition to the verbal spanking Casey received at the hands of the committee, he was also forced into a substantive concession. He agreed to put in writing a detailed inventory of the kinds of information the CIA would provide the Intelligence Committee in the future to comply with the legal requirement that Congress be kept fully informed of covert operations.[53] A month later, on June 6, 1984, Casey reluctantly signed an agreement that came to be known as the "Casey Accords." In it, he pledged to provide not only the presidential finding but also the more detailed scope paper (setting out the aims, methods, and potential risks) for each new covert operation "prior to the implementation of the actual activity." Casey promised to inform the committee if new activities under an existing finding were authorized by the NSC or the president, if they involved U.S. personnel, or if they were politically sensitive. Finally, he agreed to give the committee a comprehensive annual briefing on all covert operations and special briefings on any operation that was of particular interest to the senators.[54]

The Intelligence Committee had a hard time getting Casey to agree to such "sunshine" procedures, and there was much self-congratulation when he finally obliged. But coercing Casey into promising to reveal secrets he didn't believe the Congress had a need to know did not improve Congress's relations with the CIA. On the contrary, it made Casey more sour than ever about congressional oversight and drove covert operations deeper underground. When the administration began trading arms for hostages with Iran in 1985, Casey told the intelligence committees nothing about the operation, his signed agreement notwithstanding.

Why had Casey been so reluctant to inform an essentially friendly committee of the harbor mining? Casey's general attitude toward congressional oversight was partly to blame, but timing also played a role. Support from the Senate committee was crucial to continuing the contra aid program, and the majority in favor of aid was tenuous. Had the committee known of the U.S. role in the mining and the UCLA raids before they voted on the $21 million package, it might have been defeated. In the House Intelligence Committee, where a solid majority already wanted to close down the contra program, it made little difference what they knew about the mining.

Finally, the House committee was simply more diligent. It insisted on being briefed earlier and its members probed deeper because they knew that was the only way to get Casey to divulge the facts. On the Senate side, Goldwater and Moynihan saw themselves as partners of the intelligence community rather than watchdogs, even though Casey treated the relationship as adversarial. Some staff aides on the Senate committee felt that Goldwater and Moynihan did not want to know too much about covert operations, and so the committee exhibited a "certain passivity."[55] Passivity was not the way to get the truth out of Bill Casey.

Firestorm

Public and congressional reaction to the mining of Nicaragua's harbors and the U.S. decision to withdraw from the World Court was almost uniformly negative. The *New York Times* called the administration's actions "illegal, deceptive and dumb." The *Miami Herald* blasted the mining as "unacceptable terrorism." Among the major papers, only the *Wall Street Journal* defended the mining.[56] In a CBS–*New York Times* poll, 67 percent of the public disapproved of the U.S. "helping the opponents of the [Nicaraguan] government to lay mines in the harbors of Nicaragua." Only 20 percent approved.[57]

The intensity of the opposition to the mining stunned the administration. "Everybody's reaction was that this was a logical next step," said an official involved in the decision. "No one expected there would be a public outcry."[58] In retrospect, however, it was not so difficult to understand. Mining another country's harbors is traditionally regarded as an unequivocal act of war, and it violated the principle of freedom of navigation long championed by the United States. And while the CIA was laying mines in Nicaragua's harbors, the United States was warning Iran that it would be a violation of international law and an act of belligerency if Iran endangered commerce in the Persian Gulf by mining the Strait of Hormuz.

At the United Nations, thirteen members of the Security Council, including France and the Netherlands, voted for a resolution condemning the United States for "the escalation of acts of military aggression" and calling for an end to "all threats, attacks, and overt and covert hostile acts against the sovereignty, independence, and territorial integrity of Nicaragua, in particular, the mining of its main ports." Great Britain abstained, and the United States vetoed the resolution.[59]

Public opposition to the mining was heightened by the administration's decision to withdraw from the World Court. When intelligence sources tipped off U.S. officials that Nicaragua was planning to file a complaint against the United States, the Department of State quickly informed the World Court that Washington would refuse to recognize its jurisdiction over Central American matters for the next two years. "We do not wish to see the Court abused as a forum for furthering a propaganda campaign," the State Department explained.[60]

The withdrawal was of dubious legality. When the Senate ratified President Harry S Truman's declaration accepting compulsory jurisdiction before the court in 1946, it added a passage requiring six months' advance notice before the United States could temporarily suspend the court's jurisdiction. The Senate intended to proscribe any suspension designed to avoid specific litigation— which is just what the State Department had in mind in the Nicaraguan case. By acting without the requisite six months' notice, the administration was violating a duly ratified treaty which constitutionally had the force of domestic law.[61]

Washington's withdrawal notwithstanding, Nicaragua filed its complaint charging that the United States was "training, supplying, and directing military and paramilitary actions against the people and Government of Nicaragua, resulting in extensive loss of lives and property."[62] On May 10, the court issued an interim judgment that it would hear the Nicaraguan case. By a unanimous 15–0 vote it ordered the United States to "immediately cease and refrain" from mining or blocking Nicaragua's harbors, and by a vote of 14–1, with the U.S. judge dissenting, it ordered Washington to respect "the sovereignty and political independence of Nicaragua" and to halt "any military or paramilitary activities which are prohibited by principles of international law."[63]

Although the administration refused to defend itself on the merits of the issue before the court, it argued publicly that mining Nicaragua's harbors was consistent with international law because it was an act of "collective self-defense." Nicaragua was aiding guerrillas in El Salvador; therefore, El Salvador's friends had a right to use force against Nicaragua to get it to stop.[64]

There were problems with this argument. First, the mining was not intended to interdict arms; it was explicitly aimed at crippling the Nicaraguan economy. Second, El Salvador had not accused Nicaragua of aggression in any international forum, nor was there any bilateral self-defense agreement between El Salvador and the United States. The State Department would not even say that El Salvador had asked the United States privately to help repel Nicaraguan aggression.[65]

Both the OAS Charter and the 1947 Rio Treaty of Reciprocal Assistance (signed by the United States and most of Latin America) require that victims of aggression lodge a formal complaint, thereby setting in motion the hemisphere's collective security mechanisms. In the meantime, individual members may use force to defend themselves. But neither El Salvador nor the United States ever brought the issue of Nicaragua's alleged aggression to the OAS.[66]

Article 51 of the U.N. Charter requires that members availing themselves of the right of self-defense must "immediately" report their actions to the Security Council. Washington never did that either. Perhaps the United States could have made a persuasive case that Nicaragua was violating international law by aiding the Salvadoran guerrillas. But Washington had no intention of using the established mechanisms of the international system to seek redress, because it was unwilling to allow its own actions to be bound by international law. An administration official summed up the quality of the State Department's legal case concisely: "Unfortunately, it's bullshit."[67]

On April 10, the Senate voted 84–12 in favor of a resolution condemning the mining of Nicaraguan ports. Even Republican Majority Leader Howard Baker voted for it. "We got a bipartisan vote from the Senate, but it was bipartisan the wrong way," lamented a State Department official.[68]

When a similar resolution was brought before the House, however, Republicans rallied to defend their president. Minority Leader Robert Michel (R-Ill.) led off, arguing that the only purpose of the resolution was to "embarrass"

Ronald Reagan. Its main promoters were the "professional Reagan-haters" among the Democrats, who were turning the House into a "partisan side-show." That set the tone for most of the Republican speeches.

Donald J. Pease, an Ohio Democrat who did not usually involve himself much in the debate over Central America, saw the mining of Nicaragua's harbors in a different context. "The mining incident reveals a dangerous mind-set in the CIA, the Defense Department and the Reagan White House," Pease warned. "All are apparently so obsessed with routing Marxism out of Nicaragua that they believe the ends justify the means. They apparently believe that any act, even an unlawful one, is justified if it serves the end of fighting Marxism. . . . The last time an American president exhibited that mindset . . . the issue was a domestic one, but the episode, which we remember as Watergate, was disastrous for our nation. How much more dangerous it will be for our nation if that mind-set is applied to the international arena."[69] He could not have been more prescient.

The saga of the mining of Nicaragua's harbors ended with the final House vote on the resolution, which passed easily, 281–111. The president was unmoved. "If it is not binding, I can live with it," he said of the resolution.[70] A month later, when Reagan was asked about the mining, his account of it was completely fanciful. "Those were homemade mines that couldn't sink a ship. They were planted in those harbors where they were planted by the Nicaraguan rebels," he blithely asserted. "And I think that there was much ado about nothing."[71]

Dear Comandante

Reagan's response to the verbal beating he took over the mining was a series of speeches excoriating Congress for its lack of bipartisanship. "Unfortunately," Reagan said at Georgetown University, "many in the Congress seem to believe they are still in the troubled Vietnam era, with their only task to be vocal critics, not responsible partners."[72]

Taking their cue from the president, conservative Republicans in the House opened their own attack on the Democrats, explicitly questioning their loyalty. Newt Gingrich (R-Ga.) instigated the assault, with help from his Conservative Opportunity Society—a caucus of young, militant House Republicans who scorned the tradition of comity across party lines. To these Young Turks, comity and good manners had gotten the Republican minority nowhere. They believed in trench-warfare politics—protracted, brutal, and dirty. "A number of you are old enough to have been a rifleman in Vietnam," Gingrich told a college Republican club in 1978. "This is the same business. You're fighting a war. It's a war for power. . . . Don't try to educate."[73]

The only way to break the Democratic majority in the House, the Gingrich conservatives concluded, was to tear down the House as an institution—defaming it in the public eye so that angry voters would throw out incumbents wholesale. Gingrich and his supporters rarely tried to legislate. They had no patience for the careful bargaining and compromise needed to build bipartisan legislative majorities. Instead, they relished their role as ideological shock troopers of the Republican right, railing against the tyranny of the Democratic majority while exploiting the rules whenever possible to obstruct the normal business of the House. Republican leader Robert Michel was uncomfortable with such rabid partisanship, but he lacked the courage to stand up to Gingrich.[74]

In early 1984, Gingrich and his allies seized on the issue of Central America to bludgeon the Democrats. On March 20, ten leading Democrats (including Jim Wright, Michael Barnes, Edward Boland, and Stephen Solarz) had written a letter to Nicaraguan leader Daniel Ortega commending him for scheduling elections in 1984 and for "taking steps to open up the political process." They urged Ortega to take further measures to ensure "truly free and open elections," such as allowing contra forces to return to the country and participate. The letter itself was not unusual or distinctive. Members of Congress frequently wrote to foreign leaders calling on them to take various actions. In urging Ortega to hold a free election, the Democrats' letter was fully consistent with U.S. policy.

Gingrich, however, saw the letter as a prop he could exploit. During the debate on the House resolution condemning the harbor mining, Gingrich accused the letter writers of supporting the Sandinistas and interfering with the conduct of U.S. foreign policy because their letter began by noting that the signers were all opponents of contra aid. To have such prominent Democrats— "the foreign policy establishment of the Democratic Party in the House," Gingrich called them—express their opposition to U.S. policy was tantamount to giving aid and comfort to the enemy.[75]

The fact that the letter was signed only by opponents of contra aid was intentional. The original idea for it came from contra leader Alfonso Robelo, who believed that the Sandinistas might hold fair elections if they were pressured to do so by foreigners who were not their sworn enemies. "He felt that because we had voted against funding for the contras and precisely because we were known as opponents of this covert operation against Nicaragua, there was a possibility that we might have a measure of credibility with the leadership of Nicaragua," Solarz explained.

For Gingrich, that was beside the point. He and his allies harped on what came to be called the "Dear Comandante" letter (because of its salutation to Ortega), denouncing it at every opportunity for weeks on end. The letter was "almost certainly illegal and unconstitutional," Gingrich charged. It was "an effort to educate the Marxist regime into the art of manipulating American opinion," because it pointed out that a free election would improve the climate for U.S.-Nicaraguan relations. Gingrich's conservative partner Robert Walker (R-Pa.) called it "a bootlicking letter," and Henry Hyde (R-Ill.) accused the Democrats of making an "obsequious and fawning" appeal to Ortega.[76]

In early May, Gingrich and friends broadened their attack by reading into the *Congressional Record* a lengthy document entitled "What's the Matter with Democrat Foreign Policy?" Assembled by Republican House staff, the document was a compilation of foreign policy statements made by Democrats over the years that purported to show that they were soft on Communism.[77]

The Democrats named in the document were especially offended by how it was used. After the House completes its normal business, members are allowed to take the floor and speak for up to an hour under "special orders." This enables members to make lengthy statements for the *Congressional Record* that they could not make during regular legislative debate, when speeches are typically limited to five minutes. Since the House television cameras continue to run during special orders, members can acquire videotapes of their speeches for news programs back in their districts. In addition, sixteen million people across the United States regularly watch the live House proceedings, including special orders, on C-SPAN (Cable Satellite Public Affairs Network).[78]

When Gingrich first launched his attack on the "Dear Comandante" letter, he and two of his closest allies, Walker and Vin Weber (R-Minn.), began monopolizing the time for special orders by signing up weeks in advance. Then they used the time to attack the patriotism of various Democrats without the usual courtesy of warning their victims in advance so they could be on hand to reply. But that was not the worst of it. The Republicans, speaking to an empty chamber, postured as if the full House was in session listening to them. They challenged various Democrats by name to stand and defend themselves against charges that amounted to treason, as if the Democrats were in the chamber. Then the Republican speakers baited the absent Democrats for having nothing to say in reply. The tapes of these phony confrontations were then shipped to various news media across the country.

Gingrich and his friends could get away with this charade because the television cameras in the House remained immovably focused on the rostrum. But when various Democrats complained to Speaker Tip O'Neill, he ordered the House cameras to occasionally pan the empty chamber, exposing the Republican ruse.[79]

The Republicans complained they had been held up to "public ridicule."[80] The Democrats were unapologetic. "The gentleman [Gingrich] has written letters and made speeches, written letters to newspapers throughout the country impugning the acts of members of Congress," Jim Wright countered. "The gentleman just seems intent on repetitiously questioning the good will and good faith and patriotism of his colleagues."

Tempers grew short. Various Republicans denounced O'Neill for his television trick and then refused to yield to him so he could reply. When he finally got the floor, O'Neill was fuming. "You deliberately stood in the well before an empty House and challenged these people, and you challenged their Americanism," he said to Gingrich, "and it is the lowest thing I have ever seen in my thirty-two years in the House." Trent Lott (R-Miss.), another Gingrich ally, immediately demanded that the Speaker's "words be taken down"—that he be rebuked for unparliamentary language—and the chair reluctantly agreed. It was the first time a Speaker had been rebuked since 1797. "I was expressing my opinion," O'Neill said later. "As a matter of fact, I was expressing my opinion very mildly, because I think much worse than what I said."[81] In his campaign to polarize the House and break down the traditional bonds of civility that he believed benefited only the majority, Newt Gingrich was making good progress.

Congress Tries to Stop the War

While the firestorm raged over the mining of Nicaragua's harbors, the administration's $21 million aid package for the contras was going nowhere. The House delegation to the conference committee on the urgent supplemental appropriation bill refused to compromise on the issue of contra aid. Senate Republican conferees proposed putting a small amount of money for the contras in the CIA contingency fund "so the president can use it . . . to wind up this operation," as Senator Ted Stevens of Alaska put it.

In the House, Edward Boland was skeptical. "I'm not prepared to believe that the contingency fund is going to be used for phasing it down," he replied. "This is an item that is not negotiable from this side of the table."[82] The issue went back to the full House and Senate in disagreement.

"We must vote again," Boland told the House on May 24, 1984, "and demonstrate to the other body our unstinting commitment to end this deadly war."[83] Boland's motion prohibiting contra aid passed, 241–177.

In the Senate, contra supporters did not have the stomach to continue the fight. After the mining of Nicaragua's harbors and the House vote reaffirming its opposition to any further contra aid, the Senate leadership was ready to give in and drop the $21 million aid package from the urgent supplemental. Senate Republicans were under considerable pressure to pass the bill as the 1984 election campaign grew near because it contained funds for a smorgasbord of popular domestic programs—child nutrition, housing, anticrime programs, and summer jobs. Faced with the prospect of losing the supplemental appro-priations bill because of the Nicaraguan aid provision, the Senate leadership surrendered to the House by dropping contra aid. Since, by that time, the $24 million appropriated the preceding November had been exhausted, the legal expenditure of U.S. funds to aid the contras came to an end.[84]

The battle over Nicaragua was by no means finished, however. The presi-dent was adamant in his refusal to accept the congressional verdict. "We're not going to give up on that fight," he told supporters on June 29. "Those people who shut off that aid are supporting a totalitarian dictatorship in Nicaragua."[85] Having lost its bid for more aid during FY 1984, the administration shifted the fight to the pending legislation for FY 1985.

The House Intelligence Committee had reported the FY 1985 intelligence authorization bill (H.R. 5399) back in April 1984, after adding a ban on further contra aid authored by Boland. The Senate Intelligence Committee took up the FY 1985 intelligence bill in May 1984 and, despite the rancor that had been generated by the mining of Nicaragua's harbors, it voted to give the admin-istration the $28 million it requested.[86] However, in one last effort to force the administration to adhere to the limited objectives in the September 1983 find-ing, the committee again wrote conditions governing expenditure of the funds into the classified annex to the bill. They barred use of the money for the purpose or effect of overthrowing the Nicaraguan government or forcing a change in its composition.[87]

Faced with an erosion of support for the contras, the Republican leadership in the Senate, acting at the administration's behest, blocked the intelligence authorization bill from coming to the floor. It was better to have no intel-ligence authorization bill at all than to have one that limited or ended funding for the contras. In September, with the fiscal year running out, funds for the intelligence community had to be included in the omnibus FY 1985 continuing resolution. The House added the Boland language prohibiting contra aid to its version of the continuing resolution. The Senate version of the continuing resolution included $28 million in contra aid, as originally requested by Rea-gan and approved by the Intelligence Committee in May.[88]

Once more, House and Senate conferees met to argue about contra aid, just as they had in November 1983 on the defense and intelligence bills and in May 1984 on the urgent supplemental. A year earlier, the House conferees had agreed to $24 million in continued funding for the war—something less than half the level requested by the administration. They adamantly refused to accept a similar compromise for FY 1985. "We are not about to agree," Boland insisted. "The House has voted four times to stop this war in Nicaragua."[89]

The issue deadlocked the conference committee for several days until a compromise was finally devised. Although $14 million was appropriated for aid to the contras, none of the funds could be expended before March 1985. Even then, they would be released only if the president specifically requested them and his request was approved by a joint resolution of Congress. Both chambers would have to approve the request or the administration would get nothing. In the meantime, the Boland language prohibited any funding for the contras: "During fiscal year 1985, no funds available to the Central Intelligence Agency, the Department of Defense, or any other agency or entity of the United States involved in intelligence activities may be obligated or expended for the purpose or which would have the effect of supporting, directly or indirectly, military or paramilitary operations in Nicaragua by any nation, group, organization, movement, or individual."[90]

There was no ambiguity about what the Boland language was intended to do. "Let me make very clear that this prohibition applies to all funds available in fiscal year 1985 regardless of any accounting procedure at any agency," Boland explained to his colleagues. "It clearly prohibits any expenditure, including those from accounts for salaries and all support costs. . . . To repeat, the compromise provision clearly ends U.S. support for war in Nicaragua."[91]

Contra aid ended because the Republicans disdained the ferocious political struggle required to save it. Rather than fight for an unpopular policy in the midst of Reagan's reelection campaign, the White House postponed the confrontation, hoping that the 1984 election results would give it a stronger hand in 1985.[92] Not only did the Republicans expect Reagan to win reelection, reinvigorating his mandate and influence on Capitol Hill, but they also hoped his coattails would carry enough seats in the House to restore an ideological majority of Republicans and conservative Democrats who would resume contra aid. In the interim, the urgency of getting additional funds from Congress had given way to confidence that the contras could survive temporarily without new appropriations. Other resources had been found.

No one was more responsible for the passage of the Boland amendment than Bill Casey himself. In his hatred for congressional oversight, he ignored the early warnings of congressional distress over the Nicaragua program. He pressed full speed ahead, stretching the limits of the law. Eventually, the contra war's expansive scope and purpose became clear to all from the headlines in the daily press. Alexander Haig had been right in that regard; a full-scale guerrilla war could not be kept secret, and neither could Washington's instigation of it.

When members of the intelligence committees realized they had been deceived, their willingness to grant the administration discretion in running covert operations against Nicaragua diminished accordingly. Some, like Senator Moynihan, tried to tighten the reins by insisting on a new presidential finding to limit the operation. Others, like Ed Boland, had already concluded that no limits, formal or informal, could be enforced on an administration that refused to regard congressionally imposed restraints as legitimate. The only sure way to control what Casey and company did in Nicaragua was to prohibit them from doing anything.

The mining of Nicaragua's harbors was the last straw. Moderate members of Congress who thought that Boland's ban on contra aid was too extreme, that something less drastic might bring the administration to heel, saw that they were wrong. The mining prompted the defection of key Senate moderates to the anti-contra camp, demoralized administration supporters, and broke the Republican leadership's will to fight to save Reagan's program. But winning even so major a battle as this did not mean that congressional Democrats had won the war—or ended the one in Nicaragua.

CHAPTER 16

Peace Offensive

As the 1984 presidential campaign got under way, Ronald Reagan looked vulnerable on foreign policy. In January, polls showed that although his overall popularity remained remarkably high at 59 percent, a majority disapproved of his handling of foreign policy, particularly in Lebanon and Central America. Ever since Carter had portrayed Reagan as trigger-happy during the 1980 campaign, the electorate had harbored concerns that Reagan might get the nation into war. In May 1984, Reagan himself was moved to deny that "I somehow have an itchy finger and am going to blow up the world."[1]

Reagan's campaign managers were determined to defuse the foreign policy issue by honing the president's image as a peacemaker and statesman. In January, he declared 1984 "a year of opportunities for peace," and promised dialogue with the Soviets.[2] In April, he went to China to show that he could talk cordially with the leaders of a major Communist power. In June, he went to London for an economic summit of Western leaders, stopping off in Ireland to visit his ancestral hometown and in France to speak at the fortieth anniversary celebration of the D-day invasion of Normandy. In September, Reagan addressed the U.N. General Assembly in a speech that was downright dovish. He spoke not of the "Evil Empire" but of "our fellowship as members of the human race, our oneness as inhabitants of the planet." He spoke of the yearning for peace and ended by quoting Mahatma Gandhi.[3]

Central America posed a particular problem for the Reagan campaign. Unlike the Marines in Lebanon, who could be withdrawn (and were), or arms control talks, which could be fine-tuned from Washington, Central America's simmering conflicts might erupt into a crisis without warning. When Tony Motley replaced Thomas Enders in July 1983, both George Shultz and James Baker told him his main job was to prevent Central America from becoming a campaign issue.[4] The White House's biggest fear was that the Salvadoran guerrillas would launch their annual fall offensive just as the campaign entered the home stretch. If the Salvadoran army began to wobble, as some Pentagon officials feared it might, Reagan would face the hard choice of escalating the war dramatically, or watching the regime in San Salvador crumble.[5]

Nicaragua was also a problem. White House pollster Richard Wirthlin was especially worried about contra aid, which his numbers told him was "pure poison" with the electorate. "He would go bananas at just the mention of the word contras," recalled White House aide Kenneth Khachigian. In late 1983, Wirthlin's polls found that only 37 percent of the public had read or heard about Nicaragua, but of those who had, only 18 percent supported Reagan's handling of the issue. Some 75 percent of those polled feared that the war in Nicaragua would lead the United States into another Vietnam.[6]

Throughout the spring, Reagan tried to walk a political tightrope between resolute action to advance his Central America policy and repeated denials he had any intention of sending U.S. troops to war. After the invasion of Grenada, such assurances were not wholly convincing. Not only was the Grenada invasion quick and easy, but the American public was thrilled by it. Despite initial misgivings in the Joint Chiefs of Staff, the dreaded Vietnam syndrome made no appearance. The Pentagon's post-Vietnam skittishness about using military force in the Third World receded a bit. "We make a lot of cautionary comparisons about Vietnam, and they're valid," said a U.S. Army general. "But there's this big difference. Central America is winnable."[7]

Within a few months of the Grenada invasion, the Pentagon began drawing up detailed contingency plans for direct military action in both Nicaragua and El Salvador.[8] By April 1984, rumors of war became so intense that George Shultz, Caspar Weinberger, William Casey, and Robert McFarlane released an unprecedented joint statement declaring unequivocally that the United States was not on the verge of intervening in the region.[9]

Meanwhile, U.S. military exercises in the region went forward apace. The Big Pine II exercises begun in July 1983 did not end officially until February. The next large exercise planned for Honduras was code-named "Granadero I," which literally meant grenadier, but the allusion to Grenada was obvious. It lasted through the spring, involving 3,500 U.S. troops. At the same time, the navy held its annual Ocean Venture exercise in the Caribbean, lasting almost three weeks and involving some 30,000 U.S. personnel. Once these operations were finished, the Pentagon took a lower profile until after the U.S. elections. But small, less conspicuous exercises involving a few hundred troops continued throughout the year, both in Honduras and off Nicaragua's coasts.[10]

The exercises, the rapid buildup of U.S. advisers in Honduras, and the frenetic pace of military construction in the region convinced many in Congress that the groundwork was being laid for direct intervention, administration denials notwithstanding. In May 1984, House Democratic Whip Thomas Foley offered an amendment to the defense authorization bill that would have prevented Reagan from sending U.S. forces into combat in El Salvador or Nicaragua unless Congress declared war, or the troops were needed to rescue American citizens.

Noting that he was simply codifying Ronald Reagan's own pledge not to intervene, Foley nevertheless argued that the rapid buildup of military infrastructure in Honduras threatened to draw the United States into a war. The overwhelming support Foley got for his amendment (it passed 341–64) was a measure of Congress's nervousness about Central America. A few weeks later, however, the Senate defeated (63–31) an effort by Edward Kennedy and Mark Hatfield to add a similar amendment to the Senate version of the defense bill. When the bill went to conference, the disagreement was resolved by making the Foley amendment advisory to the president rather than binding.[11]

Contadora

Latin Americans also worried that the escalation of U.S. military involvement in Central America foreshadowed direct intervention and responded by intensifying their diplomacy. The most important effort was the Contadora process, inaugurated in January 1983, when the foreign ministers of Mexico, Venezuela, Colombia, and Panama met on the Panamanian island of Contadora to discuss a joint peace initiative.[12]

Each of the four participating countries brought different interests to the Contadora process, but all were united by their fear of regional war and direct U.S. military intervention.[13] Colombia's new president, Belisario Betancur, was intent upon settling Colombia's perennial guerrilla conflict through negotiation and compromise, and he firmly believed that a similar strategy would work in Central America. Venezuela was following a two-track policy, cooperating covertly with the United States to support the Christian Democrats in El Salvador and Edén Pastora's contras, while also promoting diplomacy. The rickety

Panamanian government hoped to boost its international stature by joining the peace initiative launched by its larger and more respectable neighbors.

Mexico's motives were the most complex. Miguel de la Madrid had just assumed the presidency at a moment of deep economic crisis. Educated at Harvard, de la Madrid was a technocrat less inclined toward anti-Americanism than his predecessor, José López Portillo. In light of Mexico's dependence on Washington to solve its economic problems, the new president also had a strong incentive to reduce bilateral tensions, and no issue was more contentious than Central America.[14] But despite de la Madrid's inclination to be amiable, the Mexicans still had real disagreements with Washington.

For de la Madrid, the dilemma was how to continue pressing Washington to change course while at the same time reducing the irritation that Central America caused in bilateral relations. The solution was to multilateralize Mexican diplomacy. By initiating the Contadora peace process, Mexico was able to spread the risk of annoying Washington among its three partners.[15]

Initially, the United States was ambivalent about Contadora. In principle, the administration endorsed the idea of negotiations; it could hardly do otherwise without arousing congressional ire. But Washington wanted only broad multi-issue, multilateral negotiations in which its regional allies—especially Honduras—could block any agreement the United States regarded as unfavorable.[16] Indeed, a multilateral negotiating process in which the United States could exercise an effective veto by proxy was better than a continuation of Mexico's independent diplomatic initiatives. Finally, the Contadora process provided a convenient excuse for refusing to talk bilaterally with the Sandinistas.[17] Despite repeated pleas from the Contadora countries that bilateral negotiations be resumed, Washington's perennial refrain was that such talks would undermine Contadora.

As the Contadora nations tried to broker a regional settlement, they quickly discovered that the Central Americans were at odds over even the most basic procedural questions. Nicaragua wanted to negotiate bilateral nonaggression pacts and set up joint border patrols with Honduras and Costa Rica to prevent contra infiltration. Honduras, reflecting Washington's view, opposed bilateral accords, insisting instead that all regional issues be negotiated simultaneously and multilaterally—a formula that promised to be so complex and difficult that some observers took it to be a veiled attempt to block any settlement whatsoever.[18]

The first major breakthrough came in September 1983, when the five Central American states surprised everyone by signing a Document of Objectives, formalizing the agenda for negotiating a binding treaty. The document set out twenty-one points of agreement covering political, economic, and security issues.[19] The political and security provisions represented a significant success for the United States. They paralleled quite closely the points Washington advocated at the October 1982 meeting of the Central American Forum for Peace and Democracy, which was composed wholly of U.S. allies.[20]

Nevertheless, as Contadora gained international legitimacy and congressional support, administration officials became increasingly worried about Washington's ability to control it. "The president will express his support for the Contadora principles, but he wants the Contadora nations to act in good faith," explained a high official. "We don't want them to play into the hands of the Sandinistas and give them the respectability they badly need in the eyes of the world."[21]

In October 1983, Nicaragua presented to the Contadora nations and the United States four draft treaties for implementation of the Document of Objectives: a multilateral treaty for all the Central American nations; a bilateral treaty between Nicaragua and the United States; a bilateral treaty between Nicaragua and Honduras; and a treaty regarding the civil war in El Salvador.[22] In the proposed treaty with Washington, Nicaragua agreed to halt all aid to regional insurgents and prohibit the use of its territory for foreign military bases that would endanger the security of the United States. In return Washington would stop aiding the contras, lift economic sanctions against Nicaragua, and cease all military exercises in Nicaragua's vicinity. Within twenty-four hours, Washington summarily rejected the drafts.[23]

Shortly after Nicaragua submitted the draft treaties, the United States invaded Grenada. Reagan's willingness to send U.S. forces into combat and the broad public support for the invasion in the United States clearly worried the Sandinistas. In the wake of the invasion, the Sandinistas asked Salvadoran revolutionary leaders living in Nicaragua to leave the country and sent home approximately a thousand Cuban advisers. They eased press censorship, opened a new dialogue with the church hierarchy, released some three hundred Miskito Indians who had been imprisoned for political reasons, and offered an amnesty to all contras except the top leadership. Privately, they communicated to Washington that they had slowed the flow of arms through Nicaraguan territory to the Salvadoran guerrillas and were seeking a reciprocal gesture from the United States.[24]

None was forthcoming. Rather than seeing the Nicaraguan moves as an opportunity for diplomacy, the administration took them as proof that the Sandinistas were weakening and, with continued pressure, could be deposed. "Everyone is saying now that the peace offer from Nicaragua . . . shows the hard-line is working," an administration official explained. Washington's response was to step up the policy of pressures rather than reduce it.[25] Publicly, the administration told the Sandinistas they should negotiate with the contras. "We do not talk to puppets," replied Nicaraguan Foreign Minister Miguel D'Escoto. "We would rather talk to the puppeteers."[26] The United States, however, had nothing to say.

The Mexican Persuasion Campaign

While Washington and Managua were sparring bilaterally, diplomats from the Contadora countries tried to draft a regional peace treaty to implement the September Document of Objectives. It was slow going. After a month of diplomatic pressure from the Contadora countries, Nicaragua softened its opposition to language calling for democratization. But no sooner had Nicaragua dropped its objections than Honduras discovered new ones. "The Hondurans suddenly started to behave as though they were looking at the twenty-one points for the first time," a Latin diplomat complained. "It seemed that this was an obstructionist tactic."[27] It was. In a private meeting, Honduran President Roberto Suazo Córdova assured NSC staff aide Oliver North that he regarded Contadora strictly as propaganda: "We participate just for export."[28]

Concerned about the lack of progress, Mexico launched a major effort in March 1984 to push Contadora forward. The Mexicans had long been convinced that U.S. intransigence was the main obstacle to a regional accord. "The United States says it supports Contadora," a Mexican diplomat complained, "but in reality its actions contradict its declarations."[29]

In Washington, administration hard-liners were getting fed up with Mexico's truculence. Ever since 1982, when falling oil prices left Mexico unable to service its huge international debt, the Mexicans had been dependent on Washington's financial help. Why not exploit Mexico's plight by making U.S. economic cooperation contingent on a change in Mexico's Central America policy?[30]

Pragmatists at the State Department replied that Washington's bilateral relations with Mexico were too important to jeopardize over Central America. Moreover, direct pressure would only provoke a nationalist backlash. The pragmatists prescribed a less confrontational approach: simply continue expressing Washington's views on Central America and let the natural dynamics of Mexican politics produce a retreat from activism on Central America in response to the domestic crisis.[31]

State's strategy was to pry at the cracks in the Mexican government, quietly reinforcing those who favored a more conservative foreign policy. U.S. officials in all fields of endeavor gently reminded their Mexican counterparts, at every opportunity, that the differences between the two countries over Central

America presented an obstacle to developing deeper cooperation. The Mexicans got the message.[32]

Hard-liners brought up the issue once more during the Central American policy review that led to National Security Decision Directive (NSDD) 124 in February 1984. This time, they won a mandate to launch a "Mexican persuasion campaign," as it was dubbed by its author, NSC staff aide Constantine Menges. The plan called for Washington to "intensify its diplomatic efforts" to get Mexico to "reduce its material and diplomatic support for Communist guerrillas and its economic and diplomatic support for the Nicaraguan government."[33] Some hard-liners wanted the persuasion campaign to include the threat of economic pressure.[34]

Constantine Menges was such a hard-liner that the pragmatists inside the administration referred to him as "Constant Menace" and "Menges Khan."[35] Even Dewey Clarridge, who saw himself as "a good anti-Communist activist" and regarded the American "liberal-left" as a variant of totalitarianism, thought Menges was "an extremist."[36] When first appointed National Intelligence Officer (NIO) for Latin America, Menges gave a briefing to the Senate Foreign Relations Committee that was an ideological diatribe tracing all the region's problems to Havana. Senators Paul Tsongas (D-Mass.), Clairborne Pell (D-R.I.), and Christopher Dodd (D-Conn.) complained to Casey that Menges had "seriously violated" the CIA's obligation to provide objective intelligence information.[37]

Menges's antipathy toward Mexico was long-standing. For years, he had argued that the Mexican government was an "enemy" of democracy in Central America.[38] Menges was especially angry at Mexico's dominant role in Contadora, which he interpreted, not incorrectly, as an effort to derail U.S. policy— or at least the hard-line version of it. He described the Contadora group's efforts to draft a regional treaty as the "cunning Mexican-Cuban-Nicaraguan false treaty trap . . . the political front in the Communist war for control of Central America."[39]

In early 1984, the administration's internal battle over Mexico spilled over into the CIA. While serving as the CIA's National Intelligence Officer (NIO) for Latin America, Menges had convinced Casey of his Mexican doomsday scenario: If Communism triumphed in Central America, Mexico itself could easily be destabilized, sending millions of "feet people," as Casey called them, streaming northward into the United States.[40] The prospect of collapse in Mexico was a strong argument in favor of the hard-liners' contention that Washington needed to stand firm in Nicaragua and El Salvador.

Complaints from career CIA officers finally led Casey to replace Menges in late 1983.[41] But before he left for his new post on the NSC staff, he initiated a National Intelligence Estimate to assess Mexico's potential for instability. It was unfinished when John R. Horton, a highly respected twenty-seven-year veteran of the CIA Operations Directorate, replaced Menges. As the new NIO for Latin America, Horton was responsible for overseeing the preparation of estimates, although the Mexican estimate was drafted by another senior analyst, Brian Latell. Latell concluded that the Mexican government was increasingly out of touch with the public and rapidly losing support. The situation was dangerously unstable, with real potential for revolutionary upheaval. Moreover, Latell hinted, the Cubans and Soviets were already working to exploit Mexico's vulnerability.[42]

Horton felt the draft was exaggerated and alarmist, based more on Latell's intuition than solid intelligence information. Casey loved the report because it confirmed his prejudices.[43] "Bill Casey wanted that estimate to read that Mexico was falling apart and was going to be a disaster down there," recalled Deputy CIA Director John McMahon. "The intelligence we had . . . did not support that."[44]

Casey was furious when Horton tried to tone down the estimate's more speculative passages. "He wanted it to come out a certain way," Horton explained. "There was constant pressure on me to redo it. I refused to do it, so he finally had the thing rewritten over my dead body, so to speak." The estimate went through nine drafts.[45]

The National Foreign Intelligence Board, comprised of the heads of all the government agencies dealing with intelligence matters, met to review the Mexico estimate in April 1984. Casey argued that the report ought to put a probability on the likelihood of Mexico collapsing within the next few years. He proposed that the chances were 50–50. No one agreed with him. He dropped the bidding to a 20 percent chance and managed to get just enough support to insert these odds in the estimate. Some of the military intelligence agencies were so appalled that they formally dissented from the finding, insisting that their dissent be recorded on the front page of the estimate. Disgusted with Casey's efforts to "jigger estimates to conform with policy," Horton resigned at the end of May.[46]

All this was prelude to de la Madrid's Washington summit meeting with Reagan on May 15, 1984. The meeting began with uncharacteristically sharp statements by both presidents criticizing each other's stance in Central America. After expressing appreciation for Mexico's efforts on behalf of Contadora, Reagan highlighted what he saw as the region's main problem—Communism. "These totalitarians have been pouring gasoline onto the fire by pumping massive supplies of weapons into Central America and encouraging tyranny and aggression," Reagan asserted. "Responsible governments of this hemisphere cannot afford to close their eyes to what is happening or be lulled by unrealistic optimism."

De la Madrid countered by warning of the growing danger of "a generalized war" in Central America. "Every country in the continent must do its utmost to restore peace and avoid war by respecting and upholding the sovereign right of its people to decide their own destiny and by rejecting interventionist solutions of any kind," he said.[47] The two presidents then retreated to a forty-five-minute private meeting that focused mainly on Central America. Neither of them pulled any punches. The following day, May 16, de la Madrid addressed a joint session of Congress and was discreetly but unmistakably critical of Reagan's policy.[48]

Despite the harsh exchanges, or perhaps because of them, the Reagan–de la Madrid summit ended with the two sides agreeing to take some new initiatives to reduce bilateral friction. Mexico promised to upgrade its relations with El Salvador, where José Napoleón Duarte had just won the presidential election. Washington agreed to reconsider bilateral talks with Nicaragua.[49]

Manzanillo

On June 1, 1984, while on his way back from Duarte's inauguration in San Salvador, Secretary of State Shultz made a surprise stop in Nicaragua and met for two and a half hours with Daniel Ortega—the first high-level talks between the two governments since 1981. The meeting went well, and they agreed to designate special representatives to continue the dialogue. "We are proceeding on the premise that a negotiated solution is possible," Shultz said on the way home, "and that practical reasons exist on all sides to reach an agreement."[50]

The opening of negotiations with Nicaragua had various salutary effects for the Reagan administration. It responded to Mexico's direct request for a U.S.-Nicaraguan dialogue and produced a change in Mexican policy toward El Salvador as a quid pro quo.[51] By making the administration appear more reasonable, the negotiations repaired some of the political damage done in Congress by the mining of Nicaragua's harbors. Once negotiations began, they became a new rationale for continuing contra aid. A cut-off of aid, the administration argued, would weaken the U.S. bargaining position.[52]

Finally, the talks allowed Reagan to emphasize his desire for negotiations in Central America just as the U.S. presidential campaign began, thus undercutting Democratic plans to exploit the unpopularity of Reagan's policy. The strategy began paying dividends immediately; Democratic front-runner Walter Mondale had planned to give a major speech during the first week of June blasting Reagan's Central America policy, but canceled it in the wake of Shultz's trip.[53]

The administration could realize all these gains from the talks with Nicaragua without actually reaching any agreement. Given the timing of the initiative, both the Sandinistas and the Democrats had doubts about Shultz's sincerity. Puzzled by the sudden shift in U.S. policy, Nicaraguan Foreign Minister Miguel D'Escoto wondered aloud if perhaps it was all a "publicity stunt."[54] Nevertheless, the talks went on through the summer and fall of 1984 at the Mexican resort of Manzanillo. Washington was represented by veteran diplomat Harry Shlaudeman, who had replaced Richard Stone as special envoy for Central America in February 1984. Nicaragua was represented by Vice Foreign Minister Victor Tinoco.

Back in Washington, Shultz's trip reignited the battle between officials who wanted an agreement with the Sandinistas and those who did not. Within the State Department, the prevailing view on Nicaragua had not changed from Enders's days: the contras were a useful tool to pressure the Sandinistas into making major concessions, but they could never win the war. Assistant Secretary of State Motley called the contras "the biggest bargaining chip out there." But pressure, if not accompanied by diplomacy, was pointless. Bargaining chips had no value if you never cashed them in.[55]

Through negotiations, Motley hoped to extract foreign policy concessions from the Sandinistas on the three main issues Shultz had raised in Managua: Sandinista support for the Salvadoran guerrillas; Nicaragua's military relationship with Cuba and the Soviet Union; and the size of the Sandinista armed forces. State was willing to settle for some minimal Sandinista concessions on the issue of internal democratization, which the pragmatists regarded as secondary.[56]

The hard-liners still opposed negotiations entirely, fearing that the Sandinistas would sign an agreement to get rid of the contras but never live up to it. Once the contras were disbanded, Washington would have no effective leverage to force Sandinista compliance other than the direct use of U.S. military force—something that neither Congress nor the American people would countenance. Washington would then be stuck with another Cuba.

Ever since Enders had been fired for hinting at a negotiated settlement in Nicaragua (and El Salvador), this split in the administration had paralyzed the State Department's efforts to move forward on the negotiating track. By early 1984, however, the hard-liners' control over foreign policy had begun to wane. The replacement of Clark by McFarlane and the subsequent eclipse of Kirkpatrick weakened the hard-line coalition. Shultz, who proved he was tough by pushing hard for the invasion of Grenada, had gradually regained the dominant position in the administration's confused foreign policy process.

Enders's replacement, Tony Motley, unexpectedly reinforced the pragmatist camp, to the great disappointment of the hard-liners. They had assumed a Republican Party stalwart and political appointee like Motley would feel ill at ease among the striped-pants boys at Foggy Bottom and would remain loyal to the White House. Instead, Motley went native. Unlike the hard-liners, Motley was not an ideologue; he was a pragmatic businessman whom one journalist described as "unencumbered by deep philosophical beliefs."[57] Although he was no intellectual, Motley was smart enough to realize that his personal familiarity with Brazil (where he had been ambassador before moving into Enders's job) was of little help in understanding Central America. He relied heavily on the team of midlevel foreign service officers that Enders had assembled, especially his deputy on Central America, Craig Johnstone.

In early 1984, encouraged by Nicaragua's apparent willingness to make concessions after the Grenada invasion, Motley and his aides developed a detailed negotiating strategy. When President de la Madrid urged Reagan to resume talks with the Sandinistas, and Reagan replied that it was "a great idea," Motley had a presidential imprimatur to put his plan into action.[58] But success depended upon stealth. If the hard-liners got wind of State's diplomatic initiative before it was launched, they might talk Reagan into changing his mind.

So the State Department hatched the plan for Shultz's trip to Managua without telling the hard-liners until the last possible moment. With McFarlane's connivance, Shultz got Reagan to agree to the trip. Motley finally briefed Casey, telling him the whole thing was just a "public relations stunt" designed to appease Congress. Weinberger and Kirkpatrick were briefed shortly thereafter. But the second-level officials in the hard-liners' camp—Fred Iklé at the Pentagon and Constantine Menges and Oliver North at the National Security Council—were not told about the trip until Shultz's plane touched down in Managua.[59]

The hard-liners were justifiably angry that such a major initiative could be taken without a full discussion of its implications in either the Restricted Inter-Agency Group (RIG) on Latin America (a reorganized version of the Inter-Agency Core Group) or the National Security Council. "It looks like Shultz doesn't feel he has to talk with any of us now that he has his private get-togethers with the boss," Casey complained.[60] Routed by State's surprise attack, the hard-liners fell back to their second line of defense: the debate over Harry Shlaudeman's negotiating instructions.

The State Department developed a detailed, step-by-step approach in which concessions by Nicaragua would be phased in and matched by reciprocal gestures from the United States and its Central American allies. The hard-liners drafted alternative instructions designed to "cause a breakdown at the very outset of the talks," according to Shultz.[61] McFarlane was forced to hold an NSC meeting on June 25, 1984, to discuss Shlaudeman's instructions, just as he was beginning the talks with Tinoco in Mexico. The meeting, which Menges characterized as "the stormiest I ever attended," ran an hour longer than planned.[62] Shultz defended the negotiating plan; Weinberger, Casey, and Kirkpatrick argued that it made too many concessions.

The hard-liners wanted to scuttle the negotiation entirely. Kirkpatrick warned that bilateral talks with Nicaragua might frighten U.S. allies like Honduras into seeking a separate peace with the Sandinistas and thus "totally unravel our entire position in the region."

Reagan sought a middle ground. The negotiations should go forward, he decided, but primarily for domestic political reasons. "If we are just talking about negotiations with Nicaragua, that is too far-fetched to imagine that a Communist government like that would make any reasonable deal with us," Reagan said, "but if it is to get Congress to support the anti-Sandinistas, then that can be helpful."[63] Shlaudeman was told not to present the State Department plan to the Sandinistas.

State's instinct was not to junk its carefully crafted plan, but to argue that it continued to be a useful policy instrument, consistent with the decisions of the June 25 NSC meeting. The hard-liners insisted that the president had rejected the plan. Since they were unable to come to any accommodation, a second NSC meeting had to be called on July 27. It, too, was marked by sharp exchanges—"heated and acrimonious" was how Shultz recalled it. The hard-liners argued for ending the talks; Shultz countered that without a negotiating track, "we would be absolutely sunk with Congress." The president was not ready to abandon Manzanillo completely, but neither was he enthralled with State's strategy. When Weinberger read aloud from the U.S. concessions listed under step one of the plan, Reagan angrily rejected them with a sharp "No!"[64] State's plan would have to be redrafted.

The hard-liners insisted on toughening the language on Nicaraguan democracy and deleting almost all the U.S. concessions. Kirkpatrick was especially intent on pushing democracy, though she acknowledged that this would make it difficult to get an agreement. "Kirkpatrick knew if the plan had democracy in it, it would fail," recalled a senior U.S. diplomat. "That was the fundamental cynicism of Manzanillo."

"She did everything she could do to subvert Manzanillo," another U.S. diplomat observed. In a private conversation with Sandinista party official Julio López in July, Kirkpatrick reportedly conveyed the impression that the Manzanillo talks were largely designed for domestic U.S. consumption. As in the case of her private conversations with Argentine officials during the Falklands war, Kirkpatrick denied that she had said anything that would undermine U.S. policy. Still, López dutifully reported her comments to the Nicaraguan Foreign Ministry, where they contributed to the Sandinistas' skepticism about Washington's sincerity.[65]

At the National Security Council, staff aide Oliver North also refused to accept any negotiating plan that included significant U.S. concessions. "His attitude was that 'we don't want a negotiated end that doesn't give us everything we want. So there can be no negotiated end,'" a State Department official explained. "I think he felt his mission was to undermine everything we did."[66]

The infighting produced a negotiating plan in which the Sandinistas were to make all the concessions. It called for Nicaragua to send home all Cuban and Soviet advisers, including civilians, in three stages over ninety days. The reciprocal U.S. concession: "The U.S. military presence in Central America takes Nicaraguan actions into consideration in each stage." Washington would halt aid to the contras only after Nicaragua expelled all Salvadoran FDR-FMLN personnel, banned even political activity on their behalf, and put "an end to foreign logistics support" for the Salvadoran guerrillas.

In exchange for Nicaragua closing down its FMLN support facilities, the contras would agree not to mine Nicaragua's harbors or attack petroleum facilities—CIA operations that had already been halted two months earlier because of congressional outrage. When Nicaragua negotiated limits on offensive weapons and troop levels with its neighbors and began implementing them, then "the U.S. presence and exercises" in the region would be "readjusted to reflect the advances made."

Finally, the Nicaraguans would have to hold "free and fair democratic elections" in which all contestants were guaranteed "equal and fair access to the media." The Sandinistas would have to negotiate a cease-fire with the contras and give them amnesty so they could participate in the election. In return, Washington suggested that El Salvador would allow the FDR-FMLN to participate in the 1985 National Assembly elections under the same conditions. The only specific U.S. concessions listed anywhere in the plan concerned economic relations. As the peace plan moved through its four stages, Washington would restore normal trade relations, stop blocking loans to Nicaragua in international financial institutions, and restore bilateral economic assistance.[67]

Even the officials negotiating on the U.S. side realized the shortcomings of the plan that finally emerged from the administration's internal debates. The State Department hoped the Nicaraguans would offer some positive response to the U.S. plan, thereby setting in motion a real bargaining process. If the

Nicaraguans asked Washington for clarifications on what it meant for the United States to "take into consideration" Nicaraguan concessions, then State might be able to revive the specific reciprocal actions that the hard-liners had managed to delete from the original plan. Once it began, the negotiation might develop its own momentum and be difficult for the hard-liners to stop. The Nicaraguans, however, found the U.S. proposal so outrageous that they dismissed it.[68] Shlaudeman's negotiating instructions were so strict that he was not allowed to explore with Tinoco how the U.S. plan might be modified to better meet Nicaragua's concerns. "No one will tell Shlaudeman what the endgame is, what the road map to a final agreement is," said one administration official. "The reason is that the administration doesn't really want a settlement with the Sandinistas. No one knows whether the United States should invade Nicaragua, but people don't want to foreclose that option by signing some kind of agreement."[69] The talks stalled.

Blocking Contadora's Draft Treaty

While the Manzanillo talks drifted, the Contadora countries were still trying to fashion a regional peace treaty. Fearful of what Reagan might do once he no longer had to worry about the electoral consequences of using military force, they badly wanted to conclude an agreement before the U.S. election, even if the final accord had some weak spots.

A draft treaty was circulated to the Central American governments in June, but because it went out just as the Manzanillo talks commenced, Washington paid little attention to it. Nicaragua registered the strongest disagreement with the draft because it still contained commitments on democracy.[70]

On September 7, the Contadora countries presented a revised version of the final treaty.[71] Most observers expected the Sandinistas to reject it. One by one, the other Central Americans indicated that the latest draft was acceptable, with some minor modifications. Then on September 21, 1984, the Sandinistas surprised everyone by agreeing to sign the accord. The Reagan administration was stunned.[72]

The Sandinistas' political acumen in agreeing to sign was immediately apparent: they had cast themselves as peacemakers. Reagan had been portraying the Sandinistas as the source of regional turmoil. A major rationale for the contra war was to force Nicaragua to negotiate seriously with its neighbors. If a Contadora agreement was actually signed, the logic of U.S. support for the contras would crumble. Administration officials denounced Nicaragua's offer to sign the treaty as a hypocritical publicity stunt. Some actually advocated that Nicaragua be punished for agreeing to sign the treaty.[73]

The State Department voiced two substantive complaints about the agreement. First, its security provisions were one-sided and incomplete. The treaty banned foreign military bases, schools, and exercises—which meant that the recently expanded U.S. military presence in Honduras would have to be dismantled. It required the immediate withdrawal of foreign advisers involved in training or operations—which meant most of the U.S. advisers in El Salvador and Honduras. But it stipulated a phased withdrawal of advisers involved in "maintenance"—which meant most of the Cuban advisers in Nicaragua. The treaty provided for an immediate freeze on all arms acquisitions pending the negotiation of a second treaty setting limits on the size of regional armies. This, the State Department claimed, would put the Salvadoran government "in an untenable position vis-à-vis the guerrillas." Finally, the treaty required an end to all support for "irregular forces or armed bands" operating against neighboring states. Support for the contras would come to an end and they would be forced out of Honduras, but "the weak verification and enforcement provisions make it highly questionable that Nicaragua would feel compelled to actually end its support for the Salvadoran insurgency," State explained. The second principal flaw in the treaty, according to the administration, concerned the provisions on democracy. In substance, the accord was fine; the problem was verification. There were no real means to hold the signatories to their commitments.[74]

The weaknesses Washington identified in the treaty were real enough. At root, however, the Reagan administration's objections to the Contadora treaty and its fury at Nicaragua for agreeing to it stemmed not from any specific provision of the accord. The hard-liners were just not prepared to accept an accord that halted U.S. efforts to overthrow the Sandinistas. "We simply could not trust their keeping up their end of the bargain if the present group remains in power," a U.S. official explained.[75]

Nicaragua's agreement to sign the treaty was conditional on its not being modified. Washington countered by pressuring the other Central Americans to reverse their initial acceptance of the text and insist upon revisions. Unless the requisite changes were made, Shultz warned, the United States would regard the treaty as "just a piece of paper."[76]

At the end of September, Reagan sent a personal letter to the heads of state of Washington's Central American allies (Costa Rica, Honduras, El Salvador, and Guatemala), whom the administration had dubbed "the Core Four." In it, he argued that the draft agreement did not represent a genuine settlement and would be harmful. He urged them to tell the Contadora countries that further negotiations were required.[77] A week and a half later, Secretary Shultz made a swing through Central America to lobby against the draft treaty on his way to the inauguration of Panamanian President Nicolás Ardito Barletta. One by one, the Core Four fell into line.[78] In October, they held a foreign ministers meeting in Tegucigalpa to revise the Contadora draft in accord with Washington's complaints. Nicaragua boycotted the meeting.[79]

The Contadora countries, Mexico in particular, bitterly resented Washington's campaign to derail the treaty. They denied that the September document was intended to be a working draft, as Washington claimed. "Everyone treated it as a final document from the beginning," insisted one diplomat.[80] Nevertheless, once Washington convinced the Core Four to refuse to sign without modifications, there was little the Contadora countries could do except reopen the negotiations.

By October 20, 1984, when Reagan's National Security Council met to review the situation in Central America, the threat of peace had been averted. By virtue of "intensive consultations," the background paper for the meeting reported, "we have effectively blocked Contadora group efforts to impose the second draft of the Revised Contadora Act."[81] A few weeks later, Deputy National Security Adviser John M. Poindexter, in a note to his boss, Robert McFarlane, tersely summed up the administration's real position on diplomacy: "Continue active negotiations but agree to no treaty, and agree to work out some way to support the contras either directly or indirectly. Withhold true objectives from staffs."[82]

The bilateral negotiations between Nicaragua and the United States at Manzanillo died almost as soon as Nicaragua agreed to sign the Contadora treaty. The U.S. bargaining position at Manzanillo called for major concessions by Nicaragua in return for only vague promises by Washington. The Contadora draft, on the other hand, required major reductions in the U.S. military posture in Central America. From the Nicaraguan point of view, the Contadora treaty was far superior. When Shlaudeman and Tinoco met on September 25, the Nicaraguans put forward the Contadora draft agreement as their bargaining position in the bilateral talks. After two more negotiating sessions in October and December, Washington suspended the meetings.[83] On January 18, 1985, the United States informed Nicaragua that they would not be resumed.

The State Department claimed the United States was ending the bilateral sessions because they were interfering with Contadora.[84] In reality, the bilateral talks ended because U.S. policy toward Nicaragua was hardening in the wake of Ronald Reagan's reelection, and there was no longer any need for the pretense of diplomacy. "The talks . . . broke down in good part because the administration was moving to a position where nothing would do but the liquidation, lock, stock, and barrel, of the Nicaraguan government," recalled State Department official Frank McNeil.[85]

The Manzanillo talks suffered the same fate as Enders's 1981 diplomatic initiative. Within the administration, the hard-liners were not strong enough to prevent pragmatists at the State Department from launching a diplomatic foray, but they retained enough influence to veto any real U.S. concessions at the bargaining table. In both instances, Washington insisted that Nicaragua comply with unilateral demands. The Nicaraguans refused, and the administration reacted by breaking off the talks and denouncing Nicaragua for not being serious about a diplomatic settlement. But Manzanillo served its political purpose by defusing Nicaragua as an issue in the presidential campaign—until the last few weeks.

The CIA's "Murder Manual"

On October 15, six days before the second presidential debate, the Associated Press reported that the CIA had written a manual for the contras, entitled *Psychological Operations in Guerrilla Warfare*. The ninety-page book of instructions focused mainly on how "Armed Propaganda Teams" could build political support within Nicaragua for the contra cause through deceit, intimidation, and violence.[86]

The manual originated, indirectly, from a June 1983 trip to Honduras by Bill Casey, Dewey Clarridge, and other top CIA officials. Casey came away convinced that the contras were getting nowhere because they were fighting a conventional war instead of a guerrilla insurgency. They ran around the countryside occasionally ambushing Sandinistas, but they had no political program and were making no effort to build a popular base. "It was decided that the rebels needed an adviser on psychological warfare to help them better understand what they were fighting for and how to motivate the [Nicaraguan] people," said an official familiar with the decision.[87]

To advise the contras, the CIA dispatched a contract employee who went by the name of John Kirkpatrick. He was a retired U.S. Army major who had worked for the paramilitary branch of the CIA (the International Activities Division). Kirkpatrick was a bit eccentric. He dressed entirely in black and called himself "the Priest of Death." His aim, he explained, was to create a cult of death among the contras to make them better fighters. The contras, unimpressed, nicknamed him "the Umpire." Kirkpatrick reminded contra leader Edgar Chamorro of "a character out of a Graham Greene novel. He drank too much and cried all the time."[88]

While touring contra base camps in 1983, Kirkpatrick heard numerous stories from rank-and-file combatants of forced recruitment, mistreatment by their officers, atrocities against civilians, rapes, and summary executions of prisoners. He decided to write a manual to teach the contras how to use violence more selectively against the Sandinistas and their sympathizers, in order to avoid alienating the general population. "He didn't want us to use a shotgun approach," explained Edgar Chamorro, who helped Kirkpatrick translate the manual into Spanish. "He wanted us to select our targets." The manual he produced was adapted almost word for word from lesson plans on armed psychological operations used in 1968 to train Green Berets at the John F. Kennedy Special Warfare School at Fort Bragg.[89]

The manual was amateurish in many ways—repetitive, self-contradictory, and filled with allusions to Aristotle and Socrates that were not likely to resonate with the illiterate peasants who composed the contra army's rank and file. The manual's central message stressed the need for every guerrilla to be "persuasive in face-to-face communications," and to try to win over the population rather than using indiscriminate violence.[90]

But despite its "hearts and minds" prescriptions, the tenor of the manual was one of callous manipulation and deceit. It called for placing secret cadres in civic groups like labor unions who could then "begin to manipulate the objectives of the groups" in order to provoke violence. The manual outlined strategies for the "involuntary recruitment" of people by blackmail.[91]

The most controversial recommendations concerned the use of violence. The manual described how contra "shock troops" could provoke violence at urban mass demonstrations: "These men should be equipped with weapons (knives, razors, chains, clubs, bludgeons) and should march slightly behind the innocent and gullible participants." Agitators would lead the demonstrators "to a confrontation with the authorities, in order to bring about uprisings or shootings, which will cause the death of one or more persons, who would become the martyrs . . . for the cause." The manual recommended hiring "professional criminals" for especially unpleasant jobs.[92]

One passage sounded like a prescription for assassination. In a section entitled "Selective Use of Violence for Propagandistic Effects," the manual read: "It is possible to neutralize carefully selected and planned targets such as court judges, justices of the peace, police and State Security officials, CDS [Sandinista Defense Committee] chiefs, etc." Targeted individuals should be chosen based in part on "the degree of violence possible without causing damage or danger to other individuals in the area of the target."[93]

The *Washington Post* dubbed the psychological warfare booklet the CIA's "murder manual," and the label stuck.[94] The Democrats reacted immediately both to the manual's prescriptions for violence and its explicit call for overthrowing the Nicaraguan government—a purpose still proscribed by the guidelines under which the Senate had approved contra funding. Tip O'Neill called the manual "nothing short of outrageous," and demanded Casey's resignation.[95]

As with the mining of Nicaragua's harbors, there was an element of willful ignorance in the shocked reaction congressional Democrats evinced toward the CIA manual. The intelligence committees had not been briefed on the manual itself, but they knew very well what the contras were doing. The Nicaraguan government reported contra attacks almost daily, including the resulting casualties. From 1981 to 1984, 854 civilians had been killed in contra attacks, including 329 local civil servants and 89 adult education teachers.[96] It was obvious from these figures that the contras were targeting low-level government officials in the countryside, just as the manual described, and stories of contra atrocities were legion.

The White House was frantic to dispose of the "murder manual" issue before the second presidential debate. The most direct strategy was to acknowledge the manual's faults, launch an investigation, and in the meantime deny that any senior official—especially the president—had anything to do with it. The White House launched two investigations: one by the CIA's own inspector general and one by the President's Intelligence Oversight Board.[97]

National Security Adviser McFarlane explained that the manual was the work of "a low-level contract employee of the CIA working in the region," and that if any U.S. officials were involved in the "development and approval" of the manual, they would be fired.[98] Other senior officials put out the word that the manual was "the work of an overzealous freelance" and had never been cleared by anyone at the CIA. When it turned out that the manual had, indeed, been reviewed in Washington, administration officials argued that the objectionable passages were expurgated in the reviewing process.[99] That wasn't true either.

The first question directed to Reagan in the October 21 presidential debate on foreign policy was about the CIA manual. Didn't it amount to "our own state-supported terrorism?" the reporter asked. Reagan's reply was an odd mix of fact and fiction. He explained that once the manual had been written, "it was turned over to the agency head of the CIA in Nicaragua, to be printed, and a number of pages were excised. . . . And he sent it on up here to CIA where more pages were excised before it was printed. But some way or other there were twelve of the original copies that got out down there and were not submitted for this printing process by the CIA." If his investigation found any U.S. official guilty of wrongdoing, Reagan promised, "they will be removed." Then he changed the subject.[100]

Although the manual had been reviewed at CIA headquarters, there had been no major excisions, as Reagan claimed and as CIA briefers initially told the Senate Intelligence Committee. In fact, only a single line about hiring professional criminals was edited out. The passage advocating assassination was left intact.[101]

Moreover, the assertion that only twelve unedited manuals were distributed in the region was wrong, and the White House had to back away from it immediately. In addition to three thousand copies of the manual printed by the CIA, the contras themselves printed two thousand unedited copies, but then tore out the two pages that advocated hiring criminals and provoking violence to create martyrs. They, too, left the passage on assassination intact. Most of the manuals were distributed to contra combatants, except for about a hundred that were sent aloft by balloons to be randomly dropped into Nicaragua as a way of scaring the Sandinistas.[102]

From the outset, Bill Casey thought that the administration was "too defensive" and "too ready to apologize" for what he regarded as a legitimate element of the covert operation against Nicaragua.[103] But so long as the outcome of the presidential campaign was in any doubt—and it was, until Reagan disposed of the "age issue" in the second debate—the administration's strategy was to keep the manual out of the news as much as possible. Any spirited defense of it would simply stoke the fires of publicity.

As the campaign came to a close with Ronald Reagan far ahead, however, the administration became less contrite. In a letter to the House and Senate Intelligence Committees, Casey insisted that the main purpose of the manual was "education."[104] Ronald Reagan's view of the manual also changed. Speaking to reporters on November 3, he contradicted his own admission during the debate that the manual "was a direct contravention of my own executive order in December of 1981 that we would have nothing to do with . . . political assassinations." Now he insisted there was "nothing in that manual that talked assassination at all." The reference to "neutralizing" Sandinista officials, he explained, simply meant that "you just say to the fellow who's sitting there in the office, 'You're not in the office anymore.'" In his first press conference the morning after the election, Reagan dismissed the furor over the manual with the same phrase he had used to describe the mining of Nicaragua's harbors—"much ado about nothing."[105]

That was the conclusion reached by the CIA and Intelligence Oversight Board investigations, too. Both found that there had been no laws or executive orders violated. The incident involved nothing worse than "poor judgment and lapses in oversight at lower levels of the agency."[106] For these, the reports urged disciplinary action against six low- and midlevel CIA officers. Despite his earlier pledge to fire any officials responsible for the manual, Reagan accepted the mild punishments recommended. Three CIA officers received reprimands, two were temporarily suspended without pay, and "John Kirkpatrick's" contract was terminated. In the end, Casey reversed the reprimand of the Central America

Task Force chief Vincent M. Cannistraro because he had received a commendation in September 1983 for his management of the Nicaragua operation.[107]

Dewey Clarridge, division chief for operations in Latin America, denied to Congress that he had any role in the creation of the manual—until he was confronted with proof that he had supervised it. Casey promoted him to division chief for Europe. Several of the CIA officers who were singled out for punishment felt they were made scapegoats to protect higher officials, particularly Clarridge and Casey himself.[108]

The House Intelligence Committee conducted its own inquiry of the manual after the November election and found that it violated the Boland amendment prohibiting U.S. assistance for the purpose of overthrowing the Nicaraguan government. "At least seven or eight times in the manual, there is a reference to overthrowing the Sandinistas," Boland noted.[109] But with Congress adjourned until January, Ronald Reagan basking in the glow of his landslide victory over Walter Mondale, and funding for the contras already halted, the Democrats on the Intelligence Committee were not of a mind to push the issue of the manual any further.[110]

Committee member Norman Mineta argued unsuccessfully that the committee should refer its report to the Justice Department for possible prosecution. After all, the manual had been approved at CIA headquarters and it clearly violated the Boland amendment. It was dangerous, Mineta warned, to allow the administration "to pick and choose which laws they will obey."[111] His colleagues thought him an alarmist.

The Other Election

Just two days before the U.S. presidential election, Nicaragua held its first elections since the overthrow of Somoza. The issue of elections had long been a point of conflict between the Sandinistas and the conservative wing of the anti-Somoza coalition. The conservatives pressed for immediate elections after Somoza was ousted in 1979; the Sandinistas argued that the nation's energies should first be devoted to economic reconstruction.

During the first two years after the fall of Somoza, the political tug of war between the government and the "civic opposition" erupted into periodic crises, as the two sides tested each other's political strength. But each crisis subsided with a dialogue followed by limited concessions aimed at keeping alive the hope of eventual accommodation.

This pattern of confrontation and conciliation was ruptured in 1982 with the beginning of the contra war, which strengthened the hand of hard-liners on both sides. Many opponents of the Sandinistas had been willing to seek accommodation because the only alternative was exile. When Washington committed itself to the contra war, however, hard-liners in the civic opposition could credibly argue that the United States would eventually remove the Sandinistas. A strategy of accommodation was unnecessary.

To Sandinista hard-liners, the opposition's intransigence and its collaboration with the contras seemed to prove that civic opponents were nothing but *vendepatrias*—a fifth column willing to sell out their country to the United States. The Sandinistas' tolerance for internal opposition declined as the war intensified.[112]

Small to begin with, the opposition political parties were hamstrung by censorship, harassment, and emergency laws banning outside rallies or demonstrations. The laws didn't prevent mobs of Sandinista supporters (*turbas*) from demonstrating outside the homes and offices of opposition leaders, sometimes breaking up their meetings. Police frequently detained opposition politicians for questioning, warning them to mend their counterrevolutionary ways. Outspoken businessmen had their property confiscated.

Only the Catholic Church enjoyed limited immunity from such constraints, and Archbishop Miguel Obando y Bravo soon emerged as the leading critic of the Sandinista regime. His homilies at mass criticized the government for curtailing political liberties, for challenging the authority of the church, and for drafting young men into the army to fight the contras. Obando never had a critical word to say about the contras, even when stories of their atrocities multiplied.[113]

Obando's opposition was not haphazard or confined to an occasional speech. He consciously assumed the role of chief opposition spokesman and mobilized the apparatus of the church to confront government policies. In the early 1980s, the church received overt funds from U.S. AID and covert funds from the CIA to help finance its antigovernment activities. In 1984, Obando traveled abroad soliciting private funds to organize "leadership training" courses to mold "pastoral cadres" from members of the church laity disenchanted with the government. The church, Obando told businessmen in New York, was the best bulwark against the consolidation of Sandinista rule.[114]

In a country that was 95 percent Catholic, the church had enormous authority and Obando was an undeniably popular leader. The dark-skinned son of a peasant family, he had the common touch. As a priest, he had traveled the mountains on a mule, bringing religious services to remote rural parishes. As archbishop, he had been a critic of Somoza. When Somoza tried to curry favor by giving him a Mercedes-Benz, Obando raffled it off and donated the proceeds to the poor. When numerous priests and nuns supported the Sandinistas during the insurrection against Somoza, Obando did not rebuke or discourage them. On the contrary, he condemned the National Guard's human rights abuses.[115]

But Obando was no revolutionary. Fundamentally a conservative, he regarded the rise of liberation theology as a threat to the institutional authority of the church. When he began to criticize the Sandinista government in 1980, some priests and nuns—including five priests serving in government posts—refused to break their solidarity with the revolution. They began to speak of the "popular church"—members of the clergy and laity who embraced liberation theology and the revolution, regardless of what Obando or the other bishops thought. The more outspoken Obando became in his criticism of the regime, the more the Sandinistas denounced him and tried to bolster the "popular church."[116]

Challenging the archbishop's authority to speak for the church was a battle the Sandinistas were fated to lose, as they discovered in March 1984 when Pope John Paul II visited Nicaragua. The pope's own experience in Poland had made him a staunch anti-Communist and had given him an appreciation of how powerful a political weapon the church could be in a devoutly Catholic country. He sided openly with Obando, commanding the Nicaraguan faithful to obey their bishops and denouncing the idea of a popular church as "absurd and dangerous." During his open-air mass in Managua, Sandinista supporters placed strategically in the crowd repeatedly interrupted the pope with chants of "Popular Power!" and "We Want Peace!" More than once the pontiff angrily demanded, "Silence!" but to no avail.[117]

The pope's visit was a political disaster for the Sandinistas. Not only did it sully their international reputation, but it also solidified the Vatican's support for Obando's confrontational politics. In 1985, Obando was made a cardinal, and on his way back from the installation ceremony in Rome, he stopped in Miami to say mass for exiled contra leaders. Inside Nicaragua, the pope's visit cast the conflict between church and state in sharp relief. For the first time, many of the faithful felt compelled to choose between their faith and loyalty to the revolution.[118]

Led by the church, the civic opposition hammered away at three main issues: the denial of civil liberties, the deterioration of the economy, and the military draft. After two years of strong growth recovering from the insurrection against Somoza, the economy went stagnant in 1982 and began to contract in 1983. Basic food commodities were rationed to insure more equal distribution, but even then some goods were unavailable due to shortages. Government subsidies and the rising costs of the war produced a fiscal deficit that the government closed by printing money, triggering a rise in inflation. In 1984, the annual rate was 50 percent. As the growing trade deficit produced shortages of hard currency, imported inputs to the domestic economy grew scarce, curtailing production and increasing unemployment to nearly 20 percent.[119] The Sandinistas did their best to blame the economic crisis on the war and Washington's policy of economic strangulation, but many people blamed the government.

No one was quite sure how much the Sandinistas' popular support was eroded by these complaints, but the opposition certainly had a good set of issues to run on when elections were finally scheduled for November 4, 1984. Yet few people on either side thought the Sandinistas could be defeated, even in a fair election, let alone one in which they could take full advantage of their incumbency. Even the U.S. embassy expected the Sandinistas to win at least a plurality of the vote.[120] For both the Sandinistas and their opponents, the 1984 election was more important for influencing international audiences than for allocating political power inside Nicaragua.[121]

The Sandinistas urgently needed to improve their international image. The limitations on political liberty they imposed had disillusioned Latin American and Western European democrats.[122] With the country running an annual balance-of-payments deficit of $500 million and the Soviets unwilling to give the Sandinistas a blank check, economic aid from Latin America and Europe was indispensable.[123] A reasonably fair election might reopen their coffers.

The elections were also aimed at Washington. A key reason for holding elections, explained Bayardo Arce, the member of the Sandinista National Directorate in charge of the campaign, was to "take away from American policy one of its justifications."[124] Arce represented the radicals within the Sandinista leadership who regarded elections not as an exercise in democracy but as a "nuisance" forced on them by international circumstances.[125] The Sandinistas scheduled their elections just two days before the U.S. balloting so that a reelected Reagan, freed from the political constraints imposed by his own campaign, would have a harder time justifying an attack on Nicaragua.[126]

Like the Sandinistas, the civic opposition also saw the elections as a battle for international legitimacy. Badly fragmented into ten different parties, none of which had much real organization or grassroots support, the opposition was no match for the highly organized and disciplined Sandinista Front. "They have no leaders, no program, and so few members that they would have a hard time coming up with poll watchers in an election," said one Western ambassador in Managua.[127]

Awareness of their own weakness led to a division of opinion within the civic opposition about whether or not they should participate in the elections. Some argued that even if they lost, the campaign would give them an unprecedented opportunity to present their message to the Nicaraguan people and establish an important precedent—that political power is subject to periodic elections. A rejectionist group argued that participation played into the hands of the Sandinistas by ratifying their legitimacy. The precedent of elections would be worth little if the Sandinistas were able to consolidate their rule. The election should be boycotted.[128]

The rejectionists were found mostly in the Democratic Coordinator (Coordinadora Democrática), a united front of the most conservative opposition groups which included four political parties, two trade union federations, and the private enterprise association COSEP (Superior Council of Private Enterprise—Consejo Superior de la Empresa Privada). Opposition parties outside the Coordinadora, such as the Independent Liberals (Partido Liberal Independiente) and the Popular Social Christian Party (Partido Popular Social Cristiano), both of which had cooperated with the Sandinista government to some degree, argued for participation.[129] In Nicaragua and abroad, attention focused on whether or not the Sandinistas could entice the reluctant Coordinadora parties into the election.

The Reagan administration was also of two minds about the elections. At the State Department, Tony Motley and Craig Johnstone saw the elections as an opportunity to remove the issue of democracy from the bilateral agenda at Manzanillo. Hard-liners like Joe Fernandez at the CIA and Oliver North at the National Security Council saw the elections as a danger, because they might weaken the administration's political will to remove the Sandinistas once and for all.[130]

The State Department's strategy was to urge the Coordinadora to bargain for the best campaign conditions they could get, wage a vigorous campaign, and hope for a strong enough showing to force the Sandinistas to moderate their policies. If the strategy worked, the issue of democracy would no longer be on the table at Manzanillo, and the negotiators could focus on resolvable security issues.

To this end, Craig Johnstone recruited Arturo Cruz to be the Coordinadora's candidate.[131] Cruz was an international civil servant who had spent much of his adult life in Washington, D.C. Nevertheless, he had stayed in touch with his country's politics and was a member of "Los Doce"—the twelve intellectuals who in 1977 spoke out against Somoza and in favor of the Sandinista Front. After the triumph of the revolution, Cruz was appointed president of the Central Bank. When Alfonso Robelo and Violeta Chamorro resigned from the governing junta in 1980, Cruz was selected as one of their replacements.

Frustrated that all important decisions were made in the National Directorate of the Sandinista Front rather than in the junta, he resigned quietly in March 1981 and became the new Nicaraguan ambassador to the United States.

His differences with the Sandinistas continued to grow, however, and he resigned as ambassador eight months later. Behind the scenes, he became active in exile politics, advising Edén Pastora and helping ghostwrite Pastora's speech announcing his break with the Sandinistas.[132]

Cruz was an unlikely candidate for the presidency of Nicaragua. Having lived abroad for so long, he had no political base at home and little name recognition. Moreover, he was not much of a politician. A quiet self-effacing intellectual, he was thoroughly uncharismatic and lacked the extroversion normally associated with successful campaigners. He tended to read his speeches in a low voice with his nose buried in the text.[133]

But none of this mattered much, since no one expected Cruz to win. Cruz had two great assets: he was respected among the conservative political leaders of the Coordinadora (so they could all agree on his candidacy), and he was highly respected in Latin America, Europe, and the United States—especially among liberals and social democrats. If the Nicaraguan election was a battle for international legitimacy, having Cruz at the top of the Coordinadora ticket was an invaluable asset. The Sandinistas would have to bend over backward to keep him in the race.

When the Sandinistas first began to discuss arrangements for the election, the Coordinadora threatened a boycott unless the Sandinistas met nine demands. Among other things, it called for cutting all ties between the Sandinista party and the armed forces, repeal of the agrarian reform, lifting the state of emergency, ending all censorship, amnesty for all prisoners (including former members of Somoza's National Guard), and a "national dialogue" between the Sandinistas and the opposition, including the contras.[134]

The Sandinistas did not take such proposals seriously. They were willing to make concessions that would allow the opposition to campaign more freely, but nothing more. They eased press censorship, retaining it only for news related to the military situation. They relaxed the state of emergency so that registered political parties could hold rallies and distribute campaign literature. They gave the opposition limited access to the mass media and they provided public funds to all parties to help defray the costs of the campaign.[135]

From the State Department's viewpoint, the Coordinadora's nine demands were unrealistic, so Craig Johnstone set about rewriting them, deleting everything that did not have a direct bearing on the conduct of the campaign.[136] But while the State Department was urging Cruz and the Coordinadora to be more flexible, CIA officers in the field and NSC staff members in Washington were advocating just the opposite. "I know the CIA was all against it," a Nicaraguan close to contra leader Alfonso Robelo recalled. "They were transmitting this loudly and clearly."[137] Administration hard-liners had particularly good connections with the businessmen at COSEP, which had been receiving CIA funds since Jimmy Carter initiated covert aid to the Sandinistas' internal opponents in 1979. In fact, virtually every element of the opposition—the press, the church, the private sector, and Arturo Cruz himself—was being funded by the CIA, either directly or indirectly. When it came to wielding influence in this milieu, the State Department was no match for Casey's covert operatives. "The other guys [at CIA] were able to run it by their complete penetration of the opposition," a senior U.S. diplomat said ruefully. "None of these people is independent anymore."[138]

As election day drew nearer, the Sandinistas and the Coordinadora remained at an impasse. Cruz campaigned, but he refused to formally register as a candidate. With the help of European Social Democrats, Colombian President Belisario Betancur and former Venezuelan President Carlos Andrés Pérez made one last-ditch effort to bring the Coordinadora into the election. They were able to get Cruz and Sandinista Comandante Bayardo Arce together for face-to-face negotiations in Rio de Janeiro during an October 1984 meeting of the Socialist International. Pérez mediated the talks. Cruz put forward the Coordinadora's reduced list of demands, as suggested by the State Department: freedom of the press; freedom of assembly without fear of being attacked by Sandinista mobs; freedom to campaign on military bases; access to voter registration lists and election returns; and international observation of the balloting. In addition, Cruz wanted the election postponed so that he could mount at least a three-month campaign.[139]

Arce agreed to all the procedural demands, but in exchange for postponing the election, he wanted a pledge that the contras would end the war if the election was fair. Cruz, of course, had no power to commit the contras to anything.[140] Nevertheless, he was ready to accept the proposal, but claimed he could not speak on behalf of the Coordinadora. In several calls to Managua, he tried to convince his erstwhile allies that Arce's deal was worth taking. But the hard-liners in COSEP, led by Enrique Bolaños, were intransigent. Cruz, Bolaños felt, had agreed to "a bunch of foolish things." The Coordinadora refused to accept Arce's proposal.[141]

Back in the meeting with Arce, Cruz offered to sign the agreement contingent on a vote of confidence from the Coordinadora. If he could just have a few days to return to Managua, he was confident he could win over the rejectionists. Failing that, he would resign as the Coordinadora's candidate. Accusing Cruz of stalling, Arce refused to extend the impending deadline for candidate registration. Either Cruz signed the agreement on behalf of the Coordinadora, or there was no deal. Cruz would not sign, and the talks collapsed.[142]

In Managua, some opposition leaders frankly admitted that they never had any intention of participating in the election; their only debate had been whether to refuse to register from the outset, or to start campaigning and then withdraw, charging the Sandinistas with creating conditions that prevented a fair contest.[143]

The summer-long minuet over whether or not Cruz would run produced some strange partners. Cruz and his moderate friends in the Coordinadora seemed to honestly want an agreement that would allow him to run in a reasonably free contest. The pragmatists in the State Department supported him, and the pragmatists in the Sandinista Front were anxious to accommodate him, too. But lined up against them were the rejectionist element in the Coordinadora, the radicals in the Sandinista leadership, and the hard-liners in the Reagan administration. "The administration never contemplated letting Cruz stay in the race," one U.S. official admitted, "because then the Sandinistas could justifiably claim that the elections were legitimate."[144] As so often happened in Central America, the people spoiling for a fight outmaneuvered the people seeking conciliation.

Once Cruz was irrevocably out of the race, the U.S. embassy launched an intensive lobbying campaign to get the three rightist opposition parties not aligned with the Coordinadora to withdraw as well. The new U.S. ambassador, Harry Bergold (who replaced Quainton in May 1984), was a reluctant demolition man. Having served previously as ambassador to Hungary, Bergold recognized that Nicaragua was a long way from the "totalitarian dungeon" described by Ronald Reagan.[145] Although the election had serious flaws, he still felt it was better to have an election than not. Sometimes the voters could surprise you. But Bergold's views didn't carry any more weight in Washington than Quainton's had. He, too, was regarded as soft because his reporting failed to conform to the hard-liners' preconceptions about Nicaraguan reality. Washington's strategy now was to wreck the elections as completely as possible.[146]

On October 20, Bergold and his political counselor visited Independent Liberal Party candidate Virgilio Godoy and expressed Washington's displeasure with the elections. Two days later, Godoy voted with a majority of his party's convention delegates to withdraw from the race, although his name remained on the ballot.[147]

The Democratic Conservative Party was also visited by U.S. diplomats who urged it to join the boycott, but the party's leaders and its convention were sharply divided. Presidential candidate Clemente Guido led the faction that wanted to remain in the race, whereas a majority of the delegates appeared to favor withdrawal. As the party convention prepared to vote on the issue, a mob of young people invaded the hall and broke up the meeting before the vote could be taken. The identity of the invaders was a matter of dispute. Party leaders who wanted to quit the race accused the mob of being Sandinistas. The young people themselves, along with the party leaders who wanted to stay in the race, insisted that they were members of the party's own youth group. They accused the pro-withdrawal leaders of having been bribed by the CIA. Guido stayed in the race, but his party split in two.[148]

Washington also urged other countries not to send official observers to the Nicaraguan election, and only Holland refused to comply. Nevertheless, over four hundred unofficial observers from some forty countries witnessed the election on November 4, in which 75 percent of registered voters participated. There was general agreement that the balloting was orderly and the count honest.[149] Among the observers, criticism of the process focused on the fairness of campaign conditions. The opposition parties were hobbled by their poor organization, and mobs of Sandinista activists harassed them during the campaign. Nevertheless, most of the observers concluded that the elections were reasonably fair by Central American standards.

Though the Sandinistas won handily, they did not do as well as expected. Tomás Borge had said that if the FSLN won less than 70 percent of the vote, it would "be enough to make one cry" and would force the party to "reconsider" its program.[150] Daniel Ortega received 67 percent of the presidential vote, Guido came in second with 14 percent, and Godoy finished third with 9.6 percent. In the assembly elections, the Sandinistas won 63 percent of the vote and sixty-one of the ninety-six seats.[151]

In taking a third of the vote, the conservative opposition showed surprising strength, given the fact that the Coordinadora boycotted the race, and the parties that participated did so halfheartedly. A high-ranking U.S. diplomat in Managua lamented that if the opposition had participated fully, it might have done even better and initiated a real process of democratization. The election, he said, was "a terrible missed opportunity," and it was not all the fault of the FSLN. "I give 60 percent of the blame to the Sandinistas and the rest to COSEP [the Superior Council of Private Enterprise]."[152]

Arturo Cruz, who on election day declared that the balloting was a "totally illegitimate and ridiculous . . . farce," later said he regretted not staying in the race.[153] But there were no second thoughts back in Washington. George Shultz pronounced the balloting "sham elections on the Soviet model," and the State Department spokesman called it "just a piece of theater."[154]

For the most part, the Reagan administration succeeded in preventing the Nicaraguan election from giving the Sandinista government any greater legitimacy. This was certainly true in the United States, where the *New York Times* editorialized that "only the naive believe that Sunday's election in Nicaragua was democratic."[155] In both Europe and Latin America, social democrats looked askance at the election because the Sandinistas had failed to entice Cruz into the race. The extent of their disappointment was evident by the attendance at Daniel Ortega's inauguration. Fidel Castro was the only head of state who came. Carlos Andrés Pérez declined his invitation, writing that friends of Nicaragua "feel cheated because sufficient guarantees were not provided to assure the participation of all political forces."[156] Five more years of war would pass before Nicaraguans would have a second opportunity to resolve their conflicts at the ballot box.

The MiGs of November

The struggle to define Ronald Reagan's second-term policy toward Central America began the night he was reelected. As the ballots were being counted, administration hard-liners leaked word to the press that a Soviet freighter was about to deliver MiG fighters to the Sandinistas in defiance of repeated U.S. warnings that such an acquisition would be intolerable.

Washington first became concerned about the Sandinistas acquiring MiGs in 1980, when eighty Nicaraguans went to Bulgaria for pilot training and the Sandinistas began lengthening and hardening the runway at the Punta Huete airstrip north of Managua, making it capable of accepting high-performance fighter aircraft.[157] Administration officials decided early on that they would not tolerate the introduction of MiGs, as Secretary of State Alexander Haig warned Foreign Minister Miguel D'Escoto during their December 1981 meeting in St. Lucia.[158] At the same time, Washington warned the Soviet Union not to provide MiGs to Nicaragua.

One of the decisions Reagan made on November 16, 1981, in NSDD 17 was to develop "contingency plans to deal with unacceptable military actions by Cuba," including the delivery of Cuban MiGs to Nicaragua. A briefing paper for an NSPG meeting on July 12, 1982, argued that "the arrival of MiGs in Nicaragua would not only tilt the regional military balance even further, but would be a major political/psychological shock demanding a prompt U.S. countermove." The paper reviewed U.S. response options up to and including military action to destroy the planes and "a blockade quarantine" of Nicaragua modeled on the blockade of Cuba during the 1962 missile crisis.[159] In September, Reagan and his senior foreign policy team agreed that if Nicaragua acquired MiGs, the United States would attack and destroy them. George Shultz again warned the Soviet Union of Washington's determination.[160]

As the contra war escalated, the Sandinistas grew increasingly anxious to build a modern air force to interdict contra air resupply operations being run out of El Salvador and Honduras. Sandinista leaders frequently declared their right and intention to acquire jets. They had the will to step across the line Washington had drawn in the sand, but they lacked the capability. The Soviet Union had promised in 1981 to provide them with MiGs, but reneged in the face of U.S. protests. The Sandinistas lacked the funds to buy comparable fighters anywhere else.[161]

Washington's warnings grew more intense as the Punta Huete airfield neared completion in 1984. "We would not allow advanced performance aircraft" in Nicaragua, said a ranking U.S. official. "It would raise the issue of Nicaragua as a Soviet military base." Just a few weeks before the 1984 U.S. election, Defense Minister Humberto Ortega (Daniel Ortega's brother) declared that both the pilots and the airfield would be ready to receive "MiGs or planes of the MiG type" by early 1985.[162]

On October 2, 1984, a U.S. intelligence satellite photographing the Soviet Black Sea port of Nikolayev spotted the freighter Bakuriani and what appeared to be 12 MiG-21 aircraft in crates on a nearby dock. Cloud cover obscured the port for several days, and when the weather cleared, the freighter had left port and the crates were gone. Since the Bakuriani was the only ship in port able to carry such large cargo below decks, intelligence analysts came to the preliminary conclusion that the crates must have been put aboard. Their suspicions were heightened when the Bakuriani sailed around Cape Horn rather than taking the shorter route through the Panama Canal, where its cargo would have been subject to inspection. A potential crisis began to develop when it became clear that the freighter's destination was Nicaragua.[163]

At the State Department, George Shultz wanted to take up the issue of the MiGs privately with the Soviets, again warning them in no uncertain terms that delivery was unacceptable. If the Soviets had miscalculated U.S. resolve, they could still avoid a crisis by deciding not to unload the MiGs. There would be no public test of wills, and the danger of escalation would be minimized. In 1970, Henry Kissinger had cut short Soviet plans to build a nuclear submarine base at Cienfuegos, Cuba, with such quiet diplomacy. For administration hard-liners, however, the impending arrival of the MiGs offered intriguing possibilities. If it became public, it could trigger a confrontation reminiscent of the Cuban missile crisis. The MiGs could become the casus belli that the hard-liners wanted to resolve the Nicaragua problem once and for all. "The crates seemed to offer a hope for bringing on the military action against Nicaragua that the [NSC] junior staffers desired," thought George Shultz.[164]

On election night, as Ronald Reagan was rolling over Walter Mondale, CBS

News quoted Defense Department sources saying that Soviet MiGs might be en route to Nicaragua. NBC News soon confirmed the story from "intelligence sources," who said that the administration regarded the shipment "as a direct challenge."[165] Further confirmations came from the White House. The story was repeated all evening long as the election coverage continued; indeed, the MiGs provided more drama than the election itself.

Terrified that Reagan was concocting the crisis as an excuse to invade Nicaragua, the Sandinistas immediately denied that they had received any MiGs. As the public sense of crisis mounted, the State Department warned the Soviets that delivering MiGs to Nicaragua would have grave implications for U.S.-Soviet relations. The Soviets also gave assurances that there were no MiGs on the Bakuriani.[166]

The freighter arrived in Nicaragua on November 7. As it unloaded its cargo of small arms and naval patrol boats, the likelihood that it was carrying MiGs diminished rapidly. Embarrassed U.S. officials quickly backtracked, explaining that they had never been sure that the crates sighted on the dock in the Soviet Union contained MiGs or that the crates had, in fact, been loaded onto the Bakuriani. All the evidence had been circumstantial.[167] By Friday, November 9, it was clear that the "crisis of the mystery MiGs," as it was jokingly referred to, had all been a big mistake—an "intelligence hype," State Department official Frank McNeil said later.[168] But, ominously, the crisis didn't end.

For administration hard-liners, the atmosphere of tension had too many benefits to be allowed to dissipate so quickly. To keep the Nicaraguans on edge, the Pentagon began flying SR-71 Blackbird spy planes over the port of Corinto and the capital Managua at such low altitudes that they produced frightening sonic booms. Many Nicaraguans thought they were being bombed. Nicaragua lodged a formal protest, but the United States publicly denied it was violating Nicaraguan airspace, even as U.S. officials admitted privately that the aim of the flights was to sow fear and panic.[169]

The administration also announced seven new military exercises in Central America and the Caribbean, all to begin within a few weeks. One of the largest, Composite Training Exercise 1-85, which involved twenty-five U.S. warships including the battleship *Iowa*, was already under way in the Caribbean, within striking distance of Nicaragua. At the same time, a land exercise, Operation Quick Thrust, began in the southern United States, involving fifteen thousand combat troops drawn from the 24th Infantry Division and the 82nd and 101st Airborne Divisions. No one needed to remind the Sandinistas these were the units most likely to spearhead an invasion and that U.S. troops had been positioned for the invasion of Grenada under the pretext of exercises.[170]

The drumbeat of anti-Nicaraguan rhetoric continued as well. Administration sources who had originally claimed there was "credible evidence" of MiGs on the Bakuriani now insisted they had "very credible evidence" of a massive Soviet military buildup in Nicaragua reminiscent of the one in Cuba prior to the missile crisis.[171] On NBC's *Meet the Press*, Secretary of Defense Weinberger claimed the Soviet Union had unleashed a "tremendous increased flow of offensive weaponry" to the Nicaraguans with the aim of "intimidating their neighbors."[172]

The Sandinistas were convinced that the MiG scare, the SR-71 overflights, the exercises, and the overblown rhetoric were all prelude to an invasion. They put the armed forces on full alert, mobilized the militia, and postponed the beginning of the coffee harvest—a costly decision for a country desperately short of hard currency.[173]

Administration officials evinced surprise that the Nicaraguans were so worried. "I don't know why they are doing this," George Shultz said in a press conference at an OAS meeting in Brazil. "As far as invasion fears, they seem to be self-inflicted wounds."[174]

In addition to frightening the Sandinistas and disrupting their economy, the MiG crisis had other payoffs for administration hard-liners. It diverted attention from Nicaragua's election and put U.S. allies on notice that despite the Nicaraguan vote, Washington's policy of hostility was unmitigated. The MiG scare also marked the beginning of a new public relations strategy at home, portraying Nicaragua as a base for the projection of Soviet military power into the Western Hemisphere and, consequently, as a direct threat to the security of the United States. By invoking the Soviet menace, the administration hoped to stir up public opinion and soften up Congress for a new round of voting on contra aid. "What we need to do," a Pentagon official explained, "is translate concern about the military buildup in Nicaragua into support for renewed aid to the rebels."[175]

The potential power in this new line of argument was demonstrated by the near universal silence from congressional Democrats during the MiG scare. Even perennial Reagan critics like Senator Christopher Dodd went out of their way to endorse the use of force against Nicaragua if the Sandinistas received jet aircraft.[176]

Most important, the MiG scare gave the hard-liners leverage in their internal struggle against State Department pragmatists, like Tony Motley and Craig Johnstone, who still wanted to reach a diplomatic accord with the Sandinistas. "Some of those who want us to adopt a harder line have long wished that MiGs would be delivered because they know that would tilt the policy in their direction," explained an administration official. "The arrival of MiGs would break the bureaucratic tie ballgame over Nicaragua. The next best thing to delivery of the MiGs was the possibility that they might arrive any day."[177]

The flood of charges and countercharges between Managua and Washington gave hard-liners the perfect atmosphere for defining U.S. policy toward Nicaragua during Reagan's second term: the Sandinistas would have to go. The basic aim of U.S. policy—"the bottom line," one official called it—had been clearly defined.[178]

CHAPTER 17

Project Democracy

Bill Casey was not about to let the contras be defeated by Congress. Long before the October 1984 aid cut-off, Casey began making contingency plans to keep the war going even if Congress refused to fund it. As early as 1983, when Congress cut Reagan's contra aid request in half, approving only $24 million for fiscal year 1984, Casey shifted various costs of the war to the CIA's general overhead accounts. For example, $1 million of the $1.2 million cost of outfitting the mother ships from which the Unilaterally Controlled Latino Assets (UCLAS) attacked Nicaraguan oil facilities and laid mines was not charged against the $24 million ceiling established by Congress. Neither were the stipends for "family living expenses" paid to some contra leaders, nor the cost of printing instruction manuals for the contras. The salaries of some CIA operatives working with the contras in Honduras were charged to general CIA payroll accounts.[1]

After an investigation, the House Intelligence Committee concluded that the CIA had overspent the 1983 ceiling by about 4 percent, but the issue was less the amount of money involved than the principle. "We drew a line in the sand this year," said one committee member, referring to the spending limit. "If they stepped over this one, how can we stop them from stepping over another line?"[2]

After the $24 million was exhausted, the law prohibited spending any additional funds to support "military or paramilitary operations in Nicaragua."[3] Edward Boland and the House Intelligence Committee meant to prohibit funding groups involved in such operations—that is, the contras. The stipulation about military and paramilitary operations was included to distinguish the contras from the internal political opposition to the Sandinistas, which was also being funded covertly by the CIA. The administration, however, interpreted the law to mean that it could continue funding the contras' nonmilitary activities. Using this loophole and the CIA's "reserve for contingencies" fund, the administration spent over $10 million annually to finance contra political operations. The House Intelligence Committee objected, but the Republican majority on the Senate committee accepted it, so the practice continued.[4]

The logical place for Casey to seek alternative sources of funding was the Department of Defense. Not only was Defense awash in money from huge budget increases in the first Reagan administration, but it also had its own covert operations apparatus, so deeply buried in the Pentagon bureaucracy that it was largely immune to congressional oversight. Casey's strategy was to simply draw on the Pentagon's vast stock of weapons to get around congressional spending limits in both El Salvador and Nicaragua. The CIA would request arms and equipment from the Pentagon for use in covert operations. By law, the CIA had to repay the Pentagon for this equipment. But to stretch the CIA budget, the Pentagon would declare the equipment surplus and give it to the CIA free or at nominal cost. "The concept is called bailment," an administration official explained. "It's basically a device to maximize the resources you can get relative to the aid ceiling."[5]

In El Salvador and Honduras, the CIA served as a conduit for military aid that the Pentagon could not provide directly because of congressional spending limits. At one point, the Pentagon planned to give El Salvador a fleet of helicopters as part of a "covert operation" that appeared to have no other purpose than to evade these limits. The nominal surplus cost of the aircraft was $20 million; their real value was at least three or four times that amount. Had the transfer gone forward, it would have constituted a 30 percent covert increase in El Salvador's military aid. The scheme was scrapped when Democrats on the House Intelligence Committee objected, but smaller transfers went forward.[6]

In Nicaragua, the Pentagon subsidized the CIA's secret war through the same mechanism. The transfers of equipment were so extensive that Secretary of the Army John O. Marsh began to worry that they were an improper effort to avoid congressional oversight. Other senior Pentagon officials shared his concerns. On May 9, 1983, Marsh wrote a lengthy memo to Secretary Caspar

Weinberger warning him that such transfers, especially for projects in Central America, "raise some difficult policy and legal questions." Marsh himself had stopped one suspect transfer by insisting that Congress be notified of the planned covert operation. The CIA aborted the project rather than tell Congress about it.[7]

Weinberger brushed Marsh off, replying that it was the CIA's job to review the legality of covert operations, not the Pentagon's.[8] Weinberger was Casey's ally in the administration's internecine battles over Central America and was not about to undercut Casey's ability to maneuver around the shoals of congressional hostility.

In July 1983, when Reagan decided to escalate the U.S. military presence in Central America, he explicitly instructed the Defense Department to "provide maximum possible assistance to the Director of Central Intelligence in improving support to the Nicaraguan resistance forces."[9] The CIA immediately requested that the Pentagon give it $28 million worth of military supplies "free of charge." Part of this flood of materiel was to accommodate a planned expansion of the contra army, and part was to be stockpiled against the possibility of a cut-off in congressional aid. Pentagon officials dubbed the request the CIA's "Christmas list."[10] They tried to block or at least delay it, arguing that there was inadequate authority for the transfer under the 1981 presidential finding and that the CIA could not legally have the equipment for free. However, when CIA scaled down its request to only $12 million, the Pentagon approved it.[11]

The flow of materiel to the contras under this project, code-named "Elephant Herd," continued for sixteen months, even after Congress banned all contra aid in October 1984. The CIA argued that since the equipment had been declared surplus and without value, giving it to the contras did not involve the expenditure of U.S. government funds and therefore did not violate the Boland amendment. "We gave the agency pretty much anything they wanted," said Colonel Richard C. Lawrence, who was director for Central American affairs at the Pentagon. "In war, they're a fourth branch of the service."[12]

Operation Elephant Herd came to light in September 1984 when the contras used two Cessna O2A light planes acquired through the program to attack a Sandinista training base. Press attention was drawn to the incident because two U.S. private citizens (from an Alabama-based group called Civilian-Military Assistance) were killed during the attack when their helicopter was shot down. The *Washington Post* traced the ownership of the Cessnas back to the New York Air National Guard. The Pentagon had declared a number of the observation planes "excess" at the end of 1984, sold two to the Salvadoran air force for $47,000 each, and transferred three others to the CIA at no cost under the auspices of Elephant Herd. The CIA then outfitted them with weapons and passed them along to the contras.[13]

The CIA's contra program also benefited directly from the expansion of U.S. military exercises in Honduras in 1983 and 1984. Army engineers built airfields along the Nicaraguan border, and when the exercises were finished, turned the bases over to the CIA and contras for use as forward supply depots. Despite promises by both Secretary of Defense Weinberger and Deputy Assistant Secretary Nestor Sanchez that U.S. troops would not leave behind any equipment when the exercises were over, they left tons of it, thereby supplementing the regular military aid programs for both the Honduran armed forces and the contras.[14]

The Seven Days in May Syndrome

In addition to helping fund CIA operations in Central America, the Pentagon itself undertook a series of covert projects, or "special operations," as the military referred to them. One of its foremost special operations units was the army's Intelligence Support Activity (ISA), which originated during planning for the Iran hostage rescue mission in 1980. The unit was so secret that it had at least three alternative code names—Royal Cape, Powder Keg, and Granite Rock—to confuse anyone who might hear mention of it. Pentagon insiders referred to it simply as "the Activity." The congressional intelligence committees were not informed of the ISA's existence until 1981 and then were told only because they stumbled upon one of its operations.[15] During the early 1980s, the ISA became deeply involved in Central America. It trained contras, gathered intelligence, developed a network of spies throughout the region, and sent "pathfinder" teams into Nicaragua to set up safe houses and mark landing zones to prepare the way for a U.S. invasion.[16]

In February 1981, the U.S. Army formed a Special Operations Division, commanded by Colonel James E. Longhofer, to coordinate the Pentagon's growing array of covert programs. The operations officers quickly developed a reputation for circumventing regulations. "We intentionally ignored the bureaucracy," one officer explained. "We had to. Because whenever we dealt with the normal bureaucracy it was immediately a giant roadblock." Others in the Pentagon called the gung-ho Special Operations people "the crazies in the basement."[17]

One of the new division's first projects was the creation of "Seaspray," a joint Army-CIA aviation unit organized in March 1981 to move men and materiel quickly for covert operations. It eventually grew to have fourteen aircraft, none of which were bought through normal procurement channels or approved by

Congress. Most of Seaspray's operations were in Central America.[18] In 1982, the Army Special Operations Division created another special element, "Yellow Fruit," to handle operational security for the various operations the division had under way.

One of the division's most successful ventures was code-named "Queens Hunter." Seaspray acquired small planes for the division to use on signal intelligence gathering missions over El Salvador in the months before the 1982 Constituent Assembly elections. The ISA provided the signal intelligence specialists and Yellow Fruit provided a safe house in Honduras where the operation was based. The tactical intelligence that Queens Hunter collected on guerrilla field operations was so good that the project, originally planned to last just a few months, was extended for three years.[19]

Impressed by the success of Queens Hunter, the CIA proposed that the Special Operations Division take on another project, "Rooks Landing," in which Seaspray helicopters would trail small planes flying from Nicaragua to El Salvador. The CIA was still searching for irrefutable proof that the Sandinistas were smuggling arms to the Salvadoran guerrillas. The Pentagon refused to provide pilots for the operation on the grounds that flights over Nicaragua could constitute a violation of the War Powers Resolution. The CIA went ahead anyway, using civilian employees. In October 1984, four of them were killed when their plane crashed on a mission in El Salvador.[20]

Elements of the army's Task Force 160 helicopter assault unit were reportedly deployed to Central America beginning in 1982. Its main mission was the quick insertion and extraction of commando units behind enemy lines. In Central America, it ferried contras from their Honduran bases into Nicaragua and back again, assisted the CIA's sabotage attacks on Nicaraguan oil facilities, and flew unspecified missions in El Salvador.[21]

In September 1982, Casey requested that Colonel Longhofer be detailed to the CIA as liaison officer between the Agency and the Special Operations Division. Longhofer started his new job the following month, working on operations in Central America.[22] In late July 1983, just as the House was voting on the Boland-Zablocki bill to cut off contra aid, Longhofer and Rudy Enders, chief of the CIA's paramilitary operations, visited the Virginia offices of Yellow Fruit, the Special Operations Division's security unit. They brought a black binder containing a thirty- to forty-page contingency plan for clandestinely continuing aid to the contras if Congress prohibited it. "The whole purpose of the plan," said Yellow Fruit intelligence officer William T. Golden, "was to circumvent the Boland amendment." The plan was not on letterhead stationery, and nowhere was the author identified. But based on the plan's language and format, Golden believed it was drafted at the CIA.[23]

The plan described how U.S. military assistance programs to other countries could be inflated, with the understanding that the recipients would pass the excess equipment along to the contras. Additional funds would be raised from a variety of other sources and channeled into offshore bank accounts. The plan also detailed the need for an air resupply operation to deliver provisions to the contras both in their base camps and inside Nicaragua. As part of the resupply operation, an airfield would be built in Costa Rica.

If Congress banned aid to the contras, the Special Operations Division would take over from the CIA and implement the contingency plan. The division was the perfect locus for such a project. It had virtually unlimited resources because its budget was not set by Congress. Its funds came from various places in the Defense Department budget, reprogrammed to the division in small amounts that fell below the limit requiring congressional notification and review.[24]

Longhofer was the army's Oliver North. He envisioned creating a whole series of special "black" (covert) army units, known collectively as the Operational Support Element, to assist CIA operations around the world—a precursor to North's "off the shelf . . . stand alone" covert operations capability. "If there was anything similar to a Seven Days in May syndrome," an army investigator later said of Longhofer's plans, "this was it."[25]

As Congress began limiting the CIA's aid to the contras in 1983, initial steps were taken to implement the contingency plan. A Swiss bank account was opened and a survey of the Costa Rican airfield site begun.[26] But the operation aborted before it got off the ground when the army opened an investigation of financial improprieties in the Special Operations Division. Investigators found gross misuse of funds, with some $324 million unaccounted for. Yellow Fruit's commander was court-martialed for forgery, theft, and obstruction of justice and sentenced to ten years in prison. For failing to report the misdeeds at Yellow Fruit, Longhofer was court-martialed for dereliction of duty and sentenced to two years. In all, thirty-six officers were disciplined as a result of the investigation.[27]

After the scandal, the Special Operations Division could no longer serve as a mechanism for continuing the contra war in the absence of congressional funding. But looking back on it, army investigators were convinced that the Yellow Fruit plan was the original blueprint for the contra resupply operation that Oliver North later directed from the National Security Council. Secretary of the Army Marsh thought so, too, even though he couldn't prove it.[28] Indeed, many of the same people were involved, except that most of them retired from active duty after the Special Operations corruption scandal. Typically, they opened consulting firms to provide the government with the same services.

"All the Pentagon's covert operators were taking off their uniforms and remaining in place," explained a former CIA officer, "and each perceived himself to be acting as an unofficial covert officer of the government." North, who was the NSC official in charge of overseeing Pentagon special operations, took on the added task of supervising the special operations of the contras' so-called "private benefactors."[29]

We Get By with a Little Help from Our Friends

From the start, support from other countries was an essential component of Reagan's covert war against Nicaragua. Argentina provided advisers and training early in the war, and Honduras provided surplus weapons and bases. When Congress became skittish, the administration naturally looked to allies abroad to take on a greater role. A draft of NSDD 124 prepared by Oliver North and Constantine Menges in early 1984 specifically proposed "immediate efforts to obtain additional funding of $10–$15 million from foreign or domestic sources," to supplement the $24 million in contra aid Congress had provided for fiscal year 1984. Rather than have the president explicitly authorize an effort that could be interpreted as circumventing the law, National Security Adviser Robert C. McFarlane dropped the language about soliciting contra aid from U.S. allies. But he did not drop the idea.[30] According to some administration officials, McFarlane verbally briefed the president on a plan to raise money from third countries and private sources, and Reagan approved it.[31]

No country was a closer ally of the United States than Israel, and the Israelis had experience in Central America. When Jimmy Carter's human rights policy led to a cut-off of military aid to Guatemala, Honduras, El Salvador, and Nicaragua, the Israelis became alternate arms suppliers for the region. By the mid-1980s, Israel was selling arms to all the Central American governments except Nicaragua and had an estimated one hundred military advisers in the region.[32]

In 1983, Casey asked the Pentagon to see if Israel would be willing to donate arms to the contras from the stocks of Soviet-made weapons captured from the Palestine Liberation Organization (PLO) during the invasion of Lebanon. Major General Richard V. Secord, not yet retired, handled the negotiations. Under the auspices of Operation Tipped Kettle, the Israelis donated $10 million worth of equipment, which the CIA delivered to the contras. Casey informed the intelligence committees that Israel had donated the arms, but failed to mention what he did with them. In 1984, when funds for the contras were running short and Congress was unwilling to provide emergency supplemental aid, Casey successfully sought Israeli help once again, in Operation Tipped Kettle II. This time, Washington promised it would find a way to compensate the Israelis for their cooperation.[33]

The Israelis, however, were sensitive about their involvement in Nicaragua. On the one hand, the conservative Likud Party government agreed ideologically with Reagan's tough anti-Communist stance and wanted to do everything possible to cooperate. On the other hand, Israel's strongest supporters in Congress were liberal Democrats who almost unanimously opposed the contra war. Fearful of getting caught in the cross fire between Reagan and Congress, the Israelis wanted to help the administration, but not too conspicuously.[34] In early 1984, when McFarlane approached Israeli Foreign Ministry official David Kimche about providing financial support and training for the contras—in effect taking over management of the operation from the United States—Kimche said no.[35]

In May 1984, McFarlane approached Saudi Arabian Ambassador Prince Bandar Bin Sultan and described the administration's predicament. The Nicaragua program was very important to the president, McFarlane explained, but appropriated funds were exhausted. Bandar took the hint and a few days later agreed, "as a humanitarian gesture," to provide the contras with $1 million monthly through the end of 1984. Oliver North directed Nicaraguan Democratic Force (FDN) leader Adolfo Calero to set up an offshore bank account for the contras into which the Saudis could deposit the funds. A few days later McFarlane advised Reagan of the Saudi decision by slipping a note inside the president's daily briefing book, so no other officials would know of the arrangement. On the note, Reagan wrote back, "Good news!"[36]

The idea of developing third-country funding sources for the contras was widely discussed inside the administration as the prospects for congressional funding faded. After the House rejected the administration's request for $21 million in emergency funds in May 1984, State Department and CIA officials working on Nicaragua drew up a plan proposing that the administration solicit help from half a dozen countries around the world. This plan, prepared under the direction of Assistant Secretary of State for Latin America Tony Motley, called for a National Security Planning Group (NSPG) meeting and an explicit presidential decision to set the operation in motion. Moreover, it also called for notifying the congressional intelligence committees that the solicitations were being made.[37]

On June 25, 1984, with Reagan in attendance, the NSPG considered the idea of third-country funding in detail. Casey argued that Reagan himself should solicit help from friendly heads of state, offering them increased U.S. economic aid as an incentive. Both Weinberger and U.N. Ambassador Jeane Kirkpatrick endorsed the plan. "If we can't get the money for the anti-Sandinistas [from Congress]," Kirkpatrick said, "then we should make the maximum effort to find the money elsewhere."[38]

George Shultz opposed the idea. In an earlier conversation, Shultz noted, James Baker had warned that such activity would be "an impeachable offense." Constitutionally, Shultz explained, "the U.S. government may raise and spend funds only through an appropriation of Congress." Moreover, he argued, the administration should be careful to conduct itself "so that we maximize the chance of persuading Congress to come back on board and give support." Soliciting third-country aid would "cut against" that strategy by seeming to circumvent the law.

Casey insisted that no laws would be broken if the aid went directly from the donor to the contras; Washington would do nothing more than make the requests and facilitate the transfers. Besides, the September 1983 presidential finding on Nicaragua specifically authorized the administration to "seek support of other governments."

The NSPG decided to ask for a legal opinion, with White House adviser (and future attorney general) Edwin Meese noting that someone should be sure to advise the Department of Justice in advance of what conclusion they wanted it to reach. Neither Reagan, Casey, nor McFarlane told the other officials in the meeting that Israel and Saudi Arabia had already been solicited and that the Saudis had begun sending money.[39] Ronald Reagan was well aware of how politically sensitive such solicitations were. If word of their efforts to finance the contras through third countries leaked to the press, the president warned, "we'll all be hanging by our thumbs in front of the White House until we find out who leaked."[40]

In the end, Shultz's reservations were ignored and the hard-liners' plan to seek third-country aid for the contras was implemented. In early 1985, the administration devised what McFarlane called a "very secret" plan to provide increased economic and military aid to Honduras, El Salvador, and Guatemala as an "incentive" for them to continue their support for the contras.[41]

Such incentives were especially important after Congress cut off contra aid in October 1984. Few of Washington's Central American allies were willing to continue backing the contras if the United States was withdrawing. The Hondurans were especially skittish; President Roberto Suazo Córdova threatened to halt Honduran support unless he received a clear signal of Washington's continuing commitment to the war.[42] In January 1985, McFarlane traveled to Central America to reassure Washington's allies that the Reagan administration was determined to continue backing the contras, Congress notwithstanding. The Hondurans wanted more than mere assurances. Shortly after McFarlane's return, on February 7, 1985, the NSC Crisis Pre-Planning Group (CPPG) met to develop "a strategy for enticing the Hondurans to [provide] greater support" for the contras.[43]

The CPPG recommended that Reagan make several foreign aid offers "as an incentive to the Hondurans for their continued support" for the contras. Specifically, the United States should expedite the delivery of military equipment, release $174 million in economic assistance funds that had been held up because of the Honduran government's economic policies, and increase the CIA's covert support for Honduran internal security forces by $4.5 million.[44]

The Hondurans were to be advised of these enticements first by a presidential letter from Reagan to Suazo. The message would then be reiterated by an emissary who would spell out the "conditions" attached to this aid, specifically, "continued Honduran support" for the contras. "The CPPG did not wish to include this detail of the quid pro quo arrangement in written correspondence," the U.S. government acknowledged later.[45]

On February 19, 1985, President Reagan approved the CPPG's plan, and later in the month he sent Suazo a letter informing him of the aid decision. A February 20 memo outlined how Reagan's decision would be implemented: The administration would thank Suazo for Honduras's continuing support for the contras and guarantee "that our appreciation manifests itself in more than just words." In the margin, Deputy National Security Adviser John Poindexter wrote, "Add that we want VP to also discuss this matter with Suazo."[46]

Vice President George Bush was scheduled to visit Honduras in mid-March, providing an occasion for reinforcing the administration's message. On March 16, 1985, Bush met with Suazo and discussed both the contras and U.S. assistance to Honduras. Bush expressed Washington's appreciation for Honduras's continuing support of Reagan's regional policy, particularly the contras, and he reminded Suazo of the recent U.S. aid concessions to Honduras. "You don't have to be clairvoyant," Tony Motley said, describing the unspoken dimension of Bush and Suazo's conversation. Motley admitted that the United States used its aid program as leverage to keep the Hondurans cooperating on the contra program, but, he insisted, "that isn't a quid pro quo."[47] Later, the fact that Bush had not explicitly stated that U.S. aid was contingent on Honduran support for the contras enabled him to deny that he had been part of any quid pro quo arrangement.[48]

As expedited U.S. military aid began to flow in March 1985, the Hondurans assured Washington that they would allow the contras' logistical system to operate freely in Honduras. They also promised to continue providing false end-user certificates for contra arms purchases so that the original seller of the weapons would believe they were being sold to a legitimate government. In addition, the Honduran military provided the contras with aircraft and loaned them ammunition when they ran short.[49]

The quid pro quo deal did not solve the problem of Honduran reluctance permanently, however. Just a few weeks after Bush's visit, the Honduran armed forces commandeered a shipment of surface-to-air missiles en route to the contras. The jealous Hondurans had nothing comparable and wanted to keep the missiles for themselves. At McFarlane's suggestion, President Reagan called President Suazo personally on April 23 to ask that the arms shipment be released. Suazo agreed, but asked for yet another increase in U.S. aid, which Reagan approved a few weeks later.[50]

Guatemala, like Honduras, also wanted some compensation for supporting U.S. policy, especially since it had been cooperating even though Congress refused to give it any military aid. As CIA Central American Task Force chief Alan Fiers wrote in a January 1985 briefing memo for McFarlane, Guatemala would help "provided that it receives a quid pro quo from the United States in the form of foreign assistance funds . . . or some other form of assistance."[51] (Fiers had taken over from Dewey Clarridge as the principal coordinator of the contra war at CIA and, like Clarridge before him, worked directly for Casey.)

Guatemala agreed to provide some equipment and false end-user certificates, leading Oliver North to recommend in March 1985 that in return for this "extraordinary assistance," the United States should resume military aid to the Guatemalan armed forces despite their continuing record of human rights abuses. Although the resumption of aid would be justified publicly as "assisting Guatemala's progress toward democracy," the Guatemalan military would be advised that the aid was actually a payment for "their cooperation on the [contra] resistance issue."[52] McFarlane approved the plan, and the administration subsequently provided $5 million worth of military equipment to Guatemala—the first military aid since 1977. A year later, to ensure Guatemala's continuing cooperation, the CIA launched a "public relations/media operation" designed to improve Guatemala's international image.[53]

In El Salvador, President José Napoleón Duarte agreed to allow the contras to continue using Ilopango air base as the hub of their logistics operation, which meant providing storage facilities, maintenance, and fuel for the contras' transport planes (fuel illegally diverted from the U.S. military aid program for El Salvador). Later, when the Iran-contra scandal broke, Duarte would deny knowing anything about the resupply operation at Ilopango.[54]

In Panama, General Manuel Antonio Noriega had been a CIA asset for two decades. Casey met with him in August 1984 in Panama City to ask him to help the contras. Noriega allowed the rebels to set up training camps, provided planes and pilots from his drug smuggling operations to move contra arms, dispatched Panamanian commandos on sabotage missions into Nicaragua, and made a cash donation to the cause.[55]

In August 1986, Noriega offered to have the entire leadership of the Sandinista party assassinated if the administration would help clean up his image in the United States, where press reports had revealed his involvement in the drug trade. But wholesale assassination was too much even for Oliver North. At a September 1986 meeting with Noriega in London, North and John Poindexter suggested that Panama undertake commando raids against economic targets in Nicaragua instead.[56]

Casey, meanwhile, had also been pursuing the possibility of South African support for the contras. In April 1984, he sent Dewey Clarridge to Pretoria to discuss a South African promise to help, but Clarridge held off because of the political furor caused by the mining of Nicaragua's harbors. In the end, nothing came of the offer because South Africa was reluctant to deal directly with the contras and insisted on being reimbursed by Washington.[57]

In mid-1984, the People's Republic of China offered to help the contras, presumably because the Sandinistas were receiving aid from China's arch-enemy, the Soviet Union. The Chinese were asked to ship surface-to-air missiles to the contras via Guatemala (the same missiles the Honduran military tried to commandeer).[58]

Nevertheless, as 1984 drew to a close, the funding situation for the contras was dire. Saudi support, which comprised almost all the cash the contras received after U.S. aid ran out, was slated to finish at year's end. Several other countries had been approached, but none was willing to make the sort of major effort required to keep the contras in the field until the administration could roll back the Boland amendment. The Central Americans were cooperative but anxious. Most of them were receiving large amounts of foreign aid from Washington and feared that Congress would cut them off if it discovered they were conspiring with the administration to circumvent the law. Other countries harbored the same concerns. At Oliver North's request, retired major general John K. Singlaub contacted South Korea and Taiwan for help in January 1985, but both were worried about the diplomatic repercussions of becoming involved. South Korea begged off and Taiwan donated a paltry $2 million.[59]

In desperation, McFarlane went back to the Saudis again in early 1985 to see if they would be willing to extend their aid. Prince Bandar was annoyed, but understood the importance of investing in a valuable friendship. "You can stop twisting my arm," he told Secord, who called to follow up on McFarlane's request. "I have decided to take it up with the head of state." In February, Saudi king Fahd visited Reagan in Washington and informed him privately that the Saudis would provide an additional $24 million for the contras. In all, the Saudis contributed $32 million to the contra cause between July 1984 and March 1985.[60]

Press reports about the administration's efforts to secure third-country aid for the contras appeared almost simultaneously with the first solicitations. The initial report that Israel was donating arms came in July 1983, just a few weeks after the initiation of Operation Tipped Kettle. Reports that Washington would seek help from the Saudis actually appeared even before McFarlane first met with Prince Bandar in May 1984.[61] Administration officials dismissed the press reports as absurd; one senior State Department official called it "off the wall thinking" and "out of the question."[62]

Administration denials notwithstanding, the press reports prompted the House Intelligence Committee to hold hearings on May 2, 1984. Asked about Israeli and Saudi aid to the contras, Casey simply lied, saying, "We have not been involved in that at all." Asked if "any element of our government" had approached "any element of another government" seeking aid for the contras, Casey answered, "No, not to my knowledge."[63]

In late 1984, another round of press stories on third-country aid to the contras prompted another round of congressional inquiries. Tony Motley was grilled about third-country aid by the Senate Foreign Relations Committee. He acknowledged that the Boland amendment banned soliciting contra aid from third countries. "Even if today we wanted to go to third countries to encourage or solicit, we could not because there is a prohibition," he said. Wary that the administration might be looking for loopholes in the law, Senator Christopher Dodd pressed Motley for his unequivocal assurance that the law would be obeyed. "We are going to continue to comply with the law," Motley assured him. "I am not looking for any loopholes. . . . Nobody is trying to play games with you." Motley, however, did not speak for everyone.[64]

In all, the efforts to raise funds for the contras from Washington's allies produced about $45 million in cash between 1984 and 1985 from Saudi Arabia, Israel, and Taiwan, plus an inestimable amount of in-kind assistance from Honduras, Guatemala, and El Salvador. That was a sizable war chest—more, in fact, than the CIA had provided during the first two years of the war. But it was far less than what the contras needed to defeat the Sandinistas.

The Little Dictator Is Retired

While Casey and McFarlane were busy laying plans to keep the contras alive, one of Washington's most intrepid allies passed suddenly from the scene. On March 31, 1984, Honduran general Gustavo Alvarez and his three top commanders were deposed by their fellow officers and sent into exile. The United States was taken totally by surprise. Alvarez was Washington's man—"a model professional," U.S. Ambassador John Negroponte once called him.[65] The CIA had helped him rise to the top of the Honduran military, and he had helped the CIA wage war against Nicaragua. Alvarez was personally close to both Negroponte and CIA Station Chief Donald Winter, who asked Alvarez to be the godfather of his child. Washington's allegiance to General Alvarez was so conspicuous that his enemies in the Honduran officers corps were careful to keep the United States completely in the dark about their plot. Even after Alvarez was deposed, relations between the CIA and the new top military commanders were strained until Winter was replaced as station chief.[66]

The coup was also a political embarrassment to the Reagan administration's effort to portray Honduras as a democracy. Ambassador Negroponte tried to pretend that President Suazo had been the protagonist in ousting Alvarez, but Suazo actually had nothing to do with it. "The president was told after it was a completed fact," admitted José Azcona Hoyo, a leader of Suazo's Liberal Party and his eventual successor as president.[67]

Various reasons lay behind Alvarez's removal, some related to the growing U.S. presence in Honduras, others strictly internal to the armed forces.[68] Historically, the Honduran military had been run collegially—"a parliamentary army," one Honduran analyst called it—with senior officers meeting regularly in the Superior Council of the Armed Forces to thrash out policy differences. When Alvarez took over as armed forces commander, he ignored the council and, together with a handful of cronies, ran the military from the top down. The catalyst for the coup was reportedly Alvarez's unilateral decision to increase the time between promotions in rank from three to five years—an action that naturally caused consternation among the junior officers. Corruption was another motive. Corruption was nothing new in the Honduran military, but Alvarez kept too much for himself. Just as he refused to share power with his fellow officers, he also refused to share the graft.[69]

A more serious concern, especially among younger officers, was the repression that Alvarez unleashed against political dissidents. Honduran officers prided themselves on not resorting to the brutal violence against civilians regularly used by their Salvadoran and Guatemalan colleagues. Alvarez, however, was a convert to the doctrine of the "national security state," a view he picked up from the Argentines. He believed that the only defense against international Communism was a garrison state that brooked no opposition whatsoever.[70]

Finally, Alvarez was deposed because many of his fellow officers felt he was too quick to do Washington's bidding and received too little in return. "They're perfectly willing to be seen as friends of the United States," said a senior U.S. diplomat in Honduras, "but they're very anxious not to be seen as puppets of the United States."[71]

Perhaps the most emotional issue for the Hondurans was the Regional

Military Training Center (RMTC), which Washington convinced the Hondurans to establish in 1983 so that the Pentagon could train Salvadoran soldiers without increasing the number of U.S. military advisers in El Salvador. El Salvador and Honduras were traditional enemies. In 1969, they fought the "Soccer War," which did not formally end until October 30, 1980. Within the military, air force general Walter López Reyes, a hero of the Soccer War, led the opposition to the RMTC. When Alvarez was overthrown, Walter López took his place as commander of the armed forces.

López and the new leaders of the Honduran military regarded the contras as a security problem. The exiles had virtually taken over provinces along the Nicaraguan border, driving out the Honduran farmers who lived there. Locals had begun referring to the region as "New Nicaragua." So long as Honduras allowed the contras to use its territory, there was always a danger of war with the Sandinistas. And if Washington decided to withdraw its support for the contras, Honduras would be stuck with them. "What am I going to do with 12,000 fighters here?" López asked.[72]

López also worried that the contras might act as shock troops in a counter-coup to bring Alvarez back to power.[73] Alvarez had been their unstinting patron, and the contras were among his staunchest supporters. López's fears were by no means irrational. In November 1984, the FBI broke up a coup plot hatched by exiled Honduran businessmen and officers loyal to Alvarez. General José Abdenego Bueso Rosa, Alvarez's chief of staff, was arrested in Florida with seven others for plotting to assassinate President Suazo and overthrow the civilian government. Seized at the time of their arrest was $10 million worth of cocaine, which they planned to sell in the United States to finance the coup. Bueso Rosa was convicted of conspiracy to murder and sentenced to five years in prison.[74]

As Alvarez's chief of staff, Bueso Rosa had helped the CIA organize the contras' logistical apparatus in Honduras, so he had many friends in the Reagan administration. Although he was a ringleader of the plot, he was made eligible for parole immediately. One of his principal co-conspirators, by contrast, was sentenced to a total of 130 years.[75]

Behind the scenes, Oliver North, Dewey Clarridge, General Paul Gorman, and Assistant Secretary of State Elliott Abrams were all urging the Justice Department to reduce Bueso Rosa's sentence because he was a "friend" of the United States. North tried to get him pardoned outright, lest he "break his longstanding silence about the Nic[araguan] resistance and other sensitive operations." The Justice Department replied that Bueso Rosa had already gotten off easily; it did agree, however, to transfer him from a federal penitentiary to a minimum security facility at Eglin Air Force Base.[76]

The United States took care of General Alvarez, too. Nestor Sanchez and Fred Iklé arranged to have him hired by the Pentagon as a consultant on "low intensity conflict," which paid $50,000 over two years.[77] Eventually, Alvarez became an evangelical Christian and returned to live in Honduras, where he was assassinated by leftist guerrillas on January 25, 1989.

With Alvarez out of power, the Hondurans began to reassess their relationship with the United States.[78] In August 1984, the Honduran government presented Ambassador John Negroponte with a list of demands: they wanted a 100 percent increase in economic aid, a 33 percent increase in military aid, a security pact committing Washington to Honduras's defense in the event of war, a reduced schedule of joint exercises (because the Hondurans could not afford them), and changes in the RMTC so that more Hondurans than Salvadorans would be trained. In exchange, the Hondurans would continue to allow Salvadorans to attend the RMTC and allow the contras to use Honduras as their base. Washington would not accept the terms, so in September, the Hondurans refused to allow the incoming class of Salvadoran RMTC trainees into the country. Training the Salvadorans was the only reason that Washington had opened the center in the first place, so in June 1985, the RMTC was closed.

The Hondurans never carried through on their threat to throw the contras out, although General López restricted their area of operations along the border. At various times in 1985 and 1986, the Hondurans held up shipments of arms to the contras in hopes of extracting new concessions from Washington, but they always reopened the spigot once they had struck the best deal possible.

The Quiet American

In early 1984, while Casey and McFarlane were raising money for the contras from foreign countries and private donors, they were also making plans to move the management of the war under deeper cover if Congress cut off U.S. funding. In March, McFarlane suggested that a member of the NSC staff meet with the CIA officers running the war to begin familiarizing himself with the operation. Casey agreed.[79] For this difficult and sensitive task, McFarlane chose an aide whom he described as "like a son" to him—Lieutenant Colonel Oliver L. North.[80]

Oliver North grew up in small-town America, the son of a prominent local businessman in Philmont, New York. His parents were patriotic, God-fearing people who passed their conservative values along to young Larry, as North was known then. North was a model young man—both an altar boy and a Boy Scout. He often wore a sports coat and tie to high school, and his classmates voted him the "nicest looking and most courteous" member of the class of 1961.[81] Neither a great student nor a great athlete, North succeeded by dint of gritty determination rather than exceptional talent. A charmer with a winning smile, he also displayed a tendency to curry favor with those in authority.

After a year at the State University of New York at Brockport, North found his calling during a summer training program at the Marine base in Quantico, Virginia. The following year, he won appointment to the Naval Academy at Annapolis. The strict hierarchy and orderliness of the military suited North perfectly. "I loved being in an environment where everybody got up in the morning headed in the same direction," North wrote later.[82]

North absorbed the ethos of the Naval Academy, including the can-do attitude expressed in the pamphlet, "A Message to García," distributed to all incoming students. During the Spanish-American War (1898), President William McKinley dispatched a naval officer to Cuba with a message for Cuban general Calixto García, who was also fighting the Spanish. Without even knowing who García was, the officer set out across the Cuban wilderness through hostile territory and delivered the message. Mission accomplished, no questions asked.[83]

Halfway through North's plebe year, a near-fatal automobile accident left him with severe back and leg injuries that normally would have prevented him from returning to Annapolis or joining the armed forces. But North refused to let the injuries kill his dream of becoming a Marine. He talked his way back into Annapolis, even though he had to repeat his first year. He took up boxing, made it to the academy finals, and then won the championship by narrowly defeating his heavily favored opponent. "Ollie," said classmate Keith Haines, "was the original Rocky."[84]

Despite his all-American image, North was not above breaking the rules to get what he wanted. To be sure that the Marines would accept him despite his residual injuries from the auto accident, North reportedly broke into the academy administration building to remove the medical records from his file.[85] North also had a habit of developing father-son relationships with authority figures, beginning with the academy's boxing coach and later with his commanding officers. "We always felt he was overrated, but his superiors always seemed to like him," said an officer who served with North. "He was a pretty good apple-polisher."[86]

From Annapolis, North went to Vietnam to command an infantry platoon. By all accounts, he was a fine combat officer who looked out for his men and inspired strong loyalty from them. Wounded several times, he won a Silver Star, a Bronze Star, and two Purple Hearts.[87]

Back in the United States in 1974, North suffered a mental breakdown when his wife, Betsy, told him she wanted a divorce because he was more married to the Marine Corps than to her. According to one account, a former commander found North "babbling incoherently and running around naked, waving a .45 pistol" and threatening to kill himself. North was hospitalized for ten days for "delayed battle stress," but the commander reportedly had the hospitalization expunged from North's service record so as not to damage his career.[88]

Released from the hospital, North was assigned a staff job in the Manpower Division at Marine headquarters in Washington. There, North developed a reputation for getting things done by bending the rules—misrepresenting the instructions of his superiors and sometimes invoking their authority without their permission. His briefings were not balanced presentations on an issue, but slanted efforts at salesmanship.[89]

In August 1981, North won a plum assignment to serve a stint on the staff of the National Security Council. North worked on a variety of military issues, but during 1982 he came to focus more and more of his attention on Central America, assisting Roger Fontaine, the NSC senior staff aide for Latin America. In 1983, North took on a more prominent role, often attending inter-agency meetings on Fontaine's behalf. North also developed a polished briefing on Central America that he gave to groups assembled by Faith Ryan Whittlesey's White House public liaison operation. "He was universally viewed as our star briefer on the subject," said one of Whittlesey's aides.[90]

When Fontaine left the White House in 1983, North became the top Latin American staff aide by default (a position he later shared with Constantine Menges, who moved to the NSC staff from the CIA in late 1983). Although he had no expertise or experience in Latin America and didn't speak Spanish, North was assigned as the NSC's liaison to the Kissinger Commission. On the commission's trip through Central America, North jokingly referred to himself as "the advance man for the U.S. invasion."[91]

North gained status when his mentor, Robert McFarlane, replaced William Clark as national security adviser in October 1983. At year's end, he accompanied Vice President George Bush on his trip to El Salvador to demand a reduction in death squad violence as the price of increased U.S. military aid.[92]

North's ignorance about Latin America produced some amusing moments. Once, while briefing NBC News anchor Tom Brokaw, North showed Brokaw aerial reconnaissance photographs of Nicaragua and pointed out a baseball field. "The interesting thing here is the baseball diamond," North said knowingly. "Nicaraguans don't play baseball. Cubans play baseball." Brokaw thought North was kidding; baseball had been Nicaragua's national pastime ever since the U.S. Marines occupied the country in the early twentieth century. But North was serious.[93]

North's understanding of the foreign policy process was unencumbered by nuance. He was a Marine, working on the president's staff. The president was the commander-in-chief. Whatever the commander-in-chief wanted done, North would do it, no questions asked. If there was a modern-day Message to Garcia, North would carry it, overcoming any obstacle, including Congress, to accomplish his mission. "This lieutenant colonel is not going to challenge a decision of the commander-in-chief," he said, explaining his attitude. "If the commander-in-chief tells this lieutenant colonel to go stand in the corner and sit on his head, I will do so."[94]

At the NSC, North developed a reputation for hyperbole, usually in the service of his own image. "Ollie was about 30 to 50 percent bullshit," a White House colleague said later. "He was notorious for constantly exaggerating his role in things." He doctored his résumé, claiming that he had been engaged in Special Operations in Vietnam and had later been a Special Operations instructor when in fact he had done neither.[95] In 1985, testifying under oath as a character witness for an NSC colleague accused of fraud, North lied shamelessly about his background, claiming to have been a Special Forces company commander in Vietnam (he was a regular infantry platoon commander) and to have been a premedical student at the University of Rochester before attending Annapolis (he was a freshman at the State University of New York).[96]

North bragged to people outside the White House about how close he was to President Reagan and how he met privately with the president in both the Oval Office and Reagan's living quarters, sometimes praying with him. He made up a story about flying combat missions in El Salvador when he didn't even know how to fly a plane. He claimed he accompanied Secretary of State Alexander Haig in 1982 on his shuttle diplomacy to avert the Falklands/Malvinas war. And he claimed that in 1986, he called the president of Costa Rica on the telephone and read him the riot act for not being steadfast enough in support of the contras. None of it was true.[97] "I never took anything he said at face value," said CIA Central America Task Force chief Alan Fiers, "because I knew that he was bombastic and embellished the record, and threw curves, speedballs, and spitballs to get what he wanted."[98]

North also liked to play the martyr. He relished telling people that he worked twelve and sixteen hours a day, rarely saw his family, and hardly ever got a good night's sleep. Even when giving mundane background briefings, he insisted that his name not be used because he would be in personal danger if the Cubans and Soviets identified him. "He thought there was a KGB plot to discredit him, publicize him, ruin him," recalled colleague Neil Livingstone. When North's dog died of natural causes, he told everyone it had been poisoned by leftists.[99]

It was not entirely clear if North actually believed these delusions of grandeur, or if they were just ploys to persuade others of his importance. "He had a great deal of difficulty distinguishing between truth and fantasy," wrote NSC consultant Michael Ledeen, who worked with North on the arms sales to Iran. "He misled himself as effectively as he dazzled his audience."[100] Jacqueline Tillman, a former aide to Jeane Kirkpatrick, warned a colleague that North should not be on the NSC staff. "I've concluded that not only is he a liar, but he's delusional, power-hungry, and a danger to the president and the country," she said.[101]

"Ollie North. God, the man could speak a blue haze of bullshit," recalled the CIA's National Intelligence Officer for Latin America John Horton. "And at times, I was convinced he was mad."[102]

Body and Soul

In early 1984, McFarlane told North that the president wanted him to hold the contras together "body and soul" until Reagan could win new funding from Congress. That, as North later described his assignment, meant "to keep them together as a viable political opposition, to keep them alive in the field, to bridge the time between . . . when we would have no money and the time when Congress would vote again."[103]

Shortly after McFarlane assigned him to look after the contras, North traveled to Tegucigalpa, Honduras, with Dewey Clarridge, then chief of the Latin American division in the CIA's Operations Directorate and the architect of the Nicaraguan operation. Clarridge, dressed in a crisp safari jacket, introduced North, in combat fatigues, to the assembled contra leaders. "If something happens in Congress, we will have an alternative way," Clarridge promised them, "and to assure that, here is Colonel North. You will never be abandoned. . . . Colonel North will take charge if need be."[104]

"Our goals and yours are the same," North told the contras. "Like you, we want to see a democratic Nicaragua. Although the Congress has cut off the CIA, President Reagan wants you to know that we will find a way to help you. I can promise you that you will not be abandoned."[105]

Over the next few months, as appropriated funds for the war ran out, North assembled the essential pieces of a contra support operation that he could coordinate out of the NSC. In April, he recruited a young conservative activist, Rob Owen, as his aide-de-camp. Owen operated as North's courier, carrying military intelligence, munitions lists, cash, and letters back and forth between North and his various collaborators in Central America.[106] North himself could not travel to the region often enough to run a war without attracting undue attention from the press. "Exercise absolute stealth," McFarlane warned North on the eve of one trip to confer with Adolfo Calero about the FDN's logistical problems.[107] Owen, however, was nondescript—just another one of the many young North Americans rummaging around in Central America looking for adventure.

North also needed an arms dealer. At Casey's suggestion, he called Richard Secord, the retired air force general who had handled Operation Tipped Kettle.[108] Secord had spent most of his military career in special operations. He spent a tour flying combat missions in South Vietnam in the early 1960s before being sent to help manage the CIA's secret war in Laos, mounting covert air missions into North Vietnam. In 1973, Secord was assigned to the Defense Security Assistance Agency and then went to Iran as head of the U.S. Air Force military advisory group. After the Shah was overthrown, Secord was appointed deputy commander of a second hostage rescue mission, Operation Honey Badger, which was never launched. In planning for the mission, Secord helped create some of the Pentagon's "black" special operations units, including the Intelligence Support Activity, that would later be deployed in Central America. Like many special operations officers, Secord was contemptuous of normal rules and procedures. "The unconventional warfare instrument of national policy is so important," he wrote in his master's thesis at the Naval War College, "that bureaucratic obstacles should be dismissed out of hand."[109]

In 1981, Secord became the first military officer ever named deputy assistant secretary of defense for the Middle East. From there, however, his promising career hit a brick wall. While in Teheran, Secord had become acquainted with Edwin P. Wilson, a former CIA contract employee who was later convicted of shipping munitions to Libyan leader Muammar el-Qaddafi. During its investigation of Wilson, the FBI also examined whether Secord had profited from the Libyan deal. Wilson himself implicated Secord in another scheme, claiming Secord was a "silent partner" in a private arms export company that was convicted of overcharging the Pentagon for military sales to Egypt.

In neither case was Secord ever charged with any wrongdoing, but he was passed over for promotion to three-star general in 1983. Bitter and convinced that his career was finished, he retired and opened a private consulting firm.[110] Secord did not sever all ties with the Pentagon, however. He remained a consultant to the Intelligence Support Activity and a member of the Pentagon's Special Operations Policy Advisory Group, a high-level panel tasked with developing the new doctrine of Low Intensity Warfare.[111]

When North approached him in July 1984, Secord agreed to buy arms for the contras and ship them to Central America using a front company. Adolfo Calero would place an order with Secord, who would buy the arms in Europe and have them shipped to either Honduras or El Salvador, where the contras had storage facilities. Calero paid Secord with the money from Saudi Arabia, which was being deposited in Calero's bank account in the Cayman Islands.

North and McFarlane obtained the necessary end-user certificates from Guatemala and Honduras. In all, Calero paid Secord $11 million between December 1984 and July 1985.[112] Secord and his business partner Albert Hakim were not providing their services pro bono (though Calero thought they were); their profit margin on the weapons averaged 38 percent.[113]

North diligently reported all these activities to both Casey and McFarlane. Sometimes McFarlane vetoed North's wilder ideas, trying to guide and season the young Marine. Casey, on the other hand, appeared less emotionally involved. He ran North like a case officer running an agent in the field, giving North advice and receiving reports from him, yet all the while remaining at arm's length from the operation, preserving the CIA's deniability in case the operation was ever blown.[114]

Building the Enterprise

In mid-1985, several motives led Casey and North to reorganize the contra resupply effort into what came to be known as "the Enterprise." One was the contras' incompetence. Despite North's efforts, by the summer of 1985, the contras' logistical system was breaking down. They had used almost all the Saudi money to purchase arms, without setting aside enough to finance deliveries to the front.[115] The backlog was so bad that the warehouse at the contras' main supply depot at El Salvador's Ilopango air base couldn't hold all the arms that Secord's company was delivering. "When the agency [CIA] was pulled out of this program, these guys didn't know how to buy a Band-Aid. They knew nothing of logistics, the CIA had been doing all that," said a U.S. official. The contras, Secord said, lacked the "unglamorous . . . sinews of war."[116]

North was also unhappy about the FDN's unwillingness to share its supplies with rebels trying to establish a "southern front" along the Nicaraguan border with Costa Rica.[117] Elementary military strategy dictated that forcing the Sandinistas to divide their troops between two fronts would benefit all the rebels, but the passion of the contras' internecine rivalries outweighed all logic. In addition, Rob Owen had reported to North his suspicion that some of the Saudi money was being siphoned off through corruption. "In the past it has been too easy to sell goods and too many people have learned how to make a good living off the war," Owen wrote to North on April 1, 1985.[118]

On July 1, North and Secord met Calero and contra military commander Colonel Enrique Bermúdez in Miami to review the state of the war. North was very critical of the contras' performance. The Nicaraguans were insulted, but in the end, everyone agreed they needed an airlift capability to drop supplies to contra forces inside Nicaragua.

North turned to Secord to organize it. Rather than continue channeling funds to the contras, North and Secord decided to take full control of the operation themselves by redirecting the Saudi money straight to Secord and Hakim. That way, the FDN could not steal it, waste it, or withhold it from rebels in the south. Secord, always the cold professional, dubbed the resulting network of companies "the Enterprise." North, more effusive, called it "Project Democracy."[119]

The Enterprise's first mission was to create an air resupply operation for the contras, which required planes, crews, an air base, and an emergency backup airfield. To provide the planes and crews, Secord enlisted retired air force colonel Richard Gadd. Like Secord, Gadd had made his career in special operations, retiring in 1982 to form a private company that provided covert transport facilities to the Pentagon's special operations. It was Gadd who procured the planes and helicopters used for the Central American operations by Seaspray, Yellow Fruit, and the Intelligence Support Activity. When North first recruited Secord to buy arms for the contras in 1984, Secord hired Gadd to ship them.[120] For the contra resupply operation, Gadd recruited about twenty people, including pilots, cargo handlers, and maintenance crews, most of them veterans of Air America, the CIA-owned airline that operated in Southeast Asia during the Vietnam War. The Enterprise eventually bought five planes of its own and leased others when necessary from Southern Air Transport, a private company that had been CIA-owned from 1960 to 1973 and that continued to do contract work for the Agency.[121]

The Enterprise needed a main base from which to operate, and the Salvadoran air force base at Ilopango was ideal. The contras already had a working relationship with the Salvadoran military, which let them fly arms shipments into Ilopango and store them there until they could be flown to forward supply bases in Honduras.[122] In September 1985, North wrote to Felix Rodriguez to ask for his help in getting permission for the Enterprise to use Ilopango as its main operational base—storing and servicing its planes, housing its pilots, and stockpiling its supplies.[123]

Felix Rodriguez was a Cuban exile who fought at the Bay of Pigs in 1961 and then worked for the CIA in Latin America and Southeast Asia. He was an adviser to the Bolivian Rangers who captured and killed Cuban revolutionary hero Ernesto "Che" Guevara in 1967. In the 1970s, he served in Vietnam under CIA officers Rudy Enders and Donald Gregg, who later became Vice President George Bush's national security adviser. While in Vietnam, Rodriguez devised a rapid response helicopter tactic for combating guerrillas.[124] Shot down several times and badly injured, Rodriguez retired from the CIA, but not from his lifelong vocation as an anti-Communist.

In the 1980s, the front line of the struggle against Communism was in

Central America. Early in the decade, Rodriguez helped raise money for the contras from private donations and shipped them nonmilitary supplies. In 1983, Rodriguez called on his old friend Donald Gregg at the White House, asking Gregg to get him into Central America to carry on his private war.[125] With Gregg's introduction, Rodriguez was able to meet with every senior administration official who dealt with the region: North at the NSC, Nestor Sanchez at the Pentagon, General Gorman at South-Com, Tony Motley at the State Department, and Ambassador Thomas Pickering in El Salvador. He even had a brief meeting with Vice President George Bush. Despite Pickering's and Gorman's displeasure at being saddled with an unpredictable and uncontrollable "no-pay mercenary," Rodriguez's White House connections landed him a position advising the Salvadoran air force and flying helicopter missions out of Ilopango. He became a close adviser to Salvadoran air force commander General Juan Raphael Bustillo, one of the most right-wing officers in the Salvadoran military and a supporter of Roberto D'Aubuisson.[126]

When Oliver North needed someone to negotiate with the Salvadoran military over the use of Ilopango for the Enterprise, he turned to Felix Rodriguez. Rodriguez was glad to help. Not only did he arrange for use of the base, but he also served as a conduit for contra payoffs to General Bustillo, and he acted as unofficial liaison between the Enterprise's air crews and the Salvadorans.[127]

Secord had two other Bay of Pigs veterans working for him on the ground in El Salvador: Raphael Quintero and Luis Posada Carriles. When North first asked Secord to help the contras buy arms, Secord brought in Quintero, a former CIA officer, because, as Secord put it, "I am not a Latin American expert."[128] In fact, Secord had never even been to Central America. Quintero, like Secord, was an acquaintance of arms dealer Edwin Wilson. In 1983, Quintero testified in court that Wilson paid him a $30,000 advance on a $1 million contract to assassinate a Libyan dissident living in Egypt. Quintero later backed out of the deal.

Luis Posada also worked for the CIA after the Bay of Pigs, handling logistics and demolitions on commando raids into Cuba between 1961 and 1967. But Posada's secret war against Castro did not end when the CIA's did. In 1976, he was arrested in Venezuela for blowing up a Cubana airline passenger plane, killing all seventy-three people aboard. After nine years in a Venezuelan prison, he escaped in August 1985 and showed up in El Salvador shortly thereafter. Under the alias "Ramón Medina," he handled administrative affairs for the Enterprise, setting up safe houses, arranging ground transportation, and paying the air crews' living expenses.[129]

The Enterprise's operation at Ilopango was aided by the good offices of Colonel James J. Steele, commander of the U.S. Military Group in El Salvador.

Steele and his subordinates helped smooth relations with the Salvadoran military, authorized refueling and maintenance of the Enterprise planes by the Salvadoran air force, provided intelligence on Sandinista air defenses, and helped Enterprise pilots plot their courses. When new crew members arrived in San Salvador, they were given the name of Steele's deputy, Lieutenant Colonel David H. Rankin, as a contact if they needed help. According to Secord, all of this was done with the knowledge and approval of Pickering's successor, U.S. Ambassador Edwin G. Corr. The CIA station chief in El Salvador refused to have anything to do with this scheme, believing that it violated the Boland amendment.[130]

Gadd provided the planes and crews; Rodriguez and Steele handled liaison with the Salvadorans. But the Enterprise still needed an emergency landing strip and refueling base in Costa Rica so it could fly supplies to the contras fighting on the southern front. In July 1985, Lewis A. Tambs, one of the authors of the 1980 Santa Fe report, was appointed ambassador to Costa Rica. "Before I went," Tambs recounted, "Ollie said when you get down there you should open the southern front"—an order that Tambs said was confirmed by Assistant Secretary of State Elliott Abrams and Alan Fiers, head of the CIA's Central American Task Force. Tambs took these marching orders to heart. When he arrived in San José, he brought together the embassy's senior officers and, according to CIA Station Chief Joe Fernandez, told them he "really had only one mission in Costa Rica, and that was to form a Nicaraguan resistance southern front."[131]

Fernandez, who went by the pseudonym Tomás Castillo, was the key to Tambs's plans. A native Spanish speaker, Fernandez had spent most of his decade-long career with the CIA in Latin America. Operating out of Washington as the Agency's chief liaison with the contras between 1981 and 1984, he had recruited the FDN's leadership and helped them stage their inaugural press conference in 1982. He had presided at meetings of the contra leadership, mediated their internal disputes, and purged the FDN's ranks of some notorious National Guard officers. He had carried suitcases full of cash to Honduras and handed out stacks of $100 bills to pay the contra leaders their "family expense" money, meticulously collecting signed receipts for every dollar. Unlike his derring-do boss, Dewey Clarridge, Fernandez was "an organization man," recalled contra leader Edgar Chamorro—not the sort to strike off wildly on his own. But Fernandez was a hard-liner who did not believe that any accommodation with the Sandinistas was possible. "They're Communists," he told Chamorro. "They're evil."[132]

When the scandal over the CIA's "murder manual" exploded in October 1984, Fernandez was one of the officials reprimanded. After that, he was sent as station chief to Costa Rica, where he developed a close working relationship with Costa Rican security chief Benjamín Piza. Through Piza, Fernandez was able to maintain President Luis Alberto Monge's cooperation in allowing contras to operate from Costa Rican territory. Washington was so grateful to Piza that he and his wife were granted a brief audience and picture-taking ceremony with Ronald Reagan.[133]

Fernandez became the link between North and Tambs. Whenever Tambs wanted to communicate with Washington about the southern front, he cabled through the "back channel"—that is, through the CIA rather than through the Department of State, so that only North, Abrams, and Fiers would get the cables. North, in turn, communicated directly with Fernandez.[134]

When the Enterprise needed to build an airstrip in Costa Rica as an emergency landing field for the resupply flights, North instructed Tambs to negotiate an arrangement with the Costa Ricans. Tambs got the Costa Ricans to agree, on the condition that planes would land there only after their missions, so that they would be empty while on Costa Rican soil. In this way, Costa Rica could preserve the fiction of its neutrality.[135] The land was purchased by one of Secord's front companies, and by April 1986 the airstrip was operational.

Once the Enterprise's resupply flights were under way in February 1986, Fernandez regularly cabled Washington for intelligence and weather information, which he then passed along to the Enterprise. He also collected information on what supplies the contras on the southern front needed and passed that intelligence back to Washington. To avoid any appearance of violating the Boland amendment, Fernandez and other CIA officers in the San José embassy worked out a charade. They would meet with contra military commanders, but instruct them that they must not ask directly for any equipment. By late 1985, intelligence sharing with the contras had become legal once again, so the contras simply described their needs, the information was passed along, and, lo and behold, the supplies appeared. "You wouldn't believe how much you can do under the heading of intelligence sharing," marveled one contra leader.[136]

This, then, was the infrastructure that North and Secord built for their Enterprise: five planes and crews assembled and managed by former military officers recently retired from Pentagon special operations; a main base at Ilopango airfield in El Salvador, coordinated by the U.S. Military Group and three Cuban-American CIA veterans; an emergency airfield in Costa Rica arranged by the U.S. ambassador; and an intelligence clearinghouse run by the CIA station chief in San José. To tie the network together while at the same time maintaining its secrecy, North, at Casey and Poindexter's suggestion, requisitioned highly secret KL-43 encryption devices from the National Security Agency to scramble telephone communications. He sent them to Secord,

Gadd, Steele, Fernandez, William J. Cooper (one of the operation's chief pilots operating out of Ilopango), and Southern Air Transport (which was leasing planes and crews to Secord), even though most of the recipients did not have the requisite security clearances to handle the sensitive technology. No one at the National Security Agency seemed to think it was odd that a lieutenant colonel on the NSC staff would need such equipment.[137]

A Neat Idea

In early 1986, North hit upon a new way to raise money for the contras. A few months earlier, McFarlane had brought North into the developing U.S. policy of trading arms for hostages with Iran. With U.S. approval, Israel had already sold the Iranians antitank missiles in exchange for an Iranian pledge to release American hostages and a U.S. pledge to replenish Israel's arms stocks. North was assigned to arrange the replenishment and to facilitate a shipment of antiaircraft missiles from Israel to Iran. He enlisted Secord's help to move the missiles. To defray Secord's expenses, Israel paid $1 million to one of Secord's companies, of which only $150,000 was spent on the arms sale. With Israel's permission, North and Secord used the rest for the contras.[138]

North realized that the arms-for-hostages operation could become an on-going source of "residuals"—profits—to finance not only the contras, but a whole series of "off the books" covert operations that would not depend on appropriated funds and therefore could be run without notifying Congress. He saw nothing improper in this scheme. "I don't think it was wrong," he testified. "I think it was a neat idea."[139]

In January 1986, North proposed that future arms sales to Iran be made directly from U.S. weapons stocks (thus avoiding the problem of replenishing Israeli supplies) and that they be arranged through Secord. The administration would sell the weapons to Secord, who would then sell them to the Iranians at inflated prices. Profits from the sales would create a "reserve fund" for extralegal covert operations. On January 17, 1986, President Reagan signed a presidential finding approving this reorganization of the arms sale operation, though he subsequently denied knowing that it was intended to generate profits that could be diverted to the contras.[140]

North was not operating outside channels. He dutifully sought Poindexter's permission for the diversion and after a few minutes' thought, Poindexter approved it. He regarded the diversion as simply the logical extension of existing policy, no different in principal than NSC efforts to keep the contras alive by soliciting help from third countries or private donors.[141]

CIA Director Casey was also "very enthusiastic" about the plan, North recalled. He savored the irony of using the Ayatollah's money to overthrow the

Sandinistas, calling it "the ultimate covert operation."[142] Casey was especially interested in developing a permanent "off-the-shelf" mechanism for running covert operations without congressional scrutiny. The need for such a capability was something Casey discussed frequently, according to North. "Director Casey had in mind, as I understood it, an overseas entity that was capable of conducting operations or activities of assistance to U.S. foreign policy goals, that was a stand-alone [entity] . . . self-financing, independent of appropriated monies and capable of conducting activities similar to the ones that we had conducted here."[143]

In ten months, arms sales to Iran produced $16.1 million in profits, of which $3.8 million were spent on the contra war. The generation of profits that could be diverted to the contras and other covert operations was so important to North and Poindexter that it became one of their chief motivations for continuing the arms sales to Iran, even though the policy was not very successful in winning the release of American hostages.[144]

North called the diversion "the deepest darkest secret" of the whole contra support operation, "the secret within a secret."[145] Yet for such a deep secret, North had trouble keeping it to himself. Not only did he tell Casey (though Poindexter had told him to stop briefing Casey on his operations), but he also told McFarlane (who had retired from the government) and CIA Central American Task Force Chief Alan Fiers, for no apparent reason other than to brag about it. It was a neat idea, alright, and North was proud of it.

CHAPTER 18

Getting Back in the Game

As the second Reagan administration began, Nicaragua stood at the top of the president's foreign policy agenda. With donations of arms and money from U.S. allies, the contras managed to survive after CIA funds ran out in 1984. But private funding was not a long-term substitute for the backing of the United States. By the end of 1984, the contras' military fortunes had begun to deteriorate. Most contra combatants had withdrawn to their base camps in Honduras; those who remained inside Nicaragua were being pushed back toward the border by the Sandinista army. The Hondurans' discomfort at hosting the contras continued to mount, and they hinted that unless Washington recommitted itself to the contra army soon, they might forcibly disperse it.

It was urgent, therefore, that the United States "get back in the game," as one White House aide put it.[1] That meant convincing Congress to lift the Boland prohibition and release the $14 million set aside for the contras just before the 1984 election. Under the 1984 law, a majority vote in both houses of Congress was required to free the funds. That would be an uphill fight. Despite his landslide reelection, Reagan's coattails were shorter in 1984 than they had been four years earlier. A majority of the Senate still favored contra aid despite the loss of two Republican seats, but the fourteen seats the Republicans gained in the House were not enough to overcome the Democratic majority against aid..

Some administration officials were reluctant to begin the new term with a bruising and probably losing battle over Nicaragua, but there was no other way to save the policy.[2] In a strategy meeting on March 8, 1985, administration officials resolved that President Reagan himself would have to draw "a line in the dust." "Our fundamental approach," a senior State Department official explained, "is going to be to hype this issue as much as we can to make Congress accountable for their votes."[3]

Testifying before Michael Barnes's House Subcommittee on Western Hemisphere Affairs in January 1985, Assistant Secretary of State Tony Motley struck a combative stance. Reagan's critics, he said, as he looked up at the panel that included some of the most vocal ones, "were wrong about El Salvador, wrong about Grenada and they are wrong about Nicaragua—and for the same reasons." Pressure had to be maintained to get the Sandinistas to bargain seriously, he insisted. "People and nations do not move to the negotiating table simply because it's a nice piece of furniture."[4]

Secretary of State George Shultz was even tougher during testimony to the House Foreign Affairs Committee in February. The Sandinistas were "a bad news government," he said, and Washington had a "moral duty" to help the contras. "I see no reason why we should slam the door on people just because they have been taken behind the Iron Curtain."[5] A few days later, in a major address to the Commonwealth Club in San Francisco, Shultz declared that lasting peace in Central America would be impossible unless the Nicaraguan government was forced to change. "Those who would cut off these freedom fighters," he said in defense of the contras, ". . . are in effect consigning Nicaragua to the endless darkness of Communist tyranny."[6]

Shultz and Motley were merely supporting players in the campaign scripted by the White House. Ronald Reagan was cast in the lead, taking a more aggressive role in promoting contra aid than ever before. In his State of the Union speech on February 6, 1985, no foreign adversary was reviled as savagely as Nicaragua.[7] On February 16, in the first of several weekly radio addresses devoted to the contra cause, Reagan called the Sandinistas "a Marxist-Leninist clique that broke the hearts of the freedom-loving people of their country by imposing a brutal dictatorship." Not only were they "a satellite of the Soviet Union and Cuba," but they were also "exporting drugs to poison our youth and linking up with the terrorists of Iran, Libya, the Red Brigades and the PLO." Only "our brothers," the contras, could stop them.[8]

On February 21, 1985, the president made headlines when he finally admitted during a news conference that his aim in Nicaragua was not to interdict arms (as specified in the December 1981 presidential finding) or to pressure the Sandinistas into negotiations (as specified in the September 1983 finding), but to get rid of the Sandinista regime. Asked directly by Sam Donaldson of ABC News if the goal of U.S. policy was "to remove" the existing government, Reagan answered, "Well, remove in the sense of its present structure, in which it is a Communist totalitarian state, and it is not a government chosen by the people."

"Is the answer yes, then?" came the follow-up.

"Not if the present government would turn around and say, 'All right. . . . Uncle,'" Reagan explained. In response to another question, he elaborated: "You can say we're trying to oust the Sandinistas by what we're saying." When asked how this position squared with the Boland amendment's prohibition on seeking the overthrow of the Nicaraguan government, Reagan seemed to think that the law was merely a proposal still pending before Congress.[9]

Speaking in early March to his "old friends" at the twelfth annual convention of the Conservative Political Action Conference, Reagan made another emotional plea on behalf of the contras. "They are the moral equivalent of the Founding Fathers and the brave men and women of the French Resistance," he declared.[10]

The main purpose behind Reagan's tough talk was to "turn up the heat" on congressional Democrats by implying that a vote against contra aid was a vote against everything good and decent. "Members of Congress will have to stand up and be counted," warned a high White House official.[11] Naturally, the Democrats did not enjoy being pilloried as apologists for the Sandinistas' alleged Communism, terrorism, drug smuggling, and genocide.

Some administration officials were not pleased with the polarization that Reagan's harsh rhetoric produced. The Republicans, after all, were still the minority party in the House of Representatives, where the White House needed the Democrats' cooperation on a whole range of issues. "It's pretty hard to ask Democrats to go along with you on Tuesday when you have painted them as the party of surrender on Saturday," explained one official. Michael Deaver, in particular, worried about exposing the president on an issue that remained highly unpopular with the public and which seemed to be a loser.[12]

During Reagan's first term, Deaver would have had the support of Chief of Staff James Baker and Communications Director David Gergen, both of whom recoiled from involving the president any more than absolutely necessary in anything Central American. But Baker had traded jobs with Treasury Secretary Donald T. Regan, Gergen had been replaced by hard-liner Patrick Buchanan, and Deaver had announced he would also be leaving shortly. So much had the tenor of the staff changed that Ed Rollins, who was among the more conservative people in the White House during the first term, was now jokingly referred to as the "house liberal."

The first-term White House team had tried to protect Reagan from his wilder instincts, always with an eye to the polls and the prospects for reelection in 1984. With the team dispersed and reelection behind him, Reagan was free to be Reagan. "He's liberated, he wants to get into the fight," said a ranking White House aide.[13] And no issue pulled at Ronald Reagan's emotions more than the cause of the Nicaraguan contras. "He means it when he says he isn't going to lose a country to Communism on his watch," explained an administration official, "and he would like to see Nicaragua become a democracy again."[14] Never mind that Nicaragua under Somoza had never been much of a democracy.

The real force behind Reagan's tough rhetoric was Buchanan, who controlled the speechwriters and chaired an ad hoc White House working group to manage the contra aid campaign. Buchanan was the foremost representative of the Republican right on the White House staff. A staunch Catholic with a Jesuit high school and university education, Buchanan was an abrasive, fanatically conservative political street brawler. He was so far right, quipped Don Regan, that he gave "new meaning to the term 'hard-core.'" White House Press Secretary Larry Speakes called Buchanan "blindly reactionary."[15]

Buchanan's bombastic rhetoric was saturated with contempt for his opponents, especially civil rights advocates, feminists, and liberals. As a columnist for the small, conservative *St. Louis Globe-Democrat* in the 1960s, Buchanan published attacks on Martin Luther King based on derogatory information leaked to him by the FBI.[16] During his years as a speechwriter in the Nixon administration, he was best known for his attacks on his erstwhile profession; he wrote Vice President Spiro Agnew's 1969 speech accusing the media of being controlled by a "small and unelected elite" of East Coast liberals. After Nixon resigned, Buchanan returned to journalism and quickly became the most prominent conservative commentator on both radio and television. His commentaries betrayed a fondness for fascists. He described Spain's General Francisco Franco and Chile's General Augusto Pinochet approvingly as "soldier-patriots," and he insisted that Senator Joe McCarthy had been maligned by the liberal press.[17]

Like other administration hard-liners, Buchanan believed that Ronald Reagan was their ultimate weapon. Unleashed, his formidable communication skills would swing the American public behind the contra program, send the Congress scurrying for cover, and save the day. Buchanan wanted to flood the airwaves with Ronald Reagan in the weeks leading up to the congressional vote on contra aid, climaxing with a massive anti-Communist rally of Cuban-Americans at the Orange Bowl in Miami and a televised address to the nation.

For the time being, however, Deaver was still keeper of the presidential image. He blocked both the television address and the Orange Bowl rally and cut back the number of Reagan's speeches and appearances during the contra aid fight. Still, Buchanan's speechwriters wrote Reagan's lines, so they controlled the tenor of the debate. It was Buchanan who penned the line comparing the contras to America's founding fathers.[18]

Contra Atrocities

While the Reagan administration tried to focus attention on Nicaragua's military buildup and its ties to various U.S. enemies, opponents of contra aid were more interested in the character of the political movement that Reagan wanted to fund. The issue of contra human rights abuses came to the fore in early 1985 when several human rights groups issued reports on the subject just as the debate over contra aid went into full swing.

Stories of contra atrocities were not new; gruesome accounts of rape, torture, and murder had been filtering out of Nicaragua for well over a year. But because most contra attacks occurred in the remote, rugged regions along the Honduran border, journalists and human rights groups found it difficult to confirm the anecdotes.

The administration, however, knew from the start that the contras were murdering civilians. Just a few months after the contras' first major operation in 1982, the Defense Intelligence Agency reported that "insurgent incidents" over the preceding months included "the assassination of minor government officials."[19] In early 1984, CIA division chief for operations in Latin America Dewey Clarridge admitted to the House Intelligence Committee staff that the contras had killed "civilians and Sandinista officials in the provinces, as well as heads of cooperatives, nurses, doctors, and judges."[20]

Edgar Chamorro, a former member of the Nicaraguan Democratic Force's (FDN) directorate, was candid about it. "It was premeditated policy to terrorize noncombatants to prevent them from cooperating with the government," he acknowledged. "Hundreds of civilian murders, mutilations, tortures, and rapes were committed in pursuit of this policy, of which the contra leaders and their CIA superiors were well aware." Arturo Cruz, Washington's favorite contra leader, also admitted that contra forces in the field had committed "damnable atrocities."[21]

Some contra field commanders were unashamed of their behavior. Comandante Suicida (Commander Suicide, formerly National Guard sergeant Pedro Pablo Ortiz Centeno) bragged about leading assassination teams into Nicaragua in 1980 to murder Nicaraguan and Cuban teachers in the government's literacy campaign. After a bloody rampage in 1983, Suicide was arrested and executed by the contras' Argentine military advisers.[22]

In December 1984, a top contra field commander, José Efrén Mondragón Martínez, quit in part because the high command was unwilling to do anything to halt atrocities. "They are kidnapping and killing people who just want to work," said Mondragón in disgust. Interviewed in the field, rank-and-file contra troops readily admitted routinely executing captured Sandinista civilian officials, soldiers, and militia members.[23]

But contra commander Colonel Enrique Bermúdez and his civilian ally Adolfo Calero adamantly denied all the atrocity stories. Calero denounced such reports as an "orchestrated campaign to make resistance fighters appear as atrocious terrorists." Bermúdez insisted that the reports had been concocted by a "Sandinista propaganda machine."[24]

Three major reports dealing with contra human rights abuses were released in 1985. The most extensive, by Americas Watch, concluded that both the Sandinistas and the contras had been guilty of abuses against civilians, but noted "a sharp decline" in violations by the government after 1982. Contra violations, however, had continued unabated. Contra forces had "attacked civilians indiscriminately; . . . tortured and mutilated prisoners; . . . taken hostages; . . . and committed outrages against personal dignity," meaning rape. A report by the Lawyers Committee for International Human Rights found the contras guilty of "killings, beatings, and violent harassment of unarmed civilian noncombatants."[25]

By far the most controversial assessment was the so-called Brody report, based on the independent investigations of Reed Brody, a former New York assistant attorney general. At the suggestion of Paul Reichler, the Nicaraguan government's legal representative in the United States, Brody had undertaken an investigation of contra abuses applying evidentiary standards appropriate for a court of law. In four months, Brody gathered 145 sworn affidavits from eyewitnesses to twenty-eight incidents of contra human rights violations. The Nicaraguan government cooperated with his investigation, providing temporary housing, office space, occasional transportation, and some clerical assistance—all of which Brody acknowledged in his final report.[26]

Brody found "a distinct pattern" of contra human rights abuses involving "attacks on purely civilian targets . . . premeditated acts of brutality, including rape, beatings, mutilation and torture . . . individual and mass kidnappings . . . [and] assaults on economic and social targets." Excerpts from the affidavits were gruesome.[27]

Once his report had been completed, Brody sought to enlist the help of two well-known human rights groups, the Washington Office on Latin America and the International Human Rights Law Group, to distribute it. Since neither group knew Brody, they commissioned an independent investigation to verify his work. Two lawyers with established reputations in human rights and international law conducted several dozen interviews in Nicaragua, ten of them with people interviewed by Brody. They found that his affidavits in those cases were accurate, and their new interviews substantiated Brody's basic conclusions. Three other spot checks were conducted on Brody's affidavits by Americas Watch, CBS News, and the *New York Times*. All confirmed the accuracy of his research.[28]

Administration officials privately conceded that the reports of contra atrocities were true, while discounting their importance. "It seems to be what you would expect to have in a war," offered one State Department official. But not all the contras' actions were so easily dismissed. "The contras have a tendency to kidnap young girls," admitted a senior government official who followed intelligence reports on contra activities. In fact, the sexual abuse of women captives and even female contra combatants was epidemic in contra base camps.[29]

Publicly, however, the State Department stonewalled, refusing to acknowledge that contra human rights abuses were a serious problem. "We have no firm knowledge of what's going on in the field," claimed one State Department official, adding that the intelligence community had not been assigned to collect that sort of information—the same excuse used when the administration pleaded ignorance about death squad violence in El Salvador during the early 1980s.[30] In fact, the CIA knew perfectly well what was going on from the extensive network of spies it had recruited within the ranks of the contras.[31]

The Brody report was especially troublesome because it contained so many heartrending stories expressed in the victims' own words. It was also the most vulnerable to attack, because it originated from a suggestion by the Nicaraguan government's lawyer. As soon as Brody's report was issued, the administration denounced it as "bought and paid for by the Sandinistas."[32]

Reagan himself excoriated the report on "so-called atrocities" by the contras. Opposition to his Nicaragua policy in general was the result of the Sandinistas and their "misguided sympathizers" in the United States "running a sophisticated disinformation campaign of lies and distortion."[33] Reagan described the enemy as ten feet tall. "We've been subjected in this country to a very sophisticated lobbying campaign by a totalitarian government, the Sandinistas," he said in an interview on April 1, 1985. "There has been a disinformation program that is virtually worldwide, and we know that the Cubans and the Soviets have such a disinformation network that is beyond anything that we can match."[34] Journalists never pressed Reagan for any evidence of this vast conspiracy. Few of them took his complaint seriously. The idea that Reagan's opponents could outmatch his ability to get his message on Nicaragua out to the American people was, on the face of it, absurd.

By far the most dramatic and horrifying evidence of contra atrocities came not from opponents of the contras but from a fervent supporter. And it came not in the form of debatable testimony, but on film. Frank Wohl, a Northwestern University student, Marine ROTC graduate, and self-described anti-Communist activist (nicknamed "Killer Rat"), was traveling with a contra patrol in Nicaragua when they captured a civilian whom they accused of being an informer. They made the man dig a grave with his bare hands and lie down in it; then they slit his throat. Wohl captured the gruesome tableau in a series of color photographs, which he sold to *Newsweek* magazine for $15,000.[35]

The State Department's Office for Public Diplomacy tried to control the damage done by Wohl's photographs by implying that they were faked. The contras' uniforms looked too clean for guerrillas on patrol, Director Otto Reich argued.[36] At the White House, Oliver North charged that Wohl was actually a Sandinista sympathizer who had staged the photos. A Pentagon official claimed that the killers couldn't be contras because they were wearing combat boots; the contras usually went into battle barefoot, he said with a straight face. CIA officials insisted that the contras did not normally carry knives. In fact, almost any photograph of contra combatants showed that they had both boots and knives.[37] But such denials put Ronald Reagan's conscience to rest. When Speaker Tip O'Neill mentioned the *Newsweek* photos to Reagan as proof of the contras' atrocities, Reagan replied, "I saw that picture, and I'm told that after it was taken, the so-called victim got up and walked away."[38]

The contra leadership, the CIA, and the White House all knew that the photographs were real. Adolfo Calero himself had given Wohl permission to visit the FDN's base camps. After the story broke, both North and the CIA officers overseeing the contra operation demanded an investigation to find out who was responsible for letting Wohl go out on patrol and take such grisly pictures. There was no investigation of the murder.[39]

The debate over contra human rights abuses was so intense because it struck to the very heart of the administration's justification for the contra war. By 1985, administration officials were claiming that support for the contras was a moral imperative: the Sandinistas were evil Communists and the contras were honest democrats. But if the contras were raping and murdering innocent civilians in their quest for power, the moral rationale for backing them would be seriously deflated. "It makes the whole problem a lot more ambiguous," admitted contra supporter Senator Richard G. Lugar (R-Ind.), "because you're trying to find out which guys are wearing the white hats and which guys are wearing the black hats."[40]

An Apple with a Razor Blade

As the time drew near for Reagan to officially request that Congress release the $14 million in contra aid set aside in 1984, the White House still did not have the votes to win.[41] On April 4, 1985, therefore, Reagan announced a peace initiative to accompany his request: He called on the Sandinistas to accept a cease-fire and negotiations with the contras on the terms proposed a month earlier by the three top civilian contra leaders—Arturo Cruz, Alfonso Robelo, and Adolfo Calero (whom Oliver North referred to as the "Three A's")—in their "San José Declaration" of March 1. To give the Sandinistas an incentive to open talks with the contras, Reagan promised that for sixty days he would use the $14 million for only nonlethal aid. After that, however, if the Sandinistas refused to talk or if they were not bargaining in good faith, he would resume military aid.[42]

Reagan had just won a close vote in the House on the MX missile with exactly the same tactic. Contra aid, like the MX missile, was the stick necessary to bring our adversaries to the bargaining table, he argued. If Congress took away the stick, there could be no successful negotiations. "This is an idea we learned directly from the MX experience," explained a White House official. "Congress will not vote against ongoing negotiations."[43]

The peace proposal was a hoax. The San José Declaration had actually been written by Cruz, Calero, and Oliver North in North's Miami hotel room in February. "The only reason Calero agreed to sign was because the criteria established for the Sandinistas were, he knew, impossible for them to meet," North told National Security Adviser Robert McFarlane. "All agreed that the objective was . . . to galvanize the internal opposition and convince the U.S. Congress that the opposition was led by reasonable men."[44]

"Now if the Sandinistas turn this down," explained former White House communications director David Gergen, "the administration will be able to cast them as wearing the black hat, and that will enhance the prospects for passage [of contra aid]."[45]

Democrats were generally unimpressed by the ploy. Tip O'Neill called it a "dirty trick" aimed at "hoodwinking the American people." Reagan had done it, O'Neill insisted, only because he didn't have the votes to get his $14 million otherwise. Even Republican David Durenberger did not see the new plan as a relaxation of the administration's hard line. It was, he said, "an apple with a razor blade in it."[46]

The Sandinistas dismissed the proposal immediately. Foreign Minister Miguel D'Escoto denounced it as "not only ridiculous, but insolent . . . a gun pointed to our head." Asked if his government would negotiate with the contras as Reagan demanded, Vice President Sergio Ramírez replied, "Never, never, never."[47]

The credibility of Reagan's peace plan was also undercut by the administration itself in a classified report to Congress that outlined plans for a wider war. According to the 1984 law that fenced off the $14 million in contra aid, Reagan had to submit a report to Congress justifying his request for release of the money. The report spelled out three options for dealing with the Nicaraguan threat: "containment," which meant accepting a Communist Nicaragua and aiding neighboring states to inoculate them against Sandinista subversion; continued pressure to force the Sandinistas to change; or the "direct application of U.S. military force."

Containment, the report estimated, would cost four to five billion dollars annually—about four times the $1.2 billion Washington was already spending in the region. Moreover, it wouldn't work. "The flaws in the containment approach . . . would appear to dictate eventual success of Sandinista-inspired insurgency throughout the region," the report concluded.

Therefore, if contra aid was not resumed, the only available means for putting pressure on the Sandinistas would be lost, "placing us in an 'accommodationist-or-military response' dilemma at some later date." That is, the United States would have to send in the Marines. The unclassified version of the report did not say this explicitly; the classified version did. While the use of U.S. troops had been ruled out for the time being, the classified report said, it "must realistically be recognized as an eventual option, given our stakes in the region, if other policy alternatives fail."[48]

As the classified version of the report to Congress revealed, Reagan planned not just to continue the contra war, but to escalate it. The report envisioned doubling or tripling the size of the contra army to a force of between 25,000 and 35,000 men, making it larger than the regular Honduran army. The cost would run to $100 million annually, more than Washington's military aid program in Honduras and only slightly less than the program in El Salvador.[49]

The inconsistency between the expansion of the war proposed in the report and Reagan's peace plan produced a credibility gap. To close it, the administration set about collecting endorsements for the peace plan. A "key part" of the White House's lobbying strategy, according to a senior official, was to show "that Nicaragua's neighbors support the plan, so Congress should as well."[50] But the Contadora countries, in particular, all opposed contra aid. The administration was so anxious to demonstrate international support that it misrepresented their views, using their remarks approving a cease-fire to claim that they supported Reagan's whole policy. The Latin Americans were enormously un-happy with what one diplomat called the "manipulation" of their statements, and they said so privately.[51]

Normally, when the Contadora countries publicly criticized U.S. policy, the administration claimed that the public statements were belied by private ex-pressions of support. Now, when the Contadora governments were privately telling anyone who would listen that their public statements did not mean what the Reagan administration was pretending they meant, State Department officials insisted that the public remarks were "more authoritative" than any-thing said privately.[52]

The administration's public relations campaign seemed inexplicably gaffe-prone. On April 16, with the campaign in high gear, Reagan told a visiting group of U.S. religious leaders that Pope John Paul II had recently sent him a "verbal message . . . urging us to continue our efforts in Central America." Reagan expanded on the claim the following day, telling reporters that the pope had been "most supportive of all our activities in Central America," including military aid programs.[53]

Reagan apparently made up the pope's endorsement out of whole cloth. The administration tried to back away gracefully from the president's claim, but the Vatican could not let it stand. The next day it issued a statement saying, "There have been no . . . messages from the Holy Father" about Central America addressed to Ronald Reagan or anyone else in the United States government.[54]

On April 15, Reagan kicked off two weeks of intensive effort by attending a $250-a-plate Nicaraguan Refugee Fund dinner. His speech was a variation on his now-familiar broadside against the Sandinistas and the Democrats, ending with the shout, "Viva Nicaragua Libre!"[55] Then eight-year-old Patricia Guerra, who was introduced as an example of the sort of refugee child the fund was helping, presented Reagan with a gift. Reagan, always alert to a good photo opportunity, picked up Patricia and kissed her for the cameras. Despite the irony of Patricia's surname (*guerra* in Spanish means "war"), the picture of the president holding the little refugee girl was perfect.

But Patricia, it turned out, was not a refugee at all. Her parents were inter-national civil servants who had been living in the United States for over fifteen years. Her mother worked at the World Bank, her father at the Inter-American Development Bank. Patricia herself was born in Washington, D.C., and at-tended private school. The dinner's organizers insisted that it was all an inno-cent mistake.[56]

There was, however, a real refugee child in the audience, eleven-year-old Maritza Herrera, who had been wounded in Nicaragua two months before and never given proper medical care. By their own admission, her pro-contra sponsors in Washington were so busy shuttling her between press conferences and fund-raisers that almost a week went by before they could fit a doctor's appointment into her schedule. The doctor took one look at her shattered, infected, and withering arm and hospitalized her immediately.[57]

Responsibility for most of the events in the administration's elaborate public relations campaign fell to Oliver North at the NSC and to the Office of Public Diplomacy at the Department of State. They stage-managed visits to Washington by the "Three A's," contra field commanders, Sandinista defectors, Nicaraguan émigrés, European parliamentarians, and Central American businessmen. They coordinated activities with various conservative lobby groups and worked to get administration officials and their supporters on network television and radio. They ghostwrote articles and op-ed pieces for senior administration officials and others. The White House conducted market research, commissioning an opinion poll "to see what turns Americans against the Sandinistas," so administration spokesmen could "review and restate themes based on results."[58]

Even the contras' military plans were "timed to a vote at the end of April," North told McFarlane. To demonstrate their potency, the contras would endeavor to carry out "special operations against highly visible military targets in Nicaragua" on the eve of the congressional vote. They never managed it, although on March 6, 1985, British mercenaries hired by North did blow up an arms depot in Managua, doing extensive damage to a nearby hospital in the process—one of the few attacks against the Sandinistas in the capital city.[59]

The Dance of Legislation

Administration officials weren't the only ones lobbying Congress as the 1985 contra aid votes approached. Everyone saw the 1985 votes as a watershed, so lobbying by contra aid opponents was more intense than ever. "The pageantry involves computers and postcards, sit-ins and videotapes, clown shows and photos of bloody corpses, Nobel Laureates and Hollywood actors," wrote *Washington Post* reporter Joanne Omang. "Mountains of paper, thousands of speeches and probably millions of telephone calls."[60]

Twenty-eight church groups cooperating through the Inter-Religious Task Force on Central America mobilized their constituents across the country to make their voices heard in Congress. The churches were the most potent lobbyists, and virtually all the established denominations opposed contra aid—the National Council of Churches, United Methodists, American Friends Service Committee, Presbyterians, Mennonites, American Baptist Churches, United Church of Christ, the National Conference of Catholic Bishops, and assorted Catholic religious orders.[61] "Taking on the churches is really tough," admitted Tony Motley at the State Department. "We don't normally think of them as political opponents, so we don't know how to handle them. . . . They are really formidable."[62]

Various secular groups were also hard at work. The American Civil Liberties Union opposed contra aid because it opposed all covert action in principle. Common Cause joined the anti–contra aid effort, providing seasoned lobbyists, as did the Committee for a Sane Nuclear Policy. Opponents of contra aid rounded up twenty-six Nobel laureates, forty-six Rhodes scholars, and forty-eight Hollywood celebrities to sign letters to Congress. Veterans of the Abraham Lincoln Brigade raised money to buy ambulances for Nicaragua, and in California, someone protested Reagan's war by mining San Francisco Bay with two dozen fake mines made of beach balls and Styrofoam cups.[63] "Our resource," said Cindy Buhl, a staff member at the Coalition for a New Foreign and Military Policy, which helped coordinate the anti–contra aid effort, "was the pressure of masses of people."[64]

Before 1985, the opponents of contra aid had the field largely to themselves. Most conservative organizations were focused on domestic issues and had virtually no presence in the contra aid debates of 1982, 1983, and 1984. In 1985, however, the conservative movement discovered Nicaragua, in large part because of Reagan's proselytizing.

Citizens for Reagan, a 100,000-member group formed in 1981 to pressure Congress on behalf of Reagan's domestic policies, was the spearhead of the right's lobbying effort. Another group, Citizens for America, headed by failed New York gubernatorial candidate Lewis E. Lehrman, spent some $300,000 on advertising and lobbying.[65] Conservative activists built a mock Nicaraguan prison camp on the lawn of the Capitol. College Republicans launched an abortive fund-raising scheme, dubbed "Save the Contras," mimicking Save the Children poster campaigns. "Only 53 cents a day will support a Nicaraguan freedom fighter," the poster promised. The campaign was halted when Save the Children complained, but not before Oliver North got a copy of the poster to hang in his office.[66]

Some Miami-based contras dreamed up their own poster campaign. René Quiñones, a former lawyer for Somoza, produced an "I Love Nicaraguan Freedom Fighters" poster featuring "sultry María," a contra combatant holding an M-16 rifle and wearing a tank top. "She would be our Ramba," Quiñones remarked (referring to the 1985 hit movie *Rambo*), "representing Christ, sex appeal, and *la lucha* [the struggle]." As it turned out, María was actually a hotel receptionist in Miami who had entered the United States illegally after working with Miskito Indian contra forces. But it was the symbolism that was important. "Our María stands for a return to values, for Nicaragua and the American way," Quiñones explained, adding, "The best touch was when we wet the shirt so that her sex appeal could show through."[67]

"Humanitarian Aid"

Despite an impressive game plan and substantial resources, Reagan's public diplomacy campaign didn't make much headway. At first, the Democratic leadership was terrified that Reagan's peace proposal might sway undecided members of the House. The MX defeat was still fresh in their minds and no one underestimated the persuasive powers of the newly reelected president. But as the vote drew closer, the margin against contra aid seemed unchanged. House Republican leader Robert H. Michel told the White House flatly that a straight request to release military aid was "dead in the water." It would lose by seventy votes in the House—a deficit too big for any public relations campaign to overcome.[68]

This dilemma produced some last-minute bargaining by the White House with moderate and conservative Democrats. Reagan promised that none of the $14 million would be used for lethal aid, regardless of whether or not the Sandinistas agreed to negotiate with the contras. The White House hoped that a "nonlethal" aid package would have a greater chance of approval because it could be portrayed as a new option on which members of Congress had not yet established a voting record.

Senate Democratic leader Robert C. Byrd (D-W.Va.) was also looking for a compromise. He disliked the Nicaragua issue because it divided his party along ideological lines and left Democrats open to charges of being soft on Communism. In 1984, the administration had split the Democrats, winning the support of enough conservatives and moderates to pass its $21 million contra aid request in the Senate. Byrd had gone along with the White House on that vote. In 1985, he wanted to find a formula that would unite the Democrats and also be acceptable to the White House. Senate Democrats would be stronger for it, no one could accuse the party of pursuing partisan advantage over national interest, and U.S. policy toward Nicaragua would be put on sounder footing. The difficulty, of course, lay in finding a proposal that both Ronald Reagan and liberals such as Christopher Dodd could support.

First, Byrd brought together the Democratic senators who had been most actively involved with the contra aid issue. In several hours of discussion, they hammered out a proposal they could all agree on. That by itself was a "miracle," several of the participants said afterward. The Democrats were willing to accept Reagan's promise to use the $14 million only for nonlethal supplies, so long as the money was not channeled through the CIA. They also wanted Reagan to resume the bilateral Manzanillo talks with Nicaragua.[69]

The day before the Senate was scheduled to vote on releasing the $14 million, Byrd and the Democrats took their proposal to the White House, met briefly with Reagan and Bush, and then spent the next eight hours in marathon negotiations with McFarlane. Although the Democrats' proposal was hardly different from what Reagan himself was proposing, the White House refused to accept it because of the demand for a resumption of bilateral negotiations. Casey was the principal opponent of the compromise. He had no more faith in negotiating with the Democrats than with the Nicaraguans. His view, according to McFarlane, was that "there simply wasn't going to be any possibility of bipartisanship," so trying to promote it was "a waste of time."[70]

After the White House talks collapsed, George Shultz opened negotiations with several individual Democrats. To satisfy Senator Lloyd Bentsen (D-Tex.), Reagan promised in a letter to "favorably consider economic sanctions against Nicaragua," because Bentsen thought economic sanctions ought to precede military ones. To satisfy Senator Sam Nunn (D-Ga.), Reagan promised to use U.S. aid to "investigate allegations" of contra atrocities and "take appropriate action against those found to be guilty."[71] In the final version of the letter, Reagan restated his pledge to use the $14 million only for nonlethal supplies, and he seemed to relent on the issue of talks. "I intend to resume bilateral talks with the Government of Nicaragua," Reagan wrote, "and will instruct our representatives in those talks to press for a cease-fire as well as a church-mediated dialogue between the contending Nicaraguan factions."[72]

This concession didn't concede much. Despite promising bilateral talks, Reagan merely pledged to tell the Sandinistas they should negotiate with the contras. Moreover, the letter was not binding. "We're not voting on letters," Senator John Glenn reminded his colleagues. But the letter was enough of a fig leaf for most southern Democrats; they voted to give Reagan his $14 million. On the closest Senate vote on contra aid to date, the White House won, 53–46. "This," complained Democratic leader Byrd, "is no way to legislate."[73]

In the House, the situation was more complex. Fearing that Reagan's peace plan might erode the majority against funding the contras, the Democratic leadership sought to devise a positive alternative to it. This would give moderate and conservative Democrats in the House something to vote for, so they could not be accused of abandoning the contras.

The result was H.J. Res. 247, sponsored by Michael Barnes, Lee Hamilton (D-Ind.), who was Boland's successor as chairman of the Intelligence Committee, and Jim Jones (D-Okla.), a respected moderate. The Barnes-Hamilton proposal, as it was known, continued the ban on military aid for the contras, but also provided $10 million for the International Red Cross and the United Nations to aid Nicaraguan refugees and $4 million to help finance the Contadora peace process. It was an amendment aimed at ending the war.

If the Democrats were going to propose an alternative program, they had to allow the Republicans to put forward one of their own. Sponsored by Minority Leader Michel, it provided $14 million in direct, nonlethal aid (so-called "humanitarian" aid) to the contras to be administered by the Agency for International Development rather than the CIA.[74] The Republicans hoped that by limiting aid to nonlethal supplies and prohibiting CIA involvement, they could regain enough votes to keep the covert war going. Despite the administration's displeasure with the ban on CIA involvement, Reagan endorsed the Michel plan as the best alternative available. Barnes-Hamilton, he said, was "a shameful surrender" that would turn freedom fighters into homeless refugees.[75]

The tone of the debate on the House floor was set by Republican leader Michel, who began by avowing, "The issue here is do you want to help the forces of democratic pluralism in Nicaragua, or do you want to consolidate the power for a Marxist-Leninist dictatorship?" If the Democrats cut aid to the contras, he warned, it would be the "de facto handing over of Nicaragua to the allies of the Soviet Union."[76] Newt Gingrich called his adversaries on the other side of the aisle "ostrich Democrats" who promised "peace through weakness." He then startled his colleagues by pulling out an automatic weapon—captured in El Salvador, he said, but since rendered harmless. When Bill Richardson (D-N.Mex.) called Gingrich a demagogue, the Republicans accused Richardson of using unparliamentary language. Gingrich, however, didn't relent. "It is your wing of the [Democratic] party which is killing freedom in Central America," he railed at Richardson. "You cripple freedom, you weaken America."

The Democrats were subdued in their replies. No one had a kind word for the Sandinistas, and most speakers were at pains to say that they shared Reagan's desire to establish democracy in Nicaragua and end the Sandinistas' interference in El Salvador. It was simply Reagan's method that they disliked. The argument most often raised against contra aid was the conduct of the contras themselves.

One of the most thoughtful speeches came not from a Democratic opponent of contra aid, but from a liberal Republican, Jim Leach of Iowa. Leach focused on the Reagan administration's disregard for international law, as exemplified by its refusal to meet Nicaragua in the World Court. He compared the administration's presumptive attitude of great power entitlement to the Athenian destruction of the island of Melos, described by Thucydides in *The*

Peloponnesian War. The rule of law, Leach warned, was the only guarantee against the doctrine that might makes right.[77]

The House procedure adopted for consideration of the various contra aid proposals was somewhat convoluted. First, the House would vote on the resolution releasing the $14 million in military aid to the contras. If that was defeated, the House would then take up the two alternatives, voting first on the Barnes-Hamilton proposal and then on Michel's proposal. Finally, the House would have to vote again, for final passage of whichever alternative had been adopted in the first round of voting.

The House leadership's strategy was designed, first and foremost, to assure a solid victory against the resolution releasing the $14 million in military aid. In that, it succeeded. The resolution was defeated 248–180. But from there, the strategy began to unravel. The first vote on the Barnes-Hamilton proposal produced a much narrower victory than the Democrats anticipated, 219–206. On the next vote, Michel's Republican proposal was barely defeated 215–213, with the winning margin provided by members changing their votes just moments before the final tally was announced. Michel slapped the back of his seat angrily in frustration when the result was posted.

But the real shock came on the vote for final passage of the Barnes-Hamilton bill. To everyone's surprise, it was overwhelmingly defeated (303–123) by an unlikely coalition of Republicans and liberal Democrats. The liberal Democrats had voted in favor of it earlier only because its defeat then would have made the passage of Michel's amendment more likely. Once the Michel proposal had been defeated and the choice was between Barnes-Hamilton and no aid at all, the liberals voted for no aid. "We're back where we wanted to be in the first place, even though we had to take this circuitous route to get there," said Congressman Norman Y. Mineta (D-Calif.).[78]

Although Barnes-Hamilton provided no contra aid, liberals worried that its passage would provide a legislative vehicle that the Senate could use to go to conference committee and insist upon direct "humanitarian" aid to the contras. Since the Senate had approved release of the $14 million and Michel's proposal for nonlethal aid had failed so narrowly, the liberals feared that the end result of this process would be a compromise that restored contra aid. By voting against Barnes-Hamilton, they deprived the Senate of the chance to negotiate because there was no House bill to go to conference. "I don't want to send a vehicle over there," said Congressman Robert T. Matsui (D-Calif.), explaining his vote against Barnes-Hamilton. "Why go to conference at all? There's a possibility that some military aid could come out of it."[79]

The Democratic leadership was shocked by the defeat of Barnes-Hamilton.

They had known many liberals would vote against it on final passage, but they never dreamed the Republicans would. On the face of it, the logical strategy for the Republicans was to support Barnes-Hamilton on final passage, even though they despised it, in order to create a vehicle for conference with the Senate. But Barnes-Hamilton became "a victim of two extremes," explained Majority Leader Jim Wright. "A lot of liberal Democrats didn't want anything and the Republicans acted in a fit of pique."[80]

The Republicans simply refused to vote for what they regarded as tantamount to surrender in the war with Nicaragua. "For many of us there was a very strong feeling that the bill was so bad that we didn't want our names put to it," said Congressman Dick Cheney (R-Wyo.). "I would rather vote for nothing than perpetuate a fig leaf."[81] But the Republican position also had a certain logic. The defeat of Barnes-Hamilton strengthened the Republicans' hand for the passage of their own aid package later. The whole purpose behind Barnes-Hamilton had been to give moderate and conservative Democrats "political cover"—some politically defensible positive alternative that did not abandon the contras. The failure of Barnes-Hamilton left those Democrats feeling betrayed by their liberal colleagues and vulnerable. Now, they were open to Republican blandishments.

"A number of people would've looked at the [Michel] proposal in a different light if they had known what was going to happen on the final vote," said Dave McCurdy of Oklahoma, a leader among the moderate Democrats. "I would have voted for it." No sooner had Barnes-Hamilton been defeated than McCurdy began talking with other angry Democrats about drafting an alternative proposal of their own. He began talking to the White House as well.[82]

The press headlined the House votes as a total defeat for Reagan's Nicaragua policy because all the aid proposals had failed. In fact, the closeness of the votes showed that the administration's position was stronger than anyone had anticipated. Michel's proposal had come within two votes of passing, and a dozen moderate Democrats were already pledging to vote with the administration next time. "I intend to return to Congress again and again to seek a policy that supports peace and democracy in Nicaragua," Reagan promised. "We must continue to support the fight for freedom in Nicaragua."[83]

"This doesn't end it," said Tip O'Neill after the votes. "I wish it did."[84]

Back in the USSR

The Republicans began plotting a new effort to secure nonlethal aid for the contras almost as soon as the April votes were over. Since they needed to pick up only two votes in the House to pass Michel's amendment, the prospects for nonlethal aid looked excellent. They looked even better the day after the House voted, when the newspaper headlines reported that Nicaraguan president Daniel Ortega would soon be traveling to Moscow.[85]

Ortega had made half a dozen trips to Moscow over the preceding four years and the political reverberations in Washington had always been slight. Thus the Sandinistas were wholly unprepared for the firestorm touched off by the April journey. Earlier trips received little attention because they never coincided with any of the periodic upsurges of congressional action on contra aid. But the April trip was announced just as the acrimonious debate in the House climaxed, so it became a front-page story.

The trip was a political disaster for opponents of contra aid. Reagan had charged that the Sandinistas were Communists and Soviet puppets. Ortega's trip seemed to prove him right. Some members of Congress believed that the trip was intentionally timed to insult and embarrass them. Others felt betrayed because they had gone out on a political limb for Nicaragua, and the Sandinistas had unthinkingly cut it off. "There's huge anger at Ortega," explained contra aid opponent Charles E. Schumer (D-N.Y.). "People regard his trip as a personal rebuke to Congress."[86]

Even among members whose response was less personal, Ortega's trip left a strong conviction that the Sandinistas could not be relied upon to act with even a modicum of political acumen. At any moment they were liable to do something that would make it untenable for a member of Congress to be seen as their defender. "He embarrassed us, to be perfectly truthful," said Tip O'Neill. In the Senate, Byrd and Republican leader Bob Dole (R-Kan.) cosponsored a resolution condemning Ortega's trip; it passed by voice vote without dissent.[87]

The fact that Ortega went to the Soviet Union in search of desperately needed oil was neither widely understood nor relevant to the political effect the trip had in Washington. From the Sandinistas' viewpoint, however, the need to find oil was paramount, and the furor in Washington was a regrettable but unavoidable price.[88]

The great irony of the infamous Moscow trip was that it came about because of the administration's success in pressuring Mexico to cut off its supply of cheap oil to the Sandinistas, leaving them no place to go but the Soviet Union. In 1981, Mexico and Venezuela, the two largest oil-producing countries in the Caribbean Basin, agreed to provide oil on concessionary terms to ten nations in the region. Venezuela halted oil shipments to Nicaragua in September 1982, ostensibly because the Sandinistas were in arrears on their payments, although other recipients also fell behind without suffering a cut-off.[89] Mexico took over as Nicaragua's sole supplier. As Nicaragua's hard currency reserves dwindled, the Mexicans granted the Sandinistas a 100 percent line of credit.

One explicit aim of U.S. policy was to put an end to this free fount of oil—
"to encourage Mexico to align its oil policy . . . with that of Venezuela," as a July
1983 NSC briefing paper said.[90] At the same time, Mexico came under pressure
from the International Monetary Fund to stop giving away oil to Nicaragua.
With IMF assistance on Mexico's foreign debt suddenly held hostage to its oil
policy, the Mexican Finance Ministry and PEMEX, the state-owned oil corporation, began advocating a reduction in credits for the Sandinistas.[91] In July 1983,
Mexico informed Nicaragua it would have to begin paying just like other
recipients. Privately, the Mexicans admitted that they had given in to Washington's pressure.[92]

By 1984, Mexico had extended over a quarter of a billion dollars in credits to
Nicaragua for oil. In August, the Mexicans told Nicaragua that they could no
longer provide oil at concessionary rates and the Sandinistas should seek a
second supplier. Nicaragua went to the Soviet Union, which provided 45 percent of its petroleum that year. In April 1985, Mexico informed the Sandinistas
that they would have to begin paying 80 percent of the cost of its oil in cash.
The Sandinistas didn't have the money, so they turned to the only country
willing to give them oil on credit—the Soviet Union.[93]

Making the Economy Scream

In the wake of the House's rejection of any contra aid program, Reagan
needed to demonstrate his resolve not to let Congress derail U.S. support for
the contras. Already demoralized by military setbacks, the contras might disintegrate if they thought that Washington was retiring from the war for good.
Washington's Central American allies also needed reassurance that the United
States would remain steadfast. The Hondurans, in particular, wanted proof
that despite Congress, U.S. support for the contras was undiminished.

As soon as the votes in the House were counted, the administration began
an urgent review of "the full family of measures" it could take to demonstrate
that it remained resolute.[94] On May 1, as the president arrived in Bonn, Germany, to laud the virtues of free trade at an economic summit with the European allies, the White House announced that the United States was imposing a
full trade embargo on Nicaragua.[95]

The trade embargo was the final step in the Reagan administration's strategy to destabilize the Sandinista government by crippling the Nicaraguan
economy—a strategy begun in April 1981 when Reagan cut off bilateral economic assistance.[96] By 1982, Washington was also lobbying against new loans
to Nicaragua both from private commercial banks and multilateral lending
agencies such as the World Bank and the Inter-American Development Bank.[97]

Washington's pressure on the banks was extremely effective. After 1979,

Nicaragua received a total of only $12 million in new private commercial bank loans.[98] In the two years from August 1979 to June 1981, before Washington began pressing the multilateral banks to halt loans to Nicaragua, the Inter-American Development Bank provided Nicaragua with $193 million and the World Bank provided $91 million. From late 1981 to 1984, Nicaragua received only $34 million from the IDB and $16 million from the World Bank.[99] After 1984, Nicaragua got nothing from either of them because it stopped making debt service payments on prior loans. The Sandinistas' decision to halt the payments was not unreasonable. During the first half of the decade, Nicaragua paid the private commercial banks and the multilaterals a total of $423 million in debt service and received almost no new capital.[100]

The imposition of a full trade embargo was a logical step in Washington's economic war. Hard-liners in the Defense Department, CIA, and National Security Council staff had wanted to impose an embargo for some time, but State, Commerce, and Treasury were all opposed on the grounds that it would violate the General Agreement on Tariffs and Trade (GATT) and harm relations with allies in both Latin America and Europe. The Commerce Department, in particular, worried that Washington would get a reputation as an unreliable trade partner, hurting administration efforts to expand trade with China and other countries with whom Washington had less than amiable political ties.[101]

Finally, some administration officials believed that an embargo would be counterproductive. Economic sanctions are rarely effective unless they can be applied multilaterally, and virtually no other country was likely to join a U.S. embargo against Nicaragua. The people likely to be hurt most were Nicaraguan businessmen, the backbone of the civic opposition to the Sandinistas. The Sandinistas, however, could use an embargo as an excuse to blame the country's mounting economic problems on the United States, just as Fidel Castro had been doing in Cuba for three decades.[102]

In 1983 and 1984, these arguments were enough to overcome the hard-liners' demands for an embargo. But after the House votes in early 1985, the administration needed to demonstrate its resolve. Imposing a trade embargo was something that could be done immediately, and it was one of the few sanctions short of direct military action that the administration had not already imposed. The symbolic importance of the embargo thus came to weigh more heavily than its practical effect, and Reagan approved it.[103]

Reaction to the embargo among major U.S. allies was uniformly negative. Participants at the Bonn summit warned that it would increase regional tensions. Among the Atlantic allies, Britain, Germany, Spain, and Portugal all openly opposed the embargo and affirmed their intention to continue trading with Nicaragua. Canada, France, Italy, Sweden, and the Netherlands went so far as to extend new trade credits to Nicaragua to offset the effects of the embargo—a significant setback for Washington's two-year diplomatic effort to convince the European allies to reduce their aid.[104] Mexico called the trade ban "economic coercion . . . not compatible with the objectives of the Contadora Group," and then reversed its decision to stop selling Nicaragua oil on credit.[105]

In May 1985, all the governments of Latin America supported a resolution in a meeting of the Latin American Economic System (SELA) that called on the United States to lift the embargo and urged SELA members to take actions to counter the embargo's effects. The OAS Permanent Council adopted a similar resolution, and the thirteen nations in the Caribbean Community called on Washington to end the embargo. When Assistant Secretary of State Motley was asked during congressional hearings if any countries had expressed support for the embargo, he could name only El Salvador—and even El Salvador did not join it.[106]

At the United Nations, the Security Council voted 11–1 (with three abstentions) for a resolution criticizing the embargo. U.S. allies France, Denmark, and Australia voted in favor, while Britain abstained; Washington's lone "no" vote vetoed the measure. In the General Assembly, a similar resolution passed 84–4.[107]

The impact of the trade embargo on Nicaragua was significant but not crippling. As relations with Washington deteriorated during the early 1980s, the Sandinistas anticipated economic sanctions and diversified Nicaragua's foreign trade as much as possible to blunt their impact. In 1980, 30.4 percent of Nicaraguan trade was with the United States. By 1984, that had been reduced to 14.9 percent, although Washington was still Nicaragua's largest single trading partner. Trade with Western Europe and Japan had grown from 20.6 to 35.1 percent, and trade with the Soviet bloc jumped from only 1.0 to 15.4 percent. The Nicaraguan government estimated that the embargo cost the country about $50 million annually.[108]

However, the cumulative impact of the embargo, the evaporation of external capital from the international banks, and the costs of the contra war proved to be fatal for an economy that had never really recovered from the insurrection against Somoza. To be sure, the economic policies of the Sandinista government and its ongoing feud with the private sector discouraged investment, thereby exacerbating the country's economic plight. But Nicaragua, like Chile in the early 1970s, was an underdeveloped agricultural export economy, dependent on international markets for both goods and capital. When Washington undertook to cut off Nicaragua from the outside world, its economy could not survive the severance. By the end of 1985, Nicaragua was suffering a severe recession (its gross domestic product contracted by 5.9 percent in 1985) combined with rapidly increasing inflation (320 percent in 1985 and soon to get much worse) from which it would not begin to recover before the end of the decade.[109]

As the standard of living in Nicaragua sank, the Reagan administration tried to detach itself from responsibility for the resulting misery. In May 1985, the State Department released a report on U.S. economic sanctions that concluded, "Depressed economic conditions in Nicaragua were, of course, due to disastrous economic policies adopted by the Sandinistas, and not to any actions by the United States."[110]

McCurdy Democrats

After announcing the trade embargo against Nicaragua, White House strategists focused on how to force another congressional vote on contra aid. Although the White House came up a few votes short in April, its aggressive strategy of harping on the evils of the Sandinista government had borne fruit. As Reagan himself noted with satisfaction, virtually no one in Congress had a good word to say about the Sandinistas. The administration had finally succeeded in "gluing the black hats" on them, as NSC official Walter Raymond recommended.[111]

In the wake of Ortega's Moscow trip, the Republicans wasted no time exploiting the Democrats' chagrin, accusing them of weakness and pro-Communist sympathies. "Whatever way they want to frame it," Reagan said of the House Democrats, ". . . they really are voting to have a totalitarian Marxist-Leninist government here in the Americas, and there is no way for them to disguise it."[112] Such rhetoric was intended to soften up the moderate Democrats who had stuck with their liberal colleagues for the April votes, but had been angered by the defeat of the Barnes-Hamilton amendment and by Ortega's trip to Moscow. While berating their party in public, Reagan began quiet backroom bargaining with the moderates to entice them into the Republicans' tent.

The disaffected Democrats, about two dozen in all, were organized into an informal caucus by Congressman Dave McCurdy, who became their leader and spokesman. As a moderate conservative from Oklahoma and member of the Intelligence Committee, McCurdy was influential among southern Democrats. In 1983, he helped line up their support for the Boland-Zablocki bill, and until 1985 he had voted consistently against contra aid.

But McCurdy was increasingly uneasy about the Sandinistas. If left to themselves, he was convinced they would continue to consolidate a Marxist-Leninist regime at home and export revolution to their neighbors. Though he doubted that aiding the contras was an effective way to pressure the Sandinistas into changing, it worried him that liberal Democrats seemed to have no alternative strategy for diverting the Sandinistas from their chosen path.[113]

Like many moderate and conservative Democrats, McCurdy deferred to the leadership in April, reluctantly voting against Reagan and for Barnes-Hamilton, even though he was uncomfortable with the votes both ideologically and politically. When the House leadership was unable (or in more Machiavellian reconstructions, unwilling) to keep the liberals from deserting Barnes-Hamilton wholesale and sending it down to defeat on final passage, McCurdy and his fellow southerners felt betrayed.[114] That same night McCurdy began drafting his own plan for giving nonlethal aid to the contras and quickly lined up over a dozen Democrats as cosponsors, most of them other moderates who had previously opposed contra aid. With the House so closely divided on the issue, McCurdy's small group constituted the margin of victory on any future vote, and he emerged as a central figure in the subsequent maneuvering.

And he relished it. McCurdy was one of the new generation of House members, first elected in 1980, just five years out of law school. He didn't think much of the seniority system and was not afraid to buck the leadership when it suited him. In January 1985, he helped Les Aspin (D-Wis.) become chairman of the House Armed Services Committee by displacing the aging chairman, Melvin Price (D-Ill.), and jumping over three more senior colleagues. "I wasn't going to wait 20 years until I had a voice in the way this place operated," McCurdy explained.[115] Smart, brash, and eager to hold center stage, Dave McCurdy was a power to be reckoned with. He was also surprisingly naive when it came to dealing with the political operatives in the Reagan White House.

In search of a contra aid proposal that could pass both houses of Congress, the administration opened discussions with McCurdy's group in the House and with southern Democrats led by Sam Nunn and Lloyd Bentsen in the Senate. The senators were easy to please. They accepted a proposal incorporating everything Reagan wanted. It repealed the Boland amendment and also provided $14 million in nonlethal aid for fiscal year (FY) 1985 and $24 million for FY 1986, to be distributed however Reagan chose—which meant through the CIA.

McCurdy tried to drive a harder bargain. He wanted to use the contra aid package as leverage on everybody. In exchange for his support, he hoped to force the White House to resume negotiations with the Sandinistas and, ultimately, to abandon its goal of overthrowing the regime. He wanted to force the contras to clean up their human rights record and become more democratic by conditioning aid on reform. Finally, he hoped the approval of nonlethal aid would pressure the Sandinistas to negotiate seriously with Washington and, through Contadora, with their neighbors. McCurdy proposed a contra aid package that was similar to the one Republican leader Michel offered in April.[116]

The administration launched its new drive for contra aid in the Senate, in the hope that victory there might yield some momentum carrying over into the House. Having failed in April to find a compromise that the White House would accept, Senator Byrd abdicated any leadership role, leaving the Democrats with no organized strategy for confronting the new aid request. The administration and its Republican allies stayed in the background during the debate, allowing conservative Democrats to take the lead. After rejecting several amendments by liberals, the Senate passed Nunn's proposal, 55–42.[117]

"They were not thinking about Nicaragua or El Salvador," Christopher Dodd said afterward, reflecting on how his colleagues had voted. "They were thinking about going home and giving a speech to the Veterans of Foreign Wars. The primary concern is that senators don't want the president to point an accusing finger at them and say, 'You lost Central America.' "[118]

In the House, the Democratic leadership sought to rebuild the coalition of liberals and moderates that produced the narrow victory against contra aid in April. To reassure southerners that they need not be afraid of their constituents, the leadership commissioned a special opinion poll in eleven southern states. The results were mixed: 51 percent opposed the use of U.S. troops to oust the Sandinistas and "prevent Communism from spreading in Central America." But when asked if they favored "humanitarian aid" for rebels fighting to overthrow the "Communist Sandinista government," 67 percent were in favor. Asked to choose between sending military aid, "humanitarian aid," and no aid at all, a plurality of 37 percent favored no aid, but 19 percent were willing to send military aid and 30 percent nonmilitary aid.[119]

National polls showed stronger opposition to Reagan's policy. ABC–*Washington Post* surveys in March and June 1985 found 72 percent and 71 percent of the public opposed to U.S. involvement in "trying to overthrow the government in Nicaragua." A June CBS–*New York Times* poll found 66 percent opposed to providing the contras with military supplies, and a Lou Harris poll found that opposition to "arming and supporting" the contras ranged from 53 percent to 73 percent in a series of surveys conducted throughout the spring.[120] But the polls didn't provide much solace to the nervous southerners. "Last November, we lost an election 1 to 49," said Virginia Democrat Dan Daniel, alluding to the fact that Walter Mondale carried only his home state of Minnesota. "One of the reasons we lost was because we were perceived to be soft on defense. . . . We can no longer temporize or compromise with Communism on our doorstep."[121]

The Democratic leadership's June 1985 proposal was a slightly revised version of the Barnes-Hamilton amendment: it extended the Boland prohibition on military aid to the contras, but provided $14 million in refugee aid to be channeled through international relief organizations. Few Democrats had any illusions that it would pass, given the defection of the McCurdy group.

The Democrats' best hope was a proposal to simply extend the existing Boland amendment banning military aid to the contras without regard to fiscal year, thus making it a permanent feature of the law. This was the amendment the Democrats were most confident of winning since the Boland language had passed by substantial margins three times since 1983. It was also a poison pill for the Republicans; if they wanted nonlethal aid for the contras, they would have to accept a permanent ban on military aid to get it.

Finally, the Democrats offered a proposal by Richard Gephardt (D-Mo.) to postpone any aid to the contras for six months to give the Contadora peace process time to work. This proposal required yet another vote before money could be expended. The strategy behind it was simple enough—to allow Ortega's Moscow trip to fade from memory and give the Democrats time to regroup.

The new version of the Michel proposal that had been worked out by McCurdy and the White House provided $27 million in nonlethal aid for the contras so long as it was not administered through the CIA or Department of Defense.[122] In addition to these restrictions, McCurdy also received a letter from President Reagan forswearing any intent to overthrow the Nicaraguan government, pledging to resume bilateral negotiations with the Sandinistas, and committing the administration to remove human rights violators from the contras' ranks. Much was made of the letter, which McCurdy and Michel both circulated to their colleagues on the eve of the vote. McCurdy argued that Democrats "ought to stand up and declare a victory" because he had convinced Reagan to abandon his aim of toppling the Sandinistas and to embrace negotiations instead.[123]

On June 12, the issue was joined once again in the House on a series of amendments to a supplemental appropriations bill.[124] The debate was unusually civil (with a few exceptions—most notably the indomitable Henry Hyde, who called the Boland amendment "a marvelous Christmas present to give to the comrade *comandantes*"). The Republicans needed the votes of moderate Democrats and so refrained from stoking the fires of partisanship. The verbal bomb throwers of Gingrich's Conservative Opportunity Society remained silent, letting the McCurdy Democrats carry the debate against their own leadership.

Contra aid opponents suffered a debacle, losing four successive votes by wide margins. The extension of the Boland prohibition on military aid was defeated 232–196. Gephardt's proposed delay did even worse, failing 259–172. For members who felt a political need to be on record favoring some sort of policy toward Nicaragua, delay was worthless. The revised Barnes-Hamilton proposal was rejected, 254–174, and the Republican proposal passed, 248–184.

When the minor differences between the House and Senate versions of the proposal had been worked out in conference committee, the Congress authorized and appropriated $27 million in nonlethal assistance for the contras for the remainder of FY 1985 and the first half of FY 1986.[125] Shortly thereafter, the legal flow of U.S. aid to the contras resumed for the first time in over a year.

Speaker Tip O'Neill was despondent over the loss, calling it "a sad day for America." He had worked especially hard to defeat Reagan's policy because he believed it was leading toward the direct involvement of U.S. troops. "He is not going to be happy until he has our Marines and our Rangers down there for a complete victory," O'Neill said of Reagan. "He can see himself leading a contingent down Broadway with paper flying out the windows, with a big smile on his face like a kind of Grade B motion picture actor coming home the conquering hero. It's unbelievable, but that's the way he talks and that's the way he thinks."[126]

Of the thirty-one House members who changed their votes between April and June, seventeen were southern Democrats. Asked to explain the defections, O'Neill found it hard to fathom. "I don't know. I can't explain it," he said wearily. "They're afraid. They're afraid of Ronald Reagan. They think Reagan is supreme."[127]

O'Neill was especially angry at John P. Murtha (D-Pa.), who gave a stirring speech in support of the Republican proposal, lambasting his Democratic colleagues. When he concluded, the Republicans applauded heartily and Bob Michel rushed to the microphone to shake Murtha's hand. O'Neill watched dejectedly from the back of the House chamber. "He is one of my dearest friends in the House," O'Neill said of Murtha. "I am upset. I am very, very upset with him. And McCurdy, he put the knife in us."[128]

McCurdy, flush with victory, didn't care whether the Speaker was angry at him. "It doesn't break my heart," he shrugged, noting that O'Neill had already announced his intention to retire at the end of the term.[129]

The final defeat of the year for opponents of contra aid came on the intelligence authorization bill, which allowed the CIA to resume "intelligence sharing" with the contras, equip them with sophisticated communications equipment in order to receive that intelligence, and train them to use the equipment. Once again, McCurdy played the central role, sponsoring the provision that renewed direct CIA involvement in the war.[130]

Although the new rules on intelligence sharing were adopted without much fanfare, they were just as important—perhaps more important—than the resumption of nonlethal aid. The advice and intelligence provided under the act was not supposed to directly facilitate the planning of contra military operations, but the administration interpreted the law loosely. The President's Intelligence Oversight Board deemed that anything not expressly prohibited was allowable. Thus it concluded that military advisers could be deployed to provide "generic military training" under the rubric of "humanitarian assistance," because although the law defined humanitarian assistance as excluding lethal equipment, it made no mention of advice.[131]

In practice, the new rules meant that the CIA could begin providing tactical intelligence to the contras again. U.S. intelligence coverage of Nicaragua was so complete that Washington knew where individual Nicaraguan military units were and where they were going. By relaying this information to contra units in the field, Washington enabled them to avoid clashing with superior forces and to set deadly ambushes.

The new rules also allowed CIA paramilitary advisers to return to the contra camps in Honduras, ostensibly to facilitate intelligence sharing. Once they were at the front, some officers provided other forms of assistance as well, including advice on combat operations and even flying contra troops and supplies into Honduras and Nicaragua on CIA helicopters.[132] Intelligence sharing with the contras also proved to be a critical link in the quasi-private contra resupply network set up by Oliver North. All told, the CIA used the intelligence sharing provision to provide the contras with $13 million worth of equipment and services over the next year.[133] As Susan Benda of the American Civil Liberties Union said, it was a loophole "big enough to run a war through."[134]

The Letter and Spirit of the Law

While Congress and the White House were grappling over whether or not to give the contras nonlethal aid, Oliver North was keeping the contras together "body and soul" as per his instructions. But too many people were involved in North's activities for them to remain secret for long. As early as January 1985, the *Miami Herald* reported that North had helped the contras purchase surface-to-air missiles. In June, the *Herald*'s Washington correspondent, Alfonso Chardy, identified North as the White House liaison with the contras and with private aid donors.[135] North was worried enough that he planned to send someone to warn Chardy that "if he printed any derogatory comments" about the contras, he "would never again be allowed to visit FDN bases or travel with their units." North urged Poindexter to begin using lie detectors to find out who on the NSC staff had been leaking word of the contra operation to the press.[136]

The dam broke in August when anonymous administration officials told the *New York Times* that North was giving the contras "tactical" military advice and helping them raise funds. "Our policy is to support them, and that's his job," said a senior official. Another candidly admitted that North had taken over from the CIA managers of the contra program. "When the right people can't manage the operation," he said, "you have to look for other alternatives."[137] The day after the *New York Times* story, Reagan responded to the news reports by saying, "We're not violating any laws," but he did not disavow the substance of the stories. This nondenial denial was conscious. "The facts were the facts, and we couldn't argue with them," White House Press Secretary Larry Speakes later conceded.[138]

The press reports of North's activities spurred congressional inquiries. On August 16, Congressman Michael Barnes wrote to McFarlane that the reports raised "serious questions regarding the violation of the letter and the spirit of U.S. law." Congress intended the Boland amendment to halt U.S. aid to the contras, Barnes reminded McFarlane. "It would be stretching the integrity of the law to suggest that this prohibition was not intended to cover the NSC [National Security Council]." Barnes requested a full report on North's activities and all pertinent documents. Lee Hamilton, chairman of the House Intelligence Committee, sent McFarlane a similar letter on August 20.[139]

As the first step toward formulating a reply, McFarlane ordered an internal review of NSC documents. The search was intentionally narrow (though NSC officials were initially tempted to "bury Mr. Barnes" in a blizzard of useless telephone and meeting logs). The search turned up ten to twenty documents relevant to the congressional requests, six of which McFarlane regarded as "troubling" because they "seemed to raise legitimate questions about compliance with the law," he said later. North was more candid, admitting that the documents "clearly indicated that there was a covert operation being conducted in support of the Nicaraguan Resistance," just as the press was alleging.[140] McFarlane and North planned to alter the documents to eliminate the incriminating passages, and North drafted the necessary changes.[141]

But McFarlane did not offer the documents to Barnes; he simply ignored the request for documents in the hope that an unequivocal denial of wrongdoing would suffice. "I want to assure you that my actions, and those of my staff, have been in compliance with both the spirit and the letter of the law," he wrote to Barnes. "None of us has solicited funds, facilitated contacts for prospective potential donors, or otherwise organized or coordinated the military or paramilitary efforts of the resistance." McFarlane assured Barnes that reports of a covert NSC operation to maintain U.S. support for the contras were absolutely untrue. "There has not been, nor will there be, any such efforts by the NSC staff."[142]

Barnes refused to be so easily put off. On September 30, he wrote back to McFarlane, insisting that the White House provide the documents requested. "Barnes is really a troublemaker," McFarlane's deputy, John Poindexter, groused.[143] Hoping to sidestep a confrontation rather than provoke one, McFarlane invited Barnes to his White House office and showed the congressman a stack of documents on his desk. The documents were too sensitive to leave the White House, McFarlane insisted, but Barnes could read them, then and there.[144] McFarlane judged, correctly, that Barnes would refuse such a limited offer. But Barnes was still not mollified. In a third letter, he suggested to McFarlane that the sensitive nature of the documents could be protected by turning them over to the House Intelligence Committee. McFarlane refused, finally falling back on executive privilege.[145]

McFarlane's reply to Lee Hamilton and the Intelligence Committee was a variation on the letter to Barnes. On September 10, McFarlane met with the committee and repeated his denial of the press reports. "I for one am willing to take you at your word," Hamilton told McFarlane at the end of the meeting.[146]

Besides Barnes, whose efforts came to naught, none of the committee chairmen in the House or Senate followed up on the reports of North's misdeeds. Politics lay behind this lack of vigor. Just a few weeks before the stories about North broke in the press, Congress had voted to overturn the yearlong ban on contra aid by approving $27 million in nonlethal assistance. The political tide seemed to be moving in Reagan's direction on the Nicaragua issue, just as it had the previous year on El Salvador. In the wake of their legislative defeat, even the liberals, who remained adamantly opposed to the contra war, had little stomach for mounting a fight over Oliver North. If North was guilty of doing what the press reports said he was doing, most of his activities were probably now legal anyway under the new law that allowed intelligence sharing with the contras.

"Congress didn't seem to care that the law was being broken," recalled Congressman Jim Leach, one of the few Republican opponents of contra aid. "I think the Democrats basically let the country down when it became clear the president was extremely popular. They were afraid to take him on."[147]

One substantive change came out of the congressional inquiries. North stopped reporting his activities through the official NSC documents system so there would be no paper trail in the future.[148]

CHAPTER 19

High Noon

Ronald Reagan's 1985 victory restoring legal U.S. aid to the contras was a great triumph, but $27 million in nonlethal aid would not alter the military balance in Nicaragua. To win back Nicaragua from the Soviet camp, Reagan would have to defeat the congressional Democrats and restore lethal aid. In that battle, 1986 was to be the decisive year. Reagan could not postpone the showdown because the contras' military situation was deteriorating. If Congress refused to fully fund the war in 1986, CIA Director Casey warned, the administration would have to "scrap our present policy and move ahead with final alternatives." That meant liquidating the war, resettling the contras as refugees, and spending "hundreds of millions" of dollars on aid for the rest of Central America—or using U.S. troops to invade Nicaragua and solve the problem once and for all.[1]

Two factors accounted for the contras' poor showing in 1985. One was a shortage of arms and ammunition due to the congressional ban on lethal military aid.[2] The other was the growing skill of the Sandinista army. In 1982 and 1983, the Sandinistas had believed that contra attacks were merely the prelude to a U.S. invasion. Rather than commit their best forces to battling the contras in remote border regions, they kept their regular military units in the country's heartland along the Pacific coast to repel the expected invasion. They

439

sent hastily formed militia units and ill-trained draftees against the contras and took heavy casualties.

In 1984, however, the Sandinistas began to regard the contras as a serious military threat. Regular army units armed with heavy artillery and commanded by veterans of the war against Somoza were committed to the front. Special counterinsurgency units, the Irregular Warfare Battalions (Batallones de Lucha Irregular), were formed to hunt down the contras and drive them back across the Honduran border. The Sandinistas also acquired Mi-8 and Mi-24 helicopters from the Soviet Union, allowing their troops greater mobility and close air support during combat. In short, they did everything that the United States had been urging the Salvadoran government to do in its counterinsurgency war.[3]

The effectiveness of this strategy was demonstrated in two battles that sent the contras reeling. In August 1985, 1,000 contras attacked and briefly captured the small town of La Trinidad. It was the first town they had ever taken, but their triumph was short-lived. As they withdrew, they were caught by Sandinista Mi-24 helicopter gunships and decimated. As many as 150 were killed and another 50 captured. The same thing happened in December in Chontales province in north-central Nicaragua when the contras attacked the village of Santo Domingo.[4]

The Sandinistas were not content to simply react to contra attacks. During the summer of 1985, they launched offensives against contra strongholds, north and south. In the south, they overran all of the principal base camps of Edén Pastora's forces, driving him back into Costa Rica. In the north, they pushed the Nicaraguan Democratic Force's (FDN) fighters back toward the Honduran border and seized the high ground overlooking the contras' favorite infiltration routes. By fall, the Sandinistas enjoyed the strongest military position they had held since the start of the war, and they proclaimed the "strategic defeat" of the contra army.[5]

Despite such setbacks, CIA officials overseeing the contra program were confident they could bring the contras to the verge of victory if only they could win congressional approval for a large lethal aid package. With adequate funding, the CIA would double the size of the contra army to some 30,000 fighters. The contras would then open operations in new areas of the country, especially the cities, where their absence had long been embarrassingly obvious. U.S. military advisers would begin a training program for contra troops modeled on the Pentagon's program in El Salvador. And although U.S. advisers would not go into combat, non-U.S. employees of the CIA (the famous UCLAS who helped mine Nicaragua's harbors in 1984) might serve as combat advisers inside Nicaragua itself.[6] The expanded contra army would finally be able to take and hold territory, establishing an alternative civil administration—perhaps even a provisional government that could seek international recognition.[7]

The plans were nothing if not grandiose, and even within the administration, most intelligence analysts thought they were a pipe dream. In a December 1984 memo to Bill Casey, his deputy, Robert Gates, began by writing, "It is time to talk absolutely straight about Nicaragua. . . . Based on all the assessments we have done, the contras, even with American support, cannot overthrow the Sandinista regime."[8]

A February 1985 National Intelligence Estimate, "Nicaragua: Prospects for Sandinista Consolidation," concluded that the contras would not be able to prevent the Sandinistas from consolidating power, and a February 1986 estimate, "Nicaragua: Prospects for Insurgency," found that the contras' military prospects were limited in light of improving Sandinista counterinsurgency techniques.[9] But for administration hard-liners, the dream of rolling back a Communist revolution obscured better judgment. "The president does not want to leave this problem to his successor," Admiral Poindexter told Senator Jim Sasser (D-Tenn.). "He wants to get rid of the Sandinistas now."[10]

Another reason for Reagan's eagerness to resume lethal aid was the ongoing need to reassure U.S. allies in Central America of Washington's steadfastness. In December 1985, National Security Adviser John Poindexter traveled secretly to the region to tell them that, as Oliver North put it, the United States intended "to pursue a victory" in Nicaragua and would not be "forced to seek a political accommodation with the Sandinistas." Poindexter, accompanied by North and Elliott Abrams, covered Panama, Costa Rica, Honduras, El Salvador, and Guatemala in a single day, spending an hour and a half on the ground in each country, beginning in Panama at 7:30 A.M. and finishing in Guatemala at 6:00 P.M.[11]

In Honduras, Poindexter sought to reestablish the government's willingness to let contra supply flights use Honduran airfields. President Roberto Suazo Córdova had banned the resupply missions in October 1985 when a flight carrying supplies from the State Department's Nicaraguan Humanitarian Assistance Office (NHAO) landed in Tegucigalpa with an NBC News television crew aboard, thereby shattering the fiction that Honduras was not a staging area for the contras. Suazo was also angry at Washington's refusal to support his political maneuvers to remain in office beyond the end of his term.[12]

Within the armed forces, Commander Walter López Reyes, a nationalist who was uncomfortable with Honduras's subservience to U.S. policy, demanded better compensation for the military's cooperation. "From previous meetings with López, it is obvious that the Hondurans perceive the USG [United States government] is 'using' Honduras for its own political ends,"

North wrote to Poindexter, briefing him for the December trip. "They have learned that we withhold our assistance . . . in order to force concessions from them. They are now using the same tactic with us. . . . López and his colonels recognize that the only leverage they have over us is their covert support for the Nicaraguan resistance."[13]

Although President Suazo never did allow the resumption of contra supply flights, his successor José Azcona Hoyo relented. The resupply operation through Honduras resumed within days of the new president's inauguration in January 1986.[14] The CIA helped smooth the way by arranging the ouster of General López. His fellow officers replaced him in early 1986 with a more conservative and cooperative commander, Colonel Humberto Regalado Hernández.[15] Although the new governing team in Honduras was more disposed to cooperate with Washington, they could not ignore the growing anxiety, both in the armed forces and in civil society, that the United States would eventually abandon the contras and leave Honduras holding the bag.

The Hondurans' worries about the future of the contras were common throughout the region. Without a clear, definitive commitment to the contras from Washington, none of the Central Americans were eager to wager their future on the outcome of the Nicaraguan war. And the only unambiguous signal from the United States that would convince U.S. allies was a signal from Congress.

Preparing for Battle

Administration officials began plotting their campaign to resume military aid shortly after Congress approved nonlethal aid.[16] Events in Nicaragua bolstered their hopes. In October 1985, President Daniel Ortega announced a new state of emergency which effectively suspended all civil liberties for a year. Ortega justified the decree as a necessary response to Washington's resumption of contra aid and its recruitment of "agents of imperialism" within the civic opposition.[17]

Administration hard-liners could barely conceal their glee at the political boon the state of emergency produced. The Sandinistas acted like Reagan's "unpaid lobby," quipped Elliott Abrams. "I find complete consensus that the Sandinistas are really reprehensible people."[18]

On December 14, 1985, Reagan used his weekly radio address to describe Nicaragua as "an imprisoned nation . . . condemned to unrelenting cruelty . . . by a dictator in designer glasses and his comrades, drunk with power." The contras needed help, Reagan said. "If we fail them in their hour of need, we fail ourselves as the last, best hope of liberty."[19] Reagan called the Sandinistas "thugs"—an insult penned by Patrick Buchanan that had been edited out of a similar speech in early 1985 because Michael Deaver thought it unpresidential. Now Deaver was gone, and there was no one to moderate Buchanan's wilder instincts.

On February 25, Reagan submitted to Congress a request for $100 million in unrestricted aid for the contras. Along with the money, he sought repeal of the ban on lethal military aid and on CIA involvement in the war—compromises he had been forced to accept as the price of getting nonlethal aid in 1985. "You can't fight attack helicopters piloted by Cubans with Band-Aids and mosquito nets," Reagan said.[20] By requesting such a large amount of money—twice as much as any previous contra aid request—the president signaled his determination to break the back of congressional opposition. This time there was to be no compromise, none of "the usual temporizing and quibbling" over half-measures.[21]

As in 1985, administration strategists differed on how the campaign for lethal aid should be waged. "Early on there was internal disagreement over whether this was an issue you heat up with television, or an issue you work the corridors of Congress," a White House aide explained. Hard-liners such as Buchanan, Casey, Weinberger, Poindexter, and North "wanted to heat it up."[22]

Buchanan's main opposition came from Chief of Staff Donald Regan, who, like James Baker before him, worried that a public venting of the contra aid issue would damage Ronald Reagan politically. But unlike Baker, Regan was not forceful in shaping the administration's political agenda. Faced with the president's obvious emotional commitment to the contras, he let Reagan be Reagan.

Other personnel changes had also eliminated potential voices of moderation. At the State Department, the affable Tony Motley resigned after Washington withdrew from the Manzanillo talks and was replaced by the acerbic Elliott Abrams. Like Jeane Kirkpatrick, Abrams was a neoconservative who relished ideological combat with his former colleagues on the liberal left. He described himself as a "gladiator" defending Reagan's Central American policy.

Abrams had the perfect neoconservative pedigree. Although he had opposed the war in Vietnam, he remained a loyal supporter of Hubert Humphrey when the Democrats split over the war in 1968. As a consequence, he was removed as chairman of the Harvard chapter of Americans for Democratic Action. When Students for a Democratic Society led a strike at Harvard in 1969, Abrams climbed to the opposite side of the barricades, chairing the Ad Hoc Committee to Keep Harvard Open. It was, he said, "one of my proudest moments." The bitter political battles of Abrams's college years were a formative experience. "I've been a counter-revolutionary for a long time," he told a reporter in 1986. Abrams married the daughter of Norman Podhoretz and Midge Decter, the high priest and priestess of neoconservatism.[23]

Abrams's first government experience was on Capitol Hill, where he worked for Senators Daniel Patrick Moynihan and Henry Jackson, whose staff was a breeding ground for young neoconservatives. In 1980, Abrams campaigned for Ronald Reagan and formally became a Republican the following year. As reward, Reagan appointed Abrams assistant secretary of state for international organizations, making him, at thirty-three, the youngest assistant secretary of state in the twentieth century.[24]

When Reagan's nominee for assistant secretary of state for human rights, Ernest W. Lefever, was forced to withdraw in 1981 (his nomination faced broad opposition because he had publicly opposed every piece of human rights legislation passed in the 1970s), Abrams was shifted to the Human Rights Bureau. He approached human rights with a theory similar to Jeane Kirkpatrick's distinction between "moderately authoritarian" and "totalitarian" regimes. Communist governments were the worst human rights violators in the world, Abrams believed, so virtually anything done to prevent Communists from coming to power (or to overthrow them) was justifiable on human rights grounds.[25] This theory fit neatly into the Cold War presumptions that framed Reagan's foreign policy and allowed the administration to rationalize supporting murderous regimes so long as they were anti-Communists. In practice, it was little different from Henry Kissinger's realpolitik that discounted human rights issues entirely.

Abrams spent considerable time defending the human rights record of the government in El Salvador, invariably insisting that things were getting better. When independent human rights groups questioned that conclusion, Abrams attacked their objectivity, accusing them of Communist sympathies. "He practices the Doberman pincher school of diplomacy," said State Department veteran Frank McNeil, himself a target of Abrams's wrath.[26]

In April 1985, when Tony Motley resigned from the Latin American bureau, Abrams was promoted to take his place. By that time, Nicaragua had replaced El Salvador at the top of the U.S. foreign policy agenda, and Abrams was wholly committed to driving the Sandinistas out of power by military force. "I want to be the first guy to reverse a Communist revolution," he told a colleague shortly after taking over for Motley. Abrams could envision no scenario in which U.S. interests would be adequately safeguarded by a negotiated agreement. The State Department's intermittent efforts to find one were over. Abrams's unswerving commitment to the contra cause earned him the nickname "contra commander-in-chief."[27]

At the NSC, an enervated Robert McFarlane resigned as national security adviser in December 1985, after months of sniping with Don Regan. He was replaced by his deputy, John M. Poindexter. McFarlane was obviously no moderate when it came to the contras, but his experience on Capitol Hill had taught him that the best way to pacify recalcitrant members of Congress was by stroking rather than insulting them.

Poindexter, on the other hand, had no use for politics or politicians, and no understanding of either, though he was, in some ways, a brilliant man. He graduated first in his class of nine hundred at the Naval Academy (class of 1958) and was also class brigade commander. The only other officer in history to achieve this dual distinction was Douglas MacArthur. Poindexter went on to earn a doctorate in nuclear physics from the California Institute of Technology and served as assistant to three secretaries of the navy.[28]

Poindexter joined the NSC staff in June 1981 as military assistant to National Security Adviser Richard V. Allen. Blessed with a photographic memory, Poindexter was thorough and meticulous, "a bureaucrat's bureaucrat," said one of his colleagues.[29] When McFarlane took over as national security adviser from William Clark in 1983, he made Poindexter his deputy. Yet Poindexter's knowledge was narrow and technical. He knew little about international political affairs and seemed unaware of his own ignorance. General Brent Scowcroft, who had been President Gerald Ford's national security adviser (and would assume the same position under President George Bush), warned McFarlane that Poindexter was in over his head and should be sent back to the navy. Scowcroft's advice went unheeded.[30]

When Poindexter himself took over as national security adviser in December 1985, his operating style, according to a former official, was "secretiveness applied to all issues." Reclusive, he sat in his office behind a closed door, communicating with subordinates through the computerized memo system. Often, he ate all three meals there.[31] He was taciturn, cerebral, and extremely serious. "He was never a little boy," Poindexter's mother commented. "He was born an old man."[32]

The ambiguity and unpredictability of politics offended the physicist's sense of order. Poindexter had "an aversion" to politics, in the words of a friend; he avoided dealing with members of Congress and journalists whenever possible. Yet he was not merely a technocrat; he held an extremely conservative ideological worldview. "Poindexter thought the press was unpatriotic," observed White House Deputy Press Secretary Larry Speakes. Indeed, Poindexter thought nothing of lying to the press in the interests of national security. When reporters heard rumors of the impending invasion of Grenada in 1983, they asked Speakes if an assault was imminent. Speakes relayed Poindexter's unambiguous, one-word response: "Preposterous." U.S. troops went ashore the following day.[33]

In 1986, Poindexter devised a "disinformation program" aimed at destabilizing Muammar el-Qaddafi's government in Libya. Part of the plan involved planting false stories in the U.S. press, including reports that Libya was increasing its international terrorist activities and that Washington was contemplating a military response. When the scheme was uncovered, State Department spokesman Bernard Kalb, a veteran journalist, resigned in protest. But Ronald Reagan was unabashed. "We would just as soon have Mr. Qaddafi going to bed every night wondering what we might do," he said in defense of the plan.[34] Poindexter was not rebuked.

With Don Regan serving as White House chief of staff, Poindexter as national security adviser, and Abrams as point man for Central America at the State Department, there was no one left to temper Ronald Reagan's instinctive enthusiasm for the contra war. "He wants to make the members [of Congress] vote in the great white light of public attention on this issue," said a White House official.[35]

On January 10, 1986, the National Security Council decided that they would make an all-out, highly public effort to win lethal aid. Ronald Reagan would play Gary Cooper in *High Noon*, preparing for the showdown with the black-hatted Sandinistas, and the Democrats would be cast as the cowardly townspeople, too foolish to see that civilization itself was put at risk by their short-sighted selfishness.

Which Side Are You On?

Branding critics of contra aid unpatriotic had helped win nonlethal aid in 1985. As the 1986 debate began, administration officials returned to the same theme with a vengeance. In mid-February, Reagan began inviting groups of legislators to the White House to lobby them. At these meetings, CIA Director Casey passed out a "highly classified report" entitled "Sandinista Disinformation and Public Manipulation Campaign." The report, which Casey collected at the end of each meeting, purportedly described an elaborate Nicaraguan effort to deceive U.S. reporters and manipulate the congressional debate. Certain Americans were alleged to be confederates in this scheme.[36]

Elliott Abrams described the plan as "elaborate and skillful." "What you have here is a Communist government, allied with the Soviet Union, undertaking a very well organized effort with the help of certain Americans to change a vote in Congress. That is not a federal crime," Abrams said, implying that perhaps it ought to be, "but it is something that Congressmen appear to wish to know about."[37]

By implication, anyone who criticized Reagan's policy might be acting as an agent or pawn of the Sandinistas. Most Democrats were afraid to protest such tactics. In the first place, they worried that Casey's report might be at least partially true. Since it had been passed around only at Reagan's White House meetings with Republicans and swing Democrats, most liberal opponents of contra aid had not actually seen it and were in no position to evaluate it. And even if the report proved to be little more than administration propaganda, it was effective because it reinforced the Democrats' fear of being tarred as soft on Communism.

When someone finally leaked the report to the press, it turned out to be based on a lobbying strategy paper prepared for the Nicaraguan government by its public relations firm in New York, Agendas International, a small two-person operation run by former Maryknoll priests. There was nothing covert in the strategy paper; it suggested all the standard lobbying tactics that any government might pursue to influence a piece of U.S. legislation—meeting with key members of Congress, making Nicaraguan officials available to the media in order to get their point of view across, and so forth.[38] The Sandinista public relations strategy that Reagan officials portrayed as an intelligence deception operation was far less elaborate and sophisticated than their own.

Ironically, the Nicaraguan government had actually decided not to expend much effort trying to influence the 1986 contra aid debate. Experience had convinced them it was futile. In 1985, the Sandinistas had treated the vote on nonlethal aid as a critical turning point in the war—not because a few million dollars were so important, but because a vote to aid the contras symbolized congressional endorsement of Reagan's policy. Deputy Foreign Minister Victor Tinoco spent considerable time in Washington explaining Nicaragua's position to members of Congress and the media prior to the 1985 vote, and President Ortega himself toured the country.[39]

In the end, none of those efforts seemed to make much difference, and any benefits were wiped out by Ortega's trip to Moscow. By 1986, the Sandinistas had concluded that lobbying was fruitless. The Reagan administration had had such success demonizing them that they could not get a sympathetic hearing from anyone in the United States except the grassroots left. Ortega was overheard saying that U.S. hostility would continue, "even if we were little angels."[40] Consequently, the Sandinistas decided to take a low profile in the 1986 debate. They did not send senior officials to lobby Congress, they did not promise new concessions if aid was defeated, and they did not even follow the lobbying plan drafted by their public relations firm.[41]

No sooner had the flap over the CIA's disinformation report subsided than Patrick Buchanan let loose another blast at Reagan's opponents. In a March 26, 1986, opinion piece for the *Washington Post* and in subsequent television interviews, Buchanan accused Democrats who opposed Reagan's Nicaragua policy of being Soviet allies and "useful idiots." Whether or not Nicaragua became the "next appendage of the Soviet Empire" depended on how the Democrats voted on contra aid, Buchanan avowed. If the Congress deserted the contras, all of Central America would fall, unleashing a flood tide of twenty million refugees on the United States. "Which side are you on?" Buchanan demanded. "With the vote on contra aid, the Democratic Party will reveal whether it stands with Ronald Reagan and the resistance—or Daniel Ortega and the Communists."[42]

That was too much. Buchanan's hyperbole was too crude and strident, too obviously an attempt at intimidation. It hurt the administration where it could least afford it—among undecided Democrats and moderate Republicans. When Shultz met with twenty swing voters in the House shortly after Buchanan's bare-knuckle assault, "He got an earful that the McCarthy-type line was not the way to do it," recalled one White House official.[43]

Ronald Reagan, however, refused to disown Buchanan's vitriolic attacks. "I like what he says," the president answered when asked if he would tell Buchanan to tone it down.[44] Nevertheless, the barbs subsided shortly after Senator Nancy Kassebaum (R-Kan.), a moderate supporter of contra aid, took the Senate floor to criticize the White House for abandoning "reasoned and rational debate." The administration was distorting the issue, she argued, by presenting it as a conflict between "Republicans in white hats and Democrats wrapped in red banners," and by questioning the patriotism of anyone opposed to the president's policy. "I find this simplistic reasoning to be highly offensive," she concluded.[45] If Kassebaum's sense of offense translated into a vote against contra aid, the administration stood at risk of losing in the Senate. After her speech, Buchanan held his tongue.

Reagan on the Stump

Pat Buchanan had assumed Jeane Kirkpatrick's role as the administration's ideological shock trooper, but Ronald Reagan was still the main force. At a White House strategy meeting on March 1, 1986, Reagan resolved to make a "flat-out effort" to win the $100 million in lethal aid, playing an even more active role than he had in 1985.[46] Two days later, the president kicked off the new public diplomacy effort by meeting with the "Three A's" (Adolfo Calero, Arturo Cruz, and Alfonso Robelo) and declaring that without U.S. aid, the contras would be wiped out. Their defeat, Reagan warned, would constitute a "strategic disaster" for the United States, providing "a privileged sanctuary for terrorists and subversives just two days driving time from Harlingen, Texas." (Texans were somewhat amused by this, since Harlingen is a good 2,000 miles from Nicaragua—a lot of driving for two days, even by Texas standards.)[47]

In the two and a half weeks before the House voted on the $100 million request on March 20, Reagan gave eleven speeches in support of the contras.

Speaking to Jewish leaders on March 5, he accused the Sandinistas of anti-Semitism and warned that Nicaragua could become "a permanent staging ground for terrorism, a home away from home for Qaddafi, Arafat, and the Ayatollah." Criticism of the contras was "disinformation," Reagan insisted— "an orchestrated campaign to slander the freedom fighters. . . . If we don't want to see the map of Central America covered in a sea of red, eventually lapping at our own borders, we must act now."[48]

On March 13, Reagan visited the lobby of the State Department to inaugurate an exhibit of Communist bloc arms captured from the Salvadoran rebels. George Bush, Caspar Weinberger, George Shultz, and Elliott Abrams all turned out for the occasion to listen as their boss accused the Sandinistas of "run[ning] drugs to poison our children." Again, Reagan attributed criticism of the contras to a Communist plot: "The Communists have surrounded their aggression with a well-managed campaign of lies, distortion and . . . disinformation." The gravity of the drama was marred only by the fact that Weinberger fell asleep in the midst of it.[49]

The following day, speaking to a group of visiting local elected officials, Reagan characterized the Sandinistas as "part of the 20th century's answer to Murder, Incorporated." The contras got their name, Reagan explained, because they were against the Sandinista revolution. "God bless them for being that way," he exclaimed. If opposing Communism made them contras, "it makes me a contra, too." In celebration of that remark, the contras passed out buttons and T-shirts to their supporters with the slogan, "I'm a contra, too."[50]

It was difficult to judge the impact of this rhetorical blitzkrieg on members of Congress. All of it was aimed at those few dozen swing voters who continued to hold the balance of power. The administration's confrontational style and demonization of the Sandinistas was obviously not designed to convince wavering members by dint of logic. It was intended to scare them. The White House wanted Congress to know how deeply committed Reagan was to winning in Nicaragua. A vote against him was a vote the White House would remember. It might even be a vote, the administration warned, that could cost you your job in the next election.

A credible threat of political retaliation, however, depended upon the administration's ability to move public opinion. And the public was less fickle (or perhaps simply less interested) than the swing members of Congress. Despite Reagan's campaign, the public remained opposed to aiding the contras, as it had been all along. Trying to change their mood "was like trying to push water uphill," lamented one administration official.[51] In March and April 1986, all the major polling firms asked whether or not people supported Reagan's $100 million aid proposal. Opponents were always in the majority, outnumbering supporters almost two to one.[52] If anyone out there was listening to Reagan's verbal barrage against the Sandinistas, they were unmoved.

The Peace Scare

One of the major obstacles to winning congressional support for the $100 million contra aid request was Reagan's continuing disdain for diplomacy. Moderate Democrats agreed that something had to be done to blunt the Sandinista threat, but they were reluctant to reenlist wholeheartedly in the proxy war until diplomatic avenues had been exhausted. Reagan's rhetoric and the size of his lethal aid request made him appear too eager to charge down the warpath without giving peace a chance.

In 1985, to win Congressman Dave McCurdy's support for nonlethal contra aid, Reagan had promised to resume bilateral talks with Nicaragua. Once the nonlethal aid package had passed, Reagan reneged. The promise had been carefully couched, administration officials explained. The president had not agreed to talk with the Sandinistas about bilateral issues; he had merely agreed to consult with U.S. allies, including the contras, "as to how and when the United States could resume useful direct talks with Nicaragua."[53] Having consulted, the administration did not feel that bilateral talks would make any sense unless the Sandinistas agreed to talk to the contras first. So there would be no talks.

This position was arguably consistent with the text of the letter Reagan had signed, but it was just as certainly at odds with what the moderate Democrats thought Reagan had promised them—a serious effort to resolve the conflict by negotiations. "Is he the president of the United States," asked a frustrated aide to one of the key swing Democrats, "or a used car salesman?"[54]

In January 1986, McCurdy and thirty swing Democrats asked Reagan to delay his military aid proposal until he had made one last effort at serious diplomacy. Eighteen senators followed with a similar appeal. If Reagan wanted bipartisan support for his policy, he had to prove he sincerely wanted a negotiated settlement, McCurdy warned. "If they just seek more military aid, I'd have a lot of trouble voting for it."[55]

The Sandinistas had been trying to cajole Washington into resuming bilateral negotiations ever since the cancellation of the Manzanillo dialogue.[56] Washington's stock excuse for refusing was that a bilateral dialogue with Nicaragua would disrupt the multilateral Contadora process. Administration officials held tenaciously to this position, even when the Contadora nations themselves called for a resumption of the bilateral talks.[57]

Contadora, meanwhile, had been paralyzed ever since Washington sabotaged the September 1984 draft treaty by convincing its regional allies to reject it. Frustrated by their inability to broker an agreement, the Contadora governments gradually became discouraged. Within each of the four countries, conservative political forces demanded that the process be terminated rather than strain relations with the United States. This was especially true in Mexico, where the debt crisis and the economic dislocation caused by an earthquake that hit Mexico City in September 1985 made the government particularly vulnerable. "We are not discarding Contadora," said a source close to President Miguel de la Madrid, "but there are other subjects more pressing."[58]

To counterbalance U.S. pressure on the four original Contadora countries, the Sandinistas were able to enlist Brazil, Uruguay, Peru, and Argentina to form a Contadora Support Group (Grupo de Apoyo).[59] The establishment of the Support Group in the summer of 1985 formally involved all the principal South American democracies in the peace process. Their first major initiative in August 1985 was to again call upon Washington to resume bilateral talks with Nicaragua. Again, Washington refused.[60] Administration officials continued to insist that they would support a "good agreement," by which they meant an agreement requiring Nicaragua to reorganize its political system. But, as the briefing paper for a September 1985 meeting of U.S. ambassadors to Central America said of Contadora, U.S. policy held that "collapse would be better than a bad agreement."[61]

As Reagan launched his campaign for $100 million in contra aid, the Contadora peace process seemed moribund. But the Latin Americans, realizing how vital it was to keep alive a viable peace process as an alternative to Reagan's war policy, refused to give up. In early February 1986, the eight Contadora foreign ministers assembled once again in Washington to ask the Reagan administration to halt contra aid and resume talks with the Sandinistas. Shultz informed the foreign ministers that U.S. policy would not change. The Sandinistas would have to open negotiations with the contras before Washington would consider a new dialogue, and the request for military aid would go forward. The Latins were openly angry at what one of them called the administration's "stone wall." The Colombian foreign minister denounced U.S. policy publicly as "intransigent and extreme."[62]

Yet in the inner councils of the administration, the diplomatic pressure brought to bear by the eight Latin nations had some effect. Shultz was loath to simply reject their appeal. As a gesture to rejuvenate the diplomatic process, he proposed to other administration officials that they proceed with plans to win congressional approval for military aid, but offer to delay disbursement pending the resumption of the Contadora negotiations. The moratorium on lethal aid would be extended as long as the talks were making progress. Although this formula was similar to the peace plan Reagan himself had put forward in 1985, hard-liners in the White House and the Defense Department vetoed it, "in part out of fear that the Sandinistas would accept it this time," according to a State Department official.[63]

George Shultz had always been the cabinet officer most willing to accept a diplomatic accord with Nicaragua, but he was not willing to invest his political capital in trying to change Ronald Reagan's mind about the Sandinistas. At opportune moments, he tried to prod the administration toward some sort of diplomatic opening, but he never staked his job on it. For the most part, he left Nicaragua to the righteous certainty of Elliott Abrams.

By its obdurate opposition to Contadora, the White House wielded a double-edged sword. On the one hand, opposing diplomacy damaged Reagan's credibility with moderate Democrats in the House and made them less likely to vote for lethal aid. But, paradoxically, Reagan's intransigence also weakened the liberal Democrats. House moderates would vote against Reagan only if the Democratic leadership could offer a viable alternative, and Contadora was the only one available. When the peace process stalled, so did the Democrats' drive to halt contra aid. "If the talks break down," warned swing Democrat Bill Richardson, "the vote to stop aid to the contras is lost."[64]

The relationship between the Democrats and the Contadora countries was symbiotic; both were afraid to stand up to the Reagan administration on their own. The Latin Americans feared economic retribution; the Democrats feared political retribution. The Latins opposed contra aid, but had little influence over Washington. They relied upon the Democrats to end war by cutting off its funding. The Democrats, for their part, could point to Contadora's position as legitimation of their own opposition to the war. Certainly Latin Americans knew more about Central America than the United States did, the Democrats could argue. If the eight major democracies in Latin America all regarded contra aid as counterproductive, they were probably right. But with Contadora stalled, the Democrats could not realistically offer diplomacy as an alternative to Reagan's war.

On March 7, 1986, Reagan sought to disarm critics who accused him of lax efforts on the diplomatic front by appointing a veteran negotiator and troubleshooter, Ambassador Philip Habib, as his third special envoy to Central America. "I want to emphasize today that there can be a diplomatic solution for Central America," Reagan said, introducing his envoy. But that did not mean any change in U.S. policy. "Let there be no misunderstanding," Reagan quickly added. "Ambassador Habib's efforts to achieve a diplomatic solution must be accompanied by an increasing level of pressure on the Nicaraguan Communists"—more contra aid.[65]

Habib, an accomplished diplomat, was fresh off the plane from the Philippines, where he successfully arranged the departure of Ferdinand Marcos—a policy triumph that won universal praise. By appointing Habib, Reagan hoped that the bipartisan support for his policy in the Philippines might rub off on Nicaragua.

Although no one doubted Habib's competence, the timing of his appointment, coming just before Congress voted on Reagan's request for military aid, was a bit obvious. Like Richard Stone, Reagan's first special envoy who was appointed in 1983 to mollify congressional opponents of aid to El Salvador, Habib was widely assumed to be as much an ambassador to Congress as to Central America. He confirmed those suspicions by spending his first few days in the new post lobbying on Capitol Hill. Even within the administration, some officials saw the appointment cynically. "There's no real interest in negotiations," a senior official observed. "This administration believes that a negotiated settlement with these guys [the Sandinistas] . . . would be a life-time insurance policy for the revolution."[66]

One of Habib's tasks was to convince Congress that Latin American opposition to Reagan's proposal for military aid was not as widespread as it appeared to be. This was no easy matter, since the eight Contadora foreign ministers had just been in Washington pleading for a change in U.S. policy. In fact, even the Central American countries had begun distancing themselves from the United States. Costa Rica, Honduras, and Guatemala all had new presidents, and they were all less enthusiastic about Reagan's policy than their predecessors.

In Costa Rica, Oscar Arias had won a narrow come-from-behind victory by campaigning hard on a pledge to maintain Costa Rican neutrality vis-à-vis the war in Nicaragua. Now he was speaking openly against contra aid and trying to negotiate an agreement with Nicaragua to establish a civilian border patrol to prevent incursions from either side. Washington opposed any such agreement, arguing that it would make a comprehensive Contadora accord more difficult to achieve—even though the Contadora foreign ministers were helping negotiate the border agreement. The real reason for Washington's opposition was that border patrols would interfere with the war.[67]

In Honduras, Roberto Suazo Córdova had been replaced as president by José Azcona Hoyo, who criticized U.S. policy during his campaign and made a major issue of the need to get the contras out of Honduran territory. Meanwhile, Vinicio Cerezo in Guatemala continued to resist Washington's efforts to recruit Guatemala to its anti-Sandinista front, preferring instead to bolster his political stature at home by garnering prestige as a regional peacemaker. He, too, spoke openly of his opposition to contra aid. Only José Napoleón Duarte in El Salvador continued to toe the line without complaint.

The Reagan administration was so annoyed at the Central Americans, especially Arias and Azcona, that Habib was sent to warn them to stop speaking out against contra aid, lest they complicate their relations with the United States. "They have been told they have been embarrassing the president and that this could cost them," explained a Western diplomat in the region.[68]

Win One for the Tipper

The March 1986 fight over Reagan's $100 million contra aid request was cast as the final epic battle between Reagan and Speaker Tip O'Neill, who had announced his intention to retire at the end of the session. O'Neill was a veteran New Deal liberal who believed in the power of government to cure social ills. Ronald Reagan's crusade to dismantle the welfare state was an attack on everything the Speaker had spent his life building. Like many professional politicians who came into contact with Ronald Reagan, O'Neill was appalled by his shallowness, his ignorance of issues, and his habit of substituting anecdotes and hoary conservative bromides for analysis. Yet despite O'Neill's lifetime of political experience and his party's solid majority in the House, Reagan had beaten him in every major domestic policy battle. During the budget fights of 1981, a constituent back home asked O'Neill what was happening on the Hill. "I'm getting the shit whaled out of me," he replied. Much as he disliked Reagan's philosophy, the Speaker came to have a grudging respect for the president's political ability.[69]

At first, O'Neill did not take an active role in the issue of contra aid. Like his close friend Edward Boland, he hoped the issue would not become terrain for partisan confrontation. O'Neill came to Congress believing that "when it comes to foreign policy, you support your president."[70] And although Vietnam tempered such reflexive deference to the executive, foreign policy was still an area where O'Neill did not relish a test of strength between the branches of government.

Central America, however, was special. Because of friends and family, O'Neill knew more about the history of U.S. intervention in the region than most politicians. A childhood friend, Eddie Kelly, went to Nicaragua with the Marines during the intervention of 1927–33, was wounded, and returned thoroughly disillusioned. "He said, 'We're taking care of the property and rights of United Fruit. I got stabbed for United Fruit,'" O'Neill recalled. "That always stuck in my head. We kept that nation in servitude for years, we exploited them. . . . We ought to allow them to make their own free choice of government."[71]

O'Neill stayed current on events in Central America through his friends among the Maryknoll sisters, many of whom served as missionaries in the region. O'Neill's beloved aunt, Annie Tolan (Sister Eunice), was a founder of the order in 1919 and stayed with it until her death in 1983 at age ninety-one.

When Maryknoll sisters told O'Neill horror stories of contra atrocities, or that the Sandinistas, whatever their faults, were trying to build a better life for their countrymen, he believed them. "I have faith and trust when they come and talk to me. I have complete trust."[72]

Reagan might convince other members of Congress that the contras were democrats, but not Tip O'Neill. "The president calls them 'freedom fighters,' but that's ridiculous," O'Neill said flatly. "In reality, they're a small ragtag army of racketeers, bandits, and murderers who are led by some of the same people who ran the National Guard under Somoza. They were thrown out of office and now we're trying to put them back in."[73]

Moreover, the Speaker was convinced that Reagan and administration hard-liners were intent upon overthrowing the Sandinistas, even it meant involving U.S. troops directly in a war. Just weeks after Reagan's inauguration, Secretary of State Alexander Haig, with his usual braggadocio, told O'Neill that the United States should just go in and clean out Nicaragua.[74]

In 1964, O'Neill had suppressed his doubts about the Tonkin Gulf resolution and voted for it. His conscience never forgave him. "Of all the votes I cast during 34 years in the House of Representatives," he recalled, "[it is] the only one I really regret." Now he saw another president pushing the United States down the road to war. As Speaker, he felt an obligation to try to stop it. Reagan's request for $100 million in lethal aid for the contras was, in O'Neill's mind, "the Central American equivalent of the Gulf of Tonkin Resolution."[75]

With less than a year remaining before he retired, the battle over lethal aid would be the Speaker's last chance to halt the march to war in Central America and the last chance to best his old nemesis, Ronald Reagan. While Reagan gave speech after speech lambasting the Sandinistas, O'Neill drew upon his considerable prestige to swing wavering members to the Democrats' side. The motto in the Democratic whip organization was "Win one for the Tipper."

The key to the Democrats' strategy was to win back the votes of moderates like Dave McCurdy who had switched to Reagan's camp in 1985 after Ortega's trip to Moscow. In January, an Associated Press survey of thirty-three swing voters found thirteen of them opposed to lethal aid, seventeen undecided, and only three in favor.[76] In theory, then, it was possible for the Democratic leadership to reassemble a majority against Reagan's proposal.

Reagan's allies on Capitol Hill warned that unless he showed some flexibility, he would lose.[77] Surprisingly, as administration officials were forced toward some sort of compromise, the one person they did not want to deal with was Dave McCurdy. The consensus among Republicans was that they had given up too much to get his support in 1985—agreeing to limit contra aid to nonlethal supplies and to prohibit CIA involvement in its delivery. By 1986, with the Sandinistas making major gains on the battlefield, these limitations loomed large, and McCurdy was now demanding further concessions.

McCurdy was angry that Reagan had not made good on the promise in his June 1985 letter to reopen bilateral negotiations with Nicaragua. To McCurdy, this looked like duplicity, and he was embarrassed at having gotten nothing but a worthless letter in exchange for helping Reagan win a major victory on nonlethal aid. In 1986, he was not about to support the resumption of lethal aid without extracting some specific and enforceable commitments from the White House. Following the example set by his friend Les Aspin (D-Wis.) on the issue of the MX missile, McCurdy sought to mold administration policy by making Reagan negotiate for his support.[78]

The White House, however, resolved to win without McCurdy. Reagan proposed a superficial "compromise" of his own in hopes of splitting the undecided House moderates. He offered to delay lethal aid for sixty days, during which time he would encourage the Sandinistas to open negotiations with the contras aimed at forming a "consensus government." If they refused, the full lethal aid package would be disbursed. Reagan was not willing to put even this minor concession into law, however. Instead, he proposed to simply write another letter to Congress spelling out his intentions. "Beware of letters," warned Congressman Bill Richardson, one of the Democrats who had supported Reagan's nonlethal aid in 1985 on the strength of Reagan's letter promising bilateral talks. "Beware of compromises unless they're in legislative language."[79]

Spurned by the White House, McCurdy had no place to go but back into the Democratic fold. More than anything, he wanted to remain a key player on the Nicaragua issue, and his leverage depended upon allying with one side or the other; by themselves, his moderates were far too few to carry any proposal. In exchange for opposing Reagan's $100 million lethal aid request in March, Speaker O'Neill promised McCurdy an opportunity to present his own compromise plan in April. McCurdy agreed, and most of the conservative Democrats who had followed him into Reagan's camp in June 1985 followed him right back out again in March 1986.

The House vote on March 20 was a simple up or down vote on the aid proposal submitted by the White House, with no amendments allowed. The debate lasted two days, but had few new wrinkles.[80] A number of Republicans echoed Buchanan's charge that Democratic opponents of contra aid were pro-Communist. The Democrats indignantly denied it and carefully laced their remarks with harsh comments about the Sandinistas to prove their anti-Communist bona fides. For the most part, however, members on both sides simply recapitulated their standard briefs. "The arguments haven't changed since 1982 when we first discussed this matter on the House floor," Ed Boland acknowledged. "Neither have the facts."[81] In the end, Reagan's package was defeated, 222–210. Forty-six Democrats supported Reagan's proposal; sixteen Republicans opposed it.

The vote represented a major political loss for the president because he had invested so much time and prestige on it. But Reagan was unbowed. Echoing his statement a year earlier when nonlethal aid was initially rejected by the House, he called defeat of the $100 million package "a dark day for freedom," and pledged to continue the legislative struggle. "This vote must be reversed," he declared.[82]

The day after the vote, Reagan again hosted the Three A's at the White House and then, sporting a button that said, "If you like Cuba, you'll love Nicaragua," he appeared briefly before an assemblage of conservative activists and contra aid supporters. "We intend to bring this back to the House as many times as it takes to win," the president promised. Turning to the contra leaders, he declared, "We're in this together. . . . You are the future of Central America." Adolfo Calero, overcome by Reagan's profession of unflagging faith, raised his fist and shouted, "Viva Reagan!"

"Viva Reagan!" the audience shouted back.[83]

The War Flares Up

On the same day the House rejected Reagan's request for $100 million, the first of several hundred Nicaraguan troops entered Honduras to attack contra base camps ten miles inside the border. Although the assault force was larger than usual, such incursions were a regular occurrence. Sandinista troops, usually numbering no more than a few dozen, had crossed the frontier in pursuit of the contras on literally hundreds of occasions. Nor was this the first big operation. In May 1985, about a thousand Sandinista troops had attacked the main contra camp at Las Vegas, prompting the Honduran government to relocate the camp further from the border.[84] Another cross-border raid in September 1985 wounded half a dozen Honduran soldiers and killed at least one. The Hondurans responded with an airstrike against Sandinista artillery units on the Nicaraguan side of the border, shooting down a Nicaraguan helicopter in the process. Washington's reaction to the 1985 incursion was mild. After the initial denunciations, nothing more was said about the incident. On Capitol Hill, the September 1985 clash passed virtually unnoticed.

What distinguished the 1986 incursion from earlier ones was its timing, coming just after the House vote against contra aid. Perhaps the Sandinistas had simply given up on the idea that Congress could actually end the war and therefore decided to try to end it themselves by routing the contras on the battlefield. Or perhaps Washington's relatively mild response to previous incursions lulled the Sandinistas into thinking that another cross-border raid would have little effect. To the White House, the attack was a godsend. Like Ortega's 1985 trip to Moscow, it could be used to shame the moderate Democrats into changing their votes on contra aid.

Elliott Abrams broke the story on March 25, telling reporters that over 1,000 Nicaraguan troops had entered Honduras. At the White House, Larry Speakes put the number of troops at 1,500, and unnamed administration officials claimed the real number was 2,000.[85] At the State Department, spokesman Charles Redman called the incursion "the deepest, largest, most serious Nicaraguan penetration of Honduran territory ever." But he put the number of Sandinista troops at just 800, which matched the Pentagon's intelligence estimates.[86]

The administration's inability to get its numbers straight was not the only cause for skepticism about the Nicaraguan "invasion" of Honduras, as both Shultz and Weinberger called it. Evidence that the administration was hyping the incident for political purposes came from the Hondurans themselves. They were inclined to ignore the incursion, as they usually did with cross-border raids, both to avoid a confrontation that could lead to war with Nicaragua and to maintain the fiction that there were no contra camps in Honduras. This was a convenient fiction for the Sandinistas as well; they freely admitted launching an offensive against contra bases, but denied that their troops had crossed the frontier. "The Honduran government denies the presence of counterrevolutionary camps on its territory," said Daniel Ortega. "If such camps do not exist in Honduras, then the fighting must be going on inside Nicaragua."[87]

The Nicaraguan and Honduran governments had decided to handle the risk of border conflicts by establishing secret, back-channel communications with each other. The Hondurans supplied the Sandinistas with intelligence on contra military operations in exchange for advance warning of Sandinista border raids. That way, Honduran troops could be moved away from the area to avoid incidents between the two regular armies.[88] Thus, the Hondurans evinced a certain evenhandedness: they pretended not to see the contra camps on their territory, and they pretended not to see the Sandinista attacks on the camps.

In Washington, however, this was wholly unacceptable. The administration had denounced a Nicaraguan invasion of Honduras. The Hondurans would now have to ask for help, whether they wanted to or not. At first, Honduras denied any incursion was taking place. When a U.S. official asked President José Azcona to send Washington a letter requesting emergency military aid, he refused.[89]

"You have got to tell them to declare there was an incursion!" Abrams's deputy William Walker shouted at Ambassador John Ferch's deputy over the telephone.[90] Ferch then went to Azcona and explained reality. "You don't have a choice in this one. You've got to get a letter up there right now," Ferch instructed the Honduran president. "They're going bonkers up there. This is absurd, but you've got to do it."[91]

Washington's leverage was straightforward. "My understanding," explained a U.S. official, "is that we said to them, 'If you do not admit a problem down there at your border, then perhaps you don't need our help and our money.'" Azcona sent the letter.[92]

In response to the Honduran request for assistance, Reagan invoked his emergency powers to send $20 million in military aid, along with U.S.-piloted helicopters to ferry Honduran troops to the border area, which they had been assiduously avoiding. By this time, the Sandinistas had already withdrawn.[93]

Throughout the crisis, Azcona refused to interrupt his Easter vacation. Various Honduran officials spoke privately to the press, accusing Reagan of inflating the incident in order to win votes in Congress, thereby forcing the Hondurans into a confrontation they did not want. "The United States' interest was that this situation have the connotations of an international incident," said a senior Honduran official. "We had no interest in this. We can't lend ourselves to a two-hour political debate in Washington that leads us into a confrontation with Nicaragua." A headline in the Honduran press said it all: "Washington Tells Hondurans We Are at War."[94]

In light of the Hondurans' reluctance to play up the incursion, the U.S. press reacted skeptically to administration efforts to portray it as a massive invasion.[95] The skepticism was justified. When a CIA intelligence assessment concluded that the incursion was a routine raid, Casey insisted that the paper be redrafted to conclude that the Sandinistas' aim was "to knock out the contras" while Congress debated whether or not to help them. Casey also directed that a "sanitized version" of the report be given to the White House public diplomacy apparatus for use in the United States.[96]

After Abrams fired him in July 1986 for being "lukewarm" in his support for the contras, Ambassador John Ferch admitted that the administration had concocted the Honduran crisis.[97] Ferch, a career foreign service officer with extensive experience in Latin America, had been fired because he treated Honduras as a sovereign country rather than a satrapy, whereas Abrams wanted "somebody down there to be strong enough and proconsul enough that no Honduran government is going to object to anything." Rather than accept a new assignment, Ferch retired. "I really don't think I want to have anything to do with the Foreign Service," he said in disgust.[98]

Although the political impact of the incursion was muted by the general impression that the administration had intentionally stoked it into a crisis, it still scared the Democrats. It still reminded them of Ortega's trip to Moscow.

Speaker Tip O'Neill labeled the incursion "a terrible blunder" by Ortega, whom he castigated as "a bumbling, incompetent Marxist-Leninist."[99]

The incursion probably accounted for the administration's surprise victory in the Senate. On March 27, while fighting was still under way along the Nicaraguan-Honduran border, the Senate voted 53–47 to approve Reagan's $100 million contra aid request with only slight modifications.[100] That put the issue back in the House. As the price for McCurdy's support in March, Speaker O'Neill had promised him a later opportunity to present an alternative contra aid plan of his own. After Republicans scuttled an attempt to bring McCurdy's proposal to the House floor in April, O'Neill scheduled the final showdown on contra aid for June.[101]

Clean Boots and Dirty Hands

Although only a few weeks separated the House votes on contra aid in March and June, events in Central America were moving quickly. Three issues—contra corruption, contra drug-smuggling, and the Contadora peace process—that had been slowly percolating in the background suddenly came to the fore as the debate entered its final stages, and they all seemed to favor the Democrats.

Back in 1985, to be sure the State Department was abiding by the limitations on how it could spend the $27 million in nonlethal aid approved by Congress, Michael Barnes's subcommittee had asked the General Accounting Office (GAO) to oversee distribution of the funds by the State Department's Nicaraguan Humanitarian Aid Office (NHAO).[102] The GAO presented the preliminary results of its inquiry in early March 1986, and its report sent a shock wave across Capitol Hill. Of the $27 million, $17.3 million could not be adequately accounted for. The GAO was careful to specify that it had no hard proof the money had been stolen; it simply could not track where it had gone.[103] Money spent in Central America (over half of the total) was not being monitored by the NHAO. It was simply transferred into the bank accounts of foreign firms acting as brokers for the contras, where the audit trail abruptly ended. When GAO officials tried to go to Central America to verify unaudited expenditures, the administration refused to permit it, citing diplomatic sensitivities.[104]

Democrats were outraged, especially since the law providing the $27 million explicitly required the administration to "establish appropriate procedures to ensure that any humanitarian assistance . . . is not diverted for acquisition of weapons."[105] On the face of it, the State Department appeared to be simply ignoring the law because it was inconvenient.

Administration officials insisted they were doing the best they could. The Hondurans were so uncomfortable about the presence of the contras that they refused to allow any NHAO personnel to be stationed in Honduras. Thus verification of the contras' claimed expenditures could only be accomplished by reports from CIA officers in the field. Based on those reports, administration officials insisted that most of the money spent in Central America was buying appropriate items. NHAO director Robert W. Duemling said that the amount being lost to contra corruption amounted to "tiddlywinks."[106] But because the classified CIA reports involved intelligence sources and methods, the administration refused to show them to the GAO or to Barnes's subcommittee. They could only be seen by the Intelligence Committee, which could not reveal what the reports said.[107]

Had there been an atmosphere of trust between Congress and the executive branch, perhaps the dubious nature of the NHAO's auditing procedures would have been excused as the inevitable consequence of running an overt aid program for a purportedly covert army in a country trying to pretend the army wasn't there. But between Reagan and the Democrats, there was no trust at all.

Moreover, the contras did not have a spotless record. Many Democrats were convinced that if the NHAO's laxity gave the contras an opportunity to steal from the till, they would. According to former FDN director Edgar Chamorro, senior contra commanders began skimming money from the funds provided by the CIA during the early 1980s. Complaints from contra field commanders echoed Chamorro's charges. In September 1981, six commanders accused military chief Enrique Bermúdez and his cronies of stealing $50,000. The six were purged from the FDN. In early 1984, yet another revolt against corruption broke out when forty-two contra commanders signed a petition demanding the ouster of Bermúdez and seven of his top aides. The CIA was so concerned that it conducted polygraph examinations of the entire FDN general staff with the sole exception of Bermúdez himself, then forced him to reorganize his command. Nevertheless, the CIA backed Bermúdez when he again purged the dissident commanders.[108]

By 1986, some thirty contra field commanders had either quit the FDN or been ousted over corruption. "I think the entire leadership is corrupt," said Gerardo Martínez, former commander of the contras' elite "Jeane Kirkpatrick Task Force." People at the top, he said bitterly, were "living a high life" at the expense of troops in the field. "They have clean boots and dirty hands," the field commanders said of their erstwhile leaders living in Tegucigalpa and Miami.[109]

The nonlethal aid program offered unprecedented opportunities for corruption. The contras could submit phony or inflated receipts as a way of generating money for military purchases, as occasionally happened. But more substantial profits could be made in currency manipulation because of the difference between the official exchange rate and the black market exchange rate. When the contras submitted bills to the NHAO for the dollar value of goods purchased in local currency, they used the official exchange rate. Then they converted the dollars provided by the NHAO on the black market, generating far more local currency than they would have at the official rate. Thus they could buy the requisite goods and still have a tidy sum left over.

North's aide, Robert Owen, who nominally worked for the NHAO, estimated that the FDN was regularly making a 37 percent profit on such currency manipulation. "This does not even take into account the false receipts," he wrote in a memo to North in March 1986. The problem, Owen explained to North, was the people Calero had around him. "Unfortunately, they are not first rate people; in fact, they are liars, and greed and power motivated. . . . THIS WAR HAS BECOME A BUSINESS TO MANY OF THEM," he typed in capital letters. "If the $100 million is approved and things go on like they have these last five years, it will be like pouring money down a sink hole."[110]

The issue of contra corruption seemed tailor-made for the Democrats. It was yet another indication of the contras' moral weakness, they argued, and the administration's antagonism toward the GAO investigation was yet another example of its willingness to skirt the law to keep the war going. Moreover, by 1986, the domestic budget deficit was moving to the forefront as the nation's premier economic problem. The draconian Gramm-Rudman-Hollings automatic budget-cutting procedures had been adopted, and Congress was slashing almost every discretionary domestic program. Foreign aid, never a popular item with the voters, was an obvious target for cuts, and most voters regarded contra aid as just another category of foreign assistance. Among the majority of the public who consistently opposed contra aid, the most frequent reason cited was that the money could be put to better use at home.[111]

The administration stonewalled on the corruption issue, accusing the Democrats of making a mountain out of a molehill. When the GAO issued an interim report on the eve of the final June 1986 vote on Reagan's $100 million request, Shultz and Abrams both blasted it. "Obviously, it was something concocted by people in the Congress who are opposing us on this vote," Shultz asserted. "It was a put-up job." Abrams took the same line, arguing that the report was nothing more than "a smear campaign" by Democrats trying to defeat contra aid.[112]

When a group of journalists asked Ronald Reagan about the contra corruption charges, he blamed Congress, implying that it had forced the administration to create an ineffective accounting system. "I don't see why their investigation has not revealed, as yet, that they were so concerned that the agencies of the executive branch might not be trustworthy in the handling of this money, that in the passing of this money, that in the passing of the $27 million, they laid down the strict rules as to exactly how that money must be delivered and spent," said the president to his bewildered listeners. "And we followed those rules," he continued. "I think they ought to give us back control of that because they didn't do too well." Moreover, he added, the stories of contra corruption were mostly untrue anyway: "Much of this we have found is part of the disinformation campaign tending to discredit them."[113]

Denials of the charges of contra corruption were as disingenuous as the denials of contra human rights abuses. The CIA knew that corruption had been an ongoing problem in the FDN for years, North knew from Owen's reports that the NHAO was being defrauded, and the State Department's own investigators had turned up evidence that some NHAO money had been diverted to purchase weapons and ammunition. None of this was shared with Congress.[114]

Surprisingly, the corruption issue seemed to have little impact on swing voters in the House. In part, this was because of the circumstantial nature of the evidence; the NHAO's inadequate supervision of the program made it impossible to know how much money had been stolen. As one administration official said with relief, there was no "smoking gun" of large-scale theft.[115] If a swing member wanted to look the other way on contra corruption, the evidence was not compelling enough to prevent it. Moreover, as in the case of El Salvador, many members regarded corruption as an inevitable part of the overhead cost of any foreign assistance program. If the basic aims of the program served U.S. interests, then a certain amount of corruption was tolerable.

Smuggling Drugs to Finance the War

The charge that the contras had been smuggling drugs was potentially more damaging. As early as 1984, rumors implicated members of Edén Pastora's command in drug trafficking. But the source of the accusations—the Nicaraguan government—made it easy for Washington to summarily dismiss the charges as "a big disinformation campaign," even though officials in the intelligence community knew they were true.[116]

In December 1985, two reporters for Associated Press, Brian Barger and Robert Parry, broke the story of the contra drug connection. Quoting U.S. law enforcement officials and American citizens working with the contras, Barger and Parry detailed how contra commanders in Costa Rica were assisting the Colombian cartel. The contras provided airstrips and refueling services for drug planes and shipped drugs across Costa Rica to Atlantic seaports where they were loaded on shrimp boats destined for the United States.[117]

Even conservative Republicans in Congress demanded that the charges of contra drug smuggling be thoroughly investigated. After several months, the administration sent Congress a three-page report acknowledging, "Individual members of the resistance . . . may have engaged in such activity [drug trafficking] but it was, insofar as we can determine, without the authorization of resistance leaders." Any other accusations of contra drug smuggling were, according to Elliott Abrams, "simply charges whose purpose is to defeat the aid proposals in Congress."[118]

The contras' involvement was deeper than the White House let on. The CIA had known since 1984 that contras on the southern front were smuggling drugs. "It is not a couple of people. It is a lot of people," CIA Central America Task Force chief Alan Fiers testified later. "There was a lot of cocaine trafficking around Edén Pastora."[119] The other main contra group operating from Costa Rica, led by Fernando "El Negro" Chamorro, was also involved with the traffickers, according to North's aide, Robert Owen.[120]

General Manuel Noriega, head of Panama's armed forces, was a key link in the contras' drug connection. A paid CIA asset for more than twenty years, Noriega gladly purchased weapons for the contras and had his pilots deliver them to contra camps in Costa Rica. The planes, however, carried both guns and drugs. The guns were off-loaded in Costa Rica, where the planes refueled and then flew the drugs on to the United States.[121]

Circumstantial evidence suggested even closer ties between the contras and the traffickers. Five of the firms hired by the NHAO to ship nonlethal aid to the contras were involved in drug trafficking, and two of the brokers the NHAO used to handle currency transactions were under investigation as laundering operations for drug money.[122] While such connections were highly suggestive, there was no solid proof implicating senior contra leaders in the drug trade.[123]

El Casi

The persistent reports of contra human rights abuses, corruption, and drug smuggling convinced some administration officials that the FDN needed new leadership if it was ever going to establish credibility inside Nicaragua or on Capitol Hill. The continuing control of FDN military forces by former members of Somoza's National Guard made even other Nicaraguan exiles loath to associate with them. "The people of Nicaragua remember the Guard for murder, torture and the bombardment of cities," Edén Pastora said, explaining why he wouldn't join forces with the FDN. "The memory makes people's hair stand on end. The very words are a curse."[124]

No one denied that the FDN had been dominated by former guardsmen at its founding, but the State Department insisted that over the years, the contras had evolved into a truly mass movement in which the guardsmen were only a small minority. In fact, though rank-and-file contra soldiers were mostly poor peasants, the FDN command structure was still controlled by former guardsmen. Of the thirteen members of the FDN general staff, twelve (including the commander, Bermúdez) were former National Guard officers. Five of the six regional commanders and all of the thirty task force commanders were former guardsmen. Even Adolfo Calero's colleagues Arturo Cruz and Alfonso Robelo were uneasy with the taint of the Guard.[125]

Administration officials were divided over whether to push for changes in the rebel leadership. Hard-liners like Undersecretary of Defense for Policy Fred Iklé, CIA Central America Task Force chief Alan Fiers, and Oliver North at the NSC wanted to stick with Bermúdez and Calero. They knew them, had worked with them for years, and trusted them, blemishes notwithstanding. At the State Department, Elliott Abrams hoped to promote more attractive contra figures like Cruz and Robelo.[126]

From the beginning of the contra program, the United States had been deeply involved in trying to forge unity among the various contra factions, to make them both more effective in the field and more credible abroad. In 1981, the CIA helped create the FDN out of several diverse splinter groups, and in 1983 it picked a new FDN directorate. From 1982 to 1984, Dewey Clarridge tried unsuccessfully to broker the unification of the FDN in the north with Pastora's group in the south. Failing that, the CIA enticed Alfonso Robelo to split with Pastora in 1984 and, in early 1986, drove Pastora out of the war entirely by bribing most of his field commanders to desert him in exchange for U.S. aid.[127]

By 1985, Washington had become more interested in the contras' civilian political front. In June, just before the final House vote on the $27 million nonlethal aid package, Oliver North brokered a shotgun marriage among Cruz, Robelo, and Calero, who signed a pact creating the United Nicaraguan Opposition (Unidad Nicaragüense Opositor, UNO), with themselves as directors.[128] From the beginning, the alliance of the Three A's was unequal. Neither Cruz nor Robelo had any troops under his command, or any significant political following inside Nicaragua. Their only asset was their good standing in Washington. Calero, on the other hand, headed the FDN and its army of some 12,000 combatants.

FDN leaders were contemptuous of Cruz and Robelo, regarding them as collaborators for having served briefly in the Sandinista government.[129] Bermúdez treated UNO as just a public relations front created to win support from Congress. Indeed, UNO was essentially powerless because decisions among the Three A's were made by consensus, so Calero could block anything he disliked. "No one tells the FDN what to do," confirmed Calero's deputy Aristedes Sánchez, "not UNO, not anyone."[130]

By October 1985, just three months after UNO's creation, Cruz was threatening to quit because UNO was nothing but a paper organization designed to take advantage of his good name without giving him any real power.[131] Robelo was discontented as well. "Cruz and I were integrated into the FDN to clean their face," he complained. In addition to progress on human rights, Cruz and Robelo demanded control over the FDN's finances because they suspected corruption.[132]

By March 1986, nothing had changed, and Cruz was again threatening to resign. Abrams, who was directing the campaign for the $100 million aid package, worried that if Cruz quit, the swing members of the House would kill the package. The moderates, especially McCurdy's group, respected Cruz and Robelo, but they regarded Calero and the FDN as reactionaries likely to restore a Somoza-style dictatorship. "If Cruz walks," McCurdy warned, "they might as well kiss support to the rebels goodbye."[133]

Throughout his tenure with UNO, Cruz played Hamlet. He threatened resignation, reconciled with Calero, threatened again, and reconciled again. It was, for him, a familiar pattern. Cruz always seemed to have excruciating difficulty making political commitments. Among Nicaraguans, he was nicknamed "El Casi"—the Almost. As a young man, Cruz graduated from Nicaragua's military academy, but refused to join the National Guard. Instead, he went abroad to study economics, but never finished his doctorate. In 1981, when differences with the Sandinistas led him to resign from the governing junta, he took the job as Nicaraguan ambassador to the United States rather than leave the government. But after only a few months, he resigned from that post, too. He quickly became a confidential adviser to Edén Pastora, but could not bring himself to openly identify with the contras. In January 1982, he spurned Dewey Clarridge's efforts to recruit him as the political leader of the FDN (the job eventually given to Adolfo Calero); nevertheless, in 1983, he went on the CIA's payroll.[134] In 1984, he accepted the internal opposition's nomination to run against Daniel Ortega for the presidency, but then could not decide whether to stay in the race. In early 1985, he declared himself in favor of contra aid, but disclaimed any intention of joining the contras. Then just a few months later, he joined Robelo and Calero to form UNO. Now, in May 1986, with the June vote looming on the $100 million aid package, he was threatening to resign.

Abrams met with the Three A's on April 14, 1986, and warned them that they were in danger of losing the $100 million aid package unless they stopped bickering and moved ahead quickly with reforms. The FDN felt betrayed. Weren't they the ones that had built a 12,000-man army? What had Cruz and Robelo ever accomplished? "You could say that we're being penalized for success,"

Calero said unhappily. Other FDN officials reacted less diplomatically. "We're being stabbed in the back," said one.[135]

At Abrams's urging, the Three A's signed the "Miami agreements," in which Calero promised to make many of the changes Cruz had been demanding. Cruz agreed not to resign.[136] But try as it might, the State Department could not make its reforms stick in the face of resistance from the CIA and Oliver North. "We're trying, but we don't have people on the ground," Abrams's deputy William Walker told a pro-reform contra leader.[137] After the House vote in June, the State Department lost interest in pressing Calero to reform, and nothing changed. "The FDN still has the troops," a U.S. official said, explaining the inability of UNO's civilian directorate to exert any control over the movement. Among the contras, political power still grew out of the barrel of a gun.[138]

"Pentagon Predicts Big War if Latins Sign Peace Accord"

The administration's internal differences broke into the open in late May 1986, just weeks before the scheduled final round of voting on contra aid. But it was not the issue of contra reform that provoked the embarrassing display of disunity; it was the old disagreement over diplomacy.

At the behest of the Contadora countries, the Central Americans had resumed negotiations in early April 1986, but found themselves deadlocked. In June, the Contadora foreign ministers submitted a third draft treaty, warning the Central Americans that this would be the last. The Nicaraguans agreed to sign, but only on the condition that the United States pledge to abide by the accord. Costa Rica, Honduras, and El Salvador all rejected the draft on the grounds that it provided no guarantee of democratization in Nicaragua.[139]

After almost four years of Contadora negotiations, the gap between Nicaragua and the other countries still appeared unbridgeable. With considerable skill, Washington had used its leverage to shift Contadora's agenda away from security issues and toward "democracy." The same issue that administration hard-liners had used to torpedo the bilateral talks between Washington and Managua had been turned against the multilateral diplomatic process with similar effect.

Despite the dearth of progress, "No one dares to declare the process officially dead," admitted a Contadora diplomat.[140] To give up on diplomacy was to admit the inevitability of wider war. With the Contadora nations unwilling to see the process fail and the United States unwilling to let it succeed, the Contadora negotiations seemed destined to continue interminably—like a hopelessly comatose patient whose family cannot bear to turn off the life-support equipment.

The administration was anxious to pin the blame for Contadora's failure on the Sandinistas. In April, Ambassador Philip Habib wrote a letter to Representative Jim Slattery (D-Kan.) portraying the administration's position on Contadora as eminently reasonable. In the letter, which the State Department also transmitted to the Contadora nations as an official statement of U.S. policy, Habib pledged that Washington would, "as a matter of policy," abide by the terms of an accord that was being fully respected by all the signatories. Most important, he interpreted the draft accord as requiring an end to contra aid "from the date of signature" of the agreement.[141]

To be sure, there were various escape clauses carefully crafted into the letter, and the United States would make its own determination as to whether Nicaragua was abiding by the accord. Nevertheless, the Habib letter represented yet another indication that some State Department officials were still willing to trade the contras for a negotiated settlement with Nicaragua.

The Habib letter exploded like a bomb inside the Reagan administration, leading to open warfare. Congressional conservatives acted as point men for administration hard-liners, accusing Habib of "selling out" the contras.[142] Congressman Jack Kemp (R-N.Y.) and Senator Jesse Helms (R-N.C.) complained directly to Reagan, and Kemp even urged Reagan to fire the envoy. Publicly, the White House defended Habib, but an unnamed "senior administration official" repudiated the Habib letter, saying that Washington would not end its support of the contras until Nicaragua had fully implemented any agreement.[143]

This internal battle escalated when the Defense Department released a study entitled "Prospects for Containment of Nicaragua's Communist Government." The report was an attempt by the hard-liners to discredit the Contadora process. It argued that if a Contadora agreement was signed, Nicaragua would violate it and the United States would have no choice but to intervene directly with 100,000 troops at a cost of $9.1 billion the first year. The *New York Times* headline reporting on the study captured its Orwellian premise: "Pentagon Predicts Big War if Latins Sign Peace Accord."[144]

The State Department denounced the Pentagon report as having "no standing as a United States Government document." Undersecretary of Defense Fred C. Iklé, who had directed the study, called the State Department "plain wrong," insisting that the document had been cleared with senior officials both at State and in the White House.[145] President Reagan did little to reduce the chaos, assuring the hard-liners that he would never abandon the contras, while simultaneously expressing confidence in Habib, whose letter pledged that Washington *would* abandon the contras if a Contadora agreement was signed. The whole episode reinforced congressional skepticism about the coherence of administration policy and the sincerity of the White House's claims to support a regional diplomatic settlement.

The House Decides

As the June 1986 House vote on Reagan's $100 million contra aid proposal approached, the Democrats were reasonably confident. Stories of contra corruption, drug smuggling, and disunity seemed to weaken the administration's position. The diplomatic stalemate in Contadora undercut the Democrats' calls for a diplomatic approach rather than a military one, but the brouhaha between administration hard-liners and pragmatists over the Habib letter had cast the White House as an enemy of diplomacy. It was difficult to imagine that anyone would have swung to the administration's side on the merits of the issue.

But Reagan was in search of just seven votes. Enormous pressure was brought to bear on the sixteen House Republicans who had voted against the president in March. The White House posed the issue as one of party loyalty, hinting that the president (whose popularity stood at a near-record 67 percent) would remember this benchmark vote when he was deciding which Republican candidates to campaign for in the fall.[146] Still, whip counts showed that Reagan could not convince enough of the dissident Republicans to build a majority; he would have to seek out some of the Democrats in the McCurdy group as well. After negotiating unsuccessfully with McCurdy himself, the White House set out to splinter his group, picking off just enough members to win.

The need to target moderate Democrats dictated a change in strategy. The harsh partisan rhetoric that characterized the debate earlier in the year was replaced by a conciliatory call for bipartisanship. Reagan's public denunciations of the Sandinistas were replaced by quiet, one-on-one lobbying of swing voters. The day before the vote, Reagan gave a speech to the nation from the White House. Pat Buchanan had wanted Reagan to give a prime-time television address, as he did on the eve of the House vote in March, but senior White House aides in Chief of Staff Don Regan's office—"the mice," Buchanan called them—vetoed that idea. If the president was going to lose, as it appeared he might, better not to call attention to it. Instead of scheduling the address in prime time, they scheduled it at noon. None of the networks broadcast it.[147]

The climactic debate on contra aid was joined on June 25.[148] The Republicans proposed Reagan's $100 million aid package once again. McCurdy offered a plan allowing only $30 million in nonlethal aid to be distributed to the contras immediately; $70 million in lethal aid would be delayed for six months, at the end of which Congress would vote again on whether to release it; and Washington would provide $350 million in economic aid to strengthen Central

America's "democracies." By holding off lethal military aid, the Democrats hoped to give the Contadora countries more time to produce a peace agreement. Although liberals were not happy about providing any aid, they grudgingly agreed to back the McCurdy plan because it was the best they could hope to pass.

One serious weakness of the McCurdy plan was that it required yet another congressional vote on military aid, scheduled for October—just a few weeks before congressional elections. Few members wanted to go through another bitter debate, and since many swing members worried about the political repercussions of their contra aid votes, they certainly did not want to cast a decisive one at the height of a campaign. "They want to get it behind them," McCurdy admitted. "They're tired of jumping through the hoop."[149]

The rhetoric in the House was more restrained than usual; all sides put forward their most moderate and reasonable advocates in order to avoid alienating any wavering voters. Throughout the chamber, as the debate wound toward a conclusion, members on both sides of the debate shared Majority Whip Tom Foley's sense that this was "a truly historic occasion," tantamount to a declaration of war.[150]

The first vote was the critical one—a choice between the administration's proposal and McCurdy's. Reagan won, 221–209. To Speaker O'Neill, the loss was a bitter disappointment, but he tried to be philosophical about it. "While we lost, we did the right thing," he said. "We followed the will of the American people. You can't do more than that."[151]

Fifty-one Democrats voted with the president and only eleven Republicans voted against him. Eleven members who had opposed Reagan in March sided with him in June and gave him his margin of victory. Five were Republicans who simply gave in to partisan pressure from the White House. The remaining six were Democrats, several of whom were on the Armed Services Committee, including its chairman, Les Aspin, whose vote almost certainly influenced those of his committee colleagues. For Aspin, the motive was largely ideological; his seat was safe and his constituents were more likely to oppose contra aid than support it. Privately, Aspin had favored contra aid for over a year, but hesitated to break ranks for fear of further complicating his relations with the party leadership and the liberals, relations already strained by his championing of the MX missile.[152] At the moment of truth, however, Aspin cast his vote for contra aid on the Republican side of the House and then stood around joking with the grateful Republicans while his own party went down to defeat.[153] It was a spectacle his Democratic colleagues would not soon forget.

Ronald Reagan was chiefly responsible for the victory. He lobbied the swing voters personally, making phone calls right up until the vote, and he won commitments from eight of the eleven who switched. "When a president gets to the point that he can pinpoint 20 people and work face to face with them, he's hard to stop," admitted Tip O'Neill.[154]

On June 26, the day after the House passed Reagan's $100 million aid package, the World Court announced its verdict on Nicaragua's complaint against the United States. On fifteen counts, the court found the United States in violation of international law for arming the contras, attacking Nicaragua directly (the UCLA attacks in 1983 and 1984), mining Nicaragua's harbors, embargoing Nicaraguan trade, and violating Nicaraguan airspace with reconnaissance overflights. The court called on the United States to "immediately cease and to refrain from all such acts" and to "make reparation to the Republic of Nicaragua for all injury caused" by U.S. actions. The State Department was unimpressed. "The Court's decisions are not self-enforcing," said spokesman Charles Redman. "It doesn't have the power to order anything."[155]

The Sandinistas' reaction to the House vote came swiftly. The following day, the Nicaraguan government announced the "indefinite suspension" of the opposition newspaper *La Prensa*. The day after that, June 27, the government refused to allow Monsignor Bismark Carballo, director of the Catholic radio station, back into the country after a trip abroad, and a week later, it expelled Bishop Pablo Antonio Vega, the most outspoken critic of the government next to Cardinal Miguel Obando y Bravo himself. "We have tolerated things that no country in our situation . . . would tolerate," Comandante Bayardo Arce said. "We have been permitting citizens to act openly as agents of a country that is at war with [our] country." They would no longer tolerate such "traitors." Anticipating the coming escalation of the war, the Soviet Union agreed to triple the size of Nicaragua's helicopter fleet.[156]

Back in Washington, the Reagan administration moved quickly to add the contra aid package to the military construction bill in the Senate, the next necessary step toward final approval. Senate opponents of contra aid had little hope of defeating it. In March, the Senate had voted 53–47 for essentially the same package. But Reagan's victory in the House had a sobering effect on Senate Democrats, who were accustomed to relying on the House to put the brakes on U.S. policy. Now they were the last bulwark against a major escalation of the war, and the realization galvanized them to action.

Led by freshmen Tom Harkin (D-Iowa) and John Kerry (D-Mass.), Senate liberals organized a filibuster and quickly picked up the support of senior members Alan Cranston (D-Calif.), Edward Kennedy (D-Mass.), and Intelligence Committee vice chairman Patrick Leahy (D-Vt.). Not all opponents of contra aid thought a filibuster was a good idea, however. Senator Christopher Dodd, whose credentials as an opponent of contra aid were unimpeachable (he sponsored the first effort in the Senate to cut off contra aid in December 1982), opposed the filibuster. He feared it would allow Reagan to brand the Democrats as "obstructionist" and thereby damage their chances for regaining control of the Senate in the upcoming 1986 election. Better to give Reagan a vote on contra aid, Dodd argued, regain control of the Senate, and then launch a concerted effort to stop the war.[157]

Moderate Democrats such as Jim Sasser and Minority Leader Robert Byrd were reluctant to fight the gritty battle required to sustain a filibuster. Byrd's opposition made it especially difficult for the liberals to hold their moderate Democratic colleagues. Finally, moderate Republicans who opposed contra aid were loath to engender the wrath of their leadership by blocking a final vote on contra aid when its proponents clearly had majority support.[158]

Nevertheless, the administration was sorely worried since a dozen determined senators could wage a protracted battle delaying final passage of the contra aid package for days or weeks. As the Senate moved into August and members became anxious to adjourn for the fall campaign, pressure would mount on the Republican leadership to negotiate a compromise. But any change from the bill passed by the House meant that the contra aid package would have to go to conference committee (further delaying it), and then the conference reports would have to come back to the House and Senate, giving contra aid opponents yet another chance to kill it.

To prevent a Democratic filibuster on contra aid, Majority Leader Bob Dole tied it to the issue of economic sanctions against South Africa. Senator Kennedy wanted to pass a tough sanctions bill before the August recess. Whenever Kennedy tried to attach sanctions to pending legislation, Dole threatened to attach contra aid as well, thus forcing the Democrats to accept contra aid as the price for getting sanctions against South Africa. Dole was also willing to trade one issue off against the other, offering to forego a sanctions filibuster if the Democrats would abandon the contra aid filibuster.

At first the liberals refused, and the Senate remained deadlocked. Gradually, Democratic opponents of the contra aid filibuster—Byrd, Daniel Inouye, Sasser, and Dodd—talked all but the most dedicated liberals into abandoning the struggle. Their ranks dwindling, the liberals sought to negotiate the best surrender terms possible. Instead of a filibuster aimed at stopping contra aid, they would settle for an extended debate in which they could fully explain their opposition to Reagan's Nicaragua policy and, hopefully, educate the American people.[159]

Debate in the Senate was more solemn than usual. One after another, Democrats implored their colleagues to reject a headlong rush into another quagmire.[160] Mark Hatfield, one of the few Republicans as adamantly opposed to contra aid as the liberal Democrats, was beside himself with anger over the impending escalation of the war. He denounced "that fraternity of compulsive interventionists" controlling the administration's foreign policy. "Here we are, once again, old men creating a monster for young men, young Americans, to destroy," Hatfield continued. "What a waste of life. What utter disregard for the lessons of history."[161]

Reagan's Republican supporters said little in rebuttal. Knowing they had the votes to prevail, the Republicans were anxious to get the debate over with as quickly as possible. During three days, the Democrats offered more than a dozen amendments to the contra aid package. All of them were defeated. On August 12, the Senate rejected 54–46 a motion by Sasser and Dodd to strike the contra aid program from the military construction bill, and the following day it formally approved the contra aid portion of the bill, 53–47. Eleven Democrats sided with the administration, and eleven Republicans broke ranks to oppose the package. When the House and Senate worked out their differences over other issues in the bill after the August recess, Reagan had his $100 million for the war in Nicaragua.

How Reagan Won

With the House vote in June and the Senate vote in August, the Congress had come full circle—from the two-year-long battle to control the covert war, culminating in the October 1984 cut-off of funds, through the administration's successful two-year struggle to restore the program. Reagan's victory was impressive. At the height of opposition to the contra war in 1984 and early 1985, House Democrats held more than a sixty-vote margin over the White House. Reagan gradually eroded the opposition coalition around its ideological edge, peeling off moderates a few at a time. He was persistent, refusing to take no for an answer. Time after time, he returned to Congress with new contra aid proposals, eventually wearing down the margin and wearing out his opponents. "It was a personal victory for the president," Mike Barnes said of Reagan's triumph. "He just kept coming back and coming back."[162] The few dozen swing voters were the subject of extraordinary presidential attention—and pressure. Reagan badgered them, threatened them, courted them, and promised them favors. It was, said one White House official, "the Vince Lombardi school of legislative strategy—three yards at a time."[163]

The administration played heavily on the tried and true themes of anti-Communism: the Sandinistas were Marxist-Leninists, puppets of Havana and Moscow. Unless stopped by Washington, they would export revolution to their neighbors, toppling dominoes south to the Panama Canal and north to the Texas border. The litany of Sandinista crimes recited by administration spokesmen was boundless: they had done away with all human rights, committed genocide against the Miskito Indians, driven the Jewish community into exile with anti-Semitic pogroms, smuggled drugs to poison the youth of America, and allowed Nicaragua to become a base for international terrorism.

The demonization of Nicaragua became so extreme that it caricatured itself. Few people who followed the issue took the charges literally—especially since the administration could rarely adduce much concrete evidence to back them up. But even though the exaggerated rhetoric was discounted, it had effect. It skewed the terms of debate, shifting the ground from the question of the effectiveness and propriety of the contra war to the issue of the Sandinista government's character.

This proved to be a fatal shift for Reagan's opponents. The Sandinistas, under the mounting pressures of war, acted in ways that gave ammunition to Reagan's campaign of vilification. They moved into closer political and military alliance with Cuba and the Soviet Union and tightened internal controls against the civic opposition. Many Democrats argued that these developments were consequences of Reagan's war, but that did not make the events any less disturbing. Whenever the Sandinistas did something that was politically embarrassing for the Democrats, such as Ortega's trip to Moscow in 1985 and the incursion into Honduras in 1986, opponents of the covert war felt the ground slip out from under them.

The Democrats tried to deflect the administration's assault on the Sandinistas' character by shifting the debate back to the merits of Reagan's policy, where the Democrats generally had the better of the argument. In hopes of doing this, they began conceding the evils of the Sandinista government. A floor statement during the June 1986 debate by Majority Whip Thomas Foley (D-Wash.), an ardent opponent of contra aid, was typical. "What we decide tonight is not whether we agree with the Government of Nicaragua; it has no support in this body," Foley declared. "I agree with the characterizations that have been made by the president . . . concerning the decline of respect for human values, for religious freedom, and for freedom of the press that are the sad, daily chronicle of the abuses of the Government in Managua."[164]

But the Democrats ended up conceding the argument without managing to shift its terms. Once they accepted Reagan's premise, their posture was unavoidably defensive. If the Sandinistas were as bad as Reagan said—or even half as bad—then certainly the United States needed to do something about them. Reagan promised to do something; he would pressure them to behave, and the Communists would understand force. As an alternative, the Democrats offered support for the Contadora negotiations. Contadora, however, was stalled. Whatever the merits of their case, the Democrats sounded soft. As

David Halberstam wrote of the decisionmaking that led to Vietnam, the advocates of force always had "the manhood argument" on their side.

The Democrats also tried to counter Reagan's attack on the Sandinistas by examining the moral character of the contras. The issue of contra human rights abuses was powerful in 1985, but by 1986 it had lost much of its punch. The administration neutralized it by denying the accuracy of reports about contra atrocities and then countering with stories of Sandinista atrocities.[165] Rather than trying to sort fact from fiction, many moderates accepted the conventional wisdom that both sides had reprehensible human rights records. Human rights was replaced in 1986 by the issue of contra corruption, which the Democrats also hoped would reveal the contras' moral turpitude. It had surprisingly little effect.

Both the human rights and corruption issues suffered from the serious flaw of being tangential. Most Democrats did not oppose the contra war because of human rights abuses or corruption. The core of opposition to the war was based on the belief that it was ineffective and immoral. The Democrats debated the peripheral issues because they hoped to find something that would convince undecided colleagues who did not share their basic convictions. But by focusing on peripheral issues rather than on the war itself, the Democrats left themselves vulnerable to Reagan's pledges to reform the contras.

The significance of the contra aid debate went well beyond Nicaragua. Reagan's support of the contras was the most visible and controversial manifestation of the Reagan Doctrine, which represented a reorientation of U.S. foreign policy away from the containment doctrine that had guided it since World War II and toward a more aggressive and potentially risky "roll back" policy— using military force to subvert Communist governments around the world.

Reagan's quest for bipartisan acquiescence to his Nicaragua policy was, in large measure, an attempt to return to the pre-Vietnam era of congressional-executive relations when presidents made foreign policy and Congress rubber-stamped it. Reagan was still intent upon exorcising the Vietnam syndrome from the national psyche. In the flush of its 1986 victory, the administration bragged of a new bipartisanship behind its policy, but its majority remained razor thin, its opponents still willing and able to do battle. No one believed that $100 million would end the war in Nicaragua, so it was inevitable that Reagan would soon return to Congress for yet another increase in aid, yet another step up the ladder of escalation, and the battle would be joined once again.

CHAPTER 20

Iran-Contra

As Ronald Reagan was winning $100 million for the contras, the secret of Oliver North's operation was unraveling. In Miami, U.S. Attorney Leon Kellner had launched an investigation into contra gunrunning and drug trafficking, which was beginning to impinge on the Enterprise.[1] At the same time, reporters who had begun tracking North's activities in 1985 were gradually putting the pieces together. "Colonel's Actions May Have Broken Contra Aid Ban," read the headline on Alfonso Chardy's April 30, 1986, story in the *Miami Herald*. In June, Chardy wrote several follow-up pieces that identified North as the principal architect of the contras' private aid network and Robert Owen as North's "messenger boy."[2] Chardy and the *Herald* won a Pulitzer Prize for uncovering the Enterprise, and other journalists were not far behind on the trail.[3]

The new reports of North's activities prompted another round of congressional inquiries. In letters to three House committees, National Security Adviser John M. Poindexter reiterated Robert McFarlane's 1985 denials, assuring the Congress that "the actions of the National Security Council staff were in compliance with both the spirit and the letter of the law." Later, Poindexter would argue this was not a lie because he did not believe the Boland amendment applied to the NSC staff. He was unapologetic about the deception: "My objective all along was to withhold from the Congress exactly what the NSC staff was doing in carrying out the president's policy."[4]

Poindexter's assurances notwithstanding, the House Intelligence Committee interviewed North on August 6, 1986. He denied everything. All he did in his role as liaison with the contra leadership, he claimed, was to apprise them of the legal restrictions imposed by the Boland amendment, assess their long-term viability, and give them advice on human rights. Press reports to the contrary were the fruits of a "Soviet disinformation campaign."[5] Later, North would admit that all of this was untrue, but the committee believed him, and it decided not to investigate any further.[6] When Poindexter heard about the meeting, he sent North a computer message reading, "Well done."[7]

Even though Congress was easily put off, the conspirators were worried about the increasingly widespread knowledge of their operation. Owen was particularly nervous about the Miami investigation. "If and when I am contacted by the FBI I will not answer any questions without an attorney present," he wrote to North. "Even then, I will not answer any questions. It is the only way I can see to stem the tide."[8]

Back in Washington, North too had a sense that things were coming unglued. In May, he told Poindexter there was an "urgent need" to turn the contra support network over to the CIA, lest it be exposed. "The more money there is . . . the more visible the program becomes . . . and the more inquisitive become people like Kerry, Barnes, Harkins [*sic*], et al.," he warned. Still, North didn't want Poindexter to think he was burned out. "I am not complaining," he wrote, "and you know that I love the work, but we have to lift some of this onto the CIA so that I can get more than 2–3 hours of sleep at night."[9]

The Fat Lady Sings

It was broad daylight on October 6, 1986, when the big C-123 cargo plane nicknamed "The Fat Lady" came lumbering across the Nicaraguan–Costa Rican border carrying 10,000 pounds of arms and ammunition for contra troops inside Nicaragua. For security's sake, such a mission should have been flown at night, but the troops on the ground had been unable to accurately identify their own position or mark a proper drop zone. The only way the supply plane could make contact with them was to fly in daylight so the soldiers could see it coming.[10] That meant the Sandinistas could see it, too.

Nineteen-year-old José Fernando Canales had only been in the Sandinista army a few months when the C-123 appeared in the sky over his position. Aiming his Soviet-made shoulder-launched surface-to-air missile just as he had been trained, he fired, and the missile swept upward toward the big, slow-moving target above him. The heat-seeking SAM-7 struck the plane's wing, and Canales watched in amazement as it plummeted to earth. "I thought I was dreaming," he said of his triumph.[11]

Inside the plane, only cargo handler Eugene Hasenfus was wearing a parachute. The Enterprise did not provide them, and Hasenfus's fellow crew members razzed him no end about wearing the one his brother had given him. But when the Sandinista missile hit, sending the plane careening toward the ground, Hasenfus was able to dive out the open cargo door and save himself. The other three men on board—two former CIA pilots and a Nicaraguan radioman—died on impact.

Sandinista troops found Hasenfus the next day, not far from the crash site, sleeping in a makeshift hammock fashioned from his life-saving parachute. In captivity, Hasenfus exhibited the same instinct for survival that led him to wear the chute. He had taken the job dropping supplies to the contras because he needed the money, not out of any ideological conviction. "This is not my war," he declared, and proceeded to tell both the Sandinistas and the news media everything he knew about the Enterprise.[12] He knew a lot. He described how he had been recruited for the job by old buddies from the CIA's secret air war in Southeast Asia. He detailed the operations at Ilopango, El Salvador, including the managerial role of the Cuban Americans and the patronage of Colonel James J. Steele, the U.S. Military Group commander. He confirmed that the emergency airfield in Costa Rica was part of the network. The only thing he didn't know for sure was who ran the operation from "Top Floor," the Enterprise's code word for Washington. He thought it was the CIA, since almost everyone involved seemed to have worked for the Agency at one time or another. But he knew one thing for sure. "It's in our government someplace," he avowed. "It's there."[13]

The wreckage of Hasenfus's plane contained an intelligence bonanza for the Sandinistas. The pilot had all his flight logs with him, documenting runs from Miami, Ilopango, Palmerola air base in Honduras, and Aguacate, the contras' forward base along the Honduran-Nicaraguan border. Other documents tied the crew members to Rob Owen, the State Department's Nicaraguan Humanitarian Assistance Office (NHAO), and Southern Air Transport, the former CIA proprietary company that supplied some of their planes.[14]

Within two weeks, reporters had acquired phone records in El Salvador showing numerous calls between the safe house that Hasenfus said was used by the Enterprise's flight crews and the offices of North, his partner in the Enterprise Richard Secord, Joe Fernandez (CIA station chief in Costa Rica), and

Southern Air Transport. The supersecret KL-43 encryption devices that allowed the principals in the Enterprise to communicate over regular phone lines left a trail of long-distance records that now linked the conspirators inextricably.[15]

Despite such damning evidence, the administration immediately and unequivocally denied any involvement with the Hasenfus flight. Secretary of State George Shultz insisted that the plane was "hired by private people" who were "not from our military, not from any U.S. government agency. . . . They had no connection with the U.S. government at all."[16]

Elliott Abrams thought the best defense was a good offense. Not only did he categorically deny any U.S. government connection with the contra resupply network, he praised the "private benefactors" profusely. On television shortly after Hasenfus was captured, a reporter asked Abrams, "Mr. Secretary, can you give me categorical assurances that Hasenfus was not under the control, the guidance, the direction, or what have you of anybody connected with the American government?"

"Absolutely," Abrams answered. "That would be illegal. We are barred from doing that and we are not doing that. This was not in any sense a U.S. government operation." Abrams repeated such denials over and over.[17]

Two days after Hasenfus was captured, Abrams chaired a Restricted Inter-Agency Group (RIG) meeting called to formulate a damage control plan. According to notes from the meeting, the participants decided to ask either the contras or retired general John Singlaub to "assume responsibility" for the plane. The cover stories, explained one official, were intended "to deflect attention from the White House." Over the next two days, senior administration officials spread word to the press that the flight belonged to Singlaub. This cover story had not been cleared with Singlaub, however, and it collapsed when he denied any involvement with the flight. The contras were more cooperative; within a week they were claiming the plane as their own.[18]

In the aftermath of the Hasenfus flight, Abrams was summoned to testify before the Western Hemisphere Subcommittee and the Intelligence Committee in the House, and the Foreign Relations Committee in the Senate. During the last two appearances, he was accompanied by the chief of the CIA's Central American Task Force, Alan Fiers, and the CIA's deputy director for operations, Clair George. Abrams took the lead in denying absolutely that there was any government link to the "private benefactors."[19]

Later, both Fiers and George would claim to have been shocked at Abrams's denials. They knew of North's role, and they assumed that as chairman of the RIG, Abrams did, too.[20] "I was surprised that Abrams made that statement,"

George admitted later. "The question is, should I leap up and say, 'Hold it, Elliott. . . .' I didn't have the guts to do it."

Fiers kept quiet, too. "I could have been more forthcoming, but I frankly was not going to be the first person to step up and do that. . . . So long as others who knew the details, as much as I, who knew more than I, were keeping their silence on this, I was going to keep my silence. . . . I was a member of the administration team. I wasn't going to break ranks with the team."[21]

Five years later, in 1991, Fiers and Abrams admitted that they had known more than they acknowledged at the time. Rather than face felony charges of perjury for giving false testimony to Congress, they pleaded guilty to reduced misdemeanor charges of misleading Congress. Clair George refused to cooperate with Iran-contra special prosecutor Lawrence E. Walsh and was indicted on ten felony counts of perjury, making false statements, and obstructing Congress.[22]

The downing of Hasenfus's plane marked the end of the Enterprise's contra resupply operation. Between press revelations and congressional inquiries, the whole project had become too public. As Secord moved the planes and pilots out of Ilopango, Casey told North to destroy the paper trail. "This whole thing is coming unravelled," Casey said. "Get rid of things. Clean things up." North began shredding documents to eliminate any record of the network.[23]

In the wake of the Hasenfus shoot-down, no one in Washington had much doubt that the White House was covertly supporting the contras in defiance of the Boland amendment. Senior administration officials were admitting as much to the press on background, but for the record, they continued to maintain the fiction that all the reports detailing operations of the Enterprise were untrue.

The Democrats, for their part, felt stymied. They were certain that North and other officials were operating near the edge of the law if not outside it, but congressional Republicans blocked any investigation. In the House, Republicans and conservative Democrats prevented an inquiry by the Intelligence Committee. In the Senate, Chairman Richard G. Lugar of the Foreign Relations Committee refused to give Senator John Kerry subpoena power to pursue his investigation of drug smuggling by the contras and their "private benefactors." So long as administration officials were willing to lie and refuse to produce relevant documents, the Democrats could not obtain definitive proof of what everybody in Washington knew.

Perhaps the new Congress elected in November 1986 would have launched a serious investigation of Oliver North's Enterprise on the strength of the Hasenfus revelations alone. But before it had that opportunity, a small magazine in Lebanon triggered the biggest political scandal in Washington since Watergate.

Things Fall Apart

On November 3, the day before the 1986 congressional elections, the Lebanese magazine *Al Shiraa* reported that the United States had been selling arms to Iran to secure the release of U.S. hostages in Lebanon. The story was soon picked up by the U.S. press, but for a week, administration officials, including Reagan himself, either refused to comment on the allegation or denied it. The story would not disappear, however, and on November 13, Reagan went on national television to admit that he had sold arms to Iran after all, though he continued to deny he had traded arms for hostages.[24]

Over the next week, administration officials scrambled to recover from the worst public relations catastrophe of Reagan's presidency. On November 19, Reagan held a disastrous news conference, during which he was defensive, unsteady, and made several fundamental factual errors about the Iran initiative, prompting the White House to issue corrections almost immediately.[25] Reagan's poor performance was due in part to the inability of senior officials to agree on what exactly had transpired during the approach to Iran—or what they were willing to admit. On Friday, November 21, Reagan's longtime aide Edwin Meese, now attorney general, offered to undertake an informal inquiry to determine the facts. Reagan agreed.[26]

Shortly after hearing of the impending inquiry, North told McFarlane that he was going to have a "shredding party" over the weekend. North began destroying evidence of both the Iran and contra operations that afternoon, shredding a stack of documents a foot and a half high. The destruction of documents continued throughout the weekend, so heavy at times that it jammed North's shredding machine. He also had his secretary, Fawn Hall, collect the original copies of six contra-related documents that McFarlane had identified as problems during the 1985 congressional inquiries. North altered these by eliminating references to military and logistical assistance to the contras and fundraising from third countries. He then directed Hall to prepare new doctored documents to replace the originals. Poindexter and Secord, in their respective offices, also began destroying documents.[27]

On Saturday, November 22, Meese's aides went to North's office to examine his files and came across an eight-page memorandum entitled "Release of American Hostages in Beirut," which described the arms sales to Iran. There were several versions of the memo, but only one included a paragraph on Nicaragua: "The residual funds from this transaction are allocated as follows: . . . $12 million will be used to purchase critically needed supplies for the Nicaraguan Democratic Forces."[28] Profits from the arms sales were being diverted to the contras.

Meese's aides realized immediately that they had uncovered a bombshell. So did Meese. "Oh, shit," said the attorney general when his aides told him what they had found.[29] But it was not clear from the memo whether or not that particular arms deal with Iran had been consummated. To find out, Meese had to ask North.

The attorney general and his aides interviewed North the following day, and he was visibly surprised when his interrogators showed him the diversion memo. "Oh, shit," he thought. "This was precisely the kind of document I had shredded."[30] Meese asked North if he had told the president about the diversion, and North replied that Poindexter was the person who dealt with the president. North then proceeded to give a false account of the diversion, claiming that it had been the Israelis' idea and that they had paid the money directly into contra bank accounts. North didn't mention Secord.[31]

Although North seemed surprised that Justice Department investigators had found the diversion memo, Meese took no steps to secure the remaining documents in North's files. That night, North stayed at the office until 4:30 in the morning, shredding.[32] At this point, North was not concealing his operation from the Sandinistas or congressional liberals; he was concealing it from the attorney general, who was conducting an investigation at the personal behest of the president.

Meese informed Reagan of the diversion on Monday, November 24. The president reacted, by his own recollection, with "surprise, shock, and disbelief." Chief of Staff Donald Regan, who was at the meeting, thought Reagan's surprise was genuine.[33] CIA Director Casey tried to convince Reagan not to disclose the diversion, on the grounds that it would destroy congressional support for the contras, but that view was quickly overruled. As Meese admitted later, he feared the diversion could lead to Reagan's impeachment if the press uncovered it before the administration announced it.[34]

On the morning of November 25, Regan informed Admiral Poindexter that he would have to submit his resignation. Later that day, after informing the cabinet and congressional leaders of the diversion, Reagan went before the White House press corps. He announced that he had not been "fully informed" about one aspect of the Iran initiative, which was "seriously flawed." Consequently, Admiral Poindexter had resigned as national security adviser, and Lieutenant Colonel Oliver North had been "relieved of his duties" on the NSC staff. After these brief and cryptic remarks, Reagan turned the floor over to Meese to drop the bomb. "Certain monies" received from the arms sales to Iran "were taken and made available to the forces in Central America which are opposing the Sandinista government there," Meese explained.[35]

As he sat watching the press conference on television, Oliver North had no idea that he was about to be fired. He was, to say the least, stunned. His reaction shifted from shock to anger when a reporter asked if any laws had been broken and Meese replied, "We are presently looking into the legal aspects of it as to whether there's any criminality involved."[36]

North had known all along that if the full story of the Enterprise leaked, it would unleash a political firestorm. He was perfectly willing to be the "fall guy," protecting Poindexter and Reagan. In fact, North and Casey had discussed the need for such a contingency plan. "I was simply willing to take the fall if somebody needed a political scapegoat," North later testified. "I was to be dropped like a hot rock when it all came down." But North expected his liability would be merely political, not criminal. He was not willing to go to jail for carrying out the mission given to him by Casey, McFarlane, Poindexter, and, he believed, the president. "I never in my wildest dreams or nightmares envisioned that we would end up with criminal charges."[37]

Later in the day, after Meese's press conference, Reagan called North and disclaimed any awareness of the diversion. "I just didn't know," he said. Reagan didn't scold North for acting improperly, or ask who had authorized North's actions. Instead, he praised him. "Ollie, you're a national hero," Reagan said, adding, "This is going to make a great movie one day." The president reaffirmed his characterization of North as a hero repeatedly over subsequent months.[38]

The revelation of the diversion set in motion a bevy of official investigations. On December 1, 1986, Reagan appointed a Special Review Board chaired by former Republican senator John Tower to examine what had gone wrong with the NSC system in the Iran-contra affair. That same day, the Senate Intelligence Committee launched a preliminary investigation of its own.[39] In January, both the House and Senate created special select investigating committees. Operating together as the Iran-contra Committee, they conducted an extensive joint investigation lasting through most of 1987. On December 19, 1986, the Justice Department appointed a special prosecutor, Lawrence E. Walsh, to investigate possible criminal liability.

At the height of the turmoil over the Iran-contra revelations, one of the central players was suddenly and unexpectedly removed from the stage. On December 15, 1986, CIA Director William Casey suffered a seizure and collapsed at his office. Doctors discovered a brain tumor. Confined to the hospital, his health deteriorating, Casey resigned six weeks later. Casey, who so hated congressional meddling in intelligence matters, escaped the indignity of having to explain his role in Oliver North's Enterprise under the klieg lights of a televised congressional investigation. On May 6, the day after the Iran-Contra committee began holding public hearings, Bill Casey died.

Moratorium

The political aftershocks of the Iran-contra revelations were disastrous for Ronald Reagan. Most Americans did not believe him when he denied trading arms for hostages or knowing about the diversion of funds to the contras.[40] Reagan, who for years had managed to portray himself as a "citizen politician," above the venality and dishonesty of professional politics, now looked like just one more dissembling political operator. Stripped of his most valuable asset—his credibility—Reagan's popularity plummeted. From early November to early December, it fell 21 points from 67 percent approval to 46 percent, the steepest descent the polls had ever recorded—worse, even, than the collapse of Nixon's support during Watergate.[41]

Reagan's decline was all the more dramatic because for six years he had maintained consistently high ratings, defying the conventional wisdom that presidential popularity inevitably declines over time because the complexities of governing compel presidents to make enemies faster than they make friends. Until now, neither gaffes nor scandals had shaken the public's confidence in Reagan, leading Congresswoman Patricia Schroeder to dub him the "teflon president." By December 1986, his teflon had worn perilously thin.

The scandal's effect was magnified by its timing, coming as it did close on the heels of the Democrats' victory in the 1986 midterm elections. Despite an exhausting personal campaign effort by Reagan himself—he traveled over 24,000 miles and made fifty-five appearances in twenty-two states—the Republicans lost eight seats, giving the Democrats control of the Senate, 55–45. The 1986 election demonstrated dramatically that Reagan's popularity was not transferable to other Republicans—he had "teflon coattails," quipped Senator John Glenn.[42]

The election debacle also made Republicans less willing to take unpopular stands at the behest of the White House. Few officeholders were eager to climb out on a limb by defending arms sales to the Ayatollah or secret aid for the contras, both of which were highly unpopular. As the Iran-contra scandal engulfed the White House, Ronald Reagan's friends lost faith in the power of his political charm and his adversaries ceased to fear him. "The contras are on their own," said Dave McCurdy. "The power of the president, the personality of the president, is not going to carry the day for them again."[43]

Reagan and his allies on Capitol Hill tried to insulate the contra aid program from the spreading contagion of the scandal, insisting that the merits of the policy were unchanged. But inevitably, the scandal tainted the entire policy. Members who continued to voice their support for contra aid ran the risk of appearing to condone the deception and lawbreaking associated with it. Most administration officials were pessimistic about the contras' prospects for survival. "If you wanted to bet the smart money," said one, "you'd bet that this thing is going to go down the tubes."[44]

Ronald Reagan, however, was undaunted. On December 4, 1986, he declared "unflinching" dedication to the contra cause, insisting that the Iran-contra scandal was irrelevant. In his State of the Union message, he affirmed that contra aid would be one of his main foreign policy priorities during his last two years in office.[45] In February, the administration announced it would ask Congress for another $105 million for the contras in the new fiscal year (FY 1988).[46]

The Democrats were equally determined that 1987 would be the year they definitively ended contra aid. Both the new Speaker of the House, Jim Wright, and the new Senate majority leader, Robert Byrd, promised that the issue would be a top priority. Les Aspin nearly lost his chairmanship of the powerful House Armed Services Committee because he had voted for Reagan's $100 million contra aid package in June 1986—proof of the passion that the issue generated among Democrats.[47]

The first postscandal test of strength between Reagan and his opponents came in early March 1987, when Congress had a chance to block dispersal of the final $40 million from the $100 million package approved the previous summer. The 1986 law provided for this review, although it was essentially hollow because Congress had no real hope of stopping the funds. Even if both the House and Senate voted against dispersal, Reagan could veto their resolution of disapproval, so the contras would ultimately get their $40 million. Nevertheless, the March 1987 votes were an important bellwether—dress rehearsals for the real showdown later in the year when Reagan would need a majority to pass his new $105 million aid request.

To make the most of the March vote, House Democrats decided to replace the simple yea or nay vote on releasing the remaining $40 million with a resolution calling for a six-month "moratorium" on further contra aid until the administration made a full accounting of how previous aid had been spent. The moratorium resolution was the idea of David Bonior (D-Mich.), who had just been elected chief deputy whip in reward for his management of the Democrats' fight against contra aid in 1986. Even though Reagan won that battle, Bonior's deft integration of legislative strategy, press relations, and lobbying by grassroots groups won high praise.[48] First elected to Congress in 1976 from a blue-collar district in Michigan, Bonior was a low-key, diligent insider—a member who focused on the hard work of legislating rather than showy public relations. In 1981, he was selected to sit on the Rules Committee, and in 1985 he was chosen to be one of seven deputy whips in the Democratic leadership organization. But Bonior was not just an organization man. He spoke his mind, even when it put him at odds with majority opinion in his district (which was less liberal than he), or with his liberal colleagues.[49]

Central America, especially Reagan's proxy war against Nicaragua, aroused Bonior's passion. The policy, he believed, was not just bad politics—it was illegal and immoral. In 1983, Tip O'Neill appointed Bonior to direct a special Speaker's Task Force on Central America. He ran the task force for the next five years, becoming the chief legislative strategist for the Democratic leadership on Central American issues. When Mike Barnes left the House in 1986, Bonior succeeded him as the House's foremost opponent of Reagan's policy.

Bonior's strategy was to make the March 1987 vote the easiest possible vote for opponents of contra aid and the hardest for supporters. By putting an anticorruption spin on the resolution, he provided excellent political cover for moderates whose constituents favored the contra cause. House members who voted to release the $40 million without an accounting risked looking like patsies if the stories about contra corruption proved to be true. He had another aim as well. "It can build a nice bridge to moderates voting 'no' later," he told Wright. Bonior understood the need to offer moderates who had supported Reagan in 1986 a way to vote against contra aid that could not be characterized as inconsistent with their earlier position.

Majority Leader Thomas Foley opposed Bonior's plan because it required changing the rules in a way that verged on unfairness. The 1986 law called for a simple resolution of approval or disapproval, and although it was within the power of the House to substitute the moratorium resolution instead, it was not altogether fair play. At the very least, Foley warned, such jiggering with the rules would enrage the Republicans and damage the collegiality of the House.[50]

But on the issue of contra aid, there was not much collegiality left after two years of red-baiting by Newt Gingrich and friends. Wright sided with Bonior. The decision was exemplary of Wright's approach to the speakership. To Tip O'Neill, the House was like a living thing, with its own mind and momentum. A Speaker might influence and guide it, but ultimately the House would work its will. To Wright, the House was more like a machine. An effective leader, like a skilled machine operator, could pull the right levers and turn the right wheels to make the machine do his bidding. The rules were one important lever, and Wright was not averse to using them.

Foley was right about the Republicans. They complained bitterly that the moratorium resolution was unfair, and in retaliation they agreed at their caucus meeting to attack the Democrats for being soft on Communism. Virtually every Republican who rose to speak against the moratorium resolution began by declaring, "I do not want to be recorded as handing Central America over to the Soviets."[51] Many said worse.

Debate from the Democratic side focused mainly on the Iran-contra scandal as dramatic confirmation of the corruption of the contras and of Reagan's policy as a whole. "The determination to carry on the contra war despite the overwhelming opposition of the American people, has led this administration to set up a secret government, a private foreign policy," Bonior declared. "The drive to wage this war has led the administration to bypass our system of checks and balances, to ignore the Constitution of the United States, and to subvert the law of the land."[52]

On March 11, 1987, the moratorium resolution was approved, 230–196, with seventeen Republicans voting in favor of it and forty conservative Democrats voting against. Passage by such a wide margin represented a significant gain in strength for contra aid opponents; they had lost the June 1986 vote on Reagan's $100 million aid package 221–209. On an issue where most members had a well-defined, consistent position established over literally a dozen roll calls, gaining twenty-one votes was a major achievement.

The Senate, unlike the House, could not easily change its rules to substitute a moratorium resolution for the simple resolution of disapproval on releasing the $40 million. Although the Democrats had won control of the Senate, the election produced a net gain of only two votes against contra aid. Several of the defeated Republicans had been contra aid opponents, and several of the victorious Democratic challengers in the South were contra aid supporters. When the resolution of disapproval came up on March 18, it lost 52–48.[53]

Casi Fué (Almost Gone)

The Iran-contra scandal was not the only thing eroding the contras' support on Capitol Hill. Their image problem was aggravated by their internal bickering, which flared up again early in 1987. The feud between Adolfo Calero and United Nicaraguan Opposition (UNO) co-directors Arturo Cruz and Alfonso Robelo had subsided temporarily after they signed the Miami agreements in June 1986, in which Calero pledged to surrender significant control over the contra army to the UNO directorate. He never did. He refused to allow his co-directors to see the Nicaraguan Democratic Force's (FDN) financial records, and he resisted imposing sanctions on contra officers accused of human rights abuses. FDN military commanders, meanwhile, said openly that they would not take orders from UNO.[54]

When Cruz visited a main base camp of the FDN in Honduras, he was introduced not as a leader of the movement, but as a "guest of the FDN." On the bulletin board, he found an article describing him and Robelo as the "true enemies" of Nicaraguan democracy. "We are struggling in two directions," one of UNO's top leaders conceded, "against the Sandinistas and among ourselves. And sometimes the struggle is more passionate among ourselves."[55] In late January 1987, Cruz finally decided that UNO was beyond redemption and began telling friends and reporters that he was going to resign. He cleaned out his desk in the UNO office in Miami.[56]

"There is no single leader that has more credibility than Arturo Cruz," Elliott Abrams acknowledged. "Nobody's irreplaceable, but he comes as close as you can get." Abrams pleaded with Cruz to stick it out, promising that the State Department would continue to back his demands for reform. But Cruz insisted his mind was made up; he really had decided to quit. "I have been under pressure, but the most important pressure is my own conscience," he told an interviewer. "So I'm going, I'm going." But he didn't go. For weeks on end, Cruz talked about quitting, but didn't quit. While Cruz equivocated, Robelo got into the act, threatening that he, too, would resign unless Calero was forced out and the UNO directorate was given the power to replace FDN military commanders like Bermúdez.[57]

With the flood of Iran-contra revelations endangering congressional support for the contra program, the administration could ill afford to have UNO fall apart. The specter of Cruz and Robelo's resignations once again galvanized the government into pressing Calero to accede to demands for reform. Calero was much weaker than he had been a year before. Not only was he implicated in the Iran-contra scandal, but his principal patrons inside the government—North, Poindexter, and Casey—had all been replaced. Midlevel CIA operatives still preferred Calero to the opportunist Robelo or the intellectual Cruz, but Shultz, Abrams, and the new national security adviser, Frank C. Carlucci, were all convinced that contra reform was an unavoidable prerequisite for sustaining contra aid in Congress.[58] In a meeting on February 12, 1987, Abrams told Calero he would have to resign from the UNO directorate to preserve any hope of further U.S. aid.[59]

Four days later, Calero resigned. Conservatives were bitter about the administration's willingness to jettison an old friend. Senator Jesse Helms charged that Calero's ouster had been "forced by high officials in the State Department who are seeking a capitulation to the Communists"—not something Elliott Abrams was accused of very often.[60] But in reality, Calero had not given up a great deal. He would remain president of the FDN, which would retain its own command structure. Since UNO had never been more than a facade pasted on the FDN to prettify it for Congress, Calero would continue to control the contra movement. The rest, a U.S. official conceded, was "cosmetics."[61]

Cosmetic or not, the stratagem seemed to work. After a bit of caviling, both Robelo and Cruz agreed to remain on the UNO directorate. Exiled *La Prensa* editor Pedro Chamorro (eldest son of Pedro Joaquín Chamorro, whose assassination in 1978 sparked the insurrection against Somoza) took Calero's seat. Chamorro was selected by an assembly of delegates from various Nicaraguan exile groups meeting in Costa Rica. The assembly was as divided as the old directorate had been. After two days of bitter debate and factional deadlock, they finally chose Chamorro only when an official from the U.S. embassy in San José warned them that Washington would cut off the assembly's finances unless they came to a decision. That seemed to concentrate their minds.[62]

The storm had not quite passed, however. On March 9, just two days before the House was scheduled to vote on release of the $40 million, Arturo Cruz changed his mind again and, without telling anyone in advance, announced his resignation. Stunned administration officials tried to downplay the significance of his departure, and George Shultz denigrated Cruz for quitting.[63] But there was no gainsaying the damage done to the contras' image.

Cruz was an honest, well-intentioned man of enormous naïveté who didn't belong in politics. Every political operator he met seemed to take advantage of him. He ended up with his reputation sullied by the revelation that he had been on both the CIA's and Oliver North's payroll. Cruz began taking money from the CIA in 1983 but had to be taken off its accounts in early 1985 because he was lobbying Congress in support of contra aid, something for which CIA money could not legally be used.[64] When members of the House Intelligence Committee complained, North simply shifted Cruz over to the Enterprise's payroll, which paid him $7,000 monthly until North was fired in November 1986. North entitled one of his memos to McFarlane discussing these financial arrangements "Cruz Control."[65]

"It doesn't look real good to have a guy we've been putting forward as a key Nicaraguan leader drawing a salary from Ollie North," admitted a State Department official. "One of our vulnerabilities all along has been the charge that these leaders were chosen by the United States and not by Nicaraguans. Unfortunately, the charge is true."[66]

Stalling for Time

After losing the March moratorium vote in the House, the White House decided to delay the president's request for the new $105 million lethal aid package until the fall.[67] This had two virtues. First, it put off the vote until after the flood of Iran-contra disclosures and associated congressional hearings. Second, it gave the contras time to try to redeem their reputation by making some dramatic military gains using the $100 million approved in 1986.

The Iran-contra scandal cast new doubts on the contras' viability by revealing how utterly dependent on the United States they actually were. During the congressional debates in 1985 and 1986, the White House argued that the contras had proved their stamina by surviving and even growing during the ban on U.S. support.[68] In reality, however, almost all of the allegedly "private" support received by the contras was sent to them through the back door by the administration—solicited from foreign governments, diverted from the Iranian arms deal, or raised by private aid campaigns set up and run by the White House. In all, the administration raised some $47.8 million, not counting $10 million Elliott Abrams solicited from the Sultan of Brunei that was mislaid. The contras themselves had been able to raise only a million dollars in private donations. Financially at least, they were a wholly owned subsidiary of the United States.[69]

And despite the resumption of official U.S. support in 1986, they still weren't very effective. No contra forces had managed to establish themselves along the populous Pacific coast. The southern front had essentially collapsed with Pastora's withdrawal from the war in May 1986, and even the Atlantic coast was quiet as a result of Sandinista promises of autonomy for the rebellious Miskito Indian minority.[70] In the cities, the contras were unable to establish any underground movement to carry out sabotage, or even to paint anti-Sandinista graffiti on the walls. Occasional attempts to build an urban infrastructure were always quickly routed by the Nicaraguan security police. "It would be one thing not to have blown up Daniel Ortega's house after five years," a Western diplomat observed. "But they haven't even gotten anyone to spray-paint mean things about his mother."[71]

In the field, the contra army still did not behave like a guerrilla force. It had no political program beyond anti-Communism and did little political organizing even in regions like Chontales where it had some base of support. Despite persistent U.S. advice to the contrary, the rebels loved to attack peasant cooperatives and state farms, the symbols of everything they hated about the Sandinista regime. Attacks on the farms produced civilian casualties, often women and children. When the contras successfully occupied a farm, their modus operandi was to burn down all the peasants' houses and kidnap the able-bodied men, forcibly recruiting them into the contra army.[72] Apart from the adverse publicity such behavior produced in the American press, this was no way to win the hearts and minds of the Nicaraguan peasantry. In January 1987, General Paul Gorman (retired after his stint as South-Com commander) told Congress that the contras were nothing more than a "cross-border raiding party" with no chance of defeating the Sandinista army.[73]

The contras' continuing failure to register any significant political or military success made them look like a dubious investment. To win additional support from Congress, they needed to prove that they were more than a paper organization with offices in Miami and Tegucigalpa and bank accounts in Switzerland and the Cayman Islands. As Elliott Abrams put it, if the contras wanted more U.S. aid, they would "have to get it themselves with their performance on the ground."[74]

In January 1987, the contras began infiltrating en masse into northern and central Nicaragua. By midyear, their Honduran camps were largely deserted, and some eight to ten thousand soldiers were in the field. With $100 million in U.S. aid, they were now the best-trained and best-equipped guerrilla army in Latin American history. Several hundred field commanders had received specialized military instruction in the United States from the CIA and U.S. Army Special Forces, and hundreds more were scheduled for training throughout the year. Contra troops headed into combat sporting new uniforms, heavy mortars and machine guns, sophisticated "Red Eye" surface-to-air missiles, and portable computerized radio encoding equipment. Back in Honduras, the contras had a room full of computers for decoding Sandinista military communications intercepted for them by the United States. Washington's U-2 spy planes and other "national technical means" blanketed Nicaragua, tracking every move of the Nicaraguan armed forces and relaying the information to contra forces in the field.[75]

The CIA resumed control of the contras' logistics, operating several resupply flights each week out of Aguacate air base in Honduras and new installations built on Honduras's Tiger and Swan Islands—safe from prying reporters and Sandinista border raids.[76] CIA advisers picked the contras' military targets and trained contra demolition specialists for commando missions against Nicaragua's economic infrastructure. They especially targeted the power grid—a strategy inspired by the Salvadoran guerrilla attacks on electrical lines and substations. The CIA briefed the commandos using old blueprints of the targeted installations, most of which had been built by either the U.S. Army Corps of Engineers during the occupation of Nicaragua in the 1920s and 1930s, or the U.S. Agency for International Development during the Alliance for Progress in the 1960s.[77]

To improve their image in Washington, the contras once again began allowing journalists to visit their camps and accompany them into the field.[78] The trips did not always produce the desired effect. In April and May, some eight hundred contras tried to establish a base area and supply depot in the north-central Bocay river valley. The Sandinistas sent several thousand troops to drive the contras back into Honduras. During the battle for the Bocay valley, *Newsweek* correspondent Rod Nordland and photographer Bill Gentile spent a month with the contras. The contras, Nordland reported, "were more like a rabble on the loose than a guerrilla army in enemy country." When they came upon peasant homes in the mountains, they stole whatever food the peasants had. "Why not make me a gift of this chicken," a heavily armed contra trooper asked a terrified peasant. "No one ever refused," Nordland noted.

The contras were a fearsome bunch. The field commander of the group Nordland and Gentile accompanied was nicknamed "Attila," and others called themselves by such names as "Dragon," "Mercenary," and "Exterminator." Many sported skull-and-crossbones tattoos. The local peasants were scared to death of them. Frequently, the contras forced peasants to act as guides, walking "point" in front of the column of troops. The peasants, Nordland reported, felt "like human mine detectors."

"The contras were great at retreating," Nordland wrote. "Attacks, they never quite managed." In the month he and Gentile spent with them, they never attacked anything. They simply ignored the targets assigned to them by the central command because they were too heavily defended. One of Gentile's photographs showed the contras using a helicopter with a Red Cross emblem to move military supplies—a violation of the Geneva Convention. These "new contras," as some pundits were touting them, still looked a lot like the old National Guard.[79]

As the summer of 1986 approached, the contras were fighting more than they had in the two years since legal U.S. aid was cut off, but they weren't fighting any better. There were no signal victories to convince Congress that the contras were on the threshold of triumph, or to divert attention from the spectacle of the Iran-contra investigation.

Capitol Offenses

Through the winter of 1986 and into the spring of 1987, the Iran-contra affair dominated the headlines as reporters uncovered the fantastic story bit by bit, like archaeologists slowly unearthing a buried city brimming with artifacts. After five months of investigation, sorting through thousands of documents, and interviewing hundreds of witnesses, the House and Senate investigators began joint public hearings on May 5, 1987. Forty days of televised sessions stretched from May to August, exploring the dark corners of both the contra resupply operation and the Iran initiative. Like the Watergate hearings before them, the Iran-contra hearings held the Washington political community in rapt attention.

The Democratic leadership in both the House and Senate wanted to focus the Iran-contra investigation on fundamental constitutional issues rather than rehashing the merits of U.S. policy toward Nicaragua. After all, the Democrats had lost the debates on the merits of contra aid in 1985 and 1986. If the public concluded that they were using the investigation to batter the president for partisan advantage, a backlash could develop that would do more damage to the investigators than to the White House. "The idea was, if we stuck to process and constitutional questions, they were so important it would be easy to carry the day for us," explained David Bonior. "We didn't want to debate the policy itself."[80]

House Republicans took the opposite tack. From the beginning, their approach was intensely partisan. They regarded the proceedings as little more than a Democratic excuse to finish off the contras and render Ronald Reagan a premature lame duck. Their strategy was to protect the president, defend his Nicaragua policy, and attack the investigation they were supposedly conducting.[81]

The first witness was General Richard Secord. Testifying without immunity, he displayed a confident military bearing and was stubbornly unrepentant. His only regret was that the contra resupply operation had become public. The luster of Secord's patriotism was tarnished a bit by the fact that he amassed several million dollars in profit from being such a good patriot, but he offered to donate it to a fund for the contras, set up as a memorial to the late CIA Director Bill Casey.[82]

Robert McFarlane was at least appropriately contrite. He tried to take full responsibility for the Iran-contra scandal on his own shoulders, but it was a diffuse sort of responsibility, based simply on the fact that he had been national security adviser. When it came to specific misdeeds, he consistently denied knowing much of anything about what North had been doing.[83] Although McFarlane testified that he had briefed Ronald Reagan regularly on how the contras were faring and what the NSC was doing on their behalf, no one thought to ask him exactly what he told the president. He did say, though, that Ronald Reagan had a "far more liberal interpretation" about what could legally be done to help the contras under the Boland prohibition than McFarlane himself had.[84]

McFarlane's testimony raised so many questions about Reagan's role in the contra support operation that the White House changed its damage control strategy. Before McFarlane testified, Reagan insisted that he had not known the NSC staff was actively supporting the contras. That was what he told the Tower Board.[85] Two days after McFarlane finished testifying, Reagan offered a revised account of his knowledge. "As a matter of fact, I was very definitely involved in the decisions about support to the freedom fighters," he told a group of newspaper editors. "It was my idea to begin with."[86] The White House began claiming that Reagan and the NSC staff were not bound by the Boland amendment and therefore had done nothing illegal by continuing to support the contras.[87]

Elliott Abrams testified that although he knew North was "involved" with Secord's network, he believed that North was simply "monitoring" it, not actively coordinating it. And even though Secretary Shultz had warned him that North was a "loose cannon" and advised Abrams to keep an eye on him ("monitor Ollie," Abrams wrote in his notes), Abrams claimed that he never suspected what North was really doing. Nor did he ever ask North point-blank whether there was any truth in the flurry of newspaper reports about his efforts on behalf of the contras.[88]

There was, admittedly, a degree of willful ignorance behind this behavior. "Everybody involved in the RIG [Restricted Inter-Agency Group] knew that Ollie was somehow connected with this but did not know how," Abrams admitted. "Most of us were careful not to ask North a lot of questions, other than once in awhile to say is this all okay, is this stuff legal—once in awhile."[89]

In light of the many press accounts of North's adventures, some committee members found Abrams's ignorance a bit too convenient. His credibility was not helped by his admission that he had misled the Senate Intelligence Committee about third-country support for the contras.[90] During the hearing, Congressman Jack Brooks (D-Tex.) called Abrams's testimony "the wildest story I ever heard." Outside it, he called Abrams "a lying son of a bitch."[91]

Apart from appearances by a few supporting players, Abrams's testimony ended the first phase of the Iran-contra hearings. After a two-week break, the hearings would resume with the main attractions: Oliver North and John Poindexter, the two people who could answer the "Watergate question" of what Ronald Reagan knew.

On balance, the first phase of the hearings went reasonably well from the Democrats' point of view. Along with moderate Republicans Warren Rudman of New Hampshire, William S. Cohen of Maine, and Paul S. Trible of Virginia, they had tried with lawyerly dispassion to establish a factual record, relying on the slow accumulation of evidence to settle the issue of how high up in the administration the scandal reached. Witnesses had given the committee a detailed portrait of how the Enterprise came into being and how it worked. McFarlane and Abrams, the only senior administration officials to testify in the first phase of the hearings, both agreed that what had been done was wrong and probably illegal.

Republican conservatives, following the maxim that the best defense is a good offense, ignored the scandal and tried to turn the hearings into an advertisement for Reagan's Nicaragua policy. Instead of asking serious questions, they gave long soliloquies demonizing the Sandinistas, lionizing the contras, and implying that doubters were either cowards or Communists. They invited the witnesses to wax eloquent on the same themes. There was scant difference between the arguments heard from the witness stand and the Republican side of the dais.

The Democrats ignored the Republicans' fulminations. They did not contest the witnesses' laudatory accounts of the contras or the Republicans' assault on the right of Congress to participate in formulating foreign policy. Instead they went doggedly in pursuit of the facts, defending their passive response to Republican provocations by pointing out that the hearings were producing an inexorable accumulation of evidence against an ever-widening array of administration officials. This, they argued, was the heart of the matter. The Republicans' perorations were designed to distract attention from the culpability of their colleagues in the executive branch. It would be foolish to take the bait, engage the Republicans in verbal fisticuffs, and thereby allow the hearings to be transformed into a new contra aid debate.

Olliemania

This rationale for the Democrats' quiescence seemed reasonable enough until the coming of Lieutenant Colonel Oliver L. North. North's long-awaited appearance dramatically changed the atmosphere of the hearings and, for the first time, gave them a larger audience than the daytime soap operas.[92] North appeared in his Marine uniform bedecked with six rows of decorations: the all-American boy turned military hero. Over six days of testimony he took the committee and the nation on a roller coaster of emotion. He was defiant, proud, smug, indignant, and droll, shifting moods as easily as a veteran actor. Throughout his performance, he played the role of persecuted hero—the loyal and obedient Marine who took on the tough job of defending freedom by keeping the contras alive, succeeded against all odds, and was now being pilloried by the same bumbling politicians whose vacillation had endangered the freedom fighters in the first place.

North was the first witness to effectively challenge the very premise of the investigation. Secord had defended his own role, but did not offer a spirited defense of the policy underlying the contra resupply operation. McFarlane admitted that the operation was wrong and accepted responsibility for it, if not blame. Abrams, too, acknowledged it was wrong but claimed to have known nothing about it. North, however, was unapologetic. "I am going to walk from here with my head held high and my shoulders straight because I am proud of what we accomplished. I am proud of the efforts we made, and I am proud of the fight we fought," North said.[93]

Rather than accept blame, North counterattacked, accusing the Congress of endangering national security by interfering with the president's foreign policy. "Plain and simple, Congress is to blame because of its fickle, vacillating, unpredictable, 'on again, off again' policy toward the Nicaraguan Democratic Resistance," he charged.[94]

North freely admitted lying to Congress about his activities, with just a touch of remorse. "I want you to know that lying does not come easy to me," he said, "but I think we all had to weigh in the balance the difference between lives and lies." Congress could not be told the truth, he maintained, because it could not keep a secret, and if word of the operation had leaked, the lives of the people in the field would have been at risk.[95]

North also swore he had proper authorization for everything he did. "I realize there's a lot of people around that think there's a loose cannon on the gun deck of state at the NSC," North said with a hint of bitterness. "That wasn't what I heard while I worked there. I've only heard it since I left. People used to walk up to me and tell me what a great job I was doing. . . . I never carried out a single act, not one, . . . in which I did not have authority from my superiors."[96]

"I am not trying to drag in a whole bunch of people in the Ollie North dragnet here," North said, but then he did exactly that. In addition to Casey, McFarlane, and Poindexter, North named Elliott Abrams, CIA Central American Task Force chief Alan Fiers, and the late Vice Admiral Arthur Moreau (the Joint Chiefs of Staff representative on the RIG) as having had detailed knowledge of his operations. Others who had a general knowledge of his activities included CIA Deputy Director for Operations Clair George, former CIA Latin American division chief Dewey Clarridge, and former South-Com commander General Paul Gorman. At one point, North said, he had briefed a full RIG meeting on his activities.[97] He was convinced that his efforts were also "fairly well known" to senior officials like Shultz, Weinberger, and Joint Chiefs of Staff chairman General John Vessey, "although they may all deny it."[98] They did.

To the millions of Americans who watched North testify, he looked like an authentic American hero—an unabashed patriot, fearless soldier, and faithful family man. He seemed to embody all the values that his commander-in-chief, Ronald Reagan, had built a political career on. And like "the old man" himself, North was superb in front of an audience. People liked his willingness to take responsibility for what he had done. They liked his loyalty and unshakable commitment to his beliefs. They especially liked his defiance of the investigators. Here was a man of action, cutting through the red tape of a vaguely corrupt bureaucracy in order to get the job done. In a society grown too soft and decadent to defend itself against the forces of evil, rugged individualists like Oliver North would save us from our enemies. It was the plot of a thousand westerns and cop shows, from John Wayne to Clint Eastwood, and it struck a deep chord of resonance among the viewing public.

Sympathy for North surged; some 50,000 telegrams and letters of support poured in to Congress from all across the country. At the start of each new day of interrogation, North's lawyer piled the messages on the corner of the witness table—an ever-present, silent rebuke to the committee from the American people. Each day, supporters gathered outside the Capitol to cheer North as he entered and left the arena. A whole room filled with the flowers sent by well-wishers, and during breaks in the proceedings, congressional aides begged to have their pictures taken with North in the hearing room. Young men flocked to barbershops to get close-cropped "Ollie North" haircuts. "Ollie Takes the Hill: The Fall Guy Becomes Folk Hero," *Newsweek*'s cover proclaimed. The appearance of Ollie North T-shirts confirmed that the errant lieutenant colonel had become America's newest celebrity.[99]

Once the public's sympathy for North became apparent, few committee members wanted to risk appearing to persecute him. The conservative Republicans fawned over North and took the opportunity of his meteoric rise to celebrity to press their attack on the investigation itself.[100] Toward the end of North's appearance, some of the Democrats finally jettisoned their legalistic strategy and began lecturing him (and the viewing audience) on the rule of law, which North had so nonchalantly shredded. Maine senator George Mitchell reminded North that he and his friends held no monopoly on patriotism. "Please remember . . . that it is possible for an American to disagree with you on aid to the contras and still love God and still love this country as much as you do."[101]

After listening to North's opinion that the president was supreme in foreign policy and could ignore intelligence oversight laws by simply using the NSC staff, Lee Hamilton tried to explain to North that his conception of the foreign policy process left no room for checks and balances or accountability—the sinews of democracy. "You have an extraordinarily expansive view of presidential power," Hamilton observed. "I do not see how your attitude can be reconciled with the Constitution of the United States." Moderate Republicans Rudman and Cohen sounded the same theme. "I guess the last thing I want to say to you, Colonel," Rudman concluded, "is that the American people have the constitutional right to be wrong."[102]

The Buck Stops Here

Although North's testimony was by far the most dramatic, it did little to resolve the central question of the investigation—what did the president know and when did he know it. On that issue, North passed the buck to Admiral John Poindexter. Poindexter could hardly have drawn a sharper contrast to North. In his six days at the witness table, North displayed a gamut of emotions from indignation to wry amusement. Poindexter was emotionless, answering questions for five days with nary a crack in his taciturn demeanor. North, in his uniform, played the America hero to the hilt. Poindexter chose to wear civilian clothes to the hearing because he regarded his role at the NSC as separate from his duties as a navy admiral. North's testimony was a dramatic roller coaster as he jousted with the committee. Poindexter was almost boring because he stated his views matter-of-factly and professed not to recall many of the most critical events. He was, in short, anticlimactic.

Yet Poindexter's testimony was more chilling than North's. North's behavior could be understood, if not excused, as the excesses of a midlevel official who became too emotionally involved in his work. But Poindexter, who authorized North's actions, was a technician whose judgment was not clouded by emotional fervor. His decision to circumvent the will of Congress was cold and calculated. And, if his testimony was to be believed, he did it all on his own authority.

When North proposed the diversion of funds from the Iranian arms sales to the contras, Poindexter approved it on the spot, without seeking legal advice from either the White House counsel or the attorney general. "The thought never crossed my mind," he said. Poindexter also testified that he had decided not to tell the president about the diversion. The reason, he explained, was to give the president "deniability" so that if the operation was ever uncovered, Reagan could honestly claim to have known nothing about it. "The buck stops here with me," Poindexter told the committee. "I made the decision and I felt that I had the authority to do it. I was convinced that the president would in the end think it was good idea."[103]

The admiral insisted that he had not usurped the rightful role of the president. After all, the president had been "steadfast" in his support for the contras and had made it clear that he wanted to do everything possible to keep them fighting, regardless of congressional efforts to shut the war down. "I was aware that the president was aware of third-country support, that the president was aware of private support, and . . . it was obvious to me that this fell in exactly the same category," Poindexter said of the diversion. "I believe the president would have approved the decision at the time if I had asked him."[104]

The White House immediately denied that Reagan would have done any such thing. Reagan himself told the press that if it had been suggested to him, he would have yelled so loud that "you would have heard me without opening the door to the office." But the admiral's belief that he had done Reagan's bidding was unshaken. "I would have expected him to say that," Poindexter said of the president's denials. "That is the whole idea of deniability."[105]

Beyond the issue of the diversion, Poindexter was extraordinarily vague about what Ronald Reagan knew of the NSC's contra support activities. He acknowledged briefing the president regularly "on most all aspects of all the projects that Colonel North was involved with," including third-country and private efforts to keep the contras alive. "He understood the contras were being supported and that we were involved in—generally in coordinating the effort," Poindexter affirmed. And Reagan knew that North was the "chief action officer" in charge of the operation.[106] But whenever the committee tried to elicit more precise details about Reagan's knowledge, they ran into the dead end of Poindexter's faulty memory.

Poindexter's blindness to the legal dimension of what he and North had done went beyond their belief that the Boland amendment didn't cover the NSC staff. For Poindexter, in particular, the issue was more basic. Supporting the contras was one of Ronald Reagan's most fervent commitments. As part of the personal staff of the commander-in-chief, Poindexter was responsible for seeing to it that Reagan's policy was effectively implemented. Congress had no right to interfere.

Though Poindexter didn't wear his uniform to the hearings, his belief in the military chain of command and unquestioning obedience to orders defined his conception of the national security adviser's role—indeed, of the whole foreign policy process. He seemed deeply frustrated that foreign policy could not be made and carried out with the precision of a military operation. Congress and the press refused to simply salute the commander-in-chief and fall in line behind him. Instead, they were insubordinate and obstructionist. Even when they lost the political battle over contra aid, the Democrats did not accept defeat, but kept looking for ways to reverse the verdict. It was this aspect of politics, the messiness of it, the fact that victories were almost never complete or permanent, that Poindexter seemed to find intolerable. He could no more countenance loyal opposition to Reagan's foreign policy than he could countenance a subordinate officer's refusal to obey orders. Like a ship's captain faced with mutineers, Poindexter would have relished hanging the Congress and most of the Washington press corps from the yardarm.

To Take Care That the Laws Are Faithfully Executed

All the Democrats and three of the eleven Republicans signed the final report of the Iran-contra committee. The other Republicans, all conservative hard-liners, wrote a lengthy dissent.[107] The majority report condemned Reagan's foreign policy apparatus for "secrecy, deception, and disdain for the rule of law." To avoid accountability to Congress and to other administration officials, a "cabal of zealots" who "believed that they alone knew what was right" had run a covert foreign policy in violation of both stated U.S. policy and the law. These officials—chief among them Casey, McFarlane, Poindexter, and North—"viewed the law not as setting boundaries for their actions, but raising impediments to their goals."[108]

The majority rejected the argument that the NSC was justified in circumventing the Boland amendment because it had been modified over time, or because its scope was imprecisely defined. "A law is no less a law because it is passed by a slender majority," they wrote, "or because Congress is open-minded about its reconsideration."[109] They also noted half a dozen other laws that North and his colleagues had violated.

This litany of malfeasance posed a direct danger to American democracy, the majority concluded. By usurping Congress's power of the purse in order to carry out activities "in direct contravention of the will of Congress," the administration had "undermined a cardinal principle of the Constitution" and set the nation on "a path to dictatorship."[110]

The majority report held Reagan accountable for the misdeeds of his subordinates, whether or not he actually knew what they were doing. It noted that Reagan still had not condemned North and Poindexter's behavior, thus leaving "the impression that he does not find these actions objectionable." While the Boland amendment was in force, "the president created, or at least tolerated an environment where those who did know of the diversion certainly believed with certainty that they were carrying out the president's policies."[111] The president, the report argued, has "a responsibility for cultivating a respect for the Constitution and the law by his staff." In that, Ronald Reagan failed, and in so doing, he failed to discharge his oath of office—to take care that the laws are faithfully executed.[112]

The Republicans, in their minority report, argued that the Democrats were making a mountain out of a molehill. "The worst that can be said of these people," the minority report wrote of North and company, "is that they adopted one side of a reasonable dispute over interpretation. . . . There was no constitutional crisis, no systematic disrespect for the 'rule of law,' no grand conspiracy, and no administration dishonesty or coverup."[113] In their report, the Republican minority took the same stance they had held throughout the investigation—they defended Ronald Reagan tooth and nail, conceded almost nothing, and pilloried their Democratic colleagues.

The root of the Iran-contra affair, they argued, was not anything the administration had done (though they allowed as how the diversion was a mistake). Rather, the problem was Congress. Congressional Democrats had passed myriad Boland amendments, all of which the Republicans regarded as unconstitutional infringements on the president's prerogatives in foreign policy. Congress had no business trying to constrain the president beyond the water's edge, and the safety of the nation was endangered when it tried. The Iran-contra affair resulted from the administration's "legitimate frustration with abuses of power and irresolution by the legislative branch."[114]

The Republican minority advocated what Henry Hyde characterized as "presidential monarchism" in the realm of international affairs—an extreme theory of presidential supremacy.[115] They even insisted that the president's implicit foreign policy power superseded the Congress's constitutionally explicit power of the purse, the power Congress invoked when it cut off contra aid. If Congress transgressed the president's prerogatives, the Republicans argued, he was justified in ignoring it.[116] Reagan's defenders took no cognizance of the fact that he had not challenged the constitutionality of the Boland amendment when it was passed. If the president believed the amendment was unconstitutional, he could have vetoed it, or challenged it in the courts. He did neither. Instead, the White House assured Congress it was obeying the law when it was not.

The Republican minority report was testimony to how deeply the issue of Nicaragua had divided the government. In defense of their president and his policy, eight members of Congress put forth a brief for crippling their own institution by diminishing its core power over the expenditure of public funds and excluding it from meaningful participation in foreign policy. For the sake of achieving "democracy" in Nicaragua, they were prepared to fundamentally alter the balance of power and weaken the system of checks and balances between the branches of their own democracy. This apologia for the Reagan administration's misdeeds was an embarrassment to moderate Republicans, whose sense of civic responsibility went beyond narrow partisan loyalty. It was, said committee member Warren Rudman, "pathetic."[117]

The Iran-contra investigation never fully resolved the question of what Ronald Reagan knew about North and Poindexter's schemes. If the president had authorized the diversion, most committee members agreed, he was guilty of an impeachable offense. Yet almost no one in either party wanted to put the nation through a wrenching constitutional crisis, especially since Reagan had only a year left in office. Committee Chairman Daniel Inouye felt this most strongly. Unless a "smoking gun" surfaced—a document or firsthand testimony directly implicating the president in the diversion—the committee decided early on that it would reprimand Reagan, but would not take issue with his protestations of ignorance.[118]

If Reagan did know about the diversion, any "smoking gun" had long since disappeared in Ollie North's "smoking shredder."[119] But apart from the diversion, there was considerable evidence that Reagan knew a great deal about the contra support operation. As early as 1983, Reagan signed a draft National Security Decision Directive (NSDD) specifying that if Congress refused to appropriate adequate funding for his Central America policy, the executive branch would find the funds elsewhere. The NSDD was derailed only when George Shultz pointed out that, constitutionally, "you cannot spend money that is not appropriated."[120]

Some of the earliest press reports on North's activities, based on sources inside the administration, said that McFarlane had orally briefed the president on NSC plans to raise funds for the contras from third countries and private donors and had received Reagan's approval.[121] No one on the Iran-contra committee explicitly asked McFarlane if this report was true, but at least one piece of documentary evidence corroborated it. In early 1984, after a conversation about the contras with McFarlane, North jotted down in his notebook, "Pres. has approved funding plan."[122]

McFarlane did tell the committee that Reagan directed him to keep the contras together "body and soul," and he testified that he regularly briefed the president on what was being done for the rebels.[123] Poindexter, too, said he briefed Reagan on all aspects of the contra support operation except the diversion.

Throughout the period covered by the various Boland amendments, Reagan was consistently defiant about his commitment to continue supporting the contras. At a press conference in April, a reporter asked Reagan whether he would "look for some other avenue to help the contras" if Congress cut off aid.

"Well, we're not going to quit and walk away from them no matter what happens," Reagan replied.[124] He meant it. In May 1986, Reagan told Poindexter, "I don't want to pull out our support for the contras for any reason. This would be an unacceptable option. . . . If we can't move the contra package [through Congress] before June 9, I want to figure out a way to take unilateral action."[125] In November, when Reagan and Meese briefed congressional leaders on the diversion, just before announcing it publicly, the president told them that while he had not authorized the use of the arms sale profits to support the contras, "it wasn't contrary to policy."[126]

Although the Iran-contra committee didn't know it, because the administration "inadvertently" failed to turn over the relevant documents, Reagan approved a plan in 1985 to give U.S. aid to Honduras, Guatemala, and Costa Rica in exchange for their support of the contras. The investigating committee was also unaware that Reagan had approved an airdrop of weapons to contras inside Nicaragua in October 1985, while the Boland amendment prohibited such aid. That was not as dramatic as the diversion, but it was just as clearly a violation of the law—a small, but unmistakable smoking gun that the committee failed to uncover.[127]

In 1987, the United States marked the two hundredth anniversary of the Constitution with a bitter debate over the fundamental principles of government. The Iran-contra scandal revealed a complex web of covert operations mounted outside the law. Bill Casey's attitude that legal restraints were obstacles for sharp lawyers to evade had become the guiding philosophy of Ronald Reagan's White House. Oliver North was no loose cannon. His Nicaraguan capers were no aberration; they were the forerunner of a string of unauthorized covert operations to be conducted by North and Casey's "off-the-shelf, self-sustaining, stand-alone" enterprise. To avoid the messy uncertainty of democratic debate and accountability in foreign policy, administration hard-liners were building a permanent secret government. "If you carry this to its logical extreme," said Senator Rudman, "you don't have a democracy anymore."[128]

Iran-contra was often compared to Watergate. But unlike the Watergate scandal, which produced a virtual consensus within the political establishment that what Richard Nixon and his co-conspirators had done was wrong, the Iran-contra scandal deepened the existing partisan divide between liberal Democrats and conservative Republicans. Most Republicans, as the minority report on the investigation exemplified, refused to acknowledge that the Reagan administration had done anything improper. To them, the fight against Communism in Nicaragua was a higher imperative that justified Reagan's actions. Some Republicans, like Pat Buchanan and Newt Gingrich, went even further, accusing the Democrats of being on the wrong side in this apocalyptic battle between Democracy and Communism, Good and Evil.

Democrats did not have much to be proud of, either. They had reason to know what North was doing as early as 1985, and by 1986 there was no doubt whatever.[129] Yet they were unwilling to look too closely at the White House's shenanigans. Had they discovered hard proof of North's intrigues, they would have been compelled to do something about them. Too many Democrats preferred to look the other way, rather than provoke a crisis of constitutional dimensions with so popular a president as Ronald Reagan. Of course, turning a blind eye to the administration's misdeeds did not make them disappear; if anything, it gave North and company a sense of invulnerability. Congressional Democrats summoned up the courage to hold Reagan accountable only after his political magic evaporated and his popularity collapsed because he traded arms for hostages with the Ayatollah.

Surprisingly, the Iran-contra scandal did not resolve the issue of contra aid. It tipped some swing voters toward the Democrats, as the House vote on the aid moratorium showed. But the scandal did not kill the contra program outright. The margin between contra aid supporters and opponents remained narrow, and the disenchantment with the Sandinistas remained high. House moderates were still searching for a middle ground. When the smoke cleared from the scandal, Ronald Reagan's reputation had been irreparably damaged and the partisan division over Nicaragua was deeper and more bitter. But the issue was still unresolved.

CHAPTER 21

Giving Peace a Chance

The Contadora peace process finally died a quiet death in late 1986. In November, both Honduras and Costa Rica suspended their participation when Nicaragua filed complaints against them in the World Court for harboring the contras. In a last, desperate attempt to reinvigorate the talks, the Contadora countries sought help from the OAS and the United Nations. General Secretaries João Baena Soares of the OAS and Javier Pérez de Cuellar of the U.N. agreed to lead a special delegation to the Central American countries to try to break the deadlock. The Reagan administration roundly condemned the new initiative and called for a special OAS meeting to censure Soares for undertaking it without explicit authorization from the OAS membership. To stiffen the resolve of Washington's allies, Reagan dispatched his special envoy, Philip Habib, to the region just before the general secretaries' trip.[1]

De Cuellar and Soares made no breakthrough. The problem, as Argentine Foreign Minister Dante Caputo explained with unusual candor, was that the United States was "not in favor of one of the fundamental points in the efforts of Contadora to achieve peace," specifically, the need to end "outside support for irregular forces." Contadora, said Costa Rican Foreign Minister Madrigal Nieto, "is a corpse that nobody dares to bury."[2]

Having scuttled Contadora, the Reagan administration was in need of a peace plan it could endorse in order to maintain the fiction that it was interested in a political settlement of the war. It embraced a plan devised by Costa Rica's new president, Oscar Arias Sánchez.

Arias was an unabashed intellectual. Before earning a law degree in Costa Rica, he attended Boston University, the University of Essex in England, and the London School of Economics. His temperament was cold and aloof, his speaking style quiet and unemotional—not a combination seemingly advantageous to a prospective politician. By his own admission, he was timid and shy—"a man of books" rather than social skills. At five feet eight inches tall, he was physically unimposing and walked with a slouch that made him look even shorter.[3]

Yet Arias's rise to the presidency was meteoric. In 1972, just five years out of law school, he became minister of national planning. He was elected to Congress in 1978, took over as general secretary of the National Liberation Party, and captured the party's presidential nomination in 1985 by leading a youthful revolt against the old guard. Then he won a stunning come-from-behind victory in the general election by promising to keep Costa Rica out of Nicaragua's war. At forty-four, he was Costa Rica's youngest president ever.[4]

An unassuming man, Arias disdained pomp and circumstance, often driving himself around in a Jeep with no entourage whatsoever. But he was fiercely proud of his own intellectual achievements and his country's tradition of peace and social democracy. "Tell them," he said to an American interviewer, "that the president of Costa Rica is a man who could be president of any European country."[5]

The United States worried about Oscar Arias even before he was elected. Running as a peace candidate, Arias reaffirmed Costa Rica's neutrality. "Costa Rica will not be converted into a dormitory for the contras," he pledged. "I am not going to look the other way."[6] Arias's opponent, Raphael Angel Calderón Fournier, ran as a hard-line anti-Communist, sympathetic to the contras. Privately, he promised U.S. officials that if elected he would abandon the policy of neutrality and enlist Costa Rica in the anti-Sandinista crusade. In exchange, Washington secretly aided Calderón's campaign.[7]

Shortly after his election, Arias criticized U.S. support for the contras, arguing that the money would be better spent promoting economic development among Washington's allies. Such heresy brought a quick response. Even before Arias had taken the oath of office, Elliott Abrams, John Galvin (the new U.S. South-Com commander), and a senior CIA official traveled to Costa Rica to complain. Not wishing to be accused of interfering in Washington's domestic policy disputes, Arias kept quiet about contra aid until after the congressional votes in early 1986.[8]

But when it came to Costa Rica's role, he would make no concessions. Upon assuming office in May, Arias insisted that contra base camps be closed, that contra combatants leave the country, and that senior contra officials in Costa Rica refrain from anything more than political proselytizing or face expulsion. He also demanded that the airstrip at Santa Elena built in 1985 as part of North and Secord's contra resupply Enterprise be closed. "We'll have to squeeze his balls," Abrams remarked when told of Arias's lack of cooperation. Despite Ambassador Lewis Tambs's promise that the strip would be closed, the Enterprise continued using it.[9]

When the Costa Ricans found out the field was still operational, they planned a press conference to denounce it. Secord sent an urgent message to warn North and seek White House intervention with Arias. "Boy needs to be straightened out by heavy weights," he wrote.[10] On instructions from Abrams, Tambs called Arias and warned him that unless he canceled the press conference, his upcoming official visit to Washington would be put "at risk." North's notes on the incident were blunt. Tambs was to tell Arias that if the airstrip was revealed, he would "never set foot in W[hite] H[ouse]" and "never get five cents of $80 m[illion]" in pending economic aid. The threat worked only temporarily. The press conference was finally held September 25, and Costa Rican police occupied the airstrip to ensure that it remained closed. Arias's invitation to Washington was postponed.[11]

Throughout 1986, Washington pressured Arias to be more cooperative. "Abrams was breathing fire," recalled a Costa Rican official. "The meetings were not very pleasant, and sometimes they got very uncomfortable." The dignified Arias was insulted by Abrams's imperious tone. "Not even [Margaret] Thatcher, the closest ally you have, supports your policy," he said to Abrams during a face-to-face confrontation. "Doesn't that tell you something?" The administration, however, was not interested in debating the pros and cons of contra aid with little Costa Rica. It simply wanted Arias to cooperate.[12]

Although the Costa Ricans refused to admit it publicly, both Tambs and Abrams repeatedly hinted that U.S. economic aid depended on Costa Rica's cooperation. "The United States does not intend to have Costa Ricans ask us for money and then treat us badly," Philip Habib warned Arias.[13] During 1986, $40 million in economic aid was held up, purportedly on technical grounds. But Arias refused to cave in. "Friendship should not mean being servile," Arias said in explanation of his differences with Washington. "A friend who does everything you want is not a friend, but a slave."[14]

Twice Arias refused to meet privately with CIA Director William Casey because he didn't want to be pressured about the contras. During a secret trip to Central America in the fall of 1986, Casey stopped in Costa Rica and demanded a meeting. Arias refused, instead sending his foreign minister to listen to Casey's lecture about why the Costa Ricans should be more cooperative. In December, Arias was in Washington when Casey summoned him to the CIA. Again, Arias refused to be ordered around like an underling. He made Casey come to his hotel, and rather than meet with him privately, Arias assembled the entire Costa Rican delegation to chat with the chagrined director. Casey had wanted "a meeting in the shadows," recalled Arias's ambassador to the United States, Guido Fernández, and Arias turned it into "a tea party."[15]

Arias's uncooperativeness did not indicate any sympathy for the Sandinistas. On the contrary, Arias shared Ronald Reagan's contempt for their Marxist ideology and denial of domestic civil liberties. "What you call democracy isn't called democracy here nor in any part of the world," Arias bluntly told Daniel Ortega at the first Central American presidential summit in May 1986. So Arias needed no prodding from Washington to demand that, as part of any peace agreement, the Sandinistas firmly pledge to establish democracy.[16] Like Reagan, Arias worried that Contadora focused too much on foreign policy issues. Regional peace, he insisted, could only come from "an authentic, pluralistic and participatory democratic process."

Arias also resented the tendency of the Contadora countries to patronize the smaller, poorer Central Americans. He was no more inclined to yield to diplomatic pressure from Mexico City or Buenos Aires than from Washington.[17] When Contadora officials gathered for Arias's inauguration, he asked them to endorse democracy as an essential element in any peace accord. The diplomats spurned him, issuing a statement of their own that downplayed the democracy issue. From that point on, Arias was determined to wrest control of the diplomatic process away from Contadora and put it into the hands of the Central Americans themselves. He began developing a peace plan of his own.[18]

In addition to the Contadora provisions on national security, Arias included in his plan a timetable for the democratization of Nicaragua in exchange for an end to the contra war. The Sandinistas would have to agree to allow full exercise of civil liberties, open a dialogue with their internal opponents, give the contras amnesty, and hold free elections overseen by foreign observers at the end of Ortega's regular term. In exchange, an immediate ceasefire would be instituted and all foreign assistance to the contras would stop.[19] In Washington, administration officials were not much impressed by the Arias plan. "It's not that big a deal," said one. "It won't transform the situation."[20]

Although Arias's demand for democracy in Nicaragua echoed Ronald Reagan's, he disagreed fundamentally with Reagan's strategy of military pressure. Arias did not believe the contras could win, so they offered no real hope of replacing the Sandinistas with a more democratic government. "You can't overthrow the Sandinistas with $100 million or even with $200 million or $400 million," he explained. "The more you give the contras, the more Ortega gets from the Soviets." The contras merely increased the danger of war between Nicaragua and its neighbors and gave the Sandinistas a rationale for militarizing the country, restricting domestic liberties, and cozying up to Cuba and the Soviet Union.[21]

The Nicaraguans denounced Arias's plan, yet in its details, it demanded few things that the Sandinistas had not already said they were willing to do. They would not have to open talks with the contras, as Washington had been demanding; they would simply have to dialogue with their internal opponents, which they had done intermittently (albeit without much progress) since 1980. They would not have to change their constitution or electoral calendar; they would simply have to assure that the balloting scheduled for 1990 was free and fair. Moreover, since the Arias plan postponed the nettlesome issue of regional arms reductions, the Sandinistas would not have to limit the size of their army or the flow of military aid from Cuba and the Soviet Union. In the near term, to achieve an end to the contra war, all the Sandinistas had to do was lift the state of emergency and declare another amnesty. The closer the Sandinistas looked at the Arias plan, the better it looked.[22]

The same calculus made the Reagan administration increasingly dubious about the plan, despite its focus on democracy. "The fear is that the plan would let the Sandinistas off the hook by cutting off the contras on day one, while the Sandinistas wouldn't have to do anything until later," a U.S. official explained.[23] Instead, Washington wanted to keep the contras in the field until the Sandinistas created a democracy to Reagan's liking. Then the Sandinistas would have to negotiate directly with the contras to end the war.

But with Contadora defunct, the Arias plan was, as a Costa Rican diplomat said, "the only game in town."[24] If Reagan hoped to win further military aid for the contras, he could not afford to appear too hostile to the one remaining diplomatic option. So administration officials publicly praised the Arias initiative while quietly urging their regional allies to demand extensive revisions before signing it—the same strategy Washington had used to scuttle Contadora.[25]

If Arias had any doubts about the depth of administration antipathy toward his plan, they were dispelled in June 1987 when he was invited to the White House for what he thought would be a simple courtesy call. Instead he was confronted with an angry phalanx of top U.S. officials—President Reagan, Vice President Bush, National Security Adviser Frank Carlucci, Chief of Staff Howard Baker, Deputy Secretary of State John C. Whitehead, Elliott Abrams, and

Philip Habib. Reagan lectured Arias for fifteen minutes on the evils of the Sandinistas, the need to preserve the contras, and the "loopholes" in Arias's peace plan.[26]

His quiet demeanor notwithstanding, Oscar Arias was not easily cowed. He retorted by lecturing Reagan for thirty minutes on the failings of U.S. policy. "I told him the U.S. has been left completely alone on aid to the contras," Arias recalled. " 'You're totally isolated,' I said. 'Nobody is backing Washington. . . . By no one, I mean Contadora, the Latin American Support Group, Western Europe. You're betting on war. Why don't we bet on peace?' "[27]

Reagan hung tenaciously to his conviction that only military force could dislodge the Sandinistas. When Arias tried to point out that the contras were not strong enough to win, Reagan countered that reports of the contras' weakness were the product of "disinformation" spread by the "press and leftist groups." Communists, Reagan insisted, had never in history left power voluntarily.

"We all know history, Mr. President," Arias replied, "but no one is obliged to repeat it."[28]

The Wright-Reagan Plan

While Oscar Arias was plotting a path to peace in Central America, the Reagan administration was trying to devise a way to convince Congress to continue funding the contra war despite the Iran-contra scandal. Even after Oliver North's electrifying testimony to the Iran-contra committee, the prospects for winning additional military aid appeared bleak. Elliott Abrams, his credibility shattered by the scandal, had lost effectiveness as a lobbyist. "I wouldn't trust Elliott Abrams any farther than I could throw Oliver North," said Senator David Durenberger (R-Minn.).[29]

Reagan needed someone new to lead the next charge up Capitol Hill. In July 1987, he named Tom Loeffler special White House congressional liaison just for the contra aid issue. Loeffler was an easygoing veteran Republican congressman who had been chief deputy whip before giving up his House seat in 1986 to make an unsuccessful run for the Republican gubernatorial nomination in Texas. His specialty was wooing southern conservative Democrats, and he had played a key role in winning the support of the "boll weevils" for Reagan's 1981 budget victories. As an added advantage, he was also a friend of fellow Texan Jim Wright, the new Speaker.[30]

Loeffler's experience in Congress made him a good vote counter, and he quickly determined that a majority of the House no longer supported military aid for the contras. To revive its prospects, the White House needed to demonstrate that it was not, in principle, hostile to diplomacy.[31] Within the administration, this was still a delicate matter, because the hard-liners were opposed to any diplomatic accord that left the Sandinistas in power. Although some of the most vociferous hard-liners—Casey, Poindexter, and North—were gone, the new White House staff was by no means comprised of doves. Frank Carlucci, Reagan's new national security adviser, was generally supportive of the contras, having been chastened by right-wing Republican attacks when he expressed private doubts about their ability to win the war.[32] Carlucci's assistant for Latin America, José Sorzano, was a conservative Cuban American, a former aide to Jeane Kirkpatrick and a staunch contra supporter. At the State Department, Elliott Abrams was still in charge of coordinating U.S. policy on Central America, even if he was persona non grata at the other end of Pennsylvania Avenue. And at Defense, Caspar Weinberger remained adamantly opposed to any diplomatic settlement.

Reagan's new chief of staff, Howard Baker, was more inclined toward pragmatism. His own lobbying efforts had saved the Senate contra aid vote in March, but he recognized that Reagan's political weakness made another victory unlikely. As former Senate majority leader, he too could count votes.[33] Moreover, Baker was a moderate Republican uncomfortable with the bitter partisanship of the contra aid issue. Like Jim Wright, he preferred the tradition of a bipartisan foreign policy and was willing to compromise to achieve it.

When Baker first accepted the White House job, Wright warned him that Congress would approve no further aid to the contras. Reagan ought to actively press for a diplomatic settlement with Nicaragua while the contras were still an effective fighting force.[34] Baker was receptive. But if Ronald Reagan floated a new peace initiative, who would believe he was sincere? In past years, Reagan had offered several bogus peace proposals on the eve of congressional votes, reneged more than once on promises to resume bilateral talks with Nicaragua, and consistently praised multilateral diplomatic efforts in public while scuttling them behind the scenes. "The president doesn't have any credibility," Loeffler admitted privately. If Reagan launched a new peace initiative on his own, "it would be dismissed as empty rhetoric."[35] A peace plan would have to be bipartisan if it was to be taken seriously either in Central America or in Congress.

With this in mind, Baker sent Loeffler to visit his old friend Jim Wright with an unusual offer—a joint Wright-Reagan peace initiative.[36] Loeffler played to Wright's vanity. Wright believed that the Speaker of the House, as leader of a coequal branch of government, had just as much right to set the national policy agenda as the president. Loeffler was offering Wright the chance to act with the president on an equal footing. "It would be precedent-setting, enormously important," Loeffler said temptingly. "It would involve the speaker of the House in foreign policy in a new way. What significance for the speakership!"

Wright was enticed, but suspicious. "My antenna went up, that they were just trying to use me," he later told some Democratic colleagues. "I don't trust Reagan," Wright said bluntly. "Even if he means something when he says it, who knows if he'll remember." Wright wanted assurances from both Howard Baker and George Shultz that the administration was really behind the idea.

Loeffler insisted that the president was serious; Nancy Reagan had been urging him to negotiate with Nicaragua so that he would be "remembered as the president who made peace."[37] Wright agreed to explore the idea further to see if they could come up with a common proposal.

The rest of the Democratic leadership was deeply skeptical. "Why now?" asked David Bonior, the Democrats' chief deputy whip. The administration would soon launch a new bid for contra aid, he noted. "They've lied to us so often. My instinct is this is a setup."

Majority Whip Tony Coehlo felt the same way. "They know now they can't win in the House. The symbolism of the speaker would be spectacular for them. If the Sandinistas turn the plan down, then Reagan's on TV pushing contra aid and we're trapped." Dave McCurdy, who had been snookered by Reagan's peace promises in 1985, also thought the Loeffler proposal was a trick.[38]

Wright understood the danger. No issue engaged the passions of House Democrats more than contra aid. Almost a third of the caucus belonged to Bonior's Nicaragua Task Force, and fifty-three Democrats attended a strategy meeting in July when the next round of voting was still two months away. If Wright went along with the White House and their bipartisan initiative failed, his ability to defeat Reagan's new military aid request would be fatally weakened. House liberals would see it as a betrayal, and Wright's influence in his own party would be crippled.

Yet Wright felt compelled to test Reagan's sincerity. For years, the Democrats had lambasted the administration's hostility to diplomacy. "I'm the speaker of the House, and they're saying they want peace," Wright told his skeptical colleagues. "What am I supposed to do, walk away from that? . . . If there's any real chance for peace, we have to take that chance."[39]

Despite the political dangers, Wright very much wanted to play the role of peacemaker. Against the advice of almost everyone else in the House leadership and most of his staff, he decided to join Ronald Reagan in a bipartisan initiative. But he covered his flanks. To minimize the danger of the plan blowing up in his face, Wright laid down certain conditions. First and foremost, his cooperation on the peace initiative did not imply that the Democrats would support contra aid if the plan failed. "There can be absolutely no linkage between this and contra aid," Majority Leader Tom Foley told Howard Baker emphatically. "No connection! No implication that if this fails, the speaker is expected to support contra aid."[40] Yet both sides knew that if the plan failed, Reagan would seek more military aid, arguing that diplomacy alone was not enough to tame the Sandinistas. Having endorsed a bipartisan peace plan, the Democrats would be hard pressed to claim that Reagan's diplomacy had been half-hearted.[41]

Jim Wright himself drafted what came to be known as the Wright-Reagan plan. The final version, unveiled by President Reagan on August 5, 1987, called for a cease-fire in Nicaragua, the suspension of both military aid to the contras and Soviet bloc aid to the Sandinistas after the cease-fire, negotiated limits on foreign military advisers and the size of military establishments throughout Central America, the immediate lifting of Nicaragua's state of emergency and restoration of civil liberties, amnesty for the contras, and national reconciliation between the Sandinistas and their domestic opponents. Once all this was accomplished, Washington would lift the trade embargo and include Nicaragua in its regional economic aid program. At Wright's insistence, the plan also declared that the United States "has no right to influence or determine the identity of the political leaders . . . nor the social and economic system" in Nicaragua.[42]

Administration officials were as divided over the Wright-Reagan plan as the Democrats. Some believed the whole thing was essentially cosmetic—designed to appeal to Congress, while at the same time including elements guaranteed to provoke rejection by Nicaragua.[43] "The calculation was that you were going to hook Jim Wright," explained a senior administration official. "Wright would be on record for democracy in Nicaragua, not just containment, and the Nicaraguans would reject the plan." Consequently, in the next round of contra aid voting, "Wright's opposition to contra aid would be pro forma, and many swing voters would be freed up. There would be no threats from the speaker. And we'd get more contra aid."[44]

There were indications, however, that Howard Baker wanted the diplomatic initiative to succeed. He kept the hard-liners—including Weinberger—in the dark about his contacts with Wright until the plan was so far along that they couldn't stop it. His decision to approach Wright was made without a formal inter-agency review or NSC meeting to discuss it. The contras were not told about the plan until after it had been announced publicly.[45]

Even before the plan was announced, the hard-liners were trying to move away from it. When Wright met with Reagan in the Oval Office just before the president unveiled the plan, Reagan handed him a piece of paper and said, "This is our interpretation of what the agreement means."[46] When Wright read the memorandum later, he was furious. It included twenty-one points of interpretation that construed the peace plan as harshly as possible. It said, for example, that the Sandinistas would have to open negotiations with the contras to achieve a cease-fire—something the Sandinistas had consistently refused to do. It construed "national reconciliation" to mean that Ortega would have to step down as president before the end of his term and hold new elections. And it stated that the United States reserved the right to take military action against Nicaragua, including additional contra aid, unless the Sandinistas agreed to the entire plan within two weeks and implemented it completely by September 30. "By either accident or design, the 21 points amounted to a shotgun blast at the nervous dove of peace," Wright wrote later.[47]

When he called Howard Baker to complain, Baker insisted the memorandum was not a statement of U.S. policy and that Wright should just forget it. "That was written by Cap Weinberger on his own, and it doesn't represent anybody else in the White House," Baker said. "I don't think the president even had a chance to read it all the way through. It does not represent our position, and I think you'd do us all a favor if you just got rid of it." Even though the president himself had given Wright the memo, he took Baker's advice.[48]

But that was not the end of the confusion. Hard-liners leaked the twenty-one points to the press, in hopes of provoking the Sandinistas into summarily rejecting the whole plan.[49] White House spokesman Marlin Fitzwater implied that the Sandinistas had to choose between accepting the peace plan or facing bipartisan support for more contra aid. The peace plan, he said, "is tied to the [aid] request. Peace and funding are all tied together." Baker and Loeffler tried to reassure Wright that the problem was simply lower-level officials who had not been properly briefed yet. But it was obviously more than that. Both Abrams and NSC staff aide José Sorzano were working actively behind the scenes to derail the initiative, backstopped by conservative Republicans in Congress.[50]

Esquipulas: The Central Americans Take Control

The Wright-Reagan plan was announced just as the five Central American presidents arrived in Esquipulas, Guatemala, for a summit meeting to discuss the Arias peace plan. Administration officials expected the U.S. proposal to displace the Central Americans' agenda. Instead, the presidents ignored Washington's plan and insisted on discussing their own. In this, they were encouraged by the Democrats. When Costa Rican Ambassador Guido Fernández asked Wright whether the Central Americans would have to accept the Wright-Reagan plan without modification, Wright replied, "Certainly not. We wouldn't presume to dictate the terms of a settlement between your countries."[51]

At 4:30 in the morning on August 7, 1987, Wright's phone rang. It was Guido Fernández. "President Arias wanted you to be the first to know," he said. "The five presidents have just signed off on an agreement in principle." Wright was so exhilarated, he was unable to get back to sleep.[52]

The peace agreement signed at Esquipulas closely followed Arias's draft. Each government pledged itself to democratic pluralism, free elections, and a concerted effort to end internal fighting by seeking a cease-fire with its armed opponents, instituting an amnesty for them, and initiating a process of political reconciliation and dialogue. Each country promised to refrain from providing support or refuge for armed insurgents, and together they called upon other governments to do the same.[53]

The plan was obviously not airtight. As U.S. officials pointed out, there was no guarantee that the Sandinistas would keep their end of the bargain once the contras had disappeared. On the other hand, the Sandinistas had no guarantee that the contras would accept a cease-fire or that the United States would stop aiding them. Nevertheless, the accord established a workable framework for peace if all sides were willing to make a sincere effort to implement it.

The Democrats were jubilant. In an instant, the political trap of the Wright-Reagan plan had been transformed into an actual peace agreement. Wright, whom many House Democrats thought had been duped by the White House, was suddenly a hero whose foresight and willingness to take a risk for peace had paid off. Now it was the White House that found itself checkmated in the diplomatic chess game.

"When the Sandinistas signed, we were caught by surprise," one U.S. official admitted. "We had no backup plan."[54] Abrams and Sorzano had assured their colleagues that the Sandinistas would never sign the agreement, so the White House expected the summit to either collapse in discord or produce an innocuous communiqué that settled nothing. Their expectation was not unreasonable. All summer long the Sandinistas had been saying that the Arias plan violated Nicaraguan sovereignty by making internal political affairs subject to international negotiations. "That is unacceptable," Ortega himself said just before leaving for Esquipulas.[55] In the end, Ortega signed because the Esquipulas agreement offered the prospect of ending the contra war.[56]

Washington also had assurances from both Salvadoran president José Napoleón Duarte and Honduran president José Azcona that they would not sign the Arias proposal at the summit. But Arias locked the presidents in a room without any aides and wouldn't let them leave until the negotiations were concluded—a trick he learned from a biography of Franklin D. Roosevelt. "I didn't want them going downstairs and talking to the generals and foreign ministers," Arias said later. "That would have been the end of everything."[57]

Ultimately, it was self-interest that led Duarte and Azcona to sign. Duarte changed his mind because the final agreement recognized the legitimacy of existing governments. Still struggling against the FMLN guerrillas, he found the agreement too good to pass up. Azcona was the last holdout. In essence, the other presidents shamed him into signing by threatening to blame him for the summit's collapse and paint him as a puppet of the United States.[58]

Ironically, the Wright-Reagan plan, which administration officials thought would derail the Arias initiative, spurred the Central Americans to sign a pact of their own. On the one hand, the U.S. plan implied new flexibility toward diplomacy and therefore reduced Central American fears of retribution if they signed an accord. On the other hand, Washington's arrogance in expecting the Central Americans to lay aside their own work and simply accept the U.S. plan injured their pride and made them more intent upon resolving their differences among themselves.[59]

Within the Reagan administration, the Esquipulas accord was greeted with very mixed feelings. Pragmatists such as George Shultz and Philip Habib wanted to embrace the agreement; any weak spots in it could be repaired by stepping up U.S. diplomatic activity. "A constructive process was under way," Shultz recalled, "and I felt we could work with Esquipulas II."[60] The hard-liners regarded Esquipulas as an unmitigated disaster. Caspar Weinberger complained that the agreement called for demobilizing the contras while the Sandinistas remained in power and did not include a timetable for new elections. George Bush criticized the accord because it gave Nicaragua "too much of what Communist leader Daniel Ortega wanted." The administration, he implied, would stick with the Wright-Reagan plan. "We are not going to leave the contras twisting in the wind."[61]

But the political imperative of being in favor of peace was too strong to resist. Messages of support for the Esquipulas agreement streamed in from all over the world. The eight Contadora countries endorsed the plan enthusiastically and pledged to help verify it. The U.N. General Assembly passed a resolution by acclamation giving the plan the "firmest support." Both Cuba and the Soviet Union praised the plan and promised to abide by it.[62]

Administration officials felt trapped. How could they argue for continued contra aid when the Sandinistas had signed an agreement that met all of Washington's explicit demands and satisfied Nicaragua's democratic neighbors? How could they ignore the Central Americans' call for an end to all outside aid to insurgents? Stopping such assistance was "an indispensable element to achieve permanent and lasting peace in the region," the five Central American presidents had agreed.[63]

The administration finally settled upon an Alice-in-Wonderland explanation of its attitude toward the Esquipulas accord. "We want to try to work with it and we are not against it," a senior administration official insisted. But he went on to argue that Washington would keep aiding the contras, even though that violated a central tenet of the peace agreement.[64] So Washington would support the Central American peace agreement—except for the part about ending the war.

On August 10, the internal tug of war over Esquipulas came to a head when Reagan again sided with the hard-liners and refused to allow Habib to travel to Central America to follow up on the Esquipulas accord. Despite the backing of both Shultz and Baker, the diplomatic track was still closed. "The rightwing ideologues did not want a negotiated settlement that would end contra aid," Shultz concluded.[65]

Four days later, Habib resigned as special envoy, since there was no real role for diplomacy in Reagan's policy. "Habib failed to realize that he was just a symbol," Abrams explained. "[He] wanted to get something negotiated."[66]

On August 22, Reagan demonstrated his continuing support for the contras by recording a speech for broadcast over their clandestine radio station. In it, he implicitly criticized the Esquipulas agreement because it called for a simultaneous cease-fire and restoration of civil liberties in Nicaragua. The Sandinistas, Reagan said, could not be trusted to keep their end of the bargain. "The Sandinistas have told us this before, and no one believes the Sandinistas any more. Simultaneity must mean freedom up front, or no deal."[67]

By autumn, the administration's willingness to pay even lip service to the Esquipulas agreement had worn thin. On September 10, Shultz told the Senate Foreign Relations Committee that the administration would seek $270 million in new contra aid for fiscal year 1988.[68] A few days later, Reagan called the Esquipulas agreement "fatally flawed."[69]

At a meeting of U.S. ambassadors to Central America, Elliott Abrams instructed them to inform their host governments that the United States had deep reservations about the Esquipulas accord. Abrams called it "more a preliminary agreement than a final peace treaty"—the same line the administration had used to derail the 1984 Contadora agreement. Attendees at the meeting were given copies of the 1973 Paris Peace Accords that provided for the U.S. withdrawal from Vietnam, to show how ambiguities in a treaty could be exploited by Communists.[70]

Apart from verbal sniping, the administration's main strategy for derailing the Esquipulas plan was to pressure Honduras to obstruct its implementation. After U.S. ambassador Everett Briggs expressed Washington's reservations about the accord, the Honduran foreign minister failed to appear for the first day of a Central American foreign ministers' meeting on treaty compliance.

When the minister finally arrived, he declared, "There are no contra camps in Honduras. Therefore Honduras has no commitment to dismantle them." He went on to call the peace treaty "a group of joint intentions," rather than obligations.[71] The Hondurans would do nothing to force the contras out of the country.[72]

Congressional Diplomacy

While administration hard-liners were working to subvert the Esquipulas agreement, Democrats on Capitol Hill were doing everything possible to bolster it. Ironically, the administration itself had put Wright in position to play a major diplomatic role by involving him in the Wright-Reagan plan. Like the sorcerer's apprentice, the White House could not control Wright once it had set him loose.

From the beginning, Wright had hoped that the bipartisan initiative would act as a catalyst, prompting the Central Americans to devise a peace plan of their own. Once the Esquipulas agreement was signed, he quickly endorsed it and declared that it superseded the Wright-Reagan plan. Then he called on Reagan to suspend all requests for new contra aid while the Esquipulas process was under way.[73]

House Democrats immediately began developing a strategy to defend the Esquipulas agreement. They would pressure the White House to comply with the accord and try to insulate the Central Americans from administration pressure to make them back away from it.[74] To strengthen Arias's hand, Wright invited him to address a joint session of Congress—a rare honor for a foreign dignitary. But protocol demanded that the White House consent, and administration hard-liners would not allow it. Instead, Wright arranged for Arias to speak to the Democratic caucus in the House chamber. The caucus would invite both their Republican colleagues and the Senate, so Arias would end up speaking before the full Congress. The White House objected to this arrangement as well. When Wright refused to withdraw the invitation, the administration warned Arias that his appearance would be a breach of protocol because he would be acting in a political role, bolstering Reagan's congressional opponents. Arias came anyway, spoke on September 22, and received a standing ovation.[75] Just as the White House feared, Arias was unequivocal in his opposition to the contras. "Believe me," he declared, "they are not the solution; they are the problem."[76]

On August 25, Wright invited the five Central American ambassadors to lunch with the House Democratic leadership to impress upon them how committed the Democrats were to the success of the peace accord. "The speaker wants to make this a focus of his speakership," Democratic whip Tony Coehlo told the guests. "The administration will be in office 17 more months," he added pointedly. "The speaker will serve ten years."[77]

In October, the Honduran vice president told Foley, Coehlo, and Bonior that the civilian government was under pressure from the armed forces to delay complying with the peace plan. "Our military has a lot to say about what happens," the vice president explained. "You may have more influence on our military than we do." Wright reminded President Azcona and senior Honduran officers that Democrats still controlled the military aid budget, adding, "We would look with very great disfavor on anything that slowed the peace process."[78]

Wright was fighting fire with fire. The Reagan administration habitually threatened reluctant Central Americans with reduced aid in order to extract cooperation with the contra war; now the Democrats wielded the same sword in support of the peace process. For the Central Americans, who heard one version of U.S. policy from administration hard-liners, another from the pragmatists, and yet a third from House Democrats, American politics must have seemed strange indeed.

Wright was most active in promoting cease-fire talks in Nicaragua. The Esquipulas plan called for governments facing armed rebellion to make every effort to achieve a cease-fire, but it did not require talks between a government and its armed adversaries. To comply with the cease-fire provisions of the peace plan, the Sandinistas announced a unilateral cease-fire and initiated contacts with local contra commanders to try to achieve a mutually agreed upon cease-fire piecemeal.[79] They refused to talk directly with the contra leadership. Though this strategy met the letter of the peace accord, it was widely regarded as insufficient. Few local contra commanders were willing to agree to a separate peace, so the fighting continued apace.

The Reagan administration, which had been demanding that the Sandinistas negotiate with the contras since 1985, quickly seized on this issue as the sine qua non of Nicaraguan compliance. If the Sandinistas refused to negotiate with the contras, there would be no cease-fire. The Sandinistas would then be in violation of the Esquipulas accord. "If any part fails, the entire structure fails," Shultz said of the agreement. "If no cease-fire is negotiated, if no full amnesty is implemented, the other measures are in abeyance."[80]

In one sense, talking with the contras was not such a big concession. The Sandinistas were already talking with local contra commanders and with the leadership of the Miskito Indian rebels on the Atlantic coast. Cardinal Miguel Obando y Bravo, who conferred regularly with both Sandinista and contra leaders, was carrying messages back and forth. But for years, the Sandinistas had made it a point of principle that they would not negotiate with the contras because they were merely, as Comandante Bayardo Arce put it, "mercenary puppets." To now accede to demands for talks would look like a major concession signaling the regime's weakness. Moreover, Sandinista hard-liners were upset with Ortega for conceding too much at Esquipulas; they were adamantly opposed to further concessions.[81]

Cardinal Obando, whom the Sandinistas had selected as head of the national reconciliation commission mandated by the Esquipulas accord, added his voice to those insisting on negotiations. So did several Western European countries to whom the Sandinistas were looking as potential sources of foreign aid.[82] The definitive voice, however, was that of Arias. "Now, more than ever, I am going to insist that a negotiated cease-fire in Nicaragua is indispensable if we are to achieve a lasting peace in Central America," he said in October 1987. He went on to endorse President Azcona's position that if the Sandinistas refused, Honduras would be under no obligation to close the contra camps along its border.[83]

In Washington, House Democrats were also anxious to see the Sandinistas and the contras work out a cease-fire. Wright urged both sides to at least open indirect cease-fire talks, using Cardinal Obando as an intermediary. The contras, who called Obando "our Cardinal" because of his stinging criticism of the Sandinistas, readily agreed.[84] At first, the Sandinistas rejected the idea. Despite Obando's open hostility to the Sandinistas, Ortega had chosen him to head the national reconciliation commission as a way of demonstrating the government's good faith. To the Sandinistas, that was concession enough. They opposed using Obando as an intermediary because they did not regard him as an honest broker.

Instead, they wanted Jim Wright. The Speaker was astonished when Nicaragua's vice minister of foreign relations, Victor Tinoco, asked him to mediate the cease-fire talks. "No, no," Wright demurred. "I *have* a job." No one was better suited to the role than Obando, Wright insisted. Reluctantly, the Sandinistas agreed to accept the cardinal.[85]

Before agreeing to serve as mediator, Obando asked Wright to meet with him and Ortega to discuss the terms of Obando's role. On November 12, 1987, Ortega came to Wright's office to preview the cease-fire proposal he intended to submit to the contras through Obando. When Wright criticized a passage that accused Washington of trying to "sabotage" the Esquipulas agreement, Ortega agreed on the spot to drop the offending paragraph. David Bonior suggested that the Nicaraguans should be more precise about the terms of a proposed amnesty and should give an unequivocal commitment to lift the state of emergency. Again, Ortega agreed. The Democrats were astonished.

"These emissaries were so unexpectedly accommodating it almost seemed they would have let us change [the proposal] in just about any way we chose to specify," Wright recalled.[86]

The Reagan administration, however, was less accommodating. For Obando to undertake the mediator's role would give the cease-fire talks credibility and undercut the administration's main rhetorical weapon against the Sandinistas—that they refused to talk to the contras. To let Obando know that the administration did not approve of him serving as mediator, Elliott Abrams informed him that if he met with Wright, he could not meet with any senior administration official during his visit to Washington.[87]

When Wright heard about the threat, he offered to withdraw from the meeting between Obando and Ortega, but they both wanted him to attend. Wright then called Shultz and offered to back out if the secretary has strong objections to his participation. Shultz hinted that he disapproved of Wright's involvement, but did not ask him to withdraw.[88]

Wright then met with Obando, Ortega, and the papal nuncio at the Vatican embassy in Washington. Obando wanted to know whether he would be free to take an active role as mediator, proposing solutions when the two sides were at odds, or whether he would be merely a messenger. Ortega was noncommittal until Wright took Obando's side. The cardinal would need the power to participate actively in the talks, Wright said. "If I were the Cardinal, I would insist on that." Ortega reluctantly agreed. Wright also endorsed Obando's insistence that he control the scheduling of meetings and the support staff. Again, Ortega conceded. Obando agreed to act as the intermediary in the cease-fire talks, and the war in Nicaragua came one step closer to ending.[89]

Before the day was out, unnamed administration officials, among them Elliott Abrams, were denouncing Wright to the press. Abrams called Wright's meetings with Ortega an "unbelievable melodrama" that dealt "a serious setback" to the chances for peace.[90] "This was not forward movement," Abrams said. "This was screwing up the process. The notion that serious negotiations will be advanced if prominent Americans are dragged into it is ridiculous on its face." Another administration official called Wright an "egomaniac" who was "in over his head and didn't understand what was going on."[91]

Wright countered by accusing the administration of obstructing the peace process. Some officials, he charged, "are literally terrorized that peace might break out." The Central Americans preferred dealing with him because they "have the unfortunate impression that the administration treats them as inferiors, by scorning them, lecturing them, holding them up to public ridicule, and refusing to see them." While Wright insisted that he was not negotiating with the Sandinistas, he would continue to meet with whomever he wanted. "I don't need the permission of the administration," he told NBC's Tom Brokaw. "I represent the American people, too."[92]

Wright understood that the attacks against him were aimed mainly at the peace process. Still, he had a hard time not taking it personally. He called the White House and demanded to meet with Reagan and Shultz. "If you people have got anything to say to me, say it to my face," he told Howard Baker. On November 16, Wright met Reagan, Shultz, Weinberger, Carlucci, and Baker at the White House. "Mr. Reagan was angrier than I had ever seen him," Wright recalled. He blasted Wright for deserting the Wright-Reagan plan after Esquipulas was signed. "We started with the Wright-Reagan plan. Now we've got the Wright-Ortega plan," the president charged.[93]

Carlucci argued that the Sandinistas could be trusted only when they were at the point of a bayonet. Then he asked if Wright would help the White House win $30 million in new military aid for the contras. Wright was flabbergasted at the audacity of the request after the White House's personal attacks against him. They seemed to think they could get their way by bullying. Given the attitudes in Congress, Wright told Carlucci, they would be lucky to get even humanitarian aid.[94]

A few days later, former Democratic Party chairman Robert Strauss, Washington's premier political fixer, called Wright to say that George Shultz wanted to call a truce. Wright was willing, but wary. "They think they have a right to excoriate people to bring them into line," he told Strauss. "Well, they've got a different animal now. If they want a truce, OK, but I'm not afraid of the bastard [Reagan]. . . . This is latter-day McCarthyism. If they refer to the Wright-Ortega plan again, they'll have a fight."[95]

Shultz and Wright hammered out a six-point statement of their common views toward Central America and appeared publicly together to announce their reconciliation. "The speaker and I, as is well known, had a little tiff," said Shultz, but all was forgiven. Nothing had really changed, though. When reporters asked Wright if he had agreed to stop meeting with the Central Americans, Wright's answer was a flat, unequivocal, "No."[96]

Continuing Conflict

Reagan's bitterness about Wright's activist role in promoting the Nicaraguan cease-fire talks was primarily a product of his frustration at having lost control of events. In October, Oscar Arias was awarded the Nobel Prize for Peace, giving added impetus to the Esquipulas accord. By November, every Central American government was conferring with Wright, and it was not unusual for Sandinista representatives and contra representatives to meet with the Speaker on the same day. The administration, meanwhile, was floundering. Divided internally, it was ambivalent about the Esquipulas plan, but had no credible alternative. By focusing singlemindedly on military aid for the contras when everyone else was talking about peace, the administration made itself irrelevant.

By November 1987, Reagan had already floated and withdrawn two military aid proposals: the $105 million proposal for fiscal year 1988 made early in the year and then postponed to avoid the Iran-contra hearings, and a $270 million aid proposal announced by Shultz in early September, but never formally submitted to Congress because, as one administration official said, "We knew we'd get our rear ends kicked."[97] Despite the unfriendly political atmosphere on Capitol Hill, the administration could no longer delay; the $100 million in contra aid passed in 1986 was running out.

Wright was unwilling to provide the contras with any further military aid. Not only would the House Democratic caucus have risen in rebellion at the idea, but Wright agreed with Oscar Arias that further military aid would doom the peace process. The Sandinistas had made major political concessions in order to end the contra war. If Washington continued to fuel the fighting regardless, the Sandinistas would have no incentive to abide by the Esquipulas accord, and every excuse to abrogate it.

But Wright was less antagonistic toward the contras than many of his fellow Democrats. He knew and respected many of the contras' political leaders and he distrusted the Sandinistas. The existence of the contras was politically useful because it provided leverage against the Sandinistas; if they reneged on the Esquipulas agreement, the war could be resumed. So while Wright opposed further military aid for the rebels, he was not opposed to nonmilitary assistance (so-called "humanitarian aid" of food, medicine, clothing, and shelter) that would allow the contras to hold together in the field.[98] This put him at odds with a majority of House Democrats, who opposed any contra aid whatsoever.

In early October, Wright used his control over House procedures to add $3.5 million in nonmilitary aid for the contras to the short continuing resolution lasting until November 9. To avoid a direct vote on the aid, Wright added the funds by putting them in the rule that governed floor debate on the bill. It was exactly the sort of maneuver that the Republicans bitterly denounced when done at their expense. Now that Wright was using the same tactic to outflank the liberals, the Republicans voiced no objection—except to complain that $3.5 million was not enough.[99]

The liberals were angry not only that Wright would support more contra aid, but that he did it by such procedural legerdemain. Three extensions of the short continuing resolution (taking it through December 21) contained another $3.2 million for the contras.[100] The liberals mounted no opposition to these extensions, preferring to hold their fire for the debate over the "long" continuing resolution covering the rest of fiscal year 1988.

Congress took up the long continuing resolution in late November. The House version included no aid for the contras. The Senate version, however, provided $16 million in food, clothing, and medical supplies.[101] The Senate action dashed the liberals' hopes for finally cutting off all contra aid; some compromise amount was certain to emerge from the House-Senate conference committee. Reagan and the Republicans swore they would do whatever was necessary to assure an extension of contra aid, even if it meant stopping the government by deadlocking the conference committee. House Republicans had lost every major floor vote in 1988 because of Wright's hardball leadership style; they were determined to win on the contras. "This is the president's last year and he isn't going to lose the contras on his last vote," warned Howard Baker. "He is willing to stay here through Christmas."[102]

House Democrats who opposed any extension of contra aid also labored under the burden that both Arias and the Sandinistas were willing to countenance nonmilitary assistance. Arias said so openly, declaring that aid in the form of food and medicine was consistent with the Esquipulas agreement, even though it clearly contradicted the actual text of the accord. Privately, the Sandinistas were also willing to go along with "humanitarian" aid because they believed it was inevitable.[103]

Less than a week before Christmas, the conference committee finally arrived at an agreement. The continuing resolution would provide $14 million for the contras until February 3, 1988, at which time the House would vote on whether to allow any further aid. Although the new funds could purchase only nonmilitary items, they could also be used to finance the delivery of military supplies the contras already had. The military deliveries would stop for a week beginning January 12, 1988, however, so that the United States would not be violating the Esquipulas agreement while the Central American presidents were holding their summit meeting to review progress on the accord. If Reagan certified that the peace process was stalled because of Nicaraguan intransigence, military deliveries could resume January 19.[104]

In almost every particular, the Democrats gave in to the Republican position. "It's a pig," Robert Mrazek (D-N.Y.) said of the compromise. "It's dressed up in a tuxedo, but it's still a pig and I'm not going to vote for it."[105] Most of the liberals felt the same way, including Bonior, who refused to support the compromise even though he was chief deputy whip. The leadership didn't even try to convince the liberals to support the bill, and in the end, 128 Democrats voted against it. A majority of Republicans supported the bill, however, and it passed by just a single vote, 209–208.[106]

Crippled politically by the Iran-contra scandal, Ronald Reagan was lucky he managed to keep the contras alive in 1987. His strategy of enlisting Speaker Wright in a joint diplomatic initiative seemed at the time like a masterstroke. The Sandinistas would balk at accepting U.S. demands for democracy, as they always had before, so the initiative would fail. Wright's participation would make it harder for him to oppose a new dose of contra aid. But the president was soon hoist with his own petard. The Wright-Reagan plan encouraged the Central Americans to make peace, but on their own terms, not Washington's. Reagan rejected Esquipulas, but Jim Wright embraced it with fervor. Wright's extraordinary activist role was possible because the administration's hostility to the accord left a diplomatic vacuum. Wright stepped in and played the role that Philip Habib had not been allowed to play. He could do it because the Central Americans regarded him as an honest broker. Everyone trusted him. And no one, not even the contras, trusted the Reagan administration.

CHAPTER 22

The Last Hurrah

Despite the Iran-contra scandal and the Esquipulas peace accord, it was by no means certain that the Democrats could prevent Ronald Reagan from eventually resuming lethal military aid to the contras. After nearly four years and over a dozen votes on contra aid, most members of Congress had long since made up their minds about the policy. For them, each new contra aid vote was routine; they were either for it or against it, regardless of the details of any particular aid package. What made Congress, or rather the House of Representatives, so fickle about the issue was the close balance between the pro-contra and anti-contra blocs. Seventy percent of the members of the House who sat in the 98th, 99th, or 100th Congresses (1983–88) had perfect records either for or against contra aid in as many as nineteen major floor votes. The solidly pro-contra and anti-contra blocs were almost the same size, with 192 members always in favor of aid and 185 always opposed. Over six years, only 158 swing members (29.5 percent) changed sides even once. By 1987–88, only a few dozen House members were willing to even consider changing their vote.[1]

With the pro-contra and anti-contra blocs so evenly matched, every vote was guaranteed to be close. By 1988, no event was powerful enough to erode the cohesion of the opposing camps. Both sides courted the scant middle—the few dozen House members who were perennially undecided. A shift by even a few of them meant the difference between stopping contra aid and resuming a massive flow of arms, between ending the war in Nicaragua and escalating it.

On the face of it, events seemed to have strengthened the anti-contra forces considerably. The Iran-contra scandal revealed the lawlessness of administration policy, and Esquipulas validated the viability of a diplomatic alternative. But the swing members, many of whom were southern Democrats, were an unpredictable lot, easily spooked by the administration's anti-Communist rhetoric. As the last year of Ronald Reagan's presidency began, it was still unclear whether Congress would end contra aid once and for all.

The Esquipulas peace process emerged as the determining factor. As long as the Sandinistas complied with the accord, congressional moderates were unlikely to upset the diplomatic apple cart by voting to renew lethal aid. The administration's only hope was to convince swing members that the peace process was failing for lack of Sandinista compliance.

But who would judge compliance? Throughout the fall and winter of 1987–88, the Reagan administration tried furiously to claim that prerogative for itself. Whatever the Sandinistas did, administration spokesmen denounced it as insincere or inadequate. When the Nicaraguans created a national reconciliation commission that included an opposition party leader, a neutral Protestant clergyman, and their arch-adversary Cardinal Miguel Obando y Bravo as chair, the State Department denounced them for having "stacked the commission in their favor." When the Sandinistas allowed the Catholic radio station to resume broadcasts and *La Prensa* to resume publication, the State Department called it "cosmetic gestures."[2]

The Sandinistas argued that compliance should be judged under the terms established in the accord itself: by the International Committee of Verification and Follow-Up, composed of the general secretaries of the U.N. and OAS, the foreign ministers of the five Central American signatories, and the foreign ministers of the eight Contadora countries. The verification commission was scheduled to report on compliance when the five Central American presidents met for a follow-up summit in January 1988.[3]

For Congress, however, the authoritative judge of Nicaragua's compliance was Oscar Arias. Both liberals and moderates trusted Arias's judgment because of his diplomatic skill in crafting the accord, because he was a staunch anti-Communist, and because he refused to bend to pressure from the Reagan administration. Senator Christopher Dodd spoke for many on Capitol Hill when he concluded, "If Oscar Arias says there has been compliance, there is compliance."[4]

Arias in the role of Solomon made both Reagan and the Sandinistas exceedingly nervous. Administration officials worried that Arias would accept minimal Sandinista compliance rather than see his vaunted peace plan disintegrate. Then Congress would end contra aid, the rebel army would collapse, and the Sandinistas would be free to renege on their commitment to democracy. In the end, Arias might wail about the Sandinistas' bad faith, but it would be too late.

Consequently, the administration set out to undermine Arias. The State Department held up the delivery of some $140 million in economic assistance to Costa Rica, allegedly on technical grounds. Privately, U.S. officials warned the Costa Ricans that U.S. aid was tied to their cooperation in the peace process.[5] Administration officials and Republicans in Congress complained that Costa Rica's ambassador to the United States, Guido Fernández, was lobbying Congress against contra aid. Under pressure from the State Department, Arias recalled him.[6] The Republicans also went after John Biehl, a Chilean employee of the United Nations Development Program who was acting as a personal adviser to Arias. Biehl and Arias had been friends since their student days at the University of Essex in England. Senator Robert Kasten (R-Wis.) wrote to the U.N., warning that Biehl's continued employment could jeopardize Washington's funding of the agency. Someone then leaked the letter to Arias's conservative opponents in Costa Rica, who hounded Biehl until he resigned and returned to Chile.[7]

Meanwhile, the Republican Institute for International Affairs, the Republican affiliate of the quasi-public National Endowment for Democracy (NED), funneled $433,000 to Arias's political opponents in the Social Christian Party. One of the projects that NED helped pay for was a Social Christian magazine that regularly attacked Arias and his policies, including the Esquipulas peace accord.[8]

"Arias, more than any other Latin leader, singlehandedly undid U.S. policy in Nicaragua," said Elliott Abrams's assistant Robert W. Kagan, explaining the administration's intense dislike for the Costa Rican president. When Arias won the Nobel Peace Prize, "all of us who thought it was important to get aid for the contras reacted with disgust, unbridled disgust."[9]

The Sandinistas were unhappy with Arias, too. After all, he regarded them as an ideological enemy. On paper, his peace plan was advantageous to Nicaragua, but the Sandinistas quickly discovered that the peace process had a life of its own. Complying with the letter of the accord would not be good enough; to avert a resumption of military aid to the contras, they would have to comply with the accord as interpreted by Oscar Arias. And Arias interpreted it to require things that were not in the actual text—most especially, negotiations with the contras.

After being pressured into accepting indirect talks with the contras in the fall of 1987, with Cardinal Obando as intermediary, the Sandinistas found themselves on a slippery slope. The contras continued to insist on direct talks, and Obando endorsed their position.[10] With the January 1988 Central American presidents' summit fast approaching, little progress had been made toward ending the Nicaraguan war, and the Sandinistas were being cast as the intransigent party. In late December, Ortega suggested that the Sandinistas might be willing to open direct low-level technical talks with the contras, but pressure from Sandinista hard-liners forced him to back away from the proposal. Shortly thereafter, even the indirect talks were suspended.[11]

The January summit of the Central American presidents loomed as a critical benchmark for assessing implementation of the Esquipulas agreement. Just days before the presidents convened, Elliott Abrams and General Colin Powell, Reagan's new national security adviser, traveled to Costa Rica, Honduras, El Salvador, and Guatemala. They urged the four presidents to denounce the Sandinistas at the summit for noncompliance with the Esquipulas accord. Otherwise, Powell warned, Congress might cut off contra aid. If that happened and the contras collapsed, the Central Americans would have to fend for themselves; U.S. aid would dry up.[12]

To counter the administration's lobbying, the House Democratic leadership continued its own diplomacy. On January 14, the day before the summit convened, Majority Leader Tom Foley and Majority Whip Tony Coelho invited the five Central American ambassadors to lunch. Foley told them that the summit needed to produce tangible progress toward peace if contra aid was to be definitively ended. Coelho reminded them that Democrats controlled the foreign aid spigot and wanted to see the peace process succeed.[13] Senator Christopher Dodd led a congressional delegation to Managua a few days before the summit to warn the Sandinistas that they had to make significant concessions to revitalize the peace process, or risk a resumption of lethal contra aid. "We gave them a very clear message," said a member of the delegation. "Either they agree to some direct talks [with the contras], or they are going to be hit with another $50 million or $100 million in new aid for the contras."[14]

When the Central American presidents met in Costa Rica on January 15, 1988, Daniel Ortega avoided a confrontation by finally agreeing to open direct talks with the contras. He also announced that the Sandinistas would lift the state of emergency limiting the civic opposition's political liberties, hold free elections, and give up political power if they lost.[15]

The announcement that the Sandinistas would finally meet the contras face to face should have been a great triumph for the rebel movement. They had been demanding direct negotiations for years, thinking that if the Sandinistas agreed, the rebels' legitimacy would be greatly enhanced. If the Sandinistas continued to refuse, they would appear intransigent. For the contras, the demand for talks seemed like a no-lose proposition—until the Sandinistas agreed to it.

By early 1988, the contras' top priority was winning a renewal of military aid from the United States. When Ortega agreed to direct negotiations, the Sandinistas fulfilled the principal demand that everyone—the Reagan administration, congressional Democrats, Western European social democrats, and the other Central American governments—had been making of them since the Esquipulas agreement was signed. Peace talks between the Sandinistas and the contras would dramatically reduce the chances of Congress approving further military aid. Knowing this, the contras panicked and at first refused to participate. That was so obviously contrived, however, that it damaged the contras' credibility, and within forty-eight hours they had reconsidered. Both sides, it appeared, would have to be dragged to the bargaining table kicking and screaming.[16]

Selling Insurance

Not surprisingly, the Reagan administration was unimpressed by Ortega's concessions. White House Press Secretary Marlin Fitzwater announced that Reagan would request additional contra aid even if the Sandinistas agreed to a cease-fire and granted a full amnesty to all dissidents, contras, and former National Guardsmen. "Our basic strategy doesn't change," explained a senior State Department official. "It is to persuade Congress that Ortega cannot be trusted and that there is a need to maintain aid as an insurance policy."[17]

Eight days later, on January 27, 1988, Reagan notified Congress that he would seek a new contra aid package including $36.25 million in both lethal and nonlethal supplies and $20 million to replace any of the airplanes delivering supplies to the contras if they were shot down. In addition, he asked for "passive air defense equipment" (primarily radar) to be leased to the contras at no cost. The value of such equipment was about $7 million, making the total package worth $63.25 million.[18]

Administration officials called it a bare-bones package, greatly scaled back from the $270 million requested in 1987.[19] Upon close inspection, however, the new request was larger than it appeared. In 1987, Reagan had requested $270 million to last for eighteen months; the new $63.25 million request covered just four months and gave the president the right to return to Congress using "fast-track" procedures to get more money in July. The two proposals represented almost identical annual funding rates (the 1987 request amounted to $180 million annually; the 1988 request, $189.75 million annually), both of which were nearly twice the peak amount of $100 million the contras received in 1986.

Congressional debate on the president's aid package revolved around one main issue: would resuming lethal aid to the contras enhance the prospects for peace or demolish them? The Democrats pointed out that seven years of contra aid had extracted few concessions from the Sandinistas, whereas just seven months of the Central American peace process had produced many. The Esquipulas agreement called upon all outside countries to halt aid to insurgent movements. When the Central American presidents met in January 1988, they reiterated that appeal.[20] "We cannot credibly say we support the agreement and then act in direct contradiction to its terms," argued Congressman Matt McHugh (D-N.Y.). "How can we expect the Sandinistas to take the myriad steps required of them when we refuse to do the one thing asked of us?"[21]

The Republicans countered that only military pressure had brought the Sandinistas to the bargaining table in the first place, and only continued pressure would force them to live up to the peace accord. "We must keep the pressure on the Sandinistas so that they can't reverse course," Reagan said in late January 1988. "Only the freedom fighters can do that, only they can be our insurance policy for democracy in Central America." Regardless of what the Esquipulas accord actually said, Reagan insisted that continued military aid for the contras was fully consistent with it. "Some say that if you're for aid to the freedom fighters in Nicaragua you're against the peace process," the president noted during one of his weekly radio addresses to the nation. "Phooey!"[22]

But Reagan was losing the one audience that counted—the moderate swing members of the House. In late January, nineteen of them wrote to the president asking him to delay his request for new contra aid lest it disrupt the direct talks between the Sandinistas and the contras.[23] As the February vote approached, the White House had still not put together a majority. The Democrats understood from bitter experience that a president could always sway a handful of members. "I suspect he can buy a few votes for a project here and there," said David Bonior. Asked if administration officials were engaged in that sort of horse trading, a White House aide replied, "I hope so."[24]

The floor debate on Reagan's contra aid package began at 10:00 in the morning on February 3, 1988, and ran uninterrupted for over twelve hours.[25] The tone was even harsher than usual. Opening for the Republicans, Dick Cheney of Wyoming charged that contra aid opponents were either trying to "embarrass the president" for selfish partisan reasons, or they "do not want to insist that the Sandinistas comply with the peace process." Lawrence Coughlin of Pennsylvania called the liberal Democrats "gutless wonders" and "bleeding hearts" who always "blame America first."

Opponents of contra aid gave as good as they got. Democrat Ted Weiss of New York accused Reagan of waging "a cruel and incessant war on the people of Nicaragua. In pursuit of an ideological obsession, spurred on by radical right-wing fanatics, the president, his top cabinet-level officers, and their underlings have engaged in every immoral, unethical, and illegal activity imaginable."

In an unusual move, Speaker Wright closed the debate for the Democrats. If Washington expected to hold Nicaragua accountable for its compliance with Esquipulas, Wright asked, "do we not have the responsibility to comply ourselves? . . . The five Central American presidents have joined together and have asked us not to send any more destructive weapons into their region. Let us heed their plea." The House did so, rejecting Reagan's aid proposal, 219–211.[26]

Reagan had built his Nicaragua policy so completely around the contras that when the House voted down his aid package, he was left with nothing but the shell of a policy. "As of today, the entire spectrum of U.S. policy in Central America . . . is in shambles," a White House official admitted after the House vote. "It's back to the drawing boards."[27] But administration officials had been wedded to the contras for so long, they suffered a poverty of imagination; they simply could not conceive of fundamentally changing the policy. Despite long odds, they clung to the hope that some bolt from the blue would shift the congressional mood once again and make a resumption of the war possible. In Central America, the CIA maintained its air base and logistics infrastructure, just in case. It also continued to pay for the contras' political activities and provide "family support" payments to their leadership.[28]

Throughout the region, people interpreted the House vote as the death knell for the contras. The day after the vote, Alfonso Robelo resigned from the contra leadership and returned to private life. General Humberto Regalado, commander of the Honduran armed forces, washed his hands of the contras, declaring that the program "belongs to the United States." Even in the U.S. intelligence community, analysts doubted that the contras would survive for long without a new infusion of aid. The operation was "on its last legs," one analyst concluded. "It's an end game."[29]

The Democratic Alternative

As usual, to keep the moderate swing Democrats on board, Jim Wright had to promise them he would propose an alternative aid program after Reagan's plan was defeated. Wright put David Bonior in charge of crafting something that would satisfy the moderate Democrats' need for political cover without offending the liberals' adamant opposition to any contra aid. Needless to say, it was not an easy assignment. "Our goal is to find something that is 60 percent acceptable to 52 percent of the members, and I think we have a 75 percent chance of doing that," quipped liberal Barney Frank (D-Mass.). To draft the alternative, Bonior assembled a task force including the most prominent moderates and the most committed liberals. If they could agree on a plan, they could then sell it to their respective constituencies in the House.[30]

The package Bonior's task force came up with provided $16 million in direct aid for the contras, but restricted it to food, clothing, shelter, medical supplies, and field radios (so that contra units could be apprised if a cease-fire was signed). No further military aid could be delivered, not even what remained in the pipeline from the $100 million approved in 1986.[31]

Bonior's bill attracted some unexpected supporters. The Sandinistas discreetly let it be known that they did not oppose it; they recognized that some aid program would be passed, and Bonior's proposal was acceptable because it excluded military aid. Costa Rican Foreign Minister Rodrigo Madrigal Nieto, speaking for President Arias, said that the Democratic plan would not harm the peace process, even though it obviously violated the Esquipulas accord's injunction against providing any aid to insurgents. The most surprising endorsement, however, came from the contras themselves. Even though they badly wanted military aid, nonmilitary aid was better than nothing. Without new resources, the whole contra army might collapse. Despite White House opposition, the contras conferred with the Democrats about what should go into Bonior's proposal.[32]

Ronald Reagan, however, was unmoved. If adopted, the Democratic plan would lead to the "rapid debilitation of the resistance and further encouragement of Sandinista intransigence," he charged. House Republicans devised an alternative of their own, a slightly revised version of the administration plan rejected by the House in February.[33]

As the vote approached, Reagan went back on the stump, condemning the Democrats for selling out America's allies.[34] On Capitol Hill, both Republicans and Democrats were turning their attention to the procedural rules under which the two alternative aid packages would be considered. As in 1985 and 1986, the rules were crucial. Republican leader Robert Michel was convinced that if he could just get a straight yes or no vote on the Republican package, it would win. After all, Reagan's proposal had almost won in February, and Michel's revised version of it made just enough concessions to the moderates to gain the handful of additional votes needed to prevail. That, at least, was the firm conviction on the Republican side.

Moderate Democrats opposed giving the Republicans a vote on their alternative because it meant one more vote they would have to cast against the contras. "The next vote has got to be on our proposal," said a southerner in a Democratic whip meeting. "I can't have several votes in a row against contra aid."[35] To assure the support of the swing voters, the Democratic proposal would have to be voted on first.

That could be arranged one of two ways. A "king of the mountain" rule—used often in the House—would allow votes on both proposals, and whichever passed last would win. That would satisfy the moderates, but it would lose some liberals. To vote on the Democratic proposal under such a rule meant that liberals would have to cast an unabashed vote in favor of contra aid (albeit the limited aid contained in the Democratic proposal)—something they had consistently refused to do. In 1985 and 1986, the leadership carefully structured the rules so that the liberals were always voting on a Democratic proposal that *reduced* the amount of contra aid in a pending Republican proposal. To the liberals, that was barely palatable. A king of the mountain rule provided no such cover, and without it, some liberals would oppose the Democratic plan. Since the House was so closely divided, the defection of a few liberals could easily defeat the Democratic proposal. Then the moderates would vote for Reagan's plan, just as they had in 1985, and the administration would emerge victorious.

The only way to satisfy both the moderates and the liberals was to vote first on the Democratic plan (so the moderates could vote *for* a contra aid proposal rather than having to cast another vote against one), but to have the Democratic plan be proposed as an amendment to the Republican proposal (so the liberals would be voting to limit the aid in the pending proposal, rather than voting in favor of a contra aid proposal per se). A rule structured in this way, however, meant that the Republican plan would start out as the pending legislation, with the Democrats' plan as a substitute amendment. If the Democratic proposal passed, the Republican plan would be replaced without ever coming up for a simple yes or no vote.

With fewer than ten votes separating the two sides, the Democrats could not chance a rule that might split their moderate and liberal coalition. The Democratic majority on the Rules Committee made the Republican proposal the pending legislation, thus giving the Democratic alternative the first vote.[36] The Republicans were livid. On the floor Michel argued in vain for the House to reject the Democratic rule. "We were promised a fair shot at a substitute," he said angrily. "We got a shot, all right, a shot to the head."[37] The Democrats responded that Michel had only been promised the right to present a Republican alternative, not to have the rule structured to his advantage.

After the controversy over the rule, debate on the Democratic proposal was predictably bitter.[38] The angry Republicans accused the Democrats of sending

U.S. troops into danger by insisting that the Pentagon rather than the CIA deliver aid to the contras. The Democrats pointed out that their amendment explicitly prohibited U.S. military personnel from entering Nicaragua, or even from approaching closer than twenty miles to the border. The Republicans also accused the Democrats of giving foreign aid to the Sandinistas because the bill's relief fund for children included victims inside Nicaragua. The Democrats countered that their bill channeled the children's assistance through "nonpolitical private and voluntary organizations and international relief organizations"—hardly a foreign aid program for the Sandinistas.

Wright finally lost his temper at the repetition of such disingenuous accusations. "I had not intended to get into this debate," he began, "but for anyone to stand in the well of this House and say that the plan our colleagues put together carefully gives money to the Ortega brothers to distribute in any way they want to is just lying or he doesn't understand it." Between the Republicans' anger over the rule and the Democrats' anger over the Republicans' willful misreading of the Bonior proposal, precious little remained of the comity of the House.

The partisan animosity generated by the whole process inevitably hurt the Republicans, since they were still the minority. The Bonior proposal was adopted, 215–210, on a vote that divided the House along party lines more sharply than any contra aid vote in the previous five years. Only three Republicans broke ranks to back the Democratic proposal.[39]

The first vote was only half the battle, however. The Democrats had successfully disposed of the Republican proposal by replacing it with their own. That made the Bonior plan the pending legislation. The Democrats still had to hold a majority together for the vote on final passage of the bill. The leadership knew from the outset that the vote on final passage would be a problem. Some liberals would vote for Bonior's proposal the first time, because it was the lesser evil compared to the Republican plan. But they would not vote for it on final passage when the alternative was no aid at all. This was precisely the problem that had led to the defeat of the Barnes-Hamilton alternative in 1985 and paved the way for the resumption of contra aid on a new vote a few weeks later.

This time, at least, the leadership was aware of the danger and lobbied the liberals hard to keep them from opposing the Democratic plan on final passage. The fact that Bonior led the task force that drafted the plan helped enormously. No one had been a more active or consistent opponent of the contra war than Bonior, so when he pronounced the alternative plan reasonable, most liberals trusted him. In addition, the major human rights and peace groups that had worked against contra aid for years reluctantly endorsed Bonior's proposal. Consequently, unlike 1985, most of the liberals agreed to hold their noses and vote for the Bonior plan on final passage.

Two dozen die-hard liberals were unmoved. No amount of reasoning would convince them to abandon their principled opposition and cast a pragmatic vote for nonmilitary aid in order to keep the moderates happy. Wright warned Michel that he needed a dozen Republican votes to assure final passage of the Bonior plan, or else the contras would end up with nothing. Moderate Democrats who had sided with the Republicans on earlier contra aid votes canvassed the Republican side of the chamber, beseeching them to put aside their rancor toward the Democrats and vote for the Bonior plan.[40] The Republicans refused. Better, they thought, to let the Democratic package be defeated, leaving the moderates with no political cover. That way, the American people would see clearly the Democrats' vile betrayal of the contras and their abandonment of Nicaragua to Communism. "You will bear the guilt you deserve for being an accessory to the murder of freedom and democracy in the hemisphere," Henry Hyde said bitterly.

Only five Republicans supported the Bonior plan on final passage, not enough to make up for the twenty-six liberals who opposed it. Just as Wright warned, the bill was defeated, 216–208. "I'm very happy," Ronald Reagan exclaimed when he heard the news.[41] Reagan and the House Republicans would not settle for half a loaf.

When a similar coalition of liberals and Republicans defeated the Barnes-Hamilton bill in 1985, moderate Democrats felt betrayed. This time, however, most of the liberals had supported the bill on final passage, even though they disliked it. The vast majority of the votes against final passage of the Bonior proposal were cast by Republicans, even though the vote left the contras stranded in the field. To many moderates, it looked as if the Republicans' partisan hatred of the Democrats had become more important than the contra cause itself. Unlike 1985, the moderates did not rally to the Republican camp, leaving the Republicans with the worst of both worlds: no contra aid, and no majority to win it later.

The contras were stunned. They felt abandoned, not so much by the Democrats as by their erstwhile Republican allies. "The White House felt it was better to leave our forces up in the air than vote with the Democrats," said contra leader Alfredo César. "The bottom line is the resistance has been hurt in the field."[42]

Sapoá

During January and February, the direct talks between the contras and the Sandinistas had produced no substantive progress. In late February, Cardinal Obando, in his role as mediator, submitted a surprise peace proposal that essentially incorporated the contras' negotiating position. When the Sandinistas refused to accept it on the spot, Obando denounced them for intransigence and suspended the talks.[43]

This odd behavior, which threatened to derail the negotiations, came just on the eve of the congressional vote on contra aid. The coincidence of events heightened the Sandinistas' suspicions about Obando's motives. Tired of dealing with a mediator who acted more like a member of the opposing delegation, the Sandinistas opted for another diplomatic bold stroke. On March 2, 1988, they invited the contras to send a delegation to Nicaragua to meet directly with high-level Sandinista officials, including Defense Minister Humberto Ortega— but without a mediator. The meeting was set for March 21, in the small border town of Sapoá.

The contras came to Sapoá intent upon pressing an agenda of political reforms—issues the Sandinistas had repeatedly said they would never discuss. The Sandinistas insisted that the only agenda at Sapoá would be the mechanics of a cease-fire. With such incompatible demands separating the adversaries, no one expected much progress. Yet after just two days of talks, the contras and Sandinistas announced agreement on a comprehensive cease-fire and political settlement of the war. Humberto Ortega signed the March 23 accord for the Nicaraguan government; Adolfo Calero, Alfredo César, and Aristedes Sánchez signed for the "Nicaraguan Resistance." In an emotional moment, members of both delegations stood at attention for the Nicaraguan national anthem.[44]

The Sapoá agreement embodied most of the demands the contras brought to the bargaining table. The Sandinistas agreed to a general amnesty for both the contras and the remaining members of Somoza's National Guard still imprisoned for war crimes. Exiles would be allowed to return to the country without fear of prosecution and could participate fully in national political life. The contras would be allowed to send delegates to the "national dialogue" between the Sandinistas and the internal opposition over how to carry out the Esquipulas agreement. And the Sandinistas renewed their pledge to abide by the Esquipulas accord.

In exchange, the contras recognized the legitimacy of the Sandinista government, agreed to a sixty-day cease-fire, and pledged to move their combatants into mutually agreed upon cease-fire zones. They also pledged to solicit no outside assistance other than "exclusively humanitarian aid channeled through neutral organizations." Significantly, they did not agree to disarm; that, along with a final cease-fire, would be the subject of further talks.

The contras' motives in signing the accord seemed straightforward. On paper at least, they won most of the political guarantees they had sought, and they gave up little. Moreover, without military aid from Washington, the contras' leverage over the Sandinistas would diminish rapidly. The sooner they signed an agreement, the more they were likely to get from it. "For us not to have accepted this treaty would have left us politically dead," said a senior contra official. "There was no help left in Washington."[45]

The Sandinistas' motives for conceding so much were harder to divine. The contras posed no serious military threat; most of them were already moving back toward their Honduran base camps for want of supplies.[46] Further military aid from Washington seemed unlikely. If the Sandinistas simply stalled the negotiations, the withering contra army would have had less and less bargaining power. The key factor, however, was the domestic economy. Under the terms of the Esquipulas agreement, the Sandinistas would have to hold national elections by late 1990. Unless they could begin to revive the economy, their reelection would be in peril. And the sine qua non for economic recovery was ending the war.

By 1988, the Nicaraguan economy was in collapse. The government's political feud with the private sector had led to disinvestment, and its economic policies created disincentives for producers, especially in agriculture.[47] These internal problems were aggravated by Washington's economic pressure—the virtual elimination of loans from international financial institutions and the U.S. trade embargo. Economic aid from the Soviet Union never came close to covering the resulting losses.

Even without the contra war, the Nicaraguan economy would have faced a serious crisis in the mid-1980s. The war tipped it into chaos. The cost of physical damage due to the fighting and lost production due to, for example, the disruption of transportation, displacement of people from the war zones, and interruption of energy supplies amounted to $2 billion between 1980 and 1986.[48] But the most significant cost was the diversion of resources from economic development to defense. By 1986, 55 percent of the government's budget was devoted to fighting the war, a figure that held constant through 1988.[49] With production declining, tax revenues could not begin to cover the costs of the conflict, so the government closed the fiscal gap by simply printing money. That, of course, unleashed inflation.

In 1987, the inflation rate was 1,300 percent. The government took its supplies of old 20 and 50 cordoba bank notes and simply printed three more zeros on them to make 20,000 and 50,000 cordoba notes. In 1988, the government's austerity measures, intended to control inflation by reducing public spending, triggered a severe recession. The economy contracted 15 percent, and the fiscal deficit actually widened. Inflation raged completely out of control, reaching 33,600 percent—hyperinflation of the sort experienced by only a few nations in history. As money became worthless, the economy was reduced to primitive barter, further dislocating production and exchange. By the end of the year, the gross domestic product had fallen by a third and per capita consumption had fallen by more than 50 percent from 1979 levels.[50] So despite the contras' military weakness, the Sandinistas were willing to make significant political concessions at Sapoá because peace was a precondition for economic stabilization.

Once again, diplomatic developments caught the Reagan administration unawares. "You can believe me, we had nothing to do with this," said an administration official of the Sapoá agreement. "It came as a complete surprise."[51] Just as in 1984, when a Contadora agreement was almost reached, and in 1987, when the Esquipulas accord was signed, administration officials had been certain that nothing would come of the Central Americans' efforts at the bargaining table. They were shocked that the contras would take such audacious action without clearing it first with their handlers in Washington.

Administration hard-liners were appalled by the Sapoá agreement. They could hardly condemn the accord in public, however, without appearing to be so enamored of the war that they were prepared to fight to the last Nicaraguan. Nevertheless, they blamed the Democrats for having forced the contras into a bad bargain. "The freedom fighters were cut off by Congress," explained Elliott Abrams. "They had to sign some kind of agreement because Congress had just smashed them into a corner."[52]

In response to the cease-fire, the House leadership introduced a slightly modified version of the Bonior proposal that had been narrowly defeated just a few weeks earlier. It provided $17.7 million in food, clothing, shelter, and medical supplies for the contras, $17.7 million for children who were victims of the war, and $10 million to finance the verification commission created by the Sapoá accord. This time, the administration reluctantly agreed to support the bill because contra forces in the field were desperate for supplies. The bill passed, 345–70. The following day, the Senate approved the House package, 87–7.[53]

Behind the scenes, the administration's response to the Sapoá agreement replicated its response to the 1984 Contadora accord and 1987 Esquipulas accord. While paying grudging lip service to diplomacy, the administration set about sabotaging the agreement. Elliott Abrams lobbied the contra leadership not to sign a final accord. When Jim Wright called George Shultz to complain, the secretary told him that the contras needed to maintain military pressure on the Sandinistas and therefore should refuse a permanent cease-fire.[54]

Not everyone in the contra camp thought the agreement was a good bargain, either. When Calero, Sánchez, and César appeared before the fifty-four-member contra assembly on March 26, some members criticized them for signing, arguing that they had won little more than promises. The chief critic was military commander Enrique Bermúdez. A few weeks after the Sapoá agreement, the two contra military representatives who attended the talks and approved the agreement were expelled from the movement by pro-Bermúdez commanders.[55]

The disagreement among the contras over Sapoá precipitated yet another internal crisis in the movement. In April 1988, forty-nine rebel field officers, including fifteen of the twenty-eight top regional commanders, signed a petition demanding Bermúdez's ouster.[56] Calero, long an ally of Bermúdez in their battles with contra "liberals" Alfonso Robelo and Arturo Cruz, sided with this "rebellion in the rebellion," in order to maintain his personal control over the negotiating process. Calero and fellow contra director Pedro Joaquín Chamorro Jr. tried to convince the other three members of the five-member executive directorate to remove Bermúdez as military commander and put Calero himself in direct charge of the contra army.

The CIA, however, still supported Bermúdez. Although both Calero and Bermúdez had worked with the Agency for years, the CIA preferred Bermúdez because he had proved himself a reliable commander and, like administration hard-liners, he opposed the Sapoá agreement.[57] When Pedro Chamorro urged the contra directorate to replace Bermúdez, Aristedes Sánchez called John Mallet, the former deputy CIA station chief in Honduras who had worked with the contras since early in the war. Over a speakerphone in front of the entire directorate, Mallet berated Chamorro as "stupid" and "an imbecile" for thinking that the civilian directorate could remove the contras' military commander. Another CIA officer was more diplomatic, but no less adamant. "I admire your idealism," the officer told Chamorro, "but let's be realistic." The CIA had selected the members of the directorate and paid their salaries, so it expected them to do as they were told. Bermúdez stayed.[58]

The contra field commanders, a tougher lot, were not so easily persuaded. Even though CIA contacts told them that it was "official U.S. policy to support Bermúdez," they refused to drop their complaints. When CIA efforts to bribe them didn't work either, the Agency asked the Honduran armed forces to round up the dissident officers and expel them from Honduras. After half a dozen of them had been kicked out, the rest gave in and signed a loyalty oath to Bermúdez.[59]

Predictably, the negotiations for a permanent cease-fire made no progress. In June, the contras rejected a Sandinista proposal and countered by demanding a major reorganization of the existing political system, including the abolition of the Sandinista Defense Committees (a neighborhood-level Sandinista political organization) and the replacement of the entire Supreme Court. And they demanded that the Sandinistas accept their proposal within two hours. When the Sandinistas refused, the contras walked out.[60] In private, contra officials admitted that Bermúdez had scuttled the talks intentionally in the hope their failure would prompt renewed military aid from the United States. "We broke off the . . . talks. They were strangling us," a contra official said. "So long as we were talking, we had no chance for a revival of military aid. Now we may."[61]

The contras' decision to quit the negotiations may have been precipitated by a vote in the House just a week and a half before the final round of talks. On May 26, Henry Hyde and Dick Cheney offered a surprise amendment to the intelligence authorization bill for fiscal year 1989 deleting all restrictions on aid to the contras. Had the amendment passed, it would have freed the administration to use the CIA's contingency fund to resume military aid.

By springing the amendment on the unsuspecting Democrats, the Republicans hoped to gather the votes of wavering moderates before the Democratic leadership could mobilize its whip organization. Offering surprise amendments was not the normal way of doing business in the House. "When inquiries were made, we were told by Republican staff that this would not come up," David Bonior said. "It went beyond surprise," added a House Democratic aide. "They flatly lied about it."[62] Such deceit was an extraordinary breach of House protocol. On the floor, Hyde personally apologized to Intelligence Committee Chairman Louis Stokes (D-Ohio) for misleading him, but added, "We had to do what we had to do."[63]

A spirited debate ensued. Unlike previous debates, it was largely unscripted because most members were caught off guard, without prepared speeches. "The issue," said Tom Foley, "is not about helping the peace process but abandoning it. . . . What we are doing is sending a clear signal that we have lost confidence in the negotiations." That was a signal the moderate members of the House were not willing to send; they still had hope that the talks would succeed. Hyde's amendment was defeated, 214–190.

Enrique Bermúdez was right to conclude from this episode that the Congress would never approve new military aid as long as the peace process was alive. His mistake was thinking that Congress would resume aid if the contras killed it. Ronald Reagan was game for one last try, but with the collapse of the peace talks, Republican leader Robert Michel advised the White House that the prospects for winning military aid were "very negative."[64]

Congressional support for the contras also faded in proportion to their disintegration as a fighting force. Delivery of the humanitarian aid approved by Congress in March was delayed for several months by a dispute between the Sandinistas and the contras over what agency could distribute supplies to contra units inside Nicaragua. Eventually, most contra combatants withdrew to Honduras where they could be resupplied by U.S. AID.

"It is a disaster," said a State Department official. "It is a defeat. You've got to admit it." As the dream of military victory evaporated, the administration settled on the limited aim of keeping a few thousand contra combatants in the field to continue harassing the Sandinistas. "Those 2,000 hard-core guys could keep some pressure on the Nicaraguan government, force them to use their economic resources for the military and prevent them from solving their economic problems," the State Department official explained. "And that's a plus."[65]

Another U.S. official was dubious about the prospects for holding even that much of the contra army together. "We may not be capable of keeping 2,000 troops in the field," he worried. "We may end up simply trying to avoid having to airlift them all to Florida."[66] Around Washington, analysts and government officials began discussing the problem of "contra disposal." In the field, the CIA began to disengage as well, closing the command and logistics bases on Swan Island and Aguacate, Honduras. "The agency is striking its tents," lamented one administration official who didn't want to give up on the contras. "The problem is, we're still in them."[67]

Patriotas or *Vendepatrias*?

With the contras in decline, the Reagan administration shifted its attention to the civic opposition inside Nicaragua or, as the Sandinistas called it, the "internal front" in Washington's war. The United States had been covertly financing internal opponents of the Sandinistas since 1980. Within weeks after the Sandinista triumph on July 19, 1979, President Carter signed a presidential finding authorizing the CIA to provide covert financial support to moderate political groups, including the Superior Council of Private Enterprise (COSEP), *La Prensa*, and non-Sandinista trade unions. The purpose of this program, budgeted "in the low millions," according to one U.S. intelligence official, was to bolster the political center and right.[68]

President Reagan expanded the CIA's covert support for the civic opposition, first in his March 9, 1981, finding and then again in his December 1, 1981, finding that initiated the contra war. The scope paper accompanying Reagan's September 19, 1983, finding continued the program of "financial and material support" for "Nicaraguan opposition leaders and organizations."[69] Virtually every element of the opposition—the press, the church, the private sector, trade unions, and political parties—received financial support from the CIA, though they may not all have been aware of their benefactor's identity. "We've always had the internal opposition on the CIA payroll," explained one U.S. official.[70] By the mid-1980s the annual budget for this program was more than $10 million annually. In the eleven months from December 1984 to October 1985, the CIA spent $13 million on the civic opposition.[71]

The Catholic Church was also a recipient of covert funding from the CIA. In fact, when Congress insisted that covert aid to the church be halted, for fear it would ruin Obando's reputation, Casey told his Central America Task Force chief, Alan Fiers, to arrange a private alternative. A corporate contractor was directed to overbill the CIA for legitimate contracts and then funnel the residuals to the church.[72] Oliver North sent about $160,000 to the civic opposition, mostly to the Catholic Church. Roy Godson, a political warfare specialist who worked at the NSC, raised the money from conservative donors and channeled most of it through the Heritage Foundation. Obando also had access to an account in the Cayman Islands controlled by the CIA and contras.[73] When these transactions came to light during the Iran-contra investigation, Obando's aide, Bismark Carballo, defended the prelate's actions, saying, "In Nicaragua, everyone receives money from outside."[74]

Not only was Reagan's covert aid program larger than Carter's, but its aim was different. Carter's program had been designed to strengthen moderates as a political counterweight to the Sandinistas, in the hope that the government would evolve in a democratic direction. Most Reagan officials did not believe such an evolution was possible. To them, CIA support for the civic opposition was an ancillary part of the contra war. Internal opposition to the Sandinistas would weaken the regime's ability to prosecute the war and hasten its defeat.

The main source of overt assistance to the civic opposition was the quasi-public National Endowment for Democracy, which funneled about $2 million into Nicaragua between 1984 and 1988. *La Prensa* received about half of that; the rest went to the constituent groups of the opposition coalition that boycotted the 1984 election, including two small trade union federations.[75] In the early 1980s, these two union federations (which together included only about five thousand workers, or 2 percent of the organized labor force) also received funds from the AFL-CIO's American Institute for Free Labor Development (AIFLD). After the fall of Somoza, AIFLD tripled its budget for Nicaraguan programs, to about $500,000 annually; by 1982, it had forty-four projects under way. The Sandinistas kicked AIFLD out of the country in 1982.[76]

La Prensa was the linchpin of the civic opposition. Making no pretense of objectivity, it vilified the Sandinista government at every opportunity, just as it had vilified Somoza in the late 1970s. CIA funding of *La Prensa* began in 1980 when conservatives in the paper's management (publisher Jaime Chamorro and owner Violeta Chamorro) took control away from its progressive staff and turned the paper's editorial policy sharply to the right. The United States then financed the rebuilding of *La Prensa*'s plant, purchased new presses, and provided a supply of newsprint.[77]

As in the case of the Catholic Church, CIA money was channeled through third-party "cut outs" to disguise its source; the paper's management may not have known who its real patron was.[78] During the mid-1980s, in addition to the funds provided by the National Endowment for Democracy, *La Prensa* also received aid from the Inter-American Press Association, the Friedrich Naumann Foundation in West Germany, a group of Venezuelan businessmen, and Norwegian newspapers. In the United States, the conservative Americares Foundation donated newsprint.[79]

The Sandinistas believed *La Prensa* had been suborned by the CIA to serve as an instrument of psychological warfare, just as *El Mercurio* had been in Chile in the early 1970s.[80] Whether or not the CIA directed *La Prensa*'s antigovernment campaign, the paper openly identified with the contras. "Our fight is the same as the FDN's," said Jaime Chamorro. "It's like the difference between the infantry and an air force; two arms of the same thing. . . . The contras are fighting with arms, and we are fighting in another way."[81] In the weeks leading up to the 1986 House votes on Reagan's $100 million contra aid package, five *La Prensa* staff members published op-ed pieces in U.S. newspapers denouncing the Sandinistas. Jaime Chamorro's April 3, 1986, column in the *Washington Post* openly endorsed Reagan's contra aid request.[82]

When *La Prensa* staff members grew weary of fighting with the pen, they often picked up the sword. Most of the contras' press spokesmen were former *La Prensa* reporters. In 1982, editorial page editor Humberto Belli came to the United States and, with the help of the CIA, published a book denouncing the Sandinistas' persecution of the church. In late 1984, editor Pedro Joaquín Chamorro Jr. himself went into exile, joined the contras, and was appointed to replace Adolfo Calero on the UNO directorate in 1988.[83]

The Sandinistas regarded the entire civic opposition as traitors. They called them *vendepatrias*—literally, "country-sellers." As the contra war escalated, so did the Sandinista government's restrictions on their civil liberties. Despite Washington's overt and covert support for the civic opposition, most U.S. officials regarded it as a sideshow. Divided, disorganized, and confronted by Sandinista security police and officially sanctioned mobs (*turbas*), the civic opposition pestered the Sandinistas more than it threatened them. Among the hard-liners in Washington, the idea that it could ever challenge the Sandinistas for power was widely derided. The contras were the main event.

After the Esquipulas peace accord was signed, however, the civic opposition took on new importance. How the Sandinistas treated their domestic opponents was an important indicator of their willingness to create a pluralist democracy as promised in the accord. Consequently, the Reagan administration stepped up its support for the internal opposition, according to one administration official, urging them "to push to the limit and beyond the limit of Sandinista toleration."[84]

To oversee this policy, Reagan named Richard H. Melton as the new U.S. ambassador to Nicaragua in late 1987. Melton was a career foreign service officer, but he was ideologically at home in the milieu of Reagan's State Department. When Elliott Abrams took over for Tony Motley as assistant secretary of state for inter-American affairs in July 1985, he brought in Melton as his office director for Central America. Melton went to Nicaragua with the aim of stirring up the domestic opposition. When the Sandinistas lifted restrictions on its right to hold demonstrations, the U.S. embassy openly promoted the opposition rallies. By encouraging the civic opposition to be as aggressive as possible, the U.S. embassy hoped to provoke the Sandinistas into repressive actions that would isolate Nicaragua internationally, scuttle the peace accord, and win a renewal of contra aid.[85]

The opposition needed no great encouragement from the United States to lambaste the Sandinistas. Once the government began relaxing legal constraints on free expression, the civic opposition roared to life. A new, broad coalition of opposition parties, the Group of Fourteen, was formed in 1987, including most of the parties from the Democratic Coordinating Committee that boycotted the 1984 election and most of the parties (even some of the leftist ones) that had participated. The number of demonstrations and strikes by discontented workers grew rapidly. With the Nicaraguan economy disintegrating, the civic opposition saw an unprecedented opportunity to rally public opinion to its side.

The Sandinistas saw that possibility, too. Fearful that Washington's financial support would transform the opposition into a formidable foe, the Sandinistas sought to limit its activities by harassment and intimidation.[86] Opposition leaders were detained, usually for no more than a day or two, and warned against taking advantage of their newly restored civil liberties. Public rallies by the opposition were sometimes broken up by Sandinista mobs.

On July 10, 1988, a coalition of opposition parties mounted a major antigovernment demonstration in the town of Nandaime. About five thousand people marched and then rallied to listen to speeches by prominent opposition leaders. According to *New York Times* reporter Stephen Kinzer, the Sandinista police seemed intent on antagonizing the crowd. After some mutual pushing and shoving, demonstrators began pelting the police with sticks, rocks, and bottles. The police responded with volleys of tear gas and waded into the crowd swinging their nightsticks. Thirty-eight people were arrested and scores suffered minor injuries.[87]

The day after the Nandaime demonstration, the Nicaraguan government expelled Ambassador Melton and seven other U.S. diplomats for interfering in Nicaragua's internal affairs by encouraging antigovernment protests. The

United States had a "Melton plan" for destabilizing Nicaragua, the Sandinistas charged, and they were not going to sit idly by while he carried it out. The government also arrested six prominent opposition leaders for inciting violence at Nandaime and temporarily closed *Radio Católica* and *La Prensa*. Washington retaliated by expelling Nicaraguan Ambassador Carlos Tunnermann and seven of his staff.[88]

In Washington, the Sandinista crackdown was universally denounced. The Senate passed a resolution, 91–4, condemning the Nicaraguan government for "brutally suppressing a peaceful demonstration." The House approved a similar resolution, 385–18.[89] Speaker Wright called Melton's ouster "a gravely serious and lamentable act of bad judgment and bad faith" by the Sandinistas and "a setback to the peace process." But privately, Wright, like many Democrats, was suspicious about what Melton had been doing. On June 21, just three weeks before the Nandaime demonstration, the CIA had briefed the House Intelligence Committee on a new, long-term covert plan to destabilize the Sandinista government by stepping up support to the internal opposition.[90] "The CIA . . . was drilling people in the local political opposition on how to put on protest demonstrations—the bigger and noisier, the better," Wright later wrote in his memoirs.[91]

Two months later, in September, Wright gave public voice to his belief that the Reagan administration was trying to scuttle the Esquipulas peace process by provoking Sandinista repression. "We have clear testimony from CIA people that they have deliberately done things to provoke an overreaction on the part of the government of Nicaragua," he said in response to a question at a press conference. "I do not believe it is the proper role of our government to try to provoke riots."[92]

The administration jumped on Wright immediately for revealing classified information. White House Press Secretary Marlin Fitzwater accused him of always being "more than eager" to side with the Sandinistas against the United States.[93] Wright replied that his comments had been based on public information, not the CIA briefing, which he had not attended. And he refused to back down. The administration was "seeking to disrupt the domestic tranquility in Nicaragua," he charged, and U.S. agents had "assisted in organizing the kinds of anti-government demonstrations that have been calculated to stimulate and provoke arrests."[94]

In essence, Wright was correct. "There's enough truth in Wright's accusations that they cannot be flatly denied," an administration official admitted.[95] But that did not stop House GOP leaders from demanding that the Ethics Committee investigate Wright's statements, adding another charge to the inquiry already under way as a result of Republican Newt Gingrich's yearlong media campaign against Wright for financial improprieties.

As support for Reagan's Nicaragua policy melted in the House, Republicans both in the administration and on the Hill focused their frustration and anger on Wright personally—in part because he had played such a central role in promoting the peace process, and in part because the Republicans could not best his no-holds-barred approach to the legislative struggle. Gingrich seized on the issue of contra aid to rally other House Republicans behind his one-man crusade to discredit Wright and drive him out of the Speaker's chair. The best way to attack the Democrats on Central America, Gingrich told the Republican caucus, was to ruin Jim Wright.[96]

"They are not just out to embarrass and discredit you, Jim," veteran Washington pol Robert Strauss warned Wright. "They are out to destroy you."[97]

Bentsen's Umbrella

The riot at Nandaime gave Ronald Reagan one final opportunity to seek a resumption of military aid to the contras, though not everyone in the administration was eager to continue the fight. The 1988 presidential election campaign was moving into high gear with Vice President George Bush as the Republican nominee. His campaign manager, James Baker, was still as allergic to Central America as he had been during his tenure as White House chief of staff during Reagan's first term. He remained convinced that Nicaragua was political poison, a view reinforced by Richard Wirthlin's polling for the White House, which still showed the public opposed to contra aid by a margin of two to one. "The reality," explained an administration official, "is that we are going into a sensitive period of the election and we want to keep the lid on."[98]

To avoid associating George Bush's candidacy too closely with the contra program, Reagan himself did not put forward a new aid package. Instead, Senate minority leader Bob Dole took the lead, and Reagan endorsed his proposal.[99] Forcing a Senate vote on contra aid had the added political benefit of embarrassing the Democrats. Their presidential nominee, Massachusetts governor Michael Dukakis, was an outspoken opponent of contra aid, but his choice for vice president, Senator Lloyd Bentsen (D-Tex.), was a consistent contra supporter. If the Republicans could force a vote on military aid before the Democratic convention, Bentsen would be in a tough spot. If he voted against aid, he could be pilloried for opportunism. If he voted for it, he might spark a rebellion against his nomination by rank-and-file delegates at the Democratic convention, virtually all of whom would be adamant contra aid opponents.

When Dole brought his proposal to the Senate floor on August 10, 1988, it was nearly identical to the administration package approved by the Senate in February.[100] To counter Dole's proposal and provide a "Bentsen umbrella" to protect the Democratic vice presidential candidate from embarrassment, Senate Democrats drafted a plan of their own. It provided for $27 million in food, medicine, and clothing until March 1989 and $5 million in relief for war victims.

As the 100th Congress moved toward recess for the national presidential conventions, both sides in the debate over contra aid were worn out. Except for a few Republican hard-liners, still eager to blame the Democrats for betraying Central America to Communism, the Senate's final debate over contra aid was anticlimactic. Senator William Armstrong (R-Colo.) decried the Democrats' amendment as "the Dunkirk for the contras. It is the end of the Reagan Doctrine," he lamented. "It is the end of the Monroe Doctrine in Central America."

As the debate drew to a close, it was clear that conservative southern Democrats who had always given Reagan the margin of victory on past contra aid proposals would vote with the Democratic leadership this time. Sensing that the impending vote would probably mark the end of Reagan's proxy war, Senator Dole became reflective. "For some reason, the American people have never appreciated our policy in Nicaragua. Maybe it is the fault of the administration. Maybe it is the fault of Congress," he mused. "And so we find ourselves today . . . split down the middle. There is no way we can prevail . . . without the votes of some of my Democratic friends"—votes Dole knew he didn't have. On August 10, 1988, the Senate voted 57–39 to adopt the Byrd amendment rather than the Dole amendment, thus ending Ronald Reagan's last hope of resuming military aid to the contras.

On October 14, with the presidential election just three weeks away and Congress preparing to adjourn, Reagan acknowledged that his hopes for military aid would not be fulfilled. "Our policy in Nicaragua remains the same," he bravely affirmed.[101] But the contras would be getting nothing beyond humanitarian aid. "Face it, the aid isn't coming," an administration official said flatly. "The contras are defeated." Even Elliott Abrams had to admit that U.S. policy was entering the "post-contra era."[102]

So ended Reagan's crusade to roll back Communism in Nicaragua, to "win one" for the United States. The policy of covert and overt war by proxy, of economic strangulation and diplomatic isolation, had laid waste to Nicaragua. It had also polarized American politics and prompted the worst political scandal since Watergate. But as Ronald Reagan prepared to leave office, Daniel Ortega was still the president of Nicaragua.

The departure of Ronald Reagan brought no rejoicing in Managua. The revolution had survived its tenth year, but just barely. The economy had collapsed into depression and hyperinflation. Nothing but privation and austerity lay on the horizon—austerity that had already destroyed the revolution's proudest advances in education and health care. In the first few years after the fall of Somoza, government vaccination campaigns virtually eliminated communicable diseases such as polio and diphtheria. By 1988, they were all returning. Infant mortality, which fell sharply in the revolution's early years, began to rise again. Starvation appeared.[103]

The year came to a close with Hurricane Joan hitting Nicaragua's Atlantic coast in late October, destroying 98 percent of the buildings in Bluefields, the main coastal city. In just a few hours, 130-mile-per-hour winds wiped out Nicaragua's Caribbean fishing industry, most of its banana plantations, 15 percent of its forests, and 20 percent of the coffee crop. Estimates of the loss ranged from $400 to $800 million. Nicaragua's prostrate economy had no capacity to absorb the shock. Not only did the Reagan administration refuse to provide ordinary disaster relief to Nicaragua, but it tried to discourage other donors from helping. "We don't trust the Sandinistas enough to give them aid," a White House official explained. "We don't know how they would make use of it."[104]

Despite the urgency of Nicaragua's economic problems, the Sandinistas could not shift major resources from defense because the war did not end. Most of the contras had gone back to Honduras, but a few thousand remained in the countryside launching hit-and-run attacks on outlying communities. The truce negotiated at Sapoá had eroded to the point that armed clashes were killing an average of fifteen Nicaraguans daily. Honduras still showed no sign of fulfilling its obligations under the Esquipulas agreement by closing the contras' base camps, so it appeared that the war of attrition might continue indefinitely.

And despite Congress's rejection of Reagan's pleas for military aid, Washington showed no sign of changing its policy. The administration still rejected Nicaraguan pleas for bilateral talks to normalize relations and pledged its fealty to the contras. In November, George Bush won the presidency handily, and his initial remarks on Nicaragua gave the Sandinistas no reason for optimism. "I will press to keep pressure on the Sandinistas to keep their commitment . . . to democracy and freedom," Bush promised. Pressure, his advisers explained, meant more military aid for the contras.[105]

IV Denouement

In a free society like ours a policy is bound to
fail which deliberately violates our pledges and
our principles, our treaties and our laws. . . . The
American conscience is a reality. It will make
hesitant and ineffectual, even if it does not prevent,
an un-American policy. . . . In the great struggle
with Communism, we must find our strength
by developing and applying our own principles,
not in abandoning them.

—Walter Lippmann

CHAPTER 23

A Kinder, Gentler Policy?

When George Bush succeeded Ronald Reagan, promising a "kinder, gentler" America, most observers expected a shift in Washington's approach to Latin America as well. Although Bush had been a loyal supporter of Reagan's policies, he nevertheless seemed more pragmatic than his mentor. Unlike Reagan, Bush seemed to harbor no deep feelings about Central America. As vice president, he conducted crucial diplomatic missions to El Salvador in 1983 (to pressure the army to reduce human rights abuses) and to Honduras in 1985 (to cajole the Hondurans to continue backing the contras), but he was never a prominent public defender of the policy. He hardly mentioned Central America during his campaign.

Opinion among the Washington policy elite also favored a less strident approach. Crucial hemispheric issues such as narcotics trafficking and international debt had been left to fester while everyone's attention was focused on the small countries of Central America. Participants on both sides of the policy debate had grown weary of the poisonous partisan wrangling.

Bush's initial appointments confirmed expectations that he would be more pragmatic than Reagan. As national security adviser, he selected General Brent Scowcroft, who had held the same post under President Gerald Ford and won acclaim for his professional, nonideological management of foreign policy. As

553

secretary of state, Bush appointed his campaign manager and friend of many years, James Baker, whose primary interest in Central America was to get this "bleeding sore" off the national agenda as rapidly as possible so that Bush could attend to the historic changes under way in Eastern Europe and the Soviet Union.[1]

As assistant secretary of state for inter-American affairs, Baker chose Bernard Aronson, a lifelong Democrat and former speechwriter for Walter Mondale who became interested in Central America in the mid-1980s and helped the Reagan White House lobby congressional Democrats for contra aid. He and three friends (Bruce Cameron, Penn Kemble, and Robert Leiken) came to be known as "Ollie's Liberals," because they cooperated with the White House efforts to lobby Congress on behalf of contra aid.[2] Aronson spoke no Spanish, had no expertise on Latin America, and had no experience in administration, policymaking, or diplomacy. His one asset was his ability to converse easily with moderate Democratic representatives.[3]

The Treaty of Washington

After selecting an assistant secretary for Latin America who looked more like an ambassador to Capitol Hill, Baker's first major policy initiative was aimed not at a foreign country but at Congress. On March 2, 1989, Baker met with Speaker Jim Wright to propose a diplomatic plan for Nicaragua. "We want to wind this thing down," the secretary told Wright. "We are willing to substitute negotiations for military action." But Bush could not just abandon the contras because he would receive "flack from the right-wing" of the Republican Party. Baker proposed to continue nonmilitary aid to the contras for a year, combined with real support for the Esquipulas peace process.[4] After twenty-two days of negotiations among administration officials and congressional leaders from both parties, an accord was finally drafted. Like two punched-out prizefighters staggering in a clinch, Congress and the new administration embraced, ending the eight-year fight over contra aid. As much out of exhaustion as conviction, they decided to call it a draw.[5]

Dubbed "the Treaty of Washington" by one senior administration official, the formal agreement was signed on March 24, 1989. It did not really resolve the policy differences over Nicaragua; it simply suspended them for a year, until after the 1990 Nicaraguan elections.[6] With no hope of convincing Congress to resume military aid, the White House gave up on Ronald Reagan's quest for a contra victory. The partisan rancor of Reagan's approach had been its Achilles' heel. "We all have to admit that the policy basically failed . . . because we were not united," Baker acknowledged. Now Bush would support the Esquipulas peace process "in good faith" and refrain from military pressure on the Sandinistas during the period leading up to Nicaraguan elections.[7] Still, Bush and Baker insisted that the United States must not abandon the contras, because their existence would help to assure that the Sandinistas lived up to their commitments under the Esquipulas agreement.

As their part of the bargain, the Democrats agreed to continue nonmilitary aid, thereby keeping the contras together, "body and soul" as Reagan used to say, in case the Nicaraguan elections went awry. Under the bipartisan plan, the contras would get $4.5 million in nonmilitary aid monthly through the end of February 1990 ($66.6 million in total), provided that they did not launch any military attacks before the elections.[8] To assure that both the contras and the administration lived up to the bargain, four congressional committees (the Foreign Affairs and Appropriations Committees in the House and Senate) were given the right to review the situation in November 1989. If any one of them voted to halt further contra aid, Bush promised to abide by their decision.[9]

The differences between Bush's and Reagan's policies toward Nicaragua were subtle, but real. Bush had the same maximum objective as Reagan—to replace the Sandinistas with a conservative pro-U.S. regime. Bush continued Reagan's policy of hostility unchanged—the threatening military exercises, the trade embargo, and the efforts to block economic aid from Europe, Latin America, and the international banks.[10]

Reagan had had no fallback position from his maximum objective. The continued existence of the Sandinista government was simply unacceptable; nothing short of its removal would do. Bush, on the other hand, was prepared to coexist with the Sandinistas if they lived up to their commitments under the Esquipulas agreement—that is, if they held free elections and stopped aiding the Salvadoran guerrillas. With no hope of removing the Sandinistas by military force, diplomacy was the only alternative. "We talked about diplomacy [during the Reagan years]," a senior administration official admitted, "but it began as a cover story for what we were really trying to do. What has happened since then is that the cover story has become real."[11]

In the wake of the bipartisan agreement with Congress, the Bush administration pursued three objectives in Nicaragua: keep the contras together as an effective fighting force; mount a multifaceted diplomatic strategy to force the Sandinistas to hold a free and fair election in February 1990; and provide the internal opposition with the resources needed to seriously challenge the Sandinistas in the campaign.[12]

Contra Demobilization

In February 1989, the five Central American presidents held another summit in Tesoro Beach, El Salvador. In a new accord, the Sandinistas agreed to change their constitution and advance the date of national elections from November to February 1990. They also promised complete freedom for the opposition to organize and campaign, along with extensive international observation to guarantee the fairness of the process. In return, the other presidents called, yet again, for the demobilization of the contras.[13]

Washington was unmoved. Shortly after the Tesoro accord, Baker dispatched Undersecretary of State Robert M. Kimmit to warn the Hondurans that if they pressed for immediate demobilization, they would damage Bush's efforts to win more nonmilitary aid from Congress. The contras might then be stranded in Honduras without U.S. assistance. That, of course, was the outcome the Hondurans feared most; the next day, Honduras announced its support for continued contra aid while plans for their demobilization were being formulated.[14]

Another Central American summit was scheduled for August 1989 in Tela, Honduras, to review progress on Nicaraguan electoral preparations and contra demobilization. In the days leading up to the summit, Washington lobbied furiously to block a new call for demobilization. The State Department arranged a meeting for contra commanders with the presidents of Costa Rica, Guatemala, and El Salvador so the contras could plead their case in person. Bush himself called both President José Azcona in Honduras and President Oscar Arias in Costa Rica to lobby against demobilization.[15]

But on the eve of the summit, the Sandinistas came up with another diplomatic coup. Knowing that Washington was trying to focus the summit on electoral conditions inside Nicaragua rather than on contra demobilization, the Sandinistas preempted the electoral issue. On August 4, they signed a sweeping accord with their internal opponents, settling almost all the outstanding disputes over the conduct of the upcoming election. "Ninety-five percent of our demands have been met," said an opposition leader emerging from the final negotiating session. In exchange for Sandinista concessions, the opposition endorsed the government's call for demobilization of the contras and repudiated any covert (i.e., CIA) interference in the election campaign.

With the issue of election procedures resolved, the Tela summit focused entirely on the contras. Rejecting the Bush administration's best efforts to dissuade them, the five presidents agreed that the contra army should be demobilized and disbanded by the first week of December.[16] Despite massive infusions of economic and military aid over the preceding decade, not one of Washington's four allies could be relied upon to hold fast against an accord that repudiated a key element of U.S. policy. After a decade of regional strife, Washington's allies all preferred a separate peace with Nicaragua.

The Tela agreement put George Bush on the horns of a dilemma. On the one hand, he opposed contra demobilization; on the other, he had agreed in the bipartisan accord with Congress that he would support the Central American peace process. Tela made these two positions incompatible. Bush's solution was simply to ignore the obvious inconsistency and declare support for the Tela agreement, with the caveat that he disagreed with the demobilization deadline. When a United Nations official visited the contra camps in Honduras and urged them to accept demobilization, he was vigorously denounced by Secretary of State Baker.[17]

Not only did the contras refuse to demobilize, but they stepped up the fighting. Although most contras were in their Honduran camps, some two to three thousand remained inside Nicaragua, occasionally attacking isolated farms and ambushing government patrols. These attacks intensified in October 1989, disrupting election registration in several dozen towns.

At the end of October, all the elected heads of state in the Western Hemisphere, including George Bush, assembled in San José, Costa Rica, to celebrate one hundred years of Costa Rican democracy. No one expected much serious business would transpire, but no one imagined that Daniel Ortega would spoil the party by announcing an end to his government's unilateral cease-fire with the contras. In the nineteen months that the cease-fire had been in place, over seven hundred Nicaraguans had been killed by the contras, Ortega declared. He denounced the recent slaying of eighteen army reservists on their way to register to vote as "the straw that broke the camel's back."[18]

The Costa Ricans complained that Ortega's bad manners had ruined the summit's festive atmosphere. President Bush delighted in condemning Ortega, referring to him derisively as that "little man," and threatening to resume military aid to the contras.[19] But Ortega was not just being truculent. He hoped the unpopular announcement would force the Central American presidents to face the fact that there had been no progress toward demobilization. All the concessions made by the Sandinistas since the first Esquipulas agreement in 1987 had been aimed at ending the contra war, yet the war continued. By lifting the cease-fire, Ortega issued a stark reminder that the Sandinistas' compliance with the Esquipulas, Tesoro, and Tela accords was not irreversible.

In Washington, the timing of Ortega's announcement rescued Bush from a looming confrontation with congressional Democrats. Under the bipartisan accord, Congress could have exercised a veto over additional contra aid in November 1990. Many liberals felt that the ongoing contra attacks and Bush's refusal to accept the Tesoro and Tela calls for contra demobilization constituted violations of his agreement with Congress. They were prepared to push for a cut-off of even nonmilitary aid to the contras. But Ortega's repudiation of the cease-fire reinforced Bush's insistence that the Sandinistas were belligerent and could not be trusted. When the time came to review the contra program, the Democrats meekly agreed to continue it.[20]

Strange Bedfellows

Keeping the contras together and threatening the Sandinistas with the "bogeyman" of renewed military aid, as one White House official called it, was not Washington's only leverage.[21] Economic pressure was equally important. The Sandinistas had agreed to hold free elections in order to end the war, not because they were losing it, but because it was destroying their economy. Peace would open the way for new economic assistance from Western Europe. Consequently, James Baker made a point of urging the Europeans to withhold any significant aid until after the Nicaraguan election—a strategy that served the dual purpose of ensuring that the Sandinistas would honor their pledge to make the elections fair and preventing them from easing the population's misery. Most European donors postponed new economic assistance until after the election.[22]

Washington was also able to muster unexpected leverage from the Soviet Union. Since 1987, the Soviets had been providing the Sandinistas with about $750 to $800 million annually—$450 to $500 million in military assistance and $300 million in economic assistance, including virtually all of Nicaragua's petroleum imports.[23] Bush and Baker decided to make Central America a key test of the Soviet Union's "new thinking" in foreign policy. In March 1989, Bush wrote a letter to Soviet President Mikhail Gorbachev warning that a continuation of Soviet aid to Nicaragua would "inevitably affect the nature of the [U.S.-Soviet] relationship."[24] Gorbachev replied on May 6, announcing that the Soviets had suspended military aid at the end of 1988 because U.S. policy had shifted from military pressure to diplomacy. Military aid from Soviet allies, especially Cuba, continued to flow, however. When Baker visited Moscow in May, he pushed hard for an end to Soviet aid. If Moscow cooperated, Baker pledged that Washington would accept the results of a free election in Nicaragua even if the Sandinistas won.[25]

Anxious to prevent Central America from interfering with the improvement of East-West ties, Gorbachev made it clear to the Sandinistas that he wanted the 1990 election to proceed fairly and on schedule. Not only did the Soviets halt military aid, but they also refused a Sandinista request for emergency economic aid on the eve of the election. "They wanted money to put consumer goods in the stores, so they could portray the economic situation as improving and attract voter support," said Yuri Pavlov, the senior official for Latin America in the Soviet Foreign Ministry. "We didn't think it was a good investment."[26]

The Washington-Moscow concordat on Nicaragua was an astonishing development. After all, it was the fear of Soviet penetration that had animated U.S. policy in Central America since 1981, when Secretary of State Alexander Haig swore that Washington would draw the line there against the spread of international Communism. The specter of Soviet bases dotting the region, directly threatening the security of the United States and the NATO alliance, constituted the Pentagon's main rationale for building up the Salvadoran and Honduran militaries and for waging war by proxy against Nicaragua. Now suddenly, the archenemy, the "Evil Empire" itself, was cooperating with Washington's plans to bring Nicaragua back into the orbit of the United States.

Campaign Contributions

The final element in U.S. policy was support for the internal opposition. In 1984, the Reagan administration had convinced the main opposition parties to boycott Nicaragua's election and then denounced it as a "Soviet-style" sham. Five years later, Washington's strategy was to contest the 1990 election as vigorously as possible.

The collapse of the economy had badly eroded the Sandinistas' popular support. If the internal opposition could unify behind a single candidate and put forward a credible political program, it stood an excellent chance of winning. Previously, however, the opposition had proved utterly unable to take advantage of the public's disaffection with the Sandinistas. It remained splintered in over a dozen miniparties, many based on nothing more than feuding personalities.

To prepare the opposition for the campaign, U.S. officials helped forge a new unified anti-Sandinista coalition, the National Opposition Union (Unión Nacional Opositor, UNO), that included fourteen of the twenty-two non-Sandinista parties. Centripetal forces were intense within the diverse coalition, which included both ultrarightists and Communists. UNO nearly fell apart when it deadlocked over who should head its ticket. The rightist parties wanted Enrique Bolaños, president of the Superior Council of Private Enterprise (COSEP); the moderates wanted Virgilio Godoy, leader of the Independent Liberal Party. As a compromise, they settled on Violeta Barrios de Chamorro, the publisher of *La Prensa* and widow of editor Pedro Joaquín Chamorro, whose murder in January 1978 sparked the insurrection against Somoza.[27]

Violeta Chamorro, like Corazon Aquino in the Philippines, was the perfect unity candidate. Drawn into politics by the murder of her activist husband, she carried none of the partisan baggage that weighed down other politicians. Even though she had resigned from the Sandinista governing junta in 1980 because of the leftward drift of the revolution, and even though her newspaper relentlessly defamed the Sandinistas, she nevertheless projected an aura of being above the political fray. She seemed so unconcerned with either political strategy or policy that even her closest supporters wondered if she had the capacity to govern the country.[28]

Washington also urged exiled contra political leaders to return to Nicaragua to join in the electoral battle. The CIA gave them a not-so-subtle shove by cutting off funds for their political operations abroad and offering to finance their relocation to Nicaragua.[29] Few took up the challenge, although one who did, Alfredo César, emerged as a top adviser to Chamorro during her campaign.

Besides advice, the Bush administration also provided material assistance to UNO. The White House's preference was to proceed covertly.[30] The manipulation of foreign elections was, after all, a well-established technique in the CIA's repertoire. By aiding conservative parties, the Agency had helped prevent the French and Italian Communist Parties from winning elections in post–World War II Europe.[31] As recently as 1984, it had helped José Napoleón Duarte win the presidency of El Salvador.

Congressional Democrats, however, objected that when the covert aid was disclosed—as it surely would be—the recipients would be discredited as disloyal agents of a foreign power. Besides, the opposition parties themselves had repudiated covert foreign involvement in the election process in their August agreement with the Sandinistas on election procedures.

Faced with a Democratic move to ban covert election aid, James Baker promised that assistance to the opposition would be handled overtly. The administration gave "absolute assurances" that the CIA would not interfere in the election, Senate Intelligence Committee Chairman David Boren told his colleagues. "It's not going to happen. There's not a glimmer, not a crack, not a loophole of any kind . . . that would allow anything to go on."[32]

Senator Boren underestimated the CIA's ingenuity. It had already given the internal opposition $5 million in 1989 as part of its ongoing program of political support, from an account budgeted at $10 to $12 million annually.[33] After Baker's promise to Congress, the CIA launched a $6 million "regional" operation to boost the UNO coalition—training UNO activists in Costa Rica, running foreign press operations to defame the Sandinistas, and funding an anti-Sandinista radio station to broadcast into Nicaragua from Costa Rica. Agency officials justified the program by arguing that they had promised Congress not to conduct covert operations to influence the election *in* Nicaragua; they had not promised to abstain from operations *outside* Nicaragua. Finally, the CIA gave some $600,000 to former contra leaders to use in the election campaign.[34]

The bulk of U.S. aid to the UNO coalition was overt, however, channeled through the National Endowment for Democracy (NED). NED had been providing aid to Nicaraguan opposition trade unions and media since 1985, with little pretense of being nonpartisan. As one of NED's directors, Sally Shelton-Colby, described its operations in Nicaragua, "The whole thrust of this program is to help the opposition coalesce and overcome their historical differences, and develop a national political structure with a view to getting their message into all corners of Nicaragua."[35]

Still, NED's charter explicitly prohibited it from giving money to finance the campaigns of candidates for public office, so its funds had to be channeled to opposition trade unions and political parties rather than the Chamorro campaign itself. Recipients were not supposed to use the money for the campaign, but could use it for voter registration and education, poll watching, and "party building" activities. These were distinctions without much difference; no one had the slightest doubt that the aid was intended to enhance UNO's ability to challenge the Sandinistas at the polls. None of the NED money, for example, went to conservative parties that refused to join the UNO coalition, though they were not demonstrably less "democratic" or needy than the recipients of NED's largesse.[36]

In all, NED provided $11.6 million to the opposition ($3.9 million appropriated for fiscal year 1989 and $7.7 million for 1990)—a program that dwarfed previous NED election support programs in Chile and the Philippines.[37] Not counting CIA aid or the undisclosed amount provided to UNO by the Republican Party, NED alone spent $7 for every Nicaraguan voter—at that rate, the equivalent of spending $800 million in a U.S. election.

The 1990 Elections

The Nicaraguan campaign was conducted under close international supervision by the Organization of American States, the United Nations, and former president Jimmy Carter's Council of Freely Elected Heads of Government. Sporadic fighting and rock throwing at campaign rallies escalated in November and December, climaxing in a riot at a UNO rally in the town of Masatepe in which one person was killed. The foreign observer missions (especially President Carter's) and the Nicaraguan Supreme Electoral Council stepped in quickly, however, and mediated an agreement between the Sandinistas and UNO to head off further violence. Incidents between the two campaigns subsided, although a number of Sandinista campaigners were killed by contras in conflicted areas.[38]

As the election approached, the Bush administration maintained a tough anti-Sandinista stance. At every opportunity, spokesmen denounced the electoral procedures as unfair. Every problem was magnified, every advance minimized or ignored. Just days before the vote, Secretary of State Baker insisted that the administration would make its own judgment on the fairness of the election; it would not necessarily accept the conclusions of international observers. Even if the Sandinistas won a fair election, Baker continued, Washington would not move quickly to improve relations. It would take time to assure that democracy was being consolidated in Nicaragua and that the Sandinistas had stopped aiding the Salvadoran guerrillas. Only then would rapprochement be possible.[39] A Sandinista victory, Washington was telling the Nicaraguan electorate, would mean more war and economic misery.

Despite this rhetoric, administration officials expected the Sandinistas to win and were prepared to live with it. Assistant Secretary of State Aronson had already begun discussions with Nicaraguan vice minister of foreign affairs Victor Tinoco about a step-by-step process for normalizing relations between the two countries after the anticipated Sandinista victory.[40]

The expectation of a Sandinista triumph was widely shared. In the months before the election, several major independent public opinion polls showed Ortega running far ahead of Chamorro; only Chamorro's own polls showed her leading. Some reporters had doubts about the polling results because they seemed to contradict the population's widespread discontent with the economy, but in most cases, the doubts were submerged by the extraordinary Sandinista campaign, which was far more extensive and sophisticated than UNO's.[41]

Sandinista organizers, banners, and assorted paraphernalia were everywhere, while UNO was virtually invisible until just before the election. Sandinista rallies were routinely much larger than UNO's, culminating in the final FSLN rally of 200,000 people on February 21—almost five times the size of UNO's closing rally.[42] In most elections, such stark differences in the quality of two campaigns would be enough to settle the outcome. In Nicaragua, however, the campaign itself meant very little.

The election was a referendum on ten years of Sandinista rule, and no campaign could overcome the government's record of economic disaster. The Sandinistas tried to defuse the economic issue by appealing to nationalism, linking UNO with the contras and the United States. By focusing on the war, the Sandinistas hoped to escape, Houdini-like, from the political consequences of the country's economic collapse. It didn't work.

On February 25, 1990, 86 percent of Nicaragua's registered voters turned out to cast their ballots under the watchful eyes of some two thousand foreign observers. To the surprise of almost everyone—the Sandinistas, the Bush administration, most of the press corps, and even many top UNO officials—Chamorro and the UNO coalition won a stunning victory. Chamorro took 54.7 percent of the popular vote for president, to Daniel Ortega's 40.8 percent, and

UNO won fifty-one seats in the ninety-three-member National Assembly, to thirty-nine for the Sandinistas.[43]

After the election, Washington's first priority was to ensure that the Sandinistas honored the result and transferred power to Chamorro. The transition proceeded with surprising smoothness. The stunned Sandinistas accepted defeat, albeit grudgingly, and prepared to transform themselves from governing party into loyal opposition. Transition teams from the outgoing and incoming administrations negotiated agreements on key issues, such as control over the armed forces and maintenance of the agrarian reform program. The main obstacle to a peaceful transition was the continued existence of the contra army, which Washington had so vigorously resisted demobilizing.[44]

Both the UNO transition team and the Bush administration urged the contras to disarm and repatriate to Nicaragua, but the contras themselves were reluctant to lay down their weapons while the Sandinistas retained control of the armed forces. Negotiating with the contras was no easy matter. In February, field commanders had finally succeeded in ousting Enrique Bermúdez as commander-in-chief, and central control over the contra army disintegrated forthwith.[45] Nevertheless, the Chamorro transition team opened talks with the contra field commanders. As the inauguration approached, between three and six thousand contra combatants were in Nicaragua, threatening to remain armed indefinitely.

On April 19, the Sandinista government, the Chamorro transition team, and the contra commanders signed new agreements for a cease-fire and demobilization of the contra army beginning on inauguration day and concluding three weeks later, by June 10.[46] The contras agreed to turn over their arms to United Nations forces who would insure their safety. Chamorro promised to provide war veterans with land and economic assistance to reenter civilian life. By the end of June 1990, Nicaragua's long and bloody conflict had finally come to an end.

On April 25, 1990, Violeta Chamorro was inaugurated president in the national stadium, which seemed a microcosm of the Nicaraguan polity. Sandinista supporters and UNO supporters sat on opposite sides of the field, jeering at one another, but refraining from violence. As bitter as Nicaragua's political rivalries were, everyone had had enough of the war.[47]

The Bush administration rejoiced at Chamorro's election, lifted the economic embargo Reagan had imposed in 1985, and asked Congress to provide $300 million in economic assistance for the new government in 1990 and another $241 million in fiscal year 1991.[48] In Congress, there was broad agreement that the United States, having financed the contra war for nearly a decade, had a responsibility to help pay for economic reconstruction. But with new demands on the limited foreign aid budget coming from Eastern Europe and Panama, debate developed over how much aid Washington could afford to spend in Nicaragua. With the Sandinistas out of power, Nicaragua's importance in Washington faded fast. When Chamorro came to the United States in April 1991 and addressed a joint session of Congress to request desperately needed economic aid, so few members showed up to listen that the leadership had to scour the halls for staff members and pages to fill the empty seats. "Like Andy Warhol's 15 minutes of fame, issues seem to suffer the same plague," lamented Senator Christopher Dodd. "A few months ago, Nicaragua was the hot international issue. Now it's been forgotten."[49]

The Decline and Fall of José Napoleón Duarte

As Nicaragua moved off the American political agenda, El Salvador reappeared. El Salvador had not been a focal point of partisan debate in the United States since Christian Democrat José Napoleón Duarte was elected president in 1984. But as Duarte's term in office drew to an end, the fragility of his regime became increasingly apparent. Despite good intentions, he had failed to win either the war or the peace. He managed to hang on to his office despite the oligarchy's hatred and the military's distrust, but he could claim little substantive progress beyond mere survival.

In March 1988, El Salvador held elections for its National Assembly and municipal governments. They were the electorate's first opportunity in three years to render a verdict on the Christian Democratic Party's (PDC) performance. Washington expected some Christian Democratic losses, but was surprised by the magnitude of the party's defeat. The PDC lost its majority in the National Assembly and most of the country's mayoralty contests to the rightist National Republican Alliance (ARENA). Ambassador Edwin G. Corr, who had replaced Thomas Pickering in 1985, was such a booster of the Christian Democrats that he saw Duarte's government through rose-colored glasses. Corr had "a penchant for excluding bad news . . . from the cable traffic," the State Department inspector general later concluded, thus leaving his superiors badly uninformed about the depth of Duarte's difficulties.[50] To make matters worse, shortly after the PDC's electoral debacle, Duarte was diagnosed with terminal liver cancer. The disease and its treatment rendered him a caretaker president for the final year of his term.[51]

The dual shocks of electoral defeat and Duarte's incapacity capped a three-year decline in the political fortunes of the Christian Democrats. The March election also marked the exhaustion of the Reagan administration's seven-year effort to win the war by combining large-scale military aid with support for a moderate reformist government. Since Jimmy Carter's presidency, Washington's strategy for holding back the tide of revolution in El Salvador had been based upon Duarte and the Christian Democrats. By 1988, that strategy, like the political health of the PDC and physical health of its leader, was spent.

While inefficiency and corruption corroded the Christian Democrats' popular image, the PDC lost its social base among the urban and rural poor because Duarte failed to live up to the "social pact" he made with them during his 1984 presidential campaign.[52] Instead of a negotiated peace, Duarte continued the war. Despite $1 billion in U.S. military aid, the war went grinding on through hundreds of small engagements and acts of economic sabotage, punctuated by an occasional dramatic guerrilla assault. The Salvadoran army was no closer to eradicating the insurgency in 1988 than when the war began.

Instead of the promised social reforms, Duarte imposed an austerity program whose cost fell mainly on his own constituents. The primary impetus for the program came from the United States, which threatened to curtail essential economic aid unless Duarte reduced his government's fiscal deficit and devalued the currency. Unable to pass a tax increase to raise revenues because of rightist opposition, Duarte was forced to cut spending, increasing unemployment. The cumulative damage from capital flight, guerrilla sabotage, and the 1986 earthquake left El Salvador with over 50 percent unemployment and underemployment, 40 percent inflation, and a standard of living far below what it had been a decade before. Economic aid from the United States—$2 billion since 1981, $328 million in 1988 alone—kept the economy afloat, but real recovery could not begin until the war ended.[53]

Popular disenchantment with the Christian Democrats also produced alienation from the electoral process. Only half the registered voters participated in the 1988 election (down from an 83 percent turnout in 1982 and 70 percent in 1985).[54] The guerrillas of the Farabundo Martí National Liberation Front (FMLN) saw these disillusioned voters as a potential base of support, but were not very adept at organizing them. The revival of urban political activism during Duarte's administration, especially by trade unions, produced sharp confrontations with the government over economic issues, but most of the newly mobilized groups resisted efforts by the guerrillas to politicize them further.

The guerrillas' civilian allies, the politicians from the Revolutionary Democratic Front (FDR), returned from exile in late 1987 after the Esquipulas peace accord and quickly set about building an electoral alliance on the left. The Democratic Convergence (Convergencia Democrática) was composed of the newly organized Social Democratic Party, Guillermo Ungo's National Revolutionary Movement (affiliated with the Socialist International), and Rubén Zamora's Popular Social Christian Movement.

The Convergence planned to participate in the upcoming 1989 presidential election, even though ARENA seemed poised to triumph. Poorly organized and underfunded, the Convergence had no chance of winning, but it hoped to get some 10 percent of the vote. If the contest between ARENA and the Christian Democrats was close and a runoff was required, a strong showing would enable the Convergence to demand concessions in return for its endorsement in the second round of voting. The Convergence nominated Guillermo Ungo, the veteran social democrat who ran as Duarte's vice president in 1972.[55]

Without Duarte's dominant personality to lead them, the Christian Democrats split over their presidential nomination. Duarte's longtime political fixer, Julio Adolfo Rey Prendes, quit to form his own party after losing the nomination to Washington's perennial favorite, Fidel Chávez Mena.

On the right, ARENA nominated Alfredo Cristiani, the soft-spoken, U.S.-educated coffee grower who took over leadership of the party from Roberto D'Aubuisson after the ARENA's disastrous defeats in the 1984 and 1985 elections. Cristiani ran on a platform that echoed the 1984 program of the Christian Democrats: He promised economic recovery and a quick end to the war. He even pledged to negotiate peace with the guerrillas—an amazing policy reversal for ARENA that reflected how desperately the population wanted peace.

On March 19, 1989, Cristiani swept to a decisive first ballot victory, winning 53.8 percent of the vote to Chávez Mena's 36.6 percent. Ungo managed a paltry 3.8 percent. The Christian Democrats simply could not recover from the liability of their own record, and the Democratic Convergence could not shake its association with the guerrillas.[56]

Back to the Future

George Bush had been in office just two months when Cristiani won the Salvadoran presidency. A decade of Washington's efforts to promote a stable centrist regime had instead produced victory by the extreme right. Even though Cristiani represented a more moderate, less violent faction of ARENA than D'Aubuisson, the victors were still unquestionably the political representatives of the Salvadoran upper class. ARENA in power was not likely to undertake policies of social and economic reform that would address the deeper grievances that gave rise to the Salvadoran insurgency in the first place.

In Washington, both congressional and executive officials worried that extremists in the army or in ARENA itself might see Cristiani's triumph as a mandate for repression and reactivate the death squads. Political killings had never entirely stopped, and the harassment and persecution of trade unionists and other civic leaders continued throughout Duarte's presidency. Nevertheless, the wholesale slaughter that characterized El Salvador in the early 1980s had subsided.[57]

Concern about the rise of ARENA prompted the first congressional debate about El Salvador since 1984. As in the early 1980s, liberals proposed making military aid conditional on the government's human rights performance and its willingness to seek a negotiated end to the war. In the summer of 1989, the House of Representatives added these certification requirements to the foreign aid authorization and appropriation bills. But like the earlier certification, the president was given the power to decide whether the conditions had been met.[58]

In the Senate, the Appropriations Committee reported a foreign aid bill that included even more detailed certification conditions than the House had approved. But during the floor debate, Christopher Dodd surprised his colleagues by arguing the administration's case. Although Dodd had been one of Reagan's toughest critics on El Salvador in the early 1980s, he was now convinced that Cristiani sincerely wanted a political solution to the war. "I believe at this moment we ought to give President Cristiani an opportunity to succeed, to say we appreciate and support what he is doing, and we stand behind him," Dodd declared. The conditionality provision was soundly defeated, 68–32. Instead, the Senate passed an amendment cosponsored by Dodd and Robert Kasten (R-Wis.) that gave El Salvador the full $90 million in military aid requested by the Bush administration. Late in the year, the House-Senate conference committee accepted the aid levels and weak conditions passed by the House. The consensus on El Salvador had wobbled a bit, but in the end it held—at least for the time being.[59]

Having weathered the congressional debate, Bush was inclined to simply continue Reagan's policy of supporting the incumbent regime in San Salvador. So long as the Cristiani government permitted no egregious deterioration in the human rights situation, the administration could portray ARENA as nothing more than supply-side Christian Democrats. The situation on the ground seemed under control.

Washington's status quo policy rested on two key assumptions: that the Salvadoran armed forces, bolstered by U.S. military aid, were gradually winning the war; and that the Salvadorans were slowly building a democracy to replace the nation's traditional military dictatorship.[60] Strengthened by U.S. aid, the Salvadoran armed forces kept the guerrillas off-balance and prevented them from launching major offensives. Adjusting to the army's new capability, the guerrillas had returned to small-unit hit-and-run tactics—a strategy that allowed them to continue a war of attrition without exposing themselves to the government's superior firepower. But this strategy made the war less visible. From Washington, it appeared that the tide of battle had shifted in the government's favor.

On the political front, the guerrillas seemed to be in retreat as well. Cristiani's election marked the sixth successful balloting since 1982, all conducted despite guerrilla opposition and sporadic efforts at disruption. The civilian politicians on the left in the Democratic Convergence had finally decided to participate in the March 1989 presidential election, thereby giving the process broader legitimacy. Then they lost decisively, undercutting the left's claim to represent a significant sector of the population. Finally, the election itself crystallized the growing division between the politicians on the left and the guerrilla combatants when the Democratic Convergence decided to stay in the election even after the guerrillas called on their supporters to boycott it.

The guerrillas themselves recognized that circumstances had changed since the early 1980s. Few of them still believed that defeating the government on the battlefield was possible. No matter how well the guerrillas performed, Washington could always counter by pouring more resources into the armed forces. Endless war was not a viable strategy; the weary population was losing patience with both sides. A January 1989 opinion poll found that 68 percent of Salvadorans favored a negotiated end to the fighting. Even guerrilla factions that had resisted talks earlier in the decade were ready to pursue negotiations seriously.[61]

As president, Cristiani kept his campaign promise by reopening negotiations in September 1989. But with both military and political events apparently moving in the government's favor, Cristiani's representatives were not disposed to make any concessions. As in earlier sessions, the government's position was not negotiable: the guerrillas should simply lay down their arms and join the existing political process. Despite major concessions offered by the FMLN, the talks remained stalled.[62]

El Salvador's Tet Offensive

The FMLN concluded that negotiations would achieve nothing until the government was convinced that the only alternative to a negotiated compromise was perpetual bloody stalemate. To shock the government out of its intransigence, the FMLN launched a major urban offensive.[63] Attacks began on November 11, 1989, when guerrillas occupied six poor neighborhoods along the northern rim of San Salvador. When the army was unable to dislodge the guerrillas by ground assault, the high command began to worry that it was losing control of the situation. The air force unleashed its full firepower, bombing and rocketing poor neighborhoods, producing over a thousand civilian casualties, and leaving thousands more homeless. The guerrillas dug in, fought the army house to house in some neighborhoods, and after two weeks withdrew in orderly fashion to their strongholds in the north.

The most dramatic confrontation of the offensive developed at the Sheraton hotel, where twelve U.S. Special Forces advisers were trapped when guerrillas overran the wealthy neighborhood of Escalón. An army counterattack left the guerrillas surrounded but still in control of the hotel—except for the one floor where the Green Berets had barricaded themselves in. Both sides judged, under the circumstances, that discretion was the better part of valor, and no one opened fire. While the Catholic Church began negotiations to resolve the stalemate, President Bush deployed some two hundred elite U.S. troops from Delta Force to rescue the advisers if need be. Overnight, however, the dozen or so guerrillas occupying the hotel slipped away despite a cordon of several hundred Salvadoran soldiers. The Green Berets quickly went back to Honduras, where they were officially stationed (so that they wouldn't count against the fifty-five-adviser limit).[64]

At the height of the offensive, some Salvadoran officers feared they might be on the verge of losing the war. Frustrated and angered by the guerrillas' unexpected strength, senior officers decided to settle accounts with people they regarded as guerrilla collaborators—journalists, relief workers, clerics, and intellectuals. Censorship was imposed on domestic media outlets, and journalists were harassed and fired at by troops. Death squads went back on the prowl, murdering prominent members of the revitalized popular organizations. Government security forces raided churches and refugee relief offices of all denominations, ransacking files and arresting dozens of staff members, including foreign-born missionaries, many of whom were deported.[65] In the heat of the war, the army's vaunted human rights improvement was evaporating.

After a meeting of the high command on the night of November 15, Colonel Guillermo Alfredo Benavides called together three lieutenants for a special mission. "This is a situation where it's them or us," he told his subordinates. "We are going to begin with the ringleaders. Within our sector we have the university, and Ellacuría is there."[66]

Benavides was head of the military academy, but during the offensive, he was named commander of a special security zone that included the academy, the Defense Ministry, and the armed forces' joint command headquarters. It also included the Jesuit-run Central American University. The Salvadoran right had long hated the Jesuits, who were regarded as the "intellectual authors" of the insurgency because of their concern for the poor. No single Jesuit was more despised by the right than university rector Ignacio Ellacuría, an internationally known theologian and vocal advocate for a negotiated end to the war. Both Duarte and Cristiani had sought Ellacuría's help in finding a settlement, and at times (during the kidnapping of Duarte's daughter, for example) he had served as a formal mediator between the government and the FMLN.

On Benavides's orders, several dozen soldiers from a special elite commando unit of the U.S.-trained Atlactl Battalion occupied the university campus in the early morning hours of November 16. They rousted Ellacuría and five other Jesuits from their beds, forced them to lie face down on the ground in their backyard, and then executed them. The soldiers also murdered the Jesuits' housekeeper and her fifteen-year-old daughter, so as not to leave any witnesses. The unit then staged a phony firefight, scrawled graffiti on the walls implicating the FMLN in the killings, and withdrew. When word of the murders reached a meeting of senior Salvadoran intelligence officers a few hours later, the assembled group let out a spontaneous cheer.[67]

The Bush administration's instinctive reaction to the guerrilla offensive was to denigrate it as a "desperation move" and proclaim that the armed forces had everything under control.[68] President Bush absolutely rejected any suggestion that military aid to El Salvador be reduced or subjected to conditions because of the killing of the Jesuits or the ferocity of the aerial attacks. On the contrary, when Cristiani requested emergency military aid to replenish depleted stocks, Bush promised to speed up weapon deliveries.[69]

U.S. Ambassador William Walker even defended the government's raids on religious and relief groups, comparing them to the internment of Japanese Americans during World War II. And although the State Department condemned the murder of the Jesuits and demanded a full investigation, Walker's first instinct was to believe the cover story that the guerrillas had done it.[70]

In January, however, a U.S. military adviser reported that a Salvadoran colleague had told him that Benavides had ordered the killings. Shortly thereafter, Cristiani admitted that the murders were the work of the army and ordered the arrest of five enlisted men and four officers—including Colonel Benavides and the three lieutenants he sent on the mission.[71]

If the Bush administration evinced relatively little public concern over the implications of the offensive, the same was not true for Congress. Stunned by the intensity of the FMLN attacks, some members began to wonder whether the picture of political and military success painted by the State Department since 1984 was anything more than a Potemkin village. Congress was especially horrified by the murder of the Jesuits. Several of the victims were internationally prominent scholars, and the university was a routine stop for U.S. visitors seeking a cogent analysis of El Salvador's *coyuntura*. Even Republicans who opposed placing any conditions or limits on aid to the Cristiani government demanded a full and rapid investigation of the killings. In the House, the new Speaker, Thomas Foley, appointed Rules Committee chairman Joe Moakley (D-Mass.) to head a task force to follow progress in the investigation.[72]

Although many in Congress raised their voices in bitter protest over the slayings and the indiscriminate air attacks, neither the House nor the Senate was willing to take any immediate punitive action. Members were too angry at the guerrillas for launching the attacks and too fearful that the army might be tottering. While the offensive was under way, the House narrowly refused (on a vote of 215–194) to consider a proposal to temporarily withhold 30 percent of the $85 million in military aid approved for El Salvador in FY 1990, pending an investigation of the Jesuits' murders. A similar move also failed in the Senate.[73] But El Salvador was moving back toward the top of the foreign policy agenda.

Like the 1968 Tet offensive in Vietnam, the FMLN's offensive was less a military success than a political one. Although it did not fundamentally alter the military balance, it mocked conventional wisdom in Washington. The strength and tenacity of the offensive shattered the illusion that the Salvadoran army was winning the war, and the army's brutal response shattered the illusion that the trappings of Salvadoran democracy constrained the men in uniform.

The offensive clearly demonstrated that the guerrillas were far from being defeated. The military was able to regain control of occupied neighborhoods only by virtue of its willingness to strafe and bomb guerrilla positions regardless of civilian casualties. The offensive also revealed a greater degree of political support for the FMLN than many observers expected, though less than the guerrillas themselves had hoped. The attack did not spark a massive popular insurrection; the instinct of most civilians was to flee the combat zones any way they could. But the FMLN had managed to infiltrate as many as two thousand combatants and tons of arms into the city and conceal them until the offensive was launched—operations that could not have been carried out without significant civilian collaboration.[74]

The offensive also wrecked the regime's pretense of democracy. Despite the steady decline in the number of death squad killings since the dirty war of the early 1980s, the attitude of the military had not really changed. They still couldn't distinguish between dissent and sedition. When their backs were to the wall, the armed forces reverted to type, treating everyone from the center of the political spectrum to the left as subversive. The cold-blooded murder of the Jesuits symbolized the core problem of El Salvador: the military had no respect for the rule of law, and civilian political institutions had no way to hold it accountable.

Behind the public facade of confidence displayed by U.S. officials during the November offensive, some were shaken enough by events to seriously contemplate negotiations as a way out. In February 1990, General Maxwell R. Thurman, head of the U.S. Southern Command, told the Senate Armed Services Committee that the Salvadoran army would not be able to achieve a military victory over the FMLN and that the war ought to be ended at the negotiating table. The State Department also began voicing support for new negotiations facilitated by the good offices of U.N. Secretary General Javier Pérez de Cuellar.[75] Secretary Baker, looking back, acknowledged that the rebel offensive proved to be a "catalyst for negotiations."[76]

For the first time since Carter's presidency, the United States seemed genuinely open to a settlement that was not merely a disguised FMLN surrender. "El Salvador needs peace, and the only path to peace is at the negotiating table," Assistant Secretary Aronson told Congress in January. "Let both sides commit to come to the bargaining table . . . and stay and negotiate in good faith until the war is over."[77]

In April 1990, the government and the guerrillas resumed negotiations with new seriousness. Cristiani and the moderate right seemed genuinely interested in reaching a settlement. Unlike the traditional oligarchy, this "modernized" segment of the private sector believed that its economic interests could be safeguarded in a democratic system. ARENA's victories in the 1988 and 1989 elections seemed to prove them right. But the consolidation of an ARENA electoral majority required, first and foremost, reactivation of the economy. That was impossible without peace, and the strength of the guerrilla offensive proved that peace could not be won through military victory. If Cristiani could manage to both end the war and begin economic recovery, ARENA's political fortunes would be bright indeed. If the war went on indefinitely, however, ARENA would risk the same fate as Duarte's Christian Democrats—continued economic crisis and an eventual debacle at the polls.

Within the armed forces, however, hard-liners still opposed any negotiated concessions to the FMLN. That problem was mitigated to some degree when Cristiani's ally Colonel René Emilio Ponce, the army chief of staff, managed to send air force commander General Juan Raphael Bustillo into diplomatic exile as military attaché to Israel. Bustillo, the leader of the far right faction in the officers corps, was Ponce's main rival for the position of minister of defense. Several months after ousting Bustillo, Ponce won the cabinet post, giving Cristiani a much freer hand to negotiate.[78]

International circumstances also favored a diplomatic settlement. The collapse of Communism removed the Salvadoran conflict from the East-West struggle. In fact, during 1990 and 1991, Moscow and Washington became partners in an effort to resolve the conflict, just as they cooperated on the Nicaraguan elections. The Soviets urged the FMLN to show flexibility at the bargaining table and, behind the scenes, pressured the Cubans and the Sandinistas to stop shipping Soviet-supplied arms to the guerrillas.[79]

In addition, the demise of Communism weakened the ideological underpinnings of the guerrillas' revolutionary socialism, making them more willing to participate in a political system based on pluralist democracy and a modified market economy. Finally, the electoral defeat of the Sandinistas in February 1990 robbed the Salvadoran guerrillas of their main regional ally and complicated their logistical situation. "We cannot deny reality," said a guerrilla commander. "The FMLN is feeling the need to end the war."[80]

The changing international environment put pressure on the Salvadoran government as well. In 1981, Ronald Reagan had invoked national security as the rationale for committing the United States to El Salvador, arguing that the indigenous civil conflict there had been transformed by Cuba and the Soviet Union into a case of "indirect Communist aggression." Washington had an overriding security interest in preventing a guerrilla victory, Reagan argued, regardless of the imperfect human rights record of the government. If the guerrillas won, they would establish a Communist regime, ally themselves with Nicaragua, Cuba, and the Soviet Union, and export violence to their neighbors. With the end of the Cold War, such security concerns evaporated, making Congress and the executive branch less willing to accept the Salvadoran army's depredations, or finance an interminable war.

The new attitude in Congress was not long in appearing. Repentant for his opposition to renewed certification in the fall of 1989, Senator Christopher Dodd introduced a bill in 1990 designed to give both the government and the guerrillas incentives to bargain seriously. Dodd's bill (cosponsored by Senator Patrick Leahy) cut military aid by 50 percent immediately and required an end to all remaining military aid unless the government made a serious effort to investigate the Jesuits case and to reach a negotiated settlement of the war. On the other hand, the bill allowed President Bush to restore full military aid if the FMLN refused to negotiate in good faith or launched an offensive that threatened the government's survival.[81]

The Dodd-Leahy bill picked up support in April when Congressman Moakley's task force issued an interim report on the investigation of the Jesuits' murder. The inquiry was at a "virtual standstill," the task force charged, and the Salvadoran military showed little interest in examining the possibility that senior officers had ordered the killings. Critical evidence had been destroyed in an apparent cover-up attempt. Moreover, the report concluded, this case was symptomatic of the broader pathology of Salvadoran politics. Moakley himself recounted his conversations about the killings with senior Salvadoran officers during a trip in February. "They said it was a stupid thing to do, but no one had any sorrow in their hearts."[82]

On May 22, the House voted by a surprisingly wide margin (250–163) to attach the Dodd-Leahy language to the supplemental foreign aid authorization that included funds for Panama and Nicaragua. "Enough is enough," said Moakley during the floor debate. "The time to act has come. They killed six priests in cold blood. I stood on the ground where my friends were blown away by men to whom the sanctity of human life bears no meaning."[83]

Shortly after attaching the Dodd-Leahy language, the House rejected the foreign aid bill on final passage, so the military aid cut did not become law. But it was a somber warning to the Bush administration that Congress was finally fed up with the war in El Salvador. The House had reached a "watershed," Speaker Foley said.[84]

In June, the House approved the regular FY 1991 foreign aid appropriations bill with the Dodd-Leahy language, and in October, the Senate voted 74–25 to add the Dodd-Leahy amendment to its version of the bill, despite President Bush's threat to veto the measure. In conference committee, the Democrats refused to compromise.[85] In the end, the veto threat was a bluff; the foreign aid bill had many provisions that Bush liked, and he signed it. For the first time since the war in El Salvador began, Congress had significantly cut the amount of military aid flowing to the government, from $85 million to $42.5 million. For Salvadoran rightists who never really believed Washington would abandon them, the 50 percent aid reduction was sobering evidence that the well was finally beginning to run dry.

Just two months after the Dodd-Leahy language became law, President Bush invoked an escape clause in the bill and restored full military aid to El Salvador on the grounds that the FMLN was engaging in terrorism and receiving military support from abroad. Two developments prompted Bush's action. During 1990, the FMLN had begun purchasing shoulder-launched surface-to-air missiles on the international arms market and from sympathetic officers in the Sandinista army in Nicaragua. The missiles significantly altered the military balance, preventing the Salvadoran air force from flying close combat support for troops on the ground and limiting the army's air mobility. After several helicopters were brought down by missiles, some Salvadoran pilots refused to fly during daylight. A surge of fighting in the countryside late in 1990 demonstrated that without air power, the army might soon find itself in dire straits.[86]

The broader aim of restoring military aid was to reassure the skittish Salvadoran military forces that the United States remained committed to their survival. Nevertheless, the administration did not actually disburse the renewed aid for another six months. Despite having opposed the Dodd-Leahy provision, administration officials were happy to use it as leverage to push forward both the investigation of the Jesuits case and the peace process.[87]

Talk, Talk Is Better Than War, War

With active mediation by U.N. Secretary General Javier Pérez de Cuellar and his personal representative, Alvaro de Soto, the new Salvadoran talks made real progress. Both the government and the guerrillas seemed finally to have come around to Winston Churchill's admonition that "talk, talk is better than war, war." In July 1990, the two sides signed a preliminary agreement to end human rights abuses against civilians and prisoners and to have U.N. observers monitor compliance once a cease-fire was in place.[88] Then, however, the talks deadlocked around the issue of reforming the Salvadoran military. The FMLN demanded major reductions in the size of the army, a separate civilian police force to replace the existing security forces (the Treasury Police, National Police, and National Guard), and a "purification" of the armed forces by removing officers guilty of human rights abuses.[89]

In August 1990, the FMLN escalated its demands (partly in response to complaints from guerrilla field commanders that their negotiators were giving away too much), insisting on the removal not just of human rights abusers in the military but of the entire high command. They also insisted on "exemplary punishment" for past human rights violations and proposed not just a reduction in the armed forces, but its complete elimination, leaving El Salvador with only a police force, like Costa Rica.[90] Not surprisingly, the army summarily rejected that idea. Hopes that the war might end soon enough for the FMLN to participate in the March 1991 legislative elections were disappointed.

The March election, however, gave new impetus to the peace process. The leftist Democratic Convergence did surprisingly well, winning 12 percent of the vote (about three times its vote in the 1989 presidential election) and eight seats in the new National Assembly. The success of the Convergence showed the guerrillas that the electoral system offered real possibilities for the left, and it confirmed Cristiani's belief that ARENA's political health depended upon ending the war.

Within a month, the negotiations produced a major agreement on constitutional changes that strengthened the independence of the judiciary, reorganized the security forces into a single civilian-controlled police force, and created a Truth Commission to investigate the human rights abuses of the

1980s. Although the changes would not take effect until a cease-fire was signed, agreement on these political issues left military reform as the main substantive stumbling block to a final settlement.[91]

The April accord led the FMLN to abandon its demand that the entire armed forces be eliminated along with the guerrilla army. Its fallback position was more practical; it called for a reduction in the size of the military from 56,000 to the prewar level of 12,000. However, the guerrillas still wanted the removal of officers guilty of serious human rights abuses and the merger of FMLN combatants into the regular army.[92]

The deadlock over military reform was finally broken in September 1991, during a marathon negotiating session in New York attended by President Cristiani and all five of the FMLN's principal military commanders. Under pressure from Washington, Cristiani made significant concessions, agreeing to reduce the size of the armed forces by half and to create an independent civilian commission (the Ad Hoc Commission) to review the human rights records of individual officers.[93] In exchange, the guerrillas agreed to accept participation in the new civilian police force rather than the military. With the signing of that agreement on September 25, all the fundamental political and military issues dividing the two sides had been resolved in principle. However, the delicate details of implementation, especially the cease-fire, still remained to be hammered out. And like the earlier accords, the compromises agreed to in September would not actually take effect until a cease-fire was in place.

Just one day after the agreement was signed, the Jesuits case went to trial. For the first time in modern Salvadoran history, two officers were convicted for the politically motivated murder of civilians. Most significant, Colonel Benavides, the highest-ranking officer charged, was found guilty of ordering the killings. In January 1992, the two officers convicted were given maximum sentences of thirty years in prison. Yet Salvadoran justice remained imperfect. Seven other soldiers directly involved in the killings were acquitted despite their own confessions and overwhelming physical evidence against them. Three officers convicted of perjury and conspiracy for covering up army complicity in the murders were given suspended sentences.[94] The price for getting the army to accept Benavides's conviction was that the rest of the participants be exonerated and that the investigation proceed no further.

In December, the Salvadoran negotiators returned to New York in hopes of crafting a final accord before the January 1, 1992, retirement of U.N. Secretary General Pérez de Cuellar, whose personal interest in the process had been an important stimulus. A "group of friends" (Mexico, Venezuela, Colombia, and Spain) pressured the FMLN commanders to make concessions, and the United States pressured the Salvadoran government. Despite opposition from the right wing of his own party and from hard-liners in the military, President Cristiani again came to New York personally, along with Defense Minister Ponce, to push the talks forward.

In the final hours before Pérez de Cuellar's departure, the two sides announced that they had reached a settlement. When the final accord was signed in Mexico City on January 16, Cristiani came down from the dais and shook hands with FMLN's high command, a gesture that moved some of the battle-hardened guerrillas to tears. "The conflict," said Cristiani, "is behind us."[95] In San Salvador, thousands of FMLN supporters rallied to celebrate, surprising many people by their numbers. As if to punctuate the coming of peace, on February 21 news came of Roberto D'Aubuisson's death from throat cancer.[96]

The peace agreement ran to more than eighty pages and established an elaborate timetable for implementing various elements of the accord. A cease-fire would take effect February 1, after which the 6,000 to 8,000 FMLN combatants and the 63,000 government soldiers would gather in separate zones. The FMLN would gradually demobilize, completing the process by October 31. The armed forces would begin its 50 percent force reduction by disbanding the rapid deployment battalions and the security forces. The cease-fire and demobilization would be overseen by 1,000 U.N. peacekeepers.[97]

Credit for the accord was widely shared. Cristiani had pursued peace doggedly, despite resistance from the right. The FMLN had given up its demands for powersharing and social reform, settling for changes in the armed forces and participation in a democratic polity. The Bush administration had lobbied the Salvadoran government and military hard to get them to sign an agreement. Congressional Democrats deserved a measure of credit, too. The Dodd-Leahy 50 percent cut in military aid in 1990 and the threat of even more drastic cuts in 1991 forced the Bush administration to adopt more aggressive diplomacy—just as the congressional cut-off of contra aid had forced it to support the peace process in Nicaragua.

The only clear loser in the Salvadoran settlement was the armed forces. It had to accept a 50 percent cut in manpower, the dismantling of its elite battalions and security forces, the loss of its intelligence functions to civilian agencies, the loss of its jurisdiction over internal security to a civilian police force, a purge of the officer corps by the civilian Ad Hoc Commission, and investigations of past human rights violations by the Truth Commission. In addition, with the end of the war, the flow of U.S. military aid—a lucrative source of graft—would quickly subside.

"This is the closest that any process has ever come to a negotiated revolution," commented U.N. mediator Alvaro de Soto.[98] The peace process promised a truly revolutionary shift in the basic dynamic of Salvadoran politics.

Since 1931, when General Maximiliano Hernández Martínez seized power and exterminated some 10,000 to 30,000 peasants in El Salvador's first anti-Communist crusade, the military had been the dominant force in Salvadoran politics. Through the years, they suffered civilians just barely. At the core of the state, behind the thin veneer of party politics and elections, stood the army. Above the rule of law and beyond all civilian authority, the army was El Salvador's Leviathan. The oligarchy had willingly surrendered authority to it in the 1930s in the vain hope that military authoritarianism could protect them from class war. In the 1970s, the war came anyway, accelerated by the very repression that the rich had hoped would maintain order. With beneficent aid from the United States, the Salvadoran army grew immense and increasingly autonomous. For the civilians to tame it would be a historic achievement. As the conservatives of ARENA and the radicals of the FMLN searched for common ground upon which to base a peace agreement, one point of accord was their common interest in harnessing the armed forces.

Return to Normalcy

The principle difference between George Bush's approach to Central America and Ronald Reagan's was in the degree of importance they attributed to the region. For Reagan, Central America was the focal point of his tough new foreign policy. It was the place where Washington would draw the line against the spread of Communism in the Third World, where the post-Vietnam decline of American power would be reversed. George Bush, on the other hand, seemed to regard Central America's problems as the troublesome bequest of his predecessor rather than as issues of intrinsic significance. His main priority was to get Central America off the foreign policy agenda so he could concentrate on important matters such as U.S.-Soviet relations, Eastern Europe, the Middle East, and the Persian Gulf War.

The low priority Bush accorded to Central America did not mean that his goals differed fundamentally from Reagan's. On the contrary, in Nicaragua he too sought the ouster of the Sandinistas, and in El Salvador the survival of the U.S.-crafted regime. Bush was no less willing than Reagan to pursue his aims by resorting to force, as the 1989 invasion of Panama and continuing military aid to El Salvador demonstrated. But Central America's subordinate place on Bush's agenda meant that he was not willing to pay a heavy political price to achieve his aims.

As a result, U.S. policy took a more pragmatic turn. Bush was willing to accept compromises when necessary to prevent his policy from stirring up controversy with Congress. By simply conferring with Congress, Bush and Secretary of State Baker were able to diffuse the visceral bitterness evoked by

Reagan. Congressional Democrats were so delighted at the contrast with Reagan's habit of ignoring or denouncing them that they demanded relatively small concessions from Bush as the price for striking bipartisan agreements.

As George Bush ended his term in office, his Central American policy seemed to be remarkably successful compared to Reagan's. Bush encouraged a diplomatic-electoral process that defeated the Sandinistas in Nicaragua, where Reagan's military strategy had failed. Bush came around, albeit belatedly, to support a diplomatic settlement in El Salvador, where Reagan had vainly pursued military victory. As the Central American wars sputtered to an end, the network news programs stopped covering it, the columnists stopped writing about it, the pollsters stopped asking about it, and Congress stopped debating it. For better or worse, the region resumed its traditional place near the bottom of the U.S. foreign policy agenda.

The end of the Cold War was certainly a key factor in the declining urgency Central America's conflicts held for Washington. With the "new thinking" of Mikhail Gorbachev's foreign policy, U.S. policymakers could no longer see Central America as pivotal in the global struggle between the superpowers. Indeed, Gorbachev was anxious to settle the region's brushfire wars—even on terms favorable to Washington—to eliminate them as an obstacle to superpower concordat.

For conservative Republicans, compromise on Nicaragua and El Salvador became a bit easier to swallow when it no longer signaled the retreat of American power in the face of a Soviet challenge in our own backyard. Once the end of the Cold War had drained the regional crisis of its symbolic content, all that remained were five small countries of little economic or strategic import, riven by domestic conflicts. Nothing, save habit, impelled Washington to remain at the center of the region's turmoil. It was easier to declare victory and retreat from engagement after our global adversary had already abandoned the field.

CHAPTER 24

Why Were We in Central America?

For decades, Central America had been a backwater of U.S. foreign relations, a region so unimportant that Washington often assigned its least promising diplomats there. Then suddenly, in the 1980s, the United States became so obsessed with the small countries of the isthmus that they dominated not just hemispheric policy, but all of foreign policy. Central America occasioned the most bitter domestic political debate since Vietnam and ignited a scandal that rivaled Watergate. How could the United States have become so alarmed about such a small place?

In part, it was an accident of timing. Ronald Reagan came to Washington in 1981 determined to restore America's global stature by taking the offensive in the Cold War. At that very moment, the accumulated grievances from decades of social inequality and political repression in Central America exploded in revolutionary violence. Historically, Washington had sided with the region's elites, subordinating democracy and human rights to the exigencies of national security and stability. The revolutionaries, most of them Marxists, saw the United States as an imperialist nemesis and looked to Washington's global adversaries for support.

To Reagan, the Marxist ideological bent of Central America's radicals and their willingness to solicit Soviet aid branded them as enemies. Urged on by

Secretary of State Alexander Haig, Reagan declared Central America the place to draw the line against the expansion of Soviet influence in the Third World, a test case of Washington's assertive new foreign policy. Over the next eight years, U.S. policy never wavered from the core premise that Central America's wars were Cold War battles that Washington could not afford to lose. "Central America is the most important place in the world," Jeane Kirkpatrick solemnly avowed in 1981.[1]

In this Manichean struggle between good and evil, anything short of victory amounted to defeat. Negotiated solutions were not good enough; you could not negotiate with Communists, administration officials said repeatedly. You could not bargain with the devil. In El Salvador, the objective was to prevent the Salvadoran guerrillas from seizing power by force, or gaining any share of power at the bargaining table. In Nicaragua, administration hard-liners were not content with containment. They wanted to reverse Communism in the Third World, and Nicaragua became the test case for the Reagan Doctrine.

Reagan's political appointees tended to be committed ideologues of the Republican right, eager to unleash the military power of the United States, both overtly and covertly, in hopes of rolling back the "Evil Empire" at the periphery. Not everyone in the government shared this zest for fomenting "low intensity conflicts." Foreign policy professionals generally saw the Reagan Doctrine as reckless. Pragmatic by instinct, they tended to be more cautious about embroiling Washington in multiple brushfire wars around the world.

The balance of power between pragmatists and hard-liners shifted to and fro as Reagan's staff played musical chairs through two secretaries of state, two U.N. ambassadors, four White House chiefs of staff, and six national security advisers. But despite having more government experience and foreign policy expertise than most of the hard-liners, pragmatists (such as Thomas Enders, Deane Hinton, Philip Habib, and George Shultz) could never quite get the upper hand. In the end, the hard-liners always prevailed, even after their chieftains (Alexander Haig, William Clark, Jeane Kirkpatrick, William Casey, John Poindexter, and Caspar Weinberger) departed, because they accurately reflected the emotional commitment of the president himself. Ronald Reagan was the premier hard-liner, pursuing victory in Central America as single-mindedly as Ahab pursued the whale.

Did Washington Win This Time?

How successful was Ronald Reagan's policy? Assessments were as sharply divergent in hindsight as they were when the policy was first formulated. Conservatives were quick to credit the president with having saved Nicaragua from the Sandinistas and El Salvador from the guerrillas of the Farabundo

Martí National Liberation Front (FMLN). Liberals retorted that both the Nicaraguan elections and the Salvadoran peace accord were produced by diplomacy, not the military initiatives favored by Reagan. Both were half right.

During the protracted debates over contra aid, the conservatives warned that the Sandinistas were Communists who would never hold a free election or surrender power peacefully; they could be driven out only at the point of a bayonet. If liberal Democrats refused to give the contras military aid, conservatives insisted, they were condemning the Nicaraguan people to the "the endless darkness of Communist tyranny."[2] When liberals replied that diplomacy was more likely to produce Sandinista concessions, conservatives derided them for the foolish prattle of weaklings. As it turned out, the hard-liners were wrong on every count—wrong about the consequences of ending military aid to the contras, wrong about the efficacy of diplomacy, and wrong about the Sandinistas' willingness to accept free elections. Had the hard-liners prevailed, continuing contra aid, Nicaragua would have remained a garrison state at war.

On the other hand, liberals were reluctant to acknowledge that the duress Ronald Reagan and the contras inflicted on Nicaragua was the main reason the Sandinistas held an election in 1990 and lost it. The contras never came close to winning a military victory, but the war and Washington's financial pressure destroyed the Nicaraguan economy. Had the Nicaraguan economy been in better shape, perhaps the Sandinistas would not have felt compelled to change their constitution and advance the electoral timetable by almost a year. Had the economy been in better shape, perhaps they would not have lost.

A certain unintended symbiosis emerged from the bitter battles between liberals and conservatives over Nicaragua. When the Iran-contra revelations led Congress to halt military aid, the White House had to shift policy away from relying exclusively on the ineffectual exile army. Unable to continue the war, President Bush had no alternative but to accept a diplomatic approach as outlined in the Esquipulas peace process. To Bush's great surprise, it worked.

But Washington's strategy carried a heavy price for Nicaraguans. Some 30,000 died in the contra war—proportionate to population, this was more than the United States lost in the Civil War, World War I, World War II, Korea, and Vietnam *combined*.[3] Over a hundred thousand Nicaraguans were turned into refugees. Millions suffered economic privation as real wages fell 90 percent, inflation spun out of control, and unemployment afflicted a third of the labor force. Even with international help, it would take a generation for the Nicaraguan economy to recover. In official Washington, these costs were downplayed amid the euphoria of the Sandinistas' defeat. But if Ronald Reagan wanted credit for having saved Nicaragua, he also had to take responsibility for having destroyed much of it in the process.

In El Salvador, too, the verdict on U.S. policy was mixed. As in Nicaragua, Reagan failed to win a military victory. Despite over a billion dollars in military aid, the Salvadoran armed forces could not defeat the guerrillas. While the two sides fought to a stalemate, some 80,000 people died, most of them innocent civilians killed by the military and the government's security forces, armed and bankrolled by Washington. Three billion dollars in U.S. economic aid prevented El Salvador's economy from collapsing like Nicaragua's, but the war still took its toll—over a billion dollars in lost production and destroyed infrastructure, another billion lost to capital flight.[4] In 1991, though the Salvadoran economy was growing at a healthy 3.5 percent rate, a third of the population was unemployed and 90 percent lived in poverty, not earning enough to adequately feed a family of four.[5]

Yet Washington succeeded in denying the guerrillas victory, which they almost certainly would have won in the early 1980s if the Salvadoran government had not received massive U.S. aid. By giving the government the wherewithal to avoid defeat, the Reagan administration met its minimum objective. When the two sides finally sat down to negotiate an end to the war, the FMLN won key concessions from the armed forces, but they received no guaranteed share of political power in return for laying down their arms.

Could a similar outcome have been attained in the early 1980s if the Reagan administration had been willing to accept a diplomatic settlement? Both the guerrillas and the armed forces still thought they could win the war then, so finding sufficient common ground to sustain a settlement would have been difficult. Nevertheless, the possibility of a negotiated settlement was visible as early as 1981. Sobered by the failure of their "final" offensive, the guerrillas made their first serious peace proposal that year—a proposal similar in many regards to the agreement signed a decade later. Christian Democrats in the government were disposed to begin talks in 1981, but the army wouldn't let them. Mexico and the Socialist International were prepared to press the guerrillas to make compromises for peace, and European Christian Democrats were willing to do the same with the government. The missing piece was the United States. Only Washington had the power to force the Salvadoran military to make the concessions necessary to stop the war, but the Reagan administration had no interest in a negotiated settlement. Only after a decade of inconclusive combat was Washington willing to acknowledge that military victory was unattainable. Once the United States put itself squarely behind the negotiating process, the armed forces fell into line, albeit grudgingly.

In El Salvador, even more than in Nicaragua, congressional opposition forced changes in the president's policy that ultimately helped it succeed. To win aid increases from Congress, Reagan embraced José Napoleón Duarte, despite conservatives' initial suspicions about the Christian Democrats' "communitarianism." The certification requirements imposed by Congress in 1981 forced the administration to pay attention to agrarian reform and human rights, despite Reagan's initial instinct to downplay both. Although the facts of Reagan's certifications were questionable, the need to certify led the administration to pressure the Salvadoran regime into undertaking real change, if only to make the semi-annual ordeal of certification less onerous. Eventually, U.S. pressure produced significant reductions in the number of political murders. That, in turn, created enough political space for the reemergence of an unarmed, dissident politics—an essential first step in the process of moving El Salvador's conflict off the battlefield and into the political arena. Toward the end of the war, Congress's decision to cut military aid by 50 percent in 1991 and the threat to cut it even further in 1992 compelled the Bush administration to support a compromise peace agreement.

In the end, Washington neither won nor lost the wars in Central America; it grew tired of fighting them and, with the waning of the Cold War, settled for diplomatic solutions not fundamentally different from ones it had resisted for years.

The Past Is Prologue

"Too often in our history, we have turned our attention to Latin America in times of crisis, and we have turned our backs when the crisis passed," said Deputy Secretary of State Clifford Wharton in early 1993. "That is shortsighted and self-defeating. This administration will not make that mistake." Wharton was giving the first Latin American policy address of Bill Clinton's presidency. But the circumstances belied the message. Wharton was standing in for Secretary of State Warren Christopher, who had been scheduled to give the speech, but was called to Europe on more urgent business—conferring with NATO about the escalating war in Bosnia. The history of U.S.–Latin American relations was ever thus: until a Latin country erupted in crisis, someplace else was always more important. As the wars that swept Central America in the 1980s subsided, Washington's attention drifted away, Wharton's brave rhetoric notwithstanding.

Nothing was a better indicator than the foreign assistance budget. In the mid-1990s, scarce foreign aid dollars flowed away from Central America, toward Eastern Europe and the former Soviet states. For fiscal year (FY) 1998, President Clinton requested just $169 million in economic assistance for all of

Central America—down 86 percent from the peak level of $1.2 billion in 1985. Military assistance virtually disappeared; none of the Central American countries were slated for any in FY 1996, other than a few hundred thousand dollars in military training funds—a total of just $1.6 million regionwide.[6]

Costa Rica "graduated" from AID programs in 1996 and thus was slated for no economic assistance at all. Nicaragua and El Salvador suffered dramatic declines in aid despite the danger that economic difficulties could undermine their fragile democratic institutions. Nicaragua, which received almost $300 million in 1990 after the Sandinistas lost the election, was slated for just $24 million in FY 1998. El Salvador, which received almost $500 million annually in the late 1980s and $230 million as recently as 1993, was slated for just $35 million.[7]

For Central Americans, Washington's shifting priorities came as a shock. After the tumultuous 1980s, when U.S. foreign policy seemed to hinge on events in Central America, the disinterest of the 1990s was disquieting. "It is as though a hurricane passed through," a Honduran businessman said, "and all that is left is the bad aftermath"—an aftermath that the United States expected the Central Americans to clean up themselves.[8]

Vital Interests and the War at Home

Washington's abrupt loss of interest in Central America suggested that perhaps it had not been quite so "vital" to U.S. national security as Ronald Reagan proclaimed. No doubt the Soviet Union saw the region as a point of vulnerability for the United States in the 1980s and was happy to stir up trouble there. But the Soviets were never eager for a direct confrontation with Washington in its own backyard, where all the geostrategic advantages lay with the United States. They were reluctant to supply the Salvadoran guerrillas with arms and gave the Sandinistas significant military aid only after the contra war began.[9] Moreover, the Soviets were always stingy with economic assistance; their financial help fell well below what the Sandinistas needed to prevent economic decay. Much as the Soviets may have enjoyed seeing Washington squirm in Central America, they had no interest in paying for another Cuba. Such an adventure was just too expensive.

But the Reaganites were reacting as much to the symbolic threat posed by the Soviet Union as to the actual threat. Here was a region, close to home, where the United States had traditionally held sway. Suddenly, it was rising in rebellion against regimes that historically aligned themselves with Washington, rebellions led by insurgents who identified ideologically with the rival superpower. Could the United States defend its interests in Central America, or would this region, like Southeast Asia before it, slip into the orbit of the enemy? And if the erosion of American power and influence could not be halted here, in our own backyard, where would it end?

The memory of Vietnam was fresh when Central America erupted in revolution. To conservative Republicans, the Vietnam syndrome was the Achilles' heel of American national security. Could they reestablish an activist, interventionist posture or would liberal Democrats ratify the nation's post-Vietnam reluctance to entangle itself in other people's insurgencies? If the advocates of intervention could not maintain domestic support for the use of force abroad, the United States would be unable to meet the Soviet challenge in the Third World, with catastrophic consequences.

Liberal Democrats thought Reagan was exaggerating the threat to U.S. security posed by the upheavals in Nicaragua and El Salvador, just as President Lyndon B. Johnson had exaggerated the importance of Vietnam. As Reagan became more and more committed to the Salvadoran regime and the Nicaraguan contras, Democrats worried that the president was taking America down another slippery slope. Unlike the Cold War liberals, who stifled their doubts about Johnson's war, the Democrats of the 1980s were determined to use the power of Congress to prevent "another Vietnam" in Central America.

That was something Ronald Reagan would not tolerate. The Reagan Republicans refused to acknowledge the legitimacy of congressional activism in international affairs. To them, foreign policy was the president's job, and he would brook no interference. Washington itself had become a crucial front in every brushfire war. The struggle for Central America was more likely to be lost in the halls of Congress than on the battlefields of the region itself—just as the war in Vietnam had been lost in Washington, according to conservative mythology. Convinced that the global stakes were enormous, the Reaganites were determined to prevail over congressional resistance by any means necessary.

Add to these high stakes a slightly conspiratorial mentality, a touch of the paranoid style in American politics, and some conservatives became convinced that domestic opposition was being fueled clandestinely by America's global enemies. To them, the line between loyal opposition and treason became indistinct. The epic struggle between good and evil was no longer simply the United States versus the Soviet Union. Some of "us" had joined "them," or acted as if they had, which amounted to the same thing. The battle lines were no longer drawn along national boundaries, but between Democrats and Republicans, between liberals and conservatives, between Congress and the White House. One result was the corrosion of civility in the foreign policy debate, epitomized by the Republican right's incessant red-baiting of opponents. Another was the erosion of the rule of law caused by the executive branch's flagrant flouting of statutes that did not comport with policy.

From Reagan's first weeks in office, he treated Congress as an adversary to be subdued. To evade congressional scrutiny of his aid program for El Salvador, he invoked presidential emergency powers to send military assistance without congressional approval. When Congress imposed certification requirements on aid, he blithely certified that things were getting better regardless of the facts. When Congress refused to fund police training for the Salvadoran security forces, Reagan went ahead anyway, using the regular military aid program and pretending the police were actually regular military units. He refused to comply with laws governing the deployment of U.S. military advisers to El Salvador and Honduras, and he used the CIA to send U.S. soldiers into covert combat in El Salvador and Nicaragua without complying with the War Powers Resolution. When Congress refused to fund the construction of new military bases in Honduras, the Pentagon built them anyway under the cover of military exercises.

Nowhere was Reagan's contempt for Congress more manifest than on the issue of contra aid. From the beginning, administration officials lied to Congress about the real intent of the not-so-secret war against Nicaragua. Despite repeated assurances, the operation was never aimed at interdicting arms smuggled from Nicaragua to the Salvadoran guerrillas. When Congress passed the Boland amendments to halt contra aid, the administration simply ignored the law, using every artifice to continue the war—rerouting money from the Pentagon, soliciting funds from foreign countries, and diverting profits from Iranian arms sales. And through it all, administration officials lied about what they were doing—publicly, privately, repeatedly, and egregiously.

From 1983 on, the White House's secret efforts on behalf of the contras were carried out by a clandestine foreign policy apparatus under the Orwellian code name Project Democracy. By setting up this secret network, the Reagan administration subverted the constitutional balance between the branches of government and thereby posed a greater threat to democracy in the United States than Nicaragua ever could. Moreover, when the Iran-contra scandal revealed how deceitful the White House had been, neither Reagan nor most of the responsible officials were contrite. On the contrary, they defended their actions as necessary to defeat Communism in Central America—an imperative that took precedence over telling the truth to Congress or obeying the law. Most Republicans endorsed this rationale, praising the inauguration of the new Imperial Presidency.

In point of fact, the Democrats were much less implacable foes of Reagan's Central America policy than one would think from reading the president's speeches. Liberals in Congress tried mightily to block Reagan from taking the nation down a path that they believed led to disaster, but they were not in full command of their party. On foreign policy issues, conservative southern Democrats invariably sided with Reagan, often giving him an ideological majority that rendered the Democrats' partisan majority meaningless. At critical junctures—the 1984 House votes on military aid to El Salvador and the 1985 and 1986 House votes on contra aid—divisions among the Democrats handed victory to the White House.

Despite consistent public opposition to Reagan's policy, Democratic leaders in Congress were slow to mobilize the party to challenge the president precisely because the issue exacerbated the Democrats' internal ideological split. Some Democratic leaders were themselves ambivalent about the policy. Jim Wright opposed Reagan on Nicaragua more effectively than anyone—so much so that angry Republicans attacked him mercilessly and drove him from the Speaker's chair in 1989. But Wright supported the president on El Salvador. Senate Democratic leader Robert Byrd vacillated between support and opposition, never taking an active role in the Central America debate, wishing it would simply go away. But even among Democrats who consistently opposed Reagan's policy, many were reluctant to stand up to the popular president for fear they would be tarred with having lost Central America to Communism. Senator Joseph McCarthy was thirty years dead, but his ghost was still enough to give Democrats a fright.

In short, Congress largely failed in its institutional responsibility to serve as a check on executive behavior. Democrats were reluctant to protest too vehemently or look too closely at what the White House was doing, even when they knew it was improper; Republicans made transparently partisan excuses for their president. The foreign policy process would have been healthier had Democrats brought more backbone to it and Republicans brought more conscience.

The press and public also proved imperfect bulwarks against executive malfeasance. Except for a few investigative journalists who gave Reagan headaches, most of the media reported the Central America story from the official point of view. Administration efforts at elaborate public relations campaigns to manage the press or, failing that, to intimidate it succeeded more often than not.

Throughout Reagan's eight years in the White House, polls showed that a large majority of the public opposed every aspect of his Central American policy. In fact, administration officials suffered from a Vietnam syndrome of their own—the fear that direct military action might trigger the sort of mass public opposition that made the war in Vietnam untenable. Significant organized grassroots opposition to Reagan's policy from the religious community and the peace movement foreshadowed what might happen if direct involvement produced significant U.S. casualties. But so long as U.S. troops stayed out, most voters paid little attention to Central America, and the White House could ignore the polls.

One lesson of the experience in Central America was that values expressed in policies abroad invariably seep into politics at home. The only way to assure that foreign policy remains consistent with American values is to subject it to the same close public scrutiny and debate as domestic policy. Although the foreign policy process has become more open than in the heyday of the Imperial Presidency, it was not democratic enough to prevent Ronald Reagan from disregarding the law. Congress, the press, and—most especially—the voting public need to pay more attention to foreign affairs, not less. Only their vigilance can hold presidents to account when ideological certainty convinces them that they alone understand the national interest and that the ends of securing it justify the means.

Like Vietnam, the Central American crisis ended without policymakers reaching any consensus about how the United States should deal with similar conflicts in the future. To be sure, with the end of the Cold War, those issues seemed less compelling. Third World struggles that Washington once viewed as proxy wars with Moscow ceased to have any larger meaning, and successful interventions elsewhere—in Grenada, Panama, and the Persian Gulf—boosted America's confidence in its ability to go to war and win.

Yet much of the Third World, Latin America not excepted, still holds the tinder for social upheaval—privileged classes and political elites unresponsive to the majority's demands for democracy and social justice. If the past is any guide, the United States is unlikely to stand aloof from such conflicts, especially in its own backyard. Although the imperative of superpower rivalry is gone, other interests—in immigration, narcotics interdiction, oil supplies, humanitarian aid, or "promoting democracy"—tend to pull Washington in. And like Banquo's ghost, the questions raised first in Vietnam and again in Central America will reappear: What national interests are compelling enough to justify the use of force abroad; how can we use force in ways consistent with the laws of war and our own sense of moral decency; and how can we do it without undermining the foundations of our own democracy?

In the end, Central America proved not to be another Vietnam, at least not in the way that people feared in 1981. Neither the worst nightmares of the conservative Republicans—a Communist Central America toppling dominoes from Panama to Mexico—nor those of the liberal Democrats—a quagmire on our doorstep—came to pass. Washington avoided the slippery slope in part just by knowing it was there.

We went to war in Central America to exorcise the ghosts of Vietnam and to renew the national will to use force abroad. These imperatives, more than the Soviet threat, Fidel Castro's menace, or the Nicaraguan and Salvadoran revolutions, shaped U.S. policy—how it was conceived, struggled over, and executed. Central America's misfortune lay in being the stage upon which this American drama was played out.

Notes

Abbreviations Used in the Notes

GOVERNMENT DOCUMENTS

Iran-Contra Chronology
  U.S. Congress, *Report of the Congressional Committees Investigating the Iran-Contra Affair: Appendix C, Chronology of Events*, H. Rept. 100-433, S. Rept. 100-216, 100th Cong., 1st sess. (Washington, D.C.: Government Printing Office, 1988).
Iran-Contra Depositions
  U.S. Congress, *Report of the Congressional Committees Investigating the Iran-Contra Affair: Appendix B, Depositions, Volumes 1–27*, H. Rept. 100-433, S. Rept. 100-216, 100th Cong., 1st sess. (Washington, D.C.: Government Printing Office, 1988).
Iran-Contra Documents
  U.S. Congress, *Report of the Congressional Committees Investigating the Iran-Contra Affair: Appendix A, Source Documents, Volumes 1 and 2*, H. Rept. 100-433, S. Rept. 100-216, 100th Cong., 1st sess. (Washington, D.C.: Government Printing Office, 1988).
Iran-Contra Hearings
  U.S. Congress, *Iran-Contra Investigation: Testimony, Volumes 100-1 to 100-13*, Joint Hearings before the Senate Select Committee on Secret Military Assistance to Iran and the Nicaraguan Opposition, and the House Select Committee to Investigate Covert Arms Transactions with Iran, 100th Cong., 1st sess. (Washington, D.C.: Government Printing Office, 1987).
Iran-Contra Report
  U.S. Congress, *Report of the Congressional Committees Investigating the Iran-Contra Affair*, H. Rept. 100-433, S. Rept. 100-216, 100th Cong., 1st sess., November 17, 1987 (Washington, D.C.: Government Printing Office, 1988).
Iran-Contra Testimonial Chronology
  U.S. Congress, *Report of the Congressional Committees Investigating the Iran-Contra Affair: Appendix D, Testimonial Chronology: Witness Accounts Supplemented by Documents, Volumes 1–5*, S. Rept. 100-216, 100th Cong., 1st sess. (Washington, D.C.: Government Printing Office, 1988).
Reagan Papers
  Public Papers of the Presidents of the United States: Ronald Reagan, 1981–1989 (Washington, D.C.: Government Printing Office, 1982–89).

ARCHIVES AND MEDIA

CQ Weekly Report	*Congressional Quarterly Weekly Report*
CSM	*Christian Science Monitor*
LAT	*Los Angeles Times*
MH	*Miami Herald*
NSA	National Security Archive
NYT	*New York Times*
PROFS	Professional Office System (NSC computerized message system)
UPI	United Press International

WP   *Washington Post*
WSJ   *Wall Street Journal*

CHAPTER ONE

1. "Inaugural Address, January 20, 1981," *Reagan Papers, 1981*, pp. 1–4.

2. Reagan on August 18, 1980, quoted in Cannon, *Reagan*, p. 271. On opinion among both the mass public and the political elite, see Holsti and Rosenau, *American Leadership in World Affairs*, and Rielly, *American Public Opinion*.

3. Reagan coined the term "Evil Empire" in a March 8, 1983, speech to Evangelical ministers in Orlando, Florida. Cannon, *President Reagan*, p. 316.

4. Franck and Weisband, *Foreign Policy by Congress*; Crabb and Holt, *Invitation to Struggle*.

5. Public Law (PL) 93-189, Sec. 30, 87 Stat. 714.

6. See Johnson, *Season of Inquiry*.

7. See Schoultz, *Human Rights*.

8. Francis X. Clines, "Sun Smiles on the President, Blowing Kisses and Happy," *NYT*, January 21, 1981; Pete Early and Thomas Morgan, "National Pride Unites Throng of Revelers at Inauguration," *WP*, January 21, 1981.

9. Pete Early and Thomas Morgan, "National Pride Unites Throng of Revelers at Inauguration," *WP*, January 21, 1981.

CHAPTER TWO

1. Reagan first used this comparison in "Remarks on Central America and El Salvador at the Annual Meeting of the National Association of Manufacturers, March 10, 1983," *Reagan Papers, 1983*, book 1, pp. 372–77.

2. Bulmer-Thomas, *Political Economy of Central America*, pp. 1–10.

3. Berman, *Under the Big Stick*, pp. 43–46.

4. Ralph Lee Woodward Jr., *Central America: A Nation Divided*, pp. 136–48.

5. Quoted in Blachman, LeoGrande, and Sharpe, *Confronting Revolution*, pp. 329–50. For a detailed history of the Monroe Doctrine, see Perkins, *History of the Monroe Doctrine*.

6. The next two sections are adapted from LeoGrande, "Revolution in Nicaragua," *Foreign Affairs*, Fall 1979.

7. Berman, *Under the Big Stick*, p. 169.

8. Macaulay, *Sandino Affair*; Selser, *Sandino*.

9. Quoted in LaFeber, *Inevitable Revolutions*, p. 67.

10. Smallwood, *Writings of Will Rogers*, p. 134.

11. The best history of the relationship between Somoza and the United States is Millet, *Guardians of the Dynasty*.

12. Pastor, *Condemned to Repetition*, pp. 3–4.

13. Millet, *Guardians of the Dynasty*, p. 252.

14. Booth, *End and Beginning*, pp. 67–82; Eric Morgenthaler, "Somoza Combines Politics, Business, Military to Rule Nicaragua as Undisputed Strongman," *WSJ*, October 22, 1973.

15. Booth, *End and Beginning*, chaps. 6–7; Chamorro, *Dreams of the Heart*, pp. 99–103.

16. Millet, *Guardians of the Dynasty*, pp. 258–59. On the early history of the Sandinistas, see also Nolan, *Ideology of the Sandinistas*; and for a first-person account, Cabezas, *Fire from the Mountain*.

17. LeoGrande, "Cuba," in Blachman, LeoGrande, and Sharpe, *Confronting Revolution*, pp. 229–55. Sandinista defector Roger Miranda says that the FSLN received no more than a few thousand dollars in aid from Cuba prior to late 1978. Miranda and Ratliff, *Civil War in Nicaragua*, p. 97.

18. Diederich, *Somoza*, p. 129.

19. "University of Notre Dame: Address at Commencement Exercises at the University, May 22, 1977," *Public Papers of the Presidents of the United States: Jimmy Carter 1977*, book 1, pp. 954–62.

20. Carter, *Keeping Faith*, p. 145. Regarding the ability of the human rights issue to build a domestic consensus behind foreign policy, see the results of Carter's pollster, Patrick Caddell, reported in Elizabeth Drew, "Reporter-at-Large: Human Rights," *New Yorker*, July 18, 1977.

21. Lake, *Somoza Falling*, pp. 28, 76; Pastor, *Condemned to Repetition*, p. 50.

22. Schoultz, *Human Rights*, p. 257. According to Wade Matthews, the State Department's director of Central American affairs in 1977–78, Carter officials saw Central America as "a great testing ground" for the human rights policy. Quoted in Morley, *Washington, Somoza, and the Sandinistas*, p. 96.

23. In March 1977, a publication of the U.S. Foreign Service reported, "During 1976, the government inflicted heavy blows on the local guerrilla organization and now faces no serious threat from that quarter." Quoted in Diederich, *Somoza*, pp. 141–42.

24. For an excellent history of U.S. relations with Nicaragua during the Nixon and Ford administrations, see Morley, *Washington, Somoza, and the Sandinistas*.

25. Alan Riding, "U.S. Neutrality Heartens Nicaragua Rebels," *NYT*, February 5, 1978.

26. Christian, *Nicaragua*, pp. 48–51. The text of the statement is in Leiken and Ruben, *Central American Crisis Reader*, pp. 172–73.

27. The differences among the three tendencies are explained in interviews with three Sandinista factional leaders, in "Sandinista Perspectives," *Latin American Perspectives*, Winter 1979.

28. It was never established with certainty who killed Chamorro. Five men were arrested and tried for the crime, one of whom claimed that a Cuban-American businessman, Pedro Ramos, ordered the murder, presumably because of exposés *La Prensa* had run about his business dealings. Some Chamorro family members doubted that explanation, however, and suspected Somoza's son of having organized the assassination. Christian, *Nicaragua*, pp. 54–56.

29. Sandinista leader Humberto Ortega admitted that the Sandinistas had only a "limited capacity" to assert leadership over this mass opposition movement in early 1978. He explains Sandinista strategy from October 1977 to July 1979 in detail in Borge et al., *Sandinistas Speak*, pp. 53–84.

30. Ambassador Solaun reported on the moderates' dependence on the United States and their frustration with U.S. inaction in U.S. Department of State cable, Managua 4609, September 24, 1978, "Perceived Needs of Nicaragua's for U.S. Intervention" (NSA Nicaragua collection).

31. The policy positions of the various bureaus and individuals are based mainly on two excellent detailed discussions of the Carter administration's deliberations, written by people involved in them: Lake, *Somoza Falling*, and Pastor, *Condemned to Repetition*. See also "U.S. Risks Toppling an Ally in Nicaraguan 'Test Case,'" *MH*, February 8, 1978; "Arms Cut-off Sparks Policy Fight," *MH*, February 24, 1978.

32. "Crisis in Nicaragua," *WP*, August 29, 1978. See also the description of this policy disagreement by U.S. Ambassador Mauricio Solaun in Diederich, *Somoza*, p. 165.

33. Murphy's influence with the Carter administration stemmed from his chairmanship of the House Merchant Marine and Fisheries Committee, which had jurisdiction over legislation needed to implement the Panama Canal treaties. Lake, *Somoza Falling*, pp. 231–41; Pastor, *Condemned to Repetition*, pp. 114–15, 149–52; John M. Goshko, "Murphy Visited Somoza During Resignation Talk," *WP*, June 30, 1979.

34. Both Pastor and Lake discuss the letter in detail: Lake, *Somoza Falling*, pp. 84–90;

Pastor, *Condemned to Repetition*, pp. 66–71. Pastor opposed sending it, as did the State Department Human Rights Bureau; the Latin American Bureau was equivocal. Brzezinski prevented these objections from reaching Carter, who sent the letter not realizing that most administration officials working on Latin America opposed it. The text of the letter, dated June 30, 1978 (although it was not delivered until mid-July), is in Somoza, *Nicaragua Betrayed*, pp. 276–77.

35. On Somoza's reaction to the letter, see Somoza, *Nicaragua Betrayed*, pp. 136–40; on the opposition's reaction, see Booth, *End and Beginning*, pp. 161–63.

36. Booth, *End and Beginning*, pp. 164–67. For a detailed report on the National Guard's atrocities during and after the September insurrection, see Organization of American States, Inter-American Commission on Human Rights, *Report on the Situation in Nicaragua*.

37. The positions in this debate are described in Lake, *Somoza Falling*, pp. 115–17, 134–35; and Pastor, *Condemned to Repetition*, pp. 82–85.

38. Pastor, *Condemned to Repetition*, pp. 94–97, 103.

39. Lake, *Somoza Falling*, p. 116.

40. State Department spokesman Hodding Carter argued that the United States should not call publicly for Somoza's resignation for fear of a negative domestic reaction, especially from Congress. Ibid., pp. 173, 179, 209.

41. On the efforts of the mediation group, see [William Bowdler], "Report to the Secretary of State on the Work of the International Commission of Friendly Cooperation and Conciliation for Achieving a Peaceful Solution to the Grave Crisis of the Republic of Nicaragua" (typescript). The author expresses appreciation to Ambassador Viron P. Vaky for providing this document.

42. See, for example, Pastor, *Condemned to Repetition*, p. 107; Lake, *Somoza Falling*, p. 155.

43. Bowdler's instructions are described in Lake, *Somoza Falling*, pp. 143–44.

44. Diederich, *Somoza*, p. 205.

45. On the mediation, see Pastor, *Condemned to Repetition*, pp. 101–19; Lake, *Somoza Falling*, pp. 141–67; [Bowdler], "Report to the Secretary of State on the Work of the International Commission," pp. 3–15. Appendices to the Bowdler report include all the written proposals that were exchanged between the two sides during the mediation. U.S. Ambassador Mauricio Solaun, who left Nicaragua shortly after the failure of the mediation, concluded that Somoza rejected U.S. demands because he knew Washington was "unwilling to go all the way against him" to force him out of power. Diederich, *Somoza*, p. 243.

46. Lake, *Somoza Falling*, pp. 148, 160, 166–67; Pastor, *Condemned to Repetition*, p. 102. See also Alan Riding, "U.S. Strategy in Nicaragua Keeps Time Bomb Ticking," *NYT*, December 12, 1978.

47. Dickey, *With the Contras*, p. 44.

48. Lake, *Somoza Falling*, pp. 168–80; Pastor, *Condemned to Repetition*, pp. 121–24; John M. Goshko, "Administration Softens Stance on Somoza Rule," *WP*, January 31, 1979.

49. Lake, *Somoza Falling*, pp. 166, 213; Pastor, *Condemned to Repetition*, p. 140. See also John M. Goshko, "More Pressure to Oust Somoza Weighed," *WP*, June 13, 1979.

50. Lake, *Somoza Falling*, p. 155; Karen DeYoung, "Nicaragua Expects to Win IMF Loan," *WP*, May 11, 1979. Pastor (*Condemned to Repetition*, p. 129) explains U.S. support for the loan as an effort to avoid politicizing IMF decisions, though he admits this was not entirely consistent with the administration's attitude in November.

51. Goshko, "More Pressure to Oust Somoza Weighed," *WP*, June 13, 1979.

52. Committee for Freedom and Justice in the Americas, "Congress Asks: Please, Mr. President, Not Another Cuba!," *NYT*, June 18, 1979.

53. Pastor, *Condemned to Repetition*, p. 144.

54. Vance's statement, along with those of other U.S. officials at the OAS meeting, is in "Western Hemisphere: Nicaragua," *U.S. Department of State Bulletin*, August 1979, pp. 55–61.

55. The purpose of the peacekeeping force is confirmed by Pastor, *Condemned to Repetition*, pp. 134–35, and by U.S. Department of State cable, State 153522, June 13, 1979, "OAS Action on Nicaragua" (NSA Nicaragua collection). The cable explained to U.S. diplomatic posts that the purpose of the peacekeeping force was to eliminate "the potential for a Castroite takeover of Nicaragua."

56. John M. Goshko, "OAS Weighs Nicaragua Move," *WP*, June 23, 1979; John M. Goshko, "OAS Votes for Ouster of Somoza," *WP*, June 24, 1979. Vaky admitted that the Cuban role was a secondary one on June 26 when he told a congressional committee: "This is fundamentally a Nicaraguan crisis. And Cuba is not the only, or even the most important of the supporters of the anti-Somoza rebellion." "Reassessing Cuba's Role in Nicaragua," *CSM*, June 27, 1979.

57. Pastor, *Condemned to Repetition*, pp. 124–28; Booth, *End and Beginning*, pp. 127–34; Charles A. Krause, "Nicaraguan War Polarizes Left, Right in Latin America," *WP*, June 23, 1979; Karen DeYoung, "Somoza Reported Meeting Latin Allies," *WP*, July 14, 1979. According to Alan Riding, Mexico also provided the Sandinistas with a small quantity of arms. Riding, *Distant Neighbors*, pp. 351–52. For a detailed discussion of the Panamanian and Venezuelan roles, see Dinges, *Our Man in Panama*, pp. 100–113.

58. This was the gist of a May 2, 1979, CIA report, "Cuban Support for Central American Guerrilla Groups," that leaked to the press. See Graham Hovey, "U.S. Study Says Cuba Plays Cautious Role in Nicaragua," *NYT*, July 4, 1979. The text of the report was eventually published in the *Congressional Record*, May 19, 1980, pp. 11653–55. Pastor (*Condemned to Repetition*, p. 84) cites another CIA estimate from September 1978 that the Sandinistas had received little outside aid up to that time. Sandinista defector Roger Miranda confirms this (Miranda and Ratliff, *Civil War in Nicaragua*, p. 97). Former Sandinista Arturo Cruz Jr. (*Memoirs of a Counter-Revolutionary*) says that 181 Sandinistas went to Cuba for training after the September insurrection.

59. Frente Sandinista de Liberación Nacional, Dirección Nacional, "Acuerdos de Unidad," March 1979, in Gilbert and Block, *Sandinistas: Key Documents*, pp. 68–73.

60. McNeil, *War and Peace in Central America*, pp. 112–14; Pastor, *Condemned to Repetition*, pp. 124–28; Mitchell A. Seligson and William J. Carroll III, "The Costa Rican Role in the Sandinistas' Victory," in Walker, *Nicaragua in Revolution*, pp. 332–36. In 1981, the Costa Rican Congress investigated Costa Rica's role in military assistance for the Sandinistas, identifying twenty-one Cuban arms shipments through Costa Rica in May and June 1979. Asemblea Legislativa, *Informe Sobre el Tráfico de Armas*, Comisión de Asuntos Especiales, May 14, 1981 (San José, Costa Rica).

61. U.S. Central Intelligence Agency, "Cuban Support for Central American Guerrilla Groups," May 2, 1979, in *Congressional Record*, May 19, 1980, pp. 11653–55.

62. Brzezinski, quoted in Pastor, *Condemned to Repetition*, pp. 148, 162.

63. Pastor, *Condemned to Repetition*, pp. 142–48; Lake, *Somoza Falling*, pp. 224–26.

64. The text of the resolution is in "Western Hemisphere: Nicaragua," *U.S. Department of State Bulletin*, p. 58.

65. Pastor, *Condemned to Repetition*, chap. 9; Lake, *Somoza Falling*, chap. 12. No sooner had the plan been formulated than it was leaked to the press. See Graham Hovey, "Two U.S. Diplomats Off to Nicaragua in Growing Bid to Replace Somoza," *NYT*, June 28, 1979. Once again there were divisions in the government over what U.S. strategy should be. Vaky and Ambassador Pezzullo did not think Washington could fashion a credible alternative to the provisional government, and urged that the United States focus on trying to influence the junta. Pastor and his boss, Brzezinski, won the argument, however.

66. U.S. Department of State cable, Managua 2914, June 30, 1979, "National Guard

Survival." Washington's instructions to Pezzullo reflect the same priority given to maintaining the Guard. See U.S. Department of State cable, State 168715, June 20, 1979, "Nicaragua Scenario." Both are quoted in Kornbluh, *Nicaragua*, pp. 16–17. Pastor (*Condemned to Repetition*, pp. 174–78) is also explicit about U.S. hopes of maintaining the National Guard intact.

67. Quoted in Lake, *Somoza Falling*, pp. 232–35. Pezzullo's account of the meeting is in Pezzullo and Pezzullo, *At the Fall of Somoza*, pp. 11–16, and in his report back to Washington, U.S. Department of State cable, Managua 2857, June 27, 1979, "Somoza—the First Visit" (NSA Nicaragua collection). Somoza taped his meetings with Pezzullo and published extensive excerpts in Somoza, *Nicaragua Betrayed*, pp. 334–72.

68. Pezzullo and Pezzullo, *At the Fall of Somoza*, p. 108.

69. Lake, *Somoza Falling*, pp. 226–28; Karen DeYoung, "Somoza Reported Close to Resigning," *WP*, July 6, 1979; Karen DeYoung, "Somoza Agrees to Quit, Leaves Timing to U.S.," *WP*, July 7, 1979. On Fidel Castro's advice, the Sandinistas were willing to expand the junta, but the moderates already on the junta, Alfonso Robelo and Violeta Chamorro, objected. Pastor, *Condemned to Repetition*, pp. 167–68; Chamorro, *Dreams of the Heart*, pp. 158–59.

70. Diederich, *Somoza*, p. 287.

71. Fearing extradition back to Nicaragua, Somoza moved from Miami to Paraguay, where he was assassinated on September 17, 1980, by Argentine leftist guerrillas working for the Nicaraguan Ministry of the Interior. Martha Honey, "Contra War Mystery Bomber Identified," *San Francisco Chronicle*, August 2, 1993.

72. Somoza's action was prompted by a call to him from Deputy Secretary of State Warren Christopher reminding him that his entry into the United States was part of the transition deal that Urcuyo had broken. Lake, *Somoza Falling*, pp. 254–56; Christian, *Nicaragua*, p. 135. Somoza's account of the conversation with Christopher is in Somoza, *Nicaragua Betrayed*, pp. 390–91.

73. The junta included three Sandinistas: Daniel Ortega Saavedra, a founding member of the FSLN and a Tercerista representative on the National Directorate; Moisés Hassan Morales, radical head of the United People's Movement (Movimiento Pueblo Unido, MPU)—a grassroots community organization of students, workers, and urban poor; and Sergio Ramírez Mercado, a socialist academic and member of Los Doce. The junta's moderates were Violeta Barrios de Chamorro, the widow of Pedro Joaquín Chamorro, and millionaire Alfonso Robelo Callejas, former head of the Supreme Council of Private Enterprise, Nicaragua's largest umbrella organization for the business community. Most of the cabinet members were well-known Nicaraguan professionals and business leaders. Robelo and Chamorro resigned in early 1980 when the subordinate role of the junta became clear. Chamorro, *Dreams of the Heart*, pp. 200–201.

74. On the social and economic policies followed by the Sandinistas, see Booth, *End and Beginning*, chaps. 9–10; Walker, *Nicaragua in Revolution*; Walker, *Nicaragua: The First Five Years*; Walker, *Revolution and Counterrevolution in Nicaragua*; Colburn, *Post-Revolutionary Nicaragua*; Vilas, *Sandinista Revolution*.

75. On the ideological divisions within the FSLN, see Gilbert, *Sandinistas*.

76. Smith, *Closest of Enemies*, p. 181; Marlise Simons, "Castro Advises Nicaraguans to Avoid His Errors," *WP*, November 9, 1980; "Cuba Sends Advisers to Nicaragua, but Counsels Caution," *NYT*, July 9, 1980.

77. Gilbert, *Sandinistas*, pp. 31–33.

78. Author's interviews with various private sector representatives, Managua, Nicaragua, November 1980, January 1982, and August 1983. For a detailed discussion of the views of the private sector, see Gilbert, *Sandinistas*, pp. 105–27.

79. Author's interview with an official of the Superior Council of Private Enterprise (Consejo Superior de Empresa Privada, COSEP), Managua, Nicaragua, November 1980.

80. Morley, *Washington, Somoza, and the Sandinistas*, p. 238.

81. Pastor, *Condemned to Repetition*, pp. 192–93.

82. Steve Frazier, "Political Standoff Stymies Nicaragua," *WSJ*, January 8, 1981.

83. Author's interview with a midlevel State Department official, September 1979. This comment has also been attributed to former Venezuelan President Carlos Andrés Pérez. See Terry Karl, "Mexico, Venezuela, and the Contadora Initiative," in Blachman, LeoGrande, and Sharpe, *Confronting Revolution*, pp. 271–94. For a more mundane but authoritative statement of this strategy, see U.S. Department of State cable, State 210125, August 12, 1979, "U.S. Central American Policy" (NSA Nicaragua collection).

84. Karen DeYoung, "House Unit Votes $9 Million in Aid for Nicaragua," *WP*, September 12, 1979.

85. U.S. Senate, S. 2012, Hearings before the Committee on Foreign Relations, 96th Cong., 1st sess., December 6 and 7, 1979, pp. 77–80.

86. John M. Goshko, "U.S. Debates Aid to Latin American Rightists to Bar Takeovers," *WP*, August 2, 1979.

87. *Congressional Record*, February 27, 1980, pp. H2009–20.

88. John Felton, "Delay in Foreign Aid Funding Is Creating Fiscal, Policy Headaches," *CQ Weekly Report*, July 12, 1980, pp. 1956–57.

89. U.S. House of Representatives, *U.S. Intelligence Performance on Central America*, p. 7. On the available intelligence, see Pastor, *Condemned to Repetition*, pp. 216–18; U.S. Department of State, *"Revolution Beyond Our Borders,"* pp. 20–21.

90. Pastor, *Condemned to Repetition*, pp. 216–18; John M. Goshko, "Aid for Nicaragua the Focus of Fierce Internal Policy Dispute," *WP*, August 8, 1980.

91. "Presidential Determination No. 80-26, September 12, 1980," 45 *Federal Register* 62779. See also U.S. House of Representatives, *Review of the Presidential Certification of Nicaragua's Connection to Terrorism*.

92. U.S. Department of State, *"Revolution Beyond Our Borders,"* pp. 20–21.

93. Within a week after the triumph of the revolution, senior Nicaraguan officials traveled to Havana, where they were hailed as the guests of honor at Cuba's annual Twenty-sixth of July celebration. Nicaragua's relationship with Cuba blossomed quickly as Cuba sent several thousand teachers, hundreds of medical experts, and scores of technical advisers, including some military personnel, to help Nicaragua reconstruct. LeoGrande, "Cuba," in Blachman, LeoGrande, and Sharpe, *Confronting Revolution*, pp. 229–55.

94. Pastor, *Condemned to Repetition*, pp. 194–97.

95. Ibid., pp. 211–12. Pastor also describes how the United States resisted the temptation to support a coup plot hatched by exiles and some members of the internal opposition, including businessman Jorge Salazar, who was shot and killed by Sandinista security agents when the plot was uncovered (pp. 221–24).

96. "Nicaragua: An Unfinished Revolution," *Newsweek*, July 28, 1980.

97. Pezzullo and Pezzullo, *At the Fall of Somoza*, p. 34.

98. John M. Goshko, "U.S. Debates Aid to Latin American Rightists to Bar Takeovers," *WP*, August 2, 1979.

99. See the statement by Assistant Secretary Viron P. Vaky in U.S. House of Representatives, *Central America at the Crossroads*.

100. The next three sections are adapted from William M. LeoGrande and Carla Anne Robbins, "Oligarchs and Officers: The Crisis in El Salvador," *Foreign Affairs*, Summer 1980, pp. 1084–1103.

101. Armstrong and Shenk, *El Salvador*, pp. 6–7.

102. Weeks, *Economies of Central America*, p. 47; Melvin Burke, "El Sistema de Plantación y la Proletarización del Trabajo Agrícola en El Salvador," *Estudios Centroamericanos* (September–October 1976), pp. 473–86. On the problem of population pressure in the countryside, see also Durham, *Scarcity and Survival in Central America*. On the origins of the plantation system in El Salvador during the final decades of the nineteenth century, see Browning, *El Salvador*.

103. The war, touched off by a soccer game, was actually the result of Honduran efforts to expel illegal Salvadoran immigrants. Anderson, *War of the Dispossessed*.

104. For a history of this period, see Anderson, *Matanza*.

105. For post–World War II political histories of El Salvador, see Armstrong and Shenk, *El Salvador*; Baloyra, *El Salvador in Transition*; Montgomery, *Revolution in El Salvador*; and Dunkerley, *Long War*.

106. Bulmer-Thomas, *Political Economy of Central America*, chaps. 9–10; Williams, *Export Agriculture*.

107. There were three major confederations of popular organizations: the Popular Revolutionary Bloc (Bloque Popular Revolucionario, BPR); the United Popular Action Front (Frente de Acción Popular Unificada, FAPU); and the Popular Leagues of the 28th of February (Ligas Populares 28 de Febrero, LP-28), named for the day in 1977 when security forces killed over a hundred demonstrators. Each of these confederations was politically allied with one of the major guerrilla groups: the BPR was affiliated with the Popular Liberation Forces (FPL), the Popular Leagues with the Revolutionary Army of the People, and the FAPU with the Armed Forces of National Resistance (FARN). On the history of developments on the left, see Montgomery, *Revolution in El Salvador*, chap. 5.

108. On the role of the church in the 1970s, see Lernoux, *Cry of the People*, pp. 61–80.

109. It was the Christian Federation of Salvadoran Peasants (Federación Cristiana de Campesinos Salvadoreños). See Montgomery, *Revolution in El Salvador*, pp. 97–118.

110. For a biography of Romero, see Sobrino, *Monseñor Romero*.

111. Etchinson, *United States and Militarism*, pp. 95–96.

112. U.S. Agency for International Development, *U.S. Overseas Loans and Grants*, p. 47.

113. Lernoux, *Cry of the People*, p. 76.

114. Pastor, "Continuity and Change in U.S. Foreign Policy," *Journal of Policy Analysis and Management* (1984).

115. The text of the law is in Organization of American States, Inter-American Commission on Human Rights, *Report on the Situation of Human Rights in El Salvador*, pp. 40–47.

116. Devine's reaction to the Public Order Law is in Alan Riding, "El Salvador's Dissidents Disappointed at U.S. Silence," *NYT*, May 8, 1978. He describes his opposition to Carter's human rights policy and his reaction to the rising tide of violence in El Salvador in Devine, *El Salvador*, pp. 40–59, 65–95. His personal security concerns were confirmed by a senior intelligence official working on Latin America at the time (author's interview, Washington, D.C., March 1992).

117. Organization of American States, Inter-American Commission on Human Rights, *Report on the Situation of Human Rights in El Salvador*; Fox, *Report on Mission to El Salvador*; U.S. Department of State, *Report on Human Rights Practices in Countries Receiving U.S. Aid*, February 8, 1979; Amnesty International, *Report for 1978*. These figures cover all of 1978 and the first nine months of 1979, until Romero was overthrown.

118. Pastor, "Continuity and Change in U.S. Foreign Policy," *Journal of Policy Analysis and Management*. For Vaky's account of his trip, during which he urged a new election schedule, see Dickey, *With the Contras*, p. 60.

119. Alan Riding, "Salvadoran Junta Tells of Plans; Curfew Is Set as Strife Continues," *NYT*, October 17, 1979.

120. Ibid.

121. Dunkerley, *Long War*, pp. 132–45.

122. Laurie Becklund, "Salvador Junta Unable to Keep Promises," *LAT*, November 5, 1979; Devine, *El Salvador*, pp. 148–49.

123. A U.S. military report described Salvadoran military values thus: "These values are loyalty to the institution, anti-Communism, and love of country, perhaps in that order. . . . Loyalty to the institution has become an overpowering value." Brigadier General Fred F. Woerner, "Report of the El Salvador Military Strategy Assistance Team (Draft)," Department of Defense, November 1981 (NSA El Salvador collection), pp. 42–43.

124. U.S. Department of State cable, San Salvador 06140, untitled, October 24, 1979 (NSA El Salvador collection).

125. Devine, *El Salvador*, p. 146. See also Montgomery, *Revolution in El Salvador*, p. 196; Bonner, *Weakness and Deceit*, p. 166; James Nelson Goodsell, "El Salvador Blames U.S. for Junta's Near Collapse," *CSM*, January 7, 1980.

126. Bonner, *Weakness and Deceit*, p. 162; Baloyra, *El Salvador in Transition*, pp. 86–96.

127. Bonner, *Weakness and Deceit*, p. 183. In September, an embassy cable described the Christian Democrats as "a party in search of a constituency." U.S. Department of State cable, San Salvador 6756, September 30, 1980, "Political Situation in El Salvador, Late September" (NSA El Salvador collection). Duarte himself conceded that the PDC "had been practically eliminated as a grassroots organization" over the previous decade and that his junta was virtually without popular support. Duarte, *Duarte*, pp. 110–11, 179.

128. U.S. Senate, *Nomination of Robert E. White*, p. 13.

129. *Transcript of the Luncheon Meeting on U.S. Policy toward El Salvador, February 26, 1981*.

130. "Special Coordinating Committee Meeting, January 28, 1980. Subj: U.S. Policy to El Salvador and Central America," minutes of the meeting (NSA El Salvador collection); "Summary of Conclusions, SCC [Special Coordinating Committee] Meeting on El Salvador and Honduras, February 15, 1980" (NSA El Salvador collection); Briefing Memorandum to the Secretary, from John A. Bushnell, ARA Acting, March 13, 1980, "Situation in El Salvador and MTTS" (NSA El Salvador collection).

131. U.S. Department of State cable, San Salvador 06664, November 20, 1979, "Security Assistance for El Salvador"; U.S. Department of State cable, San Salvador 07097, December 11, 1979, "The Military of El Salvador in Its Moment of Crisis"; and U.S. Department of State cable, San Salvador 00274, January 11, 1980, "Briefing of New Revolutionary Governing Junta on Proposed USG Assistance Programs" (NSA El Salvador collection). See also Bonner, *Weakness and Deceit*, pp. 165–66.

132. The text of Romero's letter to Carter is in U.S. Senate, *Nomination of Robert E. White*, pp. 39–40. The Pentagon's counterinsurgency planning is described in Minutes of Special Coordination Committee Meeting (NSC), January 28, 1980, "U.S. Policy in El Salvador and Central America" (NSA El Salvador collection).

133. Christopher Dickey, "Oligarch Takes Stand Against Salvadoran Land Reform," *WP*, April 4, 1980. The U.S. Military Group commander, Colonel John D. Waghelstein, made this same point in Manwaring and Prisk, *El Salvador at War*, p. 193.

134. U.S. Department of State cable, San Salvador 01336, February 22, 1980, "Rightist Coup Imminent in El Salvador"; U.S. Department of State cable, San Salvador 01375, February 24, 1980, "The Rightist Coup That Was and Yet May Be" (NSA El Salvador collection). See also Alan Riding, "U.S. Is Said to Block Coup in El Salvador," *NYT*, February 25, 1980. The promise of U.S. military aid was recalled by Héctor Dada, who was a member of the junta at the time. Arnson, *El Salvador*, p. 49.

135. Under no-cost lease arrangements, the United States lends equipment to foreign governments at no cost. Since leases do not require the expenditure of funds, they can be undertaken by the executive branch without congressional approval and in excess of appro-

priated levels of foreign military assistance. On Cheek's arguments for military aid, see Briefing Memorandum to the Secretary, from John A. Bushnell, ARA Acting, March 13, 1980, "Situation in El Salvador and MTTS" (NSA El Salvador collection). Cheek is quoted in Alan Riding, "U.S. Aid to Salvador Army: Bid to Bar 'Another Nicaragua,'" *NYT*, February 23, 1980.

136. Briefing Memorandum to the Secretary, from John A. Bushnell, ARA Acting, March 13, 1980, "Situation in El Salvador and MTTS" (NSA El Salvador collection).

137. Alfonso Chardy, "U.S. May Send Troops to Train Soldiers in El Salvador," *MH*, May 9, 1980.

138. Bonner, *Weakness and Deceit*, p. 164; Christopher Dickey, "Salvadorans Training at U.S. Sites in Panama," *WP*, October 9, 1980.

139. Dickey, "Salvadorans Training at U.S. Sites in Panama," *WP*, October 9, 1980. See also U.S. Department of State cable, San Salvador 9544, July 16, 1980, "Training at the School of the Americas" (NSA El Salvador collection).

140. Department of the Army Memorandum to Director, Security Assistance Training Management Office, Fort Bragg, N.C., from Cpt. Jorge E. Rodriguez, December 29, 1980; Memorandum to Roberta Cohen, HA, from Robert Jacobs, HA/HR, "Salvador Working Group," October 29, 1980; U.S. Department of State cable, San Salvador 08006, November 17, 1980, "Operation Golden Harvest" (NSA El Salvador collection).

141. Memorandum to James Cheek, ARA, from Roberta Cohen, HA, October 3, 1980, "Helicopters for El Salvador"; U.S. Department of State cable, San Salvador 06729, September 29, 1980, "JRG Provides Written Response on Helicopter Offer" (NSA El Salvador collection).

142. On the loss of influence of the progressive officers, see U.S. Department of State cable, San Salvador 6756, September 30, 1980, "Political Situation in El Salvador—Late September" (NSA El Salvador collection).

143. The texts of six letters of resignation, including Dada's, are included in Revolutionary Democratic Front, *El Salvador*, pp. 12–19.

144. Christopher Dickey, "Salvadorans Pay Tearful Homage to Slain Archbishop," *WP*, March 26, 1980.

145. Shirley Christian, "Reformist Colonel Ousted in El Salvador," *MH*, December 8, 1980.

146. Bonner, *Weakness and Deceit*, p. 204. The text of D'Aubuisson's planned announcement is in U.S. Department of State cable, San Salvador 03268, May 8, 1980, "Draft Manifesto of Major D'Aubuisson for Use in Aborted Rightwing Coup" (NSA El Salvador collection).

147. Dunkerley, *Long War*, p. 150; Baloyra, *El Salvador in Transition*, pp. 106–11; Montgomery, *Revolution in El Salvador*, pp. 159–70. The divisions in the military are described in U.S. Central Intelligence Agency, "Arrest of Rightist Coup Plotters," May 8, 1980 (NSA El Salvador collection).

148. Montgomery, *Revolution in El Salvador*, pp. 177–78; Christopher Dickey, "Military Dispute Imperils El Salvador's U.S.-Nurtured Junta," *WP*, September 5, 1980. This was also the conclusion of a detailed U.S. military study of the Salvadoran armed forces. Woerner, "Report of the El Salvador Military Strategy Assistance Team (Draft)" (NSA El Salvador collection), p. 46.

149. "Platform of the Democratic Revolutionary Front (April 1980)," in Armstrong and Shenk, *El Salvador*, pp. 254–59.

150. Sam Dillon, "New Words Try to Soften Image for D'Aubuisson," *MH*, March 25, 1984.

151. Christopher Dickey, "Behind the Death Squads," *New Republic*, December 26, 1983.

152. On the origins of ORDEN and ANSESAL, and the CIA's role, see McClintock, *American Connection*, pp. 204–22.

153. Conservative politician and 1984 presidential candidate Francisco Guerrero described how this system operated. His account and Medrano's are in Anderson and Anderson, *Inside the League*, pp. 193–94. According to a former official of the Salvadoran Treasury Police, ANSESAL was responsible for the murder in March 1977 of Father Rutilio Grande, the first priest killed by the death squads. Allan Nairn, "Behind the Death Squads," *Progressive*, May 1984. See also James LeMoyne, "A Reminder of a Painful U.S. Role in El Salvador," *NYT*, December 6, 1987.

154. Stephen Kinzer, "Death Squads in El Salvador: Ex-Aide Accuses Colleagues," *NYT*, March 3, 1984; Nairn, "Behind the Death Squads," *Progressive*, May 1984. The CIA's profile of D'Aubuisson described him as "relatively intelligent" but "egocentric, reckless and perhaps mentally unstable." U.S. CIA, National Foreign Assessment Center, "El Salvador: The Role of Roberto D'Aubuisson," March 4, 1981 (NSA El Salvador collection).

155. Laurie Becklund, "Death Squads: Deadly 'Other War,' " *LAT*, December 18, 1983. The CIA concluded D'Aubuisson led the death squad. U.S. CIA, Directorate of Intelligence, National Intelligence Estimate, "El Salvador: Controlling Rightwing Terrorism," February 1985 (NSA El Salvador collection).

156. Pyes, *Salvadoran Rightists*. This series of articles originally published in the *Albuquerque Journal* was the product of a ten-month investigation by Pyes and Laurie Becklund of the *Los Angeles Times* (Becklund, "Death Squads: Deadly 'Other War,' " *LAT*, December 18, 1983). It is by far the most detailed portrait of the Salvadoran far right, told mostly in the words of participants. See also Dennis Volman, "Salvador Death Squads, a CIA Connection?," *CSM*, May 8, 1984.

157. Nairn, "Behind the Death Squads," *Progressive*, May 1984.

158. "Red Privada," *Excelsior* (Mexico City), May 13, 1982. Both the Christian Democratic Party and D'Aubuisson's former boss, Colonel Santiváñez, accused D'Aubuisson of ordering Zamora's murder. Baloyra, *El Salvador in Transition*, pp. 112–13; Kinzer, "Death Squads in El Salvador," *NYT*, March 3, 1984.

159. Craig Pyes, "U.S. Cables Reveal Salvador Archbishop Assassination Plan," *Albuquerque Journal*, April 15, 1983. See also the testimony of former ambassador Robert White in U.S. House of Representatives, *Situation in El Salvador*, pp. 40–55.

160. U.S. House of Representatives, *Situation in El Salvador*, pp. 40–55.

161. Some of the captured documents are reprinted in ibid.

162. U.S. Department of State cable, San Salvador 08084, November 19, 1980, "[subject heading excised]"; U.S. Department of State cable, San Salvador 09718, December 21, 1981, "Assassination of Archbishop Romero" (NSA El Salvador collection). See also Pyes, "U.S. Cables Reveal Salvador Archbishop Assassination Plan," *Albuquerque Journal*, April 15, 1983; Laurie Becklund, "U.S. Cables Reportedly Tie Salvador Right to Slaying," *LAT*, April 15, 1983.

In May 1982, in a conversation with a U.S. citizen, D'Aubuisson's longtime friend and colleague Captain Eduardo Alfonso Avila admitted planning the Romero assassination. Avila had been, along with D'Aubuisson, one of Medrano's "*tres asesinos*" in the intelligence department of the National Guard. The U.S. embassy received other indications of Avila's involvement in Romero's assassination as well. (Craig Pyes, "Salvadoran Army Officer Implicated in Slaying of Archbishop," *Albuquerque Journal*, May 19, 1983.) In 1985, the U.S. embassy in San Salvador developed another informant who corroborated this account, according to documents declassified in 1993. (Guy Gugliotta, "D'Aubuisson Kept U.S. on Its Guard," *WP*, January 4, 1994.)

In 1990, one of the participants in the assassination also implicated D'Aubuisson. (U.S. Department of State cable, San Salvador unnumbered, May 17, 1990, "Saravia Revelations" [NSA El Salvador collection]) In 1993, the United Nations Truth Commission investigating the thousands of political murders committed during the war in El Salvador specifically accused D'Aubuisson of ordering Romero's murder. (United Nations, *From Madness to Hope*.)

163. Pyes, *Salvadoran Rightists*, p. 6.

164. U.S. Department of State cable, San Salvador 0096, January 6, 1981, "Millionaires' Murder Inc.?"; U.S. CIA, National Foreign Assessment Center, "El Salvador: The Role of Roberto D'Aubuisson," March 4, 1981; U.S. CIA, "Controlling Rightwing Terrorism," February 1985 (NSA El Salvador collection).

165. Legal Department of the Archdiocese of San Salvador, *Repression Carried Out by the National Army*. During the period that Duarte was on the junta, 147 PDC activists were killed. U.S. House of Representatives, *Presidential Certification on El Salvador (Volume II)*, p. 472. Duarte himself acknowledged that the armed forces continued to use "brute force and terror" against dissidents despite pleas by civilian junta members to stop. Duarte, *Duarte*, pp. 105–8.

CHAPTER THREE

1. Howell Raines, "Reagan Calls Arms Race Essential to Avoid 'Surrender' or 'Defeat,'" *NYT*, August 19, 1980. For a discussion of how the Reagan team saw Carter's foreign policy, see Meese, *With Reagan*, pp. xiv–xv, 231; Weinberger, *Fighting for Peace*, p. 21; Haig, *Caveat*, pp. 29–30.

2. Quoted in Dugger, "Reagan and the Imperial Presidency," *Nation*, November 1, 1980.

3. Fontaine, DiGiovanni, and Krugar, "Castro's Specter," *Washington Quarterly* (Autumn 1980).

4. Committee of Santa Fe, *A New Inter-American Policy for the Eighties*.

5. Kirkpatrick, "Dictatorships and Double Standards," *Commentary*, November 1979.

6. Sanders, *Peddlers of Crisis*, p. 282. For a critique of Kirkpatrick's article, see Farer, "Reagan's Latin America," *New York Review of Books*, March 19, 1981.

7. Committee of Santa Fe, *A New Inter-American Policy for the Eighties*, pp. 6, 9.

8. Fontaine, DiGiovanni, and Krugar, "Castro's Specter," *Washington Quarterly*. Specifically, Fontaine argued that Carter's policy was drawn largely from the reports of the Commission on U.S.–Latin American Relations—a bipartisan group of prominent U.S. citizens convened under the chairmanship of Ambassador Sol Linowitz—and that several people involved with the commission had joined the Carter administration to work on Latin American issues. Fontaine then noted that several people involved with the Linowitz group were also involved in preparing another policy report for the Institute for Policy Studies, a left-liberal think tank, and that the two sets of recommendations overlapped on some issues. Fontaine implied that people from the institute had smuggled their ideas into the Linowitz report, and from there into the Carter administration. The capstone of the indictment was Fontaine's unsubstantiated claim that the Institute for Policy Studies was infiltrated by Cuban and Soviet intelligence agents. The Linowitz Commission produced two reports: *The Americas in a Changing World* and *The United States and Latin America: Next Steps*. On the influence of these reports within the Carter administration, see Lake, *Somoza Falling*, pp. 21, 32.

9. Quoted in Nairn, "Reagan Administration Links with Guatemala's Death Squads," *Covert Action* (April 1981).

10. Christopher Dickey, "Central America," *WP*, November 3, 1980; "Latin America: Back to Square One with Reagan?," *Newsweek*, August 18, 1980.

11. Gerald F. Seib and Steve Frazier, "Central America Strife Grows, Posing Problem for Reagan Team," *WSJ*, December 23, 1980.

12. Bonner, *Weakness and Deceit*, p. 212.

13. Alan Riding, "Reagan Impact Felt in Central America," *NYT*, November 16, 1980; Alan Riding, "Rightist Offensive Seen in Latin Region," *NYT*, November 30, 1980.

14. Kenneth A. Briggs, "Clerics in U.S. Seek Reagan Rights Vow," *NYT*, December 18, 1980; "A Talk with Ronald Reagan," *Newsweek*, December 29, 1980.

15. "Marines Hurl Gas as U.S. Envoy Eludes Rightists in El Salvador," *WP*, May 13, 1980; "Salvadoran Junta, Armed Forces Agree to Prosecute Top Right-Wing Figures," *WP*, May 14, 1980.

16. Bernard Gwertzman, "Reagan Favors Linking Arms Talks to Soviet Behavior Around World," *NYT*, November 7, 1980.

17. Juan deOnis, "Reagan Aides Promise Salvadorans More Military Aid to Help Fight Rebels," *NYT*, November 29, 1980.

18. Duarte, *Duarte*, p. 159. See also Roy Gutman and Susan Page, "Central America: The Making of U.S. Policy," *Newsday*, July 31, 1983.

19. Christopher Dickey, "Arrest of Leftists Blunts Hopes of Salvador Accord," *WP*, November 28, 1980; Christopher Dickey, "Killings Signal Shift to Right in El Salvador," *WP*, November 29, 1980.

20. Bonner, *Weakness and Deceit*, p. 214.

21. Ibid., pp. 215, 218. In June 1980, the Carter administration devised a plan with Omar Torrijos in Panama to end the Salvadoran conflict by creating a coalition government. Johnson, *Sleepwalking through History*, p. 248.

22. "Cauldron in Central America," *NYT*, December 7, 1980.

23. Pyes, *Salvadoran Rightists*, p. 39.

24. Lawyers Committee for International Human Rights, *Justice in El Salvador: A Case Study*, Update, February 1, 1983, reprinted in U.S. Senate, *Presidential Certification on Progress in El Salvador*, p. 448.

25. This account of the kidnapping and murder of the four churchwomen is based on two U.S. government investigative reports, the first by the Bowdler and Rogers mission, described below, and the second by independent jurist Harold Tyler: William D. Rogers and William G. Bowdler, "Report to the President of Special Mission to El Salvador" (NSA El Salvador collection); Harold R. Tyler Jr., "The Churchwomen Murders: A Report to the Secretary of State," December 2, 1983 (typescript).

26. Ann Carrigan and Bernard Stone (producers and directors), *Roses in December: The Story of Jean Donovan*, 2nd of December Films, Inc., 1982.

27. The Tyler report mistakenly confuses Santiago Nonualco with another nearby town, San Pedro Nonualco.

28. Bonner, *Weakness and Deceit*, pp. 74–76.

29. Allman, *Unmanifest Destiny*, pp. 1–5; Christopher Dickey, "Four U.S. Catholics Killed in El Salvador," *WP*, December 5, 1980.

30. Allman, *Unmanifest Destiny*, pp. 1–5.

31. Not all aid was halted, however. Military aid from FY 1980 that was still "in the pipeline" (i.e., that had not yet been delivered) was not interrupted, and training programs for Salvadoran soldiers continued through mid-January 1981. Memorandum for the President, from Secretary of State Edmund S. Muskie, January 8, 1981, "Security Assistance to El Salvador" (NSA El Salvador collection).

32. John Goshko, "U.S. Halts Salvadoran Aid," *WP*, December 6, 1980.

33. Juan deOnis, "U.S. Officials Fly to El Salvador to Investigate Murders," *NYT*, December 7, 1980.

34. U.S. Department of State cable 335609, December 20, 1980, "U.S. Policy and El Salvador" (NSA El Salvador collection). See also Baloyra, *El Salvador in Transition*, pp. 114–16.

35. The mission's broader political agenda is laid out in "Scope Paper: What Could Be Accomplished by the Rogers/Bowdler Mission" (NSA El Salvador collection). It describes the "the real objective of the Rogers mission" as finding a way "to dismantle the whole structure of repression." See also Bonner, *Weakness and Deceit*, pp. 217–23.

36. U.S. Department of State cable 335609, December 20, 1980, "U.S. Policy and El Salvador" (NSA El Salvador collection); Duarte, *Duarte*, pp. 131–32.

37. U.S. Department of State cable, State 329627, December 13, 1980, "Instructions for Ambassador"; U.S. Department of State cable, State 333786, December 17, 1980, "Resumption of U.S. Economic Assistance to El Salvador"; and U.S. Department of State cable, State 333735, December 18, 1980, "Instructions for Ambassador" (NSA El Salvador collection). Specifically, the three conditions for resuming military aid were "(1) the progress of the murder investigation, (2) progress in implementing the military aspects of the JRG restructuring, and (3) prospects for the reduction of the level of violence." Memorandum for the President, from Secretary of State Edmund S. Muskie, January 8, 1981, "Security Assistance to El Salvador" (NSA El Salvador collection).

38. Gerald F. Seib and Steve Frazier, "Central America Strife Grows, Posing Problem for Reagan Team," *WSJ*, December 23, 1980.

39. "Cauldron in Central America: What Keeps the Fire Burning?," *NYT*, December 7, 1980.

40. John Hall, "Ambassador Kirkpatrick: Reagan-Appointed Democrat Speaks Her Mind on World, Domestic Politics," *Tampa Tribune*, December 25, 1980.

41. Letter to William P. Ford, from David E. Simcox, Director El Salvador Working Group, ARA, Department of State, April 16, 1981 (NSA El Salvador collection). In a letter to Senator Charles Percy, Kirkpatrick insisted she had merely said the nuns were *perceived* to be activists. The nuns, "two of whom I said were reported to have just returned from Nicaragua and to have ties in the Santanista [*sic*] junta, were perceived not just as nuns . . . but as political activists on behalf of the Frente." However, the reporter who originally interviewed her had the conversation on tape. Letter to Senators Charles Percy and Clairborne Pell, from Jeane J. Kirkpatrick, in U.S. Senate, *Situation in El Salvador*, pp. 235–36.

42. Bonner, *Weakness and Deceit*, p. 80. Eventually five Salvadoran National Guardsmen were convicted of killing the women.

43. Menges, *Inside the National Security Council*, pp. 43–44.

44. Fontaine, DiGiovanni, and Krugar, "Castro's Specter," *Washington Quarterly*. See also the interview with Fontaine in Don Bohning, "How Reagan Might Change Latin Policies," *MH*, August 24, 1980.

45. Pastor, "Continuity and Change in U.S. Foreign Policy," *Journal of Policy Analysis and Management* (1984).

46. Cord Meyer, "Confusing Signals to El Salvador," *Washington Star*, December 13, 1980. The report was written by Pedro Sanjuan and John Carbaugh, an aide to Senator Jesse Helms.

47. Pedro A. Sanjuan, "Interim Report on the Bureau on [*sic*] Inter-American Affairs and Related Bureaus and Policy Areas, Department of State" (typescript); Juan deOnis, "Reagan's State Department Latin Team Asks Curbs on 'Social Reformers,'" *NYT*, December 4, 1980.

48. Bonner, *Weakness and Deceit*, pp. 218–19; Christopher Dickey, "Envoy Assails Reagan Aides on El Salvador," *WP*, December 10, 1980; "U.S. Envoy in Salvador Charges Reagan Team Is Undercutting Him," *NYT*, December 10, 1980; "An Ambassador Under Fire," *Newsweek*, December 22, 1980.

49. "State Department Is Critical of Reports on Reagan's Aims," *NYT*, December 11, 1980.

50. Christopher Dickey, "Second Ambassador Joins Criticism of Reagan Team," *WP*, December 13, 1980.

51. "State Department Official Blasts Reagan Transition Team," *Washington Star*, December 12, 1980; John M. Goshko, "Policy Dispute on Latin America Jars Transition," *WP*, December 13, 1980.

52. Marlise Simons, "Reagan's Aides Snub Carter Staff on Mexican Visit," *WP*, December 29, 1980.

53. In his exposé of covert operations in Latin America, former CIA officer Philip Agee

called AIFLD a "CIA-controlled labor center financed through AID." Agee, *Inside the Company*, p. 600. Despite AIFLD's repeated denials of any CIA connection, former *Wall Street Journal* reporter Jonathan Kwitny established beyond reasonable doubt, based on interviews with a number of former CIA officials, that AIFLD was closely involved with CIA operations during the 1960s. Kwitny, *Endless Enemies*, pp. 339–54.

There was no direct evidence that Hammer or Pearlman were working with the CIA, although an odd incident shortly after their murder raised the issue. In January 1981, Solicitor General Wade H. McCree Jr., testifying on the need for a law that would make it a crime to reveal the names of CIA operatives, cited Hammer and Pearlman as examples of people who had been operating "under cover." Later he denied that he had meant to imply they were working for the CIA. Judith Miller, "Solicitor General Calls Two Americans Killed in El Salvador 'Under Cover,' " *NYT*, January 15, 1981.

54. AIFLD operated in El Salvador from 1965 until it was kicked out in 1973 for promoting agrarian reform; it resumed operations after the October 1979 coup. Christopher Dickey, "Two U.S. Aides, Salvadoran Assassinated," *WP*, January 5, 1981; Mike Sager, "Slain U.S. Adviser Had an 'Obsession' to Distribute Land," *WP*, January 5, 1981.

55. Karen DeYoung, "Assassinated Salvadoran Official Had Worked for Peaceful Change," *WP*, January 6, 1981.

56. Pyes, *Salvadoran Rightists*, pp. 13–18.

57. Ibid. See also the testimony of AIFLD official William C. Doherty Jr. in U.S. Senate, *Presidential Certification on Progress in El Salvador*.

58. "We do not support United States assistance to any Marxist government in this hemisphere and we oppose the Carter administration's aid program for the government of Nicaragua," the platform declared. "However, we will support the efforts of the Nicaraguan people to establish a free and independent government." "1980 Republican Party Platform," *CQ Weekly Report*, July 19, 1980, pp. 2030–56.

59. Alan Riding, "Central Americans Split on U.S. Voting," *NYT*, August 4, 1980.

60. "Latin America: Back to Square One with Reagan?," *Newsweek*, August 18, 1980; William R. Long, "Reagan Reaction from Nicaragua," *MH*, November 9, 1980.

61. Alan Riding, "Salvadoran Rebel Predicts Final Push," *NYT*, December 27, 1980.

62. Statement of Randolph Pherson, Central Intelligence Agency, in U.S. House of Representatives, *Impact of Cuban-Soviet Ties in the Western Hemisphere*, p. 46. "I believe that if it hadn't been for the Cubans, specifically Fidel Castro, it would not have been possible for the FMLN to achieve unity," said former guerrilla commander Miguel Castellanos, recounting Cuban pressure in 1979 and 1980. Prisk, *Comandante Speaks*, p. 23.

63. Cuba subsequently acknowledged its "material assistance" to the Salvadorans during this period. Author's interview with a senior Cuban official, Havana, April 1982. The official admitted that Cuba had provided "material" support to the Salvadoran guerrillas prior to the spring of 1980, but he contended that no aid had been provided since that time. The Salvadoran guerrillas also purchased arms from Panama that remained in the pipeline at the end of the Nicaraguan insurrection. Dinges, *Our Man in Panama*, pp. 112–14.

64. Pastor, *Condemned to Repetition*, p. 356; Krauss, *Inside Central America*, p. 68.

65. Pastor, *Condemned to Repetition*, pp. 224, 230–34. Edén Pastora told Pastor that the FSLN National Directorate debated for over a year about whether or not they should actively help the Salvadoran guerrillas (p. 217). According to Sandinista defector Roger Miranda, Bayardo Arce doubted that the Salvadorans were close enough to victory to justify a major Nicaraguan commitment; Humberto Ortega disagreed. Miranda and Ratliff, *Civil War in Nicaragua*, pp. 32–33.

66. "Before September 1980 . . . the insurgents acquired weapons predominantly through purchases on the international market and from dealers who participated in the supply of arms to the Sandinistas in Nicaragua." U.S. Department of State, *Communist Interference in*

El Salvador, p. 2. See also Pastor, *Condemned to Repetition*, pp. 224–25. Ambassador White said that the evidence of Nicaraguan aid to the Salvadoran guerrillas was "most unconvincing" until early November 1980. U.S. House of Representatives, *Foreign Assistance and Related Programs Appropriations for 1982, Part 1*, pp. 7–8. This timing is also confirmed by Sandinista defector Roger Miranda, in Miranda and Ratliff, *Civil War in Nicaragua*, p. 140.

67. Pastor, *Condemned to Repetition*, p. 225.

68. Of the $75 million economic aid package approved a few months earlier, $15 million had not yet been disbursed.

69. Pastor, *Condemned to Repetition*, p. 228. The law did not, in fact, leave Carter much alternative. Section 536(g) of the Foreign Assistance Act as amended reads: "In the event that the President transmits such a certification, but at a later date he determines that the Government of Nicaragua cooperates with or harbors any international terrorist organization or is aiding, abetting, or supporting acts of violence or terrorism in other countries, the President shall terminate assistance to the Government of Nicaragua under this chapter." From "Presidential Determination No. 80-26, September 12, 1980," 45 *Federal Register* 62799.

70. "Salvador to Hold Elections 'Soon,' but Leftists Pledge War for Power," *MH*, January 8, 1981.

71. Christopher Dickey, "U.S. Adds 'Lethal' Aid to El Salvador," *WP*, January 18, 1981. Former FMLN commander Miguel Castellanos described the assumptions behind the "final offensive," noting that his organization, the Popular Liberation Forces (FPL), did not think it would work. Prisk, *Comandante Speaks*, p. 29.

72. Memorandum for the President, from Secretary of State Edmund S. Muskie, January 8, 1981, "Security Assistance to El Salvador" (NSA El Salvador collection). See also Karen DeYoung, "State's Latin Bureau Urges Resumption of Arms Aid to Salvador," *WP*, January 10, 1981; Karen DeYoung, "Carter Decides to Resume Military Aid to El Salvador," *WP*, January 14, 1981.

73. Memorandum for the President, from Secretary of State Edmund S. Muskie, January 8, 1981, "Security Assistance to El Salvador" (NSA El Salvador collection).

74. U.S. Department of State cable 001000, January 2, 1980, "Approach to Duarte on Military Assistance" (NSA El Salvador collection).

75. U.S. Senate, *Situation in El Salvador*, pp. 204–12. Ambassador White supported the decision to resume military aid because of the guerrilla offensive, but he refused to sugarcoat it by pretending that progress had been made on the murder investigation. "It is amazing to me that the Department can state publicly that the investigation of the nuns' deaths is proceeding satisfactorily," he cabled Washington. "In my judgment there is no sign of any sincere attempt to locate and punish those responsible for this atrocity." U.S. Department of State cable, San Salvador 000483, January 19, 1981, "Investigation of Churchwomen's Death" (NSA El Salvador collection). Two days later, White said the same thing publicly. Juan deOnis, "Envoy Disputes U.S. on Salvador Deaths," *NYT*, January 22, 1981.

76. Dickey, "U.S. Adds 'Lethal' Aid to El Salvador," *WP*, January 18, 1981.

CHAPTER FOUR

1. Morris, *Haig*, p. 15.

2. Hersh, *Price of Power*, p. 56.

3. On Haig's career, see Morris, *Haig*; and Michael Getler, "Serving at the Seat of Power: A Fourth President Calls on Haig's Abilities," *WP*, December 17, 1980. For Haig's own account of his career and his comparison of himself to Marshall, see his opening statement to the Senate Foreign Relations Committee during his confirmation hearings, reprinted in "Major Points from Appearance by Haig Before Senate Committee," *NYT*, January 10, 1981.

4. Schieffer and Gates, *Acting President*, p. 26.

5. Cannon, *Reagan*, pp. 394–96. This was not a recently acquired trait. An antagonist of Haig's from his days as deputy commandant of West Point described the general's "peculiar anxiety" about any challenge to his authority. Morris, *Haig*, p. 94.

6. Grove, "Haig Running to Take Charge," *WP*, January 30, 1988.

7. Ibid.

8. For a sampling of Haigisms that includes such classics as "I caveat it that way," see Garry Wills, "What Did He Say?," *Albuquerque Journal*, May 1, 1981.

9. Duggan, "Little Engine of Alexander Haig," *Washingtonian Magazine*, November 1981.

10. Reagan, *American Life*, pp. 360–61.

11. Grove, "Haig Running to Take Charge," *WP*, January 30, 1988; Smith, *Power Game*, pp. 308–9.

12. Reagan, *American Life*, p. 360.

13. Haig, *Caveat*, p. 95. See also Don Oberdorfer, "Haig: Soviets Focus of His Global View," *WP*, December 23, 1980.

14. Haig, *Caveat*, p. 95. Haig's lack of basic knowledge about Latin America is confirmed in his memoirs. For instance, he asserts that Cuban and Soviet adventurism in Latin America ceased after Lyndon Johnson sent 20,000 troops to the Dominican Republic in 1965 (p. 125). In fact, the most active period of Cuban support for Latin American revolutionary movements began in 1966 just after the intervention and lasted until 1968. At another point, Haig asserts that in some Latin American countries, the armed forces are regarded as the "protector of liberty of the people" and the "remover of tyrants." El Salvador, he says, "belonged to this tradition." Nothing could be further from the truth. The Salvadoran armed forces seized power from a newly elected reformist president in 1931, killed upward of 30,000 peasants in the *Matanza*, and held full control of the government until 1979. Later, Haig describes Cuban vice president Carlos Raphael Rodríguez as "the guarantee in human form that the Cuban revolution will outlive Castro" (p. 134). In fact, Rodríguez was seventy-five years old in 1988, fourteen years older than Fidel Castro. Barring Castro's sudden and unexpected demise, Rodríguez was not likely to outlive him.

15. Michael Getler, "Haig Dismisses State Transition Team," *WP*, December 24, 1980; John M. Goshko, "Reagan State Department Aide Sees 'Nationalistic' Policy," *WP*, December 18, 1980.

16. "Reagan Is Replacing Top Official on Latin Policy at the State Department," *NYT*, May 28, 1983; John M. Goshko, "Clout and Morale Decline: Reaganites' Raid on the Latin Bureau," *WP*, April 26, 1987.

17. Shirley Christian, "Two Salvadoran Coalition Leaders: We Were Near Talks with U.S.," *MH*, January 29, 1981.

18. Stephen Kinzer, "U.S. Has Replaced Nearly All Its Specialists on Central America," *Boston Globe*, November 23, 1981.

19. Karen DeYoung, "Envoy Removed from Salvadoran Post," *WP*, February 2, 1981.

20. Juan deOnis, "Haig Said to Remove Ambassador to Salvador in Signal of New Policy," *NYT*, February 2, 1981; Juan deOnis, "'Experienced' Envoy to Salvador," *NYT*, February 5, 1981. In his memoirs, Haig confirmed that White was removed because he disagreed with the new administration's intention of increasing military aid and because his ouster would have "symbolic value." Haig, *Caveat*, p. 127.

21. Christopher Dickey, "The Gang That Blew Vietnam Goes Latin," *WP*, November 28, 1982.

22. The term was used by a Reagan appointee to refer to Carter's Africa policy, but the attitude toward Central America was the same. Richard Burt, "Reagan Aides Diagnose 'Regionalitis' in U.S. Africa Policy," *NYT*, December 7, 1980.

23. Dickey, "The Gang That Blew Vietnam Goes Latin," *WP*, November 28, 1982.

24. "Latin Official Named Prior to Nomination," *MH*, March 25, 1981.

25. Whittle, "Helms Loses Committee Test on Nominees," *CQ Weekly Report*, May 2, 1981, p. 755.

26. "Latin Official Named Prior to Nomination," *MH*, March 25, 1981; Edward Walsh, "Some Key Reagan Foreign Policy Aides Remain in Bureaucratic Twilight Zone," *WP*, April 14, 1981; "Reagan Said to OK Haig Choice for Latin American Affairs Post," *MH*, April 17, 1981.

27. Charles Mohr, "An 'Intimidating' Diplomat," *NYT*, March 26, 1982; Phil Keisling, "Tallest Gun in Foggy Bottom," *Washington Monthly*, November 1982.

28. Keisling, "The Tallest Gun in Foggy Bottom," *Washington Monthly*; Frank A. Aukofer, "Enders: Point Man in Central America," *Milwaukee Journal*, April 3, 1983.

29. Sydney H. Schanberg, "The Can-Do Bombardier," *NYT*, February 6, 1982; Shawcross, *Sideshow*, pp. 269–71.

30. Shawcross, *Sideshow*, pp. 271–72.

31. Ibid., pp. 275–77; Bonner, *Weakness and Deceit*, p. 246.

32. Bonner, *Weakness and Deceit*, pp. 246–47.

33. CORDS and the Phoenix program are described in Ranelagh, *Agency*, pp. 436–41. The most complete account of Phoenix is Valentine, *Phoenix Program*.

34. Snepp, *Decent Interval*, pp. 406–7; Valentine, *Phoenix Program*, pp. 417–19.

35. Diederich, *Somoza*, p. 251; Barbara Crossette, "A Team at State Is Key to El Salvador Policy," *NYT*, February 24, 1981.

36. Bonner, *Weakness and Deceit*, p. 251; Dickey, "The Gang That Blew Vietnam Goes Latin," *WP*, November 28, 1982; Hersh, *Price of Power*, pp. 584–85.

37. Robert Parry, "Reagan's Central America Team Familiar with World Hot Spots," Associated Press wire story, May 26, 1981. For extended profiles on Hinton, Quainton, Negroponte, and Chapin, see Christopher Dickey, "Proconsuls," *Rolling Stone*, August 18, 1983.

38. Bonner, *Weakness and Deceit*, pp. 251–53.

39. Stephen Kinzer, "Specialists on Central America Are Out the Door," *Boston Globe*, November 23, 1981.

40. Goshko, "Clout and Morale Decline: Reaganites' Raid on the Latin Bureau," *WP*, April 26, 1987.

41. Don Oberdorfer, "Salvador Is 'the Place to Draw the Line' on Communism, Percy Says," *WP*, February 20, 1981.

42. Haig, *Caveat*, pp. 23, 30, 95, 127, 129.

43. Barrett, *Gambling with History*, p. 207.

44. Presidential Press Secretary James Brady said quite explicitly that U.S. policy toward El Salvador was designed to "send a message to Moscow." Karen DeYoung, "El Salvador: Where Reagan Draws the Line," *WP*, March 9, 1981. See also Karen DeYoung, "El Salvador: A Symbol of World Crisis," *WP*, March 8, 1981.

45. For Reagan's views on the Vietnam syndrome, see Reagan, *American Life*, p. 451.

46. The meeting was attended by Reagan, Haig, Weinberger, Casey, Allen, Baker, and Meese. Weinberger, *Fighting for Peace*, pp. 26–31.

47. Haig, *Caveat*, p. 77.

48. Ibid., pp. 127–29; Juan deOnis, "Baker Supports Added Advisers for El Salvador," *NYT*, February 26, 1981.

49. Dickey, *With the Contras*, p. 103; Haig, *Caveat*, pp. 120–22.

50. Haig, *Caveat*, pp. 120–22, 125. Haig had absolutely no doubt that Cuba and the Soviet Union were providing the materiel for the Salvadoran insurgency, later writing, "Moscow was the banker." He dismissed as naive the idea that the guerrillas financed the war with money raised from kidnappings (*Caveat*, pp. 123–24), even though that was the conclusion

reached by analysts in the intelligence community. Gerald F. Seib, "The Influence of Cuba in Latin America," *WSJ*, February 24, 1981.

51. Reagan, *My Turn*, p. 242; Smith, *Power Game*, p. 350; Cannon, *President Reagan*, p. 196.

52. Dickey, *With the Contras*, p. 104. The *Washington Post* also reported that Haig had "strong personal feeling of animosity" toward Castro, which was a key factor in the direction of U.S. policy. Michael Getler, "Lack of Political Intelligence Data Is Hampering U.S. on El Salvador," *WP*, February 21, 1981.

53. Haig, *Caveat*, p. 131.

54. McFarlane and Smardz, *Special Trust*, pp. 177–80; Cannon, *President Reagan*, p. 345; "Reagan's Goal: Cutting Castro Down to Size," *U.S. News and World Report*, April 6, 1981.

55. Allen is quoted in Barrett, *Gambling with History*, p. 209; Baker in Schieffer and Gates, *Acting President*, p. 125.

56. Haig does not explicitly say he was advocating a blockade, only that Enders was assigned to develop a plan to "seal off the export of arms from Cuba to Central America." Haig, *Caveat*, p. 130. Enders confirmed that Haig sought a blockade in a 1986 interview with journalist Jim Lobe, which Lobe was kind enough to share with me. Other administration officials also said at the time that a blockade was under consideration. Saul Friedman, "El Salvador No Vietnam, Reagan Says," *MH*, February 25, 1981.

57. Haig, *Caveat*, pp. 128–29. Edwin Meese had some sympathy for Haig's proposal. On February 22, Meese refused to rule out a blockade of Cuba in an interview on ABC's "Issues and Answers," and threatened U.S. action against Cuba, "if the arms shipments [to El Salvador] don't cease." Lee Lescaze, "U.S. Action 'Possible' in Cuban Arms Flow, Reagan Aide Says," *WP*, February 23, 1981.

58. Don Oberdorfer, "Applying Pressure in Central America," *WP*, November 23, 1983; Haig, *Caveat*, pp. 98–99.

59. Reagan first suggested a blockade in January 1980 and reaffirmed it in his debate with George Bush on April 23. Franklin, *Cuban Foreign Relations*, pp. 31–32; Saul Friedman, "Reagan's Deep Commitment to Resist Communism," *MH*, July 1, 1983.

60. "Campaign '84: The Inside Story," *Newsweek*, November–December 1984, p. 32.

61. Haig, *Caveat*, p. 128. Among Haig's opponents was Chairman of the Joint Chiefs of Staff David C. Jones. George C. Wilson, "U.S. Military Leaders Warn Against Central America Buildup," *WP*, June 4, 1983. For Weinberger's views, see Weinberger, *Fighting for Peace*, pp. 30–34.

62. Michael Getler, "Lack of Political Intelligence Data Is Hampering U.S. on El Salvador," *WP*, February 21, 1981; Haig, *Caveat*, p. 131. One South-Com commander recalled that senior U.S. officers regarded El Salvador as a "distraction" from the strategic buildup. The war was so unpopular at the Pentagon that five officers turned down appointments as MilGroup commander in the early 1980s. Bacevich et al., *American Military Policy in Small Wars*, pp. 9, 18.

63. A Pentagon report on the state of the Salvadoran military is described in Richard Halloran, "Military Aspects of Crisis Are Underlined by Haig and a Pentagon Study," *NYT*, February 21, 1981. For an earlier assessment along the same lines, see U.S. Department of State cable, San Salvador 07097, December 11, 1979, "The Military of El Salvador in Its Moment of Crisis" (NSA El Salvador collection). An interagency review group identified five areas in which U.S. military assistance was needed: basic training, command and control, communications, intelligence collection, and naval forces to intercept arms smuggling. Robert C. Toth, "U.S. Prepares Extensive Plan for Salvador Aid," *LAT*, February 26, 1981. For an account of the Pentagon's recommendations for aid, see Juan deOnis, "U.S. Still Undecided on Amount of Aid to Salvador," *NYT*, February 15, 1981.

64. Haig, *Caveat*, pp. 125, 128.

65. Ibid., p. 130; Alexander Haig, "Where the Contra Policy Went Wrong," *CSM*, February 16, 1988.

66. DeOnis, "U.S. Still Undecided on Amount of Aid to Salvador," *NYT*, February 15, 1981.

67. "Secretary Haig: News Conference," *Current Policy*, no. 258 (U.S. Department of State, 1981).

68. John M. Goshko, "U.S. Pressing Nicaragua to Choke Off Salvador Arms," *WP*, February 6, 1981; "U.S. Drops Link to Reforms for Salvadoran Aid," *Washington Star*, February 18, 1981.

69. Haig, *Caveat*, pp. 99–100.

70. Ibid., pp. 107–9.

71. Karen DeYoung, "El Salvador: Where Reagan Draws the Line," *WP*, March 9, 1981.

72. John M. Goshko, "U.S. Prepares to Aid El Salvador in First Test of Reagan Policy," *WP*, February 14, 1981; Bernard Gwertzman, "El Salvador: A Test Issue," *NYT*, February 14, 1981.

73. U.S. Department of State, *Communist Interference in El Salvador*, Special Report No. 80, February 23, 1981.

74. Juan deOnis, "State Department Says Salvador Rebels Get Fewer Arms," *NYT*, February 24, 1981.

75. U.S. Department of State, *Aggression from the North: The Record of North Vietnam's Campaign to Conquer South Vietnam*. On parallels between the two White Papers, see Don Oberdorfer, "Using El Salvador to Battle the Ghosts of Vietnam," *WP*, March 1, 1981; Hodding Carter, "The El Salvador Crusade," *WSJ*, March 19, 1981.

76. Richard Eder, "Europe and El Salvador," *NYT*, February 21, 1981.

77. Bernard Gwertzman, "More Salvador Aid Backed in Congress," *NYT*, February 18, 1981. See also John M. Goshko, "Hill Leaders Vow Aid to Salvador to Resist Leftists," *WP*, February 18, 1981.

78. Kwitny, *Endless Enemies*, p. 362; Hallin, "White Paper, Red Scare," *NACLA Report on the Americas* (July–August 1983).

79. John Dinges, "White Paper or Blank Paper?," *LAT*, March 17, 1981; Bonner, *Weakness and Deceit*, pp. 121, 257.

80. See Kwitny, "Apparent Errors Cloud U.S. 'White Paper' on Reds in El Salvador," *WSJ*, June 8, 1981; and Robert G. Kaiser, "White Paper on El Salvador Is Faulty," *WP*, June 9, 1981. At about the same time, the *Columbia Journalism Review* published a critique of how gullibly most of the press had accepted the White Paper when it was released. Maslow and Arana, "Operation El Salvador," *Columbia Journalism Review*, May–June 1981.

81. Bonner, *Weakness and Deceit*, p. 263. For a subsequent defense of the White Paper's conclusions, see Hager, "Soviet Bloc Involvement in the Salvadoran Civil War," *Communist and Post-Communist Studies* (1995).

82. Kwitny, *Endless Enemies*, p. 369.

83. As Kaiser points out, even the Salvadoran government with whom Washington was allied did not accept this assessment; they saw it as primarily an internal problem. Kaiser, "White Paper on El Salvador Is Faulty," *WP*, June 9, 1981.

84. James Kelly, "Winning Hearts and Minds," *Time*, March 2, 1981; Robert G. Kaiser, "The Man Behind the White Paper and the Unfolding of the Story," *WP*, June 9, 1981; DeOnis, "U.S. Officials Concede Flaws in Salvador White Paper but Defend Its Conclusions," *NYT*, June 10, 1981; DeYoung, "Sleuth of the Salvador Papers," *WP*, March 14, 1981; Kwitny, "Apparent Errors Cloud U.S. 'White Paper' on Reds in El Salvador," *WSJ*, June 8, 1981.

85. Dinges, "White Paper or Blank Paper?," *LAT*, March 17, 1981. On January 26, 1981, for example, Ambassador Robert White sent José Napoleón Duarte a summary of what U.S. intelligence analysts had been able to glean from the captured documents. The summary,

intended for internal use, was far more balanced than the published White Paper. It noted the Sandinistas' ambivalence about helping the Salvadorans, and barely mentioned any role by Eastern bloc countries other than Cuba. The summary was printed in *Congressional Record*, July 15, 1981, pp. 15961–62.

86. Carothers, *In the Name of Democracy*, p. 17.

87. Section 506(a) of the Foreign Assistance Act of 1961, as amended, gave the president unilateral authority to provide military aid in the event of an "unforeseen emergency" that cannot be handled by regular aid procedures, up to a limit of $75 million per fiscal year. President Reagan's justification for invoking Section 506(a) is in "Emergency Military Assistance for El Salvador," memorandum to the president from Alexander M. Haig Jr., March 2, 1981 (NSA El Salvador collection).

88. John M. Goshko and Don Oberdorfer, "U.S. to Send More Aid, Advisers to El Salvador," *WP*, March 3, 1981; Department of State Daily Press Briefing, Monday, March 2, 1981 (NSA El Salvador collection).

89. Woodward, *VEIL*, p. 117; Don Oberdorfer and Patrick E. Tyler, "U.S.-Backed Nicaraguan Rebel Army Swells to 7,000 Men," *WP*, May 8, 1983. In April 1982, the program was expanded to include operations inside Guatemala, for which $2.5 million was allocated. Raymond Bonner, "President Approved Policy of Preventing 'Cuba-Model States,'" *NYT*, April 7, 1983.

90. Pastor, "Continuity and Change in U.S. Foreign Policy," *Journal of Policy Analysis and Management* (1984).

91. The FDR-FMLN was, by all accounts, shocked at the failure of the offensive. Its international support was seriously eroded, not only in Europe but even among staunch allies such as Nicaragua and Cuba. Both Havana and Managua began pressing the FDR-FMLN to seek a negotiated solution to the conflict. Alan Riding, "Salvadoran Rebels Find Support Ebbing," *NYT*, February 16, 1981; Alan Riding, "Nicaragua Seeking Accord in El Salvador," *NYT*, February 12, 1981; Smith, "Dateline Havana," *Foreign Policy* (Fall 1982).

92. "An Interview with Ronald Reagan," *Time*, January 5, 1981.

93. Christopher Dickey, "Rightist Says U.S. Would Back Ouster of Civilians from Salvadoran Regime," *WP*, March 4, 1981.

94. Christopher Dickey, "Diplomat Says U.S. Opposes Rightist Coup in El Salvador," *WP*, March 5, 1981; John M. Goshko, "Haig Denies Administration Would Support Coup in El Salvador," *WP*, March 5, 1981.

95. Goshko, "Haig Denies Administration Would Support Coup in El Salvador," *WP*, March 5, 1981; Juan deOnis, "Haig Opposes a Coup by Salvador's Right," *NYT*, March 5, 1981.

96. "The President's News Conference, March 6, 1981," *Reagan Papers, 1981*, pp. 206–9.

97. Hedrick Smith, "House Democrats Seeking to Limit Involvement by U.S. in El Salvador," *NYT*, March 1, 1981.

98. "Prod Soviets on Salvador, Byrd Urges," *MH*, March 1, 1981.

99. "Congressional Foes of Salvador Policy Criticize Move to Boost Aid, Advisers," *Baltimore Sun*, March 4, 1981; Bernard Gwertzman, "More Salvador Aid Backed in Congress," *NYT*, February 18, 1981; Smith, "House Democrats Seeking to Limit Involvement by U.S. in El Salvador," *NYT*, March 1, 1981.

100. For White's testimony, see U.S. House of Representatives, *Foreign Assistance and Related Programs Appropriations for 1982, Part 1*, pp. 1–25; U.S. Senate, *Situation in El Salvador*, pp. 100–190; U.S. House of Representatives, *U.S. Policy Toward El Salvador*, pp. 133–55.

101. U.S. House of Representatives, *Foreign Assistance and Related Programs Appropriations for 1982*, pp. 3–19.

102. U.S. Senate, *Situation in El Salvador*, p. 57. At another hearing, Bushnell said the

human rights abuses of the government had been "exaggerated." U.S. House of Representatives, *U.S. Policy Toward El Salvador*, p. 21.

103. For a good summary of the various human rights reports, see Americas Watch and the American Civil Liberties Union, *Report on Human Rights in El Salvador*. Bushnell's testimony is in U.S. House of Representatives, *Foreign Assistance and Related Programs Appropriations for 1982*, p. 276.

104. U.S. House of Representatives, *U.S. Policy Toward El Salvador*, p. 33; U.S. Senate, *Situation in El Salvador*, p. 90.

105. "Helping El Salvador," letter from Ambassador Murat W. Williams, *WP*, February 28, 1981.

106. See, for example, the testimony of John Bushnell in U.S. House of Representatives, *U.S. Policy Toward El Salvador*, p. 41; FBI official Francis Mullen in U.S. Senate, *Situation in El Salvador*, p. 62; and FBI official Harry Brandon in U.S. House of Representatives, *Foreign Assistance and Related Programs Appropriations for 1982*, pp. 269–70.

107. Harold R. Tyler Jr., "The Churchwomen Murders: A Report to the Secretary of State," December 2, 1983 (typescript), pp. 22, 25–26.

108. Ibid., pp. 28–32.

109. U.S. House of Representatives, *U.S. Policy Toward El Salvador*, pp. 19–20.

110. Einaudi's presentation at the American Political Science Association Annual Meeting, Washington, D.C., September 1984.

111. U.S. Senate, *Situation in El Salvador*, pp. 5, 7, 35, 83.

112. "Applicability of the War Powers Resolution and Section 21(c) of the Arms Export Control Act to the Proposed Deployment of Additional Mobile Military Training Teams to El Salvador," memorandum to the Acting Undersecretary of Defense for Policy Planning from Virginia M. Dondy, Associate General Counsel of the Department of Defense, February 12, 1981 (NSA El Salvador collection). Dondy judged that a report to Congress under the War Powers Resolution would be necessary if the advisers were posted to zonal commands since "until now the capital area has been described as the only secure area; the outlying areas have been described as unstable and the subject of terrorist incidents." She also argued that a report would be required if the advisers carried more than sidearms for personal self-defense.

113. The advisers' rules of engagement are detailed in "Application of the War Powers Resolution to El Salvador," distributed to members of Congress by the Department of State in March 1981. They are quoted extensively in Juan M. Vasquez, "U.S. Advisers' Frustration Deepens in El Salvador," *LAT*, February 11, 1983. On the applicability of War Powers, see Department of State Daily Press Briefing, Monday, March 2, 1981, p. 5.

114. U.S. Senate, *Situation in El Salvador*, p. 51.

115. This is the language of the statement that members of the armed forces signed each month to qualify for hostile fire pay, as quoted in U.S. House of Representatives, *U.S. Policy in El Salvador*, p. 28.

116. Section 21(c) of the Arms Export Control Act prohibits U.S. advisers abroad from engaging in combat activities, and requires a report to Congress if significant hostilities break out in a country hosting U.S. advisers. The administration denied the applicability of both subsections to the situation in El Salvador. Whittle, "Reagan Weighs Military Aid to Counter Soviet, Cuban 'Interference' in El Salvador," *CQ Weekly Report*, February 28, 1981.

117. U.S. Senate, *Situation in El Salvador*, pp. 30–31, 68–71.

118. Jagelski, *Legislative History of Sections 506 and 652 of the Foreign Assistance Act of 1961 (Special Security Assistance Authority)*.

119. "Economic Aid for El Salvador Increased to $126.5 Million," *CQ Weekly Report*, May 9, 1981, p. 789.

120. *Politics in America, 1984*, pp. 659–61.

121. U.S. House of Representatives, *Foreign Assistance and Related Programs Appropriations for 1982*, pp. 263–64, 283; "U.S. Embassy Fired On After Long's Visit," *LAT*, March 18, 1981.

122. Judith Miller, "Fifteen U.S. Green Berets to Aid Salvadorans," *NYT*, March 14, 1981; Whittle, "Reagan El Salvador Policy Clears First Hurdle," *CQ Weekly Report*, March 28, 1981.

123. Quoted in Judith Miller, "House Panel Approves $5 Million in Extra Military Aid for El Salvador," *NYT*, March 25, 1981. See also U.S. House of Representatives, *Foreign Assistance and Related Programs Appropriations for 1982*, pp. 281–308.

124. *The Gallup Report*, no. 199 (April 1982); Edward Walsh, "Reagan Gets First Public Opinion Backlash—on Salvador Policy," *WP*, March 27, 1981; Oberdorfer, "More U.S. Effort Yields Less Result," *WP*, March 4, 1982. For a more detailed review of polling data on Reagan's policy toward El Salvador and Nicaragua, see LeoGrande, *Central America and the Polls*.

125. John M. Goshko, "Administration to Begin New Drive for Support of El Salvador Policy," *WP*, July 9, 1981; author's interview with the director of the Latin American Program at the Foreign Service Institute, October 1981.

126. Alan Riding, "López Portillo to Reagan on Central America: Don't," *NYT*, January 4, 1981. See also Riding, *Distant Neighbors*, p. 354.

127. Alan Riding, "Mexican Leader Criticizes Efforts for Military Solution in Salvador," *NYT*, February 25, 1981; Alan Riding, "The Salvador Strategy," *NYT*, March 11, 1981. For details on Mexico's policy, see Olga Pellicer, "Mexico in Central America: The Difficult Exercise of Regional Power," in Fagen and Pellicer, *Future of Central America*, pp. 119–34; Mario Ojeda, "Mexican Policy Toward Central America in the Context of U.S. Mexican Relations," in Fagen and Pellicer, *Future of Central America*, pp. 135–60; and René Herrera Zuniga and Mario Ojeda, "Mexican Foreign Policy and Central America," in Feinberg, *Central America*, pp. 160–86.

128. Marlise Simons, "U.S.-Mexican Ties Getting New Test," *WP*, January 25, 1981.

129. Daniel Southerland, "Mexico, Venezuela Try to End Salvador Fighting," *CSM*, April 27, 1981; Frank J. Prial, "World Socialists Support Talks on Salvador," *NYT*, May 3, 1981. For a fuller discussion of Venezuelan views, see Robert D. Bond, "Venezuelan Policy in the Caribbean Basin," in Feinberg, *Central America*, pp. 187–200; and Demetrio Boersner, "Venezuelan Policies Toward Central America," in Grabendorff, Krumwiede, and Todt, *Political Change in Central America*, pp. 245–60.

130. Richard Eder, "Europe and El Salvador," *NYT*, February 21, 1981; Pierre Schori, "Peace in El Salvador," *NYT*, February 28, 1981. In his memoirs, Haig (*Caveat*, p. 130) acknowledges the Europeans' reluctance to enlist in his anti-Communist crusade in Central America.

131. Grabendorff, "Western European Perceptions of the Central American Turmoil," in Feinberg, *Central America*, pp. 201–12; Pierre, *Central America as a European-American Issue*.

132. Author's interview with Rolf Linkhohr, member of the European Parliament, Washington, D.C., February 1991. See also John Vincour, "For Europe's Left, Salvador Helps to Fuel U.S. Distrust," *NYT*, February 22, 1981.

133. "Remarks During a White House Briefing on the Program for Economic Recovery, February 24, 1981," *Reagan Papers, 1981*, p. 153.

134. Eusebio Mujal-León, "European Socialism and the Crisis in Central America," in Wiarda, *Rift and Revolution*, pp. 253–302.

135. John Vincour, "West Germans May Try to Bring Salvadorans to Bonn to Negotiate," *NYT*, February 23, 1981; Alan Riding, "Social Democrats Offer to Act as Mediators in Salvador," *NYT*, March 3, 1981; Alan Riding, "El Salvador Turns Down a Plan for Outside Mediation," *NYT*, May 7, 1981; Alan Riding, "New Salvador Mediation Effort Under Way,"

NYT, May 27, 1981; Warren Hoge, "Politicians in Salvador Are Under the Gun," *NYT*, May 31, 1981.

136. Richard Halloran, "U.S. to Train 1,500 Salvadoran Soldiers," *NYT*, December 16, 1981.

137. Martin Schram, "White House Revamps Top Policy Roles," *WP*, March 22, 1981; Kaiser, "White Paper on El Salvador Is Faulty," *WP*, June 9, 1981. El Salvador was by no means the only issue on which Haig clashed with the White House staff. See Szulc, "Dateline Washington: The Vicar Vanquished," *Foreign Policy* (Summer 1981).

138. Oberdorfer, "Applying Pressure in Central America," *WP*, November 23, 1983; Hedrick Smith, "Clark Works at Being an 'Honest Broker of Ideas,' " *NYT*, July 8, 1982.

139. Oberdorfer, "More U.S. Effort Yields Less Result," *WP*, March 4, 1982. For Reagan's denials, see "Remarks During a White House Briefing on the Program for Economic Recovery, February 24, 1981," *Reagan Papers, 1981*, pp. 152–53; "Excerpts from an Interview with Walter Cronkite of CBS News, March 3, 1981," pp. 191–96; "Press Conference, March 6, 1981," pp. 206–9.

140. Smith, *Power Game*, pp. 350–51.

141. U.S. House of Representatives, *Foreign Assistance Legislation for Fiscal Year 1982 (Part 1)*, p. 194. The following day, Haig conceded that Nicaragua had not actually been "seized" by the Soviets, but it didn't seem to alter his conception of the regional crisis. Szulc, "Confronting the Cuban Nemesis," *NYT*, April 5, 1981.

142. U.S. House of Representatives, *Foreign Assistance Legislation for Fiscal Year 1982 (Part 1)*, p. 163.

143. Department of State Press Guidance, March 19, 1981 (NSA El Salvador collection). Michael R. Donovan, "Chronology of Events Relating to the Death of Jean Donovan on December 2, 1981," in U.S. Senate, *Situation in El Salvador*, pp. 198–203. See also Al Kamen, "Haig Remarks May Hinder Nuns' Death Probe," *WP*, March 22, 1981.

144. Bonner, *Weakness and Deceit*, pp. 75–76.

145. Szulc, "Confronting the Cuban Nemesis," *NYT*, April 5, 1981.

146. Schram, "White House Revamps Top Policy Roles," *WP*, March 22, 1981.

147. Gwertzman, "Salvador Issue: Side Effects," *NYT*, March 14, 1981.

148. Oberdorfer, "Using El Salvador to Battle the Ghosts of Vietnam," *WP*, March 1, 1981.

149. Saul Friedman, "El Salvador No Vietnam, Reagan Says," *MH*, February 25, 1981.

150. Haig is quoted in Bernard Gwertzman, "Haig Claims Proof Outsiders Direct Salvador Rebels," *NYT*, March 3, 1982; Bushnell in U.S. House of Representatives, *Foreign Assistance and Related Programs Appropriations for 1982*, p. 259; Graves in U.S. Senate, *Situation in El Salvador*, p. 23; Reagan in "Remarks on Presenting the Medal of Honor to Master Sergeant Roy P. Benavidiz, February 24, 1981," *Reagan Papers, 1981*, pp. 155–58.

CHAPTER FIVE

1. Haig, *Caveat*, p. 109.

2. Pastor, *Condemned to Repetition*, pp. 218–19.

3. Christian, *Nicaragua*, pp. 225–26.

4. Pastor, *Condemned to Repetition*, p. 232.

5. Woodward, *VEIL*, p. 116; Pastor, *Condemned to Repetition*, pp. 232–33.

6. Haig, *Caveat*, pp. 122–23.

7. Quoted in Swedberg, "U.S. Economic Policy," p. 21.

8. Woodward, *VEIL*, p. 116.

9. U.S. Department of State, *"Revolution Beyond Our Borders,"* pp. 21–23.

10. Christopher Dickey, "Nicaragua Fears Aid Loss," *WP*, January 31, 1981.

11. U.S. Department of State, *"Revolution Beyond Our Borders,"* p. 22.

12. Alan Riding, "Nicaragua Seeking Accord in El Salvador," *NYT*, February 21, 1981. Closure of the radio station was confirmed by Acting Assistant Secretary of State Bushnell in

Judith Miller, "High Official Now Plays Down El Salvador," *NYT*, March 13, 1981. Closure of the airfield was confirmed by Pezzullo in Woodward, *VEIL*, p. 120.

13. Juan deOnis, "State Department Says Salvador Rebels Get Fewer Arms," *NYT*, February 24, 1981. State Department spokesman William Dyess confirmed this assessment the following day. Michael Getler, "U.S. Weighs Arms, Advisers to Bolster Salvador Regime," *WP*, February 25, 1981.

14. U.S. House of Representatives, *U.S. Policy Toward El Salvador*, pp. 42–43. See also administration testimony in U.S. Senate, *Situation in El Salvador*, pp. 10–11; and U.S. House of Representatives, *Foreign Assistance Legislation for Fiscal Year 1982 (Part 7)*, pp. 68, 71.

15. Pezzullo quoted in Swedberg, "U.S. Economic Policy," pp. 21–22. Woodward (*VEIL*, pp. 119–20) recounts a meeting between Pezzullo, William Casey, CIA Deputy Director for Operations John McMahon, CIA Director of Operations for Latin America Nestor Sanchez, and the CIA station chief in Nicaragua, in which all agreed that the arms flow to the Salvadoran rebels had been stopped.

16. Swedberg, "U.S. Economic Policy," p. 24.

17. Gutman, *Banana Diplomacy*, pp. 35–37; Dickey, *With the Contras*, p. 106.

18. Dickey, *With the Contras*, p. 106.

19. Swedberg, "U.S. Economic Policy," p. 26.

20. Gutman, *Banana Diplomacy*, p. 37.

21. The termination announcement did hold out the possibility that aid might be restored at some future date. "U.S. Suspends Economic Aid to Nicaragua: Department Statement, April 1, 1981," *U.S. Department of State Bulletin*, May 1981, p. 71; Edward Walsh, "U.S. Economic Aid to Nicaragua Is Suspended but May Be Resumed," *WP*, April 2, 1981.

22. Swedberg, "U.S. Economic Policy," p. 23.

23. "Nicaragua Denounces U.S. Aid Cut-Off," *LAT*, April 3, 1981; "Soviets Send Aid to Nicaragua," *MH*, April 26, 1981.

24. *Congressional Record*, April 2, 1981, pp. S3391, H1285–87.

25. Don Oberdorfer, "U.S., in Secret Dialogue, Sought Rapprochement with Nicaragua," *WP*, December 10, 1981.

26. Gutman, *Banana Diplomacy*, pp. 19–21.

27. "Latin America: Back to Square One with Reagan?," *Newsweek*, August 18, 1980; William R. Long, "Reagan Reaction from Nicaragua," *MH*, November 9, 1980. Fontaine favored "molding the National Guard in exile into an effective fighting force" (Lernoux, "Reagan Abrazo," *Nation*, November 29, 1980). Initially, Menges envisioned destabilizing the Sandinistas by funneling aid to their domestic opponents, the way the United States and its NATO allies covertly aided anti-Communist forces in Portugal in 1975. Menges, "Central America and the United States," *SAIS Review* (Summer 1981); and "Crisis in Central America," Memorandum from Constantine C. Menges to the National Security Council, June 1980 (NSA El Salvador collection).

28. Inter-Agency Groups (IGs) were composed of officials at the assistant secretary level, Senior Inter-Agency Groups were composed of the deputies to the heads of the agencies involved, and when the principals themselves gathered, they constituted the National Security Council.

29. Cannon, *Reagan*, pp. 379, 398–401.

30. Gutman, *Banana Diplomacy*, p. 72.

31. Joanne Omang, "Rebel Fund Diversion Rooted in Early Policy," *WP*, January 1, 1987.

32. A later version of these options is presented in Cunningham, "U.S. Strategic Options in Nicaragua," *Parameters* (March 1988).

33. Interview of Thomas Enders by journalist Jim Lobe, 1986.

34. Kotz and Kondracke, "How to Avoid Another Cuba," *New Republic*, June 20, 1981; Alan Riding, "Rightist Exiles Plan Invasion of Nicaragua," *NYT*, April 2, 1981.

35. Omang, "Rebel Fund Diversion Rooted in Early Policy," *WP*, January 1, 1987.

36. Kotz and Kondracke, "How to Avoid Another Cuba," *New Republic*, June 20, 1981; Omang, "Rebel Fund Diversion Rooted in Early Policy," *WP*, January 1, 1987.

37. Omang, "Rebel Fund Diversion Rooted in Early Policy," *WP*, January 1, 1987.

38. Ranelagh, *Agency*, pp. 510–655. On the congressional response to revelations of CIA misdeeds, see Johnson, *Season of Inquiry*.

39. Sec. 501(a) of the National Security Act of 1947 as amended, in U.S. House of Representatives, *Compilation of Intelligence Laws*, p. 211.

40. This requirement, which became law in 1974, is known as the Hughes-Ryan Amendment and is at Sec. 662 of the Foreign Assistance Act of 1961 as amended. The same law defines covert operations subject to the requirement as "operations in foreign countries other than activities intended solely for obtaining necessary intelligence." U.S. House of Representatives, *Compilation of Intelligence Laws*, p. 212.

41. Stein, "Reagan's Plans for Intelligence," *Nation*, July 12, 1980.

42. Ibid.; "1980 Republican Platform," *CQ Weekly Report*, July 19, 1980, p. 2051.

43. *Iran-Contra Report*, p. 32.

44. Persico, *Casey*, p. 53.

45. Ibid., pp. 72–73.

46. Ibid., pp. 41–42, 90.

47. Ibid., pp. 42, 91.

48. Cannon, *Reagan*, p. 275.

49. Persico, *Casey*, p. 381; Prados, *Keepers of the Keys*, p. 454.

50. Woodward, *VEIL*, pp. 148–49, 200.

51. Goldwater, *Goldwater*, p. 302.

52. Persico, *Casey*, p. 290.

53. Ibid., p. 225; Woodward, *VEIL*, p. 136.

54. Chardy and Tamayo, " 'New' CIA Deepens U.S. Involvement," *MH*, June 5, 1983. The program to mount guerrilla warfare against Soviet allies, which would later come to be called the Reagan Doctrine, was initially recommended by the campaign's CIA transition team, an especially right-wing group headed by William Middendorf (later appointed U.S. Ambassador to the Organization of American States) and run by Republican staffers from the Senate Intelligence Committee. Believing the CIA was full of liberals, the team also argued for a deep purge of CIA personnel, including civil service positions. The transition report argued that the CIA's record was replete with failures "of such enormity that they cannot help but suggest to any objective observer that the agency itself is compromised to an unprecedented extent and that its paralysis is attributable to causes more sinister than incompetence." Ranelagh, *Agency*, pp. 659–65; Woodward, *VEIL*, pp. 60, 67.

55. Don Oberdorfer and Patrick E. Tyler, "U.S.-Backed Nicaraguan Rebel Army Swells to 7,000 Men," *WP*, May 8, 1983; Leslie H. Gelb, "Argentina Linked to Rise in Covert U.S. Actions Against Sandinistas," *NYT*, April 8, 1983. In April 1982, the paramilitary program was expanded to include operations inside Guatemala, for which $2.5 million was allocated. Raymond Bonner, "President Approved Policy of Preventing 'Cuba-Model States,' " *NYT*, April 7, 1983. Carter's covert program in Nicaragua was confirmed by Senate Intelligence Committee chairman Barry Goldwater (*Congressional Record*, April 4, 1984, pp. 3765–66) and in *Iran-Contra Report*, p. 27.

56. The finding itself was just two paragraphs long, although the scope paper (which was not shared with Congress) was twenty pages. A redacted version of the finding is in *Iran-Contra Documents*, vol. 1, p. 8. Several committee members sent letters to the administration expressing their concern over the vagueness of the program's guidelines. Oberdorfer and Tyler, "U.S.-Backed Nicaraguan Rebel Army Swells to 7,000 Men," *WP*, May 8, 1983.

57. Chardy and Tamayo, " 'New' CIA Deepens U.S. Involvement," *MH*, June 5, 1983.

58. Affidavit of Edgar Chamorro submitted to the World Court, September 5, 1985, pp. 3–5. The legion was named for the date of Central America's independence from Spain in 1821.

59. U.S. Department of Defense, Defense Intelligence Agency, "Weekly Summary of Intelligence," July 16, 1982, quoted in Joanne Omang, "A Historical Background to the CIA's Nicaragua Manual," in *Psychological Operations in Guerrilla Warfare*, pp. 1–30.

60. Kornbluh, *Nicaragua*, p. 24; Christian, *Nicaragua*, pp. 228–30. See also Guy Gugliotta, "Anti-Sandinistas Claim Argentine Aid," *MH*, March 25, 1982.

61. Gutman, *Banana Diplomacy*, pp. 54–55; Alan Riding, "Nicaragua Reports a Pledge by Argentina to Quit Region," *NYT*, December 19, 1982. Edgar Chamorro said that Walters arranged for Argentina to expand its training of the contras, and that he played a major role in getting the disparate exile groups to unite. Affidavit of Edgar Chamorro submitted to the World Court, September 5, 1985, p. 5.

62. Robert C. Toth and Doyle McManus, "Contras and CIA: A Plan Gone Awry," *LAT*, March 3, 1985; Alfonso Chardy, "Secret Contra Pact Linked to Invasion of Falklands," *MH*, May 10, 1987.

63. Gutman, *Banana Diplomacy*, p. 43.

64. Schulz and Schulz, *The United States, Honduras, and the Crisis in Central America*, pp. 64–65; Gutman, *Banana Diplomacy*, pp. 29–33; Christopher Dickey, "Honduran Military Girds for War with Nicaragua," *WP*, May 5, 1981.

65. Robert C. Toth and Doyle McManus, "Contras and the CIA: A Plan Gone Awry," *LAT*, March 3, 1985.

66. Dickey, *With the Contras*, pp. 108–9.

67. Clarridge, *Spy for All Seasons*, pp. 89, 185; Persico, *Casey*, p. 265.

68. Dickey, *With the Contras*, pp. 107–8, 144–47; Clarridge, *Spy for All Seasons*, p. 160. See also David Ignatius and David Rogers, "Why the Covert War in Nicaragua Evolved and Hasn't Succeeded," *WSJ*, March 5, 1985; David Johnson, "Indicted CIA Official Cut a Dashing Figure in the World of Spies," *NYT*, November 27, 1991.

69. Persico, *Casey*, p. 266; Dickey, *With the Contras*, pp. 107, 144–47; Clarridge, *Spy for All Seasons*, p. 203. Stein moved on to become CIA inspector general in 1984 because of his opposition to the Nicaraguan covert operation. Rhodri Jeffreys-Jones, *CIA and American Democracy*, p. 239.

70. Affidavit of Edgar Chamorro submitted to the World Court, September 5, 1985, p. 5. See also Chamorro, "Confessions of a 'Contra,' " *New Republic*, August 5, 1985. Chamorro asserts that U.S. officials attended the Guatemala meeting, whereas Gutman (*Banana Diplomacy*, p. 56) expresses uncertainty about the CIA's role. On this meeting, see also Christian, *Nicaragua*, pp. 231–32.

71. Gutman, *Banana Diplomacy*, pp. 56–57; Dickey, *With the Contras*, p. 119; Clarridge, *Spy for All Seasons*, pp. 200–201, 209–10.

72. Gutman, *Banana Diplomacy*, pp. 47–48; Kotz and Kondracke, "How to Avoid Another Cuba," *New Republic*, June 20, 1981.

73. Two reporters uncovered most of the details of the Enders trip to Nicaragua and the subsequent diplomatic exchanges: Don Oberdorfer, "U.S., in Secret Dialogue, Sought Rapprochement with Nicaragua," *WP*, December 10, 1981; and Gutman, "Nicaragua: America's Diplomatic Charade," *Foreign Policy* (Fall 1984).

74. Ledeen, *Perilous Statecraft*, p. 21.

75. Dickey, *With the Contras*, p. 111.

76. Gutman, *Banana Diplomacy*, p. 66. The official was Colonel Lawrence Tracy, former aide to Deputy Assistant Secretary of Defense Nestor Sanchez.

77. Dickey, *With the Contras*, p. 110; Gutman, "Nicaragua: America's Diplomatic Charade," *Foreign Policy*.

78. Gutman, *Banana Diplomacy*, pp. 66–70; Gutman, "Nicaragua: America's Diplomatic Charade," *Foreign Policy*.

79. Gutman, *Banana Diplomacy*, p. 67.

80. Ibid., p. 68.

81. Oberdorfer, "U.S., in Secret Dialogue, Sought Rapprochement with Nicaragua," *WP*, December 10, 1981.

82. The account of this meeting is based upon a partial transcript submitted to the International Court of Justice by the government of Nicaragua ("Reporte de Reunión Entre Thomas Enders y El Comandante de la Revolución Daniel Ortega Saavedra, Agosto 12, 1981," author's translation) and the brief description in U.S. Department of State, *"Revolution Beyond Our Borders,"* pp. 22–23.

83. Woodward, *VEIL*, p. 165.

84. See, for example, Enders's August 31, 1981, letter to Ortega reiterating the U.S. position. Enders calls an end to Sandinista aid for the FMLN the "sine qua non of a normal relationship," and he notes that the United States is "deeply preoccupied" by Nicaragua's military buildup. He does not mention the issue of democracy. The text of the letter is in Bagley, Alvarez, and Hagedorn, *Contadora and the Central American Peace Process*, pp. 22–23. On the fight inside the U.S. administration, see Gutman, *Banana Diplomacy*, pp. 71–72; Krauss, *Inside Central America*, p. 143.

85. The text of the letter is in Bagley, Alvarez, and Hagedorn, *Contadora and the Central American Peace Process*, pp. 24–25. For a detailed discussion of the Neutrality Act and the legal status of contra paramilitary training camps in the United States, see the testimony by Congressman David Bonior in U.S. House of Representatives, *Foreign Assistance Legislation for Fiscal Year 1982 (Part 7)*, pp. 39–66.

86. Pastor, *Condemned to Repetition*, pp. 234–35. The Reagan administration employed a very loose interpretation of the Neutrality Act as it applied to the contras: they could plan and train to invade Nicaragua, but unless they actually launched an attack from U.S. territory, they were regarded as within the law. See, for example, the explanation of U.S. policy by Enders quoted in Jo Thomas, "Latin Exiles Focus on Nicaragua as They Train Urgently in Florida," *NYT*, December 23, 1981.

87. Oberdorfer, "U.S., in Secret Dialogue, Sought Rapprochement with Nicaragua," *WP*, December 10, 1981.

88. The text of the letter is in Bagley, Alvarez, and Hagedorn, *Contadora and the Central American Peace Process*, pp. 25–27.

89. Gutman, *Banana Diplomacy*, p. 73.

90. Letter from Nicaraguan Foreign Minister Miguel D'Escoto to Secretary of State Alexander Haig, September 19, 1981; and letter from Enders to D'Escoto, September 28, 1981, in Bagley, Alvarez, and Hagedorn, *Contadora and the Central American Peace Process*, pp. 27–30.

91. "Nicaragua Protests Naval Exercise," *MH*, September 20, 1981.

92. George deLama, "U.S. Embassy in Managua Feared Attack," *MH*, October 18, 1981; Dial Torgerson, "U.S. Embassy in Nicaragua Wary of Mob," *LAT*, October 24, 1981.

93. Emerson, *Secret Warriors*, p. 122. This plan was initially developed in early 1981, in case the decision to cut off economic aid provoked an attack on the embassy. Haig, *Caveat*, p. 145.

94. Gutman, *Banana Diplomacy*, p. 74.

95. Oberdorfer, "U.S., in Secret Dialogue, Sought Rapprochement with Nicaragua," *WP*, December 10, 1981; Roy Gutman and Susan Page, "A Fumbled Chance for Accord," *Newsday*, August 1, 1983. Gutman suggests that General Schweitzer and Defense Department deputy assistant secretary Nestor Sanchez, both hard-liners, were involved in pushing the tough arms provision through the inter-agency process (*Banana Diplomacy*, pp. 75–76).

96. Gutman, "Nicaragua: America's Diplomatic Charade," *Foreign Policy*.

97. The text of the Nicaraguan letter is in Bagley, Alvarez, and Hagedorn, *Contadora and the Central American Peace Process*, pp. 30–32.

98. On September 10, the Nicaraguan government declared a state of emergency banning strikes and limiting press freedom. Then in late October, three prominent opposition businessmen and a number of Communist labor leaders were arrested for criticizing the regime.

99. Arturo Cruz, "The Ambassador of Nicaragua Responds," *WP*, October 21, 1981; "State Faults Envoy's Description of U.S.-Nicaraguan Relations," *WP*, October 22, 1981.

100. The account of this meeting is based on Barbara Crossette, "Haig Asserts the Nicaraguans May Discuss Resuming Ties," *NYT*, December 3, 1981; Don Oberdorfer, "Haig Talks with Nicaraguan, Repeats 'Totalitarian' Charge," *WP*, December 3, 1981; Gutman, *Banana Diplomacy*, pp. 86–87.

101. Alan Riding, "Central Americans Anxious Over Effects of Reagan Policy," *NYT*, December 13, 1981.

102. Author's interview with senior Sandinista official from the International Relations Directorate, Washington, D.C., December 1983. According to Arturo Cruz Jr., who also served briefly in the same directorate, Fidel Castro advised the Sandinistas not to accept the Enders proposal. Cruz, *Memoirs of a Counter-Revolutionary*, p. 126.

103. Gutman, "Nicaragua: America's Diplomatic Charade," *Foreign Policy*.

CHAPTER SIX

1. Woodward, *VEIL*, p. 134; Memorandum for the Secretary [Alexander Haig] from the Deputy Secretary [William P. Clark] and Richard T. Kennedy, Undersecretary for Management, "Reinvigoration of Human Rights Policy," October 26, 1981 (NSA Nicaragua collection), excerpted in "Excerpts from State Department Memo on Human Rights," *NYT*, November 5, 1981.

2. Gutman, *Banana Diplomacy*, p. 60.

3. Author's interview with a senior State Department official working on Latin America, Washington, D.C., August 1983.

4. Gutman, *Banana Diplomacy*, pp. 60–61.

5. Broder, *Behind the Headlines*, p. 193.

6. Enders, "El Salvador: The Search for Peace," *U.S. Department of State Bulletin*, September 1981, pp. 70–73.

7. John M. Goshko, "Administration to Begin New Drive for Support of El Salvador Policy," *WP*, July 9, 1981.

8. Paul Heath Hoeffel, "The Eclipse of the Oligarchs," *New York Times Magazine*, September 6, 1981.

9. On the status of the agrarian reform, see Raymond Bonner, "Salvador Land Program Aids Few," *NYT*, August 3, 1981. On human rights, see Warren Hoge, "Soldiers Are the Villains in Salvador Horror Tales," *NYT*, June 5, 1981; Warren Hoge, "Slaughter in El Salvador: Two Hundred Lost in Border Massacre," *NYT*, June 8, 1981. On the lack of progress in the murder investigations, see John M. Goshko, "U.S. Is Pressing for Prosecution of Salvadorans," *WP*, May 9, 1981. On the army reneging on its December pledges, see Al Kamen, "Salvador Conflict Centers on Army's Role," *WP*, April 21, 1981.

10. Hedrick Smith, "The Salvador Caldron: Reagan Keeps His Distance," *NYT*, September 28, 1981.

11. The new administration's aim, according to a U.S. diplomat in San Salvador, was to "repair the alienation" that Carter's policy had created between the United States and the right. Bonner, *Weakness and Deceit*, p. 236.

12. On the right's demands for a role in the government and U.S. efforts to mediate

between them and the Christian Democrats, see Raymond Bonner, "Salvadoran Leader Says Biggest Threat Is from Rightist Businessmen," *NYT*, July 2, 1981; Raymond Bonner, "Salvadoran Right Seeks More Power," *NYT*, July 20, 1981. On the U.S. blocking a rightist coup, see Raymond Bonner, "In Salvador's Many-Sided Conflict, the U.S. Presence Is Potent," *NYT*, July 8, 1981.

13. Hinton acknowledged this trade-off in an interview with the press. Bonner, "In Salvador's Many-Sided Conflict, the U.S. Presence Is Potent," *NYT*, July 8, 1981. General Woerner also reported that the armed forces put up with the Christian Democrats only as a matter of convenience. Brigadier General Fred F. Woerner, "Report of the El Salvador Military Strategy Assistance Team (Draft)," Department of Defense, November 1981 (NSA El Salvador collection), p. 206.

14. Quoted in Loren Jenkins, "Arms Put U.S. Stamp on Salvadoran War," *WP*, May 7, 1981. See also U.S. Department of State, *Report of the Secretary of State's Panel on El Salvador*, July 1993, pp. 11–16.

15. Hinton made this point in an interview. Christopher Dickey, "Left Expected to Ignore Salvador Vote," *WP*, August 31, 1981. On U.S. hopes for civilizing the right, see also Bonner, "Salvadoran Right Seeks More Power," *NYT*, July 20, 1981.

16. In a speech to Salvadoran businessmen, Hinton explained that Washington had initially opposed any talks between the government and the left, but more recently had come to see negotiations over the conditions for holding elections as a way of dividing the civilian politicians of the FDR from the guerrillas of the FMLN. "Insurgent Troops Vie for Village," *MH*, August 19, 1981.

17. Raymond Bonner, "U.S. Stand Is Countered by Many in El Salvador," *NYT*, July 18, 1981.

18. Whittle, "House Liberals Retain Clout on Foreign Affairs Panel," *CQ Weekly Report*, February 7, 1981.

19. U.S. House of Representatives, *Foreign Assistance Legislation for Fiscal Year 1981 (Part 7)*, p. 71.

20. Economic Support Funds (ESF) were cash grants given to governments in which the United States had a security interest. Unlike economic development assistance, ESF aid was rarely project-specific. It simply went into the recipient's national treasury to alleviate the budgetary or balance of payments deficit. The congressional Arms Control and Foreign Policy Caucus made a detailed analysis of how U.S. aid to El Salvador was actually used during the first Reagan administration and concluded that most of it was either directly war-related (30 percent of total aid, mostly in the military assistance program) or indirectly war-related because it cushioned the economic impact of the war or financed the government's budget (44 percent of total aid). In this analysis, most ESF aid for El Salvador was indirectly war-related. Arms Control and Foreign Policy Caucus, *U.S. Aid to El Salvador*.

21. U.S. House of Representatives, *Foreign Assistance Legislation for Fiscal Year 1981 (Part 7)*, pp. 250–55.

22. Whittle, "Panel Compromises on Military Aid Request," *CQ Weekly Report*, May 2, 1981. Legislative vetoes may be exercised by either house of Congress (a "one-house veto") or both (a "two-house veto") depending on the particular statute. The original Solarz certification amendment provided for a two-house veto within thirty days after the president submitted his certification to Congress. In 1983, the legislative veto was ruled unconstitutional by the Supreme Court in *Immigration and Naturalization Service v. Chadha*.

23. U.S. House of Representatives, *Foreign Assistance Legislation for Fiscal Year 1981 (Part 9)*, p. 57.

24. U.S. Senate, *International Security and Development Cooperation Act of 1981*, pp. 75–76.

25. Smith, "The Salvador Caldron," *NYT*, September 28, 1981. Enders confirmed this in a

1986 interview with journalist Jim Lobe. In his autobiography, Duarte recalled that he received a "cool" reception from Republicans as well as Democrats. Duarte, *Duarte*, pp. 173–74.

26. Mary McGrory, "Our Recent Past Is Haunting Duarte's Effort to Win Friends," *WP*, September 24, 1981. Duarte admitted later that he knew the military was covering up responsibility for the killings. Duarte, *Duarte*, pp. 140–46.

27. The letter from Duarte is in *Congressional Record*, September 23, 1981, p. 21671. See also John M. Goshko, "Duarte Says Salvador Moving Toward Democracy," *WP*, September 24, 1981; Mary McGrory, "Pressure Over Missionaries' Deaths Is the Only Card Duarte Holds," *WP*, October 1, 1981.

28. *Congressional Record*, September 23, 1981, p. 21646. This was also the rationale behind the Senate Foreign Relations Committee's adoption of the certification conditions. The committee report explained that the purpose of the provision was to "strengthen Duarte's ability to undertake the basic reforms necessary to bring peace to his nation." The report is quoted in ibid., September 23, 1981, p. 21663.

29. Ibid., September 23, 1981, pp. 21642–43, 21671, 21676; September 24, 1981, p. 21910.

30. Whittle, "With Little Controversy, House Passes Authorization for Foreign Aid Programs," *CQ Weekly Report*, December 12, 1981.

31. On the FMLN's thinking, see Manwaring and Prisk, *El Salvador at War*, pp. 64–69, 132–41.

32. Steve Frazier, "El Salvador's Civil War Is Likely to Grind On; Civilian Casualties Rise," *WP*, May 7, 1981; Christopher Dickey, "New Tactics Alter Salvadoran Conflict," *WP*, August 30, 1981.

33. Loren Jenkins, "Arms Put U.S. Stamp on Salvadoran War," *WP*, May 7, 1981.

34. Bonner, *Weakness and Deceit*, p. 281; Drew Middleton, "Salvador Army's Troubles," *NYT*, March 5, 1983; Guy Gugliotta and Shirley Christian, "Salvadoran War: Both Sides Are All Punched Out," *MH*, October 16, 1981.

35. Bacevich et al., *American Military Policy in Small Wars*, pp. 24, 37; Juan Vasquez, "U.S. Analysts Expect Drawn-Out Fight for El Salvador Control," *International Herald Tribune*, March 13, 1981. The "defensive mentality" of the Salvadoran army is cited as one of its main weaknesses in the Woerner report. Woerner, "Report of the El Salvador Military Strategy Assistance Team (Draft)," pp. 131, 178–80.

36. Lydia Chavez, "The Odds in El Salvador," *New York Times Magazine*, July 24, 1983. See also Gugliotta and Christian, "Salvadoran War: Both Sides Are All Punched Out," *MH*, October 16, 1981.

37. Loren Jenkins, "Silent Stares of Death Routine in El Salvador," *WP*, May 3, 1981.

38. Richard Halloran, "From Washington and Salvador, Differing Views on Fighting Rebels," *NYT*, February 21, 1981; Vasquez, "U.S. Analysts Expect Drawn-Out Fight for El Salvador Control," *International Herald Tribune*, March 13, 1981.

39. Alma Guillermoprieto, "Salvadoran Guerrillas Renew Attacks," *WP*, June 12, 1981.

40. Dial Torgerson, "Salvadoran Troops Defend Cotton Crop from Rebels," *LAT*, November 4, 1982; Edward Cody, "Rebels Still Control Parts of El Salvador," *WP*, November 7, 1982.

41. Loren Jenkins, "Rebels Down First 'Huey' in El Salvador," *WP*, May 13, 1981. The Salvadoran military's strategy is described in detail in Woerner, "Report of the El Salvador Military Strategy Assistance Team (Draft)," p. 178.

42. Woodward, *VEIL*, pp. 134–35.

43. Christopher Dickey, "Salvadoran Guerrillas on the Offensive," *WP*, August 19, 1981; Christopher Dickey, "El Salvador Could Get Aid Boost," *WP*, August 21, 1981.

44. Gerald F. Seib, "El Salvador Gets More U.S. Helicopters; Haig Asserts Guerrilla Activity Has Risen," *WSJ*, August 26, 1981.

45. "Salvadoran Army Claims Victory; Rebel Leader Blasts U.S. Advisers," *MH*, August 21, 1981; Dickey, "New Tactics Alter Salvadoran Conflict," *WP*, August 30, 1981. Four U.S. colonels who studied the Salvadoran conflict concluded in 1981, "The guerrillas held the initiative and operated freely in many parts of the country, especially at night. They also exhibited a tactical competence that repeatedly embarrassed Salvadoran forces in the field." Bacevich et al., *American Military Policy in Small Wars*, p. 4.

46. Robert C. Toth and Doyle McManus, "Contras and the CIA: A Plan Gone Awry," *LAT*, March 3, 1985.

47. Don Oberdorfer, "More U.S. Effort Yields Less Result," *WP*, March 4, 1982.

48. "Role in Salvador Is Questioned," *NYT*, November 16, 1981; "The Pentagon vs. State on El Salvador," *Newsweek*, May 18, 1981.

49. By early September, U.S. military officers at the Southern Command headquarters in Panama were convinced that the Salvadoran army was already losing. "Salvador Junta Seeks More U.S. Aid," *MH*, September 10, 1981.

50. Woerner, "Report of the El Salvador Military Strategy Assistance Team (Draft)."

51. Philip Taubman and Raymond Bonner, "Salvador's Ability to Win Doubted in Report," *NYT*, April 22, 1983. In the declassified version of the Woerner report, most explicit criticism of the Salvadoran army is redacted.

52. Woerner, "Report of the El Salvador Military Strategy Assistance Team (Draft)," pp. 17, 45–48.

53. Ibid., pp. iv, 199–200.

54. "Salvadorans Report Rebel Fall Offensive," *LAT*, October 22, 1981; Raymond Bonner, "The Only Sure Outcome in Salvador Is More Death," *NYT*, November 15, 1981.

55. "Secretary Interviewed for *Newsweek*," *U.S. Department of State Bulletin*, December 1981, pp. 24–29.

56. Michael Getler, "Bush Urges the Sandinistas to Reject Totalitarian Rule," *WP*, November 17, 1981.

57. U.S. Department of State, "Soviet Bloc Assistance to Nicaragua and Cuba Versus U.S. Assistance to Central America," *Latin America Dispatch*, October 1987.

58. Michael Getler and Don Oberdorfer, "U.S. Nearing Decision on Nicaragua," *WP*, November 22, 1981.

59. Leslie H. Gelb, "Haig Is Said to Press for Military Options," *NYT*, November 5, 1981. The task force and its conclusions are also described in Smith, *Closest of Enemies*, pp. 244–46.

60. Some of the sanctions on the lower rungs of the escalatory ladder had already been implemented. In early September, the administration tightened visa restrictions on Cuban officials traveling to the United States, and announced plans to establish Radio Martí, a propaganda radio station modeled on Radio Free Europe and aimed at Cuba. Measures were also taken to tighten the U.S. economic embargo against Cuba, which had grown a bit lax since it had been imposed in 1963. John M. Goshko, "U.S., Accusing Castro of Lying to Populace, Plans New Radio to 'Tell the Truth' to Cuba," *WP*, September 24, 1981; Shirley Christian, "Reagan Has Few Options with Cuba," *MH*, September 20, 1981.

61. Haig is quoted in Don Oberdorfer, "Haig Says U.S. Is Studying Ways to Put Heat on Cuba," *WP*, October 30, 1981. See also Robert C. Toth, "U.S. Policy Expected to Keep Pressure on Cuba," *LAT*, November 28, 1981; Christopher Dickey, "Cubans Stress Preparations for 'Total War,'" *WP*, September 27, 1981.

62. John M. Goshko, "Haig Won't Rule Out Anti-Nicaragua Action," *WP*, November 13, 1981.

63. James McCartney, "Haig Says U.S. Might Intervene in Nicaragua," *MH*, November 13, 1981. For additional examples of Haig's rhetoric, see John M. Goshko, "Haig Voices Concern on Nicaragua," *WP*, November 15, 1981; and Michael Getler, "Haig Brings Concern About Nicaragua to Talks in Mexico," *WP*, November 24, 1981.

64. Gelb, "Haig Is Said to Press for Military Options," *NYT*, November 5, 1981; James McCartney, "Saber-Rattling by Haig a Clumsy Latin Policy," *MH*, December 8, 1981.

65. LeoGrande, *Central America and the Polls*.

66. "The President's News Conference, November 10, 1981," *Reagan Papers, 1981*, pp. 1031–38; Philip Taubman, "Latin Policy: Out of Focus," *NYT*, March 17, 1982. See also Steven R. Weisman, "Aides Fear Reagan's Peaceful Image Is in Peril," *NYT*, April 6, 1983.

67. Barbara Crossette, "Venezuela Warns U.S. on Nicaragua," *NYT*, November 18, 1981; Jackson Diehl, "U.S. Told to Stand Firm Against the Salvadoran Right," *WP*, November 20, 1981.

68. Marlise Simons, "Mexico Warns Against Attack on Nicaragua," *WP*, November 25, 1981; Alan Riding, "Haig Winds Up 'Cordial' Talks with Mexicans," *NYT*, November 25, 1981. In an effort to defuse the immediate tensions between Washington and Havana, the Mexicans also arranged a secret meeting between Haig and Cuban vice president Carlos Raphael Rodríguez while Haig was in Mexico City—the highest-level diplomatic meeting between the two countries since 1961. Haig read a litany of U.S. complaints against Cuba. Rodríguez replied that Cuba was willing to discuss whatever differences existed. Haig insisted that Washington wanted action, not words. The conversation ended inconclusively. Haig's account of the meeting is in Haig, *Caveat*, pp. 133–36. For Rodríguez's view, see the interview with him in Alfonso Chardy, "Cuba's Canny Old Communist," *MH*, December 18, 1983. See also Smith, *Closest of Enemies*, p. 253; Martin Schram, "Cuba Pressing for Full-Scale Negotiations, but White House Says No," *WP*, December 11, 1981. Wayne Smith reports that Washington spurned a Cuban diplomatic feeler in October 1981. Cuba's deputy foreign minister, Ricardo Alarcón, told Smith that Cuba favored a negotiated solution to the Salvadoran war and was prepared to cooperate in achieving it. Smith conveyed word to Washington, but received no response. Smith, *Closest of Enemies*, pp. 249–50.

69. Mary McGrory, "The Pentagon, Praise Be, Is Showing Restraint on El Salvador," *WP*, November 12, 1981. See also Bernard Gwertzman, "Reagan Aides at Odds: Differences Between Haig and Weinberger Seen as Affecting Conduct of Foreign Policy," *NYT*, February 15, 1982.

70. Frank Greve, "U.S. Policy for Nicaragua: No Force but Some Flexing," *MH*, November 26, 1981. See also James McCartney, "Saber-Rattling by Haig a Clumsy Latin Policy," *MH*, December 8, 1981.

71. Greve, "U.S. Policy for Nicaragua," *MH*, November 26, 1981.

72. Bernard Gwertzman, "Haig Warns 'Hours Are Growing Short,'" *NYT*, November 23, 1981; Stephen Kinzer, "Administration Debate Flares Over Central American Unrest," *Boston Globe*, November 22, 1981.

73. "Role in El Salvador Is Questioned," *NYT*, November 16, 1981.

74. Gutman, *Banana Diplomacy*, pp. 81–83; Woodward, *VEIL*, p. 173; Cannon, *President Reagan*, pp. 355–56; Toth and McManus, "Contras and the CIA: A Plan Gone Awry," *LAT*, March 3, 1985.

75. Gutman, *Banana Diplomacy*, pp. 80–81.

76. Testimony of Robert C. McFarlane, *Iran-Contra Hearings*, vol. 100-2, pp. 3–4.

77. The army study is described in Gutman, *Banana Diplomacy*, pp. 81–82. For a public version of it, see Robert Kennedy and Gabriel Marcella, "U.S. Security on the Southern Flank: Interests, Challenges, and Response," in Atlantic Council, *Western Interests*, pp. 187–241.

78. Philip Taubman, "Background Noise on Overt Covert CIA Plot," *NYT*, December 19, 1981.

79. Woodward, *VEIL*, p. 174.

80. Except as otherwise noted, this description of the NSC decisions is drawn from Don Oberdorfer and Patrick E. Tyler, "Reagan Backs Action Plan for Central America," *WP*, February 14, 1982. A summary of the ten points in NSDD 17 is in Joanne Omang and Don

Oberdorfer, " 'Military Shield' Changing Face of Region," *WP*, April 29, 1984. See also the redacted and declassified version of NSDD 17 itself, "National Security Decision Directive on Cuba and Central America," January 4, 1982 (NSA Nicaragua collection).

81. Enders's presentation is described in Gutman, *Banana Diplomacy*, p. 84; and Woodward, *VEIL*, p. 173.

82. Among the possible U.S. responses to be explored were putting "direct pressure" on Cuba by establishing a naval blockade that would cut off petroleum supplies (thereby bringing the Cuban economy to a halt) and airstrikes against Cuban installations—measures that President John F. Kennedy had rejected as too dangerous during the 1962 missile crisis. The language quoted is from an official report on the November 16, 1981, NSC meeting in which NSDD 17 was first discussed, as reported in Don Oberdorfer, "U.S. Plans for Possible Rise in Cuban Role in Nicaragua," *WP*, April 17, 1983; Don Oberdorfer, "Applying Pressure in Central America," *WP*, November 23, 1983. Clarridge confirms that the Cuba language in the NSDD was mostly "pandering to Haig." Clarridge, *Spy for All Seasons*, p. 198.

83. Woodward, *VEIL*, p. 173.

84. Patrick E. Tyler and Bob Woodward, "U.S. Approves Covert Plan in Nicaragua," *WP*, March 10, 1982; Don Oberdorfer and Patrick E. Tyler, "U.S.-Backed Nicaraguan Rebel Army Swells to 7,000 Men," *WP*, May 8, 1983.

85. Oberdorfer and Tyler, "U.S.-Backed Nicaraguan Rebel Army Swells to 7,000 Men," *WP*, May 8, 1983.

86. Tyler and Woodward, "U.S. Approves Covert Plan in Nicaragua," *WP*, March 10, 1982; Oberdorfer and Tyler, "U.S.-Backed Nicaraguan Rebel Army Swells to 7,000 Men," *WP*, May 8, 1983; Leslie H. Gelb, "Reagan Backing Covert Actions, Officials Assert," *NYT*, March 14, 1982.

87. Tyler and Woodward, "U.S. Approves Covert Plan in Nicaragua," *WP*, March 10, 1982.

88. "A Secret War for Nicaragua," *Newsweek*, November 8, 1982. See, for example, Haig's remarks calling the FMLN's attacks on the economy "straight terrorism . . . which reflects their failure and frustration in major force operations." Bernard Gwertzman, "Haig Says Rebels Are Terrorizing the Salvadorans," *NYT*, August 29, 1981.

89. Gelb, "Reagan Backing Covert Actions, Officials Assert," *NYT*, March 14, 1982; "CIA's Nicaragua Role: A Proposal or a Reality?," *NYT*, March 17, 1981.

90. Toth and McManus, "Contras and the CIA: A Plan Gone Awry," *LAT*, March 3, 1985.

91. Leslie H. Gelb, "Argentina Linked to Rise in Covert U.S. Actions Against Sandinistas," *NYT*, April 8, 1983; Philip Taubman, "CIA Is Making a Special Target of Latin Region," *NYT*, 4 December 1982.

92. Stephen Engelberg, "U.S. and the Nicaraguan Rebels: Six Years of Questions and Contradictions," *NYT*, May 3, 1987.

93. Dugger, *On Reagan*, pp. 357–58.

94. "CIA's Nicaragua Role: A Proposal or a Reality?," *NYT*, March 17, 1981; Gelb, "Argentina Linked to Rise in Covert U.S. Actions Against Sandinistas," *NYT*, April 8, 1983; Toth and McManus, "Contras and the CIA: A Plan Gone Awry," *LAT*, March 3, 1985.

95. Woodward, *VEIL*, pp. 173–74; Gelb, "Reagan Backing Covert Actions, Officials Assert," *NYT*, March 14, 1982. Gelb was able to obtain a copy of the finding and the CIA options paper that accompanied it.

96. Prados, *Keepers of the Keys*, p. 456.

CHAPTER SEVEN

1. Don Oberdorfer and Patrick Tyler, "Reagan Backs Action Plan for Central America," *WP*, February 14, 1982; "U.S. Ship Reported on Spy Mission off El Salvador," *LAT*, February 24, 1982; Leslie H. Gelb, "U.S. Aides See Need for Big Effort to Avert Rebel Victory in

Salvador," *NYT*, April 22, 1983; Alfonso Chardy and Juan Tamayo, "CIA Calls the Shots Against Nicaragua," *MH*, April 17, 1983.

2. Oberdorfer and Tyler, "Reagan Backs Action Plan for Central America," *WP*, February 14, 1982; Michael Getler and Don Oberdorfer, "NATO Plans Exercise in Florida Straits," *WP*, February 20, 1982.

3. "U.S. Plans Exercises in the Caribbean Basin," *MH*, March 30, 1982.

4. Raymond Bonner, "All of a Sudden, Honduras Has Gone on War Footing," *NYT*, August 15, 1982; "Pentagon Plans Airport Improvements in Honduras, Colombia for New Access," *MH*, March 4, 1982.

5. Raymond Bonner, "G.I.'s Join Hondurans in Touchy Region," *NYT*, August 5, 1982.

6. Christopher Dickey, "Rebels Damage Jets, Copters in El Salvador," *WP*, January 28, 1982.

7. William Chapman, "U.S. to Send More Aid to El Salvador," *WP*, February 2, 1982. The infantry trained at Fort Bragg became the Ramon Belloso Battalion. Wendell Rawls Jr., "Fort Benning Trains 490 Salvadorans," *NYT*, February 19, 1982.

8. Felton, "Caribbean Basin Proposal Faces Lengthy Hearings; Numerous Objections Cited," *CQ Weekly Report*, March 27, 1982; Whittle, "Senate Panel Votes Change in Caribbean Basin Aid Plan," *CQ Weekly Report*, May 22, 1982.

9. U.S. House of Representatives, *Making Supplemental Appropriations for Fiscal Year Ending September 20, 1982*, pp. 22–24; Felton, "House Appropriations Panel Delays Caribbean Initiative, Rejects Additional Arms Aid," *CQ Weekly Report*, May 29, 1982.

10. After the war, U.S. soldiers and diplomats who served in El Salvador acknowledged that advisers were frequently in combat and urged that they be eligible for combat decorations. Bradley Graham and Douglas Farah, "With Honors Bestowed, U.S. Veterans of Salvador War Lift Their Silence," *WP*, May 27, 1996.

11. Leslie H. Gelb, "U.S. Said to Plan $100 Million Rise in Salvadoran Aid," *NYT*, January 31, 1982; Raymond Bonner, "Envoys Are Increasingly Skeptical About the Fate of Salvador's Army," *NYT*, February 17, 1982.

12. Gelb, "U.S. Said to Plan $100 Million Rise in Salvadoran Aid," *NYT*, January 31, 1982.

13. The certification requirements are in Public Law 97-113, International Security and Development Cooperation Act of 1981, Sec. 728 (December 29, 1981), 95 Stat. 1519.

14. Text of the certification report is in U.S. House of Representatives, *Presidential Certification on El Salvador (Volume I)*, pp. 2–9. The embassy report, "A Statistical Framework for Understanding Violence in El Salvador," January 15, 1982, is also in the above volume, pp. 74–95.

15. Officially known as the "Violence Week in Review" cables, the grim-gram was begun by Ambassador Robert White in September 1980. It initially included not only summary statistics on the violence, but also a narrative of the most egregious incidents. Many of the early grim-grams have been declassified and are available at the National Security Archive.

16. U.S. House of Representatives, *Presidential Certification on El Salvador (Volume I)*, pp. 74–95. A U.S. embassy official acknowledged that the Salvadoran press was "inherently biased, not accurate, and not competent by U.S. standards." Americas Watch, *El Salvador's Decade of Terror*, p. 120.

17. "America's Secret Warriors," *Newsweek*, October 10, 1983; Don Oberdorfer and Patrick E. Tyler, "U.S.-Backed Nicaraguan Rebel Army Swells to 7,000 Men," *WP*, May 8, 1983; Leslie H. Gelb, "Argentina Linked to Rise in Covert U.S. Actions Against Sandinistas," *NYT*, April 8, 1983.

18. The Amnesty International report is quoted in U.S. House of Representatives, *Presidential Certification on El Salvador (Volume I)*, pp. 209–12; Neier's testimony is at pp. 143–44. The full report is American Civil Liberties Union and Americas Watch, *Report on Human Rights in El Salvador*.

19. John M. Goshko, "ACLU Criticizes El Salvador Over Human Rights Record," *WP*, January 27, 1982; "U.S. Is Said to Understate Salvador Deaths," *WP*, February 16, 1982.

20. Defense Minister García estimated that some 25,000 noncombatants had been killed in the war since 1979—a figure that closely matched the numbers from the human rights groups. John Dinges, "Compiling the Body Count," *WP*, January 27, 1982. Socorro Juridico of the Catholic Archdiocese counted 13,353 killings in 1981 (as compared to 8,062 in 1980); the Salvadoran Human Rights Commission counted 16,276 (up 20 percent over 1980); and the Jesuit-run Central American University counted 13,229 (as compared to 9,826 in 1980). Different sources sometimes report slightly different figures from each of these groups because the groups themselves revised their preliminary estimates as they acquired new information. "Salvadorans Are Accused of More Massacres," *NYT*, March 8, 1982.

21. Hedrick Smith, "Struggle in Salvador Pinches Washington's 'Vietnam Nerve,'" *NYT*, February 7, 1982.

22. U.S. House of Representatives, *Presidential Certification on El Salvador (Volume I)*, p. 25; Barbara Crossette, "U.S. Disputes Report of 926 Killed in El Salvador," *NYT*, February 2, 1982.

23. "AIM and Human Rights in El Salvador," letter from Juan E. Méndez, Americas Watch, *WP*, September 18, 1982. See also U.S. House of Representatives, *Presidential Certification on El Salvador (Volume I)*, p. 257.

24. Alma Guillermoprieto, "Salvadoran Peasants Describe Mass Killing," *WP*, January 27, 1982; [Raymond Bonner], "Massacre of Hundreds Is Reported in El Salvador," *NYT*, January 28, 1982.

25. Christopher Dickey, "Government Troops Kill 19 in Raid on Slum in San Salvador," *WP*, February 1, 1982; Raymond Bonner, "The Bodies in a Barrio," *NYT*, February 7, 1982. An account of the massacre is also included in Americas Watch and American Civil Liberties Union, *Supplement to the Report on Human Rights in El Salvador, July 20, 1982*, pp. 71–74.

26. U.S. House of Representatives, *Presidential Certification on El Salvador (Volume I)*, pp. 25–26. After the war, forensic pathologists unearthed many of the bodies at El Mozote, confirming the truth of the press reports. Danner, *Massacre at El Mozote*.

27. Christopher Dickey, "Two Detained for Murder of Nuns," *WP*, February 9, 1982; Jim Hoagland, "Duarte Stresses Elections as a Means to Control Army," *WP*, March 17, 1982.

28. Dickey, "Two Detained for Murder of Nuns," *WP*, February 9, 1982.

29. U.S. House of Representatives, *Presidential Certification on El Salvador (Volume I)*, p. 9.

30. Christopher Dickey, "Duarte's Party Hints at Talks After the Election," *WP*, March 28, 1982. The military regarded negotiations as equivalent to a guerrilla military victory. Brigadier General Fred F. Woerner, "Report of the El Salvador Military Strategy Assistance Team (Draft)," Department of Defense, November 1981 (NSA El Salvador collection), p. 65.

31. U.S. House of Representatives, *Presidential Certification on El Salvador (Volume I)*, pp. 97–110.

32. Rubén Zamora, "Saving Salvador," *NYT*, January 22, 1982.

33. U.S. House of Representatives, *Presidential Certification on El Salvador (Volume I)*, pp. 14, 20–21.

34. Barbara Crossette, "Congress Teams Are Being Sent to El Salvador," *NYT*, February 12, 1982.

35. U.S. House of Representatives, *Presidential Certification on El Salvador (Volume I)*, pp. 43, 45, 61.

36. William Chapman, "Doubling of Military Aid to El Salvador Is Sought," *WP*, February 9, 1982.

37. On the weaknesses of certification as a policy instrument, see Arnson, *Crossroads*, pp. 87–91.

38. Enders, quoted in William Chapman, "U.S. to Send More Aid to El Salvador," *WP*, February 2, 1982.

39. Steven V. Roberts, "Rift on Salvador Grows in Congress," *NYT*, February 4, 1982.

40. Ibid.; Margot Hornblower, "Rumbles of War Give Hill the Jitters," *WP*, March 8, 1982.

41. Smith, *Power Game*, p. 518.

42. Barbara Crossette, "Congressman Asserts Salvador Does Not Want U.S. Troops," *NYT*, February 20, 1982.

43. Ibid.

44. Christopher Dickey, "El Salvador Could Get Aid Boost," *WP*, August 21, 1981; Steven R. Weisman, "The Struggle for Backing on Strategy in El Salvador," *NYT*, March 14, 1982.

45. Christopher Dickey, "Left Expected to Ignore Salvador Vote," *WP*, September 31, 1981.

46. Author's interview with Rubén Zamora, Washington, D.C., March 1982. See also Terri Shaw, "New Aid to Salvador Called Wasted Effort," *WP*, March 1, 1982.

47. Raymond Bonner, "Salvador Election Bringing Fears of New Violence," *NYT*, February 16, 1982; Dickey, "El Salvador Could Get Aid Boost," *WP*, August 21, 1981; Christopher Dickey, "U.S. Envoy Expresses Doubts," *WP*, January 31, 1982.

48. Alan Riding, "Salvadoran Rebels' Aim Is to 'Defeat' Election," *NYT*, March 2, 1982; Christopher Dickey, "Salvadoran Rebel Leader Vows Major Offensive," *WP*, March 8, 1982; Steven R. Weisman, "The Struggle for Backing on Strategy in El Salvador," *NYT*, March 14, 1982.

49. "Behind ARENA's legitimate exterior lies a terrorist network led by D'Aubuisson henchmen and funded by wealthy Salvadoran expatriates residing in Guatemala and the United States," the CIA concluded. U.S. Central Intelligence Agency, "Controlling Rightwing Terrorism," February 1985 (NSA El Salvador collection). See also Pyes, *Salvadoran Rightists*, pp. 10–12.

50. Warren Hoge, " 'Pathological Killer' Candidate Gains," *NYT*, February 19, 1982.

51. "Salvador Tries the Ballot," *Newsweek*, February 22, 1982; Christopher Dickey, "Salvadoran Rightist Mounts Vigorous Election Campaign," *WP*, February 7, 1982. Green was the official color of the Christian Democratic Party.

52. Hoge, " 'Pathological Killer' Candidate Gains," *NYT*, February 19, 1982; Hugh O'Shaugnessy, "Yearning for Peace, but at a Price," *Financial Times* (London), March 30, 1982.

53. Hoge, " 'Pathological Killer' Candidate Gains," *NYT*, February 19, 1982.

54. Christopher Dickey, "Salvadoran Rightist Mounts Vigorous Election Campaign," *WP*, February 7, 1982.

55. Krauss, *Inside Central America*, pp. 104–5.

56. Hoge, " 'Pathological Killer' Candidate Gains," *NYT*, February 19, 1982; "U.S. Indicating Support for Salvadoran Centrists," *NYT*, March 19, 1982.

57. "We helped in the El Salvador election," CIA Director Casey acknowledged, though he insisted that the CIA's role was nonpartisan. Philip Taubman, "CIA Chief Tells of Attempt to Aid Salvador Vote," *NYT*, July 30, 1982. On support for the Christian Democrats, see *Congressional Record*, July 27, 1983, p. H5762; Bonner, *Weakness and Deceit*, p. 293. The comic book is described in Joanne Omang, "A Historical Background to the CIA's Nicaragua Manual," in *Psychological Operations in Guerrilla Warfare*, p. 24.

58. Warren Hoge, "Salvadorans Vote Today in Election U.S. Calls Crucial," *NYT*, March 28, 1982; Christopher Dickey, "As Vote Nears, El Salvador Is Tense, Calm," *WP*, March 27, 1982.

59. Hinton's declassified cable is quoted in Guy Gugliotta, "D'Aubuisson Kept U.S. on Its Guard," *WP*, January 4, 1994. The edited biographies are discussed in U.S. House of Representatives, *U.S. Intelligence Performance on Central America*, p. 14.

60. Christopher Dickey, "Turnout Heavy in El Salvador," *WP*, March 29, 1982. The guerrillas prevented voting in about 10 percent of the country's municipalities, but different guerrilla groups within the FMLN took different attitudes toward the election. The Armed Forces of National Resistance (FARN), for example, sought to actively disrupt them, whereas the Popular Liberation Forces (FPL) ignored them entirely. Raymond Bonner, "For the Left, Big Setback," *NYT*, March 30, 1982.

61. Former FMLN commander Miguel Castellanos described the disagreements among the guerrilla groups over how to respond to the elections. Prisk, *Comandante Speaks*, p. 39. In a poll conducted by the Christian Democrats, 12 percent of the public admitted supporting the FDR (Raymond Bonner, "Salvador Election Bringing Fears of New Violence," *NYT*, February 16, 1982). Duarte estimated that the left could have won 15–20 percent of the vote if it had been on the ballot, though some Christian Democrats estimated that the left's share might have gone as high as 30 percent (Raymond Bonner, "Duarte Is Seeking to Stay in Power, Defying the Right," *NYT*, April 2, 1982; Bonner, "Heavy Vote in El Salvador Can Be Read in Many Ways," *NYT*, April 4, 1982). Officials at the U.S. embassy estimated that the left would have received 15–25 percent (Lynda Schuster, "El Salvador Election, with Its Big Turnout, Is a Plus for Democracy," *WSJ*, March 30, 1982; Bonner, "Salvador Election Bringing Fears of New Violence," *NYT*, February 16, 1982).

62. The first occasion on which Reagan told this story was at a news conference on March 31, 1982, published in *Reagan Papers, 1982*, book 1, pp. 398–405. He was still telling it six years later.

63. The other parties on the right were Democratic Action (Acción Democrática) with two seats; the Popular Salvadoran Party (Partido Popular Salvadoreño) with one seat; and the Popular Orientation Party (Partido de Orientación Popular), which did not win any seats.

64. "Ordinary Salvadoran men and women in unprecedented numbers yesterday displayed awesome courage and civic responsibility," Secretary Haig told the press. "The Salvadoran people's stunning personal commitment to the power of the democratic vision is an unanswerable repudiation of the advocates of force and violence." "Transcript of Haig's Remarks," *NYT*, March 30, 1982.

65. Dickey, "Procounsuls," *Rolling Stone*, August 18, 1983.

66. Robert Parry, "Reagan's Central America Team Familiar with World Hot Spots," Associated Press wire story, May 26, 1981.

67. Dickey, "Proconsuls," *Rolling Stone*. When Hinton finally finished his tour in El Salvador in 1983, he was sent as ambassador to Pakistan—the staging area for another of the CIA's burgeoning secret wars. From there he went to Costa Rica to repair relations in the aftermath of the Iran-contra scandal, and then on to Panama in 1990 to reorganize the government in the wake of the U.S. invasion.

68. Sam Dillon, "Timing of Salvador Shuffle Worries U.S. Officials," *MH*, May 30, 1983.

69. Bonner, *Weakness and Deceit*, p. 253.

70. Rushworth M. Kidder, "Is El Salvador Governed by Bullets, or a Congress?," *CSM*, April 16, 1983; Christopher Dickey, "Hinton Predicts Long Salvadoran War," *WP*, April 28, 1983.

71. Loren Jenkins, "Duarte's Party Moves into Lead in Salvadoran Voting," *WP*, March 30, 1982.

72. Robert J. McCartney, "Fraud Alleged in 1982 Salvador Vote," *WP*, February 25, 1984. Both Duarte and D'Aubuisson subsequently admitted that the vote count was padded. Duarte, *Duarte*, pp. 181–82; Bonner, *Weakness and Deceit*, pp. 305–7.

73. Joanne Omang, "As Salvadoran Politics Boil, U.S. Envoy Shifts Attention," *WP*, April 24, 1982.

74. Warren Hoge, "Salvador Vote: U.S. Euphoria Wanes," *NYT*, April 3, 1982.

75. Michael Getler, "Senate Leaders Warn Salvadorans They Risk Losing U.S. Assistance," *WP*, April 21, 1982; Raymond Bonner, "U.S. Congressional Group Attends Talks by El Salvador's Politicians," *NYT*, April 9, 1982.

76. Joanne Omang, "Salvadoran Rightists, Christian Democrats to Discuss Coalition," *WP*, April 2, 1982.

77. Joanne Omang, "Salvador's Assembly Assumes Office but Deadlock Over Power Continues," *WP*, April 17, 1982.

78. Joanne Omang, "Salvadorans Pick Key Officials," *WP*, April 23, 1982; Joanne Omang, "'Administrator' Likely for Salvadoran Post," *WP*, April 26, 1982.

79. Juan O. Tamayo, "Magaña Performs Balancing Act amid Salvador Conflict," *MH*, March 23, 1984; Edward Cody, "Respect Vote, Salvadoran Army Told," *WP*, May 5, 1984.

80. Omang, "Salvadorans Pick Key Officials," *WP*, April 23, 1982. The high command's meeting with the politicians is described by a Salvadoran participant in U.S. Department of State cable, San Salvador 3481, April 24, 1982, "[Excised] Expresses Disaffection" (NSA El Salvador collection).

81. Richard J. Meislin, "Salvadoran Right Assumes Control of New Assembly," *NYT*, April 23, 1982; Joanne Omang, "Candidate Backed by Army Wins Salvadoran Presidency," *WP*, April 30, 1982; U.S. Department of State cable, San Salvador 3481, April 24, 1982, "[Excised] Expresses Disaffection" (NSA El Salvador collection).

82. Raymond Bonner, "Salvadoran Politicians Heatedly Picking New Team," *NYT*, April 13, 1982; Dickey, "Hinton Predicts Long Salvadoran War," *WP*, April 28, 1983.

83. Omang, "'Administrator' Likely for Salvadoran Post," *WP*, April 26, 1982; "Salvador Leader Installs Three Party Cabinet," *NYT*, May 6, 1982.

84. A detailed planning paper prepared for an April 1982 NSPG meeting on Central America noted that while "militarily, the situation has improved in El Salvador," nevertheless, the postelection government was beset by "a dangerous lack of political consensus." "National Security Council Document on Policy in Central America and Cuba," *NYT*, April 7, 1983.

85. U.S. Department of State cable, State 141668, May 22, 1982, "Program for Political Progress in El Salvador" (NSA El Salvador collection). For details on it, see John Dinges, "Red Cross Said Ready to Quit El Salvador," *WP*, July 3, 1982; and John Dinges, "To Boost Aid Case, U.S. Asks El Salvador to Alter Policies," *WP*, July 8, 1982.

86. Before the reform, 33.5 percent of this land was planted in export crops (sugar, coffee, and cotton), 25.3 percent was planted in food grains, and the rest (41.2 percent) was pasture or uncleared forest. Checchi and Company, *Agrarian Reform in El Salvador*, Report for the Agency for International Development under contract no. PDC-1406-I-00-1136-00, pp. 49–51, 96. The texts of the reform laws are in Simon, Stephens, and Diskin, *El Salvador Land Reform*, pp. 47–56.

87. Simon, Stephens, and Diskin, *El Salvador Land Reform*, p. 30. Some estimates of the cooperative leaders killed ranged as high as 240. Bonner, *Weakness and Deceit*, p. 200.

88. U.S. Agency for International Development (AID), *El Salvador: Agrarian Reform Organization Project Paper*, July 25, 1980, p. 25.

89. See the testimony by Roy Prosterman in U.S. House of Representatives, *Presidential Certification on El Salvador (Volume II)*, p. 146. See also Checchi and Company, *Agrarian Reform in El Salvador*, pp. 168–75; Serafino, *Post-Election Situation*, pp. 2–3.

90. Serafino, *Post-Election Situation*, pp. 2–3.

91. Al Kamen, "Beset by Violence and Delays, Land Reform Falters in El Salvador," *WP*, April 5, 1981. On U.S. opposition to Phase Two, see U.S. Department of State cable, San Salvador 01654, March 4, 1981, "USG Position on Phase II of Agrarian Reform" (NSA El Salvador collection).

92. Checchi and Company, *Agrarian Reform in El Salvador*, p. 129. In all, the three phases

of the agrarian reform potentially benefited only about two-thirds of the landless rural families in El Salvador, and less than half of the rural poor. Testimony by Roy Prosterman in U.S. House of Representatives, *Presidential Certification on El Salvador (Volume II)*, pp. 209, 145; U.S. AID Sector Strategy Paper, cited in Simon, Stephens, and Diskin, *El Salvador Land Reform*, p. 12.

93. Ambassador White admitted as much. Bonner, *Weakness and Deceit*, p. 198.

94. Memorandum from M. Chapin, "Difficulties with the Implementation of Decree 207 ('Land to the Tiller') in El Salvador's Agrarian Reform Program" [U.S. AID, August 1980]. AID's Latin American chief passed the memo along to Assistant Secretary of State William Bowdler, who called it "a serious indictment" of the program. Both the memo and Bowdler's attached note were declassified (NSA El Salvador collection). The diplomat is quoted in Bonner, *Weakness and Deceit*, p. 194. For a description of the shoving, see U.S. Department of State cables, San Salvador 02679, April 15, 1980, "Agrarian Reform Program Phase III," and San Salvador 02378, April 16, 1980, "Agrarian Reform" (NSA El Salvador collection).

95. A 1981 audit of the agrarian reform program sponsored by U.S. AID concluded that most of the beneficiaries of Decree 207 were still living below subsistence level because of the small size of their plots. Cited in Simon, Stephens, and Diskin, *El Salvador Land Reform*, pp. 19, 35. See also the testimony by Martin Diskin in U.S. House of Representatives, *Presidential Certification on El Salvador (Volume II)*, p. 209. For a defense of the program, see Prosterman, Riedinger, and Temple, "Land Reform and the El Salvador Crisis," *International Security* (Summer 1981).

96. Prosterman and Temple, "Land Reform in El Salvador," *Free Trade Union News*, June 6, 1980.

97. American Institute for Free Labor Development (AFL-CIO), *Preliminary Report*. The AID official is Mac Chapin ("A Few Comments on Land Tenure and the Course of Agrarian Reform in El Salvador," June 1980, typescript).

98. In a survey of renters, 86.8 percent said they did not have a written rental agreement. American Institute for Free Labor Development (AFL-CIO), *Preliminary Report*, p. 12.

99. Unión Comunal Salvadoreña, *El Salvador Land Reform Update*. This report is described in detail in Karen DeYoung, "Salvadoran Land Reform Imperiled, Report Says," *WP*, January 25, 1982. U.S. AID also noted that evictions were a serious problem; see the reports cited in Simon, Stephens, and Diskin, *El Salvador Land Reform*, p. 20.

100. Richard J. Meislin, "Duarte Struggles to Block Alliance by Rightist Rivals," *NYT*, April 1, 1982.

101. "El Salvador Suspends 'Land to the Tiller,' " *WP*, May 20, 1982. The text of the law is in Simon, Stephens, and Diskin, *El Salvador Land Reform*, p. 58.

102. Christopher Dickey, "Changes Slow Land Reform in El Salvador," *WP*, May 31, 1982.

103. U.S. Department of State, *El Salvador Agrarian Reform Monthly Report*, as cited in Simon, Stephens, and Diskin, *El Salvador Land Reform*, p. 34. The Salvadoran government estimated three to four thousand evictions; a pro–Christian Democratic peasant group, the Salvadoran Communal Union (UCS), estimated ten thousand. Serafino, *Post-Election Situation*, p. 12.

104. John M. Goshko and William Chapman, "Bid to Curb Land Reform in Salvador Stirs Critics," *WP*, May 21, 1982.

105. William Chapman, "Aid Request for Salvador Slashed," *WP*, May 27, 1982; John M. Goshko, "U.S. Denies New Salvadoran Law Will End Land Reform," *WP*, May 25, 1982.

106. U.S. Senate, *International Security Enhancement Act of 1982*, pp. 3, 30–31; Bernard Weinraub, "A Senate Panel Votes a Cut in Salvador Aid," *NYT*, May 27, 1982.

107. "U.S. Panel Delays Salvador Aid Session," *MH*, June 26, 1982; Christopher Dickey, "El Salvador Gives Farmers Land to Show Progress in Reforms," *WP*, June 5, 1982.

108. Raymond Bonner, "Salvador Evicts Peasants from Land," *NYT*, May 30, 1982; Ray-

mond Bonner, "Duarte Says Salvadoran Land Plans Have Been Stopped and Could 'Die,'" *NYT*, June 7, 1982.

109. Hinton is quoted in Raymond Bonner, "Salvadoran President Takes 'Cautious' Approach to Rightists," *NYT*, June 11, 1982. See also William Chapman, "U.S. Ambassador Asserts El Salvador Did Not Kill Land Reform Program," *WP*, June 8, 1982; William Chapman, "Plea to Restore Aid to Salvador Does Not Persuade Congress," *WP*, June 12, 1982; Bernard Weinraub, "Envoy Says Salvadoran Plan Is Intact," *NYT*, June 12, 1982.

110. Christopher Dickey, "El Salvador Gives Farmers Land to Show Progress in Reforms," *WP*, June 5, 1982; Torgerson, "U.S. Rekindles Land Reform in El Salvador," *LAT*, July 18, 1982.

111. Shirley Christian, "Salvadorans Battle Erosion of Land Reform," *MH*, June 13, 1982; U.S. House of Representatives, *Presidential Certification on El Salvador (Volume II)*, p. 479.

112. Lynda Schuster, "'Land Reform' Proves Costly to El Salvador, Mixed Blessing to Poor," *WSJ*, September 1, 1982.

113. U.S. House of Representatives, *Presidential Certification on El Salvador (Volume II)*, p. 88. The administration's certification report is on pp. 467–86.

114. Ibid., pp. 16, 23, 487.

115. Ibid., p. 26; Raymond Bonner, "With Pomp, Salvador Hands Over Land Titles," *NYT*, July 28, 1982. In the two months prior to the July 1982 certification, four thousand provisional titles were distributed; in the following two months, only two hundred were given out. Bernard Weinraub, "El Salvador's Land Program Seems to Run Out of Steam," *NYT*, September 25, 1982.

116. Suzanne Garment, "The El Salvador Rights Campaign Begins to Fade," *WSJ*, August 6, 1982.

117. U.S. House of Representatives, *Presidential Certification on El Salvador (Volume II)*, p. 19.

118. Raymond Bonner, "Reagan's Salvador Rights Report: The Balance Sheet," *NYT*, February 26, 1982.

119. U.S. House of Representatives, *Presidential Certification on El Salvador (Volume II)*, p. 219.

120. Ibid., p. 458.

121. LeoGrande, *Central America and the Polls*, table 2.

122. Barry Bearak, "Salvadoran Land Reform Seen as a Promise Unkept," *LAT*, May 31, 1982; Lynda Schuster, "'Land Reform' Proves Costly to El Salvador, Mixed Blessing to Poor," *WP*, September 1, 1982; Bernard Weinraub, "El Salvador's Land Program Seems to Run Out of Steam," *NYT*, September 25, 1982.

CHAPTER EIGHT

1. Lou Cannon and Les Lescaze, "Rocky Start in Handling Foreign Policy," *WP*, March 25, 1981.

2. Haig, *Caveat*, pp. 338–41; Cannon, *President Reagan*, pp. 200–204.

3. Whittle, "Shultz Confirmed as Secretary of State," *CQ Weekly Report*, July 17, 1982.

4. Cannon, *President Reagan*, p. 309; Schieffer and Gates, *Acting President*, pp. 212–13.

5. Shultz, *Turmoil and Triumph*, p. 234.

6. The transition report, dated June 26, 1982, is quoted in Alan Riding, "Mexican Officials Obtain U.S. Plan for the Region," *NYT*, August 16, 1982; John M. Goshko and Don Oberdorfer, "El Salvador Ascends the U.S. Agenda," *WP*, March 6, 1983; Don Oberdorfer, "U.S. Latin Policy Reflects a New Sense of Urgency," *WP*, August 7, 1983; and Joanne Omang and Don Oberdorfer, "'Military Shield' Changing Face of Region," *WP*, April 29, 1984.

7. Bernard Weinraub, "U.S. Warning Last Week Reflects Frustration with Salvadoran Regime," *NYT*, November 7, 1982.

8. Shirley Christian, "Justice Still Sought in Salvador Killings," *MH*, January 3, 1983.

9. Bernard Gwertzman, "Salvador Aid, American Ire," *NYT*, November 4, 1982.

10. Karen DeYoung, "Murder Case Is Test for U.S. in El Salvador," *WP*, October 10, 1982.

11. Bonner, *Weakness and Deceit*, p. 47.

12. Bernard Weinraub, "U.S. Warning Last Week Reflects Frustration with Salvadoran Regime," *NYT*, November 7, 1982.

13. Bonner, *Weakness and Deceit*, pp. 45–46.

14. U.S. Department of State cable 141668, May 22, 1982, "Program for Political Progress in El Salvador" (NSA El Salvador collection).

15. John E. Newhagen, "New Drive Bolsters Salvadoran Rebels' Bargaining Position," *WP*, October 20, 1982.

16. "Salvadorans Reject Rebel Call for Talks," *NYT*, October 28, 1982.

17. Americas Watch and American Civil Liberties Union, *Second Supplement*, pp. 30–36.

18. Richard J. Meislin, "U.S. Envoy Assails Salvador Seizures," *NYT*, October 24, 1982.

19. "Eight Missing Salvador Leftists Are in Military Jails, Army Says," *MH*, October 26, 1982. Even after the army admitted holding the eight men, Hinton continued to insist that the kidnappings had not been ordered by senior government officials. Terri Shaw, "Salvadoran Rebels Seek Talks, but Proposal Is Turned Down," *WP*, October 27, 1982.

20. Shaw, "Salvadoran Rebels Seek Talks, but Proposal Is Turned Down," *WP*, October 27, 1982; Edward Cody, "Rightist Backlash Dampens Hopes for Peace in El Salvador," *WP*, November 1, 1982.

21. Bernard Gwertzman, "Salvador Aid, American Ire," *NYT*, November 4, 1982.

22. Deane R. Hinton, "System of Justice in El Salvador," *U.S. Department of State Bulletin*, December 1982, pp. 68–69. This text is a more polite version of what Hinton actually said, which is quoted in U.S. Department of State, *Report of the Secretary of State's Panel on El Salvador*, p. 12.

23. Edward Cody, "U.S. Warns El Salvador on Rights Abuses," *WP*, October 30, 1982; Edward Cody, "Salvadoran Businessmen Assail U.S. Ambassador as Roman 'Proconsul,'" *WP*, November 3, 1982.

24. Richard J. Meislin, "El Salvador: The State of Siege Continues," *New York Times Magazine*, February 20, 1983; Marlise Simons, "U.S. Resolve Is Questioned on Salvadoran Aid Cut-Off," *NYT*, November 22, 1982.

25. Christopher Dickey, "Hinton Predicts Long Salvadoran War," *WP*, April 28, 1983.

26. Bernard Weinraub, "U.S. Envoy to Salvador Is Ordered to Stop Criticizing Rights Abuses," *NYT*, November 10, 1982; Arnson, *Crossroads*, p. 104.

27. Christopher Dickey, "Reagan Sees Progress in El Salvador," *WP*, December 4, 1982.

28. U.S. Department of State, *Report of the Secretary of State's Panel on El Salvador*, p. 55.

29. "Question and Answer Session with Reporters on the President's Trip to Latin America, December 4, 1982," *Reagan Papers, 1982*, book 2, pp. 1562–66.

30. The *tanda* system constituted the sinews that held the Salvadoran officers corps together—"a sort of West Point Protective Association gone berserk," wrote U.S. officers familiar with it. After surviving brutal hazings at the military academy which produced an attrition rate of 80 percent, classmates were closely bonded and looked out for one another for the rest of their careers. "Whatever an officer's personal failings—stupidity, cowardice in battle, or moral profligacy—his career is secure through the rank of colonel, after which he may depart, with his *tanda*, into honorable retirement," according to a report on the Pentagon's unsuccessful efforts to reform the Salvadoran military. Bacevich et al., *American Military Policy*, p. 26.

31. Karen DeYoung, "Murder Case Is Test for U.S. in El Salvador," *WP*, October 10, 1982; Marlise Simons, "Foes of Rightist Leader in El Salvador Take Steps to Weaken His Powers,"

NYT, November 20, 1982; Bernard Weinraub, "Two Leaders Vie for Power in El Salvador," *NYT*, November 7, 1982.

32. Christopher Dickey, "Rightist Leader Appears to Weaken in Salvadoran Power Struggle," *WP*, November 11, 1982; Marlise Simons, "Foes of Rightist Leader in El Salvador Take Steps to Weaken His Powers," *NYT*, November 20, 1982.

33. Bernard Weinraub, "Salvadoran Rebels Said to Extend Fighting to Quiet Parts of the Country," *NYT*, September 26, 1982.

34. Manwaring and Prisk, *El Salvador at War*, pp. 196–97, 273–74; Dial Torgerson, "Big Sweeps Net Few Fish in Salvador's War," *LAT*, October 10, 1982; Daniel Southerland, "Salvador Army, Rebels Stock Up for More War," *CSM*, December 20, 1982.

35. Lydia Chavez, "Low Morale Called a Growing Problem in Salvador Military," *NYT*, February 13, 1983.

36. Stephen Kinzer, "El Salvador: Rebels Make Gains in Their Latest Offensive," *Boston Globe*, November 14, 1982.

37. Dial Torgerson, "Salvadoran Troops Defend Cotton Crop from Rebels," *LAT*, November 4, 1982. See also Edward Cody, "Rebels Still Control Parts of El Salvador," *WP*, November 7, 1982.

38. Edward Cody, "Salvador's Rebels Make Gains," *WP*, December 28, 1982; "El Salvador Hints at Major Drive Against Rebels," *WP*, December 3, 1982.

39. Richard J. Meislin, "Salvador Colonel Resists an Order," *NYT*, January 8, 1983.

40. Edward Cody, "Key Salvadoran Officer Rebels," *WP*, January 8, 1983.

41. Christopher Dickey, "Job on the Line for Durable Salvadoran," *WP*, January 12, 1983.

42. Bernard Weinraub, "U.S. Said to Want Salvadoran Out," *NYT*, April 8, 1983; Sam Dillon, "García Quits, Averting a Mutiny in El Salvador," *MH*, April 19, 1983.

43. "New Choice in Salvador Likes Role of Mediator," *NYT*, April 19, 1983.

44. Bonner, *Weakness and Deceit*, p. 313; Christopher Dickey, "Rightists Gain in Salvadoran Shake-Up," *WP*, June 1, 1983. In 1984, Carranza acknowledged that death squads operated out of the Treasury Police. "The White Hands of Death," *Newsweek*, May 21, 1984.

45. Lydia Chavez, "Salvador Rebels Pushing Drive in Three Provinces," *NYT*, January 31, 1983; Sam Dillon, "U.S. Envoy: Battles in Salvadoran Province 'Critical,'" *MH*, January 27, 1983.

46. Lydia Chavez, "City's Fall Called Blow to Salvador," *NYT*, February 2, 1983.

47. Bernard Weinraub, "Reagan's Brain Trust: Font of Varied Ideas," *NYT*, December 1, 1980.

48. Jeane Kirkpatrick, "The Fate of America: Can Liberty Survive?," *New York Post*, October 24, 1983.

49. Kenworthy, "Our Colleague Kirkpatrick," *LASA Forum* (Winter 1984).

50. Steven R. Weisman, "Frustration Cited in Enders Removal," *NYT*, May 30, 1983.

51. Christopher Dickey, "U.S. Diplomats Criticize Political Interference," *WP*, June 12, 1983; Don Oberdorfer and Lou Cannon, "Enders' Ouster Signals Policy Turn on Salvador," *WP*, June 5, 1983.

52. "Salvadoran Troops Near Highway Reinforced," *LAT*, February 10, 1983.

53. Lou Cannon, "President Firm on El Salvador," *WP*, March 3, 1983.

54. Bernard Weinraub, "The Question About Salvador: Why a Crisis Now?," *NYT*, March 4, 1983; Goshko and Oberdorfer, "El Salvador Ascends the U.S. Agenda," *WP*, March 6, 1983.

55. Manwaring and Prisk, *El Salvador at War*, p. 233.

56. Shultz, *Turmoil and Triumph*, pp. 292–99; Weinraub, "The Question About Salvador," *NYT*, March 4, 1983; Leslie H. Gelb, "U.S. Aides See Need for Big Effort to Avert Rebel Victory in El Salvador," *NYT*, April 22, 1983.

57. "Analysts Disagree on Salvador Rebel Strength," *MH*, November 23, 1982.

58. Bernard Weinraub, "Friction Reported Over Latin Policy," *NYT*, March 10, 1982.

59. Shultz (*Turmoil and Triumph*, p. 290) confirms Enders's independence, though more critically in retrospect than at the time. See also Henry Trewhitt, "U.S. Quietly Softens Approach to Leftists in Central America," *Baltimore Sun*, October 8, 1982.

60. Menges, *Inside the National Security Council*, pp. 67, 108–9; Cannon, *President Reagan*, p. 376.

61. Oberdorfer and Cannon, "Enders' Ouster Signals Policy Turn on Salvador," *WP*, June 5, 1983.

62. John M. Goshko and Lou Cannon, "Reagan Has Enders Replaced at State Department," *WP*, May 28, 1983.

63. Bernard D. Gwertzman, "Shultz Replaced Latin Aides as Part of a Reagan Pact," *NYT*, June 5, 1983; Virginia Prewett and William Mizelle, "Salvadoran Commander Bucks No-Win U.S. Policy," *Washington Times*, January 14, 1983.

64. Alan Riding, "Reagan Trip: Aims at Issues," *NYT*, November 29, 1982. Yet even Shultz conceived of Central America in East-West terms, seeing the regional crisis as a case of "Soviet geographical expansion." Shultz, *Turmoil and Triumph*, pp. 265, 285.

65. Rowland Evans and Robert Novak, "Clark's Spring Offensive," *WP*, June 6, 1983. The phrase was Reagan's own. Reagan, *American Life*, p. 552.

66. Bernard Weinraub, "Rumor and Bickering on U.S. Salvador Policy," *NYT*, February 11, 1983.

67. Oswald Johnston, "Administration Certifies Salvador Rights Progress," *LAT*, January 22, 1983. On the anger of conservatives at this formulation, see Alfonso Chardy, "Reagan Conservatives Take Reins of Latin Policy," *MH*, March 15, 1983.

68. Oberdorfer and Cannon, "Enders' Ouster Signals Policy Turn on Salvador," *WP*, June 5, 1983; Morton Kondracke, "Enders' End," *New Republic*, June 27, 1983.

69. Shultz, *Turmoil and Triumph*, pp. 292–97; Philip Taubman, "Reagan Aides Look to a Larger Role in Latin Conflicts," *NYT*, June 3, 1983.

70. Briefing paper for a meeting of the National Security Planning Group (NSPG) in April 1992, the text of which appeared in "National Security Council Document on Policy in Central America and Cuba," *NYT*, April 7, 1983.

71. See Enders's testimony in U.S. House of Representatives, *Foreign Assistance Legislation for Fiscal Years 1984–1985 (Part 7)*, pp. 5, 28.

72. Interview with Thomas Enders by journalist Jim Lobe, 1986.

73. Weinraub, "Friction Reported Over Latin Policy," *NYT*, March 10, 1982; Seib, "U.S. Urges El Salvador to Offer Amnesty to Guerrillas, Set Up 'Peace Commission,' " *WSJ*, February 11, 1983. Concern about congressionally imposed negotiations was expressed in a briefing paper prepared for an April 1982 National Security Planning Group (NSPG) meeting. One of the action-items proposed was to "step up efforts to co-opt negotiations issue to avoid congressionally mandated negotiations, which would work against our interests." "U.S. Policy in Central America and Cuba Through FY 1984, Summary Paper," reprinted in "National Security Council Document on Policy in Central America and Cuba," *NYT*, April 7, 1983.

74. Oberdorfer and Cannon, "Enders' Ouster Signals Policy Turn on Salvador," *WP*, June 5, 1983; Gerald F. Seib, "U.S. Urges El Salvador to Offer Amnesty to Guerrillas, Set Up 'Peace Commission,' " *WSJ*, February 11, 1983.

75. Gelb, "U.S. Aides See Need for Big Effort to Avert Rebel Victory in El Salvador," *NYT*, April 22, 1983.

76. Shultz, *Turmoil and Triumph*, p. 305; Oberdorfer and Cannon, "Enders' Ouster Signals Policy Turn on Salvador," *WP*, June 5, 1983; Goshko and Oberdorfer, "El Salvador Ascends the U.S. Agenda," *WP*, March 6, 1983.

77. Ron Cordray, "Salvador Option: Coalition or the Marines," *Washington Times*, February 8, 1983. See also Alfonso Chardy, "Enders' Swan Song: Don't Count Out Talks with Leftists," *MH*, June 3, 1983.

78. See, for example, the exceptionally long editorial "Stay the Course in El Salvador!," *Washington Times*, February 14, 1983.

79. Bernard Weinraub, "Rumor and Bickering on U.S. Salvador Policy," *NYT*, February 11, 1983.

80. John M. Goshko, "Shultz Says U.S. Opposes Talks with Salvador Guerrillas," *WP*, February 17, 1983.

81. Lou Cannon, "President Firm on El Salvador," *WP*, March 3, 1983; Oberdorfer and Cannon, "Enders' Ouster Signals Policy Turn on Salvador," *WP*, June 5, 1983.

82. Shultz, *Turmoil and Triumph*, p. 304; Goshko and Oberdorfer, "El Salvador Ascends the U.S. Agenda," *WP*, March 6, 1983; Cannon, "President Firm on El Salvador," *WP*, March 3, 1983; Ledeen, *Perilous Statecraft*, p. 69.

83. "Senate Confirms Clark as Deputy Secretary of State," *CQ Weekly Report*, February 28, 1981; Schieffer and Gates, *Acting President*, pp. 44–45, 130; Cannon, *Reagan*, p. 167.

84. Cannon, *Reagan*, p. 125.

85. Lou Cannon and David Hoffman, "Reagan Adviser Clark Named to Succeed Watt," *WP*, October 14, 1983.

86. John M. Goshko, "A Quick Study," *WP*, December 14, 1981; "Senate Confirms Clark as Deputy Secretary of State," *CQ Weekly Report*, February 28, 1981.

87. Schieffer and Gates, *Acting President*, p. 111.

88. Deaver, *Behind the Scenes*, p. 129; "Why the Shultzes Can't Win," *Newsweek*, August 29, 1983.

89. Smith, *Power Game*, pp. 310, 321–22; Deaver, *Behind the Scenes*, p. 170.

90. Shultz, *Turmoil and Triumph*, pp. 304–7.

91. "Ex-Senator Stone Considered for 'Superspokesman' Post," *MH*, February 8, 1983.

92. Shultz, *Turmoil and Triumph*, pp. 302–3; Chardy, "Reagan Conservatives Take Reins of Latin Policy," *MH*, March 15, 1983; Oberdorfer and Cannon, "Enders' Ouster Signals Policy Turn on Salvador," *WP*, June 5, 1983.

93. Bernard Gwertzman, "White House Urges Salvador to Call Election This Year," *NYT*, March 3, 1983.

94. Bradlee, *Guts and Glory*, pp. 159–60. See also Alfonso Chardy, "New Envoy Learns Fast; Quiet Diplomacy a Virtue," *MH*, March 13, 1983.

95. Alfonso Chardy, "Stone Given Approval by Senate Panel," *MH*, May 25, 1983.

96. Shultz, *Turmoil and Triumph*, pp. 305–6; Oberdorfer and Cannon, "Enders' Ouster Signals Policy Turn on Salvador," *WP*, June 5, 1983; Gwertzman, "Shultz Replaced Latin Aides as Part of a Reagan Pact," *NYT*, June 5, 1983.

97. Goshko and Cannon, "Reagan Has Enders Replaced at State Department," *WP*, May 28, 1983.

98. Chardy, "Policy May Now Reflect Tough Talk," *MH*, June 5, 1983.

99. Dickey, "U.S. Diplomats Criticize Political Interference," *WP*, June 12, 1983; McNeil, *War and Peace in Central America*, pp. 170–71. McNeil subsequently returned to the State Department's Bureau of Intelligence and Research, where he would again tangle with Reagan hard-liners.

100. Warren Hoge, "Aide with a Direct Approach: Langhorne Anthony Motley," *NYT*, May 28, 1983; Jackson Diehl, "Enders' Successor: High-Profile, Controversial Envoy to Brazil," *WP*, June 11, 1983.

101. Shultz, *Turmoil and Triumph*, p. 307; Alfonso Chardy, "Ambassador to Nigeria Chosen to Replace Hinton in El Salvador," *MH*, June 3, 1983; Bernard Gwertzman, "Career Diplomat Chosen to Be Envoy to Salvador," *NYT*, June 3, 1983.

102. U.S. Department of State, *Report of the Secretary of State's Panel on El Salvador*, p. 26.

103. Walter S. Mossberg, "The Army Resists a Salvadoran Vietnam," *WSJ*, June 6, 1983.

104. Drew Middleton, "U.S. Generals Leery of Intervening in Central America," *NYT*, June 21, 1983.

105. George C. Wilson, "U.S. Military Leaders Warn Against Central America Buildup," *WP*, June 4, 1983.

106. "The President's News Conference, June 28, 1983," *Reagan Papers, 1983*, book 1, pp. 928–35.

107. Goshko and Oberdorfer, "El Salvador Ascends the U.S. Agenda," *WP*, March 6, 1983; Gelb, "U.S. Aides See Need for Big Effort to Avert Rebel Victory in El Salvador," *NYT*, April 22, 1983.

108. Manwaring and Prisk, *El Salvador at War*, pp. 169–70.

CHAPTER NINE

1. Richard J. Meislin, "Rights and Central America: For Many, Situation Is Grim," *NYT*, January 24, 1983.

2. U.S. House of Representatives, *U.S. Policy in El Salvador*; U.S. Senate, *Presidential Certification on Progress in El Salvador*. See also Arnson, *Crossroads*, pp. 119–20.

3. Author's interview with House Inter-American Affairs Subcommittee staff member, Washington, D.C., January 1983.

4. Richard J. Meislin, "El Salvador: The State of Siege Continues," *New York Times Magazine*, February 20, 1983.

5. Daniel Southerland, "The Irksome Yes-No Choice on El Salvador," *CSM*, January 27, 1983. "One of the useful things this will have accomplished is to focus the attention of Congress and the country on exactly what is happening in El Salvador," said Stephen Solarz, who drafted the original legislation. Gerald F. Seib, "New Reagan Assurances on El Salvador Heating Up Debate on U.S. Aid to Junta," *WSJ*, February 2, 1982.

6. Christopher Dickey, "El Salvador Certification Based on Mixed Record," *WP*, January 21, 1983; Julia Preston, "El Salvador: Fewer Killings but Little Gain in Human Rights," *CSM*, January 26, 1983; Linda Chavez, "Politics and Costs Hinder Land Program," *NYT*, January 22, 1983.

7. See, for example, Americas Watch, *U.S. Reporting on Human Rights in El Salvador*; Americas Watch, *Protection of the Weak and Unarmed*.

8. Lou Cannon, "President Firm on El Salvador," *WP*, March 3, 1983.

9. Patrick E. Tyler and Lou Cannon, "President to Appeal to Congress, Nation to Back Latin Policy," *WP*, April 21, 1983.

10. Leslie H. Gelb, "U.S. Aides See Need for Big Effort to Avert Rebel Victory in Salvador," *NYT*, April 22, 1983.

11. "Remarks at the Annual Washington Conference of the American Legion, February 22, 1983," *Reagan Papers, 1983*, book 1, pp. 264–67.

12. Bernard Weinraub, "Reagan Weighing More Advisers for El Salvador," *NYT*, March 1, 1983.

13. "Remarks and a Question-and-Answer Session with Members of the Commonwealth Club of California in San Francisco, March 4, 1983," *Reagan Papers, 1983*, book 1, pp. 330–38. See also Lou Cannon, "Salvadoran Defeat Would Peril U.S., Reagan Declares," *WP*, March 5, 1983.

14. Bernard Weinraub, "Weinberger Proposes Military Aid for Salvador Worth $110 Million," *NYT*, March 9, 1983.

15. "Remarks on Central America and El Salvador at the Annual Meeting of the National Association of Manufacturers, March 10, 1983," *Reagan Papers, 1983*, book 1, pp. 372–77. Reagan reiterated this assurance the following day to reporters, saying, "We have no inten-

tion of sending combat forces, nor have we ever been asked for combat forces." "Remarks and a Question-and-Answer Session with Reporters on Domestic and Foreign Policy Issues, March 11, 1983," ibid., pp. 387–90.

16. Felton, "$60 Million in Emergency Aid Due for El Salvador Military," *CQ Weekly Report*, February 26, 1983, pp. 425–26.

17. U.S. House of Representatives, *Foreign Assistance Legislation for Fiscal Years 1984–1985 (Part 7)*, p. 43; Alfonso Chardy, " 'Savage Battle' Predicted on Bid to Boost U.S. Aid to El Salvador," *MH*, March 14, 1983.

18. By tradition, the Foreign Operations Subcommittees of the House and Senate Appropriations Committees handled foreign aid reprogramming. As reprogramming became more and more frequent, however, the authorizing committees felt that their jurisdiction was being infringed. In 1981, the Senate Foreign Relations Committee was angry at being bypassed when the administration reprogrammed military aid for El Salvador. Jealous of its prerogatives, the committee insisted on an equal right to review all future reprogramming requests, and the administration acceded to prevent the committee from enacting a statutory restriction on reprogramming. Reagan's proposal to reprogram $60 million in military aid for El Salvador was the first occasion for the Foreign Relations Committee to exercise its new power. A discussion of how the Senate Foreign Relations Committee asserted its jurisdiction over reprogramming is in U.S. Senate, *El Salvador: Reprogramming*, pp. 37–42.

19. Felton, "Moderates' Foreign Policy Support Wanes," *CQ Weekly Report*, March 19, 1983; Margot Hornblower, "Frustration Builds in Congress Over El Salvador," *WP*, February 10, 1983.

20. *Congressional Record*, March 14, 1983, pp. S2742–43; Don Oberdorfer, "Inouye's Switch," *WP*, March 16, 1983.

21. U.S. Senate, *El Salvador Military and Economic Reprogramming*, pp. 39, 61–63.

22. The Senate Foreign Operations Subcommittee's conditions are detailed in a letter of March 23, 1983, to George Shultz from Chairman Robert W. Kasten and other members of the subcommittee. The text of the letter is in *Congressional Record*, March 29, 1984, p. S3365. See also "Conditions Placed on Military Aid," *CQ Weekly Report*, March 26, 1983, p. 607.

23. The Foreign Relations Committee's recommendations are set out in a letter of March 24, 1983, to George Shultz from Chairman Charles Percy and other members of the Senate Foreign Relations Committee. See also "Conditions Placed on Military Aid," *CQ Weekly Report*.

24. Margot Hornblower and John M. Goshko, "Key Hill Figures Put Conditions on Salvadoran Aid," *WP*, March 12, 1983.

25. Martin Tolchin, "Shaping a Response to the 'Mistake' in El Salvador," *NYT*, April 22, 1983.

26. Christopher Dickey, "Shell-Shocked City Welcomes U.S. Aid," *WP*, March 17, 1983.

27. Rowland Evans and Robert Novak, "Clark's Spring Offensive," *WP*, June 6, 1983.

28. Although congressional committees ordinarily have only fifteen days to block a reprogramming request, the administration agreed to allow Long's committee to take extra time to consider the $60 million request. It had little choice. "The 15 day deadline is only there if the administration insists on it," Long explained. "I told the administration, if you insist on the 15 days we'll simply say no. Naturally, they agreed to give us all the time we needed." Bernard Weinraub, "Delay Indicated in Reagan's Plan for Salvador Aid," *NYT*, April 7, 1983.

29. "Text of Shultz's Letter on El Salvador to Chairman of House Subcommittee," *NYT*, April 27, 1983; Felton, "Congress Directing Attention to Central America Policies," *CQ Weekly Report*, April 30, 1983.

30. Patrick E. Tyler, "American Special Envoy to El Salvador in Works," *WP*, April 17, 1983.

31. Alfonso Chardy, "U.S. May Appoint Envoy to Salvadoran Guerrillas," *MH*, April 24, 1983.

32. The subcommittee defeated a liberal Democratic motion to deny the entire $60 million request on a 6–6 tie vote, with Long voting with the Republicans against the motion. It then approved Long's motion to approve half the request by a vote of 7–6. Felton, "Congress Directing Attention to Central America Policies," *CQ Weekly Report*.

33. "Text of Shultz's Letter on El Salvador to Chairman of House Subcommittee," *NYT*, April 27, 1983.

34. "Fifteen U.S. Green Berets to Aid Salvadorans," *NYT*, March 14, 1981.

35. Philip Taubman, "Pentagon Seeking a Rise in Advisers in Salvador to 125," *NYT*, July 24, 1983.

36. Lydia Chavez, "G.I.'s in Salvador: Busy Behind Battle Scenes," *NYT*, May 26, 1983. After the war, there was broad acknowledgment that advisers had regularly engaged in combat. Bradley Graham and Douglas Farah, "With Honors Bestowed, U.S. Veterans of Salvador War Lift Their Silence," *WP*, May 27, 1996.

37. Dickey, "U.S. Relieves 3 of Salvadoran Duties," *WP*, February 6, 1983.

38. Alfonso Chardy, "Weinberger: Salvador Needs Arms Fast," *MH*, February 25, 1983.

39. Taubman, "Pentagon Seeking a Rise in Advisers in Salvador to 125," *NYT*, July 24, 1983; Drew Middleton, "More U.S. Advisers Asked in Salvador," *NYT*, May 29, 1983.

40. Bernard Weinraub, "Reagan Weighing More U.S. Advisers for El Salvador," *NYT*, March 1, 1983; Shultz, *Turmoil and Triumph*, p. 299. Shultz says he opposed increasing the number of advisers because "it played straight into the argument that El Salvador was the next Vietnam."

41. See, for example, Enders's testimony in U.S. House of Representatives, *Foreign Assistance Legislation for Fiscal Years 1984–1985 (Part 7)*, pp. 27–30.

42. Michael Getler, "Advisers' Role May Grow in El Salvador," *WP*, March 3, 1983; Juan M. Vasquez, "U.S. Advisers' Frustration Deepens in El Salvador," *LAT*, February 11, 1983; "U.S. Shift in El Salvador Denied," *NYT*, October 21, 1984.

43. Letter of March 23, 1983, to George Shultz from Chairman Robert W. Kasten and other members of the Senate Subcommittee on Foreign Operations.

44. Letter of May 4, 1983, to Robert W. Kasten from Powell Moore, assistant secretary of state for congressional relations.

45. "The First Casualty," *Newsweek*, June 6, 1983.

46. Alfonso Chardy, "General: More Advisers Needed in El Salvador," *MH*, August 2, 1984; Michael Getler and George C. Wilson, "U.S. Officials Urge Holding Trainers to 55 in Salvador," *WP*, August 17, 1983.

47. Lydia Chavez, "G.I.'s in Salvador: Busy Battle Scenes," *NYT*, May 26, 1983; Juan M. Vasquez, "U.S. Trainers Expand Role in El Salvador," *LAT*, August 14, 1983; Robert J. McCartney, "Americans and Combat: Rules Unclear in El Salvador," *WP*, October 23, 1984.

48. David Hoffman, "Reagan Likely to Retain Limit of 55 on Trainers," *WP*, August 18, 1983.

49. Author's interview with U.S. military adviser in San Vicente, El Salvador, August 1983.

50. Joanne Omang, "100 U.S. Advisers Going to Honduran Base," *WP*, May 28, 1983.

51. Ibid.

52. Schulz and Schulz, *The United States, Honduras, and the Crisis in Central America*, pp. 88–89.

53. Juan O. Tamayo, "Honduras Balks at Hosting Salvador Army Training," *MH*, April 12, 1983.

54. Doyle McManus, "CIA Trained Salvadorans, Officials Say," *MH*, July 9, 1987. This program was revealed in the course of the Iran-Contra investigation, although journalist Raymond Bonner had an inkling of it in 1983. Bonner, *Weakness and Deceit*, pp. 282–84.

55. Ironically, by the end of the decade, most U.S. military officers who had been involved with El Salvador agreed that the limit on advisers had been fortuitous because it prevented the Pentagon from "gringo-izing" the war. Bacevich et al., *American Military Policy in Small Wars*, p. 23.

56. U.S. House of Representatives, *Foreign Assistance Legislation for Fiscal Years 1984–85 (Part 7)*, pp. vii–xviii. The foreign aid authorization bill never became law. Work on it was incomplete when the new fiscal year began, so foreign aid programs were funded through the annual omnibus continuing resolution.

57. Ibid., pp. xi–xiv.

58. Ibid., p. 131. See also Felton, "Panel Cuts Reagan Proposals for Aid to Central America," *CQ Weekly Report*, April 16, 1983.

59. The vote was 19–16 against the $50 million, with five conservative Democrats voting for the aid. The full committee did not take up the FY 1984–85 foreign aid bill until later. Felton, "Reagan Plans Hill Offensive to Win Central America Aid," *CQ Weekly Report*, April 23, 1983.

60. Lou Cannon and Patrick E. Tyler, "Reagan's Speech Tonight on Central America Entails High Risks," *WP*, April 27, 1983.

61. Ibid.

62. Patrick E. Tyler and Lou Cannon, "President to Appeal to Congress, Nation to Back Latin Policy," *WP*, April 21, 1983; Cannon and Tyler, "Reagan's Speech Tonight on Central America Entails High Risks," *WP*, April 27, 1983.

63. Gerald F. Seib, "Central America Leftists Called Threat by Reagan," *WSJ*, April 28, 1983; Cannon and Tyler, "Reagan's Speech Tonight on Central America Entails High Risks," *WP*, April 27, 1983.

64. "Address Before a Joint Session of the Congress on Central America, April 27, 1983," *Reagan Papers, 1983*, book 1, pp. 601–7.

65. Patrick E. Tyler, "Support, Skepticism: Democrats Fault Focus on Military," *WP*, April 28, 1983.

66. Felton, "Reagan Takes Case to Public: Congress Directing Attention to Central American Policies," *CQ Weekly Report*, April 30, 1983; Patrick E. Tyler, "Support, Skepticism: Democrats Fault Focus on Military," *WP*, April 28, 1983.

67. Weinraub, "Mrs. Kirkpatrick Calls Dodd Speech 'Demagogic,'" *NYT*, May 1, 1983.

68. Jeane J. Kirkpatrick, "Communism in Central America," *WP*, April 17, 1983. Actually, it was Lenin who asserted that Communist revolutions were irreversible. The Brezhnev doctrine, articulated at the time of the 1968 Soviet invasion of Czechoslovakia, held that the Warsaw Pact had the right to intervene in any member country's internal affairs if the security of the entire socialist camp was endangered by internal developments. This doctrine of limited sovereignty was not unlike the Roosevelt Corollary to the Monroe Doctrine.

69. "Congressmen Attacked Over El Salvador Stand," *NYT*, May 5, 1983; Mary McGrory, "Echoes of Red-Baiting," *WP*, June 12, 1983. For a sample of congressional reaction, see *Congressional Record*, May 5, 1983, pp. H2673, H2686.

70. "Clark Blasts Backers of 'Power-Sharing,'" *MH*, May 14, 1983.

71. U.S. Department of State and Department of Defense, *Background Paper: Central America*, pp. 15–16. The document reads: "Beginning in early 1980, the Soviet bloc and Cuba complemented their subversive activities in Central America by launching a worldwide propaganda and disinformation campaign focused on U.S. policy toward El Salvador. . . . Meanwhile, the FDR-FMLN, with Soviet and Cuban support, has directed the establishment of 'Solidarity Committees' throughout Europe, Canada, Australia, and New Zealand. These serve as propaganda outlets and conduits for contributions to the guerrillas. These committees have also helped plan, in conjunction with Communist parties and local leftist groups, many of the demonstrations that have taken place in support of the Salvadoran guerrillas."

72. "Remarks Prepared for Delivery by the Honorable Fred C. Iklé, Under-Secretary of Defense for Policy . . . September 12, 1983," News Release, Office of the Assistant Secretary of Defense (Public Affairs), No. 450-83. Iklé's speech was cleared by Clark at the White House. Philip Taubman, "Pentagon Gets Tough on Latin Policy," *NYT*, September 12, 1983.

73. Philip Taubman, "Pentagon Gets Tough on Latin Policy," *NYT*, September 12, 1983.

74. David S. Broder, "New Potential for Dividing Democrats," *WP*, May 8, 1983.

75. Alfonso Chardy, "Reagan Is Stemming Erosion of Latin Policies in Congress," *MH*, May 15, 1983.

76. Felton, "Compromise Featured in El Salvador Debate," *CQ Weekly Report*, May 14, 1983.

77. U.S. House of Representatives, *International Security and Development Cooperation Act of 1983*, pp. 11, 32–36.

78. Martin Tolchin, "House Unit Ties Aid to Salvador to Start of Talks," *NYT*, May 12, 1983; Ellen Hume, "Capitol Hill Mood Shifts on Latin Aid," *LAT*, May 16, 1983.

79. U.S. Senate, *International Security and Development Cooperation Act of 1983*, pp. 17–19, 82–85; Felton, "Compromise Featured in El Salvador Debate," *CQ Weekly Report*, May 14, 1983.

80. The compromises that led to the final provisions of the continuing resolution (P.L. 98-151) are described in U.S. House of Representatives, *Congress and Foreign Policy 1983*, pp. 40–43.

81. LeoGrande, *Central America and the Polls*, pp. 34–37.

82. The data in this section are drawn from LeoGrande, *Central America and the Polls*. Wirthlin's results are described in Lou Cannon and Patrick E. Tyler, "Reagan's Speech Tonight on Central America Entails High Risks," *WP*, April 27, 1983.

83. LeoGrande, *Central America and the Polls*, pp. 29–34.

84. Margot Hornblower, "Panel Votes Most of El Salvador Aid," *WP*, May 12, 1983.

CHAPTER TEN

1. Testimony of George P. Shultz, *Iran-Contra Hearings*, vol. 100-9, p. 454.

2. Smith, *Power Game*, p. 602; Lou Cannon and David Hoffman, "Reagan Tugged by Rival Strategies," *WP*, April 17, 1983; Michael Getler, "Shultz Said Displeased by Clark Trip," *WP*, October 7, 1983.

3. Steven R. Weisman, "The McFarlane Choice," *NYT*, October 18, 1983.

4. Cannon and Hoffman, "Reagan Tugged by Rival Strategists," *WP*, April 17, 1983.

5. Steven R. Weisman, "Aides Fear Reagan's Peaceful Image Is in Peril," *NYT*, April 6, 1983.

6. Eleanor Clift, "Nancy with the Centrist Face," *WP*, January 8, 1995.

7. Michael Getler, "The Knives Have Come Out for Shultz, Clark on Policy," *WP*, April 24, 1983.

8. Schieffer and Gates, *Acting President*, pp. 159–60; Cannon, *President Reagan*, p. 382.

9. Memorandum to the President from George P. Shultz, "Managing Our Central America Strategy," May 25, 1983, in *Iran-Contra Hearings*, vol. 100-9, pp. 454–59; Memorandum to Shultz from Ronald Reagan, "Managing Our Central America Strategy," undated, in *Iran-Contra Hearings*, vol. 100-9, pp. 462–64; Shultz, *Turmoil and Triumph*, p. 307.

10. Don Oberdorfer, "Shultz's Roar on Policy-Making Got Results," *WP*, October 23, 1983; Shultz testimony, *Iran-Contra Hearings*, vol. 100-9, p. 59; Shultz, *Turmoil and Triumph*, pp. 312–13. In his memoir, Shultz places the date of this meeting in July, but his contemporary notes referred to during his Iran-Contra testimony put it in August.

11. Oberdorfer, "Shultz's Roar on Policy-Making Got Results," *WP*, October 23, 1983.

12. Schieffer and Gates, *Acting President*, p. 161; McFarlane and Smardz, *Special Trust*, pp. 254–59; Lou Cannon, "Overtaxed, Clark Sought Interior Post," *WP*, October 15, 1983.

13. Steven R. Weisman, "Clark's Move to Interior Makes External Waves," *NYT*, October 16, 1983.

14. David Hoffman, "McFarlane's Influence Is Questioned," *WP*, October 16, 1983.

15. Reagan, *American Life*, p. 448; Steven R. Weisman, "Reagan and Aides Said to Dispute Clark's Successor," *NYT*, October 15, 1983; Lou Cannon, "Reagan Appoints McFarlane Adviser on U.S. Security," *WP*, October 18, 1983.

16. Schieffer and Gates, *Acting President*, p. 161. See also Smith, *Power Game*, pp. 323–24; Cannon, *President Reagan*, pp. 428–33.

17. Michael Getler, "McFarlane Expected to Be Appointed National Security Adviser," *WP*, October 14, 1983; testimony of Robert C. McFarlane, *Iran-Contra Hearings*, vol. 100-2, pp. 11–12.

18. Mayer and McManus, *Landslide*, p. 57.

19. Schieffer and Gates, *Acting President*, pp. 221, 240.

20. Goshko, "Kirkpatrick Thought Clark Should Stay," *WP*, October 23, 1983.

21. John M. Goshko and Lou Cannon, "Kirkpatrick to Quit Government," *WP*, January 31, 1985. In January 1985, as in October 1983, Kirkpatrick lobbied for a senior post in an unusually public fashion. Leslie H. Gelb, "Kirkpatrick: In-Front-of-Scene Talks," *NYT*, January 26, 1983.

22. Margot Hornblower, "Frustration Builds in Congress Over El Salvador," *WP*, February 10, 1983.

23. Philip Taubman, "U.S. Officials Cite Cuba-Backed Drive in Urging Latin Aid," *NYT*, April 24, 1984.

24. Christopher Dickey and Robert J. McCartney, "Little Hope Seen for Salvadoran Peace," *WP*, September 4, 1983; Fabiola Santiago, "Salvador Envoy Says Peace Talks Lack Substance," *MH*, September 10, 1983.

25. Bonner, *Weakness and Deceit*, pp. 246–47. Colby himself commented on the similarity between the National Plan and CORDS in William E. Colby, "Chicken Little Is Back," *WP*, March 20, 1983. For a description of CORDS, see Valentine, *Phoenix Program*, pp. 116–87.

26. "A Plan to Win in El Salvador," *Newsweek*, March 21, 1983. For an overview of the National Plan, see Manwaring and Prisk, *El Salvador at War*, pp. 222–29.

27. Author's interview with U.S. military adviser, San Vicente, El Salvador, August 1983. See also Lydia Chavez, "Salvadorans Plan Two-Track Campaign to Defeat Rebels," *NYT*, March 17, 1983.

28. Author's interview with Colonel Rinaldo Golcher, commander of Operation Well-Being, San Vicente, August 1983. See also Lydia Chavez, "U.S. Advisers Say Salvadoran Military Is Regaining Its Momentum," *NYT*, July 16, 1983.

29. Michael Getler, "Salvadoran Troops Have Seized the Initiative, Reagan Is Told," *WP*, August 27, 1983.

30. Christopher Dickey, "El Salvador Said to Gain on Rebels," *WP*, July 18, 1983.

31. Stephen Kinzer, "Salvadoran Guerrilla Chief Says Rebels Changed Plans," *NYT*, August 27, 1983; Edward Cody, "Rebels Return to the Offensive in El Salvador," *WP*, October 7, 1983.

32. Lydia Chavez, "Salvador Rebels Make Gains and U.S. Advisers Are Glum," *NYT*, November 4, 1983.

33. Doyle McManus, "Stubborn Congress Balks at Central American Policy," *LAT*, March 11, 1984.

34. Chris Hedges, "Rebels Pull Strings on US Aid Program in El Salvador Province," *CSM*, December 9, 1983.

35. Lydia Chavez, "U.S. Pilot Program in Salvadoran Area in Danger of Failing," *NYT*, December 18, 1983.

36. Hedges, "Rebels Pull Strings on US Aid Program in El Salvador Province," *CSM*,

December 9, 1983; Robert McCartney, "Salvadoran Rebel Area Gets U.S. Aid," *WP*, December 18, 1983.

37. "Salvadoran Rebels Cut Vital Span," *WP*, January 2, 1984.

38. Chris Hedges, "Salvador Army Morale Sinks After Losses," *CSM*, January 9, 1984.

39. U.S. Department of State briefing paper, "El Salvador: Death Squads," January 23, 1984; U.S. Department of State cable, San Salvador 08447, September 16, 1983, "[excised] Renewed Threat from the Extreme Right" (NSA El Salvador collection).

40. Sam Dillon, "Salvadoran Peasants Protest Opponents of Land Reform," *MH*, September 28, 1983.

41. Edward Cody, "Death Squads Step Up Killings in El Salvador," *WP*, October 3, 1983.

42. "The Death Squads Take Aim," *Newsweek*, October 17, 1983; Sam Dillon, "U.S. Official: Communist Rebels Aiding Salvadoran Death Squads," *MH*, November 9, 1983.

43. Robert J. McCartney, "U.S. Praises Salvadoran Vote," *WP*, December 15, 1983.

44. Sam Dillon, "El Salvador Gives In to U.S. Demands," *MH*, December 19, 1983.

45. "The Death Squads Take Aim," *Newsweek*, October 17, 1983; "Another Warning to the Death Squads," *Newsweek*, December 5, 1983.

46. The document relating to this meeting was leaked and described in detail in Philip Taubman, "U.S. Said to Weigh 40 Percent Increase in Military Funds for Latin Allies," *NYT*, July 17, 1983. See also Kornbluh, *Nicaragua*, p. 159.

47. Sam Dillon, "U.S. Envoy Blasts 'Death Squads,' " *MH*, November 28, 1983.

48. Christopher Dickey, "Behind the Death Squads," *New Republic*, December 26, 1983.

49. Dillon, "U.S. Official: Communist Rebels Aiding Salvadoran Death Squads," *MH*, November 9, 1983.

50. From a conversation with a congressional delegation, quoted in U.S. House of Representatives, *U.S. Policy in Central America*, pp. 40–41.

51. On U.S. officials naming death squad members, see, for example, Lydia Chavez, "U.S. Presses Salvador to Act on Men Tied to Death Squads," *NYT*, November 5, 1983. Regarding the suspect in the Schaufelberger case, see Juan deOnis, "U.S. Thinks Salvador Rebel Is Not Navy Officer's Killer," *LAT*, November 12, 1983.

52. The text of Pickering's speech is in U.S. House of Representatives, *Situation in El Salvador*, pp. 248–57. See also "Another Warning to the Death Squads," *Newsweek*, December 5, 1983.

53. "President Opposes El Salvador Certification Legislation: White House Statement," *U.S. Department of State Bulletin*, January 1984, p. 88. In August 1984, a U.S. Circuit Court of Appeals agreed with Congress, ruling that the bill could not properly be pocket-vetoed because Congress was not out of session. Thus it had become law when President Reagan failed to sign it. The administration chose not to appeal the decision to the Supreme Court. By the time the ruling was handed down, however, fiscal year 1984 was nearly over, so the certification requirement was moot. Robert Pear, "Court Rejects Reagan Veto on Salvador," *NYT*, August 30, 1984.

54. As a result of the July 8, 1983, NSC meeting, Reagan adopted a legislative plan that called for an effort to "relieve current legislation constraints regarding 'certification.' " Memorandum to George P. Shultz, Caspar W. Weinberger, William J. Casey, and General John W. Vessey Jr. [chairman of the Joint Chiefs of Staff] from Ronald Reagan, "Central America," July 12, 1983, in *Iran-Contra Chronology*, pp. 145–51.

55. Joanne Omang, "Shultz Waits for Action on Amnesty," *WP*, December 6, 1983; "Don't Press El Salvador on Rights, Reagan Urged," *MH*, November 30, 1983.

56. Robert J. McCartney, "Salvadorans Confused by U.S. Signals," *WP*, December 2, 1983.

57. Felton, "President's El Salvador Veto Sparks Uproar Among Critics," *CQ Weekly Report*, December 3, 1983.

58. "Question-and-Answer Session with High School Students on Domestic and Foreign Policy Issues, December 2, 1983," *Reagan Papers, 1983*, book 2, pp. 1642–47.

59. "Salvadorans Confused by U.S. Signals," *WP*, December 2, 1983.

60. "U.S. Bids Salvador Expel the Leaders of Murder Squads," *NYT*, December 15, 1983.

61. The text of the toast, along with Bush's other public statements in El Salvador, are in U.S. House of Representatives, *Foreign Assistance Legislation for Fiscal Year 1985 (Part 6)*, pp. 450–54. His private meetings are described below.

62. A full account of Bush's meetings, including his talking points, are in U.S. Department of State cable, San Salvador 11567, December 14, 1983, "Vice-President Bush's Meetings with Salvadoran Officials" (NSA El Salvador collection). See also Alfonso Chardy, "U.S., Salvador Cut a Deal: Aid Rises If Abuses Drop," *MH*, January 6, 1984; "U.S. Bids Salvador Expel the Leaders of Murder Squads," *NYT*, December 15, 1983.

63. Robert J. McCartney, "Death Squad Suspects to Stay in Country," *WP*, January 10, 1984.

64. Robert J. McCartney, "U.S. Lauds Drive to Halt Death Squads," *WP*, January 8, 1984.

65. James LeMoyne, "A Salvadoran Police Chief Vows to End Rights Abuses," *NYT*, July 1, 1984.

66. The two were Major José Ricardo Pozo, head of intelligence for the Treasury Police, and Lieutenant Colonel Aristedes Alfonso Marquez, head of intelligence for the National Police. Lydia Chavez, "U.S. Presses Salvador to Act on Men Tied to Death Squad," *NYT*, November 5, 1983.

67. Robert J. McCartney, "El Salvador Transfers Death Squad Suspects," *WP*, November 30, 1983; Robert J. McCartney, "Death Squads Suspects to Stay in Country," *WP*, January 10, 1984.

68. U.S. House of Representatives, *Foreign Assistance Legislation for Fiscal Year 1985 (Part 6)*, pp. 104–5.

69. Chris Hedges, "Brief Lull in Salvador Death Squad Killings," *CSM*, April 5, 1984; Lydia Chavez, "Salvador Extending Land Purchase Program," *NYT*, December 28, 1983.

70. U.S. CIA, Directorate of Intelligence, "El Salvador: Dealing with Death Squads," January 20, 1984 (NSA El Salvador collection).

71. McCartney, "U.S. Lauds Drive to Halt Death Squads," *WP*, January 8, 1984.

72. Quoted in U.S. House of Representatives, *U.S. Intelligence Performance on Central America*, p. 11.

73. U.S. House of Representatives, *U.S. Intelligence Performance on Central America*, p. 12.

74. U.S. Senate, *Recent Political Violence in El Salvador*, pp. 11, 15. The House Intelligence Committee conducted a less detailed investigation, the results of which are summarized in Robert Parry, "House Panel Absolves CIA," *WP*, January 14, 1985. The 1985 National Intelligence Estimate acknowledged that all the security forces and various regular military units had their own death squads, and that they were responsible for most political murders. U.S. CIA, Directorate of Intelligence, National Intelligence Estimate, "El Salvador: Controlling Rightwing Terrorism," February 1985 (NSA El Salvador collection).

75. Author's interview with Colonel John D. Waghelstein, commander of the U.S. Military Group, San Salvador, January 1983.

76. On the role of expatriates in Miami, see U.S. Senate, *Recent Political Violence in El Salvador*, p. 15. The CIA identified death squads operating out of the National Guard, National Police, and D'Aubuisson's office at the National Assembly. CIA and State Department, "Briefing Paper on Right-Wing Terrorism in El Salvador," October 27, 1983 (NSA El Salvador collection).

77. U.S. Senate, *Recent Political Violence in El Salvador*, p. 9.

78. Ibid., p. 5.

79. Douglas Farah, "Salvadoran Death Squads Called Back Burner Issue for U.S.," *WP*, October 6, 1988.

80. Ibid. The Senate Intelligence Committee concluded "that in nearly all instances, contacts between U.S. agencies and Salvadoran organizations or individuals suspected of being involved in political violence have been managed satisfactorily. The Committee, however, called to the attention of the Executive Branch some instances of concern in the handling of particular relationships." U.S. Senate, *Recent Political Violence in El Salvador*, p. 6.

81. Bonner, *Weakness and Deceit*, p. 366.

82. Stephen Kinzer, "Death Squads in El Salvador: Ex-Aide Accuses Colleagues," *NYT*, March 3, 1984. Carranza's role is also discussed in Pyes, *Salvadoran Rightists*, pp. 1–5.

83. Philip Taubman, "Top Salvador Police Official Said to Be a CIA Informant," *NYT*, March 22, 1984. See also Alfonso Chardy, "Probes: Death Squads Not Linked with CIA," *MH*, June 3, 1984.

84. *In re Yamashita*, 327 U.S. 1, 66 S.Ct. 340, 90 L.Ed. 499 (1946). Yamashita was charged with having "failed to discharge his duty as commander to control the operations of the members of his command permitting them to commit brutal atrocities . . . and he thereby violated the laws of war."

85. "Warning the Death Squads," *Newsweek*, November 21, 1983.

86. James LeMoyne, "A Salvadoran Police Chief Vows to End Rights Abuses," *NYT*, July 1, 1984; Anderson and Anderson, *Inside the League*, p. 203.

87. According to Socorro Juridico, the Legal Aid office of the archbishop's diocese in San Salvador, the number of noncombatant civilians killed by the army, security forces, and paramilitary deaths squads were 8,062 in 1980; 12,501 in 1981; 5,389 in 1982; and 5,142 in 1983. Reported in *El Salvador: One Year of Repression*, p. 30; Americas Watch and the American Civil Liberties Union, *Report on Human Rights in El Salvador*, p. 279; Americas Watch and the American Civil Liberties Union, *Second Supplement*, p. 6; U.S. House of Representatives, *Situation in El Salvador*, p. 128.

88. "The institution seems committed to the agrarian and banking reforms as a necessary evil to avoid cataclysmic change to society," General Woerner wrote in late 1981. Brigadier General Fred F. Woerner, "Report of the El Salvador Military Strategy Assistance Team (Draft)," Department of Defense, November 1981 (NSA El Salvador collection), p. 206.

89. Chris Hedges, "Salvadoran Who Was Tortured Tells of Military–Death Squad Links," *CSM*, January 25, 1984.

CHAPTER ELEVEN

1. Lou Cannon and David Hoffman, "Choice of Kissinger Is Seen as a 'High-Visibility' Move," *WP*, July 20, 1983.

2. Steven R. Weisman, "Reagan Chooses Kissinger to Run New Latin Team," *NYT*, July 19, 1983. McFarlane confirms that the MX Commission was the model. McFarlane and Smardz, *Special Trust*, p. 281.

3. Lou Cannon, "Reagan Rewrites How He Viewed Kissinger," *WP*, July 22, 1983.

4. Bernard Gwertzman, "Kissinger on Central America: A Call for U.S. Firmness," *NYT*, July 19, 1983.

5. Jay Ducassi, "Choice for Latin Panel Draws Fire," *MH*, August 2, 1983; Rowland Evans and Robert Novak, "One Latin Panelist Chosen by Mistake," *WP*, August 22, 1983.

6. Quoted in Bodnar, "Kissinger Commission," p. 105.

7. Ibid., pp. 113–14.

8. Robert S. Greenberger, "A Panel's Politics: Managua Visit Pushed Kissinger Commission Toward a Harder Line," *WSJ*, January 12, 1984.

9. Doyle McManus, "Issues of Peace, War Dominate Latin Tour," *LAT*, October 16, 1983.

10. "Kissinger Report 'Magnificent,' Reagan Says," *MH*, January 14, 1984; Margaret Shapiro, "Hill Democrats Hit Latin Report," *WP*, January 12, 1984.

11. *Harris Poll Report*, January 19, 1984.

12. Felton, "Reagan Unveils Central America Aid Package," *CQ Weekly Report*, February 4, 1984.

13. Felton, "Reagan Seeks Major Program of Help for Central America," *CQ Weekly Report*, January 21, 1984; U.S. House of Representatives, *Foreign Assistance Legislation for Fiscal Year 1985 (Part 6)*, p. 25.

14. U.S. House of Representatives, *Congress and Foreign Policy 1983*, pp. 30–40.

15. U.S. House of Representatives, *Situation in El Salvador*, p. 15.

16. Doyle McManus, "U.S. to Chart Options for a Crisis in El Salvador," *LAT*, July 13, 1984.

17. "Central America: Promoting Democracy, Economic Improvement, and Peace," National Security Decision Directive 124, February 7, 1984 (NSA Nicaragua collection). See also Alfonso Chardy, "Reagan's Credibility and Congressional Opposition," *MH*, July 1, 1983.

18. Others in the administration overruled Poindexter on the grounds that there was no need to provoke a fight with Congress while there was still a chance that Congress might approve at least some of the aid Reagan had requested. Joanne Omang and Margaret Shapiro, "Debate on U.S. Latin Policies Opens in Senate," *WP*, March 29, 1984.

19. Felton, "Panel Deals Blow to Central America Package," *CQ Weekly Report*, March 3, 1984.

20. Felton, "Reagan Tactic on Central America Funds Fails," *CQ Weekly Report*, March 10, 1984; Rothman, "Senate Panel Hands Reagan Latin American Aid Victory," *CQ Weekly Report*, March 17, 1984.

21. In the Senate, bills are normally taken up by unanimous consent, which means that any senator can block a bill from coming to the Senate floor by simply objecting to the consideration of it. Although Senate rules allow a bill to be taken up if a simple majority approves a motion to consider it, such a motion is debatable and therefore can be filibustered. Consequently, if a large minority of the Senate wishes to block a bill's consideration, as the Democrats did in this case, it is extremely difficult to get the bill to the floor. Rothman, "Pact Calls for Funding Cut in El Salvador Aid Package," *CQ Weekly Report*, March 24, 1984.

22. Joanne Omang and Margaret Shapiro, "White House Reaches Deal on Latin Aid," *WP*, March 23, 1984.

23. John M. Goshko and Margot Hornblower, "Senate Leaders Predict Cut in President's Salvador Aid Request," *WP*, March 19, 1983.

24. *Congressional Record*, April 2, 1984, pp. S3587–88.

25. The corruption issue flared briefly when an auditing firm contracted by the State Department, Arthur Young & Company, found that Salvadoran central bank controls over hard currency were so lax that businessmen were able to make huge profits off the exchange rate by false invoicing. See the discussion in ibid., February 29, 1984, p. S1921.

26. Ibid., March 28, 1984, pp. S3325–26.

27. Ibid., March 29, 1984, pp. S3357–59, S3364.

28. Martin Tolchin, "House Agrees to Meet Senate on Central America Aid," *NYT*, May 10, 1984. After José Napoleón Duarte won the first-round election, however, the House leadership's opposition softened somewhat. As Congress prepared to recess for Easter in April 1984, the leadership agreed to approve $32.5 million in additional military aid—half of what the Senate had allocated in the urgent supplemental—since that was the likely outcome from the conference committee anyway.

29. The text of the draft bill passed by Barnes's subcommittee and reported to the full committee is in U.S. House of Representatives, *Foreign Assistance Legislation for Fiscal Year 1985 (Part 6)*, pp. xii–xxiii.

30. Felton, "Reagan Tactic on Central America Funds Fails," *CQ Weekly Report*, March 10, 1984.

31. Philip Taubman, "U.S. Aides Fear Salvador Setback, Even a Coup, in Election's Wake," *NYT*, February 2, 1984.

32. James Brooke, "Clear Choice Will Face Salvador Voters," *MH*, January 22, 1984; Philip Taubman, "C.I.A. Said to Have Given Money to 2 Salvador Parties," *NYT*, May 12, 1984.

33. Chris Hedges, "Salvador Right Said to Weigh Dropping D'Aubuisson," *CSM*, February 7, 1984.

34. Lydia Chavez, "The Strongest Contender, Some Say, Is Not in Salvador Race," *NYT*, March 24, 1984.

35. Carothers, *In the Name of Democracy*, p. 30; Philip Taubman, "U.S. Aides Fear Salvador Setback, Even a Coup, in Election's Wake," *NYT*, February 2, 1984; Robert J. McCartney, "Guerrero Offers Alternative to Polarization in Salvador," *WP*, March 19, 1984.

36. Chris Hedges, "Salvador Politico Works the Crowds," *CSM*, March 9, 1984. To conservatives in the Reagan administration, Guerrero's opposition to social reform was an attraction in itself; they still blanched at having to support the Christian Democrats. Carothers, *In the Name of Democracy*, p. 30.

37. On the CIA's aid to Guerrero, see Taubman, "C.I.A. Said to Have Given Money to 2 Salvador Parties," *NYT*, May 12, 1984.

38. Juan M. Vasquez, "Insults, Ambiguity Mark Salvador Presidential Race," *LAT*, February 13, 1984.

39. James Brooke, "Clear Choice Will Face Salvador Voters," *MH*, January 22, 1984; "Salvador Seeking a Way Out in Vote Today," *NYT*, March 25, 1984; Joanne Omang, "Salvadoran Vows Probe of Violence," *WP*, May 21, 1984; Richard J. Meislin, "Salvador's Right Wing Scores in Soccer Coup," *NYT*, March 19, 1984.

40. Robert J. McCartney, " 'Strong Character,' " *WP*, May 8, 1984.

41. See White's testimony in U.S. House of Representatives, *Foreign Assistance and Related Programs Appropriations for 1982, Part 1*, p. 16.

42. On Duarte's relationship to the CIA, see Woodward, *VEIL*, p. 117. On the 1982 election, see *Congressional Record*, July 27, 1983, p. H5762; Bonner, *Weakness and Deceit*, p. 293.

43. Taubman, "C.I.A. Said to Have Given Money to 2 Salvador Parties," *NYT*, May 12, 1984; Robert J. McCartney, "U.S. Seen Assisting Duarte in Sunday's Salvadoran Vote," *WP*, May 4, 1984; Krauss, *Inside Central America*, p. 93. For the record, Duarte steadfastly denied receiving any CIA funds. Duarte, *Duarte*, p. 199.

44. Sam Dillon, "U.S. Bankrolls Vote: Salvadorans Worried," *MH*, March 19, 1984; McCartney, "U.S. Seen Assisting Duarte in Sunday's Salvadoran Vote," *WP*, May 4, 1984.

45. Edward Cody, "Duarte Declared El Salvador Victor," *WP*, May 12, 1984.

46. Steven V. Roberts, "Reagan Defends Aide in Salvador Assailed by Helms," *NYT*, May 4, 1984.

47. *Congressional Record*, May 8, 1984, pp. S5406–7.

48. Joanne Omang, "Reagan Sees Hill Leaders: Pressure for Latin Aid Rises," *WP*, May 9, 1984. See also Martin Tolchin, "Helms Denies He Revealed Secrets from Senate Intelligence Panel," *NYT*, May 17, 1984; "A Little Help from Friends," *Newsweek*, May 21, 1984.

49. John M. Goshko, "D'Aubuisson's Cooperation Seen as Vital to U.S. Salvador Policy," *WP*, June 26, 1984.

50. D'Aubuisson himself told Walters that Helms's office had alerted him. U.S. Department of State cable, San Salvador 05682, May 19, 1984, "General Walters' Talk with D'Aubuisson" (NSA El Salvador collection). See also McManus and Pyes, "Assassination Plot on

U.S. Envoy to Salvador Reported," *LAT*, June 23, 1984; Joanne Omang, "U.S. Feared Slaying of Envoy Here," *WP*, June 27, 1984.

51. U.S. Department of State cable, San Salvador 05682, May 19, 1984, "General Walters' Talk with D'Aubuisson" (NSA El Salvador collection); James LeMoyne, "Salvador Right Reportedly Plotted to Assassinate U.S. Ambassador," *NYT*, June 23, 1984.

52. Leslie H. Gelb, "U.S. Uncertain About D'Aubuisson's Role in Plot," *NYT*, June 24, 1984; Doyle McManus and Craig Pyes, "Assassination Plot on U.S. Envoy to Salvador Reported," *LAT*, June 23, 1984; declassified documents quoted in Guy Gugliotta, "D'Aubuisson Kept U.S. on Its Guard," *WP*, January 4, 1994.

53. McManus and Pyes, "Assassination Plot on U.S. Envoy to Salvador Reported," *LAT*, June 23, 1984.

54. "Salvadorans Said to Plot to Kill Envoy," *WP*, October 11, 1984; Joanne Omang, "Salvadoran Travel Not Advised," *WP*, November 3, 1984. The Pickering assassination plot was not the first of its kind. In the late 1970s, U.S. intelligence had uncovered a similar plot by Salvadoran rightists angry over Jimmy Carter's human rights policy. They planned to murder U.S. Ambassador Frank Devine and blame it on leftist guerrillas. Devine, *El Salvador*, p. 18.

55. Philip Taubman, "Salvador Rightist Granted U.S. Visa," *NYT*, December 4, 1984; Lois Romano, "In the Name of RFK," *WP*, November 21, 1984.

56. *Congressional Record*, May 8, 1984, pp. S5406–7.

57. Michael Marriot, "D'Aubuisson Encounters Angry Protesters Here," *WP*, June 29, 1984; Joanne Omang, "D'Aubuisson Honored by Conservatives at Capitol Hill Dinner," *WP*, December 5, 1984.

58. Frank del Olmo, "Dirty Tricks in Central America," *LAT*, January 26, 1984.

59. Ungo, "People's Struggle," *Foreign Policy* (Fall 1983).

60. Joanne Omang, "El Salvador Faction Reported Split on Election Violence," *WP*, February 17, 1984.

61. "Remarks at the Presentation Ceremony for the Presidential Medal of Freedom, March 26, 1984," *Reagan Papers, 1984*, book 1, pp. 414–16.

62. Lydia Chavez, "Duarte Is Inaugurated in El Salvador and Promises to Curb Abuses," *NYT*, June 2, 1984.

63. "Address to the Nation on United States Policy in Central America, May 9, 1984," *Reagan Papers, 1984*, book 1, pp. 659–65.

64. *Congressional Record*, May 8, 1984, p. H3498.

65. In addition, whereas the bill that was approved by Barnes's subcommittee provided none of the $179 million in supplemental military aid requested for fiscal year 1984, and only about one-third of the military aid that Reagan had requested for fiscal year 1985, the Solarz compromise provided half the $179 million supplemental request and the entire FY 1985 request of $189.5 million. Such high levels of funding were acceptable to the Democrats only because they were accompanied by such strict certification conditions. U.S. House of Representatives, *Congress and Foreign Policy 1984*, pp. 25–27.

66. *Congressional Record*, May 10, 1984, p. H3714.

67. Ibid., May 8, 1984, pp. H3505, H3731.

68. Ibid., May 10, 1984, p. H3714.

69. Ibid., pp. H3679, H3687.

70. Ibid., pp. H3679, H3709.

71. Ibid., p. H3740.

72. On the impact of Wright's speech, see Arnson, *Crossroads*, pp. 160–61.

73. *Congressional Record*, May 10, 1984, pp. H3744, H3750–53.

74. Joanne Omang, "Latin Requests Face Further Test: House Conferees Balk at Arms Aid," *WP*, May 18, 1984.

75. "Excerpts from Salvadoran Leader's Address," *NYT*, May 22, 1984; "Duarte: 'Guerrillas Are Symptoms, Not Causes,'" *CQ Weekly Report*, May 26, 1984.

76. Barnes is quoted in Joanne Omang, "Duarte Conquers Congress on Aid to El Salvador," *WP*, May 23, 1984; Long is quoted in "Salvadoran Leader Makes Conquests on Hill," *CQ Weekly Report*, May 26, 1984.

77. The debate on the supplemental is in *Congressional Record*, May 24, 1984, pp. H4777–4840. Support for Reagan's policy in El Salvador did not carry over to Nicaragua. On the same day that the House approved the funds for El Salvador in the urgent supplemental, it voted against the $21 million in contra aid funds that the Senate had added to the bill. All five National Guardsmen convicted of killing the churchwomen were sentenced to thirty years in prison.

78. Lydia Chavez, "Salvador Frees Witness in Slaying of Two Americans," *NYT*, March 31, 1984; "Salvadoran Cleared in Three Deaths," *MH*, May 23, 1984.

79. Debate on Inouye's motion and two other amendments on El Salvador by Christopher Dodd and Edward Kennedy are in *Congressional Record*, August 8, 1984, pp. S9918–30.

80. Republicans tried to added an additional $359 million in military and economic aid for Central America, much of it for El Salvador, when the appropriations bill came to the House floor, but the motion was ruled out of order because Congress had passed no legislation authorizing the additional funds. Pressman, "Supplemental Showdown Set Over Central America Money," *CQ Weekly Report*, August 4, 1984.

81. U.S. House of Representatives, *Congress and Foreign Policy 1984*, pp. 27–28.

82. Guy Gugliotta, "A Policy of Pressure, Not Negotiation," *MH*, July 1, 1984.

83. U.S. House of Representatives, *Making Continuing Appropriations for Fiscal Year 1985, and for Other Purposes*, pp. 59, 68. Senator Dodd added a similar provision to the Senate version of the bill, without Republican objection. *Congressional Record*, October 3, 1984, p. S12829.

84. U.S. House of Representatives, *Congress and Foreign Policy 1984*, pp. 28–29.

85. James LeMoyne, "Salvadoran Right Blocks Land Plan," *NYT*, June 30, 1984.

86. Gorman is quoted in U.S. Senate, *Department of Defense Authorization for Appropriations for Fiscal Year 1985 (Part 2)*, p. 1162. McFarlane is quoted in "El Salvador Victory in the Offing, Official Says," *MH*, July 18, 1984.

CHAPTER TWELVE

1. Robert J. McCartney, "Duarte Plans to Move Slowly in Seeking Peace," *WP*, June 11, 1984.

2. "Two Salvadoran Officers with Alleged Death Squad Ties Shifted," *WP*, May 25, 1984; Lydia Chavez, "Attempts Told to Stop Salvador Killings," *NYT*, June 1, 1984; Edward Cody, "Duarte: Limited Power Over Military," *WP*, September 17, 1984.

3. James LeMoyne, "A Salvadoran Police Chief Vows to End Rights Abuses," *NYT*, July 1, 1984; Lydia Chavez, "El Salvador to Restructure Security Forces," *NYT*, June 14, 1984; Robert J. McCartney, "El Salvador Moves Against Death Squads," *WP*, June 14, 1984. According to the Legal Aid office of the Catholic Church, the number of people killed or disappeared by the army and death squads from January 1, 1979, to July 1, 1985, was 36,924.

4. U.S. CIA, Directorate of Intelligence, National Intelligence Estimate, "El Salvador: Controlling Rightwing Terrorism," February 1985 (NSA El Salvador collection).

5. Dan Williams, "Duarte's First Month a Rocky Road," *LAT*, July 2, 1984.

6. James LeMoyne, "Duarte Won't Talk with Rebels Yet," *NYT*, June 21, 1984.

7. Duarte, *Duarte*, p. 210.

8. Joanne Omang, "Reagan Praises Duarte's Peace Effort," *WP*, October 11, 1984; James LeMoyne, "Duarte Rejects Rebels' Bid for Outsiders at Talks," *NYT*, October 13, 1984.

9. James LeMoyne, "Battalion's Arrival Jolts Plan for Salvador Talks," *NYT*, October 14, 1984.

10. Robert J. McCartney and Loren Jenkins, "Duarte, Rebels Agree to Continue Contacts," *WP*, October 16, 1984.

11. Loren Jenkins, "Salvadorans Still Divided on Major Issues," *WP*, October 17, 1984.

12. "Duarte Cites His Nation's 'New Reality,'" *WP*, October 16, 1984; "Salvador Rebel Chief Sees Slow Progress in Talks," *NYT*, November 4, 1984.

13. Loren Jenkins, "Rightist Politician Lobbies in Salvadoran Barracks," *WP*, November 9, 1984.

14. Dennis Volman, "Salvador's Military Backs Away from Duarte's Peace Talks," *CSM*, January 17, 1985.

15. Duarte, *Duarte*, pp. 226–27. See also James LeMoyne, "Duarte Will Not Attend Peace Talks Next Week," *WP*, November 24, 1984; Loren Jenkins, "Salvadoran Rebels Arrive for Talks," *WP*, November 30, 1984.

16. Loren Jenkins, "Duarte Rejects Rebel Position," *WP*, December 1, 1984.

17. Loren Jenkins, "Salvadoran Cleric Puts Best Light on Talks," *WP*, December 3, 1984.

18. Dan Williams, "Hopes for Salvador Talks Fade as Duarte Assails Rebels," *LAT*, January 25, 1985.

19. Deputy Chief of Mission David Passage, quoted in Moberg, "Labor Report Due on Central America," *In These Times*, April 3–9, 1985. See also Robert J. McCartney, "U.S. Cools Support for Duarte," *WP*, March 20, 1985; Chris Norton, "As Salvador Vote Nears, Rightists Sound More Like Moderates," *CSM*, March 27, 1985; Robert J. McCartney, "The $150,000 Election Campaign Headache," *WP*, March 26, 1985.

20. The FDR-FMLN once again boycotted the elections, denouncing them as unfair, though they made no special effort to disrupt voting. William R. Long, "Guerrillas Use Fire to Oppose Salvador Vote," *LAT*, March 30, 1985.

21. Duarte describes this incident in detail in his autobiography, *Duarte*, pp. 237–40.

22. Marlise Simons, "D'Aubuisson, Salvador Rightist, Steps Down as His Party's Leader," *NYT*, September 30, 1985.

23. Tim Golden, "U.S.-Backed Salvadorans Haunt Rebels," *MH*, July 10, 1985.

24. On the inflation of estimates, see McNeil, *War and Peace in Central America*, p. 162. Former FMLN commander Miguel Castellanos says that in 1980, the Popular Liberation Forces alone had 6,000 members, but enough weapons for only 1,000. In total, about 3,000 FMLN combatants participated in the abortive 1980 final offensive. Castellanos puts the number of FMLN combatants at 10,000 in 1983, but falling to just 5,000 by 1985, due largely to desertions as the war dragged on longer than anticipated. Prisk, *Comandante Speaks*, pp. 26, 29, 110.

25. Doyle McManus, "U.S. Sending More Copters to El Salvador," *LAT*, September 5, 1985. By 1988, the size of the air force had doubled, to 135 aircraft, 72 of which were helicopters. Bacevich et al., *American Military Policy in Small Wars*, p. 32.

26. Edward Cody, "Salvadoran Army: Bigger, Tougher," *WP*, January 28, 1985.

27. James LeMoyne, "Salvadoran Air Force Gets U.S. Gunship Designed for Anti-Rebel Warfare," *NYT*, January 9, 1985.

28. Broadcast of "60 Minutes," CBS television, May 25, 1996.

29. Tim Golden, "Salvador Air Raids Hit Civilians, Tour of Rebel Area Shows," *MH*, December 15, 1985.

30. On the use of bombing and military sweeps to depopulate guerrilla zones, see Americas Watch, *Draining the Sea*, pp. 27–38; Americas Watch, *Settling into Routine*, pp. 25–31.

31. Clifford Krauss, "El Salvador Army Gains on the Guerrillas," *WSJ*, July 30, 1986; Julia Preston, "Salvadoran Refugees Returning Home," *WP*, July 28, 1986.

32. Tim Golden, "Salvador Evicting Peasants from Guerrilla Stronghold," *MH*, February 19, 1986.

33. Edwards and Siebentritt, *Places of Origin*, pp. 17–18; Americas Watch, *El Salvador's Decade of Terror*, p. 108.

34. Bacevich et al., *American Military Policy in Small Wars*, p. 44. This is an assessment of U.S. counterinsurgency policy in El Salvador written by four U.S. colonels, one of whom served in country as an adviser.

35. Dan Williams, "Salvador Villages Resist Army's Call for Militias," *LAT*, January 9, 1985; Dan Williams, "Salvador Builds Fortified Towns to Block Guerrillas," *LAT*, January 29, 1985.

36. Dan Williams, "Signs Positive but Reality Is Still Painful in Salvador," *LAT*, May 30, 1985. The government's resettlement plans are described in Edwards and Siebentritt, *Places of Origin*, pp. 61–76.

37. Manwaring and Prisk, *El Salvador at War*, pp. 269–71; Chris Hedges, "Salvador Guerrillas Switch Strategy to Evade Air Force," *CSM*, July 31, 1984; Chris Hedges, "Salvador Rebel Leaders Admit Army Has Thrown Them Off Balance," *CSM*, August 28, 1984.

38. Robert J. McCartney, "Rebel Force Damages Main Salvadoran Power Dam," *WP*, June 29, 1984; Robert J. McCartney, "Rebels Attack Near San Salvador," *WP*, March 17, 1985.

39. For an insider's description of the FMLN's strategy, see Prisk, *Comandante Speaks*, pp. 35–36. See also Edward Cody, "Salvadoran Rebels Change Tactics," *WP*, May 17, 1985; Sam Dillon, "Is Top Salvador Rebel Dead?," *MH*, April 12, 1985.

40. For a detailed discussion of the FMLN's reassessment of strategy, see Miles and Ostertag, "FMLN New Thinking," *NACLA Report on the Americas* (September 1989). The FMLN's return to small-unit tactics successfully blunted the impact of air power. "Lucrative targets all but disappeared," U.S. military officers reported. Bacevich et al., *American Military Policy in Small Wars*, p. 33.

41. Robert J. McCartney, "Rebels Optimistic Despite Army Attacks," *WP*, November 7, 1985.

42. James LeMoyne, "Rebels Reported to Seize and Kill Salvador Mayors in a New Tactic," *NYT*, May 12, 1985.

43. James LeMoyne, "Salvadoran Army Improving, but Rebels Adjust," *NYT*, January 29, 1985; McCartney, "Rebels Optimistic Despite Army Attacks," *WP*, November 7, 1985. For a detailed discussion of the FMLN's renewed emphasis on political struggle after 1984, especially in the cities, see the captured FMLN documents, "Apreciación Estratégica," written between January and March 1988, and "Organizar El 'Fuego'—Una Necesidad Imperativa para Avanzar Hacia la Victoria," January 1988.

44. Sam Dillon, "Guerrillas: We Killed Ex-General," *MH*, March 25, 1985.

45. Americas Watch, *Continuing Terror*, pp. 115–18. After the war, senior FMLN commanders said that the Zona Rosa attack had been carried out without their approval. Tim Golden, "From Suspect in Murders to a New Life in America," *NYT*, November 22, 1996.

46. Gerald M. Boyd, "Reagan Promises Marines Killers Will Not Escape," *NYT*, June 23, 1985.

47. Joel Brinkley, "U.S. Said to Have Weighed Raid on Training Camp in Nicaragua," *NYT*, July 24, 1985; Alfonso Chardy, "Central America Is Prime U.S. Target in Anti-Terror War," *MH*, July 16, 1985; Lou Cannon, "Reagan Congratulates Duarte for Arrests," *WP*, August 29, 1985.

48. Ed Offley, "Former Ranger Tells of Raid to Destroy Terrorist Camp," *Seattle Post-Intelligencer*, June 15, 1995; "U.S. Reportedly Killed 83 Guerrillas in El Salvador in '85 Retaliation," *Boston Globe*, June 16, 1995.

49. For a description of the police training programs, see Langguth, *Hidden Terrors*. For a discussion of the congressional ban on police aid, see Schoultz, *Human Rights*, pp. 179–83.

50. The special Treasury Police unit was the Cuerpo Especial Anti-Terrorista. U.S. House of Representatives, *Central American Counterterrorism Act of 1985*, p. 64; James LeMoyne, "Duarte Meets FBI on Raid Inquiry," *NYT*, June 27, 1985.

51. *Congressional Record*, July 10, 1985, pp. H5413–15.

52. George Miller, "Salvadoran Security Agents and the Law," *CSM*, September 19, 1985; Americas Watch, *El Salvador's Decade of Terror*, p. 83. D'Aubuisson's name appears in program documents as a participant, according to McClintock, *American Connection*, p. 218.

53. "Money for Latin American Police Forces Advances on Capitol Hill," *CQ Weekly Report*, December 7, 1985.

54. Marlise Simons, "Kidnappers of Duarte's Daughter Said to Demand Freedom for 34," *NYT*, September 26, 1985.

55. Edward Cody, "Duarte Denounces Kidnapping 'Barbarity,' " *WP*, September 16, 1985.

56. Joanne Omang, "Talks Opposed in Kidnapping of Duarte Kin," *WP*, September 23, 1985.

57. Marjorie Miller, "Duarte Daughter Freed in Trade with Rebels," *LAT*, October 25, 1985. For a more detailed account of the agreement, see Americas Watch, *El Salvador's Decade of Terror*, p. 66.

58. Duarte, *Duarte*, pp. 256–57; Marlise Simons, "Kidnapping Shakes Duarte's Authority," *NYT*, November 10, 1985.

59. Edward Cody, "Peace Talks' Promise Unfulfilled," *WP*, October 16, 1985.

60. Author's interview with Rubén Zamora, vice president of the FDR, Washington, D.C., July 1988. Most of this interview was printed in LeoGrande, "El Salvador After Duarte: Interview with Rubén Zamora," *World Policy Journal* (Fall 1988).

61. William R. Long, "Guerrillas Use Fire to Oppose Salvador Vote," *LAT*, March 30, 1985; Robert J. McCartney, "Split Noted in Salvadoran Rebel Front," *WP*, August 19, 1985. Part of the problem was geographic. From 1981 to 1983, the FMLN general command (i.e., the top guerrilla military commanders) operated from Managua, Nicaragua, where they could confer regularly with the civilian politicians of the FDR. After the U.S. invasion of Grenada, however, the general command relocated to El Salvador, making it much harder for FDR representatives to exert any influence on its deliberations. In July 1985, FDR and FMLN leaders met inside the country and redefined the relationship between the two left-wing organizations. The FMLN would carry out whatever military actions it felt justified, with or without the support of the FDR, and the FDR would be free to publicly criticize any action it disapproved. Prisk, *Comandante Speaks*, p. 68; James LeMoyne, "Salvador Parties Loosen Rebel Links," *NYT*, January 22, 1986.

62. U.S. House of Representatives, *Foreign Assistance Legislation for Fiscal Years 1986–1987 (Part 6)*, pp. 3–4.

63. Ibid., p. 153.

64. Ibid., pp. 121, 154; Bacevich et al., *American Military Policy in Small Wars*, p. 31. Evidence on the bombing of civilians is presented in Americas Watch and the Lawyers International Committee for Human Rights, *Free Fire*; and Americas Watch, *Draining the Sea*. The latter report, from 1985, includes excerpts from Duarte's directive to the air force regarding bombardment in civilian areas. Colonel Carlos Reynaldo López Nuila admitted that the air force refused to abide by the government's human rights directives. Americas Watch, *El Salvador's Decade of Terror*, p. 55.

65. *Congressional Record*, July 10, 1985, pp. H5408–11.

66. Doyle McManus, "House Panel OKs Curb on Salvador Aid," *LAT*, April 3, 1985. See also U.S. House of Representatives, *International Security and Development Cooperation Act of 1985*.

67. U.S. House of Representatives, *International Security and Development Cooperation Act of 1985: Conference Report*, pp. 50–51.

68. Americas Watch, *Civilian Toll, 1986–1987*, pp. 7–8.

69. Author's interview with a midlevel State Department official working on Central America, Washington, D.C., March 1985.

70. In FY 1986, El Salvador received $445.4 million ($121.7 million in military aid), and in FY 1987, $529.8 million ($111.5 million in military aid). In the last two foreign aid budgets passed during Reagan's second term (FY 1988 and FY 1989), the budget crunch caught up with Central America. Despite the lack of any significant congressional opposition, the aid allocation for El Salvador dropped to $395.6 million ($81.5 million military aid) in FY 1988 and $382.7 million ($81.4 million military) in FY 1989. U.S. Agency for International Development, *U.S. Overseas Loans and Grants*, 1990, p. 49; *U.S. Overseas Loans and Grants*, 1993, p. 97.

71. Tim Golden, "U.S. Advisers to Begin Training, Equipping Salvador Police Force," *MH*, February 15, 1986.

72. Joanne Omang, "Representative Crockett and the Volley from the Right," *WP*, February 10, 1987.

73. Marjorie Miller, "El Salvador: No End in Sight," *LAT*, January 14, 1986; Chris Norton, "Salvador: Peace Is Distant," *CSM*, November 24, 1986. The stable casualty rate of two to three thousand annually was down considerably from the July 1982–June 1983 rate of over six thousand, however.

74. Tim Golden, "Salvador Rebels Attack Strategic Base," *MH*, June 20, 1986.

75. William Branigin, "American Killed in El Salvador," *WP*, April 1, 1987; William Branigin, "Infiltrators Said to Stay in Army Base," *WP*, April 3, 1987; Tim Golden, "Intelligence Woes Plagued Salvador Military," *MH*, April 3, 1987.

76. "Six Americans Die in Salvador Copter Crash," *LAT*, July 17, 1987; "U.S. Advisers Reported Under Fire in Salvador," *NYT*, February 13, 1986.

77. Norton, "Salvador: Peace Is Distant," *CSM*, November 24, 1986; James LeMoyne, "After Parades and Promises, Duarte Flounders in El Salvador," *NYT*, February 15, 1987.

78. Bacevich et al., *American Military Policy in Small Wars*, p. 20.

79. Ponce's biography is in Arms Control and Foreign Policy Caucus, *Barriers to Reform*, pp. 13–14. His link to death squads is reported in U.S. Department of State and CIA, "Selective Study on Death Squads," October 27, 1983 (NSA El Salvador collection).

80. Douglas Farah, "Salvadoran President Comes to U.S. Bearing Heavy Domestic Burden," *WP*, January 30, 1990. For a concise statement of the rightist view, see the interview with Colonel Sigifredo Ochoa in "A Voice of Dissent from the Salvadoran Military," *WSJ*, July 17, 1987.

81. World Bank, *El Salvador*.

82. Peter Ford, "Civil War Undermines Efforts to Boost Salvador's Ailing Economy," *CSM*, May 21, 1986. See also Marjorie Miller, "Duarte, Jolted by Kidnapping Case in '85, Faces Economic Perils in '86," *LAT*, January 17, 1986; Duarte, *Duarte*, p. 271.

83. Miller, "Duarte, Jolted by Kidnapping Case in '85, Faces Economic Perils in '86," *LAT*, January 17, 1986. Duarte's "war tax" on the rich was eventually ruled unconstitutional by the Supreme Court, which had been appointed by the rightist majority in the National Assembly. "Top Salvadoran Court Rules 'War Tax' Unconstitutional," *LAT*, February 20, 1987.

84. Marjorie Miller, "Salvador Rightists Attack Duarte Over Taxes for War," *LAT*, January 12, 1987.

85. Marjorie Miller, "Thousands of Salvadorans March to Protest Duarte's Economic Austerity Plan," *LAT*, February 22, 1986.

86. James LeMoyne, "Duarte Plans Sweeping Economic Changes, but Is Meeting Stiff Opposition," *NYT*, January 17, 1986; James LeMoyne, "Duarte's Critics on the Rise at Home," *NYT*, February 10, 1986.

87. Tim Golden, "Communists Blamed for Salvador Strikes," *MH*, June 14, 1985.

88. American Institute for Free Labor Development and Freedom House, *Captured Documents*, pp. 6–8. Former FMLN commander Miguel Castellanos confirmed this strategy. Prisk, *Comandante Speaks*, p. 80.

89. James LeMoyne, "Duarte's Critics on the Rise at Home," *NYT*, February 10, 1986.

90. Smyth, "Duarte's Secret Friends," *Nation*, March 14, 1987. See also William Branigin, "Duarte Loses Support of Rival Salvadoran Unions," *WP*, July 16, 1987.

91. U.S. Senate, Democratic Policy Committee, *Foreign Aid to Central America*, FY 1981–1987, p. 61.

92. "Security Tight at 'El Bunker'—the U.S. Embassy in San Salvador," *Journal of Commerce*, July 24, 1981; Marjorie Miller, "U.S. Embassy in El Salvador Has Look of Fortress," *LAT*, August 18, 1985.

93. Joanne Omang, "U.S. Embassy in El Salvador 'a Total Loss,' " *WP*, October 20, 1986.

CHAPTER THIRTEEN

1. Gutman, *Banana Diplomacy*, p. 85; Leslie H. Gelb, "Argentina Linked to Rise in Covert U.S. Actions Against Sandinistas," *NYT*, April 8, 1983; Leslie H. Gelb, "Reagan Backing Covert Actions, Officials Assert," *NYT*, March 14, 1982. A heavily redacted text of the finding is included in *Iran-Contra Chronology*, p. 143.

2. The finding is quoted in Don Oberdorfer and Patrick E. Tyler, "U.S.-Backed Nicaraguan Rebel Army Swells to 7,000 Men," *WP*, May 8, 1983; Alfonso Chardy and Juan O. Tamayo, " 'New' CIA Deepens U.S. Involvement," *MH*, June 5, 1983. Boland is quoted in *Congressional Record*, July 27, 1983, p. H5721.

3. The committee's concerns are discussed in U.S. House of Representatives, *Amendment to the Intelligence Authorization Act for Fiscal Year 1983*, May 13, 1983; Woodward, *VEIL*, p. 176.

4. Patrick E. Tyler, "Nicaragua: Hill Concern on U.S. Objectives Persists," *WP*, January 1, 1983.

5. Woodward, *VEIL*, p. 176.

6. U.S. House of Representatives, *Amendment to the Intelligence Authorization Act for Fiscal Year 1983*, May 13, 1983; *Congressional Record*, July 28, 1983, p. H5847.

7. Tyler, "Nicaragua: Hill Concern on U.S. Objectives Persists," *WP*, January 1, 1983; Oberdorfer and Tyler, "U.S.-Backed Nicaraguan Rebel Army Swells to 7,000 Men," *WP*, May 8, 1983.

8. Oberdorfer and Tyler, "U.S.-Backed Nicaraguan Rebel Army Swells to 7,000 Men," *WP*, May 8, 1983.

9. McNeil, *War and Peace in Central America*, pp. 154–55. McNeil was U.S. ambassador to Costa Rica at the time.

10. Gutman, *Banana Diplomacy*, p. 86. In his autobiography written ten years later, Ronald Reagan still clung to the fiction that the contras were literally supposed to "halt the flow of Soviet-made arms from Cuba to Nicaragua and El Salvador." Reagan, *American Life*, p. 300.

11. Joanne Omang, "Rebel Fund Diversion Rooted in Early Policy," *WP*, January 1, 1987.

12. The text of López Portillo's speech is in Bagley, Alvarez, and Hagedorn, *Contadora and the Central American Peace Process*, pp. 101–2.

13. "Mexico Giving U.S. Latin Plan Details," *NYT*, March 6, 1982.

14. Bernard Gwertzman, "U.S. Seeking Right to Use Air Bases in the Caribbean," *NYT*, March 3, 1982.

15. Alan Riding, "Mexicans Pessimistic on Talks Between U.S. and Caribbean Leftists," *NYT*, May 10, 1982. See also Bernard Gwertzman, "Haig Is Cautious About Any Accord with Nicaraguans," *NYT*, March 16, 1982; Philip Taubman, "Latin Policy: Out of Focus," *NYT*, March 17, 1982.

16. The document, entitled "U.S. Policy in Central America and Cuba Through FY '84, Summary Paper," was leaked and printed as "National Security Council Document on Policy in Central America and Cuba," *NYT*, April 7, 1983.

17. Taubman, "Latin Policy," *NYT*, March 17, 1982.

18. Leslie H. Gelb, "Central American Talks: Much Ado About Nothing," *NYT*, March 26, 1982. For one hard-liner's objections, see Menges, *Inside the National Security Council*, p. 105.

19. Don Oberdorfer, "Mexican Tells Haig Details of Peace Plan," *WP*, March 7, 1982.

20. Smith, *Closest of Enemies*, pp. 253–54; Alfonso Chardy, "Cuba's Canny Old Communist," *MH*, December 18, 1983.

21. Don Oberdorfer, "Mexican Tells Haig Details of Peace Plan," *WP*, March 7, 1982; Bernard D. Nossiter, "Haig and Mexican Confer on Ending War in Salvador," *NYT*, March 7, 1982.

22. "Transcript of Remarks on Nicaragua," *NYT*, March 16, 1982.

23. Leslie H. Gelb, "U.S. Denies It Opposes Salvadoran Talks," *NYT*, March 25, 1982; Alan Riding, "U.S. and Nicaragua Said to Agree to Hold Direct Talks on Disputes," *NYT*, March 24, 1982.

24. John M. Goshko, "U.S. Considers Aid to Nicaragua to Ease Tensions," *WP*, April 10, 1982; Gutman, *Banana Diplomacy*, pp. 95–96; Menges, *Inside the National Security Council*, p. 105.

25. See Nicaragua's diplomatic note of May 7, included in Bagley, Alvarez, and Hagedorn, *Contadora and the Central American Peace Process*, pp. 34–39.

26. John M. Goshko, "U.S. Stalling on Negotiations with Nicaragua," *WP*, April 17, 1982.

27. William Goodfellow, "The Diplomatic Front," in Walker, *Reagan Versus the Sandinistas*, pp. 143–58.

28. Enders, "Building Peace in Central America," *U.S. Department of State Bulletin*, October 1982, pp. 66–69.

29. Cynthia Gorney, "Reagan's Latin Policy," *WP*, April 15, 1981; John M. Goshko, "U.S. Ends Opposition to Loans to Repressive Latin Regimes," *WP*, July 9, 1981.

30. See the testimony of General Ernest Graves in U.S. Senate, *Foreign Assistance Authorization for Fiscal Year 1982*, May 4, 1981.

31. Details of the "dirty war" are in the official government investigative report compiled after the restoration of democratic government in 1983: *Nunca Mas: Informe de la Comisión Nacional Sobre la Desaparición de Personas*.

32. Anthony Lewis, "Ideology and Ignorance," *NYT*, April 15, 1982; Edward Schumacher, "Latins Get Taste of Kirkpatrick Style," *NYT*, August 5, 1981; Sanders, *Peddlers of Crisis*, pp. 300–301.

33. Dugger, *On Reagan*, p. 521. Long after the horrors of the Argentine military government had been revealed and a number of the military officers responsible had been tried and convicted, Reagan was still referring to human rights violations during the dirty war as "rumors." Reagan, *American Life*, p. 358.

34. Dickey, *With the Contras*, p. 145; Horowitz and Sklar, "South Atlantic Triangle," *NACLA Report on the Americas* (May–June 1982).

35. Alan Riding, "U.S. Support for Britain Imperiling Latin Policy," *NYT*, May 16, 1982; John M. Goshko, "By Backing Britain, U.S. Upsets Its Apple Cart in Central America," *WP*, May 2, 1982.

36. Gelb, "Argentina Linked to Rise in Covert U.S. Actions Against Sandinistas," *NYT*, April 8, 1983. See also Chardy and Tamayo, " 'New' CIA Deepens U.S. Involvement," *MH*, June 5, 1983.

37. Raymont, "Argentine Miscues," *New Republic*, June 9, 1982. See also Haig, *Caveat*, pp. 267, 275; Jackson Diehl, "Argentine-U.S. Tie Unravels in Mutual Misunderstandings," *WP*,

May 9, 1982; John M. Goshko, "Did the U.S. Give Argentina a 'Wink and a Nod'?," *WP*, May 31, 1982.

38. Reagan, *American Life*, p. 358; Don Oberdorfer, "A Diplomatic Dilemma," *WP*, April 4, 1982.

39. Kirkpatrick, *Leader and Vanguard in Mass Society*, p. 228. She concluded that the Peronists were finished as a political force—a conclusion that proved a bit premature. In 1973, Peronist candidate Héctor J. Cámpora was elected president, and later that year, the aging Juan Domingo Perón himself returned triumphant from exile in Spain and won the presidency in a special election.

40. Haig, *Caveat*, pp. 268–69.

41. Ibid.; Bernard Gwertzman, "Mrs. Kirkpatrick Sees Reagan Over Her Quarrel with Haig," *NYT*, June 1, 1982; Bernard Nossiter, "Kirkpatrick Feud With Haig Is Noted," *NYT*, May 31, 1982; Goshko, "Did the U.S. Give Argentina a 'Wink and a Nod'?," *WP*, May 31, 1982. Kirkpatrick aide Allan Gerson insists that she told the Argentines that Washington would back Great Britain if diplomacy failed. Gerson, *Kirkpatrick Mission*, p. 118.

42. Margot Hornblower, "Argentines, Feeling Betrayed, Turning Hostile Toward U.S.," *WP*, May 8, 1982.

43. Lydia Chavez, "Argentine Court Finds Five Guilty for Junta Roles," *NYT*, December 10, 1985.

44. Riding, "U.S. Support for Britain Imperiling Latin Policy," *NYT*, May 16, 1982.

45. Gutman, *Banana Diplomacy*, pp. 105–6; Clarridge, *Spy for All Seasons*, p. 220; Alan Riding, "Nicaragua Reports a Pledge by Argentina to Quit Region," *NYT*, December 19, 1982; Alfonso Chardy and Juan Tamayo, "CIA Calls Shots Against Nicaragua," *MH*, April 17, 1983.

46. Gutman, *Banana Diplomacy*, p. 105.

47. Pastor, *Condemned to Repetition*, pp. 174, 196–97; Christian, *Nicaragua*, pp. 98–100, 119, 123; Garvin, *Everybody Had His Own Gringo*, p. 54. Pastora was tempted, however. During the "final offensive" against Somoza, Pastora asked the United States to have Somoza deploy the National Guard against other Sandinista columns so that his could reach Managua first. The approach was made through Costa Rica. U.S. Department of State cable, San José 2691, June 25, 1979, "Figueres' Associate Suggests USG Aid Eden Pastora" (NSA Nicaragua collection).

48. Dickey, *With the Contras*, pp. 120–23, 148–49; Christian, *Nicaragua*, pp. 310–19.

49. Doyle McManus and Robert C. Toth, "The Contras: How U.S. Got Entangled," *LAT*, March 4, 1985; Juan Tamayo, "CIA Fights with New Technology, Old Techniques," *MH*, June 5, 1983; Christian, *Nicaragua*, p. 325.

50. Gutman, *Banana Diplomacy*, p. 109. See also Clarridge's account of the recruitment in *Spy for All Seasons*, pp. 213–15.

51. Dickey, *With the Contras*, p. 149. Clarridge was so intent on recruiting Pastora that he agreed to Pastora's demand that the CIA air-drop weapons to Guatemalan guerrillas to prove its good faith. With Casey's approval, the drop was made. Clarridge, *Spy for All Seasons*, pp. 217–18; Glenn Garvin, "CIA Secretly Shipped Arms to Guerrillas in Guatemala," *MH*, March 10, 1997.

52. Christopher Dickey, "Ex-Commander Surfaces, Assails Nicaraguan Rulers," *WP*, April 16, 1982; Christian, *Nicaragua*, pp. 319–20. The text of Pastora's statement, but not his answers to questions, is in Christian, *Nicaragua*, pp. 391–94.

53. Christian, *Nicaragua*, p. 321. The CIA also expected a military coup against the National Directorate, according to Pastora supporter Arturo Cruz Jr., in *Memoirs of a Counter-Revolutionary*, p. 89.

54. Tim Golden, "Rivalries Hurt Fight for the South," *MH*, June 17, 1986.

55. Dickey, *With the Contras*, pp. 150–51; Gutman, *Banana Diplomacy*, pp. 110–11.

56. Americas Watch, *Human Rights in Honduras: Signs of "The Argentine Method,"* pp. 8–10.

57. Schulz and Schulz, *The United States, Honduras, and the Crisis in Central America*, p. 71; Philip L. Shepherd, "Honduras," in Blachman, LeoGrande, and Sharpe, *Confronting Revolution*, pp. 125–55.

58. The phrase is from a U.S. official quoted in "$10 Million in Aid Sought for Honduras," *WP*, May 16, 1981. See also Schulz and Schulz, *The United States, Honduras, and the Crisis in Central America*, p. 58.

59. Kornbluh, *Nicaragua*, pp. 137–38; Philip Taubman and Raymond Bonner, "U.S. Ties to Anti-Sandinistas Reported to Be Extensive," *NYT*, April 3, 1983.

60. U.S. Senate Democratic Policy Committee, *Foreign Aid to Central America*, FY 1981–1987; Felton, "U.S. Troops Expanding Role in Region's Wars," *CQ Weekly Report*, May 26, 1984.

61. Documents declassified in the 1990s confirmed the CIA's role. Gary Cohn and Ginger Thompson, "Special Report: Battalion 316," four-part series in the *Baltimore Sun*, June 11–18, 1995. See also Joe Pichirallo and Edward Cody, "U.S. Trains Anti-Terrorists," *WP*, March 24, 1985; Juan O. Tamayo, "Contras Linked to Murders," *MH*, January 15, 1985.

62. This was confirmed in classified congressional testimony by CIA Deputy Director for Operations Richard Stolz in June 1988. Cohn and Thompson, "Special Report: Battalion 316," *Baltimore Sun*, June 11–18, 1995.

63. William Branigin, "Honduras on Trial in Rights Court," *WP*, January 21, 1988; James LeMoyne, "Honduras' Army Tied to 200 Deaths," *NYT*, May 2, 1987; James LeMoyne, "Testifying to Torture," *New York Times Magazine*, June 5, 1988. LeMoyne's magazine article is based on a chilling interview with a Honduran woman who survived Alvarez's clandestine prisons. The essence of Caballero's story is confirmed by documents declassified in 1997. Gary Cohn, Ginger Thompson, and Mark Matthews, "Torture Was Taught by CIA," *Baltimore Sun*, January 27, 1997.

64. This was the conclusion of a 1984 Honduran armed forces investigation into the activities of the DIES. "Armed Forces Communiqué on the Missing," in Committee for the Defense of Human Rights in Honduras (Comité para la Defensa de los Derechos Humanos en Honduras), *Human Rights in Honduras, 1984*, pp. 52–53. See also Dickey, *With the Contras*, pp. 82–88, 153; Dillon, *Commandos*, pp. 99–100, 117; James LeMoyne, "Nicaragua Rebels Suspected of Link to Honduras Deaths," *NYT*, January 20, 1985. For a first-person account from a contra who claimed to have been a member of the death squad that operated under DIES orders, see Drucker, "A Contra's Story," *Progressive*, August 1986.

65. Christopher Dickey, "'Disappearances' Weaken Small Leftist Movement in Honduras," *WP*, December 13, 1981.

66. Gutman, *Banana Diplomacy*, p. 103; Schulz and Schulz, *The United States, Honduras, and the Crisis in Central America*, p. 74.

67. Author's interview with General Gustavo Alvarez Martínez, Tegucigalpa, Honduras, August 1983.

68. Dan Williams, "Assassinations by Contras in Honduras Told," *LAT*, January 15, 1985. For a first-person account by a veteran of Battalion 316, see Julia Preston, "Honduras Accused of Death Squad Operations," *WP*, November 1, 1988.

69. Americas Watch, *Human Rights in Honduras: Central America's Sideshow*. In 1994, the Honduran government released a report that attributed three to five hundred killings to the Honduran armed forces, and set the stage for the prosecution of some of those responsible. National Commissioner for the Protection of Human Rights in Honduras, *Honduras*; Larry Rohter, "Honduras Confronts Military Atrocities of the 80s," *NYT*, December 21, 1995.

70. James LeMoyne, "CIA Accused of Tolerating Killings in Honduras," *NYT*, February 14, 1986. As his tour in Honduras ended, Carter's ambassador, Jack Binns, cabled Washington about the sharp increase in "officially sponsored/sanctioned assassinations" of dissidents. The briefing book prepared for Negroponte when he replaced Binns also noted that "GOH security forces have begun to resort to extralegal tactics—disappearances and, apparently, physical eliminations—to control a perceived subversive threat." Quoted in Cohn and Thompson, "Special Report: Battalion 316," *Baltimore Sun*, June 11–18, 1995.

71. LeMoyne, "Testifying to Torture," *New York Times Magazine*. After General Alvarez was ousted in 1984, the new leadership of the Honduran armed forces tried to dismantle Battalion 316; the CIA tried to prevent it. Dennis Volman, "Killing of Honduran Army Officer Linked to Testimony in U.S.," *CSM*, November 19, 1985.

72. Christopher Dickey, "Honduran Feud Triggers Scandal," *WP*, October 15, 1982.

73. U.S. Department of State, *Country Reports on Human Rights Practices for 1983*, pp. 609–15. In 1982, the initial draft of the human rights report on Honduras included allegations of government involvement in the disappearances, but Negroponte ordered them deleted. Cohn and Thompson, "Special Report: Battalion 316," *Baltimore Sun*, June 11–18, 1995.

74. John Negroponte, "Honduras Is Well Worth Saving," *LAT*, August 12, 1983; Anne Manuel, "Death Squad Debris," *WP*, November 28, 1993.

75. Chardy and Tamayo, " 'New' CIA Deepens U.S. Involvement," *MH*, June 5, 1983.

76. Oberdorfer and Tyler, "U.S.-Backed Nicaraguan Rebel Army Swells to 7,000 Men," *WP*, May 8, 1983; Dickey, *With the Contras*, p. 146.

77. Schieffer and Gates, *Acting President*, p. 246; Woodward, *VEIL*, p. 200.

78. Woodward, *VEIL*, p. 148; Goldwater, *Goldwater*, p. 302; Persico, *Casey*, p. 275.

79. Doyle McManus and Robert C. Toth, "CIA Mining of Harbors 'a Fiasco,' " *LAT*, March 5, 1985; Fox Butterfield, "Senior Official in CIA Is Linked to North's Effort on Contra Arms," *NYT*, January 21, 1987; Weiner, *Blank Check*, p. 141.

80. William Beecher, "Military Option Rejected in Nicaragua, Cuba," *Boston Globe*, December 4, 1981; Don Oberdorfer and Patrick E. Tyler, "Reagan Backs Action Plan for Central America," *WP*, February 14, 1982.

81. Patrick E. Tyler and Bob Woodward, "U.S. Approves Covert Plan in Nicaragua," *WP*, March 10, 1982. Goldwater is quoted in "A Lot of Show, but No Tell," *Time*, March 22, 1982.

82. Woodward, *VEIL*, pp. 190–95. In fact, some administration officials admitted that the leaks were intended to intimidate the Sandinistas. Don Bohning, "Is Threat of Covert Operations a Ploy to Rattle Nicaragua?," *MH*, March 11, 1982; Patrick E. Tyler, "Senate Conducts Own Probe of Latin Unrest," *WP*, March 13, 1982; Philip Taubman, "Latin Policy," *NYT*, March 17, 1982.

83. U.S. House of Representatives, *Amendment to the Intelligence Authorization Act for Fiscal Year 1983*, June 14, 1983.

84. On the intent of the House Intelligence Committee, see U.S. House of Representatives, *Amendment to the Intelligence Authorization Act for Fiscal Year 1983*, May 13, 1983, p. 8. For the administration's interpretation of the restriction, see "The Boland Amendment," Opinion of the Intelligence Oversight Board, April 6, 1983, in *Iran-Contra Documents*, vol. 1, pp. 12–17; and the letter from William H. Taft IV, Deputy Secretary of Defense, to Henry R. Wray, Assistant General Counsel, General Accounting Office, February 2, 1984, reprinted in *Congressional Record*, February 23, 1984, pp. H886–87.

85. Clarridge, *Spy for All Seasons*, p. 215; Cruz, *Memoirs of a Counter-Revolutionary*, p. 149. Like his father, Cruz was a political ally of Pastora.

86. Robert C. Toth and Doyle McManus, "Contras and the CIA: A Plan Gone Awry," *LAT*, March 3, 1985. On Inman's concerns, see Woodward, *VEIL*, p. 205.

87. *Iran-Contra Report*, p. 32.

88. Toth and McManus, "Contras and the CIA: A Plan Gone Awry," *LAT*, March 3, 1985.

89. "A Secret War for Nicaragua," *Newsweek*, November 8, 1982. Gutman (*Banana Diplomacy*, p. 116) identified the source as Casey.

90. Oberdorfer and Tyler, "U.S.-Backed Nicaraguan Rebel Army Swells to 7,000 Men," *WP*, May 8, 1983; "A Secret War for Nicaragua," *Newsweek*, November 8, 1982.

91. David Rogers and David Ignatius, "How the CIA-Aided Rebels in Nicaragua in '84 Led Congress to End Funds," *WSJ*, March 6, 1985.

92. Oberdorfer and Tyler, "U.S.-Backed Nicaraguan Rebel Army Swells to 7,000 Men," *WP*, May 8, 1983.

93. Chardy and Tamayo, " 'New' CIA Deepens U.S. Involvement," *MH*, June 5, 1983.

94. Oberdorfer and Tyler, "U.S.-Backed Nicaraguan Rebel Army Swells to 7,000 Men," *WP*, May 8, 1983.

95. Philip Taubman, "Nicaraguan Exile Limits Role of U.S.," *NYT*, December 9, 1982; Christian, *Nicaragua*, p. 360.

96. Debate on the Harkin amendment and Boland's substitute are in *Congressional Record*, December 8, 1982, pp. H9148–59.

97. Public Law 97-377, Sec. 793. See also *Iran-Contra Report*, p. 396. The Senate debate on Nicaragua is in *Congressional Record*, December 18, 1982, pp. S15350–65.

98. Omang, "Rebel Fund Diversion Rooted in Early Policy," *WP*, January 1, 1987; Joe Pichirallo, "How North Wove Contras' Lifeline During Aid Ban," *WP*, May 4, 1987.

99. Woodward, *VEIL*, pp. 227–28.

CHAPTER FOURTEEN

1. Dickey, *With the Contras*, pp. 157–58; David Ignatius and David Rogers, "Why the Covert War in Nicaragua Evolved and Hasn't Succeeded," *WSJ*, March 5, 1985; Chamorro, "Confessions of a Contra," *New Republic*, August 5, 1985.

2. Doyle McManus and Robert C. Toth, "The Contras: How U.S. Got Entangled," *LAT*, March 4, 1985. For one example of how the administration then used the directorate as evidence to convince Congress that the contras were democratic and indigenous, see Enders, "Nicaragua," *Current Policy*, April 12, 1983.

3. Chamorro, "Confessions of a Contra," *New Republic*.

4. Ibid. Robert C. Toth and Doyle McManus, "Contras and the CIA: A Plan Gone Awry," *LAT*, March 3, 1985; Joanne Omang and Margaret Shapiro, "Punishment Urged Over CIA Manual," *WP*, November 10, 1984.

5. Chamorro, *Packaging the Contras*, p. 20; McManus and Toth, "The Contras: How U.S. Got Entangled," *LAT*, March 4, 1985.

6. James LeMoyne, "Contras Debate How to Widen Group's Appeal," *NYT*, May 23, 1986; Shirley Christian, "Sandinista Trials Slow and 'Worse Than Nuremberg,' " *MH*, January 5, 1981. A high-ranking U.S. official during the Carter administration acknowledged that Calero was a CIA asset prior to the Sandinista victory in 1979. Asked about the alleged relationship, Calero did not deny it. Joanne Omang, "Contra Chiefs Have Much to Prove with U.S. Aid," *WP*, July 14, 1986. Bermúdez had also been a CIA asset before Somoza was overthrown. James LeMoyne, "Nicaragua Rebels, in Retreat, Viewed as a Reduced Threat," *NYT*, March 6, 1986.

7. Affidavit of Edgar Chamorro submitted to the World Court, September 5, 1985, pp. 10, 18; Chamorro, "Confessions of a Contra," *New Republic*. Chamorro says that while Calero was in Nicaragua, he was the conduit through which the CIA channeled funds to Nicaraguan student and labor organizations.

8. Chamorro, "Confessions of a Contra," *New Republic*.

9. Chamorro, *Packaging the Contras*, p. 42. A subsequent investigation by the General Accounting Office (GAO) concluded that the CIA violated the law by coaching contra leaders

on how to lobby Congress. Alfonso Chardy, "Congressmen Cite More Cases of Contra Aid Misuse," *MH*, April 20, 1986.

10. Affidavit of Edgar Chamorro submitted to the World Court, September 5, 1985, p. 12; Jeane Hopfensperger, "U.S. and Contras Find Ally in Costa Rica's Three Major Dailies," *CSM*, August 18, 1986; Martha Honey, "Contra Coverage—Paid for by the CIA," *Columbia Journalism Review*, March–April 1987, pp. 31–32.

11. Chamorro, *Packaging the Contras*, pp. 34–36.

12. Don Oberdorfer and Patrick E. Tyler, "U.S.-Backed Nicaraguan Rebel Army Swells to 7,000 Men," *WP*, May 8, 1983. These figures were intentionally inflated to some extent as part of the administration's ongoing psychological warfare against the Sandinistas. Exaggerating the size of the contra army was also part of the effort to convince Congress that the covert program was a roaring success. McNeil, *War and Peace*, p. 163.

13. Richard J. Meislin, "Mexico Expels Nicaraguan Rebel After Barring a 'War' Declaration," *NYT*, April 16, 1983. The Miskito rebellion was sparked by Sandinista efforts to exert central control over the remote and traditionally autonomous Atlantic region.

14. Hinton's testimony to a closed meeting of the Senate Foreign Relations Committee, cited in Policy Alternatives for the Caribbean and Central America, *Changing Course*, p. 27.

15. Christopher Dickey, "Nicaraguan Border Town Gets Reprieve After 3rd Rebel Siege," *WP*, May 29, 1983.

16. McManus and Toth, "The Contras," *LAT*, March 4, 1985.

17. Sam Dillon, "Image, Money Woes Haunt Contras," *MH*, June 15, 1986; Ignatius and Rogers, "Why the Covert War in Nicaragua Evolved and Hasn't Succeeded," *WSJ*, March 5, 1985. Dewey Clarridge claims he never believed the contras could win on their own; either they would have to be put in power by a U.S. invasion, or traded away at the bargaining table. Clarridge, *Spy for All Seasons*, pp. 203, 232.

18. Christopher Dickey, "U.S. Diplomats in Central America See Gap Between Policy, Facts," *WP*, March 5, 1982.

19. Christopher Dickey, "The Rebels in Nicaragua Gamble on a Short War," *WP*, May 30, 1983.

20. Philip Taubman, "CIA Is Reported to Predict Ouster of the Sandinists," *NYT*, May 23, 1983. Casey denied press reports that he predicted a contra victory by December in his testimony to the intelligence committees, but it appeared that he made the comments to members informally. "Director of CIA Denies Report He Predicted Ouster of Sandinists," *NYT*, May 24, 1983.

21. Ignatius and Rogers, "Why the Covert War in Nicaragua Evolved and Hasn't Succeeded," *WSJ*, March 5, 1985; Patrick Tyler, "U.S.-Backed Rebels Can't Win in Nicaragua, CIA Finds," *WP*, November 25, 1983.

22. Sam Dillon provides the best account of the history and internal operations of the contra army. Dillon, *Commandos*.

23. Philip Taubman, "Are U.S. Covert Activities Best Policy on Nicaragua?," *NYT*, June 15, 1983.

24. Patrick E. Tyler, "Nicaragua: Hill Concern on U.S. Objectives Persists," *WP*, January 1, 1983; Alfonso Chardy, "CIA Chief Asks Continued Funding of 'Secret War' in Central America," *MH*, February 16, 1983.

25. Oberdorfer and Tyler, "U.S.-Backed Nicaraguan Rebel Army Swells to 7,000 Men," *WP*, May 8, 1983.

26. Woodward, *VEIL*, pp. 230–31; Gutman, *Banana Diplomacy*, pp. 152–53.

27. *Congressional Record*, April 28, 1983, pp. S5492–94. See also his statement in ibid., April 5, 1983, p. S4109.

28. U.S. Senate, *Report of the Select Committee on Intelligence, January 1, 1983, to December 31, 1984*, p. 5. For additional details on Leahy's report, see Woodward, *VEIL*, p. 233; Philip

Taubman, "Sandinist Factions at Issue in Hostilities, Reagan Says," *NYT*, March 30, 1983; Patrick J. Leahy, "A Makeshift Policy, Leading to War," *WP*, April 15, 1984.

29. Wyche Fowler Jr., "Conference Table Is the Place to Pursue Reagan's Goals," *LAT*, May 29, 1983; "Can Congress Keep Secrets and Keep a Rein on the CIA?," *NYT*, June 12, 1983; Martin Tolchin, "Key House Member Fears U.S. Breaks Law on Nicaragua," *NYT*, April 14, 1983.

30. Blumenthal, *Our Long National Daydream*, pp. 268–70.

31. Ibid.

32. The language of the prohibition and the subsequent quotations from the committee report are in U.S. House of Representatives, *Amendment to the Intelligence Authorization Act for Fiscal Year 1983*, May 13, 1983, pp. 1–2, 10–11, 19.

33. The administration requested $30 million in supplemental aid for the contras for FY 1983 and $50 million for FY 1984. U.S. House of Representatives, *Amendment to the Intelligence Authorization Act for Fiscal Year 1983*, June 14, 1983, p. 12.

34. U.S. House of Representatives, *Amendment to the Intelligence Authorization Act for Fiscal Year 1983*, May 13, 1983, pt. 1, p. 2. Weinberger claimed that an effective overt interdiction program would cost $300 million the first year and $100 million annually thereafter. Fred Hiatt, "Finding Justifies Covert Action," *WP*, July 27, 1983.

35. Lou Cannon, "Reagan Defends Nicaragua Role," *WP*, May 5, 1983; David Hoffman, "Miscues Worry Aides," *WP*, May 8, 1983. Perhaps Reagan's confusion about third countries stemmed from the fact that Bill Casey was already developing plans for third-country funding of the contras if Congress cut off U.S. support.

36. Edwin M. Yoder Jr., "Is Congress Serious on Nicaragua?," *WP*, April 7, 1983; "A Few Serious Thoughts," *WSJ*, April 11, 1983; "A Shield or a Land Mine?," *NYT*, July 28, 1983; "Nicaragua: Choices," *MH*, July 15, 1983.

37. In only one poll was approval of Reagan's policy higher than disapproval. Right after his speech to the joint session of Congress, approval jumped from 21 percent to 44 percent, and disapproval fell from 49 percent to 42 percent. But by the end of the year, approval had fallen back to the 25 percent range. All the polling data are drawn from LeoGrande, "Did the Public Matter?" On Wirthlin's results, see Hinckley, *People, Polls, and Policy-Makers*, pp. 79–89. Hinckley worked on the NSC staff as a polling specialist.

38. Gutman, *Banana Diplomacy*, p. 157; George Lardner Jr. and Fred Hiatt, "House Meets in Secret on War in Nicaragua," *WP*, July 20, 1983.

39. Don Oberdorfer, "CIA Planning to Back More Nicaragua Rebels," *WP*, July 14, 1983. Other options are described in Alfonso Chardy, "Diplomatic, Military Options Prepared for Managua Crisis," *MH*, April 20, 1983.

40. Leslie H. Gelb, "Central American Policy: Three Theories," *NYT*, August 19, 1983.

41. Frank Greve, "Weighing U.S. Military Options," *MH*, July 1, 1984.

42. Alfonso Chardy, "General Indicates U.S. Weakness in Latin America Is Carter Legacy," *MH*, March 2, 1984.

43. Stephen Kinzer, "The Tough U.S. General on Duty in Latin Lands," *NYT*, May 19, 1984; Loren Jenkins, "U.S. Officer Influential in Latin Region," *WP*, January 3, 1984.

44. Author's interview with a U.S. Army brigadier general, Fort Bragg, South Carolina, December 1985. See also Robert S. Greenberger, "U.S. General Is Playing Crucial Role in Setting Central American Policy," *WSJ*, June 26, 1984; James McCartney, "Powerful U.S. General Calls Signals in Central America," *MH*, May 31, 1984. Although many people attributed the reassignments of Quainton and Negroponte to Gorman's influence, there were other reasons as well. Negroponte's usefulness in Honduras diminished after General Alvarez was deposed in early 1984 because the new government would not confide in him. Quainton was said to have angered Henry Kissinger during the Kissinger Commission's trip to Central America by denying that the Sandinistas were really as bad as the administration

had portrayed them. Joanne Omang, "Two Ambassadors to Central America Expected to Be Replaced," *WP*, January 5, 1984.

45. Kinzer, "The Tough U.S. General on Duty in Latin Lands," *NYT*, May 19, 1984. For a broad review of U.S. policy aims in Costa Rica, see the leaked State Department memorandum, "U.S. Response to Costa Rica's Urgent Request for Security Assistance," May 5, 1984, in Edelman and Kenen, *Costa Rica Reader*, pp. 279–90. A network of access roads along the Costa Rican border with Nicaragua was eventually built by U.S. AID rather than the Pentagon. James LeMoyne, "In War on Want, a Military Front?," *NYT*, July 14, 1987.

46. Don Oberdorfer, "U.S. Latin Policy Reflects a New Sense of Urgency," *WP*, August 7, 1983.

47. The NSC document is described at length in Philip Taubman, "U.S. Said to Weigh 40 Percent Increase in Military Funds for Latin Allies," *NYT*, July 17, 1983; and Don Oberdorfer, "U.S. Latin Policy Reflects a New Sense of Urgency," *WP*, August 7, 1983. See also Kornbluh, *Nicaragua*, pp. 117–18.

48. Memorandum to George P. Shultz, Caspar W. Weinberger, William J. Casey, and General John W. Vessey Jr., from Ronald Reagan, "Central America," July 12, 1983, in *Iran-Contra Chronology*, p. 145. Part of the military program involved increasing aid to the contras. The contras are not mentioned in the declassified version of this document, but other documents make it clear that the redacted portion directs the Defense Department to expand its support for the contra program. See also National Security Decision Directive (NSDD) 100, "Enhanced U.S. Military Activity and Assistance for the Central American Region," July 28, 1983, in *Iran-Contra Depositions*, vol. 22, pp. 446–47.

49. Philip Taubman, "Pentagon Seeking a Rise in Advisers in Salvador to 125," *NYT*, July 24, 1983.

50. Oberdorfer, *Turn*, pp. 41–42; Fred Hiatt, "U.S. to Increase Its Military Presence in Central America," *WP*, July 21, 1983; Shultz, *Turmoil and Triumph*, pp. 310–14.

51. For detailed discussions of the exercises, see U.S. Senate, *Central America Policy*; U.S. House of Representatives, *U.S. Policy in Central America*; Richard Halloran, "Pentagon Details Honduras Action," *NYT*, July 26, 1983.

52. George Lardner Jr. and Fred Hiatt, "U.S. Envoys Hint at Possible Latin Quarantine," *WP*, July 25, 1983.

53. George C. Wilson, "U.S. Bases Considered for Honduras," *WP*, August 6, 1983.

54. Christopher Dickey, "Exercises Said to Be 'Shield' for Honduras," *WP*, July 28, 1983.

55. In one hearing, Congressman Michael Barnes asked, "Will any equipment, supplies, or facilities be left in Honduras that is not there today after our forces withdraw?" Deputy Assistant Secretary of Defense Nestor Sanchez answered, "No sir, none is being planned at this time." U.S. House of Representatives, *U.S. Policy in Central America*, p. 36. But the General Accounting Office (GAO) reported that supplies were, in fact, left behind, which was "a significant departure from past practices." See the GAO report in *Congressional Record*, June 25, 1984, pp. H6818–26.

56. Lardner and Hiatt, "U.S. Envoys Hint at Possible Latin Quarantine," *WP*, July 25, 1983. On perception management, see Gutman, *Banana Diplomacy*, pp. 144–45; Joel Brinkley, "Nicaraguan Army: 'War Machine' or Defender of a Besieged Nation?," *NYT*, March 30, 1985.

57. See, for example, Jeane Kirkpatrick's comments at the United Nations in Michael J. Berlin, "Nicaragua, at U.N., Says 4,000 Rebels Are Ready to Invade," *WP*, March 24, 1983.

58. Brinkley, "Nicaraguan Army," *NYT*, March 30, 1985.

59. Fred Hiatt, "Pentagon Outlines Plan for Exercises, Construction in Honduras," *WP*, May 12, 1984; Lou Cannon, "Maneuvers Part of New U.S. Strategy," *WP*, July 22, 1983.

60. See the speech by Senator James R. Sasser (D-Tenn.) reporting on his fact-finding trip to Honduras, in *Congressional Record*, February 8, 1984, pp. S1122–25; and the report of

the comptroller general on a GAO investigation of U.S. military exercises in Honduras requested by Congressman Bill Alexander (D-Ark.), in ibid., June 25, 1984, pp. H6818–26.

61. The GAO also found that the Pentagon used its operations and maintenance funds improperly during the exercises to train Honduran troops and to conduct civic action medical aid programs among Honduran peasants, thereby supplementing the military and economic assistance programs to Honduras without congressional approval. Ibid., June 25, 1984, pp. H6818–26.

62. O'Neill is quoted in Mary McGrory, "Imagine If the House Hadn't Voted Against the Secret War," WP, August 2, 1983. Congressional action is described in David S. Broder, "Reagan Latin Remarks Ignite Debate," WP, July 27, 1983.

63. U.S. Senate, Central American Policy, p. 12; "Shultz Vows No Attack on Nicaragua," NYT, August 8, 1983.

64. Shultz, Turmoil and Triumph, pp. 315–16.

65. "Remarks and a Question-and-Answer Session with Reporters on Domestic and Foreign Policy Issues, July 21, 1983," Reagan Papers, 1983, book 2, pp. 1066–69.

66. "The President's News Conference, July 26, 1983," ibid., pp. 1082–90.

67. Steven R. Weisman, "Reagan Denies Aim Is Bigger Presence in Latin Countries," NYT, July 27, 1983. Shultz (Turmoil and Triumph, p. 311) also concluded that "by heightening the worst fears of Congress," Big Pine assured the passage of Boland-Zablocki.

68. Taubman, "U.S. Said to Plan Military Exercises in Latin America," NYT, July 19, 1983.

69. For the debate on Boland-Zablocki, see Congressional Record, July 27, 1983, H5721–62, and July 28, 1983, H5819–81. Quotations from the debate are drawn from this transcript unless otherwise noted.

70. Congressman Thomas J. Downey (D-N.Y.) called the contras "thugs, brigands, and thieves." The Republican comments are by Robert L. Livingston (R-La.) and Mark D. Siljander (R-Mich.).

71. Don Ritter, "For Covert Action . . . ," NYT, July 19, 1983. See also his comparable comments during the floor debate, in Congressional Record, July 27, 1983, p. H5757, and July 28, 1983, pp. H5859–60.

72. Philip Taubman, "White House Says U.S. Will Still Aid Nicaragua Rebels," NYT, July 30, 1983.

73. Don Oberdorfer, "Washington's Role Troubles Congress," WP, April 3, 1983. See also Moynihan's statement in Congressional Record, April 5, 1983, pp. S4109–10.

74. Martin Tolchin, "House Panel Bars Aid for the CIA Against Nicaragua," NYT, May 4, 1983.

75. "Sanitized Version of SSCI Language from Intelligence Authorization Act of 1984," press release from the Senate Select Committee on Intelligence, May 6, 1983. Goldwater announced the amount placed in the reserve fund during a press conference. Patrick E. Tyler, "Senate Panel Compromises on Nicaragua," WP, May 7, 1983.

76. Tyler, "Senate Panel Compromises on Nicaragua," WP, May 7, 1983; Woodward, VEIL, p. 252.

77. U.S. Senate, Report of the Select Committee on Intelligence, pp. 5–6.

78. Alfonso Chardy, " 'Secret War' in Nicaragua May Expand," MH, August 7, 1983; Patrick E. Tyler, "U.S.-Backed Rebels Can't Win in Nicaragua, CIA Finds," WP, November 25, 1983; Gerald Seib, "New Reagan Strategy for Covert Activities in Nicaragua Likely to Clear Senate Panel," WSJ, September 21, 1983.

79. Moynihan's views are in Congressional Record, March 29, 1984, p. S3383; Durenberger's are in Charles R. Babcock, "Covert War in Central America Troubles a Hill GOP Overseer," WP, April 22, 1984.

80. The September 19, 1983, finding and associated scope paper are in Kornbluh and Byrne, Iran-Contra Scandal, pp. 12–17.

81. Felton, "Central America Returns to the Agenda," *CQ Weekly Report*, October 15, 1983. Moynihan's views are in Woodward, *VEIL*, pp. 276–77; *Congressional Record*, March 29, 1984, p. S3383. Durenberger's views are in Charles R. Babcock, "Covert War in Central America Troubles a Hill GOP Overseer," *WP*, April 22, 1984. Reactions of other moderates are in *Congressional Record*, April 4, 1984, pp. S3782–85.

82. *Congressional Record*, October 20, 1983, p. H8390. See also Joanne Omang, "Shultz States New Case for Covert Aid to Rebels," *WP*, September 22, 1983; and Joanne Omang, "U.S. Covert Actions Said Not Unusual," *WP*, September 23, 1983.

83. On October 20, 1983, the House approved the Boland-Zablocki language in the intelligence authorization bill, and in November it passed the defense appropriations bill containing similar language. The authorization debate is in *Congressional Record*, October 20, 1983, pp. H8389–8433. The Republicans did not challenge the defense appropriation in November.

84. Alfonso Chardy, "CIA Given $24 Million for 'Contras,' " *MH*, November 18, 1983.

85. The defense bill became P.L. 98-212 and the intelligence bill became P.L. 98-215. These acts superseded the Boland amendment of 1982, which expired at the end of FY 1983. For the text of the relevant section from P.L. 98-212, see U.S. House of Representatives, *Compilation of Intelligence Laws*, p. 345.

86. Chardy, "CIA Given $24 Million for 'Contras,' " *MH*, November 18, 1983; Alfonso Chardy, "Administration 'Pleased' by Covert Aid Extension," *MH*, November 19, 1983.

CHAPTER FIFTEEN

1. Inter-agency Task Force report and action plan, "Where Next in Central America," forwarded to McFarlane, December 20, 1983, included in *Iran-Contra Documents*, vol. 1, pp. 89–90; Memorandum to the President from Robert C. McFarlane, "Central America Legislative Strategy—Additional Funding for the Anti-Sandinista Forces," February 21, 1984, in *Iran-Contra Documents*, vol. 1, pp. 209–10.

2. "Central America: Promoting Democracy, Economic Improvement, and Peace," National Security Decision Directive 124, February 7, 1984 (NSA Nicaragua collection). See also *Iran-Contra Report*, pp. 36, 54 n. 114; Alfonso Chardy, "Reagan: Hands off Nicaragua," *MH*, June 23, 1984.

3. Memorandum to George P. Shultz, Caspar W. Weinberger, William J. Casey, and John W. Vessey Jr., from Ronald Reagan, "Central America Legislative Strategy—Additional Funding for Nicaraguan Democratic Opposition Forces," February 21, 1984, in *Iran-Contra Documents*, vol. 1, pp. 212–13.

4. The bill was H.J. Res. 493. As described earlier, the administration hoped to add $93 million in aid for El Salvador to another urgent supplemental providing funds for Africa famine relief, child nutrition, and summer jobs (H.J. Res. 492).

5. *Congressional Record*, April 4, 1984, p. S3785.

6. Joanne Omang and Margaret Shapiro, "Panel Votes Down Funds Request for Nicaragua Rebels," *WP*, March 9, 1984.

7. *Congressional Record*, March 29, 1984, pp. S3382–84.

8. H.J. Res. 492.

9. "An Interview with President Reagan on Campaign Issues," *NYT*, March 29, 1984.

10. *Congressional Record*, March 29, 1984, p. S3383. Actually, Reagan signed the finding on September 19, not September 20. It was briefed to the Intelligence Committee on September 20.

11. Ibid., April 4, 1984, p. S3760.

12. The debate is in *Congressional Record*, April 4, 1984, pp. S3758–96, and April 5, 1984, pp. S3848–53. All subsequent quotes are drawn from this source unless otherwise noted.

13. Stephen Kinzer, "Nicaraguan Port Thought to Be Mined," *NYT*, March 14, 1984; Dusko Doder, "Soviets Blame U.S. in Tanker Blast," *WP*, March 22, 1984.

14. "U.S. Denies Responsibility," *NYT*, March 22, 1984; Doder, "Soviets Blame U.S. in Tanker Blast," *WP*, March, 22, 1984.

15. Kornbluh, *Nicaragua*, p. 50.

16. *Congressional Record*, April 4, 1984, p. S3775.

17. Doyle McManus, "U.S. Didn't Mine Ports: Weinberger," *LAT*, April 9, 1984.

18. Gutman, *Banana Diplomacy*, p. 196; Shultz, *Turmoil and Triumph*, p. 308. The first report that plans were afoot to mine Nicaragua's harbors was John Wallach's article in the *San Francisco Examiner* in July 1983, reprinted in the *Congressional Record*, July 21, 1983, E3641–42.

19. Dickey, *With the Contras*, pp. 258–59.

20. Woodward, *VEIL*, p. 281; Clarridge, *Spy for All Seasons*, pp. 263–65. The CIA had originally trained contra units as commandos, but they weren't very effective. Dillon, *Commandos*, p. 133.

21. Quoted in Kornbluh, *Nicaragua*, p. 47.

22. The SEALS were probably drawn from U.S. forces stationed in El Salvador, who were training Salvadoran commandos to use "piranha" speedboats provided by the CIA to intercept arms smuggling to the Salvadoran guerrillas. Both the Salvadoran commandos and the UCLAS operated their boats from the same base on Tiger Island, just off the Honduran coast. Salvadorans were also the most numerous nationality among the UCLAS, though prior to the U.S. training program, El Salvador had no navy. Andres Oppenheimer, "Poor Islanders Fear a Role in Contra War Despite Chance of Jobs," *MH*, November 1, 1986; Frank Greve and Mark Fazlollah, "NSC Bypassed Military with Covert Operations," *MH*, July 26, 1987. Some of the UCLA operations are described in "CIA Employees Fought Nicaraguans," *WP*, December 20, 1984, although the participants are described as "CIA employees" rather than Special Forces units.

23. David Rogers and David Ignatius, "How CIA-Aided Raids in Nicaragua in '84 Led Congress to End Funds," *WSJ*, March 6, 1985; "CIA Internal Report Details U.S. Role in Contra Raids in Nicaragua Last Year," *WSJ*, March 6, 1985; Charles R. Babcock, "CIA Directly Oversaw Attack in October on Nicaragua Oil Facility," *WP*, April 18, 1984; "October 10 Assault on Nicaraguans Is Laid to CIA," *NYT*, April 18, 1984; Robert J. McCartney, "Exxon Cuts Nicaragua's Oil Supply," *WP*, October 15, 1983. The CIA's role in the harbor attacks came to light shortly after disclosure of the mining, probably as a result of Boland's offhand remark that there were "other things" besides the mining that the UCLAS had done. *Congressional Record*, April 12, 1984, p. H2918.

24. Clarridge, *Spy for All Seasons*, pp. 269–70; Woodward, *VEIL*, p. 282; Rogers and Ignatius, "How CIA-Aided Raids in Nicaragua in '84 Led Congress to End Funds," *WSJ*, March 6, 1985.

25. "Our intention is to severely disrupt the flow of shipping essential to Nicaraguan trade during the peak export period," NSC staffers wrote in a memo to McFarlane shortly after the mining began. "It is entirely likely that once a ship has been sunk, no insurers will cover ships calling in Nicaraguan ports." Memorandum to McFarlane from Oliver L. North and Constantine Menges, "Special Activities in Nicaragua," March 2, 1984, in *Iran-Contra Hearings*, vol. 100-7, pt. 3, pp. 726–27.

26. Hedrick Smith, "Britain Criticizes Mining of Harbors Around Nicaragua," *NYT*, April 7, 1984.

27. Shultz, *Turmoil and Triumph*, p. 406; Alfonso Chardy, "Contras Plotted Mexican Ship Paths," *MH*, January 12, 1988.

28. Testimony of Robert C. McFarlane, *Iran-Contra Hearings*, vol. 100-2, pp. 233–34.

29. Shultz, *Turmoil and Triumph*, pp. 308, 404. Shultz was out of the United States from

December 6 to December 13. Donald Gregg, Vice President Bush's national security adviser, described the December meeting during Senate hearings, as quoted in Daniel Patrick Moynihan, *On the Law of Nations*, pp. 135–37. There is, however, some confusion about when the final decision was made. McFarlane dates the decision to a January NSPG meeting (McFarlane and Smardz, *Special Trust*, p. 282), and Clarridge claims to have thought of the idea after a mid-January NSPG meeting (Clarridge, *Spy for All Seasons*, pp. 269–70). Clarridge claims the first mines were laid on February 7, but the Nicaraguan press first reported the existence of the mines on January 3.

30. Gutman, *Banana Diplomacy*, p. 196.

31. *Congressional Record*, April 12, 1984, p. H2918; Babcock, "CIA Directly Oversaw Attack in October on Nicaragua Oil Facility," *WP*, April 18, 1984. Casey is quoted in Joanne Omang, "A Historical Background to the CIA's Nicaragua Manual," in *Psychological Operations in Guerrilla Warfare*, pp. 1–30.

32. Bernard Gwertzman, "Moynihan to Quit Senate Panel Post in Dispute on CIA," *NYT*, April 16, 1984.

33. Bernard Gwertzman, "CIA Now Asserts It Sought Delays in Senate Briefing," *NYT*, April 17, 1984.

34. Woodward, *VEIL*, p. 320.

35. Goldwater, *Goldwater*, p. 302.

36. David Rogers, "U.S. Role in Mining Nicaraguan Harbors Is Larger Than First Thought," *WSJ*, April 6, 1984. For confirmations, see Philip Taubman, "Americans on Ship Said to Supervise Nicaragua Mining," *NYT*, April 8, 1984.

37. Goldwater, *Goldwater*, p. 305.

38. *Congressional Record*, April 10, 1984, p. S4198.

39. The full text of the letter is in "Goldwater Writes CIA Director Scorching Letter," *WP*, April 11, 1984.

40. Woodward, *VEIL*, pp. 322–23.

41. Martin Tolchin, "Senate, 84–12, Acts to Oppose Mining Nicaragua Ports," *NYT*, April 11, 1984; George Lardner Jr., "Will We Ever Harness Our Rogue Agency?," *WP*, April 22, 1984.

42. "No Place Left to Hide?," *Time*, April 30, 1984.

43. "Moynihan's Statement on Quitting Panel Job," *NYT*, April 16, 1984; Persico, *Casey*, p. 377.

44. Moynihan, *Came the Revolution*, p. 177.

45. Philip Taubman, "House Unit Says Report on Mines Arrived Jan. 31," *NYT*, April 14, 1984; Gwertzman, "Moynihan to Quit Senate Panel Post in Dispute on CIA," *NYT*, April 16, 1984.

46. Persico, *Casey*, p. 377.

47. "Text of Statement by CIA," *NYT*, April 17, 1984; Don Oberdorfer and Bob Woodward, "U.S. Says Port Mining Has Ceased," *WP*, April 12, 1984; Woodward, *VEIL*, p. 326.

48. "What's Behind Reagan Strategy in Nicaragua," *U.S. News and World Report*, April 23, 1984.

49. Helen Dewar, "Casey Apologizes to Hill for Lapse on Port Mining," *WP*, April 27, 1984; Philip Taubman, "Moynihan to Keep Intelligence Post," *NYT*, April 27, 1984.

50. Goldwater, *Goldwater*, p. 307.

51. Dewar, "Casey Apologizes to Hill for Lapse on Port Mining," *WP*, April 27, 1984.

52. Persico, *Casey*, p. 380.

53. U.S. Senate, *Report of the Select Committee on Intelligence, January 1, 1983, to December 31, 1984*, pp. 9–10.

54. "Procedures Governing Reporting to the Senate Select Committee on Intelligence (SSCI) on Covert Action," June 6, 1984, and "Addendum to Procedures Governing Reporting

to the Senate Select Committee on Intelligence on Covert Action," June 17, 1984, in *Iran-Contra Documents*, vol. 1, pp. 884–89; Johnson, *Sleepwalking through History*, pp. 278–79.

55. Gwertzman, "Moynihan to Quit Senate Panel Post in Dispute on CIA," *NYT*, April 16, 1984. Moynihan and Goldwater agreed that they would keep some especially sensitive secrets to themselves, not even sharing them with other senators on the committee. And Goldwater, for one, didn't really believe in congressional oversight of intelligence activities; in 1976, he voted against creation of the Senate committee. Goldwater, *Goldwater*, pp. 287, 301.

56. "Illegal, Deceptive and Dumb," *NYT*, April 11, 1984; "Contempt for the Rule of Law," *St. Louis Post-Dispatch*, April 18, 1984; "Mining vs. Values," *MH*, April 16, 1984; "Anatomy of a Cop-Out," *WSJ*, April 12, 1984.

57. LeoGrande, "Did the Public Matter?"

58. Gutman, *Banana Diplomacy*, p. 196.

59. Kornbluh, *Nicaragua*, p. 51.

60. Don Oberdorfer and Fred Hiatt, "U.S. to Bar Latin Role for Court," *WP*, April 9, 1984. See also Bernard Gwertzman, "U.S. Voids Role of World Court on Latin Policy," *NYT*, April 9, 1984.

61. Martin Feinrider, "World Court Snub Undermines Law and Logic," *MH*, April 15, 1984. The text of the 1946 declaration is in the *Congressional Record*, April 10, 1984, pp. S4194–97. See also Briggs, "Nicaragua v. the United States," *American Journal of International Law* (April 1985); D'Amato, "Modifying U.S. Acceptance of the Compulsory Jurisdiction of the World Court," *American Journal of International Law* (April 1985).

62. Stuart Taylor Jr., "Nicaragua Takes Case Against U.S. to World Court," *NYT*, April 10, 1984.

63. "U.S. 'Should Cease and Refrain,'" *WP*, May, 11, 1984; Deatherage, "International Court of Justice," *Harvard International Law Journal* (1985).

64. Felton, "Administration Defends Mining of Harbors," *CQ Weekly Report*, April 14, 1984. For a more extended debate on the merits of the issue, see Moore, *Secret War in Central America*, in defense of the administration, and Chayes, "Nicaragua, the United States and the World Court," *Columbia Law Review* (November 1985), against.

65. Felton, "Administration Defends Mining of Harbors," *CQ Weekly Report*; Charlotte Saikowski, "Behind U.S. Rebuff of World Court," *CSM*, April 16, 1984.

66. Administration hard-liners had wanted to lodge a complaint against Nicaragua in the OAS in 1983 as a prelude to collective sanctions, but the State Department opposed it because most of Latin America would have voted against Washington. Alfonso Chardy, "U.S. May Try for Censure of Managua," *MH*, October 6, 1983.

67. John M. Goshko and Charles Babcock, "U.S. Reasons for Mining Challenged," *WP*, April 14, 1984; Bob Woodward, "CIA Funds Run Short for Covert Operations," *WP*, April 13, 1984. The use of mining as an instrument was itself of dubious legality. The 1907 Hague Convention Relative to the Laying of Automatic Submarine Contact Mines, to which both Nicaragua and the United States were signatories, prohibited using mines "with the sole object of intercepting commercial shipping" (Article 2), or laying mines that remain operative for more than one hour, even in war time (Article 1). Article 3 required notification to ship owners and governments that mines had been laid so as to safeguard "the security of peaceful shipping." Washington complied with none of these provisions. "CIA Mining vs. More Than One World Law," *NYT*, April 21, 1984.

68. *Congressional Record*, April 10, 1984, pp. S4199–4205; Philip Taubman, "President's Secret War in Nicaragua Backfires," *NYT*, April 15, 1984.

69. *Congressional Record*, April 12, 1984, pp. H2878–2905.

70. Woodward, *VEIL*, p. 325.

71. "Interview with Brian Farrell of RTE-Television, Dublin, Ireland, on Foreign Issues, May 28, 1984," *Reagan Papers, 1984*, book 1, pp. 750–56.

72. "Remarks at the National Leadership Forum of the Center for International and Strategic Studies of Georgetown University, April 6, 1984," ibid., pp. 477–85.

73. Barry, *Ambition and Power*, pp. 162–65.

74. Ibid., pp. 158–59.

75. *Congressional Record*, April 12, 1874, pp. H2907–9 (which includes the text of the letter to Ortega); ibid., May 1, 1984, pp. H3232–38.

76. Ibid., April 24, 1984, pp. H2983–94.

77. Ibid., May 7, 1984, pp. H3434–38; May 8, 1984, pp. H3537–53.

78. "Audience Growing for TV Coverage of the House," *CQ Weekly Report*, January 12, 1985.

79. *Congressional Record*, May 14, 1984, pp. H3789–90.

80. Granat, "The House's TV War," *CQ Weekly Report*, May 19, 1984.

81. *Congressional Record*, May 15, 1984, pp. H3840–52.

82. Joanne Omang, "House Democrats Firm on Rebel Aid," *WP*, May 17, 1984.

83. The full debate, from which this and subsequent quotations are drawn, is in *Congressional Record*, May 24, 1984, pp. H4777–4806.

84. Ibid., June 25, 1984, pp. S8160–73. In exchange for dropping the $21 million for the contras from its version of the bill, the Senate required the House to drop the Boland prohibition it had added. Consequently, in its final form, the urgent supplemental had no section at all on Nicaragua. The operative legal restriction was in the continuing resolution passed the previous year, which prohibited any aid for the contras in excess of $24 million.

85. "Remarks and a Question-and-Answer Session with Elected Republican Women Officials, June 29, 1984," *Reagan Papers, 1984*, book 1, pp. 927–31.

86. *Congressional Record*, April 12, 1984, p. H2901; U.S. House of Representatives, *Report on the Activities of the Permanent Select Committee on Intelligence*, p. 15; U.S. Senate, *Report of the Select Committee on Intelligence*, p. 10.

87. Felton, "Intelligence Bills," *CQ Weekly Report*, June 16, 1984. Senator Biden tried to make the conditions even tougher, allowing the aid to be used solely for interdicting arms shipments from Nicaragua to El Salvador, but his proposal failed, 8–4. Margaret Shapiro, "$28 Million Backed for Aid to 'Contras,' " *WP*, June 14, 1984.

88. *Congressional Record*, October 3, 1984, p. S12879. When the continuing resolution came to the Senate floor, Inouye tried but failed to delete the funds, instead providing $2 million in wind-down money to extract the contras from Nicaragua and $4 million in humanitarian aid for them after they disarmed.

89. "On Foreign Aid, More Stumbling Blocks," *CQ Weekly Report*, October 6, 1984.

90. P.L. 98-473, Sec. 8066(a). The text of this provision is in U.S. House of Representatives, *Compilation of Intelligence Laws*, pp. 346–48. The expedited procedures provided that the request could not be held in committee longer than ten legislative days, after which the request would be automatically discharged and available for consideration on the floor. Amendments to the request were prohibited, as was a filibuster in the Senate.

91. *Congressional Record*, October 11, 1984, p. H12206.

92. McFarlane's testimony at North's trial, quoted in Draper, *Very Thin Line*, p. 80; Alfonso Chardy, "Reagan Seeks Deal to Fund Contras," *MH*, August 30, 1984.

CHAPTER SIXTEEN

1. Lou Cannon, "President Sees Talks Resuming," *WP*, May 23, 1984.

2. Joseph Kraft, "Running as Peacemaker," *WP*, June 5, 1984.

3. "Address to the 39th Session of the United Nations General Assembly in New York, New York, September 24, 1984," in *Reagan Papers, 1984*, book 2, pp. 1355–61.

4. Mayer and McManus, *Landslide*, pp. 15–16; Woodward, *VEIL*, p. 256.

5. Don Oberdorfer, "Cuba Eyeing Latin 'Tet,' U.S. Says," *WP*, May 14, 1984.

6. Mayer and McManus, *Landslide*, p. 15.

7. "Aides Confirm Thinking on GI's," *NYT*, April 10, 1984; Hedrick Smith, "U.S. Latin Force in Place If Needed, Officials Report," *NYT*, April 23, 1984. Two nonofficial estimates were made of what an invasion of Nicaragua would require and what it would cost. One estimated the cost for the initial assault and a five-year occupation at $10.6 billion, with 12,000 to 23,000 U.S. casualties. The other analysis estimated $12 billion in about the same time frame, with only 7,000 casualties. Theodore Moran, "The Cost of Alternative U.S. Policies Toward El Salvador," in Leiken, *Central America*, pp. 153–72; "U.S. Invasion of Nicaragua: Appraising the Cost," *Defense Monitor* (1987). Former chief of staff of the army Edward C. Meyer thought the cost would be even higher. "I'd double or triple the estimates I've seen because once you put American forces down there against Nicaraguans, the whole country would unify against the Yankee. There would be a lot more resistance than most people expect because fighting guerrillas in the countryside and in the cities is the most difficult and exasperating kind of warfare. And as it wore on, I guarantee that the stomach for it would go down not only among the American people but among any enthusiasts you might currently find in the Army." Frank Greve, "Weighing U.S. Military Options," *MH*, July 1, 1984.

8. Richard Halloran, "U.S. Said to Draw Latin Troops Plan," *NYT*, April 8, 1984; "Aides Confirm Thinking on GI's," *NYT*, April 10, 1984; Hedrick Smith, "U.S. Latin Force in Place If Needed, Officials Report," *NYT*, April 23, 1984; Greve, "Weighing U.S. Military Options," *MH*, July 1, 1984; Doyle McManus, "U.S. to Chart Options for a Crisis in El Salvador," *LAT*, July 13, 1984.

9. "U.S. Policy in Central America: White House Statement, April 10, 1984," *U.S. Department of State Bulletin*, June 1984, pp. 85–86.

10. Richard Halloran, "Arms and the Election Year," *NYT*, June 29, 1984.

11. The House debate is in *Congressional Record*, May 23, 1984, pp. H4745–48. The Senate debate is in ibid., June 18, 1984, pp. S7480–98. The compromise is described in Wayne Biddle, "Conferees Reach Accord on the Next Military Budget," *NYT*, September 26, 1984.

12. The text of their communiqué is in Bagley, Alvarez, and Hagedorn, *Contadora and the Central American Peace Process*, pp. 164–66.

13. For a good explication of the Contadora countries' motives, see Tom Farer, "Contadora: The Hidden Agenda," *Foreign Policy* (Summer 1985). For a detailed discussion of the foreign policies of the major Contadora states, see Bagley, *Regional Powers in the Caribbean Basin*.

14. James Nelson Goodsell, "Mexico Begins to Bridge Policy Gap with U.S. on Salvador, Other Issues," *CSM*, April 11, 1983.

15. Riding, *Distant Neighbors*, p. 358.

16. Stuart Taylor Jr., "U.S. Still Favors Latin Peace Talks," *NYT*, April 11, 1983; Barbara Crossette, "What Hopes for the Contadora Process?," *NYT*, June 19, 1983.

17. "U.S. Rejects Nicaraguan Offer," *NYT*, April 12, 1983. Administration officials express their candid views in the minutes of the June 25, 1984, National Security Planning Group (NSPG) meeting, released during Oliver L. North's trial, in Kornbluh and Byrne, *Iran-Contra Scandal*, pp. 69–82.

18. Alfonso Chardy, "Latin Ministers Fail to Find Peace Plan," *MH*, April 22, 1983.

19. The text of the Document of Objectives is in Bagley, Alvarez, and Hagedorn, *Contadora and the Central American Peace Process*, pp. 176–80.

20. The text of the "Declaration of San José," signed by the participants, is in ibid., pp. 155–60.

21. Lou Cannon, "Castro's Effort to End Aid 'Not Serious,' Officials Say," *MH*, August 14, 1983.

22. Texts of the four draft treaties are in Bagley, Alvarez, and Hagedorn, *Contadora and the Central American Peace Process*, pp. 60–83.

23. Hedrick Smith, "U.S. Spurns Peace Plan Offered by Nicaragua," *NYT*, October 22, 1983.

24. Edward Cody, "Fear of Attack Seen Causing Cubans to Leave Nicaragua," *WP*, January 31, 1984; Robert S. Greenberger, "Nicaragua Offers Amnesty to Some Critics as Part of Plan to Hold Elections in 1985," *WSJ*, December 5, 1983; Leslie Gelb, "Latin Diplomacy: Little Result Yet," *NYT*, April 29, 1984. Senator David Durenberger, a member of the Intelligence Committee, reported that the Cubans had advised the Sandinistas to be cautious in the wake of the Grenada invasion, and that the Sandinistas had taken his advice. *Congressional Record*, April 10, 1984, p. S4202.

25. Lou Cannon, "Aides Propound Scenarios for Central America," *WP*, July 31, 1983; Alfonso Chardy, "U.S.: Signals by Managua 'Just Words,'" *MH*, January 24, 1984. See also Hedrick Smith, "U.S. Policy on Nicaragua: Keep the Pressure On," *NYT*, December 1, 1983; Don Oberdorfer, "U.S. Officials Doubt Reports of Changes in Nicaraguan Policy," *WP*, November 26, 1983.

26. George Skelton, "U.S. Relays Peace Bid to Nicaragua," *LAT*, December 2, 1983.

27. Stephen Kinzer, "Honduras Said to Snag Latin Peace Bid," *NYT*, December 15, 1983.

28. From North's notebooks for March 1984, quoted in "The Talk of the Town," *New Yorker*, June 11, 1990.

29. Robert J. McCartney, "Mexico Says Peace Moves at an Impasse," *WP*, May 11, 1984.

30. In April 1982, a National Security Planning Group (NSPG) policy document complained about Mexico's "public and covert support for the extreme left." The administration decided to adopt "a more active diplomatic campaign" to turn Mexico around. "U.S. Policy in Central America and Cuba Through F.Y. '84, Summary Paper," prepared for NSPG meeting, April 1982, as printed in "National Security Council Document on Policy in Central America and Cuba," *NYT*, April 7, 1983.

31. Marlise Simons, "Washington Drops In on the 'Last Domino,'" *NYT*, April 17, 1983. At the July 1983 National Security Council meeting that adopted the hard-liners' aggressive new approach to Central America, the Department of Defense argued for turning the screws on the Mexicans. "DOD believes the U.S. should seek a more supportive policy from Mexico, building on U.S. financial support," a planning paper for the meeting reported. "State believes that a substantial modification in Mexican behavior is already underway and that explicitly linking U.S. financial support to further changes in Mexican behavior is not likely to improve results." Again, the State Department view prevailed. "Strategy for Central America," an NSPG discussion paper, July 6, 1983, as quoted in Kornbluh, *Nicaragua*, p. 116.

32. Roy Gutman, "Mexico's Oil Is Leverage on Nicaragua," *Newsday*, September 2, 1985.

33. "Central America: Promoting Democracy, Economic Improvement, and Peace," National Security Decision Directive 124, as quoted in Kornbluh, *Nicaragua* p. 116. See also Menges, *Inside the National Security Council*, p. 118.

34. Richard J. Meislin, "Mexican Official Condemns Mining of Nicaragua's Ports," *NYT*, April 14, 1984. Menges described the plan as an elaborate public diplomacy campaign that did not include an economic component. Menges, *Inside the National Security Council*, pp. 118–20. At about this same time, the President's Foreign Intelligence Advisory Board, a panel of private citizens charged with overseeing intelligence policy, suggested that Washington use the threat of reduced economic aid to pressure Mexico into changing its Central America policy. Robert S. Greenberger, "U.S. Encouraged by Mexican Leader's Tougher Stance Towards Sandinistas," *WSJ*, May 15, 1984.

35. Shultz, *Turmoil and Triumph*, p. 423; Doyle McManus, "Stubborn Congress Balks at Central American Policy," *LAT*, March 11, 1984; Woodward, *VEIL*, p. 257.

36. Clarridge, *Spy for All Seasons*, pp. 42, 179, 241.

37. "Three Senate Democrats Criticize Briefing by CIA on Caribbean," *WP*, December 23, 1981.

38. Menges, "Central America and Its Enemies," *Commentary*, August 1981. The same attitude suffuses Menges's memoir, *Inside the National Security Council*.

39. Menges, *Inside the National Security Council*, p. 133.

40. Woodward, *VEIL*, p. 340.

41. Cannon, *President Reagan*, p. 350.

42. Woodward, *VEIL*, pp. 340–41. The estimate was entitled "Prospects for Instability in Mexico." Jack Anderson, "Mexican Party Losing Its Grip, CIA Concludes," *WP*, August 17, 1984.

43. Philip Taubman, "Analyst Reported to Leave CIA in a Clash with Casey on Mexico," *NYT*, September 28, 1984; Omang, "Byrd Seeks Senate Probe of Charges of Report-Altering at CIA," *WP*, September 29, 1984.

44. U.S. Senate, *Nomination of Robert M. Gates to Be Director of Central Intelligence*, pp. 175–76. A subsequent CIA estimate, "Mexico: Growing Challenge to Current Stability," was produced in 1987 after Casey's death. It concluded that the government was basically stable, that Cuba and the Soviet Union were not likely to try to subvert it, and if they did, "We believe the government has the power to forestall such an effort." Jack Anderson and Dale Van Atta, "Mexico—Not Much of a Domino," *WP*, June 7, 1987.

45. Joanne Omang, "Analyst Says He Quit CIA When Casey Altered His Report to Support Policy," *WP*, September 28, 1984; U.S. Senate, *Nomination of Robert M. Gates to Be Director of Central Intelligence*, p. 175. See also John Horton, "Why I Quit the CIA," *WP*, January 2, 1985; John Horton, "The Real Intelligence Failure," *Foreign Service Journal*, February 1985. Horton reported that similar pressures were brought to bear on intelligence estimates concerning the Cuban presence in Grenada and the military competence of the Salvadoran armed forces.

46. Woodward, *VEIL*, pp. 343–44; Taubman, "Analyst Reported to Leave CIA in a Clash with Casey on Mexico," *NYT*, September 28, 1984.

47. "Excerpts from Remarks by the Two Presidents," *NYT*, May 16, 1984. See also Francis X. Clines, "Blunt Talk Marks Reagan's Welcome for Mexico's Chief," *NYT*, May 16, 1984.

48. De la Madrid's speech is in the *Congressional Record*, May 16, 1984, pp. H3965–67.

49. Shultz, *Turmoil and Triumph*, pp. 400–401; Juan M. Vasquez, "Mexico Upgrading Its Ties with Salvador Government," *LAT*, June 10, 1984.

50. Shultz, *Turmoil and Triumph*, p. 410; Joanne Omang, "Shultz Meets with Ortega in Managua," *WP*, June 2, 1984.

51. Richard J. Meislin, "Mexico Is Said to Modify Its Policy on El Salvador," *NYT*, June 3, 1984.

52. Shultz makes this point in *Turmoil and Triumph*, p. 401. See also Bernard Gwertzman, "Shultz Trip: A Serious Bid for Peace?," *NYT*, June 4, 1984.

53. Author's interview with a Mondale campaign foreign policy adviser, Washington, D.C., June 1984. See also Pastor, *Condemned to Repetition*, pp. 247–48.

54. Bill Keller, "Democrats Laud Nicaragua Move but They Question the Motives," *NYT*, June 3, 1984; Robert J. McCartney, "Managua Wary of Initiative by Washington," *WP*, June 3, 1984.

55. Joanne Omang, "Reagan Sees Hill Leaders; Pressure for Latin Aid Rises," *WP*, May 9, 1984.

56. Dennis Volman, "U.S.-Nicaragua Ties Getting Steadier?," *CSM*, July 10, 1984.

57. Robert S. Greenberger, "Motley Helps Sell U.S. Central American Policy," *WSJ*, August 13, 1984.

58. Don Oberdorfer, "Administration Seeking Agenda with Nicaragua," *WP*, June 3, 1984.

59. Gutman, *Banana Diplomacy*, pp. 209–10; Menges, *Inside the National Security Council*, p. 123.

60. Menges, *Inside the National Security Council*, p. 123.

61. Shultz, *Turmoil and Triumph*, p. 412.

62. Menges, *Inside the National Security Council*, p. 127. The following account of the meeting is based on minutes from the June 25, 1984, National Security Planning Group (NSPG) meeting, released during Oliver L. North's trial, in Kornbluh and Byrne, *Iran-Contra Scandal*, pp. 69–82. See also Shultz's account in *Turmoil and Triumph*, p. 415.

63. Reagan reiterated this point three different times in the meeting.

64. Shultz, *Turmoil and Triumph*, p. 419; Menges, *Inside the National Security Council*, p. 129.

65. Gutman, *Banana Diplomacy*, pp. 216–17.

66. Ibid., p. 216.

67. The text of the U.S. proposal is included in ibid., pp. 378–81.

68. Ibid., p. 219. The text of the Nicaraguan proposal is at pp. 382–84.

69. Philip Taubman, "Nicaraguan Talks Are Said to Stall," *NYT*, November 2, 1984.

70. "Diplomats See 'a Lot of Talk, Little Progress' with Contadora," *MH*, August 30, 1984; Richard J. Meislin, "Latins Offer a Salvador Mediation Plan," *NYT*, July 24, 1984.

71. The draft's security provisions prohibited foreign military schools or bases, banned international military maneuvers, required the withdrawal of all foreign military advisers, prohibited support for insurgent movements against other nations in the region, and placed limits on the size of military forces and the sophistication of their weaponry. The political provisions of the proposed treaty committed the five nations to developing representative pluralist democracies, ensuring honest periodic elections, and protecting human rights. Countries torn by civil strife would be required to promote national reconciliation. The full text of the agreement is in Bagley, Alvarez, and Hagedorn, *Contadora and the Central American Peace Process*, pp. 186–217.

72. See, for example, "[Salvadoran] Foreign Minister Praises Contadora Efforts," in U.S. Foreign Broadcast Information Service, *Daily Report: Latin America*, September 13, 1984, p. 3; "[Costa Rican] Government Accepts Contadora Peace Document," ibid., September 19, 1984, p. 1; and "[Honduran] Government Declaration on Contadora Document," ibid., September 20, 1984, p. 5. The Sandinistas' acceptance of the draft is reported in Philip Taubman, "U.S. Reported to Fear Sandinista Publicity Coup," *NYT*, September 24, 1984.

73. John M. Goshko, "Modify Contadora Plan, U.S. Urges Latin Allies," *WP*, October 2, 1984; Taubman, "U.S. Reported to Fear Sandinista Publicity Coup," *NYT*, September 24, 1984.

74. "Unclassified Summary of the State Department's Objections to September 7 Draft of Contadora Agreement," *International Policy Report* (Center for International Policy), November 1984, p. 5.

75. Leslie H. Gelb, "Stalemates Will Survive the Election," *NYT*, October 8, 1984.

76. Don Oberdorfer, "Shultz, Foreign Ministers Discuss Contadora Treaty," *WP*, October 6, 1984; Joanne Omang, "U.S. Plays Contadora Catch-Up," *WP*, October 15, 1984.

77. Menges, *Inside the National Security Council*, pp. 142–45.

78. Michael J. Berlin, "Salvadoran Leader Proposes Meeting with Guerrillas," *WP*, October 9, 1984; James Feron, "Honduran, at the U.N., Suggests Latin Nations Meet," *NYT*, October 10, 1984; James Feron, "Costa Rica Seeks Peace Plan Shift," *NYT*, October 11, 1984.

79. "Acta de Contadora para la paz y la cooperación en centroamerica: Versión revisada durante la reunión de cancilleres centroamericanos," Tegucigalpa, October 20, 1984 (typescript).

80. "U.S. Version of Contadora Draft Disputed," *WP*, October 3, 1984. No doubt the Contadora foreign ministers hoped the September document was close to final, but in their letter transmitting the draft to the Central Americans, they expressed their hope for quick signature, "once the improvements considered relevant are made." "Communication from

the Ministers for Foreign Affairs of the Contadora Group Addressed to the Five Central American Heads of State," in Bagley, Alvarez, and Hagedorn, *Contadora and the Central American Peace Process*, pp. 188–90.

81. "Background Paper for NSC Meeting on Central America," October 30, 1984, as described in Alma Guillermoprieto and David Hoffman, "Document Describes How U.S. 'Blocked' a Contadora Treaty," *WP*, November 6, 1984; Alma Guillermoprieto, "Torpedoing Latin Interests," *WP*, November 11, 1984.

82. PROFS note to Robert C. McFarlane from John M. Poindexter, "A Proposal for Resolving Inter-Agency Conflict," November 23, 1984, in *Iran-Contra Hearings*, vol. 100-8, pp. 414–17.

83. Gutman, *Banana Diplomacy*, p. 230.

84. Philip Taubman, "U.S. Says It Has Halted Talks with Nicaragua," *NYT*, January 19, 1985. From the beginning, the hard-liners had argued against the Manzanillo talks on the grounds that they interfered with Contadora, and Shultz countered that the main aim of the bilateral talks would be to smooth the way for a regional accord. Yet when the Contadora draft treaty appeared on the bargaining table at Manzanillo, the United States walked away. Minutes from the June 25, 1984, National Security Planning Group (NSPG) meeting, released during Oliver L. North's trial, in Kornbluh and Byrne, *Iran-Contra Scandal*, pp. 69–82.

85. McNeil, *War and Peace in Central America*, p. 180.

86. "CIA Said to Produce Manual for Anti-Sandinistas," *NYT*, October 15, 1984. The manual was published in translation as *Psychological Operations in Guerrilla Warfare*. All citations herein are to this translation. The CIA also prepared a comic book on sabotage for the contras to distribute to civilian sympathizers, the existence of which became known in June 1984. The "Freedom Fighter's Manual," as the comic book was entitled, illustrated thirty-eight ways in which people could help "liberate Nicaragua from oppression and misery" and "participate in the final battle" against the Sandinistas. The manual advised people how to sabotage electrical systems, make Molotov cocktails, set fires in factories, and disable vehicles. The book, *Manual del Combatiente por la Libertad*, was reproduced and distributed in the United States as *The Freedom Fighter's Manual*. See also [Robert Parry], "Nicaraguans Said to Get CIA Sabotage Tips," *Baltimore Sun*, June 30, 1984.

87. Robert Parry, "Latin Manual Is Linked to CIA 'Psy-War' Plan," *WP*, December 3, 1984; Joanne Omang, "Nicaragua Manual Was Censored, but Still Urged Violence," *WP*, October 23, 1984.

88. David Ignatius and David Rogers, "Why the Covert War in Nicaragua Evolved and Hasn't Succeeded," *WSJ*, March 5, 1985; Dickey, *With the Contras*, pp. 254–56; Jeffreys-Jones, *CIA and American Democracy*, p. 239.

89. Joel Brinkley, "CIA Chief Defends Manual for Nicaraguan Rebels," *NYT*, November 2, 1984; Brian Barger, "CIA Manual Said Aimed at Contra Abuses," *WP*, October 31, 1984; Joanne Omang, "CIA Manual Based on Vietnam," *WP*, October 30, 1984; Philip Taubman, "CIA Manual Is Linked to Vietnam War Guide," *NYT*, October 29, 1984.

90. Political proselytizing, the manual explained, "is simple and requires only a basic knowledge of the Socratic dialectic." It quoted Aristotle and a Huk guerrilla leader from the Philippines, and listed Cicero, Demosthenes, Robespierre, Lenin, Trotsky, Hitler, and Roosevelt as great orators. In an appendix, it reviewed the basic elements of good speaking: anaphora, reduplication, simile, antithesis, prolepsis, and preterition. *Psychological Operations in Guerrilla Warfare*, pp. 92–93.

91. Ibid., pp. 38, 62–63, 69–70, 74–77.

92. Ibid., pp. 84–87.

93. Ibid., pp. 57–58. President Gerald Ford first prohibited CIA participation in assassinations in the mid-1970s after previous attempts to kill Fidel Castro, Patrice Lumumba, and

Raphael Trujillo came to light. Both Carter and Reagan reaffirmed the prohibition. Norman Kempster, "Reagan Orders Probe of CIA Manual for Rebels," *LAT*, October 19, 1984.

94. Editorial, "The CIA's Murder Manual," *WP*, October 21, 1984.

95. Joel Brinkley, "President Orders Two Investigations on CIA Manual," *NYT*, October 19, 1984.

96. "Congress Is Widening CIA Primer Inquiry," *NYT*, October 26, 1984.

97. Joanne Omang and Lou Cannon, "Reagan Orders Investigation of Controversial CIA Manual," *WP*, October 19, 1984.

98. Joel Brinkley, "Reagan to Dismiss Officials Responsible for the Guerrilla Primer," *NYT*, October 22, 1984.

99. Joel Brinkley, "Playing by the Wrong Book in Nicaragua," *NYT*, October 21, 1984; Joanne Omang and Lou Cannon, "Reagan Orders Investigation of Controversial CIA Manual," *WP*, October 19, 1984; Joel Brinkley, "Nicaraguan Rebel Disputes U.S. Aide," *NYT*, October 20, 1984.

100. "Text of the Second Reagan-Mondale Debate," *WP*, October 22, 1984.

101. Joel Brinkley, "CIA Chief Defends Manual for Nicaraguan Rebels," *NYT*, November 2, 1984.

102. Joel Brinkley, "CIA Disputes Reagan on Primer," *NYT*, October 23, 1984; "Balloons Took CIA Manuals to Nicaragua," *WP*, December 7, 1984.

103. Memorandum to McFarlane from Oliver L. North, "FDN Manual on Psychological Warfare," October 22, 1984, in *Iran-Contra Hearings*, vol. 100-7, pt. 3, pp. 728–30.

104. "Casey's Letter on Nicaragua Manual," *NYT*, November 2, 1984.

105. "Question and Answer Session with Reporters on Foreign and Domestic Issues, November 7, 1984," *Reagan Papers, 1984*, book 2, pp. 1802–6; Francis X. Clines, "U.S. Study Found Manual Broke No Law," *NYT*, November 11, 1984.

106. The reports themselves remained classified. The quotations are from a White House summary of their findings quoted in David Hoffman, "President Agrees to Punishment in CIA Manual Case," *WP*, November 11, 1984.

107. "One of Six Accused Employees Is Absolved by CIA Chief," *WP*, November 21, 1984. Among the other CIA officers disciplined were Donald Winters, station chief in Honduras, Joe Fernandez, chief of propaganda for the Central America Task Force, Fernandez's deputy, and the officer directly in charge of supervising John Kirkpatrick.

108. Walter Pincus, "CIA Opening New Inquiry on Contra Aid," *WP*, February 9, 1987; "Aides Disciplined by CIA Are Irked," *NYT*, November 15, 1984.

109. U.S. House of Representatives, *Report on the Activities of the Permanent Select Committee on Intelligence*, p. 15; Joel Brinkley, "House Panel Calls CIA Manual Illegal," *NYT*, December 6, 1984.

110. U.S. House of Representatives, *Report on the Activities of the Permanent Select Committee on Intelligence*, p. 15.

111. Joel Brinkley, "House Panel Calls CIA Manual Illegal," *NYT*, December 6, 1984.

112. Alan Riding, "Sandinistas Say the U.S. Seeks to Overthrow Them," *NYT*, March 27, 1983.

113. Dan Williams, "Church Assumes Main Nicaragua Opposition Role," *LAT*, July 1, 1984.

114. In May 1984, Obando met with a representative of W. R. Grace and Company, whose chairman, J. Peter Grace, had long been involved in fighting the war of ideas against international Communism, sometimes in concert with the CIA. W. R. Grace, which had extensive holdings in Latin America, cooperated with efforts to destabilize the elected governments of both Joao Goulart in Brazil in 1964 and Salvador Allende in Chile in 1973, by providing assistance to conservative elements in the Catholic Church. In his meeting with

Grace's representative, John Meehan, Obando sought financial assistance for "leadership courses" he had organized to train cadres to thwart the Sandinista government. Meehan recommended that Grace and Company help Obando by sending him funds clandestinely through an "aid conduit" that would disguise the foreign source of the money. Peter Grace agreed. Memorandum from John Meehan to J. Peter Grace, "Archbishop of Managua, Nicaragua," May 9, 1984; Don Irwin, "North Tied to Church Funds in Nicaragua," *LAT*, June 8, 1987; Philip Taubman, "Managua Cleric Is Said to Train Sandinista Foes," *NYT*, August 1, 1984; Robert J. McCartney, "Church Leaders Seek Funds Citing Conflict with Sandinistas," *WP*, August 14, 1984.

115. "Embattled Archbishop," *NYT*, March 5, 1983.

116. See, for example, the denunciation by Foreign Minister Miguel D'Escoto, himself a Maryknoll priest, in Robert C. Toth, "Pope Visit May Widen Nicaragua Rift," *LAT*, January 17, 1983.

117. Alan Riding, "Pope Says Taking Sides in Nicaragua Is Peril to Church," *NYT*, March 5, 1983; Alan Riding, "Sandinists Are Indignant at Pope; Dissidents Delighted at His Politics," *NYT*, March 6, 1983.

118. On the church-state conflict in postrevolutionary Nicaragua, see Dodson and O'Shaughnessy, *Nicaragua's Other Revolution*; Betsy Cohn and Patricia Hinds, "The Manipulation of the Religion Issue," in Walker, *Reagan Versus the Sandinistas*, pp. 97–122; Gilbert, *Sandinistas*, pp. 128–52.

119. International Bank for Reconstruction and Development (IBRD), *Report and Recommendation*, p. 3.

120. Robert G. Kaiser, "Yankees Are a Sandinista's Best Enemy," *WP*, January 16, 1983. A Spanish opinion poll taken in early 1984 showed the Sandinistas winning 35 percent of the vote if they ran alone, 45 percent if they ran in coalition with parties that had been participating in government with them, and 55 percent if they ran in coalition and lowered the voting age to sixteen. Dennis Volman, "Free Elections in Nicaragua?," *CSM*, March 2, 1984.

121. Dennis Gilbert makes this point in "Nicaragua," in Blachman, LeoGrande, and Sharpe, *Confronting Revolution*, pp. 88–124.

122. Stephen Kinzer, "Disillusionment with Nicaragua Grows in Europe," *NYT*, November 16, 1983.

123. Miller, *Soviet Relations with Latin America*, pp. 192–216; Stephen Kinzer, "Soviet Help to Sandinistas: No Blank Check," *NYT*, March 28, 1984.

124. "Las elecciones son parte integral de la defensa," *Barricada* (Managua, Nicaragua), July 21, 1984, as quoted in Robinson and Norsworthy, "Elections and U.S. Intervention in Nicaragua," *Latin American Perspectives* (Spring 1985).

125. U.S. Department of State, *Comandante Bayardo Arce's Secret Speech Before the Nicaraguan Socialist Party* (PSN).

126. Hedrick Smith, "Nicaragua Elections Likely in '85 Despite New Snag, Diplomats Say," *NYT*, February 6, 1984.

127. Author's interview with a senior Western diplomat in Managua, Nicaragua, August 1983. This was no exaggeration. None of the opposition parties was able to put poll watchers at more than 10 percent of the polling stations on election day. Latin American Studies Association (LASA), *The Election Process in Nicaragua: Domestic and International Influences*, p. 13.

128. For an insider's account of this debate, see Cruz, *Nicaragua's Continuing Struggle*, pp. 7–8.

129. Edward Cody, "Sandinista Foes Doubt Pledges on Elections," *WP*, January 17, 1984; Alma Guillermoprieto, "Opposition Debates Nicaraguan Vote Role," *WP*, April 4, 1984. The Coordinadora included the Conservative Democratic Party (Partido Conservador Demó-

crata de Nicaragua, PCDN), Social Christian Party (Partido Social Cristiano, PSC), Social Democratic Party (Partido Social Demócrata, PSD), Constitutional Liberal Party (Partido Liberal Constitucionalista, PLC), Superior Council of Private Enterprise (Consejo Superior de la Empresa Privada, COSEP), and two labor federations—the Confederation for Trade Union Unity (Confederación de Unificación Sindical), which received aid from the AFL-CIO's American Institute for Free Labor Development, and the Nicaraguan Workers Central (Central de los Trabajadores Nicaragüenses), which was linked to the Social Christians.

130. Cruz, *Memoirs of a Counter-Revolutionary*, pp. 183–87.

131. Gutman, *Banana Diplomacy*, p. 233.

132. In October 1981, Defense Minister Humberto Ortega accused some businessmen of being in league with imperialism and threatened that in the event of a U.S. invasion, they would all be hanged from the lampposts. The leaders of COSEP, in response, charged the Sandinistas with preparing a "new genocide" against the Nicaraguan people. Three of the COSEP leaders were arrested and imprisoned for several months as a result. Author's interview with COSEP official William Baez, Managua, Nicaragua, January 1982. See also Gilbert, *Sandinistas*, pp. 114–17.

133. Clifford Krauss, "New Political Challenge for Sandinistas," *WSJ*, August 6, 1984.

134. Gutman, *Banana Diplomacy*, p. 238.

135. Stephen Kinzer, "Nicaragua Says It Will Relax Curbs for Election Campaign," *NYT*, July 20, 1984. *La Prensa* publisher Jaime Chamorro acknowledged that censorship was "less harsh and arbitrary" during the campaign. Chamorro, *La Prensa*, pp. 89–92.

136. Philip Taubman, "U.S. Role in Nicaragua Vote Disputed," *NYT*, October 21, 1984.

137. Gutman, *Banana Diplomacy*, p. 245; Taubman, "U.S. Role in Nicaragua Vote Disputed," *NYT*, October 21, 1984.

138. Gutman, *Banana Diplomacy*, p. 235.

139. The fullest account of the Rio meeting is in ibid., pp. 248–50. For Cruz's perspective, see Cruz, *Nicaragua's Continuing Struggle*, pp. 7–28. Cruz's reduced list of demands are in Arturo Cruz, "Can the Sandinistas Hold a Fair Election?," *WP*, September 28, 1984.

140. Gutman, *Banana Diplomacy*, p. 241. Gutman includes a transcript of the agreement that Cruz and Arce almost reached at pp. 385–87.

141. Ibid., p. 252. Cruz blamed the CIA for the Coordinator's rejection of Arce's offer. Tad Szulc, "Contras: Lost in a Jungle of Mismanagement," *LAT*, March 15, 1987.

142. John Lantigua, "Collapse of Talks Reflects Polarization of Sides in Nicaragua," *WP*, October 4, 1984; Stephen Kinzer, "Brandt Visits Managua but Fails to Settle Nicaragua Vote Dispute," *NYT*, October 15, 1984.

143. Robert J. McCartney, "Sandinista Foes Always Intended to Boycott Vote," *WP*, July 30, 1984. Gilbert (*Sandinistas*, p. 122) found the same thing in his interviews with Coordinator leaders.

144. Taubman, "U.S. Role in Nicaragua Vote Disputed," *NYT*, October 21, 1984.

145. David Hoffman and Joanne Omang, "Reagan Attacks 'Totalitarian' Nicaragua in Push for Rebel Aid," *WP*, July 19, 1984.

146. Stephen Kinzer, "Nicaraguan Parties Cite Sandinista Aid and U.S. Pressure," *NYT*, October 31, 1984.

147. LASA, *Election Process in Nicaragua*, p. 30.

148. Robert J. McCartney, "Youths Crash Party Meeting," *WP*, October 30, 1984. For an airing of the charges and countercharges about the convention and the alleged bribery, see Leiken, "Tangled Nicaragua," *New York Review of Books*, December 5, 1985; and the subsequent exchange of letters and statements by the Nicaraguan principals in "The Nicaraguan Tangle: An Exchange," *New York Review of Books*, May 8, 1986. Journalist Marc Cooper, who was covering the Nicaraguan elections for the *Village Voice*, recounts, "I was there and it wasn't some unknown mob that walked in. It was the rank and file of party delegates led by

the youth section of the Conservative Democrats." Quoted in Cockburn, "Beat the Devil," *Nation*, March 15, 1986.

149. "Election Draws Many Observers," *NYT*, November 4, 1984. The main election reports include LASA, *Election Process in Nicaragua*; Americas Watch, *Freedom of Expression and Assembly in Nicaragua*; Kerstiens and Nelissen, "Report on the Elections in Nicaragua," Report of the Netherlands Government Observers; Canadian Church and Human Rights Delegation, "Nicaragua 1984"; Parliamentary Human Rights Group, "Report of a British Parliamentary Delegation to Nicaragua"; Lord Chitnis, "The Election in Nicaragua," Report to the British Liberal Party; "Report of the Irish Inter-Parliamentary Group"; International Human Rights Law Group and Washington Office on Latin America, *Political Opening in Nicaragua*.

150. Stephen Kinzer, "Foes of Sandinistas Call Voting Law Unfair," *NYT*, March 17, 1984.

151. The Democratic Conservatives won fourteen seats, the Independent Liberals nine, the Popular Social Christians six, and the leftist parties two each. LASA, *Election Process in Nicaragua*, p. 17. The three leftist parties were the Communist Party of Nicaragua (Partido Comunista de Nicaragua), the Nicaraguan Socialist Party (Partido Socialista Nicaragüense, PSN), and the Marxist-Leninist Popular Action Movement (Movimiento de Acción Popular, Marxista-Leninista, MAP-ML).

152. Robert J. McCartney, "Vote Boycott Lamented," *WP*, November 3, 1984.

153. Stephen Kinzer, "Sandinistas Hold Their First Election," *NYT*, November 5, 1984; Pastor, *Condemned to Repetition*, p. 250.

154. Joanne Omang, "Nicaraguan Elections Hit; U.S. Latin Policies Working, Shultz Says," *WP*, August 21, 1984.

155. Editorial, "Nobody Won in Nicaragua," *NYT*, November 7, 1984.

156. An excerpt from the letter is in Leiken and Rubin, *Central American Crisis Reader*, pp. 300–302.

157. John M. Goshko, "Nicaraguans Said to Get Soviet Tanks," *WP*, June 2, 1981.

158. Gutman, *Banana Diplomacy*, p. 87; Barbara Crossette, "Haig Asserts Nicaraguans May Discuss Resuming Ties," *NYT*, December 3, 1981.

159. Don Oberdorfer, "U.S. Plans for Possible Rise in U.S. Role in Nicaragua," *WP*, April 17, 1983. See also Don Oberdorfer, "U.S. Breathes Easier Despite Latin Turmoil," *WP*, August 15, 1982; Alfonso Chardy, "Nicaragua Warned Not to Buy Jets," *MH*, September 29, 1983.

160. Shultz, *Turmoil and Triumph*, p. 121.

161. According to Major Roger Miranda Bengochea, a defector from the Nicaraguan armed forces, the Soviets initially promised to provide the MiGs by 1985, but kept putting off actual delivery. Miranda and Ratliff, *Civil War in Nicaragua*, pp. 116–19, 127–33.

162. Robert J. McCartney, "Nicaragua Says Air Base, Pilots Due by Early 1985," *WP*, September 16, 1984; Dan Williams, "U.S. Renews Its Warning on Jets for Nicaragua," *LAT*, August 18, 1984.

163. Philip Taubman, "U.S. Warns Soviets It Won't Tolerate MiGs in Nicaragua," *NYT*, November 8, 1984; Philip Taubman, "U.S. Aides Broaden Warnings to Nicaragua," *NYT*, November 9, 1984; Robert S. Greenberger, "U.S. Cautions Soviet Union on Nicaragua," *WSJ*, November 8, 1984.

164. Richard Halloran, "Pentagon Says It Would Fight Sandinista Invasion," *NYT*, November 14, 1984; Shultz, *Turmoil and Triumph*, p. 424.

165. Joanne Omang, "Nicaraguan Jet Incident Leaves Mysteries," *WP*, November 18, 1984.

166. Fred Hiatt, "U.S. Watching Soviet Cargo for Nicaragua," *WP*, November 8, 1984; Bernard Gwertzman, "Shultz Indicates Soviet Has Denied Shipping Fighters," *NYT*, November 9, 1984; Shultz, *Turmoil and Triumph*, p. 424. Both the Defense Intelligence Agency

and the Soviet affairs division of the CIA doubted that the Soviets would challenge such an explicit U.S. warning by providing MiGs. U.S. Senate, *Nomination of Robert M. Gates to Be Director of Central Intelligence*, pp. 136–37.

167. Norman Kempster, "Cargo Not MiGs, Photos Indicate," *LAT*, November 10, 1984.

168. McNeil, *War and Peace in Central America*, p. 163.

169. McCartney, "Reporters Watch Unloading of Crates," *WP*, November 9, 1984; McCartney, "U.S. Spy Plan Rattles Nicaragua," *WP*, November 10, 1984.

170. Fred Hiatt, "Seven Exercises Going On as U.S. Continues Nicaragua Pressure," *WP*, November 14, 1984.

171. Fred Hiatt and David Hoffman, "U.S. Says Soviets Seek to Improve Nicaragua Arms," *WP*, November 9, 1984; Fred Hiatt, "No MiGs Seen in Nicaragua," *WP*, November 10, 1984.

172. Fred Hiatt, "Nicaragua Buildup Called Defensive," *WP*, November 13, 1984; Joel Brinkley, "U.S. Aides Split on Plans to Press the Sandinistas," *NYT*, November 12, 1984.

173. Stephen Kinzer, "Sandinista Accuses Reagan," *NYT*, November 11, 1984.

174. Jackson Diehl, "Shultz Says No U.S. Invasion Planned," *WP*, November 13, 1984.

175. Philip Taubman, "U.S. Is Said to Be Studying Ways to Increase Pressure on Nicaragua," *NYT*, November 11, 1984.

176. Taubman, "U.S. Seeks to Sway Opinion on Nicaragua," *NYT*, November 14, 1984.

177. Taubman, "U.S. Is Said to Be Studying Ways to Increase Pressure on Nicaragua," *NYT*, November 11, 1984.

178. Philip Taubman, "Policy Rift on Nicaragua," *NYT*, November 12, 1984; Joanne Omang, "U.S. Is Hardening Stand on Nicaragua," *WP*, December 17, 1984.

CHAPTER SEVENTEEN

1. Philip Taubman, "Nicaragua Rebels Reported to Have New Flow of Arms," *NYT*, January 13, 1985.

2. T. R. Reid, "CIA Faces Inquiries on Nicaragua Rebel Spending," *WP*, June 7, 1984; Martin Tolchin, "CIA Said to Overspend in Nicaragua," *NYT*, June 14, 1984. The Republican majority on the Senate committee disagreed with the House committee's conclusion that the spending limit had been exceeded; it found nothing wrong with the Agency's accounting procedures. U.S. Senate, *Report of the Select Committee on Intelligence, January 1, 1983, to December 31, 1984*, October 10, 1983, p. 12.

3. P.L. 98-212, Section 775, in U.S. House of Representatives, *Compilation of Intelligence Laws*, p. 345.

4. Robert Parry and Brian Barger, "CIA Gave Political Aid to Contras," *WP*, April 14, 1986.

5. Doyle McManus, "U.S. Drops Covert Plan to Send Copters to El Salvador," *LAT*, May 18, 1984.

6. Ibid. For example, the CIA gave both the Salvadorans and the Hondurans high-speed patrol boats to use for arms interdiction. Philip Taubman, "U.S. Is Reported to Skirt Curbs in Latin Moves," *NYT*, May 18, 1984; Juan O. Tamayo, "Hondurans Hunt Arms in Boats Bought by the CIA," *MH*, June 5, 1983.

7. "Sensitive DOD Support to CIA Special Activities," Memorandum to Secretary of Defense Caspar Weinberger from Secretary of the Army John O. Marsh Jr., May 9, 1984, in *Iran-Contra Depositions*, vol. 17, pp. 867–70. See also Emerson, *Secret Warriors*, pp. 130–33. Marsh cited three examples of suspect projects: Operation Poker Face, in which the CIA requested the assignment of eight army officers to help train the contras; Operation Queens Hunter; and Operation Rook's Landing (see below).

8. "DOD Support to CIA Special Activities," Memorandum to Secretary of the Army John O. Marsh Jr. from Secretary of Defense Caspar Weinberger, June 13, 1983, in *Iran-Contra Depositions*, vol. 17, pp. 872–73.

9. Presidential memorandum, July 12, 1983, quoted in Department of Defense "Background Paper," July 13, 1983, in *Iran-Contra Documents*, vol. 1, p. 55.

10. *Iran-Contra Report*, pp. 34–35, 380.

11. Emerson, *Secret Warriors*, p. 133; "DOD Support for DCI," Memorandum to the Joint Chiefs of Staff from Chairman of the Joint Chiefs John W. Vessey, September 6, 1983, in *Iran-Contra Documents*, vol. 1, pp. 48–54.

12. Blaine Harden and Joe Pichirallo, "CIA Said to Supply Planes to Nicaraguan Rebels," *WP*, September 15, 1984. See also Emerson, *Secret Warriors*, p. 133; *Iran-Contra Report*, p. 35.

13. Blaine Harden and Joe Pichirallo, "CIA Said to Supply Planes to Nicaraguan Rebels," *WP*, September 15, 1984.

14. The promises are reported in Fred Hiatt, "U.S. Has Steadily Amassed Troops, Counterrevolutionaries in Latin America," *WP*, April 15, 1984; U.S. House of Representatives, *U.S. Policy in Central America*, p. 36. The fact that material was left behind nonetheless is documented in a report by the General Accounting Office (GAO), the unclassified version of which is in *Congressional Record*, June 25, 1984, pp. H6818–26. For a description of the classified version, which also discusses the facilities turned over to the contras, see Taubman, "U.S. Is Reported to Skirt Curbs in Latin Moves," *NYT*, May 18, 1984.

15. Emerson, *Secret Warriors*, pp. 51, 81; Raymond Bonner, "Secret Pentagon Intelligence Unit Is Disclosed," *NYT*, May 11, 1983.

16. Emerson, *Secret Warriors*, p. 92.

17. Ibid., pp. 42, 142; Tim Weiner, "Covert Forces Multiply, and Some Run Amok," *Philadelphia Inquirer*, February 10, 1987.

18. Emerson, *Secret Warriors*, p. 45.

19. Ibid., pp. 85–92. There were two other signal intelligence operations run out of Honduras, "Royal Duke" and "Quiet Falcon," but Queens Hunter was by far the most productive. The army's 224th Military Intelligence Battalion, based in Honduras, also conducted overflights of El Salvador. Robert S. Greenberger and Clifford Krauss, "Reagan Plan to Revive Intelligence Flights Used by El Salvador Prompts Concerns," *WSJ*, August 8, 1984; Edward Cody, "Helicopters Vital to El Salvador in Civil War," *WP*, August 18, 1986. Some U.S. military advisers on the ground in El Salvador were less impressed with the usefulness of the intelligence gathered by these operations. See Bacevich et al., *American Military Policy in Small Wars*, p. 30.

20. Emerson, *Secret Warriors*, p. 150; Felicity Barringer, "CIA Plane That Crashed Said to Be Tailing Second Craft," *WP*, October 21, 1984.

21. When the *Philadelphia Inquirer* ran an exposé on Task Force 160's role in Central America, the Pentagon flatly denied that the unit was in the region. Such denials may not have been technically false. In the past, military personnel detailed to the CIA for special operations temporarily "retired" from the armed forces, to then be "hired" by the CIA for the duration of the mission. A similar procedure was probably used in this case, since the CIA did tell Congress about two combat incidents between CIA helicopters and Nicaraguan shore defenses. When Secretary of the Army John Marsh expressed his concerns to Weinberger about Pentagon transfers of equipment to the CIA for projects in Central America, he mentioned the transfer of personnel as well. Frank Greve and Ellen Warren, "Secret Army Unit Allegedly Flies in Latin America," *Philadelphia Inquirer*, December 16, 1984; Frank Greve and Mark Fazlollah, "NSC Bypassed Military with Covert Operations," *MH*, July 26, 1987; "Panel Launches Probe of Reports of Secret Latin Missions by Army," *WP*, December 18, 1984; "CIA Employees Fought Nicaraguans," *WP*, December 20, 1984.

22. Weiner, *Blank Check*, p. 180; Emerson, *Secret Warriors*, pp. 135–36.

23. *Iran-Contra Depositions*, vol. 12, pp. 402–8, 432. The Iran-Contra investigators were never able to locate the contingency plan for using Yellow Fruit to aid the contras, and so did not pursue it further. Working under a tight deadline, the Iran-Contra Committee did

not take depositions from Rudy Enders, Lieutenant Colonel James Longhofer, or the Yellow Fruit commander, Lieutenant Colonel Dale Duncan.

24. The method used for moving funds between DOD programs is described in detail in Weiner, *Blank Check*, pp. 190–91. Oliver Kennedy, the assistant comptroller of the army, conceded that the only purpose for such a scheme was to circumvent Congress.

25. Emerson, *Secret Warriors*, p. 153.

26. Deposition of William Golden, *Iran-Contra Depositions*, vol. 12, p. 410. Golden's testimony suggested that the Swiss bank account opened by Yellow Fruit was later used by North and Secord's contra resupply operation (pp. 420–27).

27. Tim Weiner, "Covert Forces Multiply, and Some Run Amok," *Philadelphia Inquirer*, February 10, 1987; Emerson, *Secret Warriors*, pp. 155–82; Weiner, *Blank Check*, pp. 184–92.

28. Emerson, *Secret Warriors*, p. 153; Marsh deposition, *Iran-Contra Depositions*, vol. 17, pp. 860–61.

29. Deposition of Noel C. Koch, *Iran-Contra Depositions*, vol. 15, pp. 6–8; Greve and Fazlollah, "NSC Bypassed Military with Covert Operations," *MH*, July 26, 1987.

30. *Iran-Contra Report*, p. 38.

31. Robert Parry, "President Linked to Secret Aid," *WP*, October 8, 1985. Parry cites both current and former administration officials, including one senior official, who knew of the funding plan. See also Alfonso Chardy, "Sources: White House OK'd Contra Supply Network," *MH*, June 22, 1986.

32. Philip Taubman, "Israel Said to Aid Latin Aims of U.S.," *NYT*, July 21, 1983; Frank Greve, "Israel Could Fill the Gap If U.S. Latin Aid Funds Cut," *MH*, May 27, 1984. See also Hoffman, *PLO and Israel in Central America*; Hunter, *Israeli Foreign Policy*.

33. "U.S. Government Stipulation on Quid Pro Quos with Other Governments as Part of Contra Operations," introduced by the U.S. government during Oliver L. North's trial, paragraphs 1–2, in Kornbluh and Byrne, *Iran-Contra Scandal*, pp. 85–97. Secord acknowledges his role in *Honored and Betrayed*, p. 218.

34. Woodward, *VEIL*, pp. 355–57; John M. Goshko, "Israeli Technical Aid to El Salvador Part of Meetings Here," *WP*, April 21, 1984. The Sandinista government's close relations with the Palestine Liberation Organization (PLO) gave Israel another reason for helping the United States arm the contras. See, for example, U.S. Department of State, *Sandinistas and Middle Eastern Radicals*.

35. Memorandum to Howard Teicher from Robert C. McFarlane, April 20, 1984, in *Iran-Contra Hearings*, vol. 100-2, pp. 458–59; *Iran-Contra Report*, p. 38. However, the Israelis continued to support the contras discreetly. Two years later, in May 1986, then–Defense Minister Yitzchak Rabin offered to send several dozen military advisers to train contras in Costa Rica. In September, North and Rabin agreed that Israel would provide additional weapons to the contras from new stocks captured from the PLO. John Poindexter and Donald Regan briefed the president on the Israelis' generosity in preparation for his September 15, 1986, meeting with Prime Minister Shimon Peres. U.S. Senate, *Preliminary Inquiry into the Sale of Arms to Iran*, pp. 44–45; *Iran-Contra Report*, pp. 75–76.

36. *Iran-Contra Report*, p. 39; McFarlane and Smardz, *Special Trust*, p. 69; Mayer and McManus, *Landslide*, p. 79. Reagan later told McFarlane to keep the Saudi contribution secret from other administration officials, according to McFarlane's testimony at North's trial, quoted in Draper, *Very Thin Line*, p. 80.

37. "Chronology of Non-USG Support for the Nicaraguan Opposition Forces," in *Iran-Contra Hearings*, vol. 100-9, pp. 438–43.

38. Quotations from this meeting are drawn from minutes of the June 25, 1984, National Security Planning Group (NSPG) meeting, released during Oliver L. North's trial, in Kornbluh and Byrne, *Iran-Contra Scandal*, pp. 69–82. See also *Iran-Contra Testimonial Chronology*, pp. 93–97.

39. *Iran-Contra Report*, pp. 38–39. Meese said, "It's important to tell the Department of Justice that we want them to find the proper and legal basis which will permit the United States to assist in obtaining third party resources for the anti-Sandinistas. You have to give lawyers guidance when asking them a question." Minutes of the June 25, 1984, National Security Planning Group (NSPG) meeting, released during Oliver L. North's trial, in Kornbluh and Byrne, *Iran-Contra Scandal*, pp. 69–82.

40. Quoted in the minutes from the meeting, in Kornbluh and Byrne, *Iran-Contra Scandal*, pp. 69–82.

41. Johnson, *Sleepwalking through History*, p. 287.

42. "U.S. Government Stipulation on Quid Pro Quos with Other Governments as Part of Contra Operations," paragraph 46, in Kornbluh and Byrne, *Iran-Contra Scandal*, pp. 85–97.

43. The phrase is from a February 11, 1985, memo to McFarlane from North and Burghardt, as quoted in Joe Pichirallo and Walter Pincus, "Key Parts of 1985 Honduras Deal Carried Out," *WP*, May 1, 1989. The CPPG was made up of senior officials at the subcabinet level; in attendance at this meeting were Poindexter, North, Fred Iklé and Nestor Sanchez from the Pentagon, Clair George and Alan Fiers from the CIA, and others. "U.S. Government Stipulation on Quid Pro Quos with Other Governments as Part of Contra Operations," paragraphs 50–51, in Kornbluh and Byrne, *Iran-Contra Scandal*, pp. 85–97.

44. Memorandum to members of the National Security Council briefing them on the February 7 CPPG meeting, from Robert McFarlane, February 12, 1985, as quoted in Pichirallo and Pincus, "Key Parts of 1985 Honduras Deal Carried Out," *WP*, May 1, 1989.

45. "U.S. Government Stipulation on Quid Pro Quos with Other Governments as Part of Contra Operations," paragraph 51, in Kornbluh and Byrne, *Iran-Contra Scandal*, pp. 85–97; Walter Pincus and Joe Pichirallo, "Memo on Honduran Deal Cites Bush," *WP*, April 12, 1989.

46. Doyle McManus, "Bush Aware of Honduran Aide Ties," *LAT*, April 13, 1989.

47. Pincus and Pichirallo, "Memo on Honduran Deal Cites Bush," *WP*, April 12, 1989; McManus, "Bush Aware of Honduran Aide Ties," *LAT*, April 13, 1989. See also Draper, *Very Thin Line*, pp. 107–9.

48. "The word of the president of the United States, George Bush, is: there was no *quid pro quo*," he insisted in 1989 when documents on the Honduran deal were released. "Remarks and a Question-and-Answer Session with Reporters Following a Luncheon with Prime Minister Brian Mulroney of Canada, May 4, 1989," *Public Papers of the Presidents of the United States: George Bush, 1989*, book 1, pp. 514–19.

When a few documents were released in 1989, the State Department at first tried to deny there had been any linkage. Acting Assistant Secretary of State for Latin America Michael Kozak testified to Congress on April 24, 1989, that the quid pro quo plan had been "disapproved at the objection of the State Department" because it was contrary to U.S. policy. A few weeks later, however, the government released a February 7, 1985, memo from Motley to George Shultz that summarized the quid pro quo plan, and Shultz had initialed his approval. Congressman David Obey was especially angry at this discovery, since Shultz had assured him in writing in March 1987 that "the [State] Department is not aware of or [has it] participated in any attempt by the United States government to condition provision of U.S. foreign assistance on support by the recipients for the Nicaraguan democratic resistance." Stephen Engelberg, "Reagan Lapses Found on Iran-Contra Documents," *NYT*, June 4, 1989; Joe Pichirallo and Walter Pincus, "Shultz Backed Honduras Aid When Contra Support Slipped," *WP*, December 16, 1989.

49. "U.S. Government Stipulation on Quid Pro Quos with Other Governments as Part of Contra Operations," paragraphs 54–55, in Kornbluh and Byrne, *Iran-Contra Scandal*, pp. 85–97; Juan O. Tamayo, "Dealers: Israel Sent Rebels Arms," *MH*, December 1, 1986.

50. "U.S. Government Stipulation on Quid Pro Quos with Other Governments as Part of

Contra Operations," paragraphs 62–64, in Kornbluh and Byrne, *Iran-Contra Scandal*, pp. 85–97. The Hondurans were constantly angling for more aid in exchange for their cooperation. In late 1986, CIA Central American Task Force chief Alan D. Fiers traveled through the region and reported back in a memo to Casey, "They [the Hondurans] agreed to fully support the program and to allow supplies to begin moving as scheduled. They were very clear as to what they seek in return: support for the purchase of advanced aircraft, with those aircraft arriving as soon as possible (within six months). . . . The real message in Honduras is that the Hondurans want to extract the maximum possible from us in return for their cooperation." Quoted in Stephen Engelberg, "Memos Suggest U.S. Honduran Deal on Contra Aid," *NYT*, May 18, 1989.

51. Doyle McManus, "Document Tells of Bush Contra Role," *LAT*, April 7, 1989. North used almost the same language in another memo to McFarlane before McFarlane's January trip; see Draper, *Very Thin Line*, pp. 107–9.

52. Memorandum to McFarlane from Oliver L. North, "[Redacted] Aid to the Nicaraguan Resistance," March 5, 1985, in *Iran-Contra Hearings*, vol. 100-2, pp. 492–509.

53. Memorandum from Alan D. Fiers to William J. Casey reporting on Fiers's trip to Central America, October 12, 1986, as quoted in Engelberg, "Memos Suggest U.S. Honduran Deal on Contra Aid," *NYT*, May 18, 1989.

54. "U.S. Government Stipulation on Quid Pro Quos with Other Governments as Part of Contra Operations," paragraph 49, in Kornbluh and Byrne, *Iran-Contra Scandal*, pp. 85–97; North, *Under Fire*, p. 254. On the fuel diversion, see Walter Pincus, "Fuel Sent to El Salvador as Military Aid Powered North Arms Drops, GAO Says," *WP*, June 9, 1989. On Duarte's professed ignorance, see Marjorie Miller, "He Wasn't Told Salvador Base Was Used to Supply Contras, Duarte Says," *LAT*, December 11, 1986.

55. Dinges, *Our Man in Panama*, pp. 147–49, 233–53; Clarridge, *Spy for All Seasons*, p. 237; Frederick Kempe, "The Noriega Files," *Newsweek*, January 25, 1990. One source indicates that Noriega was already allowing the contras to train in Panama as early as 1983. Woodward, *VEIL*, p. 233.

56. "U.S. Government Stipulation on Quid Pro Quos with Other Governments as Part of Contra Operations," paragraphs 42–46, in Kornbluh and Byrne, *Iran-Contra Scandal*, pp. 85–97; Johnson, *Sleepwalking through History*, pp. 262–67. See also Buckley, *Panama*, pp. 44–46, 60–61.

57. *Iran-Contra Report*, p. 38. See also Stephen Engelberg, "U.S. Planned in '84 for South Africa to Help Contras," *NYT*, August 20, 1987.

58. "U.S. Government Stipulation on Quid Pro Quos with Other Governments as Part of Contra Operations," paragraphs 6 and 10, in Kornbluh and Byrne, *Iran-Contra Scandal*, pp. 85–97; *Iran-Contra Testimonial Chronology*, pp. 238–39, 248, 299.

59. *Iran-Contra Report*, pp. 44–45; Draper, *Very Thin Line*, p. 84.

60. *Iran-Contra Report*, pp. 45, 120. Reagan insisted that he did not solicit the king for aid, but that the king simply mentioned it during their conversation. However, the U.S. government's statement of facts released at the North trial suggests that Reagan may have played a less passive role. Paragraph 16 states, "President Reagan urged the head of state of Saudi Arabia to continue its support for the Resistance." Kornbluh and Byrne, *Iran-Contra Scandal*, pp. 85–97.

61. Philip Taubman, "Israel Said to Aid Latin Aims of U.S.," *NYT*, July 21, 1983; Bob Woodward, "CIA Funds Run Short for Covert Operations," *WP*, April 13, 1984.

62. Bernard Gwertzman, "House Committee, Echoing Senate, Opposes Mining," *NYT*, April 12, 1984.

63. *Iran-Contra Report*, pp. 118–19.

64. U.S. Senate, *Security and Development Assistance*, pp. 908–10. See also *Iran-Contra Report*, pp. 120–21.

65. Richard Weekes, "CIA's Friend Sent into Exile," *Manchester Guardian*, April 8, 1984.

66. Clarridge, *Spy for All Seasons*, p. 284; Christopher Dickey, "Honduran General's Ouster Surprised CIA," *WP*, December 16, 1984.

67. Juan O. Tamayo, "Suazo Gave Cue for Coup, U.S. Diplomat Says," *MH*, April 3, 1984; Lydia Chavez, "Honduras Names New Army Chief," *NYT*, April 5, 1984; Schulz and Schulz, *The United States, Honduras, and the Crisis in Central America*, pp. 98–99.

68. Leticia Salomón, "The National Security Doctrine in Honduras: Analysis of the Fall of General Gustavo Alvarez Martínez," in Peckenham and Street, *Honduras*, pp. 197–207.

69. Edward Cody, "20 Younger Officers Reportedly Behind Honduran Shake-Up," *WP*, April 2, 1984.

70. Dennis Volman, "Honduran General Ousted for 'Repression,' " *CSM*, April 2, 1984. In 1988, the families of several people who disappeared during Alvarez's reign brought suit against Honduras in the Inter-American Court on Human Rights—the first time a government had been charged in the court. The seven-judge panel unanimously ruled that the Honduran armed forces had committed torture and murder during the early 1980s, and ordered the government to pay compensation in the specific case before it. Stephen Kinzer, "OAS Tribunal Finds Hondurans Responsible for a Political Killing," *NYT*, July 30, 1988.

71. Robert J. McCartney, "Honduras to Bar Salvadoran Trainees," *WP*, September 28, 1984.

72. Dan Williams, "Honduras Reportedly Wants Change in U.S. Ties," *LAT*, July 5, 1984.

73. Juan O. Tamayo, "Honduran Military Pushes for Better Deal from U.S.," *MH*, August 14, 1984.

74. Howard Kurtz and Joanne Omang, "FBI Holds 8 in Plot on Honduras," *WP*, November 2, 1984.

75. Stephen J. Hedges, "Assassination Coup Plotter Is Sentenced," *MH*, August 9, 1986; Susan F. Rasky, "North Urged Leniency for Honduran Linked to Assassination Plot," *NYT*, February 23, 1987.

76. *Iran-Contra Report*, pp. 109–11. Bueso Rosa served forty months at Eglin before being released on parole in May 1989. Jefferson Morley and Murray Waas, "Favor for a Felon," *WP*, May 29, 1994.

77. Charles R. Babcock, "Ousted Chief of Honduran Military Was Hired as U.S. Defense Consultant," *WP*, May 10, 1987.

78. Schulz and Schulz, *The United States, Honduras, and the Crisis in Central America*, pp. 104–6.

79. Memorandum to McFarlane from William J. Casey, "Supplemental Assistance to Nicaragua Program," March 27, 1984, *Iran-Contra Hearings*, vol. 100-2, pp. 456–57.

80. Joanne Omang, "McFarlane Aide Facilitates Policy," *WP*, August 11, 1985.

81. Bradlee, *Guts and Glory*, pp. 22–24, 27.

82. North, *Under Fire*, p. 75; Bradlee, *Guts and Glory*, pp. 38–39.

83. Bradlee, *Guts and Glory*, p. 47.

84. Ibid., p. 54; North, *Under Fire*, pp. 80–81.

85. Bradlee, *Guts and Glory*, p. 62; Robert Timberg, "The Private War of Ollie and Jim," *Esquire*, March 1988.

86. Bradlee, *Guts and Glory*, p. 97.

87. Ibid., pp. 71–80.

88. Keith Schneider, "Pentagon Aides Say North Spent 10 Days in Hospital in 1974," *NYT*, December 24, 1986; Eric Alterman, "Inside Ollie's Mind," *New Republic*, February 16, 1987. The former commander was Colonel Richard C. Schulze. North denies that he was running about naked; his account of his bout with "depression" is in his autobiography, *Under Fire*, pp. 134–39.

89. Bradlee, *Guts and Glory*, pp. 111–13.

90. Ibid., pp. 158, 163.

91. Alterman, "Inside Ollie's Mind," *New Republic*.

92. Bradlee, *Guts and Glory*, pp. 165–67, 183–86.

93. Tom Brokaw, "Some Colonel Named North," *NYT*, July 7, 1987.

94. Testimony of Oliver L. North, *Iran-Contra Hearings*, vol. 100-7, pt. 1, pp. 245–46.

95. Mayer and McManus, *Landslide*, p. 68.

96. Alterman, "Inside Ollie's Mind," *New Republic*.

97. Bradlee, *Guts and Glory*, pp. 544–45.

98. Testimony of the Chief of the CIA's Central America Task Force (C/CATF) [Alan Fiers], *Iran-Contra Hearings*, vol. 100-11. See also Walter Pincus, "CIA Official Knew of Aid, Kept Silent," *WP*, August 26, 1987.

99. Bradlee, *Guts and Glory*, pp. 468, 544–45; North testimony, *Iran-Contra Hearings*, vol. 100-7, pt. 2, p. 158.

100. Ledeen, *Perilous Statecraft*, pp. 80–82. A Nicaraguan who worked with North, Arturo Cruz Jr., wrote that North "lived deeply within the world of inner fantasy." Cruz, *Memoirs of a Counter-Revolutionary*, p. 181.

101. Schieffer and Gates, *Acting President*, p. 250.

102. Persico, *Casey*, pp. 388–89.

103. North testimony, *Iran-Contra Hearings*, vol. 100-7, pt. 1, p. 267.

104. This is Edgar Chamorro's account of the meeting, in Fox Butterfield, "Senior Official in CIA Is Linked to North's Effort on Contra Arms," *NYT*, January 21, 1987. Clarridge's account is similar, although he denies he was in any sense "turning over" the CIA operation to North. Clarridge, *Spy for All Seasons*, pp. 287–88.

105. North, *Under Fire*, p. 244.

106. Letters to Oliver L. North from Robert W. Owen, January 31, 1985, and undated, in *Iran-Contra Hearings*, vol. 100-2, pp. 778–82. See also testimony of Robert W. Owen, ibid., pp. 325–28.

107. Memorandum to McFarlane from North, "Official Travel [excised] on August 31, 1984," August 28, 1984, in ibid., vol. 100-7, pt. 3, p. 991.

108. North testimony, ibid., pt. 2, p. 2.

109. Mayer and McManus, *Landslide*, p. 142.

110. Secord, *Honored and Betrayed*, pp. 59–197; Mayer and McManus, *Landslide*, pp. 141–42; air force biography of Secord, in *Iran-Contra Documents*, vol. 2, p. 157; Fox Butterfield et al., "Ex-General Provided Arms Channel," *NYT*, December 26, 1986.

111. Koch deposition, *Iran-Contra Depositions*, vol. 15, pp. 117–18.

112. *Iran-Contra Chronology*, p. 18.

113. Testimony of Albert Hakim, *Iran-Contra Hearings*, vol. 100-5, p. 194; *Iran-Contra Report*, p. 51.

114. Secord discusses Casey's role in *Honored and Betrayed*, pp. 235–50.

115. *Iran-Contra Report*, p. 60.

116. Shirley Christian, "Nicaragua Rebels Reported to Raise up to $25 Million," *NYT*, August 13, 1985; testimony of Richard V. Secord, *Iran-Contra Hearings*, vol. 100-1, p. 59.

117. *Iran-Contra Report*, p. 60.

118. Memorandum to North from Robert W. Owen, April 1, 1985, in *Iran-Contra Hearings*, vol. 100-2, pp. 799–802.

119. Secord testimony, *Iran-Contra Hearings*, vol. 100-1, pp. 57–60. See also Secord, *Honored and Betrayed*, pp. 211–12. Another motive for creating the Enterprise was to enable the NSC staff—North in particular—to undertake other covert operations (*Iran-Contra Report*, pp. 361–66). As he took over management of the contra operation in 1984, North quickly realized he needed an independent source of financing to pay for daily expenses. At Casey's suggestion, he set up an operating fund of $100,000 to $150,000, which Calero

provided in the form of traveler's checks. North used traveler's checks in the mistaken belief that they would leave no trail of receipts. North used the slush fund to pay his own expenses and to provide cash payments to some contra officials, including a Miskito Indian leader who was bribed to break off negotiations with the Sandinistas. He also spent some of the money to finance political opposition to the Sandinistas inside Nicaragua, channeling the funds through groups in Venezuela, Costa Rica, Honduras, and El Salvador (Owen testimony, *Iran-Contra Hearings*, vol. 100-2, pp. 340–41; North testimony, *Iran-Contra Hearings*, vol. 100-7, pt. 1, pp. 135–36).

120. Deposition of Richard Gadd, *Iran-Contra Depositions*, vol. 11, pp. 8–12; Emerson, *Secret Warriors*, pp. 143–44.

121. Testimony of Robert C. Dutton, *Iran-Contra Hearings*, vol. 100-3, pp. 201–7.

122. The CIA had especially good relations with Salvadoran air force commander Juan Raphael Bustillo; the Agency ran observation planes out of Ilopango during much of the war. At the CIA's request, Bustillo allowed the contras to use Ilopango beginning in 1983–84. The Salvadoran base became vital in late 1985, when the Honduran military temporarily blocked contra supply flights coming from the United States. Tim Golden, "Bay of Pigs Veteran Never Worked for Us, Salvadorans Claim," *MH*, October 14, 1986; Tim Golden, "Contras Evade Honduran Supply Ban," *MH*, January 29, 1986.

123. Letter to Felix Rodriguez from Oliver L. North, September 20, 1985, in *Iran-Contra Hearings*, vol. 100-3, pp. 553–56.

124. Emerson, *Secret Warriors*, p. 126; Rodriguez, *Shadow Warrior*, pp. 194–95.

125. Rodriguez, *Shadow Warrior*, pp. 216–19, 225; "George Bush's Iran-Contra Albatross," *U.S. News and World Report*, January 18, 1988.

126. The phrase "no pay mercenary" is Colonel James J. Steele's, in his deposition, *Iran-Contra Depositions*, vol. 26, pp. 433–35. See also Rodriguez, *Shadow Warrior*, pp. 239–44.

127. Letter to Felix I. Rodriguez from Oliver L. North, September 20, 1985, in *Iran-Contra Hearings*, vol. 100-3, pp. 556–59; Rodriguez, *Shadow Warrior*, p. 239; Frank Greve, Steve Stecklow, and Tim Golden, "U.S. Aided Suppliers, Crew Says," *MH*, January 18, 1987.

128. Secord testimony, *Iran-Contra Hearings*, vol. 100-1, pp. 49–54.

129. Alfonso Chardy, "Cuban Fugitive Tied to Contras' Supply Effort," *MH*, August 26, 1987.

130. Frank Greve, Steve Stecklow, and Tim Golden, "U.S. Aided Suppliers, Crew Says," *MH*, January 18, 1987; Robert Parry, "CIA Clears Aide Said to Help Rebels," *WP*, January 22, 1987; KL-43 message from Secord, April 10, 1986, in *Iran-Contra Hearings*, vol. 100-1, p. 418. Corr insisted that he told Steele not to do anything illegal (deposition of Edwin G. Corr, *Iran-Contra Depositions*, vol. 7, p. 872), but he was present at an August 12, 1986, meeting in Washington attended by North, Donald Gregg, Alan Fiers, and Felix Rodriguez, in which Rodriguez described the contra supply operation in detail. U.S. Senate, *Nomination of Robert M. Gates to Be Director of Central Intelligence*, p. 87.

131. Fernandez testimony to the Tower Review Board, quoted in Bob Woodward, "North Ran Contra War from White House Office," *WP*, February 27, 1987.

132. Alfonso Chardy, Sam Dillon, and Tim Golden, "By-the-Book CIA Agent Led Contras, Rebels Say," *MH*, March 1, 1987.

133. Ibid.

134. Testimony of Lewis A. Tambs, *Iran-Contra Hearings*, vol. 100-3, p. 390.

135. *Iran-Contra Report*, pp. 61–62; Tambs testimony, *Iran-Contra Hearings*, vol. 100-3, pp. 375–81.

136. James LeMoyne, "CIA Said to Guide Contras' Military Despite Ban on Aid," *NYT*, January 11, 1987.

137. North testimony, *Iran-Contra Hearings*, vol. 100-7, pt. 2, p. 18.

138. *Iran-Contra Report*, pp. 167–70, 178–79.

139. North testimony, *Iran-Contra Hearings*, vol. 100-7, pt. 1, p. 109.

140. *Iran-Contra Report*, pp. 205–9.

141. Poindexter testimony, *Iran-Contra Hearings*, vol. 100-8, pp. 35–37.

142. North testimony, ibid., vol. 100-7, pt. 1, p. 142.

143. Ibid., pp. 124, 143, 317–18; pt. 2, pp. 8–9.

144. *Iran-Contra Report*, pp. 7, 193.

145. North testimony, *Iran-Contra Hearings*, vol. 100-7, pt. 1, p. 146; North, *Under Fire*, p. 19.

CHAPTER EIGHTEEN

1. PROFS note to Robert C. McFarlane from Donald Fortier, "Contras Project," January 22, 1985, in *Iran-Contra Hearings*, vol. 100-7, pt. 3, p. 1006.

2. See the policy options laid out in memorandum to Robert C. McFarlane from Oliver L. North, "Options and Legislative Strategy for Renewing Aid to the Nicaraguan Resistance," January 15, 1985, in *Iran-Contra Documents*, vol. 1, pp. 292–99.

3. Joanne Omang, "Frontal Assault Set to Gain Latin Funds," *WP*, March 12, 1985; "White House Rejects Indirect Assistance to Nicaraguan Rebels," *NYT*, March 13, 1985.

4. Joanne Omang, "U.S. Strongly Defends Policy on Nicaragua," *WP*, January 30, 1985.

5. U.S. House of Representatives, *Foreign Assistance Legislation for Fiscal Years 1986–1987 (Part 1)*, pp. 52, 58–59.

6. Shultz, "America and the Struggle for Freedom," *U.S. Department of State Bulletin*, April 1985.

7. "The Sandinista dictatorship of Nicaragua, with full Cuban-Soviet bloc support, not only persecutes its people, the church, and denies a free press," Reagan accused, "but arms and provides bases for Communist terrorists attacking neighboring states." See "Address Before a Joint Session of Congress on the State of the Union, February 6, 1985," *Reagan Papers, 1985*, book 1, pp. 130–39.

8. "Radio Address to the Nation on Central America, February 16, 1985," ibid., pp. 172–74.

9. "The President's News Conference, February 21, 1985," ibid., pp. 197–202. Later, Reagan argued that he had not really meant that he wanted to overthrow the Sandinistas, merely that he wanted them to return to the democratic promises they had made to the OAS. "Interview with Morton Kondracke and Richard H. Smith of *Newsweek* Magazine," ibid., p. 263.

10. "Remarks at the Annual Dinner of the Conservative Political Action Conference, March 1, 1985," ibid., pp. 226–30. Originally, the convention had invited El Salvador's Major Roberto D'Aubuisson to speak the evening following Reagan's address. The State Department, however, was still annoyed at the attempts by D'Aubuisson's friends to assassinate Ambassador Thomas Pickering, and it refused to give "Major Bob" a visa. The conservatives got ex-Sandinista Edén Pastora to speak instead. Lou Cannon, "Reagan Says U.S. Owes 'Contras' Help," *WP*, March 2, 1985.

11. Lou Cannon and John M. Goshko, "Fight Over Further Aid to 'Contras' Intensifies," *WP*, February 28, 1985; Hedrick Smith, "Reagan Hurls the Harshest Broadside Yet at Nicaragua," *NYT*, February 24, 1985.

12. Lou Cannon, "Buchanan Seen Hurting President," *WP*, April 27, 1985; Michael K. Deaver, *Behind the Scenes*, p. 168.

13. Bernard Weinraub, "In His 2nd Term, Reagan Is Liberated," *NYT*, March 11, 1985.

14. Lou Cannon, "White House Seen as Grim on Nicaragua," *WP*, February 24, 1985; Steven V. Roberts, "Reagan Reported to Postpone Move on Rebel Arms Aid," *NYT*, April 19, 1985.

15. Cannon, "Reagan Says U.S. Owes 'Contras' Help," *WP*, March 2, 1985. Speakes, *Speaking Out*, p. 87.

16. Howard Kurtz, "Pat Buchanan and the Jewish Question," *WP*, September 20, 1990.

17. Patrick Buchanan, "Dusting Off 'Messianic Globaloney,'" *Washington Times*, September 18, 1989.

18. Cannon, "Buchanan Seen Hurting President," *WP*, April 27, 1985.

19. Defense Intelligence Agency, *Weekly Intelligence Summary*, July 16, 1982, quoted in Kornbluh, *Nicaragua*, p. 46.

20. Dickey, *With the Contras*, p. 257.

21. Chamorro is quoted in U.S. House of Representatives, *Foreign Assistance and Related Programs Appropriations for 1987*, p. 93. Cruz is quoted in Joel Brinkley, "Nicaragua Rebels Accused of Abuses," *NYT*, December 27, 1984.

22. James LeMoyne, "The Secret War Boils Over," *Newsweek*, April 11, 1983; Dickey, *With the Contras*, pp. 248–51; Kornbluh, *Nicaragua*, pp. 23, 39.

23. Robert J. McCartney, "A Defecting Nicaraguan Contra's Tale," *WP*, May 8, 1985; James LeMoyne, "Nicaragua Guerrillas Ponder Chances Without U.S. Help," *NYT*, March 18, 1985.

24. Brinkley, "Nicaragua Rebels Accused of Abuses," *NYT*, December 27, 1984; Joel Brinkley, "Report on Nicaragua Cites Recent Atrocities by Rebels," *NYT*, March 6, 1985.

25. Americas Watch, *Violations of the Laws of War*, pp. 4–6; Lawyers Committee for International Human Rights, *Nicaragua: Revolutionary Justice*, April 1985.

26. Joanne Omang, "Inquiry Finds Atrocities by Nicaraguan 'Contras,'" *WP*, March 7, 1985.

27. "Attacks by the Nicaraguan 'Contras' on the Civilian Population of Nicaragua: Report of a Fact-Finding Mission, September 1984–January 1985" (typescript), pp. iv–xi. The report was subsequently published as Reed Brody, *Contra Terror in Nicaragua*.

28. *Report of Donald T. Fox*, pp. 14–19; Larry Rohter, "Nicaraguan Rebels Accused of Abuses," *NYT*, March 7, 1985; Americas Watch, *Violations of the Laws of War*, pp. 8–9.

29. Joel Brinkley, "Report on Nicaragua Cites Recent Atrocities by Rebels," *NYT*, March 6, 1985. Former contra task force commander José Efrén Mondragón Martínez confirmed that contra units regularly abducted young women for sexual abuse. Robert J. McCartney, "A Defecting Nicaraguan Contra's Tale," *WP*, May 8, 1985. For a detailed discussion of sexual abuse by the contras and the unsuccessful efforts of some women in the movement to stop it, see Dillon, *Commandos*, pp. 34–36, 201, 236, 297.

30. *Report of Donald T. Fox*, pp. 20–21.

31. Dillon, *Commandos*, p. 126.

32. Omang, "Frontal Assault Set to Gain Latin Funds," *WP*, March 12, 1985. Reagan himself repeated the charge in "Remarks at a White House Meeting with Deficit Reduction Coalition, April 16, 1985," *Reagan Papers, 1985*, book 1, pp. 440–42.

33. "Remarks at a Fundraising Dinner for the Nicaraguan Refugee Fund, April 15, 1985," *Reagan Papers, 1985*, book 1, pp. 427–31; "Radio Address to the Nation on the Central American Peace Proposal, April 19, 1985," ibid., pp. 467–68.

34. "Interview with Lou Cannon, Dave Hoffman, and Lynn Downie of the *Washington Post*, April 1, 1985," ibid., pp. 379–84.

35. Geoffrey Tomb, "Student's Photo of Sandinista Execution Sparks Furor," *MH*, April 25, 1985; Dillon, *Commandos*, p. 149. The photographs were printed in "Execution in the Jungle," *Newsweek*, April 29, 1985.

36. Tomb, "Student's Photo of Sandinista Execution Sparks Furor," *MH*, April 25, 1985.

37. Dillon, *Commandos*, pp. 153–54. In the CIA's "investigation" of the incidents in the Brody report, it interviewed FDN field commanders who, naturally, denied they had committed any atrocities. The CIA concluded that FDN troops were "normally not equipped with either bayonets or combat knives" (Parry, "CIA Denies Contra Atrocities," *WP*, February 3, 1986). For proof that this was mistaken, see, for example, the half-dozen photographs of contras in Gentile, *Nicaragua*, all of whom are carrying knives and wearing boots.

38. O'Neill, *Man of the House*, pp. 440–41.

39. Dillon, *Commandos*, pp. 153–56. In 1985, Enrique Bermúdez admitted that the photographs were real.

40. Joel Brinkley, "Report on Nicaragua Cites Recent Atrocities by Rebels," *NYT*, March 6, 1985.

41. Under the terms of the 1984 compromise, Reagan's request to release the $14 million would be handled in Congress by "expedited procedure." That is, the normal process of hearings was speeded up and the president was guaranteed that both the House and the Senate would actually vote on the bill.

42. "Remarks Announcing a Central American Peace Proposal and a Question-and-Answer Session with Reporters, April 4, 1985," *Reagan Papers, 1985*, book 1, pp. 400–404.

43. Gerald M. Boyd, "Two Factors Led to Reagan's Plan," *NYT*, April 5, 1985.

44. Memorandum to Robert C. McFarlane from Oliver L. North, "Using the March 1 San José Declaration to Support the Vote on the Funding for the Contras," April 1, 1985, in *Iran-Contra Hearings*, vol. 100-7, pt. 3, pp. 1013–16.

45. Boyd, "Two Factors Led to Reagan's Plan," *NYT*, April 5, 1985.

46. Steven V. Roberts, "O'Neill Calls Plan Ruse; Republicans Optimistic," *NYT*, April 5, 1985; David Hoffman, "President Keeps Pushing 'Contra' Aid," *WP*, April 7, 1985.

47. Edward Cody and Michael Getler, "Nicaraguan Dismisses U.S. Proposal," *WP*, April 6, 1985; Joel Brinkley, "Nicaragua Scorns Reagan Proposal for Rebel Talks," *NYT*, April 6, 1985; Joel Brinkley, "Reagan's Peace Proposal: Ideas Long Opposed by Sandinistas," *NYT*, April 5, 1985.

48. The unclassified report, "U.S. Support for the Democratic Resistance Movement in Nicaragua," is in U.S. House of Representatives, *U.S. Support for the Contras*, pp. 199–215. The classified report is quoted in Hedrick Smith, "A Larger Force of Latin Rebels Sought by U.S.," *NYT*, April 17, 1985.

49. Smith, "A Larger Force of Latin Rebels Sought by U.S.," *NYT*, April 17, 1985; memorandum to McFarlane from North, "Nicaraguan Options," Tab F, "Options and Legislative Strategy for Renewing Aid to the Nicaraguan Resistance," January 15, 1985, in *Iran-Contra Documents*, vol. 1, pp. 292–99.

50. Joel Brinkley, "Charges on Latin Support Denied," *NYT*, April 18, 1985.

51. Joel Brinkley, "White House Maps Strategy on Aid to Rebels," *NYT*, April 11, 1985; Richard J. Meislin, "How Region Views Plan," *NYT*, April 17, 1985.

52. Goshko, "Latin Leaders Cited as Backing Reagan Plan," *WP*, April 13, 1985. For an example of the administration inclination to claim private support from Latin American governments despite their opposition to U.S. policy, see George Shultz's claims at a 1986 OAS meeting, and the subsequent statements of various delegations. Norman Kempster, "Shultz Finds OAS Support Against Sandinistas," *LAT*, November 12, 1986; Stephen Kinzer, "At OAS, Many Reject Contras," *NYT*, November 15, 1986.

53. "Remarks at a Conference on Religious Liberty, April 16, 1985," *Reagan Papers, 1985*, book 1, pp. 437–40; Omang, "Democrats Draft Latin Aid Options," *WP*, April 18, 1985.

54. Sara Gilbert, "Vatican Disputes Reagan Statements," *WP*, April 19, 1985.

55. "Remarks at a Fundraising Dinner for the Nicaraguan Refugee Fund, April 15, 1985," *Reagan Papers, 1985*, book 1, pp. 427–31.

56. Elizabeth Kastor, "Mistaken Identity," *WP*, April 18, 1985.

57. Karlyn Baker, "Child of War Finds Refuge," *WP*, May 12, 1985.

58. Memorandum to McFarlane from North and Fortier, "Timing and the Nicaraguan Resistance Vote," Tab A, "Chronological Event Checklist," March 20, 1985, in *Iran-Contra Documents*, vol. 1, pp. 325–36.

59. Memorandum to McFarlane from North and Fortier, "Timing and the Nicaraguan Resistance Vote," March 22, 1985, in *Iran-Contra Documents*, vol. 1, pp. 338–40; North testimony, *Iran-Contra Hearings*, vol. 100-7, pt. 2, pp. 86–87.

60. Joanne Omang, "Contra Aid Fight Nears; Hill Besieged from All Sides," *WP*, April 15, 1985.

61. Ibid.

62. Gerry Fitzgerald, "Religious Groups Orchestrate Opposition to Contra Aid," *WP*, April 23, 1985.

63. Joel Brinkley, "Both Sides Gearing for Fight on Aid to Nicaraguan Rebels," *NYT*, April 13, 1985; Omang, "Contra Aid Fight Nears; Hill Besieged from All Sides," *WP*, April 15, 1985; Sara Fritz, "Lobbying Battle Over Contra Aid Intensifies," *LAT*, April 15, 1985; "Frisco Bay Mined," *Washington Times*, May 31, 1985.

64. Cindy Buhl, presentation at the Latin American Studies Association convention, Washington, D.C., April 5, 1991.

65. Fritz, "Lobbying Battle Over Contra Aid Intensifies," *LAT*, April 15, 1985.

66. Phil McCombs, "Sandinistas Are Mocked," *WP*, April 24, 1985; Jacqueline E. Sharkey, "Republicans Raising 'Contra' Funds Complain of White House Muzzling," *WP*, March 22, 1985. The poster is reproduced in *Iran-Contra Depositions*, vol. 22, p. 855.

67. Debbie Sontag, "A War Over 'Ramba,'" *MH*, January 30, 1986.

68. Gerald M. Boyd, "Reagan Is Told House Rejects Aid to Rebels," *NYT*, April 4, 1985.

69. Steven V. Roberts, "Eight Hour Talks Fail on Accord to Aid Nicaragua Rebels," *NYT*, April 23, 1985.

70. McFarlane testimony, *Iran-Contra Hearings*, vol. 100-2, p. 157.

71. Joanne Omang and Don Oberdorfer, "Despite Votes, U.S. Role in Latin America Is Unchanged," *WP*, April 26, 1985.

72. "Letter to Senate Majority Leader Dole on the Central American Peace Proposal and United States Assistance for the Nicaraguan Democratic Resistance, April 23, 1985," *Reagan Papers, 1985*, book 1, pp. 489–90.

73. Joanne Omang and Margaret Shapiro, "Senate Approves, House Defeats 'Contra' Aid," *WP*, April 24, 1985. Reagan later reneged on his promise to resume bilateral talks with Nicaragua, claiming it had been contingent upon Congress actually approving the $14 million aid package.

74. The Republicans' use of the term "humanitarian aid" was a misnomer. Under the Geneva Convention and Protocols, humanitarian aid must be administered by parties independent of the conflict, must be distributed on the basis of need to noncombatants only, and must be available impartially to civilians on both sides. The Republican aid proposal met none of these criteria; it would have been distributed by the United States to contra combatants, and included nonlethal military supplies such as uniforms, jeeps, and aircraft.

75. "Radio Address to the Nation on the Central American Peace Proposal, April 19, 1985," *Reagan Papers, 1985*, book 1, pp. 467–68.

76. The full debate on the April votes is in *Congressional Record*, April 23, 1984, H2310–2428, and April 24, 1985, H2442–92.

77. Ibid., April 23, 1985, p. H2420.

78. Margaret Shapiro, "House Votes Down 'Contra' Aid Plans," *WP*, April 25, 1985.

79. Steven V. Roberts, "House Votes Down All Efforts to Aid Nicaragua Rebels," *NYT*, April 25, 1985. Technically, the Barnes-Hamilton resolution and the resolution passed in the Senate releasing the $14 million in military aid for the contras were unrelated and therefore could not go to conference with one another. The fear, though, was that Senate Republicans would hold Barnes-Hamilton at the desk when it came over from the House, amend it by substituting a direct aid proposal similar to Michel's, and then send *that* bill to conference with the bill passed by the House.

80. Roberts, "House Votes Down All Efforts to Aid Nicaragua Rebels," *NYT*, April 25, 1985.

81. Margaret Shapiro, "Congress Expected to Back Some Form of Aid to 'Contras,'" *WP*, April 26, 1985; Thomas D. Brandt, "House Panel Spurns New Contra Aid Plan," *Washington Times*, May 10, 1985.

82. Arnson, *Crossroads*, p. 198.

83. "Statement on the House of Representatives Disapproval of United States Assistance for the Nicaraguan Democratic Resistance, April 24, 1985," *Reagan Papers, 1985*, book 1, p. 497.

84. Shapiro, "House Votes Down 'Contra' Aid Plans," *WP*, April 25, 1985.

85. Shirley Christian, "Senator Objects to Trip," *NYT*, April 25, 1985.

86. Bernard Gwertzman, "Nicaragua Rebels Gain Some Backing," *NYT*, May 3, 1985.

87. Margaret Shapiro and Joanne Omang, "Speaker Says House May Aid Contras," *WP*, May 7, 1985. The Senate resolution is in *Congressional Record*, April 29, 1985, pp. 9694–95.

88. Stephen Kinzer, "Sandinista Says Soviet Will Meet Almost All Nicaragua's Oil Needs," *NYT*, May 21, 1985.

89. Richard Stahler-Sholk, "Foreign Debt and Economic Stabilization Policies in Revolutionary Nicaragua," in Spalding, *Political Economy of Revolutionary Nicaragua*, pp. 151–68.

90. Marlise Simons, "Mexicans Pressing Nicaragua on Oil," *NYT*, August 13, 1983.

91. Riding, *Distant Neighbors*, pp. 360–61; Sam Dillon, "Loss of Oil on Credit and Stiff Loan Markets Plaguing Sandinistas," *MH*, October 10, 1983.

92. Marlise Simons, "Mexicans Pressing Nicaragua on Oil," *NYT*, August 13, 1983; William A. Orme Jr., "Nicaragua Resolves Oil Debt," *Journal of Commerce*, February 22, 1984.

93. Kornbluh, *Nicaragua*, p. 117; John Lantigua, "Ortega Says Moscow to Supply More Oil," *WP*, May 21, 1985; Roy Gutman, "Mexico's Oil Is Leverage on Nicaragua," *Newsday*, September 2, 1985.

94. White House Press Secretary Larry Speakes, quoted in Joanne Omang, "Reagan Orders Review of Policy on Nicaragua," *WP*, April 27, 1985. In explaining the embargo, Assistant Secretary Motley listed three rationales, the first of which was to "underscore to both friends and adversaries our determination" to continue the Nicaragua policy. The second was to "affirm our opposition to Sandinista policies," and the third, "to maintain pressure on the Sandinistas." U.S. House of Representatives, *Imposition of Economic Sanctions and a Trade Embargo Against Nicaragua*, p. 5.

95. "Message to the Congress on Economic Sanctions Against Nicaragua, May 1, 1985," *Reagan Papers, 1985*, book 1, pp. 548–49.

96. That decision halted the disbursement of $15 million in Economic Support Funds, and $9.8 million in PL-480 wheat shipments. Stahler-Sholk, "Foreign Debt and Economic Stabilization Policies in Revolutionary Nicaragua," in Spalding, *Political Economy of Revolutionary Nicaragua*, pp. 151–68. Small amounts of aid continued to flow to the private sector until 1982 when the Sandinistas prohibited it on the grounds that it was designed to destabilize their government. Don Oberdorfer, "Nicaragua Bars U.S. Aid to Private Groups," *WP*, August 4, 1982. For a detailed discussion of U.S. pressures, see LeoGrande, "Making the Economy Scream," *Third World Quarterly* (June 1996).

97. Morrell and Biddle, "Central America: The Financial War," *International Policy Report*, March 1983; Morrell, "Redlining Nicaragua," *International Policy Report*, December 1985; Michael E. Conroy, "Economic Aggression as an Instrument of Low Intensity Conflict," in Walker, *Reagan Versus the Sandinistas*, pp. 57–79.

98. Stahler-Sholk, "Foreign Debt and Economic Stabilization Policies in Revolutionary Nicaragua," in Spalding, *Political Economy of Revolutionary Nicaragua*, pp. 151–68.

99. International Bank for Reconstruction and Development (IBRD), "Country Program Paper: Nicaragua," February 16, 1982 (typescript), pp. 10–11; Robert J. McCartney, "U.S. Will Oppose Loans to Nicaragua," *WP*, July 1, 1983.

100. Fitzgerald, "An Evaluation of the Economic Cost to Nicaragua of U.S. Aggression,

1980–1984," in Spalding, *Political Economy of Revolutionary Nicaragua*, pp. 195–216. The Sandinistas never sought financing from the International Monetary Fund because in May 1979, as the Somoza regime was crumbling, the IMF gave it a $63 million loan. Of that, $49 million was delivered before Somoza fled, and he took almost all of it with him; the remaining $17 was provided to the Sandinista government in August 1979. The Sandinistas agreed to pay off the $63 million loan, but they were so wary of the IMF that they never asked it for funds themselves. "The IFIs in Central America: Development or Politics?," *Center for International Policy Aid Memo*, October 1, 1982.

101. Joanne Omang, "Sanctions: A Policy by Default," *WP*, May 8, 1985.

102. Joanne Omang, "Reagan Expected to Place Sanctions Against Nicaragua," *WP*, May 1, 1985. This assessment was generally shared by even the most anti-Sandinista members of the Nicaraguan private sector, such as COSEP President Enrique Bolaños. "Nicaraguan Says Embargo Aids Sandinista Government," *NYT*, September 29, 1985.

103. Omang, "Sanctions: A Policy by Default," *WP*, May 8, 1985.

104. Clifford Krauss, "U.S. Trade Embargo Helps Nicaragua's Sandinistas," *WSJ*, October 2, 1985; Lou Cannon, "Summit Partners Criticize Sanctions Against Nicaragua," *WP*, May 4, 1985; Edward Cody, "Western Europeans Open Talks on Central America," *WP*, September 29, 1984. In a trip through Europe just after the embargo was imposed, Ortega won pledges of $190 million in loans from Western countries and $202 million from the Soviet Union and Eastern Europe. Tony Jenkins, "The U.S. Embargo Against Nicaragua: One Year Later," *Policy Focus* (1986), p. 5.

105. "Mexico Joins Critics of U.S. Embargo Against Nicaragua," *WP*, May 5, 1985.

106. "Latin Group Urges U.S. to Lift Nicaragua Embargo," *Journal of Commerce*, May 16, 1985; Reuters, "Caribbean Unit Faults U.S.," *NYT*, May 13, 1985; U.S. House of Representatives, *Imposition of Economic Sanctions and a Trade Embargo Against Nicaragua*, pp. 50, 71.

107. Reuters, "Managua Sets Austerity Measures," *WP*, May 11, 1985; "Security Council Ruling Sought," *NYT*, December 7, 1985. Nicaragua also asked GATT to rule on the legality of the embargo, as it had when Washington reduced the Nicaraguan sugar quota. The United States claimed the embargo was justified under Article 21 of the GATT agreement, which gives member states the right to "take any action which it considers necessary for the protection of its essential security interests" (quoted in U.S. House of Representatives, *Imposition of Economic Sanctions and a Trade Embargo Against Nicaragua*, p. 33).

108. Trade statistics are quoted in Jenkins, "U.S. Embargo Against Nicaragua—One Year Later," *Policy Focus* (1986). The cost estimate of the embargo is quoted in "Nicaragua Moves to Protect Assets," *Journal of Commerce*, March 16, 1987.

109. Bill Gibson, "A Structural Overview of the Nicaraguan Economy," in Spalding, *Political Economy of Revolutionary Nicaragua*, pp. 15–42.

110. Joanne Omang, "Sandinistas Mismanaged Economy, U.S. Says," *WP*, May 4, 1985.

111. Walter Raymond, a career CIA officer and specialist in media operations who was detailed to the White House to run "public diplomacy," described his aim as "gluing black hats on the Sandinistas and white hats on [the contras]." Note from Walter Raymond Jr., "Otto Reich," July 3, 1986, in *Iran-Contra Hearings*, vol. 100-9, p. 816.

112. "Interview with Foreign Journalists, April 29, 1985," *Reagan Papers, 1985*, book 1, pp. 534–40.

113. Author's interview with Congressman Dave McCurdy, Washington, D.C., May 1985.

114. Steven V. Roberts, "A Wildcatter Drills for Power," *NYT*, June 18, 1985.

115. Ibid.

116. Steven V. Roberts, "House Gets Compromise on Rebel Aid," *NYT*, May 9, 1985.

117. For the June Senate debate, see *Congressional Record*, June 6, 1985, pp. S7587–7648, and June 7, 1985, pp. S7726–59, S7796.

118. Steven V. Roberts, "Senate Would Aid Nicaragua Rebels with $38 Million," *NYT*, June 7, 1985.

119. Memorandum from the Democratic Congressional Campaign Committee, "From a Poll of 600 Registered Voters in 11 Southern States," summarizing the poll's results. See also Thomas D. Brandt, "Reagan Fails to Sell Latin Policy at Home or Abroad, O'Neill Says," *Washington Times*, June 6, 1985.

120. LeoGrande, *Central America and the Polls*, tables 25–28.

121. Margaret Shapiro, "House Votes to Aid Contras," *WP*, June 13, 1985.

122. The administration had requested $28 million in covert military aid to the contras for FY 1986, but the House Intelligence Committee had rejected the request. Margaret Shapiro, "House Votes Down Contra Aid Plans," *WP*, April 25, 1985.

123. Lou Cannon and Margaret Shapiro, "Democrats Soothed on Nicaragua," *WP*, June 12, 1985. The text of Reagan's letter to McCurdy is in *Congressional Record*, June 11, 1985, pp. H4093–94.

124. The bill was H.R. 2577. *Congressional Record*, June 12, 1985, pp. H4115–4200.

125. In the wake of the Democrats' defeat in the House, the Senate Appropriations Subcommittee on Foreign Operations added Nunn's nonlethal aid proposal to the same supplemental bill passed by the House, and it went unchallenged on the Senate floor. The Senate Intelligence Committee then added the package to the secret portion of the intelligence authorization (S. 1261). Similarly, the House added the Michel proposal (this time sponsored by McCurdy) to the foreign assistance authorization on July 10 without opposition. The final legislation is described in U.S. House of Representatives, *International Security and Development Cooperation Act of 1985: Conference Report*, pp. 63–73 and 142–46; *Making Supplemental Appropriations for the Fiscal Year Ending September 30, 1985*, p. 56.

126. Mary McGrory, "When Fear Batters Friendship," *WP*, June 13, 1985.

127. Ibid.; Margaret Shapiro, "Contra Aid Votes Presages Renewed U.S. Role," *WP*, June 14, 1985.

128. McGrory, "When Fear Batters Friendship," *WP*, June 13, 1985.

129. Roberts, "A Wildcatter Drills for Power," *NYT*, June 18, 1985.

130. *Congressional Record*, November 19, 1985, pp. H10293–98. The bill became Public Law 99-169.

131. Memorandum to John M. Poindexter from the President's Intelligence Advisory Board, "The Legality of Providing Basic Military Training for the Nicaraguan Democratic Resistance," April 8, 1986, in *Iran-Contra Documents*, vol. 2, pp. 1186–96. Democrats on the House Intelligence Committee tried to insist upon a narrow definition of what "intelligence-sharing" meant, but without much success. See the exchange of letters between House committee chairman Lee Hamilton, Senate committee chairman David Durenberger, and William Casey in *Iran-Contra Documents*, vol. 2, pp. 1198–1200.

132. In May 1987, James Adkins, who was CIA chief of base for the contra operation in Honduras, was removed from his post for allowing subordinates to provide illegal aid to the contras. Dillon, *Commandos*, p. 360. On the extent of the assistance, see deposition of "CIA Identity A," *Iran-Contra Depositions*, vol. 4, pp. 1348–49, 1357–66. This person was stationed at the CIA base at Aguacate.

133. The equipment and the training to use it cost $3 million. In addition, the United States increased its intelligence collection budget by $10 million in order to produce militarily useful intelligence for the contras. Bob Woodward, "CIA Provided Contras $13 Million in Assistance Under Reagan 'Finding,'" *WP*, January 14, 1987.

134. Author's interview with Susan Benda, Washington, D.C., November 1985.

135. "U.S. Helped Contras Get Missiles," *MH*, January 18, 1985; Alfonso Chardy, "U.S. Found to Skirt Ban on Aid to Contras," *MH*, June 24, 1985. Associated Press reporter Robert

Parry was not far behind. In October, he reported that the White House had helped organize a network of private and third-country donors to finance the contras, based on a plan drafted by North and approved by National Security Adviser Robert McFarlane and Reagan himself. Robert Parry, "President Linked to Secret Aid," *WP*, October 8, 1985. Parry had an administration source who participated in strategy meetings on how to continue financing the contras if Congress cut aid. Parry, *Fooling America*, pp. 250–52.

136. Memorandum to John M. Poindexter from Oliver L. North, "Press Revelations Regarding North's Role with Nicaraguan Resistance," June 3, 1985, in *Iran-Contra Hearings*, vol. 100-7, pt. 3, p. 750. Chardy says no such threat was ever made. Parry, *Fooling America*, pp. 251–52.

137. Joel Brinkley, "Nicaragua Rebels Getting Advice from White House on Operations," *NYT*, August 8, 1985.

138. Gerald M. Boyd, "Security Council's Nicaragua Role Defended," *NYT*, August 9, 1985; Hertsgaard, *On Bended Knee*, p. 307.

139. Letter from Michael D. Barnes to Robert C. McFarlane, August 16, 1985, in *Iran-Contra Hearings*, vol. 100-2, p. 547; letter to Robert C. McFarlane from Lee H. Hamilton, in *Iran-Contra Hearings*, vol. 100-2, p. 559.

140. *Iran-Contra Report*, pp. 122–26.

141. North did not actually substitute the altered documents for the originals until the Iran-contra scandal broke in 1987. Testimony of Robert C. McFarlane, *Iran-Contra Hearings*, vol. 100-2, pp. 73–75. The problem documents, both the originals and altered versions, are in *Iran-Contra Hearings*, vol. 100-5, pp. 1284–1372.

142. Letter to Michael D. Barnes from Robert C. McFarlane, September 12, 1985, in *Iran-Contra Hearings*, vol. 100-8, pp. 441–43. Poindexter assigned North to draft the reply to Barnes "because my objective here again would have been to withhold information" (testimony of John M. Poindexter, in *Iran-Contra Hearings*, vol. 100-8, pp. 82–83). In the end, however, the final draft of this letter was mostly McFarlane's (Draper, *Very Thin Line*, p. 119).

143. Letter from Michael D. Barnes to Robert C. McFarlane, September 30, 1985, in *Iran-Contra Hearings*, vol. 100-2, pp. 551–52; routing slip for letter from Michael Barnes, in *Iran-Contra Hearings*, vol. 100-8, pp. 425–26.

144. *Iran-Contra Report*, pp. 129–30.

145. David Ignatius, "Contra-Funding Affair Illustrates Failure of Oversight Process," *WP*, December 16, 1986; letter to Robert C. McFarlane from Michael D. Barnes, October 29, 1985, in *Iran-Contra Hearings*, vol. 100-2, pp. 553–55; draft letter from Robert C. McFarlane to Michael D. Barnes, undated, in *Iran-Contra Hearings*, vol. 100-2, p. 558; *Iran-Contra Report*, pp. 129–30.

146. *Iran-Contra Report*, p. 128.

147. Charles Green and R. A. Zaldivar, "The Contras and the Congress," *MH*, April 12, 1987.

148. Instead, he kept his superiors briefed verbally or on the NSC computerized message system (PROFS, short for Professional Office System). North testimony, *Iran-Contra Hearings*, vol. 100-7, pt. 1, p. 87.

CHAPTER NINETEEN

1. Letter to Donald T. Regan from William J. Casey, April 23, 1986, with attached fact sheet, "Situation in Nicaragua," in *Iran-Contra Hearings*, vol. 100-10, pp. 342–43.

2. Memorandum to Ronald Reagan from John M. Poindexter, "Meeting with the National Security Planning Group (NSPG), May 16, 1986," in *Iran-Contra Hearings*, vol. 100-7, pt. 3, pp. 15–18.

3. On improvements in the Nicaraguan army, see Cunningham, "U.S. Strategic Options

in Nicaragua," *Parameters: U.S. Army War College Quarterly* (March 1988). Cunningham was U.S. defense attaché in Nicaragua in 1985–86.

4. Sam Dillon, "1985 Was a Bad Year for Nicaraguan Rebels," *MH*, December 30, 1985; Marjorie Miller, "Sandinistas Hunt Contras in Low Intensity Conflict," *LAT*, June 26, 1986.

5. Author's interview with Daniel Ortega, Managua, Nicaragua, July 1987. See also Juan Tamayo, "Sandinista Offensive Routs Rebels from Strongholds," *MH*, June 19, 1985; Clifford Krauss, " 'Great Coffee War' in Nicaragua Is Being Won by Sandinistas," *WSJ*, January 21, 1986.

6. Alfonso Chardy, "CIA Is Planning to Make Contras a Fighting Force," *MH*, March 16, 1986.

7. U.S. House of Representatives, *Joint Resolution Relating to the Additional Authority*, pp. 3–6.

8. Memorandum from Robert M. Gates to CIA Director William Casey, December 14, 1984, "Subject: Nicaragua," in Kornbluh and Byrne, *Iran-Contra Scandal*, pp. 45–49. In the memo, Gates argues for a much tougher U.S. policy, including a naval blockade and U.S. airstrikes against Nicaragua.

9. U.S. Senate, *Nomination of Robert M. Gates to Be Director of Central Intelligence*, pp. 119–21. "It continues to be the assessment of the U.S. intelligence community that only U.S. forces could truly resolve the conflict in Nicaragua on a military basis," the House Intelligence Committee reported after being briefed in early 1986. U.S. House of Representatives, *Joint Resolution Relating to the Additional Authority*, p. 6.

10. Mary McGrory, "Dealing in Blood," *WP*, August 14, 1986.

11. *Iran-Contra Report*, p. 64; PROFS note to Poindexter from Oliver L. North, December 10, 1985, in *Iran-Contra Documents*, vol. 1, pp. 405–6.

12. Joanne Omang, "Aid to Contras Cloaked in Charade," *WP*, October 18, 1985; Robert J. McCartney, "Shift in Honduras Seen Facilitating Contra Aid," *WP*, January 22, 1986.

13. Memorandum to Poindexter from North, December 10, 1985, quoted in Stephen Engelberg, "Memos Suggest U.S. Honduran Deal on Contra Aid," *NYT*, May 18, 1989.

14. According to Ambassador John Ferch, he got Azcona's agreement to resume the flights at a meeting on January 30. Dan Morgan and John M. Goshko, "Costa Rican Disputes North Trial Document," *WP*, April 15, 1989.

15. Schulz and Schulz, *The United States, Honduras, and the Crisis in Central America*, pp. 135–37; Anne-Marie O'Connor, "CIA Role Seen in General's Fall," *WP*, February 9, 1986.

16. The $27 million approved in 1985 extended only through the first half of fiscal year (FY) 1986 (until March 31).

17. Edward Cody, "Nicaraguan Crackdown Seen Aimed at Church," *WP*, October 17, 1985.

18. Joanne Omang and John M. Goshko, "Reagan to Ask Military Aid for Contras," *WP*, January 15, 1986; Joanne Omang, "New Efforts Urged Against Nicaragua," *WP*, October 11, 1985.

19. "Radio Address to the Nation on Tax Reform and the Situation in Nicaragua, December 14, 1985," *Reagan Papers, 1985*, book 2, pp. 1476–77. The reference to designer glasses was to Daniel Ortega's much-publicized purchase of some $5,300 worth of eyeglasses for himself and his wife during a 1985 trip to the United States. David Hoffman, "Reagan Seeking More Aid for Contras," *WP*, December 15, 1985.

20. "Remarks and an Informal Exchange with Reporters on United States Assistance for the Nicaraguan Democratic Resistance, February 18, 1986," *Reagan Papers, 1986*, book 1, p. 216. The $100 million was to last through the second half of FY 1986 and all of FY 1987.

21. Edward Walsh and Milton Coleman, "Idea of Compromise on Contra Aid Fades," *WP*, March 12, 1986.

22. David Hoffman, "Inside the White House Contra-Aid Command Post," *WP*, March 20, 1986.

23. Blumenthal, *Rise of the Counter-Establishment*, pp. 162–63; Lloyd Grove, "The Contrary Evolution of Elliott Abrams," *WP*, January 14, 1987; Alfonso Chardy, "Latin Expert Wins Power Over Contras," *MH*, August 15, 1986.

24. Bernard Weinraub, "Reagan's Human Rights Chief: No 'Liberal Mole,'" *NYT*, October 19, 1982.

25. Ibid.

26. See, for example, Elliott Abrams, "The Silence on Nicaragua," *WP*, August 22, 1982; Eric Alterman, "The Best and the Rightest," *Tikkun* (July–August 1987). McNeil is quoted in Alfonso Chardy, "A 'Doberman' Diplomat Runs Reagan Latin Policy," *MH*, May 9, 1988.

27. Jack Beatty, "The Education of Elliott Abrams," *LAT*, July 16, 1988; Roy Gutman, "Muddled Start for 'Year of the Contras,'" *Newsday*, January 5, 1986; Joanne Omang, "New Efforts Urged Against Nicaragua," *WP*, October 11, 1985.

28. Testimony of John M. Poindexter, *Iran-Contra Hearings*, vol. 100-8, pp. 11–12.

29. Henry Allen, "The Prototypical Poindexter," *WP*, July 15, 1987.

30. Mayer and McManus, *Landslide*, p. 174.

31. Ibid., pp. 172–76.

32. Allen, "The Prototypical Poindexter," *WP*, July 15, 1987.

33. Mayer and McManus, *Landslide*, pp. 172–76; Schieffer and Gates, *Acting President*, p. 259; Cannon, *President Reagan*, pp. 625–26.

34. Woodward, *VEIL*, pp. 473–77; Mayer and McManus, *Landslide*, p. 281.

35. Joel Brinkley, "Reagan Plans to Seek Renewed Military Aid to Nicaraguan Rebels," *NYT*, February 14, 1986.

36. Gerald M. Boyd, "Nicaragua Lying, Reagan Declares," *NYT*, February 20, 1986.

37. Anthony Lewis, "'Conspiracy So Immense,'" *NYT*, February 24, 1986.

38. Bob Woodward and Lou Cannon, "CIA Document Based on Lobby Techniques," *WP*, March 1, 1986.

39. Sam Dillon, "Nicaraguans See U.S. Vote on Contras as Key to Future," *MH*, March 10, 1985.

40. Edward Cody, "Sandinistas Seen Turning Away from Liberal Allies," *WP*, February 16, 1986. According to Sandinista defector Roger Miranda, the National Directorate did not believe Reagan would stop the war even if Congress rejected his aid proposals, so they did not regard the congressional votes as very significant. Miranda and Ratliff, *Civil War in Nicaragua*, p. 38.

41. Stephen Kinzer, "Sandinista View of Contra Debate: Ortega Takes a Vacation," *NYT*, March 19, 1986; Tim Golden, "Managua Letting Others Fight Against Contra Aid," *MH*, March 11, 1986.

42. Patrick J. Buchanan, "The Contras Need Our Help," *WP*, March 5, 1986; Hoffman, "Inside the White House Contra-Aid Command Post," *WP*, March 20, 1986.

43. "Reagan's Resolve," *NYT*, March 7, 1986; Roberts, "Two House Units Bar Contra Aid Plan and One Backs It," *NYT*, March 7, 1986. Pragmatists in the administration also thought that Buchanan had cost Reagan votes. "Instead of getting Congress behind us, he antagonized them," wrote Press Secretary Larry Speakes. Speakes also claimed that Buchanan acted on his own, without clearing his article with anyone else in the White House. Speakes, *Speaking Out*, p. 88.

44. "Informal Exchange with Reporters Prior to Special Envoy Philip C. Habib's Departure for Central America, March 12, 1986," *Reagan Papers 1986*, book 1, pp. 323–25.

45. *Congressional Record*, March 6, 1986, pp. S2125–26.

46. Gerald M. Boyd, "Reagan Plans 'Flat-Out Effort' to Win Aid for Contras," *NYT*, March 2, 1986.

47. "Remarks at a White House Meeting for Supporters of United States Assistance for

the Nicaraguan Democratic Resistance, March 3, 1986," *Reagan Papers, 1986*, book 1, pp. 284–85.

48. "Remarks to Jewish Leaders During a White House Briefing on United States Assistance for the Nicaraguan Democratic Resistance, March 5, 1986," ibid., pp. 295–99.

49. "Remarks at an Exhibit of Weapons Captured in Central America, March 13, 1986," ibid., pp. 334–35; Smith, *Power Game*, p. 411.

50. "Remarks to Elected Officials During a White House Briefing on United States Assistance for the Nicaraguan Democratic Resistance, March 14, 1986," *Reagan Papers, 1986*, book 1, pp. 338–41.

51. Robert W. Merry, "Congress Shifts Toward Reagan on Aid for Contras in Nicaragua," *WSJ*, January 13, 1986.

52. LeoGrande, *Central America and the Polls*, table 27.

53. The text of Reagan's letter to McCurdy is in *Congressional Record*, June 11, 1985, pp. H4093–94.

54. Author's interview with a senior staff aide to Congressman James C. Slattery (D-Kan.), February 1986.

55. Robert Greenberger, "Congress Cautious on Military Aid Requested by Reagan for Contras," *WSJ*, January 23, 1986.

56. In February 1985, Nicaraguan vice president Sergio Ramírez traveled to Western Europe, hoping to enlist the NATO allies to urge diplomacy on Washington. West Germany, Spain, Ireland, and France all favored a resumption of the Manzanillo talks, but Washington paid them no heed. In March 1985, Daniel Ortega and Shultz met face to face in Montevideo, Uruguay, at the inauguration of President Julio Sanguinetti. Ortega again proposed resuming bilateral negotiations; Shultz refused. A week later, Ortega approached Vice President George Bush in Brasilia during the inauguration of Brazil's new civilian president, José Sarney, but he had no better luck. Tim Coone, "Nicaragua Seeks Fresh Peace Talks," *Financial Times of London*, February 20, 1985; Riding, "New Peace Backed by Latin Nations Backed by Shultz," *NYT*, March 3, 1985; Mimi Whitefield, "Nicaragua: Cuban Advisers Are Few," *MH*, March 20, 1985.

57. See Shultz's comments in Riding, "New Peace Backed by Latin Nations Backed by Shultz," *NYT*, March 3, 1985.

58. Dan Williams, "Mexicans to Lay Aside Contadora Issue for U.S. Talks," *LAT*, December 15, 1985. Washington, for its part, continued to pressure the Mexicans to change their regional policy by hinting that a cooperative attitude on the debt issue might depend upon Mexican concessions in Central America. Robert J. McCartney, "U.S. Seen as Unhappy with Mexico's Policies," *WP*, December 25, 1985; William Stockton, "Reagan Sees Mexican Today," *NYT*, January 3, 1986.

59. "Press Release Issued by the Ministers of Foreign Relations of the Contadora Group and Those of the Support Group, Integrated by Argentina, Brazil, Peru, and Uruguay, August 26, 1985," Embassy of Mexico Press Release No. 15/85. On the Nicaraguan role in engineering the Support Group, see Dan Williams, "Nicaragua Looks to Latin Meeting for Aid," *LAT*, August 24, 1985.

60. Juan deOnis, "Eight Latin American Democracies Announce Drive to Promote Peace in Central America," *LAT*, August 26, 1985.

61. Shirley Christian, "U.S. Envoys to Meet Today to Discuss Latin Peace Bid," *NYT*, September 9, 1985.

62. "Latin Ministers Urge U.S. to Halt Aid to Contras," *NYT*, February 11, 1986; "Reagan Urged to Push for Contra Aid," *WP*, February 12, 1986; Joanne Omang, "Latin Peace Talk Move Vetoed," *WP*, February 16, 1986.

63. Omang, "Latin Peace Talk Move Vetoed," *WP*, February 16, 1986.

64. "Nicaragua's 'No,'" *MH*, April 10, 1986.

65. "Remarks and a Question-and-Answer Session with Reporters on Announcing the Appointment of Philip C. Habib as Special Envoy for Central America, March 7, 1986," *Reagan Papers, 1986*, book 1, pp. 300–305.

66. Eleanor Clift and Doyle McManus, "Reagan Names Habib Central America Envoy," *LAT*, March 8, 1986. See also Shultz, *Turmoil and Triumph*, p. 951; Joanne Omang, "Troubleshooter Has a Second Mission: Pacify Increasingly Critical Congress," *WP*, March 8, 1986.

67. Tim Golden, "U.S. Effort to Isolate Nicaragua Is Losing Support in Region," *MH*, February 21, 1986.

68. William Long, "New Central American Leaders Reluctant to Back U.S. Policy on Nicaragua," *LAT*, March 21, 1986.

69. Cannon, *President Reagan*, p. 116.

70. O'Neill, *Man of the House*, p. 227.

71. Margaret Shapiro, "The Roots of O'Neill's Dissent," *WP*, June 5, 1985.

72. Ibid.; O'Neill, *Man of the House*, pp. 443–44; Philip Taubman, "The Speaker and His Sources on Latin America," *NYT*, September 12, 1984.

73. O'Neill, *Man of the House*, p. 443.

74. Ibid.

75. Ibid., p. 441.

76. Robert Parry, "Swing Votes Could Deliver Contra Aid," *WP*, January 27, 1986.

77. Joanne Omang, "18 Senators Want Contra Aid Plan Withdrawn," *WP*, February 27, 1986.

78. Steven V. Roberts, "A Wildcatter Drills for Power," *NYT*, June 18, 1985.

79. *Congressional Record*, March 19, 1986, p. H1356. See also Edward Walsh and Milton Coleman, "Idea of Compromise on Contra Aid Fades," *WP*, March 12, 1986.

80. The full debate is in *Congressional Record*, March 19, 1986, pp. H1324–1411, and March 20, 1986, pp. H1444–93.

81. Ibid., March 20, 1986, pp. H1467, H1491.

82. "Statement on House of Representatives Disapproval of United States Assistance to the Nicaraguan Democratic Resistance, March 20, 1986," *Reagan Papers, 1986*, book 1, pp. 380–81.

83. Lou Cannon, "Contra Leaders Cheer Reagan's Promise to Persist," *WP*, March 22, 198; "Remarks at White House Reception for Private Sector Supporters of United States Assistance for the Nicaraguan Democratic Resistance, March 21, 1986," *Reagan Papers, 1986*, book 1, pp. 380–81.

84. James LeMoyne, "Amid Indications of Battle, Questions About Its Scale in Honduras," *NYT*, March 29, 1986; Alfonso Chardy, "U.S. Feared Raid Would End Contras," *MH*, March 27, 1990; Edward Cody, "Honduras Limits Contras," *WP*, May 20, 1985.

85. "Statement by Principal Deputy Press Secretary Speakes on the Nicaraguan Incursion into Honduras, March 25, 1986," *Reagan Papers, 1986*, book 1, pp. 394–95; Tim Golden, "Hondurans Take Simmering Conflict in Stride," *MH*, March 26, 1986.

86. David K. Shipler, "Copters Will Go On Aiding Hondurans with Supplies," *NYT*, March 28, 1986; Joel Brinkley, "Sandinista Troops Said to Battle Contras 12 Miles Inside Country," *NYT*, March 26, 1986.

87. Stephen Kinzer, "Nicaragua Leader Warns of Risks in Use of U.S. Forces in Honduras," *NYT*, March 29, 1986.

88. Paul Glickman, "Secret Contacts on 'Contras,'" *CSM*, May 13, 1986.

89. Don Oberdorfer and Fred Hiatt, "U.S. Aides Uncertain on Size of Incursion by Nicaragua," *WP*, March 27, 1986; Steve Stecklow, "Envoy: Congress Was Fooled," *MH*, January 7, 1987.

90. Roy Gutman, "Competing in Blunders: Washington vs. Managua," *WP*, March 20, 1988; Gutman, *Banana Diplomacy*, pp. 324–25.

91. Stecklow, "Envoy: Congress Was Fooled," *MH*, January 7, 1987. See also account based on an interview with Ferch, in Schulz and Schulz, *The United States, Honduras, and the Crisis in Central America*, p. 162.

92. Alfonso Chardy, "U.S. Pushed Hondurans to Admit Raid," *MH*, March 28, 1986; James LeMoyne, "Honduran Tells of U.S. Pressure," *NYT*, April 3, 1986. The text of Azcona's letter requesting U.S. assistance is included with "Statement by Principal Deputy Press Secretary Speakes on the Nicaraguan Incursion into Honduras, March 26, 1986," *Reagan Papers, 1986*, book 1, pp. 403–4.

93. "Statement by Principal Deputy Press Secretary Speakes on the Nicaraguan Incursion into Honduras, March 25, 1986," *Reagan Papers, 1986*, book 1, p. 401. Intelligence reports regarding the Nicaraguan withdrawal are reported in *Iran-Contra Report*, p. 382. Of the $20 million in emergency aid, $19.6 arrived in Honduras after the incursion had ended. Joanne Omang, "Honduras Incursion Aid Arrives After the Fact," *WP*, April 30, 1986.

94. LeMoyne, "Honduran Tells of U.S. Pressure," *NYT*, April 3, 1986; Eleanor Randolph, "Incursion Announced Casually," *WP*, March 30, 1986.

95. For example, a *Washington Post* editorial accused the administration of "the manipulation of information to squeeze congressional votes here and there." "War Hype," *WP*, March 28, 1986.

96. *Iran-Contra Report*, pp. 382–83.

97. Ferch was called to a meeting in Washington in late 1985 and pressured to take on a more active role in directing contra operations, despite the Boland prohibition. When he asked for these instructions in writing, he was fired. Joanne Omang, "Ideology No Factor in Envoy's Firing," *WP*, July 2, 1986; Stecklow, "Ex-Envoy: Congress Was Fooled," *MH*, January 7, 1987; Mayer and McManus, *Landslide*, p. 150.

98. Roy Gutman, "U.S. Is Said to Seek Military Solution in Nicaragua," *WP*, July 25, 1986.

99. "Commander in Chief," *WSJ*, March 26, 1986.

100. *Congressional Record*, March 26, 1986, pp. S3454–92, and March 27, 1986, pp. S3564–3693.

101. The Republicans' April parliamentary maneuver is in ibid., April 16, 1986, pp. H1848–93.

102. The NHAO was created specifically to distribute the $27 million in nonlethal contra aid because the law prohibited the CIA or Pentagon from distributing it. Although Congress didn't know it at the time, the NHAO had been effectively captured by North. At his and Elliott Abrams's insistence, Rob Owen had been hired as the NHAO's "liaison" with the contras, and Richard Gadd had been hired as the NHAO's air carrier. The NHAO would pay for Gadd's planes to fly from the United States to Central America carrying nonlethal loads, the Enterprise would use the planes to move lethal supplies inside the region, and the NHAO would pay for the planes to fly back to the United States (Doyle McManus, "Use of Humanitarian Aid for Arming Contras Told," *LAT*, May 19, 1987; James LeMoyne, "How Contras Got Arms: An Account from Crew," *NYT*, December 4, 1986). Some NHAO funds were used directly to deliver arms to the contras, and NHAO planes sometimes carried "mixed loads" of both lethal and nonlethal supplies ("Nicaraguan Humanitarian Assistance Office [NHAO] Policy on 'Mixed Loads,'" in *Iran-Contra Depositions*, vol. 9, pp. 94–96; Alfonso Chardy, "Abrams Was Key to Arms Flights, Ex-Official Says," *MH*, August 14, 1987).

103. U.S. General Accounting Office, *Central America: Problems in Controlling Funds*.

104. U.S. House of Representatives, *Investigation of United States Assistance to the Nicaraguan Contras (Volume I)*.

105. U.S. House of Representatives, *Investigation of United States Assistance to the Nicaraguan Contras (Volume II)*, p. 2.

106. Joanne Omang, "Nicaragua Feels Pressure to Sign Pact," *WP*, May 16, 1986.

107. U.S. House of Representatives, *Investigation of United States Assistance to the Nicaraguan Contras (Volume II)*, p. 19.

108. Kornbluh, *Nicaragua*, p. 35; Dillon, *Commandos*, p. 127; Alfonso Chardy, "Congressmen Cite More Cases of Contra Aid Misuse," *MH*, April 20, 1986; David K. Shipler, "Ex-Officers Accuse Contra Chiefs of Siphoning Off U.S. Aid Money," *NYT*, June 21, 1986.

109. Shipler, "Ex-Officers Accuse Contra Chiefs of Siphoning Off U.S. Aid Money," *NYT*, June 21, 1986; Sam Dillon, "Ex-Rebels Seek Contra Chief's Removal," *MH*, June 25, 1986.

110. Memorandum to North ["BG"] from Robert W. Owen ["TC"], "Overall Perspective," March 17, 1986, in *Iran-Contra Hearings*, vol. 100-2, pp. 820–24. The NHAO subsequently admitted knowing that the currency transactions were yielding profits that were going into the contras' general operating budget. Robert Parry, "Contras Reported to Sell U.S. Aid Dollars for Profit," *WP*, July 8, 1986.

111. A CBS News poll in April 1986, for example, found 62 percent opposed to providing $100 million to the contras, and only 25 percent in favor. When opponents were asked the main reason for their opposition, 44 percent cited problems at home, 14 percent said the war was none of our business, and 9 percent said it was too expensive. Another April poll, by Market Opinion Research, found very similar reasons for opposition: 21 percent favored spending the money at home, and 27 percent thought the United States should not get involved. LeoGrande, "Did the Public Matter?"; Market Opinion Research, *Americans Talk Security*.

112. Alfonso Chardy, "Shultz Says GAO Study 'Concocted,'" *MH*, June 13, 1986; Bernard Weinraub, "Reagan, Seeking Aid for Contras, Warns of Russians," *NYT*, June 25, 1986. The administration released a twenty-five-page response to the interim GAO report, defending the nonlethal aid program and concluding, "All available evidence supports the conclusion that the aid, as Congress intended, is getting through." Alfonso Chardy, "U.S. Rejects Charges Contra Aid Misused," *MH*, June 26, 1986. The final GAO report did not appear until well after the contra aid debate was over. It concluded that some funds had been embezzled and some had been diverted to military uses. U.S. General Accounting Office, *Central America: Problems in Controlling Funds*.

113. "Remarks and a Question-and-Answer Session at a White House Luncheon for Regional Editors and Broadcasters, June 13, 1986," *Reagan Papers, 1986*, book 1, pp. 764–70.

114. Alfonso Chardy, "U.S. Officials Knew of Illegal Use of Funds," *MH*, October 28, 1986.

115. Ibid.

116. Joel Brinkley, "Costa Rica Said to Consider Breaking with Nicaragua," *NYT*, February 28, 1985. Documents released during the Iran-contra scandal showed that the administration knew the charges were true. See, for example, memorandum to CIA headquarters from Tomás Castillo [Joe Fernandez], "Drug Trafficking Activities by Members of Pastora's Organization," undated, in *Iran-Contra Hearings*, vol. 100-4, p. 123.

117. Brian Barger and Robert Parry, "Nicaragua Rebels Linked to Drug Trafficking," *WP*, December 27, 1985.

118. "Allegations of Misconduct by the Nicaraguan Democratic Resistance," Department of State document no. 3079c, April 16, 1986, as cited in U.S. Senate, *Drugs, Law Enforcement and Foreign Policy*, p. 37. See also Julia Preston, "Rebels Defended on Drug Allegations," *WP*, April 17, 1986. A second report released in July (after the June House vote on the $100 million aid package was safely over) admitted that "a limited number of persons having various kinds of affiliations with, or political sympathies for, the resistance groups" had been involved in drug trafficking. "Allegations of Drug Trafficking and the Nicaraguan Democratic Resistance," Department of State document no. 5136c, July 26, 1986, cited in U.S. Senate, *Drugs, Law Enforcement and Foreign Policy*, p. 37. See also Robert Parry, "Contra Drug Role Cited," *WP*, August 27, 1986.

119. Testimony of the Chief of the CIA's Central America Task Force (c/catf) [Alan Fiers], *Iran-Contra Hearings*, vol. 100-11, pp. 182–84. The Pastora group's drug activities are described in detail in U.S. Senate, *Drugs, Law Enforcement and Foreign Policy*, pp. 49–53.

120. Memorandum to North ["The Hammer"] from Owen ["TC"], "Southern Front," April 1, 1985, in *Iran-Contra Hearings*, vol. 100-2, pp. 799–802.

121. Johnson, *Sleepwalking through History*, pp. 266–73. Stansfield Turner, Director of Central Intelligence under Jimmy Carter, dropped Noriega from the cia payroll because of his drug connections. In 1981, Casey restored the relationship, paying Noriega $185,000 annually. Frederick Kempe, "The Noriega Files," *Newsweek*, January 25, 1990; Michael Isikoff, "Drug Cartel Gave Contras $10 Million, Court Told," *WP*, November 26, 1991.

122. U.S. Senate, *Drugs, Law Enforcement and Foreign Policy*, pp. 41–49; memorandum to North ["BG"] from Owen ["TC"], "Update," February 10, 1986, in *Iran-Contra Hearings*, vol. 100-2, pp. 816–17. The nhao's general practice was to continue using firms with whom the contras already had established business relationships, according to its director. Deposition of Robert W. Duemling, *Iran-Contra Depositions*, vol. 9, pp. 47–48.

123. Warren Richey, "Justice Officials Find No Crime Link to 'Contra' Leaders," *CSM*, May 9, 1986. A preliminary investigation of the drug issue by the Iran-contra congressional committees found no corroboration of "media-exploited allegations that the U.S. government condoned drug trafficking by contra leaders or contra organizations or that contra leaders or organizations did in fact take part in such activity." It added, however, that the scope of its investigation had not included "determining whether the contras have been independently or individually involved in drug trafficking." Memorandum to Lee H. Hamilton and John Nields from Robert A. Bermingham, "Allegations Re: Contra Involvement with Drug Smuggling," July 23, 1987, in *Iran-Contra Hearings*, vol. 100-11, pp. 1060–62.

124. Frank del Olmo, "Ties to Somocistas Choke U.S. Policy Goals," *LAT*, January 27, 1983.

125. The data are from two reports by the congressional Arms Control and Foreign Policy Caucus: *Who Are the Contras?* and *Contra High Command*. At the time, Elliott Abrams called the congressional report "incorrect and misleading," and the State Department circulated a report of its own in rebuttal, disputing the figures regarding the fdn's midlevel command—but not the general staff. U.S. Department of State, *Documents on the Nicaraguan Resistance*. In his memoirs, however, Abrams acknowledged that the fdn was "exclusively a right-wing preserve" of Somoza supporters. Abrams, *Undue Process*, p. 15. Cruz and Robelo's views are reported in James LeMoyne, "Contras Debate How to Widen Group's Appeal," *NYT*, May 23, 1986.

126. Abrams, *Undue Process*, p. 15. See also Alfonso Chardy, "Rebels Pick Miami Man as Director," *MH*, April 8, 1986.

127. "CIA Role Reported in Contras' Fall," *NYT*, May 30, 1986.

128. Sam Dillon, "Infighting Disrupts Contras," *MH*, February 15, 1987.

129. "None of these people can stand Robelo or Cruz," Rob Owen wrote of the fdn's leadership. "At every turn they will undermine them and do all in their power to see they are not given any power." Memorandum to North ["BG"] from Owen ["TC"], "Overall Perspective," March 17, 1986, in *Iran-Contra Hearings*, vol. 100-2, pp. 820–24.

130. Peter Ford, "Contras Greatest Challenge Is Boosting Credibility," *CSM*, January 21, 1987; Dan Williams, "Contras' Top Goals: More Troops, U.S. Funds for Weapons," *LAT*, September 6, 1985; Clifford Krauss, "Nicaragua's Contras Confront Infighting," *WSJ*, October 13, 1986; Cruz, *Memoirs of a Counter-Revolutionary*, p. 191.

131. Dennis Volman, "Rift Develops within Nicaraguan Rebel Group," *CSM*, October 15, 1985.

132. Memorandum to North ["BG"] from Owen ["TC"], August 25, 1985, in *Iran-Contra Hearings*, vol. 100-2, pp. 807–9; memorandum to North ["William"] from Owen ["TC"], April 7, 1986, "Recent Trip," in *Iran-Contra Hearings*, vol. 100-2, pp. 827–28.

133. James LeMoyne, "Rivalry Threatening to Split Contras," *NYT*, May 16, 1986; memorandum to North ["BG"] from Owen ["TC"], "Present Situation," February 27, 1986, in *Iran-Contra Hearings*, vol. 100-2, pp. 818–19.

134. Clarridge, *Spy for All Seasons*, p. 211; Stephen Kinzer, "Ex-Contra Looks Back, Finding Much to Regret," *NYT*, January 8, 1988.

135. Doyle McManus, "U.S. Moves to Reshape Leadership of Contras," *LAT*, March 13, 1986; Julia Preston, "Changes Sought in Leadership of Contras," *WP*, April 16, 1986.

136. The reforms and potential problems with them are detailed in Arms Control and Foreign Policy Caucus, *Contra "Reforms."*

137. Krauss, "Nicaragua's Contras Confront Infighting," *WSJ*, October 13, 1986.

138. McManus, "U.S. Moves to Reshape Leadership of Contras," *LAT*, March 13, 1986.

139. Julia Preston, "Nicaraguan Leader Says Contras Are No Threat," *WP*, June 22, 1986.

140. Dennis Volman, "Contadora Doggedly Pursues Central American Peace," *CSM*, June 6, 1986.

141. Letter to Congressman Jim Slattery (D-Kan.) from Ambassador Philip C. Habib, April 11, 1986, in *Congressional Record*, August 12, 1986, p. 20832. See also Morrell and Goodfellow, *Contadora under the Gun*.

142. Rowland Evans and Robert Novak, "A Box Called Contadora," *WP*, May 13, 1986.

143. Joanne Omang, "U.S. Reaffirms Desire for Latin Peace Pact," *WP*, May 23, 1986; Joanne Omang, "Habib Called Wrong, Imprecise, in Letter on U.S. Latin Policy," *WP*, May 24, 1986. Although Elliott Abrams was one of the officials who criticized the Habib letter to the press, Abrams's staff had drafted the letter and Abrams himself had approved it before it was sent. Frank McNeil, "The Road to Esquipulas," paper prepared for delivery at the meeting of the Latin American Studies Association, Washington, D.C., April 1991.

144. Leslie H. Gelb, "Pentagon Predicts Big War If Latins Sign Peace Accord," *NYT*, May 20, 1986.

145. Ibid.; Bernard Gwertzman, "State Department Assails the Pentagon Over Study of Latin Peace Talks," *NYT*, May 21, 1986.

146. Bernard Weinraub, "Reagan, Seeking Aid for Contras, Warns of Russians," *NYT*, June 25, 1986.

147. David Hoffman, "Spat Preceded Reagan's Noon Appeal," *WP*, June 25, 1986; Weinraub, "Reagan, Seeking Aid for Contras, Warns of Russians," *NYT*, June 25, 1986.

148. The legislative vehicle was the military construction appropriation bill (H.R. 5052). The full debate is in *Congressional Record*, June 25 and 26, 1986, pp. H4174–4300.

149. Edward Walsh, "Reagan Allies in Contra Vote Were Compromise, Fatigue," *WP*, June 27, 1986.

150. *Congressional Record*, June 26, 1986, pp. H4260, H4257.

151. Walsh, "Reagan Allies in Contra Vote Were Compromise, Fatigue," *WP*, June 27, 1986.

152. Author's interview with a member of Aspin's foreign policy staff, March 1986.

153. Mary McGrory, "Aspin, GOP: Comrades in Arms," *WP*, June 29, 1986.

154. Ken Fireman, "Reagan's Efforts Were a Major Factor in Aid Turnaround," *MH*, June 27, 1986; Walsh, "Reagan Allies in Contra Vote Were Compromise, Fatigue," *WP*, June 27, 1986.

155. Jonathan Karp, "Administration Dismisses Ruling," *WP*, June 28, 1986; David K. Shipler, "U.S. Assails Court Ruling and Closing of *La Prensa*," *NYT*, June 28, 1986. A summary of the court's finding is in "International Court of Justice," *Harvard International Law Review* (1987).

156. Stephen Kinzer, "Sandinistas Indefinitely Shut the Opposition Paper," *NYT*, June 28, 1986; Stephen Kinzer, "Sandinista Forces Are Said to Triple Stock of Copters," *NYT*, July 10, 1986.

157. Author's notes of Senate Democratic staff meeting, July 28, 1986.

158. Ibid.

159. Ibid., August 7, 1986.

160. *Congressional Record*, August 11, 1986, pp. S11187, S11192.

161. Ibid., August 12, 1986, pp. S11336–38.

162. Fireman, "Reagan's Efforts Were a Major Factor in Aid Turnaround," *MH*, June 27, 1986.

163. Walsh, "Reagan Allies in Contra Vote Were Compromise, Fatigue," *WP*, June 27, 1986.

164. *Congressional Record*, June 25, 1986, p. H4271.

165. U.S. Department of State, *Human Rights in Nicaragua*. The Sandinistas were certainly guilty of human rights violations, but the administration exaggerated them for political effect. For a critique, see Americas Watch, *Human Rights in Nicaragua*.

CHAPTER TWENTY

1. *Iran-Contra Report*, pp. 106–9; Sandra Dibble, "Contra Supporter Lands in Jail," *MH*, August 4, 1986.

2. Alfonso Chardy, "Colonel's Actions May Have Broken Contra Aid Ban," *MH*, April 30, 1986; Alfonso Chardy, "Despite Ban, U.S. Helping Contras," *MH*, June 8, 1986; Alfonso Chardy, "Sources: White House OK'd Contra Supply Network," *MH*, June 22, 1986. Reagan's approval was also cited in Robert Parry, "President Linked to Secret Aid," *WP*, October 8, 1985.

3. See, for example, Robert Parry and Brian Barger, "Reagan's Shadow CIA," *New Republic*, November 24, 1986. Parry recounts that he and Barger actually had the North story before Chardy, but their editors at the Associated Press were afraid to run it until after Chardy's story appeared. Parry, *Fooling America*, pp. 253–67.

4. *Iran-Contra Report*, pp. 140–42.

5. Memorandum to the files from Steven K. Berry, associate counsel for the House Intelligence Committee, September 3, 1986, summarizing North's August 6, 1986, meeting with the committee, in *Iran-Contra Hearings*, vol. 100-7, pt. 3, pp. 553–54; Lee Hamilton's testimony at Poindexter's trial, quoted in Draper, *Very Thin Line*, p. 345.

6. Testimony of Oliver L. North, *Iran-Contra Hearings*, vol. 100-7, pt. 1, p. 179.

7. *Iran-Contra Report*, pp. 141–42.

8. Memorandum to North ["William"] from Robert W. Owen ["TC"], "Recent Trip," April 7, 1986, *Iran-Contra Hearings*, vol. 100-2, pp. 827–28.

9. PROFS note to John M. Poindexter from North, "Iran and Terrorism," May 16, 1986, *Iran-Contra Hearings*, vol. 100-7, pt. 3, pp. 29–30. See a similar message in PROFS note to Poindexter from North, "Private Blank Check," June 10, 1986, in *Iran-Contra Hearings*, vol. 100-2, p. 623.

10. *Iran-Contra Report*, p. 77; Steve Stecklow, Mark Fazlollah, and Frank Greve, "Contra Relief Poorly Run, Crew Relates," *MH*, February 22, 1987.

11. Julia Preston, "Contra Supply Mission Casual," *WP*, October 19, 1986.

12. James LeMoyne, "Hasenfus Says He Does Not Know Who Ran Nicaragua Operation," *NYT*, October 20, 1986.

13. Marjorie Miller, "Caught in U.S.-Sandinista Struggle, Hasenfus Says," *LAT*, October 25, 1986.

14. Tim Golden, "Captured American Has Little to Say at Briefing," *MH*, October 8, 1986.

15. Mayer and McManus, *Landslide*, p. 276.

16. *Iran-Contra Report*, p. 145.

17. Ibid.; Joanne Omang and Joe Pichirallo, "Fliers' Network Shares Old CIA Links," *WP*, October 10, 1986; Joe Pichirallo, "U.S. Role in Contra Supply Program Remains Mysterious," *WP*, November 9, 1986.

18. Memorandum to Poindexter from Vincent Cannistraro, "Downed Plane," October 8, 1986, in *Iran-Contra Hearings*, vol. 100-7, pt. 3, p. 570; Alfonso Chardy, "'Friends' Paid for Contra Flight," *MH*, October 8, 1986; Joel Brinkley, "Contras Take Responsibility for the C-123 Supply Flight," *NYT*, October 14, 1986.

19. Testimony of Elliott Abrams, *Iran-Contra Hearings*, vol. 100-5, pp. 64–65.

20. *Iran-Contra Report*, p. 146.

21. Ibid., p. 147.

22. George was ultimately convicted on two counts, but then pardoned by President George Bush, along with Fiers, Abrams, McFarlane, and Dewey Clarridge. Walsh, *Final Report of the Independent Counsel*, Volume I, pp. 233–45. Fiers's case is described at pp. 263–82, and Abrams's at pp. 375–92. Abrams insisted that he pleaded guilty simply to avoid a trial even though he did nothing wrong. Abrams, *Undue Process*, especially pp. 103–4.

23. North testimony, *Iran-Contra Hearings*, vol. 100-7, pt. 1, pp. 19–20, 136–37; Mayer and McManus, *Landslide*, p. 287.

24. *Iran-Contra Report*, pp. 293–97.

25. Ibid., pp. 297–98.

26. Ibid., p. 306.

27. Ibid., pp. 305–7.

28. "Release of American Hostages in Beirut," undated, in *Iran-Contra Hearings*, vol. 100-9, pp. 1390–97. A detailed account of their finding the document is in Mayer and McManus, *Landslide*, pp. 334–35.

29. Bradlee, *Guts and Glory*, p. 470; Draper, *Very Thin Line*, pp. 508–9.

30. North, *Under Fire*, p. 327.

31. *Iran-Contra Report*, pp. 312–13.

32. Ibid.

33. Reagan, *American Life*, p. 530; testimony of Donald T. Regan, *Iran-Contra Hearings*, vol. 100-10, pp. 29–30.

34. Casey's fallback plan was to have Reagan admit that North and Poindexter had broken the law, but to pardon them immediately because they had acted for a good cause. *Iran-Contra Report*, p. 316; Regan, *For the Record*, pp. 40–44, 51; Draper, *Very Thin Line*, pp. 521–22.

35. "Remarks Announcing the Review of the National Security Council's Role in the Iran Arms and Contra Aid Controversy, November 25, 1986," *Reagan Papers, 1987*, book 2, pp. 1587–88. The transcript of Meese's remarks is in *Iran-Contra Hearings*, vol. 100-9, pp. 1456–74.

36. North, *Under Fire*, pp. 1–2.

37. North testimony, *Iran-Contra Hearings*, vol. 100-7, pt. 1, pp. 148, 152, 184, 236–37.

38. *Iran-Contra Report*, p. 318; North, *Under Fire*, pp. 16–17; Mayer and McManus, *Landslide*, p. 351. Reagan again called North a hero in "An Interview with the President," *Time*, December 8, 1986. When North was indicted in March 1988, Reagan declared, "I have some definite reason for still thinking that Ollie North is a hero." "Remarks and a Question-and-Answer Session with Members of the Center for the Study of the Presidency, March 25, 1988," *Reagan Papers, 1988*, book 1, pp. 386–91.

39. U.S. Senate, *Preliminary Inquiry into the Sale of Arms to Iran*.

40. A May CBS–*New York Times* poll found that 59 percent of the public thought Reagan was lying when he denied knowledge of the diversion (Steven V. Roberts, "At the White House, the TV Is Turned Off," *NYT*, July 8, 1987). In a July poll, *Time* found about the same result (Michael Weisskopf, "Majority in Polls Say North Had Top Approval," *WP*, July 13, 1987).

41. Schieffer and Gates, *Acting President*, p. 292.

42. Cannon, *President Reagan*, p. 670; Thomas M. Burnett, "Glenn: Reagan Has Teflon Coattails," UPI wire, November 5, 1986.

43. Linda Greenhouse, "Prospects for Rebel Aid Look Bleak in Congress," *NYT*, November 27, 1986.

44. Joel Brinkley, "U.S. Aides Fear Crisis Will End Contras' Effort," *NYT*, December 8, 1986.

45. "Remarks Following Discussions with President Oscar Arias Sanchez of Costa Rica, December 4, 1986," *Reagan Papers, 1986*, book 2, pp. 1603–4; "Address Before a Joint Session of Congress on the State of the Union, January 27, 1987," *Reagan Papers, 1987*, book 1, pp. 56–61.

46. Elaine Sciolino, "Contra Aid Appeal Will Be Postponed," *NYT*, February 12, 1987.

47. Linda Greenhouse, "Contra Aid Is Said to Have Bright Prospects in Senate," *NYT*, June 27, 1986; Calmes, "Aspin Makes Comeback at Armed Services," *CQ Weekly Report*, January 24, 1987.

48. Barry, *Ambition and Power*, pp. 80–81, 127–28.

49. Ibid., pp. 80–81.

50. Ibid., pp. 127–28.

51. The red-baiting phrase was Henry Hyde's idea. Steven Pressman, "House, in Symbolic Action, Votes Contra Aid Moratorium," *CQ Weekly Report*, March 14, 1987. The full debate on the moratorium resolution is in *Congressional Record*, March 11, 1987, pp. H1188–1250.

52. *Congressional Record*, March 11, 1987, pp. H1246–47.

53. The debate on the resolution of disapproval is in ibid., March 18, 1987, pp. S3329–86. The debate on cloture is in ibid., March 25, 1987, pp. S3796–97.

54. William Branigin, "Divisions Detract from Contra Advances," *WP*, January 29, 1987; Tim Golden, "Contra Leader Considers Resignation," *MH*, January 27, 1987.

55. Peter Ford, "Contras' Greatest Challenge: Boosting Credibility," *CSM*, January 21, 1987; Guillermo Martinez, "Arturo Cruz: Contra Leader at Bay," *MH*, January 29, 1987; Alfonso Chardy and Sam Dillon, "Contras' Plan Is to Step Up Raids into Nicaragua," *MH*, January 22, 1987.

56. Jim Hampton, "Deluge on Leaky UNO Umbrella," *MH*, February 1, 1987.

57. Lloyd Grove, "Arturo Cruz at the Nicaraguan Crossroads," *WP*, February 19, 1987; Elaine Sciolino, "Key Contra Criticizes Rightist's Role," *NYT*, February 14, 1987. See also Dennis Volman, "Why Cruz Quit the Contras," *CSM*, March 11, 1987.

58. Robert S. Greenberger, "Contra Leader Plans to Remain with the Group," *WSJ*, February 20, 1987.

59. Joanne Omang, "UNO's Future Hinges on Control of Contra Army," *WP*, February 18, 1987; Joanne Omang, "Contra Leader Says Internal Rift Will Be Resolved by Thursday," *WP*, February 14, 1987.

60. Joanne Omang, "Calero Quits Post in Rebel Leadership," *WP*, February 17, 1987; Sam Dillon, "Irked Conservatives Praise Contra Forced Out of Alliance," *MH*, February 18, 1987.

61. Tim Golden, "Officials: Contra to Quit Alliance," *MH*, February 16, 1987.

62. Sam Dillon, "Contra Leader Presses for Reforms," *MH*, February 19, 1987; Sam Dillon, "Cruz Retains Contra Post, Demands Military Reform," *MH*, February 20, 1987.

63. James LeMoyne, "Top Contra Quits Citing Disillusion," *NYT*, March 10, 1987; Ken Fireman, "Shultz Criticizes Cruz for Leaving Contras," *MH*, March 18, 1987.

64. "Leading Anti-Sandinista Got CIA Cash, Sources Say," *WSJ*, April 23, 1985. Cruz admitted receiving $6,000 a month from the CIA for twenty-six months, which means that he must have been put on the payroll in early 1983. Stephen Kinzer, "Ex-Contra Looks Back, Finding Much to Regret," *NYT*, January 8, 1988.

65. Memorandum to McFarlane from North, "Meeting with Arturo Cruz," March 15, 1985, in *Iran-Contra Hearings*, vol. 100-7, pt. 3, pp. 471–72; memorandum to McFarlane from North, "Cruz Control," February 27, 1985, cited in *Iran-Contra Hearings*, vol. 100-7, pt. 3, p. v. See also Lela Mayers, "Cruz Control and Intelligence Oversight," *First Principles* (May–June 1989): 8. One of North's strategies, as detailed in the March memo cited above, was to find a "legitimate publisher or foundation" that was willing to take over paying Cruz. Shortly thereafter, Cruz was given a $40,000 post as researcher at Roy Godson's National Strategy Information Center. Deposition of Roy S. Godson, *Iran-Contra Depositions*, vol. 12, pp. 301–2. See also Doyle McManus, "North's Payment of Salary to Contra Leader Reported," *LAT*, February 20, 1987.

66. "Wright Says North Aid May Compromise Contra Leader," *LAT*, February 21, 1987.

67. Elaine Sciolino, "Contra Aid Appeal Will Be Postponed," *NYT*, February 12, 1987.

68. See, for example, Assistant Secretary Motley's 1985 testimony before the Senate Foreign Relations Committee, quoted in Walter Pincus and Dan Morgan, "Using Saudi Funds, Contras Expanded Despite Aid Cutoff," *WP*, May 26, 1987.

69. Joel Brinkley, "U.S. Aides Fear Crisis Will End Contras' Effort," *NYT*, December 8, 1986. From Israel (in Operation Tipped Kettle I and II), the contras received approximately $11 million; from Taiwan, $2 million; from Saudi Arabia, $32 million; and from North's domestic fundraising, $2.8 million. In 1985, Abrams solicited $10 million for the contras from the Sultan of Brunei, but contras never received the money because it was deposited in the wrong account by mistake. Abrams testimony, *Iran-Contra Hearings*, vol. 100-5, p. 86.

70. Clifford Krauss and Frederick Kempe, "Managua Tightens Grip on Former Contra Strongholds," *WSJ*, February 6, 1987.

71. Tim Golden, "Rebels' Efforts Sputter in Cities," *MH*, June 18, 1986.

72. Marjorie Miller, "Contra Push Fails to Worry Sandinistas," *LAT*, April 19, 1987; James LeMoyne, "How Contras Recruit: The Kidnapping Way," *NYT*, June 22, 1987.

73. Lou Cannon, "Carlucci Taking Trip to Evaluate Contras," *WP*, January 29, 1987. Admiral William J. Crowe Jr., chairman of the Joint Chiefs of Staff, held a similar view; see Elaine Sciolino, "Joint Chiefs' Head Warns Contras; Shultz in Aid Plea," *NYT*, February 13, 1987.

74. Joel Brinkley, "U.S. Aides Fear Crisis Will End Contras' Effort," *NYT*, December 8, 1986.

75. Tim Golden, "Contras in Training for Major Offensive," *MH*, March 23, 1987; James LeMoyne, "New Arms Haven't Changed Contras' Ways," *NYT*, June 1, 1987; Tim Golden, "Nicaragua: U.S. Flights Spy on Us," *MH*, July 18, 1986.

76. Anne-Marie O'Connor, "Plans for Three Contras' Island Bases Told," *LAT*, October 31, 1986; Marjorie Miller, "Honduran Island Used as CIA Base for Contras," *LAT*, January 15, 1987. Swan Island was one of the Agency's old stomping grounds; it was where the CIA had set up "Radio Swan" to broadcast propaganda and coded messages into Cuba at the time of the Bay of Pigs invasion in 1961. The CIA built the contras a radio station, too: "Radio Liberación," based in El Salvador. "Contras' AM Radio Station Begins Operating," *LAT*, January 19, 1987.

77. Joel Brinkley, "CIA Gives Contras Detailed Profiles of Civil Targets," *NYT*, March 19, 1987; Alfonso Chardy, "CIA Airdropping Contra Saboteurs," *MH*, April 1, 1987.

78. Examples of resulting stories include James LeMoyne, "With Rebels in Nicaragua: Battle Ready," *NYT*, March 3, 1987; William Branigin, "Contras Hold Command Post in Watery Corner of Nicaragua," *WP*, April 19, 1987; Sandra Dribble, "With the Contras," *MH*, May 17, 1987; James LeMoyne, "New Arms Haven't Changed Contras' Ways," *NYT*, June 1, 1987; Marjorie Miller, "Contra Recruits Get Political Talks," *LAT*, June 11, 1987.

79. Rod Nordland, "The New Contras?," *Newsweek*, June 1, 1987.

80. Barry, *Ambition and Power*, p. 303. In their book about the hearings, Senators George

Mitchell and William Cohen agreed that turning the hearings into another contra aid policy debate was "a trap to be avoided." Cohen and Mitchell, *Men of Zeal*, p. 98.

81. See the opening statements by Republican committee members in *Iran-Contra Hearings*, vol. 100-1, pp. 1–39.

82. Secord testimony, *Iran-Contra Hearings*, vol. 100-1, p. 40.

83. Testimony of Robert C. McFarlane, *Iran-Contra Hearings*, vol. 100-2, pp. 36–40, 116. McFarlane makes the same claim in his memoirs (McFarlane and Smardz, *Special Trust*, pp. 77–84). North, when he testified, insisted that he fully reported everything he was doing to his superiors—first McFarlane and later Poindexter. The documentary record of NSC memoranda and computer messages supported North. For example, the six problematic NSC system documents that McFarlane located during the 1985 congressional inquiry were all memos from North to McFarlane detailing North's military support for the contras. McFarlane eventually pleaded guilty to four misdemeanor counts of withholding information from Congress and was pardoned by President Bush. North was convicted on three counts of a twelve-count indictment, but the convictions were overturned on appeal when McFarlane claimed his testimony at North's trial was tainted by his knowledge of North's immunized testimony before Congress. Walsh, *Final Report of the Independent Counsel*, Volume I, pp. 79–104, 105–22.

84. McFarlane testimony, *Iran-Contra Hearings*, vol. 100-2, p. 206.

85. *Report of the President's Special Review Board* (Tower Board), p. III-24.

86. "Remarks and a Question-and-Answer Session with Southeast Regional Editors and Broadcasters, May 15, 1987," *Reagan Papers, 1987*, book 1, pp. 512–16.

87. "The Boland amendment is tightly specific and it applies only to particular agencies," explained White House Chief of Staff Howard Baker. "All I can tell you is, it doesn't apply to the president." Gerald F. Seib, "White House Case Against Boland Amendment Attempts End Run Around Charges of Violation," *WP*, May 18, 1987.

88. Abrams testimony, *Iran-Contra Hearings*, vol. 100-5, pp. 14–15, 32.

89. Excerpt from the testimony of Elliott Abrams to the Tower Board, in *Iran-Contra Hearings*, vol. 100-5, pp. 781–82.

90. Testifying on November 25, 1986—the same day Reagan fired North and Poindexter—Abrams denied he had ever discussed the "problems of fundraising by the contras with members of the NSC staff." He also testified that as far as he knew, the contras had not received contributions from any foreign governments (U.S. Senate, *Transcript of Proceedings before the Select Committee on Intelligence: Briefing on Nicaragua*, November 25, 1986, in *Iran-Contra Hearings*, vol. 100-5, pp. 650–62). These answers did not square well with the fact that Abrams had indeed discussed third-party support with North and others, and had personally solicited a $10 million contribution from the Sultan of Brunei. On October 10, 1986, Abrams had told the Senate Foreign Relations Committee essentially the same thing. When Senator John Kerry asked whether the contras had received any aid from third countries, Abrams replied, "Not that I am aware of, and not through us." Abrams's rationale for this answer was that the money from Brunei was still in transit, so had not yet been received (Abrams testimony, *Iran-Contra Hearings*, vol. 100-5, p. 86). On December 8, 1986, Abrams appeared again before the Intelligence Committee, this time under oath, and acknowledged his role in the Brunei solicitation (U.S. Senate, *Transcript of Proceedings before the Select Committee on Intelligence: Testimony of Elliott Abrams*, December 8, 1986, in *Iran-Contra Hearings*, vol. 100-5, pp. 663–76).

91. Abrams testimony, *Iran-Contra Hearings*, vol. 100-5, pp. 104, 151, 164; Doyle McManus, "Shultz Defends Abrams, Calls Him a 'Good Guy,'" *LAT*, July 25, 1987.

92. Maureen Dowd, "A Fall Guy Yes, a Patsy No, a President's Servant Says," *NYT*, July 10, 1987.

93. North testimony, *Iran-Contra Hearings*, vol. 100-7, pt. 1, p. 192.

94. Ibid., p. 191.

95. Ibid., pt. 1, pp. 180, 183; pt. 2, p. 132.

96. Ibid., pt. 1, pp. 36, 76.

97. Ibid., pt. 1, pp. 135, 88–89, 160, 162; pt. 2, pp. 118–19, 178.

98. Ibid., pt. 1, p. 152.

99. Haynes Johnson, "Counsel Liman Seizes the Day," *WP*, July 10, 1987; North, *Under Fire*, pp. 366–67.

100. See, for example, North testimony, *Iran-Contra Hearings*, vol. 100-7, pt. 1, pp. 319–21; pt. 2, pp. 68, 130–31, 182–83.

101. Ibid., pt. 2, p. 46.

102. Ibid., pp. 127, 196.

103. Poindexter testimony, *Iran-Contra Hearings*, vol. 100-8, pp. 37–38, 204.

104. Ibid., pp. 36–39, 162.

105. Ibid., pp. 169, 183, 273.

106. Ibid., pp. 89, 101, 289.

107. The Republicans who signed the majority report were Senators Warren Rudman (N.H.), Paul S. Trible (Va.), and William S. Cohen (Maine).

108. *Iran-Contra Report*, pp. 11, 13, 18, 22.

109. Ibid., p. 15.

110. Ibid., pp. 16, 405–7.

111. Ibid., pp. 21–22.

112. Ibid., p. 420.

113. Ibid., p. 437.

114. Ibid.

115. The phrase is Hyde's, quoted in testimony of Caspar W. Weinberger, *Iran-Contra Hearings*, vol. 100-10, p. 194.

116. *Iran-Contra Report*, p. 474.

117. Quoted in *Congressional Quarterly Almanac 1987*, p. 75.

118. Several committee members and staff confirmed this decision. Seymour M. Hersh, "The Iran-Contra Committees: Did They Protect Reagan?," *New York Times Magazine*, April 29, 1990.

119. Oliver North believed that Reagan knew about the diversion, although he could offer only circumstantial evidence in support of his conclusion. North, *Under Fire*, pp. 14–15.

120. Shultz, *Turmoil and Triumph*, pp. 309–10.

121. Robert Parry, "President Linked to Secret Aid," *WP*, October 8, 1985; Alfonso Chardy, "Sources: White House OK'd Contra Supply Network," *MH*, June 22, 1986; "McFarlane: A Question of Candor," *Newsweek*, May 18, 1987.

122. Persico, *Casey*, p. 412.

123. In his memoirs, McFarlane quotes Reagan as telling him, "We've got to find a way to keep doing this, Bud. I want you to do whatever you have to do to help these people keep body and soul together. Do everything you can." McFarlane and Smardz, *Special Trust*, p. 68.

124. "Remarks Announcing a Central American Peace Proposal and a Question-and-Answer Session with Reporters, April 4, 1985," *Reagan Papers, 1985*, book 1, pp. 400–403.

125. Poindexter testimony, *Iran-Contra Hearings*, vol. 100-8, p. 51. Poindexter also describes this conversation in a PROFS note to Don Fortier, "Contra Project," May 2, 1986, in *Iran-Contra Hearings*, vol. 100-7, pt. 3, p. 1141.

126. Notes of the November 25 meeting, in *Iran-Contra Hearings*, vol. 100-9, pp. 1436–55.

127. Johnson, *Sleepwalking through History*, p. 287; Stephen Engelberg, "Reagan Lapses Found on Iran-Contra Documents," *NYT*, June 4, 1989.

128. North testimony, *Iran-Contra Hearings*, vol. 100-7, pt. 1, pp. 317–18; Carl Bernstein, "TV Anchormen Are Missing the Big Story of the Hearings," *NYT*, July 14, 1987.

129. Kenneth E. Sharpe, "What Did *We* Know and When Did We Know It?," *Baltimore Sun*, December 7, 1986.

CHAPTER TWENTY-ONE

1. Julia Preston, "Two Nations Suspend Peace Talks Role," *WP*, November 8, 1986; Joanne Omang, "U.S. Questions OAS Chief's Treaty Effort," *WP*, January 8, 1987; Peter Ford, "Expectations Low for Central American Peace Bids," *CSM*, January 13, 1987.

2. "Contadora Peace Hopes Fade," *Financial Times of London*, January 22, 1987; William Branigin, "Contadora Effort Shows No Progress," *WP*, January 22, 1987; Peter Ford, "Contadora Is 'Emperor Without Clothes,' Europeans Worry," *CSM*, February 12, 1987.

3. Julia Preston, "Oscar Arias, Defiantly," *WP*, October 30, 1987; Richard Boudreaux, "The Bashful Peacemaker," *LAT*, November 2, 1987.

4. Stephen Kinzer, "Peacemaker with Ardor," *NYT*, September 23, 1987; James LeMoyne, "Costa Rica Gets a Persistent President," *NYT*, February 4, 1986.

5. Preston, "Oscar Arias, Defiantly," *WP*, October 30, 1987.

6. Joanne Omang, "Political Tension Over Contra Activity Rises in Costa Rica," *WP*, July 19, 1986.

7. Alfonso Chardy, "U.S. Used Threats on Latin Allies," *MH*, May 10, 1987; Tim Golden, "Costa Rica Got Pressure from U.S.," *MH*, March 9, 1987.

8. Edward Cody, "U.S. Pressure on Costa Rica Reported," *WP*, April 13, 1986; James LeMoyne, "Costa Rican Vows to Be a Peacemaker," *NYT*, May 9, 1986.

9. William Branigin, "Costa Rica Pushes New Peace Plan, Cracks Down on Contras," *WP*, February 1, 1987; James LeMoyne, "Costa Rica Weighs Protest to U.S. on Use of Airstrip to Aid Contras," *NYT*, March 9, 1987; Peter Kornbluh and Martha Honey, "The Case of Ollie's Airstrip," *Nation*, February 22, 1993. The Costa Rican side of the story is recounted in the memoir of Arias's ambassador to Washington, Guido Fernández, *El Desafío de la Paz*, pp. 44, 48, 60–63.

10. KL-43 message, September 10, 1986, in *Iran-Contra Hearings*, vol. 100-1, p. 435.

11. *Iran-Contra Report*, p. 76; *Report of the President's Special Review Board* (Tower Board), February 26, 1987, pp. C11–13.

12. Golden, "Costa Rica Got Pressure from U.S.," *MH*, March 9, 1987; Fernández, *El Desafío de la Paz*, pp. 78–79.

13. Fernández, *El Desafío de la Paz*, pp. 33–34.

14. Stephen Kinzer, "Costa Rica Gets Tougher on Contras," *NYT*, September 10, 1986. The various economic pressures are reported in detail in Fernández, *El Desafío de la Paz*, pp. 104–14. See also Golden, "Costa Rica Got Pressure from U.S.," *MH*, March 9, 1987; Cody, "U.S. Pressure on Costa Rica Reported," *WP*, April 13, 1986.

15. Fernández, *El Desafío de la Paz*, pp. 50–53; Persico, *Casey*, p. 2; "Costa Rican President Says He Snubbed Casey," *WP*, March 13, 1987; Preston, "Oscar Arias, Defiantly," *WP*, October 30, 1987.

16. Sam Dillon, "Low-Key Leader Packs Wallop," *MH*, July 10, 1987; Edward Cody, "Contadora Deadline Imperiled," *WP*, May 26, 1986.

17. Fernández, *El Desafío de la Paz*, pp. 70–75; Karen DeYoung, "Costa Rican President Wins Nobel Peace Prize," *WP*, October 14, 1987.

18. Jaime Daremblum, "Costa Rican Leader Plays His Ace in the Contadora Game," *WSJ*, May 23, 1986.

19. Brook Larmer, "Latin Peace Plan Wins Wide U.S. Support," *CSM*, March 12, 1987.

20. Tim Golden and Sandra Dribble, "U.S., Costa Rica Talk Peace in Miami," *MH*, January 8, 1987.

21. Kinzer, "Costa Rica Gets Tougher on Contras," *NYT*, September 10, 1986; Cody, "U.S.

Pressure on Costa Rica Reported," *WP*, April 13, 1986; Branigin, "Costa Rica Pushes New Peace Plan, Cracks Down on Contras," *WP*, February 1, 1987.

22. Stephen Kinzer, "Nicaragua Chief Says Peace Plan Will Fail Without Shift by Reagan," *NYT*, March 18, 1987; Peter Ford, "Central American Peace Plan Seen as Promising," *CSM*, February 17, 1987.

23. Stephen Kinzer, "Costa Rican Peace Plan Draws Doubt," *NYT*, April 26, 1987.

24. Larmer, "Latin Peace Plan Wins Wide U.S. Support," *CSM*, March 12, 1987.

25. Kinzer, "Costa Rican Peace Plan Draws Doubt," *NYT*, April 26, 1987; Robert S. Greenberger, "U.S. Warms to Central America Plan, Hoping to Win More Aid for Contras," *WSJ*, April 27, 1987.

26. Arias's ambassador to the United States was at the meeting, taking notes for the Costa Rican side. His detailed account of the confrontation is in Fernández, *El Desafío de la Paz*, pp. 119–26. See also Elaine Sciolino, "Reagan Meets Costa Rican to Fault His Peace Plan," *NYT*, June 18, 1987.

27. Dillon, "Low-Key Leader Packs Wallop," *MH*, July 10, 1987.

28. Fernández, *El Desafío de la Paz*, pp. 119–26.

29. Jack Beatty, "The Education of Elliott Abrams," *LAT*, July 16, 1988.

30. Barry, *Ambition and Power*, pp. 309–10.

31. Linda Greenhouse, "Latin Peace Plan Is Put Forward by Administration," *NYT*, August 5, 1987.

32. Alfonso Chardy, "Contra Issue Spurs Bitter U.S. Battle," *MH*, August 9, 1987.

33. Ibid.

34. Wright, *Worth It All*, p. 50.

35. Barry, *Ambition and Power*, p. 328.

36. The account of this meeting is based on ibid., pp. 2–4, 311–12, 322, 343.

37. Chardy, "Nancy Reagan Pushed Peace Plan, Wright Says," *MH*, August 7, 1987. Nancy Reagan's role is confirmed in Deaver, *Behind the Scenes*, p. 38.

38. Barry, *Ambition and Power*, pp. 315, 322.

39. Edward Walsh, "Despite Skeptics, Wright Pushes Latin Peace Plan," *WSJ*, August 6, 1987; Barry, *Ambition and Power*, pp. 314, 320–21, 329.

40. Barry, *Ambition and Power*, pp. 320–21.

41. Wright acknowledged as much to George Shultz. Shultz, *Turmoil and Triumph*, pp. 957–58.

42. The text of the plan is in "U.S. Initiative for Peace in Central America," *U.S. Department of State Bulletin*, October 1987, pp. 54–56.

43. Barry, *Ambition and Power*, pp. 310–11, 502; Joel Brinkley, "Plan for Peace, or Arms?," *NYT*, August 6, 1987; Joel Brinkley, "Reagan Plan: Deeper Hole," *NYT*, August 15, 1987.

44. Fred Barnes, "White House Errors Cripple Contra Aid," *LAT*, August 18, 1987.

45. Joel Brinkley, "Plan for Peace, or Arms?," *NYT*, August 6, 1987; Rowland Evans and Robert Novak, "Another Threat to the Contras," *WP*, August 7, 1987. See also Barry, *Ambition and Power*, p. 351.

46. Barry, *Ambition and Power*, p. 343.

47. Wright, *Worth It All*, p. 108.

48. Ibid., 108–9; Barry, *Ambition and Power*, p. 344.

49. James LeMoyne, "Sandinistas and Contra Leaders Differ Sharply on Peace Proposal," *NYT*, August 7, 1987.

50. Barry, *Ambition and Power*, pp. 340–43, 351.

51. Ibid., pp. 347–48; Fernández, *El Desafío de la Paz*, pp. 129–36, 145.

52. Wright, *Worth It All*, p. 109; Barry, *Ambition and Power*, p. 358; Fernández, *El Desafío de la Paz*, p. 140.

53. *Procedimiento para Establecer La Paz Firme y Duradera en Centroamerica*. This book-let also includes an English version of the accord.

54. Alfonso Chardy and Don Bohning, "Sandinistas' Refusal Aids Contra Fund Drive," *MH*, November 2, 1987.

55. Author's interview with President Daniel Ortega, Managua, Nicaragua, July 1987. According to a former Sandinista, the National Directorate did not expect an agreement to be reached. Miranda and Ratliff, *Civil War in Nicaragua*, p. 265.

56. Kinzer, *Blood of Brothers*, pp. 350–51. Ortega's colleagues on the Sandinista National Directorate were distraught at the political concessions he made. For three days, the direc-torate did not publicly endorse the accord, while they subjected it to "very deep and very serious questioning," according to Tomás Borge, its principal opponent. Only after Ortega flew to Cuba and won Fidel Castro's blessing did the directorate give the agreement their seal of approval.

57. Ibid. See also Fernández, *El Desafio de la Paz*, p. 139.

58. Fernández, *El Desafio de la Paz*, pp. 140–41.

59. Ibid., pp. 129, 146.

60. Shultz, *Turmoil and Triumph*, p. 959.

61. Ibid., pp. 959–60; Mark Lawrence, "Wright Urges Support for Peace Accord," *WP*, August 10, 1987; Elaine Sciolino, "Weinberger Opposes Aspects of Latin Peace Plan," *NYT*, August 12, 1987.

62. Ivo Dawnay, "Contadora Group Welcomes Progress," *Financial Times of London*, August 11, 1987; "Cuba Endorses Peace Plan for Central America," *WP*, August 14, 1987; Marlise Simons, "Shevardnadze, in Brazil Backs Latin Peace Plan," *NYT*, October 1, 1987; Michael J. Berlin, "U.N. Assembly Acclaims Regional Peace Plan," *WP*, October 8, 1987.

63. *Procedimiento para Establecer La Paz Firme y Duradera en Centroamerica*, p. 16.

64. Neil A. Lewis, "U.S. Aide Calls Contras Crucial to Region's Peace," *NYT*, August 19, 1987.

65. Shultz, *Turmoil and Triumph*, p. 961.

66. Ibid.; Gutman, *Banana Diplomacy*, pp. 349–53. See also Michael Gordon, "Habib Quits Post as Special Envoy; Rift Is Reported," *NYT*, August 15, 1987; John Goshko, "Kissin-ger Calls Habib Departure Damaging," *WP*, August 16, 1987.

67. "Address to the People of Nicaragua on the Central American Peace Plan, August 22, 1987," *Reagan Papers, 1987*, book 2, pp. 975–77.

68. Neil A. Lewis, "Shultz Delivers $270 Million Plan for Contra Help," *NYT*, September 11, 1987.

69. Neil A. Lewis, "President Attacks the Peace Plan of Five Central American Coun-tries," *NYT*, September 13, 1987.

70. Neil A. Lewis, "U.S. Envoys Told to Convey Doubt Over Latin Plan," *NYT*, August 18, 1987.

71. Sam Dillon, "Central American Diplomats Achieve Scant Peace Progress," *MH*, August 21, 1987.

72. William Branigin, "Regional Peace Plan Sets Off Dispute in Honduras," *WP*, Septem-ber 23, 1987.

73. Barry, *Ambition and Power*, p. 370. See also Stephen Engelberg, "House Speaker Backs Central American Plan," *NYT*, August 8, 1987.

74. Joel Brinkley, "Wright, in Shift, Denounces Reagan Over Sandinistas," *NYT*, October 6, 1987; Tom Wicker, "Still the 'Uncle' Policy," *NYT*, October 8, 1987.

75. Wright, *Worth It All*, pp. 116, 120; Barry, *Ambition and Power*, p. 374; Fernández, *El Desafio de la Paz*, pp. 153–54; Neil A. Lewis, "Costa Rica Chief to Address Congress," *NYT*, August 26, 1987.

76. Arias's speech is in *Congressional Record*, September 22, 1987, pp. S12428–30.

77. Barry, *Ambition and Power*, p. 372.

78. Ibid., p. 493.

79. Richard Boudreaux, "Tentative Truce Takes Hold in Small Nicaraguan Zone, Raising Hopes," *LAT*, October 10, 1987.

80. Neil A. Lewis, "Wright Says Award for Arias Dooms Aid for Contras," *NYT*, October 14, 1987.

81. James LeMoyne, "Contras and Nicaraguan Cardinal Meet," *NYT*, October 26, 1987; Richard Boudreaux, "Nicaragua Hardens Peace Stance," *LAT*, October 30, 1987. For an insider's account of these divisions, see Miranda and Ratliff, *Civil War in Nicaragua*, p. 35.

82. Stephen Kinzer, "Sandinistas Pressed on 2 Key Points," *NYT*, October 26, 1987.

83. Wilson Ring, "Sandinistas Urged to Talk to Contras," *WP*, October 16, 1987; James LeMoyne, "Sandinistas Urged by Arias to Yield on Contra Talks," *NYT*, October 29, 1987.

84. Barry, *Ambition and Power*, p. 374; Robert Parry and Tamar Jacoby, "Covert Aid and the Church," *Newsweek*, June 15, 1987.

85. Wright, *Worth It All*, p. 129; Barry, *Ambition and Power*, p. 494.

86. Wright, *Worth It All*, pp. 136–38; Barry, *Ambition and Power*, pp. 497–500.

87. "A Tug of War Over Peace," *Newsweek*, November 23, 1987.

88. Wright, *Worth It All*, pp. 138–44; Barry, *Ambition and Power*, p. 502. Shultz's recollection is a bit different. He was under the impression that Wright and Obando would endorse Daniel Ortega's peace proposal in a public press conference. Shultz, *Turmoil and Triumph*, p. 964.

89. Wright, *Worth It All*, pp. 144–46; Barry, *Ambition and Power*, p. 504.

90. John Goshko, "Diplomacy by Wright, Ortega Hit," *WP*, November 15, 1987.

91. Barry, *Ambition and Power*, p. 509; Steven V. Roberts, "Reagan and Wright Caught Up in a Feud," *NYT*, November 15, 1987. Time did nothing to calm Abrams's ire; in his memoirs, he accused Wright and other congressional opponents of Reagan's policy of "plotting with the Communists against their own government." Abrams, *Undue Process*, p. 165.

92. John Goshko, "Reagan Hits Wright on Peace Talks," *WP*, November 17, 1987; Barry, *Ambition and Power*, p. 509.

93. Wright, *Worth It All*, pp. 150–51; Barry, *Ambition and Power*, pp. 511–13.

94. Wright, *Worth It All*, p. 151; Shultz, *Turmoil and Triumph*, p. 966.

95. Barry, *Ambition and Power*, p. 515.

96. The six points of agreement were that both Shultz and Wright believed that the United States had a vital interest in the region; supported the Esquipulas accord; believed negotiations should be "concentrated in Central America and continue to be guided primarily by Central Americans"; supported Obando's role as mediator; supported U.S. meetings with the region's foreign ministers if the Sandinistas opened negotiations with the contras; wanted to "work together to bring about solutions." The text of the agreement is in Wright, *Worth It All*, p. 274.

97. Alfonso Chardy and Don Bohning, "Sandinistas' Refusal Aids Contra Fund Drive," *MH*, November 2, 1987.

98. "Wright Hails Peace Plan 'Good Faith,'" *MH*, August 29, 1987.

99. *Congressional Record*, September 23, 1987, pp. H7814–22; Barry, *Ambition and Power*, p. 389.

100. *Congressional Record*, February 4, 1988, p. S566.

101. U.S. House of Representatives, *Congress and Foreign Policy 1987*, pp. 85–86. See also *Congressional Record*, December 11, 1987, pp. S17910–12. The Stevens proposal was passed using the highly unusual "standing vote," for which the final tally is not recorded.

102. Jonathan Fuerbringer, "Contra Aid Accord Set by Congress and White House," *NYT*, December 21, 1987.

103. The Esquipulas accord prohibited all forms of aid to combatants, including "military, logistic, financial, promotional, human resources, armaments, ammunitions, and equipment." It allowed aid only for repatriation and reintegration of former combatants into society. See points 5 and 6 of the accord, *Procedimiento para Establecer La Paz Firme y Duradera en Centroamerica*, p. 16. On the Sandinistas' attitude regarding humanitarian aid, see Wright, *Worth It All*, p. 128; on Arias's attitude, see Fernández, *El Desafío de la Paz*, pp. 176–77, 211–12.

104. U.S. House of Representatives, *Congress and Foreign Policy 1987*, pp. 87–89.

105. Jonathan Fuerbringer, "Contra Aid Accord Set by Congress and White House," *NYT*, December 21, 1987.

106. Barry, *Ambition and Power*, pp. 561–70; *Congressional Record*, December 21, 1987, pp. H11992–96.

CHAPTER TWENTY-TWO

1. William M. LeoGrande and Philip Brenner, "The House Divided: Ideological Polarization Over Aid to the Nicaraguan Contras," *Legislative Studies Quarterly* (February 1993): 105–36. The degree of consistency was even higher in the 98th and 100th Congresses, where only forty-four (10.0 percent) and sixty-four (14.6 percent) members were swing voters.

2. "Complaint by U.S. Over Latin Panel," *NYT*, August 27, 1987; Neil A. Lewis, "U.S. Terms Managua Moves 'Cosmetic,'" *NYT*, September 24, 1987.

3. The verification commission's report to the January summit was so detailed and technical that it received only passing attention in the United States. In one of its key passages, however, it noted: "In spite of the exhortation of the Central American presidents, the Government of the United States of America maintains its policy and practice of providing assistance, military in particular, to the irregular forces operating against the Government of Nicaragua. The definitive cessation of this assistance continues to be an indispensable requirement for the success of the peace efforts and of this procedure as a whole." Regarding the Nicaraguan government's compliance with the accord, the commission said simply, "In spite of the wartime suffering, it has made concrete steps toward initiating democratic processes." "Agreement on Procedure to Achieve a Firm and Lasting Peace in Central America: Report on Compliance," Report of the International Verification Commission, January 12, 1988, *Congressional Record*, February 4, 1988, pp. S611–12.

4. Alfonso Chardy and Don Bohning, "Sandinistas' Refusal Aids Contra Fund Drive," *MH*, November 2, 1987.

5. Martha Honey and Tony Avirgan, "Leaning on Arias," *Nation*, September 12, 1987; author's interview with Costa Rican Ambassador to the United States Guido Fernández, Atlanta, Georgia, April 1991.

6. According to Fernández, Reagan was telling swing voters in the House that Arias privately supported contra aid. Fernández got into trouble for telling the members that Reagan's "malicious distortion" of Costa Rican policy was untrue. Fernández, *El Desafío de la Paz*, pp. 176–77.

7. Stephen Kinzer and Robert Pear, "Officials Assert U.S. Is Trying to Weaken Costa Rican Chief," *NYT*, August 7, 1988; Fernández, *El Desafío de la Paz*, pp. 61–62, 109–11.

8. Robert S. Greenberger, "U.S. Group Aided Arias' Costa Rica Foes," *WSJ*, October 13, 1989; Doyle McManus, "U.S. Fund Gives $433,000 to Opponents of Costa Rican Leader's Policies," *LAT*, October 14, 1989; David Corn, "Foreign Aid for the Right," *Nation*, December 18, 1989.

9. Kinzer and Pear, "Officials Assert U.S. Is Trying to Weaken Costa Rican Chief," *NYT*, August 7, 1988.

10. Stephen Kinzer, "Nicaraguan Talks Reach an Impasse on Primate's Plan," *NYT*, December 5, 1987.

11. Larry Rohter, "Nicaraguan-Contra Talks Suspended," *NYT*, December 23, 1987.

12. National Security Adviser Frank Carlucci became secretary of defense when Weinberger resigned for personal reasons. Neil A. Lewis, "Four Latin Presidents Cautioned by U.S. on Contras' Fate," *NYT*, January 13, 1988; Fernández, *El Desafío de la Paz*, p. 113.

13. Barry, *Ambition and Power*, pp. 586–87.

14. Stephen Kinzer, "U.S. Congressmen Warn Sandinistas," *NYT*, January 13, 1988; Wright, *Worth It All*, pp. 160–61.

15. James LeMoyne, "Nicaragua Agrees to Talk Directly with the Contras," *NYT*, January 17, 1988. An inside view of the summit is provided in Fernández, *El Desafío de la Paz*, pp. 184–87.

16. George Volsky, "Contras Agree to Attend Truce Talks with the Sandinistas in Costa Rica Next Week," *NYT*, January 20, 1988.

17. Elaine Sciolino, "Reagan Will Seek Contra Arms Aid Despite New Move," *NYT*, January 18, 1988; Joel Brinkley, "U.S. to Resume Sending Arms to Contras," *NYT*, January 20, 1988.

18. *Congressional Record*, February 3, 1988, p. H174.

19. "Message to the Congress Transmitting a Request for Aid for the Nicaraguan Democratic Resistance, January 27, 1988," *Reagan Papers, 1988*, book 1, pp. 130–33.

20. "Declaración conjunta de los presidentes de Centro América," *Panorama Centroamericano* (January 1988): 7.

21. *Congressional Record*, February 3, 1988, p. H109.

22. "Remarks to Civic Leaders at a White House Briefing on Aid to the Nicaraguan Democratic Resistance, January 20, 1988," *Reagan Papers, 1988*, book 1, pp. 62–66; "Radio Address to the Nation on Administration Goals, January 23, 1988," ibid., pp. 79–80.

23. Neil Lewis, "Opposition to Contra Aid Is Growing in Congress," *NYT*, January 24, 1988.

24. Steven Roberts, "Reagan Pressing His Fight for Aid to Nicaragua Rebels," *NYT*, January 31, 1988.

25. The full debate on H.J. Res. 444 is in *Congressional Record*, February 3, 1988, pp. H89–217.

26. The next day, the Senate debated the same proposal for a few hours before approving it, 51–48, but since the House had already rejected the bill, the issue was moot. The Senate debate is in ibid., February 4, 1988, pp. S555–621.

27. Alfonso Chardy, "U.S. Policy on Contras in Disarray," *MH*, February 5, 1988.

28. Alfonso Chardy, "U.S. Readies Fallback Aid for Contras," *MH*, January 31, 1988; "Despite Vote, CIA Maintains Contra Air Base," *MH*, March 13, 1988.

29. Alfonso Chardy, "Twin Crises Plunge Latin Policy into Disarray," *MH*, February 15, 1988; Chardy, "U.S. Readies Fallback Aid for Contras," *MH*, January 31, 1988.

30. Wright, *Worth It All*, p. 161; Tom Kenworthy, "Hill Democrats Draft Nonlethal Contra Aid," *WP*, February 24, 1988.

31. Text of the Democratic proposal is in *Congressional Record*, March 3, 1988, pp. H673–75, and descriptions of its content are at pp. H643–44 and H655.

32. "Contras, Sandinistas Both Show Support for Democrats' Aid Plan," *LAT*, February 25, 1988; Peter Osterlund, "Reagan's Grip on Policy Toward Contras Slipping," *CSM*, March 2, 1988. On details of consultation between the Democrats and contras on contents of the aid package, see remarks by McCurdy and Spratt in *Congressional Record*, March 3, 1988, pp. H682, H684.

33. "Letter to Congressional Leaders on Aid to the Nicaraguan Democratic Resistance, March 3, 1988," *Reagan Papers, 1988*, book 1, pp. 281–82. The Republican aid proposal included $36.2 million in nonlethal aid to be delivered by the CIA over two months and gave

Reagan the right to send Congress a new military aid request during the summer under expedited procedures. *Congressional Record*, March 3, 1988, pp. H467–68.

34. "Remarks at the Annual Leadership Conference of the American Legion, February 29, 1988," *Reagan Papers, 1988*, book 1, pp. 271–76.

35. Barry, *Ambition and Power*, p. 591.

36. The rule and subsequent debate on it is in *Congressional Record*, March 3, 1988, pp. H643–51.

37. Barry, *Ambition and Power*, pp. 592–95; *Congressional Record*, March 3, 1988.

38. The full House debate is in *Congressional Record*, March 3, 1988, pp. H643–94.

39. Jim Leach (R-Iowa), Jim Jeffords (R-Vt.), and Connie Morella (R-Md.), the latter of whom held the seat formerly occupied by Michael Barnes.

40. Barry, *Ambition and Power*, p. 596.

41. Susan F. Rasky, "Democrats' Contra Aid Plan Defeated by House, 216–208; All U.S. Funds Now Halted," *NYT*, March 4, 1988.

42. Julia Preston, "Contra Leaders Criticize U.S. Officials' Handling of Aid Politics," *WP*, March 16, 1988.

43. Marjorie Miller, "Nicaragua Cease-Fire Talks Suspended; Future in Limbo," *LAT*, February 20, 1988.

44. Stephen Kinzer, "Sandinista-Contra Cease-Fire Termed Major Breakthrough by Nicaragua's Rival Factions," *NYT*, March 25, 1988. The agreement is in "Text of the Nicaraguan Agreement on a Cease-Fire," *NYT*, March 25, 1988.

45. James LeMoyne, "For Contras, 'No Help Left,'" *NYT*, March 26, 1988.

46. Joe Pichirallo, "Shortages Force Contras into Honduras," *WP*, April 22, 1988.

47. See, for example, Colburn, *Post-Revolutionary Nicaragua*; Gilbert, *Sandinistas*.

48. Tony Jenkins, "U.S. Embargo Against Nicaragua," *Policy Focus* (1986), p. 7; E. V. K. Fitzgerald, "An Evaluation of the Economic Cost to Nicaragua of U.S. Aggression, 1980–1984," in Spalding, *Political Economy of Revolutionary Nicaragua*, pp. 195–216.

49. Julia Preston, "Inflation Runs Away in Managua," *WP*, January 22, 1988.

50. At the end of 1988, GDP stood at 67.5 percent of its 1978 level, and per capita consumption at 46.3 percent. International Bank for Reconstruction and Development (IBRD), *Report and Recommendation*, p. 3.

51. LeMoyne, "For Contras, 'No Help Left,'" *NYT*, March 26, 1988.

52. Josh Getlin, "Wright Wants Cut-off of Soviet Aid to Nicaragua," *LAT*, March 28, 1988. See also Alfonso Chardy, "Nicaragua Takes Step Toward Peace," *MH*, March 25, 1988.

53. The House debate is in *Congressional Record*, March 30, 1988, pp. H1320–41. The Senate debate is in ibid., March 31, 1988, S3481–3505. In delivering the humanitarian aid, the Reagan administration tried to be as provocative as possible. It assigned U.S. AID the task of distributing the supplies, in defiance of the Sapoá agreement's requirement that only "neutral" organizations be involved. U.S. AID then gave the contras cash instead of goods if they simply promised to spend it only on humanitarian supplies. Despite problems with the contras' misappropriation of the $27 million in nonlethal aid money in 1985, the administration insisted that this system would somehow be "self-monitoring." Robert Pear, "U.S. Plans to Send Money to Contras," *NYT*, May 10, 1988; John Goshko, "U.S. to Send Cash for Food to Contras Inside Nicaragua," *WP*, May 14, 1988.

54. Wright, *Worth It All*, p. 170.

55. Christopher Marquis, "Pact Rouses Controversy Among Exiles," *MH*, March 27, 1988; Richard Boudreaux, "Contra Troops Uneasy Over Cease-Fire, Talks," *LAT*, April 16, 1988; "Two Contras Who Support Negotiations are 'Expelled,'" *MH*, April 20, 1988.

56. "Contra Revolt Seeks Ouster of Military Chief," *WP*, April 28, 1988.

57. James LeMoyne, "Nicaragua Rebels, in Retreat, Viewed as a Reduced Threat," *NYT*, March 6, 1986.

58. Cruz, *Memoirs of a Counter-Revolutionary*, pp. 254–55; Dillon, *Commandos*, pp. 107, 134, 225; Sam Dillon, "CIA Joins in Contra Feuding," *MH*, May 18, 1988.

59. Dillon, *Commandos*, p. 223; Julia Preston, "Broad Delegation of Contras Back at Managua Talks," *WP*, April 29, 1988; Julia Preston, "Simmering Animosities Set Stage for Contra Rebellion," *WP*, May 14, 1988; Dillon, "CIA Joins in Contra Feuding," *MH*, May 18, 1988; Wilson Ring, "Contra Dissidents Sign Loyalty Pledge," *WP*, May 19, 1988.

60. Richard Boudreaux, "Nicaraguan Peace Talks Broken Off," *LAT*, June 10, 1988.

61. Roy Gutman, "Contra Peace-Talks Ploy Disclosed," *Newsday*, July 5, 1988; Roy Gutman, "How the Contras Created Shultz's Credibility Gap," *WP*, August 7, 1988.

62. Don Phillips and Joe Pichirallo, "House Republicans Jolt Democrats on Contra Aid," *WP*, May 27, 1988; Barry, *Ambition and Power*, p. 624.

63. The full debate is in *Congressional Record*, May 26, 1988, pp. H3665–86.

64. Joe Pichirallo, "Action on Contra Aid Deferred," *WP*, June 29, 1988. But see Reagan's statement blaming the Sandinistas for the collapse of the talks: "Remarks at a Campaign Fundraising Luncheon for Representative Connie Mack in Miami, Florida, June 29, 1988," *Reagan Papers, 1988*, book 1, pp. 854–57.

65. Doyle McManus, "U.S. Lowers Its Contra Goals; Collapse Feared," *LAT*, May 28, 1988.

66. Ibid.

67. Ibid.; Alfonso Chardy, "CIA Closes Command Center in Honduras, Contras Say," *MH*, July 2, 1988.

68. Philip Taubman, "Are U.S. Covert Activities Best Policy on Nicaragua?," *NYT*, June 15, 1983. The existence of the Carter program was officially acknowledged in the *Iran-Contra Report*, p. 27. The recipients are named in Woodward, *VEIL*, p. 113; "A Secret War for Nicaragua," *Newsweek*, November 8, 1982; and Philip Taubman, "U.S. Role in Nicaragua Vote Disputed," *NYT*, October 21, 1984. Several accounts (e.g., Clarridge, *Spy for All Seasons*, pp. 196–97) date the Carter program to late 1980, suggesting there may have been a second finding that expanded the initial program.

69. The 1981 programs are described in Leslie H. Gelb, "Argentina Linked to Rise in Covert U.S. Action Against Sandinists," *NYT*, April 8, 1983; "CIA's Nicaragua Role: A Proposal or a Reality?," *NYT*, March 17, 1982. The 1983 finding and scope paper were released at Oliver North's trial and are available in Kornbluh and Byrne, *Iran-Contra Scandal*, pp. 12–17.

70. "CIA's Nicaragua Role: A Proposal or a Reality?," *NYT*, March 17, 1982; "Taking Aim at Nicaragua," *Newsweek*, March 22, 1982; Don Irwin, "North Tied to Church Funds in Nicaragua," *LAT*, June 8, 1987. The quote is from Parry, *Fooling America*, p. 297.

71. The annual budget was reported in a UPI wire story, August 7, 1988, quoted in Holly Sklar, "Dollars Don't Buy Democracy," *Nicaraguan Perspectives* (Winter–Spring 1990). The $13 million figure is from Donald Gregg's testimony to the Iran-Contra congressional investigators, quoted in Robinson, *Faustian Bargain*, pp. 29–31.

72. Walter Pincus and George Lardner Jr., "Covert CIA Operation via Church Outlined," *WP*, August 1, 1992.

73. Parry, *Fooling America*, p. 297; *Iran-Contra Report*, p. 97; deposition of Richard R. Miller, *Iran-Contra Depositions*, vol. 19, pp. 207–9, 522–23; Irwin, "North Tied to Church Funds in Nicaragua," *LAT*, June 8, 1987; "Covert Aid and the Church," *Newsweek*, June 15, 1987.

74. "Covert Aid and the Church," *Newsweek*, June 15, 1987. Some of the money raised by Godson and North also financed an unnamed human rights organization in Nicaragua, and a media operation intended to generate favorable publicity for the civic opposition in the international press. Richard R. Miller deposition, *Iran-Contra Depositions*, vol. 19, pp. 522–23.

75. A detailed breakdown of NED programs in Nicaragua from 1984 to 1989 is in U.S.

House of Representatives Arms Control and Foreign Policy Caucus, "U.S. Efforts to Promote Democracy in Nicaragua: Choices for Congress on Covert and Overt Aid," Issue Preview paper, August 3, 1989. See also Andres Oppenheimer, "U.S. Agency to Send Funds to Anti-Sandinista Groups," *MH*, July 21, 1988. The two union federations that received NED money were the Confederation of Trade Union Unity (Confederación de Unificación Sindical) and the Workers' Central of Nicaragua (Central de los Trabajadores Nicaragüenses). Weinraub and Bollinger, *AFL-CIO in Central America*, p. 29.

76. Barry and Preusch, *Soft War*, p. 508; Spalding, "U.S. Labor Intervention in Latin America," *Labor, Capital and Society* (November 1984); Jeff McConnell, "Counterrevolution in Nicaragua: The U.S. Connection," in Rosset and Vandermeer, *Nicaragua Reader*, pp. 175–90.

77. Author's interview with Xavier Chamorro, editor of *El Nuevo Diario*, Managua, Nicaragua, January 1982, describes the fight for control of the paper. On the types of aid provided by the United States, see Woodward, *VEIL*, p. 113; "Crackdown in Managua," *Newsweek*, July 25, 1988; and Nichols, "*La Prensa*," *Columbia Journalism Review*, July–August 1988 (see also correspondence and Nichols's reply, November–December 1988, pp. 67–68). In her autobiography (*Dreams of the Heart*, pp. 202–7, 239) Violeta Barrios de Chamorro confirms receiving U.S. aid. Of the charge that it came from the CIA, she says simply, "Indeed, we had many democratic friends, although we were beholden to no one" (p. 239).

78. Had they known, they would probably not have objected. Senior staff members suggested to me that the CIA ought to finance anti-Sandinista propaganda inside Nicaragua. Author's interview with senior staff members of *La Prensa*, Managua, Nicaragua, August 1983.

79. Nichols, "*La Prensa*," *Columbia Journalism Review*. Some of the funds from Europe and Latin America could have originated with the CIA. In the past, the Agency had used European foundations, the Inter-American Press Association, and private groups in Venezuela as conduits. Journalist Robert Parry argues that the CIA aided *La Prensa* initially, stopped when overt aid began, and then resumed when *La Prensa* was banned after the 1986 House vote to resume military aid to the contras. Parry, *Fooling America*, p. 299.

80. Author's interview with Comandante Bayardo Arce, member of the National Directorate of the FSLN, Managua, Nicaragua, August 1983. The CIA's use of *El Mercurio* in Chile is detailed in U.S. Senate, *Covert Action in Chile, 1963–1973*. For a comparison of the roles played by *El Mercurio* and *La Prensa*, see Fred Landis, "CIA Media Operations in Chile, Jamaica, and Nicaragua," *Covert Action Information Bulletin*, March 1982.

81. Tony Jenkins, "Nicaragua's Disloyal Opposition," *Nation*, August 12, 1986; Robinson and Norsworthy, *David and Goliath*, p. 194.

82. Nichols, "*La Prensa*," *Columbia Journalism Review*; Jaime Chamorro, "Don't Abandon the Nicaraguan People," *WP*, April 3, 1986.

83. Robinson and Norsworthy, *David and Goliath*, p. 203; Chamorro, *Packaging the Contras*, pp. 50–51.

84. Gutman, "How the Contras Created Shultz's Credibility Gap," *WP*, August 7, 1988. In early 1988, the administration sought an additional $1 million in covert aid for the internal opposition. Alfonso Chardy, "Twin Crises Plunge Latin Policy into Disarray," *MH*, February 15, 1988.

85. Robert Pear, "Abrams Wants New Envoys to Support Managua's Foes," *NYT*, July 14, 1988; "Crackdown in Managua," *Newsweek*, July 25, 1988; Julia Preston, "Ortega, Opposition Begin Dialogue," *WP*, October 6, 1987.

86. Quoted in Stephen Kinzer, "Nicaragua Detains Five More Leaders of the Opposition," *NYT*, January 20, 1988.

87. Kinzer himself was clubbed with a rifle butt. His contemporary account of the riot is

in Stephen Kinzer, "Sandinistas Stop a Protest Rally with the Rare Use of Tear Gas," *NYT*, July 11, 1988. A longer version appears in Kinzer, *Blood of Brothers*, pp. 381–85.

88. Stephen Kinzer, "Nicaragua Orders U.S. Ambassador to Leave Country," *NYT*, July 12, 1988; Andres Oppenheimer, "Sandinistas Face New Discontent," *MH*, July 17, 1988.

89. Debate on the Senate resolution is in *Congressional Record*, July 13, 1988, pp. S9495–96 and S9548–73. Debate on the House resolution is in ibid., July 14, 1988, pp. H5750–59.

90. "U.S. Expels Nicaraguan Ambassador, Seven Staffers," *WP*, July 13, 1988; Don Phillips and Joe Pichirallo, "Wright Denies Secrecy Breach," *WP*, September 23, 1988. After returning to the United States, Melton testified before the Senate Intelligence Committee, and when asked about U.S. support for the Nicaraguan opposition, he declined to discuss "intelligence activities" in public session. Parry, *Fooling America*, p. 297.

91. Wright, *Worth It All*, p. 181.

92. Susan Bennett, "Wright: CIA Admits Provoking Sandinistas," *MH*, September 21, 1988.

93. Susan Bennett, "Reagan Rebukes Wright on CIA," *MH*, September 22, 1988.

94. Don Phillips and Joe Pichirallo, "Wright Denies Secrecy Breach," *WP*, September 23, 1988; William Branigin, "Wright Sparks Managua Confrontation," *WP*, September 23, 1988.

95. Alexander Cockburn, "Wright vs. CIA: A Challenge to the Secret Government," *WSJ*, September 29, 1988.

96. Wright, *Worth It All*, p. 167.

97. Ibid., p. 210.

98. Alfonso Chardy, "CIA Closes Command Center in Honduras, Contras Say," *MH*, July 2, 1988. See also Rowland Evans and Robert Novak, "Running from the Contras," *WP*, September 9, 1988.

99. "Fanning the Flames—Again," *LAT*, July 31, 1988; "Radio Address to the Nation on Aid to the Nicaraguan Democratic Resistance, July 30, 1988," *Reagan Papers, 1988*, book 2, pp. 1002–3.

100. The proposal included $27 million in nonlethal aid, $20 million in aircraft insurance, about $7 million worth of electronic air defense equipment, $16 million in lethal aid left over from 1986, and several million in transportation costs. The full debate is in *Congressional Record*, August 10, 1988, pp. 11308–53. The Dole amendment is on pp. S11343–44; the Byrd amendment appeared on August 5, 1988, pp. S11002–4. The figure of $16 million for the unexpended remainder of the $100 million approved in 1986 is from Dole, p. S11311. Other sources put the amount at $16.5 million (see, for example, Felton, "Wright at Center of Nicaragua Policy Storm," *CQ Weekly Report*, September 24, 1988, pp. 2631–33).

101. "Statement on Aid to the Nicaraguan Democratic Resistance, October 14, 1988," *Reagan Papers, 1988*, book 2, pp. 1333–34.

102. Sam Dillon, "Contra War Over, Say Many in U.S., Central America," *MH*, November 7, 1988.

103. On the contra war, see Gilbert, *Sandinistas*, pp. 168–69; and Harvey Williams, "The Social Programs," in Walker, *Revolution and Counterrevolution in Nicaragua*, pp. 187–212.

104. Doyle McManus, "U.S. Accused of Impeding Relief Effort for Nicaragua," *LAT*, October 29, 1988; Sam Dillon, "Storm Deepens Nicaraguan Crisis," *MH*, October 30, 1988; J. D. Gannon, "Hurricane Devastation Adds to Nicaragua's Economic Troubles," *CSM*, December 5, 1988.

105. Doyle McManus, "Bush Aides Drafting New Nicaragua Policy Options," *LAT*, November 17, 1988.

CHAPTER TWENTY-THREE

1. Baker, *Politics of Diplomacy*, pp. 47, 53.

2. John M. Goshko, "Contra Backer to Get State Dept. Post," *WP*, February 1, 1989;

Gutman, *Banana Diplomacy*, p. 331. Kornbluh, "The Contra Lobby," *Village Voice*, October 13, 1987; Gutman, *Banana Diplomacy*, p. 332.

3. Baker (*Politics of Diplomacy*, pp. 51–52) confirms that he picked Aronson for his potential to build bipartisanship.

4. Wright, *Worth It All*, pp. 223–24; Barry, *Ambition and Power*, pp. 662, 708–9.

5. Baker gives a detailed account of the negotiations and how hard it was to assuage the suspicions of both liberal Democrats and hard-line Republicans. Baker, *Politics of Diplomacy*, pp. 53–58.

6. Don Bohning, "On Latin Policy, the Administration Remains Adrift," *MH*, May 7, 1989. The text of the accord is in Wright, *Worth It All*, pp. 298–99.

7. The text of Baker's statement is in "U.S. Support for Democracy and Peace in Central America," *Selected Documents No. 36* (U.S. Department of State). In his memoirs, Baker acknowledges that he and Bush would have preferred military aid for the contras but knew they didn't have the votes. Baker, *Politics of Diplomacy*, pp. 49–58.

8. Don Phillips and Helen Dewar, "Hill Approves Nonmilitary Contra Aid," *WP*, April 14, 1989.

9. "U.S. Support for Democracy and Peace in Central America," *Selected Documents No. 36* (U.S. Department of State), includes the text of bipartisan accord and remarks by President Bush and Secretary Baker at the press conference announcing it. The four-committee-veto arrangement was not part of the written agreement. It is described in Ann Devroy, "Bipartisan Accord Reached on Contras," *WP*, March 25, 1989.

10. See, for example, Doyle McManus, "Baker Urges Western Europe to Pressure Nicaragua," *LAT*, February 14, 1989.

11. Doyle McManus, "New U.S. Policy on Contras Told," *MH*, March 25, 1989.

12. Baker, *Politics of Diplomacy*, pp. 57–59.

13. Fernández, *El Desafío de la Paz*, pp. 242–43.

14. Don Oberdorfer, "Baker to Contras: No Raids," *WP*, March 15, 1989.

15. Joe Pichirallo and David Hoffman, "U.S. Wants Contras to Keep Arms until Nicaraguan Voting," *WP*, July 30, 1989; Fernández, *El Desafío de la Paz*, pp. 247–49.

16. Mary Speck, "Sandinistas, Opposition Reach Sweeping Election Agreement," *WP*, August 5, 1989.

17. John M. Goshko, "Quayle Expresses Caution on Plans to Disband Contras," *WP*, August 22, 1989; Mark A. Uhlig, "Dispute Highlights Difficulty of Disarming Contras," *NYT*, October 21, 1989.

18. Lee Hockstader, "Ortega's Move Designed to Rivet Attention on War," *WP*, October 29, 1989. The cease-fire agreed to at Sapoá lasted sixty days and was renewed several times by the two parties. When the contras failed to renew it in late 1988, the Sandinistas continued to abide by it unilaterally.

19. "The President's News Conference in San José, Costa Rica, October 28, 1989," *Public Papers of the Presidents of the United States: George Bush, 1989*, book 2, pp. 1408–14.

20. The Senate unanimously passed a resolution condemning Ortega's abrogation of the cease-fire. See *Congressional Record*, October 31, 1987, pp. S14413–16.

21. Author's interview with NSC official, Washington, D.C., August 1989.

22. Doyle McManus, "Baker Urges W. Europe to Pressure Nicaragua," *LAT*, February 14, 1989; Richard Boudreaux, "Ortega Summit Action Carries Heavy Political Risk," *LAT*, October 30, 1989.

23. Oberdorfer, *Turn*, pp. 340–41; Sam Dillon, "Soviet Ambassador Urges U.S. to Improve Ties with Nicaragua," *MH*, November 1, 1988; Julia Preston, "Soviets Raise Profile—but Not Aid—in Managua," *WP*, November 6, 1989.

24. "Anger, Bluff—and Cooperation," *Time*, June 4, 1990; John M. Goshko and David Hoffman, "Bush Urges Gorbachev to Aid Peace Effort," *WP*, March 31, 1989.

24. "Anger, Bluff—and Cooperation," *Time*, June 4, 1990; John M. Goshko and David Hoffman, "Bush Urges Gorbachev to Aid Peace Effort," *WP*, March 31, 1989.

25. Baker, *Politics of Diplomacy*, pp. 59, 81; Oberdorfer, *Turn*, pp. 338–39; "Anger, Bluff—and Cooperation," *Time*, June 4, 1990.

26. "Anger, Bluff—and Cooperation," *Time*, June 4, 1990.

27. Baker, *Politics of Diplomacy*, p. 59. The conservatives complained that the United States forced Chamorro down the throat of the opposition coalition. Parry, *Fooling America*, pp. 300–301. On the U.S. role generally, see Robinson, *Faustian Bargain*, p. 58; Richard Boudreaux, "Chamorro Vows to Unite Nicaragua," *LAT*, September 4, 1989; Stephen Kinzer, "Anti-Sandinistas Choose Candidate," *NYT*, September 4, 1989.

28. Mark A. Uhlig, "Opposing Ortega," *New York Times Magazine*, February 11, 1990.

29. Christopher Marquis, "U.S. Cuts Funds; Contras Close Miami Offices," *MH*, September 29, 1989; Mary Speck, "Candidate Chamorro Names Ex-Contra as Chief Adviser," *WP*, November 23, 1989.

30. Robert Pear, "Bush Pressing Congress to Permit CIA Role in Nicaraguan Election," *NYT*, June 11, 1989.

31. From 1965 to 1976, election manipulation was the most frequent type of CIA covert operation—32 percent of the total (media and propaganda operations constituted 29 percent, and paramilitary operations, 23 percent). U.S. House of Representatives, Report of the Select Committee on Intelligence (Pike Report), January 19, 1976, as excerpted in "The CIA Report the President Doesn't Want You to Read," *Village Voice*, February 16, 1976. Details of the CIA's efforts to influence elections in Chile during the 1960s are in U.S. Senate, *Covert Action in Chile, 1963–1973*, pp. 14–23.

32. Felton, "Hill May Force a Scaling Back of Bush Election-Aid Plan," *CQ Weekly Report*, September 30, 1989, p. 2581. See also Robert Pear, "Bush Aides Say CIA Will Avoid Secret Role In Nicaragua Election," *NYT*, October 4, 1989.

33. Some of this money was reportedly laundered through Venezuela and Costa Rica. "Secret Help," *Newsweek*, September 25, 1989; "Money Isn't Everything," *Newsweek*, October 9, 1989; UPI wire story, August 7, 1988, quoted in Holly Sklar, "Dollars Don't Buy Democracy," *Nicaraguan Perspectives* (Winter–Spring 1990); Robinson, *Faustian Bargain*, p. 92.

34. Parry, *Fooling America*, p. 302; Robinson, *Faustian Bargain*, p. 114. The $600,000 program was known as the Nicaraguan Exile Relocation Program, and was launched when the CIA terminated its monthly "family expense" money paid to contra leaders. The aim was to entice contra leaders "to go back and work in the Chamorro campaign," according to an administration official. "The CIA on the Stump," *Newsweek*, October 21, 1991.

35. Robert Pear, "U.S. to Help Anti-Sandinista Parties," *NYT*, April 25, 1989.

36. Jacqueline Sharkey, "Nicaragua: Anatomy of an Election," *Common Cause*, May–June 1990.

37. Robert Pear, "U.S. to Pare Aid in Nicaragua Vote," *NYT*, September 29, 1989; Martin McReynolds, "U.S. to Send Funds for Nicaragua Vote," *MH*, December 9, 1989.

38. Latin American Studies Association (LASA), *Electoral Democracy Under International Pressure*, Report of the LASA Commission to Observe the 1990 Nicaraguan Election, March 15, 1990, p. 28; Council of Freely Elected Heads of Government, *Observing Nicaragua's Elections, 1989–1990*, pp. 73–83.

39. Doyle McManus, "U.S. Gets Ready for Likely Sandinista Election Victory," *LAT*, February 24, 1990.

40. Robert Pear, "Clash of Experts Blurs Policy on Central America," *NYT*, August 24, 1989.

41. See, for example, the *Washington Post*–ABC News poll that showed Ortega leading by 48 percent to Chamorro's 32 percent. Richard Morin and Lee Hockstader, "Pre-Election Poll Shows Ortega Leads," *WP*, February 21, 1990. For a postelection assessment of how the polls

erred, see William A. Barnes, "Rereading the Nicaraguan Pre-Election Polls," in Castro and Prevost, *1990 Elections in Nicaragua and Their Aftermath*, pp. 41–128.

42. Lindsey Gruson, "Sandinistas Draw Mammoth Crowds," *NYT*, February 22, 1990.

43. "Results of the February 25, 1990 Election," *Barricada International* (Managua, Nicaragua), March 10, 1990. The CIA reportedly expected the Sandinistas to win by fifteen percentage points. Codevilla, *Informing Statecraft*, p. 234. The decisive issues were the terrible state of the economy, the highly unpopular military draft, and the public's doubt that the Sandinistas would be able to make peace with Washington and bring the war to a definitive conclusion. Julia Preston, "The Defeat of the Sandinistas," *New York Review of Books*, April 12, 1990.

44. Chamorro, *Dreams of the Heart*, pp. 277–80; Pastor, "Nicaragua's Choice: The Making of a Free Election," *Journal of Democracy* (Summer 1990).

45. Mark A. Uhlig, "Contras Turning to Younger Leaders," *NYT*, November 5, 1989; Mark A. Uhlig, "Contra Commander Is Reported Ousted," *NYT*, February 8, 1990.

46. Mark A. Uhlig, "Cease-Fire Begins in Nicaragua as the Contras Agree to Disarm," *NYT*, April 20, 1990. The Chamorro government had to negotiate one final agreement with the contras, on May 5, 1990, promising economic resettlement aid in exchange for disarming. "Contras Get a Slice of Nicaragua in Exchange for Giving Up Rifles," *MH*, May 6, 1990.

47. Chamorro, *Dreams of the Heart*, p. 293.

48. Eagleburger, "U.S. Assistance to Panama, Nicaragua," *Current Policy* (U.S. Department of State); Guy Gugliotta, "Criticism Muted as Nicaraguans Visit," *WP*, April 17, 1991.

49. Gugliotta, "Criticism Muted as Nicaraguans Visit," *WP*, April 17, 1991.

50. U.S. Department of State, *Report of the Secretary of State's Panel on El Salvador, July 1993*, p. 26.

51. James LeMoyne, "The Vote in El Salvador Stuns Even the Right-Wing Victors," *NYT*, March 24, 1988; Douglas Farah, "Salvadoran Party Dogged by Failures," *WP*, May 24, 1988. Duarte died of cancer on February 23, 1990.

52. For a detailed discussion of the Christian Democrats' corruption, see the description of a State Department internal report, in Clifford Krauss and Robert S. Greenberger, "Corruption Threatens Political Gains by U.S. in El Salvador," *WSJ*, September 14, 1987.

53. Chris Norton, "Salvador War Tax Causes Political Stir," *CSM*, January 9, 1987; William Branigin, "Embattled Duarte Faces New Troubles," *WP*, July 7, 1987.

54. Marjorie Miller, "Salvador Moves to Right as War, Money Woes Continue," *LAT*, March 28, 1988.

55. LeoGrande, "El Salvador After Duarte," *World Policy Journal* (Fall 1988).

56. The Convergence suffered, on the one hand, from unpopular guerrilla actions like the assassination of mayors in contested areas and the detonation of car bombs in the capital. On the other hand, the Convergence failed to attract many guerrilla sympathizers because the FMLN called for a boycott of the election. Guy Gugliotta, "Salvador Vote Result Hurts Left," *MH*, March 22, 1989.

57. For detailed accounts of the human rights situation as it evolved, see Americas Watch, *Settling into Routine*; Americas Watch, *Civilian Toll, 1986–1987*; Americas Watch, *Nightmare Revisited, 1987–88*; Americas Watch, *Year of Reckoning*.

58. The House debate on El Salvador is in *Congressional Record*, June 28, 1989, pp. H3349–70. The House bills also reduced the level of military aid slightly from what Bush had requested, from $97 million to $85 million for FY 1990.

59. The Senate debate is in ibid., September 20, 1989, pp. S11448–84.

60. For an articulation of this view, see Ambassador Edwin G. Corr's remarks in Manwaring and Prisk, *El Salvador at War*, pp. 447–53.

61. Karl, "El Salvador: Negotiations or Total War," *World Policy Journal*; Miles and Ostertag, "FMLN New Thinking," *NACLA Report on the Americas* (September 1989).

62. Lindsey Gruson, "Salvador Rebels Quit Peace Talks," *NYT*, November 3, 1989.

63. Brook Larmer, "Salvadoran Offensive Slams Door on Fragile Political Opening," *CSM*, November 21, 1989.

64. Lee Hockstader, "GIs Leave Salvadoran Hotel After Rebels Slip Away," *WP*, November 23, 1989.

65. Christopher Marquis, "Churches Protest Raids in Salvador," *MH*, November 18, 1989.

66. The following account of the murder of the Jesuits is drawn from Doggett, *Death Foretold*.

67. Douglas Farah, "U.S. Pressure in Jesuit Probe Said to Alienate Salvadoran Officers," *WP*, February 6, 1990.

68. Secretary of Defense Richard B. Cheney, quoted in Douglas Farah, "127 Dead in Salvadoran Rebel Drive," *WP*, November 13, 1989.

69. Robert Pear, "Salvadorans Ask U.S. for Arms Aid," *NYT*, November 16, 1989.

70. Americas Watch, *El Salvador's Decade of Terror*, p. 133; Robert Pear, "U.S. Envoy Wasn't Promptly Told of Evidence in Salvador Killing," *NYT*, January 16, 1990.

71. The U.S. adviser, Major Eric Buckland, was deeply torn between his loyalty to his friends in the Salvadoran military and his duty. In an affidavit to the FBI on January 11, 1990, Buckland testified that Colonel Carlos Armando Avilés had told him in late October 1989 (before the FMLN offensive) that Benavides wanted to have the Jesuits killed, but that Colonel René Emilio Ponce was trying to dissuade him. Buckland said he had not reported the incident at the time because he did not believe the threat would be carried out. After the killings, Avilés told Buckland that Benavides had, in fact, ordered the killings. This extraordinary testimony indicated that the high command knew of the plot against the Jesuits in advance, and had subsequently covered it up. On January 18, Major Buckland gave a second affidavit to the FBI recanting his detailed story about the October conversation with Avilés. Lawyers Committee for Human Rights, *The "Jesuit Case,"* pp. 43–45.

72. U.S. House of Representatives, *Congress and Foreign Policy 1989*, pp. 72–73.

73. Ibid., p. 72.

74. This was the conclusion of a Rand study done for the Pentagon. Schwarz, *American Counterinsurgency Doctrine and El Salvador*, p. 13.

75. Thurman is quoted in Michael R. Gordon, "General Says Salvador Can't Defeat Guerrillas," *NYT*, February 9, 1990. "U.S. Supports U.N. Effort to Arrange Salvadoran Peace Talks," *WP*, February 3, 1990.

76. Baker, *Politics of Diplomacy*, p. 603.

77. Testimony of Bernard W. Aronson, in U.S. House of Representatives, *El Salvador at the Crossroads*, pp. 12–59.

78. Lindsey Gruson, "Rebels in El Salvador Warn of an Increase in Fighting," *NYT*, March 17, 1990; Douglas Farah, "Salvadoran Military Begins Officer Reshuffle to Fight Corruption," *WP*, January 3, 1990. Cristiani had reportedly promised Bustillo the Defense post, but Washington opposed him for fear that his human rights record would stimulate congressional opposition. Charles Lane, "The Pilot Shark of El Salvador," *New Republic*, September 24, 1990.

79. "Anger, Bluff—and Cooperation," *Time*, June 4, 1990; David Hoffman, "Bush and Gorbachev Hail New Cooperation," *WP*, December 4, 1989.

80. Douglas Farah, "Salvadoran Rebels Isolated," *WP*, February 27, 1990.

81. The Dodd-Leahy provision is in *Congressional Record*, June 27, 1990, pp. H4274–75.

82. Speaker's Task Force on El Salvador, "Interim Report" (typescript); Felton, "Hill Group Paints Dark Picture of Rights in El Salvador," *CQ Weekly Report*, May 5, 1990, pp. 1370–71.

83. The debate is in *Congressional Record*, May 22, 1990, pp. H2654–2716.

84. Felton, "House Fires a Warning Shot Over El Salvador Policy," *CQ Weekly Report*, May 26, 1990, pp. 1670–71. The House eventually passed a supplemental foreign aid authorization for Panama and Nicaragua without the El Salvador provisions.

85. Carroll J. Doherty, "Egypt Wins, El Salvador Loses in Foreign Aid Funding Bill," *CQ Weekly Report*, October 27, 1990, pp. 3627–29. The House passed the bill in June without voting on El Salvador; the Senate debate is in *Congressional Record*, October 19, 1990, pp. S16138–59.

86. Tom Gibb, "Salvadoran Rebels Attack 11 Towns; Key Captain in Jesuits Case Is Killed," *WP*, November 21, 1990; Lindsey Gruson, "Missiles Give Salvador Rebels a New Advantage," *NYT*, December 10, 1990. The catalytic event that led Bush to resume military aid came in January 1991, when an FMLN patrol shot down a low-flying helicopter carrying three U.S. advisers. One died in the crash, but the other two were captured by the guerrillas and summarily executed. A key factor in the decision to restore military aid was Bush's desire to send the FMLN an unambiguous signal that killing U.S. personnel would have very negative consequences.

87. Clifford Krauss, "Bush to Release Military Aid to El Salvador," *NYT*, June 27, 1991.

88. The text of this agreement and all the subsequent agreements leading up to the final peace accord are in *Acuerdos de El Salvador*.

89. Chris Norton, "El Salvador Peace Talks Begin with a Ray of Hope," *CSM*, May 16, 1990.

90. Salvador Samayoa, "For Lasting Peace, Dump the Army," *LAT*, September 4, 1990.

91. David Clark Scott, "Salvadorans Agree to Reforms," *CSM*, April 29, 1991.

92. "Position of the FMLN Toward the New ARENA Government and Proposal to Achieve a Real Democracy, Peace and a New Society," April 6, 1989 (typescript). Slightly modified versions of these proposals were put forward by FMLN representatives in their meetings with government officials in September and October 1989. For these proposals, see "FMLN Proposals for Negotiating a Just and Lasting Peace in El Salvador," *Envío* (January 1990).

93. Author's interview with Rubén Zamora, Washington, D.C., June 1992.

94. Tom Gibb, "Two Salvadoran Army Officers Receive 30-Year Prison Terms," *WP*, January 25, 1992.

95. Tim Golden, "Salvador Accord Aims at Quick End to Long Civil War," *NYT*, January 2, 1992; Richard Boudreaux, "Civil War Ends in El Salvador with Signing of Treaty," *LAT*, January 17, 1992.

96. Richard Severo, "Roberto D'Aubuisson, 48, Far-Rightist in El Salvador," *NYT*, February 21, 1992. Ironically, in the final months of his life, D'Aubuisson supported Cristiani's negotiating posture and helped insulate the president from opposition among ARENA hardliners. Author's interview with Rubén Zamora, Washington, D.C., June 1992.

97. *Acuerdos de El Salvador*, pp. 48–150.

98. Tim Golden, "The Salvadorans Make Peace in a 'Negotiated Revolution,'" *NYT*, January 5, 1992.

CHAPTER TWENTY-FOUR

1. Stephen Kinzer, "Central America: In Search of Its Destiny," *Boston Globe Magazine*, August 16, 1981.

2. George P. Shultz, "America and the Struggle for Freedom," *U.S. Department of State Bulletin*, April 1985, pp. 16–21.

3. Carothers, *In the Name of Democracy*, p. 107.

4. U.S. AID estimate provided in an interview with an AID analyst at the U.S. embassy in El Salvador, August 1983.

5. Shelley Emling, "El Salvador Peace Prospects Spark Hope for Rejuvenated Business Climate," *Journal of Commerce*, January 13, 1992; Kenneth Freed, "El Salvador's Dilemma of Painful Prosperity," *LAT*, September 1, 1991.

6. U.S. Agency for International Development, "FY 1998 U.S. Economic and Military Assistance Request," *Congressional Presentation Documents*, FY 1998. The figure of $169 million includes $31 million requested for Latin American regional programs, since most of those funds were slated for supporting the peace processes in Guatemala, El Salvador, and Nicaragua.

7. U.S. Agency for International Development, "FY 1998 U.S. Economic and Military Assistance Request," ibid.

8. Tracy Wilkinson, "A Legacy of Conflict and Confusion," *LAT*, October 17, 1993.

9. C. G. Jacobsen, "Soviet Attitudes Towards Aid to and Contacts with Central American Revolutionaries," in Larkin, *Vital Interests*, pp. 289–320. This paper was originally done on contract for the State Department, and concludes that Soviet contact and aid was minimal. But see also Raymond Bonner, "Arms for the Revolution: The Bulgarian Connection," *NYT*, January 27, 1994, which details evidence of Bulgarian arms shipments to the Central American left, based on documents uncovered after the fall of the Bulgarian Communist government. Finally, for a reflection on Soviet policy written after the end of the Cold War, see Kiva Maidanik, "On the *Real* Soviet Policy Toward Central America, Past and Present," in Smith, *Russians Aren't Coming*, pp. 89–96.

Bibliography

Manuscript Collections
National Security Archive, George Washington University Library, Washington, D.C.
  El Salvador collection
  Nicaragua collection
  Iran-Contra collection

Periodicals and News Media
Albuquerque Journal
Associated Press wire service
Baltimore Sun
Barricada (Nicaragua)
Boston Globe
Christian Science Monitor
Congressional Record
Excelsior (Mexico)
Financial Times (Great Britain)
International Herald Tribune
Journal of Commerce
La Prensa (Nicaragua)
Los Angeles Times
Manchester Guardian (Great Britain)
Miami Herald
Milwaukee Journal
New York Post

New York Times
Newsday
Newsweek
Philadelphia Inquirer
Proceso (El Salvador)
San Francisco Chronicle
Seattle Post-Intelligencer
St. Louis Post-Dispatch
Tampa Tribune
Time
U.S. News and World Report
United Press International wire service
Wall Street Journal
Washington Post
Washington Star
Washington Times

Government Publications
Arms Control and Foreign Policy Caucus. *Barriers to Reform: A Profile of El Salvador's Military Leaders.* Washington, D.C.: ACFPC, 1990.
——. *The Contra High Command: An Independent Analysis of the Military Leadership of the FDN.* Washington, D.C.: ACFPC, 1986.
——. *Contra "Reforms": Are the Miami Agreements Significant?* Washington, D.C.: ACFPC, 1986.
——. *U.S. Aid to El Salvador: An Evaluation of the Past, a Proposal for the Future.* Washington, D.C.: ACFPC, 1985.
——. *Who Are the Contras?* Washington, D.C.: ACFCP, 1985.
Checchi and Company. *Agrarian Reform in El Salvador.* Report for the Agency for International Development under contract no. PDC-1406-I-00-1136-00. Washington, D.C.: U.S. AID, 1983.
Eagleburger, Lawrence. "U.S. Assistance to Panama, Nicaragua." *Current Policy*, no. 1264 (1990) (U.S. Department of State).
Enders, Thomas O. "Building Peace in Central America." *U.S. Department of State Bulletin*, October 1982, pp. 66–69.
——. "El Salvador: The Search for Peace." *U.S. Department of State Bulletin*, September 1981, pp. 70–73.
——. "Nicaragua: The Threat to Peace." Statement before the Senate Foreign Relations Committee. *Current Policy*, no. 476 (April 12, 1983) (U.S. Department of State).
Hinton, Deane R. "System of Justice in El Salvador." *U.S. Department of State Bulletin*, December 1982, pp. 68–69.

Jagelski, Jeanne. *Legislative History of Sections 506 and 652 of the Foreign Assistance Act of 1961 (Special Security Assistance Authority)*. Washington, D.C.: Congressional Research Service, 1982.

"President Opposes El Salvador Certification Legislation: White House Statement." *U.S. Department of State Bulletin*, January 1984, p. 88.

"Presidential Determination No. 80-26, September 12, 1980." 45 *Federal Register* 62779.

Public Papers of the Presidents of the United States: George Bush, 1989–1993. Washington, D.C.: Government Printing Office, 1990–93.

Public Papers of the Presidents of the United States: Jimmy Carter, 1977–1981. Washington, D.C.: Government Printing Office, 1977–81.

Public Papers of the Presidents of the United States: Ronald Reagan, 1981–1989. Washington, D.C.: Government Printing Office, 1982–89.

Report of the President's Special Review Board (Tower Board). Washington, D.C.: Government Printing Office, February 26, 1987.

"Secretary Haig: News Conference." *Current Policy*, no. 258 (1981) (U.S. Department of State).

"Secretary Interviewed for *Newsweek*." *U.S. Department of State Bulletin*, December 1981, pp. 24–29.

Serafino, Nina M. *The Post-Election Situation of Agrarian Reform in El Salvador*. Washington, D.C.: Congressional Research Service, 1982.

Shultz, George P. "America and the Struggle for Freedom." *U.S. Department of State Bulletin*, April 1985, pp. 16–21.

Transcript of the Luncheon Meeting on U.S. Policy toward El Salvador, February 26, 1981. Washington, D.C.: Members of Congress for Peace through Law, 1981.

U.S. Agency for International Development. *Congressional Presentation Documents*. Washington, D.C.: U.S. AID, annual.

———. *U.S. Overseas Loans and Grants, and Assistance from International Organizations: Obligations and Loan Authorizations*. Washington, D.C.: U.S. AID, annual.

U.S. Central Intelligence Agency. "Cuban Support for Central American Guerrilla Groups," May 2, 1979. *Congressional Record*, May 19, 1980, pp. 11653–55.

U.S. Congress. *Iran-Contra Investigation: Hearings, Volumes 100-1 to 100-13*. Joint Hearings before the Senate Select Committee on Secret Military Assistance to Iran and the Nicaraguan Opposition, and the House Select Committee to Investigate Covert Arms Transactions with Iran, 100th Cong., 1st sess. Washington, D.C.: Government Printing Office, 1987.

———. *Report of the Congressional Committees Investigating the Iran-Contra Affair*. H. Rept. 100-433, S. Rept. 100-216, 100th Cong., 1st sess., November 17, 1987. Washington, D.C.: Government Printing Office, 1988.

———. *Report of the Congressional Committees Investigating the Iran-Contra Affair: Appendix A, Source Documents, Volumes 1 and 2*. H. Rept. 100-433, S. Rept. 100-216, 100th Cong., 1st sess. Washington, D.C.: Government Printing Office, 1988.

———. *Report of the Congressional Committees Investigating the Iran-Contra Affair: Appendix B, Depositions, Volumes 1–27*. H. Rept. 100-433, S. Rept. 100-216, 100th Cong., 1st sess. Washington, D.C.: Government Printing Office, 1988.

———. *Report of the Congressional Committees Investigating the Iran-Contra Affair: Appendix C, Chronology of Events*. H. Rept. 100-433, S. Rept. 100-216, 100th Cong., 1st sess. Washington, D.C.: Government Printing Office, 1988.

———. *Report of the Congressional Committees Investigating the Iran-Contra Affair: Appendix D, Testimonial Chronology: Witness Accounts Supplemented by Documents, Volumes 1–5*. S. Rept. 100-216, 100th Cong., 1st sess. Washington, D.C.: Government Printing Office, 1988.

U.S. Congress. House of Representatives. *Amendment to the Intelligence Authorization Act for Fiscal Year 1983*. Report from the Permanent Select Committee on Intelligence to Accompany H.R. 2760, H. Rept. 98-122, pt. 1, May 13, 1983. Washington, D.C.: Government Printing Office, 1983.

——. *Amendment to the Intelligence Authorization Act for Fiscal Year 1983*. Report from the Committee on Foreign Affairs to Accompany H.R. 2760, H. Rept. 98-122, pt. 2, 98th Cong., 2nd sess., June 14, 1983. Washington, D.C.: Government Printing Office, 1983.

——. *Central America at the Crossroads*. Hearings before the Subcommittee on Inter-American Affairs, Committee on Foreign Affairs, 96th Cong., 1st sess., September 11 and 12, 1979. Washington, D.C.: Government Printing Office, 1979.

——. *The Central American Counterterrorism Act of 1985*. Hearings before the Committee on Foreign Affairs, 99th Cong., 1st sess., October 24, November 19, 1985. Washington, D.C.: Government Printing Office, 1985.

——. *Compilation of Intelligence Laws and Related Executive Orders of Interest to the National Intelligence Community*. Prepared for the Permanent Select Committee on Intelligence, July 1985. Washington, D.C.: Government Printing Office, 1985.

——. *Congress and Foreign Policy 1983*. Committee on Foreign Affairs. Washington, D.C.: Government Printing Office, 1984.

——. *Congress and Foreign Policy 1984*. Committee on Foreign Affairs. Washington, D.C.: Government Printing Office, 1985.

——. *Congress and Foreign Policy 1987*. Committee on Foreign Affairs. Washington, D.C.: Government Printing Office, 1988.

——. *Congress and Foreign Policy 1989*. Committee on Foreign Affairs. Washington, D.C.: Government Printing Office, 1990.

——. *El Salvador at the Crossroads: Peace or Another Decade of War*. Hearings before the Subcommittee on Western Hemisphere Affairs, Committee on Foreign Affairs, 101st Cong., 2nd sess., January 24, 1990. Washington, D.C.: Government Printing Office, 1990.

——. *Foreign Assistance and Related Programs Appropriations for 1981, Part 1*. Hearings before the Subcommittee on Foreign Operations, Committee on Appropriations, February 21, 26, March 11, 18, 25, April 1, 1980, 96th Cong., 2nd sess. Washington, D.C.: Government Printing Office, 1980.

——. *Foreign Assistance and Related Programs Appropriations for 1982, Part 1*. Hearings before the Subcommittee on Foreign Operations and Related Agencies, Committee on Appropriations, 97th Cong., 1st sess., February 25, March 24, April 29, 1981. Washington, D.C.: Government Printing Office, 1981.

——. *Foreign Assistance and Related Programs Appropriations for 1987*. Hearings before the Subcommittee on Foreign Operations and Related Agencies, Committee on Appropriations, 99th Cong., 2nd sess., pt. 3. Washington, D.C.: Government Printing Office, 1986.

——. *Foreign Assistance Legislation for Fiscal Year 1981, Part 7*. Hearings and Markup before the Subcommittee on Inter-American Affairs, 97th Cong., 1st sess., March 23, 26, 30, April 8, 1981. Washington, D.C.: Government Printing Office, 1981.

——. *Foreign Assistance Legislation for Fiscal Year 1981, Part 9*. Markup before the Committee on Foreign Affairs, 97th Cong., 1st sess., April 28–30, May 5–7, 12–13, 1981. Washington, D.C.: Government Printing Office, 1981.

——. *Foreign Assistance Legislation for Fiscal Year 1982, Part 1*. Hearings before the Committee on Foreign Affairs, 97th Cong., 1st sess., March 13, 18, 19, 23, 1981. Washington, D.C.: Government Printing Office, 1981.

——. *Foreign Assistance Legislation for Fiscal Year 1982, Part 7*. Hearings and Markup before the Subcommittee on Inter-American Affairs, Committee on Foreign Affairs, 97th Cong., 1st sess., March 23, 26, 30, April 8, 1981. Washington, D.C.: Government Printing Office, 1981.

———. *Foreign Assistance Legislation for Fiscal Years 1984–1985, Part 7.* Hearings and Markup before the Subcommittee on Western Hemisphere Affairs, Committee on Foreign Affairs, 98th Cong., 1st sess., March 1, 16, April 12, 13, 1983. Washington, D.C.: Government Printing Office, 1983.

———. *Foreign Assistance Legislation for Fiscal Year 1985, Part 6.* Hearings and Markup before the Committee on Foreign Affairs and Its Subcommittee on Western Hemisphere Affairs, 98th Cong., 2nd sess., February 8, 21, 22, 23, March 1, 1984. Washington, D.C.: Government Printing Office, 1984.

———. *Foreign Assistance Legislation for Fiscal Years 1986–1987, Part 1.* Hearings before the Committee on Foreign Affairs, 99th Cong., 1st sess., February 19, 20, 21, 26, March 7, 1985. Washington, D.C.: Government Printing Office, 1985.

———. *Foreign Assistance Legislation for Fiscal Years 1986–1987, Part 6.* Hearings and Markup before the Subcommittee on Western Hemisphere Affairs, Committee on Foreign Affairs, 99th Cong., 1st sess., March 5, 19, 1985. Washington, D.C.: Government Printing Office, 1985.

———. *Impact of Cuban-Soviet Ties in the Western Hemisphere.* Hearings before the Subcommittee on Inter-American Affairs, Committee on Foreign Affairs, 96th Cong., 2nd sess., March 26, 27, April 16, 17, May 14, 1980. Washington, D.C.: Government Printing Office, 1980.

———. *The Imposition of Economic Sanctions and a Trade Embargo Against Nicaragua.* Hearing before the Subcommittees on International Economic Policy and Trade, and on Western Hemisphere Affairs, Committee on Foreign Affairs, 99th Cong., 1st sess., May 7, 1985. Washington, D.C.: Government Printing Office, 1985.

———. *International Security and Development Cooperation Act of 1983.* Report of the Committee on Foreign Affairs on H.R. 2992, H. Rept. 98-192, 98th Cong., 1st sess., May 17, 1983. Washington, D.C.: Government Printing Office, 1983.

———. *International Security and Development Cooperation Act of 1985.* Report of the Committee on Foreign Affairs on H.R. 1555, H. Rept. 99-39, 99th Cong., 1st sess. Washington, D.C.: Government Printing Office, 1985.

———. *International Security and Development Cooperation Act of 1985: Conference Report.* H. Rept. 99-237, 99th Cong., 1st sess., July 29, 1985. Washington, D.C.: Government Printing Office, 1985.

———. *Investigation of United States Assistance to the Nicaraguan Contras, Volume 1.* Hearings before the Subcommittee on Western Hemisphere Affairs, Committee on Foreign Affairs, 99th Cong., 2nd sess., March 5, 6, 1986. Washington, D.C.: Government Printing Office, 1986.

———. *Investigation of United States Assistance to the Nicaraguan Contras, Volume 2.* Hearings before the Subcommittee on Western Hemisphere Affairs, Committee on Foreign Affairs, 99th Cong., 2nd sess., April 9, May 1, 8, June 11, 1986. Washington, D.C.: Government Printing Office, 1986.

———. *Joint Resolution Relating to the Additional Authority and Assistance for the Nicaraguan Democratic Resistance Requested by the President.* Adverse Report, Permanent Select Committee on Intelligence, H. Rept. 99-483, pt. 4, 99th Cong., 2nd sess., March 12, 1986. Washington, D.C.: Government Printing Office, 1986.

———. *Making Continuing Appropriations for Fiscal Year 1985, and for Other Purposes.* Conference Report to Accompany H.J. Res. 648, H. Rept. 98-1159, 98th Cong., 2nd sess., October 10, 1984. Washington, D.C.: Government Printing Office, 1984.

———. *Making Supplemental Appropriations for Fiscal Year Ending September 20, 1982, and for Other Purposes: Conference Report.* H. Rept. 97-747, 97th Cong., 2nd sess., August 13, 1982. Washington, D.C.: Government Printing Office, 1982.

————. *Making Supplemental Appropriations for the Fiscal Year Ending September 30, 1985, and for Other Purposes: Conference Report.* H. Rept. 99-236, 99th Cong., 1st sess., July 2, 1985, p. 56. Washington, D.C.: Government Printing Office, 1985.

————. *Presidential Certification on El Salvador, Volume 1.* Hearings before the Subcommittee on Inter-American Affairs, Committee on Foreign Affairs, 97th Cong., 2nd sess., February 2, 23, 25, March 2, 1982. Washington, D.C.: Government Printing Office, 1982.

————. *Presidential Certification on El Salvador, Volume 2.* Hearings before the Committee on Foreign Affairs and its Subcommittee on Inter-American Affairs, 97th Cong., 2nd sess., June 2, 22, July 29, August 3, 10, 17, 1982. Washington, D.C.: Government Printing Office, 1982.

————. *Review of the Presidential Certification of Nicaragua's Connection to Terrorism.* Hearings before the Subcommittee on Inter-American Affairs, Committee on Foreign Affairs, 96th Cong., 2nd sess., September 30, 1980. Washington, D.C.: U.S. Government Printing Office, 1980.

————. *Review of the President's Report on Assistance to the Nicaraguan Opposition.* Hearing before the Subcommittee on Western Hemisphere Affairs, Committee on Foreign Relations, 99th Cong., 1st sess., December 5, 1985. Washington, D.C.: Government Printing Office, 1986.

————. *Report on the Activities of the Permanent Select Committee on Intelligence.* H. Rept. 98-1196, 98th Cong., 2nd sess., January 2, 1985. Washington, D.C.: Government Printing Office, 1985.

————. *The Situation in El Salvador.* Hearings before the Subcommittees on Human Rights and International Organizations and on Western Hemisphere Affairs, Committee on Foreign Relations, 98th Cong., 2nd sess., January 26, February 6, 1984. Washington, D.C.: Government Printing Office, 1984.

————. *U.S. Intelligence Performance on Central America: Achievements and Selected Instances of Concern.* Staff Report of the Subcommittee on Oversight and Evaluation, Permanent Select Committee on Intelligence, September 22, 1982, 97th Cong., 2nd sess. Washington, D.C.: Government Printing Office, 1982.

————. *U.S. Policy in Central America.* Hearings before the Subcommittees on Human Rights and International Organizations and on Western Hemisphere Affairs, Committee on Foreign Affairs, 98th Cong., 1st sess., August 3, 1983. Washington, D.C.: Government Printing Office, 1983.

————. *U.S. Policy in El Salvador: Third Presidential Certification on El Salvador.* Hearings before the Subcommittees on Human Rights and International Organizations and on Western Hemisphere Affairs, Committee on Foreign Affairs, 98th Cong., 1st sess., February 4, 28, March 7, 17, 1983. Washington, D.C.: Government Printing Office, 1983.

————. *U.S. Policy Toward El Salvador.* Hearing before the Subcommittee on Inter-American Affairs, Committee on Foreign Affairs, 97th Cong., 1st sess., March 5, 11, 1981. Washington, D.C.: Government Printing Office, 1981.

————. *U.S. Support for the Contras.* Hearing before the Subcommittee on Western Hemisphere Affairs, Committee on Foreign Affairs, 99th Cong., 1st sess., April 16, 17, 18, 1985. Washington, D.C.: Government Printing Office, 1983.

U.S. Congress. Senate. *Central America Policy.* Hearing before the Committee on Foreign Relations, 98th Cong., 1st sess., August 4, 1983. Washington, D.C.: Government Printing Office, 1983.

————. *Covert Action in Chile, 1963–1973.* Staff Report of the Select Committee to Study Governmental Operations with Respect to Intelligence (Church Committee), 94th Cong., 1st sess., December 18, 1975. Washington, D.C.: Government Printing Office, 1985.

——. *Department of Defense Authorization for Appropriations for Fiscal Year 1985, Part 2.* Hearings before the Committee on Armed Services, S. Hrg. 98-724, pt. 2, 98th Cong., 2nd sess., February 2, 7, 8, 23, 1984. Washington, D.C.: Government Printing Office, 1984.

——. *Drugs, Law Enforcement and Foreign Policy.* Report by the Subcommittee on Terrorism, Narcotics, and International Operations, Committee on Foreign Relations, S. Prt. 100-165, 100th Cong., 2nd sess., December 1988. Washington, D.C.: Government Printing Office, 1989.

——. *El Salvador Military and Economic Reprogramming.* Special Hearing before the Foreign Operations Subcommittee, Committee on Appropriations, 98th Cong., 1st sess., March 22, 1983. Washington, D.C.: Government Printing Office, 1983.

——. *El Salvador: Reprogramming.* Hearings before the Committee on Foreign Relations, 98th Cong., 1st sess., March 22, 23, 24, 1983. Washington, D.C.: Government Printing Office, 1983.

——. *Foreign Assistance Authorization for Fiscal Year 1982.* Hearings before the Committee on Foreign Relations, 97th Cong., 1st sess., May 4, 1981. Washington, D.C.: Government Printing Office, 1981.

——. *International Security and Development Cooperation Act of 1981.* Report of the Committee on Foreign Relations on S. 1196, S. Rept. 97-83, 97th Cong., 1st Session. Washington, D.C.: Government Printing Office, 1981.

——. *International Security and Development Cooperation Act of 1983.* Report of the Committee on Foreign Relations on S. 1347, S. Rept. 98-146, 98th Cong., 1st sess., May 23, 1983. Washington, D.C.: Government Printing Office, 1983.

——. *International Security Enhancement Act of 1982.* Report of the Committee on Foreign Relations on S. 2608, S. Rept. 97-464, 97th Cong., 2nd sess., May 28, 1982. Washington, D.C.: Government Printing Office, 1982.

——. *Nomination of Robert E. White.* Report from the Committee on Foreign Relations, Executive Report 96-31, 96th Cong., 2nd sess., February 27, 1980. Washington, D.C.: Government Printing Office, 1980.

——. *Nomination of Robert M. Gates to Be Director of Central Intelligence.* Report of the Select Committee on Intelligence, 102nd Cong., 1st sess., October 24, 1991. Washington, D.C.: Government Printing Office, 1991.

——. *Preliminary Inquiry into the Sale of Arms to Iran and Possible Diversion of Funds to the Nicaraguan Resistance.* Report of the Select Committee on Intelligence, S. Rept. 100-7, 100th Cong., 1st sess. Washington, D.C.: Government Printing Office, 1987.

——. *Presidential Certification on Progress in El Salvador.* Hearing before the Committee on Foreign Relations, 98th Cong., 1st sess., February 2, 1983. Washington, D.C.: Government Printing Office, 1983.

——. *Recent Political Violence in El Salvador.* Report of the Select Committee on Intelligence, S. Rept. 98-659, 98th Cong., 2nd sess., October 5, 1984. Washington, D.C.: Government Printing Office, 1984.

——. *Report of the Select Committee on Intelligence, January 1, 1983, to December 31, 1984.* S. Rept. 98-665, 98th Cong., 2nd sess., October 10, 1984. Washington, D.C.: Government Printing Office, 1985.

——. *S. 2012.* Hearings before the Committee on Foreign Relations, 96th Cong., 1st sess., December 6, 7, 1979. Washington, D.C.: Government Printing Office, 1980.

——. *Security and Development Assistance.* Hearings before the Committee on Foreign Relations, S. Hrg. 99-219, 99th Cong., 1st sess., March 15, 20, 21, 22, 26, 1985. Washington, D.C.: Government Printing Office, 1985.

——. *The Situation in El Salvador.* Hearings before the Committee on Foreign Relations, 97th Cong., 1st sess., March 18, April 9, 1981. Washington, D.C.: Government Printing Office, 1981.

——. *U.S. Policy Toward Nicaragua: Aid to Nicaraguan Resistance Proposal.* Hearings before the Committee on Foreign Relations, 99th Cong., 2nd sess., February 27, March 4, 1986. Washington, D.C.: Government Printing Office, 1986.

U.S. Congress. Senate. Democratic Policy Committee. *Foreign Aid to Central America,* FY 1981–1987. Special Report No. 1, February 18, 1987. Washington, D.C.: DPC, 1987.

U.S. Department of State. *Aggression from the North: The Record of North Vietnam's Campaign to Conquer South Vietnam.* Publication 7839. Washington, D.C.: U.S. Department of State, 1965.

——. *Comandante Bayardo Arce's Secret Speech Before the Nicaraguan Socialist Party* (PSN). Washington, D.C.: U.S. Department of State, 1985.

——. *Communist Interference in El Salvador.* Special Report No. 80, February 23, 1981. Washington, D.C.: U.S. Department of State, 1981.

——. *Country Reports on Human Rights Practices for 1983.* Report Submitted to the Committee on Foreign Affairs, U.S. House of Representatives, and the Committee on Foreign Relations, U.S. Senate, 98th Cong., 2nd sess., February 1984. Washington, D.C.: Government Printing Office, 1984.

——. *Documents on the Nicaraguan Resistance: Leaders, Military Personnel, and Program.* Special Report No. 142, February 24, 1986. Washington, D.C.: U.S. State Department Bureau of Public Affairs, 1986.

——. *Human Rights in Nicaragua Under the Sandinistas: From Revolution to Repression.* Washington, D.C.: U.S. Department of State, December 1986.

——. *Report of the Secretary of State's Panel on El Salvador, July 1993.* Washington, D.C.: U.S. Department of State, 1993.

——. *Report on Human Rights Practices in Countries Receiving U.S. Aid,* February 8, 1979. Washington, D.C.: Government Printing Office, 1979.

——. *"Revolution Beyond Our Borders": Sandinista Intervention in Central America.* Special Report No. 132, September 1985. Washington, D.C.: Government Printing Office, 1985.

——. *The Sandinistas and Middle Eastern Radicals.* Washington, D.C.: U.S. Department of State, 1985.

——. "Soviet Bloc Assistance to Nicaragua and Cuba Versus U.S. Assistance to Central America." *Latin America Dispatch,* October 1987. Washington, D.C.: Government Printing Office, 1987.

——. "U.S. Support for Democracy and Peace in Central America." *Selected Documents,* no. 36. Washington, D.C.: U.S. Department of State, 1989.

U.S. Department of State and Department of Defense. *Background Paper: Central America.* Washington, D.C.: U.S. Information Agency, 1983.

U.S. Foreign Broadcast Information Service (FBIS). *Daily Report: Latin America.* Washington, D.C.: FBIS, 1984.

U.S. General Accounting Office. *Central America: Impact of U.S. Assistance in the 1980s.* Report to the Chairman, Committee on Foreign Relations, U.S. Senate, July 1989, GAO/NSIAD 89-170. Washington, D.C.: Government Printing Office, 1989.

——. *Central America: Problems in Controlling Funds for the Nicaraguan Democratic Resistance.* Report to the Chairman of the Subcommittee on Western Hemisphere Affairs, Committee on Foreign Affairs, U.S. House of Representatives, December 5, 1986, GAO/NSIAD 87-35. Washington, D.C.: Government Printing Office, 1986.

"U.S. Initiative for Peace in Central America." *U.S. Department of State Bulletin,* October 1987, pp. 54–56.

"U.S. Policy in Central America: White House Statement, April 10, 1984." *U.S. Department of State Bulletin,* June 1984, pp. 85–86.

"U.S. Support for Democracy and Peace in Central America." *Selected Documents,* no. 36. Washington, D.C.: U.S. Department of State, 1989.

"U.S. Suspends Economic Aid to Nicaragua: Department Statement, April 1, 1981." *U.S. Department of State Bulletin*, May 1981, p. 71.

Walsh, Lawrence E. *Final Report of the Independent Counsel for Iran/Contra Matters*. U.S. Court of Appeals for the District of Columbia Circuit, Division No. 86-6, August 4, 1993.

"Western Hemisphere: Nicaragua." *U.S. Department of State Bulletin*, August 1979, pp. 55–61.

Books and Articles

Abrams, Elliott. *Undue Process: A Story of How Political Differences Are Turned into Crimes*. New York: Free Press, 1993.

Acuerdos de El Salvador: En El Camino de la Paz. New York: United Nations, 1992.

Agee, Philip. *Inside the Company: CIA Diary*. New York: Bantam, 1975.

Allman, T. D. *Unmanifest Destiny: Mayhem and Illusion in American Foreign Policy—from the Monroe Doctrine to Reagan's War in El Salvador*. New York: Doubleday, 1984.

Alterman, Eric. "The Best and the Rightest." *Tikkun* 2, no. 3 (July–August 1987): 21–23.

———. "Inside Ollie's Mind." *New Republic*, February 16, 1987.

American Institute for Free Labor Development (AFL-CIO). "Preliminary Report: Survey of Beneficiaries of Decree 207." Typescript, 1980.

American Institute for Free Labor Development (AFL-CIO) and Freedom House. *The Captured Documents: Guerrilla Penetration of Salvadoran Trade Unions*. Washington, D.C.: Freedom House, 1986.

Americas Watch. *The Civilian Toll, 1986–1987*. Ninth Supplement to the Report on Human Rights in El Salvador, August 30, 1987. Washington, D.C.: Americas Watch, 1987.

———. *Draining the Sea*. Sixth Supplement to the Report on Human Rights in El Salvador, March 1985. New York: Americas Watch, 1985.

———. *El Salvador's Decade of Terror: Human Rights since the Assassination of Archbishop Romero*. New Haven: Yale University Press, 1991.

———. *Freedom of Expression and Assembly in Nicaragua during the Election Period*. New York: Americas Watch, 1984.

———. *Human Rights in Honduras: Central America's Sideshow*. New York: Americas Watch, 1987.

———. *Human Rights in Honduras: Signs of "the Argentine Method."* New York: Americas Watch, 1982.

———. *Human Rights in Nicaragua: Rhetoric and Reality*. New York: Americas Watch, 1985.

———. *Nightmare Revisited, 1987–88*. Tenth Supplement to the Report on Human Rights in El Salvador. New York: Americas Watch, 1988.

———. *Protection of the Weak and Unarmed: The Dispute over Counting Human Rights Violations in El Salvador*. New York: Americas Watch, 1984.

———. *Settling into Routine: Human Rights Abuses in Duarte's Second Year*. Eighth Supplement to the Report on Human Rights in El Salvador. New York: Americas Watch, 1986.

———. *U.S. Reporting on Human Rights in El Salvador: Methodology at Odds with Knowledge*. New York: Americas Watch, 1982.

———. *Violations of the Laws of War by Both Sides in Nicaragua, 1981–1985*. New York: Americas Watch, 1985.

———. *A Year of Reckoning: El Salvador a Decade after the Assassination of Archbishop Romero*. New York: Americas Watch, 1990.

Americas Watch and the American Civil Liberties Union. *Report on Human Rights in El Salvador, January 1982*. Washington, D.C.: ACLU Center for National Security Studies, 1982.

——. *Second Supplement to the Report on Human Rights in El Salvador, January 20, 1983.* Washington, D.C.: ACLU Center for National Security Studies, 1983.

——. *Supplement to the Report on Human Rights in El Salvador, July 20, 1982.* Washington, D.C.: ACLU Center for National Security Studies, 1982.

Americas Watch and the Lawyers International Committee for Human Rights. *Free Fire: A Report on Human Rights in El Salvador.* Fifth Supplement to the Report on Human Rights in El Salvador. Washington, D.C.: Americas Watch, 1984.

Amnesty International. *Report for 1978.* New York: Amnesty International, 1979.

Anderson, Scott, and Jon Lee Anderson. *Inside the League.* New York: Dodd, Mead, 1986.

Anderson, Thomas P. *Matanza: El Salvador's Communist Revolt of 1932.* Lincoln: University of Nebraska Press, 1971.

——. *The War of the Dispossessed: Honduras and El Salvador, 1969.* Lincoln: University of Nebraska Press, 1980.

Archdiocese of San Salvador. *Repression Carried Out by the National Army . . . the Military Corps of National Security . . . and Paramilitary Organizations.* San Salvador: Archdiocese Legal Department, 1980.

Arias Sánchez, Oscar. *El Camino de la Paz.* San José, Costa Rica: Editorial Costa Rica, 1989.

Armstrong, Robert, and Janet Shenk. *El Salvador: The Face of Revolution.* Boston: South End Press, 1982.

Arnson, Cynthia J. *Crossroads: Congress, the President, and Central America, 1976–1993.* University Park: Pennsylvania State University Press, 1993.

——. *El Salvador: A Revolution Confronts the United States.* Washington, D.C.: Institute for Policy Studies, 1982.

Asamblea Legislativa. *Informe Sobre el Tráfico de Armas.* San José, Costa Rica: Comisión de Asuntos Especiales, 1981.

Atlantic Council. *Western Interests and U.S. Policy Options in the Caribbean Basin: Report of the Atlantic Council's Working Group on the Caribbean Basin.* Boston: Oelgeschlager, Gunn and Hain, 1984.

"Audience Growing for TV Coverage of the House." *Congressional Quarterly Weekly Report,* January 12, 1985, p. 95.

Bacevich, A. J., James D. Hallums, Richard H. White, and Thomas F. Young. *American Military Policy in Small Wars: The Case of El Salvador.* Washington, D.C.: Pergamon-Brassey, 1988.

Bagley, Bruce Michael. *Regional Powers in the Caribbean Basin: Mexico, Venezuela, and Colombia.* Occasional Paper No. 2. Washington, D.C.: Johns Hopkins School of Advanced International Studies, 1983.

Bagley, Bruce Michael, Roberto Alvarez, and Katherine J. Hagedorn, eds. *Contadora and the Central American Peace Process: Selected Documents.* Boulder, Colo.: Westview, 1985.

Baker, James A., III, with Thomas M. DeFrank. *The Politics of Diplomacy: Revolution, War, and Peace, 1989–1992.* New York: G. P. Putnam, 1995.

Baloyra, Enrique A. *El Salvador in Transition.* Chapel Hill: University of North Carolina Press, 1982.

Barrett, Laurence I. *Gambling with History: Ronald Reagan in the White House.* Garden City, N.Y.: Doubleday, 1983.

Barry, John M. *The Ambition and the Power.* New York: Viking, 1989.

Barry, Tom, and Deb Preusch. *The Soft War: The Uses and Abuses of U.S. Economic Aid in Central America.* New York: Grove Press, 1988.

Berman, Karl. *Under the Big Stick: Nicaragua and the United States since 1848.* Boston: South End Press, 1986.

Blachman, Morris J., William M. LeoGrande, and Kenneth Sharpe, eds. *Confronting Revolution: Security through Diplomacy in Central America.* New York: Pantheon, 1986.

Blumenthal, Sidney. *Our Long National Daydream: A Political Pageant of the Reagan Era*. New York: Harper and Row, 1988.

——. *The Rise of the Counter-Establishment: From Conservative Ideology to Political Power*. New York: Times Books, 1986.

Bodnar, Patricia Ann. "The Kissinger Commission: Building a Consensus or Using Window Dressing for an Existing Policy." Master's thesis, Boston College, 1987.

Bonner, Raymond. *Weakness and Deceit: U.S. Policy and El Salvador*. New York: Times Books, 1984.

Booth, John A. *The End and the Beginning: The Nicaraguan Revolution*. 2nd ed. Boulder, Colo.: Westview, 1985.

Borge, Tomás, et al. *Sandinistas Speak*. New York: Pathfinder Press, 1982.

Bradlee, Ben, Jr. *Guts and Glory: The Rise and Fall of Oliver North*. New York: Donald I. Fine, 1988.

Briggs, Herbert W. "Nicaragua v. the United States: Jurisdiction and Admissibility." *American Journal of International Law* 79 (April 1985): 373–78.

Broder, David S. *Behind the Headlines*. New York: Simon and Schuster, 1987.

Browning, David. *El Salvador: Landscape and Society*. Oxford: Clarendon, 1971.

Buckley, Kevin. *Panama: The Whole Story*. New York: Simon and Schuster, 1991.

Bulmer-Thomas, Victor. *The Political Economy of Central America Since 1920*. Cambridge: Cambridge University Press, 1987.

Burke, Melvin. "El Sistema de Plantación y la Proletarización del Trabajo Agrícola en El Salvador." *Estudios Centroamericanos*, nos. 335–36 (September–October 1976): 473–86.

Cabezas, Omar. *Fire from the Mountain: The Making of a Sandinista*. New York: Plume Books, 1986.

Calmes, Jacqueline. "Aspin Makes Comeback at Armed Services." *Congressional Quarterly Weekly Report*, January 24, 1987, pp. 139–42.

Canadian Church and Human Rights Delegation. "Nicaragua 1984: Democracy, Elections and War." Report on the Nicaraguan Election, Toronto, 1984.

Cannon, Lou. *President Reagan: The Role of a Lifetime*. New York: Simon and Schuster, 1991.

——. *Reagan*. New York: Putnam, 1982.

Carothers, Thomas. *In the Name of Democracy: U.S. Policy toward Latin America in the Reagan Years*. Berkeley: University of California Press, 1991.

Carrigan, Ann, and Bernard Stone, producers and directors. *Roses in December: The Story of Jean Donovan*. 2nd of December Films, Inc., 1982.

Carter, Jimmy. *Keeping Faith*. New York: Bantam, 1982.

Castro, Vanessa, and Gary Prevost, eds. *The 1990 Elections in Nicaragua and Their Aftermath*. Lanham, Md.: Rowman and Littlefield, 1992.

Cepeda Ulloa, Fernando, and Rodrigo Pardo García-Peña. *Contadora: Desafío a la Diplomacia Tradicional*. Bogotá: Editorial la Oveja Negra, 1985.

Chamorro, Edgar. *Packaging the Contras: A Case of CIA Disinformation*. New York: Institute for Media Analysis, 1987.

Chamorro, Edgar, with Jefferson Morley. "Confessions of a 'Contra.'" *New Republic*, August 5, 1985.

Chamorro, Jaime. *La Prensa: The Republic of Paper*. New York: Freedom House, 1988.

Chamorro, Violeta Barrios de. *Dreams of the Heart*. New York: Simon and Schuster, 1996.

Chayes, Abram. "Nicaragua, the United States and the World Court." *Columbia Law Review* 85 (November 1985): 1445–82.

Christian, Shirley. *Nicaragua: Revolution in the Family*. New York: Vintage, 1986.

"The CIA Report the President Doesn't Want You to Read." *Village Voice*, February 16, 1976.

Clarridge, Duane R., with Digby Diehl. *A Spy for All Seasons*. New York: Scribner, 1997.

Cockburn, Alexander. "Beat the Devil." *Nation*, March 15, 1986.

Codevilla, Angelo. *Informing Statecraft: Intelligence for a New Century*. New York: Free Press, 1992.

Cohen, William S., and George J. Mitchell. *Men of Zeal: A Candid Inside Story of the Iran-Contra Hearing*. New York: Viking, 1988.

Colburn, Forrest D. *Post-Revolutionary Nicaragua: State, Class, and the Dilemmas of Agrarian Policy*. Berkeley: University of California Press, 1986.

Committee for the Defense of Human Rights in Honduras (Comité para la Defensa de los Derechos Humanos en Honduras). *Human Rights in Honduras, 1984*. Washington, D.C.: Washington Office on Latin America and the World Council of Churches, 1985.

Committee of Santa Fe. *A New Inter-American Policy for the Eighties*. Washington, D.C.: Council for Inter-American Security, 1980.

"Conditions Placed on Military Aid." *Congressional Quarterly Weekly Report*, March 26, 1983.

Coone, Tim. "Nicaragua Seeks Fresh Peace Talks." *Financial Times*, February 20, 1985.

Congressional Quarterly Almanac 1987. Washington, D.C.: CQ Press, 1988.

Corn, David. "Foreign Aid for the Right." *Nation*, December 18, 1989.

Council of Freely Elected Heads of Government. *Observing Nicaragua's Elections, 1989–1990*. Atlanta: Carter Center, 1990.

Crabb, Cecil V., Jr., and Pat M. Holt. *Invitation to Struggle: Congress, the President and Foreign Policy*. Washington, D.C.: CQ Press, 1988.

Cruz, Arturo, Jr. *Memoirs of a Counter-Revolutionary*. New York: Doubleday, 1989.

Cruz, Arturo J. *Nicaragua's Continuing Struggle*. Washington, D.C.: Freedom House, 1988.

Cunningham, Alden M. "U.S. Strategic Options in Nicaragua." *Parameters: U.S. Army War College Quarterly* 18, 1 (March 1988): 60–72.

D'Amato, Anthony. "Modifying U.S. Acceptance of the Compulsory Jurisdiction of the World Court." *American Journal of International Law* 79 (April 1985): 385–405.

Danner, Mark. *The Massacre at El Mozote*. New York: Vintage, 1994.

Deatherage, Scott Dean. "International Court of Justice—Interim Decision in the Case Concerning Military and Paramilitary Activities in and against Nicaragua." *Harvard International Law Journal* 26 (1985): 280–86.

Deaver, Michael K., with Mickey Herskowitz. *Behind the Scenes*. New York: William Morrow, 1987.

"Declaración conjunta de los presidentes de Centro América." *Panorama Centroamericano* (Guatemala), no. 23 (January 1988): 7.

Devine, Frank J. *El Salvador: Embassy under Attack*. New York: Vantage, 1981.

Dickey, Christopher. "Behind the Death Squads." *New Republic*, December 26, 1983.

———. "The Proconsuls." *Rolling Stone*, August 18, 1983.

———. *With the Contras: A Reporter in the Wilds of Nicaragua*. New York: Simon and Schuster, 1985.

Diederich, Bernard. *Somoza and the Legacy of U.S. Involvement in Central America*. New York: E. P. Dutton, 1981.

Dillon, Sam. *Commandos: The CIA and Nicaragua's Contra Rebels*. New York: Henry Holt, 1991.

Dinges, John. *Our Man in Panama*. New York: Random House, 1990.

Dodson, Michael, and Laura Nuzzi O'Shaughnessy. *Nicaragua's Other Revolution: Religious Faith and Political Struggle*. Chapel Hill: University of North Carolina Press, 1990.

Doggett, Martha. *Death Foretold: The Jesuit Murders in El Salvador*. Washington, D.C.: Georgetown University Press, 1993.

Doherty, Carroll J. "Egypt Wins, El Salvador Loses in Foreign Aid Funding Bill." *Congressional Quarterly Weekly Report*, October 27, 1990, pp. 3627–29.

Draper, Theodore. *A Very Thin Line: The Iran-Contra Affairs*. New York: Hill and Wang, 1991.

Drew, Elizabeth. "Reporter-at-Large: Human Rights." *New Yorker*, July 18, 1977.

Drucker, Linda. "A Contra's Story." *Progressive*, August 1986, pp. 25–28.

"Duarte: 'Guerrillas Are Symptoms, Not Causes.'" *Congressional Quarterly Weekly Report*, May 26, 1984, p. 1234.

Duarte, José Napoleón, with Diana Page. *Duarte: My Story*. New York: Putnam, 1986.

Duggan, Ervin S. "The Little Engine of Alexander Haig." *Washingtonian Magazine*, November 1981.

Dugger, Ronnie. *On Reagan: The Man and His Presidency*. New York: McGraw Hill, 1983.

———. "Ronald Reagan and the Imperial Presidency." *Nation*, November 1, 1980.

Dunkerley, James. *The Long War: Dictatorship and Revolution in El Salvador*. London: Junction Books, 1982.

———. *Power in the Isthmus: A Political History of Modern Central America*. London, Verso, 1988.

Durham, William H. *Scarcity and Survival in Central America: Ecological Origins of the Soccer War*. Stanford: Stanford University Press, 1979.

"Economic Aid for El Salvador Increased to $126.5 Million." *Congressional Quarterly Weekly Report*, May 9, 1981, p. 789.

Edelman, Marc, and Joanne Kenen, eds. *The Costa Rica Reader*. New York: Grove Press, 1989.

Edwards, Beatrice, and Gretta Tovar Siebentritt. *Places of Origin: The Repopulation of Rural El Salvador*. Boulder, Colo.: Lynne Rienner, 1991.

Emerson, Steven. *Secret Warriors: Inside the Covert Military Operations of the Reagan Era*. New York: G. P. Putnam, 1988.

Etchinson, Don L. *The United States and Militarism in Central America*. New York: Praeger, 1975.

Fagen, Richard R., and Olga Pellicer, eds. *The Future of Central America: Policy Choices for the U.S. and Mexico*. Stanford: Stanford University Press, 1983.

Farer, Tom J. "Contadora: The Hidden Agenda." *Foreign Policy* 59 (Summer 1985): 59–72.

———. "Reagan's Latin America." *New York Review of Books*, March 19, 1981.

Feinberg, Richard E., ed. *Central America: International Dimensions of the Crisis*. New York: Holmes and Meier, 1982.

Felton, John. "$60 Million in Emergency Aid Due for El Salvador Military." *Congressional Quarterly Weekly Report*, February 26, 1983, pp. 425–26.

———. "Administration Defends Mining of Harbors." *Congressional Quarterly Weekly Report*, April 14, 1984, p. 835.

———. "Caribbean Basin Proposal Faces Lengthy Hearings; Numerous Objections Cited." *Congressional Quarterly Weekly Report*, March 27, 1982, pp. 681–707.

———. "Central America Returns to the Agenda." *Congressional Quarterly Weekly Report*, October, 15, 1983, pp. 2137–39.

———. "Compromise Featured in El Salvador Debate." *Congressional Quarterly Weekly Report*, May 14, 1983, pp. 936–38.

———. "Congress Directing Attention to Central America Policies." *Congressional Quarterly Weekly Report*, April 30, 1983, pp. 819–23.

———. "Delay in Foreign Aid Funding Is Creating Fiscal, Policy Headaches." *Congressional Quarterly Weekly Report*, July 12, 1980, pp. 1956–57.

———. "Hill Group Paints Dark Picture of Rights in El Salvador." *Congressional Quarterly Weekly Report*, May 5, 1990, pp. 1370–71.

———. "Hill May Force a Scaling Back of Bush Election-Aid Plan." *Congressional Quarterly Weekly Report*, September 30, 1989, p. 2581.

———. "House Appropriations Panel Delays Caribbean Initiative, Rejects Additional Arms Aid." *Congressional Quarterly Weekly Report*, May 29, 1982, p. 1258.

———. "House Fires a Warning Shot over El Salvador Policy." *Congressional Quarterly Weekly Report*, May 26, 1990, pp. 1670–71.

———. "Intelligence Bills: Fresh Forum on Covert Aid." *Congressional Quarterly Weekly Report*, June 16, 1984, pp. 1469–72.

———. "Moderates' Foreign Policy Support Wanes." *Congressional Quarterly Weekly Report*, March 19, 1983, p. 550.

———. "Panel Cuts Reagan Proposals for Aid to Central America." *Congressional Quarterly Weekly Report*, April 16, 1983, pp. 736–38.

———. "Panel Deals Blow to Central America Package." *Congressional Quarterly Weekly Report*, March 3, 1984, pp. 518–21.

———. "President's El Salvador Veto Sparks Uproar among Critics." *Congressional Quarterly Weekly Report*, December 3, 1983, p. 2524.

———. "Reagan Plans Hill Offensive to Win Central America Aid." *Congressional Quarterly Weekly Report*, April 23, 1983, pp. 775–76.

———. "Reagan Seeks Major Program of Help for Central America." *Congressional Quarterly Weekly Report*, January 21, 1984, pp. 109–10.

———. "Reagan Tactic on Central America Funds Fails." *Congressional Quarterly Weekly Report*, March 10, 1984, pp. 542–44.

———. "Reagan Takes Case to Public: Congress Directing Attention to Central American Policies." *Congressional Quarterly Weekly Report*, April 30, 1983, pp. 819–23.

———. "Reagan Unveils Central America Aid Package." *Congressional Quarterly Weekly Report*, February 4, 1984, p. 228.

———. "U.S. Troops Expanding Role in Region's Wars." *Congressional Quarterly Weekly Report*, May 26, 1984, pp. 1238–39.

———. "Wright at Center of Nicaragua Policy Storm." *Congressional Quarterly Weekly Report*, September 24, 1988, pp. 2631–33.

Fernández, Guido. *El Desafío de la Paz en Centroamerica*. San José, Costa Rica: Editorial Costa Rica, 1989.

"FMLN Proposals for Negotiating a Just and Lasting Peace in El Salvador." *Envío* (Managua, Nicaragua) 9, 102 (January 1990): 8–12.

Fontaine, Roger, Cleto DiGiovanni Jr., and Alexander Krugar. "Castro's Specter." *Washington Quarterly* 3, 4 (Autumn 1980): 3–27.

"On Foreign Aid, More Stumbling Blocks." *Congressional Quarterly Weekly Report*, October 6, 1984, p. 2418.

Fox, Donald T. *Report on Mission to El Salvador*. New York: International Commission of Jurists, 1978.

Franck, Thomas, and Edward Weisband. *Foreign Policy by Congress*. New York: Oxford University Press, 1979.

Franklin, Jane. *Cuban Foreign Relations: A Chronology, 1959–1982*. New York: Center for Cuban Studies, 1984.

The Freedom Fighter's Manual. New York: Grove Press, 1985.

The Gallup Report, no. 199 (April 1982).

Garvin, Glenn. *Everybody Had His Own Gringo: The CIA and the Contras*. Washington, D.C.: Brassey's, 1992.

Gentile, William Frank. *Nicaragua*. New York: W. W. Norton, 1989.

Gerson, Allan. *The Kirkpatrick Mission: Diplomacy without Apology—America at the United Nations, 1981–1985*. New York: Free Press, 1991.

Gilbert, Dennis. *Sandinistas: The Party and the Revolution*. Cambridge, Mass.: Basil Blackwell, 1988.

Gilbert, Dennis, and David Block, eds. *Sandinistas: Key Documents*. Ithaca, N.Y.: Cornell University Latin American Studies Program, 1990.

Goldwater, Barry, with Jack Cassidy. *Goldwater*. New York: Doubleday, 1988.

Grabendorff, Wolf, Heinrich-W. Krumwiede, and Jorg Todt, eds. *Political Change in Central America: Internal and External Dimensions*. Boulder, Colo.: Westview, 1984.

Granat, Diane. "The House's TV War: The Gloves Come Off." *Congressional Quarterly Weekly Report*, May 19, 1984, pp. 1166–67.

Gutman, Roy. *Banana Diplomacy: The Making of American Policy in Nicaragua, 1981–1987*. New York: Simon and Schuster, 1988.

——. "Nicaragua: America's Diplomatic Charade." *Foreign Policy* 56 (Fall 1984): 3–23.

Hager, Robert P., Jr. "Soviet Bloc Involvement in the Salvadoran Civil War." *Communist and Post-Communist Studies* 28, 4 (1995): 437–70.

Haig, Alexander M., Jr. *Caveat: Realism, Reagan, and Foreign Policy*. New York: Macmillan, 1984.

Hallin, Dan. "White Paper, Red Scare." *NACLA Report on the Americas* 17, 4 (July–August 1983): 2–6.

Harris Poll Report, January 19, 1984.

Heraldo Muñoz, ed. *A la Espera de una Nueva Etapa: Anuario de Políticas Exteriores Latinoamericanas, 1988–1989*. Caracas: Editorial Nueva Sociedad, 1989.

Hersh, Seymour M. *The Price of Power: Kissinger in the Nixon White House*. New York: Summit Books, 1983.

Hertsgaard, Mark. *On Bended Knee: The Press and the Reagan Presidency*. New York: Farrar Straus Giroux, 1988.

Hinckley, Ronald H. *People, Polls, and Policymakers: American Public Opinion and National Security*. New York: Lexington Books, 1992.

Hoffman, Bruce. *The PLO and Israel in Central America: The Geopolitical Dimension*. Santa Monica, Calif.: Rand Corporation, 1988.

Holsti, Ole R., and James N. Rosenau. *American Leadership in World Affairs: Vietnam and the Breakdown of Consensus*. Boston: Allen and Unwin, 1984.

Honey, Martha. "Contra Coverage—Paid for by the CIA." *Columbia Journalism Review*, March–April 1987, pp. 31–32.

——. *Hostile Acts: U.S. Policy in Costa Rica in the 1980s*. Gainesville: University of Florida Press, 1994.

Honey, Martha, and Tony Avirgan. "Leaning on Arias." *Nation*, September 12, 1987.

Horowitz, Paul, and Holly Sklar. "South Atlantic Triangle." *NACLA Report on the Americas* 16, 3 (May–June 1982): 2–43.

Horton, John. "The Real Intelligence Failure." *Foreign Service Journal*, February 1985, pp. 22–25.

Hunter, Jane. *Israeli Foreign Policy: South Africa and Central America*. Boston: South End Press, 1987.

"The IFIs in Central America: Development or Politics?" *Center for International Policy Aid Memo*, October 1, 1982.

In re Yamashita, 327 U.S. 1, 66 S.Ct. 340, 90 L.Ed. 499 (1946).

Instituto Nicaragüense de Opinión Pública Los Nicaragüenses. *Ante las Elecciones de Febrero de 1990*. Managua, 1989.

Instituto Universitario de Opinión Pública. *Los Primero Cien Dias de Cristiani Para la Opinión Pública Salvadoreña*. San Salvador: Universidad Centroamericano José Simeón Cañas, 1989.

International Bank for Reconstruction and Development (World Bank). *El Salvador: Country Economic Memorandum*, Report No. 7818-ES, August 14, 1989.

———. *Report and Recommendation of the President of the International Development Association to the Executive Directors on a Proposed Economic Recovery Credit . . . to the Republic of Nicaragua.* Report No. P-5598-NI. Washington, D.C.: IBRD, 1991.

"International Court of Justice—Case Concerning Military and Paramilitary Activities in and against Nicaragua (Nicaragua vs. United States), 1986 I.C.J. (Judgment on Merits of June 27, 1986)." *Harvard International Law Review* 28 (1987): 146–56.

International Human Rights Law Group and Washington Office on Latin America (WOLA). *A Political Opening in Nicaragua.* Washington, D.C.: WOLA, 1984.

Jeffreys-Jones, Rhodri. *The CIA and American Democracy.* New Haven: Yale University Press, 1989.

Jenkins, Tony. "Nicaragua's Disloyal Opposition." *Nation*, August 12, 1986.

———. "The U.S. Embargo against Nicaragua: One Year Later." *Policy Focus* (Center for International Policy and Overseas Development Council), no. 3 (1986): 1–7.

Johnson, Haynes. *Sleepwalking through History: America in the Reagan Years.* New York: W. W. Norton, 1991.

Johnson, Loch K. *A Season of Inquiry: Congress and Intelligence.* Chicago: Dorsey Press, 1988.

Kagan, Robert. *A Twilight Struggle: American Power and Nicaragua, 1977–1990.* New York: Free Press, 1996.

Karl, Terry. "El Salvador: Negotiations or Total War? An Interview with Salvador Samayoa," *World Policy Journal* 6, no. 2 (Spring 1989): 321–55.

Keisling, Phil. "The Tallest Gun in Foggy Bottom." *Washington Monthly*, November 1982, pp. 50–56.

Kenworthy, Eldon. "Our Colleague Kirkpatrick." *LASA Forum*, Bulletin of the Latin American Studies Association 14, 4 (Winter 1984): 23–24.

Kerstiens, Thom, and Piet Nelissen. "Report on the Elections in Nicaragua." Report of the Netherlands Government Observers, Amsterdam, 1984.

Kinzer, Stephen. *Blood of Brothers: Life and War in Nicaragua.* New York: G. P. Putnam, 1991.

———. "Central America: In Search of Its Destiny." *Boston Globe Magazine*, August 16, 1981.

Kirkpatrick, Jeane. "Dictatorships and Double Standards." *Commentary*, November 1979, pp. 35–45.

———. *Leader and Vanguard in Mass Society: A Study of Peronist Argentina.* Cambridge, Mass.: MIT Press, 1971.

Kondracke, Morton. "Enders' End." *New Republic*, June 27, 1983.

Kornbluh, Peter. "The Contra Lobby." *Village Voice*, October 13, 1987.

———. *Nicaragua: The Price of Intervention.* Washington, D.C.: Institute for Policy Studies, 1987.

Kornbluh, Peter, and Malcolm Byrne, eds. *The Iran-Contra Scandal: The Declassified History.* New York: New Press, 1993.

Kornbluh, Peter, and Martha Honey. "The Case of Ollie's Airstrip." *Nation*, February 22, 1993.

Kotz, Nick, and Morton Kondracke. "How to Avoid Another Cuba." *New Republic*, June 20, 1981.

Krauss, Clifford. *Inside Central America: Its People, Politics, and History.* New York: Summit Books, 1991.

Kwitny, Jonathan. *Endless Enemies: The Making of an Unfriendly World.* New York: Penguin, 1984.

LaFeber, Walter. *Inevitable Revolutions: The United States in Central America.* New York: W. W. Norton, 1983.

Lake, Anthony. *Somoza Falling*. Boston: Houghton Mifflin, 1989.

Lancaster, Roger N. *Thanks to God and the Revolution: Popular Religion and Class Consciousness in the New Nicaragua*. New York: Columbia University Press, 1988.

Landis, Fred. "CIA Media Operations in Chile, Jamaica, and Nicaragua." *Covert Action Information Bulletin*, March 1982.

Lane, Charles. "The Pilot Shark of El Salvador." *New Republic*, September 24, 1990.

Langguth, A. J. *Hidden Terrors*. New York: Pantheon, 1978.

Larkin, Bruce D., ed. *Vital Interests*. Boulder, Colo.: Lynne Rienner, 1988.

Latin American Studies Association (LASA). *The Election Process in Nicaragua: Domestic and International Influences*. N.p.: LASA, 1984.

———. *Electoral Democracy under International Pressure*. Report of the LASA Commission to Observe the 1990 Nicaraguan Election. Pittsburgh: LASA, 1990.

Lawyers Committee for Human Rights. *The "Jesuit Case": The July Trial (La Vista Pública)*. New York: Lawyers Committee, 1991.

Lawyers Committee for International Human Rights. *Nicaragua: Revolutionary Justice*. New York: Lawyers Committee, 1985.

Ledeen, Michael A. *Perilous Statecraft: An Insider's Account of the Iran-Contra Affair*. New York: Charles Scribner's Sons, 1988.

Leiken, Robert S. "Tangled Nicaragua." *New York Review of Books*, December 5, 1985.

———, ed. *Central America: Anatomy of Conflict*. New York: Pergamon, 1984.

Leiken, Robert S., and Barry Ruben, eds. *The Central American Crisis Reader*. New York: Summit Books, 1987.

LeoGrande, William M. *Central America and the Polls*. Washington, D.C.: Washington Office on Latin America, 1987.

———. "Did the Public Matter? The Impact of Opinion on Congressional Support for Ronald Reagan's Nicaragua Policy." Paper prepared for presentation to the Conference of Decision-Makers on Public Opinion and U.S. Policy toward Central America, Princeton University, May 4–5, 1990.

———. "El Salvador after Duarte: Interview with Rubén Zamora." *World Policy Journal* 5, 4 (Fall 1988): 703–23.

———. "Making the Economy Scream: U.S. Economic Sanctions against Sandinista Nicaragua." *Third World Quarterly* 17 (June 1996): 329–48.

———. "The Revolution in Nicaragua: Another Cuba?" *Foreign Affairs*, Fall 1979, pp. 28–50.

LeoGrande, William M., and Philip Brenner. "The House Divided: Ideological Polarization over Aid to the Nicaraguan Contras." *Legislative Studies Quarterly* 18, 1 (February 1993): 105–36.

LeoGrande, William M., and Carla Anne Robbins. "Oligarchs and Officers: The Crisis in El Salvador." *Foreign Affairs*, Summer 1980, pp. 1084–1103.

Lernoux, Penny. *Cry of the People: The Struggle for Human Rights in Latin America*. New York: Penguin, 1982.

———. "Reagan Abrazo." *Nation*, November 29, 1980.

"Las Ligas Populares 28 de Febrero no apoyamos la junta de gobierno." *Estudios Centroamericanos*, October–November 1979, pp. 1027–28.

Linowitz Commission. *The Americas in a Changing World*. New York: Quadrangle Books, 1975.

———. *The United States and Latin America: Next Steps*. New York: Center for Inter-American Relations, 1976.

Macaulay, Neill. *The Sandino Affair*. Chicago: Quadrangle Books, 1971.

McClintock, Michael. *The American Connection: State Terror and Resistance in El Salvador*. London: Zed Books, 1985.

McFarlane, Robert C., and Zofia Smardz. *Special Trust*. New York: Cadell-Davies, 1994.

McNeil, Frank. "The Road to Esquipulas." Paper prepared for delivery at the meeting of the Latin American Studies Association, Washington, D.C., April 1991.

——. *War and Peace in Central America: Reality and Illusion*. New York: Charles Scribner's Sons, 1988.

Manwaring, Max G., and Court Prisk. *El Salvador at War: An Oral History*. Washington, D.C.: National Defense University, 1988.

Market Opinion Research. *Americans Talk Security: A Survey of American Voters' Attitudes Concerning National Security Issues*, April 1988. Detroit: Market Opinion Research, 1988.

Maslow, Jonathan Evan, and Ana Arana. "Operation El Salvador." *Columbia Journalism Review*, May–June 1981, pp. 52–58.

Mayer, Jane, and Doyle McManus. *Landslide: The Unmaking of the President, 1984–1988*. Boston: Houghton-Mifflin, 1988.

Mayers, Lela. "Cruz Control and Intelligence Oversight." *First Principles* 14, 2 (May–June 1989): 8.

Meese, Edwin, III. *With Reagan: The Inside Story*. Washington, D.C.: Regnery, 1992.

Menges, Constantine C. "Central America and Its Enemies." *Commentary*, August 1981, pp. 32–81.

——. "Central America and the United States." *SAIS Review* 2 (Summer 1981): 13–33.

——. *Inside the National Security Council: The True Story of the Making and Unmaking of Reagan's Foreign Policy*. New York: Charles Scribner's Sons, 1988.

Miles, Sara, and Bob Ostertag. "FMLN New Thinking." *NACLA Report on the Americas* 23, 3 (September 1989): 16–38.

Miller, Nicola. *Soviet Relations with Latin America, 1959–1987*. Cambridge: Cambridge University Press, 1989.

Millet, Richard. *Guardians of the Dynasty*. Maryknoll, N.Y.: Orbis Books, 1977.

Miranda, Roger, and William Ratliff. *The Civil War in Nicaragua: Inside the Sandinistas*. New Brunswick, N.J.: Transaction, 1993.

Moberg, David. "Labor Report Due on Central America." *In These Times*, April 3–9, 1985.

"Money for Latin American Police Forces Advances on Capitol Hill." *Congressional Quarterly Weekly Report*, December 7, 1985, p. 2596.

Montgomery, Tommie Sue. *Revolution in El Salvador: Origins and Evolution*. Boulder, Colo.: Westview, 1982.

Moore, John Norton. *The Secret War in Central America: Sandinista Assault on World Order*. Frederick, Md.: University Publications of America, 1987.

Morley, Morris H. *Washington, Somoza, and the Sandinistas: State and Regime in U.S. Policy Toward Nicaragua, 1969–1981*. New York: Cambridge University Press, 1994.

Morrell, Jim. "Redlining Nicaragua." *International Policy Report*, December 1985, pp. 1–7.

Morrell, Jim, and William Goodfellow. *Contadora under the Gun*. Washington, D.C.: Center for International Policy, 1986.

Morrell, Jim, and William Jesse Biddle. "Central America: The Financial War." *International Policy Report*, March 1983, pp. 1–11.

Morris, Roger. *Haig: The General's Progress*. Chicago: Playboy Press, 1982.

Moynihan, Daniel Patrick. *Came the Revolution: Argument in the Reagan Era*. New York: Harcourt Brace Jovanovich, 1988.

——. *On the Law of Nations*. Cambridge, Mass.: Harvard University Press, 1990.

Nairn, Allan. "Behind the Death Squads." *Progressive*, May 1984, pp. 1, 20–29.

——. "Reagan Administration Links with Guatemala's Death Squads." *Covert Action* 12 (April 1981): 16–21.

National Commissioner for the Protection of Human Rights in Honduras. *Honduras: The Facts Speak for Themselves*. New York: Human Rights Watch, 1994.

"The Nicaraguan Tangle: An Exchange." *New York Review of Books*, May 8, 1986.

Nichols, John Spicer. "*La Prensa*: The CIA Connection." *Columbia Journalism Review*, July–August 1988, pp. 34–35.

"1980 Republican Party Platform." *Congressional Quarterly Weekly Report*, July 19, 1980, pp. 2030–56.

Nolan, David. *The Ideology of the Sandinistas and the Nicaraguan Revolution*. Miami: University of Miami, 1984.

North, Oliver L., with William Novak. *Under Fire: An American Story*. New York: HarperCollins, 1991.

Nunca Mas: Informe de la Comisión Nacional Sobre la Desaparición de Personas. Buenos Aires: Editorial Universitaria de Buenos Aires, 1984.

Oberdorfer, Don. *The Turn: From the Cold War to a New Era*. New York: Poseidon Press, 1991.

O'Neill, Tip, with William Novak. *Man of the House: The Life and Political Memoirs of Speaker Tip O'Neill*. New York: St. Martin's Press, 1987.

Organization of American States, Inter-American Commission on Human Rights. *Report on the Situation of Human Rights in El Salvador*, November 17, 1978. Washington, D.C.: OAS, 1978.

———. *Report on the Situation in Nicaragua: Findings of an "On-site" Observation in the Republic of Nicaragua, October 3–12, 1978*. Washington, D.C.: OAS, 1978.

Pardo-Maurer, R. *The Contras, 1980–1989: A Special Kind of Politics*. New York: Praeger, 1990.

Parliamentary Human Rights Group. "Report of a British Parliamentary Delegation to Nicaragua to Observe the Presidential and National Assembly Elections." London, 1984.

Parry, Robert. *Fooling America: How Washington Insiders Twist the Truth and Manufacture the Conventional Wisdom*. New York: William Morrow, 1992.

Parry, Robert, and Brian Barger. "Reagan's Shadow CIA." *New Republic*, November 24, 1986.

Pastor, Robert A. *Condemned to Repetition: The United States and Nicaragua*. Princeton: Princeton University Press, 1987.

———. "Continuity and Change in U.S. Foreign Policy: Carter and Reagan on El Salvador." *Journal of Policy Analysis and Management* 3, 2 (1984): 175–90.

———. "Nicaragua's Choice: The Making of a Free Election." *Journal of Democracy* 1, 3 (Summer 1990): 13–25.

Peckenham, Nancy, and Annie Street, eds. *Honduras: Portrait of a Captive Nation*. New York: Praeger, 1985.

Perkins, Dexter. *A History of the Monroe Doctrine*. Boston: Little, Brown, 1963.

Persico, Joseph E. *Casey: The Lives and Secrets of William J. Casey, from the OSS to the CIA*. New York: Viking, 1990.

Pezzullo, Lawrence, and Ralph Pezzullo. *At the Fall of Somoza*. Pittsburgh: University of Pittsburgh Press, 1993.

Pierre, Andrew, ed. *Central America as a European-American Issue*. New York: Council on Foreign Relations, 1985.

Policy Alternatives for the Caribbean and Central America. *Changing Course: Blueprint for Peace in Central America and the Caribbean*. Washington, D.C.: Institute for Policy Studies, 1984.

Politics in America 1984. Washington, D.C.: Congressional Quarterly Press, 1984.

"Posición del Bloque Popular Revolucionario frente al autogolpe de la tiranía militar." *Estudios Centroamericanos*, October–November 1979, pp. 1025–26.

Prados, John. *Keepers of the Keys: A History of the National Security Council from Truman to Bush*. New York: William Morrow, 1991.

Pressman, Steven. "House, in Symbolic Action, Votes Contra Aid Moratorium." *Congressional Quarterly Weekly Report*, March 14, 1987, pp. 460–63.

——. "Supplemental Showdown Set over Central America Money." *Congressional Quarterly Weekly Report*, August 4, 1984, pp. 1876–77.

Preston, Julia. "The Defeat of the Sandinistas." *New York Review of Books*, April 12, 1990.

Prisk, Courtney E., ed. *The Comandante Speaks: Memoirs of an El Salvadoran Guerrilla Leader*. Boulder, Colo.: Westview, 1991.

Procedimiento para Establecer la Paz Firme y Duradera en Centroamérica. San José, Costa Rica: Oficina de Apoyo de la Presidencia de la Republica, 1987.

Prosterman, Roy L., and Mary Temple. "Land Reform in El Salvador." *Free Trade Union News*, June 6, 1980.

Prosterman, Roy L., Jeffrey M. Riedinger, and Mary N. Temple. "Land Reform and the El Salvador Crisis." *International Security* 6, 1 (Summer 1981): 53–74.

Psychological Operations in Guerrilla Warfare. New York: Vintage, 1985.

Pyes, Craig. *Salvadoran Rightists: The Deadly Patriots*. Reprinted from the *Albuquerque Journal*, 1983.

Ranelagh, John. *The Agency: The Rise and Decline of the CIA*. New York: Simon and Schuster, 1987.

Raymont, Henry. "Argentine Miscues." *New Republic*, June 9, 1982.

Reagan, Nancy, with William Novak. *My Turn: The Memoirs of Nancy Reagan*. New York: Random House, 1989.

Reagan, Ronald. *An American Life*. New York: Simon and Schuster, 1990.

Regan, Donald T. *For the Record: From Wall Street to Washington*. New York: Harcourt Brace Jovanovich, 1988.

Report of Donald T. Fox, Esq. and Professor Michael J. Glennon to the International Human Rights Law Group and the Washington Office on Latin America Concerning Abuses Against Civilians by Counterrevolutionaries Operating in Nicaragua. Washington, D.C.: WOLA and IHRLG, 1985.

"Report of the Irish Inter-Parliamentary Group." Dublin, 1984.

Revolutionary Democratic Front. *El Salvador: A Struggle for Democracy*. San Salvador: FDR, 1980.

Riding, Alan. *Distant Neighbors: A Portrait of the Mexicans*. New York: Alfred A. Knopf, 1985.

Rielly, John E. *American Public Opinion and U.S. Foreign Policy 1987*. Chicago: Chicago Council on Foreign Relations, 1987.

Robinson, William I. *A Faustian Bargain: U.S. Intervention in the Nicaraguan Elections and American Foreign Policy in the Post–Cold War Era*. Boulder, Colo.: Westview, 1992.

Robinson, William I., and Kent Norsworthy. *David and Goliath: The U.S. War against Nicaragua*. New York: Monthly Review Press, 1987.

——. "Elections and U.S. Intervention in Nicaragua." *Latin American Perspectives* 12, 2 (Spring 1985): 83–110.

Rodriguez, Felix I., with John Weisman. *Shadow Warrior*. New York: Simon and Schuster, 1989.

Rosset, Peter, and John Vandermeer, eds. *The Nicaragua Reader: Documents of a Revolution under Fire*. New York: Grove Press, 1983.

Rothman, Robert. "Pact Calls for Funding Cut in El Salvador Aid Package." *Congressional Quarterly Weekly Report*, March 24, 1984, p. 650.

——. "Senate Panel Hands Reagan Latin American Aid Victory." *Congressional Quarterly Weekly Report*, March 17, 1984, pp. 606–7.

"Salvadoran Leader Makes Conquests on Hill." *Congressional Quarterly Weekly Report*, May 26, 1984, pp. 1233–37.

Sanders, Jerry W. *Peddlers of Crisis: The Committee on the Present Danger and the Politics of Containment*. Boston: South End Press, 1983.

"Sandinista Perspectives: Three Differing Views." *Latin American Perspectives* 6, 1 (Winter 1979): 114–26.

Schieffer, Bob, and Gary Paul Gates. *The Acting President*. New York: E. P. Dutton, 1989.

Schoultz, Lars. *Human Rights and United States Policy toward Latin America*. Princeton: Princeton University Press, 1981.

———. *National Security and United States Policy Toward Latin America*. Princeton: Princeton University Press, 1987.

Schulz, Donald E., and Deborah Sundloff Schulz. *The United States, Honduras, and the Crisis in Central America*. Boulder, Colo.: Westview, 1994.

Schwarz, Benjamin C. *American Counterinsurgency Doctrine and El Salvador: The Frustrations of Reforms and the Illusions of Nation Building*. Santa Monica, Calif.: Rand Corporation, 1991.

Secord, Richard, with Jay Wurts. *Honored and Betrayed: Irangate, Covert Operations, and the Secret War in Laos*. New York: John Wiley, 1992.

Selser, Gregorio. *Sandino*. New York: Monthly Review, 1981.

"Senate Confirms Clark as Deputy Secretary of State." *Congressional Quarterly Weekly Report*, February 28, 1981, p. 390.

Sharkey, Jacqueline. "Nicaragua: Anatomy of an Election." *Common Cause*, May–June 1990.

Shawcross, William. *Sideshow: Kissinger, Nixon, and the Destruction of Cambodia*. New York: Washington Square Press, 1979.

Sheehan, Neil, Hedrick Smith, E. W. Kenworthy, and Fox Butterfield. *The Pentagon Papers*. New York: Bantam Books, 1971.

Shultz, George P. *Turmoil and Triumph: My Years as Secretary of State*. New York: Charles Scribner's Sons, 1993.

Simon, Laurence R., James C. Stephens Jr., and Martin Diskin. *El Salvador Land Reform, 1980–1981: Impact Audit*. Boston: OXFAM America, 1982.

Sklar, Holly. "Dollars Don't Buy Democracy." *Nicaraguan Perspectives* 18 (Winter–Spring 1990): 12–16.

Smallwood, James, ed. *The Writings of Will Rogers: Will Rogers Weekly Articles*. Vol. 3, 1927–1929. Stillwater: Oklahoma State University Press, 1981.

Smith, Hedrick. *The Power Game: How Washington Really Works*. New York: Random House, 1988.

Smith, Wayne S. *The Closest of Enemies: A Personal and Diplomatic Account of U.S.-Cuban Relations since 1957*. New York: W. W. Norton, 1987.

———. "Dateline Havana: Myopic Diplomacy." *Foreign Policy* 48 (Fall 1982): 157–74.

———, ed. *The Russians Aren't Coming: New Soviet Policy in Latin America*. Boulder, Colo.: Lynne Reiner, 1992.

Smyth, Frank. "Duarte's Secret Friends." *Nation*, March 14, 1987.

Snepp, Frank. *Decent Interval*. New York: Random House, 1977.

Sobel, Richard. *Public Opinion in U.S. Foreign Policy: The Controversy over Contra Aid*. Lanham, Md.: Rowman and Littlefield, 1993.

Sobrino, Jon. *Monseñor Romero*. San Salvador: UCA Editores, 1989.

Somoza, Anastasio, as told to Jack Cox. *Nicaragua Betrayed*. Boston: Western Islands, 1980.

Spalding, Hobart A., Jr. "U.S. Labor Intervention in Latin America: The Case of AIFLD." *Labor, Capital and Society* 17, 2 (November 1984): 136–72.

Spalding, Rose J., ed. *The Political Economy of Revolutionary Nicaragua*. Winchester, Mass.: Allen and Unwin, 1987.

Speakes, Larry, with Robert Pack. *Speaking Out: The Reagan Presidency from Inside the White House*. New York: Charles Scribner's Sons, 1988.

Stein, Jeff. "Reagan's Plans for Intelligence." *Nation*, July 12, 1980.

Swedberg, Jeffrey E. "U.S. Economic Policy toward Nicaragua under the Reagan Administration." Master's thesis, George Washington University, 1986.

Szulc, Tad. "Dateline Washington: The Vicar Vanquished." *Foreign Policy* 43 (Summer 1981): 173–86.

"The Talk of the Town." *New Yorker*, June 11, 1990.

Timberg, Robert. "The Private War of Ollie and Jim." *Esquire*, March 1988.

"Unclassified Summary of the State Department's Objections to September 7 Draft of Contadora Agreement." *International Policy Report* (Center for International Policy), November 1984, p. 5.

Ungo, Guillermo M. "The People's Struggle." *Foreign Policy* 52 (Fall 1983): 51–63.

Unión Comunal Salvadoreña. "El Salvador Land Reform Update: Land to the Tiller Program." Executive Summary, December 10, 1981. San Salvador, 1981.

United Nations. *From Madness to Hope: The Twelve-Year War in El Salvador*. Report of the Commission on the Truth for El Salvador, U.N. Doc. s/25500, April 1, 1993.

"U.S. Invasion of Nicaragua: Appraising the Cost." *Defense Monitor* 16, 5 (1987): 1–8.

Valentine, Douglas. *The Phoenix Program*. New York: William Morrow, 1990.

Vilas, Carlos M. *The Sandinista Revolution: National Liberation and Social Transformation in Central America*. New York: Monthly Review Press, 1986.

Villalobos, Joaquín. "A Democratic Revolution for El Salvador." *Foreign Policy* 74 (Spring 1989): 103–22.

———. "Popular Insurrection: Desire or Reality?" *Latin American Perspectives* 16, 3 (Summer 1989): 5–47.

Walker, Thomas W., ed. *Nicaragua: The First Five Years*. New York: Praeger, 1985.

———. *Nicaragua in Revolution*. New York: Praeger, 1982.

———. *Reagan versus the Sandinistas: The Undeclared War on Nicaragua*. Boulder, Colo.: Westview, 1987.

———. *Revolution and Counterrevolution in Nicaragua*. Boulder, Colo.: Westview, 1991.

Weeks, John. *The Economies of Central America*. New York: Holmes and Meier, 1985.

Weinberger, Caspar W. *Fighting for Peace: Seven Critical Years in the Pentagon*. New York: Warner Books, 1990.

Weiner, Tim. *Blank Check: The Pentagon's Black Budget*. New York: Warner Books, 1990.

Weinraub, Al, and William Bollinger. *The AFL-CIO in Central America: A Look at the American Institute for Free Labor Development*. Oakland, Calif.: Labor Network on Central America, 1987.

Whittle, Richard. "Helms Loses Committee Test on Nominees." *Congressional Quarterly Weekly Report*, May 2, 1981, p. 755.

———. "House Liberals Retain Clout on Foreign Affairs Panel." *Congressional Quarterly Weekly Report*, February 7, 1981, p. 263.

———. "Panel Compromises on Military Aid Request." *Congressional Quarterly Weekly Report*, May 2, 1981, pp. 752–54.

———. "Reagan El Salvador Policy Clears First Hurdle." *Congressional Quarterly Weekly Report*, March 28, 1981.

———. "Reagan Weighs Military Aid to Counter Soviet, Cuban 'Interference' in El Salvador." *Congressional Quarterly Weekly Report*, February 28, 1981, pp. 388–89.

———. "Senate Panel Votes Change in Caribbean Basin Aid Plan." *Congressional Quarterly Weekly Report*, May 22, 1982, p. 1186.

———. "Shultz Confirmed as Secretary of State." *Congressional Quarterly Weekly Report*, July 17, 1982, pp. 1691–94.

———. "With Little Controversy, House Passes Authorization for Foreign Aid Programs." *Congressional Quarterly Weekly Report*, December 12, 1981, pp. 2436–37.

Wiarda, Howard J., ed. *Rift and Revolution: The Central American Imbroglio*. Washington, D.C.: American Enterprise Institute, 1984.

Williams, Robert G. *Export Agriculture and the Crisis in Central America*. Chapel Hill: University of North Carolina Press, 1986.

Woodward, Bob. *VEIL: The Secret Wars of the CIA, 1981–1987*. New York: Simon and Schuster, 1987.

Woodward, Ralph Lee, Jr. *Central America: A Nation Divided*. New York: Oxford University Press, 1985.

World Council of Churches, *El Salvador: One Year of Repression*. New York: World Council of Churches, 1981.

Wright, Jim. *Worth It All: My War for Peace*. Washington, D.C.: Brassey's, 1993.

Index

50, 59, 232–36, 253, 261, 643 (nn. 74, 76);
assessments of military situation, 151,
186, 670 (n. 45); operations, 153, 160,
211, 247–50, 282, 627 (n. 57); use of CIA
to avoid War Powers Resolution, 211,
385
— in Honduras: operations, 297–99, 442,
657 (n. 71); support for Alvarez, 393–96
— in Iran-contra affair: creative accounting, 381–84, 677 (n. 2); and Pentagon,
382–87, 587; role in third country support for contras, 388–93; involved in
North's activities, 403–6. See also Casey,
William J.; Clarridge, Duane R.; Fernandez, Joseph; Fiers, Alan; North, Oliver
— in Nicaragua, 676 (n. 166); assessments
during Nicaraguan revolution, 23, 25, 32,
595 (n. 58); origins of contra war, 110–11,
114–18; NSDD 17 and 1981 finding, 141–46,
285–87; Pastora and southern front,
294–96, 302, 308–9, 331, 349, 440; public
relations on behalf of contra aid, 300–
302, 446–47, 459; plans for contras, 302,
303, 306–11, 314, 440–41, 465, 491, 532;
assessment of contra war, 309–10, 441,
459; September 1983 finding, 322–24;
mining Nicaragua's harbors, 330–40,
359; UCLAS, 331–33, 337, 381, 440, 471, 664
(nn. 22, 23); "murder manual," 363–67;
support for civic opposition, 368, 372,
382, 542–44, 546, 556, 560, 658 (n. 7),
715 (nn. 77–79, 84), 718 (nn. 33, 34), 719
(n. 43); support for Cruz, 372, 375, 466,
489, 703 (n. 64); knowledge of contra
corruption and drug trafficking, 413–16,
461, 463, 464, 698 (n. 116); intelligence-
sharing, 413–17, 420–26, 431–36, 688
(nn. 73, 74, 79), 691 (nn. 122, 125, 131,
133); prohibited from contra aid delivery,
422, 424, 432, 434, 443, 455; monitoring
NHAO disbursements, 460–61; opposes
contra reform, 461, 465, 467, 488, 540;
shuts down war, 542. See also Congress,
U.S.—Nicaragua debates
Cerezo, Vinicio, 453
Cerrón Grande dam, attack on, 267
Certification, on El Salvador, 180, 190, 233,
243, 328, 636 (n. 5); passage of, 130–34,
204; first review, 152–58; administration
efforts to show progress, 163–66, 176–78;

second review, 169, 171–73; influence of,
170, 282, 584, 587; third review, 199–200;
Democrats efforts to strengthen, 212,
215–16, 245–46, 253–55, 258, 647 (n. 65);
pocket veto of extension, 228–30, 642
(nn. 53, 54); efforts to revive, 273–75, 567,
573
Certification, on Nicaragua, 31, 68–69
César, Alfredo, 536, 537, 539, 560
Chalatenango, fighting in, 60, 136, 153, 184,
224, 226, 262, 266, 273
Chamorro, Edgar, 405; and origins of FDN,
115, 118, 306–8; and CIA "murder man-
ual," 363–64; on contra human rights
abuses and corruption, 413, 461
Chamorro, Fernando "El Negro," 464
Chamorro, Jaime, 543–44, 675 (n. 135)
Chamorro, Pedro Joaquín, 15; assassination
of, 18, 489, 559, 593 (n. 28)
Chamorro, Pedro Joaquín, Jr. ("Pedrito"),
489, 540, 544
Chamorro, Violeta Barrios de, 371, 543,
596 (n. 73), 715 (n. 77); elected president,
559–64, 719 (n. 43)
Chapin, Frederic, 76, 90, 315
Chardy, Alfonso, 436, 476, 692 (n. 136)
Chávez Mena, Fidel, 247, 278, 566
Cheek, James, 31, 44, 75, 76
Cheney, Dick, 426, 531, 541
Cherne, Leo, 113
Chile, 60, 72, 76, 412, 528, 561; human
rights abuses in, 43, 54; Reagan's policy
toward, 55, 291; CIA destabilization of,
80, 108, 162, 238, 430, 544, 673 (n. 114),
715 (n. 80), 718 (n. 31); support for contras, 298
China, People's Republic of, 7, 56, 347, 392,
429
Christ, Hans, 67
Christian Base Communities, in El Salvador, 37
Christian Democratic Party of El Salvador
(PDC): early history of, 36–37; in 1980
junta, 42, 44, 46–47, 62–63, 166, 599
(n. 127), 602 (n. 165); Reagan's ambivalence toward, 59, 64–65, 90–91, 127–30,
132–33, 188, 251–52, 264, 584; affiliated
unions, 66, 226–27, 279–81; and peace
talks, 99, 156, 262–63, 583; covert U.S.
support for, 114–15, 160, 248–50, 560;

murder of FDR leaders, 59–60; church-women's murders, 60–63; AIFLD murders, 66–67; El Mozote massacre by, 155, 234; kidnapping of FDR union leaders, 178–79; "grim gram," 153–54, 233, 625 (n. 15); Jesuits' murders, 569–71, 573–74, 576

Enders, Rudy, 385, 403

Enders, Thomas O.: background of, 77–79, 162; assistant secretary under Haig, 107; policy management by, 109–10, 186–88; in conflict with hard-liners, 118, 120–22, 126–27, 188–92, 194–95, 199, 218, 290, 330; relations with Congress, 126–27, 152, 189–90, 198, 206; firing of, 195–96, 221, 332

—El Salvador policy, 127–30, 152, 176–79, 198, 219, 620 (n. 16); support for democracy promotion, 126, 143–44; congressional testimony, 154–57, 171–72, 199; two-track policy, 188–92, 310–11, 356

—Nicaragua policy, 291; support for contras, 110, 144, 287, 291, 310, 356; diplomatic initiatives toward Nicaragua, 118–24, 289–91, 618 (n. 84)

Enterprise, The. See Project Democracy

ERP (Revolutionary Army of the People), 36, 598 (n. 107)

Especiales, 48. See also Death squads, in El Salvador

Esquipulas Accord: adoption of, 514–15; Reagan's reaction to, 515–18, 539; Democrat support for, 518–19, 522–23, 527, 531–32; and Sandinista talks with contras, 519–21, 528–30; Wright's conflict with Reagan over, 521–22, 546–47; verification of compliance, 527–28, 533, 711 (chap. 21, n. 103; chap. S22, n. 3); Sapoá cease-fire, 536–42, 549, 557, 717 (n. 18); Bush promise to support, 554–55, 582; implementation in El Salvador, 565. See also Arias Sánchez, Oscar; Wright, James

Ethiopia, 53, 86

Europe, Western: views on Nicaragua, 30, 370, 372–73, 376, 558, 690 (n. 104); opposes U.S. policy, 81, 87, 98–99, 125, 140, 175, 555, 695 (n. 56); U.S. efforts to influence, 98, 307; support for peace talks, 98–99, 288, 510, 520, 530, 583;

supports Duarte, 248; opposes U.S. embargo and mining of Nicaragua's harbors, 330, 332, 338, 428–30. See also Falklands/Malvinas war; NATO

"Evil Empire," 6, 347, 559, 581

Exon, James J., 157

Exxon Corporation, 331

Fahd (Saudi king), 392

Fairbanks, Richard, 223

Falklands/Malvinas war, 174, 290–94, 359, 399

FAO (Broad Opposition Front), 20, 22

Farabundo Martí Front for National Liberation. See FMLN

FARN (Armed Forces of National Resistance), 36, 598 (n. 107), 628 (n. 60)

Fascell, Dante B., 215, 246

FDN (Nicaraguan Democratic Forces), 302, 311; National Guard veterans in, 115, 145, 295–96, 298, 301–3, 310, 405, 413, 464–66, 492; negotiations with Pastora, 296; CIA seeks to improve image of, 306–10, 405; claims credit for mining, 330–31; logistical problems, 400, 402; and UNO, 464–67, 487–89, 699 (n. 129). See also Calero, Adolfo; Contras

FDR (Revolutionary Democratic Front), 62, 130, 155; origins of, 47; relations with FMLN, 48, 252, 272–73, 651 (n. 61); leadership assassinated, 59–60, 66, 130; attitude toward elections, 156, 158, 176, 189, 252; union leaders kidnapped, 178; at La Palma, 262–63; resumption of political activity, 565–66. See also Democratic Convergence; FMLN

FDR-FMLN. See FDR; FMLN

Feinberg, Richard, 19

Feldman, Tony, 306, 307

Feldstein, Mark, 194

Ferch, John, 458–59, 693 (n. 14), 697 (n. 97)

Fernández, Guido, 508, 514, 528, 711 (n. 6)

Fernandez, Joseph, 307, 371, 405–7, 478, 673 (n. 107)

Ferraro, Geraldine A., 254

Fiers, Alan: succeeds Clarridge at CIA, 391, 543; and North, 399, 408, 465; role in Enterprise, 406, 464, 479–80, 496; pardoned, 702 (n. 22)

election, 194–95, 219, 223–24, 246; and
human rights, 206, 219, 228, 231
Majano, Adolfo, 46, 63
Maldonado, Samuel, 227
Mallet, John, 540
Manifest Destiny, 11–13
Manley, Michael, 54
Manzanillo talks, 355–56, 371; efforts to
revive, 350, 423, 434, 450–51, 456, 511,
549; internal U.S. debate over, 356–60,
672 (n. 84); end of, 362–63, 443, 444, 467
Marcos, Ferdinand, 452
Maroni, Dewey. *See* Clarridge, Duane R.
Marsh, John O., 382–83, 386, 678 (n. 21)
Marshall, George C., and Marshall Plan, 73
Marshall Plan for Central America, 186,
239–40
Martínez, Gerardo, 461
Maryknoll Order, 60–62, 447, 454–55. *See
also* Churchwomen's murders
La Matanza, 34–35, 47, 59, 243
Matsui, Robert T., 425
Mauro Araujo, Américo, 271
Maximiliano Hernández Martínez Anti-
Communist Brigade, 59
Medellín Conference of Latin American
Bishops (1968), 36
Medina, Ramón (Luis Posada Carriles),
404
Medrano, José Alberto ("Chele"), 48–49,
269
Meese, Edwin, 193; conflicts with Haig, 84,
99, 107; role in foreign policy management, 109, 146, 389; as hard-liner, 141,
194, 220, 222; in Iran-contra affair,
481–83, 502
Melton, Richard H., 545–46, 716 (n. 90)
Melton Plan, 546
Menges, Constantine: as hard-liner, 58,
109, 357, 615 (n. 27); Mexican persuasion
campaign, 326, 352–54, 669 (nn. 30, 31,
34), 695 (n. 58); as CIA National Intelligence Officer for Latin America, 353;
views on Mexico, 353–54; on NSC staff,
387, 398
Mexico: history, 11–13; support for Sandinistas, 24, 595 (n. 57); opposes Reagan's
policy, 97–98; supports negotiations,
98, 123, 140, 191, 583; U.S. perceives as
domino, 139, 202, 316, 321; López Portillo

plan, 287–91, 623 (n. 68); Mexican persuasion campaign, 326, 352–54, 669
(nn. 30, 31, 34), 670 (n. 44), 695 (n. 58);
and oil shipments to Nicaragua, 332,
427–28, 430; in Contadora, 349–50, 352,
362, 451; de la Madrid Washington visit,
354–55; in "group of friends," 576–77.
See also Contadora peace process
Meyer, Edward C., 197, 668 (n. 7)
Miami Herald, 314, 337, 436, 476
"Miami Six," 50
Michel, Robert: in 1985 contra aid debate,
320, 422, 424–26, 433–35; in debate on
mining, 339; and Gingrich, 341; in 1988
contra aid debate, 533–34, 536, 541
Middendorf, William, 616 (n. 54)
Middle East, 4, 175, 578
MiG fighters, Nicaraguan acquisition of,
377–80, 676 (nn. 161, 166)
Mikulski, Barbara, 276
Military advisers, U.S. *See* Advisers, U.S.
military
Military assistance, U.S. *See individual U.S.
administrations*
Military Assistance Group, 210
Military Assistance Strategy Team, 137
Military exercises, U.S., 83–84, 146, 149,
320, 326, 351, 396, 555; equipment left
behind, 150, 317–18, 384, 678 (n. 14);
efforts to limit, 246, 351, 359, 361
—individual: *Halcon Vista*, 121–22, 123;
REDEX 2-82, 150; Ocean Venture, 150,
349; Big Pine I and II, 221, 314, 316–19,
348; Granadero I, 318, 348; Composite
Training Exercise and Operation Quick
Thrust, 378
Military Group, U.S., in El Salvador, 209,
233, 277, 404–5, 406–7, 478
Miller, George, 270–71, 303, 312
Mineta, Norman, 300, 367, 425
Mining of Nicaragua's harbors, 330–40,
664 (n. 29), 666 (n. 67)
Miskito Indians, 308–9, 351, 421, 474, 490,
519
Mitchell, George, 497
Moakley, Joe, 571, 573–74
Mobile Training Teams (MTTS), 89–90, 210
Mondale, Walter, 260, 356, 367, 377, 433, 554
Mondragón Martínez, José Efrén, 414, 686
(n. 29)